**Ordna** Survey

CW00321615

STREET

West

Yorkshire

Contents

III Key to map symbols

IV-V Key to map pages

VI-VII Route planning

VIII Administrative and post code boundaries

1 Street maps

201 Extra-large-scale maps of town centres

 201 Bradford
 202 Halifax
 204 Leeds
 216 Wakefield

217 Index of hospitals, industrial estates, railway stations, schools, shopping centres, street names and universities

PHILIP'S

First edition published 1996
Second edition published 1999
Reprinted in 2000 by

George Philip Ltd, a division of
Octopus Publishing Group Ltd
2-4 Heron Quays, London E14 4JP

ISBN 0-540-07674-0 (pocket)

© Crown copyright 1999
© George Philip Ltd 1999

**The mapping between pages 1 and 216 (inclusive) in this
atlas is derived from Ordnance Survey® OSCAR® and
Land-Line® data, and Landranger® mapping.**

Ordnance Survey, OSCAR, Land-line and Landranger are
registered trade marks of Ordnance Survey, the national
mapping agency of Great Britain.

Printed and bound in Spain by Cayfosa

Digital Data

The exceptionally high-quality mapping
found in this book is available as
digital data in TIFF format, which is
easily convertible to other bit-mapped
(raster) image formats.

The index is also available in digital
form as a standard database table.
It contains all the details found in the
printed index together with the
National Grid reference for the map
square in which each entry is named
and feature codes for places of
interest in eight categories such as
education and health.

For further information and to discuss
your requirements, please contact
Philip's on 020 7531 8440 or
george.philip@philips-maps.co.uk

Motorway (with junction number)		Railway station
Primary route (dual carriageway and single)		Glasgow Underground station
A road (dual carriageway and single)		Midland Metro
B road (dual carriageway and single)		Metrolink station
Minor road (dual carriageway and single)		London Underground station
Other minor road (dual carriageway and single)		Docklands Light Railway station
Road under construction		Tyne and Wear Metro
Pedestrianised area		Private railway station
Postcode boundaries		Bus, coach station
County and Unitary Authority boundaries		Ambulance station
Railway		Coastguard station
Tramway, miniature railway		Fire station
Rural track, private road or narrow road in urban area		Police station
Gate or obstruction to traffic (restrictions may not apply at all times or to all vehicles)		Accident and Emergency entrance to hospital
Path, bridleway, byway open to all traffic, road used as a public path		Hospital
The representation in this atlas of a road, track or path is no evidence of the existence of a right of way		Church, place of worship
		Information Centre (open all year)
Adjoining page indicators		Parking, Park and Ride
		Post Office
The map area within the pink band is shown at a larger scale on the page indicated by the red block and arrow		Important buildings, schools, colleges, universities and hospitals

Walsall Railway station

Prim Sch Important buildings, schools, colleges, universities and hospitals

River Medway Water name

Stream

River or canal (minor and major)

Water

Tidal water

Woods

Houses

House Non-Roman antiquity

VILLA Roman antiquity

Acad	Academy	Meml	Memorial
Crem	Crematorium	Mon	Monument
Cemy	Cemetery	Mus	Museum
C Ctr	Civic Centre	Obsy	Observatory
CH	Club House	Pal	Royal Palace
Coll	College	PH	Public House
Ent	Enterprise	Recn Gd	Recreation Ground
Ex H	Exhibition Hall	Resr	Reservoir
Ind Est	Industrial Estate	Ret Pk	Retail Park
Inst	Institute	Sch	School
Ct	Law Court	Sh Ctr	Shopping Centre
L Ctr	Leisure Centre	TH	Town Hall/House
LC	Level Crossing	Trad Est	Trading Estate
Liby	Library	Univ	University
Mkt	Market	YH	Youth Hostel

■ The dark grey border on the inside edge of some pages indicates that the mapping does not continue onto the adjacent page ■ The small numbers around the edges of the maps identify the 1 kilometre National Grid lines

| The scale of the maps is 3.92 cm to 1 km (2¹/₂ inches to 1 mile) | 0 — ¹/₄ — ¹/₂ — ³/₄ — 1 mile |
| | 0 — 250m — 500m — 750m — 1 kilometre |

| The scale of the maps on pages numbered in red is 7.84 cm to 1 km (5 inches to 1 mile) | 0 — 220 yards — 440 yards — 660 yards — ¹/₂ mile |
| | 0 — 125m — 250m — 375m — ¹/₂ kilometre |

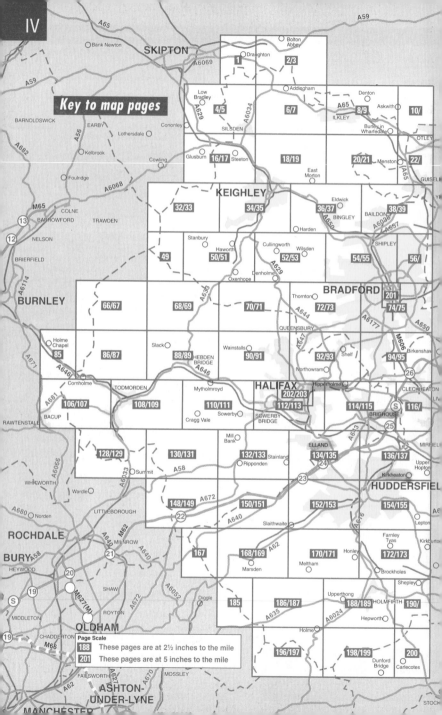

IV

Key to map pages

Page Scale

188 These pages are at 2½ inches to the mile

201 These pages are at 5 inches to the mile

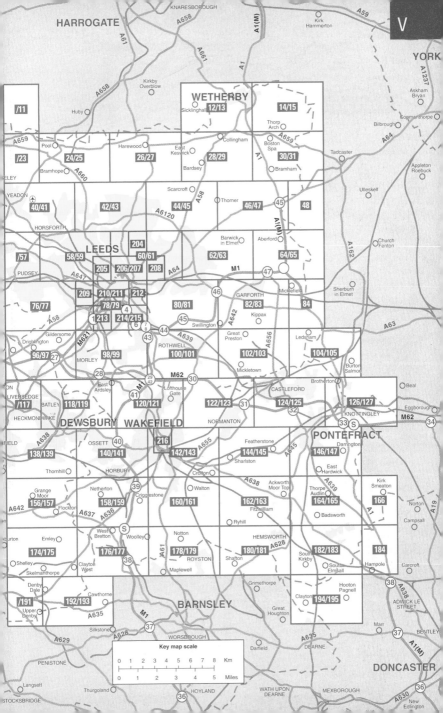

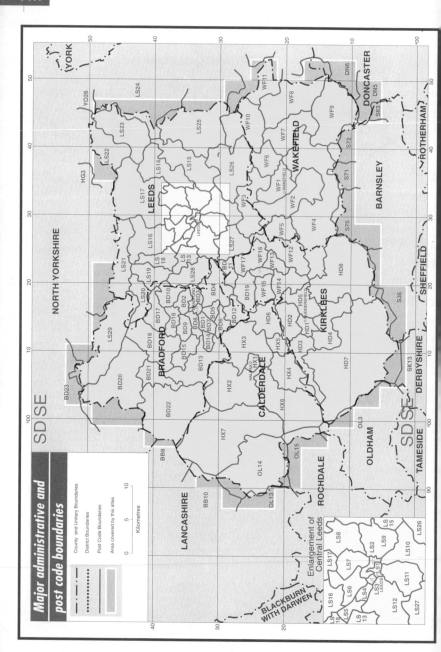

Major administrative and post code boundaries

County and Unitary Boundaries

District Boundaries

Post Code Boundaries

Area covered by this atlas

Kilometres

0   5   10

Enlargement of Central Leeds

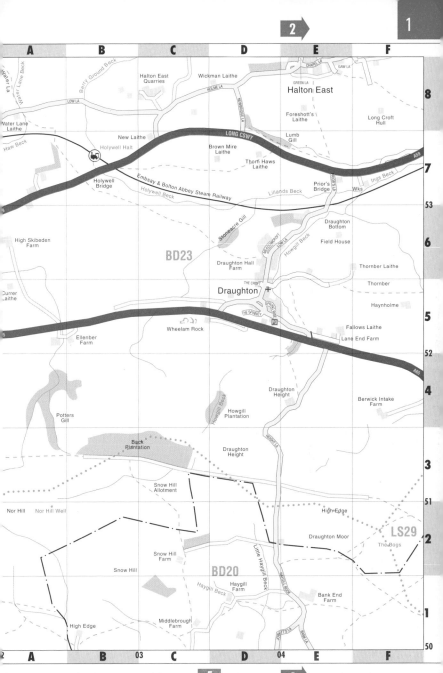

A   B   C   D   E   F

8

Halton East
Quarries
Wickman Laithe
GREEN LA
Halton East
Foreshott's
Laithe
Long Croft
Hull
LOW LA
Water Lane
Laithe
New Laithe
LONG CSWY
Lumb
Gill
Holywell Halt
Brown Mire
Laithe
Haw Beck
Thorn Haws
Laithe
A59
7
Holywell
Bridge
Embsay & Bolton Abbey Steam Railway
Holywell Beck
Lillands Beck
Prior's
Bridge
Wks
Ings Beck

53

Stoneacre Gill
Draughton
Bottom
High Skibeden
Farm
BD23
Field House
6
Currer
Laithe
Draughton Hall
Farm
Howgill Beck
Thornber Laithe
Thornber
THE CROFT
Draughton
Haynholme
5
Ellenber
Farm
Wheelam Rock
THE SPINNEY
SKIPTON RD
Fallows Laithe
Lane End Farm

52

Draughton
Height
A65
4
Potters
Gill
Howgill Plantation
Howgill Plantation
HESKETH LA
Berwick Intake
Farm
Back
Plantation
Draughton
Height
3
Snow Hill
Allotment

51

Nor Hill   Nor Hill Well
High Edge
LS29
Draughton Moor
The Bogs
2
Snow Hill
Farm
BD20
Little Haygill Beck
Snow Hill
Haygill Beck
Haygill
Farm
MIDDLE BECK
Bank End
Farm
1
High Edge
Middlebrough
Farm
JOWETT'S LA

50

A   B   03   C   D   04   E   F

A   B   C   D   E   F

8

Halton Gill
Wood

New
Laithe

Raven's Gill Dike

Raven's
Gill

Bolton
Abbey

Tithe
Barn

Struff
Wood

Hesketh
House

Hambleton
Farm

RAILWAY
COTTS

7

Embsay & Bolton Abbey
Steam Railway

HAMBLETON
COTTS

Hambleton
Quarry
(dis)

Hambleton Beck

Hambleton
Beck

The Strand

Dales Way

Hotel

Bolton
Bridge

Red Lion
Farm

Rocks Hill
Plantation

Hambleton

Huffa
Bridge

Bolton
Abbey

53

Banks
Hill

The Boyle
and Petyt
Sch

Banks

Harry Wall
Gill

Ward
Hill

6

BD23

Nettleber

Haw Pike

Beamsley
Hall

Beamsley

Berwick
West

Berwick
East

Lob
Wood

River Wharfe

Home
Farm

5

Haw
Pike

Dales Way

52

Eller Carr
Wood

Wind
Farm

Lobwood
House

BOLTON RD

Paradise
Lathe

4

A59

Chelker
Resr

Hag Head
Laithe

LS29

Farfield
Hall

Low
Park

Hare
Knoll

High
Park

Dales Way

3

Chelker House
Farm

Highfield
Farm

Syke
House

51

Upper
White Well

Highfield
House

Farfield
House

Low
Sanfitt

Wine Beck

2

Low
White Well

High
Sanfitt

Addingham Wharfedale Rd

Heathness Gill

High
Laithe

Riddings
Farm

THE ACRES 1
AYNHOLME CL 2

Addingham
Middle
Sch

Hart
House

Peak Ridding
Laithe

SKIPTON RD

Bracken Ghyll Golf
Course

Addingham First
Sch

1

Countess
Hill

Addingham
Low Moor

Round Dikes
Camp

Cross
Bank

Causeway
Foot

MOOR
LA

HEATHNESS RD

MOOR PARK
DRI

SCHOOL LA

CHAPEL
ST

50

BD20

05   A   B   06   C   D   07   E   F

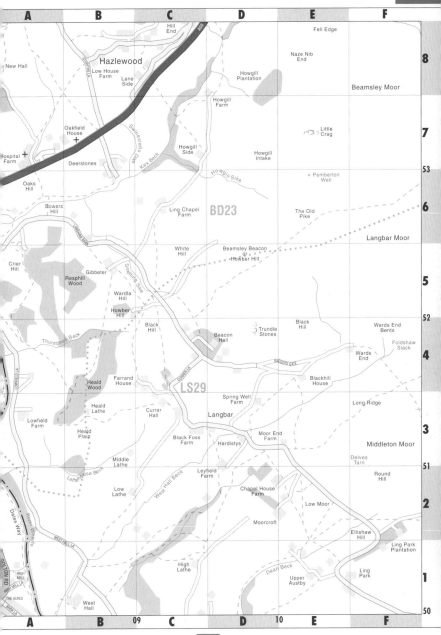

Fell Edge

Hazlewood

New Hall

Naze Nib
End

Low House
Farm
Lane
Side

Howgill
Plantation

Beamsley Moor

Oakfield
House

Howgill
Farm

Hospital
Farm

Howgill
Side

Deerstones

Little
Crag

Howgill
Intake

Oaks
Hill

Howgill Sike

Pemberton
Well

Bowers
Hill

BD23

Ling Chapel
Farm

The Old
Pike

Langbar Moor

Crier
Hill

White
Hill

Beamsley Beacon
or
Howber Hill

Gibbeter

Resphill
Wood

Wardla
Hill

Howber
Hill

Black
Hill

Trundle
Stones

Black
Hill

Wards End
Bents

Foldshaw
Slack

Thurstone's Beck

Beacon
Hall

BADGERS GATE

Wards
End

Heald
Wood

Farrand
House

LS29

Blackhill
House

Lowfield
Farm

Heald
Lathe

Currer
Hall

Spring Well
Farm

Langbar

Long Ridge

Middleton Moor

Heald
Plaip

Black Foss
Farm

Hardistys

Moor End
Farm

Delves
Tarn

Middle
Lathe

Leyfield
Farm

Round
Hill

Lathehouse Beck

West Hall Beck

Low
Lathe

Chapel House
Farm

Low Moor

Dales Way

River Wharfe

Moorcroft

Ellishaw
Hill

Ling Park
Plantation

HIGH
MILL

WEST HALL LA

High
Lathe

Dean Beck

Upper
Austby

Ling
Park

THE ACRES

BLACK LA

West
Hall

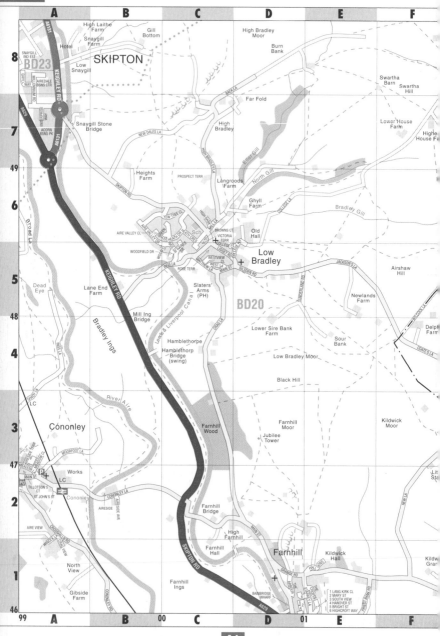

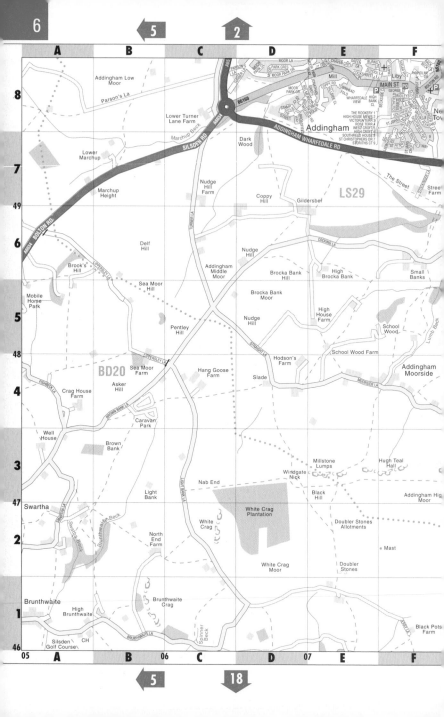

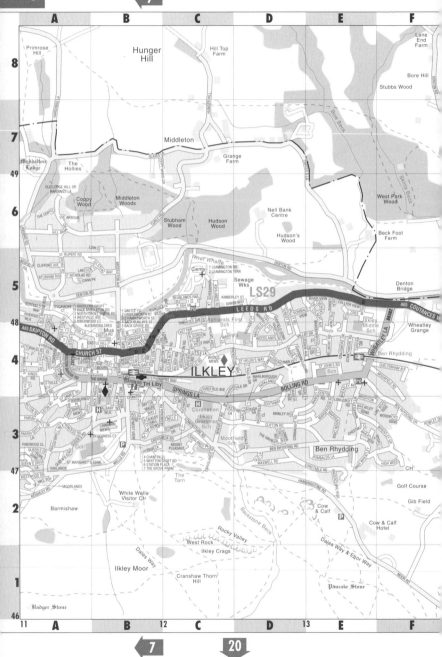

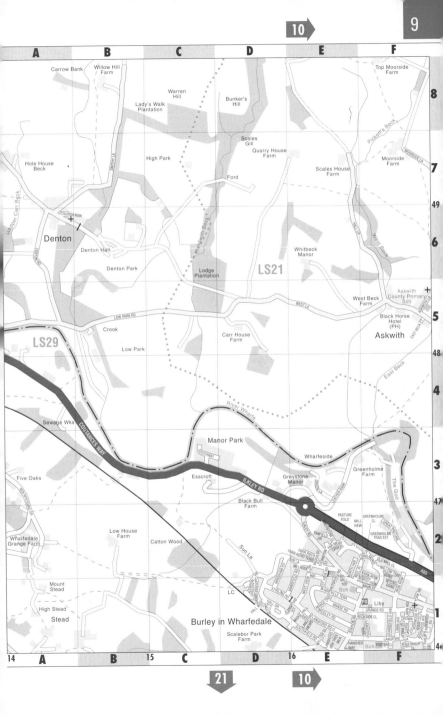

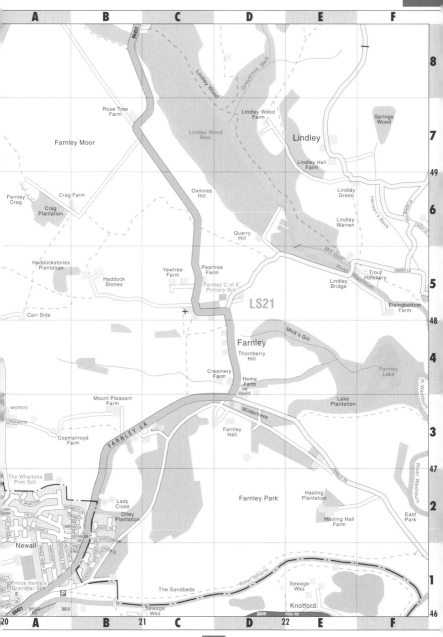

A   B   C   D   E   F

8

B6451

Lindley Wood

Greystone Beck

Rose Tree Farm

Lindley Wood Resr

Lindley Wood Farm

7

Springs Wood

Farnley Moor

Lindley

49

Lindley Hall Farm

Farnley Crag

Crag Farm

Oxmires Hill

Lindley Green

6

Crag Plantation

Lindley Warren

Hensan's Beck

COSKILLS

Haddockstones Plantation

Quarry Hill

Mill Golf

River Washburn

Trout Hatchery

Haddock Stones

Yewtree Farm

Peartree Farm

Lindley Bridge

CINDER LA

5

Farnley C of E Primary Sch

Carr Side

+

LS21

Elsingbottom Farm

48

Farnley

Mick's Gill

Thornberry Hill

4

Creamery Farm

Home Farm

Farnley Lake

THE SQUARE

Lake Plantation

R Washburn

Mount Pleasant Farm

Wilderness

3

WESTROYD

Farnley Hall

COPMANROYD

Copmanroyd Farm

FARNLEY LA

47

The Whartons Prim Sch

Farnley Park

Hasling Plantation

HEBLETT PK

2

CARR BANK

WYNBECK CR

Lady Close

WYNBECK AVE

Otley Plantation

WYNBECK CL

RIVERSIDE DR

Hasling Hall Farm

East Park

River Washburn

THE GILLS

THE CROSSWAYS

WYNBECK DR

RIVERSIDE AVE

Newall

PRINCE HENRY'S RD

TURNER CL

RIVERSIDE CL

Prince Henry's Grammar Sch

1

P

River Wharfe

The Sandbeds

Sewage Wks

B6451

Mill

BRIDGE AVE

Sewage Wks

A659 POOL RD

Knotford

46

20   A   B   21   C   D   22   E   F

A B C D E F

8

7

49

6

5

48

4

3

47

2

1

46

35 A B 36 C D 37 E F

HG3

Spofforth

Fox Heads Farm

Spofforth Park

Fox Heads Wood

Whin Lane Farm

Bowrake Farm

Royal Oak Plantation

Crag Plantation

Home Farm

HARROGATE RD

Stockeld Grange

Stockeld Park

Spring Wood

Sicklinghall Wood

Dairy Farm

Scott's Arms (PH)

HAZELDENE COTTS

Skerry Grange

Sheep Field House

Sicklinghall Rd

Linton Spring

Sicklinghall Prim Sch

THE CRESCENT

Sicklinghall

Sicklinghall Grange

Poplar House

Hill Croft Farm

LS22

Linton Spring Farm

Devonshire Whin

Devonshire Wood

Paddock House Farm

Paddock House

West Plantation

Sicklinghall House

Ebor Way

Old Wives' Wood

Lime Kiln Wood

Carlshead House

Woodhall Hotel

Ebor Way

Lawn Rein

River Wharfe

TRIP LA

LINTON COMM

Spring Wood

Ox Close

River Wharfe

Cow Wood

Whitewell House Farm

River Wharfe

Carlston Hill

Carlstonhill Farm

Woodhall Bridge

LS17

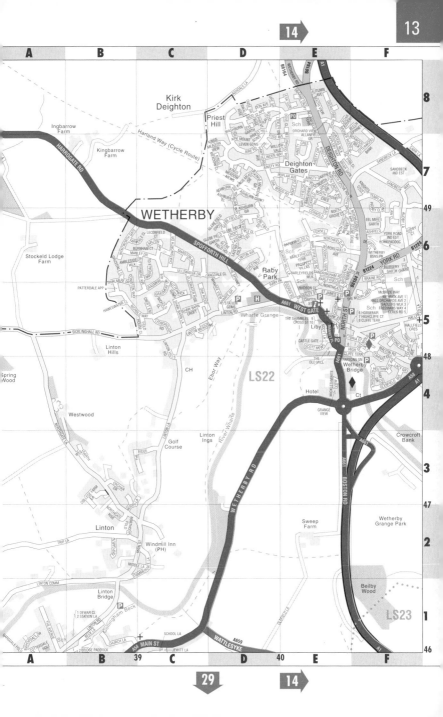

Kirk
Deighton

Priest
Hill

Ingbarrow
Farm

HARROGATE RD

Kingbarrow
Farm

Harland Way (Cycle Route)

Deighton
Gates

WETHERBY

Stockeld Lodge
Farm

SPOFFORTH HILL

Raby
Park

YORK RD

PATTERDALE APP

Linton
Hills

SICKLINGHALL RD

Wharfe Grange

WEST GATE

Castle Gate

THE SHAMBLES
CROSS ST

Liby

Wetherby
Bridge

Hotel

Wetherby
Grange Park

Crowcroft
Bank

GRANGE
VIEW

Ebor Way

River Wharfe

LS22

Westwood

Golf
Course

Linton
Ings

Linton

WETHERBY RD

BOSTON RD

Sweep
Farm

Windmill Inn
(PH)

Linton
Bridge

Collingham Beck

Beilby
Wood

LS23

1 DEWAR CL
2 STATION LA

SCHOOL LA

MAIN ST

WATTLESYKE

A659

JEWITT LA

A B C D E F

8
7
49
6
5
48
4
3
47
2
1
46

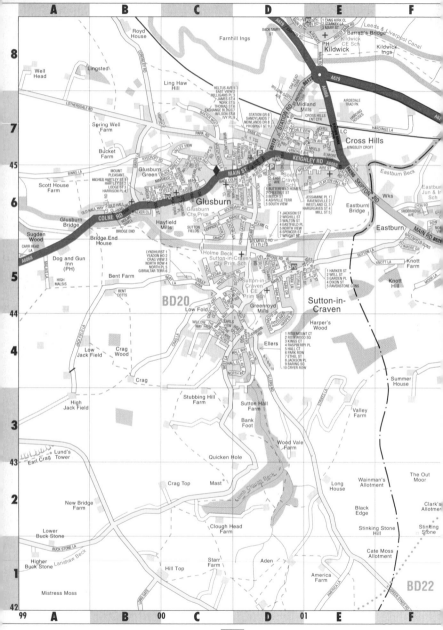

8

7

45

6

5

44

4

3

43

2

1

42

A B C D E F

Royd House

Farnhill Ings

Leeds & Liverpool Canal

Back Mary St

1 LANG KIRK CL
2 STARKEY ST
3 MARY ST

Barrett's Bridge

Kildwick
CE Sch

Kildwick
PH

Kildwick

Well Head

Lingsted

Ling Haw Hill

Spring Well Farm

Bucket Farm

KELTUS AVE 1
EAST VIEW 2
MILLIGANS PL 3
YORK ST 6
JAMES ST 4
THOMAS ST 6
EXCHANGE SQ 7
WILSON ST 8
IVY PL 9

STATION GR 6
SANDYLANDS 7
NEWLANDS DR 8
PROSPECT ST 9

AIREDALE
TRAD PK

HARDINGS LA

S Midland Mills

CROSS HILLS
ENT CTR

Cross Hills

Kingsley Croft

Scott House Farm

MOUNT PLEASANT
HIGHER HARTLEY ST 1
HARTLEY ST 2
LODGE ST 3
HARRISON PL 4

Glusburn Green

Glusburn
Cty Prim
Sch

Glusburn

1 JACKSON ST
2 WIGHILL ST
3 WALTON ST
4 EASTFIELD PL
5 NORTH VIEW
6 SPENCER ST
7 WRIGHT ST

BUTTERFIELD HOMES 1
CHESTNUT ST 2
BECK ST 3
ASHVILLE TERR 4
SOUTH VIEW 5

JESSAMINE PL 1
RAVENSVILLE 2
WESTLAND CL 3
HARGREAVES ST 4
MILL ST 5

Eastbum Beck

Eastburn
Bridge

Eastburn

Wks

Glusburn Bridge

COLNE RD

Hayfield Mills

SUTTON FIELDS

Holme Beck
Sutton-in-Craven
Cty Prim Sch

Sudgen Wood

Bridge End House

CARR HEAD

Dog and Gun Inn (PH)

Bent Farm

LYNDHURST 1
YEADON HO 2
CRAG VIEW 3
NORTH ROW 4
NORTH PL 5
GIBRALTAR TERR 6

BD20

1 HARKER ST
2 WELL ST
3 GARDEN PL
4 DIXON ST
5 RAVENSTONE GDNS

HIGH MALSIS

Low Fold

Greenroyd Mills

Sutton-in-
Craven
CE
Prim
Sch

Sutton-in-
Craven

Harper's Wood

BENT COTTS

Low Jack Field

Crag Wood

WILLOW WAY

EARLS VIEW

Ellers

1 ROSEMOUNT CT
2 ROSEWOOD SQ
3 KINGS CT
4 RASPBERRY PL
5 HALL CT
6 PARK ROW
7 ETHEL ST
8 JACKSON PL
9 BARING SQ
10 CRYER ROW

Crag

High Jack Field

Stubbing Hill Farm

Sutton Hall Farm

Bank Foot

Wood Vale Farm

Summer House

Valley Farm

Earl Crag

Lund's Tower

Quicken Hole

Lumb Clough Beck

Long House

Wainman's Allotment

The Out Moor

New Bridge Farm

Crag Top

Mast

Black Edge

Clark's Allotment

Lower Buck Stone

BUCK STONE LA

Clough Head Farm

Stinking Stone Hill

Stinking Stone

Cate Moss Allotment

Higher Buck Stone

Lanshaw Beck

Starr Farm

Hill Top

Aden

America Farm

BD22

Mistress Moss

A B C D E F

8
Silsden Golf Course
Tomling Cote Farm
Ghyll Grange
Far Ghyll Grange Farm
Brunthwaite Back

Brunthwaite Bridge (swing)
Holden Beck
Out Laith
Dirk Hill Sike

7
Holden Bridge
Howden Park Farm
Rough Holden

45
Holden Bridge (swing)
Spring Crag Wood
Robin Hood Wood
Rivock Oven

6
Low Holden Farm
Alder Carr Wood
Pinfold Hill
Mast
Rivock Edge

BD20
Holden Gate

5
Lodge Hill
Jaytail Farm
Heater

44
High Carr
Riddlesden Golf Course
Clough Beck
Marsh Farm

4
Holden Park
Carr Delph
High Wood Head
Larkfield Farm
Heights Farm

Keighley Golf Course
CH
CH
Low Wood Head
The Height

3
Low Utley
1 TURNBERRY CT
2 NURSERY CL
3 AIREVILLE ST
4 BACK AIREVILLE ST
5 ST JOHN'S CT
6 TURNVIEW CT
7 CROFT HOUSE LA
8 BACK CROFT HOUSE LA
Cemy
Leeds & Liverpool Canal
River Aire
Elam Grange

43
Syke Side
Birchwood Ave
Cemy

2
High Utley
LC
Leache's Bridge (swing)
1 BACK WAY
2 WEST BANK GR
Low Banks
21 MATTHEW CL
22 BACK RIPLEY ST
23 RICCLESDEN CT
BARLEY COTE AVE 24
BARLEY COTE AVE 25
SOUTHFIELD MOUNT 26
SOUTHFIELD AVE 27

KEIGHLEY
Greenhead Grammar Sch
Beechcliffe
Grange Middle Sch
Stockbridge

1
The Holy Family Sch
Pattie St
KEIGHLEY IND PK
1 LAWHOLME LA
2 BACK BYRL ST
3 BYRL ST
4 BACK CALEDONIA RD
5 CALEDONIA RD
6 KIRBY ST
Works
BD21
CORONATION BSNS CTR
East Riddlesden

42
High Meadow
Springfield Rd
Maple Cl
Cliffe Castle Mus
HARD INGS RD
ROTO INGS AVE
KEIGHLEY RET PK

05 A B C 06 C D 07 E F

19
8

	A	B	C	D	E	F

8

Green Gates

Gill Head

Lanshaw Delves

Green Crag

Green Crag Slack

Danger Area

Dales Way and Ebor Way

7

White Crag Moss

LS29

Twelve Apostles Stone Circle

Danger Area

High Lanshaw Dam

Lanshaw

45

White Crag

Ashlar Chair

Burley Moor

6

Square

5

BD20

Peat Edge

44

Yellow Bog

White Stones

Dales Way

Laid Stoop

Middle Beck

4

Fenny Shaw

Wicking Crag

Horncliff Well

Horncliff Beck

3

Spa Flat

Bingley Moor

Hog Hill

BD16

Cornmould Heath

Cocklake Hill

High Two Stoops

43

White Flush

Spa Dyke

Hog Hill Flat

Weecher Flat

Knaple Hill

2

Cabin Hill

Snail Green

Weecher Mouth

Weecher Brow

Low Two Stoops

Spy Hill

1

Morton Stoop

Little Graincliff

OTLEY RD

West End

Graincliff Reservoir

Eldwick Crag

Green Well Hill

Dick Hudson's or The Fleece (PH)

OTLEY RD

Eldwick Villa

OTLEY RD

Weeche Reserv

42

11	A	B	12	C	D	13	E	F

19
37

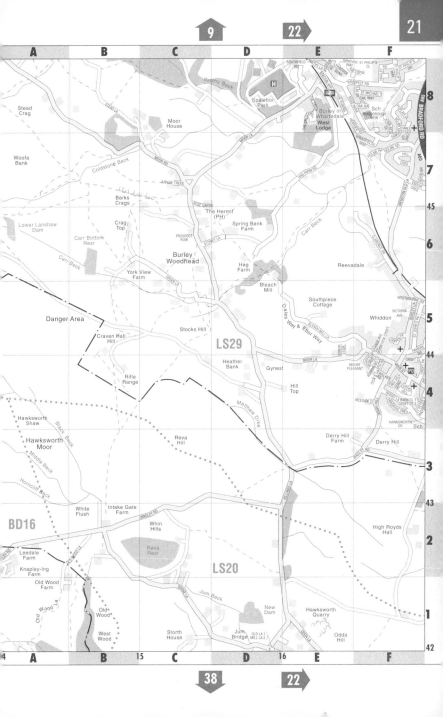

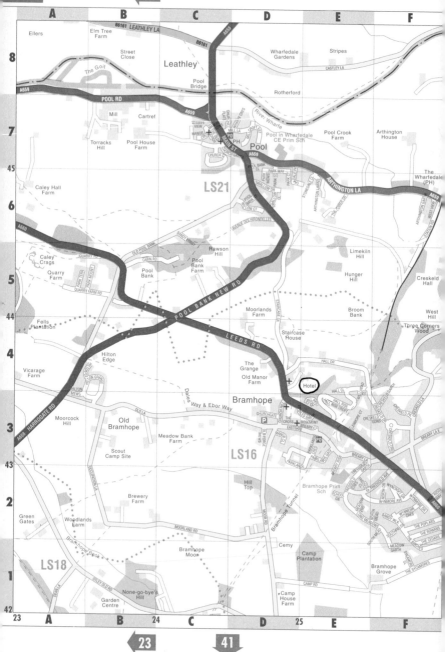

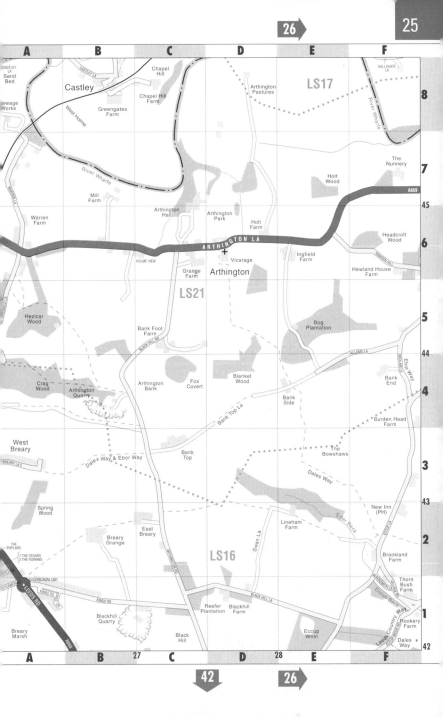

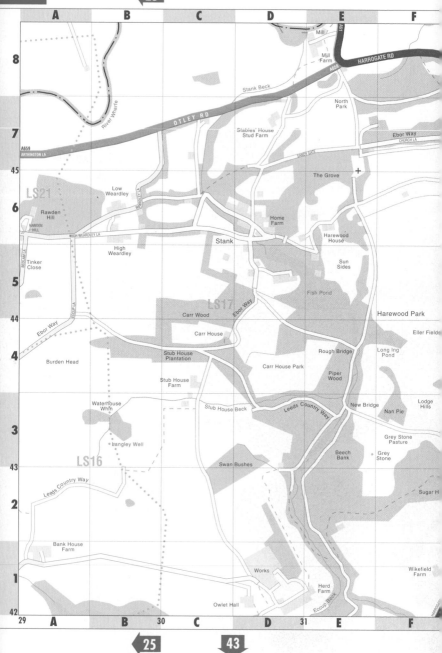

25

A   B   C   D   E   F

8

25

Mill

Mill
Farm

HARROGATE RD

A659

Stank Beck

OTLEY RD

North
Park

7

Ebor Way
CHURCH LA

A659
ARTHINGTON LA

Stables' House
Stud Farm

SANDY GATE

45

LS21

The Grove

Low
Weardley

DUBBLE LA

6

Rawden
Hill

Home
Farm

Harewood
House

RAWDEN
HILL

HIGH WEARDLEY LA

Stank

High
Weardley

Sun
Sides

BEN LANE

EGG LA

5

Tinker
Close

Fish Pond

44

LS17

Carr Wood

Ebor Way

Harewood Park

Ebor Way

Carr House

Eller Fields

4

Burden Head

Stub House
Plantation

Carr House Park

Rough Bridge

Long Ing
Pond

Piper
Wood

Stub House
Farm

New Bridge

Lodge
Hills

Waterhouse
Whfn

Stub House Beck

Leeds Country Way

Nan Pie

3

Langley Well

Grey Stone
Pasture

LS16

Beech
Bank

Grey
Stone

Swan Bushes

43

Leeds Country Way

Sugar H

2

Bank House
Farm

1

Works

Wikefield
Farm

Herd
Farm

Eccup Beck

42

Owlet Hall

29   A   B   30   C   D   31   E   F

25   43

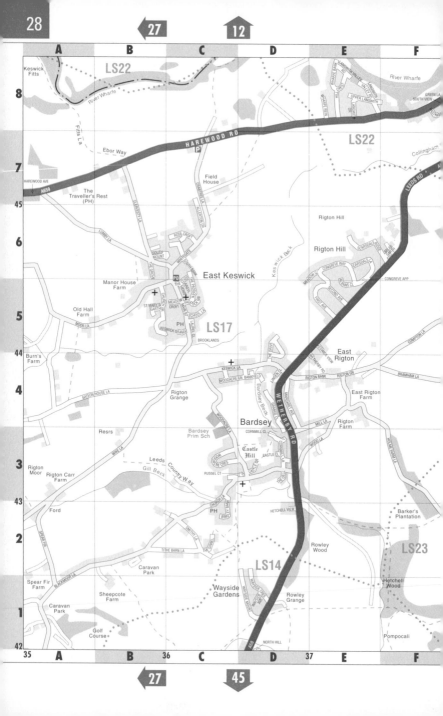

A B C D E F

8

A659
WATTLESYKE
A659

HAREWOOD RD
1 LANGWITH MEWS
2 COVERDALE GARTH
3 BISHOPDALE DRI
4 COTTERDALE HOLT
5 LINTON RD
6 DEWAR CL
7 STATION LA

MAIN ST
A659
PH

JAMES CT

8 HASTINGS CL
9 ELIZABETH CT

Collingham
Fields

Collingham

LEEDS RD

Cow Moor

LS22

Howcroft
Wood

Collingham
Moor

7

MOOR LA

45

Compton Grove

Compton La

Mast

COMPTON LA

Waver Spring
Pond

Compton

6

Dalton
Parlours

LS17

5

44

West
Woods

4

Lund
Wood

Lady
Wood

Dalton
Hill

WARRAM LA

LS23

3

Spring
Wood

DALTON LA

Old Pickhill
Rash

Hope
Hall

43

HOLME FARM LA

THORNER LA

2

Holme
Farm

Wothersome

Stubbing
Moor

Ragdale
Plantation

Bramham
Beck

TOCKER RD

Bramham
Park

Lendrick
Hills

Stubbing Moor
Plantation

Milner Beck

Terry
Lug

1

KENNELS
LA

42

A B C D E F

38

39

40

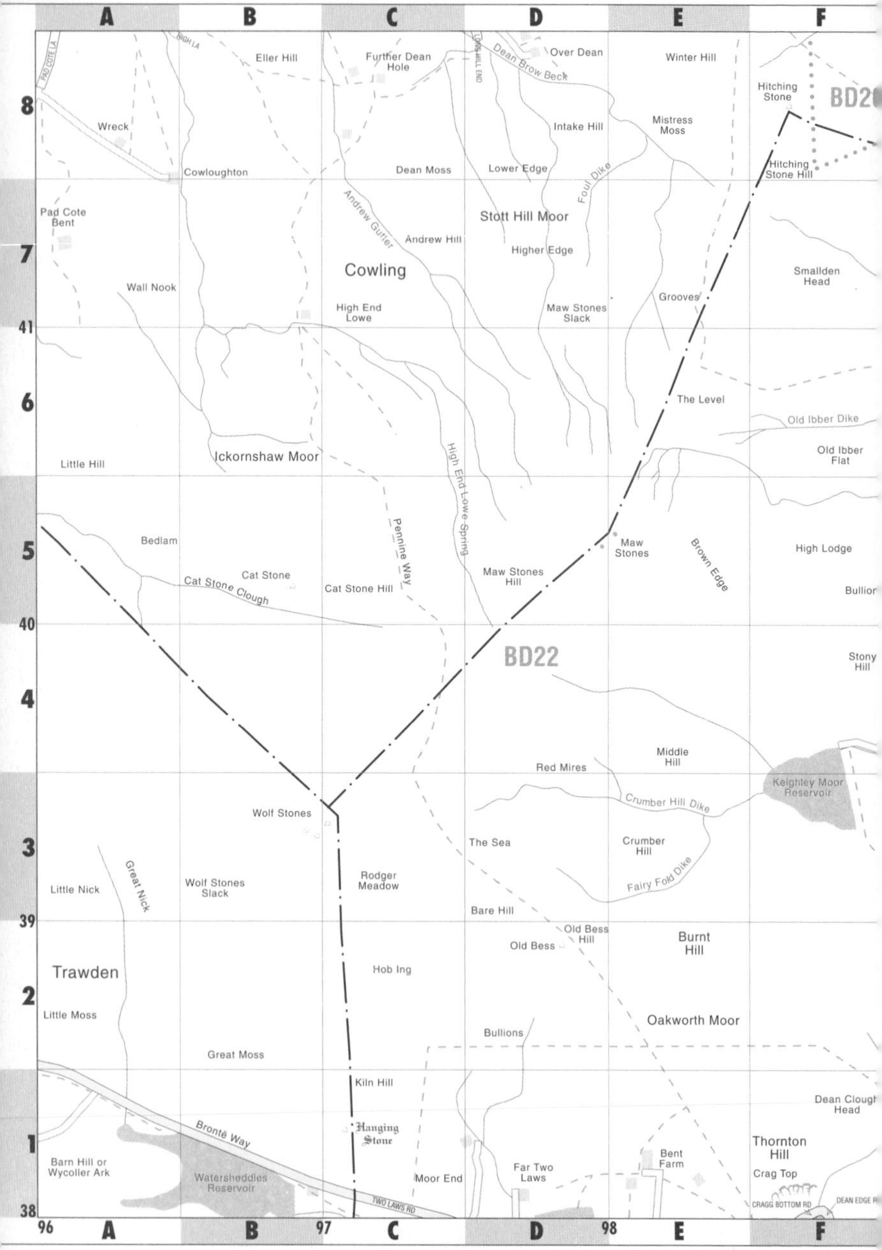
A
B
C
D
E
F
8
7
41
6
5
40
4
3
39
2
1
38
96
97
98
HIGH LA
PAD COTE LA
Eller Hill
Further Dean Hole
LONG HILL END
Dean Brow Beck
Over Dean
Winter Hill
Hitching Stone
BD20
Wreck
Intake Hill
Mistress Moss
Cowloughton
Dean Moss
Lower Edge
Foul Dike
Hitching Stone Hill
Pad Cote Bent
Andrew Gutter
Andrew Hill
Stott Hill Moor
Higher Edge
Cowling
Smallden Head
Wall Nook
High End Lowe
Maw Stones Slack
Grooves
The Level
Old Ibber Dike
Little Hill
Ickornshaw Moor
High End Lowe Spring
Old Ibber Flat
Pennine Way
Bedlam
Maw Stones
Brown Edge
High Lodge
Cat Stone
Cat Stone Clough
Cat Stone Hill
Maw Stones Hill
Bullior
BD22
Stony Hill
Middle Hill
Red Mires
Keighley Moor Reservoir
Crumber Hill Dike
Wolf Stones
The Sea
Crumber Hill
Little Nick
Great Nick
Wolf Stones Slack
Rodger Meadow
Fairy Fold Dike
Bare Hill
Old Bess Hill
Old Bess
Burnt Hill
Trawden
Hob Ing
Little Moss
Oakworth Moor
Bullions
Great Moss
Kiln Hill
Dean Clough Head
Brontë Way
Hanging Stone
Thornton Hill
Bent Farm
Barn Hill or Wycoller Ark
Watersheddies Reservoir
Moor End
Far Two Laws
Crag Top
TWO LAWS RD
CRAGG BOTTOM RD
DEAN EDGE R

49

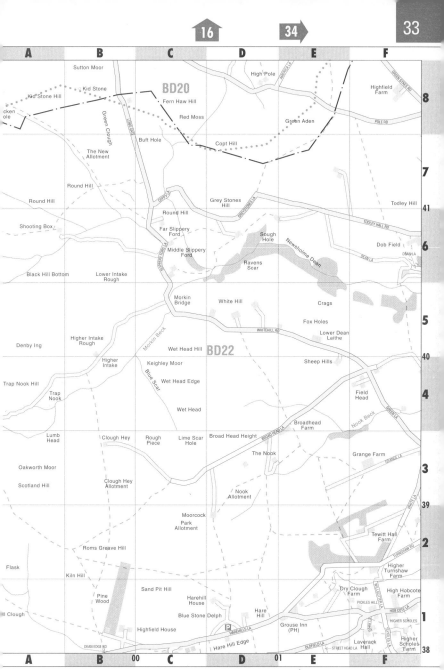

A	B	C	D	E	F

Sutton Moor

Kid Stone

BD20

Kid Stone Hill

cken ole

Fern Haw Hill

High Pole

Highfield Farm

Green Clough

Red Moss

Green Aden

POLE RD

Buft Hole

The New Allotment

Copt Hill

Round Hill

Round Hill

Round Hill

Grey Stones Hill

Todley Hill

Round Hill

Shooting Box

Far Slippery Ford

TOOLEY HALL RD

Sough Hole

Newsholme Dean

Dob Field

Middle Slippery Ford

DEAN LA

Black Hill Bottom

Lower Intake Rough

Ravens Scar

Morkin Bridge

White Hill

Crags

Fox Holes

WHITEHILL RD

Lower Dean Laithe

Higher Intake Rough

Morkin Beck

Wet Head Hill

BD22

Denby Ing

Higher Intake

Keighley Moor

Sheep Hills

Trap Nook Hill

Blue Scar

Wet Head Edge

Field Head

Trap Nook

Wet Head

GREEN LA

Lumb Head

Clough Hey

Rough Piece

Lime Scar Hole

Broad Head Height

Broadhead Farm

Nook Beck

Oakworth Moor

The Nook

Grange Farm

BROAD HEAD LA

GRANGE LA

Scotland Hill

Clough Hey Allotment

Nook Allotment

WHITE LA

Moorcock Park Allotment

Tewitt Hall Farm

Roms Greave Hill

TURNSHAW RD

Higher Turnshaw Farm

Flask

Kiln Hill

Dry Clough Farm

High Hobcote Farm

ll Clough

Pine Wood

Sand Pit Hill

Harehill House

Hare Hill

PICKLES HILL LA

HOB COTE LA

Blue Stone Delph

Grouse Inn (PH)

HIGHER SCHOLES

Highfield House

HAREHILLS LA

Hare Hill Edge

OLDFIELD LA

Laverack Hall

Higher Scholes Farm

DEAN EDGE RD

STREET HEAD LA

A	00	C	D	01	E	F

8

7

41

6

5

40

4

3

39

2

1

38

A   B   C   D   E   F

8

Coppy Hill

BD20

Whorls Farm

Green Syke Farm

Hill Clough

Far Laithe Farm

Braithwaite
1 SUNNY MOUNT
2 SOUTH VIEW
3 EXLEY HEAD VIEW
Braithwaite Sch

BD20

WESTWAY 1
BROADLANDS 2

Black Hill

RYAN

POLE RD

7

Nettle Hole

Laycock

Laycock First Sch

Guard House

Guard House Fst Sch

BD21

Calversyke Mid Sch

Nessfield Fst Sch

41

Todley Hall Farm

Lumb Hill

Goose Eye

Wood Mill Farm

Butter Clough

Intake Farm

North Beck

Works

CLIFTON

6

Clough Bank Farm

PH

Owl Hill

DEAN LA   FALLOW LA

MEADOW CRO

HOLME

NILE ST

5

Carr Laithe

True Well Hall Farm

Holme House

Park House

Bunker's Hill Farm

High Wheat Head

Browfield View

Westburn Fst Sch

Exley Head

Nessfield

40

Newsholme

Spring Wells

Lower Laithe Farm

Cemy

BD22

Branshaw Golf Course

Branshaw Moor

Brown Springs Farm

Oakba Recr Ctr

OAKWORTH RD   BD2

Oakba Sch

4

Newsholme Beck

New Laithe Farm

Branshaw Plantation

Bogthorn

Bracken Bank

THORNBANK AVE

3

Cemy   Crem

Griff Wood

Low Bank

Slack Lane Farm

Holden Park

Sykes Head
CH
1 APSLEY ST
2 ASHVILLE TERR
3 MYRTLE VIEW

KEIGHLEY RD

Bronte Mid Sch

GREYSTONES RISE   CENTRAL DR

39

Lower Turnshaw

Griff View

Lane End

Chapel Lane

Lidget

Oakworth Fst Sch

Cackleshaw
4 GREEN LA
5 HALL ST
6 CLOUGH GATE
7 LARCH CL
8 VICTORIA ST

Worth Way

Harewood Hill

Damems

BRACKEN BANK WLK 1
BRACKEN BANK CRES 2
BRACKEN BANK GR 3

2

Denby Hill

Heritage Way

Dockroyd

OAKLEIGH MEWS

1

Near Hob Cote

Green Well Farm

HEBBLE ROW

Oakworth
1 ROSEBERRY ST
2 MEADOW VIEW
3 NEW ST
4 OAKWORTH TERR

LC

Keighley & Worth Valley Rly

River Worth

Mills

VALE MILL

LONGCROFT

BACK MYRTLE TERR

BD21

HALIFAX R

LINGFIELD

38

02   A   B   03   C   D   04   E   F

33   51

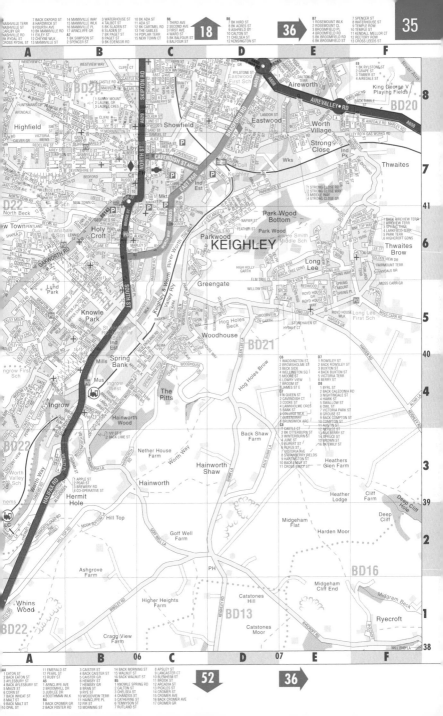

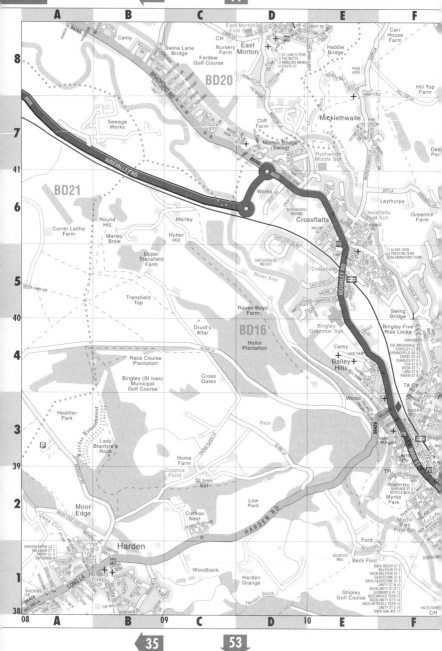

A1
1 HAZELHURST AVE
2 HAZEL BECK
3 HAZELMERE AVE

A2
1 YORK CRES
2 HEALEY LA
3 HARRIS ST
4 LEONARD'S PL
5 ASHFIELD CT

A3
1 CROSS LA
2 CHARLES ST
3 LYNDON TERR
4 NORFOLK ST
5 RUTLAND RD
6 KELL ST
7 WHITLEY ST

B
6 BACK UNITY ST S
7 OAK BANK

8 BARRAN ST
9 AMY ST
10 JARDINE RD
11 MYRTLE ST
12 SYDNEY ST
13 ELLEN ST
14 FERNBANK AVE
15 ELIZABETH ST
16 NETHER MOOR VIEW
17 EBRIDGE CT
18 AYRTON CRES

A4
1 MONK BARN CL
2 LEYBURN GR
3 WESTLEY
4 STAVELEY RD
5 STAVELEY MEWS
6 FOULDS TERR
7 PRIORY CL
8 SCARWOOD CL

F1
1 THOMPSON LA
2 COACH RD
3 ALBERT RD
4 HERBERT ST
5 FANNY ST
6 EDWARD ST
7 AMELIA ST
8 GEORGE ST
9 WILLIAM HENRY ST

A   B   C   D   E   F

8

Faweather Grange
West Wood
Intake Side Farm
Hawksworth
Hawksworth Hall Sch
OLD LA
TAVERNGATE
MAIN ST
Hawksworth C of E Primary Sch

BIRCH CLO
BD16

Ash House Farm
Potter Brow Bridge
Honey Joan Hill
Round Hill
LS20
Birkin Hill

7

Jum Beck
MILL LA
Gill Beck
Low Springs
Bradford Golf Course
Hall Croft

41

Pennythorn Hill
Sconce Crag
Low Hill
Low Springs Farm
Hawksworth Spring

6

Baildon Golf Course
Bracken Hill
LOW HILL
The Whitehouse
Lunds Farm

Acrehowe Hill

5

Windy Hill
Low Plain
Plain Side
Baildon Moor
Baildon Hill

C4
1 HIGHFIELD MEWS
2 ROCKLANDS AVE
3 ROCKLANDS PL
4 AMBLERS MEWS
5 TENTER CROFT
6 SOUTH VIEW TERR

7 STRAITS
8 TOWNGATE
9 BUNWELL FOLD
10 DELPH HILL
11 WEST GR
12 PANGUM

Hazel Head Wood
BD17

40

Ladderbanks Middle Sch
Tong Park

Hope Hill

D4
1 PERSEVERANCE ST
2 ANGEL ST
3 FLOWER MOUNT

4

Hope Farm
Dove Hall
Church Hill
The Beeches
Low Baildon
Park
BARTLE GILL VIEW
BARTLE GILL RISE
Tong Park First Sch
ST JAMES PL

3

BAILDON
Belmont Middle Sch
Baildon
Low Baildon
Hawthorn Cres
KIRKLANDS
Hoyle Court First Sch
Wks
Charlestown
River Aire
39

Midgeley Wood
Glenaire First Sch
Baildon Green
WOOD VIEW
Ferniehurst First Sch
OXFORD PL
UNION ST
OXFORD TERR
Cyprus DR 2
COTE FARM COTT
BD10

2

1 WESTLEIGH WAY
2 DEEPDALE CL
3 WESTLEIGH CL
4 BRANSDALE CL
5 ROSEDALE CL
6 BEECHTREE CT

1 KNOLL VIEW
2 LOWER GREEN
3 BANKSIDE TERRACE
4 GREEN MOUNT
5 UPPER GREEN

The Oval
Cemy
BD18

1

Higher Coach Rd
River Aire
Leeds & Liverpool Canal
Baildon Wood Bottom
Baildon Holmes
Mill
Ind Est
Wks
LEEDS RD
Perkin La

Dales Way
Mills
Recn Ctr
BD18
HELEN RD
STEAD HALL WAY

38

14   A   B   15   C   D   16   E   F

C1
1 ADELAIDE RISE
2 ALBERT ST
3 VICTORIA ST
4 WOOD ST
5 QUEEN ST
6 GEORGE ST

D2
1 IVY BANK CT
2 ROSEMONT LA
3 OAKROYD TERR
4 AIREDALE TERR

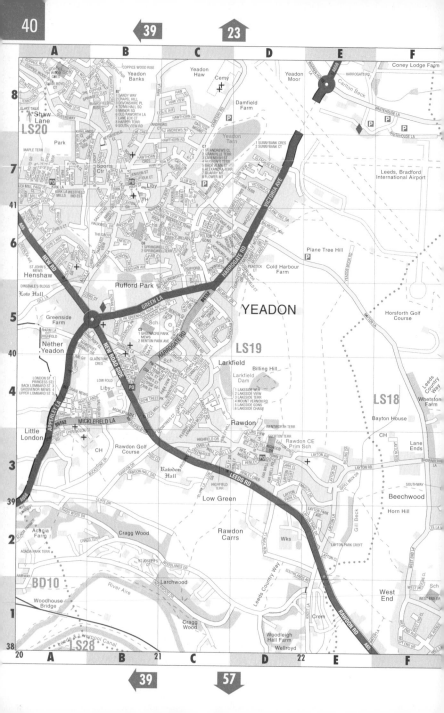

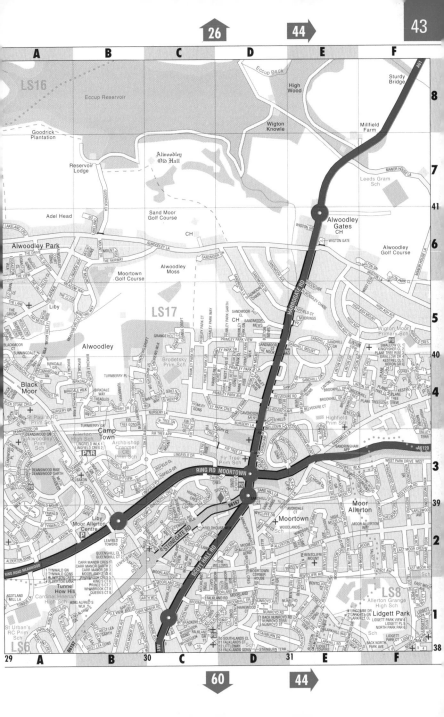

43
27

	A	B	C	D	E	F

SCHOOL LA

Leeds Golf Centre

Collier Beck

8

CH

Golf Course

Wike Ridge

Blackmoor Farm

DIAL RD

7

Wike Ridge Farm

LING LA

Sturdy Beck

Wigton Heath Farm

Shaw Hill

TARN LA

BRANDON CRES

41

Wigton Moor Whin

Brandon Hall

Hall Farm

Nursery

BRANDON CRES

6

Wigton Moor

Brandon

Brandon Grange Farm

Alwoodley Golf Course

Brandon Drain

Low Brandon Farm

Golf Course

Brandon Royd

WIKE RIDGE AVE

WIKE RIDGE VIEW

WIKE RIDGE MOUNT

WIKE

WIGTON LA

4 LONGWOOD WAY
5 SLAID HILL CT
6 CHARTWELL CT
7 BRANDON TERR
8 HARROGATE VIEW

5

CARLTON GARTH 1
OVERDALE AVE 2
RAYGILL CL 3

PLANTATION AVE

SILVERDALE

BRANDON

Slaid Hill

CH

BRIDLE PATH RD

HOLYWELL LA

HIGH ASH AVE

PLANTATION GDNS

LS17

LIBY

LUDDLE DR

ASH HILL DR

STRICKLAND

BARFIELD CRES

MIDDLETHORPE

Shadwell Park CL

MAIN ST

ASH HILL LA

40

HERON GR

OAKDENE WAY

ELMHURST

WOODLEA CT

PARK LANE

Shadwell Park GR

GATELMID DR

CHURCHFARM GARTH

ASH HILL GR

13 MIDDLETHORNE MEWS
14 MIDDLETHORNE CT

PARK CT

SHADWELL

GATESHEAD

BLIND LA

4

BRADLEY TERR

HIGHTHORNE GR

9 WOODTHORNE CROFT
10 BEECHCROFT MEAD
11 ROCHESTER MEAD
12 OAKDENE CT

Shadwell Grange Farm

Shadwell Park GR

Manor Farm

Shadwell Primary Sch

STRICKLAND

Blackwood

Oakhill

Shadwell

CHAIRVILLE GDNS

BIRCHWOOD AVE

COLLIER LA

GATELMIND LA

3

A6120

RING RD MOORTOWN

KINGSWOOD AVE

WEST PARK CHASE

Ferndale

WHINMOOR LA

WEST PARK DR W

WEST PARK DR

Woodhouse Farm

KEDLESTON RD

39

SUMMERHILL PL

WEST PARK

Greatfields Beck

RING RD SHADWELL

EARLSWOOD AVE

ROMAN

LS8

RED HALL

2

PARKVIEW

CH

Golf Course

ELMETE LA

Redhall House

1 SUMMERHILL GDNS
2 BACK ROMAN ST
3 ROMAN PL
4 BACK ROMAN PL
5 ROMAN DR
6 ROMAN MOUNT
7 WEST PARK GDNS
8 CROSS INGLEDEW CRES
9 BACK INGLEDEW CRES
10 INGLEDEW CREST

Ram Wood

Cobble Hall

1

EAST PARK

COLLETT PARK AVE

FERNWOOD

PARK COTTS

Upper Lake

Castle

Cobble Hall

Wellington Hill

RED HALL LA

DEVONSHIRE

NORTH PARK RD

GARDEN VIEW CT

Cobble Hall Golf Course

Cobble Hall Farm

RED HALL

A58

A58 WETHERBY RD

Park Villas

NEW PARK

11 PARK VILLA CT
12 ROBINWOOD CT
13 FERNWOOD CT
14 WEDGEWOOD CT

Mansion Hotel

Waterloo Lake

KINGSMEAD DR

38

St Edmund's Sch

Roundhay Park

15 WEDGEWOOD GR
16 WEDGEWOOD CT

32	A		**33**	C	**34**	E	F

43
61

| A | B | C | D | E | F |

8

Headley
Plantation

HEADLEY
COTTS

Headley
Hall

Bramham Moor

Brick House
Farm

Jackdaw Crag
Quarries

7

Spen Common

Hill of
Comfort

Crag
Wood

41

Headley Bar

Warren House
Farm

6

Hazelwood
Cottages

Beck House
Farm

Home
Farm

5

Stutton

LS24

CHANTRY LA

White Quarry
Farm

40

Castle
Farm

Peggy
Ellerton
Farm

Lowpark
Farm

4

Hazel Wood

South App

Hazelwood
Castle

Hazelwood
Park

3

SOUTH App

Lodge
Farm

Harper Rash

39

LS25

2

Hayton Wood

Mawfield
Spring

1

Bullen Wood

Newstead
Farm

Cock Beck

Castle
Wo

38

Hayton
House

| 44 A | B | 45 C | D | 46 E | F |

A B C D E F

8
West End
Moor Lodge Farm
TWO LAWS RD
CRAGG BOTTOM RD
Crag Bottom
Throstles Nest
Dean Clough
Far Dean Field Farm
Pennine Way
NEW LAITHE RD
River Worth
Bronte Way
Silver Hill
Dean Fields
Grey Stones
Old Snap
Ponden Resr
Whitestone Clough
Whitestone
7
SCAR TOP RD
37
Ponden Slack
Ponden Wood
6
The Wage of Crow Hill
Upper Ponden
Ponden Clough
Stanbury Bog
Lower Ridge Green
Bracken Hill
Ponden Clough Beck
Birch Brink
Red Mires Clough
Ponden Kirk
BD22
Middle Moor Hill
Stanbury Moor
Goaten Hill
5
Low Block Dikes
Red Mires Flat
Middle Moor
Middle Moor Clough
Blue Scar Clough
Withins Slack
36
Alcomden Stones
Lower Withins
Scar Hill
Sandy Hill
4
Boft Hole
Tang Brink Flat
Walshaw Dean
Haworth to Hebden Bridge Wlk
South Dean Beck
Withins
Crumber Dike
Crumber Red Hill
Crumber Red Dike
Black Sike Hill
Black Sike
Withins Height
Top Withins
Rough Dike
Crumber Hill
3
Greave Stone Clough
Burnt Hill Dike
Burnt Hill
Delf Hill
Pennine Way
Withins Flat
35
Burnt Hill Flat
Round Hill
Green Hole
Shoulder Nick
Rushbed Top
2
Grey Fosse Clough
Withins Height End
Dick Delf Hill
Near Oxenhope Edge
Walshaw Dean Upper Resr
Great Hill
Higher Spring Hole
Black Dike
Black Edge
Round Hill Moor
Middle Hill
HX7
Dean Stones Edge
Middle Moor
1
Lower Sough
34

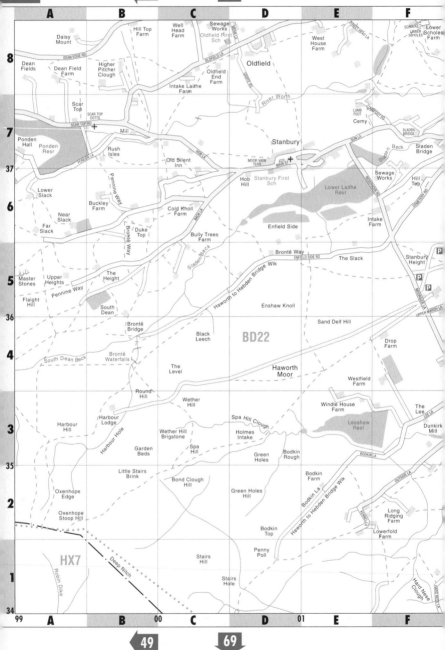

	A	B	C	D	E	F

8

Daisy Mount

Dean Fields

Dean Field Farm

Hill Top Farm

Well Head Farm

Higher Pitcher Clough

Sewage Works

Oldfield First Sch

Oldfield End Farm

Oldfield

West House Farm

SCHOLES

LOWER SCHOLES

Lower Scholes Farm

DEAN EDGE RD

OLDFIELD LA

STREET RD

STREET SIDE LA

Intake Laithe Farm

River Worth

Scar Top

7

SCAR TOP COTTS

SCAR TOP RD

Mill

LUMB FOOT

Cemy

LUMBFOOT RD

SLADEN BRIDGE

Ponden Hall

Ponden Resr

Rush Isles

Old Silent Inn

Stanbury

SUN LA

Sladen Beck

Sladen Bridge

PONDEN LA

HOB LA

MAIN ST

MOOR VIEW TERR

37

Penning Way

Lower Slack

Buckley Farm

Cold Kholl Farm

Hob Hill

Stanbury First Sch

Lower Laithe Resr

Sewage Works

Hill Top

CEMETERY RD

6

Near Slack

Far Slack

Duke Top

BACK LA

Bully Trees Farm

Enfield Side

Intake Farm

Brontë Way

Sladen Beck

5

Master Stones

Upper Heights

The Height

Brontë Way

ENFIELD SIDE RD

The Slack

Stanbury Height

P

Pennine Way

Haworth to Hebden Bridge Wlk

P

Flaight Hill

South Dean

Enshaw Knoll

UPPER MARSH LA

ROOLEY LA

P

36

Brontë Bridge

Black Leech

Sand Delf Hill

Drop Farm

4

South Dean Beck

Brontë Waterfalls

The Level

BD22

Haworth Moor

Westfield Farm

The Lee

LEE LA

Round Hill

Wether Hill

Windle House Farm

3

Harbour Hill

Harbour Lodge

Harbour Hole

Wether Hill Brigstone

Spa Hill Clough

Holmes Intake

Leeshaw Resr

Dunkirk Mill

Garden Beds

Spa Hill

Green Holes

Bodkin Rough

BODKIN LA

35

Little Stairs Brink

Bond Clough Hill

Green Holes Hill

Bodkin Farm

OXTEN LA

Oxenhope Edge

Bodkin La

Haworth to Hebden Bridge Wlk

Long Ridging Farm

2

Oxenhope Stoop Hill

Bodkin Top

Penny Poll

Lowerfold Farm

KEBBLE LA

HX7

Deep Nilch

Stairs Hill

1

Robin Dike

Stairs Hole

Herd Ness Clough

HERD NESS RD

34

| 99 | A | | 00 | B | C | | D | 01 | E | | F |

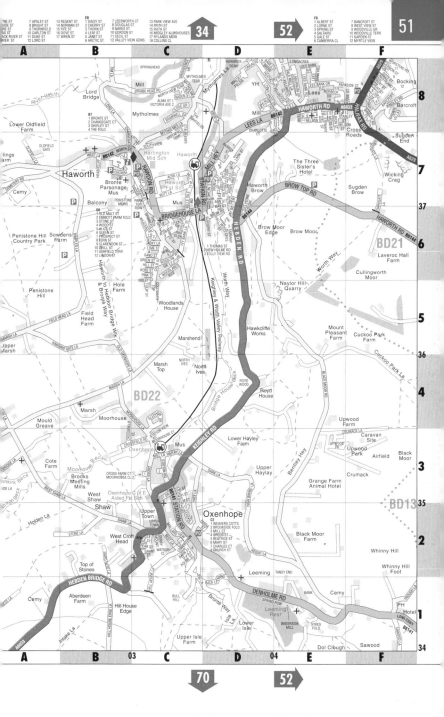

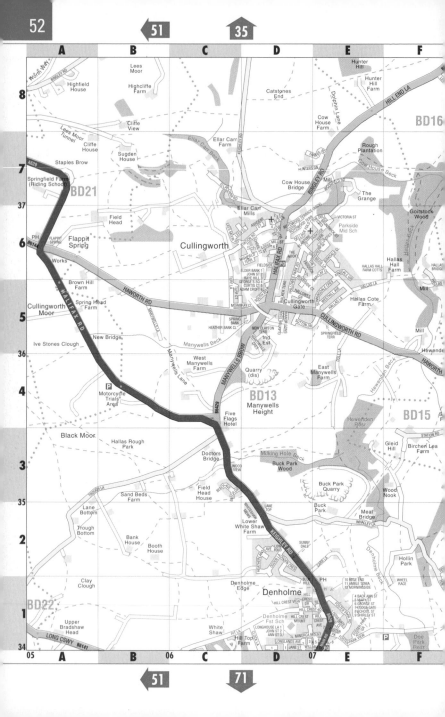

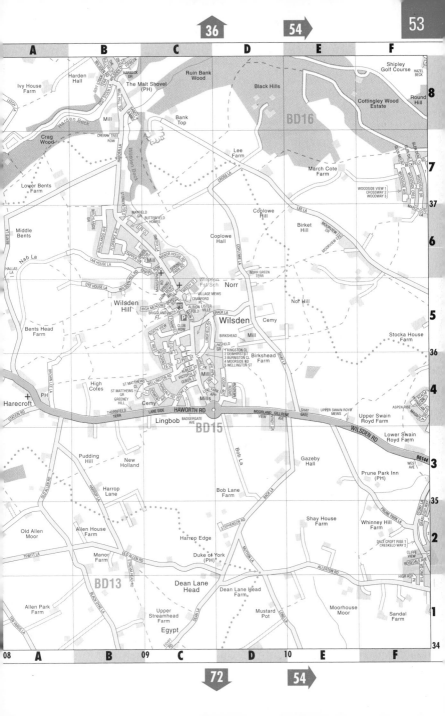

55
39

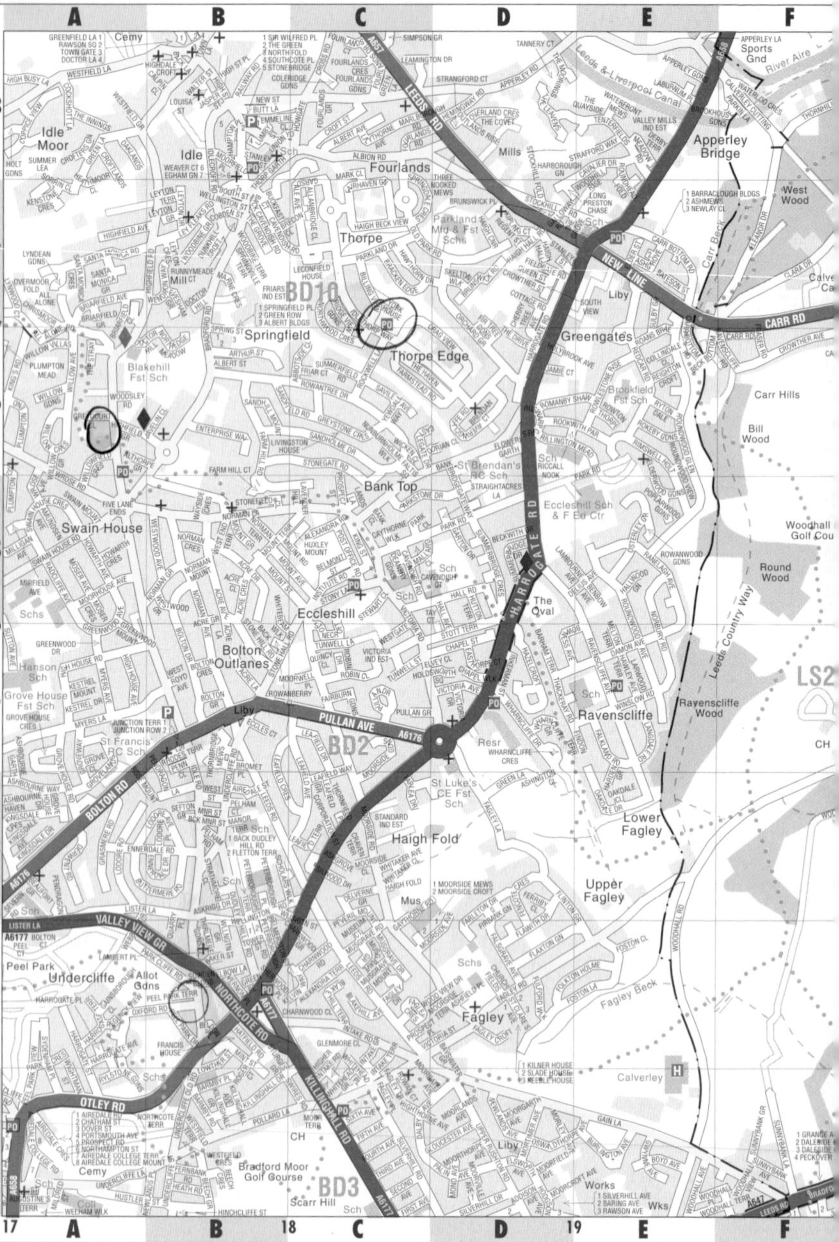
A
B
C
D
E
F
8
7
37
6
5
36
4
3
35
2
1
34
17
18
19
Idle Moor
Idle
Fourlands
Thorpe
Mills
Apperley Bridge
West Wood
Leeds & Liverpool Canal
River Aire
Sports Gnd
BD10
Springfield
Thorpe Edge
Greengates
Blakehill Fst Sch
Carr Hills
Bill Wood
Bank Top
Swain House
Eccleshill
Eccleshill Sch & F Ed Ctr
Woodhall Golf Cou
Round Wood
The Oval
Bolton Outlanes
Ravenscliffe
Ravenscliffe Wood
Leeds Country Way
LS2
BD2
St Luke's CE Fst Sch
Haigh Fold
Lower Fagley
Upper Fagley
Peel Park
Undercliffe
Allot Gdns
Fagley
Fagley Beck
Calverley
Bradford Moor Golf Course
BD3
Scarr Hill
Cemy
LEEDS RD
NEW LINE
CARR RD
HARROGATE RD
PULLAN AVE
BOLTON RD
VALLEY VIEW GR
NORTHCOTE RD
OTLEY RD
KILLINGHALL RD
A657
A658
A6176
A6177
A647

55
75

D1
1 HARKER TERR
2 HUDSON ST
3 STANHALL AVE
4 SPRINGFIELD TERR
5 CONWAY ST
6 WILSONS YD
7 DAWSON ST
8 WILLIAM ST
9 WEST TERRACE ST
10 WEST GROVE ST

D2
1 BECKBURY CL
2 BECKBURY ST
3 PROSPECT TERR
4 NEW PARK WLK
5 DONALD ST
6 PROVIDENCE ST
7 MELBOURNE ST
8 TENNYSON ST
9 ARMSTRONG ST
10 ANDREW ST

11 ARNGLIFFE GARTH
12 PROSPECT SQ
13 POPLAR SQ
14 ASHVILLE TERR
15 WEST VIEW

D3
1 GLADSTONE ST
2 OAKWELL TERR
3 MARSDEN ST
4 ANDREW ST
5 TURNER ST
6 EBENEZER ST
7 HAINSWORTH SQ
8 GAMBLES HILL
9 OLD FOLD
10 ST JOHN'S AVE

E1
1 TEMPERANCE ST
2 BODOCCK ST
3 CAVENDISH SQ
4 PROVIDENCE PL
5 PRIMROSE HILL
6 ASHFIELD GR

E2
1 BRANSBY CT
2 TURBARY AVE
3 FERN TERR
4 GROVE ST
5 NORTH VIEW TERR
6 KEIGHLEY PL

F2
1 VICTORIA TERR
2 GRANVILLE ST
3 ROSEBERY TERR
4 STANNINGLEY CT
5 HARRISONS AVE
6 BROAD LA
7 BRITANNIA ST
8 BRITANNIA CL

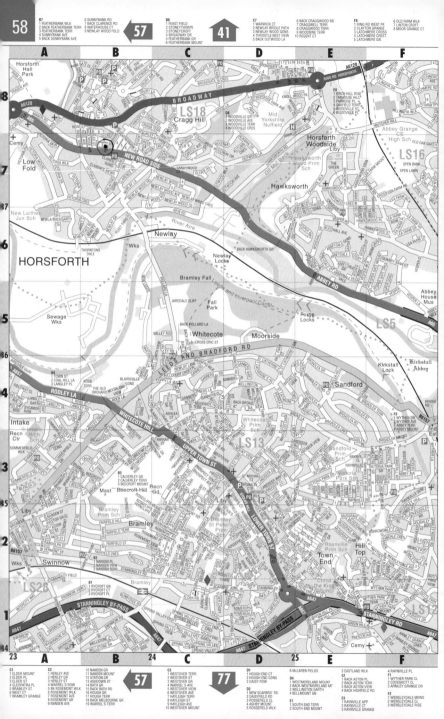

58

B7
1 FEATHERBANK WLK
2 BACK FEATHERBANK TERR
3 FEATHERBANK TERR
4 SUNNYBANK AVE
5 BACK SUNNYBANK AVE

6 SUNNYBANK RD
7 BACK CLARENCE RD
8 WATERHOUSE CT
9 NEWLAY WOOD FOLD

B8
1 FEAST FIELD
2 STONEYTHORPE
3 STONEYCROFT
4 BROADWAY DR
5 FEATHERBANK GR
6 FEATHERBANK MOUNT

C7
1 WARWICK CT
2 NEWLAY BRIDLE PATH
3 NEWLAY WOOD GDNS
4 THROSTLE NEST VIEW
5 BACK OUTWOOD LA

6 BACK CRAGGWOOD RD
7 CRAGGWELL TERR
8 CRAGGWOOD TERR
9 CRAGGWOOD TERR
10 REGENT CT

F8
1 RING RD WEST PK
2 TANHOUSE HILL
3 PARADISE PL
4 OAKFIELD TERR
5 WOODVILLE GR
6 WOODVILLE PL

E8
1 BIRCH HILL RISE
2 TANHOUSE HILL RISE
3 PARADISE PL
4 OAKFIELD TERR
5 WOODVILLE GR
6 WOODVILLE PL

F8
6 OLD FARM WLK
7 LINTON CROFT
8 MOOR GRANGE CT

57 ◄

41

C1
1 ELDER MOUNT
2 ELDER PL
3 ELDER ST
4 CLEOPATRA PL
5 BRAMLEY ST
6 WEST CT
7 BRAMLEY GRANGE

C2
1 HENLEY AVE
2 HENLEY GR
3 HENLEY ST
4 WARREL'S ROW
5 ROSEMONT WLK
6 ROSEMONT WLK
7 ROSEMONT AVE
8 ROSEMONT GR
9 NANSEN AVE

10 NANSEN GR
11 NANSEN MOUNT
12 STATION GR
13 ASHDOWN ST
14 BATH GR
15 BACK BATH RD
16 HOUGH GR
17 HOUGH TERR
18 BACK MELBOURNE GR
19 WARREL'S TERR

C3
1 WESTOVER TERR
2 WESTOVER ST
3 WESTOVER GR
4 WARREL'S AVE
5 WESTOVER VIEW
6 WESTOVER AVE
7 HAYLEIGH TERR
8 HAYLEIGH ST
9 HAYLEIGH AVE
10 WESTOVER MOUNT

D1
1 HOUGH END CT
2 HOUGH END GDNS
3 DAISY ROW

D4
1 WESTMORELAND MOUNT
2 BACK WESTMORELAND MT
3 WELLINGTON GARTH
4 BELLMOUNT GN

D3
1 NEW SCARBRO' RD
2 DAISYFIELD RD
3 ROSSEFIELD CL
4 ASHBY MOUNT
5 ROSSEFIELD WLK

6 McLAREN FIELDS

E1
1 SOUTH END TERR
2 SOUTH END MOUNT

E3
1 RAYNVILLE APP
2 RAYNVILLE CT
3 RAYNVILLE GRANGE

3 EASTLAND WLK

E9
1 BACK ASTON CT
2 BACK ASTON TERR
3 BACK ASTON VIEW
4 BACK HIGHFIELD RD

4 RAYNVILLE PL

F1
1 WYTHER PARK CL
2 COCKSHOTT CL
3 ARMLEY GRANGE DR

F2
1 WENSLEYDALE MEWS
2 WENSLEYDALE CL
3 WENSLEYDALE RISE

57 ◄

77

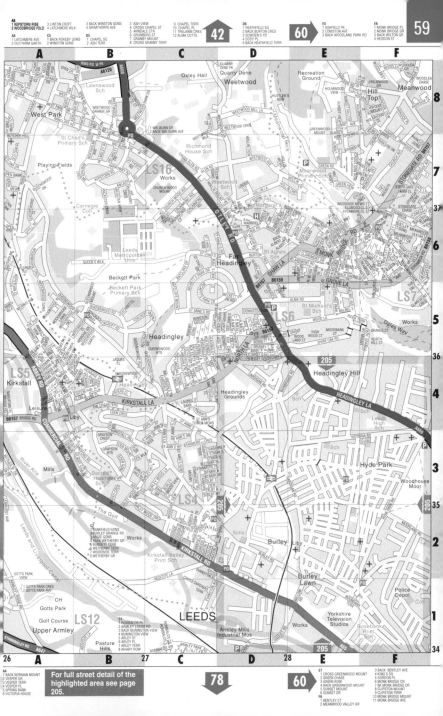

A5
1 KEPSTORN RISE
2 WOODBRIDGE FOLD

A6
1 LATCHMERE AVE
2 OLD FARM GARTH

3 LINTON CROFT
4 LATCHMERE WLK

B5
1 BACK WINSTON GDNS
2 GRIMTHORPE AVE

C5
1 BACK ROKEBY GDNS
2 WINSTON GDNS

D5
1 CHAPEL SQ
2 ASH TERR

3 ASH VIEW
4 CROSS CHAPEL ST
5 ARNDALE CTR
6 GRUNBERG ST
7 GRANBY MOUNT
8 CROSS GRANBY TERR

9 CHAPEL TERR
10 CHAPEL PL
11 TRELAWN CRES
12 ALMA COTTS

42   60   59

D6
1 HEATHFIELD SQ
2 BACK BURTON CRES
3 SOWDEN'S YD
4 ODDY PL
5 BACK HEATHFIELD TERR

60

E5
1 ASHFIELD PK
2 CONISTON AVE
3 BACK WOODLAND PARK RD

E6
1 MONK BRIDGE PL
2 MONK BRIDGE GR
3 BACK WILTON ST
4 HEDDON ST

A4
1 BACK NORMAN MOUNT
2 VESPER GR
3 VESPER TERR
4 VESPER PL
5 SPRING BANK
6 VICTORIA HOUSE

For full street detail of the highlighted area see page 205.

78

C1
1 ROMBALDS PL
2 ARMLEY GRANGE RD
3 BACK NUNINGTON VIEW
4 NUNINGTON VIEW
5 ARLEY ST
6 ARLEY PL
7 ARLEY TERR
8 AVIARY ROW

60

E7
1 CROSS GREENWOOD MOUNT
2 GREEN CHASE
3 GREEN ROW
4 BACK GREENWOOD MOUNT
5 SUNSET MOUNT
6 SUNSET DR

F6
1 BENTLEY CT
2 MEANWOOD VALLEY GR

3 BACK BENTLEY AVE
4 KING'S SQ
5 GORDON PL
6 MONK BRIDGE DR
7 BK MONK BRIDGE DR
8 CLIPSTON MOUNT
9 CLIPSTON TERR
10 MONK BRIDGE MOUNT
11 MONK BRIDGE AVE

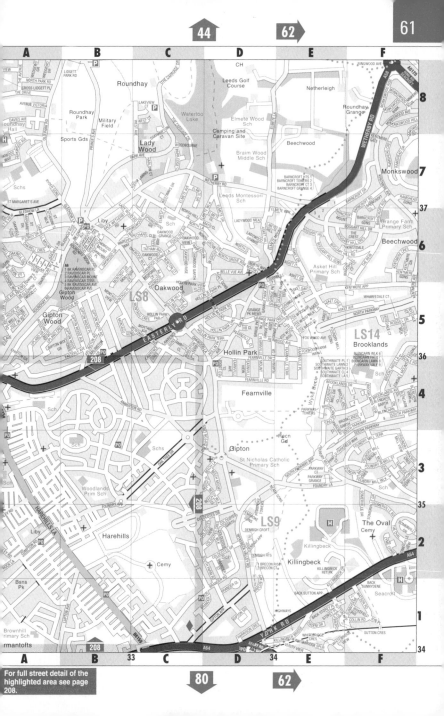

For full street detail of the highlighted area see page 208.

80   62

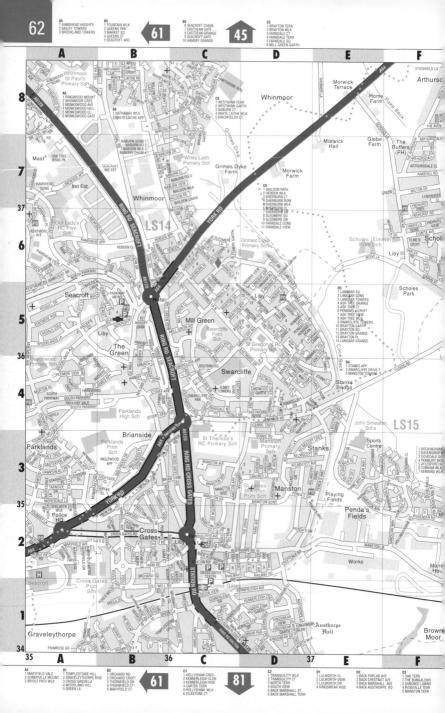

A5
1 RAMSHEAD HEIGHTS
2 BAILEY TOWERS
3 BROOKLAND TOWERS

B5
1 FOUNTAIN WLK
2 QUEENS PAR
3 MARKET SQ
4 QUEENS CT
5 SEACROFT ARC

B5
6 SEACROFT CHASE
7 EASTDEAN GATE
8 EASTDEAN GRANGE
9 SEACROFT GATE
10 HANSBY GRANGE

C5
1 BRAYTON TERR
2 BRAYTON WLK
3 FARNDALE CT
4 FARNDALE TERR
5 FARNDALE SQ
6 MILL GREEN GARTH

61 ◄   **45** ▼

A8
1 RINGWOOD MOUNT
2 WHINMOOR CRES
3 MONKSWOOD AV
4 MONKSWOOD HILL
5 MONKSWOOD CL
6 MONKSWOOD GATE

A8
1 RINGWOOD MOUNT
2 WHINMOOR CRES
3 MONKSWOOD AV
4 MONKSWOOD HILL
5 MONKSWOOD CL
6 MONKSWOOD GATE

B8
1 HATHAWAY WLK
1 WHITE LAITHE APP

C8
1 WESTWINN VIEW
2 WESTWINN GARTH
3 BALDON CT
4 WHITE LAITHE WLK
5 BIRCHFIELDS CT

C6
1 BAILDON PATH
2 HEBDEN WLK
3 SHERBURN CT
4 SHERBURN ROW
5 SHERBURN RD
6 SHERBURN WLK
7 SHERBURN SQ
8 SLEDMERE SQ
9 SLEDMERE GN
10 FARNDALE GDNS
11 FARNDALE VIEW

D5
1 LANGBAR SQ
2 LANGBAR GDNS
3 LANGBAR TOWERS
4 ASH TREE GRANGE
5 ASH TREE CT
6 PENNWELLCROFT
7 ASH TREE VIEW
8 ASH TREE WLK
9 SWARCLIFFE TOWERS
10 BRAYTON GARTH
11 BRAYTON SQ
12 BRAYTON GRANGE
13 BRAYTON PL
14 BRAYTON GRANGE

D4
1 STANKS APP
2 SWARCLIFFE DRIVE E
3 MANSTON TOWERS

1 ROCKINGHAM
2 RAVENSWOOD
3 DOVEDALE GA
4 PEMBURY MO
5 AYLSFORD SQ
6 COBHAM WLK
7 KEMSING WLK

61 ◄   **81** ▼

A2
1 MARYFIELD VALE
2 SOMERVILLE MOUNT
3 BRIDLE PATH WLK

B1
1 TEMPLESTOWE HILL
2 GRAVELEYTHORPE RISE
3 CROSS GREEN LA
4 WOODLAND HILL
5 GREEN LA

B2
1 ORCHARD RD
2 ORCHARD CROFT
3 THORNFIELD DR
4 THORNFIELD CT
5 MARYFIELD CT

C1
1 HOLLYSHAW CRES
2 KENNERLEIGH GLEN
3 KENNERLEIGH RISE
4 CARTER PAR
5 HOLLYSHAW WLK
6 SILKSTONE CT

C2
1 TRANQUILITY WLK
2 TRANQUILITY CT
3 NORTH TERR
4 SOUTH VIEW
5 BACK MARSHALL ST
6 BACK MARSHALL TERR

D1
1 LULWORTH CL
2 LULWORTH VIEW
3 LULWORTH DR
4 KINGSWEAR RISE

D2
1 BACK POPLAR AVE
2 BACK CHESTNUT AVE
3 BACK MARSHALL AVE
4 BACK AUSTHORPE RD

D3
1 OAK TREE
2 THE BUNGALOWS
3 SANDBED LAWNS
4 ROSEVILLE TERR
5 MANSTON TERR

63 47

LS15

The Ridge

Bankside Plantation

Potterton Beck

Cock Beck

Leyfield Farm

Folly Corner

Barwick Bank

The Bell

Barwick Lodge Plantation

Chantryhill Plantation

Hungerhills Plantation

Willowgarth Plantation

Cherry Strip

Old Wood

LS15

Home Farm

Aberford Park

Wilderness

Parlington Gardens

Hangings Plantation

The Terraces

LS25

Gamekeepers Cottage

PARLINGTON LA

The Staith Cottage

Bathingwell Plantation

Parlington Hollins

Fox Covert

Parlington Park

Park House Farm

Lilly Pit Cottage

Wakefield Lodge

Hook Moor Cottage

Beech Plantation

Sutton Dyke

ABERFORD RD

B1217

Hawk's Nest Bungalow

M1

Hawk's Nest Wood

The Weigh House

A642

A656

47

B1217

A658

Ridge Road Farm

Becca Banks

St John's Garth

DALE
PIM
ROH CFT
ABBS

Green Hill

HIGHFIELD RD

BECCA LA

Cock Beck

Aberford Bridge

BRIDGE CROFT

Aberford

PARLINGTON HOUSE

CATTLE LA

PARLINGTON VILLAS

BEECH VIEW

SCH

P0

Aberford CE Sch

WINDMILL RISE

White House Farm

Aberford Almshouses

Hicklam House

Hicklam Mill Farm

COLLIER LA

B1217

Dawson's Wood

Hook Moor

LOTHERTON LA

Cooper Wood

STOCKING LA

A1(M)

Football Ground

The Rein

FIELD LA

63 83

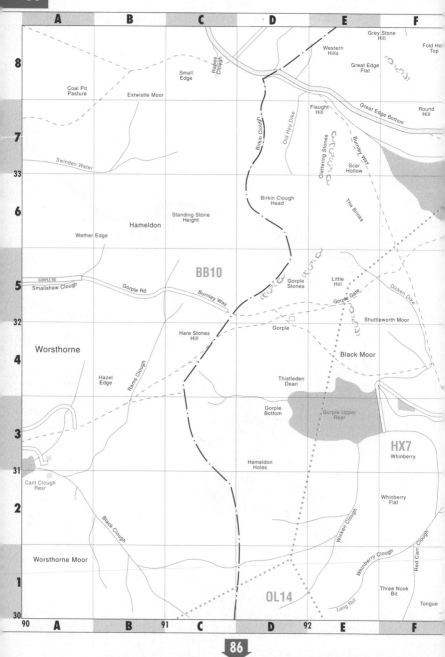

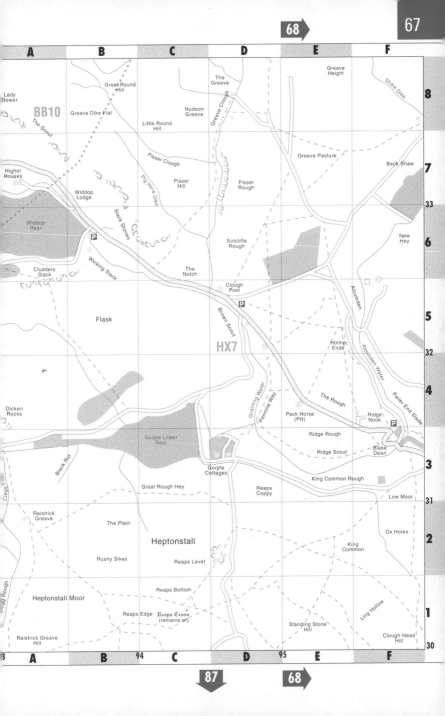

67
49

A   **B**   **C**   **D**   **E**   **F**

Shaw Dike Hill
Walshaw Dean Middle Resr
Lower Fold Hill
Black Clough

Fenny Lees

Hole Head Rushes

Black Clough Hill

White Swamp

Hole Head

The Lodge

Pennine Old Dike

Notch Brink

Old Dike Hill

Flaight Hill

7

Walshaw Dean Lower Resr

White Hill

Story Dike

Clay Dike

33

Black Nursery

Rushy Dike

Calf Hey Clough

6

The Grough

Dean Gate

High Rakes

Round Hill

Wadsworth Moor

Crumpe Hill

White Hill

Shackleton Moor

Hare Edge

5

Hoar Nib

Haworth to Hebden Bridge Walk

Rowshaw Clough

Lower Edge

Higher Edge

Navvy Head

32

Delf Brink

BABY HOUSE HILL LA

Hardibut Clough

New Laithe Moor

Jack Allotment

Knoll Flat

4

New Laithes Farm

New Cote

Rowshaw

Shackleton Knoll

Horodiddle

Nook

Black Dean

Over Wood

COPPY LA

Coppy

3

Widdop Gate

Hebden Dale

Walshaw

KILN LA

Stony Edge

SUNNY BANK RD

Haworth to Hebden Bridge Walk

Hebden Water

Dole

31

High Laithe

Black Hill

Abel Cross

Laithe

Ferny Beds

High Greenwood House

Charles Rough

2

Coppy

High Greenwood Farm

Lady Royd Edge

Hamlet

Crimsworth Dean

Hoar Royd

Walshaw Wood

Kid Stones

Turn Hill

White Mires

Pisser Clough

Lady Royd Farm

Crimsworth Dean Beck

1

Mould Grain

Hardcastle Crags

Lady Royd

Abel Cote

Abel Cote Wood

Bridge Clough

Clough Head Hill

Boothroyd Farm

30

HX7

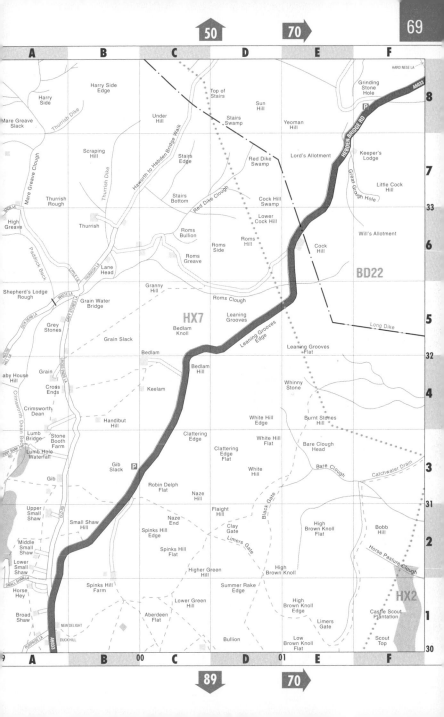

A **B** **C** **D** **E** **F**

A6033
HEBDEN BRIDGE RD
Dike Nook
HARD NESE LA
Waggon & Horses (PH)

Rough Top

Sawood Farm
Sawood
White Hill
Brontë Way
Delf Hill

8

Mast

Near Peat La

HILL HOUSE EDGE LA

Moor Close Hill

Isle La

Nan Scar

Stony Hill Clough

Foster Dike

Harden Clough

Pickles Rough

Far Peat La

Oxenhope Moor

White Moor La

White Moor

BD22

Thornton Moor Conduit

Hambleton La

7

33

Great Peat Moss

Rushworth's Allotment

Nab Water Rough

Great Clough

Little Clough

Hambleton Top

Waterloo Clough

NAB WATER LA

Nab Rough

Sawood Moss

6

Nab Water

Bentley Allotment

Buck Bean

Nab Hill

5

Long Dike

Deep Gulf

BD13

32

Spa Clough Head

Warley Moor Resr

Spa Flat

Hollin Hill

Spa Clough

Clunter Clough

Fly Landing Stages

Wind Farm

4

Catchwater Drain

Midgley Moor

Robin Rock

Skirden Edge

HX7

Ferny Brinks

Luddenden Brook

COLD EDGE RD

Knoll

Skirden Head

Ovenden Moor

3

Parcel Beds

HX2

Dean Head Stony Edge

31

Upper Dean Head Resr

Fill Belly Flat

Fill Belly

Withens Hotel (PH)

WITHENS NEW RD

2

Sheep Cote Brinks

Warley Moor

Lower Dean Head Resr

1

PADDOCK CROSS RD

Durham

Fulshaw

Long Pit

Rocking Stone

Rocking Stone Flat

WITHENS RD

30

02 **A** **B** **03** **C** **D** **04** **E** **F**

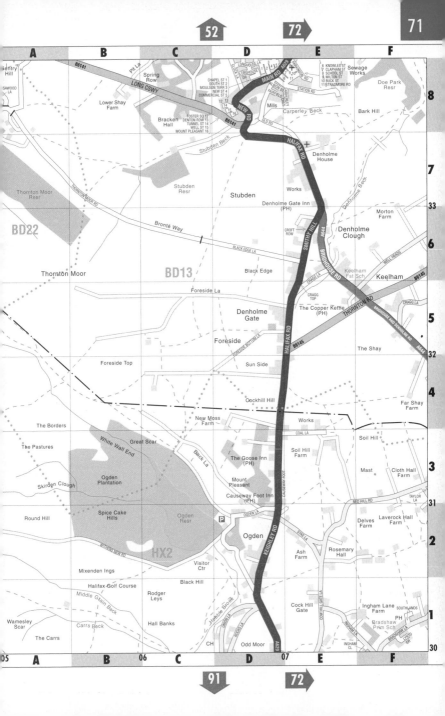

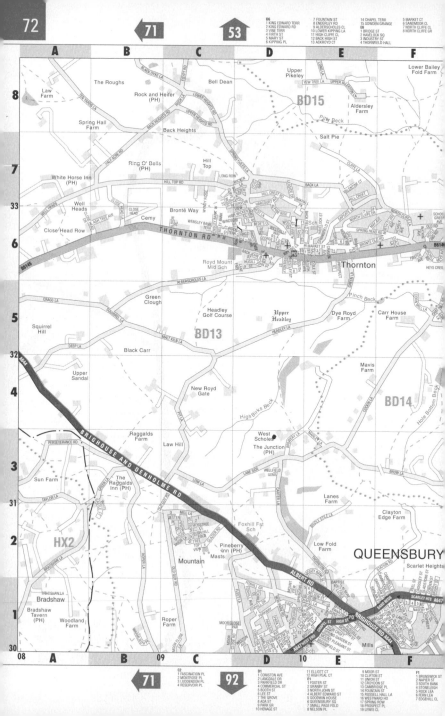

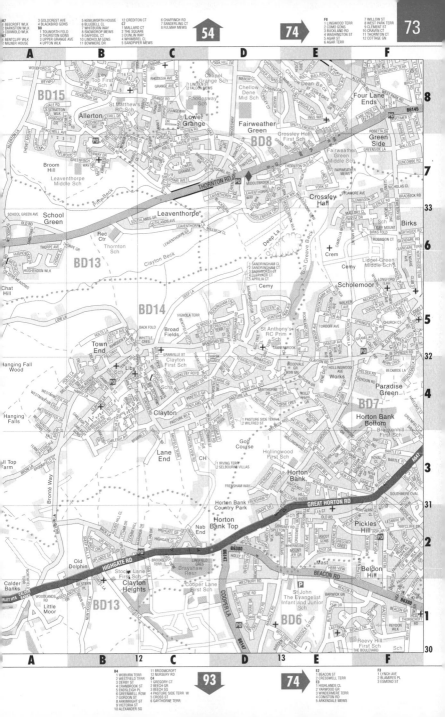

A7
1 BEECROFT WLK
2 BARKSTON WLK
3 COXWOLD WLK
B7
6 BENTCLIFF WLK
7 MILNER HOUSE

3 GOLDCREST AVE
4 BLACKBIRD GDNS
C7
1 TOLWORTH FOLD
2 THURSTON GDNS
3 UPPER GRANGE AVE
4 UPTON WLK

5 KENILWORTH HOUSE
5 BLUEBELL CL
7 WHITBURN WAY
8 SNOWDROP MEWS
9 DAFFODIL CT
10 LINDHOLM GDNS
11 BOWMERE DR

12 CREDITON CT
C7
1 MALLARD CT
2 THE SQUARE
3 DUNLIN WAY
4 WHIMBREL CL
5 SANDPIPER MEWS

6 CHAFFINCH RD
7 SANDERLING CT
8 FULMAR MEWS

F8
1 LINGWOOD TERR
2 COMO GDNS
3 BUCKLAND RD
4 WASHINGTON ST
5 AGAR ST
6 AGAR TERR

7 WILLOW ST
8 WEST PARK TERR
9 CLEMENT ST
10 CRAVEN CT
11 THORNTON CT
12 COTTAGE GN

B4
1 WOBURN TERR
2 WESTFIELD TERR
3 DERBY ST
4 CRANBROOK ST
5 ENDSLEIGH PL
6 GREENWELL ROW
7 GORDON ST
8 AINWRIGHT ST
9 VICTORIA ST
10 ALEXANDER SQ

11 BROOMCROFT
12 NURSERY RD
C4
1 GREGORY CT
2 BEECH GR
3 BEECH SQ
4 PASTURE SIDE TERR W
5 CROSS ST
6 GAYTHORNE TERR

E2
1 BEACON ST
2 CRESSWELL TERR
E3
1 HIGHLANDS CL
2 YARWOOD GR
3 WINDERMERE TERR
4 CONISTON RD
5 ARKENDALE MEWS

F3
1 LYNCH AVE
2 BLAMIRES PL
3 ESMOND ST

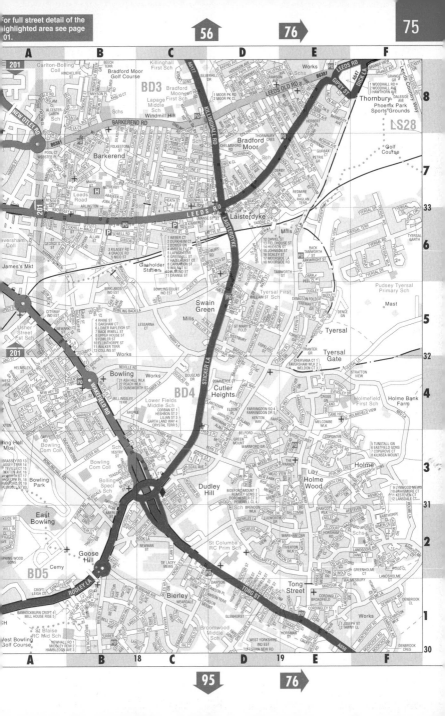

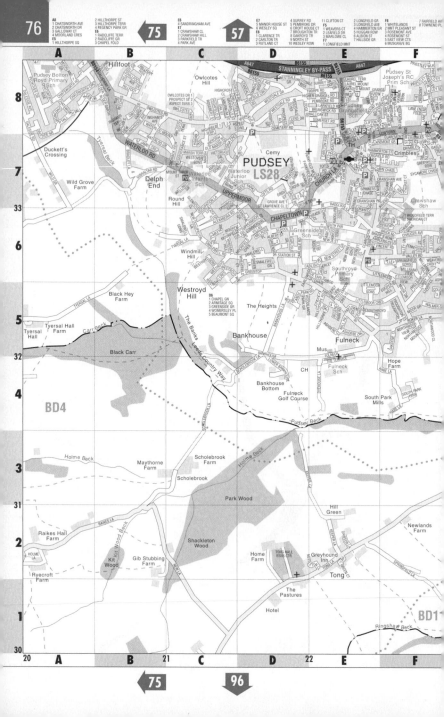

A8
1 CHATSWORTH AVE
2 CHATSWORTH ST
3 GALLOWAY CT
4 MOORLAND CRES
E5
1 HILLTHORPE SQ

2 HILLTHORPE ST
1 HILLTHORPE TERR
2 REGENCY PARK GR
E6
1 RADCLIFFE TERR
2 RADCLIFFE GR
3 CHAPEL FOLD

E6
1 SANDRINGHAM AVE
2 WESLEY SQ
E7
1 CLARENCE TR
2 CRAWSHAW HILL
3 PARKFIELD TR
4 PARK AVE

E7
3 MANOR HOUSE ST
6 WESLEY SQ
E8
1 CLARENCE TR
2 CARLTON TR
3 RUTLAND CT

4 SURREY RD
6 PEMBROKE DR
6 CROFT HOUSE CT
7 BROUGHTON TR
8 OAKROYD TR
9 NORTH ST
10 WESLEY ROW

11 CLIFTON CT
F5
1 WEAVERS CT
2 LEAFIELD DR
3 MARLOWE CL
F7
1 LONGFIELD MNT

2 LONGFIELD GR
3 LONGFIELD AVE
4 HAMMERTON GR
5 HUGGAN ROW
6 ALBION ST
7 HILLSIDE GR

F8
1 WHITELANDS
2 MNT PLEASANT ST
3 ROSEMONT AVE
4 ROSEMONT ST
5 EAST VIEW CTS
6 MUSGRAVE RG

7 FAIRFIELD A
8 TOWNEND PL

75

57

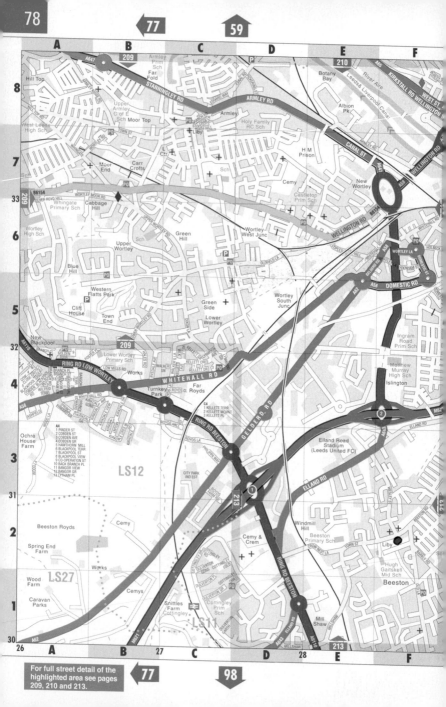

For full street detail of the
highlighted area see pages
209, 210 and 213.

For full street detail of the
highlighted area see pages
211, 212, 214 and 215.

A7
1 TEMPLE VIEW RD
2 GLENSDALE MOUNT
3 GLENSDALE ST
4 CHARLTON MOUNT
5 CHARLTON GR
6 CHARLTON ST

7 EAST PARK MOUNT
8 EAST PARK TERR
9 GARTON VIEW
10 BACK EAST PARK RD
11 RAINCLIFFE MOUNT
12 RAINCLIFFE TERR
13 ECCLESBURN TERR

79

A8
1 APPLETON WAY
2 BACK GLENTHORPE TERR
3 VINERY GR
4 VINERY RD
5 BACK ST ELMO GR
6 ST ELMO GR

61

7 CROSS IVY MOUNT
8 IVY VIEW
9 BACK IVY MOUNT
10 IVY CRES
11 BACK IVY AVE
12 BACK IVY ST
13 RAINCLIFFE ST

B8
1 DAWLISH PL
2 BACK DAWLISH MOUNT
3 BACK DAWLISH AVE
4 BACK DAWLISH RD
5 BACK VICTORIA GR
6 BACK VICTORIA AVE

7 CROSS DAWLISH GR
8 HEPTON CT

E8
1 BACK WILLIAM AVE
2 WILLIAM AVE
3 VERITY VIEW

F8
1 PRIMROSE GARTH
2 ROCK TERR
3 SELBY RD
4 LEVITA PL

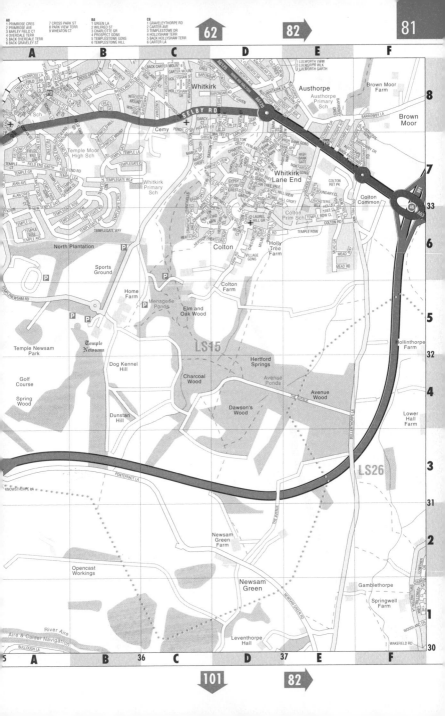

81
63

| | A | B | C | D | E | F |

8

Brown Moor

BARROWBY LA

M1

NANNY GOAT LA

Leeds Country Way

BARROWBY LA

The Elms

BARWICK RD

PARKINSON LA

Garforth

TOWN END

ABERFORD RD

STATION RD

Garforth STATION

7

Bradbury Grange

Barrowby

Barrowby Park

Barrowby Hall

SALEM PL 1
KENSINGTON TERR 2
PROVIDENCE PL 3
WOODLEIGH AVE 4
BARLEYHILL LA 5
FIDLER LA 6
FIDLER CL 7

Moor Garforth

CHAPEL LA

MAIN ST

OAK

WHITE RD
MARLOWE CT

33

Warren House

LS15

KINGSWAY GARTH

Garforth Inf Sch

QUEENSWAY

HALLDL

CYPRESS

LYNDON

WILLOW DR

BEECH DR

CHURCH

Liby

Church Garforth

A63

6

PROVIDENCE PL

LOWTHER TERR

SELBY RD

Swillington Common

Brookfield House

BARLEYHILL RD

WESTBOURN

KINGSWAY

SUMMERHILL DR

Lidgett

KINGS CROFT Sch

LIDGETT LA

LIDGETT CT

BEECH GR

LUTHER

Garforth Com Coll

GLENDALE AVE 1
PENTLAND DR 2
GLEBELANDS CL 3
HOLMAN AVE 4
MERIDEN AVE 5

WINDERMERE DR

HIGHFIELD DR

5

Waterloo Manor

HAWTHORNE TERR

Wis

RINGWAY

WESTBOURNE AVE

WESTBOURNE GR

NELSON CROFT

West Garforth

ROCKLEY GRANGE GDNS

SELBY RD

LS25

ASHROYD

ARRAN CL

ARRAN DR

A63

32

Hollinthorpe Farm

LIDGE DR

Hotel

FARNDALE CT 6
MANLEY CT 7
CARLTON DR 8
CHEVIOT CT 9
THE LEA 10
LONG MEADOW GATE 11

B6137

Field House

Southfield Bungalow

Kippax North Jun & Inf Sch

B6137

4

Hollinthorpe

Upperhall Farm

Quarry

Mount Pleasant Farm

WAKEFIELD RD

BRIGGS LA

Leeds Country Way

Brecks Farm

Brecks Wood

Kippax Beck

LEEDS RD

Sparrow Hall

BRECKS LA

3

LS26

Kippax Common

VALLEY MOUNT

GREEN AVE

31

WHITECLIFFE DR

WHITECLIFFE RISE

ASCOT RD

WESTFIELD

2

NEVILLE

CLIFFE

CHURCH LA

Swillington Prim Sch

GOODY CROSS LA

GOODY CROSS

Owlett Hall Farm

EARLSWOOD CRES

1

HILL CREST CL

THE GREAT

PLEASANCE

SPRINGWELL

LIDGE RD

ST MARY'S AVE

PRESTON

Swillington

Little Preston

7 PRIMROSE HILL DR
8 PRIMROSE HILL GR

CHURCH LN DR PARK
1 SPRINGWELL AVE
2 WOODLEY GR
3 WOODLND LA
4 WOODLN DR
5 WOODLND AVE

PRIMROSE HILL

OXFORD CRES

Townclose Wood

Townclose Hills

30

A642

38

81

39

40

102

64
84

A   B   C   D   E   F

ROTHERTON WAY
Imfield
sns Pk
WHITE ROSE
AVE

East Garforth
Prim Sch

BRIERLANDS LA
NEWRYDD

ABERFORD RD

ASH
TERR

8

Ash
Plantation

Well House
Farm

Old
Micklefield

CHURCHVILLE
TERR

East
Garforth

BAR
MOUNT

STIRLING WAY

MEADOW RD

THE
OVAL

EDINBURGH
AVE

CAERNARVON
AVE

STURTON GRANGE LA

SKIPTON CL
DOVER ST
CHEPSTOW CL
ATHLONE RISE

CONISBOROUGH
LA
APPLEBY WK
INVERNESS

CHURCH LA

CHURCHVILLE
AVE

ST MARYS
WLK

7

East
Garforth

Three Acre
Plantation

33

Cemy

1 NINELANDS VIEW
2 GREENACRE CT

HILLSIDE

WOODLANDS DR
ELDER SQUARE

Sturton Grange
Farm

Roman Ridge
Bridge

Ninelands
Prim Sch

WELLAND DR
AIREDALE DR
WITHAM WAY
FOSSE WAY

NINELANDS
SPUR

RIBBLESDALE AVE

Stub
Wood

Garforth Green Lane
Prim Sch

CRIMPLE
GN

6

DERWENT

EASTWOOD
GN
HAZELWOOD AVE

BRENT AVE

Warren
Farm

5

GARFORTH

LS25

Wtr
Twr

Garforth Cliff
Park

LONG
MEADOW
GATE

RYE HOUSE AVE

Peckfield
Quarry

32

Garforth
Cliff

SELBY RD

Peckfield
House
Farm

4

A63

Roach Grange
Farm

Roach
Hill

Limekiln
House

PECKFIELD
BAR

Warren
House

GOODCOMB
PL

SANDGATE LA

Quarryfield
Plantation

Peckfield Common

The Fruit
Gardens

Shuttocks
Wood

Warrenhouse
Plantation

3

31

The
Hills

Sandgate La

LEEDS RD

GREENFIELD
VALE

Kippax

Kippax
Greenfield
Prim Sch

MANOR GARTH

PEMBROKE
RISE

Sandgate La

Ledston Luck
Enterprise Park

RIDGE RD

Ledston
Luck

LEDSTON LUCK VILLAS

Sheepcote
Wood

2

Kippax Ashtree
Prim Sch

SANDGATE

CLIFE CRES

CHURCH LA

LEDSTON LUCK

Sheepcotes
Farm

THE GROVE

Kippax
Ashtree Prim

HIGH ST

C1
1 PARK LA
2 LONGDIKE LA
3 CORONATION BGLWS

1

THE CLOSE
WELL LA

Mount
Pleasant

THE MOUNT

BICKERDIKE
DR

HALL PARK RISE
THE WAKE

Ledston
Engine

A656

B6137

30

A   B   42   C   D   43   E   F

A1
1 THE GREEN
2 CROSS HILLS GDNS
3 CROSS HILLS CT

B1
1 ROGER FOLD
2 MALT KILN LA
3 LONGDIKE CT
4 MOUNT PLEASANT
5 MOUNT PLEASANT GDNS
6 PARK VIEW
7 HALL PARK CROFT

103
84

A B C D E F

8

Old Micklefield

Hartly Wood Cottages

LAITH STAID LA
Huddleston Hall

ST HELEN'S DR
CHURCH CL
Grange Farm

Hartly Wood

Huddleston Old Wood

7

Manor House Farm

Micklefield CE Prim Sch

1 CHURCHVILLE AVE
2 CHURCHVILLE TERR
3 ST MARY'S WLK

Micklefield

Sheep Dike Sewage Works

33

Newthorpe Farm

P
RAILWAY COTTS

Micklefield

6

PIT LA
PROSPECT TERR 1
CLIFF TERR 2
WEST VIEW 3

JOHNSTON LA

Brookfield House

Newthorpe Barrack

Newthorpe Grange

New Micklefield

Highroyds Wood

Newthorpe Beck

HALL LA

Newton Farm

5

Peckfield Quarry

Woodlands

Castle Hills

Highfield

Newthorpe Quarry

LC

The New Inn (PH)

LS25

HIGHFIELD LA

32

Micklefield Plantation

Peckfield Plantation

4

A63

SELBY RD

A63

A1(M)

WHITECOTE LA

Quarryfield Plantation

The Boot and Shoe (PH)

3

Beacon Plantation

Pointer Farm

B1222

South Milford

Whitecote Plantation

31

Wellington Plantation

Ledston Lodge

Peckfield Lodge

WESTFIELD LA

2

Ledston Park

Hundred Acre Plantation

NEW RD

Scat House Farm

Long Plantation

1

Sheepcote Farm

Old Vicarage

PASKEL

Dale Plantation

Selby Fork Hotel

A1(M)

30

WF10

44 A B 45 C D 46 E F

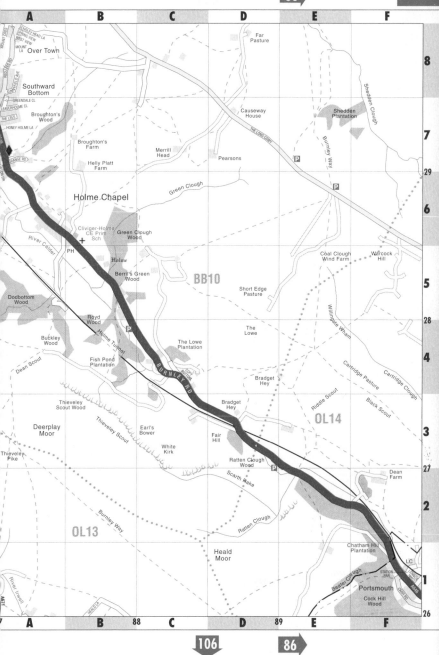

A   B   C   D   E   F

8

Sheddon
Edge

Sheddon
Top

White
Hill

HX7

BB10

Black
Hameldon

North Grain

Hoar Side

Crooker
Hill

7

Hoar Side
Top

Rush Candle Clough

29

Hoof Stones
Height

The
Lead Mine

Noah Dale Water

Stiperden
Moor

6

Lead Mine Clough

Moss Crop

Stiperden
Bar House

Stiperden
Slack

THE LONG CSWY

Moss Crop
Hill

5

Stansfield
Moor

Bent's
Pasture

Cold
Soil

OL14

28

Stiperden House
Farm

Stiperden
Bank

Hoppet

4

Coal Clough

Paul Clough

Burnley Way

Bank Top
Farm

NEW RD

Upper
Mount

Sportsman's
Arms
(PH)

Burnt Edge
Pasture

Lower Mount
Farm

Cross
Hill

Higher
Intake

NEB RD

Hawks
Stones

Keb
Bridge

3

Coal Clough
Farm

Ford

Pudsey Clough

MOUNT LA

GALE LA

SHORE LA

DEAN LA

Redmires Water

Orchan
House
Farm

Nant
Wood

27

Higher
Green End

GALE LA

Shore
Law

Dyke
Farm

BLUE BELL LA

SHORE LA

FOREST LA

Reddish Shore
Rocks

Bride
Stones

2

Whitaker
Naze

Dawk Hole
Wood

Mount
Pleasant
Farm

Shore

Blue Bell
Farm

Hudson
Bridge

Pudsey

Hartley
Royd
Farm

Hudson
Moor

Liby

BURNLEY RD

Mast

Back
Wood

Clunters

Calderdale
Way

Kit
Hill
How
Gate

STATION RD

Cornholme
Jun & Inf
Sch

A646

POR

BURNLEY RD

BURLEY HOL

CURLEW ST

Cornholme

Vale

River
Calder

A646

Cat
Hole

JUMPS LA

1

26

90   A   B   91   C   D   92   E   F

81
1 BROWN BIRKS ST
2 DAISY BANK ST
3 PEAR PL
4 PEAR ST
5 SPRING VILLAS
6 STANSFIELD TERR
7 CORNHOLME TERR
8 OAKLEIGH TERR
9 SUNNY BANK TERR
10 GLADSTONE ST

1 BURN ST
2 CARRFIELD VILLAS

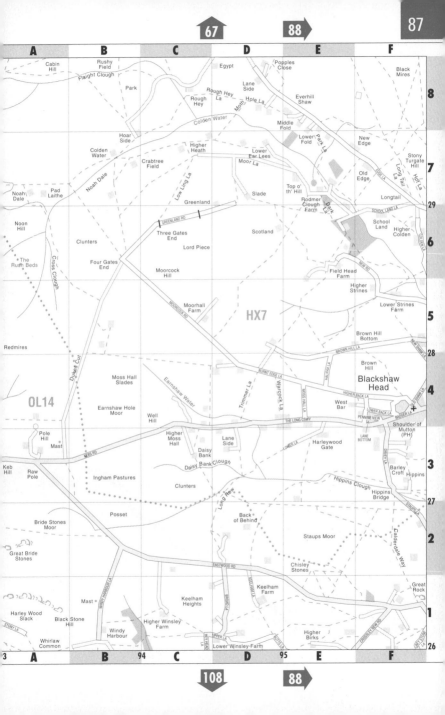

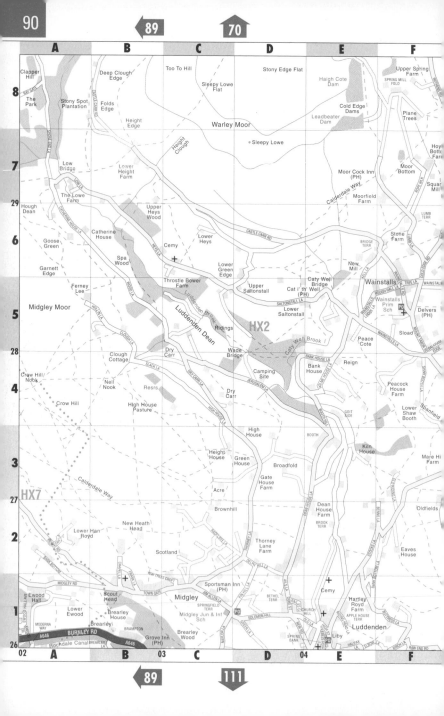

91
72

C8
1 MOOR CLOSE FARM MEWS
2 CLARENDON ST
3 SUNNY VIEW TERR
4 MYRTLE GR
5 OXFORD RD

D8
1 CONISTON AVE
2 CONISTON CL
3 LEE ST
4 HAINSWORTH MOOR GARTH
5 HAINSWORTH MOOR CRES
6 HAINSWORTH MOOR DR

| A | B | C | D | E | F |

8

Lower Warmleigh Farm

Lower Schole Croft Farm

Middle Schole Croft Farm

Oats Royd

Royd Hill

Old Harrowins

CH

Queensbury Upper Sch

Greenland Villas

West End

Hunger Hill

BRIGHOUSE RD

FORD HILL

Holmfield / Ind Est

Works

Ambler Thorn

Shibden Head Mews

Hazel Hurst Farm

Shibden Head

7

Holdsworth

HX2

1 VALLEY WAY
2 MOOR BOTTOM

29

Holy Trinity CE Senior Sch

Halifax RC High Sch

Priestley Hill

Woodleigh

Ambler Way

HALIFAX RD

BD13

6

School Cote Terr

School Cote Brow

Catherine Slack

Shibden Dale

Shibden Brook

Dunkirk Brow

Barns Hill Farm

Cut Teal La

Mills

5

Heathy La

Beechwood Ave

Holmfield

Lower Shibden Hall

Calderdale Way

Marsh Hall Farm

QUEENSBURY RD

1 BAKER ST
2 BURTON ST
3 STANLEY ST
4 ST ANDREWS CL
5 LIVINGSTONE ST N
6 SUMMERFIELD CT

Grange Ave

Station Rd

Sewage Wks

Addersgate Farm

Bunney Gr Worthowram

28

Scout Wood

Simm Carr Farm

Lands Head Farm

Little London

4

Crossley Terr

Moorside Gdns

Drakes Ind Est

Hollin Hall

Ringby Farm

Swalesmoor Inn (PH)

Swales Moor

HX3

Scout Hall

Dam Head

Foundry La

1 OLDFIELD ST
2 MAUDE ST
3 HOPKINSON ST
4 SOD HOUSE GN
5 SMITH'S TERR
6 NURSERY LA
7 BLACKHORN HOUSE

Booth Bank Farm

Pule Hill

Lee House Inn (PH)

Hollyleigh

Shibden Mill Inn (PH)

Blake Hill Farm

3

8 ATHOL ST
9 SECOND AVE
10 GRAFTON PL

New Delight Inn

BOOTHTOWN RD

Ski Slope

The Sportsman Inn (PH)

27

Boothtown

Wks

HALIFAX

Pepper Hill

Salterlee House

Salterlee Jun & Inf Sch

2

Lee Mount

Canterbury Cres

Wks

High Royd

Black Boy

Spa House Farm

Staups Common

Akroydon

Woodlands

Mus

1

Woodside

Woodside Gr

Shibden Fold

Stump Cross

Schs

ST GEORGES CRES

Lower Horley Green

GODLEY LA

BRADFORD RD A6036

LEEDS RD

26

08

| A | B | C | D | E | F |

09

10

91
113

A1
1 BRACEWELL DR
2 BRACEWELL GR
3 WHEATLEY CL
4 WHEATLEY RD
5 LEE MOUNT GDNS
6 PEABODY ST
7 ELLISON ST
8 BURTON ST
9 MATLOCK ST
10 GRANGE ST

11 LIVINGSTONE ST
12 TENNYSON ST
13 CLIFTON ST
14 LAWRENCE ST
15 OVENDEN CL
16 RUSHWORTH ST
17 GARFIELD ST
18 COLUMBUS ST
19 ASHVILLE ST
20 WASHINGTON ST
21 BRIGHTON ST

22 MELBOURNE ST
23 INGHAMS CT
24 RUSKIN TERR
25 WOODVILLE ST
26 MELROSE ST
27 CONCRETE ST
28 BATLEY ST

B1
1 FRIENDLY ST
2 BETHEL ST
3 AMY ST

A2
4 CLEVEDON PL
5 EARL TERR
6 LINCOLN WAY
7 EASTWOOD ST
8 ROBERT ST
9 OVENDEN ROAD TERR

A2
1 CHESTER CT
2 CHESTER GR
3 CHESTER CL

B1
3 CHESTER PL
4 GILMOUR ST
5 LINCOLN WAY

B2
1 TURNER'S CT
2 McBURNEY CL
3 BRUNEL CT
4 UTTLEY ST
5 SIMPSON ST
6 CATHCART ST

7 FERNFIELD TERR
8 IONA PL

C1
1 SUNNY SIDE ST
2 ALL SOULS TERR
3 ALL SOULS ST
4 SUNNY BANK TERR
5 LAURA ST
6 ADA ST
7 BACK LYTTON ST
8 WOODLANDS VIEW
9 LOWER RANGE

10 AMBLERS TERR
11 BROUGHAM RD
12 BROUGHAM ST
13 BROUGHAM TERR
14 OLD SCHOOLS GDNS
15 CHURCH SIDE CL
16 CHURCH SIDE DR
17 SCHOOL YARD VIEW

C2
1 BREWERY ST
2 ROBERT ST N
3 CLAREMOUNT TERR

4 ROYD MOUNT
5 THORN VIEW

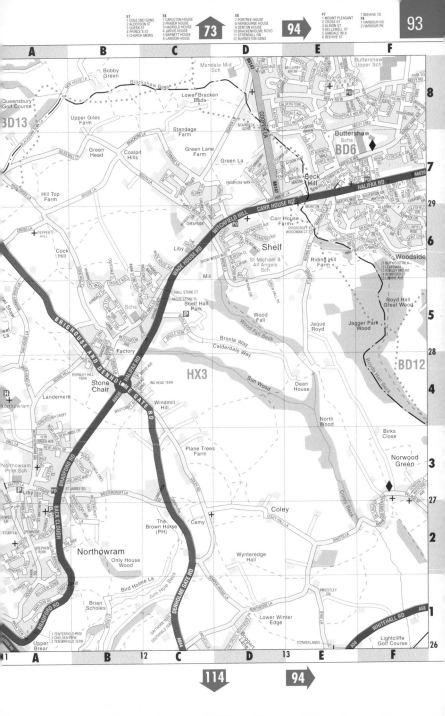

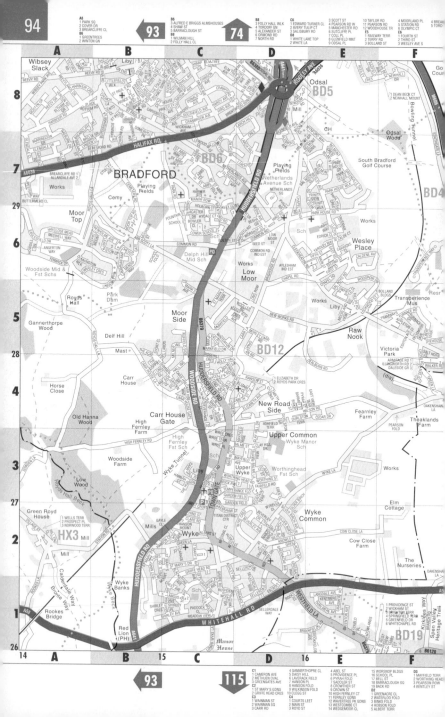

BD4

BD11

BD19

WF17

Birkenshaw

Drighlington

Birstall

Yorkshire Martyrs Collegiate Sch

Westgate Hill

Cross Lane End

Tong Lane End

Kings Arms (PH)

Shawfield Farm

Birkshaw Beck

Doles Wood

Whitely Wood

Golf Course

Manor Farm

Lumb Hall

Drighlington Jun Sch

Spring Gdns

Drighlington Inf Sch

Adwalton

Drighlington Moorside

Penfield

Springfield Farm

Birkenshaw CE County Fst Sch

Kirklees Way

Hill Top Farm

Brown Hill Farm

Birk Hill Farm

Sunnybank Farm

Heightlands Farm

Burnt Royd

Moor Fields

Fieldhead Farm

Fieldhead Jun & Inf Sch

Kirklees Way

Swincliffe

Birkenshaw Mid Sch

Birkenshaw Bottoms

Oakenshaw Moor

Thorn Hill Knowls

Wheatleys Farm

Brecks Farm

Oakwell Hall Country Park

Oakwell

Oakwell Hall

Sewage Works

St Patrick's RC Jun & Int Sch

Visitor Ctr

Spen Valley Heritage Trail

Brontë Way

Church Beck

Monk Ings

Gomersal Fst Sch

Red House Mus

Pollard Hall

Gomersal Mid Sch

Church Wood

Birstall St Peter's C of E Prim Sch

Brownhill End

Birdacre

Mills

Threelands (Amb HQ)

WESTGATE HILL ST

BRADFORD AND WAKEFIELD RD

BRADFORD RD

WHITEHALL RD

WHITEHALL RD E

WHITEHALL RD W

DEWSBURY RD

OXFORD RD

BRADFORD RD

CHURCH LA

LEEDS RD

98

A5
1 NELSON PL
2 BANK SQ
3 CHURCH WAY
4 VICTORIA GRANGE WAY
5 PROVIDENCE CT
6 VICTORIA MEWS

7 FOSTER CRES
8 FOSTER CL
9 COBDEN ST
10 COBDEN MEWS
11 FOSTER ST
12 CO-OPERATIVE ST

← 97

A6
1 ARKWRIGHT WLK
2 WINDERS DALE
3 SANDMEAD WAY
B7
1 DAFFIL GRANGE MEWS
2 HINDLE PL

↑ 78

B7
3 CLIFFORD PL
4 MOSS LEA
5 THORNVILLE
6 HODGSON PL
7 WALKER PL
8 GRANGE TERR

9 GRANGE PARK CL
10 GRANGE PARK MEWS
11 LANESIDE FOLD
C8
1 UNION ST
2 CO-OPERATIVE ST
3 FOUNTAIN ST

4 OLD SCHOOL MEWS
5 SUNNY GR
6 ALFRED ST
7 LITTLE LA
8 LITTLE LANE CT

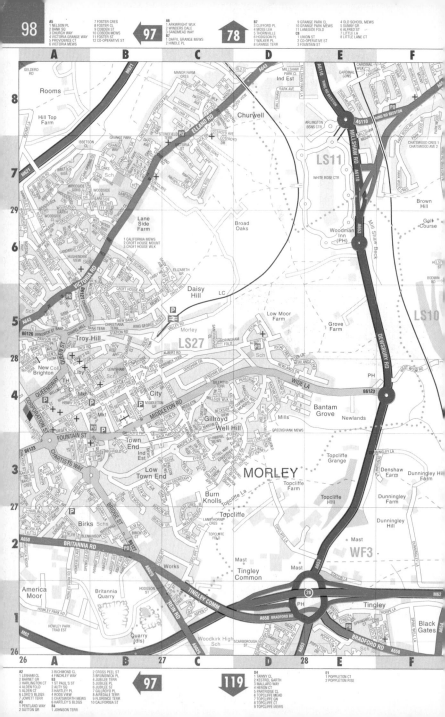

A2
1 LENHAM CL
2 BARNET GR
3 HARLINGTON CT
4 ALDEN FOLD
5 ALDEN CT
6 LORD'S BLDGS
7 JOWETT TERR
A3
1 PENTLAND WAY
2 SUTTON GR

3 RICHMOND CL
4 FINCHLEY WAY
B3
1 ST PAUL'S ST
2 AUTY SQ
3 HARTLEY PL
4 RODS VIEW
5 CHATSWORTH MEWS
6 HARTLEY'S BLDGS
B4
1 JOHNSON TERR

2 CROSS PEEL ST
3 BRUNSWICK PL
4 JUBILEE TERR
5 JUBILEE PL
6 JUBILEE ST
7 GILLROYD PL
8 AIREDALE TERR
9 FLORENCE TERR
10 CALIFORNIA ST

← 97

D4
1 TAWNY CL
2 KESTREL GARTH
3 MALLARD WAY
4 HERON CT
5 PARTRIDGE CL
6 TOPCLIFFE MEAD
7 TOPCLIFFE GN
8 TOPCLIFFE CT
9 TOPCLIFFE MEWS

↑ 119

E1
1 POPPLETON CT
2 POPPLETON RISE

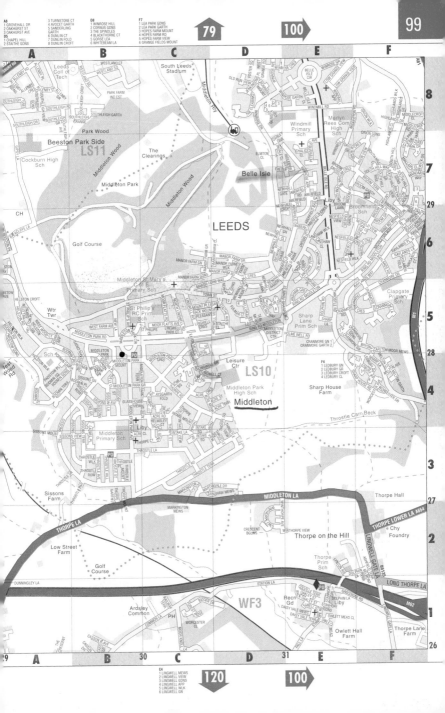

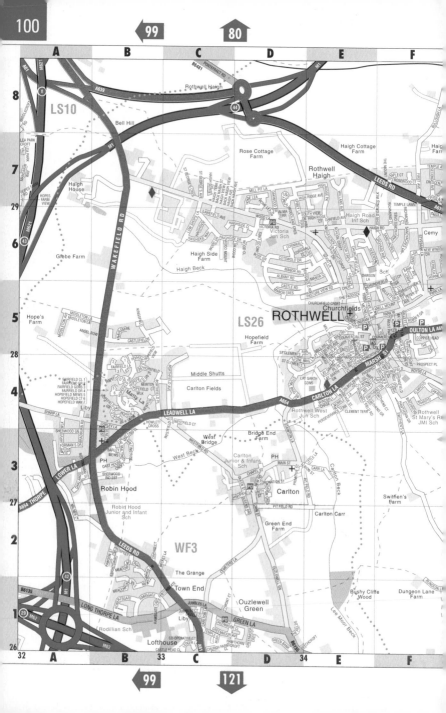

103
84

| A | B | C | D | E | F |

8

Park Lane Farm
Hastings Plantation
Hill Top Farm
PARK LA
St John's Hospital (Almshouses)
PH
HOLY ROOD LA
Park House Farm
Plaster Pits
MANOR FARM RD
Ledsham
Wormstall Wood

7

CLAYPIT LA
Capon Hill
Madbanks
LS25
Horsehock Dale

29

Lambkin Plantation
Lambkin Hill

6

Newfield Farm
JACK NEWTON LA
Newfield Plantation
Newfield La

5

Haugh Hill Plantation
Caudle Hill Plantation
Beckfield House
WF11

28

Newton Farm
Newton
Newton Abbey
CALVER HILL
NEWTON LA
P

4

Fairburn Ings Nature Reserve
P
P

3

Newton Ings
Fairburn Ings
River Aire
New Fryston
WF10
Aire Bridge

27

Spoil Heap
P
P
Sewage Works
Spoil Heap
NORTH ST
BRIDGE ST
SOUTH LA
WHELDALE LA

2

Wheldale Ings
Wheldale Farm
Well Wood
Hall Farm
Water Fryston
Sewage Works
Wheldale
WHELDALE RD
WHELDALE RD
PASCAL LN
KESWICK DR
KIRKLANDS CL
FAIRFIELD CL
ASKHAM RD
BROADWELL DR
GRANGE RD
AMBER CT
Fryston Hall Farm
LANCASTER ST

1

Whin Covert
PEMBERTON RD
STANSFIELD CL
FOSS WLK
NIDD DR
PRISCILLA LN
MACAULAY RD
ELIZABETH DR
SCHOLES LN
Sch

26

| A | B | C | D | E | F |
| 44 | | 45 | | 46 | |

103
125

A B C D E F

8

Monk
Fryston

MAIN ST   A63

A162

Pollums House
Farm

7

Monk Fryston
Lodge

BETTERAS HILL RD   LC

Hillam

29

Betteras
Hill

LUMBY LEYS LA

BUTLER LA

6

LS25

Running La

POLLUMS LA

RUNNING LA

West Park
Farm

5

1 PIPER HILL
2 CRAG TOP

ORCHARD DR

LUMFIELD LA

HILLAM LA

Ox Moor

28

Fairburn
Primary
Sch

LUMFIELD'S LA

LIMEFIELD DR

MOOR LA

ASH LA

Fairburn

Victoria
Cotts

4

WF11

NEWCASTLE FARM

TOP HOUSE FARM

RAILWAY
COTTS

BURTON COMMON LA

Burton Salmon
Primary Sch

Hall
Farm

Cow La

SCHOOL
TERR

INGS MERE
CT

GARTH END

HIGH ST

NORTH RD

ASH LA

LINDER LA

FENCOTE LA

THE INGS RD

MAIN ST

TOP
STONE
CL

Top Stone Drain

3

Bay
Horse
(PH)

LC

Plough
Inn
(PH)

NEW LA

Burton
Salmon

Fairburn Ings
Nature Reserve

POOLE ROW   Poole

27

Spoil
Heap

Brotherton
Ings

Poole
Belt

2

Water
Fryston

River Aire

Coppering
Kilns

Byram Park

1

WF10

The
Dales

Foxcliff

Byram
Hall

SHORT LA

GILL LANE

OX CLOSE LANE

DELF LANE GARTH

LOFTHOUSE GARTH

GILL STONE CL

HANOVER PL

A1

A162

P

26

47   A   B   48   C   D   49   E   F

126

OL14

OL13

BACUP

Carr and Craggs Moor

Whitworth

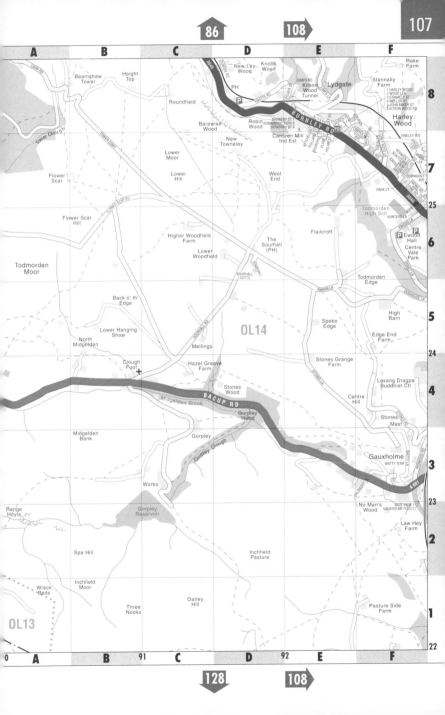

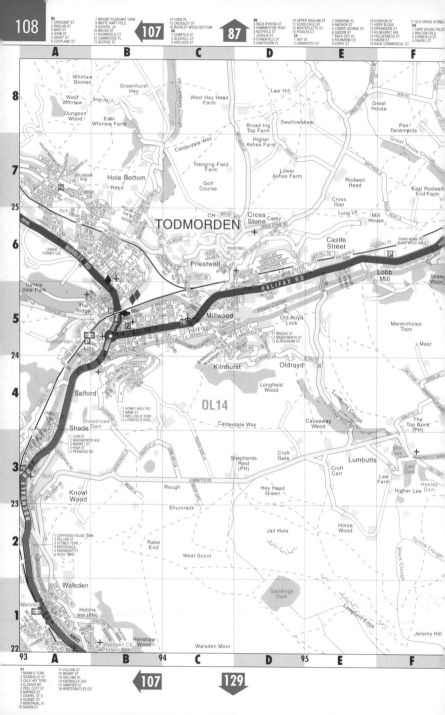

107

87

B5
1 CRESCENT ST
2 RAGLAN ST
3 BATH ST
4 JOHN ST
5 SHORT ST
6 COUPLAND ST

7 MOUNT PLEASANT VIEW
8 WHITE HART FOLD
9 SCHOOL LA
10 BROOK ST
11 ROOMFIELD CT
12 CAMBRIDGE PL
13 GEORGE ST

14 YORK ST
15 CROSSLEY ST
16 BUCKLEY WOOD BOTTOM
B6
1 COWFOLD ST
2 GLEDHILL ST
3 ADELAIDE ST

B6
4 BACK BYROM ST
5 HAMMERTON TERR
6 NUTFIELD ST
7 JOSHUA ST
8 STANSFIELD ST
9 HAWTHORN PL

10 UPPER RAGLAN ST
11 SCHOLFIELD ST
12 WHITEPLATTS ST
13 PICKLES CT
C5
5 HEY ST
6 SANWORTH ST

3 OSBORNE PL
4 ANCHOR ST
5 LOWER GEORGE ST
6 GIBSON ST
7 BACK DER ST
8 RICHMOND ST
9 EVERY ST

10 GORDON ST
11 HOPE BLDGS
12 ERRINGDEN ST
13 KILNHURST AVE
14 HOLDERNESS ST
15 HAVEN ST
16 BACK COMMERICAL ST

17 OLD CROSS STONE
D6
1 CARR HOUSE FOLD
2 WALTON FOLD
3 CORNFIELD ST
4 CHAPEL ST

TODMORDEN

Whirlaw
Stones

West
Whirlaw

Dungeon
Wood

Greenhurst
Hey

Whirlaw La

East
Whirlaw Farm

West Hey Head
Farm

Law Hill

Great
House

Broad Ing
Top Farm

Swallowshaw

Pex
Tenements

Calderdale Way

Hanging Field
Farm

Higher
Ashes Farm

Lower
Ashes Farm

Rodwell
Head

East Rodwell
End Farm

Hole Bottom

Royd

Golf
Course

Cross
Gap

Long La

Mill
House

Cross
Stone

Cemy

CH

BROAD GATE

Castle
Street

Lobb
Mill

Shaw
Wood

Priestwell

Priestwell

Centre
Vale Park

The
Ridge

Mkt

Millwood

River Calder

Old Royd
Lock

Mankinholes
Tops

Mast

Todmorden

Liby

Salford

Kilnhurst

Oldrayd

1 GREAVE ST
2 MERRYBENTS ST
3 BLACKBARN ST

OL14

Longfield
Wood

Lumbutts Clough

The
Top Brink
(PH)

1 HONEY HOLE RD
2 BANK ST
3 WELLFIELD TERR
4 LONGFIELD RISE

Shoebroad
Dam

Shade

1 LION ST
2 WADSWORTH AVE
3 MARKET ST
4 HIGH ST
5 PEXWOOD RD

Calderdale Way

Causeway
Wood

Mill
Dam

Lumbutts

Shepherds
Rest
(PH)

Croft
Gate

Croft
Carr

Lee
Farm

Mankinholes Barn

Lee Dam

Heeley
Dam

Knowl
Wood

Rough

LUMBUTTS RD

Shurcrack

Hey Head
Green

Horse
Wood

Higher Lee

1 COPPERAS HOUSE TERR
2 PELLON ST
3 STONES TERR
4 BROOKDALE
5 FARNBORO ST
6 ROCK TERR

Rake
End

West Scout

Jail Hole

Black Clough

Spinks Clough

Walsden

Gaddings
Dam

Langfield Edge

Jeremy Hill

Walsden

Hollins
Inn (PH)

Henshaw
Wood

Walsden CE
Infant Sch

Walsden Moor

93

94

95

107

129

A1
1 MONA'S TERR
2 GRANVILLE ST
3 CALF HEY TERR
4 CLOUGH RD
5 PEEL COTT ST
6 BARNES ST
7 CHAPEL ST S
8 QUEBEC ST
9 MONTREAL ST
10 SAXON ST

11 VULCAN ST
12 WHARF ST
13 HOLLINS PL
14 KNOWLSLEY AVE
15 DAMPIER ST
16 WINTERBUTLEE GR

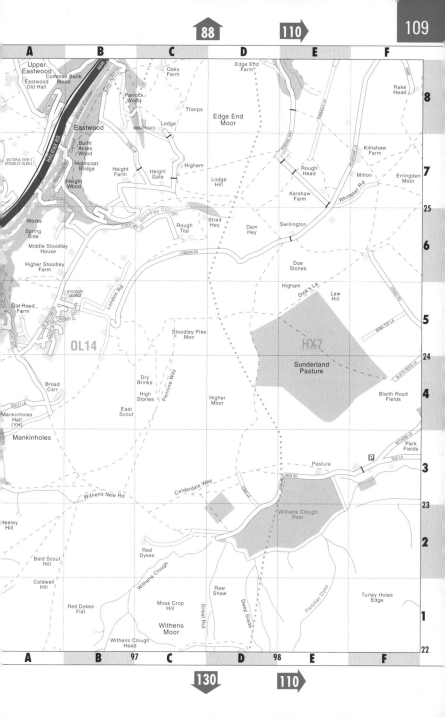

A   B   C   D   E   F

Upper
Eastwood
Common Bank
Eastwood Wood
Old Hall

Oaks
Farm

Edge End
Farm

Rake
Head

8

River Calder

Parrock
Wood

Thorps

Edge End
Moor

Eastwood

Lodge

Burnt
Acres
Wood

Holmcoat
Bridge

Height
Farm

Higham

Height
Gate

Height
Wood

Lodge
Hill

Rough
Head

Kilnshaw
Farm

Mitton

Erringden
Moor

7

Works

Stoodley Clough

Strait
Hey

Kershaw
Farm

Swillington

Whittaker Rd

25

Spring
Side

Rough
Top

Dam
Hey

6

Middle Stoodley
House

LONDON RD

Doe
Stones

Higher Stoodley
Farm

Higham

Dick's La

Law
Hill

STOODLEY
GRANGE

London Rd

Got Royd
Farm

Sunderland
Pasture

BANK TOP LA

5

24

OL14

Stoodley Pike
Mon

HX7

Broad
Carr

Dry
Brinks

Pennine Way

Higher
Moor

Blaith Royd
Fields

4

Mankinholes
Hall
(YH)

High
Stones

East
Scout

WITHENS LA

Park
Fields

Mankinholes

Pasture

P

BUD LA

3

Heeley
Hill

Calderdale Way

NEW RD

LONG LA

Withens New Rd

Withens Clough
Resr

23

Red
Dykes

2

Bald Scout
Hill

Withens Clough

Coldwell
Hill

Red Dykes
Flat

Moss Crop
Hill

Great Rut

Raw
Shaw

Deep Slade

Fletcher Dyke

Turley Holes
Edge

1

Withens
Moor

Withens Clough
Head

22

A   B   97   C   D   98   E   F

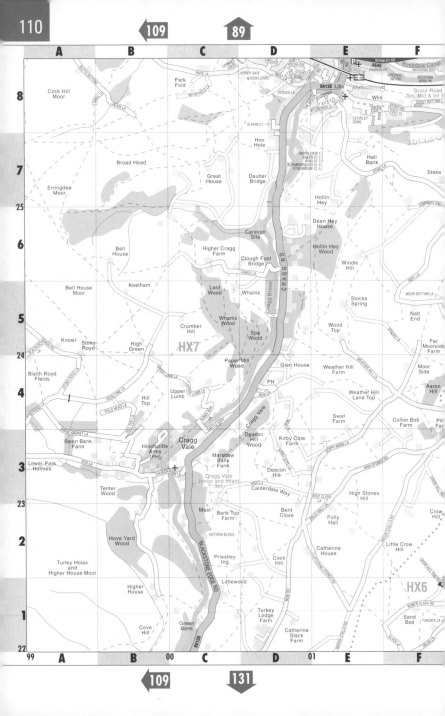

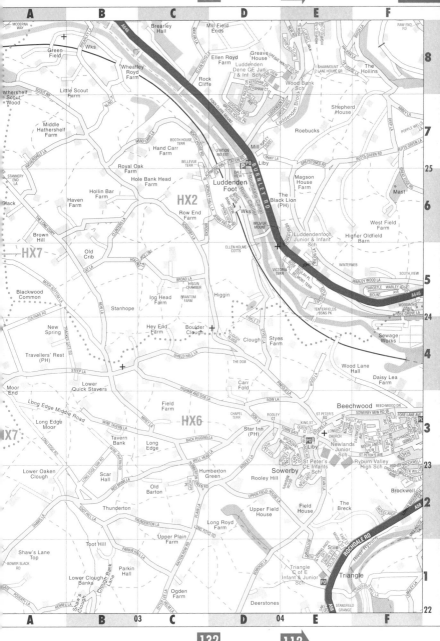

A   B   C   D   E   F

MODERNA WAY

Green Field

Wks

Wheatley Royd Farm

Little Scout Farm

Hathershelf Scout Wood

SCOUT RD

Middle Hathershelf Farm

Brearley Hall

Mill Field Ends

Ellen Royd Farm

Greave House

Rock Cliffe

Luddenden Dene CE Jun & Inf. Sch

Wood Bank Sch

The Hollins

8

Shepherd House

Roebucks

7

Hand Carr Farm

Booth House Terr

Station Ind Est

Bellevue Terr

Royal Oak Farm

Hole Bank Head Farm

Luddenden Foot

Mill

Liby

Magson House Farm

25

Hollin Bar Farm

Haven Farm

HX2

The Black Lion (PH)

Mast

6

Black

Brown Hill

Old Crib

Row End Farm

Wks

Wild/UR Mount

Luddendenfoot Junior & Infant Sch

West Field Farm

Higher Oldfield Barn

HX7

Ellen Holme Cotts

Blackwood Common

Stanhope

Ing Head Farm

Brantom Farm

Higgin Chamber

Higgin

Victoria Terr

Belmont Terr

Winterneb

SOUTH VIEW

WARLEY WOOD LA

THROSTLE

WARLEY ROYD AVE

A646

5

Hey End Farm

Boulder Clough

Clough

Styes Farm

TENTERFIELDS BSNS PK

Sewage Works

24

New Spring

Travellers' Rest (PH)

SHELD HALL LA

THE DOB

Wood Lane Hall

4

Daisy Lea Farm

Moor End

Lower Quick Stavers

STEEP LA

Field Farm

Carr Fold

HUGHAM AND DOB LA

CHAPEL TERR

ROW LA

Beechwood

BEECHWOOD DR

SOWERBY NEW RD

FORE LANE AVE

3

Long Edge Middle Road

Long Edge Moor

HX7

Tavern Bank

Long Edge

BACK RIGGING LA

Star Inn (PH)

ROOLEY CT

ST PETER'S RD

KING ST

QUEEN ST

TOWN GATE

Liby

Newlands Junior Sch

MOORLAND

ST PETER'S AVE

HX6

Lower Oaken Clough

Scar Hall

Old Barton

Humberton Green

Rooley Hill

Sowerby

St Peter's St Infants Sch

Ryburn Valley High Sch

Brockwell

23

Thunderton

UPPER FIELD HOUSE LA

Upper Field House

Field House

The Breck

2

Toot Hill

Long Royd Farm

Upper Plain Farm

ROCHDALE RD

River Ryburn

A58

Shaw's Lane Top

BOWER SLACK RD

Lower Clough Banks

Parkin Hall

PARKIN HALL LA

Clough Bank Lane

Ogden Farm

Triangle C of E Infant & Junior Sch

Stile

Triangle

STANSFIELD GRANGE

1

Deerstones

22

A   B   03   C   D   04   E   F

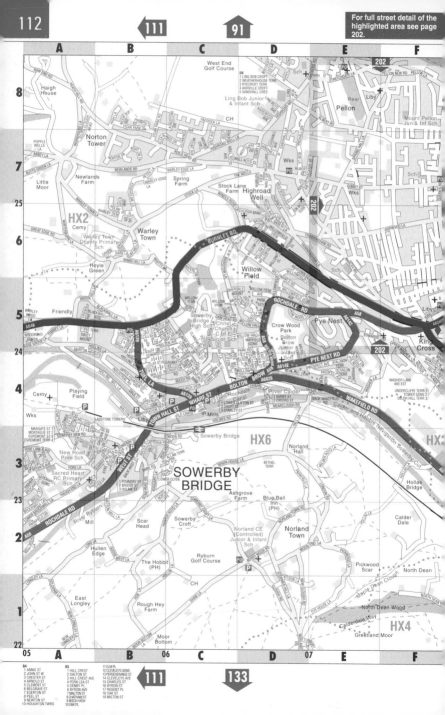

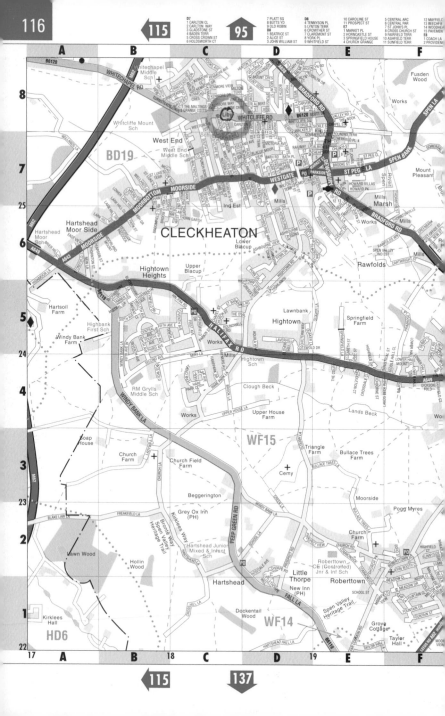

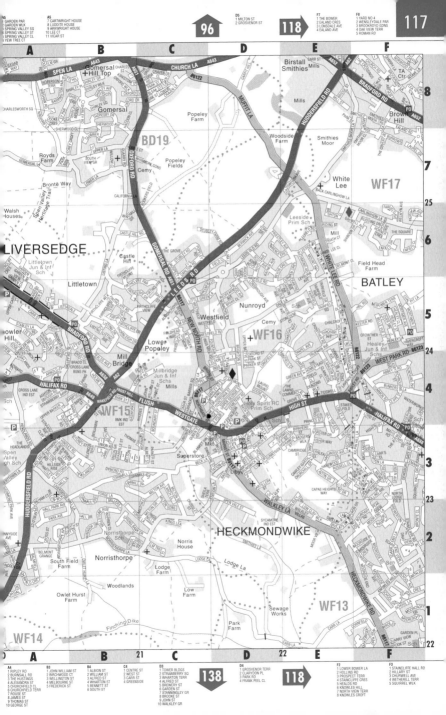

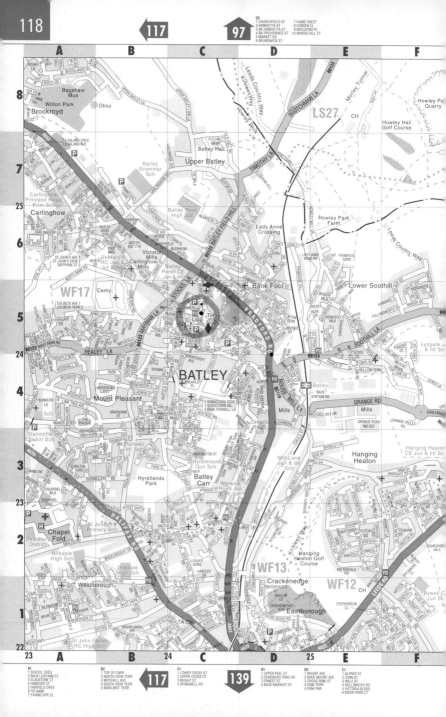

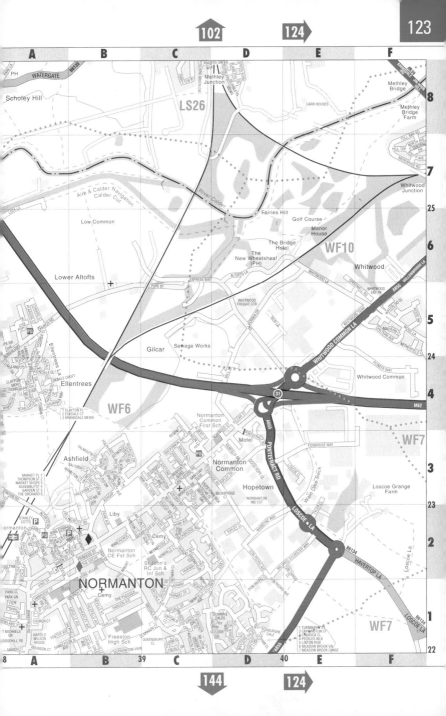

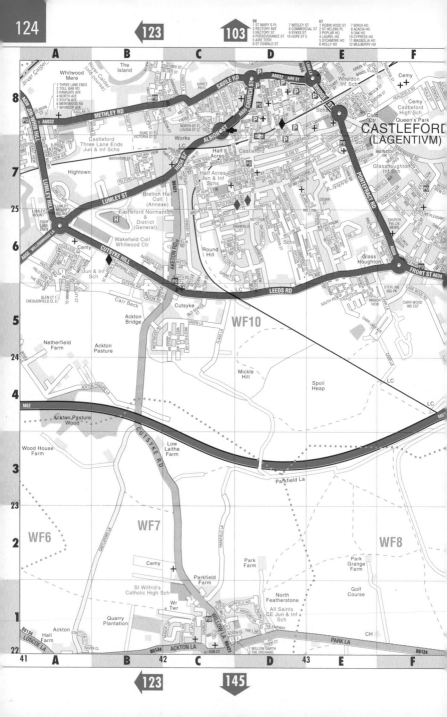

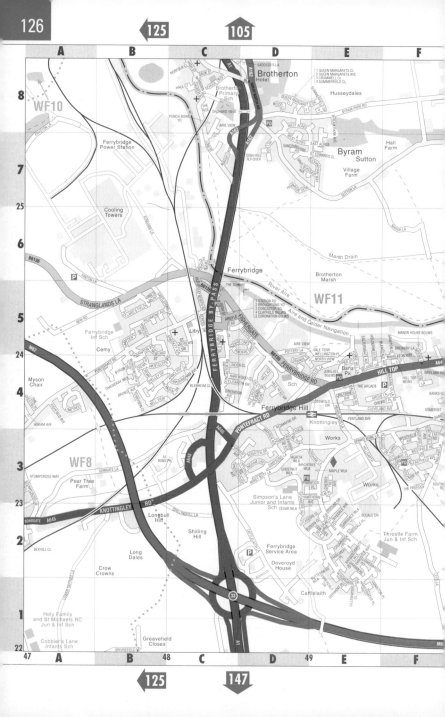

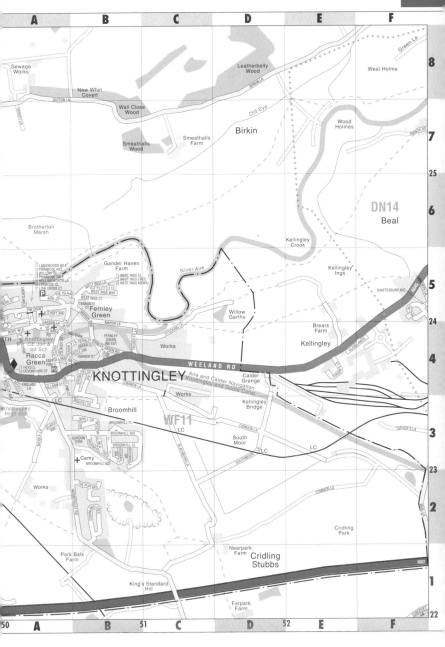

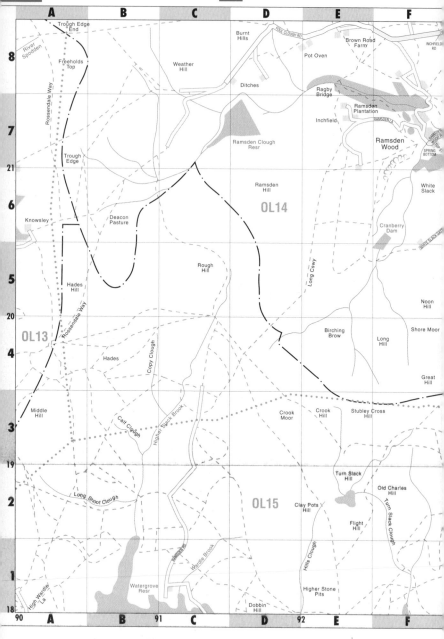

A **B** **C** **D** **E** **F**

Trough Edge End
Burnt Hills
FOUL CLOUGH RD
Brown Road Farm
INCHFIELD RD
River Spodden
Freeholds Top
Weather Hill
Pot Oven
 Diches
Ragby Bridge
Ramsden Plantation
Rossendale Way
Inchfield
RAMSDEN LA
Ramsden Wood
SPRING BOTTOM
Ramsden Clough Resr
Trough Edge
Ramsden Hill
OL14
White Slack
Knowsley
Deacon Pasture
WHITE SLACK GATE
Cranberry Dam
Hades Hill
Rough Hill
Long Cawy
Noon Hill
Rossendale Way
Shore Moor
OL13
Hades
Copy Clough
Birching Brow
Long Hill
Great Hill
Middle Hill
Call Clough
Higher Slack Brook
Crook Moor
Crook Hill
Stubley Cross Hill
Long Shoot Clough
OL15
Turn Slack Hill
Old Charles Hill
Clay Pots Hill
Turn Slack Clough
Wardle Brook
Flight Hill
Hills Clough
High Wardle La
Watergrove Resr
Higher Stone Pits
Dobbin Hill

A **B** 91 **C** **D** 92 **E** **F**

90

8 7 21 6 5 20 4 3 19 2 1 18

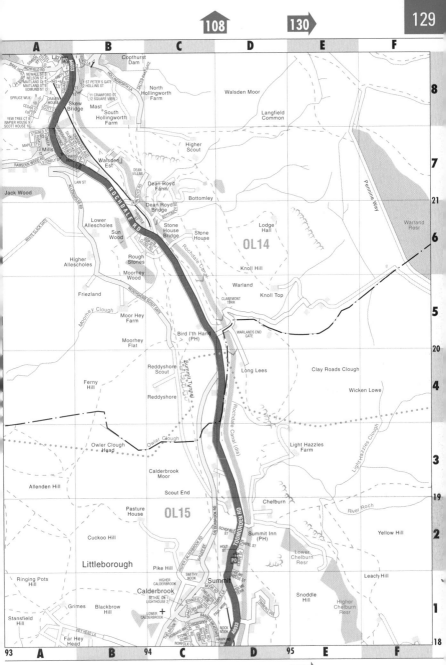

129
109

A B C D E F

8

Warland Drain
Warland Drain
Bird Nest Hill
Turley Holes and Higher House Moor

7

HX7
Blake Moor

21

Little Dove Lowe
OL14
White Holme Drain

6

White Holme Moss
Turvin Clough

Round Hills

5

Light Hazzles Resr
Little Moor Clough
Saw Gill Hollow
BLACKSTONE EDGE RD
B6138

20

White Holme Resr
Little Moor
Round Hill
Captains Mark Hill

4

Chelburn Moor
Pennine Way
Light Hazzles Edge
Toad La
Farther Hill
OL15
Cold Laughton Drain
Spoyland Moor
HX6
Knave Holes Hollow
Knave Holes Hill

3

Utley Edge
Byron Edge
Middle Hill
Nigher Hill
TURVIN RD
Black Castle Drain
Rush Bed Hill

19

Head Drain

2

Cow Head

1

Blackstone Edge Resr
Black Castle Hill
ROCHDALE RD
A58
Fairy Hill
Slate Pit Hill

18

B6138
HALIFAX RD
A58
98

96 A B 97 C D 98 E F

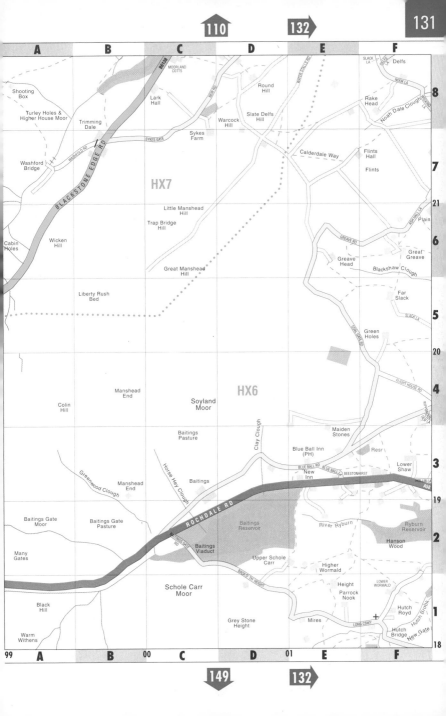

110
132

A B C D E F

8

MOORLAND COTTS

SLACK LA
Delfs
NOOK LA

Shooting Box

Lark Hall

Round Hill

Rake Head

Noah Dale Clough

Turley Holes & Higher House Moor

Trimming Dale

SYKES GATE

Sykes Farm

Warcock Hill

Slate Delfs Hill

Calderdale Way

Flints Hall

7

Washford Bridge

BLACKSTONE EDGE RD

Flints

HX7

21

Little Manshead Hill

Plain

Trap Bridge Hill

GREAVE RD

6

Cabin Holes

Wicken Hill

Greave Head

Great Greave

Great Manshead Hill

Blackshaw Clough

Far Slack

Liberty Rush Bed

SLACK LA

5

Green Holes

COAL GATE RD

20

FLIGHT HOUSE RD

Colin Hill

Manshead End

HX6

Soyland Moor

4

Baitings Pasture

Maiden Stones

Clay Clough

Blue Ball Inn (PH)

Resr

3

Greenwood Clough

Manshead End

Horse Hey Clough

Baitings

BLUE BALL RD

New Inn

Blue Ball Rd

BEESTONHIRST

Lower Shaw

A58

19

Baitings Gate Moor

Baitings Gate Pasture

ROCHDALE RD

Baitings Reservoir

River Ryburn

Ryburn Reservoir

Hanson Wood

2

Many Gates

BAITINGS GATE RD

Baitings Viaduct

Upper Schole Carr

Higher Wormald

LOWER WORMALD

Black Hill

Schole Carr Moor

BACK O' TH' HEIGHT

Height Parrock Nook

Hutch Royd

1

Warm Withens

Grey Stone Height

Mires

LONG CSWY

Hutch Bridge

New Gate

Hutch Brook

99 A B 00 C D 01 E F 18

149
132

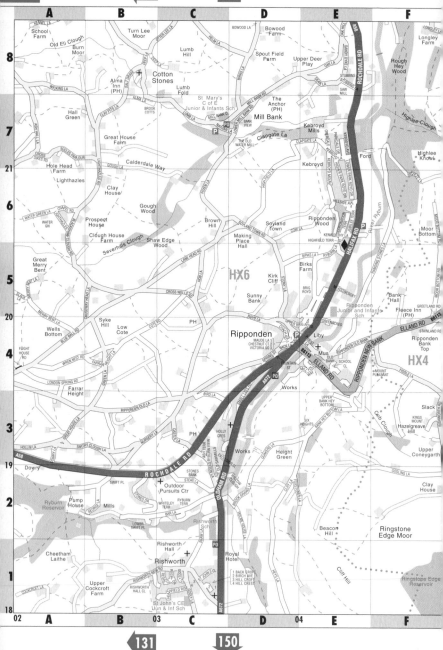

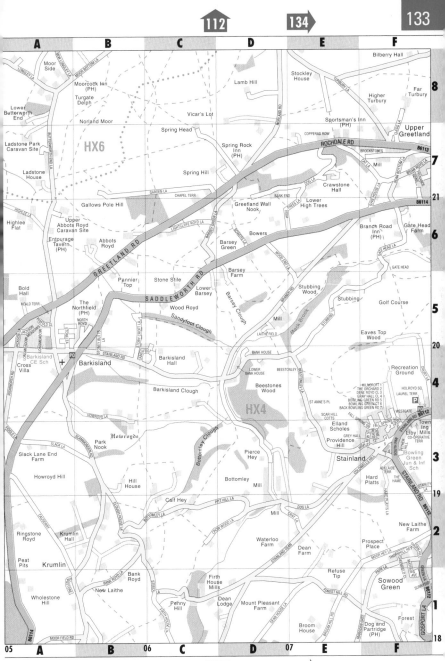

A   B   C   D   E   F

8

Bilberry Hall

Moor Side

Lonsley La
Moorcock Inn (PH)
Turgate Delph

Lamb Hill

Stockley House

Far Turbury

Higher Turbury

Lower Butterworth End

Norland Moor

Vicar's Lot

Sportsman's Inn (PH)

Upper Greetland

HX6

Spring Head

Spring Rock Inn (PH)

COPPERAS ROW

B6113

ROCHDALE RD

BROCKSTONES

Ladstone Park Caravan Site

Ladstone House

7

Spring Hill

Mill

Crawstone Hall

GARDEN LA
CHAPEL TERR

Gallows Pole Hill

Greetland Wall Nook

BANK END

Lower High Trees

B6114
21

Highlee Flat

Upper Abbots Royd Caravan Site

LIGHTCLIFFE ROYD LA

Bowers

Branch Road Inn (PH)

Gate Head Farm

6

Entourage Tavern (PH)

Abbots Royd

Barsey Green

GATE HEAD LA

GATE HEAD

GREETLAND RD

Pannier Top

Stone Stile

Barsey Farm

Golf Course

5

Bold Hall

HEALD TERR

The Northfield (PH)

SADDLEWORTH RD

Lower Barsey

Stubbing Wood

Stubbing

NORTH ROYD

Wood Royd

Barsey Clough

Eaves Top Wood

20

Sandyfoot Clough

Mill

LAITHE FIELD

STAINLAND RD

BANK HOUSE

Barkisland Hall

Recreation Ground

Barkisland CE Sch

PO

Cross Villa

Barkisland

LOWER BANK HOUSE

BEESTONLEY LA

HOLROYD SQ
LAUREL TERR

4

Barkisland Clough

Beestones Wood

St ANNE'S PL

HX4

WESTGATE

B6112

SCAR HILL COTTS

Elland Scholes

Town Ing

Lbly Mills
CO-OPERATIVE TERR

HOWROYD LA

Howroyde

Providence Hill

Stainland

Bowling Green Jun & Inf Sch

3

Park Nook

Pierce Hey

Hard Platts

ADELAIDE TERR

THE HAME

Slack Lane End Farm

BOTTOMLEY CLOUGH

Hill House

Bottomley

Mill

HANDPLATTS LA

B6112
19

Howroyd Hill

Calf Hey

PITT HILL LA

Mill

DOG LA

New Laithe Farm

2

Ringstone Royd

Krumlin Hall

CRUMB WOOD LA

Waterloo Farm

Dean Farm

Prospect Place

MOOR HEY LA

Peat Pits

Krumlin

Bank Royd

Firth House Mills

Refuse Tip

Sowood Green

1

Wholestone Hill

New Laithe

STEEL LA

Penny Hill

Dean Lodge

Mount Pleasant Farm

Broom House

FOREST HILL RD

Dog and Partridge (PH)

Forest

GOSPORT LA

B6114

MOOR FIELD RD

18

05   A   B   06   C   D   07   E   F

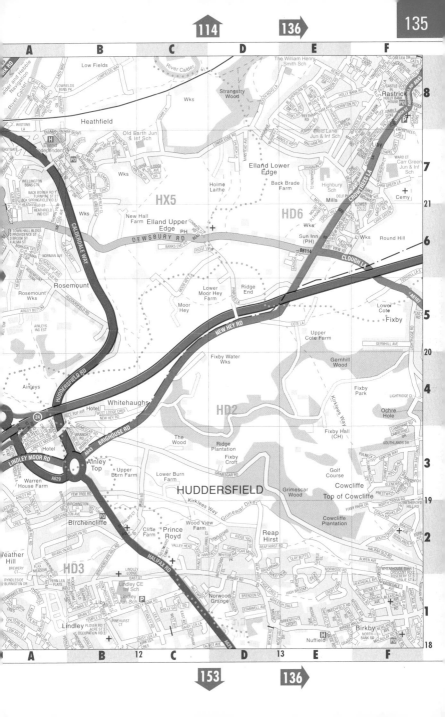

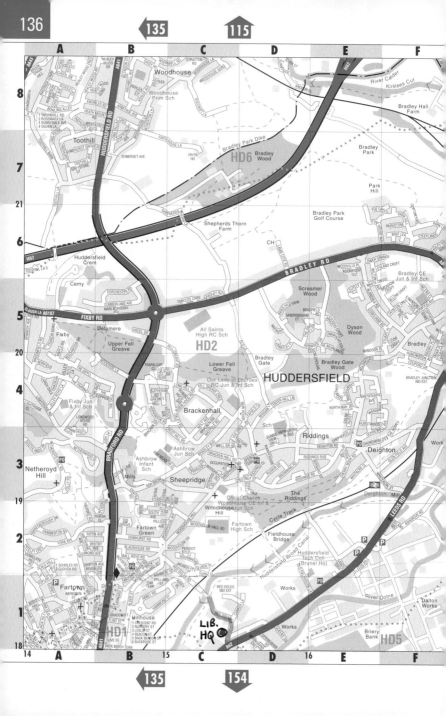

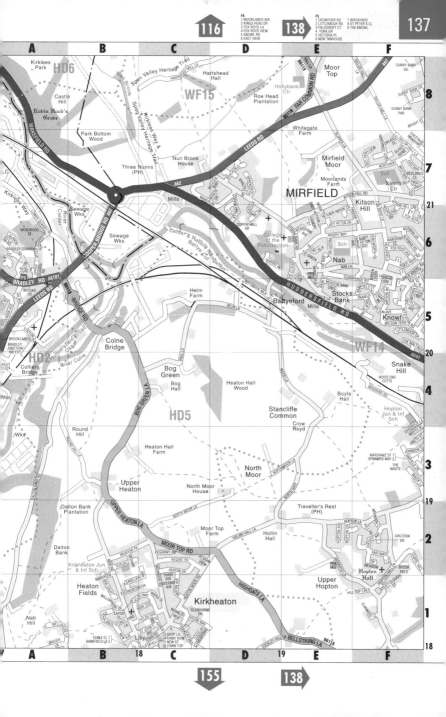

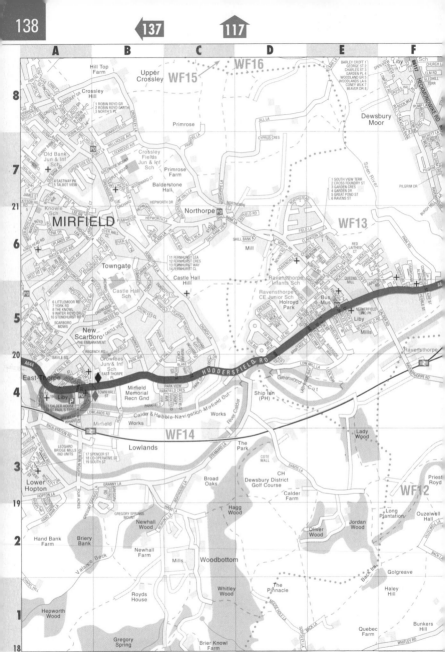

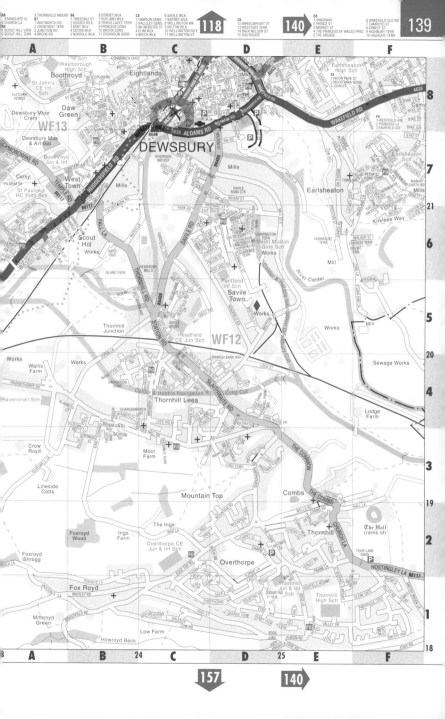

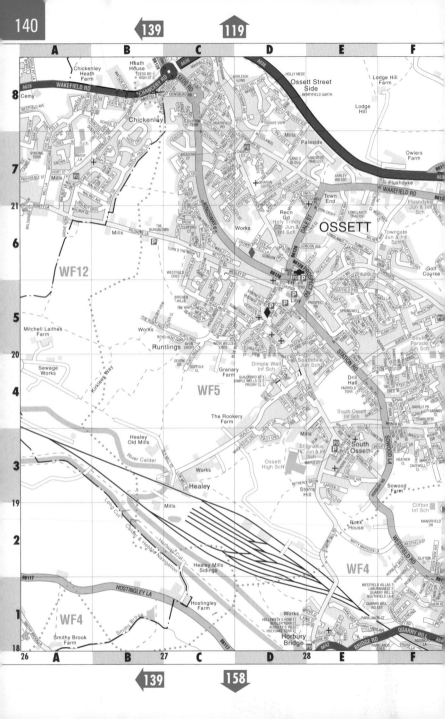

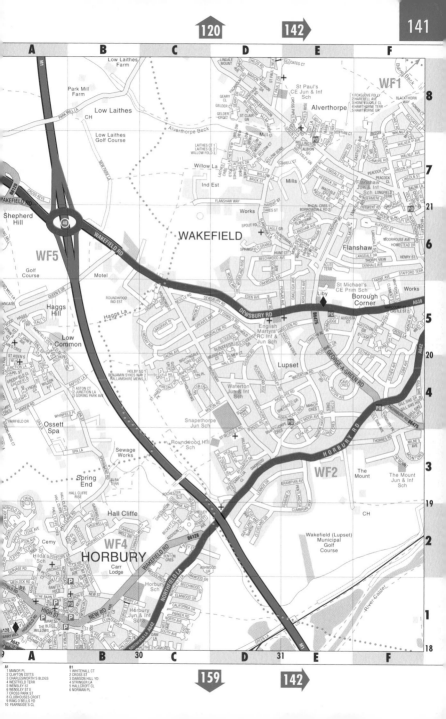

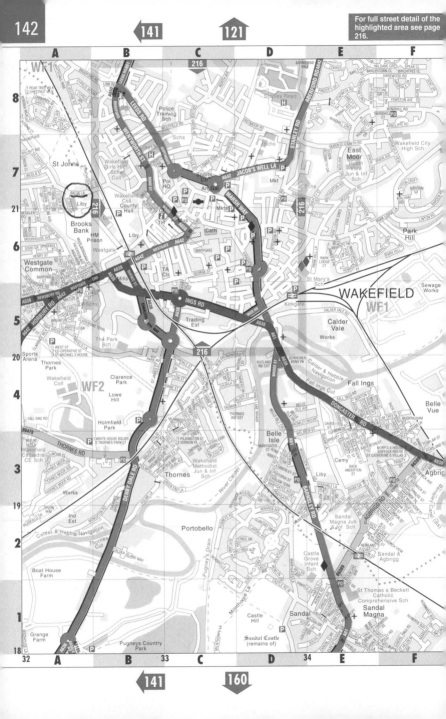

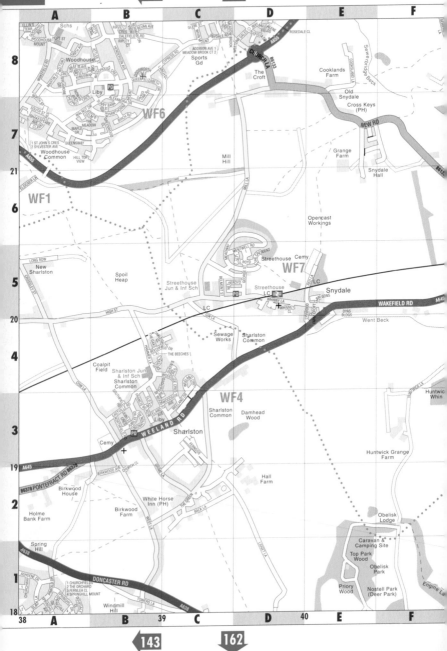

143
123

A B C D E F

8

Schs

Woodhouse

WF6

PO

Liby

ADDISON AVE 1
MEADOW BROOK CT 2

Sports
Gd

CHURCH LA

The
Croft

Old
Snydale

Cross Keys
(PH)

ROSEDALE CL

Cooklands
Farm

NEW RD

7

1 ST JOHN'S CRES
2 SYLVESTER AVE

Woodhouse
Common

HILL TOP
VIEW

QUEENSWAY

Mill
Hill

Grange
Farm

Snydale
Hall

21

WF1

6

LONG ROW

New
Sharlston

Spoil
Heap

HIGH ST

WESTWELL RD

FLOYD
CRESCENT

Streethouse

Streethouse
Jun & Inf Sch

LC

Opencast
Workings

Streethouse

Snydale

Cemy

WF7

LC

WAKEFIELD RD

A645

5

Coalpit
Field

Sharlston Jun
& Inf Sch
Sharlston
Common

THE BEECHES

Sewage
Works

Sharlston
Common

Sharlston
Common

Damhead
Wood

Went Beck

DYAS
BLDGS

Huntwic
Whin

20

4

WF4

Huntwick Grange
Farm

WEELAND RD

Liby

PO

Sharlston

19

Cemy

A645

PONTEFRACT RD

B6378

Birkwood
House

White Horse
Inn (PH)

Birkwood
Farm

Hall
Farm

Obelisk
Lodge

Caravan &
Camping Site

2

Holme
Bank Farm

BACK LA

Top Park
Wood

Obelisk
Park

18

Spring
Hill

A638

1 CHURCHFIELD
2 THE ORCHARD
3 FERNLEA CL
4 SPRINGHILL MOUNT

DONCASTER RD

Windmill
Hill

TOWERS LA

A638

Priory
Wood

Nostell Park
(Deer Park)

Engine La

38 A B 39 C D 40 E F

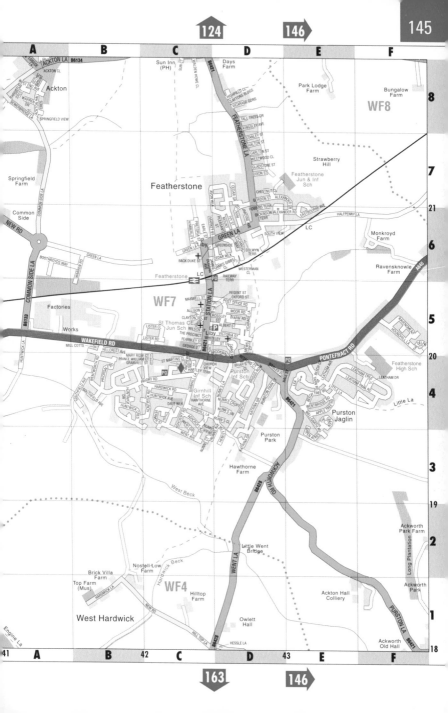

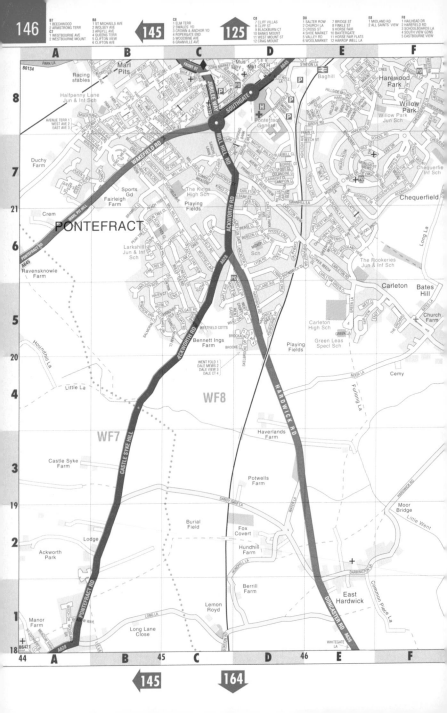

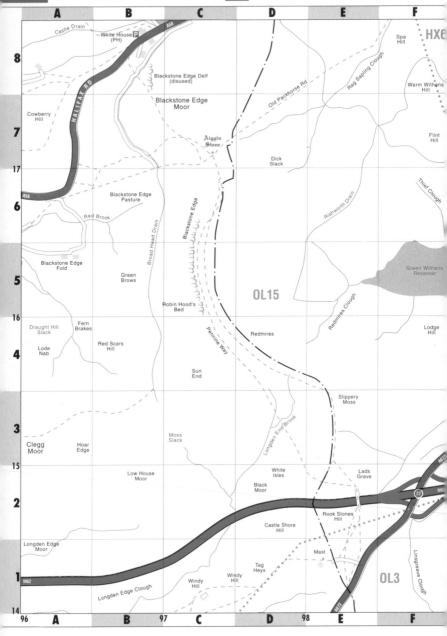

130

| | A | B | 97 | C | D | 98 | E | F |

8

7

17

6

5

16

4

3

15

2

1

14

96

HX6

Castle Drain

White House (PH)

A58

Blackstone Edge Delf (disused)

Blackstone Edge Moor

Cowberry Hill

HALIFAX RD

A58

Aiggin Stone

Old Packhorse Rd

Rag Sapling Clough

Spa Hill

Warm Withens Hill

Flint Hill

Dick Slack

Blackstone Edge Pasture

Red Brook

Blackstone Edge

Broad Head Drain

Rishworth Drain

Thief Clough

Blackstone Edge Fold

Green Brows

Green Withens Reservoir

OL15

Robin Hood's Bed

Draught Hill Slack

Fern Brakes

Red Scars Hill

Redmires Clough

Lodge Hill

Lode Nab

Pennine Way

Redmires

Sun End

Clegg Moor

Hoar Edge

Moss Slack

Slippery Moss

Longden End Brook

Low House Moor

White Isles

Lads Grave

M62

22

A672

Black Moor

Rook Stones Hill

Castle Shore Hill

Longden Edge Moor

Mast

Limsgreave Clough

M62

Longden Edge Clough

Windy Hill

Windy Hill

Tag Heys

OL3

A672

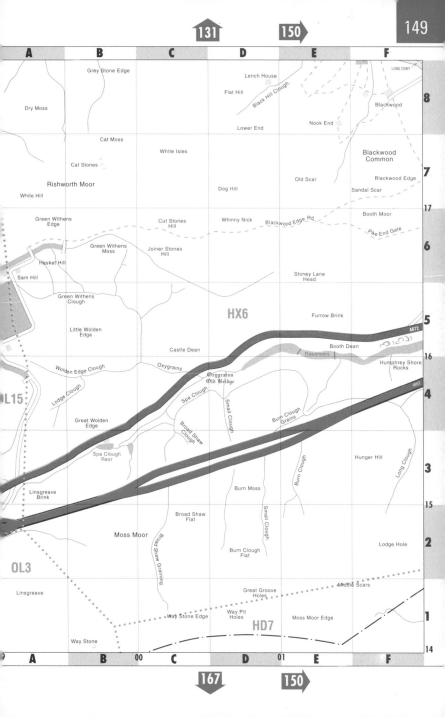

Grey Stone Edge

Lench House

Flat Hill

Black Hill Clough

Blackwood

8

Dry Moss

Lower End

Nook End

Cat Moss

White Isles

Blackwood Common

7

Cat Stones

Old Scar

Blackwood Edge

Rishworth Moor

Dog Hill

Sandal Scar

White Hill

17

Green Withens Edge

Cut Stones Hill

Whinny Nick

Blackwood Edge Rd.

Booth Moor

Pike End Gate

6

Green Withens Moss

Joiner Stones Hill

Hasket Hill

Sam Hill

Stoney Lane Head

Green Withens Clough

HX6

Furrow Brink

5

Little Wolden Edge

Castle Dean

Booth Dean

A672

Reservoirs

16

Wolden Edge Clough

Oxygrains

Humphrey Shore Rocks

OL15

Lodge Clough

Oxygrains Old Bridge

Spa Clough

Small Clough

Burn Clough Grains

M62

4

Great Wolden Edge

Broad Shaw Clough

Hunger Hill

Long Clough

3

Spa Clough Resr

Burn Clough

Linsgreave Brink

Burn Moss

Small Clough

15

Broad Shaw Flat

Lodge Hole

2

Moss Moor

Broad Shaw Graining

Burn Clough Flat

OL3

Linsgreave

Great Groove Holes

Middle Scars

1

Way Stone Edge

Way Pit Holes

Moss Moor Edge

HD7

Way Stone

14

149 132

A B C D E F

8
Pike Law
RISHWORTH NEW RD
LONG CSWY
Arkin Royd
Godly
Upper Arkin Royd
Heathfield School
Rishworth Palace
Ford
Burns Clough
Ringstone Edge Reser
Snow Hill
Pike End
Pike
Smithy Bank
RISHWORTH NEW LA
BANK BOTTOM
Far Royd
COCK PIT LA
WITHENS LA
Withens End
New Laithe
Pike End Hollows
Pike Clough
Black Hill
Esther Cliff
Near Royd
Pike Law
Royd Heights
Green Heugh

7
Rishworth Moor
Topster Hill
Turner Top
Turner Wood
Croft House
Clock Face Quarry
Plash House
Booth Moor
17
Cunning Corner Inn (PH)
Mill
Booth Dean Clough
Moselden Pasture
Picnic Area
P
Hudson Croft

6
Boan Cottage
Mount Pleasant Farm
Booth Wood
P
MOSELDEN LA
Broad Ing
WESTFIELD LA
HX4
LOWER TOP OF HEEL
Bent House
OLDHAM RD
P
HX6
Cow Gate Hill
Brown Cow Hotel (PH)
Mount Pleasant
London Pasture
Rishworth Lodge
The Derby
Green Field Lodge
Deanhead

5
A672
Booth Wood Reservoir
Stott Hall Farm
Moselden Heights
SADDLEWORTH RD
16
Hey Head Wood
High Moss
Bilberry Hill
Scammonden Water
Sailing Club

4
M62
Upper Posture
The Mosses
Black Burns Brook
NEW LA
Scammonden
Picnic Area
P
P
Upper Cars
SLEDGE GATE
Reddyshore

3
Privy Clough
Feather Team
Deanhead Reservoir
KIRKLEES WAY
Deanhead
Nont Sarah's Hotel (PH)
A640
Shrimp Hill
Head Green
Goat Hill
BURNT PLAT

15
Doe Holes
Deanhead Moor
Watermans House
WEST CARR LA

2
Lodge Greave
Deanhead Clough
Green Clough
Green Holes
The Carrs
HD3
Black Heath
HD7

1
Deanhead Moss
A640
NEW HEY RD
Slaithwaite Moor
Reaps
Bradshaw Clough
Cupwith Hill
Cupwith Reservoir
Reaps Hill

14
HD7
A6114
02 A B 03 C D 04 E F

149 168

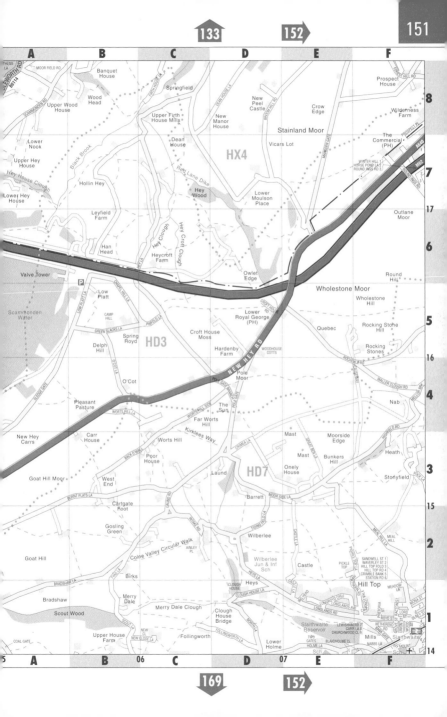

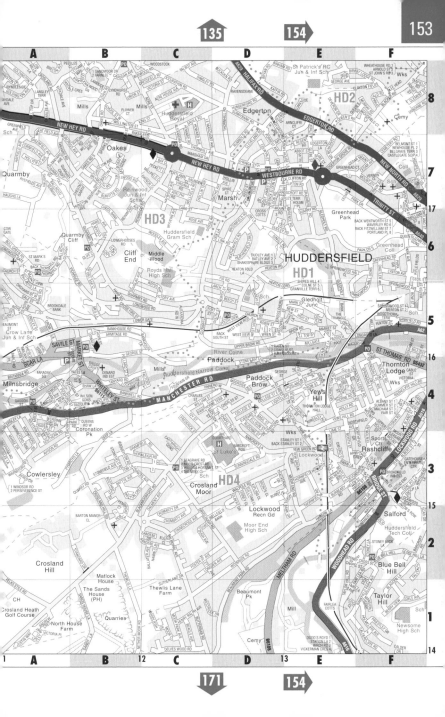

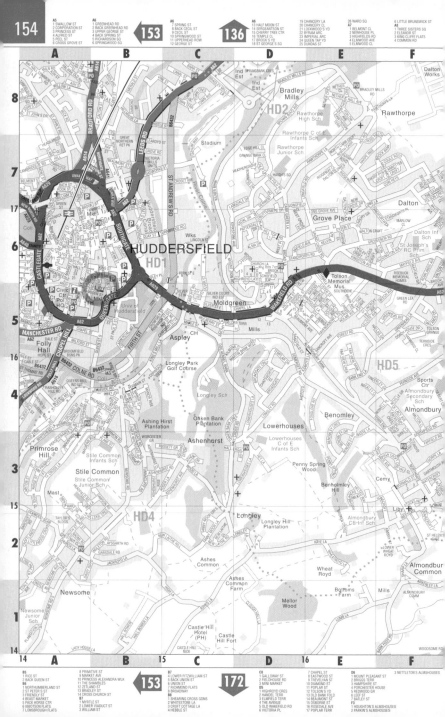

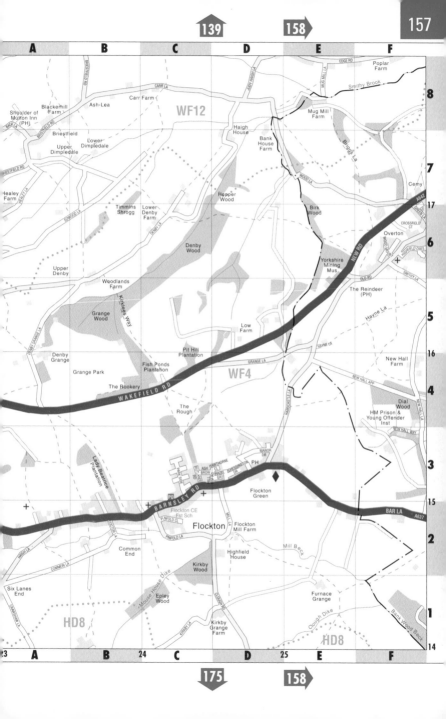

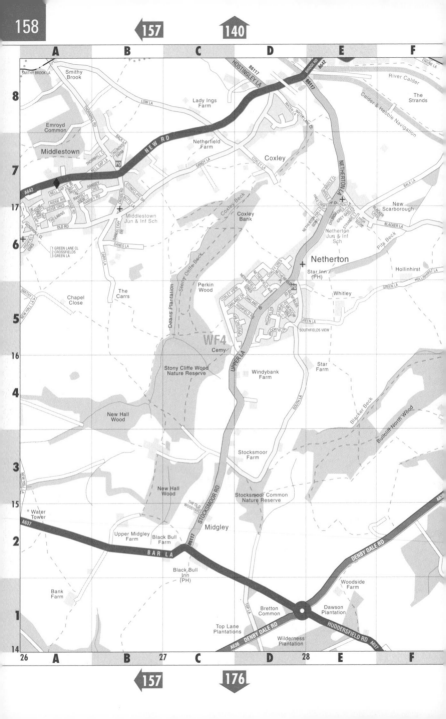

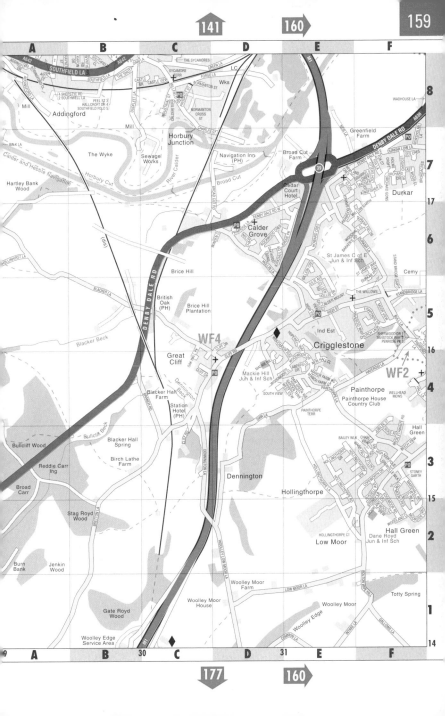

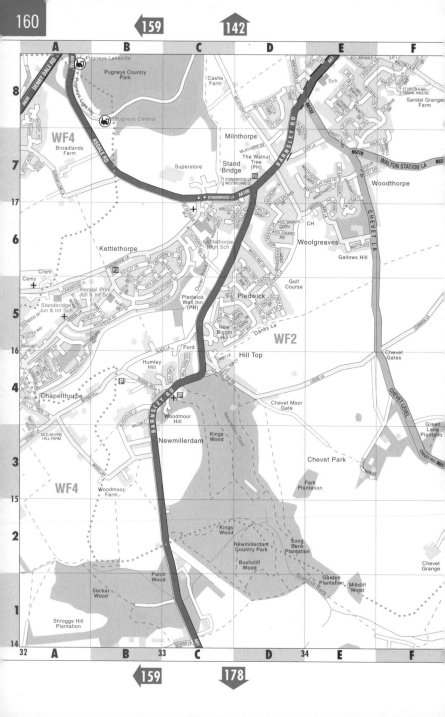

161
144

A   B   C   D   E   F

Fernlea Gl
Crofton Jun Sch
Crofton Inf Sch
Spring Mount
Hill Mount
Lanark Rise
8
Bedford Farm
PO
Glenn Way
Works
The Windmill (PH)
Foulby
Lidget Lane
DONCASTER RD
A638
Lower Lake
Foulby Farm
Nostell Park (Deer Park)
Middle Lake
Nostell Priory
Oak St
Beech Rd
Model La
New Crofton
Nostell Bridge
7
17
Upper Lake
Clay Pit
A638
Works
B6271
Vicarage
Wakefield Ind Sch
GARMIL LA
6
The Villas
Santilley La
5
Santingley Grange
Horncastle Wood
Water Tower
Garmil Head
GARMIL HEAD LA
16
WF4
Wintersett
Horncastle Hill
4
Anglers Retreat (PH)
HAW PARK LA
Reservoir Farm
BACK LA
WIND MILL LA
MIDDLE LA
B6428
3
Ferry Top
FERRY TOP LA
Horncastle Farm
NEWSTEAD LA
Horncastle View
WF9
15
Newstead Grange
Newstead Hall
2
Newstead
Horncastle View
Havercroft
COW LA
Kinsley Carr Farm
Ryhill
Cemy
Ryhill Prim Sch
PO
St James Ct
Meadow Bank
Whin View Ct
Hardie Rd
Hill Crest
Attlee Ave
Liby
1
Ryhill Ind Est
B6428
14
38 A   B 39 C   D 40 E   F

161
180

163 146

High Ackworth
PURSTON LA
B6474
A628
PONTEFRACT RD
PO
WEST HILL CL
HILL LA
ACKWORTH HOUSE CL
Court
Farm
Townend
Farm
The
Royds
Ackworth
Grange
WHITEGATE LA
Green Lane
Farm
DONCASTER RD
A639 WHITEGATE HILL

Ackworth
House
VILLA CL
WESTFIELD
BEECHWOOD DALE
YORK PL
BROWNROYD ST
LONGFIELD DR
TOWN END RD
WINDSOR
AVE
Low Ackworth
Howard
CE Jun &
Inf Sch
LINDALE AVE
South
Lodge
The
Chestnuts
Low Grange
Farm
Kennels
Farm

Ackworth
Sch
MOUNT
PLEASANT
BARNSLEY RD
A628
LOW FARM LA
Low Farm
Low Farm
WF7
Tan House Dike
RIGG LA
ACKWORTH BROOK RD
WF8
Sewage
Works

MILL LA
Mill Dam
Jun & Inf
Sch
Moor
House
Burnhill
Bridge

A638
Cemy
Sch
OAKENELL
Rockingham
Gorse
ROCKINGHAM LA
BURNHILL LA

Oak Tree
Sch
BARNSLEY RD A638
Cherry Tree
Farm
Firth Field
FIRTHFIELD LA
THORPE GILL
DALE SLACK

Shepherd's
Hill
DONCASTER RD
Ninevah
Farm
RYE HILL RD
MOOR WLK
The
Grove
BOND LA
THORPE LA
Rogerthor
Manor
(PH)

Hemsworth
Lanes
Badsworth
Common
WF9
BADSWORTH CT
1 GRANGE CT
2 BADSWORTH MEWS
3 MANOR FARM
4 NEW ROW
Hall Farm
Badsworth
CE Jun &
Inf Sch
MEW RD
MAIN ST
Brookside
Farm
BEACONSFIELD RD B6

A628
Marsh Whin
Covert
Royd Moor
Farm
ROYD MOOR LA
A628
Badsworth
Grange
Badsworth

163 182

A B C D E F

8

Wicken Clough
Hassock
Buckstones Moss
Foxstone Moss
B6114
Buckstones House
A640 NEW HEY RD
Broadrake Green
Hard Head
Blacker Edge
Chamber Clough
Buckstones

7

White Hill
Linegreave Head
Readycon Hill
White Hassock
Tom Clough
March Hill Holes
Broadrake Clough

13

March Haigh
March Hill Carr
March Haigh Rest

6

Green Brow
Dan Clough Moss
March Hill
Dan Clough
HD7
Willmer Green Clough
Berry Greave

5

Rape Hill
Rapes
RAPES HIGHWAY
Broad Wham
Station to Station Walk
Stotley Moss
Broad Greave Hill
Haigh Gutter
Little Moss
Stonepit Lee Clough

12

Denshaw Moor
Fair prings
Dowry Water
HUDDERSFIELD RD
Haigh Gutter Moss
Oldgate Moss
Fore Wham

4

Mere Clough Moss
OL3
Short Grain
Wicking Green

3

Dowry Castle Hill
Oldham Way
Denshaw
Castleshaw Moor
Blea Green
Northern Rotcher
Pennine Way
Wicking Clough
Close Moss

11

Grange Hey
Cudworth Pasture
Spa Clough
Cudworth Clough

2

Moor Lane
Bank Clough
Oaken Lee Clough
Dinner Stone
Coal Hill Slades
Millstone Edge
Thieves Clough

1

Broadhead Noddle
Broadhead
LOW GATE LA
Castleshaw Upper Resr
Lee Clough
Brown Rough
Bentley Farm
Higher Standedge

10

99 A B 00 C D 01 E F

A44

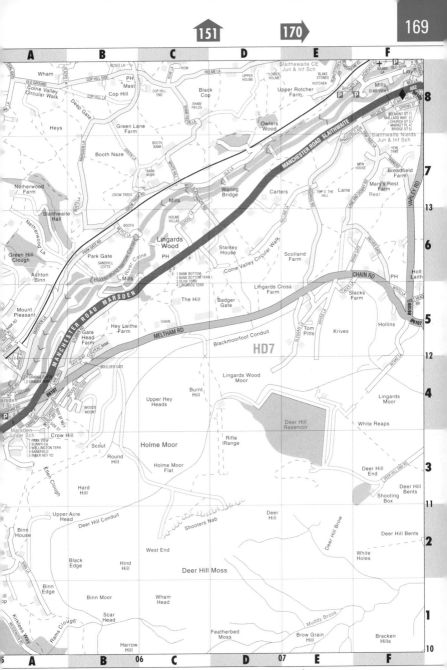

169
152

169
187

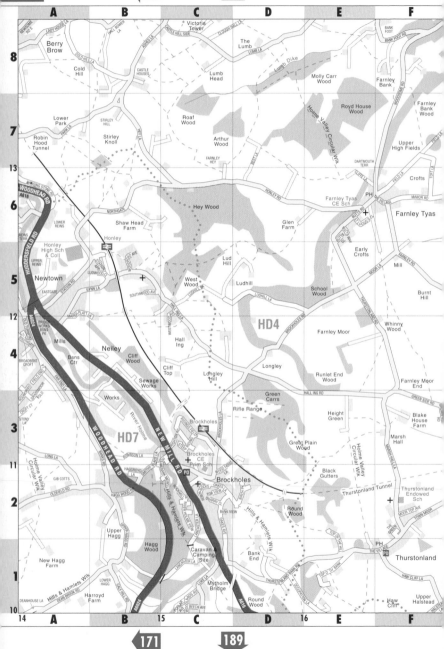

171
154

A   B   C   D   E   F

8 Berry Brow
   Cold Hill
   MILL BOWER LA
   CASTLE HILL SIDE
   Victoria Tower
   CLOUGH HALL LA
   The Lumb
   LUMB LA
   Lumb Dike
   Molly Carr Wood
   BANK FOOT
   BANK FOOT RD
   Farnley Bank
   OLD HALL LA
   CASTLE HOUSES
   ADSE LA
   Lumb Head
   Farnley Bank Wood

7 Lower Park
   STIRLEY HILL
   Robin Hood Tunnel
   Stirley Knoll
   Roaf Wood
   Arthur Wood
   FARNLEY HEY
   Holme Valley Circular Wlk
   Royd House Wood
   Upper High Fields
   DARTMOUTH TERR
   13

6 WOODHEAD RD   A616
   RING STREET RD
   Lower Reins
   NORTHGATE
   Shaw Head Farm
   Honley
   Hey Wood
   HONLEY RD
   Glen Farm
   Farnley Tyas CE Sch
   PH   THE VILLAGE
   MANOR RD
   Farnley Tyas
   HUDDERSFIELD RD

5 REINS TERR
   Newtown
   Honley High Sch & Coll
   UPPER REINS
   LUDWOOD
   EASTGATE
   GYNN LA
   SOUTHWOOD AVE
   LUDHILL LA
   West Wood
   Lud Hill
   Ludhill
   LUDHILL LA
   School Wood
   Early Crofts
   MOOR LA
   FARNLEY RD
   Mill
   Burnt Hill
   12

4 BROADBENT CROFT
   MARIA PLATT LA
   Mills
   BRIDGE WORKS BSNS PK
   Bans Ctr
   Neiley
   Cliff Wood
   Cliff Top
   Hall Ing
   HD4
   Farnley Moor
   Whinny Wood
   Farnley Moor End
   GREEN SIDE RD
   Sewage Works

3 BROADBENT GROFT
   CREST CT
   STONY LA
   Works
   River Holme
   HD7
   WOODHEAD RD
   NEW MILL RD
   Brockholes
   Longley Hill
   Longley
   HALL ING RD
   Green Carrs
   Rifle Range
   Runlet End Wood
   Height Green
   Great Plain Wood
   Marsh Hall
   Blake House Farm

11 Holme Valley Circular Wlk
   GIB COTTS
   LONG LA
   OLDFIELD RD
   ROBINSON LA
   HAGGREVD
   SANDS RD
   Brockholes CE Prim Sch
   PO
   Brockholes
   Black Gutters
   Holme Valley Circular Wlk
   Thurstonland Tunnel
   Thurstonland Endowed Sch
   MOOR TOP AVE

2 Upper Hagg
   NAGG WOOD LA
   Hagg Wood
   BANK VIEW
   TOP ROW
   QUARRY LA
   Hills & Hamlets Wlk
   Round Wood
   TOP OF THE HILL
   TOWN MOOR
   PH   THE VILLAGE
   PO
   Thurstonland

1 New Hagg Farm
   Upper Hagg
   Hagg Wood
   Caravan & Camping Site
   LANCASTER LA
   Bank End
   THURSTONLAND RD
   DIP O' TH' BANK
   Upper Halstead
   HAW CLIFF LA

10 DEANHOUSE LA
   Hills & Hamlets Wlk
   DEAN BROOK RD
   LOWER HAGG
   Harroyd Farm
   BEECH AVE
   Mytholm Bridge
   A616
   Round Wood
   CLOUGH LA
   Haw Cliff

14   15   C   16   E   F

A   B   C   D   E   F

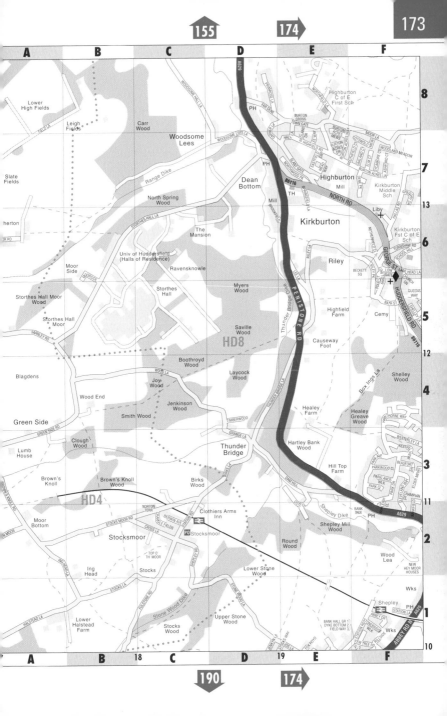

A B C D E F

8

Manor Mill Farm
Yew Tree Farm
WF4
Butts Top
Rock Wood Farm
Emley Moo

Sheep Cote

Cross Roads

MOOR LA BURTON ROYD LA

7

BURTON ACRES LA

Schs

Thorncliff

CINDER HILL

PUMP LA

Thorncliff Spring Farm

The Heater

13

HALLAS LA THORNCLIFF GREEN RD

Highfield House

Moor Head Plantation

Mast

6

Oakroyd
Lane Head

LANE HEAD LA

Common Side

Highwood

Highwood

Gryce Hall

Carr House

The Three Acres (PH)

Moor Head

High Chambe

Lane Head Farm

Roydhouse

5

Folly Hall House

CROSS LA

Standinghurst Farm

Lane End

Wool Row Farm

12

HUDDERSFIELD RD

Radcliffe Wood

PILLING TOP LA

HD8
Green House

Rough Piece Wood

Lightcliff Wood

Silver Ings

4

Wood Nook Farm

GREEN HOUSE LA

Springs Wood

Baildon Place

WESTFIELD

PH

Town End

Shelley

BARK HOUSE LA

Windmill Hill

Peace Wood

WESTERLEY LA

3

BACK LA

KIRK LA

FAR BANK

Shelley First Sch

1 WATER LA
2 DOCTOR LA

HORSE CROFT LA

Shelley Woodhouse

HUDDERSFIELD RD

SCHOOL TERR

STONELEIGH CT

11

JUBILEE

Woodhouse Farm

Skelmanthorpe Common

ABBEY RD

2

ALLEN VIEW RD

Brook Bridge

Tunnel

Round Hill

Common End

STATION RD

Long Moor

Kirklees Light Railway

SHELLEY WOODHOUSE LA

Shelley High Sch

GARRETT

1

LONG MOOR LA

Barncliffe Dike Farm

Clayton West Junction

Shelley

Mount Pleasant Farm

Cliff Hill Farm

BARNSLEY RD

COAL PIT LA

Cumberworth Common

Ponker

10

THE KNOWLE

20 A 21 B C 22 D E F

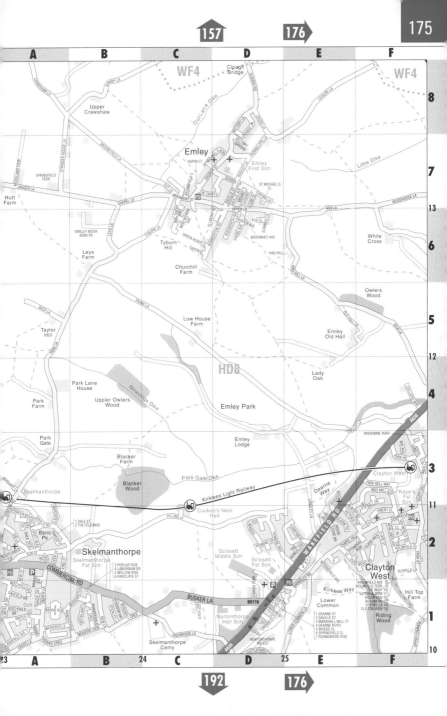

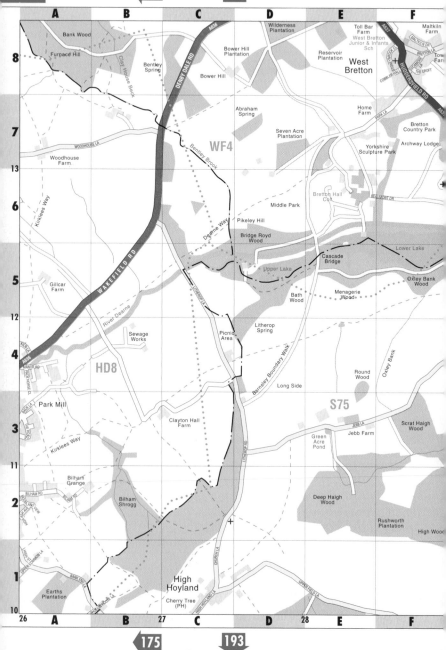

A   B   C   D   E   F

8   Bank Wood
Furnace Hill
Bentley Spring
Clay House Beck
DERBY DALE RD A636
Bower Hill Plantation
Bower Hill
Wilderness Plantation
Reservoir Plantation
Toll Bar Farm
West Bretton Junior & Infants Sch
West Bretton
Maltkiln Farm
COBBLER HALL
HUDDERSFIELD RD A637
THE CROFT

7   Abraham Spring
Bentley Brook
WF4
Seven Acre Plantation
Home Farm
PARK LA
Bretton Country Park
Archway Lodge
Yorkshire Sculpture Park

13   WOODHOUSE LA
Woodhouse Farm.
Kirklees Way
Middle Park
Pikeley Hill
Bretton Hall Coll
BEAUMONT DR

6   Dearne Way
Bridge Royd Wood
Cascade Bridge
Lower Lake

5   WAKEFIELD RD
Gillcar Farm
Upper Lake
Bath Wood
Menagerie Wood
Oxley Bank Wood

12   River Dearne
Sewage Works
Picnic Area
Litherop Spring
Burnley Boundary Walk
KENT LA   A636

4   HD8
MANOR RD
WHITE HORSE LA
Park Mill
Clayton Hall Farm
Long Side
Round Wood
Oxley Bank
S75

3   Kirklees Way
LITHEROP RD
Green Acre Pond
JEBB LA
Jebb Farm
Scrat Haigh Wood

11   Bilham Grange
BILHAM RD
Bilham Shrogg
CHURCH LA

2   BILHAM LA
SPEAR SLACK LA
Deep Haigh Wood
Rushworth Plantation
High Wood

1   UPPER COMMON LA
BANK END LA
High Hoyland
Cherry Tree (PH)
HIGH HOYLAND LA
CHURCH LA
UPPER FIELD LA

10   Earths Plantation

26   A   B   27   C   D   28   E   F

A B C D E F

8

PO

BRETTON LA
GALLOWS LA
WATER LA
COMMON LA
Wooley Edge
Service Area
BRAMPTON RD
Bimshaw
Wood
COMMON LA
WOOLLEY LOW MOOR LA
Picnic
Site
Mast
High Moor
Common
Doles
WF4
Eccle
Hill
7
Sewage
Works
Savin Royd
Wood
Beacon
Hill
Ash Farm
Woolley
SACKHOUSE LA
FUNKLE CL
FUNKLE CL
Rose
Farm
High House
Farm
WENTWORTH ST
MOLLY HURST LA
Church
Farm
13
HUDDERSFIELD RD
Dearne Way &
Barnsley
Boundary Walk
BICKHOUSE LA
Moor House
Spring
MIDDLE FIELD LA
6
Bretton
Park
Smithy
Ridge
HAIGH MEWS
Near Moor
Farm
Jobson
Wood
GIPSY LA
CLAPHOUSE
FOLD
Sewage
Works
MOORHOUSE LA
Haw Top
5
Haigh
Spoil
Heap
Barnsley Boundary Walk
12
38
Haigh
Hall
Low
Swithen
S75
Windhill
Gate
4
Sheep Lane
Head
HUDDERSFIELD RD
Riverside
Farm
Windhill
Wood
Husband
Wood
3
Swithen
House
River Dearne
Colliery
TOP
ROW
WOOLLEY COLLIERY RD
Upper
Swithen
BLUEBELL RD
LOW
ROW
Fish Pond
Halt
WALK ROYD HILL
PARK HILL
SWITHIN HILL
11
Sewage
Works
2
High
Wood
Dearne Way
Spoil
Heap
BLOOMHOUSE LA
KINGS RD
Bloomhouse
Snapethorpe
Birthwaite
Hall
HUDDERSFIELD RD
SPRING RAM
B6NS PK
FOUNTAIN
RD
Darton
Jun & Inf
Sch
1 OAKS WOOD DR
1
Cowcroft
Wood
BULLFIELD LA
Brook
Hill
Darton
STATION RD
CHURCH ST
M1
A637
BIRTHWAITE RD
ALLENDALE RD
LAMBE FLAT
PO
10

Kexbrough
Squirrel
Hall

A1
1 BLOOMFIELD RISE
2 BLOOMFIELD RD
3 OAKS FARM DR
4 PRIEST ROYD
5 CROFT CL

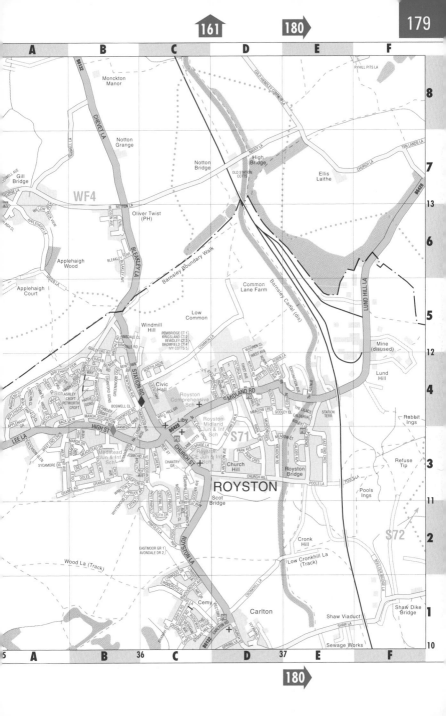

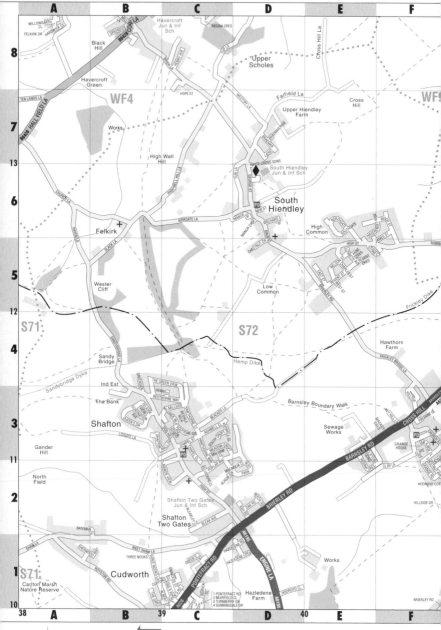

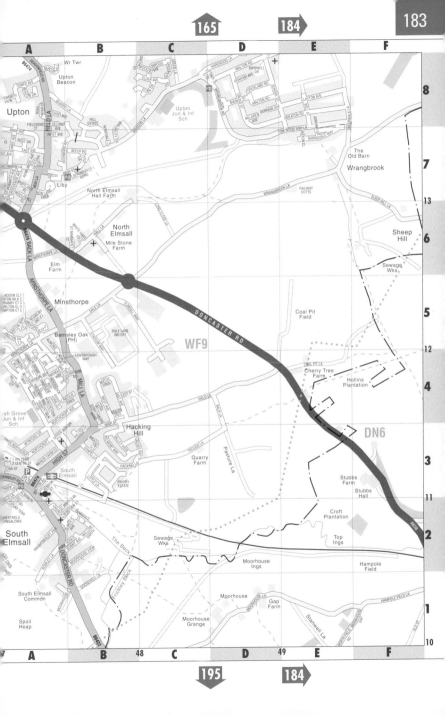

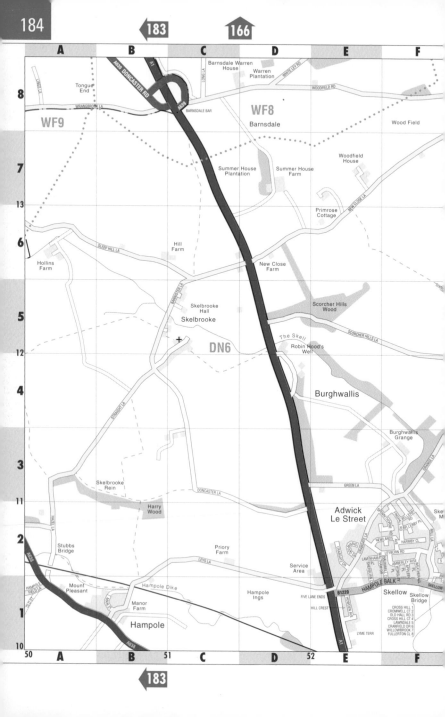

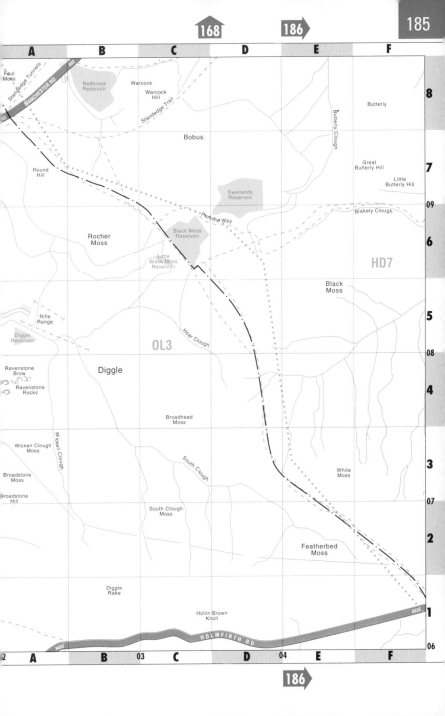

Grid labels

A B C D E F

8 7 6 5 4 3 2 1

09 08 07 06

2 03 04

Map labels

Foul Moss

Standedge Tunnels

MANCHESTER RD

A62

Redbrook Reservoir

Warcock

Warcock Hill

Standedge Trail

Butterly

Butterly Clough

Bobus

Great Butterly Hill

Little Butterly Hill

Round Hill

Swellands Reservoir

Pennine Way

09

Blakely Clough

Rocher Moss

Black Moss Reservoir

Little Black Moss Reservoir

HD7

Black Moss

Rifle Range

Diggle Reservoir

Hoar Clough

OL3

08

Ravenstone Brow

Ravenstone Rocks

Diggle

Broadhead Moss

Wicken Clough Moss

Wicken Clough

White Moss

Broadstone Moss

South Clough

Broadstone Hill

South Clough Moss

07

Featherbed Moss

Diggle Rake

Hollin Brown Knoll

A635

HOLMFIRTH RD

A635

06

A B C D E F

8

Butterley Reservoir

Holme Bank Wood

Rigg Shaw

Great Clough

Muddy Brook

The Scope

Blakeley Reservoir

Scope Moss

Meltham Moor

7

Adam Pasture

Hey Dike

Horseley Head Moss

Sike Clough

West Nab Moss

West Nab Brow

09

Hey Green

Hey Brinks

Hey Sike Head Marsh

West Nab

Wessenden Lodge

6

Holly Bank Moss

Raven Rocks

Little Hey Sike Clough

Wessenden Reservoir

Pennine Way

Great Dike Springs

Great Hey Cote Hill

5

Birken Bank

HD7

Pennine Way

Leyzing Clough

Flake Moss

08

Wessenden Brook

Lower Hills

Winter Clough

Wessenden Moor

4

Pudding Real Moss

P

Birk Moss

Wessenden Head Reservoir

A63

3

Shiny Brook Clough

Jopes Moss

Wicken Grain

Wessenden Head

Kirklees Way

Shiny Brook

07

West Grain

Loadley Clough

Reap Hill Clough

Pennine Way

2

Great Rushbed

Wessenden Head Moss

Nearmost Grain

Hoe Grain

1

P
A635

OL3

Dean Head Moss

Wessenden Head Moor

06

Dean Head Hill

05 A B 06 C D 07 E F

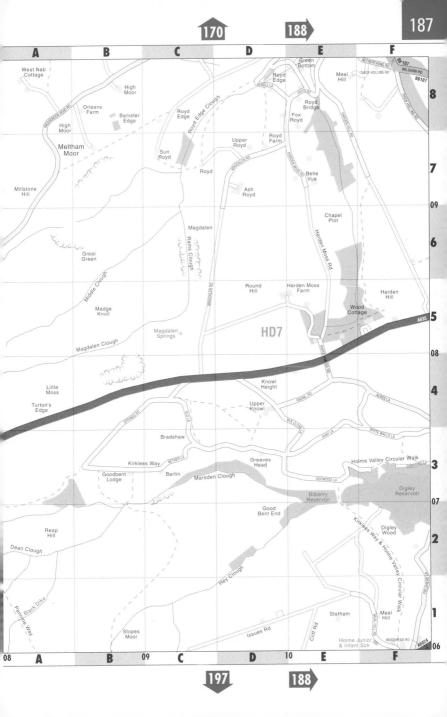

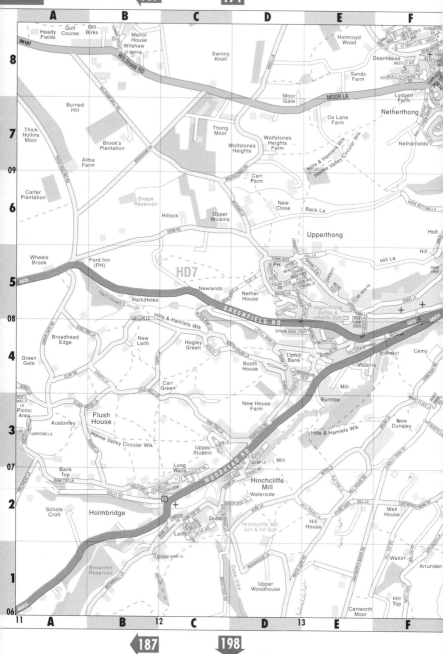

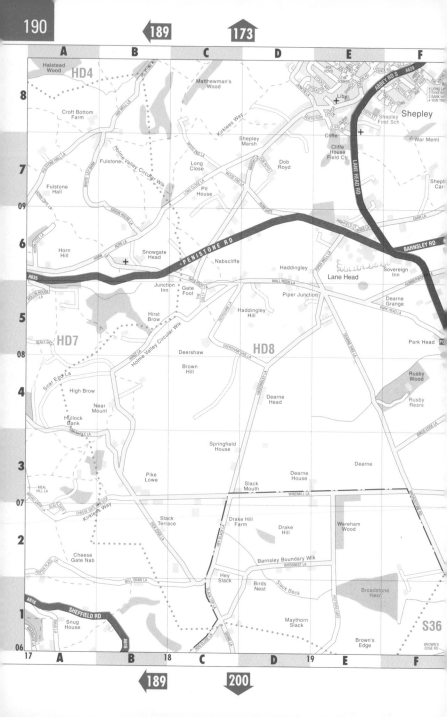

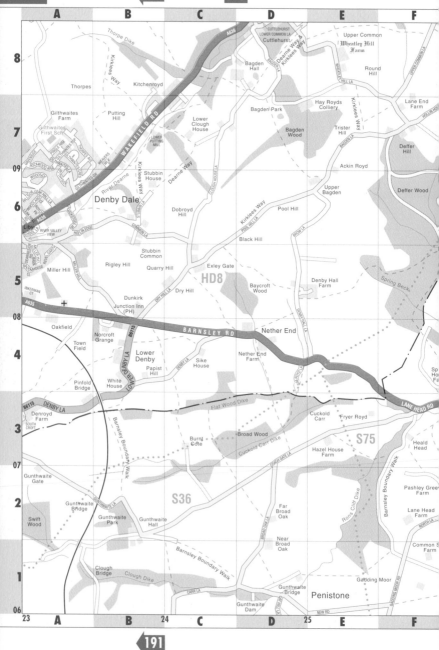

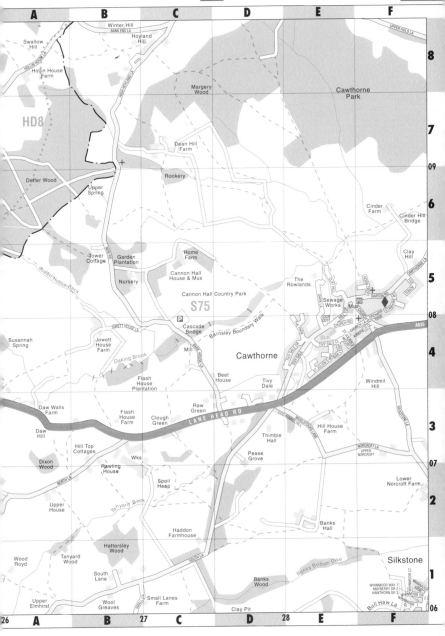

A B C D E F

8

Winter Hill
BANK END LA
Hoyland
Hill
Swallow
Hill
Hollin House
Farm

UPPER FIELD LA

Cawthorne
Park
Margery
Wood

7

HD8

Dean Hill
Farm

09

Deffer Wood
Rookery
Upper
Spring

6

Cinder
Farm
Cinder Hill
Bridge

Tower
Cottage
Garden
Plantation
Home
Farm

Clay
Hill

South House Beck

Nursery
Cannon Hall
House & Mus
The
Rowlands

5

Cannon Hall Country Park

S75

Sewage
Works
Mus
DARTON

08

Cascade
Bridge
Barnsley Boundary Walk

Susannah
Spring
Jowett
House
Farm
Daking Brook
Mill

Sch

4

Cawthorne

TIVY DALE

A635

Daw Walls
Farm
Flash
House
Plantation
Beet
House
Tivy
Dale
Windmill
Hill

Daw
Hill
Flash
House
Farm
Clough
Green
Raw
Green

LANE HEAD RD

Hill House
Farm

3

Thimble
Hall

NORCROFT LA
UPPER
NORCROFT
HAWTHORN DR

07

Hill Top
Cottages
Wks
Pease
Grove

Dixon
Wood
Rawling
House

Lower
Norcroft
Farm

Upper
House
Tanyard Beck
Spoil
Heap

2

NORTH LA

Banks
Hall

Haddon
Farmhouse

Wood
Royd
Tanyard
Wood
Hattersley
Wood

Banks Bottom Dike

Silkstone

1

South Lane

Banks
Wood

WHINMOOR WAY
MAYBERRY DR
HAWTHORN GR

Upper
Elmhirst
Wool
Greaves
Small Lanes
Farm
Clay Pit

Bull Haw La

Factory

Spoil Heap

Collieries

East Farm

West Farm

Spoil Heap

WF9

Whin Covert Plantation

FRICKLEY LA

Howell Wood Country Park

Howell Beck

Frickley Hall

Howell House

Spring Wood

Clayton Common

Wink House

Frickley Park

Frickley

Home Farm

Challenger Wood

TOP LA

SPORTSWOOD LA

CROWTREE LA

CHAPEL HILL

MAIN LA

The Green

CROW CROFT

TAN PIT LA

TEAPOT CNR

TAN PIT CL

DN5

Estate House

SELBY LA

Broadlands Farm

CHURCH FIELD RD

Lodge Farm

Clayton

Spry Wood

Bagsley Boundary Walk

Great Houghton

Thurnscoe Dike

CLAYTON LA

Knabs Hill House

Knabs Hill

STOTTS RD

S72

S63

Warehouses

Dearne High Sch

DEARNE

WHINSIDE CRES

Thurnscoe Gooseacre Jun & Mid Sch

MANOR RD

MERRILL RD

PANGBOURNE RD

LOW GRANGE RD

Hawthorne Flats

ROMAN ST

BRITTON ST

YORK ST

GRANGE CRES

Hill Prim Sch

Sewage Works

THURNSCOE LA

HOUGHTON RD

B6411

CLAYTON DR

CLAYTON AVE

WF9

Spoil Heap

Moorhouse Common

DN6

Hooton Thorn Covert

The Ashes

North Field

ELMSALL LA

LENNY BALK

Hooton Pagnell Wood

BROAD BALK

Back Field

Hooton Pagnell

Hooton Pagnell Common

Hooton Pagnell C of E Sch

HOME FARM CT

NARROW BALK

Lound Hill

Church Plantation

Redroof

Bluegate Flatt Plantation

Mapple Yard

Bread Walls Plantation

Broadrick Holt

Mapple Yard Plantation

Hooton Pagnell Hall

DN5

Black Plantation

Cemy

Cricket Ground

BUTT LA

WHITE LA

B6422 HOOTON RD

Second Plantation

BILHAM ROW

Norman Hill

Third Plantation

WATCHLEY LA

Bilham Grange

Little Watchley

Fish Pond Plantation

Bilham Lodge

Watchley Crag

Brodsworth

The Wilderness

Bilham Park

Bilham Wood

Stotfold Farm

Bilham House Farm

Summer House Plantation

Water Tower

Hickleton Spring

09

7

6

5

08

4

3

07

2

06

1

A   B   48   C   D   49   E   F

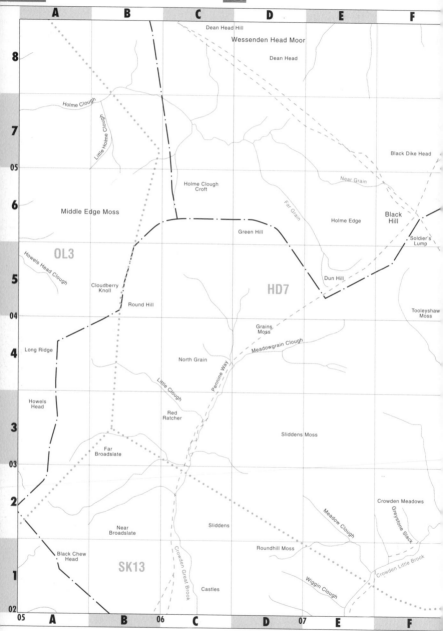

A   **B**   **C**   **D**   **E**   **F**

8

7

05

6

OL3

5

04

HD7

4

3

03

2

1

02

05 **A**   **B** 06 **C**   **D** 07 **E**   **F**

Dean Head Hill
Wessenden Head Moor
Dean Head

Holme Clough
Little Holme Clough

Black Dike Head
Near Grain

Holme Clough Croft

Middle Edge Moss

Far Grain

Holme Edge

Black Hill

Howels Head Clough

Green Hill

Soldier's Lump

Cloudberry Knoll

Round Hill

Dun Hill

Tooleyshaw Moss

Long Ridge

Grains Moss

Meadowgrain Clough

North Grain

Pennine Way

Howels Head

Little Clough

Red Ratcher

Sliddens Moss

Far Broadslate

Crowden Meadows

Greystone Slack

Near Broadslate

Sliddens

Meadow Clough

Black Chew Head

Roundhill Moss

Crowden Little Brook

SK13

Crowden Great Brook

Castles

Wiggin Clough

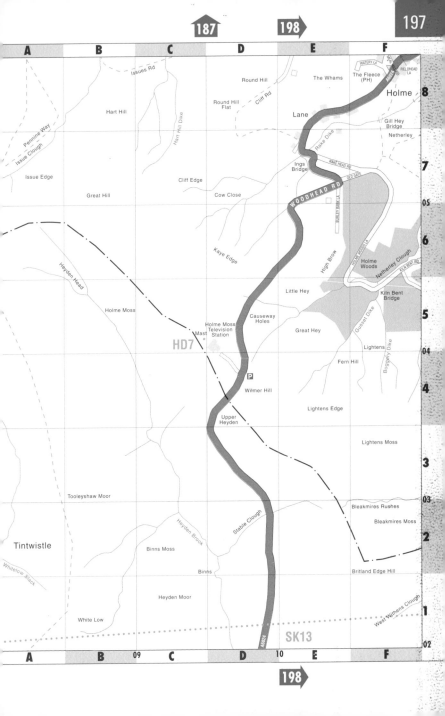

Brownhill Resr
Kirklees Way
Holme Valley Circular Walk
Netherley
Ramsden Resr
Netherley Brow
Green House Lane
Crow Hill
Moss Edge
Holme Valley Circular Walk
White Gate
Dobb Dike
Upper White Gate
Elysium
Kirklees Way
Fox Clough
Holli Hill
Kirklees Way
Raynard Clough
Riding Wood Resr
Ramsden Edge
Crossley's Plantation
Copthurst Moor
Hades
Holme Valley Circular Walk
Yateholme Cote
Peat Pit Moss
Hades Green
Yateholme Resr
Green House Hey Wood
Hades Peat Pits
Lower Flat
HD7
Cook's Study Hill
Linshaws Scar
Great Twizle Clough
Little Twizle Clough
The Rakes
Herbage Flat
Herbage Edge
Ramsden Rocks
Herbage Hill
Ruddle Clough Moss
Elbow End
Ruddle Clough
Ruddle Clough Knoll
Cook's Study Moss
Snailsden Resr
Reaps Dike
Great Twizle Hole
Great Twizle Head
Ramsden Clough
Lad Clough Knoll
Lad Clough
Reaps Moss
Upper Snailsden Moss
Herbage Moss
Twizle Head Moss
Snailsden Pike End
Snailsden Edge
Laund Moss
Bailie Causeway Moss
Swiner Clough Top
Swiner Dike
Swiner Clough
S36
Swiner Clough Moss
Grains Edge
Don Well
River Don
Ford
Grains End
West Withens Clough
Great Grains
Great Grains Clough
Black Grough
Little Grain Clough
Dead Edge Flat
SK13
Grains Moss
Withens Edge

199 190

A B C D E F

8

BARNSIDE LA
SNUG LA
Barnside
GATE HEAD LA
SHEFFIELD RD
A616
Shafts (dis)
HD7
Wood Royd Hill
GREVE LA
Upper Maythorn
POTTER LANE
HD8
BROWN'S EDGE RD
The Whams
LOWER MAYTHORN LA
UPPER MAYTHORN
Lower Maythorn
Whitley Common

7

Cote Hill
BROAD OAK RD
Victoria Inn (PH)
Victoria
Blackstone Edge
WHITLEY RD

Nab Hill
Upper Nab
SECOND LODE RD
Bedding Edge
Hepshaw Brow
Hepshaw
Sledbrook Brow
DIKE BECK
Husking Holes
Upper Whitley

05

Lower Whitley
Upper Whitley Edge
Whitley Height

6

B6106
Law Bottom Piece
Long Moors
Lower Whitley Edge
FLINTER LODE
Prince of Wales Hotel (PH)
FURNACE COTTS
Works
Crow Edge
Shiner Hill

PH
Works
Lower Whitley Farm
Kiln Hill

5

Riddlepit
FLINT LA
Slag Heap
Lumb Hills
WHITLEY TOP RD
LODE FIELD LA
Middle Cliff

04

Finkle Edge
Larches Plantation
S36
Sledbrook Hill
Sledbrook Dike

4

Topping Moor
Brook Bridge
BENTS RD
LEE LA
B6106
Sledbrook Bridge

Parsonage House
Carlecotes Hall
BROOK HILL LA
Savile House
Hillside
Low Lathe
Town Brook

3

Carlecotes
Eltack Farm
Hazlehead Bridge

03

Castle Hill
Soughley
Bracken Wood
Hazlehead
WHAMS RD

2

River Don
Cote Bank Bridge
Low Moor Ridge

Heald Common
Lower Cat Clough
Thurlstone Moors
Low Moor

1

Dick Royd
Rolly Holme
Cat Clough Hill
Reddishaw Knoll

02

Wogden Moor
Cat Clough Head
A616

17 A B 18 C D 19 E F

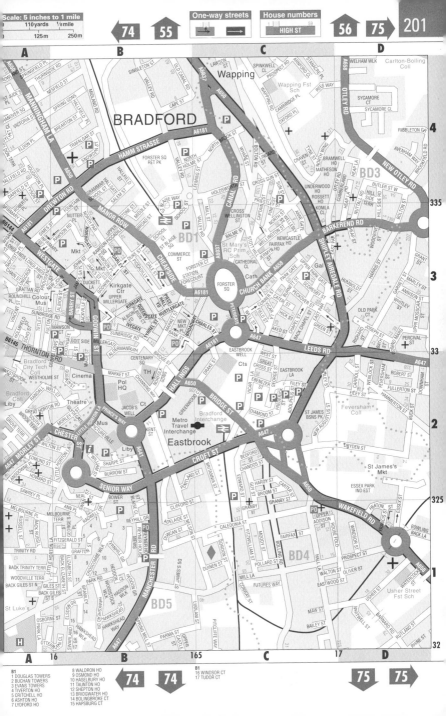

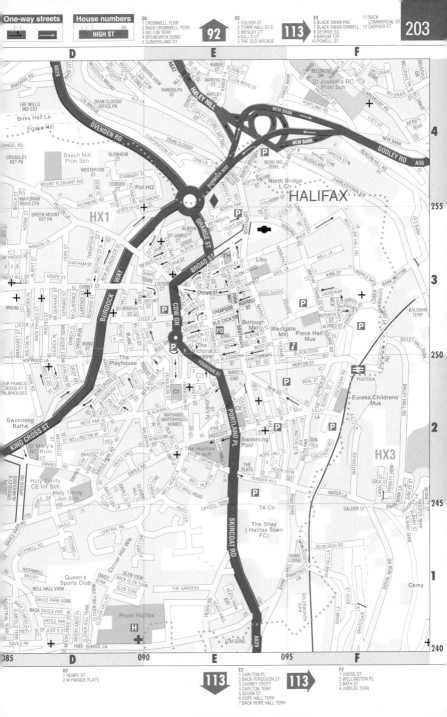

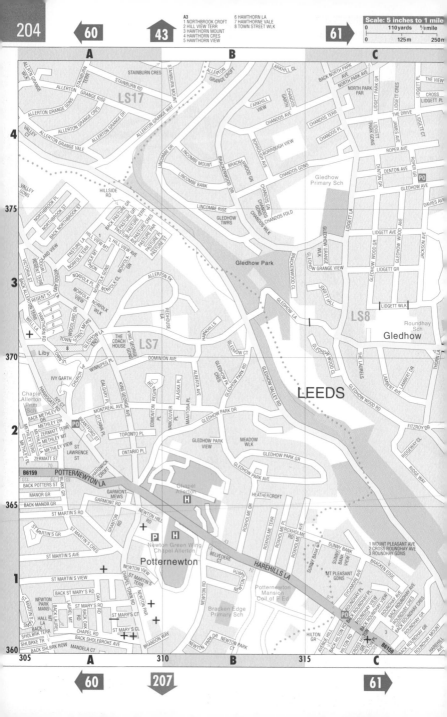

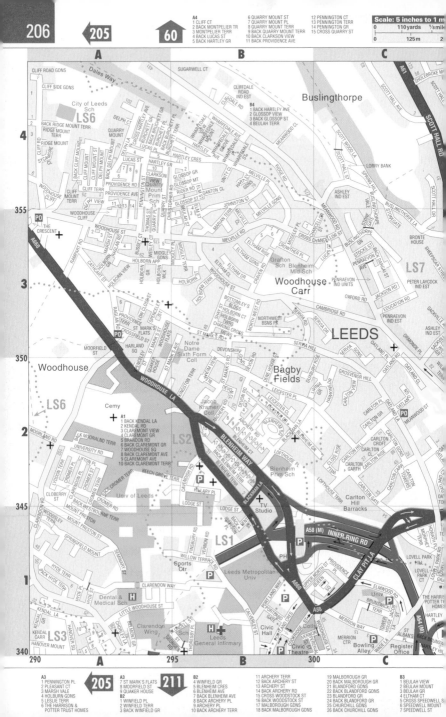

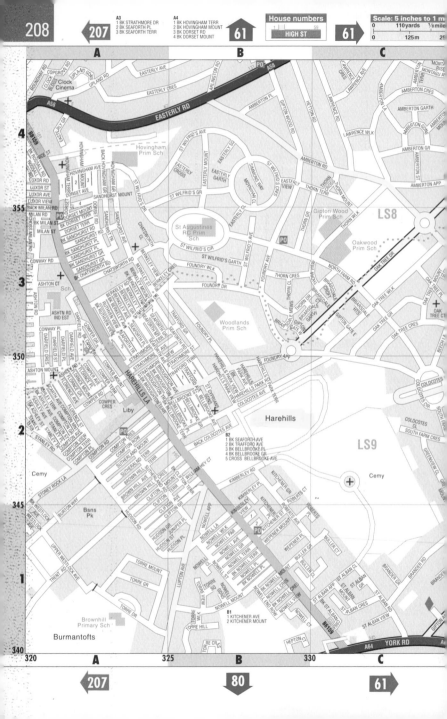

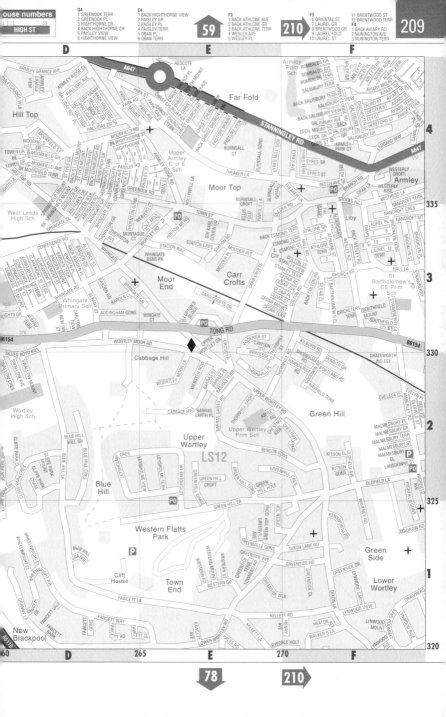

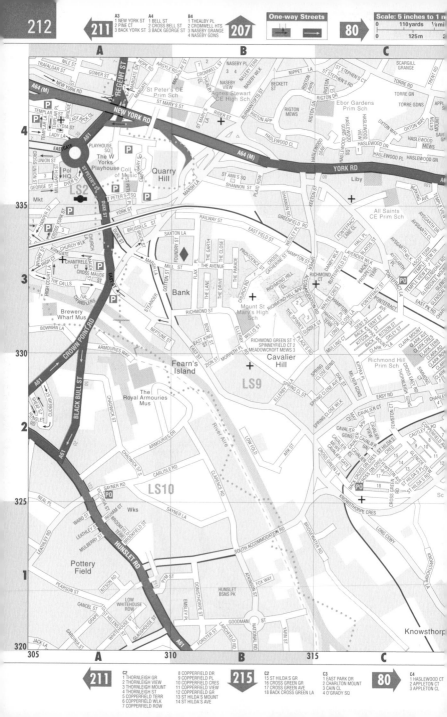

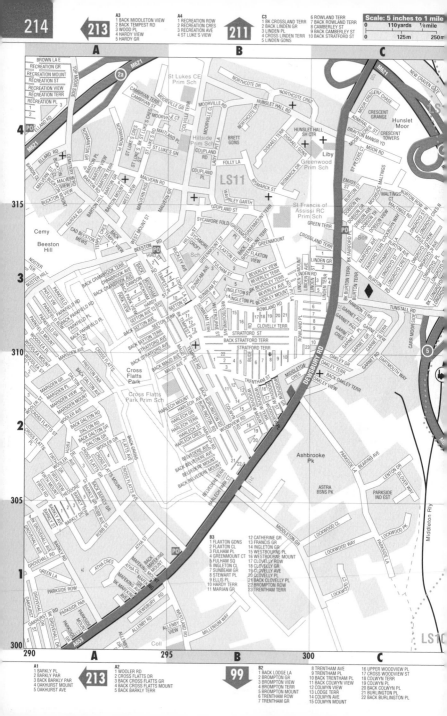

213

211

Scale: 5 inches to 1 mile

0   110yards   ⅛ mile
0   125m   250m

A3
1 BACK MIDDLETON VIEW
2 BACK TEMPEST RD
3 WOOD PL
4 HARDY VIEW
5 HARDY GR

A4
1 RECREATION ROW
2 RECREATION CRES
3 RECREATION AVE
4 ST LUKE'S VIEW

C3
1 BK CROSSLAND TERR
2 BACK LINDEN GR
3 LINDEN PL
4 CROSS LINDEN TERR
5 LINDEN GDNS

6 ROWLAND TERR
7 BACK ROWLAND TERR
8 CAMBERLEY ST
9 BACK CAMBERLEY ST
10 BACK STRATFORD ST

B3
1 FLAXTON GDNS
2 FLAXTON CL
3 FULHAM PL
4 GREENMOUNT CT
5 FULHAM SQ
6 INGLETON CL
7 SUNBEAM GR
8 STEWART PL
9 ELLIS PL
10 HARDY TERR
11 MARIAN GR

12 CATHERINE GR
13 FRANCIS GR
14 INGLETON GR
15 WESTBOURNE PL
16 WESTBOURNE MOUNT
17 CLOVELLY ROW
18 CLOVELLY GR
19 CLOVELLY AVE
20 CLOVELLY PL
21 BACK CLOVELLY PL
22 BROMPTON ROW
23 TRENTHAM TERR

213

99

A1
1 BARKLY PL
2 BARKLY PAR
3 BACK BARKLY PAR
4 OAKHURST MOUNT
5 OAKHURST AVE

A2
1 WOOLER RD
2 CROSS FLATTS DR
3 BACK CROSS FLATTS GR
4 BACK CROSS FLATTS MOUNT
5 BACK BARKLY TERR

B2
1 BACK LODGE LA
2 BROMPTON GR
3 BROMPTON VIEW
4 BROMPTON TERR
5 BROMPTON MOUNT
6 TRENTHAM ROW
7 TRENTHAM GR

8 TRENTHAM AVE
9 TRENTHAM PL
10 BACK TRENTHAM GR
11 BACK COLWYN VIEW
12 COLWYN VIEW
13 LODGE TERR
14 COLWYN AVE
15 COLWYN MOUNT

16 UPPER WOODVIEW PL
17 CROSS WOODVIEW ST
18 COLWYN TERR
19 COLWYN PL
20 BACK COLWYN PL
21 BURLINGTON PL
22 BACK BURLINGTON PL

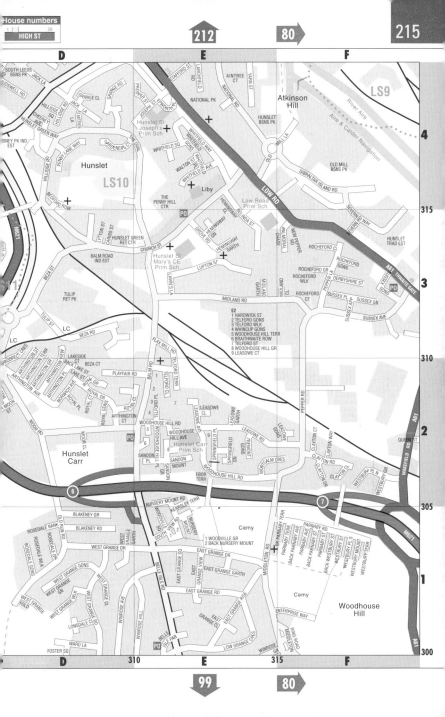

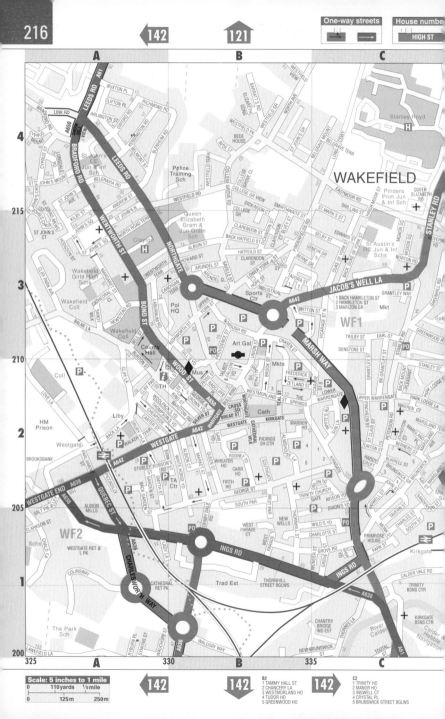

treet names are listed alphabetically and show the locality, the Postcode District, the page number and
reference to the square in which the name falls on the map page

Assembly St **5** Leeds LS2 .... **211** F3

Grid square in which the
centre of the street falls

Page number of the map
on which the street name
appears

Postcode District for
the street name

Town, village or
locality in which the
street falls.

Location Number
If present, this indicates
the street's position on a
congested area of the
map instead of the name

ull street name
his may have been
bbreviated on the map

Schools, hospitals, sports centres, railway stations, shopping centres,
industrial estates, public amenities and other places of interest are also
listed.

Abbreviations used in the index

App **Approach**	Cl **Close**	Espl **Esplanade**	Mdw **Meadows**
Arc **Arcade**	Comm **Common**	Est **Estate**	N **North**
Ave **Avenue**	Cnr **Corner**	Gdns **Gardens**	Orch **Orchard**
Bvd **Boulevard**	Cotts **Cottages**	Gn **Green**	Par **Parade**
Bldgs **Buildings**	Ct **Court**	Gr **Grove**	Pk **Park**
Bsns Pk **Business Park**	Ctyd **Courtyard**	Hts **Heights**	Pas **Passage**
Bsns Ctr **Business Centre**	Cres **Crescent**	Ho **House**	Pl **Place**
Bglws **Bungalows**	Dr **Drive**	Ind Est **Industrial Estate**	Prec **Precinct**
Cswy **Causeway**	Dro **Drove**	Intc **Interchange**	Prom **Promenade**
Ctr **Centre**	E **East**	Junc **Junction**	Ret Pk **Retail Park**
Circ **Circle**	Emb **Embankment**	La **Lane**	Rd **Road**
Cir **Circus**	Ent **Enterprise**	Mans **Mansions**	Rdbt **Roundabout**

S **South**	
Sq **Square**	
Strs **Stairs**	
Stps **Steps**	
St **Street, Saint**	
Terr **Terrace**	
Tk **Track**	
Trad Est **Trading Estate**	
Wlk **Walk**	
W **West**	
Yd **Yard**	

Town and village index

Aberford 64 E7	Clayton West 175 F2	Halton East 1 E8	Lofthouse Gate 121 D6	Silkstone 193 F1
Ackworth Moor Top . 163 E6	Cleckheaton 116 C6	Hampole 184 B1	Low Bradley 4 D5	Silsden 5 F1
Addingham 6 E8	Clifton 10 E5	Harden 36 B1	Mapplewell 178 C1	Skelmanthorpe 175 B2
Adwick Le Street 184 E2	Collingham 29 B8	Harewood 27 A7	Marsden 168 E3	Skipton 4 B8
Arthington 25 D6	Conoley 4 A3	Haworth 51 B7	Meltham 170 E3	Slaithwaite 152 A1
Askwith 9 F5	Cowling 32 C7	Hazlewood 3 B8	Menston 22 A4	South Elmsall 183 A2
Bacup 106 B4	Cridling Stubbs 127 D1	Hebden Bridge 89 B3	Micklefield 84 A7	South Hiendley 180 D6
Badsworth 164 E2	Crigglestone 159 E5	Hemsworth 181 C8	Mickletown 102 D3	South Kirkby 182 C1
Baildon 38 C3	Crofton 143 F1	Heptonstall 67 C2	Middleton 99 D4	South Milford 84 F3
Bardsey 28 D4	Cudworth 180 B1	High Hoyland 176 C1	Mirfield 138 A6	Sowerby Bridge 112 C3
Barnsley 178 F1	Cullingworth 52 C6	Hillam 105 F7	Monk Fryston 105 E8	Spofforth 12 C8
Barwick in Elmet 63 E7	Darrington 147 C5	Holme 197 F8	Morley 98 D3	Steeton 17 D5
Batley 118 C4	Dearne 194 D1	Holme Chapel 85 B6	Nesfield 7 C8	Stutton 48 C5
Beal 127 F6	Denby Dale 192 B6	Holmfirth 189 B5	Netherton 158 E6	Sutton-in-Craven ... 16 E5
Beamsley 2 F5	Denholme 52 D1	Honley 171 E4	Normanton 123 B1	Swillington 82 B1
Bickerton 15 C7	Denshaw 167 B3	Hooton Pagnell 195 C5	Northowram 93 B2	Tadcaster 31 E3
Bingley 37 C4	Denton 9 A6	Horbury 141 B2	Norton 166 F1	Thorner 45 E5
Birkenshaw 96 B5	Dewsbury 139 C7	Horsforth 41 A2	Norton 178 F6	Thornton 72 E6
Birkin 127 D7	Diggle 185 B4	Huddersfield 154 C6	Oakworth 34 D2	Thorp Arch 14 F1
Blackshaw Head 87 F4	Draughton 1 D5	Hunger Hill 8 B8	Ossett 140 E6	Thorpe Audlin 165 B4
Bolton Abbey 2 E8	Dunford Bridge 199 D1	Ilkley 8 C4	Otley 23 B8	Tintwistle 197 A2
Boston Spa 30 D7	East Ardsley 120 B7	Ingbirchworth 191 E1	Oxenhope 51 D2	Todmorden 108 C6
Bradford 74 E8	East Carlton 23 D3	Keighley 35 D6	Penistone 192 E1	Trawden 32 A2
Bradford 201 B4	East Keswick 28 C6	Kexbrough 177 A1	Pontefract 146 B6	Upton 183 A8
Bramham 30 E3	Elland 134 E6	Kippax 83 B2	Pool 24 D7	Wadsworth Moor 68 E6
Bramhope 24 D3	Emley 175 C7	Kirk Deighton 13 C8	Pudsey 76 D7	Wakefield 142 E5
Brierley 181 A3	Fairburn 105 B4	Kirk Smeaton 166 D5	Queensbury 72 F2	Wakefield 216 C4
Brighouse 115 B2	Farnhill 4 D1	Kirkburton 173 E6	Rawdon 56 C8	Walton 161 B6
Brodsworth 195 F2	Farnley 11 D4	Kirkheaton 137 C1	Ripponden 132 D4	West Bretton 176 E8
Brotherton 126 D8	Featherstone 145 C7	Knottingley 127 B4	Rothwell 100 E5	West Hardwick 145 B1
Burghwallis 184 E4	Flockton 157 C2	Leathley 24 C8	Royston 179 D3	Wetherby 13 C6
Burley in Wharfdale 9 D1	Garforth 83 B5	Ledsham 104 D8	Ryhill 162 B1	Whitley Common 200 E7
Burton Salmon 105 E3	Gildersome 97 D8	Ledston 103 E6	Saxton 65 E8	Whitworth 106 E1
Byram 126 F2	Glusburn 16 C6	Leeds 79 A7	Scarcroft 45 D8	Wighill 15 F3
Carlecotes 200 B3	Great Houghton 194 A3	Leeds 211 D3	Shafton 180 B3	Wilsden 53 D5
Castleford 124 F8	Grimethorpe 181 B1	Lepton 155 E3	Shelf 93 D6	Womersley 167 F3
Castley 25 B8	Guiseley 39 C8	Lindley 11 E7	Shepley 190 F8	Woolley 177 F7
Cawthorne 193 D4	Halifax 113 E7	Littleborough 129 B2	Sherburn in Elmet ... 65 E1	Worsthorne 66 A4
Clayton 194 C4	Halifax 203 F4	Liversedge 117 A6	Shipley 55 B7	Yeadon 40 D5
				Sicklinghall 12 C5	

A1 Bsns Pk WF11 .... 126 C3
Aachen Way HX1 .... 202 C1
Abasen Cl BD3 .... 75 B7
Abb Scott La BD12, BD6 ..... 94 B6
Abb St HD1 .... 153 D7
Abbey Ave LS5 .... 58 F3
Abbey Cl Addingham LS29 .... 7 A8
Holmfirth HD7 .... 199 B7
Abbey Ct LS18 .... 58 B6
Abbey Dr HD8 .... 173 F1
Abbey Farm Dr HD8 .... 190 F8
Abbey Gorse LS5 .... 58 F4
Abbey Grange C of E High Sch
LS16 .... 58 F8
Abbey House Mus LS5 ...... 58 F5
Abbey La HX3 .... 111 F7
Abbey Lea BD15 .... 73 C8
Abbey Mount 4 LS5 .... 58 F3
Abbey Park Sch HX2 .... 91 D6
Abbey Pl HD2 .... 136 C1
Abbey Rd Batley WF17 ...... 117 F4
Huddersfield HD2 .... 136 B1
Leeds LS5 .... 58 E5
Shepley HD8 .... 174 A2
Abbey Rd N HD8 .... 173 F1
Abbey Rd S HD8 .... 190 F8
Abbey St LS3 .... 210 C4
Abbey Terr 3 LS5 .... 58 F3
Abbey View LS5 .... 59 A5
Abbey Wlk Halifax HX3 .... 113 C4
Leeds LS5 .... 58 F5
Abbey Wlk S HX3 .... 113 D4
Abbeydale Garth LS5 ...... 58 E6
Abbeydale Gdns LS5 .... 58 E6
Abbeydale Oval LS5 .... 58 E6
Abbeydale Vale LS5 .... 58 E6
Abbeydale Way LS5 .... 58 E6
Abbot La WF4 .... 178 B6
Abbot St HD1 .... 153 E7
Abbots Pl HD2 .... 136 F5
Abbots Wood BD9 .... 55 A3
Abbotside CI BD10 .... 56 C6
Abbotsway LS25 .... 82 D6
Abbott Ct LS12 .... 210 A4
Abbott La LS12 .... 210 A4
Abbott Terr WF1 .... 142 D3
Abbott View LS12 .... 210 A4
Abbott's Ladies Home
HX3 .... 113 C3
Abbotts CI LS25 .... 64 E8
Abel St 4 BD2 .... 94 C4
Abelia Mount BD7 .... 73 F6
Aberdeen Dr LS12 .... 209 D4
Aberdeen Gr LS12 .... 209 D4
Aberdeen Pl BD7 .... 74 A5
Aberdeen Rd LS12 .... 209 D3
Aberdeen Terr
Bradford BD3 .... 73 D4
Bradford, Lidget Green BD7 .. 74 A6
Aberdeen Wlk LS12 .... 209 D3
Aberfield Bank LS10 ...... 99 E6
Aberfield Cl LS10 .... 99 E7
Aberfield Crest LS10 ...... 99 E6
Aberfield Dr
Cragglestone LS12 ...... 159 E4
Middleton LS10 .... 99 E6
Aberfield Gate LS10 ...... 99 E7
Aberfield Mount LS10 .... 99 E6
Aberfield Rd LS10 .... 99 E7
Aberfield Rise LS10 ...... 99 E6
Aberfield Wlk LS10 .... 99 E6
Aberford C of E Sch LS25 .. 64 E7
Aberford Rd Aberford LS25 .. 64 C2
Barwick in E LS15 .... 63 E7
Bradford BD8 .... 74 B8
Bramham LS23 .... 30 D2
Garforth LS25 .... 83 A8
Lofthouse Gate WF3 ...... 121 F3
Rothwell LS26 .... 101 D6
Wakefield WF1 .... 142 E8
Abingdon St Bradford BD8 .. 55 B1
Huddersfield HD2 .... 136 A1
Abraham Hill LS26 .... 100 F5
Abraham Ormerod
Day Hosp OL14 .... 108 B5
Abram St BD5 .... 74 E4
Acacia Ave WF9 .... 183 A4
Acacia Cl WF10 .... 125 D6
Acacia Dr Bradford BD15 ... 54 A4
Brighouse HX3 .... 115 A7
Castleford WF10 .... 125 D6
Acacia Gn WF8 .... 125 F1
Acacia Gr Hebden Bridge HX7 89 F1
Shafton S72 .... 180 C3
Acacia House 8 WF10 .... 124 E7
Acacia Park Cres BD10 .... 39 F2
Acacia Park Dr BD10 ...... 39 F2
Acacia Park Terr LS19 .... 40 A2
Acacia Wlk WF11 .... 126 C4
Garforth LS25 .... 83 B5
Accommodation Rd LS7 .... 60 A7
Acer Way 8 BD10 .... 115 F8
Ackroyd Ct 18 BD13 ...... 72 D6
Ackroyd St Morley LS27 .... 98 B4
Todmorden OL14 .... 86 B1
Ackton Cl WF7 .... 145 A8
Ackton Hall Cres WF7 .... 145 A8
Ackton La WF7 .... 124 C1
Acaster Dr Bradford BD12 .. 94 C6
Garforth LS25 .... 83 B5
Ackton Pastures Junior &
Infants Sch WF7 .... 124 A6
Ackworth Ave LS19 .... 40 C6

Ackworth Bridle Rd WF8 .. 164 E6
Ackworth Cres LS19 ...... 40 C6
Ackworth Dr LS19 .... 40 D6
Ackworth House Cl WF7 .. 164 A8
Ackworth Rd
Featherstone WF7 .... 145 D3
Pontefract WF7, WF8 .... 146 C5
Ackworth Sch WF7 .... 164 A7
Ackworth St BD5 .... 74 E4
Acme Terr WF1 .... 142 D3
Acorn Bsns Pk BD23 ...... 4 A7
Acorn Cl BD8 .... 93 E6
Acorn Dr LS14 .... 62 C8
Acorn Gr HD7 .... 189 D3
Acorn Pk BD17 .... 38 E2
Acorn St Halifax HX1 .... 202 C3
Keighley BD21 .... 35 B5
Acre Ave BD2 .... 56 B5
Acre Cir LS10 .... 99 C4
Acre Cl Bradford BD2 .... 56 B5
Middleton LS10 .... 99 B3
Acre Cres Bradford BD2 .. 56 B5
Middleton LS10 .... 99 C4
Acre Dr BD2 .... 56 B5
Acre Fold LS29 .... 6 E8
Acre Gr Bradford BD2 .... 56 B5
Middleton LS10 .... 99 C4
Acre House Ave HD3 .... 153 C8
Acre La
Bradford, Bolton Outlanes
BD2 .... 56 B4
Bradford, Brownroyd Hill BD6 74 C1
Haworth BD22 .... 51 C7
Heptonstall HX7 .... 88 C6
Holmfirth, Hinchcliffe Mill
HD7 .... 188 D2
Holmfirth, Snowgate Head
HD7 .... 190 B6
Meltham HD7 .... 170 F1
Acre Mount LS10 .... 99 C4
Acre Pl LS10 .... 99 C4
Acre Rd LS10 .... 99 C4
Acre Rise BD17 .... 38 C4
Acre Sq LS10 .... 99 C4
Acre St Huddersfield HD3 .. 153 C8
Middleton LS10 .... 99 C4
Acre Terr LS10 .... 99 C4
Acre The BD12 .... 94 B5
Acre Villas 4 HX7 .... 89 E1
Acrehowe Rise BD17 ...... 38 E4
Acres Hall Ave LS28 ...... 77 A6
Acres Hall Cres LS28 .... 77 A6
Acres Hall Dr LS28 .... 77 A6
Acres La Heptonstall HX7 .. 88 F4
Holmfirth HD7 .... 187 F4
Acres Rd WF3 .... 121 C8
Acres St BD21 .... 35 B6
Acute Terr WF2 .... 141 D6
Ada St Baildon BD17 ...... 38 E2
Halifax HX3 .... 92 C1
Keighley BD21 .... 35 A7
Queensbury BD13 .... 72 D1
Shipley BD18 .... 54 F8
Ada's Pl LS28 .... 57 E2
Adam Croft BD13 .... 52 D6
Adam Ct HD3 .... 135 B1
Adam St 7 Bradford BD6 .. 74 B1
Todmorden OL14 .... 108 B6
Adams Gr LS15 .... 62 E4
Addersgate La HX13 ...... 92 E4
Addi St BD4 .... 75 C3
Addingford Cl WF4 ...... 159 A8
Addingford Dr WF4 ...... 159 A8
Addingford La WF4 ...... 159 A8
Addingham First Sch LS29 .. 2 E1
Addingham Gdns LS12 .... 209 D3
Addingham Middle Sch
LS29 .... 2 F1
Addison House Bradford BD6 56 D1
Normanton WF6 .... 123 C1
Addison St Horbury WF4 .. 141 C2
Leeds LS15 .... 81 D6
Addle Croft La HD8 ...... 155 F5
Addlethorpe La LS22 .... 14 A5
Addy Cres WF9 .... 182 F3
Adel Gn LS16 .... 42 D5
Adel Grange Cl LS16 ...... 42 C2
Adel Grange Croft LS16 .. 42 C2
Adel Grange Mews LS16 .. 42 C2
Adel La LS16 .... 42 C3
Adel Mead LS16 .... 42 D4
Adel Mill LS16 .... 42 D6
Adel Park Cl LS16 .... 42 C3
Adel Park Croft LS16 .... 42 C3
Adel Park Ct LS16 .... 42 C3
Adel Park Dr LS16 .... 42 C3
Adel Park Gdns LS16 .... 42 C3
Adel Pasture LS16 .... 42 C3
Adel Prim Sch LS16 ...... 42 D3
Adel St John the Baptist
CE Primary Sch LS16 .. 42 D4
Adel Towers Cl LS16 ...... 42 D4
Adel Towers Ct LS16 ...... 42 D4
Adel Vale LS16 .... 42 D3
Adel Wood Cl LS16 .... 42 D3
Adel Wood Dr LS16 .... 42 D3
Adel Wood Gdns LS16 .... 42 D3
Adel Wood Gr LS16 .... 42 D3
Adel Wood Pl LS16 .... 42 D3
Adel Wood Rd LS16 .... 42 D3
Adelaide House BD16 .... 37 B2
Adelaide Rise 1 BD17 .... 38 C1

Adelaide St Bradford BD5 .. 201 B1
Halifax HX1 .... 202 B3
Hebden Bridge HX7 ...... 88 F3
3 Todmorden OL14 ...... 108 B6
Adelphi Rd HX4 .... 133 E3
Adelphi St HD1 .... 153 C7
Adgil Cres HX3 .... 114 A4
Administration Rd LS9 .... 80 C3
Admiral St LS11 .... 214 C4
Adolphus St BD1 .... 201 C2
Adowsley Cl WF7 .... 163 E6
Adwalton Cl BD11 .... 96 D5
Adwalton Gn BD11 .... 96 D5
Adwalton Gr BD11 .... 72 F1
Adwick Gr WF2 .... 160 D6
Adwick Pl LS4 .... 59 C2
Adwick Terr WF8 .... 125 E2
Aeron Wilkinson Ct WF9 .. 182 A2
Agar St 6 BD8 .... 73 F8
Agar Terr 6 BD8 .... 73 F8
Agbrigg Gr WF2 .... 142 E2
Agbrigg Rd WF1, WF2 .... 142 E2
Agincourt Dr WF6 .... 122 E4
Agnes St BD20 .... 18 C1
Agnes Stewart
CE High Sch LS9 .... 212 B4
Ails La HX2 .... 90 D1
Aimbry Ct HD5 .... 154 F2
Ainley Bottom HX5 ...... 135 A5
Ainley Cl HD3 .... 135 A2
Ainley Pk HD7 .... 152 E4
Ainley Pl HD7 .... 151 C2
Ainley Rd HD3 .... 135 A2
Ainley St 9 HX5 .... 134 F6
Ainleys Ind Est HX5 .... 135 A5
Ainsbury Ave Baildon BD10 .. 39 B3
Bradford BD10 .... 39 B3
Ainsdale Cl BD13 .... 92 F8
Ainsdale Ct LS71 .... 179 B5
Ainsdale Gr S71 .... 179 B5
Ainsley La HD7 .... 168 D4
Ainsty Cres LS22 .... 13 E7
Ainsty Dr LS22 .... 13 E7
Ainsty Garth LS22 ...... 13 E7
Ainsty Rd LS22 .... 13 E7
Ainsty View LS22 .... 13 E7
Aintree Cl LS10 .... 215 E4
Aire & Calder Cotts WF3 .. 122 B2
Aire Cl BD17 .... 38 B1
Aire Cres BD20 .... 16 E6
Aire Ct BD20 .... 17 E8
Aire Gr LS19 .... 40 C4
Aire Mount LS22 .... 13 D7
Aire Pl LS3 .... 205 E1
Aire Rd LS22 .... 13 D7
Aire St Bingley BD16 .... 36 F6
Bradford BD10 .... 39 A4
Brighouse HD6 .... 115 B1
Castleford WF10 .... 124 D8
Dewsbury WF13 .... 138 F5
Glusburn BD20 .... 16 E6
3 Haworth BD22 .... 51 D7
Knottingley WF11 .... 127 A5
Leeds LS1 .... 211 E3
Aire Terr WF10 .... 103 D1
Aire Valley Cl BD20 .... 4 B6
Aire Valley Dr BD20 .... 4 B6
Aire View Brotherton WF11 126 C8
Cononley BD20 .... 4 A2
Keighley BD20 .... 18 F2
Knottingley WF11 .... 126 D5
Silsden BD20 .... 5 E2
Yeadon LS19 .... 40 C6
Aire View Ave Shipley BD16 .. 54 B8
Shipley BD18 .... 55 A8
Aire View Dr BD20 ...... 36 C7
Aire View Infants Sch BD20 .. 38 A1
Aire Way HD17 .... 38 A1
Aire View Terr BD20 .... 4 B6
Airebank BD16 .... 36 F3
Aireborough L Ctr LS20 .. 39 E8
Aireburn Ave BD20 ...... 17 D5
Airedale Ave BD16 ...... 54 A7
Airedale Bsns Ctr BD23 .. 4 A8
Airedale Cliff LS13 ...... 58 C5
Airedale College Rd BD3 .. 56 A1
Airedale College Terr BD3 .. 56 A1
Airedale Cres BD3 ...... 56 A1
Airedale Croft 8 LS13 .. 57 F5
Airedale Ct LS14 .... 61 F5
Airedale Dr
Castleford WF10 .... 104 C2
Garforth LS25 .... 83 B6
Horsforth LS18 .... 57 F8
Shelf HX3 .... 93 B5
Airedale Gdns LS13 ...... 57 F5
Airedale General Hospl
BD20 .... 17 B6
3 Morley LS27 .... 98 C5
3 Rothwell LS26 .... 101 D6
Shipley BD18 .... 54 F8
Sowerby Bridge HX6 .... 112 C5
Airedale St BD20 .... 5 E1
Yeadon LS19 .... 40 C7
Airedale Terr Baildon BD17 .. 38 D2
8 Morley LS27 .... 98 B4
2 Rothwell LS26 .... 101 D6
Airedale Trad Pk BD20 .. 16 E7
Airedale View
Glusburn BD20 .... 16 D7
4 Pudsey LS13 .... 57 F5
3 Rothwell LS26 .... 101 D6
Airedale Wharf 1 LS13 .. 57 F4
Airedale & Wharfedale Coll
of Further Education
LS18 .... 57 F7
Aireside BD20 .... 4 B2
Aireside Ave BD20 ...... 4 B2
Aireside Ctr LS1 .... 211 D3
Aireside Terr BD20 ...... 4 B2
Aireval BD17 .... 36 B7
Aireview Cres BD17 ...... 38 A1
Aireview Primary Sch LS13 57 F4
Aireview Terr Keighley BD20 36 B8
Aireville Ave BD9 .... 55 B5
Aireville Cl Keighley BD20 .. 18 A2
Shipley BD18 .... 55 B4
Aireville Cres Shipley BD9 .. 55 B4
Silsden BD20 .... 5 F1
Aireville Dr BD20 .... 5 F1
Aireville Grange BD18 .... 55 B5
Aireville Mouny BD20 .... 5 F1
Aireville Rd BD9 .... 55 C5
Aireville Rise BD9 ...... 55 B5
Aireville St BD20 .... 18 A2
Aireville Terr LS29 ...... 9 E1
Aireworth Cl LS29 ...... 18 E1
Aireworth Gr BD21 ...... 35 E8
Aireworth Mills BD21 .... 35 E8
Aireworth St BD21 ...... 35 B6
Airey St HD1 .... 35 A7
Airlie Ave LS8 .... 207 F4
Airlie Pl LS8 .... 207 F4
Airville Dr BD18 .... 55 B5
Airville Gr BD18 .... 55 B5
Akam Rd BD1 .... 74 D7
Aked St BD1 .... 201 C3
Aked's Rd HX1 .... 203 D2
Aketon Dr WF10 .... 124 C6
Aketon Rd WF10 .... 124 C6
Akroyd Ct LS13 .... 203 E4
Akroyd Dr HX7 .... 89 B6
Akroyd Pl HX1 .... 203 E4
Akroyd Terr
Bradford BD2 .... 201 B1
Brighouse HD6 .... 115 A3
Castleford WF10 .... 124 C8
Cleckheaton BD19 .... 116 B8
Cudworth S72 .... 180 C1
Elland HX5 .... 134 F6
Featherstone WF7 .... 145 D5
Halifax HX1 .... 203 D3

Albert St continued
1 Haworth BD22 .... 51 F6
Hebden Bridge HX7 ...... 89 A4
7 Hebden Bridge,
Wadsworth Banks Fields HX7 89 F1
Huddersfield HD1 .... 153 F7
Keighley BD21 .... 35 B
Liversedge WF15 .... 117 C
Normanton WF6 .... 123 C
Pudsey LS13 .... 76 De
Queensbury BD13 .... 72 D
Sutton in C BD20 .... 16 E
Thornton BD13 .... 72 De
Todmorden OL14 .... 108 B6
Wilsden BD15 .... 53 C
Albert Terr
Bradford, Raw Nook BD12 .. 94 F
8 Bradford, Wyke Common
BD12 .... 94 D3
Shipley BD18 .... 37 F
Yeadon LS19 .... 40 A2
Albert View HX2 .... 202 A4
Albert Way BD11 .... 96 B4
Albert Yd HD1 .... 154 A
Alberta Ave LS7 .... 204 B2
Albion Arc LS1 .... 211 F
Albion Ave LS12 .... 210 A2
Albion Cl BD11 .... 33 D
Albion Croft WF5 .... 140 E6
Albion Ct Batley WF16 .... 117 D6
Bradford BD1 .... 201 B
Halifax HX1 .... 203 E
Wakefield WF1 .... 216 B2
Albion Fold BD15 .... 53 C
Albion Mills WF2 .... 216 A
Albion Pk LS12 .... 210 B4
Albion Pl
15 Brighouse HD6 ...... 115 A3
Guiseley LS20 .... 22 E
Leeds LS1 .... 211 F
South Elmsall WF9 ...... 183 A
Thornton BD13 .... 72 C
Albion Rd Bradford BD10 .. 56 C
Dewsbury WF12 .... 139 E
Pudsey LS28 .... 57 E2
Albion Sq WF2 .... 141 E
Albion St Baroo OL13 ...... 106 A3
Batley WF17 .... 118 D
Batley, Heckmondwike
WF16 .... 117 D
Boston Spa LS23 .... 30 D
Bradford BD1 .... 201 B3
3 Bradford, Buttershaw BD6 93 F
Brighouse HD6 .... 115 A
Castleford WF10 .... 124 C
Cleckheaton BD19 .... 116 E
Dewsbury BD10 .... 71 D
Dewsbury WF13 .... 118 C3
Dewsbury, Ravensthorpe
WF13 .... 138 F
Elland HX5 .... 135 A
Halifax HX1 .... 203 E
Haworth BD22 .... 51 E
Hemsworth WF9 .... 163 A
Huddersfield HD1 .... 154 A
Leeds LS1, LS2 .... 211 F
1 Liversedge WF15 ...... 117 B
Morley LS27 .... 98 B
Otley LS21 .... 23 B
6 Pudsey LS28 .... 76 F
Queensbury BD13 .... 72 D
Rothwell WF3 .... 100 D
Wakefield WF1 .... 216 B
Albion Terr Boston Spa LS23 30 D
Hebden Bridge HX7 ...... 88 F
Albion Way LS12 .... 210 B4
Albion Yd BD1 .... 201 B3
Alcester Garth BD3 ...... 75 B
Alcester Pl LS8 .... 207 E
Alcester Rd LS8 .... 207 E
Alcester St 12 LS8 ...... 207 E
Alcester Terr LS8 .... 207 E
Aldams Rd WF12 .... 139 C
Alden Ave LS27 .... 98 A
Alden Cl LS27 .... 98 A
Alden Cres WF8 .... 146 B
Alden Ct 1 LS27 .... 98 A
Alden Fold 1 LS27 ...... 98 A
Alder Ave Holmfirth HD7 .. 189 E
Keighley BD21 .... 35 E
Wakefield WF2 .... 142 A
Alder Carr BD17 .... 38 B
Alder Ct LS75 .... 178 A
Alder Dr HX3 .... 113 B
Alder Garth LS28 .... 76 B
Alder Gr Halifax HX2 .... 91 E6
Normanton WF6 .... 144 B
Alder Hill Ave LS7 ...... 60 A
Alder Hill Gr LS7 .... 60 A
Alder St HD1, HD2 .... 136 B
Aldermanbury BD1 ...... 201 B3
Alderney Rd WF12 .... 118 F2
Alderscholes Cl 9 BD13 .. 72 D
Alderscholes La BD13 .... 72 C
Aldersgate LS12 .... 209 E
Alderson St 8 BD6 ...... 93 E
Alderstone Rise HD3 .... 135 A
Aldersyde WF17 .... 96 E
Alderton Bank LS17 ...... 42 F
Alderton Cres LS17 ...... 42 F
Alderton Hts LS17 .... 42 F
Alderton Mount LS17 .... 42 F
Alderton Pl LS17 .... 42 F
Alderton Rise LS17 ...... 43 A
Aldonley LS15 .... 165 A
Alegar St 3 HD6 .... 115 C
Alexander Ave LS15 ...... 80 F

Alexander Cres WF7 145 E7
Alexander Ct BD20 36 D7
Alexander Rd WF7 145 D6
Alexander Sq 10 BD14 73 B4
Alexander St
5 Bradford BD6 94 B8
Leeds LS1 211 E4
Alexander Terr HX1 202 B3
Alexandra Ave 3 WF17 96 F1
Alexandra Cres
Dewsbury WF13 118 A2
Elland HX5 135 B7
Ilkley LS29 8 A4
Alexandra Dr WF6 144 B7
Alexandra Gr Leeds LS6 205 E2
Pudsey LS28 76 D6
Alexandra Rd Batley WF17 118 D4
Bradford BD2 56 C5
8 Hebden Bridge HX7 89 A3
Horsforth LS18 58 C8
Huddersfield HD3 153 C7
Leeds LS6 205 E2
Pudsey LS28 76 C6
Shipley BD18 55 A7
Alexandra Rd W HD3 153 C5
Alexandra Sq 14 BD18 54 F8
Alexandra St Bradford BD7 74 C5
Halifax HX1 203 E3
4 Liversedge WF15 117 A4
Queensbury BD13 72 E1
Alexandra Terr
Bradford BD2 56 C2
6 Yeadon LS19 40 C7
Alford Terr BD7 74 A7
Alfred E Briggs Almshouses
3 BD12 94 B6
Alfred St
4 Batley, Heckmondwike WF16 117 D3
Batley, Mount Pleasant WF17 118 B4
5 Brighouse HD6 115 B3
1 Dewsbury WF13 118 E1
Elland HX4 134 D7
Halifax HX1 202 B3
4 Huddersfield HD1 154 A5
3 Liversedge WF15 117 B4
6 Morley LS27 98 C8
Royston S71 179 E4
Alfred St E HX1 203 F3
Alfreds Way WF17 118 C5
Alice St Bradford BD8 74 D8
2 Cleckheaton BD19 116 D8
5 Haworth BD22 51 C6
Keighley BD21 35 C7
Alkincote St BD21 35 C6
All Alone BD10 56 A7
All Alone Rd BD10 56 A6
All Saint's Circ LS26 101 D6
All Saint's Dr LS26 101 C6
All Saint's Rd LS26 101 D6
All Saint's View LS26 101 C7
All Saints C of E Jun & Inf Sch WF7 124 D1
All Saints C of E Junior Sch LS21 23 A8
All Saints' CE Fst Sch BD5 74 D5
All Saints' CE Junior & Infant Sch HX3 113 C2
All Saints CE Primary Sch LS9 212 C4
All Saints' First Sch LS29 8 B5
All Saints High RC Sch HD2 136 C5
All Saints Ind Est WF8 125 E1
All Saints Rd BD7 74 C5
All Saints' View 2 WF8 146 E8
All Souls' Rd HX3 92 C1
All Souls' St 3 HX3 92 C1
All Souls' Terr 2 HX3 92 C1
Allan Haigh Cl WF2 141 D8
Allan St BD3 75 B6
Allan Terr HX6 112 C3
Allanbridge Cl BD10 56 C7
Allandale Ave BD6 94 A7
Allandale Rd BD6 94 A7
Allanfield Terr LS22 13 E8
Allen Croft BD11 96 A5
Allenby Cres LS11 99 A8
Allenby Dr LS11 99 A8
Allenby Gdns LS11 99 A8
Allenby Gr LS11 99 A8
Allenby Pl LS11 99 A8
Allenby Rd LS11 99 A8
Allenby View LS11 214 B1
Allendale Rd S75 177 D1
Allerby Gn BD6 93 F6
Allergill Pk HD7 188 D5
Allerton Ave LS17 43 D2
Allerton Bywater Prim Sch WF10 103 B5
Allerton Cl BD15 54 B1
Allerton Dr LS17 28 C6
Allerton First & Middle Sch BD15 54 B1
Allerton Gr LS17 43 D2
Allerton Grange Ave LS17 43 E1
Allerton Grange Cl LS17 60 C8
Allerton Grange Cres LS17 204 A4
Allerton Grange Croft LS8 204 B4
Allerton Grange Dr
Bradford BD15 54 B1
Leeds LS17 204 A4
Allerton Grange Gdns LS17 204 A4
Allerton Grange High Sch LS17 43 E1
Allerton Grange Rise LS17 204 A4
Allerton Grange Vale LS17 204 A4
Allerton Grange Way LS17, LS8 204 A4
Allerton Grange Wlk LS17 204 A4
Allerton High Sch LS17 43 B3
Allerton Hill LS7 60 C7
Allerton La
Bradford BD13, BD15 73 A7
Thornton BD13, BD15 73 A7
Allerton Pk LS7 204 B3
Allerton Pl Halifax HX1 202 C3
Leeds LS17 43 D2
Allerton Rd BD15 54 B1
Allerton St LS4 205 D2
Allescholes Rd OL14 129 B7
Alliance St LS12 209 D3
Allinson St LS12 210 B2
Allison Dr HD2 136 B2
Allison La BD2 55 D4
Allison St WF7 145 C5
Allison Terr WF2 120 B2
Alloe Field View HX2 91 E6
Allott Cl WF9 182 F3
Allums La LS21 25 F5
Alma Cl LS28 57 C3
Alma Cotts 12 LS6 59 D5
Alma Dr HD5 154 D6
Alma Gr Leeds LS9 207 F2
Shipley BD18 55 D8
Alma La Batley WF16 117 D6
Ripponden HX6 132 B7
Alma Pl Keighley BD21 35 C5
Leeds BD3 207 E2
Alma Rd Leeds LS6 59 E5
Todmorden OL14 108 A1
Alma St Bacup OL13 106 A2
Bradford, Cutler Heights BD4 75 D3
Bradford, Swain Green BD4 75 D5
Elland HX5 135 A6
Haworth BD22 51 C8
Keighley BD21 35 C5
Leeds LS9 207 F1
Queensbury BD13 72 D1
Rothwell LS26 101 D7
Shipley BD18 55 D8
Todmorden OL14 108 A1
Yeadon LS19 40 C7
Alma Terr Keighley BD21 35 C5
Keighley, Green End BD20 19 E1
Rothwell LS26 100 D6
Almhouses BD21 35 A3
Almond Cl WF9 183 A5
Almond St BD3 75 C6
Almond Way WF17 96 F1
Almondbury Bank HD5 154 E5
Almondbury CE Inf Sch HD5 154 F2
Almondbury Cl HD5 155 A3
Almondbury Comm HD4 154 F1
Almondbury County Junior Sch HD5 155 A4
Almondbury Secondary Sch HD5 154 F4
Almondroyd WF16 117 C5
Almscliffe Ave WF12 139 E8
Almshouse Hill LS23 30 D2
Almshouse La
Crigglestone WF2 160 B4
Wakefield WF1 216 B2
Alpha St BD21 35 D6
Alpine Cl WF17 118 B4
Alpine Rise BD13 72 D6
Alpine Terr LS26 100 D6
Alston Cl BD9 54 D1
Alston La LS14 62 A3
Alston Rd BD21 18 D1
Altar Dr Bradford BD9 55 A3
Keighley BD20 19 A1
Altar La BD16 36 C4
Altar View BD16 36 E5
Althorpe Gr BD10 56 A6
Altinkool St WF1 142 F2
Altofts Hall Rd WF6 122 F4
Altofts La WF10 123 D6
Altofts Lodge Dr WF6 122 E3
Altofts Middle Sch WF6 122 F3
Altofts Rd WF6 123 A2
Alton Ave HD5 154 F7
Alton Gr Bradford BD9 54 F3
Shipley BD18 55 B5
Alton Way S75 178 A1
Alum Ct BD9 55 A3
Alum Dr BD9 55 A3
Alvanley Ct BD8 73 D8
Alverthorpe Rd WF2 141 F6
Alvo Terr BD18 55 B6
Alwen Ave HD2 135 F2
Alwoodley Chase LS17 43 E5
Alwoodley Court Gdns LS17 43 A6
Alwoodley Ct LS17 42 F5
Alwoodley Gdns LS17 43 A5
Alwoodley Golf Course LS17 43 F6
Alwoodley La LS17 43 C6
Alwoodley Primary Sch LS17 43 A3
Amber St WF17 118 A6
Amberley Ct BD3 75 C6
Amberley Gdns LS12 209 F2
Amberley Rd LS12 209 F2
Amberley Rise DN6 184 F2
Amberley St Bradford BD3 75 C7
Leeds LS12 210 A2
Amberton App LS8 208 C4
Amberton Cl LS8 61 C5
Amberton Cres LS8 208 C4
Amberton Garth LS8 208 C4
Amberton Gdns LS8 208 C4
Amberton Gr LS8 208 C4
Amberton La LS8 208 C4
Amberton Mount LS8 208 C4
Amberton Pl LS8 208 B4
Amberton Rd LS8, LS9 208 C4
Amberton St LS8 208 C4
Amberton Terr LS8 61 C5
Amble Tonia BD13 52 E1
Ambler St Bradford BD8 55 C1
Castleford WF10 124 E7
Keighley BD21 35 D7
Ambler Way BD13 92 C7
Amblers Croft BD10 39 B2
Amblers Ct LS28 76 E6
Amblers Mews
4 Baildon BD17 38 C4
Keighley BD20 36 D8
Amblers Terr 10 HX3 92 C1
Ambleside Ave BD9 54 F2
Ambleside Dr WF2 161 A6
Ambleside Gdns LS28 76 C7
Ambleside Gr LS26 101 C6
Ambleside Rd WF10 104 E1
Ambleside Wlk LS22 13 B6
Ambleton Way BD13 92 C8
Amelia St 1 BD18 54 F8
America La Brighouse HD6 115 C2
Sutton in C BD20 16 E1
America Moor La LS27 98 A2
Amisfield Rd HX3 114 D8
Amos St HX1 202 B3
Amport Cl HD6 115 B1
Amundsen Ave BD2 56 A5
Amy St 9 Bingley BD16 37 A3
3 Halifax HX3 92 A2
Amyroyce Dr BD18 55 E7
Anaheim Dr WF1 121 D5
Ancaster Cres LS16 59 B7
Ancaster Rd LS16 59 B7
Ancaster View LS16 59 B7
Anchor Pl HD6 136 D8
Anchor St Huddersfield HD1 154 B7
4 Todmorden OL14 108 C5
Anchorage The BD16 36 F4
Anderson Ave LS8 207 E2
Anderson Ct WF10 125 C5
Anderson House BD17 38 B1
Anderson Mount LS8 207 E2
Anderson St Bradford BD8 55 C1
Pontefract WF8 125 C1
Wakefield WF2 142 A6
Anderton St Glusburn BD20 16 D7
Wakefield WF1 142 E3
Andover Gn BD4 75 E4
Andrew Cl HX3 114 A4
Andrew Cres
Huddersfield HD4 153 A1
Lofthouse Gate WF1 121 B5
Andrew St
Featherstone WF7 145 C4
10 Pudsey LS28 57 D2
4 Pudsey, Farsley LS28 57 D3
Wakefield WF1 216 A4
Andrews Gr WF7 163 F6
Anerley St BD4 75 B2
Angel Rd HX1 202 C4
Angel Row LS26 100 B5
Angel St BD17 38 D4
Angel Way BD7 74 D6
Angerton Way BD6 94 A6
Anglers Country Pk WF4 161 F5
Angus Ave BD12 94 C1
Anlaby St BD4 75 D5
Ann Pl BD5 201 B1
Ann St Denholme BD13 52 D1
Haworth BD22 51 D7
Keighley BD21 35 B6
Annat Royd La S36 191 D1
Anne Cres S72 180 E5
Anne Gate BD1 201 C3
Anne St Batley WF17 118 A7
Bradford BD7 73 F3
Anne's Ct HX3 114 A4
Annie St Haworth BD22 51 F8
Hemsworth WF9 163 A4
Keighley BD21 18 C1
Lofthouse Gate WF1 121 B4
Morley LS27 98 B4
Shipley BD18 55 C6
1 Sowerby Bridge HX6 112 B4
Annison St BD3 201 D3
Annotes Croft HD5 154 F7
Anroyd St WF13 118 A1
Anson Gr BD7 73 F2
Anston Dr WF9 183 A5
Anthony La BD16 36 B2
Antony Cl HD3 134 D1
Anvil Ct BD8 55 B1
Anvil St Bradford BD8 55 B1
Brighouse HD6 115 A3
Apex Bsns Ctr LS11 211 F1
Apex View LS11 211 E1
Apex Way LS11 211 F1
Apperley Gdns BD10 56 E8
Apperley La BD10, LS19 39 F2
Apperley Rd BD10 56 D8
Apple Cl WF17 97 A2
Apple House Terr HX2 90 E1
Apple St Keighley BD21 35 A3
Oxenhope BD22 51 C2
Apple Tree Cl
East Ardsley WF3 120 C8
Pontefract WF8 146 B6
Apple Tree Ct WF3 120 C7
Apple Tree Gdns LS29 7 F4
Apple Tree Rd WF7 145 E4
Appleby La LS25 83 B7
Appleby Pl Adwick Le S DN6 184 F2
Leeds LS15 80 E8
Appleby Way Morley LS27 98 B4
Wetherby LS22 13 E7
Appleby Wlk LS15 80 E8
Applegarth Rothwell LS26 101 C7
Wakefield WF2 160 E7
Applehaigh Gr S71 179 A4
Applehaigh La WF4 179 A6
Applehaigh View S71 179 A4
Appleshaw Cres WF2 120 F3
Appleton Cl Bingley BD16 37 B5
Bradford BD12 94 F5
3 Leeds LS9 212 C4
Appleton Ct 2 LS9 212 C4
Appleton Gr LS9 80 B7
Appleton Sq LS9 212 C4
Appleton Way LS9 212 C4
Appletree Cl LS23 30 D7
Appleyard Rd HX7 89 F1
Approach The LS15 62 F7
April Ct WF15 117 A2
Aprilia Ct BD14 73 D5
Apsley Cres BD8 55 C1
Apsley St 7 Haworth BD22 51 D7
8 Keighley BD21 35 B5
Oakworth BD22 34 D3
Apsley Terr BD22 34 D3
Aquamarine Dr HD2 136 C2
Aquila Way WF15 116 D5
Arborary La HD4, HD7 170 F6
Arbour The Farnhill BD20 4 D1
Ilkley LS29 8 A6
Arcade The 5
Dewsbury WF12 139 D8
Knottingley WF11 126 E4
Arcadia St 12 BD21 35 B5
Archbell Ave HD6 136 B8
Archbishop Cranmer CE Prim Sch LS17 43 B3
Archer Rd HD6 115 D1
Archer St WF10 124 C6
Archery Pl 9 LS2 206 B2
Archery Rd LS2 206 B2
Archery St 13 LS2 206 B2
Archery Terr 11 LS2 206 B2
Arches St HX1 203 D2
Arches The HX3 92 D1
Archibald St BD7 74 C7
Arctic Par BD7 74 A4
Arctic St 6 Haworth BD22 51 E8
Keighley BD20 18 B1
Arden Ct Horbury WF4 159 A8
Kirkheaton HD5 155 C7
Arden Rd Bradford BD8 73 C7
Halifax HX1 203 D2
Ardennes Cl BD2 55 F4
Ardsley Cl BD4 75 F2
Argent Way BD4 75 F2
Argie Ave LS4 59 B3
Argie Gdns 3 LS4 59 C2
Argie Rd LS4 59 C2
Argie Terr LS4 59 C2
Argyl Mews LS17 28 C5
Argyle Rd Knottingley WF11 126 C5
Leeds LS9 212 A4
Argyle St Bradford BD4 75 B4
Keighley BD21 35 B7
Marsden HD7 168 F4
Shipley BD18 55 B6
Wakefield WF1 142 E4
Argyll Ave 3 WF8 146 B8
Argyll Cl Baildon BD17 38 E2
Horsforth LS18 41 B4
Ark St LS9 212 B2
Arkendale Mews 5 BD7 73 E3
Arkenley La HD4 155 A2
Arkenmore HD5 154 F7
Arksey Pl LS12 209 F4
Arksey Terr LS12 209 F4
Arkwright House 9 WF15 117 A5
Arkwright St
Bradford, Clayton BD14 73 B4
Bradford, Tyersal BD4 75 E6
Arkwright Wlk 1 LS27 98 A6
Arlesford Rd BD4 75 E2
Arley Cl HD7 188 F8
Arley Gr LS12 209 F4
Arley Pl LS12 209 F4
Arley St 5 LS12 59 C1
Arley Terr LS12 209 F4
Arlington Bsns Ctr LS11 98 E8
Arlington Cres HX2 112 D4
Arlington Gr
Castleford WF10 124 F7
Leeds LS8 61 B5
Arlington Rd LS8 61 B5
Arlington St Bradford BD3 75 B6
Wakefield WF1 216 A4
Arlington Way HD5 155 A7
Armadale Ave BD4 95 B8
Armgill La BD2 55 D4
Armidale Way BD2 55 F3
Armitage Ave HD6 136 B8
Armitage Bldgs WF12 119 B6
Armitage Rd Bradford BD12 94 F4
Halifax HX1 202 B1
Huddersfield HD3 153 B5
Huddersfield, Armitage Bridge HD4 171 E8
Huddersfield, Birkby HD2 135 F1
Wakefield WF2 141 D8
Armitage Sq 2 LS28 76 D6
Armitage St
Castleford WF10 124 C8
Dewsbury WF13 138 D5
Huddersfield HD4 154 A4
Rothwell LS26 100 E4
Armley Grange Ave LS12 209 D4
Armley Grange Cres LS12 58 F1
Armley Grange Dr LS12 77 F8
Armley Grange Mount LS12 77 F8
Armley Grange Oval LS12 58 F1
Armley Grange Rise 4 LS12 77 F8
Armley Grange View LS12 209 D4
Armley Grange Wlk LS12 209 D4
Armley Grove Pl LS12 210 A3
Armley Lodge Rd LS12 209 F4
Armley Mills Ind Mus LS12 205 D1
Armley Park Ct LS12 209 F4
Armley Park Rd LS12 59 C1
Armley Prim Sch LS12 209 F4
Armley Primary Sch LS12 209 F4
Armley Rd LS12 210 B3
Armley Ridge Cl LS12 209 D4
Armley Ridge Rd
Leeds, Moor Top LS12 209 E4
Leeds, Upper Armley LS12 59 A1
Armouries Dr LS10 212 A2
Armouries Way LS10 212 A3
Armoury Ave WF14 138 A5
Armstrong Cl WF6 123 A4
Armstrong St Bradford BD4 75 D6
9 Pudsey LS28 57 D2
Armstrong Terr 2 WF8 146 B7
Armytage Cres HD1 153 F3
Armytage Rd HD6 115 D1
Armytage Way HD6 115 D1
Armytage Wlk WF9 182 C3
Arncliffe Ave 1 BD22 35 A5
Arncliffe Cres
Brighouse HD6 135 E8
Morley LS27 98 C2
Arncliffe Ct HD1 153 E7
Arncliffe Dr WF11 126 C4
Arncliffe Garth 11 LS28 57 D2
Arncliffe Gdns WF17 118 B5
Arncliffe Gr 17 BD22 35 A6
Arncliffe Grange LS17 43 D2
Arncliffe Rd Batley WF17 118 B5
Keighley BD22 35 A6
Leeds LS16 59 A8
Wakefield WF1 142 F8
Arncliffe St LS28 57 D2
Arncliffe Terr BD7 74 B6
Arndale Ctr 5 LS6 59 D5
Arndale Gr HD7 189 B4
Arndale Sh Ctr The BD18 55 B7
Arnford Cl BD3 201 C4
Arnold Ave HD2 135 F1
Arnold Pl BD8 74 C8
Arnold Royd HD6 135 E7
Arnold St Bradford BD8 55 C1
Halifax HX1 202 C3
Huddersfield HD2 135 F1
Liversedge WF15 117 A4
4 Sowerby Bridge HX6 112 B4
Arnside Ave BD20 18 E1
Arnside Cl WF10 125 D8
Arnside Cres WF10 125 D8
Arnside Rd BD5 74 E2
Arran Cl HD7 152 D5
Arran Ct LS25 82 F5
Arran Dr Garforth LS25 82 F5
Horsforth LS18 41 B4
Arrunden Ct HD7 189 B3
Arrunden La HD7 188 F2
Arthington Ave LS10 215 D2
Arthington Cl WF3 119 D7
Arthington Ct LS10 215 D2
Arthington Garth LS21 24 F6
Arthington Gr LS10 215 D2
Arthington La
Arthington LS21 25 D6
Pool LS21 24 E6
Arthington Lawns LS21 24 E6
Arthington Pl LS10 215 D2
Arthington Rd LS16 25 C2
Arthington St Bradford BD8 74 C8
Leeds LS10 215 D2
Arthington Terr LS10 215 D2
Arthington View LS10 215 D2
Arthur Ave BD8 73 D7
Arthur Dr WF17 117 F8
Arthur St Bacup OL13 106 B3
Bingley BD16 36 F3
Bradford BD10 56 B6
Brighouse HD6 115 C2
Huddersfield HD7 152 E4
Oakworth BD22 34 C2
Pudsey LS28 57 E2
Pudsey, Farsley LS28 57 D2
Wakefield WF1 142 E3
Arthursdale Cl LS15 62 F7
Arthursdale Dr LS15 62 F7
Arthursdale Grange LS15 62 F7
Artillery St WF16 117 D3
Artist St LS12 210 B3
Arum St BD5 74 C3
Arundel Cl Batley WF17 97 B2
Wakefield WF1 216 B3
Arundel St Garforth LS25 83 B8
Halifax HX1 202 B3
Wakefield WF1 216 B3
Arundel Wlk WF17 97 B1
Ascot Ave BD7 73 E2
Ascot Dr BD7 73 E2
Ascot Gdns BD7 73 E2
Ascot Gr HD6 135 E8
Ascot Par BD7 73 E2
Ascot Rd LS25 82 F2
Ascot Terr LS9 212 C3

Asdale Rd Crigglestone WF2 160 B7
Wakefield WF2 .... 160 B7
Ash Ave LS6 .... 59 D5
Ash Brow WF4 .... 157 C3
Ash Brow Rd HD2 .... 136 B3
Ash CI Brighouse HX3 .... 114 D8
Ilkley LS29 .... 7 E4
Ossett WF5 .... 140 D5
Ash Cres Leeds LS6 .... 59 D5
Lofthouse Gate WF3 .... 121 F5
Ash Croft BD6 .... 94 A8
Ash Ct BD19 .... 115 F8
Ash Gdns LS6 .... 59 D5
Ash Ghyll Gdns BD16 .... 36 F4
Ash Gr WF8 .... 125 F1
Ash Gr Bingley BD16 .... 37 A1
Birkenshaw BD11 .... 96 A6
Brighouse HD6 .... 115 C2
Cleckheaton BD19 .... 116 B6
Cleckheaton, Birdcace BD19 .. 96 A1
Darrington WF8 .... 147 C5
Horsforth LS18 .... 41 C2
Ilkley LS29 .... 8 C5
Keighley BD21 .... 35 B4
Leeds LS6 .... 205 F3
Lofthouse Gate WF3 .... 121 F2
Otley LS21 .... 22 F7
Pudsey LS28 .... 76 E6
South Elmsall WF9 .... 183 A4
Steeton BD20 .... 17 D5
Sutton in CB20 .... 16 D5
Ash Green Prim Sch HX2 ... 91 C5
Ash Grove Jun & Inf Sch
WF9 .... 183 A4
Ash Grove Rd HD7 .... 188 E5
Ash Grove Terr 6 HD6 .... 115 A1
Ash Hall La HX6 .... 132 A7
Ash Hill Dr LS17 .... 44 F4
Ash Hill Garth LS17 .... 44 F4
Ash Hill Gdns LS17 .... 44 F4
Ash Hill La LS17 .... 44 F4
Ash Hill Wlk BD4 .... 75 B4
Ash La Cinley HD8 .... 175 E7
Garforth LS25 .... 83 A8
Ash Lea Fairburn WF11 ..... 105 B4
Lofthouse Gate WF3 .... 121 F3
Ash Meadow CI HD2 .... 136 C3
Ash Mount Bradford BD7 .... 74 B5
Keighley BD21 .... 35 A5
Ash Rd Leeds LS6 .... 59 C5
Shafton S72 .... 180 D2
Ash St Cleckheaton BD19 .. 116 C7
Crofton WF4 .... 162 A7
Glusburn BD20 .... 16 D6
Huddersfield HD1 .... 154 A8
Ilkley LS29 .... 8 C5
Lofthouse Gate WF3 .... 121 F2
Oxenhope BD22 .... 51 C3
Ash Terr Bingley BD16 .... 36 F2
Garforth LS25 .... 83 A8
2 Leeds LS6 .... 59 D5
Ripponden HX6 .... 132 C3
Ash Tree App LS14 .... 62 D4
Ash Tree Ave BD13 .... 72 B6
Ash Tree Bank LS14 .... 62 D5
Ash Tree CI LS14 .... 62 D5
Ash Tree Ct 5 LS14 .... 62 D5
Ash Tree Gdns Halifax HX2 .. 91 C5
Leeds LS14 .... 62 D5
Normanton WF6 .... 122 F3
Ash Tree Gr LS14 .... 62 D5
Ash Tree Grange 4 LS14 ... 62 D5
Ash Tree Rd HX2 .... 91 C5
Ash Tree View 7 LS14 .... 62 D5
Ash Tree Wlk
Burley in W LS29 .... 9 E1
8 Leeds LS14 .... 62 D5
Ash View East Ardsley WF3 .. 120 C7
3 Leeds LS6 .... 59 D5
Ash Wlk HD7 .... 152 E5
Ashbourne Ave
Bradford BD2 .... 55 F3
Cleckheaton BD19 .... 116 D6
Ashbourne Bank BD2 .... 55 F3
Ashbourne CI BD2 .... 55 F4
Ashbourne Cres
Bradford BD2 .... 55 F3
Garforth LS25 .... 82 F5
Queensbury BD13 .... 72 D1
Ashbourne Croft BD19 .... 116 D6
Ashbourne Dr Bradford BD2 . 55 F3
Cleckheaton BD19 .... 116 D6
Pontefract WF8 .... 146 D5
Ashbourne Garth BD2 ...... 56 A4
Ashbourne Gdns
Bradford BD2 .... 55 F3
Cleckheaton BD19 .... 116 D6
Ashbourne Gr Bradford BD2 . 55 F3
Halifax HX1 .... 202 B3
Ashbourne Haven BD2 ...... 55 F3
Ashbourne Mount BD2 ..... 55 F3
Ashbourne Oval BD2 .... 55 F3
Ashbourne Rd Bradford BD2 . 55 F3
Keighley BD21 .... 35 A5
Ashbourne Rise BD2 .... 55 F3
Ashbourne View BD19 ..... 116 D6
Ashbourne Way
Bradford BD2 .... 55 F3
Cleckheaton BD19 .... 116 D6
Ashbrook CI WF5 .... 140 D7
Ashbrooke Pk LS11 .... 214 C2
Ashbrow Infants Sch HD2 .. 136 B3
Ashburn CI LS22 .... 13 D7
Ashburn Croft LS22 .... 13 D7
Ashburn Dr LS22 .... 13 D7

Ashburn Gr Baildon BD17 .... 38 C4
Wetherby LS22 .... 13 D7
Ashburn PI LS29 .... 8 A3
Ashburn Way LS22 .... 13 D7
Ashburnham Gr BD9 .... 55 B3
Ashbury Chase WF1 .... 121 A5
Ashby Ave LS13 .... 58 D1
Ashby CI WF15 .... 116 F1
Ashby Cres LS13 .... 58 D1
Ashby Mount 4 LS13 .... 58 D2
Ashby Sq LS13 .... 58 D2
Ashby St BD4 .... 75 A4
Ashby Terr LS13 .... 58 D2
Ashby View LS13 .... 58 D2
Ashcombe Dr WF11 .... 126 F3
Ashcroft Ave WF7 .... 145 C4
Ashcroft CI WF17 .... 118 B3
Ashcroft Rd WF7 .... 145 C4
Ashdale WF2 .... 142 E1
Ashdale La LS22 .... 13 D8
Ashday La Brighouse HX3 .. 114 B3
Halifax HX3 .... 114 B3
Ashdene Gildersome LS12 .... 77 D3
Todmorden OL14 .... 108 B1
Ashdene App WF4 .... 143 F1
Ashdene Ave WF4 .... 143 F1
Ashdene CI LS28 .... 76 E5
Ashdene Cres Crofton WF4 . 143 F1
Pudsey LS28 .... 76 E5
Ashdene Ct BD13 .... 52 D6
Ashdene Dr WF4 .... 143 F1
Ashdene Garth WF4 .... 143 F1
Ashdene Gr WF8 .... 125 F4
Ashdown CI
9 Bradford BD6 .... 74 B1
Halifax HX2 .... 112 D6
Ashdown Ct BD18 .... 55 A7
Ashdown Rd WF1 .... 142 E3
Ashdown St 13 LS13 .... 58 C2
Ashenhurst Ave HD4 .... 154 C3
Ashenhurst CI
Huddersfield HD4 .... 154 B3
Todmorden OL14 .... 108 A7
Ashenhurst Rd
Huddersfield HD4 .... 154 B3
Todmorden OL14 .... 108 A7
Ashenhurst Rise HD4 .... 154 B3
Ashes La Huddersfield HD4 . 154 C1
Todmorden OL14 .... 108 D7
Ashfield Bradford BD4 .... 75 D1
Dewsbury WF12 .... 139 D4
Leeds LS12 .... 78 A4
Wetherby LS22 .... 13 F6
Ashfield Ave Morley LS27 .... 97 F3
Shipley BD18 .... 55 B5
Skelmanthorpe HD8 .... 175 A1
Ashfield CI Halifax HX3 .... 91 F2
Leeds, New Farnley LS12 .... 77 F4
Leeds, Stanks LS15 .... 62 D4
Ashfield Cres Bingley BD16 .. 37 A2
Pudsey LS28 .... 57 E1
Ashfield Ct 6 BD16 .... 37 A2
Ashfield Dr Baildon BD17 .... 38 D3
Halifax HX3 .... 92 A2
Shipley BD9 .... 55 B5
Ashfield Gr 6 Pudsey LS28 . 57 E1
Shipley BD9 .... 55 B5
Ashfield Pk 1 LS6 .... 59 E5
Ashfield PI BD2 .... 56 D2
Ashfield Rd Batley WF17 ..... 97 A2
Bradford BD10 .... 39 C1
Elland HX4 .... 134 B7
Hemsworth WF9 .... 181 D5
Huddersfield HD2 .... 135 E1
Morley LS27 .... 97 F3
Pudsey LS28 .... 57 E1
Thornton BD13 .... 72 D6
Ashfield Residential Sch
BD10 .... 39 C1
Ashfield St
Huddersfield HD2 .... 136 B2
16 Keighley BD21 .... 35 B6
Normanton WF6 .... 123 C3
Ashfield Terr Bradford BD12 . 94 D4
16 Cleckheaton BD19 .... 116 E7
Elland HX4 .... 134 B8
11 Haworth BD22 .... 51 C6
Leeds LS15 .... 62 D4
Middleton WF3 .... 99 F2
Ashfield Way LS12 .... 77 F4
Ashfold CI HD8 .... 173 F2
Ashford Dr LS28 .... 76 F6
Ashford Gn BD4 .... 73 F1
Ashford Manor HD8 .... 155 D1
Ashford Pk HD7 .... 152 D5
Ashgap La WF6 .... 123 B3
Ashgrove Bradford BD7 ...... 74 D6
Bradford, Greengates BD10 .. 56 E7
Bradford, Royds Hall BD2 .... 56 C3
Ashgrove Ave 1 HX3 .... 113 E3
Ashgrove Cres LS25 .... 83 B3
Ashgrove Croft LS25 .... 83 B2
Ashgrove Mews LS13 .... 57 F4
Ashgrove Mount LS25 .... 83 B3
Ashgrove PI 3 HX3 .... 113 E3
Ashgrove Rd
Huddersfield HD2 .... 136 F2
Keighley BD20 .... 18 A2
Ashington CI BD2 .... 56 D3
Ashlands First Sch LS29 ...... 8 C5
Ashlands Rd LS29 .... 8 C5
Ashlar Gr Castleford WF10 . 124 F6
Queensbury BD13 .... 92 D8
Ashlea Ave HX6 .... 136 B8
Ashlea CI Brighouse HD6 ... 136 B8
Garforth LS25 .... 82 F5
Ashlea Ct LS13 .... 58 C3

Ashlea Dr HD6 .... 136 B8
Ashlea Gate LS13 .... 58 C3
Ashlea Gn LS13 .... 58 C3
Ashleigh S77 .... 181 A3
Ashleigh Ave
Pontefract WF8 .... 146 D7
Wakefield WF2 .... 141 E5
Ashleigh CI HD8 .... 173 F2
Ashleigh Dale HD2 .... 135 E1
Ashleigh Gdns Ossett WF5 . 140 C8
Rothwell LS26 .... 101 C6
Ashleigh Rd LS16 .... 59 A8
Ashleigh St BD21 .... 35 C8
Ashley Ave LS9 .... 208 A2
Ashley CI Cleckheaton BD19 . 96 A2
Wakefield WF2 .... 120 F2
Ashley Croft S71 .... 179 B4
Ashley Ct WF9 .... 181 F1
Ashley Gr HX7 .... 89 E1
Ashley Ind Est
Huddersfield HD2 .... 137 A4
Leeds LS7 .... 206 C3
Leeds LS7 .... 206 C4
Ashley La BD17 .... 55 B8
Ashley Rd Bingley BD16 ..... 37 A2
Bradford BD12 .... 94 C2
Leeds LS9 .... 208 A2
Leeds, Upper Wortley LS12 . 209 E2
Ashley St Halifax HX1 .... 202 B3
Shipley BD17 .... 55 B8
Ashley Terr LS9 .... 208 A2
Ashmead Batley WF17 .... 118 A3
Boston Spa LS23 .... 30 D5
Ashmere Gr HD2 .... 136 C2
Ashmere BD10 .... 56 E7
Ashmore Dr WF5 .... 119 C1
Ashmore Gdns BD4 .... 95 B8
Ashmount Bradford BD7 .... 73 D4
Ashroyd LS26 .... 100 F4
Ashtofts Mount LS20 .... 22 E1
Ashton Ave Bradford BD7 .... 73 E5
Leeds LS8 .... 207 F3
Ashton Clough Rd WF15 ... 117 A4
Ashton Cres WF3 .... 100 D3
Ashton Ct LS8 .... 208 A3
Ashton Gr LS8 .... 207 F2
Ashton Ho 6 BD5 .... 201 B1
Ashton Mount LS8 .... 208 A2
Ashton PI LS8 .... 207 F2
Ashton Rd Castleford WF10 . 124 D6
Hebden Bridge HX7 .... 89 E1
Leeds LS8 .... 208 A3
Ashton Road Ind Est LS8 . 208 A3
Ashton St Bradford BD1 ..... 74 D7
Castleford WF10 .... 124 D7
Leeds LS8 .... 207 F3
Ashton Terr LS8 .... 207 F2
Ashton View LS8 .... 207 F2
Ashtree Gr Bradford BD7 .... 73 F3
Kippax LS25 .... 83 B1
Ashville Ave LS6 .... 205 E3
Ashville Croft 4 HX2 .... 112 D8
Ashville Gdns HX2 .... 112 D8
Ashville Gr Halifax HX2 ...... 91 D1
Leeds LS6 .... 205 D3
Ashville Rd LS4, LS6 .... 205 D3
Ashville St 10 HX3 .... 92 A1
Ashville Terr Glusburn BD20 . 16 D6
Leeds LS6 .... 205 D3
Ashwell CI BD9 .... 55 A4
Ashwell La BD9 .... 55 A4
Ashwell Rd Bradford BD8 .... 55 B1
Shipley BD9 .... 55 A4
Ashwood LS14 .... 45 B1
Ashwood CI HD2 .... 136 C3
Ashwood Dr
Gildersome LS27 .... 97 C7
Keighley BD20 .... 19 A1
Ashwood Gdns LS27 .... 97 B7
Ashwood Gr
Gildersome LS27 .... 97 C7
Horbury WF4 .... 141 C2
Ashwood Grange WF4 ...... 159 E6
Ashwood St BD4 .... 75 D1
Ashwood Terr LS6 .... 205 F4
Ashwood Villas LS6 .... 205 F4
Ashworth CI WF13 .... 139 C8
Ashworth Gdns WF13 ...... 139 C8
Ashworth PI BD6 .... 74 D1
Ashworth Rd WF13 .... 139 C8
Ashworth PI BD6 .... 74 D1
Ashworth St 12 OL13 .... 106 A3
Askam Ave WF8 .... 125 F4
Askam Gn BD6 .... 93 E8
Asket Ave LS14 .... 61 F5
Asket CI LS14 .... 61 E5
Asket Cres LS14 .... 61 E5
Asket Dr LS14 .... 61 E5
Asket Garth LS14 .... 61 E5
Asket Gdns LS8 .... 61 D6
Asket Gn LS14 .... 61 E6
Asket Hill LS8 .... 61 D6
Asket PI LS14 .... 61 E5
Asket Wlk LS14 .... 61 E5
Askey Ave LS27 .... 98 B2
Askey Cres LS27 .... 98 B2
Asket Gres LS27 .... 98 B2
Askrigg Dr BD2 .... 56 B3
Askwith
County Primary Sch 9 F5
Askwith La LS21 .... 10 A6
Aspden St OL14 .... 108 B6
Aspect Gdns LS28 .... 76 D8

Aspect Terr LS28 .... 76 C8
Aspen CI Keighley BD21 ...... 35 E5
Wakefield WF2 .... 142 A8
Aspen CI Emley HD8 .... 175 C7
Morley WF3 .... 98 C1
Aspen Gr WF13 .... 139 B8
Aspen Mount LS16 .... 41 E2
Aspen Rise BD15 .... 53 F4
Aspinall St Halifax HX1 ..... 202 B2
Hebden Bridge HX7 .... 89 E1
Aspley PI HD1 .... 154 B6
Asquith Ave LS27 .... 97 F6
Asquith CI LS27 .... 97 F5
Asquith Dr LS27 .... 97 F5
Asquith St LS27 .... 97 F5
Asquith Terr LS27 .... 97 F5
Assembly St 5 Leeds LS2 .. 211 F3
Normanton WF6 .... 123 A2
Astley Ave LS26 .... 82 A1
Astley CI LS26 .... 102 C8
Astley Lane Ind Est LS26 . 102 B8
Astley Way LS26 .... 102 B8
Aston Ave LS13 .... 58 E2
Aston CI WF15 .... 116 F2
Aston Cres LS13 .... 58 E2
Aston Ct WF5 .... 141 A4
Aston Dr LS13 .... 58 E2
Aston Gdns LS13 .... 58 E2
Aston Mount LS13 .... 58 E2
Aston PI LS13 .... 58 E2
Aston Rd Bradford BD5 .... 74 E3
Leeds LS13 .... 58 D2
Aston St LS13 .... 58 D2
Aston Terr LS13 .... 58 E2
Aston View LS13 .... 58 D2
Astor Gr LS13 .... 58 A2
Astor St LS13 .... 58 A2
Astra Bsns Pk LS11 .... 214 C2
Astral CI HX3 .... 114 D8
Astral CI HX3 .... 114 D8
Astral View BD6 .... 74 A2
Atalanta Terr HX2 .... 112 E4
Atha CI LS11 .... 214 A1
Atha Cres LS11 .... 214 A1
Atha St LS11 .... 214 A1
Athelstan La LS21 .... 11 A1
Athene Dr HD4 .... 154 C3
Atherstone Rd BD15 .... 73 B7
Atherton La HD6 .... 136 B8
Athlone Dr WF12 .... 118 E2
Athlone Gr LS12 .... 209 F3
Athlone Rise LS25 .... 83 B7
Athlone St LS12 .... 209 F3
Athlone Terr LS12 .... 209 F3
Athol CI HX3 .... 92 A3
Athol Cres HX3 .... 92 A3
Athol Gdns HX3 .... 92 A3
Athol Gn HX3 .... 92 A3
Athol Rd Bradford BD9 .... 55 B2
Halifax HX3 .... 92 A3
Athol St Halifax HX3 .... 92 A3
Keighley BD21 .... 18 E1
Atholl CI WF5 .... 140 F5
Atkinson Dr WF5 .... 140 F5
Atkinson CI WF6 .... 123 A1
Atkinson La WF8 .... 125 D2
Atkinson St Leeds LS10 .... 212 B1
Shipley BD18 .... 55 B8
Atlanta St LS13 .... 58 A4
Atlas Farm Sch BD8 .... 74 C8
Atlas Mill Rd HD6 .... 115 A2
Atlas St BD8 .... 55 B1
Oakworth BD22 .... 34 C7
Attlee Ave WF4 .... 162 C1
Attlee Cres WF2 .... 160 E8
Attlee Gr WF1 .... 121 C4
Attlee St WF1 .... 144 B8
Auckland Rd BD6 .... 74 A1
Audby CI LS22 .... 14 A6
Audby La LS22 .... 13 F6
Audrey St WF5 .... 140 E4
Audsley's Yd WF4 .... 140 E1
Augusta Ct WF2 .... 141 F5
Augusta Dr WF4 .... 144 D8
Aurelia Hous BD8 .... 55 C2
Aureus Terr LS28 .... 76 C8
Austhorpe Ct LS15 .... 81 E7
Austhorpe Dr LS15 .... 81 E7
Austhorpe Gdns LS15 .... 81 E8
Austhorpe La LS15 .... 81 E8
Austhorpe Primary Sch
LS15 .... 81 E8
Austhorpe Rd LS15 .... 62 D1
Austhorpe View LS15 .... 81 D8
Austin Ave HX6 .... 114 F4
Austin Rd WF10 .... 125 D8
Austin St BD21 .... 35 B8
Austwick CI S75 .... 178 A2
Austwick St BD21 .... 35 A3
Autumn Ave Leeds LS6 .... 205 E2
Autumn Cres LS6 .... 205 E2
Autumn PI LS6 .... 205 E2
Autumn St Halifax HX1 ..... 202 B2
Leeds LS6 .... 205 E2
Autumn Terr 17 LS6 .... 205 E2
Auty Cres WF3 .... 121 F5
Auty Mews WF3 .... 121 F5
Auty News WF3 .... 98 B3
Avenel Rd BD15 .... 73 B8
Avenel Terr BD15 .... 73 B8
Avenham Way BD3 .... 201 D4
Avens CI WF8 .... 146 D7
Avenue A LS23 .... 15 B1
Avenue C W LS23 .... 15 C2
Avenue C W LS23 .... 15 C2
Avenue Cres LS8 .... 207 F4

Avenue D LS23 .... 15 B1
Avenue Des Hirondelles
LS11 .... 24 D6
Avenue E E LS23 .... 15 C1
Avenue E W LS23 .... 31 B8
Avenue F LS23 .... 15 D1
Avenue G LS23 .... 15 D2
Avenue Gdns LS17 .... 43 A5
Avenue Hill LS8 .... 207 F4
Avenue Lawns LS17 .... 42 F5
Avenue No 2 HD6 .... 115 A1
Avenue Rd Bradford BD5 ... 74 F3
Wakefield WF2 .... 142 E1
Avenue St BD4 .... 75 D1
Avenue Terr Otley LS21 ..... 22 F7
Pontefract WF8 .... 146 A8
Avenue The Barwick in E LS15 62 F8
Batley WF17 .... 117 F3
Batley, Birstall WF17 .... 96 E1
Batley, Carlinghow WF17 ... 118 A7
Bradford BD14 .... 73 B4
Brighouse HX3 .... 114 D8
Collingham LS22 .... 13 A1
Crofton WF4 .... 143 E1
East Ardsley WF3 .... 120 A8
Guiseley BD10 .... 39 E2
Harewood LS17 .... 27 A6
Horsforth LS18 .... 40 F1
4 Huddersfield HD5 .... 154 D5
Leeds LS15 .... 81 E3
Leeds, Alwoodley LS17 .... 43 A5
Leeds, Bank LS9 .... 212 B3
Leeds, Park Villas LS8 .... 44 A1
2 Leeds, Stanks LS15 .... 62 D3
Lofthouse Gate WF1 .... 121 B4
Royston S71 .... 179 E4
Rothwell LS26 .... 54 B8
Avenue Victoria LS8 .... 61 A8
Averingcliffe Rd BD10 .... 56 D6
Avery Tulip Ct 2 BD12 .... 94 C6
Aviary Gr LS12 .... 209 F4
Aviary Mount LS12 .... 209 F4
Aviary PI LS12 .... 209 F4
Aviary Rd LS12 .... 209 F4
Aviary Row LS12 .... 209 F4
Aviary St LS12 .... 209 F4
Aviary Terr LS12 .... 209 F4
Aviary View LS12 .... 209 F4
Avison Rd HD4 .... 153 A3
Avison Yd WF1 .... 216 C2
Avocet CI BD8 .... 73 C7
Avocet Garth 4 LS10 .... 99 D5
Avon CI LS17 .... 44 F4
Avon Croft WF5 .... 140 C5
Avon Ct LS17 .... 44 E5
Avon Dr LS25 .... 82 F6
Avon Wlk WF7 .... 145 C7
Avondale BD20
Lofthouse Gate WF3 .... 121 E5
Royston S71 .... 179 C1
Avondale Gr BD18 .... 55 A7
Avondale Mount BD18 .... 55 A7
Avondale PI 8 HX3 .... 113 B4
Avondale Rd BD18 .... 54 F7
Avondale St Leeds LS13 ...... 58 C1
Wakefield WF2 .... 142 C4
Avondale Way WF2 .... 142 C4
Aygill Ave BD9 .... 93 E7
Aygill Gr BD9 .... 54 B2
Aylesbury St 8 BD21 .... 35 A4
Aylesford Mount LS15 .... 62 F3
Aylesham Ind Est BD12 ...... 94 D6
Aynholme CI LS29 .... 6 F8
Aynholme Dr LS29 .... 6 F8
Aynsley Gr BD15 .... 54 B1
Ayres Dr HX4 .... 153 A3
Ayresome Ave LS8 .... 44 A2
Ayresome Oval BD15 .... 73 A7
Ayresome Terr LS8 .... 44 A2
Ayreville Dr HX3 .... 93 C6
Ayrton Cres 18 BD16 .... 37 A3
Aysgarth Ave HX3 .... 115 A6
Aysgarth CI Bradford BD12 . 94 C2
Leeds LS9 .... 212 C3
Aysgarth Cres WF17 .... 141 D3
Aysgarth Dr Leeds LS9 ..... 212 C3
Wakefield WF2 .... 141 D3
Aysgarth Fold LS10 .... 99 C4
Aysgarth PI LS9 .... 212 C3
Aysgarth Rd Batley WF17 . 118 A5
Huddersfield HD4 .... 154 B2
Aysgarth Wlk LS9 .... 212 C3
Ayton CI BD3 .... 201 C4
Ayton Rd HD3 .... 152 E6
Azealea CI BD3 .... 75 B8

Baby House Hill La HX7 ...... 69 A4
Bachelor La LS18 .... 41 C2
Back Ada St 8 BD21 .... 35 B6
Back Ada St 18 BD21 .... 35 A7
Back Aireview Terr BD21 ... 35 B6
Back Airlie PI LS8 .... 207 F4
Back Airville St BD20 .... 18 A2
Back Albert Gr LS6 .... 205 E2
Back Albert Terr 10 LS6 .... 205 E2
Back Albion St WF1 .... 216 B2
Back Alcester PI 16 LS8 .... 207 F3
Back Alcester Rd 14 LS8 .. 207 F3
Back Alcester Terr 15 LS8 . 207 F4
Back Allerton Terr 12 LS7 . 204 A3
Back Alma St LS19 .... 40 B7
Back Anderton St WF1 ...... 142 E3
Back Ann St BD13 .... 52 E1
Back Archery PI 8 LS2 ...... 206 B2
Back Archery Rd 14 LS2 .... 206 B2

ck Archery St 12 LS2 ...... 206 B2
ck Archery Terr 11 LS2 .... 206 B2
ck Armitage Rd HD4 .... 171 E8
ck Ash Gr LS6 .... 205 F3
ck Ashgrove (W) BD7 .... 74 D6
ck Ashley Ave LS6 .... 208 A2
ck Ashley St LS6 .... 208 A2
ck Ashville Ave LS6 .... 205 E3
ck Ashville Gr LS6 .... 205 E3
ck Ashville Rd LS6 .... 205 E3
ck Ashville Terr LS6 .... 205 E3
ck Ashwood Terr LS6 .... 205 F4
ck Aston Pl 1 LS13 .... 58 E2
ck Aston Rd LS13 .... 58 E2
ck Aston St LS13 .... 58 E2
ck Aston Terr 2 LS13 .... 58 E2
ck Aston View 1 LS13 .... 58 E2
ck Athlone Ave 1 LS12 ..... 209 F3
ck Athlone Gr 2 LS12 .... 209 F3
ck Athlone Terr
.... 209 F3
ck Atlanta St LS13 .... 58 A2
ck Austhorpe Rd
.... 62 D2
ck Autumn Rd 8 LS6 .... 205 E2
ck Autumn Terr 10 LS6 ..... 205 E2
ck Aviary Rd 1 LS12 .... 209 E3
ck Aylesbury St 4 BD21 ... 35 A4
ck Baker St BD18 .... 55 A8
ck Balbovan Terr 6
.... 207 F4
ck Balfour St
ngley BD16 .... 36 F2
1 Keighley BD21 .... 35 B6
ck Bank St WF10 .... 124 D8
ck Bank Terr LS8 .... 57 E2
ck Banstead St LS8 .... 207 F3
ck Barden Pl LS12 .... 209 D3
ck Barkly Gr LS11 .... 214 A2
ck Barkly Par 3 LS11 .... 214 A1
ck Barrowby View LS15 .... 81 F7
ck Bath Rd 13 LS13 .... 58 C2
ck Beacon St HD2 .... 136 A1
ck Beamsley Gr 9 LS6 ...... 205 E2
ck Beamsley Mount 4
.... 205 E2
ck Beamsley Terr 2
LS6 .... 205 E2
ck Beaumont St WF17 ...... 118 C3
ck Beech St LS6 .... 6 F8
ck Beech St BD16 .... 36 F2
ck Beech Terr HD1 .... 153 D6
ck Beechwood Gr
-HX4 .... 133 B1
ck Bellbrooke Gr LS9 .... 208 B2
ck Bellbrooke Pl LS9 .... 208 B2
ck Bellbrooke Terr LS9 ...... 208 B2
ck Belvedere Ave LS11 ..... 214 B2
ck Belvedere Mount
LS11 .... 214 B2
ck Bentley Ave 1 LS6 .... 59 F6
ck Bentley Gr LS6 .... 59 F6
ck Berkeley Ave LS8 .... 208 A3
ck Berkeley Terr LS8 .... 208 A3
ck Beverley Terr LS11 .... 214 B3
ck Blackwood Gr HX1 .... 202 B4
ck Blandford Gdns 22
-S2 .... 206 B2
ck Blandford Gr 24 LS2 ..... 206 B2
ck Blenheim Ave 1
-D8 .... ?
ck Blenheim Mount
BD8 ....
ck Blenheim Terr 1 LS2 ..... 206 B2
ck Boundary Terr LS6 .... 205 E1
ck Bower Rd HX5 .... 135 A7
ck Bowling Green Rd
-HX4 .... 133 F3
ck Bowman St WF1 .... 142 F3
ck Bradshaw Rd HD7 .... 171 F3
ck Branch Pl 10 LS12 .... 78 A4
ck Breary Ave LS18 .... 41 D1
ck Breary Terr LS18 .... 41 D1
ck Briggate BD20 .... 5 E2
ck Broad La LS13 .... 58 D4
ck Broomfield Cres
.... 205 D4
ck Broomfield Pl 4
-S6 .... 205 D3
ck Broomfield Rd
6 Keighley BD21 .... 35 B7
ck Broomfield St 6
BD21 .... 35 B7
ck Broughton Ave LS9 ...... 208 A2
ck Broughton Terr LS9 ...... 208 A2
ck Brudenell Gr LS6 .... 205 E2
ck Brudenell Mount
.... 205 E3
ck Brudenell Rd LS6 .... 205 E3
ck Brunswick St
Dewsbury WF13 .... 118 A1
1 Leeds LS2 .... 206 B3
ck Burchett Gr LS6 .... 206 A4
ck Burchett Pl LS6 .... 206 A4
ck Burley Hill LS4 .... 205 D2
ck Burley Lodge Rd LS6 ... 205 E1
ck Burley Lodge Terr
.... 205 E1
ck Burley St 5 LS3 .... 211 F3
ck Burlington Pl 22
.... 214 B2
ck Burlington Rd LS11 ...... 214 B2
ck Burton Cres 2 LS6 .... 59 D6
ck Burton Terr 1 .... 214 C3

Back Buxton St 4 BD21 ...... 35 D7
Back Byrl St BD21 .... 18 C1
Back Byrom St 4 OL14 .... 108 B6
Back Caister St 8 BD21 ...... 35 B4
Back Camberley St 9
.... 214 C3
Back Carberry Pl 20 LS6 .... 205 E2
Back Carberry Rd 20 LS6 ... 205 E2
Back Carberry Terr 22
.... 205 E2
Back Carlinghow La WF17 .. 117 E7
Back Carter Mount LS15 .... 81 C8
Back Cartmel Rd 12 BD21 .. 35 A7
Back Castle Rd HD1 .... 35 B8
Back Cavendish Rd BD10 ... 56 A7
Back Cavendish St 35 C7
Back Cavendish Terr 12
HX1 .... 202 C3
Back Cecil St 8 HD1 .... 154 A6
Back Chapel La LS6 .... 205 E3
Back Chapel St BD1 .... 201 C3
Back Charles St 10 HD6 ..... 115 A3
Back Chatsworth Rd LS8 ... 208 A3
Back Chestnut Ave 1
Leeds, Cross Gates LS15 ... 62 D2
Leeds, Hyde Park LS6 .... 205 F3
Back Chiswick Terr 24 LS6 . 205 E2
Back Christ Church View
.... 209 E4
Back Church La
Leeds, Adel LS16 .... 42 D5
Leeds, Kirkstall LS5 .... 59 A4
Back Church View
Leeds LS11 .... 213 F4
Back Churchill Gdns 28
.... 206 B2
Back Claremont Ave 6
LS3 .... 206 A1
Back Claremont Gr 6
LS3 .... 206 A1
Back Claremont St 9
LS26 .... 101 C6
Back Claremont Terr 10
.... 206 A1
Back Clarence Rd 7 LS18 ... 58 B7
Back Clarence St HX1 .... 203 D3
Back Clarendon Pl HX1 ...... 202 C2
Back Clarkson View 11
.... 206 A4
Back Clayton St LS26 .... 100 F5
Back Cliff Mount LS6 .... 206 A4
Back Clifton Rd HD1 .... 153 E7
Back Clifton Terr LS9 .... 208 B2
Back Clipston Ave LS6 .... 59 F6
Back Clough HX3 .... 93 A2
Back Clovelly Pl 21 LS11 ... 214 B3
Back Coldcotes Ave LS9 .... 208 C2
Back Colenso Mount LS11 . 213 F4
Back Colenso Rd
Keighley BD21 .... 18 E1
Leeds LS11 .... 213 F4
Back Colne Rd BD20 .... 16 D6
Back Colton Rd LS12 .... 209 F3
Back Colwyn Pl 20 LS11 ... 214 B2
Back Colwyn View 11
.... 214 B2
Back Commercial St 1
.... 203 E3
Back Commercial St 16
OL14 .... 108 C5
Back Compton St 8 LS9 .... 35 D8
Back Conway Gr LS8 .... 207 F3
Back Conway St LS8 .... 208 A3
Back Conway St LS7 .... 207 F3
Back Craggwood Rd 5
LS18 .... 58 C7
Back Cranbrook Ave LS11 . 214 A3
Back Cranbrook Terr LS11 . 214 A3
Back Croft HX6 .... 132 C1
Back Croft House La BD20 . 18 A2
Back Cromer Ave 1 BD21 ... 35 B5
Back Cromer Gr BD21 .... 35 B5
Back Cromer Terr LS2 .... 206 A2
Back Cromwell St 2
HX1 .... 203 D3
Back Cross Flatts Ave
.... 213 F2
Back Cross Flatts Cres
.... 213 F2
Back Cross Flatts Gr 3
.... 214 A2
Back Cross Flatts Mount 1
.... 214 A2
Back Cross Flatts Pl LS11 . 213 F2
Back Cross Flatts Row
LS11 .... 213 F2
Back Cross Green Cres
.... 212 C2
Back Cross Green La 18
.... 212 C2
Back Crossland Terr 1
LS11 .... 214 C3
Back Cunliffe St LS8 .... 5 B4
Back Dalton Ave LS11 ...... 214 A2
Back Dalton Gr LS11 .... 214 A2
Back Dalton Rd LS11 .... 214 A2
Back Dargai St LS2 .... 206 C3
Back Dawlish Ave LS9 ...... 80 B8
Back Dawlish Mount 2
.... 80 B8
Back Dawlish Rd LS8 .... 80 B8
Back De Lacy Mount LS5 .. 59 A5
Back Delph Mount LS6 ..... 206 A3
Back Dent St LS9 .... 212 C3
Back Der St 7 OL14 .... 108 C5
Back Devonshire La LS8 ... 44 A2
Back Dorset Mount 4
.... 208 A4

Back Dorset Rd LS8 .... 208 A4
Back Dorset Terr LS8 .... 208 A3
Back Dudley Hill Rd BD2 ... 56 B2
Back Duke of York St
WF1 .... 216 C3
Back Duke St WF7 .... 145 C6
Back Dunbar St WF1 .... 142 F4
Back East Park Rd 10 LS9 .. 80 A7
Back Eaton St 2 BD21 .... 35 A4
Back Ecclesburn St 6 LS9 .. 80 A7
Back Ecclesburn St LS9 .... 80 A7
Back Edensor Rd BD21 ..... 35 A4
Back Edinburgh Rd LS12 ... 209 D4
Back Edward Rd HD1 .... 153 D7
Back Elford Pl LS8 .... 207 F3
Back Elizabeth St
Bradford BD5 .... 201 B1
Bradford BD5 .... 201 B1
Back Ellerby La 1 LS9 .... 212 A3
Back Ellers Rd 8 LS8 .... 207 F3
Back Elmfield Terr HX1 ...... 203 D1
Back Elsworth St LS12 ...... 210 A3
Back Emily St 16 BD21 ...... 35 D8
Back Eric St Keighley BD21 . 35 C8
Leeds LS13 .... 58 B4
Back Eshald Pl LS26 .... 101 D6
Back Esmond Terr LS12 .... 59 F3
Back Estcourt Ave LS6 ...... 59 C4
Back Estcourt Terr LS6 ..... 59 C4
Back Eversley Mount HX2 .. 202 A2
Back Fairford Pl LS11 .... 214 C3
Back Featherbank Terr 2
.... 58 B7
Back Ferguson St 2 HX1 ... 203 E2
Back Field Ct BD13 .... 72 D6
Back Fitzwilliam St HD1 .... 153 F6
Back Florist St BD21 .... 18 E1
Back Fold BD14 .... 73 B5
Back Foster Rd 2 BD21 ..... 35 B4
Back Garden St
Castleford WF10 .... 124 D6
Wakefield WF1 .... 216 A2
Back Garton Rd LS9 .... 80 A7
Back Garton Terr LS9 .... 80 A7
Back Gathorne St LS8 .... 207 F3
Back George St 3 LS2 .... 212 A4
Back Gerrard St HX1 .... 203 D3
Back Giles St N
Bradford BD5 .... 74 D5
Bradford BD5 .... 201 B1
Back Giles St S
Bradford BD5 .... 74 D5
Bradford BD5 .... 201 B1
Back Gillett La LS26 .... 100 F5
Back Girlington Rd BD8 .... 54 F1
Back Gladstone St BD16 ... 36 F2
Back Glebe Terr LS16 .... 205 F4
Back Glen Terr HX1 .... 203 D1
Back Glenthorpe Terr 2
.... 80 A8
Back Glossop St LS6 .... 206 A4
Back Gn LS21 .... 98 C7
Back Gooder La 1 HD6 ...... 115 B1
Back Gordon St WF1 .... 142 F2
Back Gordon Terr LS6 .... 59 C4
Back Graham Gr LS4 .... 205 D3
Back Granby Gr LS6 .... 205 E4
Back Grange Cres LS7 ...... 207 E4
Back Grange Cres LS7 ...... 207 D4
Back Grange View LS7 ...... 207 D4
Back Grant St BD21 .... 35 A7
Back Grantley St WF1 .... 216 C2
Back Graveley St 6 LS15 ... 81 A8
Back Great Russell St BD7 . 74 D7
Back Greaves St BD5 .... 74 D3
Back Greenhead Rd 2
HD1 .... 154 A6
Back Greenhow Wlk LS4 ... 205 D2
Back Greenmount Terr
LS11 .... 214 A3
Back Greenwood Mount 4
LS6 .... 59 E7
Back Grosvenor Terr
Halifax HX1 .... 202 C3
Leeds LS6 .... 205 F4
Back Grouse St BD21 .... 35 D8
Back Grove Gdns LS6 .... 59 E6
Back Grove Rd LS29 .... 8 A4
Back Grovehall Ave LS11 .. 214 A1
Back Grovehall Dr LS11 .... 214 A1
Back Haigh Ave LS26 .... 100 C7
Back Haigh St LS26 .... 100 C7
Back Haigh View LS26 ...... 100 C7
Back Halliday Gr LS12 .... 209 D4
Back Halliday Pl LS12 .... 209 D4
Back Hambleton St WF1 ... 216 B3
Back Hamilton Ave LS7 .... 207 E4
Back Hamilton Terr LS7 .... 207 E4
Back Hamilton View LS7 ... 207 E4
Back Harehills Ave LS7 ..... 207 D4
Back Harehills Park View
.... 80 A8
Back Harehills Pl 4 LS8 ..... 207 F4
Back Hares Ave 11 LS8 ..... 207 F4
Back Hares Mount LS7 ...... 207 E4
Back Hares Terr 10 LS8 ..... 207 F4
Back Hares View LS8 .... 207 F4
Back Harold Gr LS6 .... 205 E2
Back Hartley Ave LS6 .... 206 A4
Back Hartley Gr 5 LS6 .... 206 A4
Back Hartley St LS27 .... 98 C3
Back Hatfield St WF1 .... 216 B3
Back Hawksworth Gr LS5 . 59 C5
Back Headingley Ave LS6 .. 59 C5
Back Headingley Mount
LS6 .... 59 D6
Back Heathfield Terr 5
LS6 .... 59 D6

Back Heddon Pl LS6 .... 59 E6
Back Heddon St LS6 .... 59 E6
Back Heights Rd BD13 ...... 72 B8
Back Hessle Terr 8
WF17 .... 118 C5
Back Hessle Ave LS6 .... 205 E3
Back Hessle Mount LS6 .... 205 E3
Back Hessle Terr LS6 .... 205 E3
Back Hessle View LS6 .... 205 E3
Back Highbury Terr LS6 .... 59 E6
Back Highfield Rd 4 LS13 .. 58 A4
Back Highthorne View 1
LS12 .... 209 D4
Back Highthorne Gr 4
LS12 .... 209 D4
Back Hill Top Ave LS8 .... 207 F4
Back Hill Top Mount LS8 ... 207 F4
Back Hillcrest Ave LS7 ...... 207 E4
Back Hillcrest View LS7 .... 207 E4
Back Hilton Gr 1 LS8 .... 207 F4
Back Hilton Pl LS8 .... 207 F4
Back Hilton Rd LS8 .... 207 F4
Back Hird St 8 BD21 .... 35 B6
Back Hollyshaw Terr 1
.... ?
Back Honoria St HD1 .... 136 A1
Back Hope Hall Terr 7
.... ?
Back Hovingham Gr LS8 ... 208 A4
Back Hovingham Mount 2
.... 208 A4
Back Hovingham Terr 1
.... ?
Back Hyde Gr BD21 .... 35 D8
Back Hyde Terr LS2 .... 206 B1
Back Ibbetson Pl 2 LS2 .... 206 B1
Back Ingledew Cres LS8 ... 44 B2
Back Irwell St BD4 .... 75 A5
Back Ivy Gr 2 LS9 .... 80 B7
Back Ivy Mount 9 LS9 .... 80 B8
Back Ivy St 10 LS9 .... 80 A8
Back John St BD13 .... 72 D6
Back Kelso Rd LS2 .... 205 F2
Back Kendal La 1 LS3 .... 206 A1
Back Kennerleigh Wlk
LS15 .... 62 C1
Back Kensington St
Bradford, Brown Royd BD8 . 74 A8
Bradford, Girlington BD8 ... 55 A8
Back Kensington Terr 205 F3
Back King's Ave 7 LS6 .... 205 E2
Back Kirby St BD21 .... 35 D8
Back Kirkgate BD18 .... 55 A7
Back Kitson St LS9 .... 212 A3
Back Knowl Rd WF14 .... 137 F6
Back Knowle Mount 12
LS4 .... 205 D3
Back La Badsworth WF9 ... 164 E2
Batley WF16 .... 117 D4
Birkenshaw BD12 .... 96 F7
Bradford, Clayton Heights
BD13, BD14 .... 73 B2
Bramhall, Low BD10 .... 56 D8
Bramham LS23 .... 30 D3
Burley in W LS29 .... 9 F1
Clayton DN5 .... 194 C4
Clayton West HD8 .... 176 A3
Crofton WF4 .... 144 C2
Dewsbury WF12 .... 138 F2
Dewsbury, Whitley Lower
WF12 .... 156 F7
Emley HD8 .... 175 A5
Flockton WF4 .... 156 E5
Gildersome LS12 .... 77 C3
Guiseley LS20 .... 39 D8
Halifax HX2 .... 91 D5
Haworth BD22 .... 51 C6
Hebden Bridge HX7 .... 88 F1
Heptonstall HX7 .... 88 F4
Holmfirth HD7 .... 189 A5
Hooton Pagnell DN5 .... 195 D5
Horsforth LS18 .... 58 B8
Keighley, East Morton BD20 . 19 D1
Keighley, Laycock BD22 .... 34 A3
Kippax LS25 .... 103 B4
Ledston LS15 .... 53 A8
Lepton WF14 .... 156 F4
Netherton WF4 .... 137 E5
Mirfield WF14 .... 138 C5
Ossett WF5 .... 140 D5
Otley LS29 .... 10 A1
Pudsey LS28 .... 57 D3
Ripponden HX6 .... 132 D4
Ryhill WF4 .... 162 B4
Shelley HD8 .... 174 B3
Shipley BD9 .... 55 A4
Sicklinghall LS22 .... 12 C5
Silsden BD20 .... 5 C8
Skipton BD23 .... 4 C8
Steeton with E WF9 .... 183 A6
Thornton BD22 .... 72 E7
Wadsworth Moor HX7 .... 69 A6
Wakefield WF1 .... 216 A2
Wilsden BD15 .... 53 C5
Woolley WF4 .... 162 A6
Yeadon LS19 .... 40 A6
Back La W WF1 .... 179 A4
Back Laisteridge La BD7 ... 74 C6
Back Lake St LS10 .... 215 D2
Back Lambton Gr 17 LS8 .. 207 F4
Back Landseer Ave LS13 ... 58 E3
Back Landseer Gr LS13 .... 58 E3
Back Landseer Terr LS13 .. 58 E3
Back Langdale Gdns LS6 .. 59 C4
Back Langdale Terr LS6 .... 59 C4

Back Lascelles Terr 1
.... 207 F3
Back Laurel Mount LS7 ..... 204 A1
Back Leatham St 2 WF13 .. 118 A1
Back Leeming BD22 .... ?
Back Lime St BD21 .... 35 B3
Back Linden Gr 2 LS11 ..... 214 B2
Back Lindum St BD8 .... 55 C2
Back Lodge La 1 LS11 ...... 214 B2
Back Lombard St LS19 ...... 40 A4
Back Longroyd Terr LS11 .. 214 C3
Back Lord St HX1 .... 203 D3
Back Low La LS13 .... 41 D1
Back Lucas St 4 LS6 .... 206 A4
Back Lunan Pl LS8 .... 207 F4
Back Lunan Terr LS8 .... 207 F4
Back Lyon St BD13 .... 72 F1
Back Lytton St 7 HX3 .... 92 C1
Back Mafeking Ave LS11 ... 214 A1
Back Mafeking Mount
.... 214 A1
Back Malt St 10 BD21 ...... 35 A4
Back Mannville Rd 10
BD21 .... 35 A6
Back Manor Dr LS6 .... 205 E4
Back Manor Gr LS7 .... 204 A2
Back Manor St BD2 .... 56 B3
Back Manor Terr LS6 .... 205 E4
Back Market St 3 BD6 .... 74 C1
Back Markham Ave LS9 .... 207 F4
Back Marlborough Gdns 18
.... 206 B2
Back Marlborough Gr 2
.... 206 B2
Back Marriot St 4 WF13 ... 118 D1
Back Marshall Ave 3 LS15 . 62 C2
Back Marshall St 6 LS15 ... 62 C2
Back Marshall Terr 6 LS15 . 62 C2
Back Mary St
East Ardsley WF3 .... 120 E8
Glusburn BD20 .... 16 D8
Back Masham St LS12 ...... 210 A3
Back Maud Ave LS11 .... 214 B2
Back Mayville Ave LS6 ...... 205 E3
Back Mayville Pl 6 LS6 ...... 205 E3
Back Mayville St 3 LS6 ..... 205 E3
Back Mayville Terr LS6 ..... 205 E3
Back Meadow View 12
LS6 .... 205 E3
Back Melbourne Gr 18
LS13 .... 58 C2
Back Methley Dr LS7 .... 204 A2
Back Mexborough Ave
LS7 .... 207 D4
Back Mexborough Dr LS7 .. 207 D4
Back Mexborough Gr LS7 .. 207 D4
Back Mexborough St LS7 .. 207 D4
Back Middle Cross St
.... 210 A3
Back Middleton La LS29 .... 8 A4
Back Middleton View 1
LS11 .... 214 A3
Back Midland Rd LS6 .... 205 E3
Back Milan Ave LS8 .... 207 F3
Back Milan Rd LS8 .... 207 F3
Back Milan St LS8 .... 208 A3
Back Mitchell Terr 5 BD16 . 36 F2
Back Mitford Rd LS12 .... 210 A3
Back Model Rd LS12 .... 210 A3
Back Model Terr LS12 .... 210 A3
Back Model View LS12 ...... 210 A3
Back Monk Bridge Dr 7
.... 59 F6
Back Monk Bridge St LS6 .. 59 F6
Back Montague St WF1 .... 142 F3
Back Montpelier Terr 2
.... 206 A3
Back Moorfield St HX1 ...... 202 C1
Back Moorfield Terr 1 LS12 . 209 D4
Back Moorland Terr 2 LS2 . 206 A2
Back Morning St 14 BD21 . 35 B4
Back Morritt Dr LS15 .... 80 F8
Back Mount Ave 2 WF17 ... 118 C3
Back Mount Pleasant
Middleton LS10 .... 99 C5
Wakefield WF1 .... 216 C2
Back Mount View LS6 .... 205 F4
Back Muff St BD4 .... 75 B5
Back Myrtle Ave BD16 ...... 36 F2
Back Myrtle Terr BD22 ...... 34 F1
Back Nansen St LS13 .... 58 A2
Back Nelson St LS13 .... 139 C8
Back New St 8 HD6 .... 115 A3
Back New York St 6 LS2 ... 211 F3
Back Newport Gdns 2
.... 205 D3
Back Newport Mount 1
.... 205 D3
Back Newport Pl 6 LS6 ..... 205 E3
Back Newport Rd 5 LS6 .... 207 E4
Back Newton La
Ledston WF10 .... 104 B5
Wakefield WF1 .... 103 E7
Back Nice View LS8 .... 207 F4
Back Norman Mount 1
.... 59 A4
Back Norman Pl LS8 .... 44 A2
Back Norman Terr LS8 ...... 44 A2
Back North Park Ave LS8 .. 44 A4
Back North St BD12 .... 95 A4
Back Northbrook St 1 LS7 . 204 A4
Back Northgate WF8 .... 125 D1
Back Norwood Gr LS6 ...... 205 E3
Back Norwood Pl 2 LS6 .... 205 E3

Back Norwood La **1** LS6 .. 205 E3
Back Norwood Terr LS6 .. 205 E3
Back Nowell Cres LS9 .. 208 B1
Back Nowell Mount LS9 .. 208 B1
Back Nowell Pl LS9 .. 208 B1
Back Nowell Terr LS9 .. 208 B1
Back Nunington St LS12 .. 210 A4
Back Nunington View **8** LS12 .. 59 C1
Back Nunroyd Rd LS17 .. 43 D1
Back Nursery Mount LS10 .. 215 E1
Back o' Dam HD7 .. 170 A8
Back o' Th' Height HX6 .. 131 D1
Back O' the Mill BD16 .. 36 A1
Back O'Wall HD7 .. 151 B3
Back Oak Ave BD16 .. 36 F2
Back Oak La LS7 .. 204 A1
Back Oakfield Terr LS6 .. 59 E6
Back Oakley St **4** .. 99 E1
Back Oakley Terr LS11 .. 214 C2
Back Oakwood Ave LS8 .. 61 B6
Back Oakwood Dr LS8 .. 61 B6
Back Osmondthorpe La LS9 .. 80 C8
Back Otterburn St **2** BD21 .. 35 C8
Back Outwood La **5** LS18 .. 58 C7
Back Overdale Terr **6** LS15 .. 81 A8
Back Oxford Pl LS11 .. 211 E4
Back Oxford St
East Ardsley WF3 .. 120 E8
7 Keighley BD21 .. 35 A6
Back Paget St **5** BD21 .. 35 A7
Back Parish Ghyll Rd LS29 .. 8 B4
Back Park Cres LS8 .. 44 B2
Back Park Terr LS11 .. 202 C2
Back Park View LS11 .. 214 A3
Back Park View Ave LS4 .. 205 D3
Back Parkfield Pl LS11 .. 214 A3
Back Parkfield Pl LS11 .. 214 A3
Back Parnaby Ave LS10 .. 215 F1
Back Parnaby St LS10 .. 215 F1
Back Parnaby Terr LS10 .. 215 F1
Back Pasture Gr LS7 .. 204 A3
Back Pasture Rd LS8 .. 207 F4
Back Pawson St WF3 .. 120 E8
Back Pleasant St HX6 .. 112 C4
Back Pollard La LS13 .. 58 C5
Back Pollard St HD7 .. 136 B2
Back Poplar Ave **1** LS15 .. 62 D2
Back Potternewton La LS7 .. 60 C6
Back Potters St LS7 .. 204 A2
Back Prospect Pl BD21 .. 35 B6
Back Prospect Terr **2** LS12 .. 213 C3
Back Providence Ave **11** LS6 .. 206 A4
Back Providence St **4** WF17 .. 118 C5
Back Purwell Hall Rd WF17 .. 118 C3
Back Quarry Mount Terr **9** LS6 .. 206 A4
Back Queen St
2 Elland HX4 .. 134 D6
2 Huddersfield HD1 .. 154 B5
Back Ravens St WF13 .. 139 A6
Back Ravenscar Ave **6** LS8 .. 61 A6
Back Ravenscar Pl **1** LS8 .. 61 A6
Back Raynville Mount LS13 .. 58 E3
Back Rd **19** BD12 .. 94 C4
Back Regent Park Terr LS6 .. 205 F4
Back Regent St WF1 .. 142 E3
Back Regent Terr LS6 .. 205 F2
Back Reginald Mount LS7 .. 207 D4
Back Reginald Pl LS7 .. 207 D4
Back Reginald St LS7 .. 207 D4
Back Rhodes St HX1 .. 203 D3
Back Ribble St BD21 .. 35 F8
Back Richardson St LS10 .. 95 A4
Back Richmond Mount LS6 .. 205 E4
Back Ridge Mount Terr LS6 .. 206 A4
Back Ridge St OL14 .. 108 B5
Back Ridge View LS7 .. 60 A5
Back Rigging La HX6 .. 111 C3
Back Ripley St BD20 .. 18 F1
Back Ripon St HX1 .. 202 A2
Back Ripon Terr HX3 .. 92 B1
Back River St **8** BD22 .. 51 D7
Back Roberts St **1** LS26 .. 101 C6
Back Rochester Terr LS6 .. 205 D4
Back Rokeby Gdns **1** LS6 .. 59 C5
Back Roman Gr LS8 .. 44 A2
Back Roman Pl LS8 .. 44 B2
Back Roman St LS8 .. 44 B2
Back Rose Ave LS18 .. 58 C8
Back Rosebank Cres LS3 .. 205 F2
Back Rosemont Wlk **1** LS13 .. 58 C2
Back Rossall Rd LS8 .. 208 A4
Back Rossington Gr **3** LS8 .. 207 E4
Back Rossington Pl **5** LS8 .. 207 E4
Back Rossington Rd LS8 .. 207 E4
Back Roundhay Ave LS8 .. 204 C1
Back Roundhay Cres LS8 .. 204 C1
Back Roundhay Gr LS8 .. 204 C1
Back Roundhay Pl LS8 .. 204 C1
Back Roundhay View LS8 .. 204 C1
Back Row LS11 .. 211 E2

Back Rowland Terr **7** LS11 .. 214 C3
Back Rowsley St **8** BD21 .. 35 C7
Back Rupert St BD21 .. 35 C8
Back Russell St BD5 .. 201 A1
Back Ruthven View LS8 .. 208 A3
Back Rydal St **4** BD22 .. 35 A6
Back Rylstone St **1** BD21 .. 35 E8
Back Saint Ives Mount LS12 .. 209 D4
Back Salisbury Gr LS12 .. 209 F4
Back Salisbury Terr LS12 .. 209 F4
Back Salisbury View LS12 .. 209 F4
Back Saltaire Rd N BD17 .. 55 B8
Back Sandhurst Gr LS8 .. 208 A3
Back Sandhurst Pl LS8 .. 208 A3
Back Sandhurst Terr LS8 .. 208 A3
Back Savile Gr HX1 .. 203 D1
Back Savile Pl LS7 .. 207 D3
Back Savile Rd LS7 .. 207 D3
Back School View LS6 .. 205 E3
Back Seaforth Ave LS8 .. 208 B2
Back Seaforth Pl **2** LS8 .. 208 A3
Back Seaforth Terr **8** LS9 .. 208 A3
Back Sefton Ave LS11 .. 214 A3
Back Sefton Terr LS11 .. 214 A3
Back Shaftesbury Ave LS8 .. 44 A2
Back Shaw La BD21 .. 35 D3
Back Shepherd's La LS7 .. 207 E4
Back Shepherd's Pl **9** LS7 .. 207 E4
Back Sholebroke Ave LS7 .. 204 A1
Back Sholebroke Mount LS7 .. 207 D4
Back Sholebroke Pl LS7 .. 207 D4
Back Sholebroke Row LS7 .. 204 A1
Back Sholebroke Terr LS7 .. 204 A1
Back Sholebroke View LS7 .. 207 D4
Back Sidlaw Terr LS8 .. 207 F4
Back Simpson St **1** BD21 .. 35 A7
Back Sladen St **6** BD21 .. 35 A7
Back Slaithwaite Rd WF12 .. 139 C4
Back Smith Row BD5 .. 74 C3
Back South End Gr LS13 .. 58 C1
Back South St HD1 .. 153 D5
Back Southfield Sq BD8 .. 55 C1
Back Spencer Mount **7** LS8 .. 207 E4
Back Spring Grove Wlk **4** LS6 .. 205 E2
Back Spring St **8** HD1 .. 154 A6
Back Springfield Mount LS12 .. 209 D4
Back Springfield Pl BD8 .. 55 C1
Back Springfield Rd HX5 .. 135 A7
Back St BRamham LS23 .. 30 C2
Pontefract WF8 .. 146 C8
Back St Alban Cres LS9 .. 208 C1
Back St Luke's Cres LS11 .. 214 A4
Back St Mary's Rd LS7 .. 204 A1
Back St Paul's Rd LS8 .. 55 A7
Back Stanley St
Huddersfield HD1 .. 153 E3
Leeds LS9 .. 207 F2
Back Stanmore Pl LS4 .. 59 C3
Back Stanmore St LS4 .. 59 C3
Back Station Rd
Batley WF17 .. 118 D4
Glusburn BD20 .. 16 D7
Mirfield WF14 .. 138 A6
Back Stone Hill Rd BD20 .. 56 B4
Back Storey Pl LS14 .. 61 E1
Back Stratford La LS11 .. 214 A3
Back Stratford St **10** LS11 .. 214 A3
Back Stratford Terr LS11 .. 214 A3
Back Strathmore Dr **8** LS9 .. 208 A3
Back Sunnydene LS14 .. 61 F1
Back Sutton App LS14 .. 61 E1
Back Swinton St HX1 .. 202 B2
Back Sycamore Ave LS6 .. 36 F2
Back Tamworth St BD4 .. 75 E6
Back Tempest Rd **4** LS11 .. 214 A3
Back Temple View LS11 .. 214 A3
Back Thornhill Rd HD3 .. 153 A6
Back Thornhill St LS28 .. 57 B6
Back Tower Gr LS12 .. 209 D4
Back Trafford Ave LS9 .. 208 B2
Back Trentham Pl **8** LS11 .. 214 B2
Back Trinity Terr BD5 .. 201 A1
Back Union St **5** HD1 .. 154 B7
Back Unity St N BD16 .. 36 F2
Back Unity St S **6** BD16 .. 37 A2
Back Victor Terr HX1 .. 214 A4
Back Victoria Ave **8** LS9 .. 80 B8
Back Victoria Gr **9** LS9 .. 80 B8
Back Victoria St **1** HX3 .. 203 E3
Back Wakefield Rd HX6 .. 112 E4
Back Walmsley Rd LS6 .. 205 E2
Back Walnut St **8** BD21 .. 35 C8
Back Webster St **3** WF13 .. 139 C8
Back Welburn Ave LS16 .. 59 B7
Back Wellfield Terr LS14 .. 108 A4
Back Welton Ave **10** LS6 .. 205 E3
Back Welton Gr LS6 .. 205 E3
Back Welton Mount **18** LS6 .. 205 E3
Back Welton Pl LS6 .. 205 E3
Back Wentworth St HD1 .. 154 B4
Back Wesley Rd LS12 .. 209 F3
Back Wesley St **10** LS12 .. 124 D8
Back West St HX1 .. 112 B3
Back Westbourne Terr LS2 .. 206 A2

Back Westbury St LS10 .. 215 F1
Back Westfield Rd LS3 .. 205 F1
Back Westlock Ave LS7 .. 208 A1
Back Westmoreland Mount **2** LS13 .. 58 C4
Back Weston Rd LS29 .. 8 B4
Back Westover Rd LS13 .. 58 C3
Back Wetherby Gr **5** LS4 .. 59 C2
Back Wetherby Rd LS8 .. 61 B6
Back Wheat St **3** BD22 .. 35 A4
Back Wickham St LS11 .. 214 B3
Back William Ave **1** LS9 .. 80 E8
Back William St **9** HD6 .. 115 A1
Back Wilton Gr **4** LS6 .. 59 E6
Back Winfield Gr **3** LS2 .. 206 B2
Back Winston Gdns LS6 .. 59 C5
Back Winterburn St LS11 .. 214 A3
Back Wolsley Terr **2** HX1 .. 202 B3
Back Wood St **8**
Bradford BD6 .. 74 C8
East Ardsley WF3 .. 120 D8
Back Woodbine Terr LS6 .. 59 E6
Back Woodland Park Rd **8** LS6 .. 59 E5
Back Woodstock St **16** LS2 .. 206 B2
Back York Pl LS1 .. 211 E3
Back York St **3** LS2 .. 212 A3
Backhold Ave HX3 .. 113 E2
Backhold Dr HX3 .. 113 E2
Backhold La HX3 .. 113 D2
Backhold La HX3 .. 113 E2
Backhouse La WF4 .. 177 F7
Backstone Gill La LS17 .. 27 E1
Backstone La LS29 .. 8 D4
Backstone Way LS29 .. 8 D4
Bacon Ave WF6 .. 123 C3
Bacon St LS20 .. 39 F8
Bacup Rd OL14 .. 107 D8
Baddeley Gdns BD10 .. 39 A1
Baden Powell Cres WF8 .. 146 D7
Baden St BD22 .. 51 C8
Baden Terr **4** BD19 .. 116 D7
Badger Brow HD7 .. 170 D2
Badger Gr HD4 .. 159 F7
Badger Gate HD7 .. 170 D2
Badger Hill HD6 .. 135 E6
Badger La
Blackshaw Head HX7 .. 88 B4
Brighouse HX3 .. 114 C8
Badger Wood Glade LS22 .. 13 E7
Badgergate Ave BD15 .. 53 C4
Badgers Gate LS29 .. 3 E4
Badgers Mount LS15 .. 62 F2
Badgers Way **2** BD2 .. 55 E4
Badgers Wlk WF16 .. 117 E3
Badsworth CE
Jun & Inf Sch WF9 .. 164 E2
Badsworth Ct
Badsworth WF9 .. 164 E3
Bradford BD10 .. 73 D5
Badsworth Mews WF9 .. 164 E2
Badsworth View WF9 .. 183 A8
Bagden La Denby Dale HD8 .. 192 D8
Baghill CE WF8 .. 146 F8
Baghill Gn WF3 .. 119 D6
Baghill Rd WF3 .. 119 D6
Baghill St WF8 .. 146 E8
Bagley La LS28 .. 57 E4
Bagnall Terr **2** BD6 .. 74 B1
Bagshaw Mus WF12 .. 118 A8
Baildon Ave LS13 .. 83 B3
Baildon CE First Sch BD17 .. 38 D4
Baildon Chase LS14 .. 62 C7
Baildon Cl LS14 .. 62 C6
Baildon Dr LS14 .. 62 C6
Baildon Gn LS14 .. 62 C6
Baildon Golf Course BD17 .. 38 A6
Baildon Holmes BD17 .. 38 C1
Baildon Path **1** LS14 .. 62 C6
Baildon Pl LS14 .. 62 C6
Baildon Rd Baildon BD17 .. 38 D2
Baildon Sta BD17 .. 38 E3
Baildon Wlk LS14 .. 62 C7
Baildon Wood Ct BD17 .. 38 C2
Bailes Rd LS7 .. 60 A5
Bailey Ave **3** HX2 .. 202 C4
Bailey Hall Bank **3** .. 203 F3
Bailey Hall Rd HX3 .. 203 F2
Bailey Hills Rd BD16 .. 36 E4
Bailey St BD4 .. 201 C1
Bailey Towers **1** LS14 .. 62 A5
Bailey Wells Ave BD5 .. 74 C3
Bailey's Ct LS14 .. 62 A5
Bailey's Hill LS14 .. 62 B5
Bailey's La LS14 .. 62 A5
Bailey's Lawn LS14 .. 62 A5
Bailiff Bridge
Junior & Infants Sch HD6 .. 115 B7
Bainbridge Wharf BD20 .. 4 D1
Bainbrigge Rd LS6 .. 205 D4
Baines St Halifax HX1 .. 202 C4
Rothwell LS26 .. 100 E5
Baird St BD5 .. 74 E4
Bairstow Ct HX6 .. 112 C6
Bairstow La HX6 .. 112 C6
Bairstow Mount HX6 .. 112 C5
Bairstow St **4** LS29 .. 8 A4
Bairstow's Bldgs HX2 .. 91 F4
Baitings Gate Rd HX6 .. 131 C2
Baker Cres LS27 .. 98 A3
Baker Fold **7** HX1 .. 202 C3

Baker La WF3 .. 121 D5
Baker Rd LS27 .. 98 A3
Baker St Bradford BD2 .. 56 B2
Huddersfield HD3 .. 153 D8
Morley LS27 .. 98 A3
Shipley BD18 .. 55 A8
Baker St N HX2 .. 92 A5
Baker's St **12** HX7 .. 89 A4
Bakes St BD7 .. 74 A4
Balbec Ave LS6 .. 59 E5
Balbec St LS6 .. 59 E5
Balderstone Hall La WF14 .. 138 C7
Baldovan Mount LS8 .. 207 F4
Baldovan Pl LS8 .. 207 F4
Baldovan Terr **7** LS8 .. 207 F4
Baldwin La
Bradford BD13, BD14 .. 73 A2
Queensbury BD13, BD14 .. 73 A2
Baldwin Terr HX3 .. 203 F3
Balfour St Bingley BD16 .. 36 F2
Bradford BD4 .. 75 A4
6 Keighley BD21 .. 35 B6
Balk Ave WF3 .. 122 A2
Balk Cres WF3 .. 122 A2
Balk La Bradford BD7 .. 74 A4
Denby Dale HD8 .. 191 C6
Kirkheaton HD5 .. 155 B7
Lofthouse Gate WF3 .. 122 A1
Netherton WF4 .. 158 F7
South Elmsall WF9 .. 183 A4
Wakefield WF3 .. 122 A1
Balk St WF17 .. 118 B5
Balk The Batley WF17 .. 118 C7
Mapplewell S75 .. 178 C2
Walton WF2 .. 161 B6
Balkcliffe La LS10 .. 99 A6
Balkram Dr HX2 .. 91 A5
Balkram Edge HX2 .. 91 A5
Balkram Rd HX2 .. 91 A5
Balks WF15 .. 116 F4
Ball Royd Rd HD2 .. 136 B2
Ball St BD13 .. 72 E6
Ballantyne Rd BD10 .. 39 A2
Ballater Ave HD4 .. 153 C2
Ballfield La S75 .. 177 C1
Balroyd Clough
Huddersfield HD3 .. 153 A6
Huddersfield, Quarmby HD3 .. 153 A7
Balroyd La HD3 .. 153 A5
Balm Pl LS11 .. 211 D1
Balm Rd LS10 .. 215 D3
Balm Road Ind Est LS10 .. 215 D3
Balm Wlk LS11 .. 211 D1
Balme La BD12 .. 94 D3
Balme Rd BD19 .. 116 D8
Balme St Bradford BD1 .. 201 C3
Bradford, Upper Common .. 94 D3
Balmfield WF15 .. 117 A2
Balmfield Cres WF15 .. 117 A1
Balmoral Ave HD4 .. 153 C2
Balmoral Chase LS10 .. 215 E3
Balmoral Cl WF4 .. 146 B5
Balmoral Pl WF11 .. 126 C4
Balmoral Pl HX3 .. 203 E2
Balmoral St **12** HX7 .. 89 A3
Balmoral Way LS19 .. 40 B4
Balne Ave WF2 .. 142 A7
Balne La WF2 .. 142 A7
Bamborough St WF1 .. 142 F3
Bamburgh Cl LS15 .. 62 E3
Bamburgh Rd LS15 .. 62 E3
Bancett Brow BD22 .. 51 D8
Banbury Rd WF8 .. 125 E3
Bancroft Ave HD5 .. 154 E5
Bancroft St BD22 .. 51 F8
Bangor Gr **1** LS12 .. 78 A4
Bangor Pl LS12 .. 78 A4
Bangor St LS12 .. 78 A4
Bangor Terr LS12 .. 78 A4
Bangor View **11** LS12 .. 78 A4
Bank Bradford BD10 .. 56 D6
Oxenhope BD22 .. 51 E1
Bank Ave Horsforth LS18 .. 58 B8
Morley LS27 .. 98 A5
Bank Bldgs
Hebden Bridge HX7 .. 89 C2
Meltham HD7 .. 170 E1
Bank Bottom Halifax HX3 .. 203 F3
Hebden Bridge HX7 .. 90 A2
Marsden HD7 .. 169 C6
Ripponden HX6 .. 150 D8
Bank Bottom La HX7 .. 88 B3
Bank Bottom Terr HD7 .. 169 C6
Bank Cl BD10 .. 56 C5
Bank Crest BD17 .. 38 C3
Bank Crest Rise BD18 .. 54 C7
Bank Dr BD6 .. 74 D1
Bank Edge Cl HX2 .. 91 E3
Bank Edge Gdns **1** HX2 .. 91 E3
Bank Edge Rd HX2 .. 91 E4
Bank End Elland HX4 .. 133 D7
Slaithwaite HD7 .. 152 C4
Bank End La
Clayton West HD8 .. 176 A1
High Hoyland HD8 .. 176 A1
Huddersfield HD5 .. 154 E4
Bank End Rd HD7 .. 152 C3
Bank Field Grange HX4 .. 134 C7
Bank Field Rd WF15 .. 118 C5
Bank Field St **7** WF17 .. 118 C5
Bank Foot HD4 .. 172 F8
Bank Foot La HD7 .. 171 E7
Bank Foot Pl WF17 .. 118 C5
Bank Foot Rd HD4 .. 172 E8
Bank Foot St WF17 .. 118 C5
Bank Gate HD7 .. 151 F1
Bank Gdns LS18 .. 58 B8
Bank Gr WF12 .. 140 A7

Bank Hall Gr HD8 .. 190
Bank Hey Bottom La HX6 .. 132
Bank House HX4 .. 133
Bank House Cl LS27 .. 98
Bank House La HX2 .. 90
Bank La Denby Dale HD8 .. 191
Holmfirth HD7 .. 188
Holmfirth, Liphill Bank HD7 .. 188
Holmfirth, Town End HD7 .. 189
Silsden BD20 .. 5
Bank Nook HD7 .. 169
Bank Par LS2 .. 22
Bank Rd Glusburn BD20 .. 16
Sowerby Bridge HX6 .. 112
Bank Royd La HX4 .. 133
Bank Side HD8 .. 173
Bank Side St LS8 .. 207
Bank Sq **4** LS27 .. 98
Bank St Bradford BD1 .. 201
Bradford, Brownroyd Hill BD6 .. 74
Brighouse HD6 .. 115
Castleford WF10 .. 124
Cleckheaton BD19 .. 116
Dewsbury WF12 .. 139
Hemsworth WF9 .. 181
Holmfirth HD7 .. 189
Horbury WF4 .. 141
6 Keighley BD21 .. 35
Leeds LS27 .. 211
Liversedge WF15 .. 117
Mirfield WF14 .. 137
Morley LS27 .. 98
Ossett WF5 .. 140
Shipley BD18 .. 55
Todmorden OL14 .. 108
Wakefield WF1 .. 216
Wetherby LS22 .. 13
Bank Terr
Hebden Bridge HX7 .. 88
Morley LS27 .. 98
Bank Top HX3 .. 113
Bank Top Dr BD20 .. 18
Bank Top La
Hebden Bridge HX7 .. 109
Holmfirth HD7 .. 188
Bank Top Way BD21 .. 35
Bank View Baildon BD17 .. 38
Dewsbury WF12 .. 140
Honley HD7 .. 172
Sowerby Bridge,
Luddenden Foot HX2 .. 111
Sowerby Bridge, Mill Bank HX6 .. 132
Bank View Terr LS7 .. 60
Bank Wlk BD17 .. 38
Bank Wood Rd WF8 .. 147
Banker St **1** LS4 .. 205
Bankfield Bardsey LS17 .. 28
Marsden HD7 .. 169
Shepley HD8 .. 173
Bankfield Ave
Kirkheaton HD5 .. 155
Shipley BD18 .. 54
Bankfield Cl LS27 .. 140
Bankfield Ct
Huddersfield HD5 .. 154
Mirfield WF14 .. 137
Wakefield WF2 .. 120
Bankfield Dr Holmfirth HD7 .. 188
Keighley BD22 .. 34
Shipley BD18 .. 54
Wakefield WF2 .. 120
Bankfield Gdns Halifax HX3 .. 113
1 Leeds LS4 .. 59
Bankfield Gr Leeds LS4 .. 59
Shipley BD18 .. 54
Bankfield La LS17 .. 165
Bankfield Mount BD22 .. 34
1 Leeds LS4 .. 59
Bankfield Park Ave HD4 .. 153
Bankfield Rd
Huddersfield HD1 .. 153
Keighley BD22 .. 34
Leeds LS4 .. 59
Shipley BD18 .. 54
Bankfield St BD22 .. 34
Bankfield Terr Baildon BD17 .. 38
1 Leeds LS4 .. 59
Leeds LS4 .. 59
Bankfield View HX3 .. 92
Bankfield Wlk BD22 .. 34
Bankfoot HX7 .. 88
Bankfoot First Sch BD5 .. 74
Bankholme Ct BD4 .. 75
Bankhouse LS28 .. 76
Bankhouse La Halifax HX3 .. 113
Huddersfield HD3 .. 153
Pudsey LS28 .. 76
Bankhouse Rd HD3 .. 153
Banklands BD20 .. 5
Banklands Ave BD20 .. 5
Banklands La BD20 .. 5
Banks App HD7 .. 152
Banks Ave
Ackworth M T WF7 .. 163
Huddersfield HD7 .. 152
Pontefract WF8 .. 146
Banks Cres HD7 .. 152
Banks Dr HD7 .. 152
Banks End Rd HX5 .. 135
Banks Garth WF11 .. 126
Banks Gr HD7 .. 152
Banks La Keighley BD20 .. 18
Knottingley WF11 .. 126
Banks Mount WF8 .. 146
Banks Rd Honley HD7 .. 172
Huddersfield HD7 .. 152
Slaithwaite HD7 .. 170

Banks Side HD7 152 D5
Banks St WF17 118 C4
Banksfield Ave LS19 40 B8
Banksfield Cl LS19 40 B8
Banksfield Cres LS19 40 B8
Banksfield Gr LS19 40 B8
Banksfield Mount LS19 40 B8
Banksfield Rd 8 HX7 89 E1
Banksfield Rise LS19 40 B8
Banksfield Terr HX7 89 E1
Banksfields Ave HX7 89 E1
Banksfields Cres HX7 89 E1
Bankside OL14 108 B4
Bankside Primary Sch LS8 207 F3
Bankside Terr BD17 38 B2
Banksville HD7 189 B7
Bankwell Fold BD6 74 D1
Bankwell Rd HD3 153 B4
Bankwood WF17 97 B4
Bankwood Way WF17 97 B3
Banner St BD3 75 A6
Bannerman St BD12 95 A5
Bannister La DN6 184 C5
Bannockburn Croft BD5 75 B1
Bannockburn Way WF6 122 E4
Banstead St E LS8 207 F3
Banstead St W LS8 207 F3
Banstead Terr E LS8 207 F3
Banstead Terr W 6 LS8 207 F3
Bantam Cl LS27 98 D4
Bantam Grove La LS27 98 D4
Bantree Ct BD10 39 A2
Baptist Fold BD13 72 F1
Baptist La WF5 141 B4
Baptist Pl BD1 201 A3
Baptist St WF17 118 A3
Bar Croft HD5 137 B1
Bar House La BD20 17 F3
Bar La Bramham LS23 31 A6
Garforth LS25 83 A7
Horsforth LS18 57 F8
Keighley BD20 18 F1
Lofthouse Gate WF1 121 D1
Netherton WF4 158 B2
Ripponden HX6 132 C2
West Bretton WF4 158 B2
Bar Mount LS25 83 A7
Bar St Batley WF17 118 D4
Todmorden OL14 108 A4
Barber Row HD7 152 D1
Barber Sq WF16 117 C4
Barber St 1 HD6 115 B3
Barber Wlk 7 WF13 139 C8
Barberry Ave BD3 75 E8
Barclay Cl BD13 52 E6
Barclay St LS7 207 D1
Barcroft BD22 51 F8
Barcroft Gr LS19 40 A6
Barcroft Rd HD4 154 A2
Barden Ave BD6 93 D8
Barden Cl Batley WF17 118 B5
Leeds LS12 209 D3
Barden Dr BD16 37 C4
Barden Gn LS12 209 D3
Barden Gr LS12 209 D3
Barden Mount LS12 209 D3
Barden Pl LS12 209 D3
Barden Rd WF1 142 F7
Barden St BD8 55 B1
Barden Terr LS12 209 D3
Bardsey County Primary Sch LS17 28 C3
Bardsey Cres BD3 75 A7
Bardwell Ct WF3 121 E5
Bare Bones Rd HD7 199 B5
Bare Head La HX3 92 D5
Barewell Hill S72 181 A4
Barfield Ave LS19 40 A6
Barfield Cres LS17 43 F5
Barfield Dr LS19 40 A6
Barfield Gr LS17 44 A5
Barfield Mount LS17 44 A5
Barfield Rd HX3 114 C7
Bargate HD7 152 D1
Barge St HD1 153 F4
Bargess Terr LS25 83 B1
Bargrange Ave BD18 55 B6
Bargreen HD5 137 B1
Barham Terr BD10 56 D4
Baring Ave BD3 75 D8
Baring Sq BD20 16 D4
Bark Cl HD8 174 A3
Bark House La
Cawthorne S75 193 C4
Shepley HD8 174 C3
Bark La LS29 7 A8
Barker Cl HX3 113 E3
Barker Ct HD2 135 E1
Barker House 4 HX3 113 E3
Barker Pl LS13 58 D1
Barker Rd WF4 140 F2
Barker St Liversedge WF15 117 B4
Lofthouse Gate WF3 122 B6
Todmorden OL14 108 B6
Barker's Rd WF4 159 E6
Barkerend First Sch BD3 75 A8
Barkerend Rd BD1, BD3 75 B8
Barkers Well Fold LS12 77 D4
Barkers Well Garth LS12 77 E3
Barkers Well Gate LS12 77 E3
Barkers Well Lawn LS12 77 E3
Barkisland CE Sch HX4 133 A5
Barkly Ave LS11 214 A1
Barkly Dr LS11 214 A1
Barkly Gr LS11 214 A2
Barkly Par 2 LS11 214 A1
Barkly Pl 1 LS11 214 A1
Barkly Rd LS11 214 A1
Barkly St LS11 214 A1
Barkly Terr LS11 214 A2
Barkston Wlk 2 BD15 73 A7
Barlbro' Pl HD4 153 A4
Barlby Way LS8 61 C6
Barley Cote Ave BD20 19 A2
Barley Cote Gr BD20 19 A2
Barley Cote Rd BD20 19 A2
Barley Croft WF13 138 F8
Barley Field Ct 3 LS15 81 A8
Barley Mews WF3 100 B3
Barley St BD22 35 A4
Barleycorn Cl WF3 121 E1
Barleyfield Cl WF1 142 E8
Barleyfields Cl LS22 13 E7
Barleyfields Ct LS22 13 E6
Barleyfields La LS22 13 E6
Barleyfields Rd LS22 13 E7
Barleyfields Terr LS22 13 E6
Barleyfields Wlk LS22 13 E6
Barleyhill Cres LS25 82 E6
Barleyhill La LS25 82 E7
Barleyhill Rd LS25 82 E7
Barlow Rd BD21 35 B8
Barlow St BD3 75 B7
Barmby Cl WF5 140 F4
Barmby Cres WF5 141 A4
Barmby Fold WF5 140 F4
Barmby Pl BD2 56 B1
Barmby Rd BD2 56 B1
Barmby St BD12 94 D4
Barmouth Terr BD3 55 F2
Barn Cl LS29 21 F4
Barn St BD22 51 C2
Barnaby Rd BD16 37 C4
Barnard Cl LS15 62 E3
Barnard Rd BD4 201 D1
Barnard Way LS15 62 E3
Barnbow La
Barwick in E LS15 63 B5
Leeds LS15 63 B3
Barnbrough St LS4 59 C2
Barnby Royd HD5 154 E7
Barncliffe Hill HD8 174 C1
Barncroft Cl LS14 61 F7
Barncroft Ct LS14 61 E6
Barncroft Dr LS14 61 F7
Barncroft Gdns LS14 61 F6
Barncroft Grange LS14 61 E6
Barncroft Hts LS14 61 E7
Barncroft Mount LS14 61 E6
Barncroft Rd LS14 61 F7
Barncroft Rise LS14 61 F6
Barncroft Towers LS14 61 E6
Barnes Ave WF1 121 A3
Barnes Meadows OL15 129 C1
Barnes Rd Bradford BD8 73 F7
Castleford WF10 124 D6
Barnes St 6 OL14 108 A1
Barnet Gr 2 LS27 98 A2
Barnet Rd LS12 210 A3
Barnett House 5 BD6 93 E8
Barnsdale Bar DN6 184 C8
Barnsdale Est WF10 124 B6
Barnsdale Rd Kippax WF10 103 D4
Mickletown LS26 102 E1
Barnsdale Way WF9 183 E7
Barnside La HD7 189 F1
Barnsley Beck Gr BD17 38 D3
Barnsley Rd
Ackworth M T WF7 164 A6
Brierley S72 181 A4
Clayton West HD8 175 E1
Crigglestone WF2, WF4 160 B4
Denby Dale HD8 191 C5
Flockton WF4 157 C3
Hemsworth WF9 181 C6
Notton WF4 178 E5
South Elmsall WF9 182 E3
South Kirkby WF9 182 E3
Wakefield WF1, WF2 160 D7
Woolley WF4 178 C6
Barnstone Vale WF1 121 E1
Barnswick Cl WF8 146 D6
Barnswick View LS16 41 E4
Baron Cl LS11 214 A4
Baronscourt LS15 81 D8
Baronsmead LS15 81 D8
Baronsway LS15 81 C8
Barr St HD1 154 C8
Barrack Rd LS7 207 D3
Barrack St LS7 207 D2
Barracks Fold HD7 189 E2
Barracks St WF16 117 C4
Barraclough Bldgs BD10 56 E7
Barraclough Sq 18 BD12 94 C4
Barraclough St 5 BD12 94 B6
Barran Ct LS8 207 F3
Barran St 8 BD16 37 A3
Barras Garth Pl LS12 209 E2
Barras Garth Rd LS12 209 E2
Barras Pl LS12 209 E2
Barras St LS12 209 E2
Barras Terr LS12 209 E2
Barratt's Rd WF1 216 B4
Barrett St BD20 5 D1
Barrington Cl HX3 114 A4
Barrington Par BD19 117 A8
Barrowby Ave LS15 81 E7
Barrowby Cl LS29 22 B4
Barrowby Cres LS15 81 E8
Barrowby Dr LS15 81 F7
Barrowby La Garforth LS25 82 E8
Leeds LS15 81 F8
Barrowby Rd LS15 81 F7
Barrowclough La HX3 113 F7
Barrows La BD20 17 C4
Barrowstead HD8 175 B1
Barry St BD1 201 B3
Barsey Green La HX4 133 C6
Barstow Sq WF1 216 B2
Barthorpe Ave LS17 60 B8
Barthorpe Cl BD4 75 F2
Barthorpe Cres LS17 60 C8
Bartle Cl BD7 73 F3
Bartle Fold BD7 74 A4
Bartle Gill Dr BD17 38 E4
Bartle Gill Rise BD17 38 E4
Bartle Gill View BD17 38 E4
Bartle Gr BD7 73 F3
Bartle La BD7 73 F3
Bartle Pl BD7 73 F3
Bartle Sq BD7 74 A4
Barton Ct LS15 81 D7
Barton Gr LS11 214 A4
Barton Hill LS11 214 A4
Barton Manor Cl HD4 153 B2
Barton Mount LS11 214 A4
Barton Pl LS11 214 A4
Barton Rd LS11 214 A4
Barton St Bradford BD5 74 B3
17 Brighouse HD6 115 A3
Barton Terr LS11 214 A4
Barton View LS11 214 A4
Barton Way WF9 183 A5
Barum Top 9 HX1 203 E3
Barwick Gn BD6 73 E1
Barwick in Elmet C of E Primary Sch LS15 63 E7
Barwick Rd
Barwick in E LS15, LS25 63 E2
Leeds LS14, LS15 62 D4
Basford St WF2 142 A5
Basil St Bradford BD5 74 B3
Huddersfield HD4 153 D4
Basildon Rd S63 194 C1
Baslow Gr BD9 54 F2
Bassenthwaite Wlk WF11 126 E2
Batcliffe Dr LS6 59 C6
Batcliffe Mount LS6 59 C5
Bateman Cl S72 180 B2
Bateman St BD8 55 D1
Bates Ave HX6 111 F3
Bates La WF8 146 F5
Bateson St BD10 56 E7
Bath Cl LS13 58 C2
Bath Ct WF16 117 D4
Bath Gr 14 LS13 58 C2
Bath La LS13 58 C2
Bath Pl Cleckheaton BD19 116 D7
Halifax HX3 92 B1
Bath Rd Batley WF16 117 D4
Cleckheaton BD19 116 D7
Halifax HX3 113 C4
Leeds LS13 58 C2
Leeds, Holbeck LS11 211 D2
Bath St 1 Bacup OL13 106 A2
Batley WF17 118 D5
Bradford BD3 201 D3
Dewsbury WF13 118 C1
Elland HX5 134 F6
3 Halifax HX1 203 F2
Huddersfield HD1 154 A7
Huddersfield, Rashcliffe HD1 153 F3
Ilkley LS29 8 C5
Keighley BD21 35 B7
Kirkburton HD8 173 F5
3 Todmorden OL14 108 B5
Batley Ave HD1 153 D6
Batley Boys High Sch WF17 118 C6
Batley Bsns Ctr WF17 118 B6
Batley Ct BD17 38 D4
Batley Enterprise Ctr WF17 118 B6
Batley Field Hill WF17 118 C6
Batley Grammar Sch WF17 118 B7
Batley Parish CE Jun & Inf Sch WF17 118 C6
Batley Rd Batley WF16 117 F4
East Ardsley WF3 119 E5
Wakefield WF2 120 B2
Batley St 28 Halifax HX3 92 A1
7 Huddersfield HD5 154 D6
Batley Sta WF17 118 D4
Batter La LS19 40 C4
Battinson Rd HX1 202 B4
Battinson St HX3 113 E5
Battye Ave HD4 153 B3
Battye St BD4 75 D6
Battyeford CE (C) Junior & Infants Sch WF14 137 E6
Baulk Head La OL14 108 F6
Bavaria Pl BD8 55 B1
Bawn App LS12 77 F5
Bawn Ave LS12 77 E6
Bawn Dr LS12 77 E6
Bawn Gdns LS12 77 E6
Bawn La LS12 77 E6
Bawn Path LS12 77 F6
Bawn Vale LS12 77 E6
Bawn Wlk LS12 77 F6
Bawson Ct BD19 96 A1
Baxandall St BD5 74 E3
Baxter La HX3 93 A3
Baxter Wood BD20 16 C7
Baxtergate 10 WF8 146 D8
Bay Cl HD3 153 C7
Bay Hall Common Rd HD1 154 A8
Bay Horse La Scarcroft LS14 45 A6
Thorner LS17 45 A6
Bay of Biscay BD9 54 B4
Bayford Cl HD7 199 B8
Bayldons Pl 9 WF17 118 C5
Baylee St WF9 181 E6
Bayne Dr BD4 95 B8
Bayswater Cres LS8 207 F3
Bayswater Gr Bradford BD2 56 D2
Leeds LS8 207 F3
Bayswater Mount LS8 207 F3
Bayswater Pl LS8 207 F3
Bayswater Rd LS8 207 F2
Bayswater Row LS8 207 F3
Bayswater Terr Halifax HX3 113 C3
Leeds LS8 207 F3
Bayswater View LS8 207 F3
Bayton La LS19 40 E5
Beacon Ave LS27 98 C2
Beacon Brow BD6 73 D2
Beacon Cl BD16 37 B3
Beacon Dr WF9 183 A8
Beacon Gr Bradford BD6 73 F1
Morley LS27 98 C2
Beacon Hill WF9 183 A8
Beacon Hill Rd HX3 113 E7
Beacon Pl BD6 73 E1
Beacon Rd BD6 73 E2
Beacon Rise LS29 7 E4
Beacon St Addingham LS29 7 A8
Bradford BD6 74 A1
1 Bradford, Horton Bank BD7 73 E2
Dewsbury WF13 138 E6
Huddersfield HD2 136 A1
Beacon View WF9 182 C3
Beaconfield Rd WF9 164 F1
Beaconsfield Ct LS25 82 F8
Beaconsfield Rd BD14 73 D4
Beaconsfield St
Halifax HX3 113 E6
Todmorden OL14 108 C5
Beaden Dr HD8 155 E3
Beadon Ave HD5 155 B5
Beagle Ave HD4 153 C1
Beal La DN14 127 F2
Beamshaw WF9 182 B1
Beamsley Gr Bingley BD16 37 B3
10 Leeds LS6 205 E2
Beamsley House BD18 55 B5
Beamsley La BD23 2 F6
Beamsley Mount 3 LS6 205 E2
Beamsley Pl 11 LS6 205 E2
Beamsley Rd Bradford BD9 55 B2
Shipley BD18 55 B5
Beamsley Terr 1 LS6 205 E2
Beamsley View LS29 7 E4
Beamsley Wlk BD9 55 A2
Bean St HX5 135 C6
Beancroft Rd WF10 124 D7
Beancroft St WF10 124 C6
Beanlands Dr BD20 16 C6
Beanlands Par LS29 8 C5
Beanlands Pl BD20 16 C7
Bearing Ave LS11 214 C2
Beast Fair WF8 146 C8
Beast Market 4 HD1 154 B6
Beatrice St
1 Cleckheaton BD19 116 D8
Keighley BD20 18 C1
5 Oxenhope BD22 51 C2
Beaufort Ave HD8 173 F3
Beaufort Gr BD2 56 A3
Beaufort Rd OL13 106 A7
Beaumont Ave
Huddersfield HD5 154 D5
Leeds LS8 44 A2
South Elmsall WF9 182 F3
Beaumont Cl WF3 121 F5
Beaumont Dr WF4 176 F6
Beaumont Park Rd HD4 153 D2
Beaumont Pl WF17 117 F3
Beaumont Rd BD8 55 B1
Beaumont Sq 5 LS28 76 D6
Beaumont St Batley WF17 118 C3
Emley HD8 175 C7
Huddersfield HD1 154 B7
Huddersfield, Longwood HD3 152 F5
14 Huddersfield, Moldgreen HD5 154 D5
Huddersfield, Netherton HD4 171 D7
Lofthouse Gate WF3 121 F5
Todmorden OL14 108 A6
Beauvais Dr BD20 36 B8
Beaver Dr WF13 138 F7
Beaver Terr 10 OL13 106 A3
Becca La LS25 64 E7
Beck Bottom Pudsey LS28 56 E6
Wakefield WF2 120 C3
Beck Hill BD6 93 E7
Beck La Bingley BD16 37 A4
Collingham LS22 13 B1
Liversedge WF16 117 C3
Beck Meadow LS15 63 E6
Beck Rd Bingley BD16 36 E8
Huddersfield HD1 154 A8
Leeds LS8 207 F4
Beck Rise WF9 181 D7
Beck Side 3 BD21 35 C6
Beck St BD21 35 C6
Beck View WF4 179 A6
Beckbridge Ct WF6 123 C3
Beckbridge Gn WF6 123 C3
Beckbridge La WF6 123 C2
Beckbridge Rd WF6 123 C3
Beckbridge Way WF6 123 C2
Beckbury Cl 1 LS28 57 D2
Beckbury St 2 LS28 57 D2
Beckenham Pl HX1 202 A4
Becket La WF3 100 C2
Beckett Cl WF4 141 C2
Beckett Cres WF13 138 F8
Beckett Ct LS15 81 D6
Beckett Gr WF13 138 F7
Beckett La WF13 138 F7
Beckett Park Primary Sch LS6 59 B5
Beckett Rd WF13 118 B2
Beckett Sq HD8 173 F6
Beckett St Batley WF17 118 D3
Leeds LS9 207 F1
Beckett Terr LS9 207 F1
Beckett Wlk WF13 138 F7
Beckett's Park Cres LS6 59 C5
Beckett's Park Dr LS6 59 C6
Beckett's Park Rd LS6 59 D5
Becketts Cl HX7 88 F4
Beckfield Cl BD20 16 E6
Beckfield Rd BD16 54 A7
Beckfoot Grammar Sch BD16 37 A1
Beckfoot La BD16 36 F1
Beckfoot Mill BD16 36 E1
Beckhill App LS7 60 A6
Beckhill Ave LS7 60 A6
Beckhill Chase LS7 60 A6
Beckhill Cl LS7 60 A6
Beckhill Dr LS7 60 A7
Beckhill Fold LS7 60 A6
Beckhill Garth LS7 60 A6
Beckhill Gate LS7 60 A6
Beckhill Gdns LS7 60 A6
Beckhill Gn LS7 60 B6
Beckhill Gr LS7 60 A6
Beckhill Lawn LS7 60 A6
Beckhill Pl LS7 60 A7
Beckhill Row LS7 60 A7
Beckhill View LS7 60 A6
Beckhill Wlk LS7 60 A7
Beckley Rd WF2 142 A6
Becks Ct WF12 139 F6
Becks Rd BD21 35 A6
Beckside Cl Addingham LS29 6 F8
Burley in W LS29 9 E1
Beckside Gdns HD5 155 C4
Beckside La BD7 74 A4
Beckside Rd BD7 74 A5
Beckside View LS27 98 C4
Beckwith Dr BD10 56 D5
Bedale WF3 119 D8
Bedale Ave Brighouse HD6 135 E8
Skelmanthorpe HD8 174 F1
Bedale Dr Bradford BD6 73 F1
Skelmanthorpe HD8 174 F1
Bedale Wlk S72 180 C3
Bedding Edge Rd HD7 200 A7
Bede Ct WF1 216 B4
Bede House WF1 216 B4
Bede's Cl BD13 72 D6
Bedford Ave WF4 156 E5
Bedford Cl Crofton WF4 162 A8
Featherstone WF7 145 D4
Leeds LS16 41 E3
Lepton HD8 155 E3
Bedford Ct
Featherstone WF7 145 D4
Leeds LS8 61 C6
Bedford Dr LS16 41 E3
Bedford Garth LS16 41 E3
Bedford Gdns LS16 41 E3
Bedford Gn LS16 41 E3
Bedford Gr LS16 41 E2
Bedford Mount LS16 41 E2
Bedford Row LS10 215 D4
Bedford St Bradford BD4 201 C2
Cleckheaton BD19 116 C7
7 Elland HX5 134 F6
Halifax HX1 203 D3
Keighley BD21 35 B7
Leeds LS1 211 E4
Bedford St N HX1 203 D3
Bedford View LS16 41 E3
Bedivere Rd BD8 73 D7
Bedlam La LS21 25 F4
Beech Ave Crofton WF4 162 B7
Denholme BD13 52 C3
Holmfirth HD7 172 C1
Horsforth LS18 58 C7
Huddersfield HD5 154 F5
Huddersfield, Leymoor HD7 152 E5
Leeds LS12 209 F4
Lofthouse Gate WF3 121 F4
Sowerby Bridge HX6 112 B5
Todmorden OL14 108 B6
Wakefield WF2 141 F7
Beech Cl Bacup OL13 106 A3
Bradford BD10 39 B2
Brierley S72 181 A3
Leeds LS9 61 D3
Menston LS29 22 A6
Shelf HX3 93 D6
South Kirkby WF9 182 B2
Beech Cres Baildon BD17 37 F1
Bradford BD3 56 B1
Castleford WF10 125 D5
Darrington WF8 147 C5
Leeds LS9 61 D3
Beech Croft Pontefract WF8 125 E3
Walton WF2 161 A7
Beech Ct Baildon BD17 38 B1
Castleford WF10 124 E6
Ossett WF5 140 C6
Beech Dr
Ackworth M T WF7 146 A1
Denholme BD13 52 C3
Leeds LS12 209 F4
Beech Gdns WF10 125 D6

Beech Gr Bingley BD16 .... 37 C5
Bradford BD3 .... 56 B1
2 Bradford, Clayton BD14 ... 73 C4
Brighouse HX3 .... 115 A7
Burton Salmon LS25 .... 105 E3
Cleckheaton BD19 .... 96 A1
Featherstone WF7 .... 145 E4
Hemsworth WF9 .... 163 A2
Liversedge WF16 .... 117 C5
Morley LS27 .... 97 F3
Normanton WF6 .... 144 A8
Rothwell LS26 .... 100 F6
Silsden BD20 .... 5 D1
Beech Grove Ave LS25 .... 82 E6
Beech Grove Terr
Garforth LS25 .... 82 E6
Leeds LS2 .... 206 B2
Beech Hill Otley LS21 .... 23 A8
Pontefract WF8 .... 125 E1
Beech Hill Primary Sch
HX1 .... 203 D4
Beech Junior & Infants
Sch HD7 .... 152 E5
Beech La LS9 .... 208 C3
Beech Lees LS28 .... 57 C4
Beech Mount LS9 .... 61 D3
Beech Rd Boston Spa LS23 .... 30 C8
Bradford BD6 .... 94 C7
Shafton S72 .... 180 D2
Sowerby Bridge HX6 .... 112 C4
Upton WF9 .... 183 B7
Beech Spinney LS22 .... 13 E8
Beech Sq 3 BD14 .... 73 C4
Beech St Bacup OL13 .... 106 A3
Bingley BD16 .... 36 F2
East Ardsley WF3 .... 98 E1
Elland HX5 .... 134 F6
Elland, Holywell Green HX4 . 134 A4
Glusburn BD20 .... 16 D6
Halifax HX1 .... 203 D4
Holmfirth HD7 .... 189 A5
Huddersfield HD1 .... 153 D5
Keighley BD21 .... 35 E8
Mirfield WF14 .... 138 A5
Pontefract WF8 .... 146 E7
South Elmsall WF9 .... 182 E1
Steeton BD20 .... 17 C5
Beech Terr BD3 .... 75 B8
Beech Tree Rd WF7 .... 145 E4
Crigglestone WF4 .... 159 F3
5 Sowerby Bridge HX6 ...... 112 B5
Beech Way WF17 .... 97 A2
Beech Wlk Birkenshaw BD11 . 96 B4
5 Dewsbury WF13 .... 139 C8
Leeds LS16 .... 42 C2
Leeds, Gipton LS9 .... 61 D3
Beechcroft WF1 .... 100 D1
Beechcroft Cl LS11 .... 213 D1
Beechcroft Mead LS17 .... 44 A4
Beechcroft View LS11 .... 213 D1
Beechdale Ave WF17 .... 118 A7
Beecher St Halifax HX3 .... 92 B2
Keighley BD21 .... 18 E1
Beeches End LS23 .... 30 E7
Beeches Rd BD21 .... 35 E8
Beeches The Baildon BD17 .. 38 D4
Guiseley LS20 .... 22 E2
Pudsey LS28 .... 76 B8
Beechfield Gildersome LS12 . 77 D3
Wakefield WF2 .... 160 E8
Beechfield Ave HD8 .... 175 A1
Beechfield Dr WF4 .... 144 B4
Beechfield Rd HD2 .... 135 E1
Beechfield Terr 15 BD19 ... 116 E7
Beechmount Cl BD17 .... 38 D4
Beechnut La WF8 .... 125 C1
Beechroyd LS28 .... 76 E6
Beechroyd Terr BD16 .... 36 F2
Beechtree Ct BD17 .... 38 A2
Beechwood 1
Pontefract WF8 .... 146 B7
Rothwell LS26 .... 101 D7
Beechwood Ave
Birkenshaw BD11 .... 96 D7
Bradford BD6 .... 74 B2
Halifax HX2, HX3 .... 92 A5
Keighley BD20 .... 18 E1
Leeds LS4 .... 205 D3
Mirfield WF14 .... 138 A5
Pontefract WF8 .... 146 B7
Shelf HX3 .... 93 B5
Shipley BD18 .... 54 E7
Sowerby Bridge HX6 .... 111 F3
Wakefield WF2 .... 160 E8
Beechwood Cl Halifax HX2 ... 91 F4
Horsforth LS18 .... 41 A3
Beechwood Cres
Hemsworth WF9 .... 181 C6
Leeds LS4 .... 205 D3
Pontefract WF8 .... 146 B7
Sowerby Bridge HX6 .... 111 F3
Beechwood Ct Leeds LS16 ... 42 B5
Leeds, Beechwood LS14 ...... 61 F6
Beechwood Ctr LS20 .... 207 D7
Beechwood Dale WF7 .... 164 B7
Beechwood Dr Bradford BD6 74 B2
Halifax HX2 .... 91 F5
Sowerby Bridge HX6 .... 111 F3
Beechwood Gr
Birkenshaw BD11 .... 96 D7
Bradford BD6 .... 74 B2
Halifax HX2 .... 91 F4
Horbury WF4 .... 141 C1
Huddersfield HD2 .... 136 A4

Beechwood Gr continued
Ilkley LS29 .... 7 F4
Leeds LS4 .... 205 D3
Shipley BD18 .... 54 E7
Beechwood Mount
Hemsworth WF9 .... 181 D6
Leeds LS4 .... 205 D3
Beechwood Pl LS4 .... 205 D3
Beechwood Primary Sch
LS14 .... 62 A4
Beechwood Rd
Bradford BD6 .... 74 A2
Halifax HX2 .... 91 F4
8 Leeds LS4 .... 205 D3
Mirfield WF14 .... 138 A6
Beechwood Rise LS22 .... 13 E7
Beechwood Row 8 LS4 .... 205 D3
Beechwood St Leeds LS4 ... 205 D3
Pudsey LS28 .... 76 B8
Beechwood Terr LS4 .... 205 D3
Beechwood View LS4 .... 205 D3
Beechwood Wlk LS4 .... 205 D3
Beecroft Cl LS13 .... 58 B3
Beecroft Cres LS13 .... 58 B3
Beecroft Gdns LS13 .... 58 A3
Beecroft Mount 3 LS13 .... 58 D4
Beecroft St Keighley BD21 .. 35 D7
Leeds LS5 .... 59 A3
Beecroft Wlk 1 BD15 .... 73 A7
Beehive St 6 BD6 .... 93 F7
Beehive Yd 1 BD6 .... 93 F7
Beeston Park Croft LS11 .. 213 E2
Beeston Park Garth LS11 . 213 E2
Beeston Park Gr LS11 ..... 213 E2
Beeston Park Pl LS11 ..... 213 E2
Beeston Park Terr LS11 .. 213 E2
Beeston Primary Sch
LS11 .... 213 E2
Beeston Rd LS11 .... 214 A3
Beestonley HX4 .... 133 E4
Beestonley La HX4 .... 133 E4
Bela Ave BD4 .... 75 C3
Belcross Dr HX3 .... 203 F4
Beldon Brook Gn HD8 ..... 155 D1
Beldon La BD7 .... 73 F2
Beldon Park Ave BD7 .... 73 F2
Beldon Park Cl BD7 .... 73 F2
Beldon Pl BD2 .... 56 B2
Beldon Rd BD7 .... 74 A3
Belfast St HX1 .... 202 B1
Belford Cl BD4 .... 75 D3
Belfry Ct WF1 .... 121 C5
Belfry The LS19 .... 40 C6
Belfry Way WF6 .... 123 D1
Belgrave Ave Halifax HX3 .. 203 F4
Ossett WF5 .... 140 E4
Belgrave Cl HX3 .... 203 F4
Belgrave Cres HX3 .... 113 E8
Belgrave Dr HX3 .... 113 E8
Belgrave Gdns LS19 .... 203 F4
Belgrave Gr HX3 .... 203 F4
Belgrave Mews LS19 .... 40 A4
Belgrave Mount
Halifax HX3 .... 92 D1
Wakefield WF1 .... 216 C4
Belgrave Pk HX3 .... 203 F4
Belgrave Rd Bingley BD16 ... 37 A3
Keighley BD21 .... 35 B8
Belgrave St Leeds LS2 ...... 211 F4
Ossett WF5 .... 140 E4
6 Sowerby Bridge HX6 .... 112 B5
Belgrave Terr
Huddersfield HD1 .... 153 F7
Wakefield WF1 .... 216 C4
Belgransa Rd WF1 .... 216 A4
Belinda St LS10 .... 215 E3
Bell Bank View BD16 .... 36 E4
Bell Dean Rd BD15, BD8 .... 73 B7
Bell Hall Mount 8 HX1 .... 202 C1
Bell Hall Terr HX1 .... 202 C1
Bell House Ave BD4 .... 95 B8
Bell La Ackworth M T WF7 . 163 F5
Leeds LS13 .... 58 D3
Bell Lane Jun & Inf Sch
WF7 .... 163 F5
Bell Rd LS13 .... 58 C3
Bell Sq BD20 .... 5 E2
Bell St 17 Bradford BD12 .... 94 C4
Dewsbury WF13 .... 138 E5
Halifax HX3 .... 203 F4
Huddersfield HD4 .... 154 B4
1 Leeds LS9 .... 212 A4
Upton WF9 .... 183 E8
Wakefield WF1 .... 216 A3
Bellbrooke Ave LS9 .... 208 B2
Bellbrooke Gr LS9 .... 208 B2
Bellbrooke Pl LS9 .... 208 B2
Bellbrooke St LS9 .... 208 B2
Belle Isle Ave WF1 .... 142 D4
Belle Isle Cir LS10 .... 99 E8
Belle Isle Cl LS10 .... 99 E8
Belle Isle Cres WF1 .... 142 D4
Belle Isle Dr WF1 .... 142 D4
Belle Isle Par LS10 .... 215 E1
Belle Isle Rd Haworth BD22 . 51 C7
Middleton LS10 .... 99 E7
Belle View Rise HX3 .... 93 B5
Belle Vue Bradford BD8 .... 55 D1
Ilkley LS29 .... 8 C3
Queensbury BD13 .... 92 E7
Belle Vue Ave
Barwick in E LS15 .... 62 F6
Leeds LS8 .... 61 D6
Belle Vue Boys Sch BD9 .... 54 C4
Belle Vue Cres
Huddersfield HD2 .... 136 C3
Shelf HX3 .... 93 B5

Belle Vue Ct LS3 .... 205 F1
Belle Vue Dr LS28 .... 57 C3
Belle Vue Est LS15 .... 62 F6
Belle Vue First Sch BD8 .... 55 D1
Belle Vue Girls Sch BD9 .... 54 C5
Belle Vue Rd
Barwick in E LS15 .... 62 F6
Leeds LS3 .... 205 F1
Shelf HX3 .... 93 B5
Wakefield WF1 .... 142 E2
Belle Vue St WF17 .... 117 F5
Belle Vue Terr
Guiseley LS20 .... 39 E8
Halifax HX3 .... 113 E5
Bellerby Brow BD6 .... 73 E1
Bellerby Pl DN6 .... 184 F2
Bellerby Rd DN6 .... 184 F2
Bellevue Terr WF2 .... 111 C7
Bellgreave Ave HD7 .... 189 F6
Bellhouse Cres BD4 .... 95 B8
Bellmoor View WF9 .... 181 E6
Bellmont Cl LS13 .... 58 D3
Bellmont Gdns LS13 .... 58 C4
Bellmont Gr 4 LS13 .... 58 D4
Bellmount Pl LS13 .... 58 D4
Belloe St BD5 .... 74 D4
Bellshaw St BD8 .... 73 E7
Bellstring La WF14 .... 137 E1
Bellwood Ave LS23 .... 30 D6
Belmont WF11 .... 105 C1
Belmont Ave Baildon BD17 . 38 B3
Bradford BD12 .... 94 E7
Otley LS21 .... 10 F1
Belmont Cl Baildon BD17 ... 38 B3
1 Huddersfield HD1 .... 154 A7
Belmont Cres
Bradford BD12 .... 94 E7
Shipley BD18 .... 55 A8
Belmont Gdns BD12 .... 94 D7
Belmont Gr Bradford BD6 ... 94 D7
Leeds LS2 .... 206 A1
Yeadon LS19 .... 40 C5
Belmont Grange WF15 .... 117 A2
Belmont Middle Sch BD17 . 38 B3
Belmont Mews HX1 .... 202 C2
Belmont Rd LS29 .... 8 E4
Belmont Rise Baildon BD17 . 38 B3
Bradford BD12 .... 94 E7
Belmont St Bradford BD6 .. 56 C5
Featherstone WF7 .... 144 C5
Halifax HX3 .... 113 E8
Huddersfield HD1 .... 154 A7
Slaithwaite HD7 .... 169 F8
Sowerby Bridge HX6 .... 112 C4
Wakefield WF1 .... 142 E3
Belmont Terr Halifax HX2 . 111 E5
Middleton WF3 .... 99 F2
Shipley BD18 .... 55 A8
Belmont Way WF9 .... 183 B3
Belton Cl BD7 .... 74 A3
Belton Gr HD3 .... 135 B2
Belton Rd BD20 .... 17 D8
Belton St HD5 .... 154 E5
Belvedere Ave Leeds LS17 .. 43 D4
Leeds LS15 .... 214 B2
Belvedere Cl S72 .... 180 C2
Belvedere Ct Leeds LS17 ... 43 E4
Leeds, Potternewton LS7 .. 204 B1
Belvedere Gr LS17 .... 43 D4
Belvedere Mount LS11 .... 214 B2
Belvedere Rd Batley WF17 . 118 B4
Leeds LS17 .... 43 D4
Belvedere Terr
Bradford BD8 .... 73 F8
Leeds LS11 .... 214 B2
Belvedere View LS17 .... 43 E4
Belvoir Dr WF11 .... 126 E4
Belvoir Gdns HX3 .... 113 C3
Bembridge Ct WF2 .... 141 E5
Bempton Ct 5 BD7 .... 74 B4
Bempton Gr WF17 .... 96 F2
Bempton Pl 4 BD7 .... 74 B4
Ben Booth La WF4 .... 156 F4
Ben Rhydding Dr LS29 .... 8 E3
Ben Rhydding Rd LS29 .... 8 D3
Ben Rhydding Sta LS29 ...... 8 E4
Benbow Ave BD10 .... 56 E5
Bendigo Rd WF12 .... 118 F1
Benjamin St
Liversedge WF15 .... 117 B3
Wakefield WF2 .... 142 A7
Benjamin Sykes Way WF2 141 C4
Benn Ave BD7 .... 73 F4
Benn Cres BD7 .... 73 F4
Benn La HD3 .... 152 F6
Bennet Ct LS15 .... 81 D8
Bennett Ave WF4 .... 141 C2
Bennett Ct LS21 .... 10 F1
Bennett La WF12 .... 118 F2
Bennett Rd LS6 .... 59 D5
Bennett St Halifax HX3 .... 203 F2
5 Liversedge WF15 .... 117 B4
Benns La HX7 .... 90 F2
Benny Parr Cl WF17 .... 118 E5
Benomley Cres HD5 .... 154 E4
Benomley Dr HD5 .... 154 E4
Benomley Rd HD5 .... 154 E4
Benroyd Terr HX4 .... 134 C3
Benson Gdns Leeds LS12 . 209 E2
Normanton WF6 .... 123 C3
Benson St LS7 .... 207 D2
Bent Close La HX7 .... 110 E3
Bent Cotts BD20 .... 16 B5
Bent La Holmfirth HD7 .... 199 B8
Sutton in C BD20 .... 16 C5

Bent Lea HD2 .... 136 F6
Bent Ley Rd HD7 .... 171 A3
Bent Rd HD7 .... 199 D7
Bent St HD4 .... 154 B4
Bentcliff Wlk 1 BD15 .... 73 B7
Bentcliffe Ave LS17 .... 43 E2
Bentcliffe Cl LS17 .... 43 E1
Bentcliffe Ct LS17 .... 43 E1
Bentcliffe Dr LS17 .... 43 E2
Bentcliffe Gdns LS17 .... 43 E1
Bentcliffe Gr LS17 .... 43 E1
Bentcliffe La LS17 .... 43 D2
Bentcliffe Mount LS17 ...... 43 E1
Bentfield Cotts BD14 .... 73 C5
Bentham Rd WF5 .... 178 A2
Bentley Ave HX3 .... 115 A7
Bentley Cl BD17 .... 38 B4
Bentley La LS6 .... 59 F6
Bentley Gdns LS6 .... 59 F6
Bentley La LS6, LS7 .... 59 F6
Bentley Mount Leeds LS6 .. 59 F6
Sowerby Bridge HX6 .... 112 D5
Bentley Par LS6 .... 59 F6
Bentley Primary Sch LS6 .. 59 F6
Bentley Rd WF2 .... 142 A6
Bentley St Leeds LS6 .... 59 F6
Bentley St 1 Bradford BD12 . 94 D3
Bentley St 1 BD15 .... 101 C5
Benton Cres WF4 .... 141 C2
Benton Park Ave 3 LS19 ... 40 C5
Benton Park Cres LS19 ...... 40 C5
Benton Park Dr LS19 .... 40 C5
Benton Park Rd LS19 .... 40 C5
Benton Park Sch LS19 .... 40 B5
Bents La Marsden HD7 .... 169 B6
Wilsden BD15 .... 53 A6
Bents Rd S36 .... 200 D4
Benyon Park Way LS12 .... 213 D4
Beresford Rd BD6 .... 94 B7
Beresford St BD12 .... 95 A5
Berkeley Ave LS8 .... 208 A3
Berkeley Cres LS8 .... 208 A3
Berkeley Croft S71 .... 179 B4
Berkeley Ct LS3 .... 205 E1
Berkeley Gr LS8 .... 208 A3
Berkeley Mount LS8 .... 208 A3
Berkeley Rd LS8 .... 208 A3
Berkeley St LS8 .... 208 A3
Berkeley Terr LS8 .... 208 A3
Berkeley View LS8 .... 208 A3
Berking Ave LS9 .... 212 C4
Bermondsey St LS21 .... 23 B8
Bernard St
Huddersfield HD2 .... 136 E3
Rothwell LS26 .... 101 D6
Berne Gr WF1 .... 216 B3
Berners St WF1 .... 216 C2
Berrington Way WF13 .... 34 B3
Berry Bank La HD7 .... 189 B8
Berry Brow Infant Sch
HD4 .... 171 F8
Berry Croft HD7 .... 171 F5
Berry La Halifax HX3 .... 203 F3
Horbury WF4 .... 141 B1
Keighley BD21 .... 35 B6
Berry Moor Rd HX6 .... 112 C2
Berry Rd HD7 .... 170 C3
Berry St 6 BD21 .... 35 D7
Berry View HD4 .... 153 F1
Berry's Bldgs HX2 .... 91 F7
Berry's Yd WF4 .... 141 B2
Berryfield Garth WF5 ...... 140 D8
Bertha St Keighley BD21 .... 18 A8
Pudsey LS28 .... 57 D2
Bertie St BD4 .... 75 C3
Bertram Dr BD17 .... 38 B3
Bertrand St BD5 .... 211 D1
Berwick Ave WF16 .... 117 D6
Berwick St HX1 .... 203 F3
Bescaby Gr BD17 .... 38 E3
Besha Ave BD12 .... 94 D6
Besha Gr BD12 .... 94 D6
Bessingham Gdns BD6 .... 93 F8
Best La Kirkburton HD4 .... 172 D7
Oxenhope BD22 .... 51 C2
Beswick Cl BD3 .... 75 D8
Beswick St OL14 .... 129 A7
Bethal Gn OL15 .... 129 C1
Bethel Rd BD18 .... 55 D8
Bethel St Brighouse HD6 .. 115 B2
2 Halifax HX3 .... 92 A2
Bethel Terr Halifax HX2 ..... 90 D1
Bethesda Row HX7 .... 89 A1
Betterás Hill Rd LS25 ...... 105 F7
Betula Way HD8 .... 155 E6
Beulah Gr 3 LS6 .... 206 B3
Beulah Mount 3 LS6 .... 206 B3
Beulah Pl HX2 .... 111 E6
Beulah St LS6 .... 206 B3
Beulah Terr Leeds LS6 .... 206 B4
Leeds, Cross Gates LS15 .... 62 C2
Beulah View 3 LS6 .... 206 B3
Bevan Ave WF6 .... 144 B8
Bevan Ct BD7 .... 73 F3
Bevans Gdns LS17 .... 141 C4
Bevedere Gdns LS17 .... 43 E4
Beverley Ave Bradford BD12 . 94 D2
Leeds LS11 .... 214 B2
Beverley Cl HX5 .... 135 B7
Beverley Dr HD2 .... 136 B2
Beverley Dr Bradford BD12 . 94 D2
Dewsbury WF12 .... 139 F8
Beverley Garth WF7 .... 164 A5

Beverley Gdns WF17 .... 97 B2
Beverley Mount LS11 ...... 214 B3
Beverley Pl HX3 .... 92 B1
Beverley Rise LS29 .... 7 E4
Beverley St BD4 .... 75 D5
Beverley Terr Halifax HX3 .. 92 B1
Leeds LS11 .... 214 B3
Beverley View LS11 .... 214 B3
Beverley Wlk LS25 .... 82 F6
Bevin Cl WF1 .... 121 C5
Bevin Cres WF1 .... 121 C5
Bevor Cres WF16 .... 117 D6
Bewdley Ct S71 .... 179 D4
Bewerley Cres BD6 .... 94 A6
Bewick Gr LS10 .... 99 F7
Bexhill Cl WF8 .... 125 F2
Bexley Ave LS8 .... 207 F2
Bexley Gr LS8 .... 207 F2
Bexley Mount LS8 .... 207 F2
Bexley Pl LS8 .... 207 F2
Bexley Rd LS8 .... 207 F2
Bexley Terr LS8 .... 207 F2
Bexley View LS8 .... 207 F2
Beza Ct LS10 .... 215 D2
Beza Rd LS10 .... 215 D3
Beza St LS10 .... 215 D3
Bickerdike Pl WF10 .... 103 B4
Bickerdike Terr LS25 .... 83 A1
Bickerton Way LS21 .... 10 E1
Biddenden Rd LS15 .... 62 F2
Bidder Dr WF3 .... 99 C1
Bideford Ave LS8 .... 43 F2
Bideford Mount BD4 .... 75 E3
Bierley C of E First Sch
BD4 .... 75 B1
Bierley Hall Gr BD4 .... 95 B7
Bierley House Ave BD4 ..... 75 C1
Bierley La BD4 .... 95 B8
Bierley View BD4 .... 75 C1
Big Meadow Dr LS29 .... 6 D8
Bilham La DN5 .... 195 D2
Bilham Rd HD8 .... 176 A2
Bilham Row DN5 .... 195 F3
Bill La HD7 .... 189 C2
Billam's Hill LS21 .... 10 F1
Billey La LS12 .... 77 E4
Billing Cl LS19 .... 40 D3
Billing Dr LS19 .... 40 D3
Billing View Bradford BD10 . 56 C7
Yeadon LS19 .... 40 D3
Billingbauk Dr LS13 .... 58 D1
Billingham Cl WF2 .... 141 D8
Billingsley Terr BD4 .... 75 B4
Billingwood Dr LS19 .... 40 D3
Billy La HX7 .... 89 C5
Bilsdale Grange BD6 .... 93 F8
Bilsdale Way BD17 .... 38 A4
Binbrook App LS12 .... 59 C1
Binbrook Garth LS12 .... 59 C1
Bingley Bank LS17 .... 28 C2
Bingley C of E First Sch
BD16 .... 36 F3
Bingley Five Rise Locks
BD16 .... 36 F4
Bingley Grammar Sch
BD16 .... 36 E4
Bingley Hospl BD16 .... 37 A3
Bingley Rd Baildon BD17 .... 38 B6
Bradford BD9 .... 54 F8
Cullingworth BD13 .... 35 B1
Guiseley LS29 .... 21 C2
Menston LS29 .... 21 F3
Shipley BD18 .... 54 E8
Bingley St Bradford BD8 ..... 74 A2
Leeds LS3 .... 210 C4
Bingley (St Ives)
Municipal Golf Course
BD16 .... 36 B4
Bingley Sta BD16 .... 37 A3
Binham Rd HD2 .... 153 D8
Binks Fold 8 BD12 .... 94 D2
Binks St WF1 .... 121 C4
Binn HD7 .... 170 A7
Binn La HD7 .... 169 A2
Binn Rd HD7 .... 168 F3
Binnie St BD3 .... 75 B7
Binns Hill La HX2 .... 112 B6
Binns La Bradford BD7 .... 73 F5
Glusburn BD20 .... 16 A6
Holmfirth HD7 .... 188 F5
Binns Top La HX3 .... 114 B8
Binswell Fold 8 BD17 .... 38 C4
Birch Ave Bradford BD5 ...... 74 F2
Leeds LS15 .... 81 A8
Lepton HD8 .... 155 E2
Ripponden HX6 .... 132 C1
Todmorden OL14 .... 108 A7
Birch Cl Bradford BD5 .... 74 F2
Brighouse HD6 .... 115 C3
Birch Cliff BD17 .... 38 B2
Birch Close La BD10 .... 37 F8
Birch Cres LS15 .... 81 A8
Birch Ct LS27 .... 98 B3
Birch Dr LS25 .... 83 A3
Birch Gn WF6 .... 144 B8
Birch Gr Batley WF17 .... 118 A8
Bradford BD5 .... 74 F2
Castleford WF10 .... 125 D8
Huddersfield HD7 .... 152 E5
Keighley BD21 .... 35 B4
Kippax LS25 .... 83 B3
Birch Hill Rise 1 LS18 .... 58 C8
Birch House 7 WF10 .... 124 E7
Birch La Bradford BD5 .... 74 F2
Bradford, Staygate BD5 ...... 74 F2
Birch Mews LS16 .... 42 C2
Birch Pk HD7 .... 172 D2

Birch Rd Huddersfield HD4 171 F8
Kippax LS25 83 A3
Normanton WF6 144 B7
Birch St Bradford BD8 74 A8
Morley LS27 98 B2
Wakefield WF1 142 F4
Birch Tree Gdns BD21 35 E6
Birch Way BD5 74 F2
Bircham Cl BD16 37 C5
Birchcliffe Rd HX7 89 A3
Birchdale BD16 36 F5
Birchen Ave WF5 140 C6
Birchen Hills WF5 140 C5
Birchencliffe Hill Rd HD3 135 B2
Birchenlee Cl HX7 89 F1
Birches The Bramhope LS16 24 F2
Guiseley LS20 22 E2
Birchfield Ave LS27 97 C6
Birchfield Garth LS14 62 C8
Birchfield Gr HD8 175 A1
Birchfields Ave LS14 62 C8
Birchfields Cl LS14 62 C7
Birchfields Cres LS14 62 C8
Birchfields Ct 5 LS14 62 C8
Birchfields Rise LS14 62 C8
Birchington Ave HD3 135 B2
Birchington Cl HD3 135 B2
Birchington Dr HD3 135 A2
Birchlands Ave BD15 53 B6
Birchlands Gr BD15 53 B6
Birchroyd LS26 100 F4
Birchtree Cl WF1 142 F8
Birchtree Way LS16 41 E2
Birchtree Wlk WF11 126 D3
Birchwood Ave
Batley WF17 96 F2
Keighley BD20 18 B2
Leeds LS17 44 A3
Birchwood Cl HD2 135 D2
Birchwood Ct Ilkley LS29 8 A4
2 Liversedge WF15 117 B3
Birchwood Dr BD20 18 B2
Birchwood Hill LS17 44 A4
Birchwood Mount LS17 44 A4
Birchwood Rd BD20 18 A2
Bird La HX6 132 C3
Birdale Field La LS22 29 D8
Birdcage Hill HX3 113 A3
Birdcage La HX3 113 B3
Birdcage Wlk LS21 23 A6
Birds Edge La HD8 190 F4
Birds Royd La HD6 115 C1
Birdsedge Farm Mews
HD8 191 A4
Birdsedge First Sch HD8 191 A4
Birdsnest La HD7 190 D2
Birdswell Ave HD6 115 D3
Birfed Cres LS4 59 B3
Birk House La HD8 191 B8
Birk La LS27 97 E4
Birk Lea St BD5 74 F4
Birkby Brow Cres WF17 97 B2
Birkby Hall Rd HD2 135 E1
Birkby Haven BD6 93 E8
Birkby Junior Sch HD1 136 A1
Birkby La HD6 115 D7
Birkby Lodge Rd HD2 153 F8
Birkby Rd HD2 135 D1
Birkby St BD12 94 D4
Birkdale Ave HD3 153 A8
Birkdale Cl
Cullingworth BD13 52 E6
Leeds LS17 43 B4
Birkdale Ct BD20 18 A3
Birkdale Dr LS17 43 B4
Birkdale Gn LS17 43 B4
Birkdale Gr
Dewsbury WF13 118 A1
Halifax HX2 91 F7
Leeds LS17 43 A4
Birkdale High Sch
Dewsbury WF13 118 B2
Dewsbury, Chapel Fold
WF13 118 A2
Birkdale Mount LS17 43 B4
Birkdale Pl LS17 43 A4
Birkdale Rd
Dewsbury WF13 118 B1
Royston S71 179 B5
Birkdale Rise LS17 43 A4
Birkdale Way LS17 43 B4
Birkdale Wlk LS17 43 A4
Birkenshaw CE
County Fst Sch BD11 96 B6
Birkenshaw La BD11 96 C4
Birkenshaw Middle Sch
BD11 96 B4
Birkett St BD19 116 D8
Birkhead St WF16 117 E3
Birkhill WF10 125 C8
Birkhill Cres BD11 96 B5
Birkhouse La
Brighouse HD6 115 D6
Huddersfield HD5 154 E5
Huddersfield, Yews Hill
HD1, HD4 153 E5
Birkhouse Rd HD6 115 C6
Birkin La WF11 127 D8
Birklands Rd
Huddersfield HD2 135 F2
Shipley BD18 55 B7
Birklands Terr BD18 55 B7
Birks Ave BD7 73 F5
Birks Fold BD7 73 F6
Birks Hall St HX1 202 C4
Birks Hall Terr HX1 202 C4
Birks La Huddersfield HD4 155 A3
Kirkburton HD8 173 D3
Birks La continued
Ripponden HX6 132 E5
Sowerby Bridge HX6 132 D8
Todmorden OL14 129 B8
Birks Rd HD3 153 A5
Birkshall La BD4, BD3 75 B6
Birkshead BD15 53 D5
Birksland Ind Est BD4 75 B5
Birksland Moor BD11 96 B3
Birksland St BD3 75 B6
Birkwith Cl LS14 62 B8
Birkwood Ave WF4 144 B2
Birkwood Rd WF6 122 C3
Birmingham La HD7 170 C3
Birnam Gr BD4 75 A4
Birr Rd BD9 55 B3
Birstall County Junior
& Infants Sch WF17 96 F1
Birstall La BD11 96 E5
Birstall St Peter's C of E
Primary Sch WF17 96 E2
Birthwaite Rd S75 177 B1
Bishop St BD9 55 B2
Bishop Way WF3 119 F8
Bishop's Ct HD4 171 F7
Bishopdale Dr LS22 13 A1
Bishopdale Holme BD6 93 E8
Bishopgate St LS1 211 E3
Bishops Way Meltham HD7 170 E2
Mirfield WF14 137 D7
Bisley Cl S71 179 E4
Bismarck Dr LS11 214 B4
Bismarck St LS11 214 B4
Bittern Rise LS27 98 C3
Black Abbey La BD20 16 C6
Black Brook Way HX4 134 C6
Black Bull St LS10 212 A2
Black Dyke La BD13 53 B1
Black Edge La BD13 71 D6
Black Gates Ct WF3 119 F8
Black Gates Rise WF3 119 F8
Black Hill HX7 89 B8
Black Hill La Bramhope LS16 25 D1
Keighley BD20 17 E1
Black Hill Rd LS21 25 C5
Black La HD7 170 E7
Black Moor Rd Leeds LS17 43 A2
Oxenhope BD22 51 E4
Black Rd WF4 143 B3
Black Sike La HD7 188 C5
Black Swan Ginnell 7
HX1 203 E3
Black Swan Pas 6 HX1 203 E3
Black Wlk WF8 125 E2
Black Wood Gr LS16 41 D3
Black Wood Mount LS16 41 D3
Black Wood Rise LS16 41 D3
Blackbird Gdns 4 BD8 73 B7
Blackburn Bldgs HD6 115 C2
Blackburn Cl Bradford BD8 73 D7
Halifax HX3 91 F3
Blackburn Ct 9
Pontefract WF8 146 C8
Rothwell LS26 100 F5
Blackburn House HX3 92 A3
Blackburn La WF11 127 C3
Blackburn Pl WF17 118 D5
Blackburn Rd Batley WF17 96 E1
Brighouse HD6 115 A4
Blacker Cres WF4 158 E6
Blacker La Netherton WF4 159 B5
Shafton S72 180 C3
Blacker Rd
Huddersfield HD1, HD2 153 F8
Mapplewell S75 178 C1
Blackers Ct WF12 139 B4
Blackett St LS28 57 B7
Blackgates Cres WF3 119 F8
Blackgates Dr WF3 119 F8
Blackgates Fold WF3 119 F8
Blackgates Infant Sch
WF3 98 E1
Blackgates Junior Sch
WF3 119 F8
Blackhouse Rd HD2 136 B2
Blackledge HX1 203 F3
Blackley Rd HX5 134 E4
Blackman La LS2 206 B2
Blackmires HX2 92 A5
Blackmoor Ct LS17 42 F5
Blackmoor La LS17 28 A1
Blackmoorfoot Rd
Huddersfield HD4 153 E4
Slaithwaite HD7 170 D7
Blackpool Gr LS12 78 A4
Blackpool Pl LS12 78 A4
Blackpool St 7 LS12 78 A4
Blackpool Terr 6 LS12 78 A4
Blackpool View 8 LS12 78 A4
Blackshaw Beck La BD13 93 A6
Blackshaw Clough Rd HX6 132 A6
Blackshaw Dr BD6 93 D8
Blackshaw St OL14 108 D5
Blacksmith Fold BD7 74 A4
Blacksmith La LS16 25 F1
Blacksmiths Fold HD5 154 F3
Blackstone Ave BD12 94 C2
Blackstone Edge Rd
Hebden Bridge HX7 131 B7
Ripponden HX6 130 F5
Blackthorn Way WF2 142 A8
Blackthorne Ct 4 LS10 99 D8
Blackwall HX1 203 E2
Blackwall La HX6 112 B5
Blackwall Rise HX6 112 B5
Blackwood Ave LS16 41 D3
Blackwood Gdns LS16 41 D3
Blackwood Gr HX1 202 B4
Blackwood Hall La HX2 111 D7
Blacup Moor View BD19 116 D7
Blagden La HD4 153 F1
Blairsville Gdns LS13 58 B4
Blairsville Gr LS13 58 C4
Blaith Royd La HX7 109 F4
Blaithroyd La HX3 113 E6
Blake Cres LS20 39 F8
Blake Gr LS7 204 A2
Blake Hall Dr WF14 138 C4
Blake Hall Rd WF14 138 C4
Blake Hill HX3 92 E3
Blake Hill End HX3 92 F5
Blake Law La
Brighouse WF15 115 F2
Liversedge HD6 116 A2
Blake Lee La HD7 168 B5
Blake Stones HD7 169 E8
Blakehill Ave BD2 56 C2
Blakehill First Sch BD10 56 A6
Blakehill Terr BD2 56 C2
Blakeholme Cl HD7 169 E8
Blakelaw Dr HD6 115 D3
Blakeley Gr WF2 141 F6
Blakeney Gr LS10 215 D1
Blakeney Rd LS10 215 D1
Blakeridge La WF17 118 B5
Blakestones Rd HD7 169 E8
Blakey Rd WF2 141 F8
Blamires Pl 2 BD7 73 F3
Blamires St BD7 73 F3
Blanche St BD4 75 D6
Bland St Halifax HX1 203 D3
Huddersfield HD1 153 F4
Bland's Cl WF10 124 E7
Blandford Gdns 21 LS2 206 B2
Blandford Gr 23 LS2 206 B2
Blands Ave WF10 103 A5
Blands Cres WF10 103 A5
Blands Gr WF10 103 A5
Blands Terr WF10 103 A5
Blanket Hall St WF16 117 D3
Blantyre Ct BD13 52 D6
Blayd's Yd LS1 211 F3
Blayds Garth LS26 101 A7
Blayds St LS9 212 C3
Bleach Mill La LS29 21 E5
Bleak Ave S72 180 C2
Bleak St BD19 117 C8
Bleak St Lower BD19 117 C8
Bleakley Ave WF4 179 B6
Bleakley Cl S72 180 C2
Bleakley La WF4 179 B6
Bleakley Terr WF4 179 B6
Bleasdale Ave
Huddersfield HD2 135 F1
Knottingley WF11 126 F4
Blencarn Cl LS14 61 F4
Blencarn Garth LS14 61 F4
Blencarn Lawn LS14 61 F4
Blencarn Path LS14 61 F4
Blencarn Rd LS14 61 F4
Blencarn View LS14 61 F4
Blencarn Wlk LS14 61 F4
Blenheim Ave 6 LS2 206 B2
Blenheim Cl WF11 126 C4
Blenheim Cres 5 LS2 206 B2
Blenheim Ct Halifax HX1 203 D4
Leeds LS2 206 B2
Blenheim Dr Batley WF17 118 C6
Dewsbury WF13 118 A1
Blenheim Gr LS2 206 B2
Blenheim Hill WF17 118 D7
Blenheim Middle Sch
LS6 206 B3
Blenheim Mount BD8 55 C2
Blenheim Pl BD10 39 B1
Blenheim Primary Sch
LS2 206 B2
Blenheim Rd Bradford BD8 55 C2
Wakefield WF1 216 A4
Blenheim Sq Batley WF17 118 C6
Leeds LS2 206 B2
Blenheim St
Hebden Bridge HX7 89 B3
10 Keighley BD21 35 B5
Blenheim Terr LS2 206 B2
Blenheim View LS2 206 B2
Blenheim Wlk LS2 206 B2
Blenkinsop Ct LS27 98 B2
Blind La Bickerton LS24 15 F8
Birkenshaw BD11 96 F8
East Ardsley WF3 120 A5
Halifax HX2 91 E8
Harden BD16 36 D3
Hebden Bridge HX2 111 B7
Thorner LS17 44 E4
Todmorden OL14 108 B6
Bloomfield Rd S75 177 F1
Bloomfield Rise S75 177 F1
Bloomhouse La S75 177 F1
Blucher St BD4 75 D6
Blue Ball La HX6 131 E3
Blue Ball Rd HX6 131 D3
Blue Bell Hill HD4 153 F2
Blue Bell La OL14 86 D2
Blue Butts WF5 140 D5
Blue Hill BD13 52 D1
Blue Hill Cres LS12 209 D2
Blue Hill Gr LS12 209 D2
Blue Hill Grange LS12 209 D1
Blue Hill La LS12 209 D2
Bluebell Cl 6
Bradford BD15 73 B8
Pontefract WF8 146 D7
Bluebell Ct WF17 96 E2
Bluebell Rd S75 177 E3
Bluebell Way WF9 182 F7
Bluebell Wlk HX2 111 E8
Blundell St Leeds LS1 206 B1
South Elmsall WF9 182 E3
Blythe Ave BD8 74 A8
Blythe St BD7 74 D7
Bmk Ind Est WF15 117 B4
Boar La LS1 211 F3
Boardman St OL14 108 B6
Boat La Kippax WF10 103 B3
Mickletown WF10 103 A3
Boathouse La WF14 138 C3
Bob La HX2 112 D7
Bobbin Mill Cl
Steeton BD20 17 C5
Todmorden OL14 86 B1
Bobbin Mill Ct BD20 17 C5
Bobbin St OL14 86 C1
Bodiham Hill LS25 83 B8
Bodington Hall LS16 42 C2
Bodkin La BD22 50 E3
Bodley Terr LS4 205 D1
Bodmin App LS10 99 A5
Bodmin Ave BD18 55 F7
Bodmin Cres LS10 99 B5
Bodmin Croft LS10 99 B4
Bodmin Dr WF6 123 B3
Bodmin Garth LS10 99 A4
Bodmin Gdns LS10 99 A4
Bodmin Pl LS10 99 B4
Bodmin Rd LS10 99 A5
Bodmin Sq LS10 99 A4
Bodmin St LS10 99 A4
Bodmin Terr LS10 99 A4
Bog Green La HD5 137 C4
Bog La LS15 63 A5
Boggart Hill LS14 61 E6
Boggart Hill Cres LS14 61 F6
Boggart Hill Dr LS14 61 F6
Boggart Hill Gdns LS14 61 E6
Boggart Hill Rd LS14 61 E6
Boggart La
Skelmanthorpe HD8 175 A3
Sowerby Bridge HX6 112 B3
Boland Cres BD22 34 E3
Boldgrove St WF12 140 A6
Boldmere Rd LS15 80 E7
Boldron Holt BD6 93 F8
Boldshay St BD3 75 B8
Bolehill Pk HD6 114 E6
Bolingbroke Ct 14 BD5 201 B1
Bolingbroke St BD5 74 D2
Bolland Bldgs BD12 94 F5
Bolland St 3 BD12 94 E5
Bolling Hall (Mus) BD4 75 A3
Bolling Rd Bradford BD4 201 C1
Ilkley LS29 8 D4
Bolling Rd First Sch LS29 8 E4
Bolling Specl Sch BD4 75 B3
Bolsover Cl LS25 83 B7
Bolstermoor Rd HD7 152 A4
Boltby La BD6 93 E8
Bolton HX2 91 E7
Bolton Abbey Sta BD23 2 C7
Bolton Bridge Rd LS29 8 A4
Bolton Brow HX6 112 D4
Bolton Brow
Junior & Infants Sch
HX6 112 D4
Bolton Cres BD2 56 B4
Bolton Ct BD2 56 A2
Bolton Dr BD2 56 B4
Bolton Gdns LS19 40 C6
Bolton Gr BD2 56 B4
Bolton Hall Rd Bradford BD2 55 E5
Shipley BD2 55 E5
Bolton La BD2 55 E3
Bolton Lane First Sch BD2 55 F3
Bolton Rd Addingham LS29 2 F4
Bradford BD2, BD3 55 F2
Draughton LS29 2 F4
Silsden BD20, LS29 5 F4
Yeadon LS19 40 C6
Bolton Royd Primary Sch
LS28 76 A8
Bolton St Bradford BD3 201 D3
Bradford, Low Moor BD12 94 C6
Bolton Terr BD20 5 E2
Bolton Way LS23 30 C7
Bolton Wife Hill WF4 159 F1
Bolton Woods First Sch
BD2 55 D4
Bolus Cl WF1 121 C4
Bolus La WF1 121 C4
Bonaccord Sq WF17 118 C4
Bonaccord Terr WF17 118 C4
Bond Ct LS1 211 E4
Bond St Batley WF17 118 C6
6 Batley, Birstall WF17 96 E1
Brighouse HD6 115 A3
Dewsbury WF13 139 C8
Halifax HX1 203 D2
Hebden Bridge HX7 89 A3
Leeds LS1 211 E4
Pontefract WF8 125 E2
Todmorden OL14 108 B5
Wakefield WF1 216 A3
Bondgate Harewood LS17 27 A7
Otley LS21 23 A7
Pontefract WF8 125 F2
Bonegate Ave HD6 115 B3
Bonegate Rd HD6 115 B3
Bonn Rd BD9 55 A2
Bonwick Mall BD6 93 E7
Boocock St 2 LS28 57 E1
Bookers Cl DB19 117 C7
Bookers Field BD19 117 C7
Booth Halifax HX2 90 E3
Marsden HD7 169 B6
Booth Bank HD7 169 C7
Booth Hill HX2 90 E4
Booth House La HD7 188 D4
Booth House Rd HX2 111 C7
Booth House Terr HX2 111 C7
Booth Royd BD10 39 B1
Booth Royd Dr BD10 39 B1
Booth Royd La HD6 135 D8
Booth St Bradford BD10 56 B7
Burley in W LS29 9 E2
Castleford WF10 124 D8
Cleckheaton BD19 116 D8
5 Queensbury BD13 72 D1
Shipley BD18 55 D7
Booth's Bldgs HD6 115 B7
Bootham Pk BD9 54 D2
Boothman Wlk 4 BD21 35 A5
Boothroyd Dr HD4 153 B3
Boothroyd Gn WF13 139 B8
Boothroyd Jun & Inf Sch
WF13 139 A7
Boothroyd
Junior & Infants Sch
WF13 139 A7
Boothroyd La WF13 139 A8
Boothroyds Way WF7 145 A6
Boothtown Rd HX3 92 B2
Border Cl HD3 134 F1
Borough Ave LS8 204 B4
Borough Market HX1 203 E3
Borough Rd WF1 216 B3
Boroughgate LS21 23 A8
Borrins Way BD17 38 D3
Borrough View LS8 204 B4
Borrowdale Cres LS12 58 F2
Borrowdale Croft LS19 40 B7
Borrowdale Dr WF10 104 D1
Borrowdale Rd
Batley WF12 118 E2
Wakefield WF2 141 E7
Borrowdale Terr LS14 61 F3
Boston Ave LS5 58 F3
Boston Hill HX7 89 B6
Boston Mews LS23 30 E7
Boston Rd Boston Spa LS23 30 D6
Wetherby LS22 13 E3
Boston Spa C of E
Primary Sch LS23 30 E7
Boston Spa
Comprehensive Sch LS23 30 B7
Boston Spa Junior Sch
LS23 30 D7
Boston Spa Specl Sch
LS23 30 D7
Boston St Castleford WF10 124 E8
Halifax HX1 202 B3
Sowerby Bridge HX6 112 A3
Boston Towers LS9 207 E1
Boston Wlk BD6 93 F8
Boswell Cl S71 179 B4
Bosworth Ave WF6 122 E4
Bosworth Cl BD15 54 B1
Botany Ave BD2 55 F4
Botany Dr BD20 19 E2
Botany La HD8 155 F4
Botham Hall Rd HD3 152 F5
Bottom Boat Rd WF3 122 D6
Bottomley La HX4 133 C2
Bottomley Rd OL14 129 C6
Bottomley St Bradford BD5 74 D4
Bradford, Buttershaw BD6 93 F7
2 Brighouse HD6 115 B4
Bottomley's Bldgs LS6 206 B3
Bottoms HX3 113 D3
Bottoms La BD11 96 B4
Boulder Bridge La S71 179 F1
Boulder Gate HD7 169 B4
Boulevard The Leeds LS12 213 D3
Pudsey LS28 57 D2
Boundary Ave BD20 16 D6
Boundary Cl LS15 81 E7
Boundary Ct HD7 189 D3
Boundary Dr S72 181 A3
Boundary Farm Rd LS17 43 A3
Boundary La WF6 143 F7
Boundary Pl LS7 207 E2
Boundary Rd WF13 117 F2
Boundary St Leeds LS7 207 E2
Liversedge WF16 117 C4
Boundary The BD8 54 E1
Bourbon Cl BD6 94 B8
Bourn View Cl HD4 171 D7
Bourn View Rd HD4 171 D7
Bourne Ct S75 178 C2
Bourne St BD10 39 B2
Bourne Wlk S75 178 C2
Bow Beck BD4 75 A5
Bow Gn BD7 73 D4
Bow La HX7 88 A4
Bow St Huddersfield HD1 153 F5
Keighley BD21 35 C7
Leeds LS9 212 B3
Bowbridge Rd 9 BD5 74 E4
Bowcliffe Rd LS23 30 D2
Bower Gn BD3 75 C7
Bower La WF13 117 F3
Bower Rd LS15 62 E3
Bower Slack Rd HX6 110 F1
Bower St BD5 201 B2
Bower The 1 WF17 117 F7
Bowers La HX4 133 D6
Bowes Nook BD6 93 E7
Bowfell Cl LS14 62 A4
Bowland Ave BD17 37 E1
Bowland Cl LS15 80 E7

Bowland St BD1 .... 74 D8
Bowler Cl BD12 .... 94 C6
Bowling Alley HD6 .... 136 A8
Bowling Ave WF2 .... 120 F2
Bowling Back La BD4 .... 75 B5
Bowling Com Coll
  Bradford BD4 .... 75 A3
  Bradford BD4 .... 75 A3
Bowling Court Ind Est
  BD4 .... 75 C5
Bowling Ct HD6 .... 114 F3
Bowling Dyke HX1 .... 203 E4
Bowling Green Cl HD3 .... 152 E7
Bowling Green Junior
  & Infants Sch HX4 .... 133 F3
Bowling Green Rd HX4 ...... 133 F3
Bowling Green Terr LS11 .. 211 E1
Bowling Hall Rd BD4 .... 75 A3
Bowling Old La
  Bradford BD4 .... 74 E4
  Bradford, Bankfoot BD5 .... 74 F2
Bowling Park Cl BD4 .... 74 F4
Bowling Park Dr BD4 .... 74 F3
Bowling Park First Sch
  BD5 .... 74 F3
Bowling St HD3 .... 153 A4
Bowman Ave BD6 .... 94 B7
Bowman La HX1 .... 202 C3
Bowman La LS10 .... 212 A3
Bowman Pl 8 HX1 .... 202 C3
Bowman Rd BD6 .... 94 B7
Bowman St 8 Halifax HX1 . 202 C3
  Wakefield WF1 .... 142 F3
Bowman Terr HX1 .... 202 C3
Bowmere Dr 8 BD15 .... 73 B8
Bownas Rd LS23 .... 30 C8
Bowness Ave Bradford BD10 . 56 D4
  Castleford WF10 .... 104 E1
Bowness Dr HD5 .... 154 D7
Bowood Ave LS7 .... 60 A7
Bowood Cres LS7 .... 60 A7
Bowood Gr LS7 .... 60 A7
Bowood Rd LS6 .... 111 D1
Bowwood Dr BD20 .... 36 C8
Box La WF8 .... 125 E2
Box Tree Cl BD8 .... 54 E1
Box Trees La HX3 .... 91 D3
Boxhill Rd HX5 .... 134 F7
Boxwood Rd HX5 .... 134 F5
Boy La Bradford BD4 .... 95 B7
  Halifax HX3 .... 91 D2
Boycott Dr WF7 .... 164 A5
Boycott Way WF9 .... 183 A4
Boyd Ave BD3 .... 56 E1
Boyle & Petyt Sch The
  BD23 .... 2 E1
Boyle The LS15 .... 63 D8
Boyne Dr WF2 .... 160 A5
Boyne Hill WF4 .... 160 A4
Boyne St HX1 .... 203 D3
Boynton St BD5 .... 74 E3
Boynton Terr BD5 .... 74 E3
Boys La HX3 .... 203 F1
Boys Scarr HX2 .... 111 D6
Bracewell Ave BD15 .... 73 A8
Bracewell Bank HX3 .... 92 A2
Bracewell Dr HX3 .... 92 F2
Bracewell Gr 2 HX3 .... 92 A1
Bracewell Rd HD7 .... 170 D1
Bracewell St BD21 .... 35 F7
Bracken Ave HD6 .... 115 A5
Bracken Bank Ave BD22 ..... 34 F3
Bracken Bank Cres BD22 ... 35 A3
Bracken Bank Gr BD22 .... 34 F3
Bracken Bank Way BD22 .... 34 F3
Bracken Bank Wlk BD22 .... 34 F2
Bracken Cl Brighouse HD6 . 115 A5
  Mirfield WF14 .... 137 D7
Bracken Ct Leeds LS17 .... 43 C1
  Leeds LS12 .... 210 B1
Bracken Edge
  Bradford BD10 .... 56 C7
  Leeds LS8 .... 204 C1
Bracken Edge
  Primary Sch LS7 .... 204 B1
Bracken Ghyll Dr BD20 .... 5 D2
Bracken Ghyll Golf Course
  LS29 .... 2 E1
Bracken Gr
  Huddersfield HD2 .... 136 B4
  Mirfield WF14 .... 137 D7
Bracken Hall
  Countryside Ctr BD17 ...... 37 E3
Bracken Hall Rd HD2 .... 136 C3
Bracken Hill
  Ackworth M T WF7 .... 163 D6
  Leeds LS17 .... 43 C1
  Mirfield WF14 .... 137 D7
  South Kirkby WF9 .... 182 D4
Bracken Mount BD20 .... 5 D2
Bracken Pk Bingley BD16 .... 37 C3
  Leeds LS14 .... 45 A7
Bracken Rd Brighouse HD6 . 115 A5
  Keighley BD22 .... 35 A4
  Steeton BD20 .... 17 A5
Bracken Sq HD2 .... 136 C4
Bracken St BD21 .... 35 B4
Brackenbeck Rd BD7 .... 73 F4
Brackenbed Grange HX2 .... 91 E1
Brackenbed La HX2 .... 91 F1
Brackendale BD10 .... 39 A2
Brackendale Ave BD10 .... 39 A2
Brackendale Dr BD10 .... 38 F2
Brackendale Gr BD10 .... 38 F2
Brackendale Par BD10 .... 38 F2

Brackendale Pl BD10 .... 39 A2
Brackenhill Dr BD7 .... 73 F3
Brackenhill First Sch BD7 .. 73 F3
Brackenholme Royd 10
  .... 93 E8
Brackens La HX3 .... 9 D7
Brackenwood Cl Ilkley LS29 . 8 E4
  Leeds LS8 .... 204 B3
Brackenwood Ct WF1 ...... 121 D5
Brackenwood Dr LS8 .... 204 B4
Brackenwood Gn LS8 ...... 204 B4
Brackenwood Rd WF1 .... 121 D5
Bradbeck Rd BD7 .... 73 F7
Bradburn Rd WF1 .... 100 A3
Bradbury St WF13 .... 138 E5
Bradd Cl WF15 .... 117 B5
Bradfield Cl HD2 .... 136 E5
Bradford Bsns Pk BD1 .... 55 E1
Bradford City Tech Coll
  Bradford BD7 .... 74 D7
  Bradford BD5 .... 74 E4
Bradford Forster Sq Sta
  BD1 .... 201 B3
Bradford Girls'
  Grammar Sch BD9 .... 54 E1
Bradford Golf Course LS20 . 39 A7
Bradford Grammar Sch
  BD9 .... 55 C3
Bradford &
  Heckmondwike Rd BD4 ... 95 F8
Bradford & Ilkley Com Coll
  Bradford BD7 .... 74 D6
  Ilkley LS29 .... 8 A3
Bradford & Ilkley Com Coll
  McMillan Bldg BD5 .... 74 D5
Bradford Ind Mus BD2 ...... 56 C3
Bradford Interchange Sta
  BD1 .... 201 C2
Bradford La BD3 .... 75 D7
Bradford Moor First Sch
  BD3 .... 75 C8
Bradford Moor Golf Course
  BD2 .... 56 B1
Bradford Old Rd Halifax HX3 . 92 C2
  Shipley BD16 .... 54 B7
Bradford Rd Batley WF17 .. 118 D5
  Birkenshaw BD11 .... 37 A1
  Birkenshaw BD11 .... 96 A5
Birkenshaw, Drighlington
  BD11 .... 37 A1
  Bradford, Clayton BD14 .... 73 D5
Bradford, Oakenshaw
  BD12, BD19 .... 95 B3
Bradford, Springfield BD10 . 56 B6
  Brighouse HD6 .... 115 B2
  Brighouse HD6 .... 115 B5
  Burley in W LS29 .... 21 F8
  Cleckheaton BD19 .... 116 E8
Cleckheaton, Birstall BD19 . 96 C2
  Dewsbury WF13 .... 118 D1
  East Ardsley WF3 .... 120 B8
  Gildersome LS27 .... 97 B5
  Guiseley LS29 .... 22 B3
Huddersfield HD1, HD2 ... 136 B3
  Keighley BD20, BD21 .... 18 E1
  Liversedge WF15 .... 117 B4
  Lofthouse Gate WF2 .... 120 E5
  Menston LS29 .... 22 B3
  Northowram HX3 .... 93 A1
  Northowram HX3 .... 93 A1
  Otley LS21 .... 22 D6
  Pudsey LS28 .... 57 D1
  Shipley, Frizinghall BD18 .. 55 B6
  Shipley, Nab Wood BD18 ... 54 C7
  Wakefield WF2 .... 120 F1
Bradford Royal Infmy BD9 . 54 F1
Bradford St
  Dewsbury WF13 .... 118 D1
  Keighley BD21 .... 35 C7
Bradford & Wakefield Rd
  BD4, BD11 .... 96 C7
Bradfords Cl LS23 .... 30 C3
Bradlaugh Rd BD6 .... 74 B1
Bradlaugh Terr 2 BD6 .... 74 C1
Bradley Ave
  Castleford WF10 .... 124 C8
  Silsden BD20 .... 5 D2
Bradley Carr Terr WF9 ..... 194 E8
Bradley CE Jun & Inf Sch
  HD2 .... 136 F5
Bradley Gr BD20 .... 5 D2
Bradley Grange Gdns HD2 . 136 F6
Bradley Junction Ind Est
  HD2 .... 136 F4
Bradley La Elland HX4 ...... 134 B8
  Pudsey LS28 .... 76 B7
Bradley Mills La HD1 .... 154 D8
Bradley Mills Rd HD1 .... 154 D8
Bradley Park Golf Course
  HD2 .... 136 F6
Bradley Quarry Cl HD2 ... 137 A6
Bradley Rd
  Huddersfield HD2 .... 136 D6
  Silsden BD20 .... 5 D2
Bradley Rise BD20 .... 5 D2
Bradley St Bingley BD16 .... 36 F3
  Castleford WF10 .... 124 D8
  10 Huddersfield HD1 ...... 154 B6
  Shipley BD9 .... 55 C4
Bradley Terr LS17 .... 44 A4
Bradley View HX4 .... 134 B4
Bradleys Both
  County Primary Sch BD20 . 4 C6
Bradshaw Ave HD7 .... 171 E3
Bradshaw Cl HD7 .... 171 E3

Bradshaw Cres HD7 .... 171 E3
Bradshaw Dr HD7 .... 171 E3
Bradshaw La Halifax HX2 .. 72 A2
  Marsden HD7 .... 151 A1
Bradshaw Primary Sch
  HX2 .... 71 F1
Bradshaw Rd Honley HD7 . 171 E3
  Meltham HD7 .... 188 B7
Bradstock Gdns LS27 .... 98 A6
Bradwell La WF5 .... 140 E5
Brae Ave BD2 .... 55 F3
Brae Croft S72 .... 180 D7
Braemar Dr LS25 .... 83 B8
Braemar Rise S72 .... 180 D7
Brafferton Arbor BD6 .... 93 E8
Brain Wood Middle Sch
  LS8 .... 61 D7
Braine Rd LS22 .... 13 F6
Braithwaite Ave BD22 ...... 34 F7
Braithwaite Cres BD22 ...... 34 F7
Braithwaite Dr BD22 .... 34 F7
Braithwaite Edge Rd BD22 . 34 D8
Braithwaite Gr BD22 .... 34 F7
Braithwaite Rd BD22 .... 34 E8
Braithwaite Row 6 LS10 . 215 E2
Braithwaite Sch BD22 ...... 34 E8
Braithwaite St Leeds LS11 . 210 C2
  Mapplewell S75 .... 178 C1
Braithwaite Way BD22 ..... 34 F7
Braithwaite Wlk BD22 .... 34 F7
Bramah St S71 .... 179 C1
Bramble Ave LS23 .... 30 B7
Bramble Cl Bradford BD14 . 73 C2
  Pontefract WF8 .... 146 B7
Bramble Wlk WF17 .... 96 F1
Brambles The LS29 .... 7 F4
Brambling Mews LS27 ...... 98 C3
Bramham Dr BD17 .... 38 D4
Bramham La LS23 .... 29 B3
Bramham Park LS23 .... 46 F8
Bramham Primary Sch
  LS23 .... 30 D4
Bramham Rd Bingley BD16 . 37 A4
  Boston Spa LS23 .... 30 D4
  Castleford WF10 .... 124 A6
  Thorner LS14 .... 46 C2
Bramhope Old La LS21 ...... 23 E4
Bramhope Primary Sch
  LS16 .... 24 F2
Bramhope Rd BD19 .... 116 C8
Bramleigh Dr LS27 .... 98 A6
Bramleigh Gr LS27 .... 98 A6
Bramley Cl Holmfirth HD7 . 189 D7
  Oakworth BD22 .... 34 A3
Bramley Cres LS14 .... 121 B4
Bramley Ctr LS13 .... 58 D3
Bramley Fold HX3 .... 114 D8
Bramley Gr HX3 .... 114 D8
Bramley Grange 7 LS15 ..... 45 C1
Bramley Grange Coll LS14 . 45 D1
Bramley Hill Primary Sch
  LS13 .... 58 B2
Bramley La Brighouse HX3 . 114 D8
  West Bretton WF4 .... 177 B8
Bramley St Bradford BD5 .. 74 F3
  5 Leeds LS13 .... 58 B1
Bramley Sta LS13 .... 58 B1
Bramley View HX3 .... 114 E8
Brampton HX2 .... 90 B1
Brampton Ct WF9 .... 183 A5
Bramstan Ave LS13 .... 58 A3
Bramstan Cl LS13 .... 58 A3
Bramstan Gdns LS13 .... 58 A3
Bramstan Recn Ctr LS13 ... 58 A4
Bramston Gdns 8 HD6 .... 115 A1
Bramston St HD6 .... 115 A1
Bramwell Ho BD1 .... 201 C4
Bran St 8 BD21 .... 35 B4
Branch Cl LS12 .... 78 A4
Branch End LS27 .... 97 E7
Branch La HD7 .... 135 B3
Branch Pl LS12 .... 78 A4
Branch Rd Batley WF17 ... 118 C5
  Brighouse BD19 .... 94 F1
  Crigglestone WF4 .... 159 C4
  Dewsbury WF13 .... 139 C8
  Elland HX4 .... 133 D5
Huddersfield HD2 .... 135 B4
  Leeds LS12 .... 78 A4
  Leeds, Armley LS12 .... 209 F4
Branch St
Huddersfield HD1 .... 153 D5
  Leeds LS12 .... 78 A4
Brander App LS9 .... 61 D1
Brander Cl LS9 .... 61 D1
Brander Dr LS9 .... 61 D1
Brander Gr LS9 .... 61 D1
Brander Rd LS9 .... 61 D1
Brander St LS9 .... 61 D2
Brandfort St BD7 .... 74 A5
Brandon Cres LS17 .... 44 F6
Brandon Ct LS17 .... 44 F6
Brandon La LS17 .... 44 F6
Brandon Rd 8 LS3 .... 206 A1
Brandon St LS12 .... 210 C3
Brandon Terr LS17 .... 44 C5
Brandon Way LS7 .... 204 A1
Brandy Carr Rd WF2 ...... 120 C8
Branksome Cres BD9 .... 54 F2
Branksome Ct BD9 .... 54 D8
Branksome Dr BD18 .... 54 D8
Branksome Pl LS6 .... 205 E2
Branksome St LS6 .... 205 E2
Branksome Terr LS6 .... 205 E2

Bransby Cl LS28 .... 57 E2
Bransby Ct 8 LS28 .... 57 E2
Bransby Rise LS28 .... 57 E2
Bransdale Ave Guiseley LS20 . 39 E8
  Normanton WF6 .... 123 A4
Bransdale Cl Baildon BD17 ... 38 A2
  Guiseley LS20 .... 39 E8
  Normanton WF6 .... 123 A4
Bransdale Clough BD6 .... 73 E1
Bransdale Garth LS20 .... 39 E8
Bransdale Gdns LS20 .... 39 E8
Bransdale Mews WF6 ...... 123 A4
Bransdale Wlk WF6 .... 123 A4
Branshaw Dr BD22 .... 34 E5
Branshaw Golf Course
  BD22 .... 34 D4
Branshaw Gr BD22 .... 34 E5
Branshaw Mount BD22 .... 34 E5
Branshaw Sch BD22 .... 35 A6
Branstone Gr WF5 .... 119 D1
Brant Ave HX2 .... 91 F4
Brant Bank La LS29 .... 7 D6
Brantcliffe Dr BD17 .... 38 C5
Brantcliffe Way BD17 .... 38 C5
Brantdale Cl BD2 .... 56 A4
Brantdale Rd BD2 .... 56 A4
Brantford St LS7 .... 204 A2
Branton Farm HX2 .... 111 C5
Brantwood Ave BD9 .... 54 C4
Brantwood Cl BD9 .... 54 C4
Brantwood Cres BD9 .... 54 C4
  Elland HX5 .... 134 E5
Brantwood Dr BD9 .... 54 C4
Brantwood Gr BD9 .... 54 B4
Brantwood Oval BD9 .... 54 C4
Brantwood Rd BD9 .... 54 B4
Brantwood Villas BD9 .... 54 C4
Branwell Ave WF17 .... 96 F3
Branwell Dr BD22 .... 51 C8
Branxholme Ind Est HD6 . 115 B7
Brassey Rd BD4 .... 75 A4
Brassey St HX1 .... 203 D2
Brassey Terr BD4 .... 75 A4
Brathay Gdns LS14 .... 62 A3
Bray Cl HD7 .... 73 D2
Braybrook Ct BD8 .... 55 D2
Brayside Ave HD2 .... 135 F2
Brayton App LS14 .... 62 C5
Brayton Cl LS14 .... 62 C5
Brayton Garth 10 LS14 ...... 62 D5
Brayton Gn LS14 .... 62 C5
Brayton Grange 12 LS14 .... 62 C5
Brayton Pl 11 LS14 .... 62 C5
Brayton Sq 18 LS14 .... 62 C5
Brayton Terr 1 LS14 .... 62 C5
Brayton W 21 LS14 .... 62 D5
Brazil St WF10 .... 124 C8
Bread St WF1 .... 216 B2
Break Neck HX3 .... 114 A8
Breakmoor Ave BD20 .... 5 D2
Breaks Rd BD12 .... 94 C6
Brear Ley Gdns WF15 ...... 117 A3
Brearcliffe Cl BD6 .... 94 A8
Brearcliffe Dr BD6 .... 94 A8
Brearcliffe Gr BD6 .... 94 A7
Brearcliffe Rd BD6 .... 94 A7
Brearcliffe St BD6 .... 94 A7
Brearley La HX2 .... 111 B8
Brearley St WF17 .... 118 B4
Brearton St BD1 .... 201 B4
Breary Ave LS18 .... 41 D1
Breary Cl LS16 .... 24 E3
Breary La LS16 .... 24 E3
Breary La E LS16 .... 24 E3
Breary Rise LS16 .... 24 E3
Breary Terr LS18 .... 41 D1
Breary Wlk LS18 .... 41 D1
Breck Lea HX6 .... 112 A3
Breck Willows HX6 .... 111 F2
Brecks Gdns LS25 .... 82 F3
Brecks La Kippax LS25 .... 83 C6
  Swillington LS26 .... 82 C4
Brecks Rd BD14 .... 73 C4
Brecon App LS9 .... 61 D1
Brecon Ave HD3 .... 135 A1
Brecon Cl 5 BD4 .... 75 F3
Brecon Ct LS9 .... 61 D1
Brecon Rise LS9 .... 61 D1
Bredon Ave BD18 .... 55 F7
Bredon Cl WF9 .... 181 F7
Breighton Adown BD6 ...... 93 D8
Bremner St LS21 .... 23 B8
Brendon Ct 8 BD4 .... 75 F3
Brendon Wlk BD4 .... 75 D2
Brentford Rd BD12 .... 94 C6
Brentlea Ave WF2 .... 142 B3
Brentwood Cl Batley WF17 . 118 E5
  Thorpe Audin WF8 .... 165 A8
Brentwood Gdns BD6 .... 94 D8
Brentwood Gr 8 LS12 ..... 209 F3
Brentwood St 11 LS12 .... 209 F3
Brentwood Terr 11 LS12 .. 209 F3
Bretfield Ct WF12 .... 139 F6
Brett Gdns LS11 .... 214 B4
Brettegate WF9 .... 181 C7
Bretton Country Pk WF4 . 176 F7
Bretton Hall Coll
  Wakefield WF2 .... 142 D2
  West Bretton WF4 .... 176 E6
Bretton Hall Coll (Annexe)
  WF10 .... 124 C7
Bretton La Crigglestone WF4 159 C3
  West Bretton WF4 .... 159 B2

Bretton St WF12 .... 139 D5
Brevitt St WF1 .... 142 E3
Brewerton La HX3 .... 117 F2
Brewery Ct HD3 .... 135 A1
Brewery Dr HD4 .... 153 F2
Brewery La
  Dewsbury WF12 .... 139 D8
  Knottingley WF11 .... 126 F4
  Queensbury BD13 .... 72 D3
Queensbury, Shibden Head
  BD13 .... 92 C7
Brewery Rd Ilkley LS29 .... 8 C4
  Keighley BD21 .... 35 A3
Brewery St 5 Batley WF16 117 D3
  1 Halifax HX3 .... 92 C2
  Leeds LS9 .... 208 B3
Todmorden OL14 .... 107 E8
Brewery Wharf WF14 .... 138 A4
Brewery Wharf Mus LS2 ... 212 A3
Brewery Yard HD5 .... 155 C3
Brexdale Ave LS25 .... 82 F3
Brian Ave HD5 .... 154 E5
Brian Cres LS15 .... 62 B3
Brian Pl LS15 .... 62 B3
Brian Royd La HX4 .... 133 F7
Brian St HD3 .... 135 B1
Brian View LS15 .... 62 C3
Briar Ave HD7 .... 170 C3
Briar Bank WF4 .... 163 A2
Briar Cl Batley WF16 .... 117 D5
  Elland HX5 .... 134 E5
  Pudsey LS28 .... 57 D3
Briar Dr HD3 .... 117 F2
Briar Gate LS22 .... 13 E2
Briar Gr Brierley S72 .... 181 A3
  Wakefield WF1 .... 142 E3
Briar Rhydding BD17 .... 38 D2
Briar St 8 OL13 .... 106 A1
Briar Wood BD18 .... 55 E7
Briardale Rd BD9 .... 54 B4
Briarfield Ave BD10 .... 56 A7
Briarfield Cl Bradford BD10 . 56 A7
  Ilkley LS29 .... 8 D3
Briarfield Gdns
  Gildersome LS27 .... 97 C6
  Shipley BD18 .... 55 C6
Briarfield Gr BD10 .... 56 A7
Briarfield Rd Holmfirth HD7 189 C2
  Shipley BD18 .... 55 C5
Briarlea Cl LS19 .... 39 F5
Briarlyn Ave HD3 .... 135 B3
Briarlyn Rd HD3 .... 135 B2
Briarmains Rd WF17 .... 96 F2
Briarsdale Croft LS8 .... 208 C3
Briarsdale Ct LS8 .... 208 C3
Briarsdale Garth LS8 .... 208 B3
Briarsdale Hts LS9 .... 208 C3
Briarsdale Mews LS8 .... 208 B3
Briarwood Ave
  Bradford BD6 .... 74 B1
  Keighley BD20 .... 18 F1
Briarwood Cl WF1 .... 121 D5
Briarwood Cres BD6 .... 74 B1
Briarwood Dr BD6 .... 74 B1
Briarwood Gr BD6 .... 74 B1
Brick Mill Rd LS28 .... 76 F6
Brick Row BD12 .... 94 E6
Brick St Cleckheaton BD19 . 116 C7
  Leeds LS9 .... 212 A3
  Wakefield WF2 .... 141 D7
Brick Terr HD6 .... 115 A3
Brick & Tile Terr HD6 ...... 115 A1
Brickbank HD5 .... 154 F3
Brickfield Gr HX2 .... 92 A5
Brickfield La HX2 .... 92 A5
Brickfield Terr HX2 .... 92 A5
Brickyard 7 WF14 .... 137 F5
Bride St OL14 .... 108 B6
Bridge Ave LS21 .... 23 A8
Bridge Cl Boston Spa LS23 .. 30 E8
  Clayton West HD8 .... 175 E2
  Horbury WF4 .... 140 E1
Bridge Croft HD3 .... 153 B4
Bridge Ct Hemsworth WF9 . 163 A2
  Leeds LS11 .... 211 E1
  Morley LS27 .... 98 B3
Bridge End Brighouse HD6 . 115 A1
  Clayton West HD8 .... 16 B6
Bridge End St OL14 .... 86 A1
Bridge Fold LS5 .... 59 A4
Bridge Foot LS23 .... 30 E8
Bridge Garth LS23 .... 30 E8
Bridge Gate HX7 .... 89 A3
Bridge La Holmfirth HD7 .. 189 A6
  Ilkley LS29 .... 8 C5
Knottingley WF11 .... 126 F5
  Shelf HX3 .... 93 B7
  Thorpe Audin WF8 .... 165 A8
Bridge Lanes HD7 .... 88 F3
Bridge Paddock LS22 .... 13 B1
Bridge Rd Boston Spa LS23 . 30 E8
  Brighouse HD6 .... 115 A2
  Horbury WF4 .... 140 E1
  Leeds, Holbeck LS11 .... 211 D1
  Leeds, Kirkstall LS5 .... 59 A4
  Pudsey LS13 .... 57 E5
  Silsden BD20 .... 5 D2
  Sutton in C BD20 .... 16 D5
Bridge St
  Batley, Bank Foot WF17 .. 118 C5
Batley, Birstall Smithies
  WF17 .... 117 E8
  Bradford BD1 .... 201 C2
  Castleford WF10 .... 124 E8
Huddersfield HD4 .... 171 H4

Bridge St continued
Huddersfield, Rashcliffe HD4 153 F3
Keighley BD21 .... 35 B6
Leeds LS2 .... 212 A4
Liversedge WF16 .... 117 C4
Mapplewell S75 .... 177 E1
Morley LS27 .... 98 B2
Normanton WF6 .... 123 C3
Oakworth BD22 .... 34 B2
Otley LS21 .... 23 A8
7 Pontefract WF8 .... 146 D8
Silsden BD20 .... 5 E2
Slaithwaite HD7 .... 152 A1
Sowerby Bridge HX6 .... 112 B3
1 Thornton BD13 .... 72 E6
Todmorden OL14 .... 108 B5
Wakefield WF1 .... 142 D4
Bridge Terr HX2 .... 90 E6
Bridge View LS13 .... 57 E6
Bridge Wood Cl LS18 ..... 41 D2
Bridge Wood View LS18 . 41 D2
Bridge Works Bsns Pk
HD7 .... 172 A4
Bridgegate Way BD10 ... 56 D5
Bridgehouse La BD22 ..... 51 C6
Bridgewater Ct LS6 .... 59 F6
Bridgewater Park Dr DN6 . 184 F2
Bridgewater Rd LS9 ...... 212 C1
Bridgeway BD4 .... 75 D3
Bridgland Ave LS29 .... 22 A5
Bridgwater Ho 13 BD5 .. 201 B1
Bridgwater Rd BD9 .... 55 A2
Bridle Ave WF5 .... 140 C8
Bridle Ct WF4 .... 158 E7
Bridle Dene HX3 .... 93 C5
Bridle La Netherton WF4 . 158 E7
Ossett WF5 .... 140 C8
Bridle Path Rd
Harewood LS17 .... 44 E5
Harewood LS17 .... 62 A2
Bridle Path Wlk 3 LS15 .. 62 A2
Bridle Pl WF5 .... 140 D8
Bridle St WF17 .... 118 E5
Bridle Stile HX3 .... 93 C5
Bridle Stile La BD13 .... 72 E2
Bridley Brook HD7 .... 170 A5
Bridley Dr HD7 .... 170 A8
Brier Hey Cl HX7 .... 89 F1
Brier Hey La HX7 .... 89 F1
Brier Hill Cl BD19 .... 116 A6
Brier Hill View HD2 .... 136 D5
Brier La Brighouse HD6 ... 114 E2
Ryhill WF4 .... 180 C8
Brier St Halifax HX3 .... 92 B2
Keighley BD21 .... 35 B4
Brierdene BD20 .... 5 E2
Brierlands Cl LS25 .... 83 B8
Brierlands Fold LS25 ...... 83 B8
Brierlands La LS25 .... 83 B8
Brierley C of E First Sch
S72 .... 181 A3
Brierley Cl BD18 .... 55 C6
Brierley Cres WF9 .... 182 C3
Brierley Rd
Grimethorpe S72 .... 181 A1
Shafton S72 .... 180 D2
South Hiendley S72 .... 180 E5
Briery Cl LS29 .... 7 E4
Briery Field BD18 .... 55 B5
Briery Gr WF14 .... 138 A2
Briestfield Rd WF12 .... 156 C5
Big Royd HX6 .... 132 E5
Brigg Gdns BD22 .... 34 F7
Brigg's Ave WF10 .... 124 E6
Briggate Brighouse HD6 . 115 A2
Elland HX5 .... 134 F7
Huddersfield HD5 .... 155 A7
Leeds LS1 .... 211 F3
Shipley BD17 .... 55 B8
Shipley BD18 .... 55 C7
Silsden BD20 .... 5 E2
Briggland Ct BD15 .... 53 C5
Briggs Ave BD6 .... 74 A1
Briggs Gr BD6 .... 74 A1
Briggs Pl BD6 .... 74 A1
Briggs Rd S71 .... 179 C1
Briggs Row WF7 .... 145 D4
Briggs St BD13 .... 72 E1
Briggs Terr 2 HD5 .... 154 D6
Brighouse
& Denholme Gate Rd
Northowram HX3 .... 93 B4
Queensbury HX3 .... 92 F6
Shelf HX3 .... 93 B4
Brighouse & Denholme Rd
BD13 .... 72 B3
Brighouse High Sch
Brighouse HD6 .... 115 A2
Brighouse, Hove Edge HD6 . 114 F5
Brighouse Liby
& Smith Art Gal HD6 .... 115 A3
Brighouse Rd Bradford BD12 . 94 D6
Brighouse HX3 .... 114 C7
Denholme HD7 .... 71 E6
Huddersfield HD3 .... 135 B3
Queensbury BD13 .... 92 F7
Shelf BD13, HX3 .... 92 F7
Brighouse Wood La HD6 .. 114 F3
Brighouse Wood Row HD6 114 F3
Bright St Bradford BD15 .. 54 B1
3 Bradford, Clayton BD14 . 73 B4
1 Dewsbury WF13 .... 118 C1
East Ardsley WF3 .... 120 E8
Farnhill BD20 .... 4 D1
8 Haworth BD22 .... 51 D7
Mirfield WF14 .... 138 A8
Morley LS27 .... 98 A4
Pudsey LS28 .... 57 F2

Bright St continued
Queensbury BD13 .... 72 F1
Sowerby Bridge HX6 .... 112 B5
Todmorden OL14 .... 108 A3
Brighton Ave LS27 .... 97 F5
Brighton Cl WF17 .... 117 E6
Brighton Cliff LS13 .... 58 C2
Brighton Gr Halifax HX1 . 202 C4
Leeds LS13 .... 58 D1
Brighton Rd LS29 .... 8 E3
Brighton St Batley WF16 . 117 D4
Bradford BD10 .... 39 A1
2 Halifax HX3 .... 92 A1
Shipley BD17 .... 55 B8
Todmorden OL14 .... 86 C1
Wakefield WF2 .... 142 A5
Brighton Terr BD19 .... 94 F1
Brignall Cl LS29 .... 207 F1
Brignall Garth LS9 .... 207 F1
Brignall Way LS9 .... 207 F1
Brigshaw Dr WF10 .... 102 F6
Brigshaw High Sch WF10 . 102 F7
Brigshaw La LS25, WF10 . 103 A8
Brindle Park Dr WF10 ..... 125 A6
Brindley Gr BD8 .... 73 C7
Brindley Rd BD20 .... 17 F8
Brindley Way WF2 .... 120 F4
Brisbane Ave BD2 .... 55 F3
Briscoe La HX4 .... 134 B7
Bristfield Rd WF12 .... 157 A8
Bristol Ave BD20 .... 36 B8
Bristol St Halifax HX3 .... 113 D3
Leeds LS2 .... 207 D1
Britannia Ave OL13 .... 106 A2
Britannia Bldgs LS27 ...... 97 F2
Britannia Cl 8 LS28 .... 57 F2
Britannia Ct LS13 .... 77 A8
Britannia Rd
Huddersfield HD3, HD7 .... 152 F4
Morley LS27 .... 98 A2
Slaithwaite HD7 .... 169 F8
Britannia Sq LS27 .... 97 F2
Britannia St Bingley BD16 . 37 A3
Bradford BD5 .... 201 C2
Leeds LS1 .... 211 E3
Pudsey LS28 .... 58 A2
Britannia Terr BD19 ...... 116 D8
British Liby Document
Supply Ctr The LS23 .... 15 B3
Briton St S63 .... 194 E1
Britton St S63 .... 194 E1
Britton St BD19 .... 116 F6
Broad Acres WF4 .... 160 A7
Broad Balk DN5 .... 195 E6
Broad Carr La Elland HX4 . 134 C4
Holmfirth HD7 .... 190 A2
Broad Cut Rd WF4 .... 159 D7
Broad Gate
Todmorden OL14 .... 109 A5
Cronton, Cross Stone
OL14 .... 108 D6
Broad Head La BD20 .... 33 D3
Broad Ings Way HX3 .... 93 C5
Broad La Bradford BD4 .... 75 D5
Hebden Bridge HX7 .... 88 B6
Heptonstall HX7 .... 88 B6
Holmfirth HD7 .... 188 D5
Huddersfield HD5 .... 154 D6
Leeds LS5, LS13, LS28 ...... 58 C3
Pontefract WF8 .... 125 D1
South Elmsall WF9 .... 182 E1
South Kirkby WF9 .... 194 C8
Sowerby Bridge HX2 .... 111 C5
Todmorden OL14 .... 87 D1
Broad Lane Bsns Ctr WF3 . 182 F1
Broad Lane Cl LS13 .... 58 E4
Broad Oak HD7 .... 152 E2
Broad Oak La
Brighouse HX3 .... 114 D6
Ingbirchworth S36 .... 192 D2
Broad Oak Pl HX3 .... 114 D6
Broad Oak St HX3 .... 114 D6
Broad St Bradford BD1 .. 201 B3
Dewsbury WF13 .... 139 A6
Halifax HX1 .... 203 E3
Pudsey LS28 .... 57 C3
Todmorden OL14 .... 108 B6
Broad Tree Rd HX3 .... 92 A2
Broad View WF5 .... 140 F5
Broad Way WF12 .... 139 E1
Broadacre Rd WF5 .... 140 F5
Broadbent Croft HD7 ..... 172 A4
Broadcroft Chase WF3 .. 119 E7
Broadcroft Dr WF3 .... 119 E8
Broadcroft Gr WF3 .... 119 E8
Broadcroft Way WF3 ..... 119 E8
Broadfield Cl BD4 .... 75 D1
Broadfield Ind Est HD1 .. 153 F3
Broadfield Pk HD7 .... 188 C2
Broadfield Way LS29 .... 6 D8
Broadfolds BD14 .... 73 C4
Broadgate Elland HX4 .... 134 A2
Leeds LS18 .... 41 D1
Ossett WF5 .... 140 E5
Broadgate Ave LS18 .... 41 D1
Broadgate Cres
Horsforth LS18 .... 58 C8
Huddersfield HD5 .... 154 D4
Broadgate Dr LS18 .... 41 D1
Broadgate La LS18 .... 41 C1
Broadgate Primary Sch
LS18 .... 58 C8
Broadgate Rise LS18 .... 58 D8
Broadgate Wlk LS18 .... 58 C8
Broadlands BD20 .... 35 A8
Broadlands Rd WF17 ..... 170 D3
Broadlands St BD4 .... 75 D4
Broadlea Ave LS13 .... 58 E4

Broadlea Cl LS13 .... 58 E4
Broadlea Cres
Bradford BD5 .... 74 F3
Leeds LS13 .... 58 E4
Broadlea Gdns LS13 .... 58 E4
Broadlea Gr LS13 .... 58 E4
Broadlea Hill LS13 .... 58 E4
Broadlea Mount LS13 .... 58 E4
Broadlea Pl LS13 .... 58 E3
Broadlea Rd LS13 .... 58 E4
Broadlea St LS13 .... 58 E4
Broadlea Terr LS13 .... 58 E4
Broadlea View LS13 .... 58 D4
Broadley Ave HX2 .... 91 B2
Broadley Cl HX2 .... 91 C1
Broadley Cres HX2 .... 91 C1
Broadley Gr HX2 .... 91 C1
Broadley Lathe HX2 .... 91 C2
Broadley Rd HX2 .... 91 B1
Broadmead WF10 .... 124 F8
Broadmeadows WF1 .... 121 D5
Broadowler La WF5 .... 140 F7
Broadowler La WF5 .... 140 F5
Broadstone Rd
Denby Dale HD8 .... 190 F3
Ingbirchworth S36 .... 191 A1
Broadstone St OL14 ...... 108 D6
Broadstone Way BD4 ...... 75 E3
Broadwalk LS21 .... 10 E1
Broadway Bingley BD16 .. 37 A2
Bradford BD1 .... 201 C3
Guiseley LS20 .... 39 B1
Halifax HX3 .... 113 F5
Horsforth LS18 .... 58 C8
6 Huddersfield HD1 ..... 154 B7
Leeds, Halton LS15 .... 80 F7
Leeds, Hawksworth LS5 .... 58 E7
Mapplewell S75 .... 178 B1
Pontefract WF8 .... 146 E7
South Elmsall WF9 .... 182 E1
Sowerby Bridge HX6 .... 111 E3
Wakefield WF2 .... 141 D4
Broadway Ave
Bradford BD5 .... 74 D2
Leeds LS6 .... 205 E2
Broadway Cl BD5 .... 74 D2
Broadway Dr HX6 .... 111 E3
Broadway 7 LS18 .... 58 B8
Broadway Terr WF9 ..... 182 E1
Broadwell Rd WF5 .... 140 F5
Broadwood Ave HX2 ...... 91 C1
Brock Bank HD5 .... 154 F7
Brockadale Ave WF8 ...... 146 D5
Brockholes C of E
Primary Sch HD7 .... 172 C2
Brockholes La HD7 .... 172 C3
Brockholes Rd
Honley HD4 .... 172 D4
Kirkburton HD7 .... 172 D4
Brocklebes Sta HD7 .... 172 C3
Brocklesby Dr BD15 .... 73 B8
Brocks HX2 .... 111 C6
Brockstones HX4 .... 133 F7
Brockswood Cl WF2 ...... 161 C5
Brockwell Gdns HX6 .... 112 A3
Brockwell La HX6 .... 112 A3
Brodetsky Primary Sch
LS17 .... 43 C4
Brodley Cl HX3 .... 114 C8
Brodrick Ct LS6 .... 59 D5
Broken Cross HD5 .... 154 E2
Broken Way BD5 .... 74 D2
Bromet Pl BD2 .... 56 B4
Bromfield Ct S71 .... 179 D4
Bromford Rd BD4 .... 75 E3
Bromley Ave HD7 .... 189 D7
Bromley Gr BD22 .... 34 E5
Bromley Mount WF1 ..... 142 D4
Bromley Rd Batley WF17 . 118 E3
Bingley BD16 .... 36 F4
Huddersfield HD2 .... 135 F1
Shipley BD18 .... 54 E8
Bromley St WF17 .... 118 D3
Brompton Ave BD4 .... 75 A4
Brompton Gr 2 LS11 ... 214 B2
Brompton Mount 8 LS11 . 214 B2
Brompton Rd BD4 .... 75 B4
Brompton Row 22 LS11 . 214 B2
Brompton Terr 4 LS11 . 214 B2
Brompton View 9 LS11 . 214 B2
Bronshill Gr BD15 .... 54 C1
Bronte Ave WF11 .... 126 B4
Bronte Bridge BD22 .... 50 B4
Bronte Cl Batley WF13 .. 117 F2
Bradford BD9 .... 54 E2
Cleckheaton BD19 .... 96 B1
Huddersfield HD4 .... 153 D3
Bronte Ct WF8 .... 125 D2
Bronte Dr BD20 .... 34 F3
Bronte Gr Hemsworth WF9 . 181 C6
Mirfield WF14 .... 138 A4
Bronte House LS7 .... 206 C3
Bronte House Sch BD10 .. 39 F2
Bronte Middle Sch BD22 . 34 F5
Bronte Old Rd BD13 .... 72 C6
Bronte Parsonage Mus
BD22 .... 51 B7
Bronte Pl BD13 .... 72 E6
Bronte Rd WF17 .... 96 E1
Bronte St 1 Haworth BD22 . 51 B7
Keighley BD21 .... 35 D8
Bronte Villas BD22 .... 51 F8
Bronte Way WF14 .... 138 C4
Brook Cl WF5 .... 140 F3
Brook Cotts HX6 .... 132 B7
Brook Dr HX4 .... 134 C4
Brook Field WF14 .... 137 F2

Brook Gdns
17 Dewsbury WF13 .... 139 B8
Meltham HD7 .... 170 D3
Brook Grain Hill HD6 .... 136 A8
Brook Grains La HX6 .... 132 D2
Brook Hill BD17 .... 38 D3
Brook Hill La
Carlecotes S36 .... 200 B3
Dunford Bridge S36 .... 199 F2
Brook La Cleckheaton WF15 . 116 C4
Huddersfield HD7 .... 152 D4
Huddersfield HD4 .... 42 F1
Brook Rd 4 WF12 .... 139 B7
Brook Side HD7 .... 152 A2
Brook Side Bradford BD12 . 95 B5
Castleford WF10 .... 104 C3
Dewsbury WF13 .... 117 F1
Elland HX5 .... 135 A6
11 Hebden Bridge HX7 . 89 A4
Huddersfield HD1 .... 154 A7
Huddersfield, Moldgreen
HD5 .... 154 D6
Huddersfield, Yews Hill HD1 . 153 E4
Ilkley LS29 .... 8 B8
Normanton WF6 .... 122 F3
Ossett WF5 .... 140 D5
10 Todmorden OL14 ...... 108 B5
Wakefield WF2 .... 216 B2
Brook Terr Halifax HX2 .... 92 A2
Brook The
Hebden Bridge HX7 .... 110 E8
Littleborough OL15 .... 129 C1
Brook's Yd 8 HX1 .... 154 A6
Brookdale OL14 .... 108 A2
Brookdale Ave WF5 ...... 119 D1
Brookdale Bank HD3 ..... 153 A5
Brooke Ct WF8 .... 146 D5
Brooke St 8 Batley WF17 . 118 C3
Brighouse HD6 .... 115 A1
Cleckheaton BD19 .... 116 E7
7 Keighley BD21 .... 35 C6
Brooke Terr LS10 .... 99 F7
Brookfield LS29 .... 6 C2
Brookfield Ave
Normanton WF6 .... 123 C2
Pudsey LS28 .... 57 D6
Shipley BD18 .... 55 D8
Brookfield Ct
Leeds LS8 .... 207 F4
Pudsey LS28 .... 57 D6
Brookfield Dr WF7 .... 164 C8
Brookfield First Sch BD10 . 56 E6
Brookfield Gdns LS13 .... 57 D6
Brookfield Pl LS6 .... 59 E6
Brookfield Rd Bradford BD3 . 75 A8
Leeds LS6 .... 59 E6
Shipley BD18 .... 55 D8
Brookfield St Leeds LS10 . 212 A1
Leeds LS10 .... 80 A4
Todmorden OL14 .... 86 C1
Brookfield Terr
Cleckheaton BD19 .... 95 E1
Leeds LS10 .... 212 A1
Brookfield View BD19 ..... 95 E1
Brookfield Way HD5 ...... 137 C1
Brookfields Ave BD12 .... 94 E1
Brookfields Rd BD12 ...... 94 E1
Brookfoot Ave BD11 ...... 96 A5
Brookfoot Bsns Pk HD6 . 114 E3
Brookfoot La HD6 .... 114 E3
Brookgreen HX3 .... 114 C8
Brookhill Ave LS17 .... 43 E4
Brookhill Cl LS17 .... 43 E4
Brookhill Cres LS17 .... 43 E4
Brookhill Dr LS17 .... 43 E4
Brookhill Gr LS17 .... 43 E4
Brookhouse Gdns BD10 .. 56 D8
Brookland Towers 3 LS14 . 62 A5
Brooklands Brighouse HD3 . 114 D7
East Keswick LS17 .... 28 C5
Huddersfield HD2 .... 136 F5
Brooklands Ave Elland HX4 . 134 B4
Leeds LS14 .... 62 A4
Walton WF2 .... 161 B6
Brooklands Cl WF5 .... 141 A4
Brooklands Dr Leeds LS14 . 61 F4
Yeadon LS19 .... 40 B6
Brooklands Garth LS14 .. 61 F4
Brooklands Gr LS29 .... 22 B5
Brooklands La Leeds LS14 . 61 F4
Menston LS29 .... 22 B5
Brooklands Rd WF2 ...... 161 C7
Brooklands View
Leeds LS14 .... 61 F4
Walton WF2 .... 161 C2
Brooklands Way LS29 .... 22 A5
Brooklands Wlk LS29 ..... 22 B5
Brookleigh LS20 .... 39 F8
Brooklyn Ave
Huddersfield HD5 .... 155 A6
Leeds LS12 .... 210 A3
Brooklyn Ct BD19 .... 116 D8
Brooklyn Dr BD19 .... 116 D8
Brooklyn Pl LS12 .... 209 F3
Brooklyn Rd BD19 .... 116 D8
Brooklyn St Keighley BD20 . 18 A2
Leeds LS12 .... 209 F3
Brooklyn Terr
Brighouse HD6 .... 114 E5
Leeds LS12 .... 209 F3
Brookroyd Ave HD6 ...... 115 B6
Brookroyd Gdns 3 WF17 . 118 F5

Brookroyd La WF17 .... 117 F8
Brooks Terr BD13 .... 73 B2
Brooks Yd Dewsbury WF13 . 139 B7
Huddersfield HD2 .... 137 A5
Brooksbank WF2 .... 216 A2
Brooksbank Ave BD7 ...... 73 E5
Brooksbank Dr LS15 .... 81 A8
Brooksbank Gdns HX5 .. 134 F6
Brooksbank Sch The HX5 . 134 E6
Brooksfield WF9 .... 182 D2
Brookside Collingham LS22 . 29 B8
Denby Dale HD8 .... 191 F6
Hebden Bridge HX7 .... 88 E4
Hemsworth WF9 .... 181 E7
Leeds LS17 .... 43 E5
Brookside Fold 2 BD22 .. 51 C2
Brookside St WF9 .... 182 F3
Brookside Terr WF9 ...... 182 F3
Brookway WF7 .... 145 D5
Broom Cl Mapplewell S75 . 178 A1
Middleton LS10 .... 99 E7
Broom Cres LS10 .... 99 E7
Broom Cross LS10 .... 99 E7
Broom Field La HD8 ...... 175 B7
Broom Garth LS10 .... 99 E7
Broom Gdns LS10 .... 99 E7
Broom Gr LS10 .... 99 E7
Broom Hall Ave WF1 .... 121 A2
Broom Hall Cres WF1 .... 121 A2
Broom Hill Rd HX4 .... 151 D8
Broom Lawn LS10 .... 99 E7
Broom Mount LS10 .... 99 E7
Broom Nook LS10 .... 99 E7
Broom Pl LS10 .... 99 E7
Broom Rd LS10 .... 99 E7
Broom St Bradford BD4 .. 201 C2
Cleckheaton BD19 .... 116 B6
7 Keighley BD21 .... 35 C6
Broom Terr LS10 .... 99 E7
Broom View LS10 .... 99 E7
Broom Wlk WF17 .... 118 C5
Broombank Denby Dale HD8 . 191 F5
Huddersfield HD2 .... 135 D2
Broomcroft BD14 .... 73 B4
Broomcroft Rd WF5 ...... 140 D4
Broome Ave BD2 .... 55 E3
Broomer St WF13 .... 138 D6
Broomer St WF13 .... 138 D6
Bromfield Elland HX5 .... 134 D6
Leeds LS16 .... 42 B4
Broomfield Ave HX3 ...... 113 B3
Broomfield Bsns Pk HD1 . 154 A4
Broomfield Cl HD8 .... 175 C7
Broomfield Pl
Bradford BD14 .... 73 A3
Leeds LS6 .... 205 D3
Broomfield Rd
Huddersfield HD1 .... 136 A5
Huddersfield, Marsh HD1 . 153 D6
4 Keighley BD21 .... 35 D6
Leeds LS6 .... 205 D4
Broomfield St
Keighley BD21 .... 35 B7
3 Leeds LS6 .... 205 D3
Queensbury BD13 .... 72 E1
Broomfield Terr
Cleckheaton BD19 .... 116 B7
Huddersfield HD1 .... 153 D7
Leeds LS6 .... 205 D3
Broomhill Ave Keighley BD21 . 35 A5
Knottingley WF11 .... 127 B3
Leeds LS17 .... 43 C1
Broomhill Cl Holmfirth HD7 . 189 D3
Knottingley WF11 .... 127 B3
Broomhill Cres
Knottingley WF11 .... 127 B3
Leeds LS17 .... 43 C1
Broomhill Dr
Keighley BD21 .... 35 A5
Knottingley WF11 .... 127 B3
Leeds LS17 .... 43 C1
Broomhill Gr Keighley BD21 . 35 A5
Knottingley WF11 .... 127 B3
Broomhill Mount BD21 ... 35 A5
Broomhill Pl WF11 .... 127 B3
Broomhill Sq WF11 .... 127 B3
Broomhill St BD21 .... 35 A4
Broomhill Terr WF17 .... 118 D4
Broomhill Way BD21 .... 35 B5
Broomhill Wlk
Keighley BD21 .... 35 A5
Leeds LS17 .... 43 C1
Bromsgrove HD3 .... 152 A2
Broomsdale Rd WF17 .... 118 E5
Broomwood Middle Sch
BD4 .... 75 D1
Brosmy Lea La HD7 .... 188 F7
Broster Ave BD22 .... 34 F7
Brotherton Ave WF1 ..... 142 E7
Brotherton Primary Sch
WF11 .... 126 C8
Brougham Rd 11
Halifax HX3 .... 92 C1
Marsden HD7 .... 169 A4
Brougham St 12 HX3 ...... 92 C1
Brougham Terr 13 HX3 .. 92 C1
Broughton Ave Bradford BD4 . 75 B1
Leeds LS9 .... 208 A2

Broughton Rd HD4 ... 153 B3
Broughton St HX7 ... 89 A4
Broughton Terr Leeds LS9 ... 208 A2
  7 Pudsey LS28 ... 76 E8
Broughtons Yd WF11 ... 126 C5
Brow Bottom La HX2 ... 91 B6
Brow Foot Gate La HX2 ... 112 D6
Brow Grains Rd HD7 ... 170 B2
Brow La Denby Dale HD8 ... 192 D6
  Halifax HX3 ... 92 B6
  Holmfirth HD7 ... 188 E3
  Northowram HX3 ... 92 E4
  Shelf HX3 ... 93 D6
  Thornton BD14 ... 72 F3
Brow Quarry Ind Est HX3 ... 114 D6
Brow Rd Haworth BD22 ... 51 D6
  Huddersfield HD1 ... 153 E5
Brow St BD21 ... 35 D6
Brow Top Rd BD22 ... 51 E7
Brow Wood Cres BD2 ... 55 E3
Brow Wood Rd HX3 ... 93 D6
Brow Wood Rise HX3 ... 93 D6
Browcliff BD20 ... 5 E2
Browfield Terr BD20 ... 5 E2
Browfield View BD20 ... 34 E5
Browfoot BD18 ... 55 D8
Browfoot Dr HX2 ... 112 D6
Browgate BD17 ... 38 C4
Brown Ave LS11 ... 213 E4
Brown Bank La BD20 ... 6 B4
Brown Bank Terr BD20 ... 16 B7
Brown Birks St 1 OL14 ... 86 B1
Brown Hill Ave LS9 ... 208 A2
Brown Hill Cl BD11 ... 96 A7
Brown Hill Cres LS9 ... 208 A2
Brown Hill Dr BD11 ... 96 A6
Brown Hill La HX7 ... 67 E5
Brown Hill Terr LS9 ... 208 A2
Brown La E LS11 ... 210 C3
Brown La W LS11, LS12 ... 210 B1
Brown Pl LS11 ... 213 E4
Brown Rd LS11 ... 213 E4
Brown Royd Ave HD5 ... 154 D8
Brown St 19 Keighley BD21 ... 35 D8
  Mirfield WF14 ... 137 F5
Brown's Edge Rd S36 ... 200 E8
Brown's Knoll Rd HD4 ... 173 A3
Brown's Pl WF17 ... 118 A4
Brown's St WF17 ... 118 C4
Brownberrie Ave LS18 ... 41 C3
Brownberrie Cres LS18 ... 41 B3
Brownberrie Dr LS18 ... 41 C3
Brownberrie Gdns LS18 ... 41 B3
Brownberrie La LS18 ... 41 B3
Brownberrie Wlk LS18 ... 41 C3
Brownhill Cl WF17 ... 96 F1
Brownhill Cres WF8 ... 163 A1
Brownhill Garth WF17 ... 96 F1
Brownhill Inf Sch WF17 ... 96 F1
Brownhill La HD7 ... 198 B8
Brownhill Primary Sch LS9 ... 208 A1
Brownhill Rd WF17 ... 96 F1
Browning Ave LS15 ... 113 D4
Browning Rd HD2 ... 136 D3
Browning St BD3 ... 75 B7
Brownings The HX3 ... 114 C7
Brownlea Cl LS19 ... 39 F5
Brownroyd Ave LS11 ... 179 C2
Brownroyd Hill Rd BD6 ... 74 B2
Brownroyd Rd HD7 ... 171 E4
Brownroyd St Bradford BD6 ... 74 B2
  Bradford, Shearbridge BD7 ... 74 B6
Brownroyd Wlk BD6 ... 74 B2
Browns BD20 ... 4 C6
Browsfield Rd LS29 ... 6 D8
Browsholme St 2 BD21 ... 35 C6
Brownwood Terr BD6 ... 93 F7
Bruce Gdns LS12 ... 210 B3
Bruce Lawn LS12 ... 210 B3
Bruce St HX1 ... 202 B2
Brudenell Ave LS6 ... 205 F3
Brudenell Gr LS6 ... 205 F3
Brudenell Mount LS6 ... 205 F3
Brudenell Primary Sch LS6 ... 205 E3
Brudenell Rd LS6 ... 205 F3
Brudenell St LS6 ... 205 F3
Brudenell View LS6 ... 205 F3
Brunel Cl BD9 ... 55 A2
Brunel Ct 3 HX3 ... 92 B2
Brunel Gdns 7 BD5 ... 74 E3
Brunel Rd WF2 ... 120 F4
Brunswick Ave HX1 ... 162 B2
Brunswick Arc 8 BD21 ... 35 C7
Brunswick Ct LS2 ... 207 D1
Brunswick Dr WF13 ... 118 A1
Brunswick Gdns
  Garforth LS25 ... 82 F7
  4 Halifax HX1 ... 203 D3
Brunswick Gr WF1 ... 216 B3
Brunswick House BD16 ... 37 B2
Brunswick Pl
  Bradford BD10 ... 56 D7
  3 Morley LS27 ... 98 B4
Brunswick Rd
  Bradford BD10 ... 56 D7
  Pudsey LS28 ... 76 E8
Brunswick Row LS2 ... 207 D1
Brunswick St
  8 Batley WF17 ... 118 C5
  Batley, Heckmondwike WF16 ... 117 D3

Brunswick St continued
  Bingley BD16 ... 37 B3
  Cullingworth BD13 ... 52 E6
  Dearne S63 ... 194 F1
  Dewsbury WF13 ... 118 A1
  Hebden Bridge HX7 ... 88 F3
  Huddersfield HD1 ... 154 A6
  Morley LS27 ... 98 A5
  1 Queensbury BD13 ... 72 F1
  Wakefield WF1 ... 216 C2
Brunswick Terr
  Leeds LS2 ... 206 C1
  Morley LS27 ... 98 B4
Bruntcliffe Ave LS27 ... 97 F5
Bruntcliffe Cl LS27 ... 97 F5
Bruntcliffe Dr LS27 ... 97 F4
Bruntcliffe High Sch LS27 ... 97 F4
Bruntcliffe La LS27 ... 97 E4
Bruntcliffe Rd LS27 ... 97 E4
Bruntcliffe Way LS27 ... 97 F5
Brunthwaite Bridge La BD20 ... 18 A8
Brunthwaite La BD20 ... 6 A1
Brussels St LS9 ... 212 A3
Bryan Cl HF10 ... 124 A8
Bryan Rd Elland HX5 ... 134 D6
  Huddersfield HD2 ... 135 D1
Bryan St 8
  Brighouse HD6 ... 115 A1
  Pudsey LS28 ... 57 D3
Bryan St N LS28 ... 57 D4
Bryan Terr HD3 ... 152 E6
Bryanstone Rd BD4 ... 75 D5
Bryer St WF13 ... 139 C8
Bryngate LS26 ... 101 C6
Bryony Cl LS10 ... 99 F5
Buchan Towers 2 BD5 ... 201 B1
Buck La BD17 ... 38 F3
Buck Mill La BD10 ... 39 A2
Buck St Bradford BD3 ... 201 D2
  Denholme BD13 ... 71 E8
Buck Stone Ave LS17 ... 42 F4
Buck Stone Cl LS17 ... 43 A4
Buck Stone Cres LS17 ... 43 A4
Buck Stone Dr LS17 ... 42 F4
Buck Stone Gdns LS17 ... 43 A4
Buck Stone Gn LS17 ... 42 F4
Buck Stone Gr LS17 ... 42 F4
Buck Stone La BD20 ... 16 A1
Buck Stone Mount LS17 ... 42 F4
Buck Stone Oval LS17 ... 42 F4
Buck Stone Rd LS17 ... 42 F4
Buck Stone Rise LS17 ... 42 F4
Buck Stone View LS17 ... 42 F4
Buck Stone Way LS17 ... 42 F4
Buckden BD20 ... 5 E2
Buckden Rd HD3 ... 153 D8
Buckfast Cft BD10 ... 56 B7
Buckingham Ave LS6 ... 205 E4
Buckingham Cres BD2 ... 55 F4
Buckingham Ct WF1 ... 142 F4
Buckingham Dr Leeds LS6 ... 205 E4
  Wakefield WF1 ... 142 F3
Buckingham Gr LS6 ... 205 E4
Buckingham Mount LS6 ... 205 E3
Buckingham Rd LS6 ... 205 E4
Buckingham Way
  Byram WF11 ... 126 C7
  Royston S71 ... 179 B4
Buckland Pl HX1 ... 202 A2
Buckland Rd 3 BD8 ... 73 F8
Buckle La Menston LS29 ... 22 C4
  Normanton WF6 ... 123 A2
Buckley Ave HX1 ... 214 B3
Buckley La HX2 ... 91 C2
Buckley View LS28 ... 108 A6
Buckley Wood Bottom 10
  OL14 ... 108 B5
Buckrose St HD1 ... 136 A1
Buckstone Dr LS19 ... 40 B3
Buckthorne Cl WF3 ... 120 D8
Buckthorne Ct WF3 ... 120 D8
Buckthorne Dr WF3 ... 120 D8
Buckthorne Fold WF3 ... 120 D8
Buckton Cl LS11 ... 214 A4
Buckton Mount LS11 ... 214 A4
Buckton View LS11 ... 214 A4
Bude Rd Bradford BD5 ... 74 F1
  Leeds LS11 ... 214 B3
Bugler Terr WF4 ... 140 E1
Bula Cl LS25 ... 83 B2
Bulay Rd HD1 ... 153 F4
Bull Close La HX1 ... 203 E2
Bull Gn HX1 ... 203 E3
Bull Green Rd HD3 ... 152 F6
Bull Hill BD22 ... 51 C1
Bull La Crigglestone WF4 ... 159 F5
  South Kirkby WF9 ... 182 C2
Bull Ring WF1 ... 216 B2
Bull Royd Ave BD8 ... 73 E8
Bull Royd Cres BD8 ... 73 E8
Bull Royd Dr BD8 ... 73 E8
Bull Royd La BD8 ... 73 E8
Bullace Trees La WF15 ... 116 E3
Bullenshaw Rd WF9 ... 181 D6
Buller Cl LS9 ... 208 B1
Buller Ct LS9 ... 208 B1
Buller Gr LS9 ... 208 B1
Buller St Bradford BD4 ... 75 C5
  6 Rothwell LS26 ... 101 C6
Bullerthorpe La LS15, LS26 ... 83 E4
Bullfield The BD16 ... 53 B8
Bullfields Cl WF12 ... 139 E2
Bullough La Leeds LS26 ... 81 A1
  Rothwell LS26 ... 100 F8
Bullstyle Rd WF8 ... 146 C6

Bulrush Bsns Pk WF17 ... 118 B7
Bungalow Rd BD20 ... 16 C6
Bungalows The
  Clayton West HD8 ... 175 E2
  Halifax HX2 ... 91 D1
  Halifax, Lee Mount HX3 ... 92 A4
  Halifax, Sutherhebble HX3 ... 113 E2
  Leeds LS11 ... 62 D3
  Normanton WF6 ... 123 A5
  Ossett WF5 ... 140 C6
Bunker's Hill La BD22 ... 34 D5
Bunkers Hill
  Aberford LS25 ... 64 E6
  Guiseley BD17 ... 39 B5
  Holmfirth HD7 ... 188 E3
  Wakefield WF2 ... 120 F2
Bunkers La HX7 ... 117 F4
Bunney Gr HX3 ... 92 F4
Bunny Pk HD4 ... 153 D3
Burbeary Rd HD1 ... 153 E3
Burberry Cl BD4 ... 95 C8
Burchett Gr LS6 ... 206 A4
Burchett Pl LS6 ... 206 A4
Burchett Terr LS6 ... 206 B4
Burcote Dr HD3 ... 134 B1
Burdale Pl BD7 ... 74 B6
Burdett Terr 5 LS4 ... 59 C2
Burdock Way HX1 ... 203 D3
Burfitts Rd HD3 ... 153 B7
Burgh Mill La WF13 ... 139 A7
Burhouse Ct HD7 ... 171 F4
Burkill St WF1 ... 142 D2
Burking Rd WF13 ... 139 B8
Burlees La HX7 ... 89 C2
Burleigh St 8 HX1 ... 202 B1
Burley Bank La HD7 ... 197 E6
Burley C E First Sch LS29 ... 9 E1
Burley Ct Leeds LS4 ... 205 D1
  Steeton BD20 ... 17 C7
Burley Grange Rd 2 LS4 ... 59 C2
Burley Hill Cres LS4 ... 59 B3
Burley Hill Dr LS4 ... 59 C3
Burley in Wharfedale Sta
  LS29 ... 21 E8
Burley La Horsforth LS18 ... 58 B7
  Menston LS29 ... 21 F5
Burley Lodge Pl LS6 ... 205 E1
Burley Lodge Rd LS6 ... 205 E2
Burley Lodge St LS6 ... 205 E1
Burley Lodge Terr LS6 ... 205 E1
Burley Mews BD20 ... 17 C5
Burley Middle Sch LS29 ... 9 F1
Burley Park Sta LS4 ... 205 D3
Burley Pl LS4 ... 205 E1
Burley Rd Leeds LS3, LS4 ... 205 D2
  Menston LS29 ... 22 A6
Burley St 10 Elland HX5 ... 134 F6
  Leeds LS3 ... 210 C4
  Shipley BD2 ... 55 D4
Burley St Matthias' Sch
  LS4 ... 205 D2
Burley Wlk WF17 ... 118 B5
Burley Wood Cres LS4 ... 59 C3
Burley Wood La LS4 ... 59 C3
Burley Wood Mount LS4 ... 59 B3
Burley Wood View LS4 ... 59 C3
Burley & Woodhead
  C of E Sch LS29 ... 21 F8
Burlington Ave BD3 ... 56 B2
Burlington Pl 5 LS11 ... 214 B2
Burlington Rd LS11 ... 214 B2
Burlington St Bradford BD8 ... 55 D1
  3 Halifax HX1 ... 202 B3
Burlington Works BD3 ... 56 B1
Burmantofts St LS9 ... 212 B4
Burn Rd HD2, HD3 ... 135 C3
Burned Gr HX3 ... 93 C7
Burned Rd HX3 ... 93 D7
Burnett Ave BD5 ... 74 D3
Burnett Pl BD5 ... 74 D3
Burnett Rise BD13 ... 92 C8
Burnett St BD1 ... 201 C3
Burnham Ave Bradford BD4 ... 75 C1
  Mapplewell S75 ... 178 B1
Burnham Ct LS22 ... 13 C6
Burnham Rd LS25 ... 82 F6
Burnlea Gr WF9 ... 164 F5
Burnleyville BD19 ... 96 B1
Burnroyd Ave BD20 ... 16 D6
Burns Ave WF9 ... 183 F1
Burns Ct WF7 ... 96 D2
Burns Hill LS29 ... 6 E8
Burns St HX1 ... 202 C1
Burns Way LS23 ... 30 D5
Burnsall Ave WF17 ... 118 A5
Burnsall Croft LS12 ... 209 E3
Burnsall Ct LS12 ... 209 E3
Burnsall Gdns LS12 ... 209 E3
Burnsall Grange LS12 ... 209 E4
Burnsall Mews BD20 ... 5 E2

Burnsall Rd Batley WF17 ... 118 A5
  Bradford BD3 ... 75 B7
  Brighouse HD6 ... 135 E8
  Liversedge WF15 ... 116 F4
Burnsdale BD15 ... 54 A3
Burnside Ave HX3 ... 92 A5
Burnside Cl WF17 ... 97 A1
Burnside Dr HD7 ... 188 E4
Burnt Acres La OL14 ... 109 B8
Burnt Edge La HX7 ... 87 D4
Burnt House Cl OL14 ... 108 C6
Burnt Plats La HD7 ... 151 B3
Burnt Side Rd LS12 ... 77 C2
Burnt Wood Cres WF9 ... 182 C2
Burnt Wood La WF9 ... 181 E1
Burntwood Ave WF9 ... 182 C1
Burntwood Bank WF9 ... 181 D5
Burntwood Cl WF9 ... 182 C1
Burntwood Gr WF9 ... 182 C1
Burntwood Jun & Inf Sch
  WF9 ... 182 C2
Burntwood Sports
  & Leisure Ctr S72 ... 181 C2
Burnup Gr BD19 ... 116 C7
Burnwells Ave BD10 ... 39 A2
Burr Tree Dr LS15 ... 81 D7
Burr Tree Garth LS15 ... 81 D7
Burr Tree Vale LS15 ... 81 D7
Burrage St BD16 ... 36 F3
Burras Ave LS21 ... 22 F7
Burras Dr LS21 ... 22 F7
Burras La LS21 ... 22 F7
Burras Rd BD4 ... 75 B2
Burrel Cl LS22 ... 14 A5
Burrell St WF1 ... 216 C2
Burrow St BD5 ... 201 B2
Burrows The WF17 ... 117 F7
Burrwood Terr HX4 ... 134 B5
Burrwood Way HX4 ... 134 B5
Burton Acres Dr HD8 ... 173 E7
Burton Acres La HD8 ... 173 F7
Burton Acres Mews HD8 ... 173 E7
Burton Acres Way HD8 ... 173 E7
Burton Arc 1 LS11 ... 211 C3
Burton Common La LS25 ... 105 F4
Burton Cres LS6 ... 59 D6
Burton Cross HD8 ... 173 E8
Burton Rd LS11 ... 214 C3
Burton Row LS11 ... 214 C3
Burton Royd La HD8 ... 174 A7
Burton Salmon
  Primary Sch LS25 ... 105 E3
Burton St Bradford BD4 ... 75 A4
  Halifax HX2 ... 92 A5
  Keighley BD20 ... 18 E1
  Leeds LS2 ... 207 D1
  11 Sowerby Bridge HX6 ... 112 B5
Burton Terr LS11 ... 214 C3
Burton Way LS9 ... 208 A1
Burwood Rd HD3 ... 153 C8
Busely Ct LS27 ... 97 F5
Busfield St Bingley BD16 ... 36 F3
  Bradford BD4 ... 75 B3
Bush La HD8 ... 175 D6
Busker La WF4 ... 159 C7
Buslingthorpe Gn LS7 ... 206 C4
Buslingthorpe La LS7 ... 206 C4
Buslingthorpe Vale LS7 ... 206 C4
Bussey Ct LS6 ... 206 A3
Busy La BD18 ... 38 D1
Butcher Hill
  Hemsworth WF9 ... 181 E8
  Horsforth LS16 ... 41 E2
Butcher La LS26 ... 100 E5
Butcher St Bradford BD7 ... 74 D7
  Leeds LS11 ... 211 E2
Bute Ave HD6 ... 115 A5
Bute St HD2 ... 55 D4
Butler Bank La HD7 ... 38 B8
Butler St E 8 BD3 ... 75 A7
Butler St W BD3 ... 201 D4
Butt Hill LS25 ... 83 A1
Butt La Bradford BD10 ... 56 B8
  Haworth BD22 ... 51 C7
  Holmfirth HD7 ... 189 C2
  Hooton Pagnell DN5 ... 195 E4
  Leeds LS12 ... 77 D6
Butterbowl Dr LS12 ... 77 F5
Butterbowl Garth LS12 ... 77 E5
Butterbowl Gdns LS12 ... 77 E5
Butterbowl Gr LS12 ... 77 E5
Butterbowl Lawn LS12 ... 77 E5
Butterbowl Mount LS12 ... 77 F5
Butterbowl Rd LS12 ... 77 E5
Buttercup Cl WF9 ... 182 F7
Butterfield Homes
  16 Cc6
  5 Shipley BD16 ... 54 B6
  Wilsden BD15 ... 53 B6
Butterfield La LS22 ... 212 C3
Butterfields 11 HD7 ... 189 F5
Butterley St LS10 ... 211 F2
Buttermead Cl BD6 ... 94 A7
Buttermere Ave LS22 ... 13 C6
Buttermere Croft WF2 ... 161 A6
Buttermere Dr HD5 ... 154 D6
Buttermere Rd BD2 ... 56 B3
Buttermere Wlk WF11 ... 126 E2
Butternab Rd HD4 ... 171 D8
Butternab Ridge HD4 ... 171 D8

Buttershaw Dr BD6 ... 73 E1
Buttershaw First Sch BD6 ... 93 F7
Buttershaw La Bradford BD6 ... 94 B8
  Cleckheaton WF15 ... 116 B5
Buttershaw Middle Sch BD6 ... 93 F7
Buttershaw Upper Sch BD6 ... 93 F8
Butterton Cl S75 ... 178 C1
Butterwick Gdns LS22 ... 13 C5
Butterwood Cl HD4 ... 171 D8
Butterworth End La HX6 ... 133 A7
Butterworth Hill HD3 ... 152 A7
Butterworth La HX6 ... 111 E1
Buttholme Gate BD6 ... 93 F8
Button Hill LS7 ... 207 D4
Button Pk WF8 ... 146 C7
Buttress La HX2 ... 90 F1
Butts Cl HD4 ... 172 E6
Butts Garth LS14 ... 45 F5
Butts Garth View LS14 ... 45 F5
Butts Green La HX2 ... 112 A7
Butts Green Rd HX2 ... 111 F7
Butts Hill BD19 ... 117 B8
Butts La Guiseley LS20 ... 22 C8
  Monk Fryston LS25 ... 105 D8
  Netherton WF4 ... 158 B7
  South Milford LS25 ... 105 D8
  Todmorden OL14 ... 108 E8
Butts Mount LS12 ... 210 A3
Butts Rd HD4 ... 172 E6
Butts Terr LS20 ... 22 E1
Butts The Keighley BD20 ... 36 D8
  Pontefract WF8 ... 125 D1
Buxton Ave BD9 ... 55 C4
Buxton La BD9 ... 55 C4
Buxton Pl WF1 ... 216 A4
Buxton St Bradford BD9 ... 55 B2
  8 Halifax HX3 ... 92 A1
  Keighley BD21 ... 35 C7
Buxton Way HX3 ... 91 F3
Byeway LS20 ... 22 E1
Byland HX2 ... 91 E7
Byland Ct LS23 ... 30 C2
Byland Gr BD15 ... 53 F1
Bylands Ave BD20 ... 16 E8
Byram Arc 22 WF1 ... 154 A6
Byram Park Ave WF11 ... 126 E8
Byram Park Rd WF11 ... 126 D8
Byram St HX1 ... 154 B6
Byrom St OL14 ... 108 B6
Byron Ave 6 HX6 ... 112 B5
Byron Dr WF11 ... 126 B4
Byron First Sch BD3 ... 75 B8
Byron Gr Batley WF13 ... 117 E2
  Lofthouse Gate WF3 ... 121 E6
Byron St Bradford BD3 ... 201 C4
  Halifax HX1 ... 202 B3
  Leeds LS2 ... 207 D1
  11 Sowerby Bridge HX6 ... 112 B5
Bywater The WF8 ... 146 D6
Bywell CE Jun Sch WF12 ... 118 F1
Bywell Cl WF12 ... 140 A8
Bywell Rd WF12 ... 118 F1

Cabbage Hill LS12 ... 209 E2
Cabin Rd LS21 ... 24 B5
Cable St HD1 ... 154 A4
Cad Beeston Mews LS11 ... 214 A3
Cadney Croft 11 HX1 ... 203 E2
Cadogan Ave HD3 ... 153 B8
Caenarvon Ave LS25 ... 83 B7
Caernarvon Ave LS25 ... 83 B7
Cain Cl 1 LS9 ... 212 C3
Cairn Cl HD2 ... 136 F4
Caister Gr 5 BD21 ... 35 B4
Caister St 5 BD21 ... 35 B4
Caister Way 9 BD21 ... 35 B4
Caistor Cl WF17 ... 97 A2
Caldene Ave Bradford BD12 ... 94 E6
  Hebden Bridge HX7 ... 89 D1
Calder Ave Halifax HX2 ... 202 B1
  Royston S71 ... 179 E3
Calder Bank Rd WF13 ... 139 B7
Calder Banks BD13 ... 73 A1
Calder Cl Castleford WF10 ... 125 B8
  Elland HX4 ... 134 D7
  Ossett WF5 ... 140 C5
  Wetherby LS22 ... 13 D8
Calder Coll of F Ed OL14 ... 108 B5
Calder Dr HD4 ... 171 F8
Calder Gr 3 HX7 ... 89 F1
Calder House
  1 Elland HX5 ... 134 F7
  Mirfield WF14 ... 138 A4
Calder Island Way WF2 ... 142 B2
Calder Mount WF4 ... 159 E5
Calder St Brighouse HD6 ... 115 C1
  Castleford WF10 ... 124 C8
  Todmorden OL14 ... 108 B6
  Wakefield WF1 ... 142 D4
Calder Terr Elland HX3 ... 113 A1
  Hebden Bridge HX7 ... 88 F3
  Horbury WF4 ... 159 C8
Calder Vale Rd WF1 ... 142 E5
Calder View Brighouse HD6 ... 115 A1
  Crigglestone WF4 ... 159 F5
  Ossett WF5 ... 140 B5
Calder Way BD20 ... 5 E2
Calderbrook Rd OL15 ... 129 C2

Calderclere Rd HD4 ... 153 F1
Caldercroft HX1 ... 135 B6
Calderdale Bsns Pk HX2 ... 91 F3
Calderdale Way HX5 ... 135 B6
Calderstone Ave BD6 ... 93 E8
Caldervale S71 ... 179 E4
Caldicott Cl OL14 ... 107 F3
Caledonia Ct WF2 ... 120 B2
Caledonia Rd Batley WF17 ... 118 D5
　Keighley BD21 ... 35 D8
Caledonia St BD4, BD5 ... 201 C1
Caledonian Rd WF12 ... 139 C5
Calf Hey La S36 ... 200 D7
Calf Hey Terr 3 OL14 ... 108 A1
Calf Hill Rd HD7 ... 172 B1
Calgary Pl LS7 ... 204 A2
California Dr
　Castleford WF10 ... 123 D5
　Horbury WF4 ... 141 C1
　Todmorden OL14 ... 108 A3
California La DB19 ... 117 B7
California Mews LS27 ... 98 B6
California St 10 LS27 ... 98 B4
Call La LS1 ... 211 F3
Calls The LS2 ... 212 A3
Cally Hall Farm Cotts HX7 ... 88 A4
Calmlands Rd HD7 ... 170 D1
Calpin Cl BD10 ... 56 B8
Calton Cl BD21 ... 35 F6
Calton Rd BD21 ... 35 F6
Calton St Huddersfield HD1 ... 154 B8
　Keighley BD21 ... 35 B6
Calver Ave BD21 ... 35 A8
Calver Dr BD21 ... 35 A7
Calver Rd BD21 ... 35 A7
Calverley Ave Bradford BD3 ... 75 D8
　Leeds LS13 ... 58 B3
Calverley C of E
　Primary Sch LS28 ... 57 B7
Calverley Cl Leeds LS13 ... 58 B3
　Rothwell LS26 ... 101 B5
Calverley Cutting BD10 ... 56 F8
Calverley Dr LS13 ... 58 B3
Calverley Garth LS13 ... 58 B3
Calverley Gdns LS13 ... 58 A4
Calverley Gr 1 LS13 ... 58 B3
Calverley Green Rd WF6 ... 122 F3
Calverley La Horsforth LS18 ... 58 A8
　Leeds LS13 ... 58 A3
　Pudsey LS28 ... 57 C5
　Yeadon LS28 ... 57 E2
Calverley Moor Ave LS28 ... 57 A1
Calverley Parkside
　Primary Sch LS28 ... 57 B6
Calverley Rd LS26 ... 101 C5
Calverley St LS1 ... 206 B1
Calverley Terr 2 LS13 ... 58 B3
Calverskine Middle Sch
　BD22 ... 34 F7
Calverskine St BD21 ... 35 A7
Calvert Cl LS25 ... 83 A3
Calverts Wlk WF5 ... 140 E4
Cam La HD6 ... 115 D3
Camargue Fold BD22 ... 55 F4
Cambell St BD1 ... 35 C7
Camberley Cl LS28 ... 76 E6
Camberley Mount BD4 ... 75 E4
Camberley St 3 LS11 ... 214 C3
Camborne Dr HD2 ... 135 F3
Camborne Rd HD2 ... 135 F4
Camborne Way BD22 ... 34 E5
Cambrian Bar BD12 ... 94 B6
Cambrian St LS11 ... 214 A4
Cambrian Terr LS11 ... 214 A4
Cambridge Cl LS27 ... 98 B5
Cambridge Cres WF4 ... 143 C3
Cambridge Ct LS27 ... 98 B5
Cambridge Dr Leeds LS13 ... 58 B3
　Otley LS21 ... 23 C7
Cambridge Gdns LS13 ... 58 B3
Cambridge Gr Kippax LS25 ... 83 A1
　Otley LS21 ... 23 B7
Cambridge Pl
　Bradford BD3 ... 201 C4
　10 Queensbury BD13 ... 72 E1
　2 Todmorden OL14 ... 108 B5
Cambridge Rd Batley WF17 ... 96 D2
　Huddersfield HD1 ... 154 A7
　Leeds LS7 ... 206 C3
Cambridge St Batley HD6 ... 117 E4
　Batley WF17 ... 118 C5
　Bradford BD7 ... 74 B4
　Bradford, Town End BD14 ... 73 B4
　Castleford WF10 ... 124 D7
　Guiseley LS20 ... 22 E1
　Hebden Bridge HX7 ... 88 F3
　Normanton WF6 ... 123 A1
　Otley LS21 ... 23 B7
　13 Queensbury BD13 ... 72 F1
　South Elmsall WF9 ... 182 E3
　Todmorden OL14 ... 108 C5
Cambridge Terr LS21 ... 23 B7
Cambridge Way LS21 ... 23 B7
Camden Rd WF10 ... 125 D8
Camden St HX6 ... 112 B3
Camellia Cl WF2 ... 141 D3
Camelia Mount BD7 ... 73 E6
Camelot Ct WF8 ... 146 E8
Cameron Ave 1 BD2 ... 94 C1
Camerton Gn BD5 ... 74 F2
Camilla Ct WF12 ... 139 C2
Camm La WF14 ... 138 B6
Camm St HD6 ... 115 B3
Camp Hill HD3 ... 151 B5
Camp Mount WF8 ... 146 B8
Camp Rd Bramhope LS16 ... 24 E1
　South Kirkby WF9 ... 181 F1

Camp Rise WF8 ... 146 B8
Camp Sq LS14 ... 45 F5
Campbell St Glusburn BD20 ... 16 D7
　Pudsey LS28 ... 57 E2
　Queensbury BD13 ... 72 F1
Campden Rd HX7 ... 88 E4
Campinot Vale HD7 ... 151 F1
Campion Cl WF8 ... 146 D7
Campus Rd BD7 ... 74 C6
Camroyd St WF13 ... 118 D1
Canada Cres LS19 ... 40 C4
Canada Dr LS19 ... 40 C5
Canada Rd LS19 ... 40 C5
Canada Terr LS19 ... 40 C4
Canal Ct WF3 ... 121 D6
Canal La
　Lofthouse Gate WF3 ... 121 E6
　Silsden BD20 ... 18 A7
Canal Pl LS12 ... 210 C3
Canal Rd Bingley BD16 ... 36 F5
　Bradford BD1 ... 201 C4
　Halifax HX6 ... 112 E4
　Keighley BD20 ... 18 E1
　Leeds LS12 ... 210 A4
　Pudsey LS13 ... 57 E5
　Shipley BD1, BD2 ... 55 D3
Canal St Brighouse HD6 ... 115 B2
　Halifax HX3 ... 203 F2
　Huddersfield HD1 ... 154 C8
　Leeds LS12 ... 210 B3
　Todmorden OL14 ... 108 B5
Canal Wharf LS11 ... 211 E3
Canal Wlk WF13 ... 121 F6
Canary St BD19 ... 116 D8
Canberra Cl 6 BD22 ... 51 F8
Canberra Dr BD22 ... 51 F8
Canby Gr HD5 ... 155 B5
Cancel St LS10 ... 212 A1
Canford Dr BD15 ... 54 C1
Canford Gr BD15 ... 54 C1
Canford Rd BD15 ... 54 B1
Canker La Halifax HX3 ... 92 B3
　Huddersfield HD2 ... 136 D1
Canning Ave WF2 ... 141 D8
Cannon Gr WF16 ... 117 E5
Cannon Hall Cl HD6 ... 115 D2
Cannon Hall Country Pk
　S75 ... 193 D5
Cannon Hall Dr HD6 ... 115 D2
Cannon Hall House & Mus
　S75 ... 193 C5
Cannon Mill La BD7 ... 74 A4
Cannon St Bingley BD16 ... 37 A2
　Castleford WF10 ... 124 E5
　3 Halifax HX1 ... 202 B1
　Todmorden OL14 ... 108 A3
Cannon Way WF13 ... 139 C7
Canonbury Terr LS11 ... 213 E3
Canteen Mill Ind Est
　OL14 ... 107 E8
Canterbury Ave BD5 ... 74 C4
Canterbury Cres HX3 ... 92 B1
Canterbury Dr LS6 ... 59 C4
Canterbury Rd
　Dewsbury WF12 ... 118 F1
　Leeds LS6 ... 59 C4
Capas Heights Way WF16 ... 117 D3
Cape Mills Ind Est LS28 ... 57 E3
Cape St BD1 ... 201 B4
Capel Cl LS28 ... 57 B6
Capel St Brighouse HD6 ... 115 A1
　Pudsey LS28 ... 57 B6
Caprington Ct WF6 ... 123 D1
Captain St 7 Bacup OL13 ... 106 A7
　Bradford BD1 ... 201 C4
Carberry Pl LS6 ... 205 E2
Carberry Rd LS6 ... 205 E2
Carberry Terr 22 LS6 ... 205 E2
Cardan Dr LS29 ... 8 E4
Carden Ave LS15 ... 80 E8
Carden Rd BD4 ... 75 E5
Cardigan Ave LS27 ... 98 A2
Cardigan Cl WF17 ... 118 E5
Cardigan Ct LS6 ... 205 E4
Cardigan La Leeds LS4, LS6 ... 205 E3
　Leeds, Burley LS4, LS6 ... 205 D2
　Ossett WF5 ... 141 A3
Cardigan St BD13 ... 72 F1
Cardigan Terr WF1 ... 216 B3
Cardigan Trad Est LS4 ... 205 D1
Cardinal Ave LS11 ... 98 F8
Cardinal Cl HD7 ... 170 E2
Cardinal Cres LS11 ... 98 F8
Cardinal Gdns LS11 ... 98 E8
Cardinal Gr LS11 ... 98 E8
Cardinal Heenan High Sch
　LS6 ... 205 D4
Cardinal Rd LS11 ... 213 F1
Cardinal Sq LS11 ... 213 E1
Cardinal Wlk LS11 ... 98 F8
Cardwell Terr WF12 ... 139 C6
Carforth St HD1 ... 154 C5
Carisbrooke Cres BD6 ... 94 C8
Carisbrooke La LS25 ... 83 B8
Cariss St LS10 ... 215 D3
Cark Rd BD21 ... 35 C8
Carlby Gr 8 BD22 ... 35 A6
Carlby St BD22 ... 35 A6
Carleton Cl Boston Spa LS23 ... 30 E8
　Pontefract WF8 ... 146 D7
Carleton Crest WF8 ... 146 E6
Carleton Dr LS23 ... 30 E7
Carleton Gate WF8 ... 146 D6
Carleton Glen WF8 ... 146 D6
Carleton Green Cl WF8 ... 146 E5
Carleton High Sch WF8 ... 146 E6
Carleton House 1 BD6 ... 93 E8
Carleton Park Ave WF8 ... 146 D6

Carleton Park
　Jun & Inf Sch WF8 ... 146 D6
Carleton Park Rd WF8 ... 146 D6
Carleton Rd WF8 ... 146 E6
Carleton St BD20 ... 18 C1
Carleton View WF8 ... 146 D6
Carlile St HD7 ... 170 E2
Carling Cl BD7 ... 73 F3
Carlinghow Hill WF17 ... 118 B7
Carlinghow La WF17 ... 117 F6
Carlinghow Mills WF17 ... 118 B6
Carlinghow Princess Royal
　Prim Sch WF17 ... 118 A7
Carlisle Ave LS19 ... 40 C6
Carlisle Cl WF13 ... 118 C2
Carlisle Dr LS28 ... 76 E6
Carlisle Gr LS28 ... 76 D6
Carlisle Pl BD8 ... 55 C1
Carlisle Rd Bradford BD8 ... 55 C1
　Leeds LS10 ... 212 A2
　Pudsey LS28 ... 76 D6
Carlisle St Bradford BD8 ... 55 C1
　Halifax HX2 ... 202 A4
　Keighley BD21 ... 35 D7
　Pudsey LS28 ... 57 C1
Carlisle Terr BD8 ... 55 C1
Carlrayne La LS29 ... 22 A5
Carlton App LS22 ... 13 C6
Carlton Ave Batley WF17 ... 118 B3
　Castleford WF10 ... 124 F7
　Pudsey LS28 ... 76 E7
　Shipley BD18 ... 54 F8
Carlton Carr LS7 ... 206 C2
Carlton Cl
　1 Cleckheaton BD19 ... 116 D7
　Hemsworth WF9 ... 181 C5
　Leeds LS7 ... 206 C2
　Normanton WF6 ... 123 B2
Carlton Croft Leeds LS7 ... 206 C2
　Wakefield WF2 ... 160 D6
Carlton Ct
　Cleckheaton BD19 ... 116 D8
　Leeds LS12 ... 213 E4
　Ossett WF5 ... 140 D6
Carlton Dr Baildon BD17 ... 38 C4
　Garforth LS25 ... 82 F5
　Guiseley LS20 ... 22 F2
　Shipley BD9 ... 54 F8
　Shipley, Frizinghall BD18 ... 55 A5
Carlton Garth Leeds LS7 ... 206 C2
　Leeds, Blackwood LS17 ... 44 A5
Carlton Gdns Leeds LS7 ... 206 C2
　Normanton WF6 ... 123 C2
　South Elmsall WF9 ... 182 F3
Carlton Gr 2 Bradford BD5 ... 74 D3
　Elland HX5 ... 135 C7
　Leeds LS7 ... 206 C2
　Shipley BD18 ... 55 A5
Carlton Hill LS2, LS7 ... 206 C2
Carlton House Terr HX1 ... 202 C1
Carlton Junior
　& Infant Sch WF13 ... 118 B2
Carlton La Carlton LS19 ... 23 C3
　Guiseley LS20 ... 23 C3
　Rothwell LS26 ... 100 E4
　Rothwell, Lofthouse
　WF3 ... 100 C1
Carlton Marsh
　Nature Reserve S71, S72 180 A1
Carlton Moor Mews LS10 ... 99 F5
Carlton Mount LS19 ... 40 C8
Carlton Pl 1 Halifax HX1 ... 203 E2
　Leeds LS7 ... 206 C2
Carlton Rd Batley WF16 ... 117 D4
　Dewsbury WF13 ... 118 C1
　Liversedge WF15 ... 117 A3
　Royston S71 ... 179 D1
　Shipley BD18 ... 54 E8
　South Elmsall WF9 ... 182 F3
Carlton Rise Leeds LS7 ... 206 C2
　Pudsey LS28 ... 76 E7
Carlton Row LS12 ... 209 D3
Carlton St 8 Bacup OL13 ... 106 A3
　Bradford BD7 ... 74 D6
　Castleford WF10 ... 124 D8
　Featherstone WF7 ... 145 D7
　Halifax HX1 ... 203 E2
　8 Haworth BD22 ... 51 D7
　10 Hebden Bridge HX7 ... 89 A3
　Horbury WF4 ... 141 A1
　Normanton WF6 ... 123 C2
　Otley LS21 ... 23 B7
　Wakefield WF2 ... 142 A5
Carlton Terr Batley WF17 ... 118 A3
　Dewsbury WF12 ... 139 D6
　4 Halifax HX1 ... 203 E2
　2 Pudsey LS28 ... 76 E8
　Yeadon LS19 ... 40 C7
Carlton Towers 1 LS7 ... 206 C2
Carlton View Kippax WF10 ... 102 F6
　Leeds LS7 ... 206 C2
Carlton Way 2 BD19, OL2 ... 116 D7
Carlton Wlk BD18 ... 54 F8
Carlton-Bolling Coll BD3 ... 56 A1
Carlyle Cres WF10 ... 125 B7
Carlyle Rd WF10 ... 125 B7
Carmel Rd HX3 ... 92 C2
Carmine Cl HD5 ... 154 E6
Carmona Ave BD18 ... 55 B5
Carmona Gdns BD18 ... 55 B5
Carnaby Rd BD7 ... 73 E2
Carnegie Coll LS6 ... 59 B6
Carnegie Dr BD18 ... 55 C6
Carnlea Gr WF2 ... 142 C3
Carnoustie Gr BD16 ... 54 B7

Carolan Ct HD7 ... 152 D5
Caroline St
　10 Cleckheaton BD19 ... 116 D8
　Shipley BD18 ... 54 F8
Carperley Cres BD13 ... 71 E8
Carr Bank Keighley BD20 ... 19 C1
　Otley LS21 ... 11 A2
Carr Bank Bottom LS21 ... 10 F2
Carr Bottom Ave BD5 ... 74 C2
Carr Bottom Fold BD5 ... 74 C1
Carr Bottom Gr BD5 ... 74 B2
Carr Bottom Rd
　Bradford, Brownroyd Hill BD5 74 C2
　Bradford, Greengates BD10 ... 56 E7
Carr Bridge Ave LS16 ... 41 D3
Carr Bridge Cl LS16 ... 41 D3
Carr Bridge Dr LS16 ... 41 D3
Carr Bridge View LS16 ... 41 D3
Carr Cl LS19 ... 40 D3
Carr Crofts LS12 ... 209 E3
Carr Crofts Dr LS12 ... 209 E3
Carr Field Dr HX2 ... 111 E8
Carr Gate Cres WF2 ... 120 D5
Carr Gate Dr WF2 ... 120 E5
Carr Gate Mount WF2 ... 120 D5
Carr Gr BD20 ... 19 A1
Carr Green Ave HD6 ... 135 F6
Carr Green Cl HD6 ... 135 F6
Carr Green Dr HD6 ... 135 F6
Carr Green Junior
　& Infants Sch HD6 ... 135 F7
Carr Green La
　Brighouse HD6 ... 135 F7
　Huddersfield HD5 ... 154 D6
Carr Hall La HX4 ... 134 A4
Carr Hall Rd BD12 ... 94 C3
Carr Head La BD20 ... 16 A5
Carr Hill Ave LS28 ... 57 A6
Carr Hill Dr LS28 ... 57 A6
Carr Hill Gr LS28 ... 57 A6
Carr Hill Nook LS28 ... 57 A6
Carr Hill Rd
　Denby Dale HD8 ... 191 A6
　Pudsey LS28 ... 57 A6
Carr Hill Rise LS28 ... 57 A6
Carr House Wf1 ... 216 B2
Carr House Fold 1 OL14 ... 108 D6
Carr House Gate WF2 ... 94 C4
Carr House Gr BD12 ... 94 C4
Carr House La
　Bradford BD12 ... 94 B4
　Shelf HX3 ... 93 D7
　Todmorden OL14 ... 108 D6
　West House Mount BD12 ... 94 C4
Carr House Rd
　Holmfirth HD7 ... 189 A5
　Shelf HX3 ... 93 D7
Carr Houses LS26 ... 123 E8
Carr La 1 Bingley BD16 ... 36 C8
　Bradford BD12 ... 94 D5
　Castleford WF10 ... 124 F5
　Denholme BD13 ... 52 E2
　Dewsbury WF12 ... 157 C8
　Dewsbury, Heckmondwike
　WF16 ... 117 E1
　Hemsworth WF4, WF9 ... 162 F2
　Holmfirth HD7 ... 188 B4
　Ingbirchworth S36 ... 192 C1
　Keighley, East Morton BD20 ... 36 D8
　Keighley, Riddlesden BD20 ... 19 A1
　Netherton WF4 ... 158 B6
　Rothwell WF3 ... 100 E3
　Shepley HD8 ... 190 F6
　Shipley BD18 ... 55 C7
　Slaithwaite HD7 ... 152 A1
　South Kirkby WF9 ... 182 D4
　Thorner LS14 ... 45 D5
　Wakefield WF2 ... 160 E7
　Wetherby LS22 ... 14 A7
　Yeadon LS19 ... 40 D3
Carr Lane Ave WF10 ... 124 E5
Carr Manor Ave LS7 ... 43 B1
Carr Manor Cres LS7 ... 60 B8
Carr Manor Croft LS7 ... 60 B7
Carr Manor Dr LS17 ... 60 B8
Carr Manor Garth LS17 ... 43 B1
Carr Manor Gdns LS17 ... 60 B8
Carr Manor Gr LS17 ... 60 B8
Carr Manor High Sch LS7 ... 60 A7
Carr Manor Mount LS17 ... 60 B8
Carr Manor Par LS17 ... 60 B8
Carr Manor Pl LS17 ... 60 B8
Carr Manor Primary Sch
　LS17 ... 60 B8
Carr Manor Rd LS17 ... 60 B8
Carr Manor View LS17 ... 60 C8
Carr Moor Side LS11 ... 214 C3
Carr Moor St LS10 ... 215 D2
Carr Mount Denby Dale HD8 191 A6
Carr Pit Rd HD5 ... 155 F7
Carr Rd 3 Bradford BD12 ... 94 C3
　Pudsey LS28 ... 57 A7
　Todmorden OL14 ... 107 A8
Carr Side Cres WF17 ... 118 A3
Carr St 3 Batley WF16 ... 117 C2
　Batley, Birstall WF17 ... 96 E1
　Bradford BD5 ... 74 D2
　Brighouse HD6 ... 115 A4
　Cleckheaton BD19 ... 116 D8
　Huddersfield HD3 ... 153 C7
　Keighley BD21 ... 35 B8
　Liversedge WF15 ... 117 A5
Carr Top Cl WF17 ... 118 B2
Carr Top La HD7 ... 152 D4
Carr View WF9 ... 182 C3

Carr View Rd HD7 ... 189 F2
Carr Wood Cl LS26 ... 57 A6
Carr Wood Gdns LS28 ... 57 A7
Carr Wood Ind Est WF10 ... 124 F5
Carr Wood Rd WF10 ... 124 F5
Carr Wood Way LS28 ... 57 A7
Carr's Cl WF13 ... 117 F3
Carrfield Dr LS15 ... 63 D7
Carrfield La LS15 ... 63 D7
Carrfield Rd LS15 ... 63 D7
Carrfield Villas OL14 ... 86 A1
Carrgate WF9 ... 163 B2
Carrholm Cres LS7 ... 60 B7
Carrholm Dr LS7 ... 60 B7
Carrholm Gr LS7 ... 60 B7
Carrholm Mount LS7 ... 60 B7
Carrholm Rd LS7 ... 60 B7
Carrholm View LS7 ... 60 B7
Carriage Dr
　Cleckheaton BD19 ... 96 B2
　Huddersfield HD4 ... 171 F8
Carriage Dr The
　Elland HX4 ... 134 A4
　Leeds LS8 ... 61 C8
Carriage La HX4 ... 134 C8
Carricks Cl BD12 ... 94 E6
Carrier St 12 HX1 ... 203 E3
Carrington St BD3 ... 75 C7
Carrington Terr LS20 ... 39 D8
Carroll Ct WF9 ... 182 E3
Carroll St BD3 ... 201 D2
Carrs Rd HD7 ... 169 A4
Carrs Side St No 1 HD7 ... 169 A4
Carrs Side St No 2 HD7 ... 169 A4
Carrs St HD7 ... 169 A4
Carter Ave 2 LS15 ... 81 C8
Carter La 6 Leeds LS15 ... 81 C8
　Queensbury BD13 ... 72 D3
Carter Mount LS15 ... 81 C8
Carter St Bradford BD4 ... 201 C2
　Wakefield WF1 ... 216 A2
Carter Terr 4 LS15 ... 62 C1
Carter's La LS29 ... 8 E7
Cartmel Rd BD21 ... 35 A7
Cartmel Dr LS15 ... 80 D7
Cartworth Bank Rd HD7 ... 188 F2
Cartworth La HD7 ... 189 A3
Cartworth Moor Rd
　Holme HD7 ... 198 E8
　Holmfirth HD7 ... 188 E1
Cartworth Rd HD7 ... 189 A4
Cartwright Gdns HX4 ... 153 C3
Cartwright Hall Art Gall
　BD9 ... 55 C2
Cartwright House 9 WF15 117 A5
Cartwright St BD19 ... 116 F6
Carver St BD19 ... 116 D8
Caryl Rd BD4 ... 75 A3
Cashmere St BD21 ... 35 A7
Casson Ave WF3 ... 99 B1
Casson Dr WF3 ... 120 B8
Casson Gr WF3 ... 99 B1
Casterton Gdns LS14 ... 62 A3
Castle Ave Brighouse HD6 ... 135 F8
　Huddersfield HD4 ... 154 A1
　Wakefield WF2 ... 142 D2
Castle Carr Rd Halifax HX2 ... 90 B6
　Wadsworth Moor HX2 ... 70 A1
Castle Cl Bardsey LS17 ... 28 D3
　Batley WF17 ... 97 A1
Castle Cres Dewsbury WF12 139 D1
　Wakefield WF2 ... 160 D8
Castle Croft BD16 ... 36 A1
Castle Ct 1 BD10 ... 35 C8
Castle Garth WF8 ... 125 C1
Castle Gate
　Hebden Bridge HX7 ... 110 C4
　Ilkley LS29 ... 8 B4
　Lofthouse Gate LS22 ... 122 A8
　Wetherby LS22 ... 13 E5
Castle Gr Bardsey LS17 ... 28 D3
　Harden BD16 ... 36 A1
　Ilkley LS29 ... 159 C8
Castle Grove Ave LS6 ... 59 D6
Castle Grove Dr LS6 ... 59 D6
Castle Grove Inf Sch WF2 ... 142 E2
Castle Hall Sch WF14 ... 138 C5
Castle Hall Cl HD3 ... 100 C1
Castle Head La OL14 ... 121 A8
Castle Hill Brighouse HD6 ... 135 F8
　Ilkley LS29 ... 8 B4
　Wakefield WF2 ... 141 C4
Castle Hill Fort HD4 ... 154 C1
Castle Hill Junior
　& Infants Sch OL14 ... 108 D6
Castle Hill Rd BD19 ... 117 B6
Castle Hill Side HX4 ... 172 C8
Castle Hill View HX16 ... 117 F3
Castle Houses HD4 ... 172 B8
Castle Ings Cl LS12 ... 77 D3
Castle Ings Dr LS12 ... 77 D3
Castle Ings Gdns LS12 ... 77 D2
Castle La Ripponden HX6 ... 132 C3
　Slaithwaite HD7 ... 152 B3
　Todmorden OL14 ... 108 D6
Castle Lane OL14 ... 108 D6
Castle Meadows WF4 ... 159 F3
Castle Mount WF2 ... 139 D1
Castle Par WF10 ... 124 F6
Castle Pl HD6 ... 135 F8
Castle Rd Ilkley LS29 ... 8 B4
　Keighley BD21 ... 35 B8
　Rothwell LS26 ... 100 D5
　Shipley BD18 ... 55 B7
　Wakefield WF2 ... 142 E1

Castle Rd W WF2 ..... 142 D1
Castle Sch The WF10 ..... 125 C7
Castle St Leeds S1 ..... 211 D4
  Wakefield WF2 ..... 141 F5
Castle Syke Hill WF8 ..... 146 B3
Castle Syke View WF8 ..... 146 C6
Castle Terr WF2 ..... 160 D8
Castle Vale WF8 ..... 125 F2
Castle View Honley HD7 ..... 171 F3
  Horbury WF4 ..... 159 C8
  Leeds LS17 ..... 43 B1
  Mirfield WF14 ..... 138 B5
  Pontefract WF8 ..... 125 D1
  Wakefield WF2 ..... 160 D8
Castle Wood Cl
  Harewood LS17 ..... 27 A7
  Horsforth LS18 ..... 58 D8
Castle Yd LS29 ..... 8 B4
Castlefield Ct WF10 ..... 124 D8
Castlefields LS26 ..... 100 B5
Castlefields Cres HD6 ..... 135 F8
Castlefields Dr HD6 ..... 135 F8
Castlefields Ind Est BD16 ..... 36 D5
Castlefields Infants Sch
  HD6 ..... 114 F1
Castlefields La BD16 ..... 135 F8
Castlefields Rd
  Bingley BD16 ..... 36 D6
  Brighouse HD6 ..... 135 F8
Castleford Airedale
  Jun & Inf Sch WF10 ..... 125 C7
Castleford High Sch
  WF10 ..... 124 F8
Castleford La
  Featherstone WF7 ..... 124 B2
  Knottingley WF11 ..... 126 B5
Castleford Normanton
  & District Hospl (General)
  WF10 ..... 124 B6
Castleford Rd WF6 ..... 123 C3
Castleford Sta WF10 ..... 124 D7
Castleford
  Three Lane Ends
  Jun & Inf Sch WF10 ..... 124 A8
Castleford Townville
  Inf Sch WF10 ..... 125 C7
Castleford Wheldon
  Inf Sch WF10 ..... 124 D8
Castlegate HD1 ..... 154 A6
Castlegate Dr
  Bradford BD10 ..... 56 C6
  Pontefract WF8 ..... 146 C5
Castlegate House HD7 HX5 ..... 134 F7
Castlegate Loop HD1 ..... 154 A6
Castlegate Slip HD1 ..... 154 A7
Castlemore Rd BD7 ..... 38 D2
Castleton Cl LS12 ..... 210 C3
Castleton Primary Sch
  LS12 ..... 210 B3
Castleton Rd LS12 ..... 210 B4
Castletown Dr BD13 ..... 106 B1
Castley La Castley LS21 ..... 25 B8
  Leathley LS21 ..... 24 E8
Cat Hill La S36 ..... 192 D1
Cat La Elland HX4 ..... 133 F7
  Sowerby Bridge HX2 ..... 132 B5
Cater St BD1 ..... 201 C3
Cath Ch of St Peter The
  BD1 ..... 201 C3
Cathcart St 4 Halifax HX3 ..... 92 B2
  Leeds LS6 ..... 206 A3
Cathedral Church
  of All Saints The WF1 ..... 216 B2
Cathedral Cl Bradford BD1 ..... 201 C3
  Wakefield WF1 ..... 216 A3
Cathedral Ret Pk WF2 ..... 216 A1
Cathedral Wlk WF1 ..... 216 B2
Catherine Cl HD3 ..... 135 A2
Catherine Cres 5 HX4 ..... 134 F6
Catherine Gr 2 LS11 ..... 214 B3
Catherine House La HX2 ..... 90 A6
Catherine Rd HD2 ..... 136 B4
Catherine Slack
  Brighouse HD6 ..... 114 F6
  Queensbury BD13 ..... 92 C6
Catherine St
  Brighouse HD6 ..... 115 A3
  Elland HX5 ..... 134 F6
  Hemsworth WF9 ..... 163 A4
  5 Keighley BD21 ..... 35 B5
Catlow St WF10 ..... 124 C7
Cattle La LS25 ..... 64 E7
Cattle Market St LS21 ..... 23 A8
Cattlelaith La WF11 ..... 126 D2
Caudle Hill WF11 ..... 104 F4
Cauldwell Gdns 2 BD5 ..... 74 E4
Caulms Wood Rd WF13 ..... 118 D1
Causeway Halifax HX1 ..... 203 F3
  Ripponden HX4 ..... 133 D3
Causeway Cres HD7 ..... 152 D1
Causeway Foot HX2 ..... 71 D3
Causeway Garth La WF8 ..... 165 E4
Causeway Head La HX6 ..... 132 B5
Causeway Side HD7 ..... 152 D1
Causeway Wood Rd OL14 ..... 108 E4
Cautley Rd LS9 ..... 212 C2
Cavalier App LS9 ..... 212 C2
Cavalier Cl LS9 ..... 212 C2
Cavalier Ct LS9 ..... 212 C2
Cavalier Dr BD10 ..... 56 E8
Cavalier Gate LS9 ..... 212 C2
Cavalier Gdns LS9 ..... 212 C2
Cavalier Gn LS9 ..... 212 C2
Cavalier Mews LS9 ..... 212 C2
Cavalier View LS9 ..... 212 C2

Cave Cres WF2 ..... 141 E4
Cave Hill HX3 ..... 92 F4
Cave La 4 WF3 ..... 120 E7
Cavendish Ct
  Bradford BD10 ..... 56 C5
  Leeds LS18 ..... 58 C8
  2 Keighley BD21 ..... 35 C7
Cavendish Dr Bingley BD16 ..... 37 B4
  Guiseley LS20 ..... 39 D8
Cavendish First Sch BD10 ..... 56 D5
Cavendish Gr LS20 ..... 39 D8
Cavendish Mews LS17 ..... 43 D4
Cavendish Pl LS28 ..... 57 E1
Cavendish Rd
  Bradford, Eccleshill BD2 ..... 56 C5
  Bradford, Thorpe BD10 ..... 56 E8
  Guiseley LS20 ..... 39 D8
  Leeds LS2 ..... 206 B2
Cavendish Rise LS28 ..... 77 A7
Cavendish Sq 3 LS25 ..... 57 E1
Cavendish St
  1 Halifax HX1 ..... 202 C3
  Keighley BD21 ..... 35 C7
  Leeds LS3 ..... 210 C4
  Pudsey LS28 ..... 77 A7
  3 Pudsey LS28 ..... 40 C7
Cavendish Terr 3 HX1 ..... 202 C3
Cavewell Cl WF3 ..... 140 F3
Cavewell Gdns WF5 ..... 140 F3
Cawcliffe Dr HD6 ..... 115 A5
Cawcliffe Rd HD6 ..... 115 A4
Cawley Garth WF16 ..... 117 E3
Cawley La WF16 ..... 117 E3
Cawley Lane Jun & Inf Sch
  WF16 ..... 117 E4
Cawood Haven BD6 ..... 93 E8
Cawthorne Ave HD2 ..... 136 A2
Cawthorne C of E
  Jun & Inf Sch S75 ..... 193 E4
Cawthorne La S75 ..... 193 F5
Cawthorne Rd WF2 ..... 160 B6
Caxton Rd LS21 ..... 22 E7
Caxton St LS21 ..... 13 E5
Caycroft Nook HX7 ..... 88 F5
Caygill Terr HX1 ..... 203 E2
Cayre Garth HD6 ..... 114 C5
Caythorne Wlk BD10 ..... 56 C5
Caythorpe Rd LS16 ..... 59 B7
Cecil Ave Baildon BD17 ..... 38 C4
  Bradford BD7 ..... 74 B4
  Brighouse HX3 ..... 114 E8
Cecil Gr LS12 ..... 209 E4
Cecil Mount LS12 ..... 209 F4
Cecil Rd LS12 ..... 209 E4
Cecil St 11 Haworth BD22 ..... 51 E8
  8 Huddersfield HD1 ..... 154 A6
  Leeds LS12 ..... 209 F4
Cedar Ave
  Huddersfield HD1 ..... 153 F7
  Leeds LS12 ..... 209 F3
  Ossett WF5 ..... 140 E4
Cedar Cl Huddersfield HD7 ..... 152 F5
  Leeds LS12 ..... 209 F3
  Pontefract WF8 ..... 146 C5
  Royston S71 ..... 179 A4
Cedar Covert LS22 ..... 13 E8
Cedar Ct WF10 ..... 124 C7
Cedar Dr Bradford BD12 ..... 94 E4
  Dewsbury WF12 ..... 140 B7
Cedar Gr Elland HX4 ..... 134 B7
  Featherstone WF7 ..... 145 C5
  Sutton in C BD20 ..... 16 C5
Cedar Mount
  Huddersfield HD1 ..... 153 F7
  Leeds LS12 ..... 209 F3
Cedar Pl LS12 ..... 209 F3
Cedar Rd Dewsbury WF12 ..... 140 A7
  Leeds LS12 ..... 209 F3
  Normanton WF6 ..... 144 B7
Cedar St Bingley BD16 ..... 36 E5
  Halifax HX1 ..... 202 B2
  Huddersfield HD1 ..... 153 E7
  Keighley BD21 ..... 35 B4
  Leeds LS12 ..... 209 F3
  Todmorden OL14 ..... 129 A8
Cedar Terr LS12 ..... 209 F3
Cedar Way BD19 ..... 117 A8
Cedar Wlk
  Featherstone WF7 ..... 145 D6
  Knottingley WF11 ..... 126 E2
Cedars The LS16 ..... 42 E2
Celandine Ave HD3 ..... 152 E8
Celandine Cl WF8 ..... 146 D7
Celandine Dr HD3 ..... 152 E8
Cemetery La Halifax HX6 ..... 112 A4
  Leeds LS8 ..... 188 B2
  Rothwell WF3 ..... 100 C2
Cemetery Rd Batley WF17 ..... 118 B5
  Batley, Heckmondwike
  WF16 ..... 117 D4
  Bingley BD16 ..... 36 E4
  Bradford, Birks BD7, BD8 ..... 73 F6
  Bradford, Moor Top
  BD12, BD6 ..... 94 B7
  Dewsbury WF13 ..... 139 B7
  Haworth BD22 ..... 50 F6
  Hemsworth WF9 ..... 181 C8
  Holmfirth HD7 ..... 188 F4
  Huddersfield HD1 ..... 153 F7
  Leeds LS11 ..... 214 A4
  Normanton WF6 ..... 123 C2
  Pudsey LS28 ..... 76 D8
  Ryhill WF4 ..... 162 B1
  Yeadon LS19 ..... 40 C8
Centenary Rd BD17 ..... 38 B4
Centenary Sq
  Bradford BD1 ..... 201 B2
  Dewsbury WF12 ..... 139 B4
  Leeds LS2, LS9 ..... 212 A4
Centenary St 2 LS1 ..... 211 E4

Centenary Way WF17 ..... 118 B6
Central Arc BD19 ..... 116 E7
Central Ave Baildon BD17 ..... 38 B2
  Bradford BD5 ..... 74 C4
  Cleckheaton WF15 ..... 116 B5
  Hemsworth WF9 ..... 163 A4
  Huddersfield HD2 ..... 136 B2
  Keighley BD22 ..... 34 F3
  Shipley BD18 ..... 55 B7
  South Elmsall WF9 ..... 182 F2
Central Ave E WF15 ..... 116 B5
Central Cl HD2 ..... 136 B2
Central Dr
  Castleford WF10 ..... 124 A7
  Huddersfield HD2 ..... 136 B2
  Keighley BD22 ..... 34 F3
  Royston S71 ..... 179 C3
Central Par
  8 Cleckheaton BD19 ..... 116 E7
  Leeds LS9 ..... 80 C3
Central Pk Halifax HX1 ..... 203 D1
  Leeds LS11 ..... 211 E2
Central Rd
  Huddersfield HD2 ..... 136 B3
  Leeds LS1 ..... 211 F3
Central St
  Dewsbury WF13 ..... 139 C8
  Halifax HX1 ..... 203 E3
  Hebden Bridge HX7 ..... 89 A3
  Leeds LS1 ..... 211 E4
Central Street Infant Sch
  HX7 ..... 89 A3
Central View OL13 ..... 106 A2
Centre 27 Bsns Pk WF17 ..... 97 B3
Centre St 4 Bradford BD5 ..... 74 C3
  Hemsworth WF9 ..... 181 D8
  1 Liversedge WF16 ..... 117 C4
  South Elmsall WF9 ..... 183 A3
Centuria Wlk HD3 ..... 152 E8
Century Pl BD8 ..... 55 C1
Century Rd HX5 ..... 134 F7
Ceres Rd LS22 ..... 14 A5
Chaddlewood Cl LS14 ..... 45 C1
Chadwell Springs BD16 ..... 54 A7
Chadwick Cres WF13 ..... 118 B1
Chadwick La WF14 ..... 137 F4
Chadwick St LS10 ..... 212 A2
Chadwick St S LS10 ..... 212 A2
Chaffinch Rd 4 BD8 ..... 73 C7
Chaffinch Wlk HD4 ..... 171 E7
Chain HD7 ..... 169 C5
Chain Bar Meltham HD7 ..... 170 A5
  Slaithwaite HD7 ..... 169 F6
Chain St Bradford BD1 ..... 201 A3
Chalcroft Cl WF16 ..... 117 E5
Chald La WF2 ..... 216 A1
Chalfont Rd LS16 ..... 59 B8
Challenge Way
  Batley WF17 ..... 119 A3
  Bradford BD4 ..... 75 D4
Challenger Cres S63 ..... 194 D1
Chalner Ave LS27 ..... 97 F2
Chalner Cl LS27 ..... 97 F2
Chalwood HD2 ..... 136 A4
Chancellor St LS6 ..... 206 C3
Chancery Ct 40 HD1 ..... 154 A6
Chancery La 10
  Huddersfield HD1 ..... 154 A6
  Ossett WF5 ..... 140 C8
  2 Wakefield WF1 ..... 216 B2
Chancery Rd WF5 ..... 140 B8
Chandler Cl WF17 ..... 96 E1
Chandler La WF14 ..... 171 D4
Chandlers Cl WF1 ..... 121 B5
Chandlers The LS2 ..... 212 A3
Chandos Ave LS8 ..... 204 B4
Chandos Fold LS8 ..... 204 B4
Chandos Gdn LS8 ..... 204 B4
Chandos Garth LS8 ..... 204 B4
Chandos Gdns LS8 ..... 204 B4
Chandos Gn LS8 ..... 204 B4
Chandos Pl LS8 ..... 204 B4
Chandos St 4 Bradford BD4 ..... 201 C2
  4 Keighley BD21 ..... 35 B5
Chandos Terr LS8 ..... 204 C4
Chandos Wlk LS8 ..... 204 B3
Change La HX3 ..... 113 E2
Change View OL13 ..... 106 B4
Changegate BD22 ..... 51 B7
Changegate Ct 2 BD22 ..... 51 B7
Channing Way BD1 ..... 201 B2
Chantrell Ct LS2 ..... 212 A3
Chantry Bridge Ind Est
  WF1 ..... 216 C1
Chantry Cl Ilkley LS29 ..... 8 B3
  Pontefract WF8 ..... 146 B7
Chantry Croft LS15 ..... 81 D7
Chantry Dr LS29 ..... 8 B3
Chantry Garth LS15 ..... 81 D7
Chantry Dr S71 ..... 179 C3
Chantry La LS24 ..... 48 E5
Chantry Rd WF2 ..... 141 E5
Chapel Allerton Hospl
  LS7 ..... 204 A1
Chapel Allerton
  Primary Sch LS7 ..... 204 A2
Chapel Ave Batley WF16 ..... 117 E5
  Hebden Bridge HX7 ..... 89 B3
Chapel Bank HD7 ..... 189 E8
Chapel Cl Dewsbury WF12 ..... 139 D2
  Elland HX4 ..... 134 B4
  Garforth LS25 ..... 82 E7
  West Hardwick WF4 ..... 163 A7
Chapel Croft HD6 ..... 135 F7

Chapel Fold Batley WF17 ..... 118 A3
  Bradford BD6 ..... 74 B1
  Brighouse BD12 ..... 115 C8
  Leeds, Beeston LS11 ..... 213 E2
  Leeds, Burley LS6 ..... 205 D3
  Leeds, Gildersome LS27 ..... 97 E5
  3 Leeds LS11 ..... 214 B2
  3 Pudsey LS28 ..... 76 E6
Chapel Garth WF7 ..... 164 A6
Chapel Gn 1 LS28 ..... 76 D6
Chapel Gr BD16 ..... 36 E5
Chapel Grange Sch BD15 ..... 73 D8
Chapel Hill Clayton DN5 ..... 194 C4
  Clayton West HD8 ..... 175 E2
  Huddersfield HD1 ..... 154 A5
  1 Middleton LS10 ..... 99 D5
  Mirfield WF14 ..... 137 F2
  Morley LS27 ..... 98 A5
  Slaithwaite HD7 ..... 152 D1
  2 Yeadon LS19 ..... 40 B7
Chapel Hill La HD3 ..... 151 B5
Chapel House Rd BD12 ..... 94 D7
Chapel La Badsworth WF9 ..... 164 E2
  Barwick in E LS15 ..... 63 E7
  Batley WF16 ..... 117 E4
  6 Batley, Birstall WF17 ..... 96 F1
  Boston Spa LS23 ..... 30 D5
  Bradford, Clayton Heights
  BD13 ..... 73 B2
  Bradford, Lower Grange BD15 ..... 73 C8
  Dearne S63 ..... 194 F1
  Dewsbury WF12 ..... 139 D2
  Emley HD8 ..... 175 B7
  Garforth LS25 ..... 82 E7
  Guiseley BD17 ..... 39 C5
  Halifax HX3 ..... 113 D3
  Halifax, Midgley HX2 ..... 90 B2
  Halifax, Southowram HX3 ..... 114 B4
  Halton East BD23 ..... 1 E8
  Huddersfield, Moldgreen
  HD5 ..... 154 D5
  Huddersfield, Wellhouse
  HD7 ..... 152 D4
  Ilkley LS29 ..... 8 A4
  Keighley BD21 ..... 35 B7
  Keighley, Laycock BD22 ..... 34 C7
  Kippax LS25 ..... 83 B1
  Kirk Smeaton WF8 ..... 166 C4
  Leeds, Armley LS12 ..... 209 F3
  Leeds, Chapeltown LS7 ..... 77 E5
  Leeds, Headingley Hill LS6 ..... 205 D4
  Queensbury BD13 ..... 72 E1
  Royston S71 ..... 179 C1
  South Elmsall WF9 ..... 183 B3
  Sowerby Bridge HX6 ..... 112 D4
  Yeadon LS19 ..... 40 B7
Chapel Pl 1 LS6 ..... 59 D5
Chapel Rd Bingley BD16 ..... 36 E5
  Bradford BD2 ..... 94 E6
  Bradford, Low Moor BD12 ..... 94 D6
  Leeds LS7 ..... 204 A1
  Steeton BD20 ..... 17 C5
Chapel Row BD15 ..... 53 C6
Chapel Sq 1 LS6 ..... 59 D5
Chapel St Addingham LS29 ..... 6 FB
  Bingley BD16 ..... 36 D5
  Bradford BD1 ..... 201 C3
  Bradford, Brownroyd Hill BD6 ..... 74 C1
  Bradford, Eccleshill BD2 ..... 56 D4
  Bradford, Holme Top BD5 ..... 74 D4
  Brighouse HD6 ..... 114 E5
  Cleckheaton BD19 ..... 116 E8
  Cleckheaton, Hightown
  WF15 ..... 116 C5
  Denholme BD13 ..... 71 D8
  Dewsbury WF12 ..... 139 C6
  East Ardsley WF3 ..... 120 C7
  East Ardsley, Black Gates WF3 ..... 98 F1
  Elland HX4 ..... 134 B4
  Halifax HX2 ..... 202 A4
  Huddersfield HD1 ..... 154 A5
  Huddersfield, Blue Bell Hill
  HD4 ..... 153 D2
  7 Huddersfield, Moldgreen
  HD5 ..... 154 D6
  Huddersfield, Netherton
  HD4 ..... 171 C7
  Leeds, Halton LS15 ..... 81 A8
  Leeds, Headingley LS6 ..... 59 D5
  Littleborough LS15 ..... 129 D2
  Liversedge WF15 ..... 117 C4
  Lofthouse Gate WF3 ..... 121 C5
  Mirfield WF14 ..... 138 A5
  Ossett WF5 ..... 141 A4
  Pudsey, Calverley LS28 ..... 57 B6
  Pudsey, Rodley LS13 ..... 57 E5
  Pudsey, Stanningley LS28 ..... 57 E1
  Queensbury BD13 ..... 72 E1
  Rothwell WF3 ..... 100 D3
  Ryhill WF4 ..... 162 B1
  Silsden BD20 ..... 5 E2
  Slaithwaite HD7 ..... 152 B5
  Thornton BD13 ..... 72 D6
  4 Todmorden OL14 ..... 108 D6
  Yeadon LS19 ..... 40 B8
Chapel St N 4 HX3 ..... 91 F3
Chapel St S 7 OL14 ..... 108 A1
Chapel Terr Bradford BD15 ..... 54 B1
  Honley HD7 ..... 171 F4
  Huddersfield HD4 ..... 153 C2
  8 Leeds LS6 ..... 59 D5
  Ripponden HX6 ..... 133 C2
  Sowerby Bridge HX6 ..... 111 D3
  14 Thornton BD13 ..... 72 D6
Chapel Wlk Bingley BD16 ..... 36 F3
Chapel Yd LS15 ..... 81 D6

Chapelfields WF9 ..... 182 B1
Chapelgate HD7 ..... 189 D3
Chapeltown Halifax HX1 ..... 203 D3
  Pudsey LS28 ..... 76 D6
Chapeltown Bsns Ctr LS7 ..... 207 D4
Chapeltown Rd LS7 ..... 207 D4
Chapman St Bradford BD4 ..... 75 D6
  Leeds LS9 ..... 207 E1
Charing Cross Mews LS6 ..... 206 B3
Chariot Way WF8 ..... 165 A4
Charles Ave Bradford BD3 ..... 75 D7
  Halifax HX3 ..... 114 A4
  Huddersfield HD3 ..... 153 A8
  Leeds LS9 ..... 212 C2
  Lofthouse Gate WF1 ..... 121 B5
  Wakefield WF1 ..... 142 F3
Charles Cotton Cl WF2 ..... 141 D8
Charles Ct 3 BD22 ..... 51 C2
Charles Gdns LS11 ..... 211 D1
Charles Gr LS26 ..... 101 C6
Charles St Batley WF17 ..... 118 C4
  Bingley BD16 ..... 36 F3
  Bradford BD1 ..... 201 C3
  Brighouse HD6 ..... 115 A3
  Castleford WF10 ..... 124 E7
  Cleckheaton BD19 ..... 117 B8
  Dewsbury WF12 ..... 139 E8
  Dewsbury, Dewsbury Moor
  WF13 ..... 138 F8
  Dewsbury, Ravensthorpe
  WF13 ..... 138 E5
  Elland HX5 ..... 134 F6
  Halifax HX1 ..... 203 F3
  Horbury WF4 ..... 159 D7
  Horsforth LS18 ..... 58 B7
  Huddersfield HD4 ..... 153 D4
  Morley LS27 ..... 98 B4
  Ossett WF5 ..... 140 F3
  Otley LS21 ..... 23 A7
  Pudsey LS28 ..... 57 D3
  Queensbury BD13 ..... 72 D1
  Ryhill WF4 ..... 162 A1
  Shipley BD17 ..... 55 B8
  South Hiendley S72 ..... 180 E5
  15 Sowerby Bridge HX6 ..... 112 B5
  Wakefield WF1 ..... 216 C1
Charles View WF4 ..... 159 F3
Charleston St WF7 ..... 164 A4
Charlestown Rd HX3 ..... 203 F4
Charlesworth Dr HX2 ..... 202 A4
Charlesworth Pl WF3 ..... 122 C6
Charlesworth Sq BD19 ..... 117 A8
Charlesworth St WF12 ..... 139 C4
Charlesworth Terr HX2 ..... 202 A4
Charlesworth Way WF2 ..... 216 A1
Charlesworth's Bldgs 3
  WF4 ..... 141 A1
Charleville WF9 ..... 182 E4
Charlotte Cl WF17 ..... 96 F3
Charlotte Ct BD22 ..... 51 E8
Charlotte Gr 4 Leeds LS15 ..... 81 B8
  Ossett WF5 ..... 140 E4
Charlotte St WF1 ..... 216 C1
Charlton Ct HX2 ..... 202 A4
Charlton Gr 6 Leeds LS9 ..... 80 A7
Charlton Mount 2 LS9 ..... 212 C3
Charlton Pl LS9 ..... 80 A7
Charlton Rd LS9 ..... 80 A7
Charlton St LS9 ..... 80 A7
Charnwood Bank WF16 ..... 117 E4
Charnwood Cl BD2 ..... 56 C2
Charnwood Gr BD2 ..... 56 C2
Charnwood Rd BD2 ..... 56 C2
Charterhouse Rd BD10 ..... 39 E1
Chartents Rd BD8 ..... 73 C7
Chartists Way LS27 ..... 98 A3
Chartwell Ct LS17 ..... 44 B5
Charville Gdns LS17 ..... 44 F3
Chase The Burley in W LS29 ..... 22 A7
  Garforth LS25 ..... 82 D6
  Keighley BD21 ..... 34 F8
  Lofthouse Gate WF3 ..... 122 A6
  Wetherby LS22 ..... 13 F6
  Yeadon LS19 ..... 40 A4
Chase Way BD5 ..... 74 E2
Chassum Gr BD9 ..... 55 B2
Chaster St WF17 ..... 118 A6
Chat Hill Rd BD13 ..... 72 F5
Chatham St Bradford BD3 ..... 56 A1
  Halifax HX3 ..... 203 F3
  8 Sowerby Bridge HX6 ..... 112 B5
Chatswood Ave LS11 ..... 98 F8
Chatswood Cres LS11 ..... 98 F8
Chatswood Dr LS11 ..... 213 F1
Chatsworth Ave 4 LS28 ..... 76 A8
Chatsworth Cl
  Huddersfield HD5 ..... 154 D4
  Leeds LS8 ..... 208 A3
Chatsworth Cres LS28 ..... 76 A8
Chatsworth Dr WF12 ..... 139 F7
Chatsworth Fall LS28 ..... 76 A8
Chatsworth Ind Est LS12 ..... 210 A2
Chatsworth Mews 5 LS27 ..... 98 F3
Chatsworth Pl LS28 ..... 76 A8
Chatsworth Rd Leeds LS8 ..... 208 A3
  Pudsey LS28 ..... 76 A8
Chatsworth Rise LS28 ..... 76 A8
Chatsworth St BD21 ..... 35 D7
Chatsworth Terr WF12 ..... 139 F7
Chatts Wood Fold BD12 ..... 95 B5
Chaucer Ave
  Lofthouse Gate WF3 ..... 121 E6
  Pudsey LS28 ..... 76 D8
Chaucer Cl HD7 ..... 171 F3

haucer Gdns LS28 .... 76 F6
haucer Gr LS28 .... 76 F6
haucer St HX1 .... 202 B2
heapside Batley WF17 ..... 118 D5
Bradford BD1 .... 201 B3
Cleckheaton BD19 .... 116 E7
Halifax HX1 .... 203 E3
Normanton WF6 .... 123 B2
Shelf HX3 .... 93 C6
Wakefield WF1 .... 216 A2
heddington Gr BD15 .... 73 B8
heese Gate Nab Side
HD7 .... 190 A2
heetham St 图 HX7 .... 89 A3
helburn View OL15 .... 129 C1
hellow Dene Mid Sch
BD8 .... 73 D8
hellow Grange Rd BD9 ..... 54 C3
hellow La BD9 .... 54 D1
hellow St BD9 .... 74 D2
hellow Terr BD9 .... 54 D1
hellow Way WF12 .... 139 C7
helmsford Rd BD3 .... 75 C8
helmsford Terr BD3 .... 75 C7
helsea Cl LS12 .... 209 F2
helsea Mansions HX3 ..... 93 A2
helsea Rd BD7 .... 73 F4
helsea St BD21 .... 35 B6
helsfield Ct LS15 .... 62 F3
helsfield Way LS15 .... 62 F3
helsin Gr HD7 .... 171 E4
heltenham Ave LS29 .... 8 F4
heltenham Gdns HX3 ..... 113 D4
heltenham Pl HX3 .... 113 D4
heltenham Rd BD2 .... 55 F5
heltenham St LS12 .... 210 A2
helwood Ave LS8 .... 43 E3
helwood Cres LS8 .... 43 F3
helwood Dr
Bradford BD15 .... 73 A7
Leeds LS8 .... 43 F2
helwood Gr LS8 .... 43 F3
helwood Mount LS8 .... 43 F3
helwood Pl LS8 .... 43 E3
henics Cl LS14 .... 61 E1
hepstow Cl LS25 .... 83 B7
hequerfield Ave WF8 .... 146 F8
hequerfield Cl WF8 ...... 124 A6
hequerfield Dr WF8 ...... 146 F7
hequerfield Infant Sch
WF8 .... 146 F7
hequerfield La WF8 ...... 146 F8
hequerfield Mount WF8 .. 146 F7
hequers Ct WF8 .... 146 F7
hequers Cl WF8 .... 146 F8
heriton Dr BD13 .... 72 F1
herry Cl S71 .... 179 A4
herry Ct LS19 .... 207 E1
herry Fields BD2 .... 55 E4
herry Garth WF9 .... 181 C6
herry Gr LS29 .... 7 F4
herry Hills S75 .... 178 A1
herry La HD8 .... 175 F2
herry Lea Ct LS19 .... 40 B5
herry Nook Rd HD2 ...... 136 E3
herry Rise LS14 .... 62 C8
herry Row LS9 .... 207 E1
herry St 图 Haworth BD22 .. 51 E8
Keighley BD21 .... 35 E8
herry Tree Ave
Bradford BD10 .... 56 D7
Knottingley WF11 .... 126 E3
herry Tree Cl
Huddersfield HD7 .... 152 F5
Mapplewell S75 .... 178 C1
herry Tree Cres
Pudsey LS28 .... 57 D3
Walton WF2 .... 161 B7
herry Tree Ct WF3 .... 120 C7
herry Tree Ctr 图 HD1 .. 154 A6
herry Tree Dr Elland HX4 .. 134 C7
Pudsey LS28 .... 57 D3
Walton WF2 .... 161 B7
herry Tree Gdns BD10 ... 38 F1
herry Tree Rd WF2 .... 161 B7
herry Tree Rise BD21 ... 35 C6
herry Tree Row BD16 .... 53 B7
herry Tree Wlk
East Ardsley WF3 .... 120 C7
Holmfirth HD7 .... 189 D4
herrywood Cl LS14 .... 45 B1
herrywood Gdns LS14 .... 45 B1
hervana Ct BD4 .... 75 E4
herwell Croft LS25 .... 83 B5
herwell Dr BD6 .... 93 F7
hesham St Bradford BD7 .. 74 C6
Keighley BD21 .... 35 D8
hesil Bank HD3 .... 153 B6
hesilton Ave HD3 .... 153 C7
hesney Ave LS10 .... 215 D4
hesney Pk Ind Est LS10 .. 215 D4
hesnut End LS23 .... 30 E7
hessington Dr WF4 .... 157 D3
hester Cl 图 HX3 .... 92 B1
hester Ct 图 HX3 .... 92 B1
hester Gr 图 HX3 .... 92 B1
hester Pl 图 HX3 .... 92 B1
hester Rd HX3 .... 92 B1
hester St Bradford BD5 ... 201 B2
Halifax, Woodside HX3 ...... 92 B1
Leeds LS12 .... 209 F4
图 Sowerby Bridge HX6 ... 112 B4
hester Terr HX3 .... 92 B1
hesterton Ct
Horbury WF4 .... 141 C2
Leeds LS15 .... 81 D6

Chesterton Dr HD7 .... 171 F3
Chestnut Ave Batley WF17 .. 118 A4
Boston Spa LS23 .... 30 C8
Brierley S72 .... 180 F2
Leeds, Cross Gates LS15 ... 62 D2
Leeds, Hyde Park LS6 ..... 206 B3
Todmorden OL14 .... 108 A7
Walton WF2 .... 161 A6
Wetherby LS22 .... 13 D6
Chestnut Cl Elland HX4 ... 134 B7
Featherstone WF7 .... 145 B7
Huddersfield HD4 .... 154 A2
Ilkley LS29 .... 8 E3
Keighley BD22 .... 34 F6
Chestnut Cres WF6 .... 144 A7
Chestnut Ct
Ripponden HX6 .... 132 D4
图 54 F7
Chestnut Dr Leeds LS16 .. 42 B5
South Hiendley S72 .... 180 D5
Chestnut Garth HD3 ..... 153 B7
Chestnut Gdns LS12 ..... 209 F2
Chestnut Gn WF8 .... 125 F1
Chestnut Gr
Boston Spa LS23 .... 30 C8
Crofton WF4 .... 143 F1
Hemsworth WF9 .... 181 F6
Leeds LS6 .... 205 E3
Pontefract WF8 .... 146 D6
Pudsey LS28 .... 57 B6
Shipley BD2 .... 55 E4
Chestnut Meadows WF14 .. 137 F8
图 205 E3
Chestnut Pl LS6 .... 205 E3
Chestnut Rd 图 LS6 .... 205 E3
Chestnut Rise LS12 .... 209 E2
Chestnut St Glusburn BD20 ... 16 D6
Halifax HX1 .... 202 B2
Huddersfield HD2 .... 136 D3
Leeds LS6 .... 205 E3
South Elmsall WF9 .... 182 F1
Chestnut Terr WF12 ...... 139 C3
Chestnut Way LS16 .... 42 B5
Chestnut Wlk
Knottingley WF11 .... 126 D3
Wakefield WF2 .... 142 A8
Chestnuts The WF8 ...... 126 A4
Chevet Croft WF2 .... 160 E7
Chevet Gr WF2 .... 160 E7
Chevet La WF2 .... 160 F3
Chevet La Notton WF4 ... 179 B8
Wakefield WF2, WF4 ..... 160 F6
Walton WF2 .... 161 B2
Walton, Woolgreaves
WF2, WF4 .... 160 F6
Chevet Level WF2 .... 160 F4
Chevet Mount BD15 .... 73 A8
Chevet Park Ct WF2 ...... 160 E3
Chevet Rise S71 .... 179 B4
Chevet View S71 .... 179 A4
Chevin Ave Menston LS29 ... 22 A5
Otley LS21 .... 23 B6
Chevin End Rd LS20 .... 22 D3
Chevin Forest Park LS21 .. 23 D5
Chevin Side LS21 .... 23 A6
Chevinedge Cres HX3 ... 113 D1
Chevington Ct LS19 .... 40 A3
Chevins Cl WF17 .... 117 F8
Cheviot Ave HD7 .... 170 F1
Cheviot Cl WF9 .... 181 F7
Cheviot Ct LS25 .... 82 F5
Cheviot Gate BD12 .... 94 B6
Cheviot Pl WF11 .... 126 F4
Cheviot Way HX1 .... 137 F2
Cheyne Wlk 图 BD22 ...... 35 A6
Chichester St LS12 .... 209 E4
Chickenley La WF12 ..... 140 B7
Chickenley Com Jun
& Inf Sch WF12 .... 140 A7
Chidswell Gdns WF12 .. 119 B3
Chidswell La Batley WF12 .. 119 A3
Ossett WF5 .... 119 B2
Child La WF15 .... 116 F1
Childs La BD18 .... 55 E6
Childs Rd WF12 .... 141 D8
Chiltern Ave
Castleford WF10 .... 123 F5
Huddersfield HD3 .... 135 A1
Knottingley WF11 .... 126 E4
Chiltern Cl LS25 .... 82 F5
Chiltern Ct Garforth LS25 ... 82 F5
Hemsworth WF9 .... 181 F7
Pudsey LS13 .... 57 E5
Chiltern Dr
Ackworth M T WF7 .... 163 F5
Mirfield WF14 .... 137 F2
Chiltern Rd WF12 .... 118 F1
Chiltern Way WF12 ...... 116 D5
Chilwell Cl S71 .... 178 F1
Chilwell Gdns S71 .... 178 F1
Chilwell Mews S71 .... 178 F1
Chimes The HD5 .... 155 C7
Chimney La HD8 .... 155 D4
Chinewood Ave WF17 .. 118 B6
Chippendale Ct LS29 ...... 22 B4
Chippendale Rise
Bradford BD8 .... 73 D8
Otley LS21 .... 11 A1
Chirton Gr LS8 .... 61 A5
Chislehurst Pl BD5 .... 74 C4
Chiswick St LS6 .... 205 E2
Chiswick Terr 图 LS6 ..... 205 E2
Choppards Bank Rd HD7 .. 189 A2
Choppards La HD7 .... 189 A2
Chorley La 图 LS2 .... 211 D4
Chrisharben Pk BD14 ...... 73 C4
Chrismoor BD10 .... 56 A7
Christ Church Ave LS12 .. 209 E4

Christ Church C of E
Jun & Inf Sch HX2 .... 112 D8
Christ Church C of E
Junior Sch HX6 .... 112 C5
Christ Church Mount
LS12 .... 209 E4
Christ Church Par LS12 .. 209 E4
Christ Church Pl LS12 .... 209 E4
Christ Church Rd LS12 ... 209 E4
Christ Church St 图 OL13 .. 106 A3
Christ Church Terr 图 BD5 .. 209 E4
Christ Church View LS12 .. 209 E4
Christ Church Woodhouse
CE Inf & Jun Sch
Huddersfield, Riddings HD2 ... 136 C4
Huddersfield, Sheepridge
HD2 .... 136 C3
Christ the King
RC Primary Sch LS13 ...... 58 E1
Christiana Terr LS27 .... 98 B5
Christopher Rd LS6 .... 206 A4
Christopher St 图 BD5 ...... 74 C3
Christopher Terr 图 BD5 ... 74 C3
Church App LS25 .... 82 F7
Church Ave Crofton WF1 .. 143 D7
Gildersome LS27 .... 97 C8
Horsforth LS18 .... 41 B1
Huddersfield, Lindthwaite
HD7 .... 152 E2
Huddersfield, Yews Hill HD4 .. 153 E4
Leeds LS6 .... 59 F7
South Kirkby WF9 .... 182 C2
Swillington LS26 .... 82 A2
Church Bank
Bradford BD1 .... 201 C3
Halifax, Highroad Well HX2 .. 112 D6
Sowerby Bridge HX6 ...... 112 C4
Church Bank La HX7 ..... 110 C3
Church Cl Crofton WF4 ... 143 D7
Halifax HX1 .... 203 D3
Halifax, Ovenden HX2 ..... 91 D5
Hemsworth WF9 .... 181 D7
Leeds LS14 .... 62 B4
Mapplewell S75 .... 177 E1
Mickelfield LS25 .... 84 A8
Pool LS21 .... 24 C7
Shipley HD8 .... 190 D8
Swillington LS26 .... 82 A1
Church Cres
Horsforth LS18 .... 41 B1
Leeds LS17 .... 43 B3
Netherton WF4 .... 158 E6
Swillington LS26 .... 82 B1
Yeadon LS19 .... 40 A6
Church Cswy LS23 .... 14 F1
Church Ct Bradford BD7 .. 73 F5
Keighley BD20 .... 18 F2
Normanton WF6 .... 123 A1
Ossett WF5 .... 140 D7
Yeadon LS19 .... 40 A6
Church Dr Brierley S72 .. 180 F3
East Keswick LS17 .... 28 B5
South Kirkby WF9 .... 182 C2
Church Farm Cl
Normanton WF6 .... 122 F4
Rothwell WF3 .... 100 C1
Church Farm Views LS17 .. 63 E7
Church Field Rd DN5 .... 194 E4
Church Fields BD2 .... 56 D2
Church Fields Mews
HD7 .... 124 F6
Church Garth
Castleford WF10 .... 124 F6
Pool LS21 .... 24 C7
Church Gate LS18 .... 41 B1
Church Gdns
Garforth LS25 .... 82 F6
Gildersome LS27 .... 97 C7
Bradford BD8 .... 55 C1
Bradford, Beck Hill BD6 .. 93 E7
Brighouse HD6 .... 135 F7
Brotherton WF11 .... 126 C8
Castleford WF10 .... 124 D8
Cawthorne S75 .... 193 E4
Cleckheaton BD19 .... 116 E7
Church Grange 图 BD20 .. 116 E7
Church Hill Baildon BD17 ... 38 D4
Bramham LS23 .... 30 D2
Bramhope LS16 .... 24 D3
Halifax HX2 .... 90 D1
Royston S71 .... 179 D3
Thorner LS14 .... 46 A6
Church Hill Gdns LS28 ... 57 F2
Church Hill La LS28 .... 57 F2
Church Hill Mount LS28 .. 57 F2
Church House 图 HX5 ... 134 F7
Church La Bardsey LS17 .. 28 C2
Batley WF16 .... 117 D3
Bradford BD6 .... 94 B8
图 Brighouse HD6 .... 115 A2
Brighouse, Bailiff Bridge
HD6 .... 135 D7
Brighouse, Southowram,
HX3 .... 114 C4
Brighouse, Waring Green
HD6 .... 115 A3
Cawthorne S75 .... 193 F4
Clayton West HD8 .... 175 F2
Cleckheaton BD19 .... 117 C8
Clifton LS21 .... 10 B2
Collingham LS22 .... 13 B1
Crigglestone WF4 .... 160 A4
Darrington WF8 .... 147 D5
Dewsbury, Dewsbury Moor
WF13 .... 138 F8
Dewsbury, Thornhill WF12 ... 139 E2
East Ardsley WF3 .... 120 C7

Church La continued
East Ardsley, Upper Green
WF3 .... 119 D7
Elland HX4 .... 134 A4
Featherstone WF7 .... 124 C1
Garforth LS25 .... 82 F7
Guiseley BD17 .... 39 C5
Halifax HX2 .... 91 E1
Harewood LS17 .... 26 F7
Hebden Bridge HX7 .... 88 F5
Heptonstall HX7 .... 88 F5
High Hoyland S75 .... 176 C1
Horsforth LS18 .... 41 B1
Huddersfield HD4 .... 171 B6
Huddersfield, Linthwaite
HD7 .... 152 E1
Huddersfield, Moldgreen
HD5 .... 154 D6
Huddersfield, Newsome HD4 .. 154 A2
Kippax LS25 .... 83 B1
Kirkheaton HD5 .... 155 B7
Leeds LS16 .... 59 F7
Leeds LS2 .... 212 A3
Leeds, Adel LS16 .... 42 C5
Leeds, Chapel Allerton LS7 .. 204 A2
Leeds, Manston LS15 ...... 62 D3
Liversedge WF15 .... 116 E5
Liversedge, Knowler Hill
WF15 .... 117 A5
Lofthouse Gate WF1 ..... 121 B5
Marsden HD7 .... 168 F4
Marsden, Scammonden HX4 .. 150 F5
Micklefield LS25 .... 83 F7
Mickletown LS26 .... 102 C2
Mirfield WF14 .... 138 C5
Netherton WF4 .... 158 E7
Normanton WF6 .... 123 A1
Normanton WF7 .... 144 D8
图 Pontefract WF8 .... 146 D8
Pool LS21 .... 24 C7
Pudsey LS28 .... 76 E7
Ryhill S71 .... 179 F7
Shipley HD8 .... 190 E8
Swillington LS26 .... 82 A1
Church Lane Ave WF1 .. 121 B5
Church Meadows
Batley WF17 .... 96 D1
Bramham LS23 .... 30 D3
Church Mews
Boston Spa LS23 .... 30 D8
图 Bradford BD6 .... 93 E7
Church Mount
Horsforth LS18 .... 41 B1
South Kirkby WF9 .... 182 C2
Church Pk WF15 .... 116 E2
Church Pl Garforth LS25 .. 82 F7
Halifax HX1 .... 203 D3
Church Rd Batley WF17 .. 117 F8
Bradford BD6 .... 94 B8
Cawthorne S75 .... 193 E4
Cleckheaton BD19 .... 116 E7
Horsforth LS18 .... 41 B1
Leeds LS2 .... 209 F3
Leeds, Bank LS9 .... 212 B3
Liversedge FW15 .... 116 E2
Lofthouse Gate WF3 ..... 121 F5
Normanton WF6 .... 122 E4
Sutton in C BD20 .... 16 D5
Swillington LS26 .... 102 E8
Swillington LS26 .... 107 E8
图 Church Row WF9 .... 9 A6
Church Sch The BD13 .... 72 E6
Church Side LS26 .... 102 C2
图 Church Side Cl 图 HX3 .. 92 C1
Church Side Dr 图 HX3 .... 92 C1
Church Sq LS25 .... 82 F7
Church St Addingham LS29 .. 7 A8
Batley, Birstall WF17 .... 96 E1
Batley, Heckmondwike
WF16 .... 117 D3
Batley St OL14 .... 107 D8
图 Church Vale WF12 ..... 119 A2
Cinder Hill HD8 .... 174 B7
Cinder Hill Rd OL14 ..... 108 E6
Cinder Hills Rd HD7 ..... 189 B4
Cinder La Boston Spa LS23 .. 30 E6
Castleford WF10 .... 124 C8
Lindley LS21 .... 11 F5
Cinderhills La HX3 .... 113 E3
Circle The S66 .... 146 E2
City La HX3 .... 91 E2
City of Leeds
Coll of Music LS2 .... 206 B1
City of Leeds Sch LS6 ... 206 A4
City Park Ind Est LS12 .... 78 C3
City Rd BD8 .... 74 C8
City Sq LS1 .... 211 E3
City Square Mall LS1 .... 211 F3
City Varieties Music Hall
LS1 .... 211 F4
City Vue Office Pk
LS12 .... 213 D3
Cityway Ind Est BD4 .... 75 A5
Clapgate LS21 .... 23 A8
Clapgate La HX6 .... 132 E7

Church St continued
Leeds LS10 .... 215 E3
Leeds, Kirkstall LS5 .... 59 A4
Liversedge WF15 .... 117 A5
Mapplewell S75 .... 178 C1
Mapplewell, Bloomhouse
S75 .... 177 E1
Morley LS27 .... 98 A5
Ossett WF5 .... 140 D7
图 Oxenhope BD22 .... 51 C2
Rothwell, Churchfields LS26 .. 100 E5
Rothwell, Woodlesford LS26 .. 101 C1
Royston S71 .... 179 C3
Royston, Carlton S71 ..... 179 D1
Shipley BD18 .... 55 D8
Slaithwaite HD7 .... 169 F8
South Elmsall WF9 .... 183 A2
Todmorden OL14 .... 108 E6
Wetherby LS22 .... 13 E5
Woolley WF4 .... 177 F7
Yeadon LS19 .... 40 A6
Church Terr
Clayton West HD8 .... 175 D1
Halifax HX4 .... 91 D5
Holmfirth HD7 .... 189 A5
Church Top WF9 .... 182 C2
Church View
Cleckheaton BD19 .... 116 B8
Crigglestone WF4 .... 159 F5
Featherstone WF7 .... 145 C5
Holmfirth HD7 .... 188 C2
Kippax LS25 .... 83 D2
South Kirkby WF9 .... 182 C2
Sowerby Bridge HX6 ..... 112 C4
Thorner LS14 .... 45 F6
Wakefield WF1 .... 142 E2
Church View Cl WF4 ..... 162 C1
Church View Mews LS12 .. 30 D5
Church Villas WF9 .... 182 C2
Church Way Keighley BD21 .. 35 C6
图 Morley LS27 .... 98 A5
Church Wlk Batley WF17 .. 118 A3
Dewsbury WF12 .... 139 E2
Leeds LS2 .... 212 A3
Northowram HX3 .... 93 A2
Todmorden OL14 .... 108 B1
Church Wood Ave LS16 .. 59 C7
Church Wood Mount LS16 .. 59 C7
Church Wood Rd LS16 .. 59 C8
Churchbalk Dr WF8 ...... 146 E6
Churchbalk La WF8 ...... 146 E6
Churchfarm Garth LS17 .. 44 F4
Churchfield Cl 图 WF5 ... 117 A4
Churchfield Croft
Normanton WF6 .... 122 F4
Rothwell LS26 .... 100 F5
Churchfield Gr LS26 ..... 100 E6
Churchfield La
Castleford WF10 .... 124 F7
Kirk Smeaton WF8 .... 166 F7
Rothwell LS26 .... 100 E6
Churchfield Rd LS26 ..... 100 F5
Churchfield St 图 WF1 .. 117 C5
Churchfield Terr 图 WF15 .. 117 A4
Churchfields Crofton WF4 .. 143 A1
Huddersfield HD2 .... 136 F3
Ryhill WF4 .... 162 B2
Churchfields Rd HD6 .... 115 A3
Churchgate LS16 .... 24 D3
Churchill Flats LS21 .... 24 C7
Churchill Gdns 图 LS2 .. 206 B2
Churchill Gr Batley WF16 .. 117 E3
Wakefield WF2 .... 160 B8
Churchill Rd BD13 .... 72 F6
Churchill St OL14 .... 107 D8
Churchill Way BD20 .... 16 E7
Churchside Villas LS26 .. 102 C2
Churchtown Cres OL13 .. 106 B1
Churchville LS25 .... 84 A8
Churchville Ave LS25 ...... 83 F7
Churchville Dr LS25 .... 84 A7
Churchville Terr LS25 ..... 84 A7
Churchway LS27 .... 144 A1
Churchwood Cl HD7 ..... 151 F1
Churn La HX2 .... 112 D7
Churn Milk La HX3 .... 92 A4
Churwell Ave 图 WF13 .. 117 F3
Churwell Cl WF10 .... 124 D6

Clapgate Primary Sch
LS10 .... 99 F5
Clapham Dene Rd LS15 ...... 62 B1
Clapham St BD13 .... 71 E8
Claphouse Fold S75 .... 177 A5
Clapton Ave HX1 .... 202 C2
Clara Dr LS28 .... 57 A8
Clara Rd BD2 .... 55 F5
Clara St Brighouse HD6 .... 115 A1
Huddersfield HD1 .... 154 A8
Huddersfield, Cowlersley
HD4 .... 153 A3
Huddersfield, Fartown HD1 .. 136 A1
Pudsey LS28 .... 57 D2
Clare Cres BD12 .... 94 E1
Clare Hall LA HX1 .... 203 E2
Clare Hill HD1 .... 154 A7
Clare Rd Bradford BD12 .... 94 C2
Cleckheaton BD19 .... 116 D7
Halifax HX1 .... 203 E2
Hebden Bridge HX7 .... 89 D1
Clare St HX1 .... 203 E2
Claremont Ave
8 Leeds LS12 .... 206 A1
Shipley BD18 .... 55 E6
Claremont Cres
Crofton WF4 .... 161 F8
Leeds LS6 .... 59 F5
Leeds LS6 .... 59 E6
Shipley BD18 .... 55 E6
Claremont Ct LS6 .... 59 E6
Claremont Dr LS6 .... 59 E6
Claremont Gdns
Bingley BD16 .... 37 A4
Pudsey LS28 .... 57 D2
Claremont Gr
4 Leeds LS12 .... 206 A1
Pudsey LS28 .... 76 E7
Shipley BD18 .... 55 F6
Claremont Pl LS12 .... 209 D3
Claremont Rd
Dewsbury WF13 .... 118 B1
Leeds LS6 .... 59 E6
Shipley BD18 .... 55 E6
Claremont St
7 Cleckheaton BD19 .... 116 D8
Huddersfield HD1 .... 154 A7
Leeds LS12 .... 209 D3
Rothwell LS26 .... 101 C6
Sowerby Bridge HX6 .... 112 C5
Wakefield WF1 .... 142 E4
Claremont Terr
Bradford BD6 .... 74 D6
Leeds LS12 .... 209 D3
Todmorden OL14 .... 129 C5
Wakefield WF2 .... 142 A5
Claremont View 3
Leeds LS3 .... 206 A1
6 Rothwell LS26 .... 101 C6
Claremount Rd HX3 .... 92 C2
Claremount Terr 8 HX3 ..... 92 C2
Menston LS29 .... 21 F6
Clarence Gdns LS18 .... 58 B7
Clarence Mews LS18 .... 58 B7
Clarence Rd Horsforth LS18 .. 58 B7
Leeds LS10 .... 212 B2
Shipley BD18 .... 54 F8
Wakefield WF2 .... 142 B3
Clarence St Batley WF17 ..... 118 D5
Cleckheaton BD19 .... 116 D7
Halifax HX1 .... 203 D3
Leeds LS13 .... 58 C1
Clarence Terr
Dewsbury WF22 .... 139 D6
Leeds LS28 .... 76 E8
Clarence Wlk WF2 .... 142 A5
Clarendon Ct WF1 .... 216 B3
Clarendon Pl Halifax HX1 .... 202 C2
Leeds LS2 .... 206 A2
8 Queensbury BD13 .... 92 C8
Clarendon Rd Bingley BD16 .. 37 B4
Boston Spa LS23 .... 30 C8
Leeds LS2 .... 206 A1
Clarendon St
9 Haworth BD22 .... 51 C6
Hebden Bridge HX7 .... 89 E1
Keighley BD21 .... 35 B5
Wakefield WF1 .... 216 B3
Clarendon Terr LS28 .... 76 E6
Clarendon Way LS22 .... 206 A2
Clarges St BD5 .... 74 D3
Clarion Field LS29 .... 22 D5
Clark Ave LS9 .... 212 C3
Clark Cres LS9 .... 212 C3
Clark Gr LS9 .... 212 C3
Clark La LS9 .... 212 C3
Clark Mount LS9 .... 212 C3
Clark Rd LS9 .... 212 C3
Clark Row LS9 .... 212 C2
Clark Spring Cl LS27 .... 98 A7
Clark Spring Rise LS27 .... 98 B7
Clark Terr LS9 .... 212 C3
Clark View LS9 .... 212 C2
Clarke Cres WF6 .... 144 A7
Clarke Gr WF11 .... 126 E1
Clarke La HD7 .... 170 E2
Clarke Rd WF3 .... 119 E5
Clarke St Dewsbury WF13 ..... 118 A1
Pudsey LS28 .... 57 B6
Clarkson Ave WF16 .... 117 E4
Clarkson Cl WF16 .... 117 E4

Clarkson Ct WF6 .... 123 C1
Clarkson St Dewsbury WF13 138 E6
Wakefield WF2 .... 142 A5
Clarkson View LS6 .... 206 A4
Clarydon Pl 2 WF16 .... 117 D4
Clattering Stones Rd HX7 . 110 E2
Clay Butts HD2 .... 135 E2
Clay Hill Dr BD12 .... 94 D4
Clay House La HX4 .... 134 D7
Clay La HD7 .... 152 A1
Clay Pit La LS2, LS7 .... 206 C1
Clay Pits La Halifax HX1 ...... 202 B4
Ripponden HX6 .... 132 B2
Clay St Halifax HX1 .... 202 B3
Sowerby Bridge HX6 .... 112 B4
Sowerby Bridge HX6 .... 112 C5
Clay Well HD7 .... 152 D4
Clayborn View BD19 .... 116 E6
Clayfield Bglws WF11 .... 126 C4
Clayfield Dr BD7 .... 74 A2
Claypit La Ledsham LS25 ...... 104 C7
Thorner LS14 .... 45 F5
Clayton Ave Dearne S63 ...... 194 B1
Kippax LS25 .... 83 C2
Upton WF9 .... 183 E8

Clayton C of E First Sch
BD14 .... 73 C4
Clayton (CE) First Sch
BD14 .... 73 B4
Clayton Cl LS10 .... 215 F2
Clayton Cotts 2 WF4 .... 141 A1
Clayton Ct
Featherstone WF7 .... 145 C5
Leeds LS8 .... 58 F8
Leeds LS10 .... 215 F2
Clayton Dr LS10 .... 215 F2
Clayton Fields HD2 .... 153 F8
Clayton Gr LS19 .... 40 B7
Clayton Grange 2 LS16 .... 58 F8
Clayton Hall Rd BD20 .... 16 E6
Clayton Holt WF1 .... 182 B1
Clayton Hospl WF1 .... 216 A3
Clayton La Bradford BD5 .... 74 E4
Bradford, Clayton BD14 .... 73 B4
Dearne S63 .... 194 B2
Clayton Mews WF6 .... 123 A4
Clayton Middle Sch BD14 .... 73 C4
Clayton Pl WF6 .... 123 A4
Clayton Rd Bradford BD7 .... 74 A3
Leeds LS10 .... 215 F2
Clayton St Rothwell LS26 .... 100 F5
Wakefield WF2 .... 142 A5
Clayton Terr BD13 .... 52 D5
Clayton View WF9 .... 182 B1
Clayton Way LS10 .... 215 F2
Clayton West Sta HD8 .... 175 F3
Clayton Wood Bank LS16 ..... 41 F1
Clayton Wood Cl LS16 .... 41 F1
Clayton Wood Ct LS16 .... 41 F1
Clayton Wood Rd LS16 .... 41 F1
Clayton Wood Rise LS16 ...... 41 F1
Claytons Bldgs WF7 .... 145 D8
Clearings The LS10 .... 99 D8
Cleasby Rd LS29 .... 22 B4
Cleavesty La LS17 .... 28 B6
Cleckheaton Golf Course
BD19 .... 95 A2
Cleckheaton Rd BD12 .... 94 D6
Clee Hill LS19 .... 40 A8
Cleethorpe Gr WF2 .... 142 E1
Clegg La HX4 .... 133 F7
Clegg St 10 BD12 .... 94 C3
Clement St 3 Bradford BD8 .. 73 F8
Huddersfield HD1 .... 153 F8
Huddersfield, Paddock Brow
HD4 .... 153 D4
5 Sowerby Bridge HX6 ...... 112 B4
Wakefield WF2 .... 141 F5
Clement Terr
Dewsbury WF12 .... 139 C6
Rothwell LS26 .... 100 E4
Cleopatra Pl 4 LS13 .... 58 C1
Clerk Green St WF17 .... 118 B4
Clervaux Ct BD14 .... 73 D5
Clevedon Pl 4 HX3 .... 92 A2
Clevedon Way LS17 .... 179 B4
Cleveland Ave Halifax HX3 ... 113 D4
Horbury WF2 .... 141 D2
Knottingley WF11 .... 126 E4
Cleveland Garth WF2 .... 141 D2
Cleveland Gr WF2 .... 141 D2
Cleveland Pl 3 HX7 .... 89 A3
Cleveland Rd Bradford BD9 .... 55 A3
Huddersfield HD1 .... 153 D7
Cleveland St OL14 .... 86 B1
Cleveland Way HD8 .... 173 F3
Cleveley Gdns HX7 .... 110 E8
Cleveleys Ave Leeds LS11 .... 213 F4
6 Sowerby Bridge HX6 .... 112 B5
Cleveleys Cl LS11 .... 213 F4
Cleveleys Gdns 12 HX6 ...... 112 B5
Cleveleys Mount 4 LS11 .... 213 F4
Cleveleys Rd LS11 .... 213 F4
Cleveleys St LS11 .... 213 F4
Cleveleys Terr 3 LS11 .... 213 F4
Cliff Cl HD3 .... 153 B6
Cliff Cres Halifax HX2 .... 202 A1
Kippax LS25 .... 83 C1
Cliff Ct 1 Leeds LS6 .... 206 A4
Liversedge WF15 .... 117 A3
Cliff Dr WF4 .... 159 D5
Cliff Gdns HX2 .... 202 A1
Cliff Gr WF4 .... 159 C4
Cliff Hill LS25 .... 193 E5
Cliff Hill La HX2 .... 112 B6

Cliff Hollins La BD12, BD4 .... 95 C6
Cliff House La HD7 .... 189 B6
Cliff La Brierley S72 .... 180 F2
Holmfirth HD7 .... 189 B5
Leeds LS6 .... 205 F4
Ripponden HX6 .... 132 D2
Wakefield WF1 .... 216 A2
Cliff Mount LS6 .... 206 A4
Cliff Mount St LS6 .... 206 A4
Cliff Parade WF1 .... 216 A2
Cliff Park Ave WF1 .... 216 A3
Cliff Rd Crigglestone WF4 ..... 159 D8
Holmfirth, Cliff HD7 .... 189 B6
Holmfirth, Flush House HD7 . 188 A4
Leeds LS6 .... 206 A4
Cliff Road Gdns LS6 .... 206 A4
Cliff Side Gdns LS6 .... 206 A4
Cliff St Haworth BD22 .... 51 D7
8 Pontefract WF8 .... 146 C8
Wakefield WF2 .... 141 F7
Cliff Terr Leeds LS6 .... 206 A4
Micklefield LS25 .... 84 B6
Cliff Vale Rd BD18 .... 55 B5
Cliff Villas 7 WF8 .... 146 C8
Cliff Wood Ave WF18 .... 55 B6
Cliffdale Rd LS7 .... 206 B4

Cliffdale Road Ind Est
LS7 .... 206 B4
Cliffdale Road
Light Ind Est LS7 .... 206 B4
Cliffe Ash HD7 .... 152 D4
Cliffe Ave Baildon BD17 .... 38 C3
Brighouse HX3 .... 115 A7
Harden BD16 .... 36 A1
Cliffe Castle Mus BD20 .... 18 B1
Cliffe Cl S72 .... 180 F3
Cliffe Cres BD20 .... 36 B8
Cliffe Crest WF4 .... 141 A2
Cliffe Ct BD21 .... 35 B8
Cliffe Dr LS19 .... 40 B3
Cliffe End Rd HD3 .... 153 B6
Cliffe Gdns BD18 .... 55 B6
Cliffe Hill Ct HD7 .... 189 B5

Cliffe Hill Junior School
HX3 .... 115 A6
Cliffe House Ave LS25 .... 83 A5
Cliffe La Baildon BD17 .... 38 C1
Cleckheaton BD19 .... 95 F1
Kirkburton HD4 .... 172 E6
Thornton BD13 .... 72 E7
Yeadon LS19 .... 40 C3
Cliffe La S BD17 .... 38 C1
Cliffe La W BD17 .... 38 C2
Cliffe Mill Fold BD20 .... 36 E8
Cliffe Mount BD19 .... 96 A1
Cliffe Park Chase LS12 .... 209 D2
Cliffe Park Cres LS12 .... 209 D2
Cliffe Park Cl LS12 .... 209 D2
Cliffe Park Dr LS12 .... 209 D2
Cliffe Park Mount LS12 .... 209 D2
Cliffe Park Rise LS12 .... 209 D2
Cliffe Pk HD8 .... 190 E8
Cliffe Rd Bradford BD3 .... 55 F1
Brighouse HD6 .... 115 B2
Keighley BD21 .... 35 B4
Shepley HD8 .... 190 E8
Cliffe St Batley WF17 .... 117 F4
Clayton West HD8 .... 175 F2
Dewsbury WF13 .... 118 D1
9 Hebden Bridge HX7 .... 89 A3
Keighley BD21 .... 35 B8
Littleborough OL15 .... 129 D2
Thornton BD13 .... 72 D7
Cliffe Terr Baildon BD17 .... 38 C1
Bradford BD8 .... 55 D1
Halifax, Charcoal Green HX3 . 113 C2
Keighley BD21 .... 35 C4
Sowerby Bridge HX6 .... 112 A5
Wetherby LS22 .... 13 E5
8 Wilsden Cliffe Bradford BD15 .. 53 C5
Clayton West HD8 .... 175 F2
Morley LS27 .... 97 D3
Cliffe Wood Cl BD9 .... 54 E3
Cliffestone Dr BD20 .... 36 D8
Cliffewood Rise HD8 .... 175 E2
Clifford Ave Ilkley LS29 .... 8 A5
Wakefield WF2 .... 142 D2
Clifford Ct WF5 .... 140 C6

Clifford Moor Rd LS23 .... 30 C7
Clifford Pl 3 LS27 .... 98 B7
Clifford Rd Baildon BD17 .... 38 C2
Boston Spa LS23 .... 30 E7
Bramham LS23 .... 30 D3
Ilkley LS29 .... 8 A5
South Kirkby WF9 .... 182 B2
Clifford St Bradford BD5 ...... 201 B1
Cudworth S72 .... 180 C1
Silsden BD20 .... 5 D2
South Elmsall WF9 .... 182 F2
Clifford View WF2 .... 142 D2
Clifton Ave Halifax HX1 .... 202 B2
Holmfirth HD7 .... 189 B6
Horbury WF4 .... 141 A2
Leeds LS9 .... 208 B2
Littleborough OL15 .... 129 C1
6 Pontefract WF8 .... 146 B8
Clifton Cl WF4 .... 141 A2
Clifton Comm HD6 .... 115 C3
Clifton Cres Barnsley S71 .... 178 F1
Horbury WF4 .... 141 A2
Clifton Ct 10 LS28 .... 76 E8
Clifton Dr Horbury WF4 .... 141 A2
Pudsey LS28 .... 76 E8
Clifton Forge Bsns Pk
WF11 .... 126 E4

Clifton Gdns S72 .... 180 E3
Clifton Gr LS9 .... 208 B1
Clifton Hill LS28 .... 76 E8
Clifton Infant Sch WF4 .... 140 F2
Clifton La Clifton LS21 .... 10 E5
Meltham HD7 .... 170 E2
Clifton Mount LS9 .... 208 A2
Clifton Pl Pudsey LS28 .... 76 E8
Shipley BD18 .... 55 B6
Wakefield WF1 .... 216 A4
Clifton Rd
8 Brighouse HD6 .... 115 B2
Crofton WF4 .... 143 A3
Huddersfield HD1 .... 113 C4
Horbury WF4 .... 141 A2
Huddersfield HD1 .... 153 E7
Ilkley LS29 .... 8 D3
Pudsey LS28 .... 76 E8
Clifton Side HD2 .... 136 F6
Clifton St Bradford BD8 .... 55 D1
13 Halifax HX3 .... 92 A1
Hemsworth WF9 .... 181 C6
Keighley BD22 .... 35 A6
10 Queensbury BD13 .... 72 E1
Sowerby Bridge HX6 .... 112 C4
Clifton Terr Batley WF17 ..... 118 D5
Leeds LS9 .... 208 A2
Ossett WF5 .... 140 C8
Clifton View
Clayton West HD8 .... 175 F2
8 Pontefract WF8 .... 146 B8
Clifton Villas BD8 .... 55 D1
Clipston Ave LS6 .... 59 F6
Clipstone Ave HD6 .... 136 A1
Clipston La HD6 .... 136 A1
Clipston St LS6 .... 59 F6
Clipston Terr 9 LS6 .... 59 F6
Clipstone St 2 BD5 .... 74 E2
Clive Pl BD7 .... 74 B5
Clive Terr BD7 .... 74 B5
Cliviger-Holme CE
Primary Sch BB10 .... 85 B6
Cloberry St LS2 .... 206 A2
Clock Bldgs LS8 .... 208 A4
Clock La BD13 .... 71 D8
Clock Row Ave WF9 .... 182 D3
Clock Row Gr WF9 .... 182 D3
Clock Row Mount WF9 .... 182 D3
Clock View St BD20 .... 18 B2
Clog Bridge BD20 .... 5 E1
Clog Mill & Mus HX7 .... 89 C7
Clog Sole Rd HD6 .... 114 F4
Cloisters The HX1 .... 202 C1
Close Head BD13 .... 72 B6
Close Head Dr BD13 .... 72 B6
Close Head La BD13 .... 72 B6
Close Hill La HD4 .... 153 F2
Close Lea HD6 .... 115 A1
Close Lea Ave HD6 .... 114 F1
Close Lea Dr HD6 .... 114 F1
Close Lea Way HD6 .... 114 F1
Close Rd WF10 .... 124 F7
Close St WF9 .... 181 C7
Close The Barwick in E LS15 .. 63 D6
Boston Spa LS23 .... 30 E8
Bradford BD2 .... 55 F6
Clayton DN5 .... 194 C4
Clayton West HD8 .... 175 E2
Collingham LS22 .... 29 B8
Crigglestone WF4 .... 159 E7
East Ardsley WF3 .... 120 D7
East Keswick LS17 .... 28 C5
Guiseley LS20 .... 39 C8
Kippax LS25 .... 83 A1
Leeds, Alwoodley LS17 .... 43 A5
Leeds, Bank LS9 .... 212 B3
Pontefract WF8 .... 146 F7
Royston S71 .... 179 C1
Thorner LS14 .... 46 A6
Closes Rd 2 HD6 .... 115 A1
Cloth Hall St
Dewsbury WF13 .... 139 D8
Huddersfield HD1 .... 154 A6
18 Leeds LS2 .... 211 F3
Cloudsdale Ave BD5 .... 74 E4
Clough Ave BD20 .... 17 C6
Clough Bank HX2 .... 91 B5
Clough Bank La BD22 .... 34 B6
Clough Bldgs HX6 .... 111 D4
Clough Dr Batley WF17 .... 97 A2
Lepton HD8 .... 155 D2
Slaithwaite HD7 .... 170 D8
Clough Foot La HD7 .... 169 A2
Clough Gate Flockton WF4 .... 156 D5
Oakworth BD22 .... 34 D2
Clough Gate Dr WF4 .... 156 D5
Clough Hall La HD4 .... 154 D1

Clough Head Primary Sch
HD7 .... 152 A4
Clough Hey HD7 .... 168 E4
Clough House HD7 .... 151 D1
Clough House La
Denby Dale HD8 .... 192 C6
Ripponden HX4 .... 133 B2
Slaithwaite HD7 .... 151 D1
Clough Houses BD22 .... 34 C2
Clough La Brighouse HD6 ...... 115 C6
Brighouse, Fixby HD6 .... 135 F6
Halifax HX2 .... 91 B5
Huddersfield, Fixby HD6 .... 135 F6
Huddersfield, Paddock
HD1, HD7 .... 153 C5
Lepton WF14 .... 156 C7
Liversedge WF15 .... 116 D5
Oakworth BD22 .... 34 D3
Wadsworth Moor HX2 .... 90 B5
Clough Lee HD7 .... 168 F4
Clough Pk HD8 .... 155 D2
Clough Pl HX2 .... 91 B5

Clough Rd Bacup OL13 .... 106 A4
Emley WF4 .... 157 C1
Huddersfield HD2 .... 136 E4
Slaithwaite HD7 .... 152 A7
Slaithwaite, Crimble HD7 .... 152 A4
Sowerby Bridge HX6 .... 112 C1
4 Todmorden OL14 .... 108 A4
Clough St Bradford BD5 .... 74 E1
Morley LS27 .... 98 C6
Clough The Lepton HD8 .... 155 D2
Mirfield WF14 .... 137 E4
Clough Way HD8 .... 155 D2
Clovelly Ave 10 LS11 .... 214 B3
Clovelly Gr 8 LS11 .... 214 B3
Clovelly Pl 7 LS11 .... 214 B3
Clovelly Pl 20 LS11 .... 214 B3
Clovelly Row 11 LS11 .... 214 B3
Clovelly Terr LS11 .... 214 B3
Clover Cres LS28 .... 57 A4
Clover Ct 10 LS28 .... 57 A4
Clover Hill WF15 .... 116 D5
Clover Hill Cl HX1 .... 203 D3
Clover Hill Rd HX1 .... 203 D3
Clover Hill Terr HX1 .... 203 D3
Clover Hill View HX1 .... 203 D3
Clover St Bacup OL13 .... 106 B3
Bradford BD5 .... 74 B3
Clover Wlk WF9 .... 183 A4
Cloverdale HX3 .... 93 D3
Coverville App BD6 .... 94 C2
Club Houses Halifax HX2 .... 91 F1
Huddersfield HD4 .... 171 E2
Club La Halifax HX2 .... 91 F1
Pudsey LS13 .... 57 E1
Club Row Leeds LS7 .... 204 A2
Wilsden BD15 .... 53 C4
Yeadon LS19 .... 40 C5
Club St Bradford BD7 .... 73 F5
Todmorden OL14 .... 86 B3
Club Terr WF9 .... 163 B8
Clubhouses Croft 8 WF4 .. 141 A1
Clumber Dr BD19 .... 117 E6
Cluntergate WF4 .... 141 B1
Clunters La HX2 .... 111 B8
Clutton St WF17 .... 118 E5
Clyde App LS12 .... 210 B8
Clyde Chase LS12 .... 210 B8
Clyde Ct LS12 .... 210 B8
Clyde Gdns LS12 .... 210 B8
Clyde Grange LS12 .... 210 B8
Clyde St Bingley BD16 .... 36 F4
Sowerby Bridge HX6 .... 112 C4
Todmorden OL14 .... 86 B3
Clyde Wlk LS12 .... 210 B8
Clydesdale Dr BD6 .... 93 F6
Co-op Bldgs HX3 .... 91 F1
Co-op La HD7 .... 188 D4
Co-operation St
2 Bacup OL13 .... 106 A4
Leeds LS12 .... 78 A
Co-operative Bldgs HD6 ..... 115 B
Co-operative St
Dewsbury WF12 .... 140 B
Horbury WF4 .... 141 A
Keighley BD21 .... 35 A
Mirfield WF14 .... 138 A
2 Morley LS27 .... 98 C
Morley, Churwell LS27 .... 98 A
Rothwell WF3 .... 100 C
Todmorden OL14 .... 129 A
Wakefield WF2 .... 142 A
Co-operative Terr
Elland HX4 .... 133 F
Holmfirth HD7 .... 189 C
Coach Fold HX3 .... 203 E
Coach House La LS21 .... 192 D
Coach House The LS17 .... 204 A
Coach La
1 Cleckheaton BD19 .... 116 E
Lindley LS21 .... 11 F
Thornton BD13 .... 72 F
Coach Rd Baildon BD17 .... 38 A
Brighouse HD6 .... 114 F
Gildersome LS12 .... 77 E
Guiseley LS20 .... 39 D
Huddersfield HD2 .... 135 F
Lofthouse Gate WF1 .... 121 C
Meltham HD7 .... 170 E
Ripponden HX6 .... 132 D
Coal Clough Rd OL14 .... 86 B
Coal Gate HD7 .... 151 A
Coal Gate Rd HX4 .... 131 F
Coal Hill Dr LS13 .... 57 F
Coal Hill Fold LS13 .... 57 F
Coal Hill Gate LS13 .... 57 F
Coal Hill Gdns LS13 .... 57 F
Coal Hill Gn LS13 .... 57 F
Coal Hill La LS28, LS13 .... 57 F
Coal La HX4 .... 71 E
Coal Pit La Bacup OL13 .... 106 B
Batley WF17 .... 118 A
Denby Dale HD8 .... 191 F
Halifax HX3 .... 113 E
Coate's La BD20 .... 4 F
Coates Cl WF14 .... 118 F
Coates St BD5 .... 74 F
Coates Terr BD5 .... 74 F

Cobb Ave WF2 141 F4
Cobble Hall Golf Course LS8 44 D1
Cobbler Hall WF4 176 F8
Cobbler's La WF8 147 A8
Cobbler's Lane Infants Sch WF8 126 A1
Cobbler's Lane Junior Sch WF8 147 A8
Cobbydale Ct BD20 5 D1
Cobcroft La WF11 127 F1
Cobcroft Rd HD1, HD2 136 A1
Cobden Ave 3 LS12 78 A4
Cobden Cl 8 WF17 118 C5
Cobden Ct HX1 203 D4
Cobden Gr 4 LS12 78 A4
Cobden Mews 10 LS27 98 A5
Cobden Pl LS12 77 F4
Cobden Primary Sch LS12 77 F4
Cobden Rd Leeds LS12 77 F4
Leeds, New Blackpool LS12 78 A4
Cobden St Bradford BD15 54 B1
Bradford, Clayton BD14 73 B4
Bradford, Idle BD10 56 B7
Leeds LS12 77 F4
9 Morley LS27 98 A5
Queensbury BD13 72 F1
Todmorden OL14 108 B5
Cobden Terr
Brighouse HX3 114 C8
Elland HX5 134 F5
Leeds LS12 77 F4
Cobham Par WF1 121 B4
Cobham Wlk LS15 62 F2
Cock Hill La HX3 93 B6
Cock La WF4 143 F2
Cock Pit La HX4 150 E8
Cockburn High Sch LS11 99 A7
Cockburn Way LS11 214 C3
Cockcroft Gr BD3 75 A7
Cockcroft La HX6 132 A1
Cockermouth La WF4 156 D2
Cockin La BD14 72 E4
Cocking End LS29 7 C5
Cocking La LS29 6 E6
Cockley Hill La HD5 155 D8
Cockley Meadows HD5 137 C1
Cockshott Cl 2 LS12 58 F1
Cockshott Dr LS12 58 F1
Cockshott Hill LS28 57 D3
Cockshott La
Bradford BD10 56 A8
Leeds LS12 58 F1
Cockshott Pl LS29 6 E8
Coggil St LS10 80 A2
Coiners Fold HX7 110 C8
Colbeck Row WF17 96 E1
Colbert Ave LS29 8 E5
Colby Rise LS15 80 E7
Cold Edge Rd Halifax HX2 70 D3
Halifax, Wainstalls HX2 90 F6
Cold Hiendley Common La WF2 161 D1
Cold Hill La Holmfirth HD7 189 E7
Huddersfield HD4 172 A8
Cold Royd La HD5 155 A8
Cold St BD22 51 C6
Cold Well La HD7 188 B4
Cold Well Rd LS15 62 B1
Cold Well Sq LS15 62 B1
Coldbeck Dr BD6 93 E8
Coldcotes Ave LS9 208 B2
Coldcotes Cir LS9 208 C2
Coldcotes Cl LS9 208 C2
Coldcotes Cres LS9 61 D2
Coldcotes Dr LS9 208 C2
Coldcotes Garth LS9 61 D2
Coldcotes Gr LS9 61 D2
Coldcotes View LS9 61 D2
Coldcotes Wlk LS9 61 D2
Colden Cl HX7 88 F3
Colden Junior & Infants Sch HX7 88 B6
Colden La HX7 88 A6
Colden Rd HX7 88 E4
Colders Dr HD7 170 D1
Colders Gn HD7 170 D2
Coldhill La Saxton LS24 65 E4
Sherburn in E LS25 65 E4
Coldshaw Top BD22 51 C6
Coldwell St HD7 152 D1
Coldwells Hill HX4 133 F3
Coleman St Bradford BD1 55 F1
Leeds LS12 210 C2
Colenso Gdns LS11 213 F4
Colenso Gr Keighley BD21 18 E1
Leeds LS11 213 F4
Colenso Mount LS11 213 F4
Colenso Pl LS11 213 F4
Colenso Rd LS11 213 F4
Colenso Terr LS11 213 F4
Colenso Way BD21 18 E1
Colenso Wlk BD21 18 E1
Coleridge Cl LS26 101 C3
Coleridge Cres WF2 120 F3
Coleridge Gdns BD10 56 C8
Coleridge La LS28 76 F5
Coleridge St HX1 203 E2
Coleridge Way WF8 125 D2
Coles Way BD20 18 D2
Coleshill Way BD4 95 C8
Coley Hall La HX3 93 D2
Coley Rd Northowram HX3 93 C3
Shelf HX3 93 C3
Coley View HX3 93 A2
Colinsway WF2 216 A1
Coll of Music LS9 212 A4
Coll of the Resurrection WF14 137 E6
Coll Pl 7 BD6 94 D8
Collbrook Ave BD6 94 C8
Colleen Rd WF4 159 E5
College Ct BD20 4 C5
College Farm La LS22 13 B3
College Gr Castleford WF10 124 A6
Wakefield WF1 216 B4
College Grove Cl WF1 216 B4
College Grove Rd WF1 216 B4
College Grove View WF1 216 B4
College La BD20 4 D6
College Rd Bingley BD16 37 A6
Castleford WF10 125 B7
Gildersome LS27 97 D6
Low Bradley BD20 4 D5
College St 1 Batley WF17 96 E1
Huddersfield HD4 153 D4
Todmorden OL14 86 C1
College St E HD4 153 D4
College Terr
Ackworth M T WF7 163 E6
Halifax HX1 202 B1
College View WF7 163 E6
College Wlk 6 BD21 35 C7
Collier La Aberford LS25 65 A5
Baildon BD17 38 C4
Colliers Cl BD18 54 E7
Colliers La LS17 44 E4
Colliers Way HD8 175 F4
Colliery App WF3 121 B6
Collin Moor La HX4 134 C8
Collin Rd LS14 61 F1
Collindale Cl BD10 56 E6
Collinfield Rise BD6 93 F6
Collingham Ave BD6 93 E8
Collingham Dr LS25 82 F6
Collingwood Rd WF6 123 B2
Collins Cl 18 BD22 51 E8
Collins St
Bradford, Bowling BD4 75 B4
Bradford, Low Green BD7 74 A3
Collinson St BD19 116 D8
Collyer View LS29 8 E5
Colmore Gr LS12 210 A2
Colmore Rd LS12 210 A1
Colmore St LS12 210 A2
Colne Hurst HD2 136 E4
Colne Rd Glusburn BD20 16 B6
Huddersfield HD1 154 A4
Colne Rd (Chapel La) BD22 34 C2
Colne Rd (Church St) BD22 34 B2
Colne Rd (Goodley) BD22 34 C2
Colne St Huddersfield HD1 153 E5
Huddersfield, Aspley HD1 154 C5
Colne Vale Rd HD3 153 A4
Colne Valley Bsns Pk HD7 152 D1
Colne Valley High Sch HD7 152 E1
Colne Valley Mus HD7 152 D4
Colonel's Wlk WF8 125 C1
Colour Mus BD1 74 D7
Colston Cl BD8 54 E1
Colton Croft LS15 81 D7
Colton Ct LS15 81 D7
Colton Garth LS15 81 D7
Colton La LS15 81 D7
Colton Primary Sch LS15 81 E6
Colton Rd Leeds LS15 81 C7
Leeds, Armley LS12 209 F3
Leeds, Colton LS15 81 D6
Colton Rd E LS15 81 E6
Colton Ret Pk LS15 81 E7
Colton St LS12 209 F3
Coltsfoot Cl WF8 146 D7
Columbus St 18 HX3 92 A1
Colville Terr
East Ardsley WF3 99 E1
Leeds LS11 214 B4
Colwyn Ave 14 LS11 214 B2
Colwyn Mount 15 LS11 214 B2
Colwyn Pl 19 LS11 214 B2
Colwyn Rd LS11 214 B2
Colwyn St HD1 153 D7
Colwyn Terr
Featherstone WF7 145 D6
18 Leeds LS11 214 B2
Colwyn View 12 LS11 214 B2
Colyton Mount BD15 54 A1
Combs Rd WF12 139 E2
Combs The WF12 139 E3
Comet St 4 OL13 106 A7
Commerce Ct BD4 75 D4
Commerce St BD1 201 B3
Commercial Bldgs BD12 95 B4
Commercial Rd
Dewsbury WF13 118 C1
Leeds LS5 59 A3
Skelmanthorpe HD8 175 B2
Commercial St
Batley WF17 118 C5
Batley, Heckmondwike WF16 117 E4
Brighouse HD6 115 B2
8 Castleford WF10 124 D8
Cleckheaton BD19 116 E7
Denholme BD13 71 D8
Dewsbury, Earlsheaton WF12 139 F7
Dewsbury, Ravensthorpe WF13 138 F5
Halifax HX1 203 E3
Hebden Bridge HX7 89 A3
Huddersfield HD1 154 B5
Commercial St continued
Leeds LS1 211 F4
Morley LS27 98 B4
Oakworth BD22 34 B2
4 Queensbury BD13 72 D1
Rothwell LS26 100 F5
Shipley BD18 55 B8
Slaithwaite HD7 170 A8
Todmorden OL14 108 C5
Wakefield WF1 142 D4
Commercial Villas LS28 76 D6
Common End La HD8 155 D2
Common Holme La LS29 7 E6
Common Ing La WF4 162 B2
Common La Clayton DN5 194 C5
Denby Dale HD8 192 B6
East Ardsley WF3 99 C1
Emley HD8 174 E7
Flockton WF4 157 A2
Halifax HX3 113 F5
Knottingley, Broomhill WF11 127 B4
Knottingley, South Moor WF11 127 D3
Royston S71 179 C5
Thorpe Audlin WF8 165 B3
Wakefield WF2 160 F5
Woolley WF4 177 D8
Common Rd Batley WF17 117 F4
Bradford BD12 94 C6
Brierley S72 181 B2
Elland HX5 135 C6
Hemsworth WF9 163 A2
4 Huddersfield HD1 154 A8
Lofthouse Gate WF3 121 F7
South Kirkby WF9 181 E1
Common Road Ave WF9 182 A1
Common Road Ind Est BD12 94 D6
Common Road Infant Schs WF9 182 A1
Common Side La WF7 145 A6
Common Terr HD6 115 A1
Common The WF12 139 E3
Commondale Way BD4 95 A6
Commonside Batley WF17 118 D3
Liversedge FW15 116 E2
Como Ave 3 BD8 54 F1
Como Dr BD8 73 F8
Como Gdns 2 BD8 54 F1
Como Gr BD8 54 F1
Compeigne Ave BD21 18 F1
Compton Ave LS9 208 A2
Compton Cres LS9 208 A2
Compton Gr LS9 208 A2
Compton La LS22 29 B6
Compton Mount LS9 208 A2
Compton Pl LS9 208 A2
Compton Rd LS9 208 A2
Compton Row LS9 208 A2
Compton St Bradford BD4 75 C2
10 Keighley BD21 35 D8
Leeds LS9 208 A2
Compton Terr LS9 208 A2
Compton View LS9 208 A2
Concord St Honley HD7 171 F4
Leeds LS2 207 D1
Concordia St LS1 211 F3
Concourse House Est LS11 213 F1
Concrete St 27 HX3 92 A1
Conduit St BD8 55 C1
Coney La BD21 35 C7
Coney Moor Gr LS26 102 F3
Coney Warren La WF3 121 E8
Coney Wlk WF13 138 F8
Conference Gr LS12 209 D3
Conference Pl LS12 209 D3
Conference Rd LS12 209 D3
Conference Terr LS12 209 D3
Congress Mount LS12 209 D3
Congress St LS12 209 D3
Congreve App LS17 28 E6
Congreve Way LS17 28 E6
Conisborough La LS25 83 B7
Coniston Ave
Huddersfield HD5 154 D6
2 Leeds LS6 59 E5
Mapplewell S75 178 A2
1 Queensbury BD13 72 D1
Coniston Cl Elland HX5 135 B7
2 Queensbury BD13 92 D8
Coniston Ct WF3 121 B6
Coniston Dr WF10 125 E7
Coniston Gdns
Castleford WF10 125 E7
Leeds LS15 80 E6
Coniston Gr Baildon BD17 37 F1
Bradford BD9 54 F2
Coniston House 15 HX5 134 F7
Coniston Pl WF11 126 E1
Coniston Rd Batley WF12 118 F2
4 Bradford BD7 73 E3
Meltham HD7 170 E1
Rothwell LS26 101 C7
Coniston Way
Rothwell LS26 101 C6
Wetherby LS22 13 B5
Conistone Cres WF1 142 E8
Connaught Fold HD2 136 E5
Connaught Rd LS29 8 D3
Cononley County Primary Sch BD20 4 A3
Cononley La BD20 4 B2
Cononley Rd BD20 16 B8
Cononley Sta BD20 4 A2
Consort St LS3 205 F1
Consort Terr LS3 205 F1
Consort View LS3 205 F1
Consort Wlk LS3 205 F1
Constable Gr WF3 121 E6
Constable Rd
East Ardsley WF3 119 F8
Ilkley LS29 8 E3
Constance St BD18 54 F8
Constitutional St HX1 202 C1
Convent Ave WF9 182 C2
Conway Ave LS8 207 F3
Conway Cres Batley WF17 118 C2
Meltham HD7 170 D1
Conway Dr LS8 207 F3
Conway Gr LS8 207 F3
Conway Mount LS8 207 F3
Conway Pl LS8 208 A3
Conway Rd Leeds LS8 208 A3
Wakefield WF2 141 E7
Conway St Bradford BD4 201 C1
Halifax HX1 202 C2
Leeds LS8 207 F3
5 Pudsey LS28 57 D1
Conway Terr LS8 207 F3
Conway View LS8 207 F3
Cook La WF16 117 C4
Cooke Cres BD19 117 A8
Cooke La BD21 35 C7
Cooke St 3 BD21 35 C7
Cookridge Ave LS16 41 E6
Cookridge Dr LS16 41 E6
Cookridge Gr LS16 41 E6
Cookridge Hall Golf Course LS16 41 F6
Cookridge Hospl LS16 41 E2
Cookridge La LS16 41 E7
Cookridge Primary Sch LS16 41 E4
Cookridge St LS1, LS2 211 E4
Cooksland La WF7 144 E8
Cookson Cl WF10 125 D5
Cookson St HD6 114 F3
Coombe Hill BD13 73 B2
Coombe Rd HD3 152 F5
Cooper Bridge Rd HD5, WF14 137 B6
Cooper Cl BD16 37 A5
Cooper Fields HX2 111 E6
Cooper Gr HX3 93 D7
Cooper Hill LS28 76 F5
Cooper House WF9 181 D6
Cooper La Bradford BD6 93 D8
Holmfirth HD7 189 A5
Shelf BD6, HX3 93 D8
Cooper Lane First Sch BD6 73 D1
Cooper Rd LS22 13 E5
Cooper St OL14 108 E6
Cop Hill End HD7 169 C8
Cop Hill La HD7 169 B8
Cop Hill Side HD7 169 B8
Copeland St BD4 75 D5
Copeworth Dr WF4 159 F3
Copgrove Cl BD4 75 E3
Copgrove Ct BD4 75 E3
Copgrove Rd
Bradford BD4 75 E3
Leeds LS8 61 B5
Copley Ave Halifax HX2 202 B1
Meltham HD7 170 D2
Copley Bank Rd HD7 152 C3
Copley Cl HX3 113 B1
Copley Glen HX3 113 B2
Copley Gr HX3 113 B2
Copley Hall St HX3 113 B2
Copley Hall Terr HX3 113 B2
Copley Hill Batley WF17 96 F1
Leeds LS12 210 B2
Copley Hill Trad Est LS12 210 B2
Copley Hill Way LS12 210 B2
Copley Junior & Infant Sch HX3 113 B2
Copley La Aberford LS25 65 D5
Halifax HX3 113 B2
Rothwell WF3 100 B4
Saxton LS25 65 D5
Shepley HD8 174 B1
Copley Mill House HX3 113 A2
Copley Mount HX3 113 B2
Copley St Batley WF17 118 A7
Bradford BD5 74 B3
Halifax HX3 203 E4
Leeds LS12 210 B2
Copley Terr HX3 113 B2
Copley Yd LS12 210 B2
Coplowe La BD15 53 D6
Copmanroyd LS21 11 A3
Copper Beech Cl WF8 146 E6
Copper Beech Ct WF2 161 A6
Copperas House Terr OL14 108 A2
Copperas Row HX4 133 E7
Copperfield Ave LS9 212 C2
Copperfield Cres 10 LS9 212 C2
Copperfield Dr 8 LS9 212 C2
Copperfield Gr 4 LS9 80 A6
Copperfield Mount 3 LS9 80 A6
Copperfield Pl 9 LS9 212 C2
Copperfield Row 7 LS9 212 C2
Copperfield Terr LS9 80 A6
Copperfield View 11 LS9 212 C2
Copperfield Wlk 6 LS9 212 C2
Copperfields Coll LS9 80 A6
Coppertop Mews WF8 125 E3
Coppice Cl WF1 142 E8
Coppice Dr HD4 171 D6
Coppice Head LS26 100 F5
Coppice The
Barwick in E LS15 63 D6
Glusburn BD20 16 C6
Huddersfield HD2 136 B4
Ilkley LS29 8 A6
Mirfield WF14 138 A8
Yeadon LS19 40 B8
Yeadon, Westfield LS19 39 F5
Coppice View BD10 56 A8
Coppice Way LS8 61 A6
Coppice Wood Ave BD7 74 A6
Coppice Wood Cl LS20 23 A1
Coppice Wood Cres LS19 23 B1
Coppice Wood Gr
Bradford BD7 74 A6
Yeadon LS20 40 A8
Coppice Wood Rise LS19 40 B8
Coppies The BD12 94 B4
Coppin Hall Gr WF14 137 D6
Coppin Hall La WF14 137 D6
Coppy Cl BD16 54 A6
Coppy La Haworth BD22 33 C7
Leeds LS13 58 C4
Wadsworth Moor HX7 68 F3
Coppy Nook La HX7 110 E3
Coppy Rd Addingham LS29 6 E8
Steeton BD20 17 B5
Coppy Row BD22 34 B2
Coppy Wood Dr LS29 8 B7
Copse The Bingley BD16 37 D3
Brighouse BD19 115 F7
Burley in W LS29 21 E8
Featherstone WF7 124 C1
Copt Royd Gr LS19 40 A7
Copthorne First Sch BD7 74 C5
Copthorne Gdns HD2 136 F5
Copthurst Rd HD7 198 E7
Copy Bottom BB10 85 C4
Corban St BD4 75 C3
Corby St HD2 136 A1
Cordingley Cl BD4 75 E1
Cordingley St BD4 75 E1
Corfe Cl WF17 97 B2
Corn Bank HD4 171 C6
Corn Exchange 4 LS1 211 F3
Corn Market Halifax HX1 203 E3
Pontefract WF8 146 C8
Corn Mill LS29 22 B4
Corn Mill Ct LS13 77 D7
Corn Mill La Otley LS29 10 A1
Thornton BD13 72 F5
Corn St 6 BD21 35 A4
Cornerstones Cl LS29 7 A8
Cornfield WF13 117 F1
Cornfield Ave HD3 153 A7
Cornfield St 3 OL14 108 D6
Cornholme Junior & Infants Sch OL14 86 A1
Cornholme Terr 7 OL14 86 B1
Cornmill Ave WF15 117 C3
Cornmill Cl LS17 28 D3
Cornmill Cres WF15 117 B2
Cornmill Dr WF15 117 B3
Cornmill La Bardsey LS17 28 D3
Liversedge WF15 117 B3
Cornrace View HD4 154 B4
Cornus Gdns 2 LS10 99 D8
Cornwall Ave BD20 5 C1
Cornwall Cl LS26 100 D6
Cornwall Cres
Baildon BD17 38 B4
Brighouse HD6 115 B6
Rothwell LS26 100 D6
Cornwall House 16 HX5 134 F7
Cornwall Pl BD8 55 D1
Cornwall Rd Bingley BD16 37 B2
Bradford BD8 55 D1
Keighley BD21 18 E1
Cornwall Terr BD8 55 D1
Coronation Ave
Guiseley BD10 39 D4
Kippax LS25 83 C1
Normanton WF6 122 F3
Royston S71 179 E4
Shafton S72 180 B3
Coronation Bglws
3 Kippax LS25 83 C1
Knottingley WF11 126 D4
Meltham HD7 170 E1
Coronation Bsns Ctr BD21 18 D1
Coronation Hospl LS29 8 C3
Coronation Mount BD22 34 F7
Coronation Par LS15 80 E7
Coronation Rd Crofton WF4 144 B3
Halifax HX3 113 D4
Coronation St Bradford BD12 95 A4
Castleford WF10 103 F1
Elland HX5 134 F6
Elland, Lindwell HX4 134 C7
Rothwell WF3 100 D3
Wakefield WF2 120 F1
Coronation Terr
2 Batley WF17 96 F1
Castleford WF10 125 A6
Ripponden HX6 132 E6
Coronation Way BD22 34 F8
Coronation Wlk BD22 34 F8
Corporal La HX3 92 F6
Corporation St
Bradford BD2 56 C3
Dewsbury WF13 139 D8
Halifax HX1 203 E4
2 Huddersfield HD1 154 A5
Morley LS27 98 A4
Sowerby Bridge HX6 112 B4

Corpus Christi High Sch
LS9 .... 80 E8
Corpus Christi Primary Sch
LS9 .... 80 D8
Corrance Rd BD12 .... 94 D1
Corrie St BD13 .... 72 E6
Cote CI HD8 .... 173 E2
Cote Farm Cotts BD10 ..... 38 F1
Cote Farm La Bradford BD17 38 F1
  Shipley BD10 .... 55 F8
Cote Gap BD13 .... 72 D7
Cote La Bradford BD15 .... 54 A1
  Brighouse HD2 .... 135 E5
  Holmfirth HD7 .... 199 A8
  Pudsey LS28 .... 57 C2
Cote Rd HX6 .... 132 B4
Cote The LS28 .... 57 C2
Cote Wall WF14 .... 138 D3
Cotefields Ave LS28 ...... 57 C2
Coteroyd Ave LS27 .... 98 C8
Coteroyd Dr LS27 .... 98 C8
Cotewall Rd BD5 .... 74 D3
Cotswold Ave BD18 .... 55 E7
Cotswold CI WF9 .... 181 F7
Cotswold Dr
  Cleckheaton WF15 .... 116 D5
  Garforth LS25 .... 82 F5
  Knottingley WF11 .... 126 E4
  Rothwell LS26 .... 100 D6
Cotswold Mews HD8 .... 173 F7
Cotswold Rd Rothwell LS26 100 E6
  Wakefield WF2 .... 141 D5
Cottage Gn **8** BD8 ..... 73 F8
Cottage Homes HD5 .... 155 A6
Cottage Rd Bradford BD10 . 56 D7
  Leeds LS6 .... 59 D6
Cottage The HD7 .... 171 F5
Cottam Ave BD7 .... 74 B6
Cottam Croft WF9 .... 181 E7
Cottam Terr BD7 .... 74 B6
Cotterdale BD15 .... 54 A3
Cotterdale Holt LS22 ..... 13 A1
Cotterdale View LS15 ..... 80 E6
Cotterill Rd WF11 .... 126 D3
Cottingley App LS11 ...... 213 D1
Cottingley Chase LS11 .... 213 D1
Cottingley Cliffe Rd BD16 54 C6
Cottingley County
  Primary Sch LS11 .... 78 C1
Cottingley Cres LS11 ..... 213 D1
Cottingley Dr Morley LS11 78 C2
  Shipley BD16 .... 54 A8
Cottingley First Sch BD16 54 B7
Cottingley Fold LS11 ..... 78 C2
Cottingley Gdns LS11 ..... 213 D1
Cottingley Gn LS11 .... 213 D1
Cottingley Gr LS11 .... 213 D1
Cottingley Heights LS11 .. 213 D1
Cottingley Manor Pk BD16 . 54 B7
Cottingley Moor Rd BD16 .. 54 A5
Cottingley New Rd BD16 ... 54 B7
Cottingley Prim Sch LS11 . 78 C1
Cottingley Rd
  Bradford BD15 .... 54 A4
  Morley LS11 .... 78 C2
Cottingley Sta LS11 ...... 78 C1
Cottingley Terr BD8 ...... 55 D1
Cottingley Towers LS11 ... 213 D1
Cottingley Vale LS11 ..... 213 D1
Cotton St Leeds LS9 ...... 212 A3
  Wakefield WF2 .... 142 C4
Couford Gr HD2 .... 136 F4
Coule Royd HD5 .... 154 F7
Coultas CI LS29 .... 22 A4
County Arc LS1 .... 211 F4
County CI WF17 .... 118 C6
Coupe Gr WF6 .... 122 F5
Coupland PI LS11 .... 214 B4
Coupland St Garforth LS25 82 E7
  Leeds LS11 .... 214 B4
Coupland St Leeds LS11 ... 214 B3
  6 Todmorden OL14 ... 108 B5
Court Dr LS5 .... 58 E6
Court La HX2 .... 112 D7
Court No 6 WF17 .... 118 C6
Court The Leeds LS17 ..... 42 F5
  Liversedge WF15 .... 116 E4
  Shipley BD16 .... 54 E7
Court Way The WF7 .... 164 B8
Court Yard Mews BD20 ..... 17 F6
Court Yd The WF4 .... 178 A7
Courtenay CI BD3 .... 75 E7
Courthouse St LS21 .... 23 A8
Courts Leet **8** BD12 ... 94 C4
Courtyard The
  8 Bacup OL13 .... 106 A3
  Batley WF17 .... 96 F2
  Huddersfield HD4 .... 153 D4
Cousen Ave BD7 .... 73 F5
Cousen Rd BD7 .... 73 F4
Cousin La HX2 .... 91 E4
Coutances Way LS29 .... 9 B3
Coventry St Bradford BD4 . 75 B4
  Halifax HX2 .... 202 A3
Cover Dr **8** BD6 .... 94 A8
Coverdale Garth LS22 ..... 29 A8
Coverdale Way BD17 .... 38 E4
Coverley Garth LS19 ...... 39 F7
Coverley Rise LS19 .... 39 F7
Covert The WF17 .... 117 F7
Covey Clough Ct WF14 ..... 137 F1
Cow & Calf LS29 .... 8 E2
Cow Close La BD12 .... 94 E2

Cow Close Rd LS12 .... 78 A4
Cow Gate HD3 .... 152 F6
Cow Gn HX1 .... 203 E3
Cow Hey La HX7 .... 68 D3
Cow Heys HD5 .... 154 F7
Cow Hill Gate La HX2 ..... 71 E1
Cow La Brighouse HX3 ..... 114 D4
  Crofton WF4 .... 144 A4
  Halifax HX3 .... 113 C2
  Knottingley WF11 .... 127 A4
  Ripponden HX6 .... 132 D6
  Ryhill WF4 .... 162 C1
  Wadsworth Moor HX7 ..... 88 E8
Cowcliff Hill Rd HD7 ..... 199 D8
Cowcliffe Hill Rd HD2 .... 135 F3
Cowdray Dr **8** BD19 .... 115 F8
Cowdry CI WF12 .... 139 E2
Cowfold St **8** OL14 .... 108 B6
Cowgill St **8** Bacup OL13 106 A4
  Bradford BD8 .... 55 C1
Cowhurst Ave OL14 .... 108 A7
Cowlersley Junior
  & Infants Sch HD4 ...... 152 F3
Cowlersley La HD4 .... 152 F3
Cowley Cres HD4 .... 54 D4
Cowley Rd LS13 .... 57 F5
Cowpasture Rd LS29 .... 8 C3
Cowper Ave LS9 .... 208 A2
Cowper Cres LS9 .... 208 A2
Cowper Gr LS8 .... 208 A3
Cowper Mount LS9 .... 208 A2
Cowper St
  Dewsbury WF12 .... 139 C6
  Leeds LS7 .... 207 E3
Cowper Terr LS9 .... 208 A2
Cowrakes CI HD3 .... 135 A1
Cowrakes Rd HD3 .... 135 A1
Cowroyd PI HX3 .... 203 F4
Cowslip St HD1 .... 153 D5
Cowtoot La OL13 .... 106 A4
Coxley Cres WF4 .... 158 D6
Coxley La WF4 .... 158 D7
Coxley View WF4 .... 158 C5
Coxwold Hill LS22 .... 13 E7
Coxwold View LS22 .... 13 C6
Coxwold Wlk **8** BD15 ... 73 A7
Crab Hill WF8 .... 146 C8
Crab La Crigglestone WF2 . 160 B4
  Leeds LS12 .... 209 F4
Crab Tree La WF8 .... 146 B5
Crabgate Dr DN6 .... 184 E2
Crabgate La DN6 .... 184 E2
Crabtree Ave Bacup OL13 .. 106 A1
  Batley WF12 .... 117 E5
Crabtree CI LS22 .... 29 B7
Crabtree Hill LS22 .... 29 B8
Crabtree La LS17 .... 28 C7
Crabtree St
  8 Bradford BD3 ..... 74 A4
  Halifax HX1 .... 202 B3
Crabtree Way WF3 .... 119 F7
Crack La BD15 .... 53 D5
Crackenedge La WF13 ...... 118 D1
Crackenedge Terr WF13 .... 118 D1
Cracoe Rd BD3 .... 75 B6
Crag CI Halifax HX2 ...... 91 D4
  Sutton in C BD20 .... 16 C5
Crag Ct HX2 .... 91 D4
Crag Gdns LS23 .... 30 D2
Crag Hill Ave LS16 .... 41 F6
Crag Hill Rd BD10 .... 39 A2
Crag Hill View LS16 ...... 41 F6
Crag La Halifax HX2 ...... 91 D3
  Leeds LS17 .... 42 F5
  Low Bradley BD20 .... 4 C4
  Sutton in C BD20 .... 16 C4
Crag Mount **12** WF8 .... 146 C8
Crag PI BD21 .... 35 C4
Crag Rd BD18 .... 55 C7
Crag The LS23 .... 30 D2
Crag Vale Terr BD20 ...... 16 B6
Crag View Bradford BD10 .. 56 D6
  Cononley BD20 .... 4 A1
  Sutton in C BD20 .... 16 C5
Cragg Ave LS18 .... 58 B8
Cragg Bottom Rd BD22 ..... 49 E8
Cragg Dr LS29 .... 8 F3
Cragg Hill LS18 .... 58 C8
Cragg La Bradford BD7 .... 74 A3
  Denholme BD13 .... 71 E6
  Hebden Bridge HX7 ...... 110 D6
  Thornton BD13 .... 72 A5
Cragg Rd
  Hebden Bridge HX7 ...... 109 F5
  Hebden Bridge HX7 ...... 110 A6
  Horsforth LS18 .... 58 C8
Cragg St BD7 .... 74 A3
Cragg Terr Bradford BD7 .. 74 A3
  Horsforth LS18 .... 58 B8
  Yeadon LS19 .... 40 B2
Cragg Top BD13 .... 71 E5
Cragg Vale Junior
  & InfantSch HX7 .... 110 C3
Cragg View BD20 .... 5 E2
Cragg Wood Dr LS19 .... 40 A2
Craggwell Terr **8** LS18 58 C7
Craggwood CI LS18 .... 58 C7
Craggwood Rd LS18 .... 58 C7
Craggwood Terr **8** LS18 58 C7
Cragside CI BD10 .... 38 F1
Cragside Cres LS5 .... 58 E7
Cragside Gdns LS5 .... 58 D6
Cragside Gr LS5 .... 58 D6
Cragside Mount LS5 .... 58 E7

Cragside PI LS5 .... 58 E6
Cragside Wlk LS5 .... 58 E7
Craig CI WF17 .... 118 C6
Craig-y-don WF12 .... 139 F7
Craiglands HX3 .... 114 D8
Craiglands Pk LS29 .... 8 C3
Craiglands Rd LS29 .... 8 C3
Craiglea Dr BD12 .... 94 D2
Craigmore Ct BD4 .... 75 F2
Craigmore Dr LS29 .... 8 E4
Cranberry Ave OL14 .... 129 B7
Cranborne Dr S75 .... 177 F1
Cranbourne Rd BD9 .... 54 D1
Cranbrook Ave
  Bradford BD6 .... 94 C8
  Leeds LS11 .... 214 A3
Cranbrook PI **8** BD5 ... 74 E3
Cranbrook St Bradford BD5 74 E3
  8 Bradford,Clayton BD14 74 C8
Cranbrook View LS28 ...... 77 A5
Cranewells Dr LS15 .... 81 D6
Cranewells Gn LS15 .... 81 C6
Cranewells Rise LS15 ..... 81 C6
Cranewells Vale LS15 ..... 81 C6
Cranewells View LS15 ..... 81 C7
Cranfield Dr DN6 .... 184 F2
Cranford Gdns S71 .... 179 B4
Cranford PI BD15 .... 53 C5
Crangle Fields HD4 .... 173 C2
Cranleigh Mount BD21 ..... 35 A5
Cranmer Bank LS17 .... 43 A3
Cranmer CI LS17 .... 43 A3
Cranmer Gdns Leeds LS17 .. 43 A3
  Meltham HD7 .... 170 F2
Cranmer Rd Bradford BD3 .. 75 A8
  Leeds LS17 .... 43 A3
Cranmer Rise LS17 .... 43 A3
Cranmore Cres LS10 .... 99 E5
Cranmore Dr LS10 .... 99 F6
Cranmore Garth LS10 ...... 99 E5
Cranmore Gdns LS10 .... 99 E5
Cranmore Gn LS10 .... 99 E5
Cranmore Gr LS10 .... 99 E5
Cranmore La LS10 .... 99 E5
Cranmore Rd LS10 .... 99 E5
Cranmore Rise LS10 .... 99 E5
Cranwood Dr HD5 .... 155 A6
Craven Ave Silsden BD20 .. 5 E1
  Thornton BD13 .... 72 E6
Craven CI
  Cleckheaton BD19 .... 117 C8
  Royston S71 .... 179 B4
Craven Cres LS29 .... 6 E8
Craven Ct **10** Bradford BD8 74 D8
  Halifax HX1 .... 202 C2
  Silsden BD20 .... 5 E1
Craven Dr Silsden BD20 ... 5 F1
Craven Gr BD20 .... 5 F1
Craven House OL14 .... 129 A8
Craven La BD19 .... 117 C8
Craven Pk LS29 .... 21 F5
Craven Rd Dewsbury WF13 .. 139 A6
  Hemsworth WF9 .... 181 D6
  Keighley BD21 .... 35 A8
  Leeds LS6 .... 206 B3
Craven St Bradford BD3 ... 201 C4
  Dewsbury WF13 .... 138 E6
  Huddersfield HD4 .... 153 A4
  Otley LS21 .... 23 B7
  Wakefield WF1 .... 216 A3
Craven Terr Bradford BD2 . 56 C3
  Halifax HX1 .... 202 C2
  Otley LS21 .... 23 B7
Cravendale Rd WF13 .... 138 D6
Craveford Ave BD6 .... 94 C8
Crawford Dr WF2 .... 141 F7
Crawford St Bradford BD4 . 75 A4
  Todmorden OL14 .... 129 B8
Crawley Ave WF9 .... 182 D3
Crawshaw Ave **8** LS28 .. 76 F7
Crawshaw CI **8** LS28 ... 76 F7
Crawshaw Gdns LS28 .... 76 F7
Crawshaw Hill **8** LS28 . 76 F7
Crawshaw La Emley HD8 .... 175 A8
  Flockton WF4 .... 156 F2
  Flockton, Six Lanes End WF4 157 A1
Crawshaw Pk LS28 .... 76 F7
Crawshaw Rd LS28 .... 76 F7
Crawshaw Rise LS28 .... 76 F6
Crawshaw St WF13 .... 138 F6
Crawthorne Cres HD2 ...... 136 E4
Cray La HX4 .... 133 E2
Crayford Dr WF4 .... 143 F1
Crediton Ave BD15 .... 73 B8
Crediton Ct **12** BD15 .. 73 B8
Crescent Ave
  Dewsbury WF13 .... 138 D5
  Huddersfield HD4 .... 171 D7
  Rothwell LS26 .... 100 F7
Crescent Bglws WF3 .... 99 D2
Crescent Grange LS11 ..... 214 C4
Crescent Rd
  Huddersfield, Fartown HD2 136 A1
  Huddersfield, Netherton
    HD4 .... 171 D7
  Ryhill WF4 .... 162 D1
Crescent Royd HD5 .... 155 A8
Crescent St **5** OL13 ... 108 B5
Crescent Terr LS29 .... 8 B4
Crescent The Baildon BD17 38 C2
  Bingley BD16 .... 36 E6
  Birkenshaw BD11 .... 96 A4
  Bradford BD6 .... 93 E8
  8 Brighouse HD6 .... 115 B3
  Burley in W LS29 .... 21 E8
  Castleford WF10 .... 124 F6

Crescent The continued
  Cleckheaton WF15 .... 116 D5
  Dewsbury WF13 .... 138 D5
  East Ardsley WF3 .... 120 A8
  Elland HX5 .... 134 F5
  Elland, Holywell Green HX4 134 A4
  Featherstone WF7 .... 144 D5
  Garforth LS25 .... 83 A7
  Guiseley LS20 .... 39 C8
  Halifax HX3 .... 113 F6
  Holmfirth HD7 .... 189 E6
  Ilkley LS29 .... 8 E5
  Kippax LS25 .... 83 A1
  Kirkburton HD8 .... 174 A7
  Leeds LS16 .... 42 B4
  Leeds, Alwoodley LS17 .. 42 F6
  Leeds, Whitkirk LS15 ... 81 B8
  Leeds, Woodhouse LS6 ... 206 A3
  Menston LS29 .... 22 B4
  Mickelfield LS25 .... 84 A6
  Netherton WF4 .... 158 D5
  Normanton WF6 .... 122 F4
  Otley LS21 .... 11 A2
  Pudsey LS28 .... 76 F8
  Sicklinghall LS22 ...... 12 C5
Crescent Towers LS11 ..... 214 C4
Crescent View
  Keighley BD22 .... 35 A3
  Leeds LS17 .... 42 F6
Crescent Wlk
  Bradford BD14 .... 73 D5
  Dewsbury WF13 .... 138 D5
Cresent The HX3 .... 114 D8
Creskeld Cres LS16 .... 24 F3
Creskeld Dr LS16 .... 24 F3
Creskeld Garth LS16 ...... 24 F3
Creskeld Gdns LS16 .... 24 F3
Creskeld La
  Arthington LS21 .... 25 A5
  Bramhope LS16 .... 24 F3
Creskeld Pk LS16 .... 24 F3
Creskeld Way BD15 .... 53 F2
Creskell Rd LS11 .... 211 E1
Cressfield Rd HD3 .... 153 C8
Cresswell La WF13 .... 117 F3
Cresswell Mount BD7 ...... 73 E2
Cresswell PI BD7 .... 73 E2
Cresswell Terr **8** BD7 . 73 E2
Crest Ave Bradford BD12 .. 94 C1
  Huddersfield HD5 .... 154 E5
Crest Dr WF8 .... 146 E6
Crest Hill Rd HD2 .... 136 C3
Crest Mount WF8 .... 146 E6
Crest PI HD6 .... 114 E5
Crest Rd HD6 .... 135 A3
Crest The
  Huddersfield HD2 .... 136 E6
  Kippax LS25 .... 83 A1
  Leeds LS14 .... 61 E6
  Swillington LS26 .... 82 A1
Crest View Hd6 .... 114 E5
Crestfield Ave HX5 .... 134 E6
Crestfield Cres HX5 ...... 134 E5
Crestfield Dr Elland HX5 . 134 E5
  Halifax HX2 .... 202 A1
Crestfield Rd HX5 .... 134 E5
Crestville CI BD14 .... 73 C5
Crestville Rd BD14 .... 73 C5
Crestville Terr BD14 ..... 73 C5
Crestwood CI BD5 .... 75 B1
Crewe Ave WF11 .... 126 B4
Crew Rd WF10 .... 125 D7
Crib La HX1 .... 203 E4
Cricketers App WF2 .... 120 E3
Cricketers CI WF7 .... 164 A5
Cricketers Gn LS19 .... 40 C5
Cricketers Terr LS12 ..... 209 F3
Cricketers The LS5 .... 59 B4
Cricketers Wlk
  Leeds LS15 .... 81 E7
  Steeton BD20 .... 17 D5
Cricklegate LS15 .... 81 B8
Crimble Bank HD7 .... 152 A3
Crimble CI HX3 .... 114 E7
Crimble Clough Rd HD7 .... 152 A3
Crimbles Ct LS28 .... 76 F7
Crimbles PI LS28 .... 76 F7
Crimbles Rd LS28 .... 76 F7
Crimbles Terr LS28 .... 76 F7
Crimea La HD7 .... 151 E4
Crimea St **5** OL13 ..... 106 A2
Crimple Gn LS25 .... 83 B6
Crimshaw La BD5 .... 75 A4
Crimsworth Dean HX7 ...... 68 F2
Crimsworth La HX7 .... 89 A8
Crinan Ct WF6 .... 123 A4
Cringles La BD20 .... 5 F7
Cripplegate HX1 .... 203 F3
Critchell Ho **8** BD5 ... 201 B1
Crodingley HD7 .... 189 B8
Crodingley Farm Ct HD7 ... 189 B8
Croft Ave Bingley BD16 ... 36 D6
  East Ardsley WF3 .... 120 A8
  Knottingley WF11 .... 127 A5
  Normanton, Altofts WF6 . 122 F3
  Normanton, Normanton Common
    WF6 .... 123 C3
  Otley LS21 .... 10 F1
  Pudsey LS28 .... 57 D3
  Royston S71 .... 179 B3
Croft Bridge LS26 .... 101 C5
Croft Chantry WF9 .... 163 A2
Croft CI Mapplewell S75 .. 178 A1
Croft Cottage La **3** HD1 154 B8
Croft Ct Honley HD7 ...... 171 F3
  Horsforth LS18 .... 41 C1
  Menston LS29 .... 21 F4

Croft Dr Bramham LS23 .... 30 D3
  Honley HD7 .... 171 E4
  Mapplewell S75 .... 178 B1
Croft End LS29 .... 22 A4
Croft End LS22 .... 13 C5
Croft Field BD20 .... 17 E8
Croft Fold HX3 .... 91 F3
Croft Foulds Ct LS25 ..... 82 F7
Croft Gdns HD2 .... 135 E5
Croft Head Guiseley LS20 . 22 E1
  Skelmanthorpe HD8 ...... 175 A2
Croft Head La WF11 .... 143 E6
Croft Head Terr BD20 ..... 16 C6
Croft Hill BD20 .... 16 C6
Croft House **8** HX2 .... 134 F7
Croft House Ave LS27 ..... 98 B5
Croft House CI
  Bradford BD8 .... 94 B8
  Keighley BD20 .... 18 A2
  Morley LS27 .... 98 B5
Croft House Ct LS28 ...... 76 E8
Croft House Dr LS29 ...... 7 A8
Croft House Fold LS29 .... 7 A8
Croft House Gdns LS27 .... 98 B5
Croft House Gr LS27 ...... 98 B5
Croft House La
  Huddersfield HD1 .... 153 E7
  Keighley BD20 .... 18 A2
  Morley LS27 .... 98 B5
  Otley LS21 .... 11 A2
Croft House Mews LS27 .... 98 B5
Croft House Mount LS27 ... 98 B6
Croft House Rd
  Bradford BD6 .... 94 B8
  Morley LS27 .... 98 B5
Croft House View LS27 .... 98 B5
Croft House Way LS27 ..... 98 B5
Croft House Wlk LS27 ..... 98 B5
Croft La Tadcaster LS24 .. 31 E6
  Thorp Arch LS23 .... 15 A4
Croft Leigh Ct BD5 .... 75 A1
Croft Pk LS29 .... 21 F4
Croft PI **8** HD6 .... 115 B4
Croft Rd Bingley BD16 .... 36 D6
  Bradford BD20 .... 30 D3
  Keighley BD20 .... 19 D1
Croft Rise LS29 .... 22 A4
Croft Row BD13 .... 71 E6
Croft St Birkenshaw BD11 . 96 A5
  Bradford, Broxnroyd Hill BD6 74 C1
  Bradford, Eastbrook BD1 201 C2
  Bradford, Fourlands BD10 56 C8
  8 Brighouse HD6 .... 115 A2
  Dewsbury WF13 .... 139 C8
  Glusburn BD20 .... 16 D6
  Haworth BD22 .... 51 C7
  22 Hebden Bridge HX7 89 A3
  Huddersfield HD1 .... 153 C5
  Keighley BD21 .... 35 B6
  Liversedge WF16 .... 117 C3
  Otley LS21 .... 23 B7
  Pudsey LS28 .... 57 D3
  Shipley BD18 .... 55 B8
  Sowerby Bridge HX6 ..... 112 C4
  Steeton BD20 .... 17 C5
Croft Terr Leeds LS12 .... 77 E3
Croft The Badsworth WF9 .. 164 D3
  Birkenshaw BD11 .... 96 E5
  Castleford WF10 .... 124 F6
  Collingham LS22 .... 29 A8
  Draughton BD23 .... 1 D6
  East Ardsley WF22 ...... 119 D5
  East Keswick LS17 ...... 28 B1
  Meltham HD7 .... 170 F1
  Rothwell LS26 .... 101 C6
  Otley LS21 .... 23 B7
  Pudsey LS28 .... 57 D3
  Scarcroft LS14 .... 45 D8
  West Bretton WF4 .... 176 F8
Croft Way LS29 .... 22 A4
Croft's Ct LS1 .... 211 E4
Croftdale Gr LS15 .... 62 D2
Croftlands Batley WF12 ... 118 F2
  Bradford BD10 .... 56 A8
  Huddersfield HD4 .... 154 A2
Crofton High Sch WF4 .... 161 F8
Crofton Infant Sch WF4 .. 162 A8
Crofton Junior Sch WF4 .. 162 A8
Crofton Rd Bradford BD9 . 54 F3
Crofton Rise LS17 .... 45 A4
Crofton Terr LS17 .... 45 A4
Crofts The Batley WF17 .. 117 F4
  Honley HD7 .... 175 D7
Farnhill BD20 .... 4 C5
Sutton in C BD20 ...... 16 C4
Croftside CI LS14 ..... 62 B3
Croftway LS15 .... 63 E7
Croisdale CI WF15 ..... 116 C4
Cromack View LS28 ..... 76 C7
Cromarty Ave HD4 ...... 153 C2
Cromarty Dr HD4 .... 153 C2
Cromer Ave 15 **18** BD21 35 B5
Cromer Gr **17** BD21 . 35 B5
Cromer PI **8** BD21 .. 35 B5
Cromer Rd Keighley BD21 35 B5
  Leeds LS2 .... 206 A2
Cromer St Halifax HX1 . 202 B1
  Leeds LS2 .... 206 A2
Cromer Terr Leeds LS2 . 206 A2
Cromford Gr LS25 ...... 83 B6
Crompton Dr LS27 ...... 97 F6
Cromwell CI Byram WF11 . 126 D8
  Halifax HX3 .... 92 A2

Cromwell Cres WF8 .... 146 E8
Cromwell Ct
Adwick Le S DN6 .... 184 F1
Birkenshaw BD11 .... 96 B5
Shipley BD9 .... 54 C5
Cromwell Hts 2 LS9 .... 212 B4
Cromwell Mount Leeds LS9 207 F1
Middleton LS10 .... 99 D8
Cromwell Pl WF5 .... 140 E7
Cromwell Rd
Castleford WF10 .... 125 D7
Halifax HX3 .... 114 A4
Cromwell Rise LS25 .... 103 B8
Cromwell St Dearne S63 ...... 194 E1
Cromwell's La 207 E1
Cromwell Terr 1 HX1 .... 203 D3
Cromwell View HX3 .... 114 B4
Cronkhill La S71 .... 179 D1
Crooke La BD15 .... 53 C4
Crooked La Bradford BD10 .... 39 A1
Halifax HX3 .... 92 B6
Crookes La S71 .... 179 C1
Cropper Gate LS1 .... 211 D4
Cropredy Cl BD13 .... 72 F1
Cropstones LS23 .... 30 D2
Cropton Rd S71 .... 179 B3
Crosby Ave LS11 .... 213 F4
Crosby Pl LS11 .... 211 D1
Crosby Rd LS11 .... 211 D1
Crosby St Keighley BD21 ...... 35 B8
Leeds LS11 .... 210 C1
Crosby Terr LS11 .... 211 D1
Crosby View 3 LS11 .... 211 D1
Croscombe Wlk BD5 .... 201 B1
Croset Ave LS14 .... 154 C7
Crosland Ct HD3 .... 134 F1
Crosland Edge HD7 .... 170 F4
Crosland Factory La HD4 .... 171 B5
Crosland Heath
Golf Course HD4 .... 152 F1
Crosland Hill Rd HD4 .... 153 B3
Crosland Moor Infants Sch
HD4 .... 153 D3
Crosland Rd
Huddersfield, Lidley HD3 .... 135 A1
Huddersfield, Yews Hill HD1 . 153 E4
Huddersfield, New Hey Rd HD4 171 B6
Crosland St HD4 .... 153 E4
Crosley View BD16 .... 37 C2
Crosley Wood Rd BD16 .... 37 B2
Cross Albert Pl LS12 .... 210 A2
Cross Alcester Rd 12 LS8 .... 207 F4
Cross Alma St LS9 .... 207 F1
Cross Arc LS1 .... 211 F4
Cross Aston Gr LS13 .... 58 E2
Cross Ave LS26 .... 100 F7
Cross Bank Rd WF17 .... 118 B6
Cross Bank St WF14 .... 138 A2
Cross Banks BD18 .... 55 B7
Cross Banstead St 5 LS8 .... 207 F3
Cross Bath Rd LS13 .... 58 C2
Cross Beck Rd 4 LS8 .... 207 F3
Cross Belgrave St LS2 .... 211 F4
Cross Bell St 5 LS9 .... 212 A4
Cross Bellbrooke Ave LS8 .. 208 B2
Cross Bentley La LS6 .... 59 F6
Cross Burley Lodge Rd
LS6 .... 205 E2
Cross Cardigan Terr LS4 ...... 59 C1
Cross Catherine St LS9 .... 212 B3
Cross Chancellor St LS6 ...... 206 B3
Cross Chapel St 4 LS6 .... 59 D5
Cross Chestnut Gr 6 BD19 .. 116 D7
Cross Church St
3 Cleckheaton BD19 .... 116 E7
14 Huddersfield HD1 .... 154 B6
Huddersfield, Paddock HD1 . 153 D5
Cross Cliff Rd LS6 .... 205 F4
Cross Cotts HD1 .... 153 D7
Cross Cowper St LS7 .... 207 D3
Cross Crown St 5 BD19 ...... 116 D7
Cross Dawlish Gr 7 LS9 ...... 80 B8
Cross Dikes Rd HX6 .... 132 A7
Cross Easy Rd LS9 .... 212 C2
Cross Elford St LS8 .... 207 F3
Cross Emily St 11 BD21 ...... 35 C8
Cross End Fold LS29 .... 7 A8
Cross Ends La HX7 .... 69 A4
Cross Eric St LS13 .... 58 C5
Cross Evanston Ave LS4 ...... 59 C2
Cross Farm Ct BD22 .... 51 C3
Cross Field HX4 .... 134 A4
Cross Fields HD5 .... 154 E7
Cross Firs St HD3 .... 153 B5
Cross Flatts LS11 .... 214 A2
Cross Flatts Ave LS11 .... 214 A2
Cross Flatts Cres LS11 .... 213 F2
Cross Flatts Dr LS11 .... 213 F2
Cross Flatts Gr LS11 .... 214 A2
Cross Flatts Mount LS11 .... 214 A2
Cross Flatts Pl LS11 .... 213 F2
Cross Flatts Park
Primary Sch LS11 .... 214 B2
Cross Flatts Pl LS11 .... 213 F2
Cross Flatts Rd LS11 .... 213 F2
Cross Flatts Row LS11 .... 213 F2
Cross Flatts Terr LS11 .... 213 F2
Cross Foundry St WF13 ...... 138 E5
Cross Fountaine St 3
LS2 .... 211 E4
Cross Francis St LS7 .... 207 D3
Cross Gate Rd HD7 .... 189 B2
Cross Gates Ave LS25 .... 62 C3
Cross Gates Ct LS15 .... 62 C2
Cross Gates La
Harden BD16 .... 36 C3
Leeds LS15 .... 62 B3

Cross Gates Prim Sch
LS15 .... 62 A2
Cross Gates Rd LS15 .... 62 B3
Cross Gates Sta LS15 .... 62 C1
Cross Glen Rd LS16 .... 59 C7
Cross Gn Bradford BD4 .... 75 E4
Otley LS21 .... 23 B8
Cross Granby Terr 8 LS6 .... 59 D5
Cross Grange Ave LS7 .... 207 E4
Cross Grasmere St LS12 .... 210 A3
Cross Green App LS9 .... 80 A5
Cross Green Ave 17 LS9 .... 212 C2
Cross Green Cl LS9 .... 80 A5
Cross Green Cres LS9 .... 212 C2
Cross Green Dr
Huddersfield HD5 .... 155 A6
Leeds LS9 .... 80 A5
Cross Green Garth LS9 .... 80 A5
Cross Green Cl 4 LS9 .... 212 C2
Cross Green La Leeds LS15 .. 81 B8
Leeds, Knowsthorpe LS9 .... 212 C2
Cross Green Light Ind Est
LS9 .... 80 B5
Cross Green Rd
Huddersfield HD5 .... 155 A6
Leeds LS9 .... 212 C2
Cross Green Rise LS9 .... 80 A5
Cross Green Row LS6 .... 59 E7
Cross Green Vale LS9 .... 80 A5
Cross Green Way LS9 .... 80 A5
Cross Greenwood Mount 1
LS6 .... 59 E7
Cross Grove St 6 HD1 .... 154 A5
Cross Hands La WF4 .... 163 B6
Cross Hartley Ave LS6 .... 206 A4
Cross Heath Gr LS11 .... 213 E3
Cross Henley Rd LS13 .... 58 C2
Cross Hill Adwick Le S DN6 . 184 F1
Brierley S72 .... 180 F3
Elland HX4 .... 134 A7
Fairburn WF11 .... 105 A4
Hemsworth WF9 .... 181 D7
Cross Hill Ct WF15 .... 116 C1
Cross Hills Halifax HX1 .... 203 E4
Kippax LS25 .... 83 B1
Cross Hills Cl LS25 .... 83 A1
Cross Hills Dr LS25 .... 83 A1
Cross Hilts Ent Ctr BD20 ...... 16 E7
Cross Hills Gdns 2 LS25 ...... 83 A1
Cross Hilton Gr LS8 .... 204 C1
Cross Ingledew Cres LS8 .... 44 B2
Cross Ingram Rd LS11 .... 210 C1
Cross Ivy Mount 7 LS9 .... 80 A8
Cross Kelso Rd LS2 .... 205 F1
Cross Keys WF5 .... 141 A2
Cross Keys Ct WF4 .... 141 B1
Cross La Bingley BD16 .... 36 F3
Birkenshaw BD11 .... 96 B7
Bradford BD7 .... 74 A4
Brighouse HD6 .... 115 F1
Elland HX5 .... 134 E6
Emley HD8 .... 175 D8
Guiseley LS20 .... 23 A4
Holmfirth HD7 .... 189 C2
Honley HD7 .... 171 F2
Huddersfield HD4 .... 154 A3
Kirkburton, Stocksmoor HD4 173 C2
Leeds LS12 .... 209 E3
Leeds, Farnley LS12 .... 77 E5
Oxenhope BD22 .... 51 C3
Queensbury BD13 .... 92 C8
Royston S71 .... 179 E3
Shelf HX3 .... 93 A6
Shelf, Stone Chair HX3 .... 93 B4
Shepley HD8 .... 174 B6
Skelmanthorpe HD8 .... 175 A1
Todmorden OL14 .... 108 F4
Wakefield WF2 .... 141 F5
Wilsden BD16 .... 53 D7
Cross Lane Bsns Pk
WF15 .... 117 B4
Cross Lane Prim Sch
HX5 .... 134 E5
Cross Lea Farm Rd LS5 .... 58 F7
Cross Lee OL14 .... 107 F7
Cross Lee Gate OL14 .... 107 F7
Cross Lee Rd OL14 .... 107 F7
Cross Leeds St 13 BD21 ...... 35 B7
Cross Lidgett Pl LS8 .... 204 C4
Cross Linden Terr 4 LS11 214 C3
Cross Louis St LS7 .... 207 E2
Cross Maude St LS2 .... 212 A3
Cross Milan Rd LS8 .... 208 A3
Cross Mitford Rd LS12 .... 210 A3
Cross Osmondthorpe La
LS9 .... 80 C8
Cross Park Ave WF10 .... 124 F7
Cross Park St Batley WF17 118 D5
Dewsbury WF12 .... 139 F8
7 Horbury WF4 .... 141 A1
7 Leeds LS15 .... 62 B3
Cross Pasture Rd 2 LS7 .... 207 E4
Cross Peel St 12 LS27 .... 98 A4
Cross Pipes Rd WF2 .... 141 E8
Cross Platts HX3 .... 114 C4
Cross Quarry St 16 LS6 ...... 206 A4
Cross Queen St 6 LS27 .... 98 A4
Cross Rd
Bradford, Fourlands BD10 .... 56 C8
Bradford, Girlington BD8 ...... 55 B1
Bradford, Oakenshaw BD12 . 94 F4
Dewsbury WF13 .... 139 D1
Horsforth LS18 .... 58 A8
Netherton WF4 .... 158 B7

Cross Reginald Mount
LS7 .... 207 D4
Cross Rink St 3 WF17 .... 118 D3
Cross River St BD21 .... 18 E1
Cross Roseville Rd LS8 .... 207 E3
Cross Rosse St BD18 .... 55 B8
Cross Roundhay Ave LS8 .. 204 C1
Cross Row LS15 .... 82 A6
Cross Rydal St 3 BD22 .... 35 A6
Cross Ryecroft St WF5 .... 140 C2
Cross Speedwell St 5
LS6 .... 206 B3
Cross Sq WF1 .... 216 B2
Cross St 5 Bacup OL13 ...... 106 A3
Batley WF17 .... 118 C5
2 Bradford, Buttershaw BD6 93 F7
5 Bradford, Clayton BD14 .. 73 C4
Bradford, Oakenshaw BD12 .. 95 A4
Brighouse HD6 .... 115 B4
Castleford WF10 .... 124 B8
Castleford WF10 .... 124 C8
Dewsbury WF12 .... 139 E8
Dewsbury, Savile Town
WF12 .... 139 D7
East Ardsley WF3 .... 120 E8
1 Elland, Holywell Green
HX4 .... 134 B4
11 Elland, West Vale HX4 .. 134 D7
Halifax HX1 .... 203 E3
1 Halifax HX1 .... 203 F2
Hebden Bridge HX7 .... 89 A3
Honley HD7 .... 171 F4
2 Horbury WF4 .... 141 B1
Huddersfield HD4 .... 153 E4
Leeds LS15 .... 81 A8
Liversedge WF15 .... 117 A2
Ossett WF5 .... 119 C1
6 Pontefract WF8 .... 146 D8
Rothwell LS26 .... 100 E5
Slaithwaite HD7 .... 152 A1
3 Sowerby Bridge HX6 ...... 112 B3
Wakefield WF1 .... 216 B2
Wetherby LS22 .... 13 E5
Cross St Michael's La
LS6 .... 205 D4
Cross St W HX2 .... 202 A4
Cross Stamford St LS7 ...... 207 D1
Cross Stone Rd OL14 .... 108 D6
Cross Sun St BD1 .... 201 C4
Cross Terr LS26 .... 100 E5
Cross The Barwick in E LS15 . 63 E7
Liversedge WF15 .... 116 E4
2 Queensbury BD13 .... 92 E8
Cross Union St LS2 .... 212 A4
Cross Valley Dr LS15 .... 62 B1
Cross Wellington St 1
BD1 .... 201 C3
Cross Wells Rd HX6 .... 132 C5
Cross Westfield Rd LS3 .... 205 F1
Cross Wingham St LS7 ...... 207 D2
Cross Woodstock St 18
LS2 .... 206 B2
Cross Woodview St 17
WF12 .... 139 D7
Cross York St LS2 .... 212 A3
Crossbeck Cl LS29 .... 8 B3
Crossbeck Rd LS29 .... 8 C3
Crossdale Ave BD6 .... 93 E8
Crossfield Cl BD22 .... 51 E3
Crossfield Dr WF4 .... 157 F6
Crossfield Rd BD22 .... 51 C3
Crossfield St LS2 .... 206 A3
Crossfields WF4 .... 158 A6
Crossflatts First Sch BD16 .. 36 E6
Crossflatts Sta BD16 .... 36 E6
Crossgate Mapplewell S75 . 178 B1
Otley LS21 .... 23 A7
Crosshills Mount HX4 .... 134 C7
Crosshills Rd BD20 .... 4 A2
Crossings The WF17 .... 114 F8
Crossland Rd LS27 .... 98 B7
Crossland Terr LS11 .... 214 C3
Crosslane End Est WF15 .... 117 A4
Crossley Cl Halifax HX1 .... 202 C3
Mirfield WF14 .... 138 A8
Crossley Gdns HX1 .... 202 C4
Crossley Gr WF14 .... 138 A8
Crossley Hall First Sch
BD8 .... 73 E8
Crossley Hall St BD8 .... 73 D7
Crossley Heath Sch HX4 .. 113 A4
Crossley Hill HX3 .... 113 D3
Crossley La
Huddersfield HD5 .... 155 A7
Mirfield WF14 .... 138 B8
Crossley New Rd OL14 ...... 87 F1
Crossley Ret Pk HX1 .... 203 D4
Crossley St Batley WF15 ...... 117 C2
Bradford BD7 .... 74 B5
Brighouse HD6 .... 115 B1
Crofton WF4 .... 143 F6
Featherstone WF7 .... 145 D5
Halifax HX1 .... 203 E3
Queensbury BD13 .... 72 E1
10 Todmorden OL14 .... 108 B5
Wetherby LS22 .... 13 E5
Crossley Terr Batley WF17 118 C3
13 Hebden Bridge HX7 ...... 89 A3
Crossley Terr N HX3 .... 92 A4
Crossley Terr S HX3 .... 92 A4
Crossman Dr WF6 .... 123 C3
Crossmoor Cl LS29 .... 5 C1
Crossmount St WF17 .... 118 C3
Crossroads Cotts LS24 .... 47 E5
Crossway Bradford BD16 .... 73 E6
Crossways LS29 .... 11 A2
Crow Hill End Rd HX6 .... 110 F2
Crow Hill Rd HX6, HX7 ...... 110 F2

Crow La Huddersfield HD3 .. 153 A5
Otley LS21 .... 23 A7
Crow Lane Jun & Inf Sch
HD3 .... 153 A5
Crow Nest La LS11 .... 213 E2
Crow Nest Rd HX7 .... 89 B2
Crow Nest Terr 2 WF13 .... 139 B7
Crow Nest View WF13 ...... 139 A7
Crow Tree Cl BD17 .... 38 D3
Crow Tree La BD8 .... 54 E1
Crow Trees HD7 .... 169 C7
Crow Trees Pk LS19 .... 40 B4
Crow Trees Rd HD7 .... 169 B7
Crow Wood La HX4 .... 133 D2
Crow Wood Pk HX2 .... 112 D5
Crowgill Rd BD18 .... 55 B8
Crowlees C of E Sch
WF14 .... 138 B4
Crowlees Cl WF14 .... 138 B5
Crowlees Gdns WF14 .... 138 B5
Crowlees Rd WF14 .... 138 B5
Crown & Anchor Yd 3
WF8 .... 146 C8
Crown Cl WF12 .... 140 A7
Crown Ct WF8 .... 146 C8
Crown Flatt Way WF12 ...... 118 E1
Crown Gn HX4 .... 153 A4
Crown La HD7 .... 189 A5
Crown Point Cl WF5 .... 140 C6
Crown Point Dr WF5 .... 140 C7
Crown Point Rd
Leeds LS10 .... 212 A2
Ossett WF5 .... 140 C6
Crown Point Ret Pk LS10 .. 211 F2
Crown Rd HX3 .... 92 B2
Crown St
8 Bradford, Carr House Gate
BD12 .... 94 C4
Bradford, Lister Hills BD1 .... 74 C7
Brighouse HD6 .... 115 A3
Burley in W LS29 .... 9 F1
Clayton West HD8 .... 175 D1
Cleckheaton BD19 .... 116 D7
Elland HX5 .... 134 F7
Halifax HX1 .... 203 E3
17 Hebden Bridge HX7 ...... 89 A3
Honley HD7 .... 171 F5
Leeds LS2 .... 211 F3
Ossett WF5 .... 140 E3
Crownest La BD16 .... 37 A3
Crownest Rd BD16 .... 37 A4
Crownlands La WF5 .... 140 D6
Crowther Ave LS28 .... 56 F6
Crowther Cl HD7 .... 152 A2
Crowther Fold BD16 .... 36 B1
Crowther Pl
Castleford WF10 .... 124 D7
Leeds LS6 .... 206 B3
Crowther St Batley WF16 .. 117 E5
Mirfield WF14 .... 138 A5
Morley LS27 .... 98 C5
Sowerby Bridge HX6 .... 112 B3
Crowtrees Cres BD19 .... 94 C4
Crowtrees Ct BD19 .... 94 C4
Crowtrees La
Brighouse HD6 .... 116 A5
Huddersfield, Aspley HD1 .. 154 B6
Huddersfield, Rashcliffe HD1 153 F3
Crowtrees Cts HD6 .... 135 F7
Crowtrees La HD6 .... 135 F7
Crowtrees Pk HD6 .... 135 F8
Crowtrees Rd HD7 .... 121 E5
Croydon Rd BD7 .... 73 F4
Croydon St Leeds LS11 ...... 210 C2
12 Queensbury BD13 .... 72 E1
Crumack La BD22 .... 51 F3
Crumpton Pl WF11 .... 126 E2
Cryer Row BD20 .... 16 D4
Crystal Ct 3 WF1 .... 202 C3
Crystal Pl 4 WF1 .... 216 C2
Crystal Terr BD4 .... 75 C3
Cuckoo La HX7 .... 88 F2
Cuckoo Nest HD7 .... 74 C7
Cuckoo Nest Ind Est BD7 .. 74 C7
Cuckoo's Nest Halt HD8 .. 175 C2
Cuckstool Rd HD8 .... 192 A6
Cudbear St LS10 .... 212 A2
Cullingworth First Sch
BD13 .... 52 D6
Cullingworth St WF13 ...... 118 A3
Cullingworth Village HD8 .. 175 A4
Culpans Rd HX6 .... 111 A5
Culver St 8 HX1 .... 203 E3
Cumberland Ave HD2 .... 136 B5
Cumberland Cl HX2 .... 91 E3
Cumberland Ho BD3 .... 201 D4
Cumberland Rd
Bradford BD7 .... 74 A5
Castleford WF10 .... 104 E2
Leeds LS6 .... 205 F4
Cumberworth C of E
First Sch HD8 .... 191 B6
Cumberworth La
Denby Dale HD8 .... 190 F6
Denby, Lower Cumberworth
HD8 .... 191 E7
Cumberworth Rd HD8 .... 174 F2
Cumbrian Way WF10 .... 141 E2
Cunliffe La BD17 .... 39 B5
Cunliffe Rd Bradford BD8 .. 55 D3
Ilkley LS29 .... 8 B4
Cunliffe Terr BD8 .... 55 D3
Cunliffe Villas BD8 .... 55 D3
Cure Hill BD22 .... 34 B3
Curlew Cl Castleford WF10 . 124 D6
Ilkley LS29 .... 7 E4

Curlew Ct 17 B6
Curlew Rise LS27 .... 98 D3
Curlew St BD5 .... 74 C3
Curler La LS29 .... 3 C4
Curly Hill LS29 .... 8 B6
Currer Ave BD4 .... 75 B1
Currer La LS29 .... 3 C4
Currer St BD1 .... 201 C3
Currer Wlk BD20 .... 17 B6
Curwen Cres WF16 .... 117 E6
Curzon Rd BD3 .... 75 B7
Curzon St HD2 .... 137 B2
Cut Rd Rotherton WF11 .... 105 C1
Fairburn WF11 .... 105 A4
Cuthberts Cl BD13 .... 92 D8
Cutler Heights La BD4 .... 75 D3
Cutler La LS26 .... 102 E4
Cutler Pl BD4 .... 75 D4
Cutsyke Ave WF10 .... 124 B5
Cutsyke Crest WF10 .... 124 B5
Cutsyke Hill WF10 .... 124 B6
Cutsyke Rd Castleford WF7 . 124 B3
Featherstone WF7 .... 124 B3
Cypress Fold HB18 .... 155 E3
Cypress House 10 WF10 .. 124 E7
Cypress Rd WF10 .... 144 C8
Cyprus Ave Bradford BD10 .. 38 F1
Wakefield WF1 .... 142 A8
Cyprus Cres WF14 .... 138 D7
Cyprus Dr BD10 .... 39 A1
Cyprus Gr Garforth LS25 .... 82 E7
Wakefield WF1 .... 142 A8
Cyprus Mount WF1 .... 142 A8
Cyprus Rd LS25 .... 82 E7
Cyprus St WF1 .... 216 A4
Cyprus Terr LS25 .... 82 E7
Czar St LS11 .... 211 D2

Dacre Ave WF2 .... 141 C4
Dacre Cl WF15 .... 116 F5
Daffels Wood Cl BD4 .... 95 B8
Daffil Ave LS27 .... 98 B7
Daffil Gr LS27 .... 98 B8
Daffil Grange Mews 1 LS27 98 A7
Daffil Grange Way LS27 .... 98 B7
Daffil Rd LS27 .... 98 B7
Daffodil Ct 8 BD15 .... 73 B8
Dagenham Rd BD4 .... 75 C3
Dahl Dr WF10 .... 125 C8
Daisy Bank HX1 .... 203 D1
Daisy Bank Sq 2 OL14 ...... 86 B1
Daisy Cl WF17 .... 96 E2
Daisy Croft BD20 .... 5 F1
Daisy Fold WF9 .... 182 F7
Daisy Gn HD7 .... 170 C7
Daisy Hill
5 Bradford BD12 .... 94 C3
Dewsbury WF13 .... 139 C8
Morley LS27 .... 98 C5
Sirsden BD20 .... 5 F1
Daisy Hill Ave LS27 .... 98 C6
Daisy Hill Back La BD9 .... 54 E2
Daisy Hill Cl WF13 .... 139 C8
Daisy Hill Gr BD9 .... 54 E2
Daisy Hill La BD9 .... 54 E2
Daisy Hill Middle Sch
BD9 .... 54 E2
Daisy Lea LS18 .... 152 A8
Daisy Lea La HD3 .... 135 C1
Daisy Lea LS12 .... 199 C7
Daisy Mount HX6 .... 112 A5
Daisy Pl 2 BD18 .... 54 F8
Daisy Rd HD6 .... 136 B8
Daisy Row 3 LS13 .... 58 D1
Daisy St 5 Bradford BD7 .... 74 A3
6 Brighouse HD6 .... 115 A2
Halifax HX1 .... 203 D2
1 Haworth BD22 .... 51 E8
Daisy Vale Mews WF3 .... 99 E1
Daisy Vale Terr WF3 .... 99 E1
Daisyfield Rd 2 LS13 .... 58 D2
Dalby Ave BD3 .... 56 C1
Dalby St BD3 .... 75 C8
Dalcross Gr BD5 .... 74 F4
Dalcross St BD5 .... 74 F4
Dale Ave OL14 .... 108 D5
Dale Cl Batley WF17 .... 118 C3
Denby Dale HD8 .... 191 F5
Guiseley LS20 .... 39 B8
Dale Cres BD20 .... 17 C5
Dale Croft Garforth LS25 .... 82 E8
Ilkley LS29 .... 7 E4
Dale Croft Rise BD15 .... 54 A2
Dale Ct HD2 .... 137 B3
Dale St Bradford BD1 .... 201 C3
Castleford WF10 .... 139 C4
Huddersfield HD1 .... 153 A5
Huddersfield, Folly Hall HD1 154 A5
Keighley BD21 .... 18 E1

Dale St continued
Ossett WF5 .... 140 D6
Shipley BD18 .... 55 B7
Skelmanthorpe HD8 ..... 175 A2
Sowerby Bridge HX6 ..... 112 B4
Todmorden OL14 .... 108 B5
Dale Stone CI WF11 ..... 105 C1
Dale The LS25 .... 47 E1
Dale View Halifax HX2 .... 111 D6
Hemsworth WF9 .... 181 F6
Ilkley LS29 .... 7 E4
Pontefract WF8 .... 146 D5
Silsden BD20 .... 5 E2
Steeton BD20 .... 17 C5
Dale View CI BD21 .... 35 E6
Dale View Gr BD21 .... 35 E6
Dale View Rd BD21 .... 35 E6
Dale Wlk WF7 .... 145 C4
Dalefield Ave WF6 .... 123 B1
Dalefield Rd WF6 .... 144 B8
Dales Dr LS20 .... 39 B8
Dales Way LS20 .... 39 B8
Daleside Dewsbury WF12 ... 139 C1
Elland HX4 .... 134 A7
Daleside Ave
Holmfirth HD7 .... 189 C7
Pudsey LS28 .... 76 A8
Daleside CI LS28 .... 56 F1
Daleside Gr Bradford BD12 ... 94 F4
Pudsey LS28 .... 76 A7
Daleside Rd Keighley BD20 ... 19 A1
Pudsey LS28 .... 75 F8
Shipley BD18 .... 55 E8
Daleside Wlk BD5 .... 74 F2
Daleson CI HX3 .... 93 A3
Dalesway BD16 .... 37 B5
Daleview CI BD17 .... 38 A2
Dallam Ave BD18 .... 54 E8
Dallam Gr [3] BD18 ...... 54 E8
Dallam Rd BD18 .... 54 E8
Dallam Wlk BD18 .... 54 E8
Dalmeny Ave HD4 .... 153 C3
Dalmeny CI HD4 .... 153 C3
Dalton Ave LS11 .... 214 A2
Dalton Bank Rd HD5 ...... 137 A3
Dalton Clowes HD5 .... 154 E7
Dalton Fold Rd HD5 ...... 154 E7
Dalton Gr Huddersfield HD5 ... 154 E7
Leeds LS11 .... 214 A2
Dalton Green La HD5 ..... 155 A6
Dalton Infants Sch HD5 ... 154 F6
Dalton La Collingham LS23 ... 29 E3
Keighley BD21 .... 35 E7
Dalton Rd Keighley BD21 ... 35 E7
Leeds LS11 .... 214 A2
Dalton St
[2] Sowerby Bridge HX6 ... 112 B5
Todmorden OL14 .... 108 B5
Dalton Terr Bradford BD6 ... 74 B8
Castleford WF10 .... 124 D7
Keighley BD21 .... 35 E8
Dalton Works HD5 .... 136 F1
Dam Head La HD8 .... 175 F5
Dam Head Rd HX6 .... 112 C5
Dam Hill HD8 .... 173 E3
Dam La Saxton LS24 ...... 65 F6
Yeadon LS19 .... 40 C7
Damask St HX1 .... 203 D4
Damems La BD22 .... 35 A2
Damems Rd BD21 .... 35 A3
Damems Sta BD22 .... 35 A2
Damon Ave BD10 .... 56 E4
Dampier St [1] OL14 ..... 108 A1
Damside BD21 .... 35 B6
Damside Rd HD4 .... 154 B4
Dan La BD13 .... 73 C2
Danby Ave BD4 .... 95 B8
Danby La WF2 .... 160 C4
Danby Wlk LS9 .... 212 C3
Dandy Mill Ave WF8 ..... 125 F2
Dandy Mill Croft WF8 ... 125 F2
Dandy Mill View WF8 ... 125 F3
Dane Hill Dr BD4 .... 95 C7
Dane Royd Jun & Inf Sch
WF4 .... 159 F2
Danebury Rd HD6 .... 115 B1
Danecourt Rd BD4 .... 75 F3
Danefield Terr LS21 ...... 23 B8
Danehurst WF6 .... 144 A6
Danella Cres WF2 .... 120 F3
Danella Gr WF2 .... 120 F2
Danes Ave WF4 .... 158 B6
Danesleigh Dr WF4 .... 158 B6
Daniel CI BD4 .... 75 F2
Daniel St BD3 .... 75 D7
Danny La HD7 .... 171 D7
Dansk Way LS29 .... 8 D5
Danum Dr HD7 .... 38 C2
Darbyfields HD7 .... 152 E6
Darcey Hey La HX2 .... 202 A1
Darcy Ct LS15 .... 81 C8
Darfield Cres LS8 .... 208 A3
Darfield Gres LS8 .... 208 A2
Darfield Gr [6] LS8 .... 207 F3
Darfield PI LS8 .... 208 A3
Darfield Rd LS8 .... 208 A3
Darfield St Bradford BD1 ... 201 A4
Leeds LS8 .... 208 A3
Dark La Barwick in E LS15 ... 63 D8
Batley, Birstall WF17 ...... 96 F3
Batley, Mount Pleasant
WF17 .... 118 B4
Blackshaw Head HX7 ...... 88 A3
Cawthorne S75 .... 193 E5
Halifax HX2 .... 112 B6

Dark La continued
Haworth BD22 .... 33 F1
Huddersfield HD4 .... 155 A3
Oxenhope BD22 .... 51 D3
Pontefract WF8 .... 146 C7
Darkfield La WF8 .... 125 F4
Darkwood CI LS17 .... 44 A4
Darkwood Way LS17 ...... 44 A4
Darley Ave LS10 .... 99 D7
Darley Rd HD5 .... 116 F5
Darley St Batley WF16 ... 117 D4
Bradford BD1 .... 201 B3
Keighley BD20 .... 18 B1
Darnes Ave HX2 .... 202 A1
Darning La WF8 .... 165 B5
Darnley Ave WF2 .... 142 A6
Darnley CI HD7 .... 170 E1
Darnley La LS15 .... 81 C7
Darren CI LS10 .... 59 B7
Darren St BD4 .... 75 E6
Darrington C of E Junior
& Infants Sch WF8 ... 147 D5
Darrington La WF8 .... 146 E2
Dartmouth Ave
Huddersfield HD5 .... 155 A3
Morley LS27 .... 98 A2
Dartmouth Mews LS27 ... 97 F3
Dartmouth Terr
Bradford BD8 .... 55 C2
Kirkburton HD4 .... 172 E6
Dartmouth Way LS11 .... 214 C2
Darton Hall CI S75 .... 177 F1
Darton Hall Dr S75 .... 177 F1
Darton Jun & Inf Sch S75 ... 177 F1
Darton La S75 .... 178 B1
Darton Rd S75 .... 193 F5
Darwin St BD5 .... 177 E1
Darwin St BD5 .... 74 C3
Davey La HX2 .... 87 F3
David St LS11 .... 118 C2
David St Castleford WF10 ... 124 B7
Leeds LS11 .... 211 E2
Wakefield WF1 .... 142 E4
Davies Ave LS8 .... 61 A8
Davis Ave WF10 .... 124 A6
Daw Green Ave WF4 ...... 159 C4
Daw La Crigglestone WF4 ... 159 D4
Horbury WF4 .... 159 C8
Daw Royds HD5 .... 155 A4
Dawes Ave WF10 .... 124 F6
Dawlish Ave LS9 .... 80 B8
Dawlish Cres LS9 .... 80 B8
Dawlish Gr LS9 .... 80 B7
Dawlish Mount LS9 .... 80 B8
Dawlish PI [1] LS9 .... 80 B8
Dawlish Rd LS9 .... 80 B8
Dawlish Row LS9 .... 80 B8
Dawlish St LS9 .... 80 B8
Dawlish Terr LS9 .... 80 B8
Dawnay Rd BD5 .... 74 C4
Dawson Ave BD6 .... 94 C8
Dawson Gdns [1] WF13 ... 139 C8
Dawson Hill LS27 .... 98 A5
Dawson Hill Yd [3] WF4 ... 141 B1
Dawson La Birkenshaw BD4 ... 76 E2
Bradford BD4 .... 75 C1
Rothwell LS26 .... 100 E6
Dawson Mount BD4 .... 75 C1
Dawson PI Bradford BD4 ... 75 C1
Keighley BD21 .... 35 C5
Dawson Rd
Huddersfield HD4 .... 154 B3
Keighley BD21 .... 35 C5
Leeds LS11 .... 214 A3
Dawson St
Bradford, Bierley BD4 ..... 75 C2
Bradford, Thackley BD10 ... 39 B2
East Ardsley WF3 .... 98 D1
[7] Pudsey LS28 .... 57 D1
Dawson Terr BD4 .... 75 C1
Dawson Way BD21 .... 35 C5
Dawson's Corner LS28 ... 57 C2
Dawsons Meadow LS28 ... 57 C2
Dawtrie CI WF10 .... 125 D7
Dawtrie St WF10 .... 125 D7
Day St Dewsbury WF13 ... 138 E5
Huddersfield HD1 .... 154 B5
De Lacey Mews BD4 .... 75 C2
De Lacies CI LS26 .... 101 A7
De Lacies Ct LS26 .... 101 B8
De Lacy Ave Bradford BD4 ... 95 B8
Featherstone WF7 .... 124 E1
Huddersfield HD5 .... 154 F4
De Lacy Mount LS5 .... 59 A4
De Lacy Terr WF8 .... 146 E8
De Trafford St HD4 ...... 153 D4
Deacon CI HD7 .... 152 D4
Deaconss Ct LS29 .... 8 B3
Deacons Wlk HD6 .... 117 E4
Deadmanstone HD4 .... 171 F8
Deal St Halifax HX1 ...... 203 F2
Keighley BD21 .... 35 E8
Dealburn Rd BD12 .... 94 E4
Dean Ave Holmfirth HD7 ... 188 F8
Leeds LS8 .... 61 A6
Dean Beck Ave BD6 .... 74 E1
Dean Beck Ct BD6 .... 94 F8
Dean Bridge La HD7 ...... 189 E2
Dean Brook Rd
Holmfirth HD7 .... 172 A1
Huddersfield HD4 .... 171 E8
Dean CI Bradford BD8 .... 54 D1
Wakefield WF2 .... 120 F2
Dean Clough HX1 .... 203 E4
Dean Clough Office Pk
HX3 .... 203 D4
Dean Ct Elland HX3 ...... 113 A2

Dean Edge Rd BD22 .... 50 A8
Dean End HX4 .... 134 C8
Dean Hall CI S75 .... 178 C1
Dean Head LS18 .... 41 A8
Dean House La HX2 .... 90 E2
Dean La East Carlton LS16 ... 24 A1
Guiseley LS20 .... 38 F8
Holmfirth HD7 .... 188 F8
Horsforth LS18 .... 41 A8
Keighley BD22 .... 33 F6
Sowerby Bridge HX6 ..... 132 E8
Sowerby Bridge, Sowerby
HX6 .... 111 E2
Wilsden BD13 .... 53 C1
Dean Park Ave BD11 ...... 96 E7
Dean Park Dr BD11 .... 96 E6
Dean Rd Bradford BD6 .... 94 D8
Holmfirth HD7 .... 188 C6
Dean St [8] Elland HX5 ... 134 F6
Elland, West Vale HX4 .... 134 D7
Haworth BD22 .... 51 D7
Huddersfield HD3 .... 153 B8
Ilkley LS29 .... 8 C5
Dean Villas OL14 .... 129 B7
Dean Wood View HX3 ... 113 C2
Deane The LS15 .... 80 D7
Deanery Gdns BD10 .... 56 C5
Deanfield Ave LS27 .... 97 F6
Deanfield Junior
& Infants Sch LS27 .... 97 E6
Deanhouse Gdns BD10 ... 56 C5
Deanhurst Gdns LS27 .... 97 F6
Deanhurst Ind Ctr LS27 ... 97 D6
Deanroyd Rd OL14 .... 129 B7
Deanstones Cres BD13 ... 92 E8
Deanstones La BD13 ..... 92 E8
Deansway LS27 .... 97 F6
Deanswood CI LS17 .... 43 A3
Deanswood Dr LS17 ...... 42 F3
Deanswood Garth LS17 ... 43 A3
Deanswood Gdns LS17 ... 42 F3
Deanswood Gn LS17 ...... 42 F3
Deanswood Hill LS17 ..... 43 A3
Deanswood PI LS17 .... 43 A3
Deanswood Rise LS17 .... 43 A3
Deanswood View LS17 ... 43 A3
Deanwood Ave BD15 ..... 54 A3
Deanwood Cres BD15 .... 54 A2
Deanwood Wlk BD15 ..... 54 A2
Dearden St Ossett WF5 ... 140 D5
Sowerby Bridge HX6 ..... 112 B5
Dearne Croft LS22 .... 13 E8
Dearne Dike La HD8 ..... 190 E5
Dearne Fold HD3 .... 135 B1
Dearne High Sch S63 .... 194 B1
Dearne PI HD8 .... 190 E5
Dearne Rd HD8 .... 175 E2
Dearne Royd HD8 .... 175 E2
Dearne St
Clayton West HD8 .... 175 D1
Mapplewell S75 .... 177 F1
South Elmsall WF9 .... 182 F3
Dearneside Rd HD8 ...... 191 F5
Dearnfield HD8 .... 191 C6
Dearnley St WF13 .... 138 E6
Dee Ct BD22 .... 34 C2
Deep Dale LS23 .... 14 C1
Deep La Bradford BD13 .... 73 C5
Brighouse HD6 .... 115 F2
Halifax HX2 .... 111 F7
Sowerby Bridge HX6 ..... 112 B8
Thornton BD13 .... 72 A5
Deepdale CI BD17 .... 38 A2
Deepdale La LS23 .... 14 C1
Deer Croft Ave HD3 ...... 152 F8
Deer Croft Cres HD3 ..... 152 F8
Deer Croft Dr HD3 .... 152 F8
Deer Croft Rd [2] HD3 ... 134 F1
Deer Hill Croft HD7 ...... 168 F3
Deer Hill Dr HD7 .... 168 F3
Deer Hill CI HD7 .... 170 C2
Deer Hill Dr HD7 .... 168 F3
Deer Hill End Rd HD7 ... 170 A4
Deershaw La HD7 .... 190 C5
Deershaw Sike La HD7 ... 190 C5
Defarge Ct BD5 .... 74 E2
Deffer Rd WF2 .... 160 C6
Deganwy Dr HD5 .... 137 C2
Deighton CI LS22 .... 13 F6
Deighton Gates Junior
& Infants Sch LS22 .... 13 E8
Deighton Rd
Huddersfield HD2 .... 136 E3
Wetherby LS22 .... 13 E7
Deighton Sta HD2 .... 136 E3
Deightonby St S63 ...... 194 F1
Delacy Cres WF10 .... 104 D1
Delamere St BD5 .... 74 D2
Delamere Way WF6 ..... 123 B1
Delf Hill HD6 .... 135 E7
Delf La Todmorden OL14 ... 86 D3
Wadsworth Moor HX7 ... 89 C8
Delf PI HD6 .... 135 E7
Delfs La HX6 .... 110 F1
Delius Ave BD10 .... 56 E5
Dell Croft BD20 .... 17 B6
Dell The Burley LS17 ...... 28 D3
Castleford WF10 .... 124 A6
Cullingworth BD13 .... 52 E6
Huddersfield HD4 .... 136 B4
Dellside Fold BD13 .... 52 D6
Delmont CI WF17 .... 118 A6
Delph Cres BD14 .... 73 B4
Delph Croft View BD21 ... 35 D6
Delph Ct LS6 .... 206 A4
Delph Dr BD14 .... 73 B4

Delph Gr BD14 .... 73 B4
Delph Hill [10] Baildon BD17 ... 38 C4
[5] Halifax HX2 .... 113 A4
Pudsey LS28 .... 76 E8
Delph Hill La HX2 .... 90 D2
Delph Hill Middle Sch
BD12 .... 94 C6
Delph Hill Rd HX2 .... 112 F4
Delph Hill Terr [3] HX2 ... 112 F4
Delph La Huddersfield HD4 ... 171 D7
Leeds LS6 .... 206 A4
Delph Mount LS6 .... 206 A4
Delph St HX1 .... 203 D2
Delph Terr BD14 .... 73 B4
Delph The WF7 .... 145 F5
Delph View LS6 .... 206 A4
Delph Wood CI BD16 ...... 37 C3
Delverne Gr BD2 .... 56 C3
Delves Gate HD7 .... 169 C6
Delves Wood Rd HD4 .... 153 C1
Denard Ind Est HD4 ...... 153 B4
Denbigh App LS9 .... 61 D2
Denbigh Croft LS9 .... 61 D2
Denbigh Hts LS9 .... 61 D2
Denbrook Ave BD4 .... 75 F1
Denbrook CI BD4 .... 75 F1
Denbrook Cres BD4 .... 95 F8
Denbrook Way BD4 .... 75 F1
Denbrook Wlk BD4 .... 75 F1
Denbury Mount BD4 ..... 75 E2
Denby C of E Fst Sch
HD8 .... 191 F3
Denby CI Batley WF17 .... 96 D1
Liversedge WF15 .... 116 F5
Denby Crest WF4 .... 147 D5
Denby Ct BD22 .... 34 B2
Denby Dale Rd
Wakefield WF1 .... 216 A1
Denby Dale Rd E WF4 .... 159 F7
Denby Dale Rd W WF4 ... 159 D6
Denby Dale Sta HD8 ..... 191 E6
Denby Dr BD17 .... 38 B1
Denby Grange La WF4 ... 157 A5
Denby Hall La HD8 .... 192 D4
Denby Hill Rd BD22 .... 34 B2
Denby La Bradford BD15 ... 54 B1
Denby Dale, Lower Denby
HD8 .... 192 C4
Denby Dale, Upper Denby
HD8 .... 191 F3
Denby Lane Cres WF4 .... 156 E5
Denby Mount BD22 .... 51 C2
Denby Park Dr WF4 ...... 156 E5
Denby PI [3] HX6 .... 112 B5
Denby Rd Darrington WF8 ... 147 C5
Keighley BD22 .... 35 C5
Denby St BD8 .... 74 C8
Denby View WF12 .... 139 D1
Dence Gn BD4 .... 75 E3
Dence PI LS15 .... 80 E8
Dene CI HX5 .... 134 E5
Dene Gr BD20 .... 5 E2
Dene Hill BD17 .... 37 F3
Dene Mount BD15 .... 54 C1
Dene PK HD8 .... 173 F7
Dene PI HX1 .... 203 D4
Dene Rd Bradford BD6 .... 73 D1
Denehill BD9 .... 54 D2
Deneside WF5 .... 140 C7
Deneside Mount BD5 .... 74 D2
Deneside Terr BD5 .... 74 D2
Denesway LS25 .... 83 A5
Deneway LS28 .... 57 C2
Denfield Ave HX3 .... 91 F2
Denfield Cres HX3 .... 91 F2
Denfield Dr HX3 .... 91 F2
Denfield Edge HX3 .... 91 F2
Denfield Gdns HX3 .... 91 F2
Denfield La HX3 .... 91 F2
Denfield Sq HX3 .... 91 F2
Denhale Ave WF2 .... 141 F6
Denham Dr HD7 .... 189 D4
Denham St Batley WF17 ... 118 A7
[4] Brighouse HD6 .... 115 A1
Denholme Dr WF5 .... 140 D7
Denholme First Sch BD13 ... 52 D1
Denholme Gate Rd
Brighouse HX3 .... 93 C1
Northowram HX3 .... 93 C1
Denholme Meadow WF9 ... 182 F4
Denholme Rd BD22 .... 51 C3
Denison Rd LS3 .... 211 D4
Denison St Batley WF17 ... 118 C4
Yeadon LS19 .... 40 B7
Denmark St WF1 .... 142 E4
Dennil Cres LS15 .... 62 D3
Dennil Rd LS15 .... 62 D3
Dennington La WF4 ...... 159 C3
Dennis La BD20 .... 5 A4
Dennison Fold BD4 .... 75 E5
Dennison Hill LS21 .... 23 B8
Dennistead Cres LS6 ...... 59 D5
Denshaw Dr LS27 .... 98 C4
Denshaw Gr LS27 .... 98 C4
Denshaw La WF3 .... 99 A3
Denstone St WF1 .... 216 C3
Dent Dr WF1 .... 142 F8
Dent St LS9 .... 212 C3
Denton Ave LS8 .... 204 C4
Denton Dr BD16 .... 37 C4
Denton Gdns WF7 .... 164 A5

Denton Gr LS8 .... 204 C4
Denton House [9] BD6 ... 93 E8
Denton Rd Denton LS29 ... 9 A4
Ilkley LS29 .... 8 D7
Denton Row Denholme BD13 ... 71 D8
Elland HX4 .... 134 C4
Denton Terr WF8 .... 124 E8
Denwell Terr WF8 .... 125 D3
Der St OL14 .... 108 A3
Derby PI BD3 .... 75 D7
Derby Rd Bradford BD3 ... 75 E7
Yeadon LS19 .... 40 B6
Derby St Bingley BD16 .... 36 F3
[2] Bradford, Clayton BD14 ... 73 B4
Bradford, Great Horton BD7 ... 74 B6
Queensbury BD13 .... 72 D3
Sowerby Bridge HX6 ..... 112 D4
Todmorden OL14 .... 108 D5
Derbyshire St [4] LS10 ... 212 A2
Marsden HD7 .... 168 F4
Derbyshire St LS10 ...... 215 F3
Derdale St OL14 .... 108 C5
Derry Hill LS29 .... 21 F4
Derry Hill Gdns LS29 .... 21 F4
Derry La LS29 .... 21 F4
Derwent Ave Baildon BD17 ... 37 E1
Garforth LS25 .... 82 F6
Rothwell LS26 .... 101 C6
Wilsden BD15 .... 53 C4
Derwent CI HX3 .... 89 A4
Derwent Ct BD20 .... 17 E8
Derwent Dr
Castleford WF10 .... 104 E3
Huddersfield HD5 .... 154 D2
Leeds LS16 .... 42 D4
Derwent Gr WF2 .... 141 F6
Derwent PI
Knottingley WF11 .... 126 E3
Leeds LS11 .... 211 D2
Derwent Rd Batley WF12 ... 118 F2
Bradford BD2 .... 56 A1
Honley HD7 .... 171 E3
Meltham HD7 .... 170 E1
Wakefield WF2 .... 141 F6
Derwent Rise LS22 .... 13 DE
Derwent Rd HD4 .... 35 F6
Derwentwater Gr LS6 .... 59 D5
Derwentwater Terr LS6 ... 59 D5
Derwin Ave HD4 .... 173 C2
Detroit Ave LS15 .... 81 EE
Detroit Dr LS15 .... 81 EE
Deveron Gr HD2 .... 153 EE
Devon CI LS2 .... 206 B2
Devon Gr WF5 .... 140 C4
Devon Rd LS2 .... 206 B2
Devon St HX1 .... 202 B3
Devon Way HD6 .... 115 B6
Devon Wlk [4] WF13 ... 139 B8
Devonshire Ave LS8 ... 44 A2
Devonshire CI LS8 .... 44 A2
Devonshire Cres LS8 ..... 44 A2
Devonshire Gdns LS2 ... 206 B3
Devonshire La LS8 .... 44 A2
Devonshire PI [3] LS19 ... 40 B7
Devonshire St
Huddersfield HD1 .... 153 E8
Keighley BD21 .... 35 B7
Devonshire St W BD21 ... 35 A7
Devonshire Terr BD9 .... 55 C2
Dewar CI LS22 .... 13 B1
Dewhirst CI BD17 .... 38 D2
Dewhirst PI BD4 .... 75 D6
Dewhirst Rd Baildon BD17 ... 38 D2
Brighouse HD6 .... 115 A4
Dewhirst St WF15 .... 53 C5
Dewhurst Rd HD2 .... 136 B2
Dewsbury Bus Mus WF13 ... 138 E5
Dewsbury Coll
Batley WF12 .... 118 C5
Dewsbury WF13 .... 118 C1
Dewsbury District
Golf Course WF4 .... 138 D3
Dewsbury District Hospl
WF13 .... 118 A2
Dewsbury Gate Rd WF13 ... 117 F3
Dewsbury Mills WF12 ... 139 C6
Dewsbury Moor Infant Sch
WF13 .... 117 F2
Dewsbury Mus & Art Gal
WF13 .... 139 A7
Dewsbury Rd
Brighouse HD6 .... 135 C6
Cleckheaton BD19 .... 96 B2
Cleckheaton, Marsh BD19 ... 116 E7
East Ardsley WF12 .... 119 C7
Elland HX5 .... 135 C6
Leeds LS11 .... 214 C2
Middleton LS27 .... 98 E5
Ossett WF5 .... 140 D7
Wakefield WF2 .... 141 D5
Dewsbury Sta WF13 ..... 139 C8
Deyne Rd HD4 .... 171 C7
Diadem Dr LS14 .... 62 A3
Dial St LS9 .... 212 C2
Diamond Ave WF9 .... 182 E3
Diamond St Batley WF12 ... 118 B6
Bradford BD1 .... 201 C2
Halifax HX1 .... 202 C4
Huddersfield HD5 .... 154 D5
[10] Huddersfield, Moldgreen
HD5 .... 154 D5
Keighley BD22 .... 35 A4
Diamond Terr HX1 .... 202 C4
Dib CI LS8 .... 61 D5
Dib La LS8 .... 61 D5
Dibb La LS19 .... 39 F7
Dick Dean La HX7 .... 69 A5

Dick Edge La HD7 .... 190 B2
Dick La BD3, BD4 .... 75 E6
Dick's Garth Rd LS29 .... 21 F4
Dicken's St HX2 .... 202 A3
Dickens St BD5 .... 74 E3
Dickinson Ct WF1 .... 216 B4
Dickinson Gdns **11** WF13 .. 139 B8
Dickinson St
  Horsforth LS18 .... 41 C2
  Wakefield WF1 .... 216 B3
Dickinson Terr WF7 .... 145 D6
Dickson Fold WF15 .... 116 F4
Dicky Sykes La WF7 .... 163 D5
Digby Rd LS29 .... 22 A4
Digby Rd HD7 .... 188 B2
Digby Royd La HD7 .... 188 A3
Dimple Gdns WF5 .... 140 D4
Dimple Well Infant Sch
  WF5 .... 140 D4
Dimple Wells Cl WF5 .... 140 D4
Dimple Wells La WF5 .... 140 D4
Dimple Wells Rd WF5 .... 140 D4
Dimples La Haworth BD22 ..... 51 B6
  Keighley BD20 .... 36 D8
Dineley Ave OL14 .... 108 A1
Dingle Rd HD1 .... 153 D6
Dingley Rd HD3 .... 153 C8
Dinsdale's Bldgs LS19 .... 40 A6
Dirker Ave HD7 .... 169 A5
Dirker Bank Rd HD7 .... 168 F5
Dirker Dr HD7 .... 168 F4
Dirkhill Rd BD7 .... 74 C5
Dirkhill St BD7 .... 74 B5
Discovery Rd HX1 .... 203 F2
Dish Hill Fly-over WF11 ...... 126 D8
Disney Cl HD4 .... 153 D3
Dispensary Wlk HX1 .... 203 F3
Disraeli Gdns LS11 .... 214 B4
Disraeli Terr LS11 .... 214 B4
Dixon Ave BD7 .... 73 F5
Dixon Cl Elland HX4 .... 134 B8
  Sheeton BD20 .... 17 C5
Dixon La LS12 .... 209 E1
Dixon Lane Rd LS12 .... 209 F1
Dixon St
  Featherstone WF7 .... 145 D7
  Sutton in C BD20 .... 16 E5
Dixon's Yd WF1 .... 216 C2
Dob La HX6 .... 111 D3
Dob Park Rd LS21 .... 10 E8
Dob Royd HD8 .... 190 D7
Dob The HX6 .... 111 D3
Dobb Kiln La BD16 .... 37 B1
Dobb La HD7 .... 188 C2
Dobb Top Rd HD7 .... 188 C2
Dobroyd Rd OL14 .... 108 A4
Dobson Ave LS11 .... 214 C3
Dobson Gr LS11 .... 214 C3
Dobson Pl LS11 .... 214 C3
Dobson Terr LS11 .... 214 C3
Dobson View LS11 .... 214 C3
Dobsons Wharf BD20 .... 17 E8
Dock La BD17, BD18 .... 55 C8
Dock St LS10 .... 211 F3
Dockery HD4 .... 153 F3
Dockfield Pl BD17 .... 55 C8
Dockfield Rd BD17 .... 55 C8
Dockfield Terr BD17 .... 55 C8
Dockroyd La BD22 .... 34 D2
Doctor Fold HD7 .... 171 F5
Doctor Hill Bradford BD10 ... 56 A6
  Bradford, Springfield BD10 ... 56 B7
Doctor La HD1 .... 91 E1
Doctor La Bradford BD10 ...... 39 B1
  Flockton WF4 .... 157 B2
  Mirfield WF14 .... 138 A5
  Shepley HD8 .... 174 A3
Dodd's Royd HD4 .... 171 E8
Dodge Holme Ct HX2 .... 91 D4
Dodge Holme Dr HX2 .... 91 D4
Dodge Holme Gdns HX2 .... 91 D4
Dodge Holme Rd HX2 .... 91 D4
Dodgeholme Cl HX2 .... 91 D4
Dodgson Ave LS7 .... 207 E3
Dodgson St HX5 .... 134 F5
Dodlee La HD3 .... 152 E7
Dodsworth Cres WF6 .... 144 B8
Dodworth Dr WF2 .... 160 B5
Dog Hill Dr S72 .... 180 C3
Dog Hill Dr S72 .... 180 C3
Dog Kennel Bank HD5 .... 154 C4
Dog Kennel Hill LS25 .... 83 E5
Dog Kennel La HX3 .... 113 E5
Dog La
  Elland, Stainland HX4 .... 133 C2
  Elland, Upper Greetland
  HX4 .... 133 E7
Dog Pits La OL13 .... 106 A6
Doghouse La OL14 .... 108 A5
Dogley La HD8 .... 155 D1
Dogley Villa Ct HD8 .... 155 D1
Doldram La HX4 .... 112 A1
Dole La HX7 .... 89 A1
Dole St BD13 .... 72 F6
Doles Ave S71 .... 179 B3
Doles Cres S71 .... 179 B3
Dolfin Pl HD2 .... 136 F5
Doll La BD13 .... 52 E4
Dolly La LS9 .... 207 E2
Dolphin La WF3 .... 99 F2
Dolphin Rd LS10 .... 99 E5
Dombey St HX1 .... 202 C3
Domestic Rd LS12 .... 210 C1
Domestic St LS11 .... 210 C1
Dominican Ave BD8 .... 73 C7
Dominion Ave LS7 .... 204 B3
Dominion Ind Pk HX3 .... 114 C8
Don Ave LS22 .... 13 D8

Don Ct BD20 .... 5 E1
Don Pedro Ave WF6 .... 123 D2
Don Pedro Cl WF6 .... 123 D2
Don St BD21 .... 35 B8
Don View S36 .... 199 D1
Donald Ave BD6 .... 94 C8
Donald St **5** LS28 .... 57 D2
Doncaster La DN6 .... 184 C3
Doncaster Rd
  Ackworth M T WF4 .... 163 B6
  Crofton WF4 .... 143 D2
  Darrington WF7 .... 164 B3
  Hampole WF9 .... 183 D5
  Knottingley WF11 .... 126 C4
  South Elmsall WF9 .... 183 D5
  Thorpe Audlin WF8 .... 165 C4
  Upton WF9 .... 182 E7
  Upton, Barnsdale WF8 .... 166 A1
  Wakefield WF1 .... 142 E4
  West Hardwick WF4 .... 163 B6
Doncaster Road Est WF7 .... 164 A5
Doncaster Sq WF11 .... 126 D5
Doncaster St HX3 .... 113 D3
Donisthorpe St
  Bradford BD5 .... 74 E3
  Leeds LS10 .... 212 B1
Dorchester Ave WF8 .... 146 B8
Dorchester Cres
  Baildon BD17 .... 38 F4
  Bradford BD4 .... 75 E2
Dorchester Ct BD4 .... 75 E2
Dorchester Dr Halifax HX2 .. 202 A1
  Yeadon LS19 .... 40 D6
Dorchester Rd HD2 .... 136 B5
Dorian Cl BD10 .... 56 C6
Dorman Ave WF9 .... 183 D8
Dorothy St BD21 .... 35 A3
Dorset Ave LS8 .... 208 A4
Dorset Cl Bradford BD5 .... 74 C3
  Hemsworth WF9 .... 181 D8
Dorset Gr LS28 .... 76 E8
Dorset Mount LS8 .... 208 A3
Dorset Rd LS8 .... 208 A3
Dorset St Bradford BD5 .... 74 D3
  Huddersfield HD1 .... 153 F8
  Leeds LS8 .... 208 A3
Dorset Terr LS8 .... 208 A3
Dorset Wlk **6** WF13 .... 139 B8
Dortmund Sq LS2 .... 211 F4
Dotterel Glen LS27 .... 98 C3
Doubting La WF12 .... 139 D1
Doubting Rd WF12 .... 139 D1
Douglas Ave Batley WF17 ... 118 F5
  Huddersfield HD5 .... 154 E5
Douglas Cres BD18 .... 55 D6
Douglas Dr BD4 .... 75 C4
Douglas Rd Bacup OL13 ..... 106 A1
  Bradford BD4 .... 75 C4
Douglas St Dewsbury WF12 139 C4
  Halifax HX3 .... 92 B2
  8 Haworth BD22 .... 51 D7
Douglas Towers **1** BD5 .. 201 B1
Dove Cl LS27 .... 13 E8
Dove Dr WF10 .... 125 B8
  Shipley BD18 .... 54 F8
Dovecote Cl WF4 .... 141 B2
Dovecote Dr WF10 .... 103 E6
Dovecote La WF4 .... 141 A2
Dovedale Cl Crofton WF4 .... 144 A1
  Shelf HX3 .... 93 B6
Dovedale Garth LS15 .... 62 E3
Dovedale Gdns LS15 .... 62 F3
Dovelands BD20 .... 16 D4
Dover La HD7 .... 189 B3
Dover Rd HD7 .... 189 A3
Dover St Bradford BD3 .... 56 A1
  Garforth LS25 .... 83 B7
  Todmorden OL14 .... 108 D5
Dovesdale Gr BD5 .... 74 D2
Dovesdale Rd BD5 .... 74 D2
Dowkell La LS23 .... 14 F1
Dowker St Halifax HX1 .... 202 B1
  Huddersfield HD3 .... 153 B5
Dowley Gap La BD16 .... 37 B1
Downham St BD3 .... 201 D2
Downing Cl BD3 .... 75 B7
Downing St HD7 .... 170 C8
Downland Cres WF11 .... 127 B2
Downside Cres BD15 .... 54 A1
Dowry La HX6 .... 132 A3
Dracup Ave BD7 .... 73 E5
Dracup Rd BD7 .... 73 F3
Dradishaw Rd BD20 .... 5 D1
Dragon Cres LS12 .... 210 A1
Dragon Dr LS12 .... 210 A1
Dragon Rd LS12 .... 210 A1
Drake La BD11 .... 96 F5
Drake St Bradford BD1 .... 201 C2
  Keighley BD21 .... 35 C8
Drakes Ind Est HX3 .... 92 A4
Draper Corner HX7 .... 88 E6
Draughton Gr BD5 .... 74 D1
Draughton St BD5 .... 74 D1
Dray View WF13 .... 117 F2
Draycott Wlk BD4 .... 95 C8
Drayton Manor Yd LS11 .... 214 C4
Drewry Rd BD21 .... 35 B7
Drewton Rd BD1 .... 201 B4
Driftholme Rd BD11 .... 96 F7
Drighlington Inf Sch
  BD11 .... 96 E6
Drighlington Junior Sch
  BD11 .... 96 F7
Drill Par BD8 .... 55 D1

Drill St **10** Haworth BD22 .. 51 C6
  Keighley BD21 .... 35 C7
Drinker La HD8 .... 174 D6
Drive The Bardsey LS17 ...... 28 D5
  Batley WF17 .... 118 A6
  Bingley BD16 .... 36 E6
  Bradford BD10 .... 56 D6
  Brighouse HX3 .... 114 D8
  Burley in W LS29 .... 21 E8
  Hebden Bridge HX7 .... 89 D1
  Kippax LS25 .... 83 A1
  Leeds LS8 .... 204 C4
  Leeds, Alwoodley LS17 .... 43 A6
  Leeds, Bank LS9 .... 212 B3
  Leeds, Manston LS15 .... 62 D2
  Swillington LS26 .... 82 A1
Driver Pl LS12 .... 210 B2
Driver St LS12 .... 210 B2
Driver Terr Leeds LS12 .... 210 B2
  Silsden BD20 .... 5 E2
Drivers Row WF8 .... 146 B7
Drovers Way BD2 .... 55 E4
Drub La BD19 .... 95 F2
Druggist La LS29 .... 6 F8
Druids St BD14 .... 73 C4
Druids View BD16 .... 36 D6
Drummer La HD7 .... 152 B4
Drummond Ave LS16 .... 59 C7
Drummond Cl LS16 .... 59 C6
Drummond Middle Sch
  BD8 .... 55 C1
Drummond Rd
  Bradford BD8 .... 55 C1
  Leeds LS16 .... 59 C7
Drummond Trad Est BD8 ..... 74 D8
Drury Ave LS18 .... 58 B8
Drury Cl LS18 .... 58 B8
Drury La Elland HX4 .... 133 F4
  Horsforth LS18 .... 58 B8
  Normanton WF6 .... 122 A2
Dry Carr La HX2 .... 90 C4
Dry Hill La HD8 .... 192 B5
Dryclough Ave HD4 .... 153 C2
Dryclough CE Inf Sch
  HD4 .... 153 C3
Dryclough Cl HX3 .... 113 C3
Dryclough La HX3 .... 113 C3
Dryclough Rd HD4 .... 153 C2
Dryden St Bingley BD16 .... 36 F3
  Bradford BD1 .... 201 D3
Dubb La BD16 .... 37 A3
Duchy Ave BD9 .... 54 E3
Duchy Cres BD9 .... 54 E3
Duchy Dr BD9 .... 54 E3
Duchy Gr BD9 .... 54 E3
Duchy Villas BD9 .... 54 E3
Duchywood BD9 .... 54 E3
Ducie St BD10 .... 39 B1
Duck Hill HX7 .... 69 A1
Duckett Gr LS28 .... 57 F8
Duckett La BD1 .... 201 B3
Duckworth Gr BD9 .... 54 F1
Duckworth La BD9 .... 54 F1
Duckworth Terr BD9 .... 54 F1
Dudfleet La WF4 .... 159 B8
Dudley Ave Batley WF17 ...... 97 A2
  Huddersfield HD1 .... 153 D6
Dudley Cres HX2 .... 91 D5
Dudley Dr BD9 .... 54 E3
Dudley Hill First Sch BD4 ... 75 C3
Dudley Hill Rd BD2 .... 56 A3
Dudley La HD3 .... 153 D6
Dudley St Bradford BD4 ...... 75 B3
  Bradford, Dudley Hill BD4 ... 75 C3
  Bradford, Tyersal BD4 .... 75 E5
Dudwell Ave HX3 .... 113 C2
Dudwell Cl HX3 .... 113 C2
Dudwell La HX3 .... 113 C2
Dufton App LS14 .... 62 A3
Duich Rd BD6 .... 93 E6
Duinen St BD5 .... 201 C1
Duke of York Ave WF2 .... 142 D1
Duke of York St
  Wakefield WF1 .... 216 C3
  Wakefield, Wrenthorpe WF2 120 F1
Duke St Bradford BD1 .... 201 B3
  Castleford WF10 .... 124 B8
  Dewsbury WF13 .... 138 E5
  Elland HX5 .... 134 F6
  Halifax HX2 .... 90 D1
  1 Haworth BD22 .... 51 D7
  Leeds LS9 .... 212 A3
Duke Wood Rd HD8 .... 175 F2
Dulverton Cl Morley LS11 .. 213 D1
  Pontefract WF8 .... 125 F3
Dulverton Ct LS11 .... 213 D1
Dulverton Garth LS11 .... 78 C1
Dulverton Gdns LS11 .... 78 C2
Dulverton Gn LS11 .... 213 D1
Dulverton Gr Bradford BD4 .. 75 D3
  Morley LS11 .... 78 C1
Dulverton Pl LS11 .... 78 C1
Dulverton Rise WF8 .... 125 F3
Dulverton Sq LS11 .... 213 D1
Dulverton Way WF8 .... 125 F3
Dunbar Cft BD13 .... 72 F1
Dunbottle Cl WF14 .... 138 C5
Dunbottle La WF14 .... 138 B6
Duncan Ave Otley LS21 .... 22 D6
Duncan St LS1 .... 211 F3
Duncombe Rd BD8 .... 74 A7

Duncombe St
  Bradford BD8 .... 74 A7
  Leeds LS1 .... 211 D4
Duncombe Way BD8 .... 74 A7
Dundas St Halifax HX1 .... 202 B1
  22 Huddersfield HD1 ..... 154 A6
  Keighley BD21 .... 35 D6
Dundee OL14 .... 107 D8
Dunderdale Cres WF10 ...... 104 D1
Dunford Rd
  Dunford Bridge HD7 .... 199 D3
  Holmfirth HD7 .... 189 B3
  Holmfirth, Hade Edge HD7 . 199 B7
Dungeon La LS26 .... 101 A1
Dunhill Cres LS9 .... 80 E8
Dunhill Rise LS9 .... 80 E8
Dunkhill Croft BD10 .... 56 B7
Dunkirk Cres HX1 .... 202 A2
Dunkirk Gdns HX1 .... 202 A1
Dunkirk Hill LS12 .... 209 E5
Dunkirk La HX1 .... 202 A2
Dunkirk Rise BD20 .... 18 E2
Dunkirk St HX1 .... 202 A2
Dunkirk Terr HX1 .... 202 B2
Dunlin Cl LS10 .... 99 D5
Dunlin Croft **8** LS10 .... 99 D5
Dunlin Ct LS10 .... 99 D5
Dunlin Dr LS10 .... 99 D5
Dunlin Fold **7** LS10 .... 99 D5
Dunlin Way **3** BD8 .... 73 C7
Dunn Cl WF2 .... 120 F3
Dunningley La
  Middleton WF3 .... 98 F3
  Middleton, Black Gates LS10 . 98 F2
Dunnington Wlk BD6 .... 94 A6
Dunnock Croft LS27 .... 98 C3
Dunrobin Ave LS25 .... 83 B8
Dunsford Ave BD4 .... 95 B8
Dunsil Villas WF9 .... 182 F1
Dunsley Bank Rd HD7 .... 188 F3
Dunsley Terr WF9 .... 182 A2
Dunsmore Dr HD3 .... 152 H8
Dunstan Cl WF5 .... 140 E4
Dunstarn Dr LS16 .... 42 D3
Dunstarn Gdns LS16 .... 42 E3
Dunstarn La LS16 .... 42 D2
Durban Ave LS11 .... 213 F2
Durban Cres LS11 .... 213 F2
Durham Rd BD8 .... 55 A1
Durham St Castleford WF10 124 E6
  Halifax HX2 .... 202 A3
Durkar Fields WF4 .... 159 F6
Durkar La WF4 .... 159 F6
Durkar Low La WF4 .... 160 A7
Durkar Rise WF4 .... 159 F6
Durkheim Ct BD3 .... 75 C7
Durkheim St BD3 .... 75 C7
Durley Ave BD9 .... 55 A3
Durling Dr BD18 .... 55 E7
Durlston Gr BD12 .... 94 D4
Durlston Terr BD12 .... 94 D4
Durn St OL14 .... 86 A1
Durrance St BD22 .... 34 D2
Durrant Cl LS22 .... 13 F4
Dutton Gn LS14 .... 62 A8
Dutton Way LS14 .... 62 A7
Duxbury Rise LS7 .... 206 B2
Dyas Bldgs WF7 .... 144 E5
Dye House La
  Sowerby Bridge HX6 .... 112 C1
  Wilsden BD15 .... 53 B5
Dyehouse Dr Brighouse HD6 115 E1
  Pudsey LS28 .... 76 E4
Dyehouse La Bradford BD10 39 E2
Dyer La HX3 .... 91 F2
Dyer St LS2 .... 212 A4
Dyers Ct LS6 .... 205 E3
Dyke Bottom HD8 .... 190 F8
Dyke Cl WF14 .... 138 A8
Dyke End HD7 .... 152 B3
Dyke La OL14 .... 109 B7
Dymond Gr WF15 .... 117 A3
Dymond Rd WF15 .... 117 A3
Dymond View WF15 .... 117 A3
Dyson La Holmfirth HD7 .... 189 C1
  Rippondene HX6 .... 132 C2
Dyson Pl **2** HX3 .... 113 E3
Dyson Rd HX1 .... 202 B2
Dyson St Bradford BD1 .... 74 D7
  Brighouse HD6 .... 115 A3
  Huddersfield HD5 .... 154 E6
  Shipley BD9 .... 55 A4
Dyson's Hill HD7 .... 171 E5

Eagle Gr WF2 .... 141 D6
Eagle St Haworth BD22 .... 51 E8
  Keighley BD20 .... 35 B7
  Todmorden OL14 .... 108 B6
Eaglesfield Dr BD6 .... 94 A6
Ealand Ave WF17 .... 118 A7
Ealand Cres WF17 .... 118 A7
Ealand Rd
  Batley, Brown Hill WF17 .... 117 F7
  Batley, Carlinghow WF17 .. 118 A7
Ealing Ct WF17 .... 118 A6
Earl Cowper Middle Sch
  LS7 .... 207 E4
Earl St Dewsbury WF12 ...... 140 B8
  Haworth BD22 .... 51 C7
  Hemsworth WF9 .... 163 A3
  Keighley BD21 .... 35 B8
  Wakefield WF1 .... 216 C3
Earl Terr **5** HX3 .... 92 A2
Earlised WF17 .... 97 A4
Earles Ave HD5 .... 154 E5
Earls View BD20 .... 5 D1
Earlsheaton High Sch
  WF12 .... 139 E8

Earlsheaton Infants Sch
  WF12 .... 139 F7
Earlsmere Dr LS27 .... 97 F5
Earlswood Ave LS8 .... 43 F2
Earlswood Chase LS28 .... 76 E6
Earlswood Cres LS25 .... 63 A2
Earlswood Mead LS28 .... 76 E6
Easby Ave WF17 .... 117 F4
Easby Cl LS29 .... 7 F4
Easby Dr LS29 .... 7 F4
Easby Rd BD7 .... 74 C8
Easdale Cl LS14 .... 61 F5
Easdale Cres LS14 .... 62 A5
Easdale Rd LS14 .... 61 F4
Easingwood Dr HD5 .... 137 B1
East Acres WF11 .... 126 C7
East Ardsley Primary Sch
  WF3 .... 120 D8
East Ave Glusburn BD20 ...... 16 D6
  Horbury WF4 .... 141 C1
  Huddersfield HD3 .... 135 C1
  Keighley BD21 .... 35 C8
  Pontefract WF8 .... 146 B7
  South Elmsall WF9 .... 183 B4
  Upton WF9 .... 183 A7
East Bath St WF17 .... 118 D5
East Bierley CE (controlled)
  First Sch BD4 .... 95 F7
East Bolton HX2 .... 91 E7
East Busk La LS21 .... 23 C8
East Byland HX2 .... 91 E6
East Causeway Cl LS16 .... 42 D5
East Causeway Cres LS16 ... 42 E4
East Causeway Vale LS16 ... 42 E4
East Chevin Rd LS21 .... 23 C5
East Carr Cl Huddersfield HD2 136 B2
  Pontefract WF8 .... 146 F5
East Cliffe HX3 .... 113 E6
East Cswy LS16 .... 42 D5
East Dale Cl WF9 .... 181 F7
East Dene BD20 .... 5 E2
East Down WF10 .... 125 C8
East Garforth Cp Sch
  LS25 .... 83 B8
East Garforth Sta LS25 .... 83 A7
East Grange Cl LS10 .... 215 E1
East Grange Dr LS10 .... 215 E1
East Grange Garth LS10 .... 215 E1
East Grange Rd LS10 .... 215 E1
East Grange Rise LS10 ...... 215 E1
East Grange Sq LS10 .... 215 E1
East Grange View LS10 ..... 215 E1
East King St LS9 .... 212 B3
East Lee La OL14 .... 109 A7
East Leeds High Sch LS14 ... 61 F4
East Moor Ave LS8 .... 43 F1
East Moor Cres LS8 .... 43 F2
East Moor Dr LS8 .... 44 A1
East Moor La LS16 .... 42 D4
East Moor Rd LS8 .... 43 F2
East Morton First Sch
  BD20 .... 36 D8
East Mount **3** HD6 .... 115 A3
East Mount Pl **4** HD6 ... 115 A3
East Par
  Baildon BD17 .... 38 D4
  Bradford BD1 .... 201 C3
  Ilkley LS29 .... 8 C4
  Keighley BD21 .... 35 C7
  Leeds LS1 .... 211 E4
  Menston LS29 .... 22 A4
  Sowerby Bridge HX6 .... 112 D4
  Steeton BD20 .... 17 D5
East Park Dr LS9 .... 80 A7
East Park Gr LS9 .... 80 A7
East Park Mount **7** LS9 ... 80 A7
East Park Par LS9 .... 80 A7
East Park Pl LS9 .... 80 A7
East Park Rd Halifax HX3 ..... 92 A1
  1 Leeds LS9 .... 212 C3
East Park St Leeds LS9 .... 80 A7
  Morley LS27 .... 97 F3
East Park Terr **8** LS9 .... 80 A7
East Park View LS9 .... 80 A7
East Pinfold S71 .... 179 C2
East Rd BD13 .... 72 E6
East Riddlesden Hall
  BD20 .... 18 F1
East Royd BD22 .... 34 D2
East Side Ct LS28 .... 77 A5
East Squire La BD8 .... 55 C1
East St Batley WF17 .... 118 C5
  Brighouse HD6 .... 115 A1
  Hebden Bridge, Bailiff Bridge
  HX3 .... 115 A2
  Holmfirth HD7 .... 189 C3
  Huddersfield, Leymoor HD7 152 E4
  Huddersfield, Lindley HD3 . 135 B1
  Leeds LS2, LS9 .... 212 B3
  Lofthouse Gate, Newton Hill
  WF1 .... 121 C2
  Lofthouse Gate, Stanley Ferry
  WF3 .... 122 A2
  Ryhill WF4 .... 162 D1
  South Elmsall WF9 .... 183 B4
  South Hiendley S72 .... 180 E5
  Sowerby Bridge HX6 .... 111 E1
East Terr BD22 .... 51 E8

East View Bradford BD13 .... 73 C2
Brighouse HX3 .... 115 A7
Castleford WF10 .... 124 A7
Cleckheaton BD19 .... 116 A6
Gildersome LS27 .... 97 C5
Glusburn BD20 .... 16 D7
Kippax LS25 .... 83 B2
Knottingley WF11 .... 127 A4
Leeds LS15 .... 62 C2
Micklefield LS25 .... 84 B6
6 Mirfield WF14 .... 137 F6
Ossett WF5 .... 140 C3
Pudsey LS28 .... 76 E5
Rothwell LS26 .... 101 C5
Silsden BD20 .... 5 E2
Yeadon LS19 .... 40 C6
East View Cotts 5 LS28 .... 76 F8
East View WF19 .... 40 C6
East View Terr
Bradford BD12 .... 94 E4
Otley LS21 .... 23 B7
East-Thorpe Pl WF14 .... 138 B4
Eastborough Cres WF13 .... 118 D1
Eastborough Junior
& Infants WF13 .... 139 D8
Eastbourne Ave WF7 .... 145 E6
Eastbourne Cl WF7 .... 147 A7
Eastbourne Cres WF8 .... 147 A8
Eastbourne Dr WF8 .... 147 A8
Eastbourne Rd BD9 .... 55 B5
Eastbourne Terr WF8 .... 147 A8
Eastbrook La BD1 .... 201 C2
Eastbrook Well BD1 .... 201 C3
Eastburn Junior
& Infant Sch BD20 .... 16 F6
Eastbury Ave BD6 .... 73 D1
Eastdean Bank LS14 .... 62 A6
Eastdean Dr LS14 .... 62 A6
Eastdean Gate 7 LS14 .... 62 B5
Eastdean Gdns LS14 .... 62 B5
Eastdean Gr LS14 .... 62 B6
Eastdean Grange 8 LS14 .... 62 B5
Eastdean Gr LS14 .... 62 B6
Eastdean Rise LS14 .... 62 B6
Easterly Ave LS8 .... 208 B4
Easterly Cl LS8 .... 208 B3
Easterly Cres LS8 .... 208 A4
Easterly Cross LS8 .... 208 B4
Easterly Garth LS8 .... 208 B4
Easterly Gr LS8 .... 208 A4
Easterly Mount LS8 .... 208 B4
Easterly Rd LS8 .... 61 C5
Easterly Sq LS8 .... 208 B4
Easterly View LS8 .... 208 B4
Eastfield HD8 .... 190 F8
Eastfield Ave WF11 .... 126 F3
Eastfield Cres LS26 .... 101 B6
Eastfield Dr Kirkburton HD8 .... 173 E7
Pontefract WF8 .... 125 F1
Rothwell LS26 .... 101 B6
Eastfield Gdns BD4 .... 75 E3
Eastfield Gr WF6 .... 123 C3
Eastfield La WF10 .... 124 E8
Eastfield Pl BD20 .... 16 D5
Eastfield Rd
Knottingley WF11 .... 126 F3
Mirfield WF14 .... 138 D6
Eastgate Bramhope LS16 .... 24 D3
Honley HD7 .... 134 F7
Hemsworth WF9 .... 181 E6
Honley HD7 .... 171 F5
Leeds LS2 .... 212 A4
Easthorpe Ct BD2 .... 56 D4
Eastland Wlk 8 LS13 .... 58 E1
Eastlands HD5 .... 155 A4
Eastleigh Ct WF3 .... 120 A8
Eastleigh Dr WF3 .... 120 A8
Eastleigh Gr BD5 .... 74 C3
Eastmoor Gr S71 .... 179 C2
Eastmoor Rd WF1 .... 216 C4
Easton Pl HD3 .... 153 B7
Eastville Rd WF4 .... 144 B3
Eastway WF14 .... 137 F7
Eastway Pk WF14 .... 138 A7
Eastwood Ave Halifax HX2 .... 91 E7
Sowerby Bridge HX6 .... 111 F3
Wakefield WF2 .... 141 E7
Eastwood Cl
Crigglestone WF4 .... 159 F7
Halifax HX2 .... 91 E7
Eastwood Cres Leeds LS14 .... 62 D4
Shipley BD16 .... 54 B8
Eastwood Ct 7 HX3 .... 113 A4
Eastwood Dr LS14 .... 62 D5
Eastwood First Sch BD21 .... 35 D8
Eastwood Garth LS14 .... 62 D4
Eastwood Gdns LS14 .... 62 C4
Eastwood Gr Garforth LS25 .... 83 A5
Halifax HX2 .... 91 E7
Eastwood La LS14 .... 62 D4
Eastwood Nook LS14 .... 62 D4
Eastwood Rd OL14 .... 87 D2
Eastwood St Bradford BD4 .... 201 C1
8 Brighouse HD6 .... 115 B3
7 Halifax HX3 .... 92 A2
8 Huddersfield HD5 .... 154 D5
Easy Rd LS9 .... 212 C2
Eaton Hill LS16 .... 41 F3
Eaton Mews LS10 .... 99 C5
Eaton Pl WF9 .... 181 E7
Eaton Rd LS29 .... 8 A3
Eaton Sq LS10 .... 99 C5
Eaton St 1 BD21 .... 35 A4
Eaton Wlk WF9 .... 183 A5

Eaves Ave HX7 .... 88 E4
Eaves Rd HX7 .... 88 E4
Ebberston Gr LS6 .... 205 F3
Ebberston Pl LS6 .... 205 F3
Ebberston Terr LS6 .... 205 F3
Ebenezer Pl BD7 .... 74 A4
Ebenezer St Bradford BD1 .... 201 C2
6 Pudsey LS28 .... 57 D3
Rothwell WF3 .... 100 B3
Ebor Gardens Primary Sch
LS9 .... 212 C4
Ebor Gdns WF14 .... 137 F5
Ebor La BD22 .... 51 D8
Ebor Mount Kippax LS25 .... 83 A2
Leeds LS6 .... 205 F2
Ebor Pl LS6 .... 205 F2
Ebor St LS6 .... 205 F2
Ebor Terr LS10 .... 215 E2
Ebridge Ct 7 BD16 .... 37 A3
Ebson House La HD7 .... 190 B6
Ebury Cl WF17 .... 118 D6
Ebury St WF17 .... 118 D6
Eccles Ct BD2 .... 56 B4
Eccles Parlour HX7 .... 132 A7
Ecclesburn Ave LS9 .... 80 A7
Ecclesburn Rd LS9 .... 80 A7
Ecclesburn St LS9 .... 80 A7
Ecclesburn Terr 13 LS9 .... 80 A7
Eccleshill North Middle Sch
BD10 .... 56 D6
Eccleshill Sch & Further
Education Ctr BD10 .... 56 E5
Eccup La Bramhope LS16 .... 25 F2
Harewood LS16 .... 26 A5
Eccup Moor Rd LS16 .... 42 E8
Echo St WF15 .... 116 F2
Edale Ave HD4 .... 153 F1
Edale Cl HD5 .... 137 B1
Edale Gr BD11 .... 92 C8
Edale Way LS16 .... 41 F3
Eddercliff Cres WF15 .... 117 A6
Edderthorpe St BD3 .... 75 A6
Eddison Cl LS16 .... 42 D5
Eddison St LS28 .... 57 D2
Eddison Wlk LS16 .... 42 D5
Eddystone Rise WF11 .... 126 D3
Edelshain Gr WF2 .... 160 F8
Eden Ave Ossett WF5 .... 140 D6
Wakefield WF2 .... 141 D5
Eden Cl BD12 .... 94 D3
Eden Cres LS4 .... 59 B4
Eden Dr LS4 .... 59 B4
Eden Gdns LS4 .... 59 B3
Eden Mount LS4 .... 59 B3
Eden Rd LS4 .... 59 B4
Eden Way LS4 .... 59 B3
Eden Wlk LS4 .... 59 B3
Edendale HD10 .... 124 F8
Edensor Rd BD21 .... 35 A7
Ederoyd Ave LS28 .... 57 B1
Ederoyd Cres LS28 .... 57 B1
Ederoyd Dr LS28 .... 57 B1
Ederoyd Gr LS28 .... 57 B1
Ederoyd Mount LS28 .... 57 B1
Ederoyd Rise LS28 .... 57 A1
Edgar St BD14 .... 73 D3
Edgbaston Cl LS17 .... 43 A6
Edgbaston Wlk LS17 .... 43 A6
Edge Ave WF12 .... 139 D1
Edge Cl Dewsbury WF12 .... 139 E1
Huddersfield HD4 .... 152 E4
Edge End BD13 .... 58 B1
Edge End Gdns 4 BD6 .... 93 E7
Edge End La HD7 .... 188 A4
Edge End Rd BD6 .... 93 E7
Edge Hill Cl HD5 .... 154 D7
Edge Junc WF12 .... 139 E1
Edge La Dewsbury WF12 .... 139 E1
Heptonstall HX7 .... 87 F7
Edge Rd WF12 .... 139 F1
Edge Terr HD3 .... 152 F7
Edge Top Rd WF12 .... 116 F7
Edge View Dewsbury WF12 .... 139 E1
Huddersfield HD7 .... 152 E4
Edgebank Ave BD6 .... 93 F6
Edgehey Ave HX7 .... 88 B6
Edgehill Cl 6 BD13 .... 72 F1
Edgehill Rd S75 .... 178 B2
Edgeholme La HX2 .... 112 B7
Edgemoor Cl BD4 .... 113 B4
Edgemoor Rd
Crigglestone WF4 .... 159 F2
Honley HD7 .... 171 E3
Egerton Gn HD1 .... 153 E7
Egerton Grove Rd HD1 .... 153 E7
Egerton La HD1 .... 153 E7
Egerton Rd
Huddersfield HD1 .... 153 E8
Leeds LS16 .... 59 B8
Edgware Rd HD5 .... 155 A6
Edgware Gr LS8 .... 207 F2
Edgware Mount LS8 .... 207 F2
Edgware Pl LS8 .... 207 F2
Edgware Row LS8 .... 207 F2
Edgware St LS8 .... 207 F2
Edgware Terr LS8 .... 207 F2
Edgware View LS8 .... 207 F2
Edinburgh Ave LS12 .... 209 D4
Edinburgh Gr LS12 .... 209 D4
Edinburgh Pl
Garforth LS25 .... 83 B7
Leeds LS12 .... 209 D4
Edinburgh Rd LS12 .... 209 D4
Edinburgh Terr LS12 .... 209 D4
Edlington Cl BD4 .... 75 E3
Edmonton Pl LS7 .... 204 A2

Edmund St Bradford BD5 .... 201 A2
Todmorden OL14 .... 129 A8
Edna St WF9 .... 183 A3
Edrich Cl BD12 .... 94 E6
Edroyd Pl LS28 .... 57 D3
Edroyd St LS28 .... 57 D3
Education Rd LS7 .... 206 C3
Edward Cl Dewsbury WF12 .... 139 B3
Halifax HX3 .... 114 A4
Edward Dr WF1 .... 121 C5
Edward Rd WF14 .... 137 F5
Edward St 8 Bacup OL13 .... 106 A3
Bradford BD4 .... 201 C2
Bradford, Tong Street BD4 .... 75 E1
Brighouse HD6 .... 115 C2
Brighouse, Waring Green
HD6 .... 115 A3
Hebden Bridge HX7 .... 89 A3
Leeds LS2 .... 211 F4
Liversedge, Knowler Hill
WF15 .... 117 A4
Liversedge, Littletown WF15 117 A5
Normanton WF6 .... 123 A5
Shipley BD18 .... 37 F1
Sowerby Bridge HX6 .... 112 B4
Wakefield WF2 .... 216 C3
Edward Turner Cl 7 BD12 .... 94 C6
Edwards Rd HX2 .... 202 A1
Edwin Rd LS6 .... 205 F2
Eel Holme View St BD20 .... 18 B2
Eel Mires Garth LS22 .... 13 F6
Effingham Rd BD10 .... 36 A1
Egerton Gr BD15 .... 54 A1
Egerton St HD4 .... 154 B6
Egerton Terr LS19 .... 40 D3
Eggleston Dr BD4 .... 75 F2
Eggleston St LS13 .... 57 F5
Egglestone Sq LS23 .... 30 C7
Egham Gn BD10 .... 56 B7
Egmanton Rd S71 .... 178 F1
Egremont Cres BD6 .... 93 F6
Egremont St HX6 .... 112 B3
Egremont Terr HX6 .... 112 A3
Egypt Rd BD13 .... 72 C8
Eiffel Bldgs HX7 .... 89 A3
Eiffel St HX7 .... 89 A3
Eighth Ave
Cleckheaton WF15 .... 116 B5
Leeds LS12 .... 210 B2
Rothwell LS26 .... 101 A7
Eightlands Ave LS13 .... 58 D2
Eightlands La LS13 .... 58 D2
Eightlands Rd WF13 .... 139 C8
Ekota Pl LS8 .... 207 F4
Elam Wood Rd BD20 .... 18 C3
Eland House 3 HX5 .... 134 F7
Elba Terr WF4 .... 141 A3
Elbow La Bradford BD2 .... 56 B2
Halifax HX2 .... 90 E1
Elder Ave Upton WF9 .... 183 C8
Wakefield WF2 .... 142 A7
Elder Bank BD13 .... 52 D6
Elder Cl HD5 .... 137 B1
Elder Croft LS13 .... 58 C1
Elder Dr Dewsbury WF12 .... 139 D3
Upton WF9 .... 183 C8
Elder Garth LS25 .... 83 B6
Elder Gr Huddersfield HD4 .... 171 D6
Wakefield WF2 .... 142 A7
Elder Mount 8 LS13 .... 58 C1
Elder Pl 2 LS13 .... 58 C1
Elder Rd LS13 .... 58 C1
Elder St Bradford BD10 .... 56 F7
Keighley BD21 .... 18 A2
3 Leeds LS13 .... 58 C1
Elderwood Gdns BD10 .... 56 E5
Eldon Pl Bradford BD1 .... 201 A4
Bradford, Cutler Heights
BD4 .... 75 D4
Cleckheaton BD19 .... 116 F7
Eldon Rd HD1 .... 153 D7
Eldon St Batley WF16 .... 117 D4
Halifax HX3 .... 203 E4
Ossett WF5 .... 140 E3
Todmorden OL14 .... 108 C5
Eldon Terr BD1 .... 201 A4
Eldroth Mount 10 HX1 .... 202 C1
Eldroth Rd HX1 .... 202 C1
Eldwick First Sch BD16 .... 37 C5
Eleanor Dr LS28 .... 56 F7
Eleanor St Brighouse HD6 .... 115 B3
2 Huddersfield HD1 .... 154 A8
Eleventh Ave WF15 .... 116 C5
Elford Gr LS8 .... 207 F3
Elford Pl E LS8 .... 207 F3
Elford Pl W LS8 .... 207 F3
Elford Rd LS8 .... 207 F3
Elgar Wlk WF3 .... 121 E6
Elgin Cl HD4 .... 153 C2
Elia St WF3 .... 121 E6
Elim St WF13 .... 139 C8
Eliot Gr LS20 .... 39 F8
Eliots Cl WF10 .... 125 C5
Elizabeth Ave Bradford BD12 .... 94 D4
South Hiendley S72 .... 180 E5
Elizabeth Cl BD12 .... 94 D4
Elizabeth Cres BD12 .... 94 D4
Elizabeth Ct
Castleford WF10 .... 125 C8
Collingham LS22 .... 29 A8
Knottingley WF11 .... 126 C4

Elizabeth Gdns WF1 .... 216 B4
Elizabeth Gr LS27 .... 98 C5
Elizabeth House HX2 .... 91 E3
Elizabeth St
6 Bingley BD16 .... 37 A3
Bradford BD5 .... 201 B1
Bradford, New Road Side
BD12 .... 94 D4
Elland HX5 .... 134 F6
1 Elland, West Vale HX4 .... 134 B7
Huddersfield HD4 .... 154 A3
Leeds LS6 .... 205 E3
Liversedge FW15 .... 116 E4
Oakworth BD22 .... 34 D3
Wakefield WF1 .... 142 E2
Elizabethan Ct WF8 .... 125 E2
Ella St WF9 .... 163 A4
Elland Bridge HX5 .... 134 F7
Elland C of E Sch HX5 .... 134 F7
Elland Golf Course HX5 .... 134 D5
Elland Independent Hospl
HX5 .... 135 A7
Elland La HX5 .... 135 A7
Elland Rd
Brighouse HD6, HX5 .... 114 E2
Halifax HD6, HX5 .... 114 E2
Leeds LS11 .... 213 E3
Leeds LS11 .... 213 E3
Morley LS27 .... 98 C8
Ripponden HX6 .... 132 E4
Elland Road Ind Pk LS11 .... 213 D3
Elland Road Stadium
(Leeds Utd FC) LS11 .... 213 E3
Elland St WF10 .... 103 E1
Elland Way LS11 .... 213 D3
Elland Wood Bottom
HX3, HX5 .... 113 D1
Elland-Riorges' Link
HX5 .... 135 A7
Ellar Carr Rd
Bradford BD10 .... 39 C1
Cullingworth BD13 .... 52 C7
Ellar Gdns LS29 .... 22 B6
Ellen Holme Cotts HX2 .... 111 D5
Ellen Royd La HX2 .... 111 D8
Ellen Royd St HX3 .... 203 E4
Ellen St HX3 .... 203 E4
Ellenthorpe Rd BD17 .... 37 E2
Ellerby La LS9 .... 212 B2
Ellerby Rd LS9 .... 212 B3
Ellercroft Ave BD7 .... 74 A6
Ellercroft Rd BD7 .... 74 A6
Ellercroft Terr BD7 .... 74 A6
Ellerker La LS14 .... 46 B5
Ellerker Rd LS14 .... 46 A6
Ellers Gr LS8 .... 207 F4
Ellers Rd Leeds LS8 .... 207 F4
Sutton in C BD20 .... 16 D4
Ellerton St BD3 .... 75 C7
Ellicott Ct LS29 .... 22 A4
Ellin's Terr WF6 .... 144 A8
Ellinthorpe St BD4 .... 75 B5
Elliott Cl 10 BD13 .... 72 D1
Elliott St Shipley BD18 .... 55 A8
Silsden BD20 .... 5 D1
Ellis Fold LS12 .... 209 E3
Ellis Pl 2 LS11 .... 214 B3
Ellis St BD5 .... 74 D3
Ellison St 7 Halifax HX3 .... 92 A1
Huddersfield HD4 .... 153 D4
Elliston Ave S75 .... 178 C1
Ellistones Gdns HX4 .... 134 A4
Ellistones La HX4 .... 134 A6
Ellistones Pl HX4 .... 134 A6
Ellmont Ave HD8 .... 175 D7
Elton Gr 4 BD6 .... 74 A1
Elwood Cl LS6 .... 59 F7
Elm Ave Holmfirth HD7 .... 189 C8
Kippax LS25 .... 82 F3
Lofthouse Gate WF3 .... 121 F4
Sowerby Bridge HX6 .... 112 B5
Todmorden OL14 .... 108 B6
Elm Cl Darrington WF8 .... 147 C5
Ossett WF5 .... 140 E3
Elm Cres BD20 .... 36 D8
Elm Croft LS14 .... 62 C8
Elm Ct Birkenshaw BD11 .... 96 B4
Kirkburton HD8 .... 173 F7
Elm Gdns WF10 .... 125 D5
Elm Gr Burley in W LS29 .... 21 F8
Cleckheaton BD19 .... 117 A8
Keighley, East Morton BD20 .... 36 D8
Keighley, Ingrow BD21 .... 35 B4
Liversedge WF16 .... 117 C5
Shelf HX3 .... 93 D6
Shipley BD18 .... 55 E7
Sutton in C BD20 .... 16 C5
South Elmsall WF9 .... 182 F3
Elm Pk WF8 .... 146 C6
11 Sowerby Bridge HX6 .... 112 B5
Elm Rd Dewsbury WF13 .... 138 F8
Hemsworth WF9 .... 181 E7
Shipley BD18 .... 55 D7
Elm St Bacup OL13 .... 106 A3
Crofton WF4 .... 162 B7
Elland HX4 .... 134 B4
Huddersfield HD4 .... 154 B4
Leeds LS6 .... 206 B4
Oxenhope BD22 .... 51 C3
Skelmanthorpe HD8 .... 175 A2
Elm Terr Brighouse HD6 .... 115 B5
Otley LS21 .... 23 C8
Elm Tree Ave BD6 .... 94 C8

Elm Tree Cl Batley WF15 .... 117 C3
Bradford BD6 .... 94 C8
Keighley BD21 .... 35 C6
Leeds LS15 .... 81 E6
Elm Tree Gdns BD6 .... 94 C8
Elm Tree St WF1 .... 142 F4
Elm View 3 Halifax HX3 .... 113 C4
Steeton BD20 .... 17 B6
Elm Way WF17 .... 97 A2
Elm Wood St HD6 .... 115 B3
Elmcote LS16 .... 63 E2
Elmet Dr LS15 .... 63 E7
Elmet Rd LS15 .... 63 E7
Elmet Towers LS14 .... 62 C4
Elmete Ave Barwick in E LS15 62 F8
Leeds LS8 .... 61 C2
Elmete Cl LS8 .... 61 C2
Elmete Croft LS15 .... 62 F6
Elmete Ct LS8 .... 61 C0
Elmete Dr LS8 .... 61 D0
Elmete Gr LS8 .... 61 C2
Elmete Grange LS29 .... 22 A4
Elmete Hill LS8 .... 61 D0
Elmete La LS8 .... 44 E2
Elmete Mount LS8 .... 61 D0
Elmete Rd WF10 .... 104 D3
Elmete Way LS8 .... 61 D0
Elmete Wlk LS8 .... 61 D0
Elmete Wood Sch LS8 .... 61 D8
Elmfield BD17 .... 38 D0
Elmfield Ave HX3 .... 152 F5
Elmfield Bsns Pk LS25 .... 83 A2
Elmfield Ct LS28 .... 98 A1
Elmfield Dr Bradford BD6 .... 94 D8
Skelmanthorpe HD8 .... 175 A3
Elmfield Gr LS12 .... 210 A2
Elmfield Pl LS12 .... 210 A2
Elmfield Rd Glusburn BD20 .... 16 C6
Huddersfield HD2 .... 135 E3
Leeds LS12 .... 210 A2
Morley LS27 .... 98 B2
Elmfield Terr Halifax HX1 .... 203 D1
8 Huddersfield HD5 .... 154 D5
Elmfield Way LS13 .... 58 D3
Elmhurst Cl LS17 .... 44 B4
Elmhurst Gdns LS17 .... 44 A4
Elmhurst Gr WF11 .... 126 F3
Elmore Terr BD20 .... 16 C2
Elmroyd LS26 .... 100 F4
Elms Hill HD7 .... 169 F6
Elms The Ackworth M T WF7 163 F5
Guiseley LS20 .... 22 E3
Elms View HD7 .... 169 F6
Elmsall La DN6 .... 195 C3
Elmsall St BD1 .... 74 D6
Elmsall Way Wakefield WF9 .... 183 C3
Elmsdale Cl WF9 .... 183 B2
Elmsley St BD20 .... 17 C5
Elmton Cl LS10 .... 99 D2
Elmtree La LS10 .... 215 D4
Elmwood Ave
Barwick in E LS15 .... 63 D2
4 Huddersfield HD1 .... 154 A7
Walton WF2 .... 161 B2
Elmwood Chase LS15 .... 63 D2
Elmwood Cl
5 Huddersfield HD1 .... 154 A7
Mirfield WF14 .... 137 F1
Walton WF2 .... 161 B2
Elmwood Dr Brighouse HD6 114 F3
Keighley BD22 .... 35 A4
Walton WF2 .... 161 B2
Elmwood Garth WF2 .... 161 B2
Elmwood Gr Batley WF17 .... 118 D3
Horbury WF4 .... 141 C2
Elmwood La
Barwick in E LS15 .... 63 D7
Leeds LS7 .... 206 C1
Elmwood Rd Keighley BD22 .... 34 F4
Leeds LS2 .... 206 C1
Elmwood St WF1 .... 202 C1
Elmwood Terr
Dewsbury WF12 .... 118 C1
Keighley BD22 .... 34 F4
Elphaborough Cl HX7 .... 110 D8
Elphin Ct HX7 .... 110 D8
Elsdon Gr BD5 .... 201 B1
Elsham Terr LS4 .... 59 C2
Elsicker La WF1 .... 143 F6
Elsie St BD20 .... 18 B2
Elsinore Ave HX5 .... 134 F6
Elsinore Ct HX5 .... 134 E6
Elstone View WF1 .... 121 A4
Elsworth Ave BD3 .... 56 B1
Elsworth St LS12 .... 210 A3
Elsworth Terr LS12 .... 210 A3
Eltham Cl LS6 .... 206 B3
Eltham Ct 4 LS6 .... 206 B3
Eltham Dr LS6 .... 206 B3
Eltham Gdns LS6 .... 206 B3
Elton Gr BD6 .... 94 B8
Eltham Rise LS6 .... 206 B3
Eltofts Pk LS15 .... 45 C5
Elvaston Rd LS27 .... 98 A3
Elvey Cl BD2 .... 56 D4
Elwell St WF3 .... 99 E1
Elwyn Gr BD5 .... 74 E3
Elwyn Rd BD5 .... 74 F3
Ely St Elland HX4 .... 134 D6
Leeds LS12 .... 209 F4
Embankment The
Leeds LS1 .... 211 F3
Mirfield WF14 .... 138 A5
Emblem Terr WF1 .... 142 D3
Embleton Rd LS26 .... 123 C8
Embsay & Bolton Abbey
Steam Railway BD23 .... 1 C7

Emerald St Batley WF17 .... 118 86
Huddersfield HD1 .... 154 B8
🔲 Keighley BD22 .... 35 A4
Emerson Ave BD9 .... 54 D3
Emily St BD21 .... 35 D8
Emley First Sch HD8 .... 175 D7
Emley Moor Bsns Pk
  HD8 .... 175 B6
Emm La BD9 .... 55 B3
Emmanuel Terr Hd4 .... 153 F2
Emmanuel Trad Est LS12 .. 210 C2
Emmeline Cl BD10 .... 56 B8
Emmet Cl BD11 .... 96 B5
Emmfield Dr BD9 .... 55 A4
Emmott Dr LS19 .... 40 E3
Emmott Farm Fold 🔲 BD22 51 C6
Empsall Row 🔲 HD6 .... 115 B3
Emscote Ave HX1 .... 202 C1
Emscote Gdns HX1 .... 202 C1
Emscote Gr HX1 .... 202 C1
Emscote Pl HX1 .... 202 C1
Emscote St S HX1 .... 202 C1
Emsley Cl BD4 .... 95 B8
Emsley Pl LS10 .... 212 B1
Emville Ave LS17 .... 44 C5
Enderby Wlk HX3 .... 91 F3
Enderley Rd 🔲 BD13 ...... 72 D6
Endor Cres LS29 .... 21 F7
Endor Gr LS29 .... 21 F7
Endsleigh Pl 🔲 BD14 ..... 73 B4
Enfield LS19 .... 40 86
Enfield Ave LS7 .... 207 E2
Enfield Cl WF17 .... 117 F6
Enfield Dr Batley WF17 ... 117 F6
  Bradford BD6 .... 74 A1
Enfield Par BD6 .... 74 A1
Enfield Rd BD17 .... 38 C2
Enfield Side Rd BD22 ..... 50 E5
Enfield St Keighley BD21 .. 35 B7
  Leeds LS7 .... 207 D2
Enfield Terr LS7 .... 207 E2
Enfield Wlk BD6 .... 74 A1
Engine La Horbury WF4 .... 140 F1
  Shafton S72 .... 180 D1
  West Hardwick WF4 ...... 163 A7
England Lane Jun
  & Inf Sch WF11 .... 126 F3
Englefield Cres BD4 ...... 75 E2
English Martyrs' RC Infant
  & Junior Sch WF2 .... 141 D5
Ennerdale Ave WF12 ...... 118 E2
Ennerdale Cl LS22 .... 13 C6
Ennerdale Cres WF12 ..... 118 E2
Ennerdale Dr Bradford BD2 . 56 B3
  Knottingley WF11 .... 126 E2
Ennerdale Rd Batley WF12 118 E2
  Bradford BD2 .... 56 B3
  Gildersome LS12 .... 77 D2
  Wakefield WF2 .... 141 F7
Ennerdale Way LS12 ...... 77 D3
Enoch La HX4 .... 153 F3
Enterprise Park Ind Est
  LS11 .... 213 F1
Enterprise Way
  Bradford BD10 .... 56 B6
  Castleford WF10 .... 124 C8
  Middleton LS10 .... 215 F1
  Skipton BD23 .... 4 A7
Envoy St LS11 .... 214 C4
Epsom Rd LS25 .... 82 F2
Epsom Way HD5 .... 137 C1
Epworth Pl Leeds LS10 ... 215 E4
  Oakworth BD22 .... 34 83
Eric St Keighley BD21 .... 35 C8
  Leeds LS13 .... 58 C5
  Morley WF3 .... 183 A3
Ernest St 🔲
  Dewsbury WF13 .... 139 D8
  Todmorden OL14 .... 86 C1
Erringden Rd HX7 .... 89 D1
Erringden St 🔲 OL14 ..... 108 C5
Escroft Cl BD12 .... 94 D1
Eshald La LS26 .... 101 D6
Eshald Mansions 🔲 LS26 . 101 D6
Eshald Pl LS26 .... 101 D6
Esholt Ave LS20 .... 39 D7
Esholt La Baildon BD17 .. 38 F4
  Guiseley BD17 .... 39 A4
Eshton Ave BD2 .... 94 F5
Eshton Ct S75 .... 178 A2
Esk Ave WF10 .... 125 B8
Esk Gdns LS22 .... 13 E8
Eskdale Ave
  Normanton WF6 .... 123 A4
  Shelf HX3 .... 93 85
Eskdale Cl Batley WF12 .. 118 E3
  Guiseley LS20 .... 39 E8
  Normanton WF6 .... 123 A4
Eskdale Croft Guiseley LS20 . 39 E8
  Normanton WF6 .... 123 A4
Eskdale Gr LS25 .... 83 A5
Eskdale Mount
  Hebden Bridge HX7 ..... 89 A4
  Leeds LS14 .... 61 F4
Eskdale Rd WF12 .... 141 E7
Eskdale Rise BD15 ..... 73 C8
Eskine Par BD6 .... 93 F6
Esmond St 🔲 Bradford BD7 . 73 F3
  Leeds LS12 .... 209 F3
Esmond Terr LS12 ...... 209 F3
Essex Park Ind Est BD4 . 201 D2
Essex St Bradford BD4 .. 201 D1
  Halifax HX1 .... 202 B2
  🔲 Hebden Bridge HX7 .. 89 A2
Estcourt Ave LS6 ...... 59 C4
Estcourt Dr WF8 .... 147 D4
Estcourt Gr BD7 .... 74 A5

Estcourt Rd Bradford BD7 .. 74 A5
  Darrington WF8 .... 147 C5
Estcourt Terr LS6 ...... 59 C4
Esther Ave WF2 .... 141 F4
Esther Gr WF2 .... 141 F5
Esthwaite Gdns LS15 ... 80 E6
Ethel St Keighley BD20 .. 18 B1
  Sutton in C BD20 ...... 16 D4
Etna St BD7 .... 73 F3
Eton Ave HD5 .... 154 F6
Eton St Halifax HX1 .... 202 B3
  Hebden Bridge HX7 .... 88 F3
Euden Edge Rd HD7 .... 152 A3
Eunice La HD8 .... 191 C6
Eureka Childrens' Mus
  HX1 .... 203 F2
Eurocam Tech Pk HD3 .. 74 E2
Euroway Trad Est BD4 .. 95 A7
Euston Gr LS11 .... 213 F4
Euston Mount LS11 .... 213 F4
Euston Terr LS11 ...... 213 F4
Evans Towers 🔲 BD5 ... 201 81
Evanston Ave LS4 ..... 59 C1
Evelyn Ave BD3 .... 75 E8
Evelyn Pl LS12 .... 209 F2
Evens Terr BD5 .... 74 E2
Everard St HD4 .... 153 D4
Everdale Mount
  Hemsworth WF9 ...... 181 C6
  South Elmsall WF9 .... 182 E3
Everest Ave BD18 ..... 55 E7
Everleigh St LS9 ...... 80 A7
Eversley Dr BD4 ...... 75 F4
Eversley Mount HX2 ... 202 A2
Eversley Pl HX2 ...... 202 A2
Eversley Rd HX7 ...... 89 A4
Eversley View LS14 ... 45 C7
Every St 🔲 OL14 ...... 108 C5
Evesham Gr BD10 ..... 56 B7
Ewart Pl BD7 .... 74 A3
Ewart St Bradford BD7 . 74 A3
  Queensbury BD13 ..... 72 E1
Ewood Dr HX7 .... 90 A1
Ewood Hall Ave HX7 ... 89 F1
Ewood La OL14 .... 107 F6
Excelsior Cl HX6 ..... 132 C3
Exchange HD7 .... 171 F5
Exchange Bldgs BD20 .. 16 D7
Exchange Ct BD19 .... 95 D1
Exchange St
  Cleckheaton BD19 .... 95 D1
  🔲 Elland HX5 .... 134 D6
  Normanton WF6 ...... 123 A2
  South Elmsall WF9 .... 182 F3
Exe St BD5 .... 74 C3
Exeter Dr LS10 .... 99 F7
Exeter St Halifax HX3 .. 113 D3
  Sowerby Bridge HX6 .. 112 C4
Exhibition Rd 🔲 BD18 . 54 F8
Exley Ave BD21 .... 35 A4
Exley Bank HX3 ...... 113 D2
Exley Bank Top HX3 .. 113 D1
Exley Cres BD21 ..... 35 A5
Exley Dr BD21 .... 35 A5
Exley Gdns HX3 ...... 113 D2
Exley Gr BD21 .... 35 A5
Exley Head View BD22 . 34 E8
Exley La Elland HX5 ... 134 E8
  Halifax HX5 .... 113 E1
Exley Mount Bradford BD7 . 73 F5
  Keighley BD21 .... 35 A5
Exley Rd BD21 .... 35 A5
Exley St 🔲 BD22 .... 35 A6
Exley Way BD21 ..... 35 A4
Exmoor St HX1 ...... 202 B2
Exmouth Pl BD3 ..... 55 F1
Express Way WF10 ... 123 D6
Exton Pl LS15 .... 80 E7
Eyre St Batley WF17 .. 118 D4
  Dewsbury WF12 ..... 139 B4
Eyres Ave LS12 ...... 209 F4
Eyres Gr LS12 .... 209 F4
Eyres Mill Side LS12 . 209 E4
Eyres St LS12 .... 209 F4
Eyres Terr LS12 ..... 209 F4
Eyrie App LS27 ...... 98 C3

Factory La Bradford BD4 . 75 82
  Huddersfield HD3 .... 153 B4
Factory St BD4 ...... 75 C2
Fagley Cres BD2 .... 56 B2
Fagley Croft BD2 ... 56 C2
Fagley Dr BD2 ...... 56 C2
Fagley First Sch BD2 . 56 C2
Fagley La BD2 ...... 56 B3
Fagley Pl BD2 ...... 56 C1
Fagley Rd BD2 ..... 56 C2
Fagley Terr BD2 ... 56 C1
Fair Bank BD18 .... 55 C6
Fair Lea Rd HD4 ... 153 C1
Fair Mount OL14 .. 108 A1
Fair Rd BD6 .... 74 B1
Fair St HD1 .... 153 F4
Fair View Liversedge WF15 . 116 F5
  Pontefract WF8 .... 146 E5
Fair View Cres OL13 . 106 B3
Fair Ways WF14 .... 138 B8
Fairbank Rd BD8 ... 55 A1
Fairbank Terr BD8 . 55 A1
Fairbourne House 🔲 BD6 . 93 E8
Fairbrook Rd WF2 .. 160 A4
Fairburn Dr LS25 ... 83 B6
Fairburn Gdns BD2 . 56 C4
Fairburn Ings
  Nature Reserve WF10 . 104 B4
Fairburn Primary Sch
  WF11 .... 105 A4
Fairclough Gr HX3 .. 91 F3

Fairfax Ave Birkenshaw BD11 . 97 A5
  Bradford BD4 .... 75 C1
  Featherstone WF7 ..... 124 C1
  Knottingley WF11 ..... 126 D3
  Menston LS29 .... 22 A5
Fairfax Cl LS14 .... 62 B3
Fairfax Cres Bradford BD4 . 75 C1
  Halifax HX3 .... 114 A5
Fairfax Gdns LS29 .... 22 A5
Fairfax Gr LS19 ...... 39 F7
Fairfax Ho BD1 ...... 201 C3
Fairfax Rd Bingley BD16 . 36 F5
  Cullingworth BD13 ... 52 E7
  Leeds LS11 .... 214 A3
  Menston LS29 .... 22 A5
  Pontefract WF8 ...... 146 E8
Fairfax St Bradford BD4 . 201 C1
  Haworth BD22 .... 51 D7
  Otley LS21 .... 23 B7
  Silsden BD20 .... 5 D1
Fairfax View LS18 .... 41 84
Fairfield Denholme BD13 . 71 C8
  Fairburn WF11 .... 105 A5
Fairfield Ave Batley WF16 117 E5
  🔲 Dewsbury WF12 .... 139 F8
  East Ardsley WF3 .... 119 D7
  Leeds LS13 .... 58 A2
  Normanton WF6 ...... 122 E5
  Ossett WF5 .... 140 F4
  Pontefract WF8 ...... 146 B8
  🔲 Pudsey LS28 ...... 76 F8
Fairfield Cl Castleford WF10 104 E1
  Leeds LS13 .... 58 A2
Fairfield Ct Baildon BD17 . 38 E4
  Castleford WF10 ..... 125 A7
  Garforth LS25 .... 82 D7
  Liversedge WF15 .... 116 F4
Fairfield Dr Baildon BD17 . 38 E4
  Batley WF16 .... 117 E5
  Ossett WF5 .... 140 F4
  Rothwell LS26 .... 100 B4
Fairfield Cres
  🔲 Dewsbury WF13 .... 118 A1
  Leeds LS13 .... 58 A2
Fairfield Ct Baildon BD17 . 38 E4
Fairfield Garth LS13 .. 58 D5
Fairfield Gdns Ossett WF5 . 140 F5
  Rothwell LS26 .... 100 B4
Fairfield Gr Leeds LS13 . 58 B2
  Rothwell LS26 .... 100 B4
Fairfield Hill LS13 .... 58 B2
Fairfield La LS26 .... 100 B4
Fairfield Mount Leeds LS13 . 58 B2
  Ossett WF5 .... 140 F4
Fairfield Par WF16 ... 117 E5
Fairfield Rd Bradford BD8 . 73 C8
  Bradford, Girlington BD8 . 73 C8
  Bradford, Upper Wyke BD12 . 94 D3
  Leeds LS13 .... 58 A2
  Normanton WF6 ...... 122 E5
Fairfield Rise HD8 .... 174 A5
Fairfield Specl Sch WF16 . 117 E5
Fairfield Sq LS13 .... 58 B2
Fairfield St Bradford BD4 . 75 D1
  Leeds LS13 .... 58 B2
Fairfield Terr
  🔲 Cleckheaton BD19 . 116 E7
  Dewsbury WF13 ..... 139 F8
  Leeds LS13 .... 58 B2
  Wilsden BD15 .... 53 C5
Fairfield Wlk WF5 ... 140 F4
Fairfields Castleford WF10 . 125 C7
  Denby Dale HD8 .... 191 F3
Fairfields Rd HD7 ... 188 D3
Fairford Ave LS11 ... 214 C3
Fairford Terr LS11 .. 214 C3
Fairhaven Gn BD10 . 56 C7
Fairlea Ave HD4 .... 153 E1
Fairlea Cotts HD4 .. 153 E1
Fairleigh Cres WF3 . 120 A8
Fairleigh Rd WF3 .. 120 A8
Fairless Ave HX3 ... 115 A7
Fairmoor Way WF16 . 117 E5
Fairmount BD9 ..... 55 C2
Fairmount Pk BD18 . 54 E7
Fairmount Terr
  Dewsbury WF12 .... 139 E6
  Keighley BD21 ...... 35 F6
Fairview Ave WF17 .. 117 F6
Fairview Cres WF17 . 118 A6
Fairview Ct BD17 ... 38 B1
Fairview Rd WF17 ... 118 A6
Fairview Terr HX3 .. 92 B1
Fairway Bradford BD7 . 73 F1
  Guiseley LS20 ...... 22 C1
  Normanton WF6 .... 123 C1
  Shipley BD18 .... 54 F7
  Yeadon LS19 .... 40 A2
Fairway App WF6 ... 123 C2
Fairway Ave Bradford BD7 . 73 F2
  Mapplewell S75 .... 178 C2
  Normanton WF6 .... 123 C2
Fairway Cl Bradford BD7 . 73 F1
  Guiseley LS20 ...... 39 C8
  Normanton WF6 .... 123 C1
Fairway Cres BD22 . 51 D6
Fairway Dr BD7 .... 73 F2
Fairway Gr BD7 .... 74 A2
Fairway Ind Pk WF17 . 96 F2
Fairway The
  Featherstone WF7 .. 124 D1
  Halifax HX2 .... 91 F7
  Huddersfield HD2 ... 136 A4
  Leeds LS17 .... 43 B6
  Pudsey LS28 .... 57 B1
Fairways Ct WF8 ... 147 E4

Fairways The Keighley BD20 . 18 A3
  Shipley BD20 .... 54 E5
Fairweather Green
  Middle Sch BD8 ..... 73 E7
Fairweather Mews BD8 . 73 E7
Fairy Dell BD16 ...... 54 B7
Fairway First Sch WF18 . 125 D5
Faith St WF9 .... 182 D4
Falcon Cl LS21 ...... 23 A7
Falcon Cliffe BD20 ... 17 D5
Falcon Dr WF10 ..... 124 C6
Falcon Knowl Ing S75 . 177 D1
Falcon Mews Bradford BD8 . 73 C8
  Morley LS27 .... 98 C3
Falcon Rd Bingley BD16 . 36 F5
  Dewsbury WF12 ..... 139 D6
Falcon St Bradford BD7 . 74 A4
  Halifax HX3 .... 113 D3
  Huddersfield HD4 ... 153 F2
Falconer Cl S75 ..... 177 D1
Falconers Ride HD4 . 171 E7
Falhouse La WF4 .... 156 D7
Falkland Cres LS17 .. 43 C1
Falkland Ct LS17 .... 43 C1
Falkland Gdns LS17 . 43 D1
Falkland Gr LS17 ... 43 C1
Falkland Mount LS17 . 43 C1
Falkland Rd Bradford BD10 . 56 E4
  Leeds LS17 .... 43 C1
Falkland Rise LS17 . 43 C1
Falklands Ct LS17 .. 43 C1
Fall Brow Cl BD14 .. 73 A3
Fall Ings Rd WF1 .. 142 E4
Fall La Dewsbury WF13 . 139 B6
  East Ardsley WF3 .. 120 D8
  Liversedge WF15 .. 116 D1
  Marsden HD7 ...... 168 F3
  Northowram HX3 .. 92 D5
  Sowerby Bridge HX6 . 112 C3
Fall Park Ct LS13 .. 58 D5
Fall Rd WF14 ...... 137 E8
Fall Spring Gdns HX4 . 133 F3
Fall Spring Gn HX4 . 133 F3
Fall Wood St BD22 . 51 D6
Falledge La HD8 ... 191 E2
Fallow Croft HD2 .. 136 F5
Fallow La BD22 .... 34 A6
Fallowfield Cl BD4 . 95 C8
Fallowfield Dr BD4 . 75 C1
Fallowfield Gdns BD4 . 75 C1
Fallswood Gr LS13 . 58 D4
Falmouth Ave Bradford BD3 . 55 F1
  Normanton WF6 ... 123 B3
Falmouth Cres WF6 . 123 B3
Falmouth Rd WF6 .. 123 B3
Falsgrave Ave BD2 . 56 C2
Faltis Sq BD10 .... 56 C6
Fanny Moor Cres HD4 . 154 C2
Fanny Moor La HD4 . 154 C2
Far Crest LS13 .... 58 C3
Far Dene HD8 ..... 191 E2
Far End La HD7 ... 172 A4
Far Field Ave HD7 . 189 E1
Far Field Dr HD7 .. 189 E1
Far Field La Holmfirth HD7 . 189 E1
  Meltham HD7, HD4 . 170 F5
Far Fields La HD7 . 171 A5
Far La Hebden Bridge HX7 . 90 A2
  Holmfirth HD7 ..... 189 E1
Far Low Bank BD22 . 34 83
Far Mead Croft LS29 . 9 C2
Far Moss LS17 .... 43 A5
Far Reef Cl LS18 .. 41 C2
Far Richard Cl WF5 . 140 D7
Far View HX2 ..... 91 E6
Far View Bank HD5 . 154 F4
Far View Cres HD5 . 154 E4
Far Well Fold HD3 . 40 D3
Far Well La HD4 ... 190 88
Far Well Rd LS19 . 40 D3
Faraday Sq HD3 .. 153 A4
Farcliffe Pl BD8 .. 55 81
Farcliffe Rd BD8 . 55 81
Farcliffe Terr BD8 . 55 81
Fardene St BD20 . 5 D2
Fardew Ct BD16 . 36 E4
Fardew Golf Course BD20 . 36 C8
Farehill Flats HD4 . 171 F8
Farehill Rd HD4 .. 171 F8
Farfield Ave Batley WF17 . 117 F6
  Bradford BD7 ...... 93 E7
  Pudsey LS28 ...... 57 C3
Farfield Cres BD6 . 93 F7
Farfield Ct LS17 .. 43 E5
Farfield Dr LS28 . 57 C2
Farfield Gr Bradford BD6 . 93 F7
  Pudsey LS28 ...... 57 C3
Farfield Rd Baildon BD17 . 38 D2
  Bradford BD6 ...... 94 A7
  Huddersfield HD5 . 154 F3
  Shipley BD18 ..... 55 A7
Farfield Rise LS28 . 57 C3
Farfield St 🔲
  Cleckheaton BD19 . 95 D1
Farfield Terr BD9 . 55 C3
Farlea Dr BD2 .... 56 C3
Farleton Dr BD2 .. 56 C2
Farley Cres BD22 . 34 B3
Farm Croft WF7 .. 144 E5
Farm Ct LS15 .... 62 82
Farm Gdns WF7 .. 144 E5
Farm Hill Cres LS7 . 60 A5
Farm Hill Ct BD10 . 56 B5
Farm Hill N LS7 .. 60 A6

Farm Hill Rd Bradford BD10 . 56 B6
  Morley LS27 .... 97 F5
Farm Hill Rise LS7 .. 60 A5
Farm Hill S LS7 .... 60 A5
Farm Hill Way LS7 . 60 A5
Farm La WF9 .... 163 A3
Farm Mount LS15 . 62 C2
Farm Pond Dr HD6 . 114 E5
Farm Rd Featherstone WF7 . 145 D5
  Leeds LS15 .... 62 82
Farmfield Dr WF9 .. 163 A3
Farmstead Rd BD10 . 56 C6
Farnboro St OL14 . 108 A2
Farndale App LS14 . 62 C5
Farndale Cl Leeds LS14 . 62 C5
  Wetherby LS22 ..... 13 86
Farndale Ct Garforth LS25 . 82 F5
  🔲 Leeds LS14 ...... 62 C5
Farndale Garth LS14 . 62 C6
Farndale Gdns 🔲 LS14 . 62 C6
Farndale Pl LS14 .. 62 C6
Farndale Rd Baildon BD17 . 38 A2
  Bradford BD15 ..... 53 C4
Farndale Sq 🔲 LS14 . 62 C5
Farndale View LS14 . 62 C6
Farne Ave WF2 ..... 141 F6
Farnham Cl Baildon BD17 . 38 A4
  Leeds LS14 .... 45 81
Farnham Croft LS14 . 62 C6
Farnham First Sch BD7 . 74 85
Farnham Rd BD7 .. 74 85
Farnham Way WF4 . 143 F1
Farnley HD3 ...... 135 81
Farnley C of E Primary Sch
  LS21 .... 11 D5
Farnley Cl LS29 ... 22 84
Farnley Cres LS12 . 77 F6
Farnley Hey HX4 .. 172 C7
Farnley La Farnley LS21 . 11 83
  Otley LS21 .... 11 83
Farnley Park High Sch
  LS12 .... 77 E4
Farnley Pk LS21 .. 11 E2
Farnley Rd Kirkburton HD4 . 172 F5
  Menston LS29 ..... 22 84
Farnley Tyas C of E Sch
  HD4 .... 172 E6
Farnley View BD11 . 97 A6
Farr Royd LS29 ... 9 E2
Farr Royd Terr LS29 . 9 E2
Farra St BD22 ... 51 C2
Farrar Ave WF14 . 137 F6
Farrar Croft LS16 . 42 A4
Farrar Ct LS13 ... 58 C3
Farrar Gr LS16 .. 42 A4
Farrar Height La HX6 . 132 84
Farrar La LS16 ... 42 A4
Farrar Mill La HX3 . 113 D3
Farrer La LS26 ... 101 C5
Farriers Pl WF10 . 125 86
Farringdon Cl BD4 . 75 E4
Farringdon Dr BD4 . 75 E4
Farringdon Gr BD6 . 94 A7
Farringdon Sq BD4 . 75 E4
Farrow Bank LS12 . 77 F7
Farrow Gn LS12 .. 77 F7
Farrow Hill LS12 . 77 F7
Farrow Rd LS12 .. 77 F7
Farrow St LS12 .. 77 F7
Farside Gn BD5 .. 74 B3
Farsley Farfield
  Primary Sch LS28 . 57 C2
Farsley Springbank
  Junior Sch LS28 .. 57 D3
Fartown LS28 .... 76 E5
Fartown Cl LS28 . 76 E5
Fartown Green Rd HD2 . 136 B2
Fartown High Sch HD2 . 136 C2
Farway BD4 ..... 75 E4
Fascination Pl 🔲 BD13 . 72 C2
Faugh La HX7 ... 88 C6
Favell Ave WF6 . 123 81
Faversham Wlk BD4 . 75 E4
Fawcett Ave LS12 . 209 E1
Fawcett Bank LS12 . 209 D1
Fawcett Cl LS12 . 209 D1
Fawcett Dr LS12 . 209 D1
Fawcett Gdns LS12 . 209 D1
Fawcett La LS12 . 209 D1
Fawcett Pl BD4 .. 95 C8
Fawcett Rd LS12 . 209 D1
Fawcett St WF2 .. 142 C4
Fawcett Vale LS12 . 209 D1
Fawcett View LS12 . 209 D1
Fawcett Way LS12 . 209 D1
Faxfleet St BD5 .. 74 D3
Faye Gdns BD4 .. 75 D1
Fearnley Ave WF5 . 140 D7
Fearnley Cl LS12 . 210 A3
Fearnley Cres HD8 . 173 F7
Fearnley Dr WF5 . 140 C7
Fearnley La HD7 . 189 C6
Fearnley Pl LS12 . 210 A3
Fearnley St Dewsbury WF13 . 139 B7
  Featherstone WF7 . 145 C5
Fearnsides Cl 🔲 BD8 . 141 A1
Fearnsides St 🔲 BD8 . 74 88
Fearnsides Terr 🔲 BD8 . 74 88
Fearnville Ave LS8 . 61 D4
Fearnville Cl LS8 . 61 D4
Fearnville Dr Bradford BD4 . 75 D5
  Leeds LS8 .... 61 D4

Fearnville Gr Leeds LS8 ...... 61 D4
 Royston S71 .... 179 C3
Fearnville Mount LS8 .... 61 D4
Fearnville Pl LS8 .... 61 E4
Fearnville Rd LS8 .... 61 D4
Fearnville Terr LS8 .... 61 E4
Fearnville View LS8 .... 61 D4
Feast Field LS18 .... 41 B1
Feather Bed La 8 HX4 ...... 134 D6
Feather Bd BD3 .... 75 B7
Feather St BD21 .... 35 D6
Featherbank Ave LS18 .... 58 B7
Featherbank Gr 5 LS18 .... 58 B8
Featherbank La LS18 .... 58 B8
Featherbank Mount 6 LS18 58 B8
Featherbank Terr 8 LS18 ..... 58 B7
Featherbank Wlk 1 LS18 ..... 58 B7
Featherbed Cl 4 HX4 .... 134 D6
Featherbed La
 Bickerton LS24 .... 15 E6
 Wighill LS24 .... 15 E6
Featherstone High Sch
 WF7 .... 145 F4
Featherstone Junior
 & Infants Sch WF7 .... 145 E7
Featherstone Jun 17 WF7 .... 145 D7
Featherstone Sta WF7 .... 145 C6
Federation St BD5 .... 74 F2
Feetham's Fold LS9 .... 212 B3
Felbrigg Ave BD22 .... 35 A6
Felcote Ave HD5 .... 154 E6
Felcourt Dr HD4 .... 75 E2
Felkirk Dr WF4 .... 180 A8
Felkirk View S72 .... 180 B3
Felks Stile Rd HD4 .... 153 A1
Fell Cres BD22 .... 34 F6
Fell Gr Huddersfield HD2 ... 136 C4
 Keighley BD22 .... 34 F6
Fell Greave Cres HD2 .... 136 C4
Fell Greave Rd HD2 .... 136 C4
Fell La BD22 .... 34 F6
Fellows The HD4 .... 171 C7
Fellowsides La WF5 .... 140 E5
Fellside OL14 .... 109 B5
Fellside Cl BD5 .... 74 F2
Fellwood Ave BD22 .... 51 E8
Fellwood Cl BD22 .... 51 E8
Felnex Cl LS9 .... 80 C6
Felnex Cres LS9 .... 80 C5
Felnex Rd LS9 .... 80 B5
Felnex Sq LS9 .... 80 B5
Felnex Way LS9 .... 80 C5
Fenay Bankside HD8 .... 155 D3
Fenay Bridge Rd HD8 .... 155 C4
Fenay Cres HD5 .... 155 A3
Fenay Dr HD8 .... 155 C3
Fenay La HD5 .... 155 B3
Fenay Lea Dr HD5 .... 155 C4
Fenby Ave BD4 .... 75 C3
Fenby Cl BD4 .... 75 C3
Fenby Gdns BD4 .... 75 C3
Fenby Gr BD4 .... 75 C3
Fencote Cres BD2 .... 56 D3
Fender Rd BD6 .... 73 F1
Fennec Rd BD17 .... 38 E4
Fenny Royd Est HX3 .... 114 B8
Fenton Ave LS26 .... 101 B7
Fenton Cl Rothwell LS26 ..... 101 B7
 South Kirkby WF9 .... 182 B1
Fenton Rd Halifax HX1 ...... 202 B1
 Huddersfield HD1 .... 153 F3
 Lofthouse Gate WF3 .... 121 F7
Fenton St Burley in W LS29 ... 9 F1
 East Ardsley WF3 .... 98 F1
 Leeds LS2 .... 206 B1
 Mirfield WF14 .... 138 A4
Fentonsgate WF3 .... 100 C1
Fenwick Dr BD6 .... 94 A6
Ferguson St HX1 .... 203 E2
Fern Ave HD7 .... 170 C3
Fern Bank LS21 .... 23 B8
Fern Chase LS14 .... 45 A7
Fern Cl LS17 .... 118 F5
Fern Croft
 Cleckheaton WF15 .... 116 C4
 Scarcroft LS14 .... 45 A7
Fern Ct Keighley BD20 .... 18 A2
 Wakefield WF1 .... 120 E3
Fern Gdns LS29 .... 8 A3
Fern Hill Ave BD18 .... 54 F7
Fern Hill Gr BD18 .... 54 F7
Fern Hill Mount BD18 .... 54 F7
Fern Hill Rd BD18 .... 54 F7
Fern Lea BD13 .... 72 F1
Fern Lea Flats HD3 .... 135 A1
Fern Lea Rd HD3 .... 135 A1
Fern Lea St 4 HX6 .... 112 B5
Fern Lea View LS28 .... 57 D3
Fern St Bradford BD4 .... 75 D3
 Halifax HX3 .... 92 B2
 8 Haworth BD22 .... 51 C6
 Huddersfield HD1 .... 136 A1
 Keighley BD21 .... 35 C8
Fern St E HD1 .... 154 C6
Fern Terr 13 LS28 .... 57 E2
Fern Way LS14 .... 45 A7
Fernbank Ave 14
 Bingley BD16 .... 37 A3
 Keighley BD22 .... 34 F4
 Pudsey LS13 .... 57 F3
Fernbank Cl LS13 .... 57 F3
Fernbank Dr Baildon BD17 ... 38 A1
 Bingley BD16 .... 37 B3
 Pudsey LS13 .... 57 F3

Fernbank Gdns LS13 .... 57 F3
Fernbank Pl LS13 .... 57 F3
Fernbank Rd Bradford BD3 ... 56 B1
 Pudsey LS13 .... 57 F3
Fernbank St BD16 .... 37 A3
Fernbank Terr BD16 .... 37 A3
Fernbank Wlk LS13 .... 57 F3
Ferncliffe Dr Baildon BD17 ... 38 B3
 Keighley BD20 .... 18 A2
Ferncliffe Rd Bingley BD16 ... 37 A3
 Leeds LS13 .... 58 C2
 15 Shipley BD18 .... 54 F8
Ferncliffe Terr LS13 .... 58 C2
Ferndale Ave BD14 .... 73 A3
Ferndale Gr BD9 .... 55 C4
Ferndale Pl WF9 .... 181 D6
Ferndene BD16 .... 37 B2
Ferndene Ave WF17 .... 96 F3
Ferndown Gn BD5 .... 74 D3
Ferney Lee Junior
 & Infants Sch OL14 .... 108 A6
Ferney Lee Rd OL14 .... 108 A6
Fernfield Terr 7 HX3 .... 92 B2
Fernhill BD16 .... 37 A5
Fernhurst Cl WF14 .... 138 A6
Fernhurst Cres WF14 .... 138 B6
Fernhurst Lea WF14 .... 138 B6
Fernhurst Rd WF14 .... 138 B6
Fernhurst Way WF14 .... 138 A6
Fernhurst First Sch
 BD17 .... 38 C2
Fernlea LS26 .... 100 F6
Fernlea Cl Batley WF16 .... 117 E3
 Crofton WF4 .... 162 A8
Fernlea Gr HD7 .... 152 E3
Fernleigh Ct WF2 .... 141 F5
Fernley Gdns 11 BD12 .... 94 C4
Fernley Green Cl WF11 ...... 127 B4
Fernley Green Ind Est
 WF11 .... 127 B4
Fernley Green Rd WF11 ...... 127 B4
Fernley Hill Dr WF6 .... 122 F5
Ferns The 3 OL13 .... 106 A1
Fernside 4 .... 144 C3
Fernside Ave HD5 .... 154 F4
Fernside Cl HD5 .... 155 A5
Fernside Cres HD5 .... 155 A5
Fernwood LS8 .... 44 A1
Fernwood Ct LS8 .... 44 A1
Ferrand Ave BD4 .... 95 C8
Ferrand La Bingley BD16 ...... 36 F3
 Cleckheaton BD19 .... 96 A1
Ferrand St BD16 .... 37 A3
Ferrands Cl BD16 .... 36 B1
Ferrands Park Way BD16 ..... 36 B1
Ferriby Cl BD2 .... 56 D3
Ferriby Towers LS9 .... 207 E1
Ferry La WF3 .... 121 F2
Ferry Top La WF4 .... 162 A3
Ferrybridge By-Pass WF11 126 A5
Ferrybridge Inf Sch
 WF11 .... 126 B5
Ferrybridge Power Sta
 WF11 .... 126 B7
Ferrybridge Rd
 Castleford WF10 .... 124 F7
 Knottingley WF11 .... 126 D4
 Pontefract WF8 .... 125 F3
Festival Ave BD18 .... 55 D5
Feversham Coll BD3 .... 201 D2
Feversham Fst Sch BD3 ...... 75 B7
Feversham St BD3 .... 201 D2
Fewston Ave Leeds LS9 ...... 212 C2
 Wakefield WF1 .... 142 F8
Fewston Ct LS9 .... 212 C2
Fiddle La HX4 .... 132 F4
Fiddle Hill WF12 .... 139 B4
Fidler Cl LS25 .... 82 E7
Fidler La LS25 .... 82 E7
Field Cl WF16 .... 117 D6
Field Cres 2 WF9 .... 182 F2
Field Ct BD13 .... 72 E6
Field End LS15 .... 81 A7
Field End Cl LS15 .... 81 A7
Field End Cres LS15 .... 81 A7
Field End Ct LS15 .... 81 A7
Field End Garth LS15 .... 81 A7
Field End Gdns LS15 .... 81 A7
Field End Gn LS15 .... 81 A7
Field End Gr LS15 .... 81 B8
Field End La Holmfirth HD7 188 B2
 Honley HD7 .... 172 A4
Field End Mount LS15 .... 81 A7
Field End Rd LS15 .... 81 A7
Field Head HD7 .... 152 D5
Field Head La Batley WF17 ... 96 E3
 Halifax HX2 .... 91 D7
 Hebden Bridge HX7 .... 110 B4
 Oxenhope BD22 .... 51 A5
Field Head Way HX2 .... 91 D7
Field House 64 E8
Field House Cl LS22 .... 13 C5
Field Hurst BD19 .... 115 F7
Field La Aberford LS25 .... 64 E8
 Batley WF17 .... 118 D4
 Brighouse HD6 .... 135 F8
 Dewsbury WF13 .... 138 D6
 Kirkburton HD4 .... 173 A8
 Ossett WF5 .... 140 D6
 South Elmsall WF9 .... 183 C4
 Upton WF9 .... 183 C4
 Wakefield WF2 .... 142 C3

Field Side HX1 .... 202 B4
Field St Bradford BD1 .... 201 C3
 Dewsbury WF13 .... 138 F6
Field Terr LS15 .... 81 A8
Field Top Rd HD6 .... 114 F1
Field View WF10 .... 124 A6
Field Way HD6 .... 190 E8
Fieldcroft Ct 8 WF14 .... 137 F5
Fieldedge La BD20 .... 19 A2
Fielden Sq OL14 .... 108 B4
Fielden St OL14 .... 108 E6
Fieldens Pl WF17 .... 118 A6
Fieldfares The BD20 .... 5 E1
Fieldgate Rd BD10 .... 56 D7
Fieldhead Cl WF8 .... 125 F1
Fieldhead Cres WF17 .... 96 E3
Fieldhead Ct LS23 .... 30 C7
Fieldhead Dr
 Barwick in E LS15 .... 63 F8
 Glusburn BD20 .... 16 D7
 Guiseley LS20 .... 39 C8
Fieldhead Gdns WF12 .... 119 B3
Fieldhead Gr LS20 .... 39 C8
Fieldhead Hospl WF1 .... 121 D1
Fieldhead Junior & Infants Sch
 WF17 .... 96 F3
Fieldhead La HD7 .... 187 F1
Fieldhead Paddock LS23 ...... 30 C8
Fieldhead Rd LS20 .... 39 D8
Fieldhead St BD7 .... 74 C7
Fieldhouse Cl LS17 .... 43 C2
Fieldhouse Cotts 12 HX1 ... 202 C1
Fieldhouse Dr Leeds LS17 ... 43 C2
 Slaithwaite HD7 .... 152 A1
Fieldhouse Gr LS28 .... 57 C2
Fieldhouse Lawn LS17 .... 43 C2
Fieldhouse Rd 2 HD1 .... 154 C8
Fieldhouse St BD3 .... 75 D7
 Wakefield WF1 .... 142 F3
Fieldhouse Wlk LS17 .... 43 C2
Fieldhurst Ct BD4 .... 95 C8
Fielding Gate LS12 .... 210 A4
Fielding St 2 HD7 .... 89 A3
Fields Rd Bradford BD12 ...... 94 E5
 Lepton HD8 .... 155 D2
Fields The HD5 .... 137 C1
Fields The HD5 .... 100 D1
Fields Way HD5 .... 137 C1
Fieldsend Ct WF9 .... 183 A7
Fieldsend Bglws HD7 .... 170 D7
Fieldside BD13 .... 52 D6
Fieldside Rd WF9 .... 163 B2
Fieldway Bradford BD14 .... 73 B5
 Ilkley LS29 .... 8 E4
Fieldway Ave LS13 .... 58 A4
Fieldway Chase LS26 .... 101 D5
Fieldway Cl LS13 .... 58 A4
Fieldway Rise LS13 .... 58 A4
Fife St 13 BD22 .... 51 D7
Fifth Ave Bradford BD3 .... 56 C1
 Rothwell LS26 .... 101 A7
Fifth Ave E WF15 .... 116 B5
Fifth Ave W WF15 .... 116 B5
Fifth St BD12 .... 94 E6
Filbert St HD1 .... 136 A1
Filey Ave S71 .... 179 D4
Filey St BD1 .... 201 C2
Filley Royd BD19 .... 116 E6
Fillingfir Dr LS16 .... 58 F8
Fillingfir Rd LS16 .... 58 F8
Fillingfir Wlk LS16 .... 58 F8
Finch Ave WF2 .... 160 D5
Finch St BD5 .... 74 D4
Finching Gr WF14 .... 138 A8
Finchley St BD5 .... 74 D3
Finchley Way 4 LS27 .... 98 A3
Finden Terr WF10 .... 56 E4
Fine Garth Cl LS23 .... 30 D3
Finghall Rd DN6 .... 184 F2
Fink Hill LS18 .... 58 A8
Finkil St HD6 .... 114 F5
Finkin Ave WF3 .... 121 E2
Finkin Croft WF3 .... 121 E2
Finkin La WF3 .... 121 E2
Finkle St HX4 .... 177 F7
Finkle La LS27 .... 97 D6
Finkle St Pontefract WF8 .... 125 D1
 Sowerby Bridge HX6 .... 111 D4
 Woolley WF4 .... 177 F7
Finsbury Dr BD2 .... 55 F5
Finsbury Rd LS1 .... 206 A1
Finthorpe La HD5 .... 155 A3
Fir Ave WF13 .... 138 D5
Fir Bank 6 WF13 .... 118 A1
Fir Par WF13 .... 138 D5
Fir Rd HD1 .... 153 D6
Fir St Haworth BD22 .... 51 C6
 12 Keighley BD21 .... 35 B4
 Todmorden OL14 .... 129 A8
Fir Tree App LS17 .... 43 C3
Fir Tree Cl LS17 .... 43 C4
Fir Tree Gdns
 Bradford BD10 .... 56 D7
 Leeds LS17 .... 43 B4
Fir Tree Gn LS17 .... 43 C4
Fir Tree Gr LS17 .... 43 C4
Fir Tree La LS17 .... 43 C4
Fir Tree Primary Sch LS17 ... 43 C3
Fir Tree Rise LS17 .... 43 C3
Fir Tree Vale LS17 .... 43 C3
Fir Wlk WF13 .... 138 D5
Firbank Gr LS15 .... 81 C7
Firbank Rd LS15 .... 80 E6
Firbeck BD16 .... 53 B8
Firbeck Rd LS23 .... 30 D3
Firethorn Cl BD8 .... 74 A8
Firham Cl S71 .... 179 A4

Firs The Royston S71 .... 179 A4
 Scarcroft LS14 .... 45 C7
First Ave Bardsey LS17 .... 28 E5
 Bradford BD3 .... 75 B7
 Cleckheaton WF15 .... 116 C5
 Halifax HX3 .... 113 B4
 Hemsworth WF9 .... 163 A4
 Horbury WF4 .... 140 F1
 Huddersfield, Dalton HD5 . 154 F7
 Huddersfield, Town End HD7 152 D4
 3 Keighley BD21 .... 35 B6
 Leeds LS12 .... 210 A3
 Lofthouse Gate WF1 .... 121 C2
 Pudsey LS28 .... 57 E1
 Rothwell LS26 .... 100 F7
 Royston S71 .... 179 D4
 South Kirkby WF9 .... 181 F1
 Upton WF9 .... 183 A7
 Wetherby LS22 .... 13 F6
 Yeadon LS19 .... 40 C5
First Avenue Ind Est LS28 ... 57 E1
First St BD12 .... 94 E6
Firth Ave
 6 Brighouse HD6 .... 115 A3
 Leeds LS11 .... 214 A2
Firth Cl LS11 .... 214 A2
Firth Gr LS11 .... 214 A2
Firth House La
 Brighouse HD6 .... 136 C7
 Ripponden HX4 .... 133 C1
Firth La BD15 .... 53 C5
Firth Mount LS11 .... 214 A2
Firth Rd Bradford BD9 .... 55 A3
 Leeds LS11 .... 214 A2
Firth Row BD4 .... 95 B8
Firth St Brighouse HD6 ...... 115 A1
 Huddersfield HD1 .... 154 B5
 Leeds LS9 .... 207 E1
 Shipley HD8 .... 190 E8
Firth Terr LS8 .... 207 E1
Firth View LS11 .... 214 A2
Firthcliffe Dr WF15 .... 117 B5
Firthcliffe Gr WF15 .... 117 C5
Firthcliffe La WF15 .... 117 B5
Firthcliffe Mount WF15 ..... 117 B5
Firthcliffe Par WF15 .... 117 C5
Firthcliffe Pl WF15 .... 117 C5
Firthcliffe Terr WF15 .... 117 B5
Firthcliffe View WF15 .... 117 B5
Firthcliffe Wlk WF15 .... 117 B5
Firthfield La WF9 .... 164 F4
Firthfields LS25 .... 83 A7
Firtree Ave LS25 .... 83 B6
Firville Ave WF6 .... 123 B1
Firville Cres WF6 .... 144 B8
Firwood Cl OL14 .... 108 A1
Fish St LS1 .... 211 F4
Fishbeck La BD20 .... 16 B7
Fisher Gn HD7 .... 171 F4
Fisher Gr WF5 .... 140 F4
Fisher St WF11 .... 126 E4
Fisher Way WF15 .... 117 E3
Fishergate WF11 .... 126 D5
Fishpond La WF2 .... 159 F5
Fishponds Dr WF4 .... 159 F5
Fitts La LS17 .... 27 A8
Fitzgerald St BD5 .... 201 B1
Fitzroy Dr LS8 .... 61 A6
Fitzroy Rd BD3 .... 75 C7
Fitzwilliam Jun & Inf Sch
 WF9 .... 163 B4
Fitzwilliam St
 Bradford BD4 .... 201 C1
 Hemsworth WF9 .... 163 A3
Fitzwilliam Sta WF9 .... 163 A3
Five Acres S75 .... 193 F5
Five Lane Ends
 Adwick Le S DN6 .... 184 E1
 Bradford BD10 .... 56 B6
 Holmfirth HD7 .... 188 E5
 Leeds LS16 .... 42 D8
Five Oaks BD17 .... 38 A2
Fixby Ave HX2 .... 202 A1
Fixby Jun & Inf Sch HD2 .... 136 A4
Fixby La HX4 .... 133 C6
Fixby Park Dr HD2 .... 135 F2
Fixby Rd HD2 .... 136 A5
Fixby View Yd HD6 .... 135 E6
Flanshaw Ave WF2 .... 141 E6
Flanshaw Cres WF2 .... 141 E6
Flanshaw Gr WF2 .... 141 E6
Flanshaw Jun & Inf Sch
 WF2 .... 141 F7
Flanshaw La WF2 .... 141 D6
Flanshaw Rd WF2 .... 141 E6
Flanshaw St WF2 .... 141 E6
Flanshaw View WF2 .... 141 E6
Flanshaw Way WF2 .... 141 D7
Flappit Spring BD13 .... 52 A6
Flasby St BD21 .... 35 C8
Flash La WF14 .... 138 B6
Flat La HD7 .... 189 D6
Flat House HD7 .... 170 C8
Flat La HD7 .... 188 D5
Flat Nook BD16 .... 37 A3
Flatts La HD7 .... 189 D6
Flats The HX1 .... 203 E2
Flavell Cl WF9 .... 182 B1
Flawith Dr BD2 .... 56 D2
Flax Meadow HD3 .... 135 A2
Flaxen Ct BD6 .... 93 E8
Flax Pl LS9 .... 212 B3
Flaxen Ct BD6 .... 74 D1
Flaxton Cl 2 LS11 .... 214 B3
Flaxton Gdns 1 LS11 .... 214 B3

Flaxton Gn BD2 .... 56 D2
Flaxton Pl BD7 .... 74 B6
Flaxton St LS11 .... 214 B3
Flaxton View LS11 .... 214 B3
Flea La WF8 .... 166 E4
Fledborough Rd LS22 .... 13 C5
Fleece St Bradford BD6 .... 93 F7
 Keighley BD21 .... 35 C7
Fleet La Mickletown LS26 ... 102 A3
 Queensbury BD13 .... 72 D1
 Rothwell LS26 .... 101 E5
Fleet St HD8 .... 175 D1
Fleet Thro Rd LS18 .... 58 B6
Fleming Ct HD5 .... 155 A5
Fleming St WF17 .... 118 C5
Fleminghouse La HD5 .... 155 A5
Fletcher Ave BD20 .... 5 E2
Fletcher Cres HD6 .... 135 E6
Fletcher Homes WF13 .... 139 A8
Fletcher La BD2 .... 56 B6
Fletcher Rd BD6 .... 74 B1
Fletton Terr BD2 .... 56 B2
Flexbury Ave LS27 .... 98 A3
Flight Hill HD7 .... 199 C5
Flinton House Rd HX6 .... 131 F4
Flint La HD7, S36 .... 200 A5
Flint St HD1 .... 136 B1
Flintmill La LS23 .... 14 D3
Flinton Gr BD2 .... 56 D6
Flockton Av BD4 .... 75 A4
Flockton (C of E) First Sch
 WF4 .... 157 C2
Flockton Ave BD4 .... 75 A4
Flockton Cres BD4 .... 75 A4
Flockton Dr BD4 .... 75 A4
Flockton Gr BD4 .... 75 A4
Flockton Rd BD4 .... 75 A4
Floral Ave LS7 .... 60 C6
Floreat Cl WF17 .... 118 A8
Florence Ave Leeds LS9 ...... 208 A2
 Wilsden BD15 .... 53 B6
Florence Gr LS9 .... 208 A2
Florence Mount LS9 .... 208 A2
Florence Pl LS9 .... 208 A2
Florence St Bradford BD3 .... 75 C6
 Castleford WF10 .... 124 D8
 Halifax HX1 .... 202 C3
 Leeds LS9 .... 208 A2
Florence Terr 9 LS27 .... 98 B4
Florida Rd BD15 .... 54 A4
Florist St BD21 .... 35 B6
Flounders Hill WF7 .... 163 F6
Flower Acre HX5 .... 134 F6
Flower Bank Bradford BD2 ... 55 F4
 Sowerby Bridge HX6 .... 111 F3
Flower Ct LS12 .... 62 D1
Flower Croft BD21 .... 34 F5
Flower Garth BD10 .... 56 D6
Flower Haven BD9 .... 54 D4
Flower Hill BD9 .... 54 F4
 3 Yeadon LS19 .... 40 B7
Flower Scar Rd Bacup OL13 . 38 D4
Flowerlands HX3 .... 114 E8
Floyd St BD5 .... 74 B3
Flush WF15 .... 117 C4
Flush House La HD7 .... 188 A3
Flushdyke Junior
 & Infants Sch WF5 .... 140 F7
Flockton Ct HD8 .... 173 F5
Fold La HX7 .... 88 A6
Fold The 4 Haworth BD22 ... 51 B7
 Leeds LS15 .... 62 E4
Foldings Ave BD19 .... 115 F8
Foldings Cl BD19 .... 115 E8
Foldings Ct BD19 .... 115 E8
Foldings Gr BD19 .... 115 E8
Foldings Par BD19 .... 115 E8
Foldings Rd BD19 .... 115 F8
Foldings The HD8 .... 175 A2
Foljambe St WF7 .... 142 C4
Folkestone St BD3 .... 75 C7
Folkton Holme BD2 .... 56 E2
Follett Ave HX4 .... 153 C2
Follingworth La HD7 .... 151 D1
Follingworth Rd WF17 .... 118 F5
Folly Hall HD1 .... 154 A4
Folly Hall Ave BD6 .... 94 B8
Folly Hall Cl 2 BD6 .... 94 B8
Folly Hall Gdns The BD6 ..... 94 B8
Folly Hall La HX7 .... 110 C2
Folly Hall Mount WF17 ...... 119 E8
Folly Hall Rd 1 BD6 .... 94 B8
 East Ardsley WF3 .... 119 E8
Folly Hall Wlk 3 BD6 .... 94 B8
Folly La Bramham LS23 .... 30 D2
 Leeds LS11 .... 214 B4
Folly View LS23 .... 30 D2
Folly View Rd BD20 .... 51 D6
Fontmell Cl BD4 .... 75 E2
Football LS19 .... 40 C6
Forber Gr BD4 .... 75 E5
Ford BD13 .... 92 C8
Ford Gr WF14 .... 137 E6
Ford Gate HD7 .... 188 D3
Ford Hill BD13 .... 92 D8
Ford House Sch S6 .... 205 E4
Ford St 4 Hemsworth WF9 . 163 B1
 Keighley BD21 .... 18 E1
Fore La HX6 .... 112 A3
Fore Lane Ave HX6 .... 112 A3
Foreside Bottom La BD13 .... 71 D5
Forest Ave HX2 .... 91 E4
Forest Bank LS27 .... 97 C7
Forest Cl WF1 .... 121 F1
Forest Cres HX2 .... 91 E4
Forest Gate LS21 .... 23 A7

Forest Gn HX2 .... 91 E3
Forest Hill Gdns HD3 .... 152 A8
Forest Hill Rd HX4 .... 133 E1
Forest Rd HD5 .... 154 E5
Forest Ridge WF3 .... 99 C1
Forest Way HD7 .... 171 E4
Forge La Batley WF15 .... 126 E4
Forge La Batley WF15 .... 117 C2
Dewsbury WF12 .... 139 B4
Harewood LS17 .... 27 D1
Horbury WF4 .... 159 C8
Leeds LS12 .... 210 A4
Liversedge WF15 .... 117 B3
Forge Row LS12 .... 77 D3
Forge View BD20 .... 17 C5
Forman's Dr WF3 .... 100 A3
Formby Ave HD2 .... 135 F3
Forrest Ave HD1 .... 153 D7
Forrest Ter WF12 .... 139 E6
Forrester Cl WF9 .... 163 A3
Forster Ct BD1 .... 201 C3
Forster Dr WF16 .... 117 E3
Forster Pl LS12 .... 78 B4
Forster Sq BD1 .... 201 B3
Forster Square Ret Pk BD1 .... 201 B4
Forster St LS10 .... 212 B1
Forsythia Ave WF3 .... 120 C7
Fort Ann Rd WF17 .... 118 F4
Fortis Way HD3 .... 152 E8
Fortshot La LS17 .... 27 B1
Forum View WF8 .... 165 A5
Foss Ave LS22 .... 13 D7
Foss Wlk WF10 .... 104 B1
Fosse Way LS25 .... 83 B6
Foster Ave
Huddersfield HD4 .... 153 C2
Normanton WF2 .... 123 A1
Silsden BD20 .... 5 D2
Thornton BD13 .... 72 F6
Foster Beaver Coll The BD9 .... 54 F1
Foster Cl Burley in W LS29 .... 9 F1
[8] Morley LS27 .... 98 A5
Foster Cres [7] LS27 .... 98 A5
Foster Gdns BD22 .... 34 F7
Foster La HX7 .... 89 A4
Foster Park Gr BD13 .... 52 E1
Foster Park Rd BD13 .... 52 E1
Foster Park View BD13 .... 52 E1
Foster Pk BD13 .... 52 E1
Foster Place La HD7 .... 189 F2
Foster Rd BD21 .... 35 B4
Foster St [5] Morley LS27 .... 98 A5
Foston Cl BD2 .... 56 E2
Foston La BD2 .... 56 E2
Fothergill Ave WF7 .... 163 E6
Foul Clough Rd OL14 .... 128 D8
Foulcauseway La LS21 .... 23 D7
Foulds' Terr [6] BD16 .... 37 A4
Foundry App LS9 .... 208 B3
Foundry Ave LS8, LS9 .... 208 B3
Foundry Dr LS9 .... 208 B3
Foundry Hill BD16 .... 36 F3
Foundry La Bradford BD4 .... 75 B5
Knottingley WF11 .... 127 A4
Leeds LS14, LS9 .... 61 E3
Pudsey LS28 .... 57 E2
Foundry Mill Cres LS14 .... 61 F3
Foundry Mill Dr LS14 .... 61 E3
Foundry Mill Gdns LS14 .... 61 E5
Foundry Mill Mount LS14 .... 61 F3
Foundry Mill St LS14 .... 61 F3
Foundry Mill Terr LS14 .... 61 F3
Foundry Mill View LS14 .... 61 F3
Foundry Mill Wlk LS14 .... 61 F3
Foundry Pl LS9 .... 208 B3
Foundry St
Brighouse HD6 .... 115 C1
Dewsbury WF13 .... 139 D8
Dewsbury, Ravensthorpe WF13 .... 138 E5
Halifax HX1 .... 203 E4
Leeds, Bank LS9 .... 212 B3
Leeds, Camp Field LS11 .... 211 E2
Sowerby Bridge HX6 .... 112 B3
Todmorden OL14 .... 108 A4
Foundry St N HX3 .... 91 F3
Foundry Terr BD19 .... 116 F7
Fountain Cl WF8 .... 208 B3

Fountain Cl
Liversedge WF15 .... 116 F1
Mapplewell S75 .... 177 E1
Fountain Ct S71 .... 178 E1
Fountain Dr WF15 .... 116 F1
Fountain Gr HD4 .... 153 C4
Fountain Sq S75 .... 177 E1
Fountain St Batley WF16 .... 117 D5
Bradford BD1 .... 201 B4
Bradford, Low Moor BD12 .... 94 C6
Halifax HX1 .... 203 E2
[29] Hebden Bridge HX7 .... 89 A3
Leeds LS1 .... 211 D4
Liversedge WF15 .... 116 F1
[5] Morley LS27 .... 98 C8
[14] Queensbury BD13 .... 72 E1
Ripponden HX6 .... 132 D4
[7] Thornton BD13 .... 72 D6
Todmorden OL14 .... 108 E6
Fountain Terr BD12 .... 94 D3
Fountain Way BD18 .... 55 C7
Fountain Wlk [1] LS14 .... 62 B5
Fountains Ave
Batley WF17 .... 117 F4
Boston Spa LS23 .... 30 C7

Fountains Way WF1 .... 121 F1
Four Acres WF14 .... 138 A3
Four Lane Ends
Castleford WF10 .... 124 A6
Dewsbury WF12 .... 139 F2
Guiseley LS20 .... 39 C7
Four Row HD8 .... 191 A4
Fourlands Cres BD10 .... 56 C8
Fourlands Ct BD10 .... 56 C8
Fourlands Dr BD10 .... 56 C8
Fourlands Gdns BD10 .... 56 C8
Fourlands Gr BD10 .... 56 C8
Fourlands Rd BD10 .... 56 C8
Fourteenth Ave LS12 .... 210 A2
Fourth Ave Bradford BD3 .... 56 C1
Cleckheaton WF15 .... 116 B5
[6] Keighley BD21 .... 35 A6
Lofthouse Gate WF1 .... 121 B2
Rothwell LS26 .... 101 A7
Wetherby LS22 .... 13 F5
Fourth Ct LS11 .... 211 D2
Fourth St [1] BD12 .... 94 E6
Fowler St BD4 .... 75 B5
Fowler's Pl LS28 .... 57 E2
Fowlers Garth BD22 .... 34 D1
Fox Cl HD8 .... 175 D6
Fox Covert Rd
or Whin Covert La WF8 .... 166 F2
Fox Ct Crigglestone WF4 .... 159 F7
Elland HX4 .... 134 D7
Fox Heads La LS22 .... 12 A8
Fox La Crigglestone WF4 .... 159 F7
Wakefield WF1 .... 142 D1
Fox Royd HD8 .... 173 E1
Fox Royd Ave WF14 .... 137 F6
Fox Royd Dr WF14 .... 137 F6
Fox Royd La [3] WF14 .... 137 F6
Fox Royd View WF14 .... 137 F6
Fox St Batley WF17 .... 118 D4
Bingley BD16 .... 36 F3
[5] Bradford BD5 .... 74 C3
Cleckheaton BD19 .... 116 B7
Huddersfield HD1 .... 154 A6
Fox Terr WF8 .... 125 E1
Fox Way WF13 .... 118 A3
Fox Way LS10 .... 212 B1
Fox Wood Ave LS8 .... 61 E5
Fox Wood Cl LS8 .... 61 E5
Fox Wood Gr LS8 .... 61 E5
Fox Wood Rise LS8 .... 61 E5
Fox Wood Wlk LS8 .... 61 E5
Foxbridge Way WF6 .... 123 E3
Foxcliff WF11 .... 105 D1
Foxcroft Cl Leeds LS6 .... 59 B5
Queensbury BD13 .... 92 C7
Foxcroft Dr HD6 .... 114 F1
Foxcroft Gn LS6 .... 59 B5
Foxcroft Mount LS6 .... 59 C5
Foxcroft Rd LS6 .... 59 B5
Foxcroft Way LS6 .... 59 B5
Foxdale Cl [1] OL13 .... 106 A1
Foxen La HX6 .... 132 C6
Foxglove Ave LS8 .... 61 C6
Foxglove Folly WF2 .... 141 E8
Foxglove Rd Batley WF17 .... 96 E2
Huddersfield HD5 .... 154 E4
Foxhill Baildon BD17 .... 38 B3
Wetherby LS22 .... 13 E6
Foxhill Ave Leeds LS16 .... 42 C1
Queensbury BD13 .... 72 D1
Foxhill Cl BD13 .... 72 D1
Foxhill Cres LS16 .... 42 C1
Foxhill Dr LS16 .... 42 C1
Foxhill Dr Leeds LS16 .... 42 D1
Queensbury BD13 .... 72 D1
Foxhill First Sch BD13 .... 72 D2
Foxhill Gn LS16 .... 42 D1
Foxhill Gr Leeds LS16 .... 42 D1
Queensbury BD13 .... 72 D1
Foxhills The LS16 .... 41 D4
Foxhole La LS18 .... 57 B6
Foxholes Cres LS28 .... 57 B6
Foxlands La WF6 .... 122 F5
Foxlow Ave HD5 .... 154 E8
Foxroyd La WF12 .... 139 B1
Foxstone Rise BD17 .... 38 E3
Foxstones La HX6 .... 132 D2
Foxwood Farm Way LS8 .... 61 E5
Foxwood Wlk LS22 .... 13 F7
Fraile Cl WF8 .... 146 E7
France Fold HD7 .... 171 F5
France St WF17 .... 118 E4
Frances Ave HD4 .... 153 C3
Frances Rd WF12 .... 139 F7
Frances St
[9] Brighouse HD6 .... 115 A3
[1] Elland HX5 .... 134 F6
Keighley BD21 .... 35 A8
Pudsey LS28 .... 57 D2
Francis Ave HD3 .... 153 A4
Francis Cl HX1 .... 202 C3
Francis Ct LS7 .... 207 D3
Francis Gr [3] LS11 .... 214 B3
Francis House BD1 .... 56 B2
Francis Rd WF4 .... 144 B3
Francis St
Ackworth M T WF7 .... 163 D5
Batley WF16 .... 117 E3
Bradford BD4 .... 201 D1
Castleford WF10 .... 124 C7
Halifax HX1 .... 202 C2
Huddersfield HD3 .... 153 A4
Leeds LS7 .... 207 E3
Mirfield WF14 .... 137 F5
Francis Terr WF7 .... 163 D5
Francis View WF14 .... 137 F5
Frank Cl WF12 .... 139 E2

Frank La Dewsbury WF12 .... 139 E2
Emley HD8 .... 175 C5
Hebden Bridge HX2 .... 90 B1
Frank Parkinson Ct LS20 .... 22 E1
Frank Parkinson Homes
LS20 .... 22 E1
Frank Peel Cl [4] WF16 .... 117 D4
Frank [3] BD7 .... 74 B4
Frank St Bradford BD7 .... 74 B4
Halifax HX1 .... 202 C2
Frankland Gr LS7 .... 207 E3
Frankland Pl LS7 .... 207 E3
Franklin St HX1 .... 202 B3
Fraser Ave LS18 .... 58 A8
Fraser House [2] BD6 .... 93 E8
Fraser Rd LS28 .... 56 F6
Fraser St Bradford BD8 .... 74 D8
Leeds LS9 .... 207 F1
Freakfield La WF15 .... 116 B2
Fred St BD21 .... 35 B6
Fred's Pl BD4 .... 75 C3
Frederick Ave Leeds LS9 .... 80 A6
Huddersfield HD4 .... 153 F2
Frederick Cl BD10 .... 38 F1
Frederick St Bradford BD1 .... 201 C2
East Ardsley WF3 .... 120 E8
Huddersfield HD4 .... 153 C4
Keighley BD21 .... 35 B7
[8] Liversedge WF15 .... 117 B3
Pudsey LS28 .... 57 C3
Wakefield WF1 .... 216 B2
Frederick Walker Gdns
WF17 .... 118 D4
Free School La HX1, HX3 .... 203 D1
Freely La LS23 .... 30 D2
Freeman Rd HX3 .... 114 A5
Freemans Way LS22 .... 14 A6
Freemont St LS13 .... 58 B2
Freeston Ct WF6 .... 123 B3
Freeston Dr WF6 .... 123 B3
Freeston High Sch WF6 .... 123 B1
Freestone Way WF6 .... 122 E4
Fremantle Gr BD4 .... 75 E5
Fremantle Pl LS15 .... 80 E7
Frensham Ave LS27 .... 97 F3
Frensham Dr Bradford BD7 .... 73 D3
Castleford WF10 .... 125 D6
Frensham Gr BD7 .... 73 D3
Frensham Way BD7 .... 73 D3
Freshfield Gdns BD15 .... 54 B1
Freston Ave WF1 .... 143 D7
Freston Dr WF1 .... 143 D7
Friar Ct BD10 .... 56 C6
Friar Pl HD2 .... 136 A5
Friar's Cl WF7 .... 145 D4
Friars Ind Est BD10 .... 56 B7
Friars Nook WF8 .... 146 E7
Friarwood La WF8 .... 146 D8
Frickley Bridge La S72 .... 180 F4
Frickley La Clayton WF9 .... 195 A8
South Elmsall WF9 .... 195 A8
Friendly Ave HX6 .... 112 A5
Friendly Fold Rd HX3 .... 92 A2
Friendly St [1] Halifax HX3 .... 92 A2
[8] Huddersfield HD1 .... 154 B6
Thornton BD13 .... 72 D6
Friends Adult Sch LS27 .... 98 B4
Frimley Dr BD5 .... 74 C2
Frith House HD6 .... 136 C7
Frith St [2] BD22 .... 51 E8
Frizinghall First Sch BD9 .... 55 C5
Frizinghall Middle Sch BD9 .... 55 C5
Frizinghall Rd BD9 .... 55 C4
Frizinghall Sta BD9 .... 55 C4
Frizley Gdns BD9 .... 55 A5
Frober Pl LS15 .... 80 E7
Frobisher Gr WF2 .... 141 E5
Frobisher Rd OL15 .... 129 C1
Frogmoor Ave BD12 .... 94 F5
Front Row LS11 .... 214 B3
Front St Bramham LS23 .... 30 C2
Castleford WF10 .... 124 F6
Leeds LS11 .... 211 E2
Pontefract WF8 .... 146 C8
Frost Hill WF15 .... 117 B4
Fruit St BD21 .... 35 E8
Fryergate WF2 .... 141 F7
Fryston La WF11 .... 125 F7
Fryston Rd WF10 .... 125 C7
Fulford Ave HD2 .... 136 A2
Fulford Cl S75 .... 178 A1
Fulford St WF10 .... 124 C7
Fulford Wlk BD2 .... 56 D2
Fulham Pl [3] LS11 .... 214 B3
Fulham Sq [5] LS11 .... 214 B3
Fullerton Cl DN6 .... 184 F2
Fullerton St BD3 .... 201 D2
Fullwood Dr HD7 .... 152 D4
Fulmar Ct LS10 .... 99 D5
Fulmar Mews [3] BD8 .... 73 C7
Fulmar Rd WF10 .... 124 C6
Fulneck LS28 .... 76 E5
Fulneck Boys' Sch LS28 .... 76 E4
Fulneck Cl HD2 .... 135 F3
Fulneck Girls' Sch LS28 .... 76 E5
Fulneck Golf Course LS28 .... 76 D4
Fulstone Hall La HD7 .... 190 A7
Fulstone Rd HD7 .... 173 C1
Fulton St BD1 .... 201 A3
Fulwood Gr WF2 .... 160 B6
Furnace Cotts S36 .... 200 D6
Furnace Gr BD12 .... 94 F5
Furnace Inn St BD4 .... 75 D5
Furnace La BD11 .... 96 A6
Furnace Rd Bradford BD4 .... 95 A6
Wakefield, Raw Nook BD4 .... 94 F5

Furnbrook Gdns HD5 .... 155 C8
Furness Ave Halifax HX2 .... 91 E4
Furness Cres WF2 .... 120 E2
Furness Dr Halifax HX2 .... 91 D4
Wakefield WF2 .... 120 E2
Furness Gdns HX2 .... 91 E4
Furness Gr HX2 .... 91 E4
Furness Pl HX2 .... 91 E3
Fusden La BD19 .... 96 A1
Futures Way BD4 .... 201 C1
Fyfe Cres BD17 .... 38 E2
Fyfe Gr BD17 .... 38 E2
Fyfe La BD17 .... 38 E2

Gable End Terr [5] LS28 .... 76 F7
Gables The Baildon BD17 .... 38 E3
[8] Keighley BD21 .... 35 A7
Gadding Moor Rd S75 .... 192 F1
Gagewell Dr WF4 .... 141 B2
Gagewell La WF4 .... 141 B2
Gagewell View WF4 .... 141 B2
Gain La BD2, BD3 .... 56 E1
Gainest HX2 .... 202 B1
Gainford Dr LS25 .... 82 F6
Gainsborough Cl BD3 .... 56 A2
Gainsborough Pl LS12 .... 77 E3
Gainsborough Way WF3 .... 121 E5
Gainsbro Ave LS16 .... 42 B5
Gainsbro Dr LS16 .... 42 B5
Gaisby La BD18 .... 55 D5
Gaisby Mount BD18 .... 55 D5
Gaisby Rise BD18 .... 55 D5
Gaitskell Ct LS11 .... 211 D1
Gaitskell Grange [5] LS11 .... 211 D1
Gaitskell Wlk LS11 .... 211 D1
Gale St [6] Haworth BD22 .... 51 F8
Keighley BD21 .... 35 C8
Galefield Gn BD6 .... 93 F6
Gall La OL14 .... 86 C3
Gallon Croft WF4 .... 182 E3
Galloway Ct [3] LS28 .... 76 A8
Galloway La LS28 .... 57 A1
Galloway Rd BD10 .... 56 D7
Galloway St HD1 .... 154 C8
Gallows Hill WF10 .... 125 D7
Gallus La WF4 .... 159 F7
Galsworthy Ave BD9 .... 54 D3
Gamble Hill LS13 .... 77 D8
Gamble Hill Chase LS13 .... 77 D8
Gamble Hill Cl LS13 .... 77 D8
Gamble Hill Croft LS13 .... 77 D8
Gamble Hill Cross LS13 .... 77 D8
Gamble Hill Dr LS13 .... 77 D8
Gamble Hill Fold LS13 .... 77 D8
Gamble Hill Gn LS13 .... 77 D8
Gamble Hill Grange LS13 .... 77 D8
Gamble Hill Lawn LS13 .... 77 D8
Gamble Hill Path LS13 .... 77 D8
Gamble Hill Pl LS13 .... 77 D8
Gamble Hill Rise LS13 .... 77 D8
Gamble Hill Vale LS13 .... 77 D8
Gamble Hill View LS13 .... 77 D8
Gamble Hill Wlk LS13 .... 77 D8
Gamble La LS12 .... 77 C6
Gamble Lodge [8] LS28 .... 57 D3
Game Scar La or
Goose Eye Brow BD22 .... 34 B6
Gamel View BD20 .... 17 B6
Gang The LS22 .... 209 F3
Ganners Cl LS13 .... 58 C4
Ganners Gn LS13 .... 58 C4
Ganners Gr LS13 .... 58 C4
Ganners La LS13 .... 58 C4
Ganners Mount LS13 .... 58 C4
Ganners Rd LS13 .... 58 C4
Ganners Rise LS13 .... 58 C4
Ganners Way LS13 .... 58 C4
Ganners Wlk LS13 .... 58 C4
Gannerthorpe Cl [4] BD12 .... 94 C3
Gannet Cl WF10 .... 124 C6
Ganny Rd HD6 .... 115 B2
Ganton Cl LS6 .... 206 B4
Ganton Way HD2 .... 136 F5
Gaol La HX1 .... 203 F3
Garden Ave WF15 .... 117 A6
Garden Cl Bradford BD12 .... 94 C4
Glusburn BD20 .... 16 B6
Liversedge WF15 .... 117 A6
Ossett WF5 .... 140 E3
Garden Cres WF13 .... 138 E6
Garden Dr WF13 .... 138 E6
Garden Field BD12 .... 94 D3
Garden Fold HX3 .... 114 C8
Garden House La WF3 .... 120 A8
Garden La Bradford BD9 .... 54 F3
Knottingley WF11 .... 127 A5
Ripponden HX6 .... 132 C3
Garden Par [1] WF15 .... 117 A5
Garden Pl Dewsbury WF13 .... 117 F1
Sutton in CB20 .... 16 E5
Garden Rd HD6 .... 115 A4
Garden St
[6] Batley WF16 .... 117 D3
Castleford WF10 .... 124 D6
Castleford WF10 .... 125 A6
Dewsbury WF13 .... 138 E5
[1] Haworth BD22 .... 51 D7
Huddersfield HD1 .... 153 F4
Normanton WF6 .... 123 B2
Todmorden OL14 .... 108 B6
Wakefield WF1 .... 216 A2
Garden St N HX3 .... 203 F4

Garden Terr Bradford BD9 .... 55 A3
Crigglestone WF4 .... 159 E4
Denby Dale HD8 .... 191 F5
[1] Hebden Bridge HX7 .... 89 A3
Garden View Bingley BD16 .... 37 C3
Liversedge WF15 .... 117 A6
Garden View Ct LS8 .... 44 B1
Garden Village LS25 .... 84 A6
Garden Wlk [8] WF15 .... 117 A5
Gardener's Sq HX3 .... 114 C8
Gardeners Ct LS10 .... 215 D4
Gardens Rd WF3 .... 138 F5
Gardens St BD9 .... 54 F4
Gardens The Bingley BD16 .... 37 D3
Halifax HX1 .... 203 E1
Middleton LS10 .... 99 C4
Morley LS27 .... 97 F2
Pudsey LS28 .... 57 C3
Gardiner Row BD4 .... 75 B3
Garfield Ave BD8 .... 55 B2
Garfield Pl HD7 .... 168 F4
Garfield St Bradford BD15 .... 54 A1
[17] Halifax HX1 .... 92 A1
Todmorden OL14 .... 86 C1
Garforth Ave BD20 .... 17 C6
Garforth Barleyhill
Infants Sch LS25 .... 82 E7
Garforth Cl WF6 .... 122 E3
Garforth Com Coll LS25 .... 82 E5
Garforth Dr WF6 .... 122 E3
Garforth Golf Course LS15 .... 63 E3
Garforth Green Lane
Primary Sch LS25 .... 83 B6
Garforth Infants Sch LS25 .... 82 E7
Garforth Rd BD21 .... 35 E8
Garforth St Bradford BD15 .... 54 A1
Huddersfield HD4 .... 171 C7
Garforth Sta LS25 .... 82 F8
Gargrave App LS9 .... 207 F1
Gargrave Ct HD6 .... 135 D7
Gargrave Cres WF9 .... 181 C6
Gargrave Ct LS9 .... 207 F1
Gargrave Pl
Hemsworth WF9 .... 181 C6
Leeds LS9 .... 207 F1
Wakefield WF2 .... 141 C5
Garibaldi St BD3 .... 75 E7
Garland Dr LS15 .... 81 D8
Garlick St HD6 .... 135 E6
Garmil Head La WF9 .... 162 F5
Garmil La WF4 .... 162 F6
Garmont Mews LS7 .... 204 A2
Garmont Rd LS7 .... 204 A2
Garner La Honley HD7 .... 171 D4
Kirkburton HD8 .... 173 D8
Garnet Ave LS11 .... 214 C3
Garnet Cres LS11 .... 214 C3
Garnet Gr LS11 .... 214 C3
Garnet La LS24 .... 48 F8
Garnet Pl LS11 .... 214 C3
Garnet Rd LS11 .... 214 C3
Garnet Terr LS11 .... 214 C3
Garnet View LS11 .... 214 C3
Garnett St Batley WF13 .... 117 F3
Bradford BD3 .... 201 D3
Hebden Bridge HX7 .... 89 A3
Otley LS21 .... 23 B8
Garrett Cl HD8 .... 174 F2
Garsdale Ave BD10 .... 56 C7
Garsdale Cres BD17 .... 38 C4
Garsdale Fold LS22 .... 13 A1
Garsdale Gr WF1 .... 142 F8
Garside Av HD4 .... 154 B2
Garth Ave Collingham LS22 .... 29 C8
Leeds LS17 .... 43 B1
Normanton WF6 .... 144 A8
Garth Barn Cl BD9 .... 55 A4
Garth Cl LS17 .... 43 B1
Garth End LS22 .... 29 B8
Garth Gr LS29 .... 22 A4
Garth Land Way BD4 .... 75 C3
Garth La LS17 .... 43 B1
Garth Terr LS9 .... 80 A7
Garth The Collingham LS22 .... 29 B8
Leeds LS17 .... 83 A7
Leeds LS9 .... 212 B3
Garth Wlk LS17 .... 43 C1
Garthwaite Mount LS15 .... 54 82
Garton Ave LS9 .... 80 A7
Garton Dr BD10 .... 56 D5
Garton Gr LS9 .... 80 A7
Garton Rd LS9 .... 80 A7
Garton Terr LS9 .... 80 A7
Garton View LS9 .... 80 A7
Garvey View BD5 .... 74 E4
Garwick Terr [9] HX4 .... 134 D7
Gas St [3] BD22 .... 51 D7
Gas Works La
Boston Spa LS23 .... 30 F7
Elland HX5 .... 134 F7
Gas Works Rd
Keighley BD21 .... 35 F7
Sowerby Bridge HX6 .... 112 D4
Gascoigne Ave LS15 .... 63 D6
Gascoigne Ct LS15 .... 63 E6
Gascoigne Rd
Barwick in E LS15 .... 63 D6
East Ardsley WF3 .... 99 E1
Gascoigne View LS15 .... 63 D6
Gaskell Dr WF2 .... 141 A2
Gaskell St WF2 .... 142 A5

Gasson St HD3 .... 153 A4
Gasworks St
  Huddersfield HD1 .... 154 B7
  Liversedge WF15 .... 117 B4
Gate Foot La HD8 .... 190 C5
Gate Head Elland HX4 .... 133 F6
  Marsden HD7 .... 169 B4
Gate Head La Elland HX4 ... 133 F6
  Holmfirth HD7 .... 200 A8
Gate Way Dr LS19 .... 40 A6
Gatefield Mount BD6 .... 94 B6
Gatehead Bank HD7 .... 169 B5
Gatehouse Enterprise Ctr
  HD1 .... 153 F3
Gateland Dr LS17 .... 44 E4
Gateland La LS17 .... 44 E4
Gateon House La LS17 .... 28 B4
Gatesgarth Cres HD3 .... 135 A1
Gateway BD16 .... 36 B1
Gateways WF1 .... 121 C5
Gateways Girls' Prep
  & High Sch LS17 .... 27 A6
Gathorne Cl LS8 .... 207 F3
Gathorne St Bradford BD7 .. 74 B4
  Brighouse HD6 .... 115 B3
  Leeds LS8 .... 207 E3
Gathorne Terr LS8 .... 207 E3
Gauk St Brotherton WF11 ... 126 C8
  Fairburn WF11 .... 105 A4
Gaukroger La HX3 .... 203 F1
Gauxholme Fold OL14 .... 107 F3
Gavin Cl BD3 .... 75 E7
Gaw La BD23 .... 1 F8
Gawcliffe Rd BD18 .... 55 C7
Gawthorpe Ave BD16 .... 37 A5
Gawthorpe Dr BD16 .... 37 A5
Gawthorpe Green La HD8 ... 155 E6
Gawthorpe Jun & Inf Sch
  WF5 .... 119 C1
Gawthorpe La Bingley BD16 . 37 A4
  Kirkheaton HD8 .... 155 D6
  Ossett WF5 .... 119 E2
  Wakefield WF2 .... 120 A2
Gay La LS21 .... 23 A7
Gayle Cl BD12 .... 94 C2
Gaynor St BD8 .... 74 D8
Gaythorn Terr HX3 .... 93 C1
Gaythorne Rd Bradford BD5 . 74 E3
  Bradford, Haigh Fold BD2 .. 56 C2
Gaythorne Terr ⓯ BD14 ... 73 C4
Geary Cl WF2 .... 141 D8
Geary Dr WF2 .... 141 D8
Geecroft La LS22 .... 12 B4
Geelong Cl BD12 .... 55 F3
Gelder Croft WF2 .... 141 D8
Gelder Cl WF2 .... 141 D8
Gelder La LS12 .... 209 F3
Gelder Terr HD5 .... 154 C5
Gelderd Cl LS12 .... 213 D4
Gelderd La LS12 .... 213 D4
Gelderd Pl LS12 .... 210 B2
Gelderd Rd Batley WF17 .... 97 C5
  Gildersome LS27 .... 97 C5
  Leeds LS12 .... 213 D3
Gelderd Trad Est LS12 ...... 210 B1
General Infmy
  at Leeds The LS1 .... 206 B1
Geneva Gr WF1 .... 216 C3
Genista Dr LS10 .... 99 D8
Gentian Ct WF2 .... 141 E8
George Ave HD2 .... 153 E8
George Buckley Ct WF9 .... 182 A2
George & Crown Yd WF1 ... 216 B2
George La Notton WF4 ...... 178 E6
  Rippenden HX4 .... 132 B2
George Sq ⑤ HX1 .... 203 E3
George St Addingham LS29 . 6 F8
  ⑤ Baildon BD17 .... 38 C4
  Batley WF17 .... 118 C4
  Batley, Heckmondwike
  WF16 .... 117 D4
  Bradford BD1 .... 201 C2
  Brighouse HD6 .... 115 A1
  Brighouse HD6 .... 115 C2
  Brighouse, Hipperholme
  HX3 .... 114 D7
  Cleckheaton BD19 .... 116 D8
  Denholme BD13 .... 52 D1
  Dewsbury WF13 .... 139 C8
  Dewsbury, Dewsbury Moor
  WF13 .... 138 F8
  Dewsbury, Ravensthorpe
  WF13 .... 138 E5
  Elland HX5 .... 134 F6
  ⑥ Elland, West Vale HX4 . 134 D7
  Featherstone WF7 .... 145 C5
  Featherstone, Streethouse
  WF7 .... 144 D5
  Halifax HX1 .... 203 E3
  Hebden Bridge HX7 .... 110 E8
  Hemsworth WF9 .... 181 E6
  Horbury WF4 .... 141 B1
  ⑦ Huddersfield HD1 ...... 154 A6
  Huddersfield, Lindley HD3 . 135 B1
  Huddersfield, Milnsbridge
  HD3 .... 153 B5
  Huddersfield, Paddock Brow
  HD1 .... 153 E4
  Kirkburton HD8 .... 173 F7
  ⑥ Liversedge WF15 .... 117 A4
  Lofthouse Gate WF1 .... 121 B5
  Mapplewell S75 .... 178 B1
  Normanton WF6 .... 140 D7
  Ossett WF5 .... 140 D7
  Ryhill WF4 .... 162 B2

George St continued
  Shipley BD18 .... 54 F8
  South Hiendley S72 .... 180 D6
  Sowerby Bridge HX6 .... 112 B3
  Thornton BD13 .... 72 D6
  ⑬ Todmorden OL14 .... 108 B5
  Wakefield WF1 .... 216 B2
  Yeadon LS19 .... 40 B4
George's Sq
  Cullingworth BD13 .... 52 C6
  Keighley BD21 .... 35 B6
George's St HX3 .... 91 F3
George-a-Green Rd WF2 ... 141 E4
Georgia Mews WF5 .... 140 F4
Geraldton Ave BD2 .... 55 E3
Gerard Ave LS27 .... 97 F4
Gernhill Ave HD2 .... 135 F5
Gerrard St HX1 .... 203 D3
Gervase Rd WF4 .... 141 A2
Ghyll Beck Dr Otley LS21 .. 22 D6
  Yeadon LS19 .... 40 E3
Ghyll Cl BD20 .... 17 C5
Ghyll Mews LS29 .... 8 A3
Ghyll Mount LS19 .... 39 F6
Ghyll Rd LS6 .... 59 A6
Ghyll Royd LS20 .... 39 E7
Ghyll Royd Sch LS29 .... 7 F3
Ghyll The Huddersfield HD2 . 136 A4
  Shipley BD16 .... 54 A8
Ghyll Way BD23 .... 4 A8
Ghyll Wood LS29 .... 7 E3
Ghyll Wood Dr BD16 .... 54 A8
Ghyllbank BD20 .... 5 E2
Ghyllroyd Ave BD11 .... 96 B5
Ghyllroyd Dr BD11 .... 96 B4
Gib Cotts HD7 .... 172 A2
Gib La HD8 .... 175 A2
Gibb La HX2 .... 91 B3
Gibbet St HX1, HX2 .... 202 A3
Gibraltar Ave HX1 .... 202 A2
Gibraltar Island Rd LS10 .. 215 F4
Gibraltar Rd Halifax HX1 ... 202 A2
  Pudsey LS28 .... 76 B7
Gibraltar Terr BD20 .... 16 C5
Gibriding La HD7 .... 187 F3
Gibson Ave WF2 .... 141 F7
Gibson Cl LS15 .... 81 C7
Gibson Dr LS15 .... 81 C7
Gibson Mill HX7 .... 88 C8
Gibson St Bradford BD3 .... 75 B6
  Huddersfield HD3 .... 153 C7
  ⑥ Todmorden OL14 .... 108 C5
Gilbert Chase LS5 .... 59 A3
Gilbert Cl LS5 .... 59 B3
Gilbert Gr HD4 .... 153 D3
Gilbert Mount LS5 .... 59 B3
Gilbert St LS28 .... 57 D2
Gilcar St WF5 .... 123 D4
Gildersome Birchfield
  Jun & Inf Sch LS27 ..... 97 C6
Gildersome La LS27 .... 77 B1
Gildersome Primary Sch
  LS27 .... 97 C7
Gildersome Spur LS27 ...... 97 D5
Gilead Rd HD3 .... 152 E7
Giles Hill La HX3 .... 93 A7
Giles St Bradford BD6 .... 74 A1
  Bradford BD5 .... 201 A1
  Holmfirth HD7 .... 188 E8
Gill Bank Rd LS29 .... 8 A6
Gill Beck Cl BD17 .... 38 E4
Gill Cl LS29 .... 6 D8
Gill La Guiseley LS19 .... 39 F4
  Holmfirth HD7 .... 188 E2
  Nesfield LS29 .... 9 C2
  Yeadon, Henshaw LS19 .... 40 A5
  Yeadon, Westfield LS19 ... 39 F4
Gill Sike Ave WF2 .... 141 F4
Gill Sike Bglws WF2 .... 141 F4
Gill Sike Gr WF2 .... 141 F4
Gill Sike House WF2 .... 141 F4
Gill Sike Rd WF2 .... 141 F4
Gill St WF1 .... 216 B2
Gill's Bldgs WF2 .... 142 A5
⑥ Gill's Ct HX1 .... 203 E3
Gill's Yd WF1 .... 216 B3
Gillann St WF11 .... 127 A4
Gillett Dr LS26 .... 100 F5
Gillett La LS26 .... 100 F5
Gilling Ave LS25 .... 83 B8
Gillingham Gn BD4 .... 75 E3
Gilroyd Cres WF4 .... 159 E6
Gillrene Ave BD15 .... 53 D4
Gilroyd La HD7 .... 170 D8
Gilroyd Pl ⑦ LS27 .... 98 A4
Gilroyd Terr LS27 .... 98 C4
Gills The Morley LS27 .... 98 C4
  Otley LS21 .... 11 A2
Gilstone Dr BD22 .... 51 D6
Gillygate WF8 .... 146 D8
Gilmour St ⑤ HX3 .... 92 B1
Gilpin Pl LS12 .... 210 A2
Gilpin St Bradford BD3 ...... 75 B7
  Leeds LS12 .... 210 A2
Gilpin Terr LS12 .... 210 A2
Gilpin View LS12 .... 210 A2
Gilroyd Rise BD7 .... 74 B7
Gilstead Ct BD16 .... 37 C3
Gilstead Dr BD16 .... 37 C3
Gilstead La BD16 .... 37 C3
Gilstead Middle Sch BD16 . 37 C4
Gilstead Way LS29 .... 8 B5
Gilthwaites Cres HD8 ...... 192 A7
Gilthwaites First Sch HD8 . 192 A7
Gilthwaites Gr HD8 .... 192 A6

Gilthwaites La HD8 .... 192 A7
Gilthwaites Top HD8 .... 192 A7
Gilynda Cl BD8 .... 73 E7
Gin La WF7 .... 144 C4
Ginnel The LS17 .... 28 C2
Gipsy Hill LS26 .... 101 B6
⑤ Gipsy La Leeds LS11 .... 99 A7
  Middleton LS11 .... 99 A7
  Rothwell LS26 .... 101 B6
  Wakefield WF2 .... 160 E7
  Woolley WF4 .... 177 F6
Gipsy Mead LS26 .... 101 B6
Gipsy St BD3 .... 75 B8
Gipton App LS9 .... 61 D1
Gipton Ave LS8 .... 207 E3
Gipton Gate E LS9 .... 208 C3
Gipton Gate W LS9 .... 208 B3
Gipton Sq LS9 .... 61 D1
Gipton St LS8 .... 207 E3
Gipton Wood Ave LS8 ...... 61 B5
Gipton Wood Cres LS8 ..... 61 B5
Gipton Wood Gr LS8 .... 61 B5
Gipton Wood Pl LS8 .... 61 B5
Gipton Wood Primary Sch
  LS8 .... 208 C3
Gipton Wood Rd LS8 .... 61 B5
Girlington First Sch BD8 ... 74 A8
Girlington Rd BD8 .... 55 A1
Girnhill Infants Sch WF7 . 145 C4
Girnhill La WF7 .... 145 C4
Gisbourne Rd HD2 .... 136 E5
Gisburn Rd WF1 .... 142 F8
Gisburn St BD21 .... 35 B8
Gissing Rd WF2 .... 141 D4
Glade The Pudsey LS28 ...... 57 A2
  Scarcroft LS14 .... 45 B7
Gladstonbury Ave WF1 .... 121 F1
Gladstone Cres
  ⑤ Bacup OL13 .... 106 A2
  Yeadon LS19 .... 40 B5
Gladstone Ct ⑤ WF13 .... 118 A1
Gladstone Rd
  ⑱ Halifax HX1 .... 202 C3
  Keighley BD21 .... 35 A7
Gladstone St Bacup OL13 . 106 A2
  Bingley BD16 .... 36 F2
  Bradford BD15 .... 54 B1
  Bradford, Barkerend BD3 .. 75 C7
  ③ Cleckheaton BD19 ...... 116 D7
  ③ Elland HX4 .... 134 A4
  Featherstone WF7 .... 145 D7
  Keighley BD21 .... 35 B6
  Normanton WF6 .... 123 C3
  ⑤ Pudsey LS28 .... 57 D3
  Queensbury BD13 .... 72 F1
  ⑩ Todmorden OL14 .... 86 B1
Gladstone Terr
  Castleford WF10 .... 124 E8
  Morley LS27 .... 98 A4
  Pudsey LS28 .... 57 F8
Gladstone View HX3 .... 113 E3
Gladwin St WF17 .... 118 B4
Glaisdale Cl BD20 .... 17 E8
Glaisdale Ct BD15 .... 54 A3
Glaisdale Gr HX3 .... 114 D7
Glamis Cl LS25 .... 83 B8
Glanville Terr LS26 .... 100 E5
Glasshoughton Infant Sch
  WF10 .... 124 F7
Glasshouse St LS10 .... 212 A1
Glasshouse View LS10 ..... 99 B4
Glastonbury Dr HD3 .... 152 F5
Glazier Rd BD13 .... 72 C2
Gleanings Ave HX2 .... 112 C7
Gleanings Dr HX2 .... 112 C7
Glebe Ave LS5 .... 59 B4
Glebe Cl HD8 .... 175 D7
Glebe Field Chase LS22 .... 13 D6
Glebe Field Cl LS22 .... 13 D6
Glebe Field Croft LS22 ..... 13 D6
Glebe Field Dr LS22 .... 13 D6
Glebe Field Garth LS22 .... 13 D6
Glebe Field Holt LS22 ...... 13 D6
Glebe Gate WF12 .... 139 F1
Glebe La WF11 .... 126 F4
Glebe Mount LS28 .... 76 E6
Glebe Pl LS5 .... 59 B4
Glebe St Castleford WF10 . 124 D7
  Huddersfield HD1 .... 153 E7
  Normanton WF6 .... 144 C8
  Pudsey LS28 .... 76 E6
Glebe Terr Leeds LS16 ...... 59 B6
Glebelands WF11 .... 127 C4
Glebelands Cl LS25 .... 82 F6
Glebelands Dr LS6 .... 59 D6
Gledcliffe HX3 .... 203 F4
Gleddings Cl HX3 .... 113 A3
Gleddings Preparatory Sch
  The HX3 .... 113 A3
Gledhill Rd BD3 .... 75 B6
Gledhill St ⓶ OL14 .... 108 B6
Gledhill Terr ⑦ WF13 .... 138 E8
Gledholt Bank HD1 .... 153 E5
Gledholt Rd HD1 .... 153 E6
Gledhow Ave LS8 .... 204 C4
Gledhow Ct LS7 .... 204 B3
Gledhow Dr BD22 .... 51 C4

Gledhow Grange View
  LS8 .... 204 C3
Gledhow Grange Wlk LS8 . 204 C3
Gledhow La LS7, LS8 .... 204 B3
Gledhow Mount LS8 .... 207 E2
Gledhow Park Ave LS7 ..... 204 B2
Gledhow Park Cres LS7 .... 204 B2
Gledhow Park Dr LS7 ...... 204 B2
Gledhow Park Gr LS7 ...... 204 B2
Gledhow Park Rd LS7 ...... 204 B2
Gledhow Park View LS7 ... 204 B2

Gledhow Pl LS8 .... 207 E2
Gledhow Primary Sch
  LS8 .... 204 C4
Gledhow Rd LS8 .... 207 E2
Gledhow Rise LS8 .... 61 B6
Gledhow Terr LS8 .... 207 E2
Gledhow Towers LS8 ...... 204 B3
Gledhow Valley Rd
  LS17, LS7, LS8 .... 204 B2
Gledhow Wood Ave LS8 .. 204 C3
Gledhow Wood Cl LS8 ..... 204 C3
Gledhow Wood Ct LS8 .... 61 A5
Gledhow Wood Gr LS8 .... 204 C3
Gledhow Wood Rd LS8 ... 204 C2
Gledmow Lane End LS7 ... 204 A3
Glen Ave Batley WF17 ..... 118 C6
  Todmorden OL14 .... 107 F7
Glen Ct HD10 .... 136 B6
Glen Dene Menston LS29 .. 22 B4
  Shipley BD16 .... 53 F7
Glen Field Ave HD2 .... 136 F3
Glen Garth BD21 .... 35 C6
Glen Gr LS27 .... 98 B3
Glen Lee La BD21 .... 35 D5
Glen Mount Menston LS29 . 22 B3
  Morley LS27 .... 98 B3
  Shipley BD16 .... 53 F7
Glen Mount Cl HX3 .... 91 E2
Glen Rd Baildon BD17 ...... 37 D4
  Leeds LS16 .... 59 C7
  Morley LS27 .... 98 C3
Glen Rise BD17 .... 38 A2
Glen Side Rd HD7 .... 170 A8
Glen Terr Brighouse HX3 .. 114 C7
  Halifax HX1 .... 203 D1
Glen The OL14 .... 107 F7
Glen View Halifax HX1 .... 203 D1
  Harden BD16 .... 36 B1
Glen View Rd Bingley BD16 . 37 C5
  Hebden Bridge HX7 .... 88 E4
  Shepley HD8 .... 174 A2
Glen View St OL14 .... 86 B1
Glen Way BD16 .... 36 C6
Glenaire BD18 .... 38 A1
Glenaire Dr BD17 .... 38 A1
Glenaire First Sch BD17 ... 38 A2
Glenbrook Dr BD7 .... 73 F7
Glencoe Cl LS25 .... 102 F8
Glencoe Cres LS25 .... 102 F8
Glencoe Croft LS25 .... 102 F8
Glencoe Terr Kippax LS25 . 102 F8
  Liversedge WF15 .... 117 B3
Glencoe View LS9 .... 212 C2
Glendale LS14 .... 45 C5
Glendale Ave LS25 .... 82 F6
Glendale Cl BD6 .... 94 A7
Glendare Ave BD7 .... 73 F6
Glendare Rd BD7 .... 73 F6
Glendare Terr BD7 .... 73 F6
Glendorne Dr HD5 .... 137 C1
Glendower Pk LS16 .... 42 D2
Gleneagles Cl BD4 .... 95 B8
Gleneagles Rd
  Huddersfield WF2 .... 124 D1
  Leeds LS17 .... 43 B4
Gleneagles Way HD2 ...... 135 F3
Glenfield BD18 .... 54 D6
Glenfield Ave Bradford BD6 . 94 D8
  Wetherby LS22 .... 13 F6
Glenfield Mount ⑧ BD6 . 94 D8
Glenfields LS27 .... 158 D5
Glenfields Cl WF4 .... 158 D5
Glenholm Rd BD17 .... 38 C3
Glenholm Rd W BD17 ...... 38 C2
Glenholme BD18 .... 38 E1
Glenholme Heath HX1 .... 202 A3
Glenholme Rd
  Bradford BD8 .... 55 B1
  Pudsey LS28 .... 57 D2
Glenholme Terr WF5 ...... 119 C1
Glenhurst BD4 .... 75 D1
Glenhurst Ave BD21 .... 35 C5
Glenhurst Dr BD21 .... 35 D5
Glenhurst Gr BD21 .... 35 D5
Glenhurst Rd BD18 .... 54 D8
Glenlea Cl LS25 .... 58 A3
Glenlea Gdns LS25 .... 58 A3
Glenlee Rd BD7 .... 73 F7
Glenlow Rd WF12 .... 118 F3
Glenlyon Ave BD20 .... 18 A1
Glenlyon Dr BD20 .... 18 A1
Glenmere Mount LS19 .... 40 D7
Glenmore Cl BD2 .... 56 C1
Glenmore Ct LS16 .... 24 E3
Glenn Way WF4 .... 162 A8
Glenroyd Dr BD10 .... 56 C6
Glenroyd Ave BD6 .... 94 D7
Glenroyd Cl LS28 .... 76 D7
Glenroyd Dr LS28 .... 76 D7
Glensdale Gr LS9 .... 212 C3
Glensdale Mount LS9 ...... 212 C3
Glensdale Rd LS9 .... 212 C3
Glensdale St LS9 .... 212 C3
Glensdale Terr LS9 .... 80 A7
Glenside Ave BD18 .... 38 B1
Glenside Cl ⑧ BD18 .... 38 B1
Glenside Rd BD18 .... 38 E1
Glenstone Gr BD7 .... 73 F7
Glenthorpe Ave LS9 .... 80 A8
Glenthorpe Cres LS9 .... 80 A8
Glenthorpe Terr LS9 .... 80 A8
Glenton Sq BD9 .... 55 A2
Glenview Ave BD9 .... 54 E3
Glenview Cl BD18 .... 54 C7
Glenview Dr BD18 .... 54 C6
Glenview Gr BD18 .... 54 C7

Glenview Gr BD18 .... 54 D2
Glenview Rd BD18 .... 54 D2
Glenview Terr BD18 .... 54 D2
Glenwood Ave BD17 .... 37 E3
Global Ave LS11 .... 213 E3
Globe Ct WF15 .... 117 B4
Globe Fold BD8 .... 74 C8
Globe Rd LS11 .... 211 D2
Glossop Gr LS6 .... 206 B4
Glossop Mount LS6 .... 206 B4
Glossop St LS6 .... 206 B4
Glossop View LS6 .... 206 B4
Gloucester Ave
  Bradford BD3 .... 56 D7
  Silsden BD20 .... 5 C1
Gloucester Ct LS12 .... 210 B4
Gloucester Gr WF2 .... 141 D5
Gloucester Pl WF2 .... 141 D5
Gloucester Rd
  Bingley BD16 .... 37 B2
  Wakefield WF2 .... 141 D5
Gloucester Terr LS12 ...... 210 B3
Glover Ct BD5 .... 74 E4
Glover Way LS11 .... 214 B2
Glovershaw La BD16 .... 37 E4
Glusburn County Primary
  Sch BD20 .... 16 C6
Glydegate BD5 .... 201 B2
Glyndon Ct HD6 .... 136 B8
Glynn Terr BD8 .... 74 B8
Gobind Marg BD3 .... 201 D3
Godfrey Rd HX3 .... 113 C2
Godfrey St BD8 .... 73 D2
Godley Branch Rd HX3 .... 113 C8
Godley Ct S71 .... 179 D4
Godley Gdns HX3 .... 92 F1
Godley La Halifax HX3 ..... 113 E8
  Northowram HX3 .... 92 F3
Godley Rd HX3 .... 203 F4
Godley Way HX3 .... 203 F4
Godley St HX3 .... 179 C4
Godly Cl HX3 .... 132 C8
Godwin St BD1 .... 201 B3
Goff Well La BD21 .... 35 C2
Gog Hill HX5 .... 134 F7
Goit Side Bradford BD1 .... 201 A3
  Halifax HX2 .... 90 E4
Goit Stock La BD16 .... 53 B8
Goit Stock Terr BD16 .... 53 B8
Golcar Brow Rd HD7 ...... 170 C2
Golcar Jun & Inf Sch HD7 . 152 D4
Goldcrest Ave ⑥ BD8 ..... 73 B7
Goldcrest Ct HD4 .... 171 E6
Golden Acre Cres LS16 . 25 A3
Golden Acre Pk & Gdns
  LS16 .... 42 C6
Golden Bank LS18 .... 41 C3
Golden Butts Rd LS29 ...... 8 C4
Golden Sq WF4 .... 141 B1
Golden Terr LS12 .... 78 A4
Golden View Dr BD21 ...... 35 F6
Goldfields Cl ⑪ HX4 ..... 134 B8
Goldfields Vie ⑫ HX4 .... 134 B8
Goldfields Way HX4 .... 134 B8
Goldington Ave HD3 .... 153 A8
Goldington Dr HD3 .... 153 A8
Golf Ave HX2 .... 112 C7
Golf Cres HX2 .... 112 C7
Golf La LS27 .... 118 E8
Gomersal First Sch BD19 . 96 B1
Gomersal Jun Sch BD19 ... 117 A7
Gomersal Middle Sch
  BD19 .... 96 B1
Gomersal Rd HD5 .... 117 C6
Gondal Ct BD5 .... 74 C3
Good Hope Cl WF4 .... 123 D3
Goodcomb Pl LS25 .... 83 C2
Gooder Ave S71 .... 179 C3
Gooder La HD6 .... 115 B1
Gooder St HD6 .... 115 A2
Goodman St LS10 .... 212 B1
Goodrick La LS17 .... 43 F2
Goodwin House ⑥ BD13 . 72 E1
Goodwin Pl HD2 .... 136 F5
Goodwin Rd LS12 .... 209 F2
Goodwood LS29 .... 7 F6
Goodwood Ave LS25 .... 83 A2
Goody Cross LS26 .... 82 C2
Goody Cross La LS26 .... 82 C2
Goose Cote La
  Haworth BD22 .... 34 E2
  Oxenhope BD22 .... 34 E3
Goose Cote Way BD22 .... 34 E3
Goose Eye BD22 .... 34 B6
Goose Gn HD7 .... 189 A5
Goose Hill WF16 .... 117 D4
Goose La LS20 .... 21 C1
Goose St Leeds LS14 .... 59 F6
Goosacre Ave S63 .... 194 C1
Goosefield Rise LS25 .... 82 D6
Goosehill La ⑤ WF4 .... 143 E7
Gooshill Rd WF9 .... 144 A8
Goosehill St ⓶ WF9 .... 183 B1
Gordale Cl Batley WF17 ... 118 B5
  Bradford BD4 .... 75 F3
Gordon Ave WF5 .... 140 D6
Gordon Dr LS6 .... 59 F6
Gordon La ⑤ Leeds LS6 ... 59 F6
  South Elmsall WF9 .... 182 F2
Gordon St Bradford BD5 .. 201 C1
  ⑦ Bradford, Clayton BD14 . 73 B4
  East Ardsley WF3 .... 120 E8
  Elland HX5 .... 134 F6
  Featherstone WF7 .... 145 D7
  Halifax HX3 .... 92 B2
  ⑯ Haworth BD22 .... 51 E8
  Ilkley LS29 .... 8 B4
  Keighley BD21 .... 35 B7

Gordon St continued
Slaithwaite HD7 .... 170 A8
Sowerby Bridge HX6 .... 112 A3
Sutton in C BD20 .... 16 D5
🔟 Todmorden OL14 .... 108 C5
Wakefield WF1 .... 142 F2
Gordon Terr Bradford BD10 .. 39 B1
Knottingley WF11 .... 127 B3
Leeds LS6 .... 59 F6
Slaithwaite HD7 .... 152 D2
Gordon View LS6 .... 59 F6
Gordonsfield WF7 .... 163 F5
Goring Park Ave WF5 ... 141 A4
Gorple Rd BD10 .... 66 A5
Gorse Ave BD17 .... 37 E1
Gorse Lea 🟥 LS10 .... 99 D8
Gorse Rd HD3 .... 153 C6
Gorton St WF9 .... 163 B5
Gosling La HX4 .... 132 F2
Gosport Cl HD3 .... 152 A8
Gosport La Elland HD3 .. 152 A8
Elland, Sowood Green HX4 .. 133 F1
Gosside Gr WF6 .... 123 D3
Gothic Mount WF7 .... 145 A8
Gothic St BD13 .... 72 E1
Gott St BD22 .... 51 F8
Gott's Terr BD20 .... 18 A2
Gotts Park Ave LS12 .... 58 F1
Gotts Park View LS12 .... 59 A2
Gotts Rd LS12 .... 210 C3
Gough La HX6 .... 132 B7
Goulbourne St BD21 .... 35 B6
Governor's Yd WF1 .... 216 C3
Leeds LS2 .... 212 A4
Grace Leather La WF17 .. 118 E5
Grace St Keighley BD21 .. 35 D7
Leeds LS1 .... 211 D4
Gracechurch St BD8 ...... 74 D8
Gracey La BD6 .... 73 F1
Grafton Cl Baildon BD17 .. 38 D4
Knottingley WF11 .... 126 F5
Grafton Pl HX3 .... 92 A3
Grafton Rd BD21 .... 35 A5
Grafton Sch LS6 .... 206 B3
Grafton St Batley WF17 .. 118 D3
Bradford BD5 .... 201 B1
Castleford WF10 .... 124 E5
Keighley BD21 .... 35 B5
Leeds LS7 .... 207 D1
Grafton Villas LS15 .... 62 D4
Graham Ave Leeds LS4 ... 205 D3
Upton WF9 .... 183 D8
Graham Dr WF10 .... 125 B7
Graham Gr LS4 .... 205 D3
Graham Mount LS4 .... 205 D3
Graham St Bradford BD9 .. 55 A2
Huddersfield HD1 .... 153 F5
Leeds LS4 .... 205 D3
Graham Terr LS4 .... 205 D3
Graham View LS4 .... 205 D3
Graham Wlk LS27 .... 97 D7
Grain St BD5 .... 74 B2
Gramfield Rd HD4 .... 153 C3
Grammar School St BD1 .. 201 B4
Grampian Ave WF2 .... 141 E3
Grampian Cl HD8 .... 173 F3
Granby Ave LS6 .... 59 D5
Granby Cl LS6 .... 59 D5
Granby Dr BD20 .... 18 E1
Granby Gr LS6 .... 59 D5
Granby La BD20 .... 18 E1
Granby Mount 🟥 LS6 ... 59 D5
Granby Rd LS6 .... 59 D5
Granby St Bradford BD4 .. 201 C2
Leeds LS6 .... 59 D5
🟥 Queensbury BD13 .... 72 E1
Granby Terr LS6 .... 59 D5
Granby View LS6 .... 59 D5
Grand Arc LS1 .... 211 F4
Grand Cross Rd HD5 ...... 154 E6
Grand Stand WF2 .... 152 B5
Grand Stand Rd WF2 ...... 120 F5
Grand Theatre LS1 .... 211 F4
Grandage Terr BD8 .... 74 B8
Grandmere Pl 🟥 HX3 ... 113 B4
Grange Ave Batley WF17 .. 118 B3
Birkenshaw BD4 .... 96 A8
Bradford, Lower Grange
  BD15 .... 73 C8
Bradford, Thornbury BD3 .. 75 F8
Garforth LS25 .... 82 F6
Halifax HX2 .... 91 F5
Huddersfield HD2 .... 135 F1
Ilkley LS29 .... 8 A4
Leeds LS7 .... 207 E4
Marsden HD7 .... 169 A4
Menston LS29 .... 21 F5
Shipley BD18 .... 54 E8
South Elmsall WF9 .... 183 A3
Thorp Arch LS23 .... 15 A3
Yeadon LS19 .... 40 C6
Grange Bank HX3 .... 93 C6
Grange Bank Cl HD5 ..... 154 D7
Grange Castle LS19 .... 40 D6
Grange Cl Badsworth WF9 .. 164 G2
Bardsey LS17 .... 28 D4
Brierley S72 .... 180 F3
Elland HD3 .... 152 A8
Horsforth LS18 .... 57 F8
Knottingley WF11 .... 126 D4
Leeds LS10 .... 215 D4
Grange Cotts
Cleckheaton BD19 .... 116 C8
Marsden HD7 .... 169 A4

Grange Cres Dearne S63 .. 194 E1
Keighley BD20 .... 18 E2
Leeds LS7 .... 207 E4
Yeadon LS19 .... 40 C6
Grange Croft LS17 .... 43 C5
Grange Ct Badsworth WF9 .. 164 E2
Barwick in E LS15 .... 62 F6
Halifax HX3 .... 114 A4
Leeds, Alwoodley LS17 .... 43 C5
Leeds, Headingley Hill LS6 .. 59 F5
🟦 Shipley BD18 .... 54 A7
Grange Dr Bradford BD15 .. 73 C8
Emley HD8 .... 175 D8
Horsforth LS18 .... 57 F8
Ossett WF5 .... 140 F3
Grange Est LS29 .... 8 D4
Grange Farm Primary Sch
LS14 .... 61 F6
Grange Fields Mount 🟥
LS10 .... 99 F7
Grange Fields Rd LS10 .... 99 F6
Grange Fields Way LS10 .. 99 F6
Grange Gr Bradford BD3 .. 75 F8
Keighley BD20 .... 18 E1
Grange Holt LS17 .... 43 C5
Grange House S72 .... 180 F3
Grange Hts HX3 .... 114 A4
Grange La Brighouse HD6 .. 115 E2
Burghwallis DN6 .... 184 F3
Flockton WF4 .... 157 D4
Haworth BD22 .... 33 F3
Kippax LS25 .... 83 B2
Kirkburton HD8 .... 173 F3
Grange Middle Sch BD10 .. 18 E2
Grange Mount LS19 .... 40 C6
Grange Park Ave LS8 ...... 61 D5
Grange Park Cl
Kippax LS25 .... 103 A5
Leeds LS8 .... 61 D5
🟦 Morley LS27 .... 98 B7
Grange Park Cres LS8 ..... 61 D5
Grange Park Ct LS27 ...... 98 B7
Shipley BD16 .... 54 B8
Grange Park Gr LS8 .... 61 D5
Grange Park Mews
Leeds LS8 .... 61 D5
🟦 Morley LS27 .... 98 B7
Grange Park Pl LS8 .... 61 D5
Grange Park Rd Leeds LS8 .. 61 E5
Shipley BD16 .... 54 A7
Grange Park Rise LS8 ...... 61 D5
Grange Park Terr LS8 ...... 61 E5
Grange Park Way LS27 .. 98 B7
Grange Park Wlk LS8 .... 61 D5
Grange Pk Baildon BD17 .. 38 E3
Halifax HX3 .... 113 B3
Grange Rd Batley WF17 .. 118 A3
Batley, Chidswell WF17 .... 119 A4
Bingley BD16 .... 37 B4
Bradford BD3 .... 75 C8
Brierley S72 .... 180 F2
Burley in W LS29 .... 9 F1
Castleford WF10 .... 104 E1
Cleckheaton BD19 .... 116 C8
Farnhill BD20 .... 4 D1
Holme Chapel BB10 .... 85 A7
Huddersfield HD2 .... 152 E6
Keighley BD20 .... 18 E1
Leeds LS10 .... 215 D4
Royston S71 .... 179 B3
Steeton BD20 .... 17 A5
Yeadon LS19 .... 40 C6
Grange Rd First Sch BD7 .. 74 B5
Grange Rd The LS16 .... 42 B1
Grange Rise WF9 .... 181 D7
Grange Road Ind Est
WF17 .... 118 E4
Grange St 🔟 Halifax HX1 .. 92 A1
Keighley BD21 .... 35 D7
Wakefield WF2 .... 142 A5
Grange Terr Bradford BD5 .. 73 C8
Leeds LS7 .... 207 D4
Marsden HD7 .... 169 A4
🟦 Morley LS27 .... 98 B7
Pudsey LS28 .... 76 E8
Shipley BD18 .... 55 B6
Steeton BD20 .... 17 A5
Grange The Garforth LS25 .. 83 B7
Huddersfield HD5 .... 154 F7
Grange Upper Sch BD5 .. 74 B2
Grange Valley Rd WF17 .. 118 F4
Grange View Bradford BD3 .. 75 F8
Dewsbury WF13 .... 139 D1
Hemsworth WF9 .... 181 D6
Leeds LS7 .... 207 E4
Otley LS21 .... 10 E1
Pudsey LS28 .... 76 E8
Steeton BD20 .... 17 A5
Wetherby LS22 .... 13 E4
Grange View Gdns LS17 .. 44 F1
Grangefield Ave
Batley WF17 .... 118 B3
Burley in W LS29 .... 9 F1
Grangefield Ct LS25 .... 82 F7
Grangefield Ind Est LS28 .. 57 E1
Grangefield Rd LS28 .... 57 E1
Grangefields HD2 .... 135 C1
Grangeway Bradford BD3 .. 75 C8
Hemsworth WF9 .... 181 D7
Grangewood Ct Leeds LS16 .. 42 B1
Lofthouse Gate WF1 .... 121 D5
Grangewood Gdns LS16 .. 42 B1
Granhamthorpe LS13 ..... 58 C2
Granny Ave LS27 .... 98 C8
Granny Hall Gr HD6 ...... 114 F4
Granny Hall La HD6 .... 114 F4
Granny Hall Pk HD6 ...... 114 F4

Granny La Leeds LS12 .... 209 D1
Mirfield WF14 .... 138 B3
Grant Ave LS7 .... 207 E2
Grant St Bradford BD3 .. 201 D3
Keighley BD21 .... 35 A7
Oxenhope BD22 .... 51 C6
Grantham Pl Bradford BD7 .. 74 C5
Halifax HX1 .... 92 B2
Grantham Rd Bradford BD7 .. 74 C5
Halifax HX1 .... 92 B2
Grantham Terr BD7 .... 74 C5
Grantham Towers LS7 .... 207 E1
Grantley Pl HD2 .... 136 D5
Grantley St WF1 .... 216 C2
Grantley Way WF1 .... 216 C3
Granton Rd LS7 .... 204 A1
Granton St BD3 .... 75 C7
Granville Ave 🟦 WF8 .... 146 C8
Granville Mount LS21 ...... 22 F7
Granville Pl Bradford BD5 .. 54 B1
Otley LS21 .... 22 F7
Granville Rd Leeds LS14 .. 207 E1
Otley LS21 .... 22 F7
Granville St Bradford BD14 .. 73 C5
Castleford WF10 .... 124 C5
Dewsbury WF13 .... 139 B8
🟦 Elland HX5 .... 134 F6
Featherstone WF7 .... 145 C4
Keighley BD21 .... 35 B7
Liversedge WF15 .... 117 B3
Normanton WF6 .... 123 B2
Pudsey LS28 .... 76 C8
🟦 Pudsey, Stanningley LS28 77 D7
🟦 Todmorden OL14 ...... 108 A1
Granville Terr Bingley BD16 .. 37 A3
Guiseley LS20 .... 22 F2
Huddersfield HD1 .... 153 E5
Otley LS21 .... 22 F7
Shipley BD18 .... 55 B5
🟦 Yeadon LS19 .... 40 C7
Grape St Bradford BD15 .. 54 C1
Halifax HX1 .... 203 D3
🟦 Keighley BD21 .... 35 D8
Leeds LS10 .... 212 A1
Grasleigh Ave BD15 .... 54 A3
Grasleigh Way BD15 .... 53 F2
Grasmere Ave LS22 .... 13 C5
Grasmere Cl
Huddersfield HD1 .... 104 E1
Leeds LS12 .... 210 A2
Grasmere Cres S75 .... 178 A3
Grasmere Ct LS12 .... 210 A3
Grasmere Dr Elland HX5 .. 135 B7
Wetherby LS22 .... 13 C5
Grasmere Rd Batley WF12 .. 118 E2
Bradford BD2 .... 56 A3
Brighouse BD19 .... 94 E1
Knottingley WF11 .... 126 E2
Leeds LS12 .... 210 A3
Meltham HD7 .... 170 E1
Wakefield WF2 .... 141 E7
Grasscroft HD5 .... 154 F2
Grasscroft Ave HD7 .... 171 F4
Grasscroft Rd Honley HD7 .. 171 E4
Huddersfield HD1 .... 153 E7
Grasmere Rd HD1 .... 153 F7
Grassmoor Fold HD7 .... 172 A3
Gratrix La LS26 .... 112 C5
Grattan Rd 🟦 BD1 .... 74 D7
Graveleythorpe Rd LS15 .. 62 B1
Gravelyethorpe Rise 🟦
LS15 .... 62 B1
Gray Ave BD18 .... 55 D5
Gray Ct LS15 .... 81 D8
Gray Hall Cl HX4 .... 133 F3
Gray St WF15 .... 116 E4
Gray's Rd S71 .... 179 C1
Grayrigg Cl LS15 .... 80 E7
Grayrigg Ct LS15 .... 80 D7
Grayshon Dr BD6 .... 74 A2
Grayshon St 🟦 BD11 .... 96 E5
Grayson Court LS14 .... 59 B3
Grayson Hts LS14 .... 59 B3
Grayswood Cres BD4 ...... 75 D3
Grayswood Dr BD4 .... 75 D3
Great Albion St HX1 ...... 203 E3
Great Cross St BD1 .... 201 C2
Great Edge Rd HX2 .... 111 F6
Great George St
🟥 Leeds LS1 .... 211 D4
Leeds LS1 .... 211 D4
Great Horton Middle Sch
BD7 .... 74 A4
Great Horton Rd
Bradford, Great Horton BD7 .. 74 B5
Bradford, Idle Moor BD10 .. 56 C8
Bradford, Lidget Green BD7 .. 74 A4
Bradford, Oakenshaw BD12 .. 94 F4
Bradford, Ravenscliffe BD2 .. 56 D3
Bradford, Wyke BD12 .... 94 C2
Brighouse, Clifton HD6 .... 115 F2
Brighouse, Hove Edge HD6 .. 114 E5
Burley in W LS29 .... 9 F1
Castleford, Castleford Ings
  WF10 .... 103 F1
Castleford, Cutsyke WF10 .. 124 C5
Cleckheaton BD19 .... 95 E2
Collingham LS22 .... 29 A8
Denby Dale HD8 .... 191 B2
Dewsbury WF13 .... 118 A1
Elland, Sowood Green HX4 .. 133 F1
Elland, West Vale HX4 ...... 134 C6
Featherstone WF7 .... 145 C4
Featherstone WF7 .... 145 D6
Garforth LS25 .... 83 A7
Glusburn BD20 .... 16 B7
Halifax, Bank Top HX3 ...... 113 E6
Halifax, Illingworth HX2 .... 91 E8
Halifax, Midgley HX2 .... 90 D1
Halifax, Pye Nest HX2 ...... 202 A1

Greatfield Rd WF5 .... 140 E5
Greave Cl HD2 .... 136 B4
Greave Clough Cl 🟦
OL13 .... 106 B3
Greave Clough Dr OL13 .. 106 B3
Greave House Dr HX2 .... 111 D7
Greave House Fields
HX2 .... 111 E8
Greave House La HD8 ... 155 D3
Greave House Pk HX2 ... 111 D7
Greave House Terr HD5 .. 155 D3
Greave Rd Bacup OL13 .. 106 B3
Holmfirth HD7 .... 199 A8
Ripponden HX6 .... 131 E6
Greave St OL14 .... 108 C5
Greavefield La WF8 .... 146 E5
Greaves Ave WF9 .... 141 C5
Greaves Croft HD8 .... 155 D3
Greaves Fold HX4 .... 134 C4
Greaves Rd WF13 .... 118 D1
Greaves St Bradford BD5 .. 74 D3
🟦 Todmorden OL14 .... 108 B6
Greek St Castleford WF10 .. 124 E8
Leeds LS1 .... 211 E4
Green Abbey HD7 .... 199 B7
Green Acre BD17 .... 38 D3
Green Acres
Crigglestone WF4 .... 160 A7
Featherstone WF7 .... 145 E3
Green Acres Cl HD8 ...... 175 C6
Green Ave Batley WF16 .. 117 E4
Kippax LS25 .... 82 F3
Sileston BD20 .... 5 D2
Green Balk La HD8 .... 155 F2
Green Bank WF3 .... 100 D1
Green Bank Ct BD17 ...... 38 B1
Green Chase 🟦 LS6 ..... 59 E7
Green Cl Batley WF12 .. 118 E5
Bradford BD8 .... 73 E8
Dewsbury WF13 .... 118 A2
Leeds LS6 .... 59 F7
Low Bradley BD20 .... 4 C6
Steeton BD20 .... 16 F6
Green Cliff HD7 .... 171 F5
Green Cres
Huddersfield HD7 .... 152 E5
Leeds LS6 .... 59 E7
Green Croft WF9 .... 163 E3
Green Ct Barwick in E LS15 .. 62 F7
Bradford BD7 .... 73 F5
Brighouse BD19 .... 115 F8
Green Edge HD7 .... 152 C6
Green End Bradford BD14 .. 73 C4
Brighouse HD6 .... 115 A1
Green End Cl 🟦 OL13 .. 106 A3
Green End La WF2 .... 142 C3
Green End Rd Bradford BD6 .. 94 B8
Keighley BD20 .... 19 E2
Green Gate La HD7 .... 200 A4
Green Gate Rd HD7 .... 188 A4
Green Gdns HD7 .... 152 E5
Green Hall Pk HX3 .... 93 D5
Green Head Ave BD20 .... 18 A2
Green Head Dr BD20 ...... 18 A2
Green Head La BD20 ...... 18 A2
Green Head Rd BD20 ...... 18 B2
Green Hill Halifax HX2 ... 112 B6
Huddersfield HD2 .... 136 B4
Green Hill Chase LS12 .. 209 D2
Green Hill Cl LS12 .... 58 F1
Green Hill Croft LS12 .... 209 E2
Green Hill Dr LS13 .... 58 E1
Green Hill Gdns LS12 ... 209 E2
Green Hill Holt LS12 ..... 209 E2
Green Hill La LS12 .... 209 E1
Green Hill Mount LS13 .. 58 E1
Green Hill Pl LS13 .... 58 E1
Green Hill Rd
🟥 Bacup OL13 .... 106 A1
Leeds LS12, LS13 .... 58 E1
Liversedge WF15 .... 117 A5
Green Hill Way LS13 ...... 58 E1
Green House Hill HD4 ... 174 C4
Green House La HD8 .... 174 C4
Green La
Ackworth M T WF7 .... 163 D6
Addingham LS29 .... 2 E1
Adwick Le S DN6 .... 184 E3
Baildon BD17 .... 38 A4
Baildon, Baildon Wood Bottom
  BD17 .... 38 D6
Boston Spa LS23 .... 30 F6
Bradford BD6 .... 55 C1
Bradford, Fourlands BD10 .. 56 C8
Bradford, Idle Moor BD10 .. 56 A8
Bradford, Lidget Green BD7 .. 74 A5
Bradford, Oakenshaw BD12 .. 94 F4
Bradford, Ravenscliffe BD2 .. 56 D3
Bradford, Wyke BD12 .... 94 C2
Brighouse, Clifton HD6 .... 115 F2
Brighouse, Hove Edge HD6 .. 114 E5
Burley in W LS29 .... 9 F1
Castleford, Castleford Ings
  WF10 .... 103 F1
Castleford, Cutsyke WF10 .. 124 C5
Cleckheaton BD19 .... 95 E2
Collingham LS22 .... 29 A8
Denby Dale HD8 .... 191 B2
Dewsbury WF13 .... 118 A1
Elland, Sowood Green HX4 .. 133 F1
Elland, West Vale HX4 ...... 134 C6
Featherstone WF7 .... 145 C4
Featherstone WF7 .... 145 D6
Garforth LS25 .... 83 A7
Glusburn BD20 .... 16 B7
Halifax, Bank Top HX3 ...... 113 E6
Halifax, Illingworth HX2 .... 91 E8
Halifax, Midgley HX2 .... 90 D1
Halifax, Pye Nest HX2 ...... 202 A1

Green La continued
Halifax, Shibden Dale
  HX2, HX3, HX4 .... 92 E6
Halton East BD23 .... 1 E8
Haworth BD22 .... 33 F4
Heptonstall HX7 .... 88 E5
Holmfirth HD7 .... 189 A2
Horbury WF4 .... 159 C8
Horsforth LS18 .... 58 B7
Kippax LS25 .... 82 F2
Kippax, Kippax Common
  LS25 .... 82 F3
Ledston WF10 .... 103 E6
Leeds LS11 .... 214 A1
Leeds, Cookridge LS16 ..... 42 B3
🟥 Leeds, Cross Gates LS15 .. 62 B1
Leeds, Farnley LS12 .... 77 C5
Leeds, New Wortley LS12 .. 210 B2
Leeds, Whinmoor LS14 ..... 62 A8
Liversedge WF15 .... 116 D3
Low Bradley BD20 .... 5 A6
Marsden HD7 .... 169 B7
Meltham HD7 .... 170 C1
Menston LS29 .... 22 C2
Micklefield LS25 .... 84 C2
Micklefield LS25 .... 102 F2
Netherton WF4 .... 158 E5
Netherton WF4 .... 158 F5
Netherton, Overton WF4 .. 157 F6
Notton WF4 .... 179 A5
Oakworth BD22 .... 34 D2
Otley LS21 .... 10 F1
Pontefract WF8 .... 146 D7
Pontefract, Carleton WF8 .. 146 E5
Pudsey LS28 .... 76 D6
Queensbury BD13 .... 72 B3
Ripponden HX4, HX6 ...... 150 F8
Ripponden, Syke Hill HX6 .. 132 B4
Rothwell WF3 .... 100 D1
Shelf HX3 .... 93 C6
South Kirkby WF9 .... 182 E1
Steeton BD20 .... 17 A6
Thornton BD13 .... 72 E6
Upton WF9 .... 165 C1
Wakefield WF2 .... 141 E7
Green Lane LS19 .... 40 B5
Green Lane Cl WF4 .... 158 A6
Green Lane First Sch BD8 .. 55 C1
Green Lane Terr HD7 .... 152 C6
Green Lea LS26 .... 101 C6
Green La LS13 .... 30 E7
Green Lea Mills
(Ind Units) HD5 .... 155 A6
Green Lea Rd HD5 .... 154 F6
Green Lea Special Sch
WF8 .... 146 E5
Green Meadow BD15 ...... 53 D4
Green Meadows Sch LS20 .. 22 C1
Green Mount Baildon BD17 .. 38 B2
Bradford BD4 .... 75 D3
Huddersfield HD5 .... 154 D6
Green Mount Ret Pk
HX1 .... 203 D3
Green Park Ave
Halifax HX3 .... 113 C2
Horbury WF4 .... 140 F2
Ossett WF5 .... 140 E3
Green Park Dr HX3 .... 113 C2
Green Park Gate HX3 ...... 113 C2
Green Park Rd HX3 .... 113 C2
Green Park Way HX3 .... 113 C2
Green Pk Leeds LS12 .... 43 E2
Wakefield WF1 .... 142 E6
Green Pl BD2 .... 56 B2
Green Rd Baildon BD17 .... 38 C2
Leeds LS6 .... 59 E7
Liversedge WF15 .... 117 A5
Green Row Bradford BD10 .. 56 B6
Mickletown LS26 .... 102 D1
Green Royd Elland HX4 .. 134 C6
Halifax HX2 .... 91 B4
Green Side Rd HD4 .... 173 A3
Green Slacks La HD3 ..... 151 B5
Green St Bradford BD1 ... 201 C3
Bradford, Lower Woodlands
  BD5 .... 95 B5
Castleford WF10 .... 103 D1
🟦 Elland HX4 .... 134 B4
Haworth BD22 .... 51 C6
Huddersfield HD1 .... 154 A7
Meltham HD7 .... 170 D2
🟦 Oxenhope BD22 .... 51 C6
Green Sykes Rd BD20 ..... 34 A7
Green Terr
Dewsbury WF13 .... 118 A2
Guiseley LS20 .... 39 E8
Leeds LS13 .... 214 C3
Mirfield WF14 .... 137 F6
Green Terrace Sq HX1 ... 202 C1
Green The Batley WF12 ... 96 F2
Bingley BD16 .... 37 A6
Bingley BD16 .... 37 B6
Bingley, Eldwick Beck BD16 .. 37 D6
Bingley, Micklethwaite BD16 .. 36 E7
Birkenshaw BD4 .... 95 F7
Bradford BD10 .... 56 B8
Castleford WF10 .... 125 D8
Crofton WF4 .... 144 C2
Featherstone WF7 .... 145 E4
Garforth LS25 .... 83 A7
Guiseley LS20 .... 39 E8
Horsforth LS18 .... 58 B8
Huddersfield HD2 .... 136 D5
🟥 Kippax LS25 .... 83 A1

Green The *continued*
Kirkburton SH18 ... 172 F2
Leeds, Hawksworth LS5 ... 58 E7
Leeds, Moortown LS17 ... 43 E2
Marsden HD7 ... 168 F4
Mirfield WF14 ... 137 E6
Ossett WF5 ... 140 E4
Otley LS21 ... 10 F1
Pudsey LS28 ... 57 D4
Royston S71 ... 179 C3
South Kirkby WF9 ... 182 C3
Wakefield WF2 ... 120 E3
Woolley WF4 ... 178 A7
Green Top LS12 ... 209 E1
Green Top Gdns LS12 ... 209 E1
Green Top St BD8 ... 73 E7
Green View Leeds LS6 ... 59 E7
Scarcroft LS14 ... 45 C8
Green View The S72 ... 180 C4
Green Way Glusburn BD20 ... 16 C7
Halifax HX2 ... 91 E8
Scarcroft LS14 ... 45 C8
Green Wood Pk LS6 ... 59 E7
Green's Sq HX2 ... 202 A4
Green's Sq LS25 ... 83 B1
Greenacre Ave BD12 ... 94 D2
Greenacre Cl 1 BD12 ... 94 D2
Greenacre Ct LS25 ... 83 A7
Greenacre Dr
Bradford BD12 ... 94 D2
Denby Dale HD8 ... 191 E3
Greenacre Park Ave LS19 ... 40 B5
Greenacre Park Mews 1
LS19 ... 40 C5
Greenacre Park Rise LS19 ... 40 C5
Greenacre Pk LS19 ... 40 B5
Greenacre Rd WF9 ... 183 C8
Greenacre Way BD12 ... 94 D2
Greenacre Wlk WF4 ... 162 D2
Greenacres Ossett WF5 ... 119 D1
Riponden HX6 ... 132 E4
Shelf HX3 ... 93 D6
Greenacres Ave HX3 ... 93 D6
Greenacres Cl WF5 ... 119 D1
Greenacres Dr Batley WF17 ... 97 A2
Keighley BD20 ... 18 A1
Shelf HX3 ... 93 D6
Greenacres Gr HX3 ... 93 D6
Greenaire Pl 2 BD1 ... 74 D7
Greenbank BD19 ... 116 F6
Greenbank Cl WF10 ... 124 A5
Greenbank Gr WF6 ... 122 F3
Greenbank Rd
Bradford BD15 ... 73 C8
Normanton WF6 ... 122 F3
Greenbanks Ave LS18 ... 41 C2
Greenbanks Cl LS18 ... 41 C2
Greenbanks Dr LS18 ... 41 B2
Greencliffe Ave BD17 ... 38 C3
Greencroft Ave HX3 ... 93 B3
Greendale Cl BB10 ... 85 A7
Greendale Ct HD7 ... 171 F5
Greendown Cl LS29 ... 8 D4
Greeney Hill BD15 ... 53 B4
Greenfell Cl BD22 ... 34 F6
Greenfield BD22 ... 51 C8
Greenfield Ave
Birkby HX3 ... 115 A7
Gildersome LS27 ... 97 B7
Guiseley LS20 ... 39 B7
Huddersfield HD3 ... 153 A7
Kippax LS25 ... 83 A2
Ossett WF5 ... 141 A4
Shipley BD18 ... 55 C5
Greenfield Cl
Denby Dale HD8 ... 191 F3
Elland HX4 ... 133 F2
Kippax LS25 ... 83 A2
Normanton HX3 ... 93 A3
Ossett WF5 ... 141 A4
Wakefield WF2 ... 120 F2
Greenfield Cres BD13 ... 52 E6
Greenfield Ct Keighley BD21 ... 35 A7
Leeds LS16 ... 42 B4
Greenfield Dr
6 Brighouse BD19 ... 115 F8
Gildersome LS27 ... 97 B7
Greenfield Garth LS25 ... 83 A2
Greenfield Gdns BD20 ... 16 F6
Greenfield La
Bradford, Bierley BD4 ... 95 B7
Bradford, Horton Bank Bottom
BD7 ... 73 F3
Bradford, Thackley BD10 ... 39 B1
Guiseley LS20 ... 39 B7
Greenfield Mount WF2 ... 120 F2
Greenfield Pl Bradford BD8 ... 55 C1
Brighouse HX3 ... 115 A7
Greenfield Rd
Hemsworth WF9 ... 181 D5
Holmfirth HD7 ... 188 D5
Leeds LS9 ... 212 B3
Normanton WF6 ... 122 F2
Ossett WF5 ... 141 A4
Greenfield Rise LS25 ... 83 A2
Greenfield Sch BD10 ... 39 B1
Greenfield Terr
Haworth BD22 ... 51 C8
Mickletown LS26 ... 102 E3
Todmorden OL14 ... 86 A1
Greenfield Vale LS25 ... 83 A2
Greenfield View LS25 ... 83 A2
Greenfield Way WF2 ... 120 F2
Greenfields WF16 ... 117 C5
Greenfields Way LS29 ... 21 F7

Greenfinch Gr HD4 ... 171 E7
Greenfold La LS22 ... 13 F5
Greengate Rothwell LS26 .... 101 C6
Silsden BD20 ... 5 D2
Greengate Rd
Keighley BD21 ... 35 C6
Norton WF8 ... 166 F3
Greengates Ave 3 BD12 ... 94 C1
Greengates Fst Sch
BD10 ... 56 E7
Greenhead Ave HD5 ... 154 F5
Greenhead Ct HD1 ... 153 E7
Greenhead Grammar Sch
BD20 ... 18 B2
Greenhead La
Brighouse HD6 ... 135 E6
Huddersfield HD5 ... 154 F5
Greenhead Rd
Huddersfield HD1 ... 153 F6
Leeds LS16 ... 59 B8
Greenhill Ave WF8 ... 146 E6
Greenhill Bank Rd HD7 ... 189 E5
Greenhill Cres LS12 ... 209 F2
Greenhill Dr BD16 ... 36 E7
Greenhill Ind Est HX7 ... 110 F8
Greenhill La Bingley BD16 ... 36 F6
Bradford BD3 ... 75 C7
Greenhill Middle Sch
LS13 ... 77 D8
Greenhill Mount WF14 ... 146 E6
Greenhill Prim Sch
Leeds LS13 ... 77 D8
Wakefield WF1 ... 216 C3
Greenhill Rd
Huddersfield HD3 ... 152 E7
Wakefield WF1 ... 216 C3
Greenhill St BD3 ... 75 C7
Greenhills LS19 ... 40 C3
Greenholme Cl LS29 ... 9 F2
Greenholme Ct BD4 ... 75 F2
Greenholme Trad Est LS29 ... 9 F2
Greenhouse Rd HD2 ... 136 A1
Greenhow Cl LS4 ... 205 D2
Greenhow Gdns LS4 ... 205 D2
Greenhow Pk LS29 ... 9 D1
Greenhow Rd LS4 ... 205 D2
Greenhow Wlk LS4 ... 205 D2
Greenland Ave BD13 ... 92 E8
Greenland Rd HX7 ... 87 C6
Greenland Villas BD13 ... 92 E8
Greenlaws Cl HD7 ... 188 D5
Greenlay Dr WF2 ... 120 B2
Greenlea Ave LS19 ... 39 F6
Greenlea Cl LS19 ... 39 F5
Greenlea Fold LS19 ... 39 F5
Greenlea Mount LS19 ... 39 F6
Greenlea Rd LS19 ... 39 F5
Greenmoor Ave WF3 ... 100 C1
Greenmoor Cl WF3 ... 100 C1
Greenmoor Cres WF3 ... 100 D1
Greenmount Ct 1 LS11 ... 214 B3
Greenmount La LS11 ... 214 B3
Greenmount Pl LS11 ... 214 B3
Greenmount Sch LS11 ... 214 B3
Greenmount St LS11 ... 214 B3
Greenmount Terr LS11 ... 214 B3
Greenock Pl 1 LS12 ... 209 D4
Greenock Rd LS12 ... 209 D4
Greenock St LS12 ... 209 D4
Greenock Terr 1 LS12 ... 209 D4
Greenroyd Ave
Cleckheaton BD19 ... 95 D2
Halifax HX3 ... 113 B3
Greenroyd Cl Halifax HX3 ... 113 B3
Greenroyd Croft HD2 ... 135 E1
Greenroyd Ct WF8 ... 147 C5
Greenroyd Dr BD20 ... 16 D4
Greenroyd Gr BD20 ... 16 D4
Greenroyd La Rd HD2 ... 91 E1
Greens End Rd HD7 ... 170 D2
Greens La OL13 ... 106 A3
Greenset View S71 ... 178 E1
Greenshank Mews LS27 ... 98 D3
Greenshaw Terr LS20 ... 22 D1
Greenside Bradford BD12 ... 95 A4
Cleckheaton BD19 ... 116 E7
Denby Dale HD8 ... 192 A7
Featherstone WF7 ... 145 D6
4 Liversedge WF16 ... 117 C4
Mapplewell S75 ... 178 C1
Ryhill WF4 ... 180 B8
Shafton S72 ... 180 B4
Greenside Ave
Huddersfield HD5 ... 155 A5
Leeds LS12 ... 209 E1
Mapplewell S75 ... 178 C1
Greenside Cl LS12 ... 209 F1
Greenside County Infant
Sch HD5 ... 155 A4
Greenside Cres LS15 ... 155 A5
Greenside Ct Crofton WF4 ... 162 B7
Gildersome LS27 ... 97 D7
Greenside Dr
Huddersfield HD5 ... 155 A5
Leeds LS12 ... 209 F1
Greenside Est WF14 ... 138 A7
Greenside Gr 3 LS28 ... 76 D6
Greenside La Bradford BD8 ... 73 F7
Cullingworth BD13 ... 52 E6
Greenside Mount WF14 ... 138 B7
Greenside Pk WF4 ... 162 B7
Greenside Pl S75 ... 178 C1
Greenside Rd Leeds LS12 ... 209 E1
Mirfield WF14 ... 138 B7
Greenside Terr LS12 ... 209 E1
Greenside Wlk LS12 ... 209 E1
Greensnook La OL13 ... 106 A3

Greensnook Terr 1 OL13 ... 106 A3
Greensway LS25 ... 82 E7
Greenthorpe Hill WF3 ... 77 E8
Greenthorpe Mount LS13 ... 77 E8
Greenthorpe Rd LS13 ... 77 E8
Greenthorpe St LS13 ... 77 E7
Greenthorpe Wlk LS13 ... 77 E8
Greenthwaite Ct BD20 ... 18 A1
Greenton Ave BD19 ... 94 E1
Greenton Cres BD13 ... 92 D8
Greentop Crofton WF4 ... 162 B7
Pudsey LS28 ... 76 D6
Greentrees 1 BD6 ... 94 B6
Greenups Terr HX6 ... 112 B4
Greenview WF4 ... 162 B7
Greenview Cl LS9 ... 208 C2
Greenview Mount LS9 ... 61 D2
Greenville Ave LS12 ... 209 E1
Greenville Dr BD12 ... 94 C7
Greenville Gdns LS12 ... 209 E1
Greenway Guiseley LS20 ... 39 C7
Honley HD7 ... 171 F5
Huddersfield HD3 ... 152 F5
Leeds LS15 ... 62 C1
Greenway Cl LS15 ... 62 C1
Greenway Dr BD15 ... 73 B7
Greenway Rd BD5 ... 74 E2
Greenwell Row 6 BD4 ... 73 B4
Greenwell Terr HX3 ... 114 E8
Greenwood Ave
Bradford BD2 ... 56 A4
Dewsbury WF12 ... 139 F7
Upton WF9 ... 183 C8
Greenwood Bldgs HD5 ... 155 C8
Greenwood Cl
Normanton WF6 ... 144 B7
Upton WF9 ... 183 C8
Greenwood Cres S71 ... 179 B4
Greenwood Ct
Bradford BD1 ... 201 C2
Leeds LS6 ... 59 E7
Greenwood Dr BD2 ... 56 A4
Greenwood House 5 WF1 ... 216 B2
Greenwood Mount
Bradford BD2 ... 56 A4
Leeds LS6 ... 59 E7
Greenwood Primary Sch
LS11 ... 214 C4
Greenwood Rd
Baildon BD17 ... 38 B1
East Ardsley WF3 ... 119 F7
Wakefield WF1 ... 142 E7
Greenwood Row LS28 ... 76 F7
Greenwood St
Dewsbury WF12, WF13 ... 139 B8
Dewsbury, Savile Town
WF12 ... 139 C6
5 Hebden Bridge HX7 ... 89 A3
Huddersfield HD4 ... 154 A4
Gretland Junior
& Infants Sch HX4 ... 134 B7
Gretland Rd HX4 ... 133 B6
Gregory Cres BD7 ... 73 E2
Gregory Ct 1 BD14 ... 73 C4
Gregory Dr HD8 ... 173 F7
Gregory La WF14 ... 156 A7
Gregory Rd WF10 ... 124 E5
Gregory Springs La
WF14 ... 138 B3
Gregory Springs Mount
WF14 ... 138 B2
Gregory Springs Rd
WF14 ... 138 B3
Gregory St WF17 ... 118 C5
Grenfell Dr BD3 ... 75 D8
Grenfell Rd BD3 ... 75 D8
Grenfell Terr BD3 ... 75 D8
Grenley St WF11 ... 127 A4
Grenville Wlk WF4 ... 159 F3
Gresham Ave BD2 ... 55 F4
Gresley Rd BD21 ... 35 C7
Gresley Road Ind Est
BD21 ... 35 C7
Grey Cl WF1 ... 121 B3
Grey Ct WF1 ... 121 B3
Grey Gables WF4 ... 158 E6
Grey Hall HX4 ... 133 F3
Grey Scar Ct BD22 ... 34 B2
Grey Scar Rd BD22 ... 34 A2
Grey St WF1 ... 121 B3
Grey Stone La OL14 ... 108 F8
Grey Stones La HX7 ... 69 B5
Greycourt Cl
Bradford BD10 ... 56 A6
Halifax HX1 ... 202 C1
Greyfriar Wlk BD7 ... 73 E3
Greyfriars Ave HD2 ... 136 E4
Greyhound Dr BD7 ... 74 B6
Greyshiels Ave LS6 ... 59 C4
Greyshiels Cl LS6 ... 59 C4
Greystone Ave HX5 ... 134 E5
Greystone Cl
Burley in W LS29 ... 9 E2
Greystone Cres BD10 ... 56 C6
Greystone Ct HD6 ... 136 A7
Greystone Mount LS15 ... 80 E7
Greystone Pk LS25 ... 47 E1
Greystones Cl LS25 ... 47 E1
Greystones Dr
Keighley BD22 ... 34 F3
Ossett WF5 ... 140 E3
Greystones La BD22 ... 33 D7
Greystones Mount BD22 ... 34 F2
Greystones Rd HX2 ... 111 E7
Greystones Rise BD22 ... 34 F3
Griff House La WF3 ... 120 B8
Griffe Dr BD12 ... 94 C1

Griffe Gdns BD22 ... 34 B2
Griffe Head Cres 2 BD12 ... 94 C2
Griffe Head Rd BD12 ... 94 C2
Griffe Rd Bradford BD12 ... 94 C2
Haworth BD22 ... 50 D8
Griffe View BD22 ... 34 B2
Grime La Crofton WF4 ... 144 B2
Whitley Common HD7 ... 200 D8
Grimes Dyke Primary Sch
LS14 ... 62 D6
Grimescar Meadows HD2 ... 135 D2
Grimescar Rd HD2 ... 135 D3
Grimethorpe St 1 WF9 ... 182 F2
Grimscar Ave HD2 ... 135 E1
Grimthorpe Ave 8 LS6 ... 59 C5
Grimthorpe Pl LS6 ... 59 D5
Grimthorpe St LS6 ... 59 C5
Grimthorpe Terr LS6 ... 59 D5
Grindlestone Bank HX2 ... 91 C6
Grisedale Ave HD2 ... 135 F1
Grizedale Cl LS22 ... 13 B6
Grosmont Pl LS13 ... 58 C3
Grosmont Rd LS13 ... 58 C2
Grosmont Terr LS13 ... 58 C3
Grosvenor Ave
Lepton HD8 ... 155 E3
Pontefract WF8 ... 146 B8
Shipley BD18 ... 54 F8
Upton WF9 ... 183 A7
Grosvenor Ct LS16 ... 41 D4
Grosvenor Hill LS7 ... 206 C2
Grosvenor Mews LS19 ... 40 A4
Grosvenor Mount LS6 ... 205 F4
Grosvenor Park Gdns
LS6 ... 205 F4
Grosvenor Pk LS7 ... 60 C7
Grosvenor Rd
Batley WF17 ... 118 D6
Bradford BD8 ... 55 D1
Huddersfield HD5 ... 154 F6
Leeds LS6 ... 205 F4
Shipley BD18 ... 54 F7
Grosvenor St
2 Batley WF16 ... 117 D5
Bradford BD8 ... 55 D1
Dewsbury WF12 ... 139 C5
Elland HX5 ... 134 F6
Wakefield WF1 ... 142 F3
Grosvenor Terr
1 Batley WF16 ... 117 D4
Bradford BD8 ... 55 D1
11 Halifax HX1 ... 202 C3
Leeds LS6 ... 205 F4
Otley LS21 ... 23 B8
Wetherby LS22 ... 13 E6
Grosvenor Way LS10 ... 155 E3
Grouse Moor La BD13 ... 72 C2
Grouse St 8 BD21 ... 35 D8
Grove Ave Halifax HX3 ... 92 A3
Hemsworth WF9 ... 181 E6
Leeds LS6 ... 59 E6
Pontefract WF8 ... 146 B8
Pudsey LS28 ... 76 D7
Shipley BD18 ... 55 B5
South Kirkby WF9 ... 182 C2
Grove Cl WF14 ... 156 A7
Cleckheaton BD19 ... 96 B1
Grove Convalescent
Hospl The LS29 ... 8 B3
Grove Cotts HD6 ... 114 C2
Grove Cres
Boston Spa LS23 ... 30 F7
Halifax HX2 ... 111 E7
Walton WF2 ... 161 B7
Grove Cres S LS23 ... 30 F7
Grove Croft HX3 ... 92 A2
Grove Ct Halifax HX3 ... 92 A2
Huddersfield HD3 ... 152 F6
Leeds LS6 ... 59 E6
Pudsey LS28 ... 76 D7
Grove Dr Halifax HX3 ... 91 F3
Grove Edge HX3 ... 91 F2
Grove Farm Cl LS16 ... 41 F4
Grove Farm Cres LS16 ... 41 E4
Grove Farm Croft LS16 ... 41 E4
Grove Farm Dr LS16 ... 41 E4
Grove Gdns
Boston Spa LS23 ... 30 F7
Dewsbury WF12 ... 140 A6
Halifax HX3 ... 92 A3
Leeds LS6 ... 59 E6
Grove Half Park Homes
WF11 ... 147 D8
Grove Head WF9 ... 182 B2
Grove House Cres BD2 ... 56 A4
Grove House Dr BD2 ... 56 A3
Grove House First Sch
BD2 ... 56 A4
Grove La Halifax HX3 ... 91 F3
Honley HD7 ... 171 E4
Hemsworth WF9 ... 181 E6
Knottingley WF11 ... 126 E4
Leeds LS6 ... 59 E6
South Kirkby WF9 ... 182 B2
Grove Lea Jun & Inf Sch
WF9 ... 181 E6
Grove Lea Wlk WF8 ... 146 E7
Grove Mill La HX3 ... 92 A2
Grove Mount
Pontefract WF8 ... 146 B8
South Kirkby WF9 ... 182 B2
Grove Pk Crigglestone WF4 ... 159 E6
Halifax HX3 ... 92 A3

Grove Pl Boston Spa LS23 ... 30 E7
Hemsworth WF9 ... 181 E6
Grove Rd Batley WF16 ... 117 E1
Boston Spa LS23 ... 30 E7
Elland HX5 ... 135 B3
Hebden Bridge HX7 ... 89 A4
Horbury WF4 ... 141 A3
Horsforth LS18 ... 58 C6
Huddersfield HD1 ... 154 B3
Ilkley LS29 ... 7 F4
Leeds LS15 ... 81 A7
Leeds, Headingley Hill LS6 ... 59 E5
Leeds, Hunslet LS10 ... 215 E3
Mapplewell S75 ... 178 A1
Menston LS29 ... 22 A4
Pontefract WF8 ... 146 B8
Pudsey LS28 ... 76 D7
Shipley BD18 ... 55 B5
Wakefield WF1 ... 216 C3
Grove Rise Leeds LS17 ... 42 F5
Pontefract WF8 ... 146 E8
Grove Royd HX3 ... 92 A2
Grove Sq Cleckheaton BD19 ... 96 B1
Halifax HX3 ... 91 F2
Grove St Bacup OL13 ... 106 A3
Batley, Heckmondwike
WF16 ... 117 E4
Batley, Norristhorpe WF15 ... 117 C2
Brighouse HD6 ... 115 B2
Dewsbury WF13 ... 139 C8
Halifax HX3 ... 91 F3
Huddersfield HD3 ... 152 F6
Leeds LS11 ... 211 D4
Mirfield WF14 ... 138 B6
Ossett WF5 ... 140 E5
4 Pudsey LS28 ... 57 E2
Slaithwaite HD7 ... 151 F8
South Kirkby WF9 ... 182 B2
Sowerby Bridge HX6 ... 112 D4
Wakefield WF1 ... 216 C1
5 HX1 ... 202 B3
Grove Terr
Birkenshaw BD11 ... 96 A4
Boston Spa LS23 ... 30 E7
Bradford BD7 ... 201 A2
Bradford, Idle BD10 ... 56 D7
Brighouse HD6 ... 114 D8
Cleckheaton BD19 ... 116 D8
Cudworth S72 ... 180 B1
East Ardsley WF3 ... 120 B8
East Keswick LS17 ... 28 B6
Horsforth LS18 ... 41 B1
Huddersfield HD2 ... 136 B2
Ilkley LS29 ... 8 B4
Kippax LS25 ... 83 A1
Leeds LS17 ... 42 F5
Normanton WF6 ... 123 B2
Pudsey LS28 ... 76 D7
2 Queensbury BD13 ... 72 E1
Ryhill WF4 ... 162 A1
Shelf HX3 ... 93 C6
South Elmsall WF9 ... 182 F4
Swillington LS26 ... 82 B2
Thornton BD13 ... 71 B6
Yeadon LS19 ... 40 B6
Grove Way WF9 ... 182 B2
Grove Wilmington LS7 ... 207 D2
Grovehall Ave LS11 ... 214 A1
Grovehall Dr LS11, WF11 ... 147 B8
Grovehall Par LS11 ... 213 F1
Grovehall La WF11 ... 213 F1
Grovelands BD2 ... 56 A4
Groves Hall Rd WF13 ... 138 F8
Groveville HX3 ... 93 C1
Groveway BD2 ... 56 A4
Grunberg Rd LS6 ... 59 D5
Grunberg St 6 LS6 ... 59 D5
Guard House Ave BD22 ... 35 A7
Guard House Dr BD22 ... 35 A7
Guard House First Sch
BD22 ... 34 F7
Guard House Gr BD22 ... 34 F7
Guard House Rd BD22 ... 35 A7
Guernsey Rd WF12 ... 118 F2
Guild Way HX2 ... 112 B7
Guildford Rd S71 ... 179 B5
Guildford St
8 Hebden Bridge HX7 ... 89 A2
Ossett WF5 ... 140 D4
Guillemot App LS27 ... 98 D3
Guiseley Dr LS29 ... 22 B2
Guiseley Infant Sch LS20 ... 22 E1
Guiseley Sta LS20 ... 39 D8
Guiseley Sta LS20 ... 22 D1
Guiseley Queensway
Primary Sch LS19 ... 40 A8
Gully Terr HD7 ... 189 B4
Gully The HD7 ... 190 C5
Gunson Cres WF5 ... 140 D6
Gunter Rd LS22 ... 14 A5
Gunthwaite La S36 ... 192 B2
Gunthwaite Top HD8 ... 191 F3
Gurbax Ct BD3 ... 75 F7
Gurney Cl BD5 ... 74 D4
Guy St BD4 ... 201 C2
Guycroft LS21 ... 23 A7
Guys Croft WF2 ... 141 C4
Gwynne Ave BD3 ... 75 F7
Gynn La HD7 ... 172 B5

Gypsy Ct WF10 .... 125 C6
Gypsy La LS15 .... 121 C5
Gypsy Wood Cl LS15 .... 81 D7
Gypsy Wood Crest LS15 ... 81 D7

Hacking La WF9 .... 183 B3
Hadassah St HX3 .... 113 D4
Haddingley La HD7 .... 190 D4
Haddon Ave Halifax HX3 ... 113 C3
   Leeds LS4 .... 59 C2
Haddon Cl
   Cleckheaton BD19 .... 117 B8
   South Elmsall WF9 .... 183 A5
Haddon Pl LS4 .... 59 C2
Haddon St HS4 .... 205 D2
Hag Farm Rd
   Burley in W LS29 .... 21 E7
   Menston LS29 .... 21 E7
Hag Hill HD8 .... 175 E6
Hag La HD8 .... 175 E6
Hag La HX3 .... 92 D3
Hagg La WF14 .... 138 C2
Hagg Wood Rd HD7 .... 172 B2
Haggroyd La HD7 .... 172 B2
Haigh Hall Rd WF5 .... 141 A5
Hague La WF2 .... 141 C5
Hague Cres WF9 .... 181 E5
Hague Park Cl WF9 .... 182 B3
Hague Park La WF9 .... 182 B3
Hague Park Wlk WF9 ...... 182 B3
Hague Terr WF9 .... 181 E6
Haigh Ave LS26 .... 100 C7
Haigh Beck View BD10 .... 56 C7
Haigh Cnr BD10 .... 56 D7
Haigh Croft S71 .... 179 B4
Haigh Gdns LS26 .... 100 C7
Haigh Hall BD10 .... 56 D7
Haigh Hall Rd BD10 .... 56 D7
Haigh Park Rd LS10 .... 80 B2
Haigh Rd LS26 .... 100 F6
Haigh Road Inf Sch LS26 .. 100 E6
Haigh St Bradford BD4 .... 75 B3
   16 Brighouse HD6 .... 115 A3
   Elland HX4 .... 134 B7
   Halifax HX1 .... 202 B4
   Huddersfield HD1 .... 153 F3
Haigh Terr LS26 .... 100 C7
Haigh View LS26 .... 100 C7
Haigh Wood Cl LS16 ...... 41 D2
Haigh Wood Gn LS16 ...... 41 D2
Haigh Wood Rd LS16 ...... 41 D2
Haigh's Sq HD5 .... 154 D7
Haighside LS26 .... 100 C6
Haighside Cl LS26 .... 100 D6
Haighside Dr LS26 .... 100 C6
Haighside Way LS26 .... 100 C6
Hailhead Dr WF8 .... 125 F1
Haincliffe Pl 11 BD21 ..... 35 B4
   Haines Pk LS7 .... 207 E2
Hainsworth Moor Cres 5
   BD13 .... 92 D8
Hainsworth Moor Dr 6
   BD13 .... 92 D8
Hainsworth Moor Garth 4
   BD13 .... 92 D8
Hainsworth Moor
   Middle St BD13 .... 92 D8
Hainsworth Moor View
   BD13 .... 92 D8
Hainsworth Rd BD13 ...... 92 D8
Hainsworth Sq 11 LS28 ... 57 D3
Hainsworth St Leeds LS12 . 210 B2
   Rothwell BD20 .... 100 E4
Hainworth Crag Rd BD21 .. 35 A2
Hainworth La BD21 .... 35 B3
Hainworth Rd
   Keighley, Hainworth BD21 .. 35 B3
   Keighley, The Pitts BD21 ... 35 C4
Hainworth Wood Rd BD21 . 35 B3
Hainworth Wood Rd N
   BD21 .... 35 C5
Haise Mount S75 .... 178 A1
Halcyon Hill LS7 .... 60 C8
Halcyon Way BD5 .... 74 C2
Haldane Cl S72 .... 180 F3
Haldane Cres WF1 .... 142 F8
Hales Rd LS12 .... 78 B4
Halesworth Cres BD4 ..... 75 E3
Haley Hill HX3 .... 203 E4
Haley's Yd LS13 .... 58 C3
Half Acre Rd BD13 .... 72 B7
Half Acres Jun & Inf Schs
   WF10 .... 124 C7
Half House La HD6 .... 114 D5

Half Mile LS13 .... 57 F2
Half Mile Cl LS28 .... 57 F2
Half Mile Gdns LS13 ...... 57 F2
Half Mile Gn LS28 .... 57 F2
Half Mile La LS13 .... 57 F3
Half Moon La WF1 .... 143 C6
Half Moon St 8 HD1 ...... 154 A6
Half St BD21 .... 35 B8
Halfpenny La WF8 .... 146 A8
Halfpenny Lane Junior
   & Infants Sch WF8 ..... 146 B8
Halifax Golf Course HX2 .. 71 B1
Halifax High Sch The
   Halifax HX1 .... 202 C1
   Halifax HX1 .... 203 E2
Halifax Ind Ctr The HX1 .. 202 C4
Halifax La
   Blackshaw Head HX7 .... 87 E4
   Halifax HX2 .... 111 E8
Halifax New Coll HX1 ..... 202 C2
Halifax RC High Sch HX2 . 92 A6
Halifax Rd Batley WF17 ... 118 B2
   Bradford BD6 .... 94 B7
   Brighouse HD6 .... 115 A3
   Brighouse, Hartshead Moor Top
   HD6 .... 115 E7
   Brighouse, Hipperholme
   HX3 .... 114 B8
   Cleckheaton WF15 ...... 116 C5
   Cullingworth BD13 ..... 52 D6
   Cullingworth, Cullingworth Moor
   BD13 .... 52 A5
   Denholme, Denholme Gate
   HX3 .... 71 E5
   Denholme, Stubden BD13 . 71 E7
   Dewsbury WF13 .... 139 B6
   Elland HX5 .... 134 E8
   Hebden Bridge HX7 ..... 88 C2
   Keighley BD21, BD22 .... 35 A3
   Littleborough OL15 ..... 148 A7
   Northowram HX3 .... 93 B4
   Queensbury BD13 .... 92 C7
   Ripponden HX6 .... 132 C6
   Shelf HX3 .... 93 B4
   Slaithwaite HD7 .... 152 B5
   Todmorden OL14 .... 108 D6
Halifax Sta HX1 .... 203 F2
Hall Ave Bradford BD2 .... 56 D5
   Huddersfield HD1 ...... 153 F5
   Sutton in C BD20 ...... 16 D4
Hall Bank Dr BD16 .... 36 F4
Hall Bank La HX7 .... 110 E8
Hall Bower La HD4 .... 154 B1
Hall Bower La HD4 .... 154 B1
Hall Brig DN5 .... 194 C4
Hall Cl Boston Spa LS23 .. 30 E7
   Bramhope LS16 .... 24 E4
   Burley in W LS29 .... 9 D1
   Hemsworth WF9 .... 181 D7
   Liversedge WF15 .... 117 A3
   Ossett WF5 .... 119 B1
   Sutton in C BD20 .... 16 D4
Hall Cliffe Cres WF4 ..... 141 A2
Hall Cliffe Gr WF4 .... 141 A2
Hall Cliffe Rd WF4 .... 141 A2
Hall Cliffe Rise WF4 ..... 141 B2
Hall Croft WF4 .... 158 C6
Hall Cross Gr HD5 .... 154 D3
Hall Cross Rd HD5 .... 154 D3
Hall Ct Brotherton WF11 . 126 C8
   Leeds LS27 .... 207 D4
   Sutton in C BD20 .... 16 D4
Hall Dr Bramhope LS16 ... 24 E4
   Burley in W LS29 .... 9 D1
   Liversedge WF15 .... 117 B2
   Sutton in C BD20 .... 16 D4
Hall Field La WF4 .... 180 A7
Hall Garth Rd WF8 .... 165 A4
Hall Gdns BD20 .... 4 E1
Hall Gr Leeds LS6 .... 205 F2
   Mapplewell S75 .... 178 C1
Hall Green La HX6 .... 132 B6
Hall Ing La HD7 .... 172 C5
Hall Ing Rd Honley HD4 .. 172 E3
   Kirkburton HD4 .... 172 E3
Hall Ings Bradford BD1 .. 201 B2
   Halifax HX3 .... 114 A3
Hall La Askwith LS21 ..... 9 F6
   Bradford BD4 .... 201 C1
   Dewsbury WF12 .... 139 F2
   Horsforth LS18 .... 41 A1
   Kirkburton HD8 .... 173 E7
   Ledston WF10 .... 103 F6
   Leeds LS12 .... 210 A3
   Leeds, Coleridge LS16 ... 41 F6
   Leeds, Farnley LS12 ..... 77 D5
   Leeds, Potternewton LS7 .. 207 D4
   Northowram HX3 .... 92 F4
   Shipley BD18 .... 55 D8
   Slaithwaite HD3 .... 152 B6
   South Elmsall WF9 ..... 183 B6
Hall Mews LS23 .... 30 E7
Hall Orchards Ave LS22 .. 14 A6
Hall Park Ave Crofton WF4 . 143 F2
   Horsforth LS18 .... 41 A1
   Liversedge WF15 .... 117 A2
Hall Park Cl LS18 .... 41 A1
Hall Park Croft LS25 ..... 103 B8
Hall Park Cl LS25 .... 83 B1
Hall Park Garth LS18 .... 41 A1
Hall Park Meadows LS25 . 103 B8
Hall Park Mount LS18 ... 41 A1
Hall Park Orch LS25 ..... 83 B1

Hall Park Rd LS23 .... 15 B5
Hall Park Rise
   Horsforth LS18 .... 41 B1
   Kippax LS25 .... 83 B1
Hall Pl LS9 .... 212 C3
Hall Rd Bradford BD2 .... 56 D5
   Leeds LS12 .... 209 F3
   Swillington LS26 .... 82 B1
   Wakefield WF2 .... 141 D4
Hall Rise Bramhope LS16 . 24 E3
   Burley in W LS29 .... 9 D1
Hall Rise Cl LS16 .... 24 E3
Hall Rise Croft LS16 ..... 24 E3
Hall Royd BD18 .... 55 B7
Hall Royd Sq S18 .... 57 B7
Hall St 6 Bradford BD6 .. 74 C1
   6 Brighouse HD6 ...... 115 B2
   Featherstone WF7 ..... 145 B4
   Glusburn BD20 .... 16 D7
   Halifax HX1 .... 203 D3
   Haworth BD22 .... 51 C6
   Huddersfield HD3 ...... 152 F7
   Oakworth BD22 .... 34 D2
   Todmorden OL14 ...... 108 B5
Hall St N HX3 .... 92 B2
Hall Stone Ct HD3 .... 93 C5
Hall Way WD20 .... 16 D4
Hallam Field Houses LS20 . 39 E8
Hallam La LS1 .... 10 B5
Hallam St LS20 .... 39 D8
Hallamshire Mews WF2 .. 141 C4
Hallas Bridge BD13 ...... 52 F6
Hallas Gr HD5 .... 154 F5
Hallas Hall Farm Cotts
   BD13 .... 52 E6
Hallas La Cullingworth BD13 . 52 E5
   Kirkburton HD8 .... 174 B6
   Wilsden BD13 .... 52 F5
Hallas Rd HD8 .... 173 F6
Hallbank Cl BD5 .... 74 D1
Hallbank Dr BD5 .... 74 D1
Hallcroft Cl 5 WF4 ...... 141 B1
Hallcroft Dr Addingham LS29 . 7 B7
   Kippax WF4 .... 141 B1
Hallcroft Rise S71 .... 179 B3
Halley St 8 OL13 .... 106 A7
Hallfield Ave LS25 .... 83 F7
Hallfield Cres LS25 ...... 83 F7
Hallfield Dr LS22 .... 13 F5
Hallfield La LS22 .... 13 F5
Hallfield Pl BD1 .... 201 B4
Hallfield Rd BD1 .... 201 A4
Hallfield St BD1 .... 201 B4
Hallfield Terr LS25 ...... 83 F7
Hallgate BD1 .... 201 B4
Halliday Ave LS12 .... 209 D4
Halliday Dr LS12 .... 209 D4
Halliday Gr LS12 .... 209 D4
Halliday Mount LS12 .... 209 D4
Halliday Pl LS12 .... 209 D4
Halliday Rd Garforth LS25 . 82 E7
   Leeds LS12 .... 209 D4
Halliday St LS28 .... 76 E8
Hallidays Gdns 2 WF13 . 139 C8
Halliley St WF13 .... 139 B8
Halling Pl OL14 .... 108 A4
Hallows Gr BD13 .... 52 D5
Hallows Rd BD21 .... 35 A8
Hallroyd Cres OL14 ..... 108 C5
Hallroyd Pl OL14 .... 108 C5
Hallroyd Rd OL14 .... 108 C5
Hallwood Gn BD10 ...... 56 D5
Halstead Dr LS29 .... 22 A5
Halstead Gr S75 .... 178 A2
Halstead La HD4 .... 173 A1
Halstead Pl BD7 .... 74 B3
Halsteads Way BD20 .... 17 C6
Halton CI HD5 .... 154 F4
Halton Dr LS15 .... 81 A8
Halton Moor Ave LS9 ... 80 D7
Halton Moor Rd LS15, LS9 . 80 D6
Halton Pl BD5 .... 74 B3
Halton Rd WF1 .... 142 F8
Halton St HX7 .... 145 D7
Hambledon Ave
   Bradford BD4 .... 95 B8
   Meltham HD7 .... 170 F1
Hambleton First Sch BD4 . 95 B8
Hambleton Bank HX2 ... 91 B6
Hambleton Cotts BD23 .. 2 B8
Hambleton Cres HX2 .... 91 B5
Hambleton Dr HX2 ...... 91 B5
Hambleton St WF1 ...... 216 B3
Hame The HX4 .... 133 F3
Hamel Rise WF9 .... 181 D6
Hamilton Ave LS7 .... 207 E4
Hamilton Gdns LS7 ..... 207 E3
Hamilton Pl LS7 .... 207 E3
Hamilton Primary Sch
   LS7 .... 207 E4
Hamilton St Bradford BD3 . 201 D4
Hamilton Terr Leeds LS7 . 207 E4
   Otley LS21 .... 23 B8
Hamilton View LS7 ...... 207 E4
Hamm Strasse BD1 ...... 201 B4
Hammer La WF4 .... 144 B4
Hammerstone Leach La
   HX5 .... 134 D5
Hammerstones Rd HX5 .. 134 D6
Hammerton Dr LS25 .... 83 A5
Hammerton Gr 4 LS28 . 76 F7
Hammerton Rd HD2 .... 136 A2
Hammerton St Bradford BD3 . 75 A6
   Pudsey LS28 .... 76 F7

Hammerton Terr 6 OL14 .. 108 B6
Hammond Cres BD11 .... 96 E7
Hammond Dr BD9 .... 55 A3
Hammond Rd WF11 ..... 126 D3
   Huddersfield HD2 ..... 136 B3
Hammond Sq BD9 .... 55 A3
Hammond St Halifax HX1 . 202 B2
   Huddersfield HD2 ..... 136 B3
Hampden Cl WF11 ...... 126 B5
Hampden Pl Bradford BD5 . 74 D4
   Halifax HX1 .... 203 D3
Hampden St BD5 .... 74 D4
Hample Balk OH6 .... 184 C1
Hample Field La DN6 ... 183 F1
Hampshire Cl LS29 ...... 8 D4
Hampshire St 3 HD5 ... 154 D6
Hampson St WF17 ...... 118 A7
Hampton Pl Bradford BD2 . 56 A1
   Leeds LS9 .... 212 B3
Hampton St LS9 .... 212 C3
Hamworth Dr BD22 ..... 34 D2
Hamza St WF17 .... 118 B4
Hamby Ave WF6 .... 122 F3
Hand Bank La WF14 .... 138 A2
Hand Carr La WF2 ...... 111 C7
Handel St Bradford BD7 .. 74 C7
Handel La HD7 .... 172 C6
Handsworth Rd WF2 ... 160 A4
Hanging Gate La BD22 . 51 B5
Hanging Heaton CE
   Jun & Inf Sch WF17 ... 118 F3
Hanging Royd HD7 ...... 152 D3
Hanging Stone Rd HD4 . 171 F7
Hanging Stones La HX6 . 132 F5
Hanging Wood Way BD19 . 95 C2
Hanover Gdns
   Dewsbury WF13 .... 139 B8
   Keighley BD20 .... 18 A2
Hanover Gdns
   Burley in W LS29 ..... 21 E8
   Dewsbury WF13 ...... 139 B8
Hanover House HX2 .... 202 A1
Hanover La LS3 .... 211 D4
Hanover Mount LS3 ... 206 A1
Hanover Pl Batley WF17 . 118 D5
   Brotherton WF11 ..... 105 C1
Hanover Sq Bradford BD1 . 74 D8
   Leeds LS3 .... 211 D4
Hanover St Batley WF17 . 118 C5
   Dearne S63 .... 194 E1
   Dewsbury WF13 ...... 139 B8
   Farnhill BD20 .... 4 D1
   Halifax HX1 .... 203 D2
   Keighley BD21 .... 35 C7
   Sowerby Bridge HX6 .. 112 D4
   Wakefield WF2 .... 142 A5
Hanover Way
   Burley in W LS29 ..... 21 E8
   Leeds LS3 .... 211 D4
Hansby Ave LS14 .... 62 B5
Hansby Bank LS14 ..... 62 B5
Hansby Cl LS14 .... 62 B4
Hansby Dr LS14 .... 62 B4
Hansby Gate LS14 ..... 62 B4
Hansby Gdns LS14 .... 62 B5
Hansby Grange 10 LS14 . 62 B5
Hansby Pl LS14 .... 62 B5
Hansby Way LS14 ..... 62 B5
Hanson Ave WF6 ...... 123 B1
Hanson Ct 11 BD12 ... 94 B2
Hanson Fold 8 BD12 .. 94 C3
Hanson La Halifax HX1 . 202 C3
   Huddersfield HD4 .... 153 C2
Hanson Mount BD12 .. 94 C3
Hanson Pl 10 BD12 ... 94 C3
Hanson Rd Brighouse HD6 . 135 E8
   Meltham HD7 .... 170 C1
Hanson Sch HD2 ...... 56 A4
Hanworth Rd BD12 .... 94 D6
Hapsburg Ct 11 BD5 .. 201 B1
Harbeck Dr BD16 ...... 36 B1
Harborough Gn BD10 . 56 D8
Harbour Cres BD6 .... 94 A8
Harbour Pk 8 BD6 .... 94 A8
Harbour Rd BD6 ...... 94 A8
Harclo Rd BD21 .... 35 E8
Harcourt Ave BD13 ... 72 C7
Harcourt Dr Addingham LS29 . 2 F1
   Morley LS27 .... 97 F5
Harcourt Pl LS1 ...... 211 D4
Harcourt St Bradford BD4 . 75 B3
   Wakefield WF2 .... 141 F5
Hard Ings Rd BD21 ... 18 C1
Hard Nese La
   Oxenhope BD22 ...... 50 F1
   Oxenhope, Upper Town BD22 . 51 B2
Hard Platts La HX4 ... 133 F2
Hardaker La BD17 .... 38 A2
Hardaker St BD8 ..... 74 D8
Hardaker's La WF7 .. 163 E6
Hardakers App WF7 . 163 F5
Hardcastle Ave WF8 . 125 C1
Hardcastle Crags HX7 . 68 C1
Hardcastle La
   Flockton WF4 .... 157 E4
   Netherton WF4 .... 157 E4

Harden Brow La BD16 ... 36 A1
Harden First Sch BD16 .. 36 B1
Harden Gr Bradford BD10 . 39 A1
   Keighley BD21 .... 35 C5
Harden Hill Rd HD7 ..... 187 E8
Harden La Harden BD15 . 53 B7
   Wilsden BD15 .... 53 E7
Harden Moss Rd
   Holmfirth HD7 .... 187 E4
   Meltham HD7 .... 187 E7
Harden Rd Harden BD16 . 36 D2
   Keighley BD21 .... 35 F5
Hardgate La BD23 ...... 51 F7
Hardie Cl WF3 .... 121 C8
Harding Houses BD20 .. 16 F7
Hardings La Glusburn BD20 . 16 F7
   Hunger Hill LS29 ...... 8 A8
   Ilkley LS29 .... 8 A7
Hardistry Dr WF8 ...... 146 B8
Hardistry End BD7 ..... 73 E3
Hardrow Gn LS12 ..... 210 A1
Hardrow Gr LS12 ..... 210 A1
Hardrow Rd LS12 ..... 210 A1
Hardrow Terr LS12 ... 210 A1
Hardwick Cl WF4 ..... 180 A8
Hardwick Cres WF8 .. 146 D5
Hardwick Croft LS7 .. 204 A2
Hardwick Ct WF8 ..... 146 C7
Hardwick La WF8 ..... 145 B1
Hardwick Rd
   Darrington WF7, WF8 . 146 F3
   Featherstone WF7 .... 145 C4
   Pontefract WF7, WF8 . 146 D5
Hardwick St
   8 Keighley BD21 ..... 35 A6
   Leeds LS10 .... 215 E2
Hardy Ave Bradford BD6 . 94 C8
   Morley LS27 .... 98 C8
Hardy Croft WF1 ..... 216 C2
Hardy Ct LS27 .... 98 B4
Hardy Gr 6 LS11 .... 214 A3
Hardy Pl HD6 .... 114 E5
Hardy St Bradford BD4 . 201 C2
   Bradford, Brownroyd Hill
   BD6 .... 74 C1
   Brighouse HD6 ...... 115 B3
   Leeds LS11 .... 214 A3
   Morley LS27 .... 98 B4
Hardy Terr 10 LS11 . 214 B3
Hardy View 4 LS11 . 214 A3
Hare Farm Ave LS12 . 77 D7
Hare Farm Cl LS12 .. 77 D7
Hare La LS28 .... 76 F4
Hare Park Ave LS12 . 116 C4
Hare Park Cl WF15 .. 116 C4
Hare Park La
   Cleckheaton WF15 .. 116 C4
   Crofton WF4 .... 161 EB
Hare Park Mount LS12 . 77 D7
Hare Park View WF4 . 161 F8
Hare St HX1 .... 202 C2
Harebell Ave WF12 .. 141 E7
Harecroft Rd LS21 ... 11 A1
Haredon Cl LS25 .... 178 A2
Harefield Cl BD20 ... 17 A5
Harefield Dr WF17 ... 97 A1
Harefield E LS15 .... 80 E7
Harefield Pk HD2 ... 135 D2
Harefield Rd 2 WF8 . 146 F8
Harehill Ave OL14 .. 108 A6
Harehill Rd BD10 ... 39 B1
Harehill St OL14 ... 108 A6
Harehills Ave LS7, LS8 . 207 F4
Harehills Cnr LS8 ... 207 F4
Harehills La
   Haworth BD22 ...... 33 D1
   Leeds LS7, LS8, LS9 . 208 B1
Harehills Park Ave LS9 . 208 B2
Harehills Park Rd LS9 . 208 B2
Harehills Park Terr LS9 . 208 B2
Harehills Park View LS9 . 208 B2
Harehills Pl LS8 .... 208 A3
Harehills Primary Sch
   LS8 .... 208 A3
Harehills Rd LS8 ... 207 F3
Harepark Dr WF15 .. 116 C4
Hares Ave LS8 ...... 207 F4
Hares Mount LS8 .. 207 F4
Hares Rd LS8 ...... 207 F4
Hares Terr LS8 .... 207 F4
Hares View LS8 ... 207 F4
Harewood Ave
   Batley WF16 .... 117 E3
   Halifax HX2 .... 112 D8
Harewood Cl LS17 .. 27 D7
Harewood Cl WF11 .. 126 C4
Harewood Cres BD22 . 34 E2
Harewood Ct Leeds LS17 . 43 D1
   Leeds, The Green LS14 . 62 A4
Harewood Gr WF16 .. 117 E3
Harewood Gate LS17 . 27 A7
Harewood House LS17 . 26 F6
Harewood La WF9 .. 183 D8
Harewood Mews LS17 . 27 D7
Harewood Mount
   Meltham HD7 .... 170 F2
   Pontefract WF8 ..... 146 E8
   Steeton BD20 .... 17 A5
Harewood Pl HX2 ... 202 A2

Harewood Rd
Collingham LS17 28 C7
East Keswick LS17 28 C7
Keighley BD22 34 F3
Wakefield WF1 142 F8
Harewood Rise BD22 34 F3
Harewood St Bradford BD3 75 B7
Leeds LS2 211 F4
Harewood View WF8 146 E8
Harewood Way LS13 77 B8
Hargrave Cres LS29 21 F4
Hargreaves Ave WF3 121 E5
Hargreaves Cl LS27 98 A6
Hargreaves St BD20 16 E6
Harker Rd BD12 94 C7
Harker St Knottingley WF11 127 B4
Sutton in C BD20 16 E5
Harker Terr 1 LS28 57 D1
Harland Cl BD2 55 E2
Harland Sq LS2 206 A3
Harlech Ave LS11 214 B2
Harlech Cres LS11 214 B2
Harlech Gr LS11 214 B2
Harlech Mount LS11 214 B2
Harlech Park Ct LS11 214 B2
Harlech Rd LS11 214 B2
Harlech St LS11 214 B2
Harlech Terr LS11 214 B2
Harlech Way LS25 83 B7
Harley Cl LS13 77 A8
Harley Ct LS13 77 A8
Harley Dr LS13 77 A8
Harley Gdns LS13 77 A8
Harley Gn LS13 77 A8
Harley Pl HD6 115 A1
Harley Rd LS13 77 A8
Harley Rise LS13 77 A8
Harley St
7 Brighouse HD6 115 A1
Todmorden OL14 108 B6
Harley Terr LS13 77 B8
Harley View LS13 77 A8
Harley Wlk LS13 77 A8
Harley Wood OL14 107 E8
Harlington Ct 3 LS27 98 A2
Harlington Rd LS27 98 A2
Harlock St WF1 142 E2
Harlow Ct LS8 61 C7
Harlow Rd BD7 74 A5
Harmby Cl DN6 184 F2
Harmon Cl BD4 95 C8
Harold Ave LS6 205 E2
Harold Gr LS6 205 E2
Harold Mount LS6 205 E2
Harold Pl Leeds LS6 205 E2
13 Shipley BD18 54 F8
Harold Rd LS6 205 E2
Harold Sq LS6 205 E2
Harold St Bingley BD16 36 E4
Leeds LS6 205 E2
Harold Terr LS6 205 E2
Harold View LS6 205 E2
Harold Wilson House WF6 123 A1
Harold Wlk LS6 205 E2
Harp Rd HD3 153 B5
Harpe Inge HD5 154 E7
Harper Ave BD10 39 B1
Harper Cres BD10 39 C1
Harper Gr Bradford BD10 39 B1
Sutton in C BD20 16 D4
Harper La LS19 40 B6
Harper Rock LS19 40 B6
Harper Royd La HX6 112 C2
Harper St LS2 212 A3
Harper Terr 8 LS19 40 B6
Harpers Sq BD20 16 D4
Harrap St WF2 141 D7
Harrier Cl BD8 73 B7
Harrier Way LS27 98 D4
Harriet St Bradford BD8 74 B8
Brighouse HD6 115 A4
Leeds LS7 207 D3
Harrington Ct HD7 170 F1
Harris Ct BD7 74 A4
Harris St 3 Bingley BD16 37 A2
Bradford BD1 201 D3
Harrison Cres LS9 61 D1
Harrison La HD7 170 E5
Harrison Pl BD20 16 B6
Harrison & Potter Trust Homes The
Leeds LS7 206 C1
6 Leeds, Woodhouse LS2 206 A3
Harrison Rd Crofton WF4 143 F1
Halifax HX1 203 E2
Harrison St Bingley BD16 37 A2
Leeds LS1 211 F4
Todmorden OL14 86 B1
Harrisons Ave 5 LS28 57 F2
Harrogate Ave BD3 56 A2
Harrogate Pl BD3 56 A2
Harrogate Rd
Bradford BD10, BD2 56 D5
East Carlton LS16 23 F2
Harewood LS17 27 A4
Leeds LS17 43 E5
Spofforth LS22 13 B7
Yeadon LS19 40 C5
Harrogate St BD3 56 A2
Harrogate Terr BD3 56 A2
Harrogate View LS17 44 C5
Harrop Ave LS27 98 B2
Harrop Gr LS27 98 B2
Harrop La BD15 53 B3
Harrop Terr LS27 98 B2
Harrop Well La 12 WF8 146 D8
Harrow St Halifax HX1 202 B3
South Elmsall WF9 182 E3
Harrowby Cres LS16 59 B7
Harrowby Rd LS16 59 B7
Harry La Bradford BD14 73 B4
Oxenhope BD22 51 C3
Harry St BD4 75 C3
Hart St Bradford BD7 74 B4
Huddersfield HD4 154 A2
Hart's Hole HD7 152 A5
Harthill LS27 97 D7
Harthill Ave LS27 97 D7
Harthill Cl LS27 97 D7
Harthill La LS27 97 D8
Harthill Par LS27 97 D7
Harthill Rise LS27 97 D7
Hartington Middle Sch BD22 51 C7
Hartington St
Batley WF17 118 C3
9 Keighley BD21 35 C8
Hartington Terr BD7 74 A5
Hartland Rd BD4 75 E4
Hartley Ave LS6 206 B4
Hartley Cl WF9 183 A4
Hartley Cres LS6 206 B4
Hartley Ct WF15 117 A3
Hartley Gdns LS6 206 B4
Hartley Gr Dewsbury WF13 118 C1
Leeds LS6 206 A4
Hartley Hill LS2 206 C1
Hartley Park Ave WF8 146 B8
Hartley Park View WF8 146 B8
Hartley Pl Leeds LS2 206 C1
3 Morley LS27 98 B3
Hartley St Bradford BD4 75 B5
Castleford WF10 124 C7
Dewsbury WF13 118 C1
Glusburn BD20 16 A6
Halifax HX1 202 C4
Morley, Churwell LS27 98 B7
Morley, Town End LS27 98 C4
Hartley Terr WF7 145 C4
Hartley's Bldgs 6 LS27 98 B3
Hartley's Sq BD20 19 D1
Hartlington Ct BD17 38 E3
Hartman Pl BD9 54 F2
Hartshead Hall La WF15 116 D1
Hartshead Junior Mixed & Infant Sch WF15 116 C2
Hartshead La WF15 116 C2
Hartshead Moor Sch BD19 116 A6
Hartwell Rd LS6 205 E2
Harvelin Pk OL14 109 A5
Harvest Croft LS29 9 D1
Harvey Royd HD5 155 A4
Harvey St WF1 142 E3
Harwill App LS27 98 C7
Harwill Ave LS27 98 C7
Harwill Croft LS27 98 C7
Harwill Gr LS27 98 C7
Harwill Rd LS27 98 C7
Harwill Rise LS27 98 C7
Harwood Cl
Huddersfield HD5 154 F5
Wakefield WF2 142 E1
Haselbury Ho 10 BD5 201 B1
Haselden Cres WF2 141 E5
Haselden Rd WF2 141 E5
Haslam Cl BD3 75 A8
Haslam Gr BD18 55 E6
Haslemere Cl BD4 75 D3
Haslewood Cl LS9 212 B4
Haslewood Ct 1 LS9 212 C4
Haslewood Dene LS9 212 C4
Haslewood Dr LS9 212 C4
Haslewood Gdns LS9 212 C4
Haslewood Gn LS9 212 C4
Haslewood Mews LS9 212 C4
Haslewood Pl LS9 212 C4
Haslewood Sq LS9 212 C4
Haslewood View LS9 212 C4
Hasley Rd LS29 21 F8
Haslingden Dr BD9 54 F2
Hassocks La HD7 171 D4
Hassocks Rd HD7 170 C3
Haste St WF10 124 B8
Hastings Ave Bradford BD5 74 D2
Wakefield WF2 142 D2
Hastings Cres WF10 125 B7
Hastings Ct
Collingham LS22 29 B8
Normanton WF6 122 E4
Thorner LS17 44 E4
Hastings Gr WF2 142 D2
Hastings Pl BD5 74 D3
Hastings St BD5 74 D2
Hastings Terr BD5 74 D2
Hastings Way LS22 28 F8
Hastings Wlk WF10 125 B7
Hatchet La BD12 95 A4
Hatfield Gdns S71 179 B4
Hatfield Pl WF4 162 D2
Hatfield Rd BD2 56 B2
Hatfield St WF1 216 B3
Hatfield View WF1 121 C3
Hathaway Ave BD9 54 D3
Hathaway Dr LS14 45 B1
Hathaway La LS14 62 B8
Hathaway Mews LS14 45 B1
Hathaway Wlk 1 LS14 62 B8
Hathershelf La HX2 111 A7
Hatton Cl BD6 94 D8
Haugh End La HX6 112 A3
Haugh Rd OL14 108 E6
Haugh Shaw Croft 13 HX1 202 C1
Haugh Shaw Rd HX1 202 C1
Haugh Shaw Rd W HX1 202 B1
Haughs La HD3 153 A7
Haughs Rd HD3 153 A7
Hauxley Ct LS29 8 D5
Hauxwell Cl DN6 184 F2
Hauxwell Dr LS19 40 B6
Havelock Sq 2 BD13 72 E6
Havelock St Bradford BD7 74 A4
Dewsbury WF13 138 E5
Thornton BD13 72 E6
Haven Chase LS16 41 E3
Haven Croft LS16 41 F3
Haven Ct Leeds LS16 41 F3
Pontefract WF8 146 B5
Haven Garth LS16 41 E3
Haven Gdns LS16 41 E3
Haven Gn LS16 41 E3
Haven La HX7 110 B8
Haven Mount LS16 41 E3
Haven Rise LS16 41 E3
Haven St 15 OL14 108 C5
Haven The Bradford BD10 56 C6
Leeds LS15 81 D8
Haven View LS16 41 E3
Havercroft WF5 140 E5
Havercroft Jun & Inf Sch WF4 180 B8
Havercroft La WF8 147 E5
Havercroft Rise S72 180 E6
Havercroft Way WF17 117 F5
Haverdale Rd WF4 162 C1
Haverlands The WF9 181 E6
Haveroid La WF4 159 F4
Haveroid Way WF4 159 F5
Haverthwaites Dr LS25 47 E1
Havertop La WF6 123 F2
Haw Ave LS19 40 C8
Haw Cliff La HD4 172 F1
Haw Hill View WF6 123 C3
Haw La LS19 40 B8
Haw Park La Ryhill WF4 161 F3
Walton WF2 161 B2
Haw View LS19 40 C8
Hawber Cote Dr BD20 5 F2
Hawber Cote La BD20 5 F2
Hawber La BD20 5 F1
Hawes Ave Bradford BD5 74 C2
Huddersfield HD3 153 B6
Hawes Cl WF10 125 B8
Hawes Cres BD5 74 C2
Hawes Dr BD5 74 C2
Hawes Gr BD5 74 C2
Hawes Mount BD5 74 C2
Hawes Rd BD5 74 C2
Hawes Terr BD5 74 C2
Haweswater Cl LS22 13 B5
Haweswater Pl WF11 126 E1
Hawk St 4 BD21 35 D8
Hawk's Nest Gdns E LS17 43 D4
Hawk's Nest Gdns S LS17 43 D4
Hawk's Nest Gdns W LS17 43 D4
Hawk's Nest Rise LS17 43 D4
Hawkcliffe View BD20 5 C1
Hawke Ave WF16 117 E4
Hawke Way BD12 94 E6
Hawkhill Ave Guiseley LS20 39 D8
Leeds LS15 62 B2
Hawkhill Dr LS15 62 B2
Hawkhill Gdns LS15 62 B2
Hawkhills LS7 204 B3
Hawkhurst Rd LS12 209 F2
Hawkingcroft Rd WF4 140 F1
Hawkins Dr LS7 206 C2
Hawkins Way OL15 129 C1
Hawkroyd Bank Rd HD4 171 E6
Hawksbridge La BD22 51 A3
Hawkshead Cl BD5 201 B1
Hawkshead Cres LS14 62 A3
Hawkshead Dr BD5 201 B1
Hawkshead Way BD5 201 B1
Hawkshead Wlk BD5 201 B1
Hawksley Ct LS27 98 A6
Hawkstone Ave LS20 39 C7
Hawkstone Dr BD20 18 A1
Hawkstone View LS20 39 D7
Hawkswood Ave
Bradford BD9 54 F3
Leeds LS5 58 E7
Hawkswood Cres LS5 58 E7
Hawkswood Gr LS5 58 E7
Hawkswood Mount LS5 58 E7
Hawkswood Pl LS5 58 F6
Hawkswood St LS5 58 F6
Hawkswood Terr LS5 58 F6
Hawkswood View LS5 58 E7
Hawksworth Ave LS20 39 D8
Hawksworth C of E Primary Sch LS20 38 F8
Hawksworth Cl LS29 22 A3
Hawksworth Dr
Guiseley LS20 39 D7
Menston LS29 22 A4
Hawksworth Gr LS5 58 D6
Hawksworth Hall Sch LS20 38 F8
Hawksworth La LS20 39 B7
Hawksworth Rd
Baildon BD17 38 C6
Horsforth LS18 58 D7
Hawksworth St LS29 8 B4
Hawksworth Wood Primary Sch LS16 58 E7
Hawley Cl LS27 97 F2
Hawley Terr BD10 56 E4
Hawley Way LS27 97 F2
Haworth Cl WF14 137 F6
Haworth First Sch BD22 51 C7
Haworth Gr BD9 54 E3
Haworth La LS19 40 B7
Haworth Rd Batley WF17 96 F2
Bradford BD9 54 C4
Haworth BD22 51 E8
Wilsden BD15 53 C4
Haworth Sta BD22 51 C7
Hawthorn Ave
Batley WF17 118 A3
Bradford BD3 75 E8
Crofton WF4 143 E1
Knottingley WF11 126 E3
Yeadon LS19 40 C7
Hawthorn Cl
Brighouse HD6 115 C3
Wakefield WF2 120 B3
Hawthorn Cres
Baildon BD17 38 D3
4 Leeds LS7 204 A3
Yeadon LS19 40 B7
Hawthorn Croft WF3 100 C1
Hawthorn Ct S65 143 E1
Hawthorn Dr
Bradford BD10 56 C7
Pudsey LS13 57 D6
Yeadon LS19 40 C8
Hawthorn Gr
Ackworth M T WF7 163 F5
Burley in W LS29 21 F8
Pudsey LS13 57 D5
Rothwell LS26 100 F4
Silkstone S75 193 F1
Hawthorn La 6 LS7 204 A3
Hawthorn Mill 5 LS12 78 A4
Hawthorn Mount 3 LS7 204 A3
Hawthorn Pl 9 OL14 108 B6
Hawthorn Rd Bacup OL13 106 A2
Leeds LS7 204 A3
Slaithwaite HD7 151 F1
Yeadon LS19 40 C7
Hawthorn St Bradford BD3 75 E8
Brighouse HX3 114 D8
4 Halifax HX1 202 C1
Hawthorn Terr
5 Halifax HX1 202 C1
Huddersfield HX1 154 B8
Ossett WF5 140 E3
Hawthorn Vale 7 LS7 204 A3
Hawthorn View
Baildon BD17 38 E3
5 Leeds LS7 204 A3
Hawthorne Ave
Castleford WF10 125 B6
Featherstone WF7 145 C4
Hemsworth WF9 181 D6
Shipley BD18 55 D5
Wetherby LS22 13 D7
Hawthorne Cl
Flockton WF4 157 D3
Gildersome LS27 97 D7
Lepton HD8 155 D3
Hawthorne Cres WF9 181 C6
Hawthorne Dr LS27 97 D7
Hawthorne Flats S63 194 D1
Hawthorne Gdns LS16 42 B5
Hawthorne Gr WF2 141 E7
Hawthorne Mount WF6 144 B7
Hawthorne Rise LS14 62 C8
Hawthorne St Shafton S72 180 C3
Silsden BD20 5 D1
Hawthorne Terr
Huddersfield HD4 153 C4
Swillington LS25 82 C5
Wakefield WF2 141 E7
Hawthorne View LS27 97 E7
Hawthorne Way
Keighley BD20 36 E8
Shafton S72 180 C3
Shepley HD8 173 F3
Hawthorns The
Glusburn BD20 16 C6
Lofthouse Gate WF1 121 D5
Ossett WF5 140 E3
Hawtop La WF4 177 F5
Hayburn Gdns WF17 118 B5
Hayburn Rd WF17 118 A5
Haycliffe Ave BD7 74 A2
Haycliffe Dr BD7 73 F2
Haycliffe Gr BD7 74 A2
Haycliffe Hill Rd BD5 74 B3
Haycliffe La BD5, BD6 74 B2
Haycliffe Rd BD5 74 B3
Haycliffe Terr BD5 74 B3
Hayclose Mead BD6 94 A6
Hayden St BD3 75 B6
Haydn Ave WF3 121 E6
Haydn's Terr LS28 57 E2
Hayfield Ave
Boston Spa LS23 30 C8
Huddersfield HD3 153 A7
Hayfield Cl Baildon BD17 38 E4
Holmfirth HD7 189 D4
Hayfield Terr LS12 209 F2
Hayfields The BD22 51 C8
Haygill Nook BD23 1 E1
Hayhills La BD20 5 D4
Hayhills Rd BD20 5 E2
Hayleigh Ave 9 LS13 58 C3
Hayleigh Mount LS13 58 C3
Hayleigh St 8 LS13 58 C3
Hayleigh Terr 7 LS13 58 C3
Hayley Ct HX3 203 E4
Hayne La WF4 157 E5
Haynes St BD21 35 D6
Hays La HX2 91 C7
Hayson Cl WF12 118 F1
Haythorns Ave BD20 5 D
Haythorns Mount BD20 5 D
Hayton Dr LS22 13 F
Hayton Wood View LS25 64 E
Haywain The LS29 8 D
Haywood Ave HD3 153 C
Hazebrouck Dr BD17 38 B
Hazel Ave Dewsbury WF12 140 B
Leeds LS14 62 C
Hazel Beck BD16 54 A
Hazel Cl Birkenshaw BD11 96 A
Dewsbury WF12 140 B
Hazel Cres WF12 140 B
Hazel Croft BD18 55 D
Hazel Ct Rothwell LS26 100 F
Wakefield WF2 142 A
Hazel Dr WF12 140 B
Hazel Gdns WF10 125 D
Hazel Gr Bacup OL13 106 B
Batley WF17 118 A
Brighouse HX3 115 A
Flockton WF4 157 D
Huddersfield, Brackenhall HD2 136 B
Huddersfield, Cowlersley HD7 152 F
Pontefract WF8 125 E
Sutton in C BD20 16 C
Hazel Grove Rd BD20 16 C
Hazel Hurst Gr BD13 92 D
Hazel Hurst Rd BD13 92 D
Hazel La DN6 184 A
Hazel Mount BD18 55 C
Hazel Rd WF11 126 E
Hazel Rise LS26 102 C
Hazel Wlk BD9 54 D
Hazelcroft BD2 56 D4
Hazeldene BD13 92 D8
Hazeldene Cotts LS22 12 C5
Hazelheads BD17 38 C5
Hazelhurst Ave 1 BD16 37 A1
Hazelhurst Brow BD9 54 D2
Hazelhurst Ct Bradford BD9 75 C7
Bradford, Daisy Hill BD9 54 D2
Pudsey LS28 76 F7
Hazelhurst Rd BD9 54 D2
Hazelhurst Terr BD9 54 D2
Hazelmere Ave BD16 54 A8
Hazelwood Ave
Garforth LS25 83 A5
Keighley BD20 18 F1
Hazelwood Ct WF1 121 D5
Hazelwood Gdns WF9 181 E6
Hazelwood Rd
Bradford BD9 54 C3
Hemsworth WF9 163 B1
Lofthouse Gate WF1 121 D5
Hazelwood St OL14 108 B5
Hazill Bank WF2 141 E8
Hazledene Cres S72 180 D1
Hazledene Rd S72 180 D1
Headfield C of E Jun Sch WF12 139 C5
Headfield La WF12 139 C5
Headfield Rd
Dewsbury WF12 139 D5
Huddersfield HD4 154 A3
Headfield View WF12 139 D4
Headingley Ave LS6 59 C5
Headingley Cres LS6 205 D4
Headingley Ct LS6 205 F4
Headingley Golf Course LS16 42 D6
Headingley Grounds (Cricket & Rugby League) LS6 205 D4
Headingley La LS6 205 E4
Headingley Mount LS6 59 C5
Headingley Primary Sch LS6 59 D5
Headingley Rise LS6 205 F3
Headingley Sta LS5 59 B4
Headingley View LS6 205 D4
Headland Gr BD6 73 F1
Headland La WF12 139 F6
Headlands Ave WF5 140 C5
Headlands CE Prim Sch WF15 117 A4
Headlands Cl WF15 117 B3
Headlands Gr WF5 140 C5
Headlands La
Knottingley WF11 126 E4
Pontefract WF8 125 D1
Headlands Pk WF5 140 C5
Headlands Rd
Huddersfield HD1 154 A7
Liversedge WF15 117 A4
Ossett WF5 140 C5
Headlands St WF15 117 A3
Headlands The WF15 117 A3
Headlands Wlk WF5 140 C5
Headley Cotts LS24 48 A8
Headley Golf Course BD13 72 C5
Headley La Bramham LS23 30 E1
Thornton BD13 72 D5
Headrow Sh Ctr LS1 211 F4
Headrow The LS1 211 F4
Headwall Gn HD7 152 B3
Heald Cl OL13 106 A8
Heald La OL13 106 A8
Heald St WF10 124 F8
Heald Terr HX4 133 A5
Healdfield Rd WF10 124 F8
Healds Ave WF15 117 B4
Healds Rd WF13 118 A2
Healdwood Cl WF10 125 A8
Healdwood Rd WF10 125 A8

Healey Ave BD16 .... 37 A2
Healey Cl WF17 .... 117 F5
Healey Cres WF5 .... 140 D3
Healey Croft La WF3 .... 120 B7
Healey Dr WF5 .... 140 D4
Healey Green La
 WF14, HD5 .... 155 F7
Healey Junior Infants Sch
 WF17 .... 117 F5
Healey La Batley WF17 ...... 117 F5
 Batley, WF17 .... 118 B5
 2 Bingley BD16 .... 37 A2
 Healey WF17 .... 157 A7
Healey Rd WF5 .... 140 D3
Healey St WF17 .... 117 F5
Healey Wood Cres HD6 ...... 115 A1
Healey Wood Gdns HD6 ...... 136 B8
Healey Wood Gr HD6 .... 136 B8
Healey Wood Rd HD6 .... 115 B1
Heap La BD3 .... 201 D4
Heap St Bradford BD1 .... 201 D3
 Halifax HX3 .... 113 B4
Heath Ave HX3 .... 113 B4
Heath Cl Dewsbury WF12 ..... 140 B8
 Slaithwaite HD7 .... 170 E7
Heath Cres Leeds LS11 ...... 213 E3
 Low Bradley BD20 .... 4 C6
Heath Dr Boston Spa LS23 .... 30 B7
 Low Bradley BD20 .... 4 C6
Heath Gdns HX3 .... 113 C4
Heath Gr Batley WF17 ...... 118 F5
 Keighley BD20 .... 36 D8
 Leeds LS11 .... 213 E3
 Pudsey LS28 .... 76 C6
Heath Hall HX1 .... 203 E1
Heath Hall Ave BD4 .... 75 B1
Heath Hill Rd HX2 .... 91 A2
Heath House La HD7 .... 152 B4
Heath La HX3 .... 113 C4
Heath Lea HX1 .... 203 E2
Heath Mount LS11 .... 213 E3
Heath Mount Rd HD6 .... 136 A8
Heath Park Ave HX1 .... 203 E2
Heath Pk LS29 .... 7 F3
Heath Pl LS11 .... 213 E3
Heath Rd Bradford BD3 .... 56 B1
 Dewsbury WF12 .... 140 B8
 Halifax HX1, HX3 .... 203 E1
 Huddersfield HD7 .... 152 F1
 Leeds LS11 .... 213 E3
 Slaithwaite HD7 .... 170 E8
Heath Rise LS11 .... 213 E2
Heath Royd HX3 .... 113 C4
Heath St Bingley BD16 .... 37 A3
 Bradford BD3 .... 75 C7
 Halifax HX3 .... 113 C4
 Liversedge WF15 .... 117 B2
Heath Terr BD3 .... 75 C7
Heath View Jun & Inf Sch
 WF1 .... 142 E7
Heath View St HX1 .... 203 F2
Heath Villas HX3 .... 113 C4
Heath Wlk WF12 .... 140 B8
Heathcliff BD22 .... 51 B7
Heathcliffe Cl WF17 .... 96 F3
Heathcote Ave LS14 .... 45 F5
Heathcote Rise BD22 .... 51 E8
Heathcroft Bank LS11 .... 213 E2
Heathcroft Cres LS11 .... 213 E2
Heathcroft Cres LS11 .... 213 E2
Heathcroft Rise LS11 .... 213 E2
Heathcroft Vale LS11 .... 213 E2
Heathdale Ave HD2 .... 135 F1
Heather Ave HD7 .... 170 E1
Heather Bank OL14 .... 108 B1
Heather Bank Cl BD13 .... 52 D5
Heather Cl
 Lofthouse Gate WF1 .... 121 D5
 Ossett WF5 .... 140 F3
 South Kirkby WF9 .... 182 D3
Heather Ct Batley WF17 ...... 96 E2
 Bingley BD16 .... 37 A5
 Huddersfield HD3 .... 152 F8
 Lofthouse Gate WF3 .... 121 E5
Heather Dr HX2 .... 91 A3
Heather Fold HD8 .... 174 F1
Heather Gdns Leeds LS13 ..... 77 E8
 Scarcroft LS14 .... 45 C7
Heather Gr Bradford BD9 ..... 54 B3
 Keighley BD21 .... 35 A8
 Leeds LS13 .... 77 E8
Heather Grove First Sch
 BD9 .... 54 B3
Heather Rd Baildon BD17 ..... 38 D4
 Meltham HD7 .... 170 E1
Heather Rise LS29 .... 21 F8
Heather Side HD7 .... 38 B4
Heather Vale LS14 .... 45 B7
Heather View Bingley BD16 ... 37 D5
 Ossett WF5 .... 140 D5
Heatherbank Ave BD22 .... 34 F4
Heathercroft LS7 .... 204 B2
Heatherdale Ct WF3 .... 119 E8
Heatherdale Dr WF3 .... 119 E8
Heatherdale Rd WF3 .... 119 E8
Heatherfield Cres HD1 .... 153 D6
Heatherfield Rd HD1 .... 153 D6
Heathergrove Fold HD5 ...... 154 D7
Heatherlands Ave BD20 ...... 5 D2
Heatherstones 3 HX3 .... 113 B4
 Mirfield WF14 .... 137 F6
Heathfield Ave HX5 .... 135 B7
Heathfield Cl Bingley BD16 ... 37 A4
 East Ardsley WF3 .... 119 E8
Heathfield Gr Bradford BD7 .. 73 E4
 1 Halifax HX3 .... 113 C4

Heathfield Ind Est HX5 ...... 135 A6
Heathfield La LS23 .... 30 B8
Heathfield Mews HD7 .... 152 E4
Heathfield Pl 2 HX3 .... 113 C4
Heathfield Rd
 Huddersfield HD7 .... 152 E4
 Ossett WF5 .... 140 C8
Heathfield Rise LS28 .... 132 C1
Heathfield Sch HX6 .... 150 C8
Heathfield Sq 1 LS6 .... 59 D6
Heathfield St HX5 .... 135 A6
Heathfield Terr
 Halifax HX3 .... 113 C4
 Leeds LS6 .... 59 D6
Heathfield Wlk LS16 .... 42 A5
Heathmoor Cl
 Bradford BD10 .... 56 A7
 Halifax HX2 .... 91 E6
Heathmoor Mount HX2 ...... 91 E6
Heathmoor Park Rd HX2 ..... 91 D6
Heathmoor Way HX2 .... 91 D6
Heathness Rd LS29 .... 2 D1
Heathville Infants Sch
 WF1 .... 216 C3
Heathwood Dr HD7 .... 152 C5
Heathy Ave HX2 .... 92 A5
Heathy La HX2 .... 92 A5
Heaton Ave
 Cleckheaton BD19 .... 116 C7
 Dewsbury WF12 .... 139 E8
 Keighley BD20 .... 36 C7
 Kirkheaton HD5 .... 137 C1
 Leeds LS12 .... 209 F1
Heaton Avenue First Sch
 BD19 .... 116 C7
Heaton Cl Baildon BD17 ...... 38 B4
 Bingley BD16 .... 37 B4
Heaton Cres Baildon BD17 ... 38 B5
 Bingley BD16 .... 37 B4
Heaton Dr Baildon BD17 ..... 38 B4
 Bingley BD16 .... 37 B4
 Kirkheaton HD5 .... 137 C2
Heaton Fold La HD1 .... 153 D6
Heaton Gdns HD1 .... 153 D6
Heaton Gr
 Cleckheaton BD19 .... 116 C7
 Shipley, Heaton Grove BD9 ... 55 B4
 Shipley, Windhill BD18 ...... 55 B4
Heaton Hill BD6 .... 93 E7
Heaton Middle Sch BD9 ...... 54 D4
Heaton Moor Rd HD7 .... 137 C1
Heaton Park Dr BD9 .... 55 A3
Heaton Park Rd BD9 .... 54 F3
Heaton Rd Batley WF17 ...... 118 C7
 Bradford BD8, BD9 .... 55 B2
 Huddersfield HD1 .... 153 D6
Heaton Royds Hospl BD9 .... 54 D5
Heaton Royds La BD9 .... 54 F5
Heaton Royds Sch BD18 ..... 55 A5
Heaton St
 Ackworth M T WF7 .... 163 E5
 Bradford BD4 .... 201 D1
 4 Brighouse HD6 .... 115 A2
 Cleckheaton BD19 .... 116 D8
Heaton's Ct LS1 .... 211 F3
Heatons Yd HD6 .... 115 B1
Heator La HD8 .... 191 A7
Hebb View BD6 .... 73 E2
Hebble Brook Cl HX2 .... 91 C4
Hebble Ct HX2 .... 91 D4
Hebble Dean HX2 .... 91 F1
Hebble Dr HD7 .... 189 A7
Hebble End HX7 .... 88 F3
Hebble Gdns HX2 .... 91 E1
Hebble La Halifax HX3 .... 91 F1
 Meltham HD7 .... 187 D8
Hebble Mount HD7 .... 170 E1
Hebble Row BD22 .... 34 C1
Hebble St Dewsbury WF13 ... 138 F5
 4 Huddersfield HD1 .... 154 B8
Hebble Vale Dr HX2 .... 91 D5
Hebden Appl LS14 .... 62 B6
Hebden Bridge Rd BD22 ..... 51 B1
Hebden Chase LS14 .... 62 B6
Hebden Cl LS14 .... 62 B6
Hebden Ct LS14 .... 62 B6
Hebden Path LS14 .... 62 B6
Hebden Pl LS14 .... 62 B6
Hebden Rd Haworth BD22 .... 51 D6
Hebden Royd C of E Junior
 & Infant Sch HX7 .... 88 C3
Hebden Terr HX7 .... 89 B8
Hebden Wlk 2 LS14 .... 62 B6
Heber Cl BD20 .... 17 F8
Heber St BD21 .... 35 A6
Heber's Ghyll Dr LS29 .... 7 E3
Heber's Gr LS29 .... 7 E4
Heckmondwike
 Grammar Sch WF16 .... 117 D4
Heckmondwike Rd
 Batley WF13 .... 117 F1
 Dewsbury WF13 .... 138 F8
Hector Cl 7 BD6 .... 74 C1
Heddon Cl BD5 .... 201 B1
Heddon Gr BD5 .... 201 B1
Heddon Pl LS6 .... 59 E6
Heddon St LS6 .... 59 E6
Heddon Wlk BD5 .... 201 B1
Hedge Cl BD8 .... 54 D1
Hedge Side BD8 .... 73 E8
Hedge Top La HX3 .... 93 B2
Hedge Way BD8 .... 54 E1
Hedley Chase LS12 .... 210 B3
Hedley Cres WF1 .... 121 B3
Hedley Gdns LS12 .... 210 B3
Hedley Grn LS12 .... 210 B3

Heeley Rd WF2 .... 160 A4
Heidelberg Rd BD9 .... 55 A2
Height Gn HX6 .... 112 B4
Height La Draughton BD23 ... 1 D3
 Oxenhope BD22 .... 51 D2
Height Rd HX7 .... 89 E3
Heights Bank LS12 .... 77 F7
Heights Cl LS12 .... 77 F7
Heights Dr Leeds LS12 .... 77 F7
 Slaithwaite HD7 .... 170 D8
Heights E The LS12 .... 77 F7
Heights Garth LS12 .... 77 F7
Heights La Batley WF16 ..... 117 E3
 Bingley BD16 .... 37 B6
 Bradford BD9 .... 54 D3
 Leeds LS12 .... 77 F7
 Silsden BD20 .... 5 B4
Heights Par LS12 .... 77 F7
Heights The HD7 .... 189 C3
Heights W The LS12 .... 77 F7
Heights Way LS12 .... 77 F7
Heights Wlk LS12 .... 77 F7
Helen Rose Ct BD18 .... 38 E1
Helen St Huddersfield HD1 ... 153 E3
 Shipley BD18 .... 54 F8
Helen Terr HD6 .... 114 F3
Helena Cl LS25 .... 102 F8
Helena Pl LS25 .... 102 F8
Helena St LS25 .... 102 F8
Helena Way BD4 .... 95 C8
Helene Ct HD3 .... 152 E8
Hell La WF4 .... 143 E4
Hellewell St 4 BD6 .... 93 F7
Hellewell's Rd WF5 .... 140 D1
Hellwood La LS14 .... 45 D7
Helm La Mirfield WF14 ...... 137 D5
 Sowerby Bridge HX6 .... 132 C8
Helme CE Junior
 & Infants Sch HD7 .... 170 E4
Helme La HD7 .... 170 D3
Helme Pk HD7 .... 170 D3
Helmet La HD7 .... 170 D2
Helmsley Ct LS10 .... 99 C4
Helmsley Dr LS16 .... 59 B7
Helmsley Rd
 Boston Spa LS23 .... 30 C2
 Leeds LS16 .... 59 B7
 Wakefield WF2 .... 142 F1
Helmsley St BD4 .... 75 A4
Helston Croft LS10 .... 99 A5
Helston Garth LS10 .... 99 A5
Helston Gn LS10 .... 99 A5
Helston Pl LS10 .... 99 A5
Helston Rd Middleton LS10 .. 99 A5
 Normanton WF6 .... 123 B3
Helston St LS10 .... 98 F6
Helston Way LS10 .... 99 A6
Helston Wlk LS10 .... 99 A6
Helted Way HD5 .... 154 E3
Hemingway Cl LS10 .... 99 F7
Hemingway Garth LS10 .... 215 E3
Hemingway Gn LS10 ...... 215 E3
Hemingway Rd BD10 ...... 56 D8
Hemishor Dr LS26 .... 102 E8
Hemsby Gr 7 BD21 .... 35 B4
Hemsby Rd WF10 .... 124 C6
Hemsby St 7 BD21 .... 35 B4
Hemsworth By-Pass
 WF9 .... 181 D4
Hemsworth High Sch
 WF9 .... 181 E7
Hemsworth La WF9 .... 163 A5
Hemsworth Rd WF9 .... 181 F4
Hemsworth Water Pk
 WF9 .... 163 D1
Hen Holme La BD20 .... 17 E7
Henacrewood Ct BD13 ..... 92 E7
Henage St 10 BD13 .... 72 D1
Henbury St LS7 .... 207 D1
Henconner Ave LS7 .... 60 C6
Henconner Cres LS7 ...... 60 C6
Henconner Dr LS7 .... 60 C6
Henconner Garth LS7 ..... 60 C6
Henconner Gdns LS7 ..... 60 C6
Henconner La
 Leeds, Chapel Allerton LS7 .. 60 C6
 Leeds, Gamble Hill LS13 .... 77 E8
Henconner Rd LS7 .... 60 C6
Hendal Prim Jun & Inf Sch
 WF2 .... 160 B5
Henderson Ave WF6 ...... 144 B8
Henderson Glen S71 ...... 179 A3
Henderson Pl 8 BD6 ...... 74 C1
Hendford Dr BD3 .... 75 B8
Henley Ave Bradford BD5 ... 74 E2
 Dewsbury WF12 .... 139 E2
 1 Leeds LS13 .... 58 C2
 Yeadon LS19 .... 40 D3
Henley Cl LS19 .... 40 D3
Henley Cres Leeds LS13 .... 58 C2
 Yeadon LS19 .... 40 D3
Henley Croft HD5 .... 154 E6
Henley Ct BD5 .... 74 E2
Henley Dr
 Featherstone WF7 .... 145 D3
 Yeadon LS19 .... 40 C3
Henley Gr Bradford BD5 ... 74 E2
 2 Leeds LS13 .... 58 C2
Henley Hill LS19 .... 40 C3
Henley Mount LS19 ...... 40 D3
Henley Pl LS13 .... 58 C2
Henley Rd Bradford BD5 ... 74 E2
 Dewsbury WF12 .... 139 E2
 Leeds LS13 .... 58 C2
Henley St 3 LS13 .... 58 C2
Henley Terr LS13 .... 58 C2

Henley View LS13 .... 58 C2
Henrietta St 2 WF17 ...... 118 C5
Henry ave Leeds LS12 ...... 209 F1
 Ryhill WF4 .... 180 C8
Henry Cl WF2 .... 180 C3
Henry Frederick Ave HD4 .. 171 C6
Henry Moore Ct WF10 ..... 125 B7
Henry Moore Inst LS1 ...... 211 E4
Henry Pl S64 .... 98 A4
Henry Ralph Ave HD4 ..... 153 C1
Henry Sir Batley WF17 ..... 118 C2
 Bradford BD14 .... 73 C4
 Brighouse HD6 .... 115 A4
 1 Halifax HX1 .... 203 D2
 Huddersfield HD1 .... 154 A6
 Keighley BD21 .... 35 D7
 Thornton BD13 .... 72 D6
 Wakefield WF2 .... 142 A6
Henry Terr LS19 .... 39 F7
Henshaw Ave LS19 .... 40 B6
Henshaw Cres LS19 .... 40 B6
Henshaw La LS19 .... 40 B6
Henshaw Oval LS19 ...... 40 A6
Henshaw Rd OL14 .... 108 B1
Henson Gr WF10 .... 125 B6
Hepton Ct LS9 .... 208 B1
Hepton Dr HX7 .... 88 F4
Heptonstall Junior
 & Infants Sch HX7 .... 88 F5
Hepworth Ave LS27 .... 98 B8
Hepworth Cl WF14 .... 138 B6
Hepworth Cres
 Holmfirth HD7 .... 189 C3
 Morley LS27 .... 98 B8
Hepworth Dr WF14 .... 138 C6
Hepworth Junior
 & Infants Sch HD7 .... 189 F1
Hepworth La WF14 .... 138 B6
Hepworth Rd HD7 .... 189 F3
Hepworth St WF10 .... 103 F1
Hepworths Bldgs HD2 .... 136 D3
Herbalist St LS12 .... 210 B2
Herbert Pl BD3 .... 75 E8
Herbert St Bingley BD16 ... 37 A3
 Bradford, Clayton BD14 .... 73 C3
 Bradford, Holme Top BD5 ... 74 D4
 Castleford WF10 .... 124 D7
 Halifax HX1 .... 202 B2
 Shipley, Cottingley BD16 ... 54 B6
 Shipley, Saltaire BD18 .... 37 F1
Hereford Cl WF9 .... 181 D8
Hereford St LS12 .... 209 F4
Heritage Rd WF17 .... 118 C4
Heritage Way BD22 ...... 34 C2
Hermit St BD21 .... 35 A2
Hermitage Pk HD8 .... 155 E2
Hermon Ave HX1 .... 202 C2
Hermon Gr HX1 .... 202 C2
Hermon Rd LS15 .... 81 B8
Hermon St LS15 .... 62 B1
Heron Cl Leeds LS17 ...... 43 F4
 Queensbury BD13 .... 72 C2
 Steeton BD20 .... 17 B5
Heron Ct 4 LS27 .... 98 D4
Heron Dr WF2 .... 160 C5
Heron Gr LS17 .... 43 F4
Herries Ct LS29 .... 22 B4
Herriot Mews WF10 ...... 125 B5
Herschel Rd BD8 .... 73 D7
Hertford Chase LS15 ..... 81 C6
Hertford Cl LS15 .... 81 D6
Hertford Croft LS15 ...... 81 D6
Hertford Fold LS15 .... 81 C6
Hertford Lawn LS15 ...... 81 C6
Heseltine Cl WF6 .... 123 A2
Heseltine La HX7 .... 110 B4
Heshbon St BD4 .... 75 C3
Hesketh Ave
 East Ardsley WF3 .... 119 D8
 Leeds LS5 .... 59 A5
Hesketh La WF3 .... 119 D8
Hesketh Mount LS5 ...... 59 A5
Hesketh Pl LS5 .... 59 A5
Hesketh Rd LS5 .... 59 A4
Hesketh Terr LS5 .... 59 A4
Hesley Rd WF2 .... 160 B5
Hessel Ct WF8 .... 146 B8
Hessle Ave LS6 .... 205 E3
Hessle Common La WF7 .. 163 D7
Hessle La WF7 .... 163 D8
Hessle Mount LS6 .... 205 E3
Hessle Pl LS6 .... 205 E3
Hessle Rd 7 LS6 .... 205 E3
Hessle Terr LS6 .... 205 E3
Hessle View LS6 .... 205 E3
Hessle Wlk 8 LS6 .... 205 E3
Hetchell View BD22 ...... 28 D2
Hetton Dr BD3 .... 75 D6
Hetton Rd LS8 .... 208 B4
Heuthwaite Ave LS22 .... 13 F4
Hew Clews BD7 .... 73 E3
Hexham Gn HD3 .... 152 F5
Hey Beck La WF12 .... 119 C5
Hey Cres HD7 .... 170 D2
Hey Head La
 Littleborough OL15 ...... 129 A1
 Todmorden OL14 .... 108 D7
Hey La Huddersfield HD7 ... 172 B7
 Huddersfield, Lowerhouses
 HD5 .... 154 D3
 Kirkburton HD7 .... 172 B7
 Ripponden HD3 .... 151 B6
Hey Slack La HD7 .... 190 C2
Hey St Bradford BD7 ...... 74 D6
 Brighouse HD6 .... 115 B4
 1 Todmorden OL14 ...... 108 C5
Hey's Bldgs WF6 .... 122 F4

Heybeck Wlk BD4 .... 75 F2
Heycliffe Rd HD7 .... 189 B5
Heyford Cl BD2 .... 55 D3
Heygate Cl BD17 .... 38 D4
Heygate La Baildon BD17 ... 38 D4
 Bramham LS23 .... 30 F3
Heys Ave BD13 .... 72 F6
Heys Cl WF11 .... 127 A4
Heys Cres BD13 .... 72 F6
Heys Gdns HD7 .... 189 C8
Heys La Halifax HX2 ...... 90 B6
 Ripponden HX6 .... 132 D1
 Slaithwaite HD7 .... 151 D2
Heys Rd HD7 .... 189 C8
Heys The HD7 .... 170 E4
Heysham Dr BD4 .... 75 F3
Heywood Cl HX3 .... 93 A2
Heywood Pl HX3 .... 203 D3
Heywood St 10 HX1 ..... 202 C3
Heywood St 9 HX3 ...... 203 D3
Hick La WF17 .... 118 D5
Hick St BD1 .... 201 C3
Hicks La LS26 .... 102 D3
Hicks Memorial Sch LS25 .. 84 A7
Higgin Chamber HX2 ...... 111 C5
Higgin La HX3 .... 113 E5
High Ash Leeds LS17 ...... 43 E5
 Shipley BD18 .... 55 E7
High Ash Ave
 Clayton West HD8 .... 176 A2
 Leeds LS17 .... 43 F5
High Ash Cl WF4 .... 178 F7
High Ash Dr LS17 .... 43 E5
High Ash Mount LS17 .... 43 F5
High Ash Pk BD15 .... 53 F1
High Bank BD20 .... 4 C6
High Bank Appl LS15 ..... 81 D7
High Bank Cl
 Addingham LS29 .... 6 E8
 Leeds LS15 .... 81 D8
High Bank Gate LS15 .... 81 D7
High Bank Gdns LS15 .... 81 D7
High Bank La BD18 ...... 54 E6
High Bank Pl LS15 .... 81 D7
High Bank Way LS15 .... 81 D7
High Bank Way LS15 .... 81 E7
High Banks Cl BD20 ..... 18 F2
High Binns La BD22 .... 51 D3
High Bradley La BD20 ... 4 C7
High Brook Fall WF3 .... 121 C7
High Brooms HD2 ...... 135 E1
High Bury Cl BD13 ...... 92 C8
High Busy La
 Bradford BD10 .... 56 A8
 Shipley BD18 .... 55 F8
High Cl Guiseley LS20 .... 39 B8
 Huddersfield HD5 .... 154 E3
 Slaithwaite HD7 .... 170 A8
 Addingham LS29 .... 6 B8
High Cliffe Cl 11 BD13 ... 72 D6
High Cliffe Terr LS22 .... 13 E5
High Cote BD20 .... 18 D2
High Court La LS2 .... 212 A3
High Crags First Sch
 BD18 .... 55 C6
High Crest HD7 .... 152 E2
High Croft Addingham LS29 . 6 F8
 Halifax HX3 .... 91 F3
 Queensbury BD13 ...... 72 E1
High Croft Cres HD5 .... 154 F3
High Croft Rd OL14 ..... 108 C6
High Croft Way HD20 ... 4 D1
High Cross La HX3 ...... 93 A7
High Ct Heptonstall HX7 .. 212 A3
 BD18 .... 55 C6
High End BD17 .... 39 C5
High Farm Fold WF4 .... 164 E2
High Farm Mdw WF9 ... 164 E2
High Fernley Ct 10 BD12 .. 94 C4
High Fernley First Sch
 BD12 .... 94 B3
High Fernley Rd BD12 ... 94 B3
High Field La
 Oakworth BD22 .... 34 C6
 Rippondem HX6 .... 132 D6
High Fields HX6 .... 112 A4
High Fold Baildon BD17 .. 38 C4
 Bingley BD16 .... 36 E8
 Keighley BD20 .... 34 F5
High Fold La BD20 ...... 18 A2
High Green Dr BD20 .... 5 D2
High Green Rd WF9 ..... 122 E3
High Grove La HX3 ...... 93 C4
High Holly Garth BD21 .. 35 D6
High House Ave BD2 .... 56 B5
High House Edge HD7 ... 170 C7
High House La
 Halifax HX2 .... 90 C4
 Slaithwaite HD7 .... 170 C8
High House Mews LS29 . 6 B8
High House Rd BD2 .... 56 A4
High Hoyland La LS25 .. 193 B8
High Keep Fold WF4 ... 159 F3
High La Cowling BD22 .. 32 A8
 Halifax HX2 .... 112 B8
 Hebden Bridge HX7 .... 110 D3
 Holmfirth HD7 .... 189 B3
 Huddersfield HD4 .... 154 C11
 Spofforth HG3 .... 12 A8
High Lea HD7 .... 168 F4
High Lees Rd HX2 ...... 91 B5
High Level Way HX1 .... 202 B4
High Matlsi BD20 ...... 16 A5
High Meadow BD20 ... 18 A1

High Meadows
Dewsbury WF12 .... 139 C1
Elland HX4 .... 134 C7
Wilsden BD15 .... 53 C5

High Mill LS29 .... 3 A1
High Mill La LS29 .... 3 A1
High Moor Ave LS17 .... 43 E3
High Moor Cl LS17 .... 43 E3
High Moor Cres LS17 .... 43 E3
High Moor Dr LS17 .... 43 E3
High Moor Dr LS17 .... 43 E3
High Moor Gr LS17 .... 43 E3
High Oxford St WF10 .... 124 C7
High Park Cres BD9 .... 54 E3
High Park Dr BD9 .... 54 E3
High Park Gr BD9 .... 54 E3
High Peal Ct **12** BD13 .... 72 D1
High Poplars BD2 .... 55 F4
High Rd WF12 .... 139 E7
High Ridge WF4 .... 158 E6
High Ridge Ave LS26 .... 100 E7
High Ridge Ct LS26 .... 100 E6
High Ridge Pk LS26 .... 100 E7
High Ridge Way LS16 .... 24 F2
High Royds Dr LS29 .... 22 B3
High Royds Hospl LS29 .... 22 B2

High Spring Gardens La
BD20 .... 35 A8
High Spring Rd BD21 .... 35 F6
High St
Batley, Birstall WF17 .... 96 E1
Batley, Hanging Heaton
WF17 .... 118 F3
Boston Spa LS23 .... 30 D8
Boston Spa, Clifford LS23 ..... 30 E5
Bradford, Idle BD10 .... 56 B8
Bradford, Wibsey BD6 .... 74 C1
Bramham LS23 .... 30 D2
Brighouse HD6 .... 115 B3
Brotherton WF11 .... 105 C1
Castleford WF10 .... 124 C7
Clayton West HD8 .... 175 F2
Cleckheaton BD19 .... 116 D8
Crigglestone WF4 .... 159 E5
Crofton WF4 .... 161 F8
Crofton, Sharlston WF4 ...... 144 B5
Dewsbury, Daw Green
WF12, WF13 .... 139 B7
Dewsbury, Earlesheaton
WF12 ....
Dewsbury, Overthorpe
WF12 .... 139 C1
Elland, Stainland HX4 .... 133 F3
8 Elland, West Vale HX4 ... 134 D7
Halifax HX2 .... 90 E1
Honley HD7 .... 171 F4
Horbury WF4 .... 141 A1
Huddersfield HD1 .... 153 E5
Huddersfield HD1 .... 154 A5
Keighley BD21 .... 35 B7
Kippax LS25 .... 83 B1
Knottingley WF11 .... 126 C5
Mapplewell S75 .... 178 A2
Morley LS27 .... 98 A3
Normanton WF6 .... 119 C1
Normanton, Altofts WF6 ..... 122 F3
Ossett WF5 .... 119 C1
Pudsey LS28 .... 57 D3
Queensbury BD13 .... 72 E1
Royston S71 .... 179 B3
Shafton S72 .... 180 C2
South Elmsall WF9 .... 182 A3
South Hiendley S72 .... 180 E5
Steeton BD20 .... 17 C5
Sutton in C BD20 .... 16 D4
Thornton BD13 .... 72 D6
Todmorden OL14 .... 108 A3
Upton WF9 .... 183 B7
Woolley WF4 .... 178 A7
Yeadon LS19 .... 40 C7
High Stones Rd HX7 .... 110 E3
High Street Pl BD10 .... 56 B8
High Sunderland La HX3 ...... 92 D1
High Top HX2 .... 88 B4
High Trees La HX4 .... 133 E6
High Trees Sch LS23 .... 30 E6
High View
Crigglestone WF4 .... 159 E5
Royston S71 .... 179 B3
High Weardley La LS17 .... 26 A6
High Well Hall La S72 .... 180 C7
High Wheatley LS29 .... 8 D2
High Wicken Cl BD13 .... 72 D6
High Wood LS29 .... 8 F3
High Wood Cl LS6 .... 59 E5
High Wood La HD8 .... 174 B4
High Woodlands WF3 .... 120 C7
Higham & Dob La HX6 .... 111 C3
Highbank First Sch WF15 .. 116 B5
Highbridge La HD5 .... 175 C1
Highbridge Terr BD5 .... 74 F1
Higharton C of E
(Controlled) First Sch
HD8 .... 173 E8
Highbury Cl LS6 .... 59 E6
Highbury La LS6 .... 59 E6
Highbury Mount LS6 .... 59 E6
Highbury Pl Leeds LS6 .... 59 E6
Pudsey LS13 .... 77 A8
Highbury Rd Bradford BD4 ... 75 C6
Leeds LS6 .... 59 E6
Highbury Sch HD6 .... 135 E7
Highbury St LS6 .... 59 E6

Highbury Terr
6 Dewsbury WF12 .... 139 D8
Leeds LS6 .... 59 E6
Highcliffe Ave HD2 .... 135 F2
Highcliffe Ct LS22 .... 13 F5
Highcliffe Dr HX2 .... 112 D7
Highcliffe Ind Est LS27 .... 97 E5
Highcliffe Rd Batley WF17 .. 118 C3
Morley LS27 .... 97 F4
Highcroft Batley WF17 .... 118 C3
Collingham LS22 .... 29 A8
Holmfirth HD7 .... 188 E5
Highcroft Cl LS28 .... 76 C8
Highcroft Gdns BD21 .... 35 F6
Highdale WF12 .... 118 E2
Highdale Croft BD10 .... 56 B8
Higher Ashenhurst OL14 ... 108 A7
Higher Back La HX7 .... 87 F4
Higher Brockwell HX6 .... 112 A3
Higher Calderbrook
OL15 .... 129 C1
Higher Calderbrook Rd
OL15 .... 129 C2
Higher Change Villas
OL13 .... 106 B4
Higher Coach Rd BD17 .... 37 F2
Higher Downs BD8 .... 73 D8
Higher Grange Rd LS28 ...... 76 E8
Higher Hartley St BD20 .... 16 B6
Higher Intake Rd BD2 .... 56 C1
Higher Lodge St BD20 .... 16 B6
Higher Park Royd Dr HX6 .. 132 E6
Higher Scholes BD22 .... 33 F1
Higher School St **4** BD18 ... 54 F8
Higherwood Cl BD21 .... 35 E6
Highfield Rise BD22 .... 34 E5
Highfield Bradford BD4 .... 75 D1
East Ardsley WF3 .... 98 D1
Shelf HX3 .... 93 C5
Highfield Ave
Bradford BD10 .... 56 A7
Brighouse HD6 .... 115 B8
Denby Dale HD8 .... 191 A4
Elland HX4 .... 134 B7
Leeds LS12 .... 210 A1
Meltham HD7 .... 170 D3
Pontefract WF8 .... 126 A4
Pontefract WF8 .... 146 C7
Shelf HX3 .... 93 D7
Highfield Ct
Castleford WF10 .... 124 D6
Liversedge WF15 .... 116 F2
Scarcroft BD22 .... 34 C2
Shipley HD8 .... 190 E6
Highfield Ctr WF9 .... 181 D6
Highfield Dr Batley WF17 .... 96 E2
Bradford BD9 .... 54 E4
Garforth LS25 .... 82 F5
Gildersome LS27 .... 97 D7
Halifax HX2 .... 111 E8
Kippax LS25 .... 102 F5
Liversedge FV15 .... 116 E4
Wakefield WF2 .... 141 E8
Yeadon LS19 .... 40 C3
Highfield Garth LS12 .... 210 A1
Highfield Gdns
Bradford BD9 .... 54 D4
Dewsbury WF12 .... 139 D3
Gildersome LS27 .... 97 D7
Leeds LS12 .... 209 F1
Highfield Gn Kippax WF10 .. 102 F6
Pudsey LS28 .... 57 D3
Highfield Gr Bradford BD10 .. 56 A6
Halifax HX5 .... 134 C8
Kippax WF10 .... 102 F6
Highfield Grange WF4 .... 141 A1
Highfield La
Barwick in E LS15 .... 63 E5
Batley WF13 .... 117 F4
Keighley BD21 .... 35 B8
Lepton HD8 .... 155 D5
Meltham HD7 .... 170 C3
Rothwell LS26 .... 101 C7
Slaithwaite HD7 LS25 .... 84 D5
Silsden BD20 .... 5 E2
Highfield Mews **1**
Baildon BD17 .... 38 C4
Keighley BD20 .... 19 D1
Highfield Middle Sch BD21 35 B7
Highfield Mount
Dewsbury WF12 .... 139 E1
Rothwell LS26 .... 101 C7
Highfield Pl Bradford BD8 ... 55 C1
Halifax HX1 .... 202 B2
Hemsworth WF9 .... 181 C6
Kippax WF10 .... 103 A6
Morley LS27 .... 97 F4
Highfield Primary Sch
LS12 .... 43 E4
Highfield Rd Aberford LS25 .. 64 E8
Bradford BD2, BD10 .... 56 B7
Brighouse HD6 .... 135 E8
Cleckheaton BD19 .... 116 C7
Elland HX5 .... 134 F6

Highfield Rd continued
Halifax HX2 .... 111 E8
Hemsworth WF9 .... 181 D6
Horbury WF4 .... 141 A1
Keighley BD21 .... 35 A8
Kirkburton HD8 .... 173 E7
Leeds LS13 .... 58 D2
Meltham HD7 .... 170 D3
Netherton WF4 .... 158 D5
Pontefract WF8 .... 146 C6
Pudsey LS28 .... 76 C8
Shipley BD9 .... 55 C5
Slaithwaite HD7 .... 151 F4
Highfield Rise WF2 .... 141 E8
Highfield St Keighley BD21 .. 35 B7
Leeds LS13 .... 58 D2
Pudsey LS28 .... 76 C8
Highfield Terr
Dewsbury WF12 .... 139 D3
Halifax HX1 .... 202 B2
Pudsey LS28 .... 76 C8
Shipley BD18 .... 54 E8
Ripponden HX6 .... 132 E6
Shipley BD18 .... 54 E8
Yeadon LS19 .... 40 C3
Highfield View LS27 .... 97 E7
Highfields
Huddersfield HD1 .... 153 F7
Netherton WF4 .... 158 D5
Ryhill WF4 .... 162 D2
Highfields Rd HD1 .... 153 F7
Highfold LS19 .... 40 A5
Highgate Bradford BD9 .... 54 F4
Glusburn BD20 .... 16 C7
Highgate Ave HD8 .... 155 F3
Highgate Cl BD13 .... 73 C2
Highgate Cres HD8 .... 155 F3
Highgate Dr HD8 .... 155 F3
Highgate HD8 BD13 .... 73 C2
Highgate La
Kirkheaton HD5 .... 137 D1
Lepton HD8 .... 155 E3
Highgate Rd
Bradford BD13 .... 73 B2
Dewsbury WF12 .... 139 D8
Highgate St WF17 .... 118 F3
Highgate Terr **10** WF12 ... 139 D8
Highgate Wlk HD8 .... 155 F3
Highland Cl WF8 .... 125 F3
Highland Ville HX3 .... 114 D8
Highlands Ave HD5 .... 154 F3
Highlands Cl
1 Bradford BD7 .... 73 E3
Middleton LS10 .... 99 F8
Highlands Dr LS10 .... 99 F8
Highlands Gr Bradford BD7 .. 73 E3
Middleton LS10 .... 99 F8
Highlands La HX2 .... 91 F6
Highlands Pk HX2 .... 91 F6
Highlands The
Cleckheaton WF15 .... 116 D5
Ossett WF5 .... 140 C5
Highlands Wlk LS10 .... 99 F8
Highlea Cl LS19 .... 39 F1
Highley Hall Croft HD6 ...... 115 D3
Highley Pk HD6 .... 115 E2
Highmoor BD17 .... 38 A3
Highmoor Cres HD6 .... 115 D3
Highmoor La
Brighouse HD6 .... 115 F5
Brighouse, Clifton HD6 ...... 115 E4
Cleckheaton HD6 .... 116 A6
Highmoor Wlk BD17 .... 38 A2
Highroad Well La HX2 .... 112 C7
Highroyd HD8 .... 173 C8
Highroyd Cres **1** HD5 .... 155 F3
Highroyd La HD5 .... 154 D6
Highthorne Ave LS17 .... 43 F4
Highthorne Dr LS17 .... 43 F4
Highthorne Gr
3 Leeds LS12 .... 209 D4
Leeds, Blackwood LS17 .... 44 A4
Highthorne Mount LS17 ..... 43 F4
Highthorne View **6** LS12 . 209 D4
Hightown La HD7 .... 189 A5
Hightown Rd WF15 .... 116 D6
Hightown Sch WF15 .... 116 D5
Hightown View WF15 .... 116 D5
Highway LS20 .... 40 C5
Highways LS14 .... 61 E1
Highwood Ave LS17 .... 43 C3
Highwood Cres LS17 .... 43 C3
Highwood Gr LS17 .... 43 C2
Higson Ct HD5 .... 155 A7
Hilberoyd Rd WF17 .... 118 D5
Hill Brow Cl BD15 .... 54 A1
Hill Cl Baildon BD17 .... 38 B4
Huddersfield HD1 .... 134 F1
Pontefract WF8 .... 146 D7
Hill Clough Gr BD22 .... 34 D7
Hill Cres Batley WF17 .... 97 A1
Burley in W LS29 .... 21 F7
Halifax HX3 .... 113 F5
Halifax HX3 .... 114 A5
Hill Crest Adwick Le S DN6 184 E1
Collingham LS22 .... 28 E8
Ripponden HX6 .... 132 C1
Ryhill WF4 .... 162 C1
5 Sowerby Bridge HX6 .. 112 B5
Swillington LS26 .... 82 A1
Hill Crest Ave
Denholme BD13 .... 52 D1
5 Sowerby Bridge HX6 .. 112 B5
Hillam La
Burton Salmon LS25 .... 105 E5
Hillam LS25 .... 105 E5

Hill Crest Mount BD13 ...... 52 D1
Hill Crest Rd
Denholme BD13 .... 52 D1
Thornton BD13 .... 72 D7
Hill Crest View BD13 .... 52 D1
Hill Croft Ripponden HX6 .. 132 C1
Thornton BD13 .... 72 E7
Hill End WF18 .... 147 D5
Hill End Ct Leeds LS16 .... 41 D3
Hill Dr WF7 .... 164 A8
Hill End WF12 .... 139 E8
Hill End Cl Brighouse HX3 .. 94 A2
Leeds LS12 .... 77 F8
Hill End Cres LS12 .... 77 F8
Hill End Gr BD7 .... 73 E3
Hill End La
Cullingworth BD13 .... 52 F8
Harden BD16 .... 36 A1
Queensbury BD13 .... 92 D8
2 Hill End Rd LS12 .... 77 F8
Hill Estate WF9 .... 183 B7
Hill Foot BD18 .... 54 E7
Hill Gr HD3 .... 134 F1
Hill Gr S LS10 .... 99 F7
Hill Green Ct BD4 .... 74 E5
Hill Grove Lea HD3 .... 134 F1
Hill House Edge La BD22 .... 70 B8
Hill House La
Holmfirth HD7 .... 188 E2
Oxenhope BD22 .... 51 C1
Hill House Rd HD7 .... 188 E2
Hill La HD7 .... 188 E5
Hill Lands BD12 .... 94 C5
Hill Park Ave HX3 .... 91 F1
Hill Pk WF14 .... 137 F2
Hill Primary Sch The LS6 ... 59 F8
Hill Rd Castleford WF10 .... 124 F6
Wakefield WF2 .... 160 C4
Hill Side Ave HD7 .... 189 E2
Hill Side Mount LS28 .... 57 E2
Hill Rise Ave LS13 .... 58 C4
Hill Rise Gr LS13 .... 58 C4
Hill Side Bingley BD16 .... 36 F3
Bradford BD3 .... 201 D3
Hill Side Terr BD3 .... 201 D4
Hill St **1** Bradford, Bowling BD4 .. 75 B5
Bradford, Wibsey BD6 .... 74 A1
Cleckheaton BD19 .... 116 C7
Halifax HX1 .... 203 D2
Haworth BD22 .... 51 C6
Holmfirth HD7 .... 189 E3
Leeds LS11 .... 214 B3
Leeds, New Town LS9 .... 207 E2
Hill Top Brighouse HX3 ..... 114 E7
Burley in W LS29 .... 9 E1
Castleford WF10 .... 123 F7
Cawthorne S75 .... 193 E5
Halifax HX2 .... 202 A1
Hemsworth WF9 .... 163 A3
Ilkley LS29 .... 8 A2
Knottingley WF11 .... 126 F4
Leeds LS15 .... 62 E3
Steeton BD20 .... 17 C5
Hill Top Ave Barnsley S71 .. 178 E1
Huddersfield HD2 .... 135 E4
Leeds LS8 .... 207 F4
Hill Top C of E First Sch
BD12 .... 94 C6
Hill Top Cl
East Ardsley WF3 .... 119 E6
Hemsworth WF9 .... 163 A3
Leeds LS12 .... 77 F8
Hill Top Cotts BD9 .... 54 A4
Hill Top Cres WF14 .... 137 F1
Hill Top Cl East Ardsley WF3 119 E6
Wakefield WF2 .... 160 C4
Hill Top Dr HD3 .... 153 A8
Hill Top Est WF16 .... 117 E4
Hill Top Fold HD7 .... 151 F1
Hill Top Gdns WF3 .... 119 E6
Hill Top Gn WF3 .... 119 D6
Hill Top Gr Bradford BD15 .. 54 A1
East Ardsley WF3 .... 119 E6
Hill Top Infants Sch WF2 .. 119 D5
Hill Top La Bingley BD16 ..... 36 F8
Bradford BD15 .... 54 A1
Hebden Bridge HX7 .... 110 B4
Netherton WF4 .... 145 C1
Hill Top Mews WF11 .... 126 F4
Hill Top Mount LS8 .... 207 F4
Hill Top Pl Leeds LS8 .... 207 F4
Leeds, Hyde Park LS6 .... 205 F2
Hill Top Rd Flockton WF4 . 157 D3
Hemsworth WF9 .... 163 A3
Holmfirth HD7 .... 188 F1
Huddersfield HD3 .... 134 F1
Huddersfield, Grove Place
HD5 .... 154 D6
Huddersfield, Paddock HD1 . 153 E3
Keighley BD22 .... 35 A2
Leeds LS12 .... 77 F8
Oakworth BD22 .... 34 B2
Slaithwaite HD7 .... 152 A1
Thornton BD13 .... 72 C7
Wakefield WF2 .... 160 C4
Hill Top Sch WF10 .... 125 C7
Hill Top St LS6 .... 205 F2
Hill Top View
East Ardsley WF3 .... 119 D6
Horsforth LS18 .... 41 A1
Hill Top Way BD22 .... 34 F7
Hill Top Wlk BD22 .... 34 F7
Hill View HD7 .... 91 F7
Hill View Ave LS7 .... 204 A3
Hill View Mount LS7 .... 204 A3
Hill View Terr **2** LS7 ...... 204 A3
Hillam Rd BD2 .... 55 D3
Hillam St BD5 .... 55 E7
Hillary Pl LS2 .... 206 B2
Hillary Rd BD18 .... 55 E7
Hillary St **11** LS13 .... 117 F3
Hillbrook Rise LS29 .... 7 F3
Hillcote Dr BD5 .... 74 E4
Hillcourt Ave LS13 .... 58 C4
Hillcourt Croft LS13 .... 58 C4
Hillcourt Dr LS13 .... 58 C4
Hillcourt Gr LS13 .... 58 C4
Hillcrest WF4 .... 122 E4
Hillcrest Ave
Batley WF17 .... 118 A5
Castleford WF10 .... 125 D6
Featherstone WF7 .... 145 B5
Leeds LS7 .... 207 E4
Ossett WF5 .... 140 C8
Queensbury BD13 .... 92 F8
Silsden BD20 .... 5 E1
Hillcrest Cl
Castleford WF10 .... 125 D7
Swillington LS26 .... 81 F1
Hillcrest Dr
Castleford WF10 .... 125 E6
Queensbury BD13 .... 92 F8
Hillcrest Mount
Brighouse BD19 .... 115 F7
Castleford WF10 .... 125 E6
Leeds LS16 .... 41 E4
Hillcrest Pl LS7 .... 207 E4
Hillcrest Rd
Castleford WF10 .... 125 E7
Queensbury BD13 .... 92 F8
Hillcrest Rise LS16 .... 41 E4
Hillcrest View LS7 .... 207 E4
Hillesley Rd WF12 .... 119 A3
Hillfold WF9 .... 183 B3
Hillfoot Ave LS28 .... 76 B8
Hillfoot Cres LS28 .... 76 B8
Hillfoot Dr LS28 .... 76 B8
Hillfoot Rise LS28 .... 76 B8
Hillgarth Dewsbury WF12 .. 139 D3
Knottingley WF11 .... 126 E3
Hillhead Dr WF17 .... 97 A1
Hillhouse La HD1 .... 154 B8
Hillhouse Sq LS10 .... 215 D4
Hillidge Way LS17 .... 43 B6
Hilling La
Guiseley LS20, LS29 .... 21 E3
Menston LS29 .... 21 E3
Hillside Byram WF11 .... 126 D7
Denby Dale HD8 .... 192 A6
Garforth LS25 .... 83 C6
Hillside Ave Guiseley LS20 .. 22 D3
Halifax HX2 .... 111 D7
Huddersfield HD2 .... 136 B2
Oakworth BD22 .... 34 B2
Ripponden HX6 .... 132 E6
Hillside Cl
1 Addingham LS29 .... 6 E8
Wakefield WF2 .... 141 D3
Hillside Cres
8 Bacup OL13 .... 106 A7
Brierley S72 .... 181 A2
Huddersfield HD4 .... 154 B2
Hillside Ct Menston LS29 ... 21 F4
South Elmsall WF9 .... 183 A4
Hillside Gr Brierley S72 ..... 181 A2
Oakworth BD22 .... 34 B2
7 Pudsey LS28 .... 76 F7
Hillside Mount
Brierley S72 .... 181 A2
Pontefract WF8 .... 146 E8
Pudsey LS28 .... 76 F7
Hillside Prim Sch LS11 .... 214 B4
Hillside Rd
Ackworth M T WF7 .... 164 A6
Leeds LS7 .... 146 E8
Shipley BD18 .... 55 D5
Hillside Rise Guiseley LS20 .. 22 D3
Hillside Terr BD17 .... 38 C3
Hillside View Halifax HX6 . 112 A4
Pudsey LS28 .... 77 A7
Slaithwaite HD7 .... 152 E1
Hillside Works Ind Est
WF9 .... 95 D2
Hillthorpe Dr WF9 .... 165 A5
Hillthorpe Rd LS28 .... 76 E5
Hillthorpe Rise LS28 .... 76 E5
Hillthorpe Sq LS28 .... 76 E5
Hillthorpe St **2** LS28 .... 76 E5
Hillthorpe Terr **3** LS28 .... 76 E5
Hilltop LS27 .... 180 F3
Hilltop Est WF9 .... 181 F1
Hillview Gdns HX3 .... 93 A1
Hillview Mount LS7 ....
Hillman Way WF9 .... 181 F5
Hilton Ave BD18 .... 55 C7
Hilton Cres BD17 .... 38 C2
Hilton Ct LS16 .... 24 A4
Hilton Dr BD18 .... 55 B8
Hilton Gr Bradford BD7 ...... 74 B6
Leeds LS8 .... 204 C1
Shipley BD18 .... 55 B8
Hilton Grange LS16 .... 24 B4
Hilton Mews LS16 .... 24 A4
Hilton Pl LS8 .... 207 F4
Hilton Rd Bradford BD7 ...... 74 B6
Leeds LS8 .... 207 F4
Shipley BD18 .... 55 B8
Hilton St
2 Hebden Bridge HX7 .. 89 A3
2 Leeds LS8 .... 207 F4
Hilton Terr **3** LS8 .... 207 F4
Hinchliffe Ave WF5 .... 140 F5

Hinchcliffe Mill Junior & Infants Sch HD7 ..... 188 C2
Hinchcliffe St HD3 ..... 75 B8
Hinchliffe Ave BD17 ..... 38 D2
Hind Cl HD7 ..... 170 C3
Hind St 5 Bradford BD4 ..... 74 C8
Bradford, Wyke BD12 ..... 94 C2
Hindle Pl 2 LS27 ..... 98 B7
Hindley Rd WF15 ..... 117 A3
Hindley Wlk BD7 ..... 73 D2
Hinds Cres WF9 ..... 182 F3
Hinton Cl WF8 ..... 125 E3
Hinton La WF11 ..... 126 A6
Hions Cl HD6 ..... 136 A8
Hipperholme Grammar Sch HX3 ..... 114 C8
Hipperholme & Lightcliffe High Sch HX3 ..... 114 F7
Hipswell St BD3 ..... 75 C8
Hird Ave BD6 ..... 94 C8
Hird Rd BD12 ..... 94 D6
Hird St Keighley BD21 ..... 35 B5
Leeds LS11 ..... 214 A3
Mirfield WF14 ..... 55 B8
Hirst Ave WF16 ..... 117 D6
Hirst Gr HX7 ..... 89 B3
Hirst La Holmfirth HD7 ..... 190 B5
Shipley BD18 ..... 54 E8
Hirst Lodge Ct BD2 ..... 55 F5
Hirst Mill Cres BD18 ..... 37 E1
Hirst Rd Dewsbury WF13 ..... 118 C1
Wakefield WF2 ..... 141 D5
Hirst St Kippax WF10 ..... 102 F7
Mirfield WF14 ..... 138 A3
Todmorden OL14 ..... 86 B1
Hirst Wood Cres 1 BD18 ..... 54 E8
Hirst Wood Rd BD18 ..... 54 E8
Hirstlands Ave WF5 ..... 140 C7
Hirstlands Dr WF5 ..... 140 C8
Hive St BD22 ..... 35 A6
Hoads The HD6 ..... 135 F7
Hob La Haworth BD22 ..... 50 C7
Huddersfield HD4 ..... 153 B2
Ripponden HX6 ..... 132 C5
Sowerby Bridge HX6 ..... 112 B1
Hobart Bldgs HX7 ..... 89 D1
Hobart Rd Castleford WF10 ..... 125 D8
Dewsbury WF12 ..... 118 F1
Hobb Nook La LS21 ..... 10 A7
Hoberley La LS27 ..... 44 F3
Hobson Fold 3 BD12 ..... 94 D2
Hockney Rd BD8 ..... 74 B8
Hodge La WF8 ..... 166 E6
Hodgewood La WF8 ..... 147 D6
Hodgson Ave Bradford BD3 ..... 56 D1
Leeds LS17 ..... 44 A3
Hodgson Cres LS17 ..... 44 A3
Hodgson La BD11 ..... 96 C6
Hodgson Pl 6 LS27 ..... 98 B7
Hodgson St Morley LS27 ..... 98 B7
Wakefield WF1 ..... 216 A3
Hodgson Terr WF10 ..... 139 D6
Hodroyd Cl S72 ..... 180 D1
Hodroyd Cotts S72 ..... 180 F2
Hoffman St HD3 ..... 153 A4
Hog Close La HD7 ..... 200 D8
Hogley La HD7 ..... 188 C4
Holays HD5 ..... 154 E7
Holbeck La LS11 ..... 210 F3
Holbeck Moor Rd LS11 ..... 211 D1
Holbeck Towers LS11 ..... 211 D1
Holborn App LS6 ..... 206 A3
Holborn Ct Bradford BD12 ..... 94 C6
Leeds LS6 ..... 206 A3
Holborn Gdns 4 LS6 ..... 206 A3
Holborn Gn LS6 ..... 206 A3
Holborn Gr LS6 ..... 206 A3
Holborn St LS6 ..... 206 A3
Holborn Terr LS6 ..... 206 A3
Holborn Towers LS6 ..... 206 A3
Holborn View LS6 ..... 206 A3
Holborn Wlk LS6 ..... 206 A3
Holby Sq WF17 ..... 141 C4
Holden Ing Way WF17 ..... 97 A4
Holden La Baildon BD17 ..... 38 D4
Silsden BD20 ..... 18 C6
Holden Rd 1 BD6 ..... 74 B1
Holden St BD20 ..... 34 E5
Holderness Rd WF11 ..... 126 A4
Holderness St 14 OL14 ..... 108 C5
Holdforth Cl LS12 ..... 210 B3
Holdforth Gdns LS12 ..... 210 B3
Holdforth Gn LS12 ..... 210 B3
Holdforth Pl LS12 ..... 210 B3
Holdsworth Ct 6 BD19 ..... 116 D7
Holdsworth Rd HX2, HX3 ..... 92 A6
Holdsworth Sq BD2 ..... 56 D4
Holdsworth St Bradford BD1 ..... 201 C4
Cleckheaton BD19 ..... 116 D8
Shipley BD18 ..... 55 A7
Holdsworth Terr HX1 ..... 203 F1
Hole Bottom Rd OL14 ..... 108 B7
Hole La BD20 ..... 5 D3
Holes La WF11 ..... 126 E4
Holgate Ave WF9 ..... 163 B3
Holgate Cres WF9 ..... 181 C7
Holgate Gdns WF9 ..... 181 C7
Holgate Hospital WF9 ..... 181 A6
Holgate Rd WF8 ..... 146 C5
Holgate Terr WF9 ..... 163 B3
Holgate View
Brierley S72 ..... 181 A3
Hemsworth WF9 ..... 181 C7
Holker St Bradford BD8 ..... 74 B8
Keighley BD21 ..... 35 C8
Holland Rd LS25 ..... 83 C2
Holland St WF17 ..... 118 D5

Hollas La Halifax HX3, HX6 ..... 112 F3
Sowerby Bridge HX6 ..... 112 E2
Hollerton La WF3 ..... 119 F7
Hollin Ave HD3 ..... 153 D7
Hollin Brigg La HD7 ..... 188 C2
Hollin Close La BD2 ..... 55 E3
Hollin Cres LS16 ..... 59 E7
Hollin Dr
Crigglestone WF4 ..... 159 E5
Leeds LS16 ..... 59 E7
Hollin Edge HD8 ..... 192 A6
Hollin Gate LS21 ..... 10 D2
Hollin Gdns LS16 ..... 59 E7
Hollin Greaves La HX3 ..... 92 D1
Hollin Hall HD7 ..... 152 C5
Hollin Hall Dr LS29 ..... 7 E3
Hollin Hall La
Huddersfield HD7 ..... 152 C5
Kirkheaton WF14 ..... 137 D2
Hollin Hall Rd BD18 ..... 54 E6
Hollin Head BD17 ..... 38 F4
Hollin Hill Ave LS8 ..... 61 C5
Hollin Hill La LS8 ..... 61 C5
Hollin House La
Clayton West HD8 ..... 193 A8
Holmfirth HD7 ..... 189 F5
Hollin La
Crigglestone WF4 ..... 159 D6
Leeds LS16 ..... 59 D7
Ripponden HX6 ..... 132 A3
Shipley BD18 ..... 55 D6
Sowerby Bridge HX6 ..... 112 C2
Wadsworth Moor HX7 ..... 68 B1
Leeds LS16 ..... 59 D7
Hollin Mews LS16 ..... 59 D7
Hollin Mount LS16 ..... 59 D7
Hollin Park Ave LS8 ..... 61 D5
Hollin Park Cres LS8 ..... 61 D5
Hollin Park Ct LS28 ..... 57 A6
Hollin Park Dr LS28 ..... 57 A6
Hollin Park Mount LS8 ..... 61 D5
Hollin Park Par LS8 ..... 61 C5
Hollin Park Pl LS8 ..... 61 D5
Hollin Park Rd Leeds LS8 ..... 61 D5
Pudsey LS28 ..... 57 A6
Hollin Park Terr LS8 ..... 61 D5
Hollin Park View LS8 ..... 61 C5
Hollin Rd Leeds LS16 ..... 59 D7
Shipley BD18 ..... 55 C6
Hollin Rise BD18 ..... 55 C6
Hollin St HD1 ..... 111 E1
Hollin Terr
Huddersfield HD3 ..... 153 C7
Shipley BD18 ..... 55 C6
Hollin Wood Cl BD18 ..... 54 E7
Hollin Wood La LS21 ..... 9 D7
Hollinbank La WF16 ..... 117 E5
Hollingbourne Rd LS15 ..... 62 F2
Hollings Rd BD8 ..... 74 B8
Hollings Sq BD8 ..... 74 B8
Hollings St Bradford BD8 ..... 74 B8
Shipley BD16 ..... 54 B7
Hollings Terr BD8 ..... 74 B8
Hollings The LS26 ..... 102 B3
Hollingthorpe Ave WF4 ..... 159 E3
Hollingthorpe Ct WF4 ..... 159 F3
Hollingthorpe Gr WF4 ..... 159 E3
Hollingthorpe La WF4 ..... 159 E3
Hollingthorpe Rd WF4 ..... 159 E2
Hollingwood Ave BD7 ..... 73 F4
Hollingwood Ct BD7 ..... 73 F4
Hollingwood Dr BD7 ..... 73 E4
Hollingwood First Sch BD7 ..... 73 E3
Hollingwood Gate LS29 ..... 7 F3
Hollingwood La BD7 ..... 73 E3
Hollingwood Mount BD7 ..... 73 E4
Hollingwood Rise LS29 ..... 7 F3
Hollingworth La
Knottingley WF11 ..... 127 A4
Todmorden OL14 ..... 129 B8
Hollinhirst La WF4 ..... 158 C6
Hollinhurst WF10 ..... 102 F6
Hollinroyd Rd WF12 ..... 139 E8
Hollins Ave WF13 ..... 117 F3
Hollins Bank La BD20 ..... 17 F4
Hollins Cl BD20 ..... 17 F2
Hollins Cres 10 HX7 ..... 89 A3
Hollins Glen HD7 ..... 170 A8
Hollins Gr WF10 ..... 102 F6
Hollins Hey Rd HX4 ..... 134 D4
Hollins Hill BD17, LS20 ..... 39 B6
Hollins La
Halifax, Mixenden HX2 ..... 91 C5
Keighley BD20 ..... 17 F2
Slaithwaite HD7 ..... 169 E6
Sowerby Bridge HX6 ..... 111 C5
Sowerby Bridge HX6 ..... 112 D8
Hollins Meadow OL14 ..... 108 A1
Hollins Mill La HX6 ..... 112 B4
Hollins Mount WF9 ..... 181 C7
Hollins Pk LS25 ..... 83 A1
Hollins Pl
Hebden Bridge HX7 ..... 89 A3
13 Todmorden OL14 ..... 108 A1
Hollins Rd 8 Batley WF13 ..... 117 F2
Todmorden OL14 ..... 108 A1
Hollins Row HD7 ..... 170 A8
Hollins St OL14 ..... 129 B8
Hollins The OL14 ..... 108 B6
Hollins View WF14 ..... 36 D7
Hollis Pl LS3 ..... 205 F1
Hollow The HD7 ..... 170 D8
Hollowfield Croft BD12 ..... 95 B5
Hollowgate HD7 ..... 189 A5
Holly App WF5 ..... 140 D8
Holly Ave LS16 ..... 41 D3

Holly Bank
Ackworth M T WF7 ..... 163 E6
Garforth LS25 ..... 83 B6
Guiseley LS20 ..... 39 D8
Sutton in C BD20 ..... 16 C5
Holly Bank Dr HX3 ..... 114 D8
Holly Bank Pk HD6 ..... 135 F8
Holly Bank Rd
Brighouse HD6 ..... 135 F8
Huddersfield HD3 ..... 135 C1
Holly Bush Cl LS23 ..... 30 E7
Holly Cl Crofton WF4 ..... 144 D3
Middleton LS10 ..... 99 B4
Holly Cres Crofton WF4 ..... 143 E1
Ripponden HX6 ..... 132 D3
Holly Ct East Ardsley WF3 ..... 119 E6
Guiseley LS20 ..... 39 E8
Huddersfield Chase WF3 ..... 122 B6
Holly Dene WF5 ..... 140 D8
Holly Dr LS16 ..... 41 D3
Holly Gr Batley WF17 ..... 118 B3
Brierley S72 ..... 181 A3
Halifax HX1 ..... 202 C2
Huddersfield HD3 ..... 135 C1
Holly Hall La BD12 ..... 94 C4
Holly House 6 WF10 ..... 124 E7
Holly Mede WF5 ..... 140 D8
Holly Park Br BD7 ..... 73 E4
Holly Park Gr BD7 ..... 73 E4
Holly Park Rd Boston Spa LS23 ..... 30 B8
Huddersfield HD1 ..... 153 E4
Holly St Bradford BD6 ..... 73 D2
Hensworth WF9 ..... 182 A7
Wakefield WF2 ..... 141 F7
Holly Terr HD1 ..... 154 B8
Holly Tree Cl LS15 ..... 81 E6
Hollybank Ave
Batley WF17 ..... 118 C7
Denby Dale HD8 ..... 191 C6
Hollybank Ctr WF14 ..... 137 E8
Hollybank Gdns BD7 ..... 73 F3
Hollybank Gr BD7 ..... 73 E3
Hollybank House HD6 ..... 135 F8
Hollybank Rd BD7 ..... 73 F3
Hollybush La LS17 ..... 26 D5
Hollybush Gn LS22 ..... 29 C8
Hollycroft Ave S71 ..... 179 B3
Hollycroft Ct LS16 ..... 42 A3
Hollyfield Ave HD3 ..... 153 A7
Hollyns Terr 6 HX4 ..... 134 C7
Hollynsmill HX4 ..... 134 D7
Hollyoake Ave HD7 ..... 170 C8
Hollyshaw Cres LS15 ..... 81 C8
Hollyshaw Gr LS15 ..... 81 C8
Hollyshaw La LS15 ..... 81 C8
Hollyshaw St LS15 ..... 81 C8
Hollyshaw Terr 4 LS15 ..... 81 C8
Hollyshaw Wlk 5 LS15 ..... 62 C1
Hollywell La LS12 ..... 209 E4
Holm Ave S75 ..... 82 F5
Holmcliffe Ave HD4 ..... 153 F1
Holmclose HD7 ..... 188 C2
Holmdale Cres HD7 ..... 188 F8
Holmdene Dr WF14 ..... 138 A6
Holme Ave HD5 ..... 154 E5
Holme Cl Flockton WF4 ..... 156 F5
Glusburn BD20 ..... 16 D6
Holme Croft WF4 ..... 159 F7
Holme Dr HX7 ..... 112 B6
Holme Farm La LS23 ..... 28 F3
Holme Field WF5 ..... 140 D7
Holme Ghyll BD20 ..... 16 B6
Holme Gr LS29 ..... 21 F7
Holme House La
Halifax HX2 ..... 90 E4
Keighley BD22 ..... 34 C5
Holme House Rd OL14 ..... 86 C1
Holme House St OL15 ..... 129 D1
Holme House View HX6 ..... 132 D2
Holme Ings LS29 ..... 7 C7
Holme Jun & Inf Sch HD7 ..... 187 F1
Holme La Bradford BD4 ..... 75 F1
Glusburn BD20 ..... 16 D6
Halton East BD23 ..... 1 D8
Holmfirth HD7 ..... 189 E7
Slaithwaite HD7 ..... 151 E1
Sutton in C BD20 ..... 16 D6
Wakefield WF2 ..... 142 B3
Holme Lea Dr WF5 ..... 140 C7
Holme Middle Sch BD4 ..... 75 D3
Holme Mill La BD22 ..... 34 F6
Holme Rise WF4 ..... 159 F7
Holme Pl Hebden Bridge HX7 ..... 89 A4
Huddersfield HD1 ..... 153 D7
Holme Rd HX7 ..... 112 B6
Holme St Bradford BD5 ..... 74 D4
Brighouse HX3 ..... 89 A3
Hebden Bridge HX7 ..... 89 A3
Liversedge WF15 ..... 117 B4
Oxenhope BD22 ..... 51 C2
Todmorden OL14 ..... 107 F7
Holme Styes La HD7 ..... 199 A8
Holme Top La BD5 ..... 74 D4
Holme Top St BD5 ..... 74 D4
Holme Valley Bsns Ctr HD7 ..... 171 E8
Holme Valley Memorial Hospl HD7 ..... 189 A7
Holme Valley Sports Ctr HD7 ..... 189 C8
Holme View Ave HD7 ..... 188 D5
Holme View La HD7 ..... 188 D5
Holme View Pk HD7 ..... 188 E5
Holme View Rd WF9 ..... 163 C6
Holme Villas HD7 ..... 169 D6
Holme Way WF5 ..... 140 C7
Holme Well Rd LS10 ..... 99 E5

Holme Wood Rd
Bradford BD4 ..... 75 D3
Keighley BD22 ..... 34 F6
Holme Woods La HD7 ..... 197 F6
Holme's Terr HX2 ..... 202 A4
Holmebank Mews HD7 ..... 172 C2
Holmefield First Sch BD4 ..... 75 E4
Holmefield Rd HD3 ..... 152 E6
Holmefield View BD4 ..... 75 F4
Holmes Rd HX6 ..... 112 C4
Holmes St Bradford BD1 ..... 74 D8
Leeds LS11 ..... 211 F2
Holmeside Cl HD4 ..... 171 F8
Holmfield HD8 ..... 175 F2
Holmfield Ave
Clayton West HD8 ..... 175 F2
Wakefield WF2 ..... 142 B3
Holmfield Chase WF3 ..... 122 B6
Holmfield Cl
Clayton West HD8 ..... 175 F2
Pontefract WF8 ..... 125 F4
Holmfield Cotts LS26 ..... 102 E3
Holmfield Dr
Huddersfield HD7 ..... 152 F5
Leeds LS8 ..... 44 A1
Holmfield Gdns HX2 ..... 92 A5
Holmfield Ind Est HX2 ..... 92 A7
Holmfield La
Castleford WF11, WF8 ..... 125 F5
Wakefield WF2 ..... 142 B3
Holmfield Rd
Clayton West HD8 ..... 175 F2
Sutton in C BD20 ..... 16 D5
Holmfield St BD1 ..... 201 A3
Holmfield Terr HD8 ..... 175 F2
Holmfirth High Sch HD7 ..... 189 C8
Holmfirth Junior & Infants Sch HD7 ..... 189 A4
Holmfirth Rd Diggle OL3 ..... 185 F1
Holmfirth HD7 ..... 189 E7
Meltham HD7 ..... 170 E1
Holmroyd Ave BD20 ..... 16 D6
Holmsley Ave WF9 ..... 182 A2
Holmsley Crest LS26 ..... 101 A6
Holmsley Field Ct LS26 ..... 101 C6
Holmsley Field La LS26 ..... 101 C6
Holmsley Garth LS26 ..... 101 A7
Holmsley Gr WF9 ..... 182 A2
Holmsley La Rothwell LS26 ..... 101 B6
South Kirkby WF9 ..... 181 F2
Holmsley Mount WF9 ..... 182 A2
Holmsley Wlk LS26 ..... 101 C6
Holmwood Ave LS6 ..... 59 F8
Holmwood Cl LS6 ..... 59 F8
Holmwood Cres LS6 ..... 59 F8
Holmwood Dr LS6 ..... 59 F8
Holmwood Gr LS6 ..... 59 F8
Holmwood Mount LS6 ..... 59 F8
Holmwood View LS6 ..... 59 F8
Holroyd Hill BD6 ..... 74 C1
Holroyd Mill La BD16 ..... 36 E8
Holroyd Sq HX4 ..... 133 F4
Holroyd St S57 ..... 207 D2
Holsworthy Rd BD4 ..... 75 F3
Holt Ave Huddersfield HD2 ..... 136 C4
Leeds LS16 ..... 42 A4
Holt Cl LS16 ..... 42 C4
Holt Cres LS16 ..... 42 A4
Holt Dr LS16 ..... 42 A5
Holt Farm Cl LS16 ..... 42 A5
Holt Farm Rise LS16 ..... 41 F5
Holt Garth LS16 ..... 42 A5
Holt Gdns Bradford BD10 ..... 55 F8
Leeds LS16 ..... 42 A5
Holt La Holmfirth HD7 ..... 188 F6
Leeds LS16 ..... 42 A5
Holt Lane Ct LS16 ..... 42 A4
Holt Park App LS16 ..... 42 A5
Holt Park Ave LS16 ..... 42 A5
Holt Park Cl LS16 ..... 42 A5
Holt Park Cres LS16 ..... 42 A5
Holt Park District Ctr LS16 ..... 41 F5
Holt Park Dr LS16 ..... 42 A5
Holt Park Gate LS16 ..... 42 A5
Holt Park Gdns LS16 ..... 42 A5
Holt Park Gn LS16 ..... 42 A5
Holt Park Gr LS16 ..... 41 F5
Holt Park Grange LS16 ..... 42 A5
Holt Park La LS16 ..... 42 A5
Holt Park Rd LS16 ..... 42 A5
Holt Park Rise LS16 ..... 42 A5
Holt Park Vale LS16 ..... 42 A5
Holt Park Way LS16 ..... 42 A5
Holt Rd LS16 ..... 42 A5
Holt Rise LS16 ..... 42 A5
Holt St S15 ..... 129 D2
Holt The BD18 ..... 55 C8
Holt Vale LS16 ..... 42 A5
Holt View LS16 ..... 42 A5
Holt Wlk LS16 ..... 42 A5
Holtby Gr HX3 ..... 115 A7
Holtdale App LS16 ..... 41 F5
Holtdale Ave LS16 ..... 41 F5
Holtdale Cl LS16 ..... 41 F5
Holtdale Croft LS16 ..... 41 F5
Holtdale Dr LS16 ..... 41 F5
Holtdale Fold LS16 ..... 41 F5
Holtdale Gdns LS16 ..... 41 F5
Holtdale Gn LS16 ..... 41 F5
Holtdale Garth LS16 ..... 41 F5
Holtdale Lawn LS16 ..... 41 F5
Holtdale Pl LS16 ..... 41 F5
Holtdale Rd LS16 ..... 41 F5
Holtdale View LS16 ..... 41 F5
Holtdale Way LS16 ..... 41 F5

Holts La BD14 ..... 73 B5
Holts Terr HX3 ..... 113 D4
Holy Family RC Sch
LS12 ..... 210 A3
Holy Family Sch The
BD20 ..... 18 B1
Holy Family St St Michaels
RC Jun & Inf Sch WF8 ..... 126 A1
Holy Name Prim Sch LS16 ..... 42 A3
Holy Rood La LS25 ..... 104 E8
Holy Rosary & St Anne's
RC Prim Sch LS7 ..... 207 D3
Holy Trinity C of E First Sch
BD10 ..... 37 A2
Holy Trinity C of E
Jun & Inf Sch WF5 ..... 140 D6
Holy Trinity CE Infants Sch
HX1 ..... 203 D2
Holy Trinity CE Senior Sch
HX2 ..... 92 A6
Holy Trinity Junior Sch
HX1 ..... 203 D2
Holy Trinity Primary Sch
LS16 ..... 41 D5
Holybrook Ave BD10 ..... 56 D6
Holycroft First Sch BD21 ..... 35 B6
Holycroft St BD21 ..... 35 B6
Holyoake Ave Batley WF17 ..... 118 A5
Bingley BD16 ..... 36 F1
Holyoake St OL14 ..... 86 A1
Holyoake Terr
Horbury WF4 ..... 140 E1
Slaithwaite HD7 ..... 152 D1
Holyrood Cres WF6 ..... 122 F4
Holywell Ash La BD8 ..... 55 D1
Holywell Dene WF10 ..... 125 A6
Holywell Gdns WF10 ..... 125 A6
Holywell Gr WF10 ..... 125 A6
Holywell Green Junior
& Infant Sch HX4 ..... 134 B4
Holywell Hall BD23 ..... 1 B7
Holywell La
Castleford WF10 ..... 125 B6
Thorner LS17 ..... 44 D5
Holywell Mount WF10 ..... 125 B6
Home Farm Ct DN5 ..... 195 C5
Home Lea LS26 ..... 100 C7
Home Lea Dr LS26 ..... 100 D6
Home View Terr BD8 ..... 55 B1
Homefield Ave LS27 ..... 98 A2
Homepaddock House LS22 ..... 13 F6
Homes The HD2 ..... 136 F3
Homestead Dr WF2 ..... 141 F6
Homestead The WF16 ..... 117 E4
Honey Hole Cl OL14 ..... 108 B4
Honey Hole La BD10 ..... 85 A7
Honeysuckle Cl WF2 ..... 141 E7
Honeysuckle Dr WF7 ..... 139 D3
Honley C of E (Controlled)
Infant Sch HD7 ..... 171 F5
Honley C of E (Controlled)
Junior Sch HD7 ..... 171 F5
Honley High Sch & Coll
HD7 ..... 172 A5
Honley Rd HD6 ..... 172 D6
Honley Sta WF14 ..... 141 A1
Honley Sta HD7 ..... 172 B5
Honoria St HD1 ..... 136 A1
Hood St Huddersfield HD4 ..... 171 F8
South Elmsall WF9 ..... 182 C1
Hooton Cres WF4 ..... 162 A1
Hooton Pagnell C of E Sch
DN5 ..... 195 C5
Hooton Rd DN5 ..... 195 F4
Hoowood La HD7 ..... 187 E3
Hopbine Ave BD5 ..... 74 E2
Hopbine Rd BD5 ..... 74 E2
Hope Ave Bradford BD5 ..... 74 C2
Shipley BD18 ..... 55 D8
Hope Bldgs 11 OL14 ..... 108 B4
Hope St W WF10 ..... 124 D8
Hope Hall St HX1 ..... 203 E2
Hope Hall Terr 8 HX1 ..... 203 E2
Hope Hill View BD16 ..... 54 A7
Hope La WF4 ..... 158 A2
Hope Pl BD21 ..... 35 B5
Hope Rd LS9 ..... 212 A4
Hope St Castleford WF10 ..... 124 D8
Dewsbury WF13 ..... 118 B1
Halifax HX1 ..... 203 D3
21 Hebden Bridge HX7 ..... 89 A3
Huddersfield HD3 ..... 153 B5
Huddersfield, Folly Hall
HD3 ..... 154 A4
manton WF6 ..... 144 A8
Mapplewell S75 ..... 178 C1
Morley LS27 ..... 98 A4
Ossett WF5 ..... 140 F3
Ryhill WF4 ..... 180 C8
Sowerby Bridge HX6 ..... 112 C3
Wakefield WF1 ..... 216 B3
Hope Terr HD7 ..... 152 D3
Hope View BD18 ..... 55 D7
Hopefield Chase LS26 ..... 100 B4
Hopefield Cl LS26 ..... 100 B4
Hopefield Cres LS26 ..... 100 B4
Hopefield Ct
East Ardsley WF3 ..... 120 C7
Rothwell LS26 ..... 100 B4
Hopefield Dr LS26 ..... 100 B4
Hopefield Gdns LS26 ..... 100 B4
Hopefield Gn LS26 ..... 100 B4
Hopefield Gr LS26 ..... 100 B4

Hopefield Mews LS26 .... 100 B4
Hopefield Pl LS26 .... 100 B4
Hopefield View LS26 .... 100 B4
Hopefield Way Bradford BD5 75 B1
Rothwell LS26 .... 100 B4
Hopefield Wlk LS26 .... 100 B4
Hopes Farm Mount **3** LS10 99 F7
Hopes Farm Rd LS10 .... 99 F7
Hopes Farm View LS10 .... 100 A7
Hopetown Wlk WF6 .... 123 C3
Hopewell Pl **4** LS6 .... 205 E2
Hopewell St WF17 .... 118 B6
Hopewell Terr LS25 .... 83 B1
Hopewell View LS10 .... 99 D5
Hopewell Way WF4 .... 159 E5
Hopkin St SD4 .... 75 E1
Hopkinson Dr BD4 .... 95 C8
Hopkinson Rd HD2 .... 136 B4
Hopkinson St HX3 .... 91 F3
Hopkinsons Bldgs HX3 .... 91 F3
Hopps's Rd BD20 .... 16 C7
Hopton Ave Bradford BD4 .... 75 B1
Morfield WF14 .... 137 E2
Hopton Dr WF14 .... 137 E2
Hopton Hall La WF14 .... 137 F1
Hopton Jun & Inf Sch
WF14 .... 137 F2
Hopton La WF14 .... 137 F2
Hopton Mews LS12 .... 209 E3
Hopton New Rd WF14 .... 138 A3
Hopwood Bank LS18 .... 41 C2
Hopwood La LS18 .... 41 C2
Hopwood Gr WF10 .... 125 B7
Hopwood La HX1 .... 202 C2
Hopwood Rd LS18 .... 41 C2
Horace Waller VC Par
WF12 .... 119 A2
Horbury Bridge C of E
Jun & Inf Sch WF4 .... 140 E1
Horbury Jun & Inf Sch
WF4 .... 141 C1
Horbury Mews WF4 .... 140 F2
Horbury Rd Ossett WF5 .... 140 E3
Wakefield WF2 .... 141 E3
Horbury Sch WF4 .... 141 C1
Horley Green La HX3 .... 92 E2
Horley Green Rd HX3 .... 113 E8
Horn Cote La HD7 .... 190 A6
Horn Croft S75 .... 193 F5
Horn La Holmfirth HD7 .... 190 A6
Ingbirchworth S36 .... 191 B1
Silsden BD20 .... 5 C4
Hornbeam Ave WF2 .... 142 A8
Hornbeam Cl BD15 .... 53 F4
Hornbeam Gn WF8 .... 125 F1
Hornbeam Way LS14 .... 62 C8
Hornby St HX1 .... 202 B1
Hornby Terr HX1 .... 202 B1
Horncastle St **3** BD19 ...... 116 E7
Horncastle View WF4 .... 162 D2
Horne St Halifax HX1 .... 203 D3
Wakefield WF2 .... 142 C4
Horner Ave WF17 .... 117 F6
Horner Cres WF17 .... 117 F6
Hornes La S75 .... 178 C1
Hornsea Dr BD15 .... 53 C4
Horse Bank Dr HD4 .... 153 E3
Horse Croft La HD8 .... 174 B3
Horse Fair WF8 .... 125 D1
Horse Fair Flats WF8 .... 125 D1
Horse Pond La HD3 .... 152 A7
Horsefair LS22 .... 13 E5
Horsehold La HX7 .... 88 E2
Horsehold Rd HX7 .... 88 E2
Horsfall St Halifax HX1 .... 202 C1
Morley LS27 .... 97 F6
Todmorden OL14 .... 108 E6
Horsforth Featherbank
Infants Sch LS18 .... 58 B7
Horsforth Golf Course
LS18 .... 40 F5
Horsforth New Rd LS13 ...... 57 E6
Horsforth Sch & Further
Education Ctr LS18 .... 41 B1
Horsforth St Margaret's
C of E Primary Sch LS18 41 B1
Horsforth Sta LS18 .... 41 C3
Horsham Ct BD22 .... 34 E5
Horsham Rd BD4 .... 75 E2
Horsley St **5** BD6 .... 74 C1
Horsman St BD4 .... 75 E1
Horton Bank Ctry Pk
BD7 .... 73 E2
Horton Cl LS13 .... 57 F4
Horton Garth LS13 .... 57 F4
Horton Grange Rd BD7 .... 74 B5
Horton Hall Cl BD5 .... 74 D5
Horton Park Ave BD5, BD7 .. 74 C5
Horton Pl HX2 .... 91 E6
Horton Rise LS13 .... 57 F4
Horton St Halifax HX1 .... 117 D3
Halifax HX1 .... 203 F2
Ossett WF5 .... 140 C6
Hospital La LS16 .... 41 F3
Hospital Rd BD20 .... 19 A1
Hostingley La WF12 .... 140 B2
Hothfield St BD20 .... 5 D1
Hothfield Street Junior Sch
BD20 .... 5 D1
Hough HX3 .... 93 A1
Hough End Ave LS13 .... 58 D1
Hough End Cl LS13 .... 58 D1
Hough End Cres LS13 .... 58 C1

Hough End Ct **1** LS13 ...... 58 D1
Hough End Garth LS13 .... 58 C1
Hough End Gdns **2** LS13 . 58 D1
Hough End La LS13 .... 58 C1
Hough Gr **16** LS13 .... 58 C1
Hough La LS13 .... 58 C2
Hough Side Cl LS28 .... 77 B7
Hough Side High Sch
LS13 .... 77 B8
Hough Side La LS28 .... 77 A7
Hough Side Rd LS28 .... 77 A7
Hough Terr **17** LS13 .... 58 C2
Hough Top LS13 .... 77 B8
Hough Tree Rd LS13 .... 77 C8
Hough Tree Terr LS13 .... 77 C8
Houghley Ave LS12 .... 58 F2
Houghley Cl LS13 .... 58 E2
Houghley Cres LS12 .... 58 F3
Houghley La LS12, LS13 ...... 58 E1
Houghley Pl LS12 .... 58 F2
Houghley Rd LS12 .... 58 F2
Houghley Sq LS12 .... 58 F2
Houghton Ave WF11 .... 126 B5
Houghton Pl BD1 .... 201 A4
Houghton Rd S72 .... 194 A1
Houghton St HD6 .... 115 B3
Houghton Twrs **10** HX6 .. 112 B4
Houghton's Almshouses **7**
HD5 .... 154 F3
Houldsworth Ave WF16 ..... 117 E7
Hoults La HX4 .... 134 C8
Houndhill La WF7 .... 145 F5
House Grove Dr HD8 .... 175 E2
Hovingham Ave LS8 .... 208 A4
Hovingham Gr LS8 .... 208 A4
Hovingham Mount LS8 .... 208 A4
Hovingham Primary Sch
LS8 .... 208 A4
Hovingham Terr LS8 .... 208 A4
Howard Ave
Huddersfield HD3 .... 153 C7
Leeds LS15 .... 80 F7
Howard CE Jun & Inf Sch
WF7 .... 164 B7
Howard Cres WF14 .... 159 E6
Howard Ct LS15 .... 80 F7
Howard Pk BD19 .... 116 E7
Howard Pl WF17 .... 118 C3
Howard Rd HD3 .... 153 C7
Howard St Batley WF17 .... 118 C3
Bradford BD5 .... 201 A2
Halifax HX1 .... 202 C4
Ossett WF5 .... 140 D7
Wakefield WF1 .... 216 B3
Howard Villas BD19 .... 116 E7
Howard Way
Littleborough OL15 .... 129 C1
Meltham HD7 .... 170 E1
Howards Dean BD22 .... 51 D8
Howarth Ave BD2 .... 56 A5
Howarth Dr BD2 .... 56 A5
Howarth La HD1 .... 153 E3
Howarth Pl LS7 .... 206 C1
Howbeck Ave BD20 .... 19 A1
Howbeck Dr BD20 .... 36 A8
Howcans La HX3 .... 92 B5
Howden Ave
Adwick Le S DN6 .... 184 E1
Keighley BD20 .... 18 A2
Howden Cl Bradford BD4 ..... 75 F1
Huddersfield HD4 .... 152 F2
Mapplewell S75 .... 177 F1
Howden Clough High Sch
WF17 .... 97 B1
Howden Clough Ind Est
WF17 .... 118 F8
Howden Clough Rd LS27 .... 97 D3
Howden Gdns LS6 .... 205 E2
Howden Pl LS6 .... 205 E2
Howden Rd BD20 .... 5 F1
Howden Way WF1 .... 142 E6
Howdenbrook HX3 .... 93 E7
Howell La DN5 .... 194 A4
Howell Wood Country Pk
WF9, DN5 .... 194 A7
Howes La HX3 .... 92 F2
Howgate BD10 .... 56 C8
Howgate Rd HD7 .... 169 F8
Howgill Gn BD6 .... 94 A6
Howlett Cross LS26 .... 100 B4
Howley Hall Golf Course
LS27 .... 118 F8
Howley Mill La WF17 .... 118 D7
Howley Park Cl LS27 .... 97 F2
Howley Park Rd LS27 .... 97 F2
Howley Park Rd E LS27 ...... 98 A1
Howley Park Trad Est
LS27 .... 97 F2
Howley St WF17 .... 118 D6
Howley Wlk LS27 .... 118 E6
Howroyd La
Dewsbury WF12 .... 156 A7
Rippondon HX4 .... 133 B4
Howroyd's Yd WF5 .... 119 C1
Howson Cl LS20 .... 22 F1
Hoxton Mount LS11 .... 213 F3
Hoxton St BD8 .... 74 A8
Hoylake Ave HD2 .... 135 F3
Hoyland Rd WF2 .... 160 B5
Hoyland Terr WF9 .... 182 A2
Hoyle Court Ave BD17 .... 38 E3
Hoyle Court Dr BD17 .... 38 E3
Hoyle Court First Sch
BD17 .... 38 E3
Hoyle Court Rd BD17 .... 38 E3
Hoyle Fold BD22 .... 34 D2
Hoyle House Fold HD7 .... 152 D1
Hoyle Ing HD7 .... 152 D1

Hoyle Ing Rd BD13 .... 72 F6
Hoyle Mill Rd WF9 .... 163 B2
Hubberton Green Rd HX6 ... 111 C2
Hubert St Bradford BD3 ...... 75 B6
Halifax HX2 .... 112 D7
Huddersfield HD3 .... 134 E1
Hud Hill HX3 .... 93 B4
Huddersfield Gram Sch
HD3 .... 153 C6
Huddersfield New Coll
HD3 .... 152 F7
Huddersfield Rd
Batley WF17 .... 117 E8
Bradford BD12 .... 94 C4
Brighouse HD6 .... 136 B7
Denshaw OL3 .... 167 A4
Dewsbury, Ravensthorpe
WF13 .... 138 D4
Dewsbury, West Town
WF13 .... 138 B1
Elland HX5 .... 135 A4
Halifax HX3 .... 113 C4
Holmfirth HD7 .... 189 A6
Holmfirth, New Mill HD7 ..... 189 E7
Honley HD7 .... 172 A5
Huddersfield HD3 .... 135 A4
Ingbirchworth S30 .... 191 E1
Kirkburton HD8 .... 174 A4
Meltham HD7 .... 171 A5
Shepley HD8 .... 174 A4
Skelmanthorpe HD8 .... 174 D2
West Bretton WF4 .... 177 A6
Huddersfield Royal Infmy
HD3 .... 153 B7
Huddersfield Sta HD1 .... 154 A6
Huddersfield Tech Coll
Huddersfield HD4 .... 153 F2
Huddersfield Tech Coll
(Annexe) HD1 .... 154 A6
Huddersfield Tech Coll
(Brunel Ho) HD2 .... 136 C2
Huddersfield Tech Coll
HD1 .... 154 A6
Huddleston St WF2 .... 139 F8
Hudroyd HD5 .... 154 F3
Hudson Ave Bradford BD7 .. 74 B3
Notton WF4 .... 179 B6
Hudson Cl **1** Bradford BD7 74 B3
Wetherby LS22 .... 13 E5
Hudson Cres BD7 .... 74 B3
Hudson Gdns BD7 .... 74 B4
Hudson Gr LS9 .... 208 A1
Hudson Mews LS22 .... 30 E7
Hudson Mill Rd HX7 .... 88 A5
Hudson Pl LS9 .... 208 A1
Hudson Rd LS9 .... 208 A1
Hudson St Bradford BD3 ..... 75 D7
Leeds LS9 .... 208 A1
2 Pudsey LS28 .... 57 D1
Todmorden OL14 .... 86 C1
Hudson The BD12 .... 94 F4
Hudson's Terr **8** LS19 ...... 40 C7
Hudswell Rd LS10 .... 215 D4
Hudswell St WF1 .... 142 E3
Huggan Row **5** LS28 .... 76 F7
Hugh Gaitskell Middle Sch
LS11 .... 213 D2
Hugh St WF10 .... 124 D7
Hughenden View LS27 .... 98 A6
Hughendon Dr BD13 .... 73 A6
Hughendon Wlk BD13 .... 73 A6
Hugill St BD13 .... 72 D6
Hulbert Croft HD5 .... 154 F4
Hulbert St BD16 .... 37 A2
Hull St LS27 .... 98 A4
Hullen Rd HX5 .... 134 D6
Hullenedge Gdns HX5 .... 134 C6
Hullenedge La HX5 .... 134 D6
Hullenedge Rd HX5 .... 134 C6
Hullett Cl HX7 .... 89 F1
Hullett Dr HX7 .... 89 F1
Hulme Sq WF10 .... 104 D1
Hulme St HX6 .... 112 B3
Humber Cl Castleford WF10 125 B8
Slaithwaite HD7 .... 152 D1
Humboldt St BD1 .... 201 D3
Hume Crest **7** WF17 .... 118 C5
Humley Rd WF2 .... 160 B5
Humphall La WF8 .... 146 D2
Hungate La LS26 .... 122 E8
Hunger Hill Halifax HX1 ...... 203 E2
Ilkley LS29 .... 8 B4
Morley LS27 .... 98 A3
Hunger Hills Ave LS18 .... 41 A1
Hunger Hills Dr LS18 .... 41 A1
Hungerford Rd HD3 .... 153 D8
Hunslet Bsns Pk LS10 .... 212 B1
Hunslet Carr Primary Sch
LS10 .... 215 E2
Hunslet Green Ret Ctr
LS10 .... 211 F3
Hunslet Green Way LS10 .... 215 D4
Hunslet Hall Rd LS11 .... 214 B4
Hunslet Hall Sh Ctr LS11 .... 214 B4
Hunslet La LS10 .... 211 F2
Hunslet Moor Primary Sch
LS11 .... 214 C3
Hunslet Rd Leeds LS10 ...... 211 F2
Leeds, Pottery Field LS10 ... 212 A1
Hunslet St Joseph's
Primary Sch LS10 .... 215 E4
Hunslet St Mary's CE
Primary Sch LS10 .... 215 E3
Hunslet Trad Est LS10 .... 215 F3
Hunston Ave HD3 .... 153 A7
Hunsworth La
Birkenshaw BD19, BD4 .... 95 E4
Cleckheaton BD19 .... 95 E4

Hunt Ct WF2 .... 141 E6
Hunt St Castleford WF10 .... 124 B8
Castleford, Castleford Ings.
WF10 .... 103 D1
Incline The HX3 .... 113 E8
Hunt Yd **3** BD7 .... 74 A4
Hunter Hill Rd HX2 .... 91 A5
Hunters Cl BD9 .... 54 C4
Hunters Ct BD13 .... 52 E7
Hunters La HD4 .... 107 F6
Hunters Meadow BD20 .... 5 E2
Hunters Park Ave BD14 ...... 73 E5
Hunters Wlk LS22 .... 13 E7
Huntingdon Ave HD2 .... 136 F4
Huntingdon Rd HD6 .... 115 C1
Huntock Pl HD6 .... 114 F5
Huntsman Fold WF2 .... 141 D6
Huntsman's Cl HD4 .... 171 D8
Huntsman's Way WF9 .... 164 E2
Huntsmans Cl Bingley BD16 . 37 C5
Keighley BD20 .... 35 A8
Huntwick Ave WF7 .... 145 C4
Huntwick Cres WF7 .... 145 B4
Huntwick Dr WF7 .... 145 B4
Huntwick La
Featherstone WF7 .... 145 A5
West Hardwick WF7 .... 144 F3
Huntwick Rd WF7 .... 145 C4
Hurst Knowle HD5 .... 155 A4
Hurst La WF14 .... 138 B4
Hurst Rd HX7 .... 89 A4
Hurstville Ave BD4 .... 95 F6
Hurstwood HD2 .... 136 E4
Husler Gr LS7 .... 207 D3
Husler Pl LS7 .... 207 D3
Hustings The **3** WF15 .... 117 A4
Hustler St BD3 .... 56 A1
Hustler's Row LS6 .... 59 D8
Hustlergate BD1 .... 201 B3
Hutchinson La **1** HD6 .... 115 B2
Hutchinson's Pl LS5 .... 59 A3
Hutson St BD5 .... 74 D4
Hutton Dr Barnley WF16 ..... 117 E4
South Elmsall WF9 .... 183 A4
Hutton Middle Sch BD2 ..... 56 C5
Hutton Rd BD5 .... 74 C2
Hutton Terr Bradford BD2 ... 56 D5
Pudsey LS28 .... 76 E7
Huxley Mount BD2 .... 56 C5
Hydale Cl Bradford BD12 .... 94 C6
Keighley BD21 .... 35 E5
Hyde Park Cl LS6 .... 205 F2
Hyde Park Cnr LS6 .... 205 F3
Hyde Park Pl LS6 .... 205 F3
Hyde Park Rd Halifax HX1 .. 202 C1
Leeds LS6 .... 205 F3
Hyde Park Terr LS6 .... 205 F3
Hyde Pk Halifax HX1 .... 202 C2
Wakefield WF1 .... 142 E6
Hyde Pl LS2 .... 206 A1
Hyde St Bradford BD10 .... 39 B1
Leeds LS2 .... 206 A1
Hyde Terr LS2 .... 206 A1
Hydro Cl LS29 .... 8 F3
Hyman Wlk WF9 .... 183 A4
Hyne Ave BD4 .... 75 C1
Hyrst Garth WF17 .... 118 B2
Hyrst Wlk WF17 .... 118 C3
Hyrstlands Rd WF17 .... 118 C3
Hyrstmount Junior Sch
WF17 .... 118 B3

Ibbetson Cl LS27 .... 98 A7
Ibbetson Croft LS27 .... 98 A7
Ibbetson Ct LS27 .... 98 A7
Ibbetson Dr LS27 .... 98 A7
Ibbetson Oval LS27 .... 98 A7
Ibbetson Rd LS27 .... 98 A7
Ibbetson Rise LS27 .... 98 A7
Ibbotroyd Ave OL14 .... 108 A7
Ibbotson Flats **6** HD1 .... 154 B6
Ibbotson St **1** WF1 .... 142 F3
Ida & Robert Arthington
Hospl LS16 .... 42 C3
Ida St Bradford BD5 .... 74 C3
Leeds LS10 .... 80 A2
Iddesleigh St BD4 .... 75 D6
Ideal L Ctr BD5 .... 74 D2
Idle CE First Sch BD10 .... 39 B1
Idle Rd BD2 .... 56 B5
Idlecroft Rd BD10 .... 39 A1
Idlethorp Way BD10 .... 56 C7
Ilbert Ave BD4 .... 75 C1
Ilford St LS27 .... 98 B4
Ilkley Golf Course LS29 ...... 7 D6
Ilkley Grammar Sch LS29 ... 8 C3
Ilkley Hall Mews LS29 .... 8 B3
Ilkley Hall Pk LS29 .... 8 B3
Ilkley Middle Sch LS29 .... 8 E4
Ilkley Rd Addingham LS29 .. 6 F6
Burley in W LS29 .... 9 D3
Keighley BD20 .... 19 C5
Otley LS21 .... 22 F7
Ilkley Sta LS29 .... 8 B4
Illingworth Ave Halifax HX2 . 91 E7
Normanton WF6 .... 122 E3
Illingworth Cl Halifax HX2 .. 91 E7
Yeadon LS19 .... 40 A4
Illingworth Cres HX2 .... 91 E7
Illingworth Dr HX2 .... 91 E7
Illingworth Gdns HX2 .... 91 E7
Illingworth Gr HX2 .... 91 E7
Illingworth Rd
Bradford BD12 .... 94 F4
Halifax HX2 .... 91 E8
Illingworth Way HX2 .... 91 E7
Imperial Arc **22** HD1 ...... 154 A6

Imperial Ave WF2 .... 120 F2
Imperial Rd HD1, HD3 .... 153 D7
Inchfield Rd OL14 .... 129 A8
Incline The HX3 .... 113 E8
Independent St BD5 .... 74 C3
Industrial Ave WF17 .... 96 D1
Industrial Rd HX6 .... 112 A4
Industrial St Bacup OL13 ... 106 A2
Bingley BD16 .... 36 F3
Brighouse HD6 .... 115 B3
11 Brighouse, Scholes
BD19 .... 115 F8
Horbury WF4 .... 159 C8
Huddersfield HD4 .... 154 A4
Keighley BD22 .... 35 A6
Leeds LS9 .... 207 F1
Liversedge FW15 .... 116 E4
Todmorden OL14 .... 108 C5
Wakefield WF1 .... 216 B3
Industrial Terr Halifax HX1 . 203 D1
Huddersfield HD5 .... 155 A5
Industry St
3 Thornton BD13 .... 72 E6
Todmorden OL14 .... 108 A1
Infirmary Rd WF13 .... 118 B1
Infirmary St Bradford BD1 .. 201 A3
Leeds LS1 .... 211 E4
Ing Field BD12 .... 95 A4
Ing Head HD7 .... 151 E1
Ing Head La HD4 .... 173 A2
Ing Head Terr HX3 .... 93 B4
Ing La HD4 .... 154 A3
Ing St BD3 .... 75 D7
Ingdale Dr HD7 .... 189 B6
Ingfield Ave
Huddersfield HD5 .... 154 D6
Ossett WF5 .... 140 E6
Ingham Cl Halifax HX2 .... 91 F8
Mirfield WF14 .... 138 C4
Ingham Croft WF14 .... 138 C4
Ingham Garth WF14 .... 138 C5
Ingham La HX2 .... 71 E1
Ingham Rd WF12 .... 139 D3
Ingham St LS10 .... 212 A1
Ingham's Ave LS28 .... 76 B8
Ingham's View LS28 .... 76 B8
Inghams La **2** BD13 .... 92 A1
Inghams Terr LS28 .... 76 B8
Inghead Gdns HX3 .... 93 B4
Ingle Ave LS27 .... 97 F6
Ingle Cres LS27 .... 98 A5
Ingle Ct LS27 .... 97 F6
Ingle Gr LS27 .... 98 A5
Ingle Dean HX7 .... 88 C8
Ingle Row LS7 .... 204 A2
Ingleborough Dr LS27 .... 98 C3
Inglebrook Prep Sch
WF8 .... 125 D1
Ingleby Pl BD7 .... 74 A6
Ingleby Rd BD7, BD8 .... 74 A4
Ingleby St BD8 .... 74 A4
Ingledew Cres LS8 .... 44 B2
Ingledew Ct LS17 .... 43 D4
Ingledew Dr LS8 .... 44 B2
Ingleton Cl **6** LS11 .... 214 B3
Ingleton Dr LS15 .... 80 E7
Ingleton Gr **10** LS11 ...... 214 B3
Ingleton Pl LS11 .... 214 B3
Ingleton Rd HD4 .... 154 B2
Ingleton St LS11 .... 214 B3
Inglewood S75 .... 178 A1
Inglewood App LS14 .... 62 A3
Inglewood Ave HD2 .... 135 C2
Inglewood Dr Leeds LS14 ... 62 B3
Otley LS21 .... 22 F7
Inglewood Pl LS14 .... 62 B3
Ingram Cl LS11 .... 210 C1
Ingram Cres
Knottingley WF11 .... 126 D3
Leeds LS11 .... 213 F4
Ingram Ct **1** LS11 .... 211 D1
Ingram Gdns LS11 .... 210 C1
Ingram Par LS26 .... 100 E5
Ingram Parade LS26 .... 100 E5
Ingram Road Primary Sch
LS11 .... 210 C1
Ingram Row LS11 .... 211 E2
Ingram Sq **16** HX1 .... 202 C2
Ingram St Halifax HX1 .... 202 C2
Keighley BD21 .... 35 B3
Leeds LS11 .... 211 E2
Ingram View LS11 .... 210 C1
Ingrow First Sch BD21 .... 35 A4
Ingrow La BD21, BD22 .... 35 A4
Ingrow West Sta BD21 .... 35 B4
Ings Ave LS20 .... 22 D2
Ings Cl **1** WF4 .... 162 C1
South Kirkby WF9 .... 182 B3
Ings Cres Dewsbury WF12 .. 139 C2
Guiseley LS20 .... 22 D2
Leeds LS9 .... 80 B7
Liversedge WF15 .... 117 B4
Ings Croft HX3 .... 93 C6
Ings Ct LS20 .... 22 C1
Ings Dr Low Bradley BD20 .. 4 C5
Mickletown LS26 .... 102 E3
Ings Holt WF9 .... 182 C4
Ings La Castleford WF10 .... 103 F2
Cononley BD20 .... 4 A3
Dewsbury WF12 .... 139 C2
Guiseley LS20 .... 22 C2
Ledston WF10 .... 103 E4
Low Bradley BD20 .... 4 C5
Shelf HX3 .... 93 A4
Wighill LS24 .... 31 F8
Ings Mere Ct WF11 .... 105 A4
Ings Mill Ave HD8 .... 175 F3

Ings Mill Dr HD8 175 F2
Ings Mill Yd WF16 117 D4
Ings Rd Batley WF17 118 A6
Batley, Heckmondwike WF16 117 D4
Dewsbury WF13 118 E1
Hemsworth WF9 163 B1
Huddersfield HD5 155 A4
Leeds LS9 80 B8
Liversedge WF15 117 B5
Steeton BD20 17 B7
Wakefield WF1 216 B1
Ings The Brighouse HX3 115 A6
Clayton West HD8 175 F2
Ings View Castleford WF10 125 B8
Mickletown LS26 102 E3
Ings Villa WF15 117 C2
Ings Way Bradford BD8 73 E8
Ingbirchworth S36 191 D1
Lepton HD8 155 F3
Silsden BD20 17 F8
Ings Way W HD8 155 E3
Ings Wlk WF9 182 D3
Ingswell Ave WF4 179 A7
Ingswell Dr WF4 178 F7
Ingwell Ct 3 WF1 216 C2
Ingwell St WF1 216 C2
Ingwell Terr BD19 116 E7
Inholmes La LS24 15 C4
Inkerman Ct HD8 192 A5
Inkerman St
6 Bacup OL13 106 A2
Bradford, Cutler Heights BD4 75 D4
Bradford, Ravenscliffe BD2 56 D4
Inkerman Way HD8 191 F5
Inner Hey HD7 169 A4
Inner Hey Yd HD7 169 A4
Inner Ring Rd LS1, LS2 206 C1
Innings The BD10 56 A8
Institute Rd BD2 56 C5
Institute St BD20 16 C6
Intake HD7 152 E5
Intake Cl WF3 121 F5
Intake Gr BD2 56 C2
Intake High Sch LS13 58 A4
Intake La
Lofthouse Gate WF3 121 F5
Meltham HD4 170 F7
Middleton LS10 99 C3
Ossett WF5 140 E5
Pudsey LS13 57 F3
Slaithwaite HD7 169 F4
Steeton BD20 17 B4
Thorner LS14 45 D3
Woolley WF4 177 E8
Yeadon LS19 40 D3
Intake Mount LS10 99 C4
Intake Rd Bradford BD2 56 C2
Pudsey LS28 77 A8
Slaithwaite HD7 151 C2
Intake Sq LS10 99 C3
Intake Terr BD2 56 C2
Intake The LS25 83 B1
Intake View LS10 99 C3
Intercity Way LS13 58 A1
Invargarry Cl LS25 83 B8
Inverness Rd LS25 83 B7
Invertrees Ave LS19 40 C4
Iona Pl 8 HX3 92 B2
Iona St HX3 92 C1
Ireland Cres LS16 41 F3
Ireland St BD16 36 E3
Ireland Terr BD16 36 E3
Ireland Wood Primary Sch LS16 42 A4
Ireton St BD7 74 B6
Iron Row LS29 9 F1
Iron St BD19 116 C7
Ironwood App LS14 62 A3
Ironwood Cres LS14 62 A3
Ironwood View LS14 62 A4
Irvin Terr WF10 124 C7
Irving St HX1 202 B1
Irving Terr BD14 73 C3
Irwell St BD4 75 A5
Irwin App LS15 80 F7
Irwin Ave WF1 142 F7
Irwin Cres WF1 142 E7
Irwin St LS28 57 D2
Isaac St BD8 74 B8
Island The WF11 127 A5
Island View WF12 139 B6
Isles St BD8 73 F8
Ivanhoe Rd BD7 74 B5
Ive House La HX2 111 E8
Ivegate Bradford BD1 201 B3
Yeadon LS19 40 B7
Iver Way BD18 55 A7
Ives St BD17 55 B8
Iveson App LS16 41 F2
Iveson Cl LS16 41 F2
Iveson Cres LS16 41 F2
Iveson Ct LS16 41 F2
Iveson Dr LS16 41 F2
Iveson Garth LS16 42 A2
Iveson Gdns LS16 41 F2
Iveson Gn LS16 41 F2
Iveson Gr LS16 41 F2
Iveson Lawn LS16 42 A2
Iveson Primary Sch LS16 42 A2
Iveson Rd LS16 41 F2
Iveson Rise LS16 42 A2
Ivory St LS10 211 F1
Ivy Ave LS9 80 B8
Ivy Bank Ct 1 BD17 38 D2
Ivy Bank La BD22 51 C6
Ivy Chase LS28 77 B7
Ivy Cl WF1 142 E8
Ivy Cotts S71 179 D4
Ivy Cres Brighouse HX3 114 E7
Leeds LS9 80 A7
10 Leeds LS9 80 A8
Ivy Ct LS7 204 A2
Ivy Farm Cl S71 179 D1
Ivy Garth LS7 204 A2
Ivy Gdns WF10 125 D5
Ivy Gr Leeds LS9 80 B8
Shipley BD18 54 F7
Wakefield WF1 142 E8
Ivy House Rd BD5 74 E1
Ivy La Boston Spa LS23 30 C7
Bradford BD15 54 A1
Halifax HX2 91 D6
Wakefield WF1 142 E8
Ivy Mount Leeds LS9 80 A8
Slaithwaite HD7 151 F1
Ivy Pl Glusburn BD20 16 D7
Leeds LS13 58 D4
Ivy Rd Keighley BD21 35 E6
Leeds LS9 80 B8
Shipley BD18 54 E7
Ivy St Brighouse HD6 114 F3
Featherstone WF7 145 D6
Halifax HX1 202 C1
Huddersfield, Moldgreen HD4, HD5 154 C5
Huddersfield, Paddock HD4 153 C4
Keighley BD21 35 B8
Leeds LS9 80 A8
Ivy St S Halifax HX1 202 C1
Keighley BD21 35 B3
Ivy Terr Brighouse HD6 114 F3
Brighouse, Lydgate HX3 114 E7
Keighley BD21 35 F6
South Elmsall WF9 183 A3
Ivy View 8 LS9 80 A8

Jacinth Ct HD2 136 C2
Jack Bridge HX7 88 A5
Jack Close Orch S71 179 C4
Jack Field La BD20 16 A4
Jack Hill HD2 136 A1
Jack La Batley WF17 118 D2
Leeds, Mint LS11 211 E1
Leeds, Pottery Field LS10, LS11 212 A1
Jack Royd HX3 91 F2
Jackdaw La LS23 30 C8
Jackie Smart Ct LS7 207 E3
Jackie Smart Rd 1 BD5 74 E4
Jackman Dr LS18 58 D7
Jackroyd La
Huddersfield HD4 154 B2
Mirfield WF14 137 E2
Jackson Ave LS8 204 C3
Jackson Hill La BD13 92 F7
Jackson House WF9 181 D6
Jackson La HX4 133 A5
Jackson Meadows HX4 133 A5
Jackson Pl BD20 16 D4
Jackson Rd LS7 206 C3
Jackson St Bradford BD3 75 A6
Sutton in C BD20 16 D5
Jackson's La
Darrington WF8 165 E7
Dewsbury WF13 139 A1
Low Bradley BD20 4 E5
Jacky La BD22 51 C6
Jacob Kramer Coll LS2 206 B2
Jacob Kramer Coll (Art) LS2 206 B1
Jacob St Bradford BD5 74 D4
Leeds LS2 206 C1
Jacob's Row HD4 153 F3
Jacob's Well BD1 201 B2
Jacob's Well La WF1 216 C3
Jacques Gr BD20 5 F1
Jade Pl HD2 136 C2
Jaggar La HD7 171 F4
Jagger Green Dean HX4 134 B3
Jagger La Emley HD8 174 E7
Huddersfield HD5 155 A8
Jail Rd WF17 117 F5
Jail Yd LS26 100 F5
Jakeman Cl WF3 119 E8
Jakeman Ct WF3 119 E8
Jakeman Dr WF3 119 E8
James Ave Leeds LS8 204 C4
Steeton BD20 17 A5
James Cl LS25 83 A7
James Ct LS22 29 B8
James Duggan Ave WF7 145 D6
James Gate BD1 201 B3
James Gibbs Cl WF7 145 D6
James La HD7 171 A6
James St Batley WF17 118 B4
Birkenshaw BD11 96 A6
Bradford BD15 54 C1
Bradford BD1 201 B3
Brighouse HD6 115 A4
Castleford WF10 103 D1
Dewsbury WF13 118 B1
Elland HX5 135 A6
Elland, Holywell Green HX4 134 B4
Glusburn BD20 16 D7
Huddersfield HD7 152 D4
8 Liversedge WF15 117 A4
Mirfield WF14 138 A7
Oakworth BD22 34 B2
Slaithwaite HD7 152 A1
South Hiendley S72 180 F6
Thornton BD13 72 D6
Yeadon LS19 40 B4
James St E 8 BD21 35 C6
Jamie Ct BD10 56 D6
Jane Hills BD17 55 A8
Jane St Denholme BD13 52 D1
Shipley BD18 54 F8
Janesway LS25 82 F2
Janet St 5 BD22 51 E8
Jaques Cl LS6 59 B4
Jardine Ave WF7 145 D6
Jardine Rd 10 BD16 37 A3
Jarratt St BD8 55 B1
Jarratt St E BD8 55 B1
Jarrom Cl BD4 75 D4
Jarvis House 4 BD6 93 E8
Jarvis Sq WF3 100 A3
Jarvis Wlk WF3 100 A3
Jasmin Terr BD8 74 C8
Jason Terr WF17 97 A2
Jasper St Bradford BD10 56 B8
Halifax HX1 202 B3
Javelin Cl BD10 56 B6
Jay House La HD6 115 D5
Jay St BD22 51 D6
JB Priestley Liby BD7 74 C6
Jean Ave LS15 81 A7
Jebb La Cawthorne S75 176 E3
High Hoyland S75 176 F3
Jenkin Dr WF4 140 F1
Jenkin La WF4 140 F1
Jenkin Rd WF4 141 A1
Jenkinson Cl LS11 211 D1
Jenkinson Lawn LS11 211 D1
Jenkinson St WF17 118 C2
Jenkinsons Pl LS10 99 D8
Jenkyn La HD8 190 D8
Jennetts Cres LS21 22 F7
Jennings Cl BD20 17 F8
Jennings Pl BD7 74 A4
Jennings St 7 BD7 74 A4
Jenny La Baildon BD17 38 D4
Mirfield WF14 138 B7
Jensen Ave WF13 117 F3
Jepson La HX5 134 F6
Jer Gr BD7 73 E2
Jer La BD7 73 E2
Jeremy La WF16 117 D4
Jermyn St BD1 201 C3
Jerry Clay Dr WF2 120 E2
Jerry Clay La WF2 120 D2
Jerry Clay La Junior & Infants Sch WF2 120 E2
Jerry Fields Rd HX2 111 D6
Jerry La Silsden BD20 6 F1
Sowerby Bridge HX6 112 A3
Jersey Cl WF12 118 F2
Jerusalem La HX2 90 D4
Jerusalem Rd HD7 170 B7
Jerusalem Sq HX3 114 B4
Jervaulx Cl LS23 30 C7
Jervaulx Cres BD8 74 D8
Jerwood Hill Cl HX3 92 D1
Jerwood Hill Rd HX3 92 D1
Jesmond Ave S71 179 C3
Jesmond Gr Bradford BD9 54 F2
Dewsbury WF13 118 B1
Jessamine Ave LS11 213 F2
Jessamine Pl BD20 16 E6
Jessamine St WF13 138 D5
Jesse St BD8 73 D7
Jessop Ave HD5 155 A3
Jessop Fold HD7 171 F5
Jessop St Castleford WF10 124 D8
Wakefield WF2 142 C4
Jester Pl BD13 72 C2
Jew La BD22 51 C1
Jewitt La LS22 29 C7
Jill La WF14 138 D8
Jilley Royd La HD2 136 A4
Jim Allen La HX2 90 C1
Jim La HD1 153 D6
Jin Whin Ct WF10 124 A8
Jin-Whin Hill WF10 124 A8
Jinnah Ct BD8 74 D8
Jinny Moor La LS26 101 E8
Joan Royd WF16 117 D6
Joba Ave BD3 75 B7
Joffre Ave WF10 124 E6
John Baker St OL14 107 E8
John Booth Cl WF15 116 F2
John Carr Ave WF4 141 A2
John Escritt Rd BD16 37 A2
John Haigh Rd HD7 170 A8
John Jamieson Sch LS8 61 C5
John Naylor La HX2 111 E5
John Nelson Cl 9 WF17 96 F1
John O'Gaunts Wlk LS26 100 F6
John Ormsby V C Way WF12 119 A2
John Smeaton Com High Sch LS15 62 E3
John Smeaton Middle Sch LS15 62 E3
John Smeaton Sports Ctr LS15 62 E3
John St Baildon BD17 38 C1
5 Batley, Birstall WF17 96 E1
9 Batley, Heckmondwike WF16 117 D3
Bradford BD1 201 B3
Bradford, Clayton BD14 73 C4
Bradford, Tong Street BD4 75 E1
Brighouse HD6 115 A3
Castleford WF10 124 C6
Cullingworth BD13 52 D6
Denholme BD13 52 D1
Dewsbury WF13 118 C2
2 Dewsbury, Eastborough WF13 118 E1
Dewsbury, Ravensthorpe WF13 138 E5
Elland HX5 134 F6
John St continued
Elland, Lindwell HX4 134 C7
Halifax HX1 203 E3
Huddersfield HD3 153 B4
Leeds LS6 205 E3
Oakworth BD22 34 D2
Shipley BD18 55 A8
South Elmsall WF9 182 F2
Thornton BD13 72 D6
4 Todmorden OL14 108 B5
Wakefield WF1 216 C2
Yeadon LS19 40 B4
John St W 2 HX6 112 B4
John Street Mkt BD1 201 B3
John William St
3 Cleckheaton BD19 116 D8
13 Elland HX5 134 F6
Huddersfield HD1 154 A6
1 Liversedge WF15 117 B3
Liversedge, Mill Bridge WF15 117 C4
John's Cres WF2 120 E2
Johnny La LS21 23 A6
Johns Ave WF3 121 C6
Johns La HX5 134 F4
Johnson St Bingley BD16 36 F3
Bradford BD3 75 D7
Mirfield WF14 138 A3
Johnson Terr 1 LS27 98 B4
Johnston St Leeds LS6 206 B4
Wakefield WF1 216 C2
Jonathan Garth LS29 6 E8
Jons Ave WF9 182 A2
Jos La HD8 190 E8
Jos Way HD8 190 E8
Joseph Ave HX3 93 A2
Joseph Crossley's Almshouses HX1 202 C2
Joseph Priestley Coll LS26 101 B7
Joseph Priestly Coll LS27 98 B4
Joseph Priestly Institute of Further Education LS27 98 B2
Joseph St Bradford BD3 201 D3
Bradford, Tong Street BD4 75 E1
Leeds LS10 215 E4
Joseph Wright Ct BD10 39 A1
Josephine Rd HD4 153 A3
Joshua St 7 OL14 108 B6
Jowett House La S75 193 B4
Jowett Park Cres BD10 39 A2
Jowett St BD1 74 C7
Jowett Terr 7 LS27 98 A2
Jowett's La BD20 5 D8
Jubilee Ave
Lofthouse Gate WF1 121 C4
Normanton WF6 144 A8
Shepley HD8 174 A2
Jubilee Bglws WF11 126 E4
Jubilee Cl WF9 181 F6
Jubilee Cres
Birkenshaw BD11 97 A7
Crofton WF4 144 B3
Lofthouse Gate WF1 121 C4
Jubilee Croft BD11 96 F7
Jubilee Ct WF9 163 A4
Jubilee Dr 3 BD21 35 A5
Jubilee La HD4 153 A3
Jubilee Mount HD6 114 F2
Jubilee Pl 5 LS27 98 B4
Jubilee Rd Crofton WF4 144 B3
Halifax HX3 113 D3
Jubilee St Bradford BD1 55 D1
Crigglestone WF4 159 F3
Halifax HX3 203 F2
9 Hebden Bridge HX7 89 E1
6 Morley LS27 98 B4
Jubilee St N HX3 92 A3
Jubilee Terr
4 Halifax HX3 203 F2
4 Morley LS27 98 B4
Ripponden HX6 132 E6
Jubilee Trees LS29 21 C7
Jubilee Way
Pontefract WF8 146 C8
Shipley BD18 55 D8
Judy Haigh La WF12 157 D8
Judy La HD2 136 B3
Julian Dr BD13 73 C2
Julian St HD5 154 E5
Julie Ave WF4 159 E5
Jumb Beck Cl LS29 21 F8
Jumble Dyke HD6 135 F8
Jumble Hole Rd OL14, HX7 88 B1
Jumble Wood HD8 155 D3
Jumbles Ct WF3 100 C1
Jumbles La WF3 100 C1
Jumples HX2 91 D4
Jumples Cl HX2 91 D4
Jumples Crag HX2 91 D4
Jumples Ct HX2 91 D4
Jumps La
Hebden Bridge HX7 88 F1
Todmorden OL14 107 E8
Jumps Rd OL14 107 E8
Junction 1 Ret Pk LS11 213 D2
Junction Houses WF10 103 C1
Junction La WF5 141 A4
Junction Rd 3
Dewsbury WF13 139 B7
Shipley BD17 55 C8
Junction Row BD2 56 B4
Junction St LS10 211 F2
Junction Terr BD2 56 B4
June St 4 BD21 35 C8
Juniper Cl BD8 74 B8
Juniper Gr HD4 171 D6
Juniper Grove Mews HD4 171 D6
Juniper Pl LS9 208 B1
Justin Way HD4 153 A1

Kaffir Rd HD2 153 D8
Karnac Rd LS8 207 F4
Karon Dr WF4 141 B1
Kateholm OL13 106 A7
Katherine St 10 BD18 54 F8
Katrina Gr WF7 145 D4
Kay Cl LS27 97 F7
Kay St Shipley BD18 55 C5
Wakefield WF1 216 C2
Kaycell St BD4 75 B2
Kaye Hill BD13 52 D6
Kaye La Huddersfield HD5 154 E2
Huddersfield, Linthwaite HD7 152 E3
Kaye St Batley WF16 117 D3
Dewsbury WF12 139 D6
Kaye's First Sch HD8 175 F2
Kearsley Terr LS10 215 E2
Keat St HD4 153 E4
Keats Ave OL14 108 D6
Keats Cl WF8 125 D2
Keats Dr WF16 117 E2
Keats Gr WF3 121 E6
Kebble Ct BD19 117 B7
Keble Garth LS25 83 C2
Kebroyd Ave HX6 132 E7
Kebroyd La HX6 132 E7
Kebroyd Mount HX6 132 E6
Kebs Rd OL14 86 E3
Kedleston Rd LS8 43 F3
Keeble House BD2 56 D2
Keel Moorings LS13 57 F5
Keeldar Cl BD7 74 B3
Keelham First Sch BD13 71 F5
Keelham La Keighley BD20 18 A2
Todmorden OL14 87 D1
Keenan Ave WF9 182 E1
Keeper La Birkenshaw BD4 76 E2
Notton WF4 178 D5
Keeton St LS9 212 C4
Keighley Cl HX2 91 E6
Keighley Coll (Annex) BD21 35 D7
Keighley Dr HX2 91 E4
Keighley Golf Course BD20 18 A4
Keighley Ind Pk BD21 18 C1
Keighley Pl 6 LS28 57 E2
Keighley Preparatory Sch BD21 18 C1
Keighley Rd Bingley BD16 36 E5
Bradford BD8 55 C3
Cullingworth BD13 52 C7
Denholme BD13 52 D2
Glusburn BD20 16 E6
Halifax HX2 91 E5
Harden BD16 36 A2
Haworth BD22 34 E3
Hebden Bridge HX7 89 A4
Ilkley LS29 7 F2
Low Bradley BD20 4 B5
Oxenhope BD22 51 D3
Shipley BD9 55 C3
Silsden BD20 17 D8
Skipton BD23 4 A8
Steeton BD20 17 E5
Wadsworth Moor HX7 89 B8
Keighley Rd (Lidget) BD22 34 D2
Keighley Ret Pk BD21 18 C1
Keighley Sta BD21 35 D7
Keighley & Worth Valley Rly BD22 34 E1
Keir Hardy Cl WF16 117 C4
Kelburn Gr BD22 34 B3
Kelcliffe Ave LS20 22 E1
Kelcliffe Gr LS20 22 E1
Kelcliffe La LS20 22 E2
Keldholme Cl LS13 57 F5
Keldholme Rd 2 LS13 57 F5
Keldregate HD2 136 E4
Kell Beck LS21 10 F2
Kell La Halifax HX2 90 E6
Northowram HX3 92 F2
Kell St 6 BD16 37 A3
Kellett Ave LS12 78 C4
Kellett Cres LS12 78 C4
Kellett Dr LS12 78 C4
Kellett Gr LS12 78 C4
Kellett La LS12 209 E1
Kellett Mount 2 LS12 78 C4
Kellett Pl 3 LS12 78 C4
Kellett Rd LS12 209 E1
Kellett Terr 1 LS12 78 C4
Kellett Wlk LS12 78 C4
Kelloe St BD19 95 D1
Kelmore Gr BD6 93 E7
Kelmscott Ave LS15 62 D3
Kelmscott Cres LS15 62 D3
Kelmscott Garth LS15 62 E4
Kelmscott Gdns LS15 62 E3
Kelmscott Gn LS15 62 D3
Kelmscott Gr LS15 62 D3
Kelmscott La LS15 62 D3
Kelsall Ave LS6 205 E2
Kelsall Gr LS6 205 E2
Kelsall Pl LS6 205 E2
Kelsall Rd LS6 205 E2
Kelsall Terr LS6 205 E2
Kelsey St HX1 202 B4
Kelso Ct LS3 205 F1
Kelso Gdns LS2 205 F1

Kelso Gr HD5 .... 155 A6
Kelso Hts LS6 .... 205 F2
Kelso Pl LS2 .... 205 F2
Kelso Rd LS2 .... 205 F2
Kelso St LS2 .... 205 F1
Keltus Ave BD20 .... 16 D7
Kelvin Ave Halifax HX2 ...... 112 D6
 Huddersfield HD5 .... 154 E6
Kelvin Cres HX2 .... 112 D6
Kelvin Rd HX5 .... 134 E6
Kelvin Way BD2 .... 56 C2
Kemp's Bridge WF2 .... 142 A6
Kemps Way HD7 .... 189 C3
Kempton Rd LS25 .... 83 A2
Kemsing Wlk LS15 .... 62 F2
Ken Churchill Dr WF4 ..... 141 A3
Kendal Bank LS3 .... 205 F1
Kendal Carr LS3 .... 206 A1
 Leeds LS3 .... 205 F1
Kendal Croft WF10 .... 125 E7
Kendal Dr Castleford WF10 .. 125 D8
 Crofton WF4 .... 143 C2
 Leeds LS15 .... 80 E7
Kendal Garth WF10 .... 125 E7
Kendal Gdns WF10 .... 125 E7
Kendal La LS3 .... 206 A1
Kendal Rd ⓶ LS3 .... 206 A1
Kendal Rise Crofton WF4 .. 143 C2
 Walton WF2 .... 161 A6
Kendal St BD21 .... 35 D6
Kendall Wlk LS3 .... 210 C4
Kendall Ave BD18 .... 54 E8
Kendall Mellor Ct ⓫ BD21 .. 35 B7
Kendell St LS10 .... 211 F3
Kenilworth Ave LS27 .... 97 D6
Kenilworth Cl WF14 .... 137 F6
Kenilworth Dr HX3 .... 115 A1
Kenilworth Gdns LS27 .... 97 D7
Kenilworth House ⓺ BD15 .. 73 B8
Kenilworth St BD4 .... 75 B4
Kenley Ave BD6 .... 74 A2
Kenley Mount BD6 .... 74 A2
Kenley Par BD6, BD7 .... 73 F2
Kenmore Ave BD19 .... 116 C8
Kenmore Cl BD19 .... 116 C8
Kenmore Cres Bradford BD6 .. 74 A2
 Cleckheaton BD19 .... 116 C8
Kenmore Dr Bradford BD6 .... 74 A2
 Cleckheaton BD19 .... 116 C8
Kenmore Gr Bradford BD6 ... 74 A2
 Cleckheaton BD19 .... 116 C8
Kenmore Rd Bradford BD6 ... 74 A2
 Cleckheaton BD19 .... 116 C8
 Lofthouse Gate WF2 .... 120 F5
Kenmore View BD19 .... 116 C8
Kenmore Way BD19 .... 116 C8
Kenmore Wlk BD6 .... 74 A2
Kennedy Ave HD2 .... 136 A5
Kennedy Cl WF12 .... 118 F3
Kennel La Oxenhope BD22 .... 50 E2
 Sowerby Bridge HX6 .... 132 A8
Kennels La LS14 .... 46 B8
Kennerleigh Ave LS15 .... 62 D1
Kennerleigh Cres LS15 ...... 62 D1
Kennerleigh Dr LS15 .... 62 C1
Kennerleigh Garth LS15 .... 62 D1
Kennerleigh Glen ⓼ LS15 .. 62 C1
Kennerleigh Gr LS15 .... 62 D1
Kennerleigh Rise ⓫ LS15 .. 62 C1
Kennerleigh Wlk LS15 .... 62 C1
Kennet La LS25 .... 83 A6
Kenneth St LS11 .... 210 C1
Kennion St BD5 .... 201 C1
Kensington Ave LS14 .... 46 A6
Kensington Cl Batley WF17 118 B4
 Halifax HX3 .... 113 A4
Kensington Ct LS6 .... 205 F3
Kensington Gdns HX5 ...... 134 E6
Kensington Rd Halifax HX3 . 113 A3
 Wakefield WF1 .... 216 A4
Kensington St Bradford BD8 . 55 A1
 ⓬ Keighley BD21 .... 35 B6
Kensington Terr
 Garforth LS25 .... 82 E7
 Leeds LS6 .... 205 F3
Kenstone Cres BD10 .... 56 A7
Kent Ave Pudsey LS28 .... 77 A7
 Silsden BD20 .... 5 D1
Kent Cl LS28 .... 77 A7
Kent Cres LS28 .... 77 A7
Kent Dr LS28 .... 77 A7
Kent Mews BD16 .... 37 B2
Kent Rd Bingley BD16 .... 37 B2
 Pudsey LS28 .... 76 F6
Kent St Bradford BD1 .... 201 B2
 Halifax HX1 .... 203 D2
Kent Wlk ⓫ WF13 .... 139 B8
Kentmere App LS14 .... 61 F5
Kentmere Ave
 Brighouse BD12 .... 94 E1
 Garforth LS25 .... 83 B6
 Leeds LS14 .... 61 F7
Kentmere Cl LS14 .... 61 F6
Kentmere Cres LS14 .... 61 F6
Kentmere Gate LS14 .... 61 F7
Kentmere Gdns LS14 .... 61 F6
Kentmere Gn LS14 .... 61 F6
Kentmere Rise LS14 .... 62 A5
Kenton Dr WF4 .... 160 A8
Kenton Way BD4 .... 75 D4
Kenworthy Cl LS16 .... 42 A5
Kenworthy Garth LS16 .... 42 A5

Kenworthy Gate LS16 .... 42 A5
Kenworthy Gdns LS16 .... 42 A5
Kenworthy La HX6 .... 132 E6
Kenworthy Rise LS16 .... 42 A5
Kenworthy Vale LS16 .... 42 A5
Kenya Mount BD21 .... 34 F8
Kenyon La HX2 .... 112 D7
Kenyon St WF9 .... 183 A3
Kepler Gr LS8 .... 207 E2
Kepler Mount LS8 .... 207 E2
Kepler Terr LS8 .... 207 E2
Kepstorn Cl LS5 .... 59 A5
Kepstorn Rd LS16 .... 59 B7
Kepstorn Rise ⓫ LS5 .... 59 A5
Keren Gr WF2 .... 120 E2
Kerr Mackie Primary Sch
 LS8 .... 61 A8
Kerry Garth LS18 .... 41 B1
Kerry Hill Horsforth LS18 ...... 41 C1
 Horsforth LS18 .... 58 B8
Kerry St LS18 .... 41 B1
Kershaw Ave WF10 .... 125 B7
Kershaw Cres HX2 .... 111 D7
Kershaw Ct HX2 .... 111 D8
Kershaw Dr HX2 .... 111 D8
Kershaw La WF11 .... 126 E3
Kershaw Rd OL14 .... 108 A1
Kershaw St BD3 .... 75 D7
Kertland St WF12 .... 139 C7
Kester Rd WF17 .... 117 F5
Kesteven Cl BD4 .... 75 F2
Kesteven Ct BD4 .... 75 F2
Kesteven Rd BD4 .... 75 F2
Kestrel Bank HD4 .... 171 E7
Kestrel Cl LS17 .... 43 F4
Kestrel Dr Bradford BD2 .... 56 A4
 Wakefield WF2 .... 160 B5
Kestrel Garth ⓶ LS27 .... 98 D4
Kestrel Gr LS17 .... 43 F4
Kestrel Mount BD2 .... 56 A4
Kestrel View HD8 .... 173 F3
Keswick Ave HD3 .... 135 A1
Keswick Cl Halifax HX3 .... 113 E4
 Todmorden OL14 .... 107 F7
Keswick Dr Castleford WF10 104 E2
 Wakefield WF2 .... 141 E7
Keswick Grange LS17 .... 28 C5
Keswick La LS17 .... 28 C4
Keswick Rd LS75 .... 178 A3
Keswick St BD4 .... 75 D5
Keswick View LS17 .... 28 C5
Kettle La HD7 .... 169 B6
Kettlethorpe Hall Dr WF2 160 C6
Kettlethorpe High Sch
 WF2 .... 160 C6
Kettlethorpe Rd WF2 .... 160 C5
Kettlewell Dr BD5 .... 74 B3
Kew Hill HD3 .... 134 F3
Kew Hill Bottom HD3 .... 134 F3
Key Hill La S72 .... 180 F3
Key Syke La OL14 .... 108 C5
Khalig Ct BD3 .... 75 B8
Khus Wlk BD21 .... 35 C4
Kidacre St LS10 .... 211 F1
Kiddal La LS15 .... 46 E3
Kidroyd HD5 .... 154 D4
Kidroyd La HD5 .... 154 E4
Kilburn Cl HD5 .... 154 D5
Kilburn La WF13 .... 118 C1
Kilburn Rd LS12 .... 209 F3
Kilby St WF1 .... 216 A3
Kildare Cres BD15 .... 54 A1
Kildare Terr LS12 .... 210 B2
Kildwick CE Sch BD20 .... 16 E8
Killingbeck Bridge LS14 .... 61 E2
Killingbeck Dr LS14 .... 61 E2
Killingbeck Hospl LS14 ...... 61 E2
Killingbeck Ret Pk LS14 ..... 61 E2
Killinghall Ave BD2 .... 56 B1
Killinghall Dr BD2 .... 56 B1
Killinghall Fst Sch BD3 .... 56 C1
Killinghall Gr BD2 .... 56 B1
Killinghall Rd BD2, BD3 .... 56 C1
Kiln Bent Rd HD7 .... 198 A6
Kiln Brow HD7 .... 152 E4
Kiln Ct HD3 .... 134 E1
Kiln Fold HD6 .... 115 D3
Kiln Hill HD7 .... 170 A8
Kiln Hill La BD20 .... 5 B5
Kiln La Emley HD8 .... 175 F5
 Wadsworth Moor HX7 .... 68 D3
Kilncroft HX4 .... 133 F3
Kilner Bank HD5 .... 154 C7
Kilner House BD2 .... 56 D2
Kilner Rd BD6 .... 74 A1
Kilnhouse Bank La HD7 ...... 188 B1
Kilnhurst Ave ⓭ OL14 .... 108 C5
Kilnhurst La OL14 .... 108 C5
Kilnhurst Mount OL14 .... 108 D5
Kilnhurst Rd OL14 .... 108 C5
Kilnsea Mount BD4 .... 75 E3
Kilnsey Fold BD20 .... 5 D2
Kilnsey Hill WF17 .... 142 E8
Kilnsey Mews BD17 .... 38 B3
Kilnsey Rd Bradford BD3 ...... 75 B6
 Wakefield WF1 .... 142 E8
Kilnshaw La HX7 .... 109 F7
Kilpin Hill La WF13 .... 117 F3
Kilroyd Ave BD19 .... 95 D2
Kilroyd Dr BD19 .... 95 D2
Kimberley Pl Halifax HX3 ...... 92 A4
 Leeds LS9 .... 208 B2
Kimberley Rd LS9 .... 208 B2
Kimberley St Bradford BD4 .. 75 C6
 Brighouse HD6 .... 115 B3
 Dewsbury WF12 .... 139 B4
 Featherstone WF7 .... 145 C6

Kimberley St continued
 Halifax HX3 .... 92 A4
 Ilkley LS29 .... 8 C5
 Wakefield WF1 .... 142 D3
Kimberley View LS9 .... 208 B1
Kimberly Cl WF8 .... 165 B5
Kinder Ave HD4 .... 153 F2
Kineholme Dr LS21 .... 22 D6
Kineton Ave OL14 .... 108 C6
King Alfred's Dr LS6 .... 43 A1
King Alfred's Gn LS6 .... 43 A1
King Alfred's Way LS6 .... 43 A1
King Alfred's Wlk LS6 .... 43 A1
King Charles St Leeds LS1 .. 211 F4
 ⓫ Leeds LS1 .... 211 F4
King Charles Wlk ⓷ LS1 ... 211 F4
King Cl LS17 .... 43 A4
King Cliff Rd HD1, HD2 ...... 136 A1
King Cliffe Flats ⓷ HD1 .... 154 A8
King Cross Rd HX1 .... 202 B1
King Cross St HX1 .... 203 D2
King Dr LS17 .... 42 F5
King Edward Ave
 Horsforth LS18 .... 41 C1
 Kippax WF10 .... 102 F6
King Edward Cres LS18 ...... 41 C1
King Edward Rd ⓶ BD13 .... 72 D6
King Edward St
 Dewsbury WF12 .... 139 B3
 Halifax HX1 .... 203 E3
 Hemsworth WF9 .... 181 E6
 Leeds LS1 .... 211 F4
 Normanton WF6 .... 123 A2
 Sutton in CB WF10 .... 16 D5
King Edward Terr ⓫ BD13 .. 72 D6
King Edwin's Ct LS8 .... 61 A5
King George Ave
 Horsforth LS18 .... 41 C1
 Leeds LS7 .... 204 A2
 Morley LS27 .... 98 B6
King George Croft LS27 ...... 98 B5
King George Gdns LS7 ...... 204 A3
King George Rd LS18 .... 41 C1
King George St WF1 .... 121 B3
King George V
 Playing Fields BD21 .... 35 F8
King James's Sch LS14 ...... 155 A2
King La Leeds LS17 .... 42 E6
 Leeds LS17 .... 43 B3
King Royd La WF7 .... 163 C6
King St Batley WF16 .... 117 D4
 Birkenshaw BD11 .... 96 B4
 Bradford BD2 .... 56 C5
 Brighouse HD6 .... 115 B2
 Castleford WF10 .... 124 E5
 Cleckheaton BD19 .... 116 E8
 Elland HX5 .... 135 A6
 Halifax HX1 .... 203 F3
 Hebden Bridge HX7 .... 110 E8
 Hebden Bridge, Mytholm HX7 . 88 E3
 Hemsworth WF9 .... 163 B1
 Horbury WF4 .... 140 E1
 Huddersfield HD1 .... 154 B6
 Huddersfield, Oakes HD3 .... 153 C8
 Keighley BD21 .... 35 B6
 Leeds LS1 .... 211 E3
 Mirfield WF14 .... 138 A4
 Morley LS27 .... 98 A3
 Normanton WF6 .... 123 A1
 Normanton, Altofts WF6 ...... 122 F4
 Ossett WF5 .... 140 E4
 Pontefract WF8 .... 146 C8
 ⓷ Ripponden HX6 .... 132 C1
 Silsden BD20 .... 5 E1
 Skelmanthorpe HD8 .... 175 A2
 Sowerby Bridge HX6 .... 111 E3
 Todmorden OL14 .... 108 D6
 Wakefield WF1 .... 216 B2
 Yeadon LS19 .... 40 C7
 Yeadon, Little London LS19 .. 40 A4
King's Ave LS6 .... 205 E3
King's Bridge Rd HD4 .... 154 B4
King's Cres WF8 .... 146 F6
King's Croft Gdns LS17 ...... 43 D1
King's Ct LS17 .... 43 C1
King's Dr Batley WF17 .... 96 F2
 Bradford BD2 .... 55 F6
King's Gate BD1 .... 55 E1
King's Mead WF8 .... 146 B7
King's Mill La HD1 .... 154 B5
King's Mount
 Knottingley WF11 .... 126 B5
 Leeds LS17 .... 60 C8
King's Pl LS6 .... 205 D4
King's Rd Bingley BD16 .... 36 E6
 Bradford BD2 .... 55 F6
 Cudworth S72 .... 180 C1
 Leeds LS6 .... 205 E2
King's Sq ⓫ LS6 .... 59 F6
King's Sq LS20 .... 22 F2
Kingfisher Cl
 Cripplestone WF4 .... 159 F7
 Leeds LS17 .... 43 F4
Kingfisher Gr Bradford BD8 . 73 C7
 Huddersfield HD4 .... 171 E7
 Wakefield WF2 .... 160 D5
Kingfisher Mews LS27 .... 98 C3
Kingfisher Way LS17 .... 43 F4
Kings App LS13 .... 58 E2
Kings Ave Castleford WF10 . 125 A7
 Ilkley LS29 .... 8 A8
 Normanton WF6 .... 122 F5
Kings Chase LS26 .... 99 F6
Kings Cl Ackworth M T WF7 163 D5
 Ilkley LS29 .... 7 E4
 Ossett WF5 .... 140 C7
 Otley LS21 .... 23 C7
 Pontefract WF8 .... 146 C7

Kings Croft Garforth LS25 .... 82 D6
 Ossett WF5 .... 140 C8
 South Kirkby WF9 .... 182 B3
Kings Ct Batley WF17 .... 96 E1
 Hemsworth WF9 .... 163 B1
 Sutton in CB BD20 .... 16 D4
Kings Dr Bramhope LS16 ...... 25 A1
 Normanton WF6 .... 122 F5
Kings Gr BD16 .... 36 E6
Kings Head Dr ⓶ WF14 .... 137 F6
Kings Head Rd WF14 .... 137 F6
Kings High Sch The WF8 .. 136 C7
Kings Lea Batley WF15 .... 117 C2
 Halifax HX3 .... 113 B3
Kings Mead LS26 .... 101 A6
 Ossett WF5 .... 140 C8
Kings Mead LS26 .... 101 A6
Kings Meadow Cl LS22 .... 13 D7
Kings Meadow Dr LS22 ...... 13 D7
Kings Meadow Gr LS22 ...... 13 D7
Kings Meadow Mews LS22 . 13 D7
Kings Meadow View LS22 .. 13 D7
Kings Mount HX4 .... 132 F3
Kings Paddock WF5 .... 140 C7
Kings Rd Bramhope LS16 ...... 25 B1
 Ilkley LS29 .... 7 F4
 Normanton WF6 .... 122 F6
Kings View HX3 .... 114 A4
Kingsbury Pl HX1 .... 202 B3
Kingsdale Ave
 Birkenshaw BD11 .... 96 B4
 Bradford BD2 .... 56 A3
Kingsdale Cres BD2 .... 56 A3
Kingsdale Ct LS14 .... 61 E6
Kingsdale Dr BD2 .... 56 A3
Kingsdale Gdns BD11 .... 96 B4
Kingsdale Gr BD2 .... 55 F3
Kingsfield LS26 .... 100 B5
Kingsland Ct S71 .... 179 D4
Kingsley Ave
 Birkenshaw BD11 .... 96 B4
 Bradford BD2 .... 55 E3
 Crofton WF4 .... 143 E2
 Featherstone WF7 .... 145 D8
 Huddersfield HD1 .... 153 E4
 Knottingley WF11 .... 126 C5
 Leeds LS16 .... 42 B5
 Lofthouse Gate WF1 .... 121 B5
 Sowerby Bridge HX6 .... 111 F3
 Wakefield WF2 .... 160 D6
Kingsley Cl
 Birkenshaw BD11 .... 96 B4
 Crofton WF4 .... 143 E2
 Lofthouse Gate WF1 .... 121 B5
 Wakefield WF2 .... 160 D6
Kingsley Cres Baildon BD17 .. 38 C2
 Birkenshaw BD11 .... 96 B4
Kingsley Croft BD20 .... 16 E7
Kingsley Dr Birkenshaw BD11 96 B4
 Leeds LS16 .... 42 B5
Kingsley Garth WF1 .... 121 B5
Kingsley Pl HX1 .... 202 C2
Kingsley Rd LS16 .... 42 B5
Kingsmead Leeds LS14 .... 62 A8
 Ossett WF5 .... 140 C8
Kingsmead Dr LS14 .... 44 F1
Kingsmill Cl LS27 .... 97 D5
Kingston Ave HD5 .... 154 E6
Kingston Cl Halifax HX1 ..... 202 B2
 Wilsden BD15 .... 53 C5
Kingston Ct HX1 .... 202 B2
Kingston Dr Halifax HX1 .... 202 B2
 Normanton WF6 .... 123 C1
Kingston Gdns LS15 .... 62 B2
Kingston Gr BD10 .... 39 B1
Kingston Rd BD10 .... 39 B1
Kingston St HX1 .... 202 B2
Kingston Terr Halifax HX1 .. 202 B2
 Leeds LS2 .... 206 B2
Kingsway Batley WF17 .... 96 E2
 Bingley BD16 .... 37 A2
 Birkenshaw BD11 .... 96 F6
 Bradford BD2 .... 55 F6
 Keighley BD20 .... 19 A1
 Leeds LS15 .... 81 C8
 Lofthouse Gate WF3 .... 121 F2
 Mapplewell S75 .... 178 A1
 Normanton WF6 .... 144 A8
 Ossett WF5 .... 140 C6
 Pontefract WF8 .... 125 D3
Kingsway Cl WF5 .... 140 C7
Kingsway Cres LS17 .... 43 D1
 Ossett WF5 .... 140 C7
Kingsway Dr LS29 .... 8 A4
Kingsway Garth LS25 .... 82 B2
Kingswear Cl LS15 .... 62 D1
Kingswear Cres LS15 .... 62 D1
Kingswear Garth LS15 .... 62 D1
Kingswear Glen LS15 .... 62 D1
Kingswear Gr LS15 .... 62 D1
Kingswear Par LS15 .... 62 D1
Kingswear Rise ⓫ LS15 ...... 62 D1
Kingswear View LS15 .... 62 D1
Kingswell Ave WF1 .... 121 C4
Kingswood Ave LS8 .... 44 B3
Kingswood Cres LS8 .... 43 F3
Kingswood Dr LS8 .... 43 F3
Kingswood Gdns LS8 .... 43 F3
Kingswood Gn HX3 .... 92 F1
Kingswood Gr LS8 .... 44 A3
Kingswood Pl ⓼ BD7 .... 74 A4
Kingswood Rd LS12 .... 77 F4
Kingswood Terr ⓽ BD7 .... 74 A4
Kinnaird Cl Batley WF12 .... 118 F5
 Halifax HX5 .... 134 E4

Kinsley House Cres WF9 .... 163 A2
Kinsley Jun & Inf Sch
 WF9 .... 163 B2
Kinsley St WF9 .... 163 B2
Kipling Cl HD4 .... 153 D3
Kipling Ct BD10 .... 56 D7
Kipling Gr WF8 .... 125 D3
Kippax Ashtree Prim Sch
 LS25 .... 83 B1
Kippax Greenfield
 Primary Sch LS25 .... 83 A2
Kippax Mount LS9 .... 212 C3
Kippax North Junior
 & Infants Sch LS25 .... 82 F4
Kippax Pl LS9 .... 212 C2
Kipping La BD13 .... 72 D6
Kipping Pl ⓫ BD13 .... 72 D6
Kirby Cote La HX7 .... 110 D3
Kirby Row HD5 .... 137 C1
Kirby St BD21 .... 35 C3
Kirk Beeston Cl LS11 .... 213 F2
Kirk Bridge La HD7 .... 189 D7
Kirk Cl WF12 .... 140 B8
Kirk Cross Cres S71 .... 179 C2
Kirk Dr BD17 .... 38 D4
Kirk Hills LS14 .... 46 A5
Kirk La Brighouse HX3 .... 114 C8
 Yeadon LS19 .... 40 A7
Kirk La Mills LS19 .... 40 A7
Kirk Lea Cres HD3 .... 135 C1
Kirk Smeaton C of E
 Prim Sch WF8 .... 166 D6
Kirkbourne Gr BD17 .... 38 E2
Kirkbridge Way WF9 .... 182 F3
Kirkburn Pl BD7 .... 74 B6
Kirkburton C of E Fst Sch
 HD8 .... 173 F6
Kirkburton Middle Sch
 HD8 .... 174 A7
Kirkby Ave LS25 .... 83 A5
Kirkby Cl WF9 .... 182 C3
Kirkby La Emley HD8, WF4 .. 175 B8
 Sicklinghall LS22 .... 12 A5
Kirkby Leas HX1 .... 203 E2
Kirkby Rd WF9 .... 181 E5
Kirkbygate WF9 .... 181 E5
Kirkdale WF10 .... 125 C8
Kirkdale Ave LS12 .... 78 A4
Kirkdale Cres LS12 .... 78 B3
Kirkdale Dr
 Cripplestone WF4 .... 159 D6
 Leeds LS12 .... 78 A4
Kirkdale Gdns LS12 .... 78 A4
Kirkdale Gr LS12 .... 78 A4
Kirkdale Mount LS12 .... 78 B3
Kirkdale Terr LS12 .... 78 B3
Kirkdale View LS12 .... 78 B3
Kirkfield Ave LS14 .... 46 A6
Kirkfield Cl S75 .... 193 F4
Kirkfield Cres LS14 .... 46 A6
Kirkfield Dr LS15 .... 81 D7
Kirkfield Gdns LS15 .... 81 D7
Kirkfield La LS14 .... 46 A5
Kirkfield View LS15 .... 81 D7
Kirkfield Way S71 .... 179 C2
Kirkfields BD17 .... 38 E3
Kirkgate Batley, Birstall**
 WF17 .... 96 D1
 Batley, Hanging Heaton**
 WF17 .... 118 F3
 Bradford BD1 .... 201 B3
 Farnhill BD20 .... 16 E8
 Huddersfield HD1 .... 154 B6
 Leeds LS2 .... 211 F3
 Otley LS21 .... 23 A7
 Shipley BD18 .... 55 A8
 Silsden BD20 .... 5 E1
 Wakefield WF1 .... 216 C2
Kirkgate Arc LS21 .... 23 A7
Kirkgate Bsns Ctr WF1 .... 216 C1
Kirkgate Ctr BD1 .... 201 B3
Kirkgate La S72 .... 180 C6
Kirkgate Sta WF1 .... 216 C1
Kirkham Ave WF2 .... 120 B3
Kirkham Rd BD7 .... 74 B5
Kirkham St LS13 .... 57 F5
Kirkhamgate Junior
 & Infants Sch WF2 .... 120 B2
Kirkhaw La WF11 .... 126 B6
Kirkheaton Jun & Inf Sch
 HD5 .... 137 B1
Kirklands Holmfirth HD7 ..... 189 D7
 Liversedge WF15 .... 117 A4
Kirklands Ave
 Baildon BD17 .... 38 E2
 Yeadon LS19 .... 40 A8
Kirklands Cl Baildon BD17 ... 38 E2
 Yeadon LS19 .... 40 A8
Kirklands Gdns BD17 .... 38 E2
Kirklands La BD17 .... 38 E3
Kirklands Rd BD17 .... 38 E3
Kirklea HD8 .... 190 E1
Kirklees Cl LS28 .... 57 E4
Kirklees Croft LS28 .... 57 E4
Kirklees Dr LS28 .... 57 D4
Kirklees Garth LS28 .... 57 D4
Kirklees Light Rly HD8 .... 175 D3
Kirklees Rd LS28 .... 57 D4
Kirklees Rise LS28 .... 57 D4
Kirkley Ave BD12 .... 94 C1
Kirkroyds Infants Sch
 HD7 .... 189 D7
Kirkstall Abbey LS5 .... 58 F5
Kirkstall Ave LS5 .... 58 F3
Kirkstall Gr BD8 .... 73 D7
Kirkstall Hill LS4, LS5 .... 59 B3

Kirkstall Ind Pk LS4 .... 205 D1
Kirkstall La LS5 .... 59 B4
Kirkstall Mount LS5 .... 58 F3
Kirkstall Rd LS4 .... 59 C2
Kirkstall St Stephen's C of E
  Primary Sch LS4 .... 59 A4
Kirkstall Valley Primary Sch
  LS4 .... 59 C2
Kirkstone Ave HD5 .... 154 C6
Kirkstone Dr
  Cleckheaton BD19 .... 117 B8
  Halifax HX2 .... 112 C8
Kirkthorpe La WF1 .... 143 C6
Kirkwall Ave WF3 .... 80 B7
Kirkwall Dr BD4 .... 75 E2
Kirkwood Ave LS16 .... 41 D4
Kirkwood Cl LS16 .... 41 D4
Kirkwood Cres LS16 .... 41 E5
Kirkwood Dr
  Huddersfield HD3 .... 153 B8
  Leeds LS16 .... 41 E5
Kirkwood Gdns LS16 .... 41 E5
Kirkwood Gn HD3 .... 153 B8
Kirkwood Gr
  East Ardsley WF3 .... 119 F8
  Leeds LS16 .... 41 D4
Kirkwood La LS16 .... 41 D5
Kirkwood Rise LS16 .... 41 E5
Kirkwood View LS16 .... 41 E5
Kirkwood Way LS16 .... 41 E5
Kismet Gdns BD3 .... 75 C8
Kistyaen Gdns HD7 .... 170 C3
Kit La BD20 .... 5 C6
Kit Wood Cl BD4 .... 75 F2
Kitchen Fold HD7 .... 170 A8
Kitchener Ave LS9 .... 208 B1
Kitchener Gr LS9 .... 208 B2
Kitchener Mount LS9 .... 208 B1
Kitchener Pl LS9 .... 208 B1
Kitchener St Bradford BD12 .. 95 A5
  Leeds LS9 .... 208 B1
  [8] Horsell LS26 .... 101 C6
Kitson Cl LS12 .... 209 F2
Kitson Gdns LS12 .... 209 F2
Kitson Hill Cres WF14 .... 137 F6
Kitson Hill Rd WF14 .... 137 F7
Kitson La HX6 .... 112 D1
Kitson Rd LS10 .... 212 A1
Kitson St East Ardsley WF3 .. 98 D1
  Leeds LS9 .... 212 C3
  Shipley BD18 .... 55 C7
Kitson Wood Rd OL14 .... 107 E8
Kliffen Pl HX3 .... 113 D4
Knaresborough Dr HD2 .... 136 A2
Knavesmire LS26 .... 100 B5
Knight St Halifax HX1 .... 202 B2
  Huddersfield HD1 .... 154 B7
Knight's Fold BD7 .... 74 A4
Knights Croft LS22 .... 13 F7
Knightsbridge Wlk BD4 .... 95 B8
Knightsclose LS15 .... 81 C8
Knightsclose La LS26 .... 100 E6
Knightscroft Dr LS26 .... 100 E6
Knightscroft Par WF8 .... 183 A2
Knightshill LS15 .... 81 D8
Knightsway Garforth LS25 .. 82 E6
  Leeds LS15 .... 81 D8
  Rothwell WF3 .... 100 B2
  Wakefield WF2 .... 160 C6
Knoll Cl WF5 .... 140 E7
Knoll Gdns BD17 .... 38 B1
Knoll La HD7 .... 188 D8
Knoll Park Dr BD17 .... 38 B1
Knoll Pk WF3 .... 120 D7
Knoll View BD17 .... 38 B2
Knoll Wood Pk LS8 .... 58 D8
Knott La Steeton BD20 .... 16 F5
  Yeadon LS19 .... 40 E1
Knottingley C of E (C)
  Primary Sch WF11 .... 127 A4
Knottingley Cty Jun
  & Inf Sch WF11 .... 127 A3
Knottingley High Sch
  WF11 .... 127 A3
Knottingley Rd WF8 .... 126 B2
Knottingley Sta WF11 ...... 126 E4
Knotts Rd OL14 .... 108 A1
Knotty La HD8 .... 156 A3
Knowl Gr WF14 .... 138 A5
Knowl Rd Holme HD7 .... 187 C4
  Huddersfield HD7 .... 152 E4
  Mirfield WF14 .... 138 A5
Knowl The [4] WF14 .... 137 F5
Knowl Top HX7 .... 88 C6
Knowle Ave
  Huddersfield HD5 .... 154 E5
  Leeds LS4 .... 205 D3
Knowle Gr [10] LS4 .... 205 D3
Knowle La Bradford BD12 .. 94 D2
  Meltham HD7 .... 171 A2
Knowle Mount LS4 .... 205 D3
Knowle Park Ave HD8 ...... 190 F8
Knowle Pl [11] LS4 .... 205 D3
Knowle Rd Leeds LS4 .... 205 D3
  Slaithwaite HD7 .... 152 A1
Knowle Sch WF14 .... 138 A6
Knowle Spring Rd [1] BD21 .. 35 B5
Knowle Terr LS4 .... 205 D3
Knowle The HD8 .... 190 F8
Knowle Top Dr HX3 .... 114 E8
Knowle Top Rd HX3 .... 114 E8
Knowler Cl WF15 .... 117 A5
Knowler Hill WF15 .... 117 A5
Knowler Way WF15 .... 117 A5
Knowles Ave BD4 .... 75 D2
Knowles Croft [6] WF13 .... 117 F2
Knowles Hill [5] WF13 ...... 117 F2
Knowles Hill Rd WF13 ...... 117 F1

Knowles La Batley WF17 .... 118 B4
  Bradford BD4 .... 75 D2
  Cleckheaton BD19 .... 96 B2
Knowles Rd Brighouse HD6 .. 114 F3
  Brighouse HD6 .... 136 B8
Knowles St Bradford BD4 .... 75 C2
  Denholme BD13 .... 71 D8
Knowles View BD4 .... 75 D2
Knowlwood Rd OL14 .... 108 A3
Knowsley Ave [6] OL14 .... 108 A1
Knowsley St BD3 .... 75 A6
Knowsthorpe Cres LS9 ..... 212 C1
Knowsthorpe Gate LS9 .... 80 B5
Knowsthorpe La Leeds LS9 .. 80 B4
  Leeds, Cross Green LS9 .... 80 B4
Knowsthorpe Rd LS9 .... 80 C4
Knowsthorpe Way LS9 ..... 80 B4
Knox St LS13 .... 57 D5
Knutsford Gr BD4 .... 75 E2
Komla Cl BD1 .... 201 C3
Krives La HD7 .... 169 E5
Kyffin Ave LS15 .... 80 E8
Kyffin Pl BD4 .... 75 E5

Laburnum Cl WF3 .... 120 C7
Laburnum Ct
  Castleford WF10 .... 124 E6
  Horbury WF4 .... 140 F1
Laburnum Dr BD17 .... 38 D4
Laburnum Gr
  Brighouse HX3 .... 115 A6
  Cleckheaton BD19 .... 96 A1
  Haworth BD22 .... 51 E8
  Horbury WF4 .... 140 F1
  Huddersfield HD7 .... 152 F5
  Skelmanthorpe HD8 .... 175 A1
Laburnum Pl Bradford BD8 .. 55 C1
  Bradford, Apperley Bridge
  BD10 .... 56 E8
Laburnum Rd Batley WF13 .. 117 E2
  Shipley BD18 .... 55 D5
  Wakefield WF1 .... 216 A3
Laburnum St Bradford BD8 .. 55 C1
  Pudsey LS28 .... 57 D1
  Pudsey, Owlcotes Hill LS28 .. 76 C8
Laburnum Terr HD1 .... 154 B8
Lacey St Dewsbury WF13 .. 139 B8
  Horbury WF4 .... 141 C2
Lacy Ave OL14 .... 108 A1
Lacy Gr LS22 .... 13 F4
Lacy Way WF1 .... 181 C7
Lacy Way HX5 .... 135 A8
Ladbroke Gr BD4 .... 75 E1
Ladderbanks La BD17 .... 38 A4
Ladderbanks Middle Sch
  BD17 .... 38 E4
Ladstone Towers HX6 ...... 112 B4
Lady Ann Rd WF17 .... 118 E5
Lady Balk La WF8 .... 125 D3
Lady Beck Cl LS2 .... 212 A4
Lady Cl WF5 .... 140 C8
Lady Elizabeth Hastings
  C of E Sch LS22 .... 13 A1
Lady Elizabeth Hastings
  CE Sch LS23 .... 14 E1
Lady Elizabeth Hastings
  PrimSch WF10 .... 103 E6
Lady Heton Ave WF14 ...... 137 F6
Lady Heton Dr WF14 .... 137 E6
Lady Heton Gr WF14 .... 137 E6
Lady House La HX4 .... 172 A8
Lady La Bingley BD16 .... 37 A5
  Leeds LS2 .... 212 A4
  Wakefield WF2 .... 160 D6
Lady Lane Park Sch BD16 .. 37 A5
Lady Park Ave BD16 .... 37 A5
Lady Pit La LS11 .... 214 B3
Lady Wood Rd LS8 .... 61 B6
Ladybower Ave HD4 .... 152 F2
Ladyroyd Dr BD4 .... 95 E6
Ladysmith Rd BD13 .... 72 C8
Ladywell Cl BD5 .... 74 E3
Ladywell La WF15 .... 116 B3
Ladywood Grange LS8 ...... 61 D6
Ladywood Mead LS8 .... 61 D6
Ladywood Terr HX1 .... 202 C4
Ladywood Way WF13 .... 138 E4
Lafflands La WF4 .... 162 B1
Lairum Rise LS23 .... 30 D5
Laisterdyke BD4 .... 75 D6
Laisterdyke Middle Sch
  BD3 .... 75 C6
Laisteridge La BD5, BD7 .... 74 C5
Laith Cl LS16 .... 41 F3
Laith Garth LS16 .... 41 F3
Laith Gdns LS16 .... 41 F3
Laith Gn LS16 .... 41 F3
Laith Rd LS16 .... 41 F3
Laith Staid La LS25 .... 65 F1
Laithe Ave HD7 .... 188 C2
Laithe Bank Dr HD7 .... 188 C2
Laithe Cl HD20 .... 5 D1
Laithe Field HX4 .... 133 D5
Laithe Gr BD6 .... 74 B1
Laithe Rd BD6 .... 74 B1
Laithecroft Rd WF17 .... 118 E5
Laithes Chase WF2 .... 141 F7
Laithes Cl WF2 .... 141 F7
Laithes Cres WF2 .... 141 E7
Laithes Croft WF12 .... 139 E2
Laithes Dr WF2 .... 141 D7
Laithes Fold WF2 .... 141 F7
Laithes View WF2 .... 141 D7
Lake Lock Dr WF3 .... 122 A6
Lake Lock Gr WF3 .... 122 A5

Lake Lock Rd WF3 .... 122 A6
Lake Row BD4 .... 75 B5
Lake St Bradford BD4 .... 75 B5
  Keighley BD21 .... 18 E1
  Leeds LS10 .... 215 D2
Lake Terr LS10 .... 215 D2
Lake View
  Crigglestone WF2 .... 160 C4
  Halifax HX3 .... 203 D4
  Huddersfield HD4 .... 171 E8
  Pontefract WF8 .... 125 C3
Lake Yd WF3 .... 122 A5
Lakeland Cres LS17 .... 43 A6
Lakeland Dr LS17 .... 80 D6
Lakeland Dr LS17 .... 43 B6
Lakeland Way WF2 .... 161 A6
Lakeside Keighley BD20 .... 19 E2
  Marsden HD7 .... 169 A4
Lakeside Chase LS19 .... 40 C4
Lakeside Cl LS29 .... 8 B5
Lakeside Ct
  Huddersfield HD3 .... 153 B8
  Leeds LS10 .... 215 D2
Lakeside Est WF4 .... 162 B2
Lakeside Gdns LS19 .... 40 C4
Lakeside Ind Est LS12 ...... 77 E7
Lakeside Mdws WF8 .... 125 D3
Lakeside Rd LS12 .... 77 E6
Lakeside Terr LS19 .... 40 C4
Lakeside View LS19 .... 40 C4
Lakeside Wlk LS19 .... 40 C4
Lakeview Cl LS8 .... 61 C8
Lamb Cote Rd HD2 .... 136 D6
Lamb Hall Rd HD3 .... 152 E8
Lamb Inn Rd WF11 .... 127 A4
Lambe Flatt S75 .... 177 C1
Lambert Ave LS8 .... 204 C2
Lambert Cl HX4 .... 134 D7
Lambert Dr LS8 .... 204 C2
Lambert Pl BD2 .... 56 A4
Lambert St [2] HX4 .... 134 D7
Lambert Terr LS18 .... 41 E1
Lambourne Ave BD10 .... 56 E5
Lambrigg Cres LS14 .... 62 A4
Lambton Gr LS8 .... 207 F4
Lambton Pl LS8 .... 207 F4
Lambton St LS8 .... 207 F4
Lambton Terr LS8 .... 207 F4
Lambton View LS8 .... 207 F4
Lamma Well Rd HD7 .... 189 A2
Lampards Cl BD15 .... 54 A2
Lamplands WF17 .... 118 D6
Lanark Dr LS18 .... 41 B4
Lanark Rise WF4 .... 162 A8
Lancaster Cl WF8 .... 146 D6
Lancaster Cres HD5 .... 154 F4
Lancaster Ct [4] BD21 ...... 35 B5
Lancaster La HD7 .... 172 C1
Lancaster St
  Castleford WF10 .... 104 D1
  Dearne S63 .... 194 E1
Lancastre Ave LS5 .... 58 F3
Lancastre Gr LS5 .... 58 F3
Land St LS28 .... 57 D3
Land's Bldgs WF5 .... 140 D7
Landmark Ct LS11 .... 213 F3
Landor St BD21 .... 35 D8
Lands Beck Way WF15 ...... 116 F4
Lands Head La HX3 .... 93 A4
Lands La Bradford BD10 .... 56 C5
  Guiseley LS20 .... 22 E1
  Leeds LS1 .... 211 F4
Landscove Ave BD4 .... 75 F2
Landsdown Ave WF9 .... 182 A1
Landseer Ave
  East Ardsley WF3 .... 119 E8
  Leeds LS13 .... 58 D3
Landseer Cl LS13 .... 58 D3
Landseer Cres LS13 .... 58 D3
Landseer Dr LS13 .... 58 D3
Landseer Gdns LS13 .... 58 D3
Landseer Gn LS13 .... 58 D3
Landseer Gr LS13 .... 58 D3
Landseer Mount LS13 ...... 58 D3
Landseer Rise LS13 .... 58 D3
Landseer Terr LS13 .... 58 D3
Landseer View LS13 .... 58 D3
Landseer Wlk LS13 .... 58 D3
Landsholme Ct BD4 .... 75 F2
Landsmoor Gr BD16 .... 37 C5
Lane Bottom HX7 .... 88 F5
Lane Cotts S71 .... 179 C3
Lane Court No 1 [6] HD6 .. 115 B3
Lane Court No 2 [7] HD6 .. 115 B3
Lane & Dowry Rd HD7 ...... 169 F7
Lane End WF4 .... 157 D3
Lane End Croft LS17 .... 43 D5
Lane End Ct LS17 .... 43 D5
Lane End Fold LS28 .... 76 F8
Lane End La [3] OL13 ...... 106 A1
Lane End Mount LS28 ...... 76 F8
Lane End Pl LS11 .... 211 E1
Lane End Rd OL13 .... 106 A1
Lane Ends Cl Bradford BD8 .. 73 F8
  Hemsworth WF9 .... 163 A4
Lane Ends Gn HX3 .... 89 C4
Lane Ends La HX7 .... 89 C4
Lane Ends Terr HX3 .... 114 D8
Lane Fox Ct [7] LS19 .... 40 B6
Lane Hackings HD8 .... 191 E6
Lane Hackings Gn HD8 .... 191 E6
Lane Head HX7 .... 88 E5

Lane Head Cl S75 .... 178 A2
Lane Head La Halifax HX2 .. 91 D8
  Kirkburton HD8 .... 173 F6
Lane Head Rd
  Cawthorne S75 .... 193 D3
  Ripponden HX6 .... 132 C5
  Shepley HD8 .... 190 E7
Lane Head Rise S75 .... 178 A2
Lane House Gr HX2 .... 111 E8
Lane Ings HD7 .... 169 A4
Lane Side Bacup OL13 ...... 106 A4
  Queensbury BD13 .... 72 D3
  Wilsden BD15 .... 53 C4
Lane Side Cl BD12 .... 94 C4
Lane Side La HD5 .... 155 D7
Lane The Leeds LS20 .... 212 B3
  Leeds, Alwoodley LS17 .... 42 F5
Lane Top Denholme BD13 .. 71 D8
  Huddersfield HD7 .... 152 E1
Lanes The LS28 .... 76 F8
Laneside Elland HX4 .... 134 A4
  Kirkburton HD8 .... 174 A6
  Morley LS27 .... 98 B7
Laneside Cl LS27 .... 98 B7
Laneside Fold [1] LS27 .... 98 B7
Laneside Gdns LS27 .... 98 B7
Laneside St OL14 .... 108 A4
Lang Kirk Cl BD20 .... 4 E1
Langbar App LS14 .... 62 D6
Langbar Ave BD9 .... 54 D3
Langbar Cl LS14 .... 62 D6
Langbar Garth LS14 .... 62 D6
Langbar Gdns [2] LS14 .... 62 D6
Langbar Gn LS14 .... 62 D6
Langbar Gr LS14 .... 62 D5
Langbar Pl LS14 .... 62 D6
Langbar Rd Ilkley LS29 .... 8 A4
  Leeds LS14 .... 62 D5
Langbar Sq [1] LS14 .... 62 D5
Langbar Towers [3] LS14 .. 62 D5
Langbar View LS14 .... 62 D6
Langcliffe Cl S75 .... 178 A2
Langdale Ave Bradford BD8 .. 73 E8
  Brighouse BD12 .... 95 B6
  Leeds LS6 .... 59 C4
Lofthouse Gate WF1 .... 121 D5
  Normanton WF6 .... 123 A4
Langdale Cl
  Castleford WF10 .... 104 E2
  Wetherby LS22 .... 13 D6
Langdale Cres HX2 .... 91 E1
Langdale Ct BD16 .... 37 A4
Langdale Dr
  Ackworth M T WF7 .... 164 C7
  Huddersfield HD5 .... 154 D7
  Normanton WF6 .... 123 A4
  [2] Queensbury BD13 ...... 72 D1
  Wakefield WF2 .... 141 F6
Langdale Gdns LS6 .... 59 C4
Langdale Mews WF6 .... 123 A4
Langdale Mount WF2 ...... 161 A6
Langdale Prim Sch LS26 .. 100 D6
Langdale Rd Bradford BD10 .. 56 C6
  Rothwell LS26 .... 101 B6
Langdale Sq WF2 .... 141 F6
Langdale St HX5 .... 134 F6
Langdale Terr LS6 .... 59 C4
Langford Cl WF4 .... 156 E6
Langford La LS29 .... 9 E1
Langford Mews LS29 .... 9 E1
Langford Rd LS29 .... 9 E1
Langlands Rd BD16 .... 54 A7
Langlea Terr HX3 .... 114 C8
Langley Ave Bingley BD16 .. 37 A4
  Bradford BD4 .... 75 C1
  Leeds LS13 .... 58 A4
Langley Cl LS13 .... 58 A4
Langley Cres Baildon BD17 .. 38 E4
  Leeds LS13 .... 58 A4
Langley Garth LS13 .... 58 A4
Langley Gr BD16 .... 37 A4
Langley La Baildon BD17 .. 38 E4
  Clayton West HD8 .... 175 E2
  Clayton West HD8 .... 175 E4
Langley Mount LS13 .... 58 B4
Langley Pl LS13 .... 58 B4
Langley Rd Bingley BD16 .. 37 A4
  Leeds LS13 .... 58 A4
Langport Cl BD13 .... 72 F1
Langsett Croft HD2 .... 136 E5
Langsett Rd WF2 .... 160 B5
Langthorne Cres LS27 ...... 97 F4
Langthwaite Grange
  Ind Est South Kirkby WF9 .. 182 D2
Langthwaite La WF9 .... 182 D2
Langthwaite Rd WF9 .... 182 D2
Langton Ave BD4 .... 201 D1
Langton St HX5 .... 112 B5
Langwith Ave LS22 .... 29 A8
Langwith Dr LS22 .... 28 E8
Langwith Mews LS22 .... 29 A8
Langwith Valley Rd LS22 .. 28 E8
Lansdale Ct BD4 .... 75 F2
Lansdowne Ave WF10 ...... 124 F7
Lansdowne Cl Baildon BD17 .. 38 F3
  Batley WF17 .... 118 C6
Lansdowne Pl BD5 .... 201 A2
Lansdowne St LS12 .... 209 F2
Lanshaw Bank BD23 .... 1 D1
Lanshaw Cl LS10 .... 99 E6
Lanshaw Cres LS10 .... 99 E5

Lanshaw Pl LS10 .... 99 E6
Lanshaw Rd LS10 .... 99 E6
Lanshaw Terr LS10 .... 99 E6
Lanshaw View LS10 .... 99 E6
Lapage Middle Sch BD3 .. 75 C8
Lapage St BD3 .... 75 C7
Lapage Terr BD3 .... 75 C6
Lapwing Cl BD8 .... 73 B7
Larch Ave BD17 .... 189 C8
Larch Cl Batley WF17 .... 97 A2
  Kirkburton HD8 .... 173 A1
  Liversedge WF15 .... 117 C3
  Normanton WF6 .... 144 B8
  Oakworth BD22 .... 34 D2
Larch Ct WF10 .... 124 E6
Larch Dale HD2 .... 136 A4
Larch Dr BD6 .... 94 D7
Larch Gr BD6 .... 36 F5
Larch Hill BD6 .... 94 D7
Larch Hill Cres BD6 .... 94 D8
Larch La LS25 .... 83 B7
Larch Rd HD1 .... 153 D5
Larch St BD21 .... 35 B4
Larch Wood LS14 .... 45 C7
Larchfield Rd LS10 .... 212 B1
Larchmont BD14 .... 73 C4
Lark Hill WF17 .... 118 A8
Lark Hill Ave BD19 .... 116 B6
Lark Hill Cl BD19 .... 116 B6
Lark Hill Dr BD19 .... 116 B6
Lark St Bingley BD16 .... 36 F3
  Haworth BD22 .... 51 D7
  Keighley BD21 .... 35 B7
  Oakworth BD22 .... 34 D2
Larkfield Ave LS19 .... 40 C4
Larkfield Cres LS19 .... 40 C4
Larkfield Dr LS19 .... 40 C4
Larkfield Mount LS19 ...... 40 C4
Larkfield Rd Pudsey LS28 .. 76 F8
  Yeadon LS19 .... 40 C4
Larkfield Terr BD21 .... 35 E5
Larkhill Cl LS8 .... 204 B4
Larkhill Gn LS8 .... 43 E1
Larkhill Rd LS8 .... 43 E1
Larkhill View LS8 .... 204 B4
Larkhill Way LS8 .... 43 E1
Larks Hill WF8 .... 146 B6
Larkshill Jun & Inf Sch
  WF8 .... 146 B6
Larkspur Way WF2 .... 141 E7
Larwood Ave BD10 .... 56 B6
Lascelles Hall Rd HD5 .... 155 C6
Lascelles Mount [4] LS8 .. 207 F3
Lascelles Pl WF16 .... 207 F3
Lascelles Rd LS8 .... 207 F3
Lascelles Rd E LS8 .... 207 F3
Lascelles Rd W LS8 .... 207 F3
Lascelles St LS8 .... 207 F3
Lascelles Terr [3] LS8 ..... 207 F3
Lascelles View [3] LS8 .... 207 F3
Lassingham Gn BD6 .... 73 E1
Lastingham Rd LS13 .... 57 F5
Latchmere Ave LS16 .... 58 F8
Latchmere Crest [4] LS16 .. 58 F8
Latchmere Cross [3] LS16 .. 58 F8
Latchmere Dr LS16 .... 58 F8
Latchmere Gdns LS16 ...... 59 A8
Latchmere Gn [5] LS16 .... 58 F8
Latchmere Rd LS16 .... 58 F8
Latchmere View [3] LS16 .. 58 F8
Latchmere Wlk [4] LS16 .. 59 A8
Latchmore Rd LS12 .... 213 E4
Latchmore Road Ind Est
  LS12 .... 213 E4
Latham Ct BD19 .... 96 B2
Latham La BD19 .... 96 A2
Latham Lea BD19 .... 96 B2
Latimer St BD3 .... 75 D6
Launceston Dr BD4 .... 75 F2
Laund Rd Huddersfield HD3 .. 134 E1
  Marsden HD7 .... 151 D3
  Slaithwaite HD7 .... 151 D3
Launton Way BD5 .... 74 D4
Laura St [8] Brighouse HD6 .. 115 A1
  [3] Halifax HX3 .... 92 C1
  Leeds LS12 .... 210 C2
Laurel Bank
  Brighouse BD12 .... 115 C8
  [1] Halifax HX1 .... 202 C1
Laurel Bank Cl HX2 .... 92 A6
Laurel Cl East Keswick LS17 .. 28 C4
  Elland HX5 .... 134 E6
  Shelf HX3 .... 93 C6
Laurel Cres Halifax HX2 .... 91 F3
  Keighley BD21 .... 35 B8
Laurel Ct WF5 .... 140 A7
Laurel Dr WF17 .... 118 A7
Laurel Fold [9] LS12 .... 209 F3
Laurel Gr [5] Brighouse WF17 .. 117 F7
  Bingley BD16 .... 36 A1
  Keighley BD21 .... 35 B8
  [7] Leeds LS12 .... 209 F3
  Silsden BD20 .... 5 D1
Laurel Hill Ave LS15 .... 81 D7
Laurel Hill Croft LS15 ...... 81 D7
Laurel Hill Gdns LS15 ...... 81 D7
Laurel Hill Gr LS15 .... 81 D7
Laurel Hill View LS15 ...... 81 D7
Laurel Hill Way LS15 .... 81 D6
Laurel House [4] WF10 .... 124 E7

Laurel Mount Batley WF16 . 117 D4
10 Halifax HX1 .... 202 A2
Leeds LS7 .... 204 A1
Pudsey LS28 .... 76 E8
Laurel Pk BD15 .... 53 C4
Laurel Pl Leeds LS12 .... 209 F3
Middleton LS10 .... 99 B3
Laurel St Bradford BD3 .... 75 C6
Halifax HX1 .... 202 C1
10 Leeds LS12 .... 209 F3
Laurel Terr Elland HX4 .... 133 F4
Leeds LS12 .... 209 F3
Pudsey LS28 .... 76 E8
Laurels The Bingley BD16 ..... 37 A3
Dewsbury WF12 .... 139 F7
Leeds LS8 .... 204 C3
Laurence Ct LS26 .... 101 D7
Lavender Croft WF16 .... 117 E4
Lavender Ct HD4 .... 171 D6
Lavender Hill BD10 .... 56 C5
Lavender Wlk LS9 .... 212 C3
Lavenham Pl DN6 .... 184 E2
Laverack Field **8** BD12 .... 94 C3
Laverhills WF15 .... 116 D6
Laverock Cres HD6 .... 114 F5
Laverock La HD6 .... 114 F5
Laverock Pl HD6 .... 114 F5
Laverock Rd BD4 .... 75 B4
Lavinia Terr BD14 .... 73 C4
Law Cl LS22 .... 13 F6
Law Common Rd
Carlecotes HD7 .... 199 E5
Dunford Bridge HD7 .... 199 E5
Law La HX3 .... 114 A5
Law Slack Rd HD7 .... 199 D6
Law St Batley WF17 .... 117 F8
Bradford BD4 .... 75 C2
Cleckheaton BD19 .... 116 D8
Todmorden OL14 .... 129 B7
Lawcliffe Cres BD22 .... 51 D8
Lawefield Ave LS26 .... 100 C6
Lawefield Gr WF2 .... 142 A5
Lawefield La WF2 .... 142 A5
Lawefield Jun Sch WF2 ...... 142 A5
Lawefield La WF2 .... 142 A5
Lawkholme Cres **4** BD21 ..... 35 C7
Lawkholme La BD21 .... 35 C8
Law Ave LS29 .... 9 F1
Lawn Rd LS29 .... 9 F1
Lawn's La LS10 .... 215 E3
Lawndale DN6 .... 184 F2
Lawndale Fold S75 .... 177 F1
Lawns Ave LS12 .... 77 D3
Lawns Cl Gidersome LS12 ...... 77 D3
Normanton WF6 .... 122 E4
Lawns Cres LS12 .... 77 D3
Lawns Croft LS12 .... 77 D3
Lawns Dene LS12 .... 77 D3
Lawns Dr LS12 .... 77 D3
Lawns Gn LS12 .... 77 D3
Lawns Hall Cl LS16 .... 42 B3
Lawns La Gidersome LS12 ...... 77 D4
Leeds LS12 .... 77 D4
Lofthouse Gate WF2 .... 120 E6
Lawns Mount LS12 .... 77 D3
Lawns Park Primary Sch
LS12 .... 77 E5
Lawns Sq LS12 .... 77 D3
Lawns Terr
East Ardsley WF3 .... 120 D7
Gidersome LS12 .... 77 D3
Lawns The Batley WF16 ..... 117 E4
Ilkley LS29 .... 8 A4
Netherton WF4 .... 158 A6
Lawns View LS12 .... 129 E2
Lawnswood Gdns LS16 .... 42 B2
Lawnswood Rd BD21 .... 35 A5
Lawnswood Sch LS16 .... 59 B8
Lawrence Ave Leeds LS8 ..... 208 C4
Pontefract WF8 .... 146 B7
Lawrence Cres
Batley WF16 .... 117 D6
Leeds LS8 .... 61 C5
Lawrence Dr BD7 .... 73 E2
Lawrence Gdns LS8 .... 61 C5
Lawrence Rd Halifax HX3 .... 113 A3
Huddersfield HD1 .... 153 E6
Leeds LS8 .... 208 C4
Lawrence St **14** HX1 .... 92 A1
Lawrence Wlk LS8 .... 208 C4
Lawson House **8** BD6 .... 93 E8
Lawson Rd HD6 .... 115 B2
Lawson St Bradford BD3 ..... 201 C4
Leeds LS12 .... 209 E3
Lawton St HD4 .... 154 A3
Lay Garth LS26 .... 100 D5
Lay Garth Cl LS26 .... 100 E5
Lay Garth Gdns LS26 .... 100 E4
Lay Garth Gn LS26 .... 100 E4
Lay Garth Mead LS26 .... 100 E4
Lay Garth Pl LS26 .... 100 E4
Lay Garth Sq LS26 .... 100 E4
Laycock First Sch BD22 ...... 34 C7
Laycock La BD22 .... 34 C7
Laycock Pl LS7 .... 207 D3
Laygarth Dr HD5 .... 155 C6
Laythorp Terr BD20 .... 19 D1
Laythorpe Ct WF8 .... 147 A7
Layton Ave LS19 .... 40 E3
Layton Cl LS19 .... 40 E2
Layton Cres LS19 .... 40 D3
Layton Dr LS19 .... 40 E3
Layton La LS19 .... 40 E2
Layton Mount LS19 .... 40 D3

Layton Park Ave LS19 .... 40 E2
Layton Park Cl LS19 .... 40 D3
Layton Park Croft LS19 .... 40 E2
Layton Park Dr LS19 .... 40 E2
Layton Rd LS18, LS19 .... 40 E3
Layton Rise LS18 .... 40 E3
Lazenby Dr LS22 .... 13 D6
Lazenby Fold LS22 .... 13 D6
Le Marchant Ave HD3 .... 153 C8
Lea Ave HX3 .... 113 C4
Lea Cl HD6 .... 115 A4
Lea Croft Boston Spa LS23 ... 30 D5
Otley LS21 .... 23 A7
Lea Ct BD7 .... 73 E2
Lea Dr HD8 .... 190 F8
Lea Farm Cres LS5 .... 58 F6
Lea Farm Dr LS5 .... 58 F6
Lea Farm Gr LS5 .... 58 F6
Lea Farm Mount LS5 .... 58 F6
Lea Farm Pl LS5 .... 58 F6
Lea Farm Rd LS5 .... 58 F7
Lea Farm Row LS5 .... 58 F6
Lea Farm Wlk LS5 .... 58 F7
Lea Gdns HD7 .... 189 F4
Lea La Featherstone WF7 ... 145 E4
Huddersfield HD4 .... 171 C6
Lea Mill Park Ct LS19 .... 40 A7
Lea Mill Park Dr LS19 .... 40 A7
Lea Park Cl LS10 .... 99 F7
Lea Park Croft LS10 .... 100 A7
Lea Park Dr LS10 .... 99 F7
Lea Park Garth **2** LS10 ..... 99 F7
Lea Park Gdns **1** LS10 ...... 99 F7
Lea Park Gr LS10 .... 99 F7
Lea Park Vale LS10 .... 100 A7
Lea Rd WF17 .... 117 F8
Lea Rise HD7 .... 171 F3
Lea Side Gdns HD3 .... 152 E7
Lea St Huddersfield HD1 .... 154 A8
Huddersfield, Fartown HD1 . 136 A1
Huddersfield, Prince Royd
HD3 .... 153 A5
Lea The LS25 .... 82 F5
Lea View WF17 .... 117 F8
Leabank Ave LS25 .... 83 A5
Leach Cres BD20 .... 18 E2
Leach Rd BD20 .... 18 E2
Leach Rise BD20 .... 18 E2
Leach Way BD20 .... 18 E2
Leadenhall St **10** HX1 .... 202 B1
Leadwell La LS26 .... 100 C4
Leaf St Castleford WF10 ..... 124 C7
6 Haworth BD22 .... 51 E8
Leafield Ave Bradford BD2 .. 56 C4
Huddersfield HD3 .... 152 E6
Leafield Bank HD3 .... 152 E6
Leafield Cl
Huddersfield HD3 .... 136 D4
Leeds LS17 .... 43 B2
Leafield Cres BD2 .... 56 B3
Leafield Dr Bradford BD2 ..... 56 C4
Leeds LS17 .... 43 B2
2 Pudsey LS28 .... 76 F5
Leafield Gr BD2 .... 56 C3
Leafield Grange LS17 .... 43 B2
Leafield Pl LS19 .... 39 F7
Leafield Terr BD2 .... 56 C3
Leafield Way BD2 .... 56 C3
Leafland St HX1 .... 202 C3
Leafsway BD6 .... 93 F6
Leah Pl LS12 .... 210 C2
Leak Hall La HD8 .... 192 A6
Leak Hall Rd HD8 .... 191 F6
Leake St WF10 .... 124 E7
Leamington Dr BD10 .... 56 E8
Leamington Rd LS29 .... 8 C5
Leamington St BD9 .... 55 B2
Leamington Terr
Dewsbury WF12 .... 139 D6
Ilkley LS29 .... 8 C5
Learoyd St HD1 .... 154 B7
Leas Ave HD7 .... 188 F7
Leaside Dr BD13 .... 72 D7
Leasowe Ave LS10 .... 215 E2
Leasowe Cl LS10 .... 215 E2
Leasowe Garth **1** LS10 .... 215 E2
Leasowe Gdns LS10 .... 215 E2
Leasowe Rd LS10 .... 215 E2
Leatham Ave WF7 .... 145 E4
Leatham Cres WF7 .... 145 F4
Leatham Dr WF7 .... 145 F4
Leatham Park Rd WF7 .... 145 F4
Leather Bank LS29 .... 9 E5
Leathley Ave LS29 .... 22 B4
Leathley Cres LS29 .... 22 B4
Leathley La Leathley LS21 ... 24 B8
Menston LS29 .... 22 B4
Leathley Rd Leeds LS10 ..... 212 A1
Menston LS29 .... 22 B4
Leathley St LS10 .... 212 A1
Leavens The BD10 .... 56 D8
Leaventhorpe Ave BD8 .... 73 D7
Leaventhorpe Cl BD8 .... 73 D7
Leaventhorpe Gr BD13 .... 73 C6
Leaventhorpe La BD8, BD13 73 C6
Leaventhorpe Middle Sch
BD15 .... 73 B7
Leaventhorpe Way BD8 .... 73 D7
Leaveholme Cl BD10 .... 81 A7
Leavington Cl BD6 .... 94 B6
Leconfield Ct LS22 .... 13 C6
Leconfield House BD10 .... 56 C7
Ledbury Ave **4** LS10 .... 99 F4
Ledbury Croft **8** LS10 .... 99 F4
Ledbury Dr LS10 .... 99 F4
Ledbury Gn **1** LS10 .... 99 F4

Ledbury Gr **2** LS10 .... 99 F4
Ledgard Bridge Mills
Ind Units WF14 .... 138 A3
Ledgard Dr WF4 .... 159 F7
Ledgard Way LS12 .... 209 F4
Ledgate La LS25 .... 105 E4
Ledger La
Lofthouse Gate WF1 .... 121 B4
Rothwell WF3 .... 100 C1
Ledger Lane Junior
& Infants Sch WF1 .... 121 B4
Ledgerwood WF1 .... 121 B4
Ledger Pl WF1 .... 121 B4
Ledston Ave LS25 .... 83 A5
Ledston Luck Cotts LS25 ..... 83 E2
Ledston Luck Enterprise Pk
LS25 .... 83 D2
Ledston Luck Villas LS25 ..... 83 D2
Ledston Mill La
Ledston WF10 .... 103 E4
Ledston WF10 .... 103 E7
Lee Bank WF3 .... 98 B1
Lee Beck Gr WF3 .... 100 A4
Lee Bottom Rd OL14 .... 109 A5
Lee Bridge HX3 .... 203 D4
Lee Brig WF6 .... 122 F3
Lee Brigg First Sch WF6 .... 122 E3
Lee Cl BD15 .... 53 C6
Lee Clough Dr HX7 .... 89 F1
Lee Ct Keighley BD21 .... 35 F6
10 Liversedge WF15 .... 117 A5
Lee Cres WF4 .... 159 F7
Lee Dr LS12 .... 139 C4
Lee First Sch BD22 .... 51 E8
Lee Hall Rd WF12 .... 139 C3
Lee Holm WF12 .... 139 C5
Lee House Rd WF12 .... 139 C5
Lee La Haworth BD22 .... 51 D8
Pudsey LS28 .... 57 B1
Lees Mill La HD7 .... 152 B1
Lees Moor Rd BD13 .... 52 C6
Lees Rd **6** HX7 .... 89 A4
Lees St BD13 .... 85 A7
Lees Yd **4** HX7 .... 89 A3
Leeside Ave HD2 .... 136 C4
Leeside Prim Sch WF16 ..... 117 E6
Leeside Rd WF16 .... 117 E6
Leesworth Ct **7** BD22 .... 51 E8
Legrams Ave BD7 .... 73 F5
Legrams La BD7 .... 74 A6
Legrams Mill La BD7 .... 74 A6
Legrams St BD7 .... 74 C7
Legrams Terr BD7 .... 74 C7
Leicester Cl LS7 .... 206 B2
Leicester Gr LS7 .... 206 B2
Leicester Pl LS7 .... 206 B2
Leicester St BD4 .... 75 A4
Leicester Terr **8** HX3 .... 113 B4
Leigh Ave WF3 .... 120 A8
Leigh Rd WF3 .... 120 A8
Leigh St Ackworth M T WF7 163 D5
Sowerby Bridge HX6 .... 112 C5
Leigh View WF3 .... 120 A8
Leighton La **4** LS1 .... 211 D4
Leighton Pl **1** LS1 .... 211 E4
Leighton St **3** LS1 .... 211 E4
Leisure La HD8 .... 175 E8
Leith Ct WF12 .... 139 E1
Leith St BD21 .... 35 B8
Lemans Dr WF13 .... 117 F3
Lemington Ave HX1 .... 202 C2
Lemon St Bradford BD5 .... 74 C3
Halifax HX1 .... 202 C2
Lemon Tree Cl WF8 .... 146 B6
Lenacre La WF4 .... 156 D1
Lenham Cl **11** LS27 .... 98 A2
Lennie St BD21 .... 35 B6
Lennon Dr BD8 .... 74 B8
Lennox Dr WF2 .... 141 D3
Lennox Rd Leeds LS4 .... 205 D1
Todmorden, Cornholme
OL14 .... 86 A1
Lenny Balk DN5 .... 195 E7
Lens Dr BD17 .... 38 C4
Lentilfield St HX3 .... 92 A2
Lentilfield Terr **6** HX3 .... 92 A2
Lenton Dr LS11 .... 214 C2
Lenton Villas BD10 .... 39 A1
Leodis Ct LS11 .... 211 E2
Leonard St Bingley BD16 ..... 37 A2
Bradford BD12 .... 94 D2
Huddersfield HD2 .... 136 B1
Leonard's Pl **4** BD16 .... 37 A2
Leopold Gdns LS7 .... 207 E3
Leopold Gr LS7 .... 207 D3
Leopold Primary Sch LS7 ... 207 E3
Leopold St Leeds LS7 .... 207 E3
Ossett WF5 .... 141 A4
Lepton CE Jun & Inf Sch
HD8 .... 155 D3
Lepton Jun & Inf Sch
HD8 .... 155 D2
Lepton La HD8 .... 174 A8
Lepton Pl LS27 .... 97 D7
Lesley Way HD4 .... 153 A1
Leslie Ave LS19 .... 40 C8
Leslie St HD2 .... 136 A1
Leslie Terr **5** LS6 .... 206 A3
Lesmere Gr BD7 .... 73 F2
Lessarna Ct BD4 .... 75 C5
Leven Gdns LS22 .... 13 D7
Levens Bank LS15 .... 80 E6
Levens Cl LS15 .... 80 E6
Levens Garth LS15 .... 80 E6
Levens Pl LS15 .... 80 E6
Leventhorpe Cotts LS26 .... 101 E8
Leventhorpe **11** LS26 .... 101 C5
Leventhorpe Way LS26 ...... 101 C5

Leeds Rd continued
Mickletown LS26 .... 102 B3
Northowram HX3 .... 114 A8
Ossett, Chickenley WF5 ...... 140 C8
Ossett, Gawthorpe WF5 ...... 119 C1
Otley LS21 .... 23 D6
Pool LS16 .... 24 D1
Rothwell LS26 .... 100 F7
Rothwell, Robin Hood
LS26, WF3 .... 100 B2
Shipley BD18 .... 55 D8
Wakefield WF1 .... 216 A4
Yeadon LS19 .... 40 D3
Leeds Road Hospl BD3 .... 75 B7
Leeds St BD21 .... 35 C8
Leeds Sta LS1 .... 211 E3
Leeds Univ LS2 .... 206 A2
Leef St **6** HD5 .... 154 D6
Leefield Rd WF17 .... 117 E6
Leeke Ave WF4 .... 141 A2
Leeming St BD1 .... 201 C4
Lees Ave WF12 .... 139 C4
Lees Bank Ave BD22 .... 51 E8
Lees Bank Dr BD22 .... 51 E8
Lees Bank Hill BD22 .... 51 E8
Lees Bank Rd BD22 .... 51 E8
Lees Bldgs HX3 .... 114 C7
Lees Ct Cullingworth BD13 ... 52 C6
Huddersfield HD5 .... 154 D7
Lees Cres WF4 .... 159 F7
Lees Dr WF12 .... 139 C4

(continued)

Lever St **5** Bradford BD6 ..... 74 A1
Todmorden OL14 .... 108 B5
Levita Gr BD4 .... 75 D4
Levita Pl Bradford BD4 .... 75 E5
4 Leeds LS15 .... 80 F8
Levin Gr WF10 .... 125 D8
Lewin Gr **10** BD13 .... 72 E1
Lewis St HX1 .... 203 D4
Lewisham Ct LS27 .... 98 B4
Lewisham Gr LS27 .... 98 B4
Lewisham Rd HD7 .... 152 A1
Lewisham St LS27 .... 97 E3
Lexington Cl BD4 .... 95 B8
Ley Fleaks Rd BD10 .... 56 B7
Ley La LS12 .... 210 A4
Ley Top First Sch BD15 .... 73 B8
Ley Top La BD15 .... 73 C8
Leybrook Croft WF9 .... 181 E7
Leyburn Ave Batley WF16 ... 117 E6
Brighouse HX3 .... 114 E8
Leyburn Gr
2 Bingley BD16 .... 37 A4
Shipley BD18 .... 55 A7
Leyburn Rd DN6 .... 184 F2
Leyburne St BD8 .... 55 C1
Leyden Rise BD15 .... 73 B8
Leyfield **1** BD17 .... 38 B3
Leyfield Bank HD7 .... 189 C7
Leygards La HD7 .... 170 C1
Leyland Croft HD2 .... 136 E6
Leyland Rd Batley WF17 ...... 96 E1
Castleford WF10 .... 125 D8
Leylands Ave BD9 .... 54 F3
Leylands Gr BD9 .... 54 F3
Leylands La Bradford BD9 ... 54 F3
Keighley BD21 .... 35 D6
Leylands Rd LS2 .... 207 D1
Leylands Terr BD9 .... 54 F3
Leymoor Rd HD7 .... 152 E5
Leys Cl BD10 .... 39 A1
Leys La Boston Spa LS23 .... 14 C2
Emley HD8 .... 175 B6
Hampole DN6 .... 184 C2
Kirk Smeaton WF8 .... 166 C7
Knottingley WF11 .... 126 F1
Leys Rd WF8 .... 147 E6
Leys The WF9 .... 182 C1
Leysholme Cres LS12 .... 209 D2
Leysholme Dr LS12 .... 209 D2
Leysholme Terr LS12 .... 209 E2
Leysholme View LS12 .... 209 E2
Leyside Dr BD15 .... 54 B1
Leyton Cres BD10 .... 56 B7
Leyton Dr BD10 .... 56 B7
Leyton Gr BD10 .... 56 B7
Leyton Terr BD10 .... 56 B7
Libbey St BD8 .... 55 C1
Lichen Cl BD7 .... 74 A3
Lichfield Mount BD2 .... 55 F4
Lichfield Rd WF12 .... 139 F8
Lickless Ave LS18 .... 41 D1
Lickless Dr LS18 .... 41 D1
Lickless Gdns LS18 .... 41 D1
Lickless Terr LS18 .... 41 D1
Lidgate Cl WF12 .... 118 C2
Lidgate Cres LS25 .... 83 B5
Lidgate Gdns WF13 .... 118 C2
Lidgate La Dewsbury WF13 118 C2
Shafton S72 .... 180 B3
Lidget Ave BD7 .... 73 F5
Lidget Green First Sch
BD7 .... 73 F6
Lidget Green Middle Sch
BD7 .... 73 F6
Lidget Hill LS28 .... 76 E7
Lidget La WF4 .... 144 D1
Lidget Pl BD7 .... 74 A5
Lidget Rd BD20 .... 4 C5
Lidget St HD3 .... 135 B1
Lidget Terr Bradford BD14 .. 73 D4
Bradford, Scholemoor BD7 . 73 F5
Lidgett Ave LS8 .... 204 C3
Lidgett Cres LS8 .... 204 C4
Lidgett Ct Garforth LS25 ... 82 E6
Leeds LS8 .... 204 C4
Lidgett Gr LS8 .... 204 C3
Lidgett Hill LS8 .... 204 C3
Lidgett La Garforth LS25 .... 82 E6
Leeds LS8 .... 204 C3
Skelmanthorpe HD8 .... 174 F1
Lidgett Mount LS8 .... 43 E1
Lidgett Park Ave LS8 .... 204 C4
Lidgett Park Ct LS8 .... 43 F1
Lidgett Park Gdns LS8 ...... 204 C4
Lidgett Park Gr LS8 .... 204 C4
Lidgett Park Mews LS8 .... 44 A1
Lidgett Park Rd LS8 .... 44 A1
Lidgett Park View LS8 .... 43 F1
Lidgett Pl LS8 .... 204 C4
Lidgett Rise HD8 .... 174 F1
Lidgett Towers LS8 .... 43 E1
Lifton Pl LS2 .... 206 A2
Light Bank La BD20 .... 6 C3
Light La WF2 .... 141 D8
Lightcliffe CE Prim Sch
HX3 .... 114 E8
Lightcliffe Golf Course
HX3 .... 114 E8
Lightcliffe Preparatory Sch
HX3 .... 114 D7
Lightcliffe Rd
Brighouse HD6 .... 115 A4
Huddersfield HD4 .... 153 D4
Lightcliffe Royd La HX4 .... 133 C6
Lightenfield La HD4 .... 171 C6
Lightfoot Ave WF10 .... 124 C6
Lightfoot Cl WF10 .... 124 D6

Lighthazles Chapel Rd
HX6 .... 132 A6
Lighthazles Rd HX6 ...... 132 B6
Lighthouse OL15 .... 129 C1
Lightowler St 10 HX1 .... 202 C3
Lightowler Rd HX1 .... 202 C3
Lightowler St 10 BD6 .... 74 C1
Lightridge Cl HD2 .... 136 A4
Lightridge Rd HD2 .... 135 F5
Lilac Ave Knottingley WF12 .. 126 E2
Wakefield WF2 .... 142 C3
Lilac Cl Addingham LS29 .... 7 A8
Brighouse HD6 .... 115 C3
Lilac Gr Bradford BD4 ..... 75 D6
Cleckheaton BD19 .... 96 A1
Shipley BD18 .... 55 D5
Lilac St HX3 .... 92 A1
Lilac Wlk HX3 .... 152 E5
Lilacs The Guiseley LS20 .. 22 E1
Royston S71 .... 179 E4
Liley La Kirkheaton WF14 .... 155 F8
Lepton WF14 .... 156 C6
Lilian St BD4 .... 75 C3
Lillands Ave HD6 .... 114 F2
Lillands La HD6 .... 114 F2
Lillands Terr HD6 .... 114 F2
Lilley St WF9 .... 181 D6
Lilly Terr WF9 .... 182 B2
Lilly La HX3 .... 203 F2
Lilly St HX6 .... 112 B3
Lily Croft BD8 .... 55 B1
Lily St Bradford BD8 ...... 55 B1
Todmorden OL14 .... 107 E8
Lilycroft First BD9 .... 55 B2
Lilycroft Rd BD9 .... 55 B2
Lilycroft Wlk BD9 .... 55 A2
Lilythorne Ave BD10 ..... 56 C8
Lime Ave Hebden Bridge HX7 .. 88 F3
Holmfirth HD7 .... 189 C8
Todmorden OL14 .... 108 A6
Lime Cl BD20 .... 18 A1
Lime Cres
South Elmsall WF9 .... 182 E1
Wakefield WF2 .... 142 F1
Lime Gr BD16 .... 37 C4
Lime Gr Huddersfield HD7 .. 152 E5
Royston S71 .... 179 C1
South Elmsall WF9 .... 182 E1
Yeadon LS19 .... 40 A4
Lime Pit La WF3 .... 121 F4
Lime St Bingley BD16 ...... 36 F3
Bradford BD7 .... 74 B4
Cleckheaton BD19 .... 116 C7
Haworth BD22 .... 51 C6
Huddersfield HD1 .... 35 B7
Keighley BD21 .... 35 B7
Ossett WF5 .... 140 E4
Todmorden OL14 .... 108 A6
Lime Tree Ave Batley WF17 118 A4
Boston Spa LS23 .... 30 D8
Leeds LS17 .... 43 E2
Pontefract WF8 .... 146 B8
Lime Tree Ct WF9 .... 181 C6
Lime Tree Gdns LS23 ...... 30 E7
Lime Tree Gr LS11 .... 96 A7
Lime Tree Sq BD18 .... 54 D8
Lime-Tree Cres LS23 ...... 83 C1
Limers Gate OL14 .... 106 E4
Limes Ave Halifax HX3 ... 113 C4
Mapplewell S75 .... 178 C2
Limes Cl S75 .... 178 C2
Limetrees HD8 .... 126 A4
Limewood App LS14 .... 62 A7
Limewood Rd LS14 .... 62 A6
Linburn Cl S71 .... 179 A4
Lincoln Ave Batley WF16 . 117 D5
Liversedge WF15 .... 116 F2
Lincoln Cl BD8 .... 55 C1
Lincoln Cres WF9 .... 183 A4
Lincoln Ct HD5 .... 155 A7
Lincoln Dr WF15 .... 117 A2
Lincoln Gn
Huddersfield HD5 .... 155 A4
Liversedge WF15 .... 116 F2
Lincoln Green Rd LS9 ..... 207 E1
Lincoln Rd Bradford BD8 ... 118 F1
Leeds LS9 .... 207 E1
Lincoln St Bradford BD8 .. 73 C8
Castleford WF10 .... 124 E8
Huddersfield HD1 .... 154 C6
Todmorden OL14 .... 86 B1
Wakefield WF2 .... 142 A7
Lincoln Towers LS9 ...... 207 F1
Lincoln Way HX3 .... 92 B1
Lincoln Wlk LS25 .... 83 C2
Lincombe Bank LS8 .... 204 B4
Lincombe Dr LS8 .... 204 B4
Lincombe Mount LS8 .... 204 B4
Lincombe Rise LS8 .... 204 B4
Lincroft Ave HX5 .... 154 E5
Lincs World WF15 .... 116 E4
Lindale Ave WF7 .... 164 C7
Lindale Cl LS10 .... 99 D7
Lindale Garth WF2 .... 120 C2
Lindale Gr WF2 .... 120 C2
Lindale La WF2 .... 120 C2
Lindale Mount WF2 .... 120 D1
Linden Ave Bradford BD3 .. 75 F8
Leeds LS11 .... 214 B3
Todmorden OL14 .... 108 A6
Linden Cl Barnsley LS17 .. 214 B3
Brighouse HD6 .... 115 C3
Castleford WF10 .... 125 D6
Dewsbury WF12 .... 140 B7
Knottingley WF11 .... 126 C4

Linden Ct LS16 .... 59 D7
Linden Gdns 5 LS11 ..... 214 C3
Linden Gr LS11 .... 214 C3
Linden Mount LS11 .... 214 B3
Linden Pl
11 Hebden Bridge HX7 .... 89 A4
3 Leeds LS11 .... 214 C3
Linden Rd Elland HX5 .... 134 E6
Halifax HX3 .... 113 C4
Hebden Bridge HX7 .... 89 A4
Hebden Bridge, Hawks Clough
HX7 .... 89 D1
Huddersfield HD2 .... 135 F1
Leeds LS11 .... 214 C3
Linden Rise BD21 .... 35 E5
Linden St LS11 .... 214 C3
Linden Terr
Ackworth M T WF7 .... 163 D5
Leeds LS11 .... 214 C3
Pontefract WF8 .... 146 C8
Linden Way LS22 .... 13 D7
Lindholm BD15 .... 73 B8
Lindisfarne Rd BD18 ...... 54 F7
Lindley Ave HD3 .... 135 A2
Lindley Dr BD7 .... 73 F2
Lindley Lodge HD3 .... 135 B1
Lindley Moor Rd HD3 ... 134 E2
Lindley Rd Bradford BD5 .. 74 D3
Elland HX5 .... 134 F6
Lindley St HD3 .... 153 A5
Lindley St 12 BD22 .... 51 C6
Lindrick Cl Cudworth S72 .. 180 C1
Normanton WF6 .... 123 D1
Lindrick Gr HX2 .... 91 F7
Lindrick Way HX2 .... 91 F7
Lindrick Wlk HX2 .... 91 F7
Lindsay Acre WF3 .... 120 A8
Lindsay Ave WF2 .... 141 C5
Lindsay Rd LS25 .... 83 B2
Lindsey Ct 5 LS9 .... 207 E1
Lindsey Gdns LS9 .... 207 E1
Lindsey Mount LS9 .... 207 E1
Lindsey Rd LS9 .... 207 E1
Lindwell Ave 5 HX4 ...... 134 C7
Lindwell Gr 5 HX4 .... 134 C7
Lindwell Pl 1 HX4 .... 134 C7
Linefield Rd WF17 .... 118 D5
Lineham Ct WF15 .... 117 A2
Lineholme Ave OL14 ...... 107 E7
Linfit Fold HD7 .... 170 A8
Linfit La Kirkburton HD8 .. 174 B8
Lepton HD8 .... 156 C1
Slaithwaite HD7 .... 170 B8
Ling Bob HX2 .... 112 D8
Ling Bob Croft HX2 .... 91 D1
Ling Bob Junior
& Infant Sch HX2 .... 112 D8
Ling Croft LS23 .... 30 B8
Ling La LS14 .... 45 B7
Ling Park App BD15 .... 53 C4
Ling Park Ave BD15 .... 53 C4
Ling Royd Ave HX2 ...... 112 D8
Lingamore Leys S63 ..... 194 D1
Lingard St BD1 .... 201 C4
Lingards Terr HD7 .... 169 E7
Lingdale Rd BD6 .... 94 B5
Lingfield App LS17 .... 43 B3
Lingfield Bank LS17 .... 43 B3
Lingfield Cl LS17 .... 43 C3
Lingfield Cres
Bradford BD13 .... 73 C2
Leeds LS17 .... 43 B3
Lingfield Dr
Cullingworth BD22 .... 35 A1
Leeds LS17 .... 43 B3
Lingfield Gate LS17 .... 43 B3
Lingfield Gdns LS17 .... 43 B3
Lingfield Gn LS17 .... 43 B3
Lingfield Gr LS17 .... 43 C3
Wilsden BD15 .... 53 D5
Lingfield Hill LS17 .... 43 B3
Lingfield Mount LS17 ...... 43 B3
Lingfield Rd Leeds LS17 .... 43 B3
Wilsden BD15 .... 53 C5
Lingfield Terr BD13 .... 73 C2
Lingfield View LS17 .... 43 B3
Lingfield Wlk LS17 .... 43 B3
Lings La DN6 .... 184 A8
Lingwell App LS10 .... 99 C4
Lingwell Ave LS10 .... 99 C5
Lingwell Chase WF3 ...... 121 C6
Lingwell Cres LS10 .... 99 C5
Lingwell Ct
Lofthouse Gate WF3 .... 121 A5
Middleton LS10 .... 99 C4
Lingwell Gate Cres WF1 .. 121 B5
Lingwell Gate La
East Ardsley WF3 .... 120 F8
Lofthouse Gate WF1 .... 121 A6
Middleton WF3 .... 99 F2
Lingwell Gdns 3 LS10 .... 99 C4
Lingwell Gn 5 LS10 .... 99 C4
Lingwell Gr LS10 .... 99 C4
Lingwell Mews 1 LS10 ... 99 C4
Lingwell Nook La
Lofthouse Gate WF3 .... 121 C6
Lofthouse Gate, Lingwell Gate
WF3 .... 121 A8
Lingwell Park Ct LS10 ..... 99 C4
Lingwell Rd LS10 .... 99 C4
Lingwell View 2 LS10 ..... 99 C4
Lingwell Wlk 4 LS10 ...... 99 C4
Lingwood Ave BD8 .... 54 F1
Lingwood Cl HD7 .... 189 D7
Lingwood Rd BD8 .... 73 F8
Lingwood Terr 1 BD8 ..... 73 F8

Link Rd Dewsbury WF12 ... 139 D7
Huddersfield HD1 .... 153 D6
Wakefield WF1 .... 216 A4
Link The Pontefract WF8 .. 146 C6
Swillington LS26 .... 81 F1
Links Ave BD19 .... 95 D2
Links The WF7 .... 124 D1
Links View S75 .... 178 B2
Linkway BD16 .... 54 A7
Linnburn Mews LS29 .... 8 B3
Linnet Cl Bradford BD8 ..... 73 C7
Mirfield WF14 .... 138 A8
Linnet Ct LS27 .... 98 D3
Linnet Gr WF2 .... 160 D5
Linnet St BD21 .... 35 C8
Linnhe Ave BD6 .... 93 F6
Linshaws Rd HD7 .... 198 E5
Linthwaite Ardron
Meml CE Jun & Inf Sch
HD7 .... 152 E1
Linthwaite Bsns Ctr HD7 . 152 D1
Linthwaite Junior
& Infant Sch HD7 .... 152 D1
Linton Ave Batley WF17 ... 118 A5
Leeds LS17 .... 43 F4
Silsden BD20 .... 5 E2
Wetherby LS22 .... 13 D6
Linton Cl Leeds LS12 .... 43 F4
Liversedge WF15 .... 116 F5
Linton Comm LS22 .... 13 A1
Linton Cres LS17 .... 43 F4
Linton Croft 3 LS16 .... 59 A8
Linton Dr LS17 .... 43 F4
Linton Gr Batley WF16 .... 117 E3
Brighouse HD6 .... 135 E8
Leeds LS17 .... 43 F4
Linton Hills Rd LS22 .... 13 C4
Linton La Collingham LS22 . 13 C4
Spofforth LS22 .... 13 C4
Linton Meadows LS22 ..... 13 C5
Linton Rd Collingham LS22 . 13 B1
Leeds LS17 .... 43 E4
Wakefield WF1 .... 142 F6
Wetherby LS22 .... 13 D5
Linton Rise Leeds LS17 .... 43 F4
Normanton WF6 .... 123 D1
Linton St BD4 .... 74 F4
Linton View LS17 .... 43 E5
Lint Cott S75 .... 193 E4
Lint St OL14 .... 108 A3
Lintel St WF5 .... 140 E4
Liphill Bank Rd HD7 ...... 188 D4
Lippersley La LS29 .... 6 B6
Lipscomb St HD3 .... 153 B5
Lisbon Sq 6 LS1 .... 211 D4
Lisbon St LS1 .... 211 D4
Lisheen Ave WF10 .... 124 E6
Lishen Gr WF10 .... 124 E7
Lisker Ave LS21 .... 23 B7
Lisker Dr LS21 .... 23 B7
Lismore Rd BD20 .... 35 B8
Lister Ave BD4 .... 75 B3
Lister Cl WF1 .... 145 C5
Lister Ct BD13 .... 93 C4
Lister Hill LS18 .... 41 C2
Lister La Bradford BD2 ..... 56 A3
Halifax HX1 .... 202 C3
Lister Lane Sch BD2 .... 56 A3
Lister Rd WF7 .... 145 C5
Lister St
Bradford, Dudley Hill BD4 .. 75 E1
Bradford, Tong Street BD4 .. 75 E1
Brighouse HD6 .... 115 A3
Castleford WF10 .... 124 C8
Elland HX5 .... 134 F7
Huddersfield HD5 .... 154 E5
Ilkley LS29 .... 8 A4
Keighley BD21 .... 35 B6
Lister View BD8 .... 55 C1
Lister Wlk LS27 .... 97 F6
Lister's Rd Halifax HX3 ... 113 E8
Listerdale WF15 .... 117 B5
Listerhills Ind Est BD7 .... 74 C7
Listerhills Rd BD7 .... 74 C7
Listers Ct LS29 .... 8 A4
Listing Ave WF15 .... 117 B5
Listing Cl WF15 .... 117 B5
Listing Dr WF15 .... 117 B5
Listing La BD19, WF15 ... 117 B6
Litell Royd WF7 .... 144 D5
Litherop La HD8 .... 176 C5
Litherop Rd S75 .... 176 D3
Little Baines St HX1 .... 202 C3
Little Bradley HX4 .... 134 C6
Little Brunswick St 6
HD1 .... 154 B6
Little Cake HD7 .... 189 C2
Little Church La LS26 ..... 102 C2
Little Cote BD10 .... 39 A1
Little Cross St 8 BD5 ...... 74 E2
Little Fountain St LS27 .... 98 A3
Little Green La WF16 ..... 117 C5
Little Hew Royd BD10 ..... 39 B1
Little Horton Gn BD5 ...... 74 D5
Little Horton La
Bradford BD5 .... 201 B2
Bradford, Holme Top BD5 .. 74 D4
Little King St LS1 .... 211 E3
Little La Bradford BD9 ...... 54 F1
Featherstone WF7 .... 145 E4
Holmfirth HD7 .... 188 E5
Holmfirth, Wooldale HD7 .. 189 C6
Ilkley LS29 .... 8 E1
Keighley BD20 .... 19 E1
7 Morley LS27 .... 98 C8

Little La continued
Rothwell WF3 .... 100 E3
South Elmsall WF9 .... 183 B3
South Elmsall, Moorthorpe
WF9 .... 182 F3
Upton WF9 .... 183 B7
Wadsworth Moor HX7 ...... 69 B6
Little Lane Ct 3 HD7 ...... 98 C8
Little London HX3 .... 92 F4
Little Moor Pl LS12 .... 209 E3
Little Neville St LS1 .... 211 E3
Little Pk BD10 .... 39 F1
Little Queen St LS1 .... 211 D4
Little St BD22 .... 51 C8
Little Wood Dr BD19 .... 95 D2
Little Woodhouse HD6 ... 115 A2
Little Woodhouse St LS2 . 206 A1
Little Woodhouse
CE Jun & Inf Sch
Littlefield Gr WF5 .... 140 E6
Littlefield Rd WF5 .... 140 E5
Littlefield Wlk BD6 .... 94 B8
Littleholme St OL14 ...... 108 A3
Littlelands BD16 .... 37 C3
Littlemoor Cres LS28 ...... 76 E5
Littlemoor Cres S LS28 ... 76 E5
Littlemoor Gdns Halifax HX2 91 E6
Pudsey LS28 .... 76 E5
Littlemoor Gr HX4 .... 137 F5
Littlemoor La LS14 .... 45 F5
2 Mirfield WF14 .... 137 F5
Pudsey LS28 .... 76 F6
Littlemoor View LS28 ..... 76 F6
Littlethorpe Hill WF15 ... 116 D1
Littlethorpe Rd WF15 ..... 116 D2
Littletown Jun & Inf Sch
WF15 .... 117 A6
Littleway LS17 .... 43 C1
Littlewood Cl BD6 .... 94 C7
Littlewood Croft HD4 ..... 154 A2
Litton Croft WF1 .... 142 F7
Litton Rd BD22 .... 35 A6
Litton Way LS14 .... 62 B8
Littondale Cl BD17 .... 38 C4
Liversedge Hall La WF15 . 117 A3
Livingston House BD10 .... 56 C6
Livingstone Cl BD2 .... 55 F6
Livingstone Rd Bradford BD2 55 F5
Shipley BD2 .... 55 D6
Livingstone St 11 HX3 .... 92 A1
Livingstone St N HX3 .... 92 A5
Livinia Gr S17 .... 206 C2
Lloyd St OL14 .... 108 B6
Lloyds Dr BD12 .... 94 C3
Lobley St WF16 .... 117 E4
Locarno Ave BD9 .... 54 E2
Locherbie Gn BD15 .... 54 B1
Lochy Rd BD6 .... 93 F6
Lock La Castleford WF10 ... 103 D1
Lock Rd Normanton WF6 .. 122 F6
Lock St Dewsbury WF12 .. 139 D4
Halifax HX3 .... 203 F2
Todmorden OL14 .... 108 A3
Lock View BD16 .... 36 E4
Lock Way WF13 .... 138 E4
Lockbridge Way HD3 ..... 153 B4
Locks The BD16 .... 36 D3
Locksley Rd HD6 .... 115 D1
Lockwood Ave WF14 ..... 138 B7
Lockwood Cl LS11 .... 214 C1
Lockwood Ct LS11 .... 214 C1
Lockwood Pk LS11 .... 214 C1
Lockwood Rd HD1 .... 153 F3
Lockwood Scar HD4 ...... 154 A2
Lockwood St
Bradford, Brownroyd Hill
BD6 .... 74 A6
Bradford, Raw Nook BD12 . 94 E5
5 Shipley BD18 .... 54 F8
Lockwood Sta HD1 .... 153 E3
Lockwood's Yd 2 HD1 ... 154 A6
Lode Pit La BD16 .... 37 D4
Lodge Ave
Castleford WF10 .... 125 C7
Elland HX5 .... 135 C7
Lodge Cl HD4 .... 153 E1
Lodge Dr Elland HX5 .... 135 C7
Mirfield WF14 .... 138 C4
Lodge Farm Cl WF12 ..... 139 D4
Lodge Farm Gdns WF6 .. 122 F3
Lodge Gate BD13 .... 52 E1
Lodge Gate Cl BD13 .... 52 E1
Lodge Hill BD17 .... 37 F3
Lodge Hill Cl WF5 .... 140 D8
Lodge Hill Rd WF5 .... 140 D8
Lodge Hill Wlk LS12 .... 77 E3
Lodge La Crofton WF4 ..... 143 E2
Leeds LS11 .... 214 B3
Liversedge WF15 .... 117 C2
Wakefield WF2 .... 160 E4
Lodge Pl HX5 .... 135 C7
Lodge Rd LS28 .... 76 D8
Lodge St Cullingworth BD13 52 D6
Glusburn BD20 .... 16 B6
Haworth BD22 .... 51 C7
Hemsworth WF9 .... 181 D8
Leeds LS2 .... 206 B1
Skelmanthorpe HD8 .... 175 A2
Lodge Terr 13 LS11 ...... 214 B2
Lodge The HD7 .... 152 E2
Lodges Cl WF4 .... 162 C2
Lodore Ave BD2 .... 56 A3
Lodore Pl BD2 .... 56 A3
Lodore Rd BD2 .... 56 A3
Loft St BD8 .... 73 F8
Lofthouse Gate Junior
& Infants Sch WF1 .... 121 D6

Lofthouse Pl LS2 .... 206 B2
Lofthouse Terr LS2 .... 206 C2
Logwood St HD1 .... 154 A4
Lombard St Halifax HX1 .. 202 B1
Leeds LS15 .... 80 F7
Yeadon LS19 .... 40 A4
Lombardi Ct WF5 .... 140 F4
Lombardy Cl HD7 .... 171 F3
Lombardy Garth WF2 .... 142 A8
Lomond Ave LS18 .... 41 B4
Londesboro Gr LS9 .... 80 A7
Londesboro Terr LS9 ...... 80 A7
London La LS19 .... 40 A4
London Rd Slaithwaite HD7 152 A1
Sowerby Bridge HX6 .... 112 E3
Todmorden OL14 .... 109 C6
London Spring Rd HX6 .. 132 A4
London St LS19 .... 40 A4
Long Cl BD12 .... 94 B4
Long Close La
Holmfirth HD8 .... 190 C7
Leeds LS9 .... 212 C3
South Elmsall WF9 .... 183 C6
Long Crest WF8 .... 146 E6
Long Croft S75 .... 178 B1
Long Croft St HD7 .... 152 E4
Long Cswy Denholme BD13 71 C8
Dewsbury WF12 .... 139 D3
Halton East BD23 .... 1 D7
Leeds LS9 .... 212 C1
Leeds, Adel LS16 .... 42 D3
Lofthouse Gate WF3 .... 121 F5
Ripponden HX6 .... 131 F1
Todmorden OL14 .... 108 F3
Wakefield WF1 .... 216 C4
Long Cswy The
Blackshaw Head HX7 .... 87 E4
Hebden Bridge HX2 .... 111 A6
Holme Chapel BB10 .... 85 D7
Sowerby Bridge HX2 .... 111 A6
Long Dam La WF4 .... 162 A8
Long Edge Low Rd HX6 . 111 B2
Long Edge Rd HX6 .... 111 A3
Long Fallas Cres HD6 ..... 136 B8
Long Gate Haworth BD22 .. 33 B8
Ripponden HX6 .... 150 A8
Sutton in C BD20 .... 33 B8
Long Grove Ave LS16 .... 154 E6
Long Hey La OL14 .... 108 C3
Long Heys HX4 .... 134 C6
Long Hill End BD22 .... 32 D8
Long Hill Rd HD2 .... 136 C4
Long House Rd HX2 .... 91 C6
Long Ing Rd HD7 .... 199 A7
Long La Ackworth M T WF7 146 B1
Barwick in E LS15 .... 63 F5
Bradford BD15 .... 53 D1
Clayton West HD8 .... 175 F3
Dewsbury WF12 .... 139 F6
Flockton WF4 .... 156 L1
Halifax, Bank Top HX3 ..... 113 F6
Halifax, Wheatley HX2, HX3 91 E2
Harden BD16 .... 36 A1
Hebden Bridge HX7 .... 88 E1
Hebden Bridge HX7 .... 109 D3
Huddersfield HD5 .... 154 E7
Kirk Smeaton WF8 .... 166 D3
Pontefract WF7, WF8 ...... 145 F5
Queensbury BD13 .... 92 E7
Shipley HD8 .... 173 E2
Shipley BD9 .... 54 E5
Sowerby Bridge HX6 .... 112 A2
Long Lee Ferst Sch BD21 . 35 F5
Long Lee La BD21 .... 35 E5
Long Lover La HX1 .... 202 B4
Long Mdws LS29 .... 9 F2
Long Meadow Ct LS25 .... 83 A5
Long Meadow Gate LS25 . 82 F5
Long Meadows
Bradford BD2 .... 55 E4
Bramhope LS16 .... 24 E2
Garforth LS25 .... 82 F5
Long Moor La HD8 .... 174 B1
Long Preston Chase BD10 . 56 D7
Long Reach HX2 .... 91 A3
Long Ridge HD6 .... 136 A7
Long Row Bradford BD12 .. 94 C5
Crofton WF4 .... 144 A5
Horsforth LS18 .... 41 C2
Thornton BD13 .... 72 C7
Long Row E 2 BD5 .... 74 E3
Long Royd Dr BD17 .... 38 E4
Long Royd La HD8 .... 191 B8
Long Royd Rd HX6 .... 111 C2
Long Shaw La OL14 .... 108 A3
Long St BD4 .... 75 B5
Long Thorpe La WF3 ..... 100 A1
Long Tongue Scrog La
Kirkheaton HD5 .... 155 E7
Lepton HD5 .... 155 F6
Long Wall HX5 .... 134 E6
Longacre WF10 .... 124 D6
Longacre La BD22 .... 51 E8
Longacres BD22 .... 34 C2
Longbottom Ave
Silsden BD20 .... 5 F1
Sowerby Bridge HX6 .... 111 E3
Longbottom Terr HX3 ... 113 D4
Longcauseway WF13 ..... 139 D8
Longclose Ind Est LS9 ... 207 E2
Longcroft Huddersfield HD5 154 F2
Keighley BD21 .... 35 C6
Longcroft Link 3 BD1 ..... 74 D7
Longcroft Pl BD1 .... 201 A3

Longcroft Rd LS29 .... 8 E3
Longdale Dr WF9 .... 182 E4
Longden Ave HD4 .... 153 D2
Longdike Ct **3** LS25 .... 83 B1
Longdike La LS25 .... 103 C8
Longdon Ave HD8 .... 155 E3
Longdon Wlk HD8 .... 155 E3
Longfellow Gr WF3 .... 121 E6
Longfield Elland HX4 .... 134 B4
  Hepinstall HX7 .... 88 F4
Longfield Ave
  Huddersfield, Grove Place
  HD5 .... 154 D7
  Huddersfield, Leymoor HD7 .. 152 E5
  Northowram HX3 .... 93 A1
  3 Pudsey LS28 .... 76 F7
Longfield Cl
  Huddersfield HD5 .... 154 D7
  Todmorden OL14 .... 108 B4
Longfield Ct WF16 .... 117 E4
Longfield Dr
  Ackworth M T WF7 .... 164 C7
  Bradford BD4 .... 75 C3
  Leeds LS13 .... 81 A8
  Mapplewell S75 .... 178 B1
  Pudsey LS13 .... 57 F5
Longfield Garth **3** LS13 ... 57 F5
Longfield Gr
  2 Pudsey LS28 .... 76 F7
  Todmorden OL14 .... 108 B4
Longfield La OL14 .... 108 B3
Longfield Mount **1** LS28 .. 76 F7
Longfield Rd Batley WF16 .. 117 D4
  Pudsey LS28 .... 76 F7
  Todmorden OL14 .... 108 B5
Longfield Rise OL14 .... 108 B4
Longfield Terr Pudsey LS28 . 76 F7
  Todmorden OL14 .... 108 B4
  Wakefield WF2 .... 141 F7
Longfield Way OL14 .... 108 B4
Longford Terr BD7 .... 73 F5
Longhouse Dr BD13 .... 71 D8
Longhouse La BD13 .... 71 D8
Longlands Ave
  Denholme BD13 .... 52 D1
  Slaithwaite HD7 .... 151 E1
Longlands Bank HD7 .... 189 B8
Longlands Cl WF5 .... 140 E6
Longlands Dr
  Haworth BD22 .... 51 D8
  Mapplewell S75 .... 178 B1
Longlands La LS22 .... 12 C4
Longlands Rd Batley WF13 . 118 A2
  Ossett WF5 .... 140 E6
  Slaithwaite HD7 .... 151 E1
Longlands St BD1 .... 201 A3
Longlands Trad Est WF5 .... 140 E6
Longley Edge La HD7 .... 189 B1
Longley Edge Rd HD7 .... 189 B1
Longley La Holmfirth HD7 .. 189 A1
  Huddersfield HD4 .... 154 D2
  Sowerby Bridge HX6 .... 111 F1
Longley Park Golf Course
  HD1, HD5 .... 154 C4
Longley Rd HD5 .... 154 C4
Longmeadow HX4 .... 133 A5
Longroyd BD10 .... 55 F8
Longroyd Ave LS11 .... 214 C3
Longroyd Cres Leeds LS11 . 214 C3
  Slaithwaite HD7 .... 151 E1
Longroyd Cres N LS11 ...... 214 C3
Longroyd Farm WF4 .... 158 B7
Longroyd Gr LS11 .... 214 C3
Longroyd La HD1 .... 153 F5
Longroyd Pl
  Huddersfield HD1 .... 153 E5
  Leeds LS11 .... 214 C3
Longroyd St LS11 .... 214 C3
Longroyd St N LS11 .... 214 C3
Longroyd Terr LS11 .... 214 C3
Longroyd View LS11 .... 214 C3
Longroyde Cl HD6 .... 114 F1
Longroyde Gr HD6 .... 115 E8
Longroyde Junior Sch
  HD6 .... 114 F1
Longroyde Rd **3** HD6 ... 115 E1
Longside La WF7 .... 74 C6
Longsight Terr WF5 .... 178 A1
Longside La BD16 .... 163 B1
Longwood Ave BD16 .... 36 C5
Longwood Cl
  East Ardsley WF3 .... 119 E8
  Leeds LS17 .... 44 B5
Longwood Cres LS17 .... 44 B5
Longwood Ct WF3 .... 119 E8
Longwood Edge Rd HD3 .. 152 E7
Longwood Fold WF3 .... 119 E8
Longwood Garth WF3 .... 119 E8
Longwood Gate HD3 .... 152 F6
Longwood House Rd HD2 . 136 A3
Longwood Rd
  East Ardsley WF3 .... 119 E8
  Huddersfield HD3 .... 153 C5
Longwood Vale WF3 .... 119 E8
Longwood View BD16 .... 36 C5
Longwood Way LS17 .... 44 B5
Longwoods Wlk WF11 ...... 127 A5
Lonsbrough Ave WF16 ...... 117 D5
Lonsbrough Flats **7** HD1 . 154 B6
Lonsbrough Way WF9 ...... 183 A4
Lonsdale Ave **3** WF17 ... 117 F7
Lonsdale Cl LS10 .... 215 D1
Lonsdale Meadows LS23 ... 30 D7
Lonsdale Rd WF1 .... 216 A4
Lonsdale Rise WF3 .... 119 E8

Lonsdale St BD3 .... 75 B8
Lord La BD22 .... 51 B8
Lord St Batley WF13 .... 117 F4
  Dewsbury WF12 .... 140 B7
  Halifax HX1 .... 203 E3
  12 Haworth BD22 .... 51 D7
  Huddersfield HD1 .... 154 B6
  Keighley BD21 .... 35 C7
  Leeds LS12 .... 210 C2
  Slaithwaite HD7 .... 151 F1
  Sowerby Bridge HX6 .... 112 C5
  Todmorden OL14 .... 108 A1
  Wakefield WF1 .... 142 F3
Lord Terr LS12 .... 210 C2
Lord's Bldgs **6** LS27 ...... 98 A2
Lord's La HD8 .... 173 B5
Lordsfield Pl BD4 .... 75 D1
Loris St BD4 .... 75 D1
Lorne First Sch BD4 .... 75 B4
Lorne St Bradford BD4 .... 75 B3
  2 Haworth BD22 .... 51 F8
  Keighley BD21 .... 35 E8
Lorry Bank LS7 .... 206 C4
Loscoe Cl WF6 .... 123 E3
Loscoe La
  Featherstone WF6, WF7 ... 124 A1
  Normanton WF6 .... 123 E2
Lothersdale Rd BD20 .... 16 A7
Lotherton Hall LS25 .... 65 B5
Lotherton La Aberford LS25 . 65 A6
  Aberford LS25 .... 65 B5
Lotherton Way LS25 .... 83 A8
Loughrigg St BD5 .... 74 E3
Loughrigg Wlk WF7 .... 163 E6
Louis Ave BD5 .... 74 C4
Louis Ct LS7 .... 207 D3
Louis Gr LS7 .... 207 E3
Louis Le Prince Ct LS8 ..... 207 F3
Louis St LS7 .... 207 D3
Louisa St Bradford BD10 .... 56 B8
  Castleford WF10 .... 124 C8
Lound La SN5 .... 195 F5
Lovaine Gr WF2 .... 142 D1
Love La Castleford WF10 .. 124 C6
  Halifax HX1 .... 203 D1
  Ossett WF5 .... 140 C6
  Pontefract WF8 .... 146 B8
  Rothwell LS26 .... 100 E5
  Wakefield WF2 .... 216 A2
Love Lane Terr WF8 .... 146 C8
Lovell Park Cl LS7 .... 207 D1
Lovell Park Ct LS7 .... 207 D1
Lovell Park Gate LS7 .... 206 C1
Lovell Park Grange LS7 ... 207 D1
Lovell Park Hill LS7 .... 207 D1
Lovell Park Hts LS7 .... 207 D1
Lovell Park Mews LS7 ...... 207 D1
Lovell Park Rd LS2, LS7 ... 206 C1
Lovell Park Towers LS7 .... 206 C1
Lovell Park View LS7 .... 207 D1
Lovell View WF4 .... 162 A8
Low Ash Ave BD18 .... 55 D7
Low Ash Cres BD18 .... 55 D7
Low Ash Dr BD18 .... 55 D7
Low Ash First Sch BD18 ... 55 D6
Low Ash Gr BD18 .... 55 D7
Low Ash Rd BD18 .... 55 E7
Low Bank Dr BD22 .... 34 B3
Low Bank La BD22 .... 34 B2
Low Bank St LS28 .... 57 D3
Low Cl **6** Bingley BD16 .... 37 B2
  Ilkley LS29 .... 8 B5
Low Cliff Wlk WF16 .... 117 E2
Low Close St LS2 .... 206 A3
Low Cross St WF11 .... 127 A5
Low Farm La LS26 .... 102 E8
Low Farm La WF7 .... 164 A6
Low Fields Ave LS11 .... 213 E4
Low Fields Rd LS12 .... 213 E4
Low Fields Way LS11 .... 213 E4
Low Fold Baildon BD17 .... 38 C4
  Bradford BD2 .... 55 F2
  Brighouse BD19 .... 115 F8
  Denholme BD13 .... 52 D2
  Steeton BD20 .... 17 C5
  Yeadon LS19 .... 40 B4
Low Gate Kirkburton HD8 . 173 F6
  South Elmsall WF9 .... 183 A3
Low Gate La OL3 .... 167 A1
Low Gipton Cres LS8 .... 61 D3
Low Gn Ackworth M T WF7 . 164 B7
  Knottingley WF11 .... 127 B4
  Yeadon LS19 .... 40 C3
Low Grange Cres LS10 ..... 215 E1
Low Grange Rd S63 .... 194 C1
Low Grange View LS10 ..... 99 E8
Low Green **3** BD7 .... 74 A3
Low Green Terr BD7 .... 74 A3
Low Hall Cl LS29 .... 22 A4
Low Hall Pl LS11 .... 211 D2
Low Hall Rd Menston LS29 . 22 A4
  Yeadon LS18 .... 57 E8
Low Hill BD17 .... 38 D3
Low Hills La HD3 .... 135 A1
Low House Dr BD20 .... 17 E8
Low House Fold WF15 ..... 116 F4
Low La Batley WF17 .... 96 F1
  Bradford BD14 .... 73 B4
  Brighouse HD6 .... 115 C6
  Draughton BD23 .... 1 E6
  Halton East BD23 .... 1 B8
  Halton East BD23 .... 1 B8
  Horsforth LS18 .... 41 D1
  Netherton WF4 .... 158 B8
  Queensbury BD13 .... 72 C3
  Silsden BD20 .... 18 A6
  Silsden, Silsden Moor BD20 . 5 C5

Low La continued
  Thornton BD14 .... 73 A5
  Wadsworth Moor HX2 .... 90 A7
Low Laithes Golf Course
  WF5 .... 141 B7
Low Mill La
  Addingham LS29 .... 7 B8
  Dewsbury WF13 .... 138 E4
  Keighley BD21 .... 35 D7
Low Mill Rd WF5 .... 140 C3
Low Mills Rd LS12 .... 78 B4
Low Moor CE First Sch
  BD12 .... 94 E6
Low Moor Cres WF4 .... 159 F3
Low Moor La WF4 .... 159 E1
Low Moor Side LS12 .... 77 D3
Low Moor Side La LS12 ..... 77 C2
Low Moor St BD12 .... 94 D6
Low Moor Terr HX2 .... 112 D7
Low Moorside LS12 .... 77 E3
Low Moorside Ct LS12 ...... 77 D3
Low Park Rd LS29 .... 9 B5
Low Platt La HD3 .... 151 B5
Low Rd
  Dewsbury, Dewsbury Moor
  WF13 .... 138 F8
  Dewsbury, Earlsheaton
  WF12 .... 139 E7
  Dewsbury, Overthorpe
  WF13 .... 139 C1
  Huddersfield HD4 .... 171 F8
  Leeds LS10 .... 215 F3
Low Row S75 .... 177 E3
Low Shops La LS26 .... 100 C6
Low Spring Rd BD21 .... 35 F6
Low St Brotherton WF11 ... 126 C7
  Dewsbury WF13 .... 118 C1
  East Ardsley WF3 .... 120 A1
  Keighley BD21 .... 35 C7
Low Town HD8 .... 173 F6
Low Way Boston Spa LS23 ... 30 D6
  Bramham LS23 .... 30 D2
Low Well Rd **5** BD5 .... 74 D3
Low Whitehouse Row
  LS10 .... 212 A1
Low Wood BD15 .... 53 D4
Low Wood Ct BD20 .... 18 B3
Low Wood Rise LS29 .... 8 F3
Lowcroft LS22 .... 29 A8
Lowdale WF12 .... 118 E2
Lowell Ave BD7 .... 73 F5
Lowell Gr LS13 .... 77 A8
Lowell Pl LS13 .... 77 A8
Lower Ashgrove BD5 .... 74 D6
Lower Back La HX7 .... 87 F4
Lower Bank House HX4 ... 133 D4
Lower Bankhouse LS28 ...... 76 D4
Lower Basinghall St LS1 .. 211 E3
Lower Bentley Royd HX6 . 112 A4
Lower Bower La **1** HX17 . 117 F2
Lower Brockwell La HX6 .. 111 F2
Lower Brunswick St LS2 . 207 D1
Lower Calderbrook OL15 . 129 C1
Lower Cambridge St
  WF10 .... 124 E8
Lower Clay Pits HX1 .... 202 B4
Lower Clifton St HX6 .... 112 C4
Lower Clyde St HX6 .... 112 B3
Lower Common La HD8 .... 175 E1
Lower Constable Rd LS29 ... 8 D3
Lower Cross St
  1 Dewsbury WF13 .... 118 C1
  Halifax HX1 .... 203 F3
Lower Crow Nest Dr HX3 . 115 B7
Lower Denby La HD8 .... 192 B4
Lower Edge Rd
  Brighouse HD6 .... 135 D7
  Elland HX5 .... 135 D7
Lower Exley HX3 .... 113 D1
Lower Fields Middle Sch
  BD4 .... 75 C4
Lower Finkil St HD6 .... 114 F5
Lower Fitzwilliam St **4**
  HD1 .... 154 B7
Lower Fold Brighouse HD6 . 135 F6
  Halifax HX1 .... 203 E3
  Honley HD7 .... 171 F5
Lower Furney Lee OL14 .... 108 A6
Lower George St
  3 Bradford BD6 .... 74 B1
  6 Todmorden OL14 ...... 108 C5
Lower Globe St BD8 .... 74 C8
Lower Grange HD2 .... 136 E6
Lower Grange Cl BD8 .... 73 C7
Lower Grattan Rd **1** BD1 . 74 D7
Lower Greave Rd HD7 ..... 188 B8
Lower Green BD17 .... 38 B2
Lower Green Ave **1**
  BD19 .... 115 F8
Lower Hagg HD7 .... 172 B1
Lower Hall Cres WF15 ..... 116 F4
Lower Hall Cl HD5 .... 154 D3
Lower Hall Dr WF15 .... 116 F4
Lower Hall Mount WF15 .. 116 F4
Lower Hall Rd HD5 .... 155 C6
Lower Haughs HD7 .... 152 B5
Lower Heights Rd BD13 .... 72 C8
Lower Hey HD7 .... 170 D2
Lower Highfield HX2 .... 91 A3
Lower Holme Baildon BD17 . 38 C1
  Honley HD7 .... 172 C2
Lower House Cl BD10 .... 55 F8
Lower House La HD8 .... 156 B2
Lower Kipping La **18** BD13 . 72 D6

Lower Kirkgate HX1 .... 203 F3
Lower La Birkenshaw BD4 ... 95 D5
  Blackshaw Head HX7 .... 87 B3
  Bradford BD4 .... 75 C4
  Cleckheaton BD19 .... 117 B7
  Honley HD7 .... 171 E4
Lower Laith Ave OL14 ..... 108 C5
Lower Langwith LS22 .... 29 A8
Lower Lark Hill BD19 ...... 116 B7
Lower Maythorn La HD7 . 200 D8
Lower Meadows HD7 .... 188 D5
Lower Mickletown LS26 ... 102 F3
Lower Mill Bank Rd HX6 . 132 D7
Lower Newlands HD6 .... 115 B3
Lower North St WF17 ...... 118 B4
Lower Northcroft WF9 .... 183 A3
Lower Northfield La WF9 . 182 C3
Lower Oxford St WF10 .... 124 D7
Lower Park Gn BD10 .... 5 C1
Lower Park Royd Dr HX6 . 132 E6
Lower Peel St WF13 .... 118 C1
Lower Putting Mill HD8 .. 192 B7
Lower Quarry Rd
  HD5 .... 137 A6
Lower Range **3** HX3 .... 92 C1
Lower Rayleigh St BD4 ...... 75 A5
Lower Rd HX4 .... 150 F5
Lower Reins HD7 .... 172 A6
Lower Rushton Rd BD3 ...... 75 E7
Lower Sandhills LS14 .... 45 E3
Lower Scholes BD22 .... 50 F8
Lower School St
  Bradford BD10 .... 94 C6
  3 Shipley BD18 .... 54 F8
Lower Skircoat Gn HX3 ... 113 C2
Lower Smithy HX7 .... 88 A5
Lower Swift Pl HX6 .... 132 B2
Lower Taythes La WF8 ..... 126 A1
Lower Town Bradford BD5 . 74 C4
Lower Town End Rd HD7 . 189 C7
Lower Town St LS13 .... 58 D2
Lower Viaduct St **2** HD1 . 154 B7
Lower Warrengate WF1 ... 216 C2
Lower Wellgate **8** HX4 . 134 C2
Lower Wellhouse Rd HD7 . 152 D3
Lower Wellington Rd LS29 ... 8 B4
Lower Westfield Rd BD9 ... 55 A1
Lower Wheat Royd HD5 ... 154 F2
Lower Whitegate Rd HX4 . 154 B3
Lower Wood HX4 .... 131 F1
Lower Wormald
  Primary Sch LS12 .... 78 B4
Lower Wortley Rd LS12 ... 209 E1
Lower Wyke Gn BD12 ...... 115 B8
Lower Wyke La BD12 .... 115 C8
Lower York St WF1 .... 216 B3
Lowerhouses HD7 .... 152 E2
Lowerhouses La HD5 .... 154 D3
Lowerhouses Rd HD3 ...... 153 B6
Lowertown BD22 .... 51 C2
Lowestwood La HD7 .... 152 D2
Loweswater Ave BD6 .... 93 F6
Loweswater Rd WF11 ...... 126 E2
Lowfield Cl BD10 .... 3 A4
Lowfield Cres **3** 118 F8
Lowfields Bsns Pk HX5 .... 135 A8
Lowfields Cl HX5 .... 135 A8
Lowfields Rd LS11 .... 213 E4
Lowfields Way HX5 .... 135 A8
Lowlands Rd WF14 .... 138 B4
Lowood La WF17 .... 96 F3
Lowry Rd WF3 .... 99 E8
Lowry View **6** BD21 .... 35 C6
Lowther Ave LS25 .... 82 E6
Lowther Cres LS26 .... 82 A2
Lowther Dr LS25 .... 82 E6
Lowther Gr LS25 .... 82 E6
Lowther Rd LS25 .... 82 E6
Lowther St Bradford BD2 ... 56 B2
  Leeds LS8 .... 207 F4
Lowther Terr LS25 .... 82 A6
Lowtown LS28 .... 76 F8

Lowtown Junior
  & Infants Sch LS28 .... 76 F7
Loxley St WF17 .... 118 A7
Loxley Gr LS22 .... 13 D8
Lucas Ct SM6 .... 206 C3
Lucas Pl LS6 .... 206 A4
Lucas St LS6 .... 206 A4
Luck La HD1, HD3 .... 153 D6
Ludgate Hill LS2 .... 211 F3
Lucy Hall Dr BD17 .... 37 F3
Lucy La HD4 .... 155 E5
Luddenden Dene CE Jun
  & Inf Sch HX2 .... 111 D8
Luddenden La HX2 .... 111 D7
Luddendenfoot Junior
  & Infants Sch HX2 .... 111 E5
Luddenden Pl **3** BD13 ... 72 C2
Luddenden Rd **8** WF15 . 117 A5
Ludhill La HD4 .... 172 D5
Ludlam St BD5 .... 201 B1
Ludlow Ave LS25 .... 83 B7
Ludolf Dr LS17 .... 44 E4
Ludwell Cl WF12 .... 139 F1
Ludwood Cl HD7 .... 172 B5
Lugard Rd BD3 .... 75 D8
Luke La Holmfirth HD7 .... 172 C1
  Honley HD7 .... 172 C1
Luke Rd BD5 .... 74 C4

Lulworth Ave LS15 .... 81 D8
Lulworth Cl **1** LS15 .... 62 D1
Lulworth Cres LS15 .... 62 D1
Lulworth Dr LS15 .... 81 D8
Lulworth Garth LS15 .... 81 D8
Lulworth Gr BD4 .... 75 D2
Lulworth View LS15 .... 81 D8
Lulworth Wlk LS15 .... 62 D1
Lumb Bottom BD11 .... 96 F7
Lumb Foot BD22 .... 50 E7
Lumb Gill La LS29 .... 7 B6
Lumb Hole Waterfall HX7 ... 69 A3
Lumb La Bradford BD8 .... 74 D8
  Halifax, Boothtown HX2 ... 202 B1
  Halifax, Wainstalls HX3 ...... 90 F6
  Huddersfield HD4 .... 172 D8
  Liversedge WF15 .... 116 F2
  Sowerby Bridge HX6 .... 132 C7
Lumb Rd HX7 .... 88 D5
Lumb Terr HX2 .... 90 F6
Lumbfoot Rd BD22 .... 50 F7
Lumbrook Cl HX3 .... 93 C2
Lumbrook Cl HX3 .... 93 C3
Lumbutts La OL14 .... 108 F4
Lumbutts Rd OL14 .... 108 E3
Lumby Cl LS25 .... 76 F5
Lumby Leys La LS25 .... 105 A8
Lumby St BD10 .... 56 B8
Lumley Ave
  Castleford WF10 .... 124 A7
  Leeds LS4 .... 205 D3
Lumley Gr LS4 .... 205 D3
Lumley Hill WF10 .... 124 A7
Lumley Mount
  Castleford WF10 .... 124 A6
  Leeds LS4 .... 205 D3
Lumley Mount Bglws
  HD8 .... 124 A6
Lumley Pl LS4 .... 205 D3
Lumley Rd Batley WF12 ... 118 E2
Lumley St Castleford WF10 . 124 B7
  Leeds LS4 .... 205 D3
Lumley Terr LS4 .... 205 D3
Lumley View LS4 .... 205 D3
Lumley Wlk LS4 .... 205 D3
Lunan Pl LS8 .... 207 F4
Lunan Terr LS8 .... 207 F4
Lund Dr WF16 .... 117 E3
Lund Hill La Royston S71 . 179 F5
  Ryhill S71 .... 179 F5
Lund La BD22 .... 34 B6
Lund St Bingley BD16 .... 36 F3
  Bradford BD8 .... 55 C8
Lunnfields La LS25, WF11 . 105 C4
Lupset Cres WF2 .... 141 E3
Lupton Ave LS9 .... 208 B1
Lupton Flats **1** LS6 .... 55 E1
  Leeds LS10 .... 215 E3
Lupton's Bldgs LS12 .... 209 E3
Lustre St BD21 .... 35 A7
Luther Pl HD2 .... 153 E8
Luther St LS13 .... 57 E5
Luther Way BD2 .... 55 F1
Luton St Halifax HX1 .... 202 B3
  Huddersfield HD4 .... 152 F3
  Keighley BD21 .... 35 B7
Luttrell Cl LS16 .... 42 A2
Luttrell Cres LS16 .... 42 A2
Luttrell Gdns LS16 .... 42 A2
Luttrell Pl LS16 .... 42 A2
Luttrell Rd LS16 .... 42 A2
Lutyens The LS29 .... 7 F4
Luxor Ave LS8 .... 207 F4
Luxor Rd LS8 .... 207 F4
Luxor St LS8 .... 207 F4
Luxor View LS8 .... 207 F4
Lydbrook Pk HX3 .... 113 A2
Lyddon Terr LS2 .... 206 A2
Lydford Ho **7** BD5 .... 201 B1
Lydgate Leeds LS9 .... 207 F1
  Northowram HX3 .... 93 A3
Lydgate Cl HD7 .... 189 D6
Lydgate Dr Holmfirth HD7 . 189 D7
  Lepton HD8 .... 156 A3
Lydgate Jun & Inf Sch
  WF17 .... 118 F5
Lydgate Pk HX3 .... 114 E7
Lydgate Pl LS28 .... 57 A7
Lydgate Rd Batley WF17 . 118 F5
  Shepley HD8 .... 190 F8
Lydgate Sch HD7 .... 189 D7
Lydgate St LS28 .... 57 A7
Lydget Ct BD20 .... 18 A2
Lydgetts HD7 .... 188 D5
Lydia St LS2 .... 212 A4
Lyme Chase LS14 .... 61 F2
Lyme Terr DN6 .... 184 E1
Lymington Dr BD4 .... 75 E3
Lynch Ave **3** BD7 .... 73 F3
Lyncroft BD2 .... 55 F4
Lynda Gr WF5 .... 141 A4
Lyndale LS25 .... 103 A8
Lyndale Cres WF16 .... 117 A4
Lyndale Dr Shipley BD18 .. 55 F7
  Wakefield WF2 .... 120 E2
Lyndale Gr WF10 .... 123 C1
Lyndale Mews WF11 .... 105 D1
Lyndale Rd BD16 .... 37 C5
Lynden Ave BD18 .... 54 E8
Lyndean Gdns BD10 .... 56 A7
Lynden Ct BD5 .... 74 C2
Lyndhurst Ave HD6 .... 136 A7

Lyndhurst Cl LS15 .... 62 F7
Lyndhurst Cres LS15 ...... 62 F7
Lyndhurst Gr BD15 .... 54 C1
Lyndhurst Grove Rd HD6 .. 136 A7
Lyndhurst Rd
  Barwick in E LS15 .... 62 F6
  Brighouse HD6 .... 136 A8
  Huddersfield HD3 .... 153 B8
Lyndhurst View LS15 .... 62 F6
Lyndon Ave Bramham LS23 ... 30 C3
  Garforth LS25 .... 82 E7
Lyndon Cl LS23 .... 30 C3
Lyndon Cres LS23 .... 30 C3
Lyndon Rd LS23 .... 30 C3
Lyndon Sq LS23 .... 30 C3
Lyndon Terr 3 BD16 .... 37 A3
Lyndon Way LS23 .... 30 C3
Lyndum Gr LS25 .... 83 A2
Lyndum Rd Dr Bradford BD9 ... 54 C3
  Cleckheaton WF15 .... 116 B5
Lynfield Mount BD18 .... 55 E8
Lynfield Mount Hosp BD9 .. 54 D2
Lynndale Ave
  Glusburn BD20 .... 16 D7
  Huddersfield HD2 .... 135 F1
Lynnfield Gdns LS15 .... 62 F6
Lynnwood Gdns LS28 .... 76 C7
Lynsey Gdns BD4 .... 95 B7
Lynthorne Rd BD9 .... 55 C4
Lynton Ave Boston Spa LS23 ... 30 D8
  Bradford BD9 .... 54 F2
  Huddersfield HD1 .... 153 F6
  Middleton WF3 .... 99 E2
Lynton Dr Bradford BD9 ..... 54 F2
  Keighley BD20 .... 18 F1
  Shipley BD18 .... 55 A7
Lynton Gr Bradford BD9 ..... 54 F2
  Halifax HX2 .... 71 F1
Lynton Terr 5 BD19 .... 116 D8
Lynton Villas BD9 .... 54 F2
Lynwood Ave Leeds LS12 ... 209 F1
  Rothwell LS26 .... 101 D6
  Shipley BD18 .... 55 E8
Lynwood Cl
  Birkenshaw BD11 .... 96 B4
  Featherstone WF7 .... 144 E4
  Knottingley WF11 .... 127 A5
Lynwood Cres Halifax HX1 .. 202 B1
  Hemsworth WF9 .... 163 A4
  Leeds LS12 .... 209 F1
  Pontefract WF8 .... 146 D6
  Rothwell LS26 .... 101 D6
Lynwood Ct Bradford BD10 .. 56 A7
  Keighley BD22 .... 34 E5
Lynwood Dr Royston S71 ... 179 C2
  Wakefield WF2 .... 160 C6
Lynwood Garth LS12 .... 209 F1
Lynwood Gr LS12 .... 78 C4
Lynwood La S71 .... 179 C2
Lynwood Mews BD4 .... 75 F2
Lynwood Mount LS12 .... 209 F1
Lynwood Rise LS12 .... 209 F1
Lynwood View LS12 .... 209 F1
Lyon Rd Pontefract WF8 ... 146 D6
  Steeton BD20 .... 17 C5
Lyon St Queensbury BD13 .. 72 F1
  Thornton BD13 .... 72 D7
Lytham Cl WF6 .... 123 D1
Lytham Dr BD13 .... 73 B2
Lytham Gr LS12 .... 78 A4
Lytham Pl LS12 .... 78 A4
Lytham St HX1 .... 202 B3
Lytham Way HD3 .... 153 B8
Lytton Rd BD8 .... 73 F8
Lytton St LS10 .... 215 D3

Mabel Royd BD7 .... 73 F5
Mabel St HX7 .... 89 E1
Mabgate LS9 .... 212 A4
Mabgate Gn LS9 .... 212 A4
Mabgate Mills Ind Ctr
  LS9 .... 207 E1
Macaulay Rd HD1 .... 135 F1
Macaulay St LS9 .... 207 E1
Macham St HD1 .... 153 F4
Mackey Cres LS21 .... 11 D4
Mackie Hill Cl WF4 .... 159 D4
Mackie Hill Jun & Inf Sch
  WF4 .... 159 D4
Mafeking Ave LS11 .... 214 A1
Mafeking Gr LS11 .... 214 A1
Mafeking Mount LS11 ..... 214 A1
Magdale Rd HD7 .... 187 C6
Magdalen Cl LS15 .... 42 A3
Magdalene Fields WF6 .... 144 D8
Magdalene Rd WF2 .... 141 D5
Magna Gr WF2 .... 142 E1
Magnolia Cl S27 .... 180 D2
Magnolia Dr BD15 .... 53 F4
Magnolia House 1 WF10 .. 124 E7
Magpie La LS27 .... 98 C3
Maidstone St BD3 .... 75 C7
Mail Cl LS15 .... 62 E3
Main Ave HD4 .... 152 F3

Main Gate HD7 .... 189 E2
Main Rd Denholme BD13 .... 71 D8
  Farnhill BD20 .... 16 E8
  Keighley BD20 .... 36 D8
  Steeton BD20 .... 16 F6
Main St Aberford LS25 ...... 64 E7
  Addingham LS29 .... 6 E8
  Badsworth WF9 .... 164 E2
  Barwick in E LS15 .... 63 D7
  Barwick in E, Scholes LS15 .. 62 F6
  Bingley BD16 .... 36 F3
  2 Bradford, Carr House Gate
    BD12 .... 94 C4
  Bradford, Wesley Place
    BD12 .... 94 E6
  Burley in W LS29 .... 9 F1
  Burton Salmon LS25 ..... 105 E3
  Collingham LS22 .... 29 B8
  Collingham, Linton LS22 .. 13 C2
  Cononley BD20 .... 4 A2
  East Ardsley WF3 .... 120 D7
  East Keswick LS17 .... 28 C5
  Farnhill BD20 .... 4 D2
  Garforth LS25 .... 82 E7
  Guiseley, Esholt BD17 ..... 39 C5
  Guiseley, Hawksworth LS20 .. 38 F8
  Hampole DN6 .... 184 B1
  Haworth BD22 .... 51 C7
  Haworth, Stanbury BD22 .. 50 D7
  Kippax WF10 .... 103 B4
  Kirk Smeaton WF8 .... 166 D6
  Ledston WF10 .... 103 E6
  Low Bradley BD20 .... 4 C5
  Menston LS29 .... 22 A4
  Mickletown LS26 .... 102 D3
  Monk Fryston LS25 .... 105 F8
  Pool LS21 .... 24 C7
  Rothwell WF3 .... 100 B6
  Shipley BD16 .... 54 B6
  Sicklinghall LS22 .... 12 C5
  South Hiendley S72 ...... 180 D6
  Sutton in CB BD20 .... 16 D5
  Tadcaster LS24 .... 31 E7
  Thorner LS14 .... 45 F5
  Thorner, Shadwell LS17 .. 44 E4
  Thorp Arch LS23 .... 15 A4
  Upton WF9 .... 183 D8
  Wilsden BD15 .... 53 C5
Mainspring Rd BD15 .... 53 C5
Maister Pl BD22 .... 34 B3
Maitland Cl Bradford BD15 .. 73 B7
  Todmorden OL14 .... 129 A8
Maitland Pl LS11 .... 214 A4
Maitland St OL14 .... 129 A8
Maize St 8 BD21 .... 35 A4
Maizebrook WF16 .... 117 F1
Major St Todmorden OL14 .. 108 C5
  Wakefield WF2 .... 142 B3
Makin St WF2 .... 142 A5
Malais La BD20 .... 16 A5
Malham Ave Bradford BD9 .. 54 C3
  Brighouse HD6 .... 135 E8
Malham Cl Leeds LS14 ..... 62 A4
  Shafton S72 .... 180 C3
Malham Dr Batley WF17 .. 118 A5
  Liversedge WF15 .... 116 F1
Malham Rd Brighouse HD6 .. 135 E7
  Wakefield WF2 .... 142 F7
Malham Sq WF1 .... 142 F7
Mallard Ave WF3 .... 142 A5
Mallard Cl 1 BD8 .... 73 C7
Mallard Rd WF10 .... 124 C6
Mallard View BD22 .... 51 C2
Mallard Way
  2 Morley LS27 .... 98 D4
  Slaithwaite HD7 .... 169 F8
Mallards The BD20 .... 5 E1
Mallinson St WF13 .... 118 A1
Mallory Cl BD7 .... 73 F6
Malmesbury Cl
  Bradford BD4 .... 75 E1
  Leeds LS12 .... 209 F2
Malmesbury Gr LS12 ...... 209 F2
Malmesbury Pl LS12 ...... 209 F2
Malmesbury St LS12 ...... 209 F2
Malmesbury Terr LS12 .... 209 F2
Malsis Cres BD21 .... 35 A6
Malsis Rd BD21 .... 35 B5
Malt Kiln Croft WF2 .... 142 E1
Malt Kiln La
  2 Kippax LS25 .... 83 B1
  Thornton BD13 .... 72 C5
Malt St 8 BD22 .... 51 C8
Maltby Cl LS15 .... 81 D7
Malthouse Cl LS14 .... 45 C8
Malting Cl WF3 .... 100 B3
Malting Rise WF3 .... 100 B3
Maltings Cl LS11 .... 214 C4
Maltings Rd Halifax HX2 .. 91 D2
  Leeds LS11 .... 214 C3
Maltings The
  Cleckheaton BD19 .... 116 C8
  Leeds LS6 .... 205 E2
  Mirfield WF14 .... 137 F5
  Pontefract WF8 .... 125 D1
  Rothwell WF3 .... 100 B3
Maltkiln Dr WF4 .... 176 F8
Maltkiln La WF10 .... 124 E8
Malton Rd WF9 .... 183 D8
Malton St
  Halifax, Woodlands HX3 .. 92 C2
  7 Sowerby Bridge HX6 .. 112 B5
Malvern Brow BD9 .... 54 D2
Malvern Cl WF10 .... 123 F5
Malvern Cres BD20 .... 18 E3

Malvern Gr Bradford BD9 .. 54 D1
  Leeds LS11 .... 214 B4
Malvern Rd Bradford BD9 .. 54 D2
  Dewsbury WF12 .... 118 F1
  Huddersfield HD4 .... 154 B4
  Knottingley WF11 .... 126 E4
  Leeds LS11 .... 214 A4
Malvern Rise
  Huddersfield HD4 .... 154 B3
  Leeds LS11 .... 214 A4
Malvern St LS11 .... 214 A4
Malvern View LS11 .... 214 A4
Manchester Rd
  Bradford BD5 .... 74 D3
  Huddersfield HD4 .... 153 C4
  Marsden HD7 .... 168 B3
Manchester Rd Marsden
  HD7 .... 168 E4
Manchester Rd
  (Slaithwaite) HD7 .... 170 A8
Manchester Road
  Clough Head HD7 .... 168 C4
Manchester Road
  (Linthwaite) HD7 .... 152 D1
Manchester Sq LS21 ...... 23 A8
Mandale Gr BD6 .... 93 D8
Mandale Middle Sch BD6 .. 93 D8
Mandale Rd BD6 .... 93 D1
Mandarin Way LS10 .... 99 F7
Mandela Ct LS7 .... 204 A1
Mandeville Cres BD6 .... 93 F8
Mangrill La LS14 .... 46 E6
Manitoba Pl LS7 .... 204 A2
Mankinholes Bank OL14 .. 108 F3
Manley Ct LS25 .... 82 F5
Manley Dr LS22 .... 13 C6
Manley Gr LS29 .... 8 D4
Manley Rd LS29 .... 8 E4
Manley Rise LS29 .... 8 D3
Manley St HD6 .... 115 A3
Mann's Bldgs WF17 .... 97 B2
Mannheim Rd BD9 .... 55 B2
Manningham La BD1, BD8 .. 55 D1
Manningham Middle Sch
  BD8 .... 55 C1
Mannville Gr BD22 .... 35 A6
Mannville Pl 16 BD22 ...... 35 A6
Mannville Rd BD22 .... 35 A6
Mannville St 18 BD22 ..... 35 A6
Mannville Terr BD7 .... 74 D6
Mannville Way 14 BD22 .. 35 A6
Mannville Wlk 15 BD22 ... 35 A6
Manor Ave Leeds LS6 ..... 205 E4
  Ossett WF5 .... 140 F3
Manor Cl
  Badsworth WF9 .... 164 E2
  Birkenshaw BD11 .... 96 E7
  Bradford BD8 .... 73 D8
  Bramhope LS16 .... 24 D3
  Halifax HX2 .... 113 B4
  Kirk Smeaton WF8 ...... 166 D5
  Notton WF4 .... 178 F7
  Ossett WF5 .... 140 F3
  Rothwell LS26 .... 100 E6
  Yeadon LS19 .... 40 B7
Manor Cres Pool LS21 ... 24 C7
  Rothwell LS26 .... 100 D5
  Wakefield WF2 .... 141 E4
  Walton WF2 .... 161 A8
Manor Croft
  Hebden Bridge HX7 ...... 89 B3
  Leeds LS15 .... 81 C7
  South Hiendley S72 .... 180 D6
Manor Ct Fairburn WF11 .. 105 A4
  Leeds LS15 .... 81 C7
  Ossett WF5 .... 140 F3
  Otley LS21 .... 23 A8
  3 Shipley BD16 .... 54 A7
  Thorner LS17 .... 44 F4
Manor Dr Crofton WF4 ... 162 A7
  Featherstone WF7 ...... 124 C1
  Flockton WF4 .... 157 D3
  Halifax HX3 .... 113 B4
  Hebden Bridge HX7 ..... 89 B3
  Leeds LS6 .... 205 E4
  Mirfield WF14 .... 137 D7
  Ossett WF5 .... 140 F3
  Royston S71 .... 179 B3
  Shipley BD16 .... 54 B7
  Skelmanthorpe HD8 .... 175 A1
  South Hiendley S72 .... 180 D6
Manor Farm Cl WF9 ...... 164 E2
Manor Farm Cres
  Featherstone WF7 ...... 124 C1
  Leeds LS10 .... 99 D6
Manor Farm Ct WF4 ...... 159 E4
Manor Farm Dr
  Batley WF17 .... 118 F5
  Leeds LS10 .... 99 D6
  Morley LS27 .... 98 C8
Manor Farm Est WF9 ..... 183 A3
Manor Farm Gdns LS10 .. 99 C6
Manor Farm Gn LS10 ..... 99 C6
Manor Farm Gr LS10 ..... 99 C6
Manor Farm Rd
  Crigglestone WF4 .... 159 E4
  Leeds LS10 .... 99 D6
Manor Farm Rise LS10 ... 99 D6
Manor Farm Way LS10 .. 99 D6
Manor Farm Wlk LS10 ... 99 D6
Manor Fold 6 BD10 ...... 54 B6
Manor Garth
  Ledsham LS25 .... 104 D8
  Leeds LS15 .... 81 C7
  Walton WF2 .... 161 A8
Manor Garth Rd
  Dewsbury WF12 .... 139 F7
  Kippax LS25 .... 83 B2

Manor Gdns Batley WF12 .. 119 A2
  Cullingworth BD13 .... 52 D5
  Pool LS21 .... 24 C7
  Thorner LS14 .... 46 A6
Manor Gr Castleford WF10 .. 124 E5
  Leeds LS6 .... 204 A2
  Ossett WF5 .... 140 F3
  Royston S71 .... 179 B3
  South Kirkby WF9 .... 182 A1
Manor High Rd WF2 .... 141 E4
Manor Heath Rd HX3 .... 113 B4
Manor House 3 WF1 ...... 216 C2
Manor House Bglws
  WF11 .... 126 F5
Manor House Croft LS16 .. 42 D3
Manor House La LS17 .... 43 F7
Manor House Mus & Art Gal
  LS29 .... 8 B4
Manor House Rd BD15 ... 53 C6
Manor House St 5 LS28 .. 76 E7
Manor La Ossett WF5 .... 140 F3
  Shipley BD18 .... 55 B7
Manor Mill La LS11 ...... 213 E1
Manor Occupation Rd
  S71 .... 179 B4
Manor Park Ave
  Kippax WF10 .... 103 B5
  Pontefract WF8 .... 125 F3
Manor Park Gdns BD13 .. 96 B3
Manor Park Rd LS29 ..... 22 A4
Manor Park Way HD8 ... 155 D2
Manor Pk Batley WF12 ... 119 B3
  Bradford BD6 .... 73 D8
  Darrington WF8 .... 147 D5
  Ledston WF10 .... 103 E6
  Mirfield WF14 .... 137 D7
  Oakworth BD22 .... 34 C2
  Scarcroft LS14 .... 45 C7
Manor Pl 1 WF4 .... 141 A1
Manor Rd Batley WF17 .. 118 F5
  Beal DN14 .... 127 F6
  Clayton West HD8 ...... 176 A4
  Dearne S63 .... 194 C1
  Dewsbury WF13 .... 139 B7
  Horbury WF4 .... 141 A1
  Horsforth LS18 .... 58 A8
  Huddersfield HD7 .... 152 D4
  Keighley BD20 .... 18 A2
  Kirkburton HD4 .... 172 F6
  Leeds LS11 .... 211 E2
  Morley LS27 .... 98 B5
  Ossett WF5 .... 140 F4
  Rothwell LS26 .... 100 D6
  Shipley BD16 .... 54 B7
  Wakefield WF2 .... 141 F5
  Walton WF2 .... 161 A7
Manor Rise
  Huddersfield HD4 ...... 154 B4
  Ilkley LS29 .... 8 D4
  Skelmanthorpe HD8 ... 175 A1
  Walton WF2 .... 161 A8
Manor Sq Otley LS21 ... 23 A8
  8 Yeadon LS19 .... 40 B7
Manor St Bradford BD2 .. 56 B3
  Brighouse BD19 .... 115 F6
  Dewsbury WF12 .... 139 D8
  Huddersfield HD4 ...... 154 B4
  Leeds LS7 .... 207 D2
  Otley LS21 .... 23 A8
Manor Terr Bradford BD2 .. 56 B3
  Kippax LS25 .... 83 B1
  Leeds LS6 .... 205 E4
Manor View
  Castleford WF10 .... 124 E5
  Leeds LS6 .... 205 E4
  Pudsey LS28 .... 76 E7
  Shafton S72 .... 180 C2
Manor Way Batley WF17 .. 118 A4
  Sutton in C BD20 .... 16 C5
Manorcroft WF6 .... 123 B2
Manorfield LS11 .... 213 F3
Manorfield Dr WF4 ...... 141 A2
Manorfield Inf Sch
  WF17 .... 118 A4
Manorfields Ave WF4 .... 162 A8
Manorfields Ct WF4 ..... 162 A8
Manorley La BD6 .... 93 E6
Manorstead HD8 .... 175 A1
Manscombe Rd BD15 .... 54 C1
Manse Cres LS29 .... 9 E1
Manse Dr HD4 .... 153 A3
Manse Rd LS29 .... 9 E1
Manse St BD3 .... 75 C7
Manse Way BD20 .... 16 D6
Mansel Mews BD4 .... 75 E2
Mansfield Ave BD16 .... 37 C5
Mansfield Pl LS6 .... 59 D6
Mansfield Rd Bradford BD8 .. 55 C2
  Burley in W LS29 .... 9 E1
Mansion Gdns HD4 ..... 153 F1
Mansion La LS8 .... 44 B1
Manston App LS15 ...... 62 C3
Manston Ave LS15 ...... 62 C3
Manston Cres LS15 ..... 62 C3
Manston Dr LS15 .... 62 C3
Manston Gdns LS15 .... 62 D3
Manston Gn LS15 .... 62 D3
Manston Gr LS15 .... 62 C2
Manston La LS15 .... 62 E2
Manston Rise LS15 ..... 62 D3
Manston Terr 4 LS15 .. 62 D3
Manston Towers 3 LS14 .. 62 D4

Manston Way LS15 .... 62 C3
Manygates Ave WF1 ..... 142 D3
Manygates Cres WF1 .... 142 D3
Manygates Ct WF1 ...... 142 D3
Manygates La WF1, WF2 .. 142 D2
Manygates Pk WF1 ...... 142 D3
Manywells Brow BD13 .. 52 C4
Manywells Cres BD13 .. 52 B5
Manywells La BD13 ..... 52 B5
Maple Ave Bradford BD3 .. 75 E8
  Huddersfield HD7 ...... 152 F5
  Oakworth BD22 .... 34 D2
  Pontefract WF8 .... 146 C5
Maple Cl Castleford WF10 .. 124 B5
  Kirkheaton HD5 .... 137 C1
Maple Croft
  Leeds, Farnley LS12 .... 77 D5
  Leeds, Moortown LS17 .. 43 C7
Maple Ct Leeds LS11 ... 213 F2
  Ossett WF5 .... 140 E3
Maple Dr Leeds LS11 ... 77 D5
  Pontefract WF8 .... 146 D6
  Wetherby LS22 .... 13 E7
Maple Fold LS12 .... 77 D5
Maple Gr Cleckheaton BD19 .. 96 A1
  Gildersome LS12 .... 77 D5
  Huddersfield HD2 .... 136 A5
  Keighley BD20 .... 18 A1
  Normanton WF6 .... 144 A7
  Pontefract WF8 .... 146 D5
Maple Rd Dewsbury WF12 .. 140 B7
  Mapplewell S75 .... 178 A1
Maple Rise LS26 .... 100 F4
Maple St 7 Halifax HX1 .. 202 B1
  Huddersfield HD5 ...... 154 C5
  Todmorden OL14 .... 129 A7
  Wakefield WF2 .... 141 F8
Maple Terr LS19 .... 39 F7
Maple Way LS14 .... 62 C8
Maple Wlk
  Dewsbury WF12 .... 140 B7
  Knottingley WF11 ..... 126 E3
Maplin Ave HD3 .... 134 F1
Maplin Dr 9 HD3 .... 134 F1
Mapplewell Cres WF5 .. 140 E5
Mapplewell Dr WF5 .... 140 E5
Mapplewell Prim Sch
  S75 .... 178 B1
  Mapplewell S75 .... 178 C1
Marbridge Ct BD6 ..... 74 B2
March Cote La BD16 .. 54 A6
March St WF6 .... 123 A1
Marchant St WF10 .... 124 C8
Marchbank Rd BD3 ... 75 C8
Marchwood Gr BD14 .. 73 D5
Marcus Way HD3 ...... 134 D1
Mardale Cres LS14 ... 62 A3
Mardale Rd WF12 .... 118 E2
Margaret Ave LS17 ... 28 D4
Margaret Cl LS27 ..... 98 B5
Margaret St Halifax HX1 .. 203 D3
  Keighley BD21 .... 35 A8
  Lofthouse Gate WF1 .. 121 A4
  Wakefield WF1 .... 216 A3
Margate 2 LS26 ...... 101 C6
Margate Rd BD4 ..... 75 A4
Margate St HX6 ...... 112 A3
Margerison Cres LS29 .. 8 E3
Margerison Rd BD11 .. 97 A5
Margetson Rd BD11 .. 97 A5
Margram Bans Ctr HX1 .. 203 D4
Maria St LS29 .... 8 B5
Marian Gr 11 LS11 .. 214 B3
Marian Rd LS6 ...... 206 B3
Marian Terr LS6 .... 206 B3
Marie Cl HD5 .... 155 C6
Marina Cres LS27 ... 97 F3
Marina Terr HD7 .... 152 E5
Marine Villa Rd WF11 .. 126 F4
Marion Ave WF4 .... 141 D8
Marion Cl WF9 ..... 182 C2
Marion Dr BD18 .... 55 C7
Marion Gr WF2 ..... 141 D8
Marion St Bingley BD16 .. 37 A3
  Bradford BD7 .... 74 C7
  Brighouse HD6 .... 115 A3
  Marizon Gr VH1 .... 216 C3
Mark Bottoms La HD7 .. 188 F6
Mark Cl BD10 .... 56 C8
Mark La Leeds LS2 .. 211 F4
  Todmorden OL14 .... 108 A7
Mark St Bradford BD5 .. 74 E3
  Huddersfield HD1 ... 153 E5
  Liversedge WF15 ... 117 B4
  Wakefield WF1 ...... 142 C4
Market Ave 9 HD1 ... 154 B6
Market Ct 5 BD13 .. 72 E6
Market Pl
  1 Cleckheaton BD19 .. 116 E7
  Dewsbury WF13 ..... 139 D8
  Huddersfield HD1 ... 154 A6
  Keighley BD21 ...... 35 C7
  Meltham HD7 .... 170 D2
  Normanton WF6 .... 123 A2
  Otley LS21 .... 23 A8
  Pontefract WF8 .... 146 D8
  Pudsey LS28 .... 76 E7
  Slaithwaite HD7 ... 169 F8
  Wetherby LS22 .... 13 E5
Market Shops WF13 .. 123 A2
Market Sq
  5 Batley WF17 ..... 118 C5
  3 Leeds LS14 ...... 62 B5
  Shipley BD18 ...... 55 B7

Market St
Batley, Birstall WF17 ... 96 E1
Batley, Heckmondwike WF16 ... 117 D3
Bingley BD16 ... 36 F3
Bradford BD1 ... 201 B2
Bradford BD1 ... 201 B3
4 Bradford, Brownroyd Hill BD6 ... 74 C1
Brighouse HD6 ... 115 B2
Cleckheaton BD19 ... 116 E7
3 Dewsbury WF13 ... 139 D8
Featherstone WF7 ... 145 C6
Halifax HX1 ... 203 E3
Hebden Bridge HX7 ... 89 A3
Hemsworth WF9 ... 181 D7
Holmfirth HD7 ... 189 A5
Huddersfield HD1 ... 154 A6
Huddersfield, Milnsbridge HD3 ... 153 B5
Huddersfield, Paddock HD1 .. 153 E5
Keighley BD21 ... 35 C7
Normanton WF6 ... 123 A2
Otley LS21 ... 23 A8
Shipley BD18 ... 55 B7
Steeton BD20 ... 17 D5
Thornton BD13 ... 72 E6
Todmorden OL14 ... 108 A3
Wakefield WF1 ... 216 B2
Market St Arc 2 LS1 ... 211 F3
Market Wlk HD7 ... 168 F4
Markfield Ave BD12 ... 94 C5
Markfield Cl BD12 ... 94 C5
Markfield Cres BD12 ... 94 D5
Markfield Dr BD12 ... 94 C5
Markham Ave Leeds LS8 ... 207 F4
Yeadon LS19 ... 40 C5
Markham Cres LS19 ... 40 C5
Markham Croft LS19 ... 40 C5
Markham St Batley WF17 ... 118 B4
Wakefield WF2 ... 142 A6
Markington Mews LS10 ... 99 C3
Markington Pl LS10 ... 99 C3
Marl Pit Hill WF8 ... 146 A6
Marland Rd BD21 ... 35 E8
Marlbeck Cl HD7 ... 171 F3
Marlborough Ave
Byram WF11 ... 126 D7
7 Halifax HX3 ... 113 B4
Marlborough Croft WF9 ... 182 F4
Marlborough Ct LS29 ... 22 B4
Marlborough Gdns
Dewsbury WF13 ... 118 B2
17 Leeds LS2 ... 206 B2
Marlborough Gr
31 Hebden Bridge HX7 ... 89 A3
Ilkley LS29 ... 8 D3
19 Leeds LS2 ... 206 B2
Marlborough Grange
8 LS1 ... 211 D4
Marlborough House
9 HX5 ... 134 F7
Marlborough Rd
Bradford BD8 ... 55 C1
Bradford, Fourlands BD10 ... 56 C8
Hebden Bridge HX7 ... 89 A3
Huddersfield HD2 ... 136 B5
Shipley BD18 ... 55 A7
Marlborough Sq LS29 ... 8 D3
Marlborough St
Keighley BD21 ... 35 D8
Leeds LS1 ... 211 D4
Ossett WF5 ... 140 C5
Wakefield WF2 ... 142 A6
Marlborough Terr HX7 ... 89 A3
Marlborough Towers 7 LS1 ... 211 D4
Marlborough Villas LS29 ... 22 B4
Marlbro' Terr 5 WF13 ... 118 B2
Marldon Rd HX3 ... 93 A1
Marley Cl BD8 ... 73 E8
Marley Ct BD16 ... 36 D7
Marley Gr LS11 ... 213 F3
Marley La BD13 ... 72 E3
Marley Pl LS11 ... 213 F3
Marley Rd BD21 ... 35 F8
Marley St Bradford BD3 ... 201 D3
Keighley BD21 ... 35 C6
Leeds LS11 ... 213 F3
Marley Terr LS11 ... 213 F3
Marley View Bingley BD16 ... 36 D7
Leeds LS11 ... 213 F3
Marling Rd HD2 ... 135 B3
Marlo Rd WF12 ... 119 A2
Marlott Rd BD18 ... 55 E8
Marlow Cl HD5 ... 154 F6
Marlow St BD21 ... 35 E8
Marlowe Cl 3 LS28 ... 76 F5
Marlowe Ct Garforth LS25 ... 82 F7
Guiseley LS20 ... 22 D1
Marlpit La WF8 ... 147 B5
Marmion Ave BD8 ... 73 C7
Marne Ave BD14 ... 73 C3
Marne Cres BD10 ... 56 B7
Marquis Ave BD12 ... 95 B5
Marriner Rd BD21 ... 35 C6
Marriner's Dr BD9 ... 55 B4
Marriner's Wlk BD21 ... 35 C5
Marriot Gr WF2 ... 142 F1
Marsden Ave LS11 ... 214 A2
Marsden Ct 3 LS28 ... 57 D3
Marsden Gate HX4 ... 151 E7
Marsden Golf Club HD7 ... 168 E1
Marsden Gr LS11 ... 214 A2
Marsden Infants Sch HD7 169 A4
Marsden Junior Sch HD7 . 169 A4
Marsden La Marsden HD7 .. 169 A5
Marsden, Booth Naze HD7 ... 169 B7
Marsden Mount LS11 ... 214 A2
Marsden Pl LS11 ... 214 A2
Marsden St HD8 ... 175 A2
Marsden Sta HD7 ... 168 F4
Marsden View LS11 ... 214 A2
Marsett Way LS14 ... 62 B8
Marsh LS28 ... 76 C7
Marsh Croft WF11 ... 126 C7
Marsh Delves HX3 ... 113 F6
Marsh Delves La HX3 ... 113 F6
Marsh End WF11 ... 127 B5
Marsh Gdns HD7 ... 171 F4
Marsh Gr BD5 ... 74 C3
Marsh Grove Rd HD3 ... 153 D8
Marsh Hall La HD4 ... 172 F3
Marsh La Birkenshaw BD11 ... 96 A5
Blackshaw Head HX7 ... 88 B3
Byram WF11 ... 126 F6
Halifax HX3 ... 113 F6
Knottingley WF11 ... 127 B4
Leeds LS9 ... 212 B4
Oxenhope BD22 ... 51 B4
Shepley HD8 ... 190 D7
Marsh Lea Grove WF9 ... 181 F7
Marsh Platt La HD7 ... 172 A5
Marsh Rd Castleford WF10 .. 124 A6
Holmfirth HD7 ... 189 D3
Marsh Rise LS28 ... 76 C7
Marsh St Bradford BD5 ... 74 D3
Cleckheaton BD19 ... 116 E6
Honley HD7 ... 171 F4
Leeds LS6 ... 206 A3
Rothwell LS26 ... 100 F5
Marsh Terr LS28 ... 76 C7
Marsh Vale 3 LS6 ... 206 A3
Marsh Way WF1 ... 216 C3
Marshall Ave
Crigglestone WF4 ... 159 F3
Leeds LS15 ... 62 D2
Marshall Cres LS27 ... 98 B2
Marshall Dr WF9 ... 182 F3
Marshall Mill Ct HD8 ... 175 E1
Marshall St Keighley BD20 ... 18 B1
Leeds LS11 ... 211 E2
Leeds, Cross Gates LS15 ... 62 C2
Lofthouse Gate WF3 ... 121 F5
Mirfield WF14 ... 138 A3
Morley LS27 ... 98 B4
Yeadon LS19 ... 40 B7
Marshall Terr LS15 ... 62 C2
Marsham Gr HD3 ... 153 C7
Marshfield First Sch BD5 ... 74 C2
Marshfield Pl BD5 ... 74 D3
Marshfield St BD5 ... 74 D3
Marshway HX1 ... 202 C4
Marsland Ave WF1 ... 216 C2
Marsland Ct BD19 ... 95 D2
Marsland Pl Bradford BD3 ... 75 D7
Wakefield WF1 ... 216 C2
Marsland St WF1 ... 216 C2
Marsland Terr WF1 ... 216 C2
Marston Ave LS27 ... 98 A3
Marston Cl BD13 ... 72 F1
Marston Ct WF10 ... 124 A6
Marston Mount LS9 ... 207 E1
Marston Way LS22 ... 13 C6
Marston Wlk WF6 ... 122 E4
Marten Dr HD4 ... 171 D7
Marten Gr HD4 ... 171 E7
Marten Rd BD5 ... 74 C3
Martin Bank Wood HD5 ... 154 D5
Martin Cl LS27 ... 98 C4
Martin Ct LS15 ... 81 D8
Martin Frobisher Dr WF6 .. 122 F3
Martin Frobisher First Sch WF6 ... 122 F4
Martin Gr WF2 ... 160 E6
Martin Green La HX4 ... 134 A7
Martin St Batley WF17 ... 96 E1
Brighouse HD6 ... 115 B3
Normanton WF6 ... 144 A8
Martin Terr LS4 ... 59 C2
Martindale Dr LS13 ... 58 E1
Martingale Dr LS10 ... 99 D3
Martlett Dr BD5 ... 74 F2
Marton Ave WF9 ... 181 C6
Marton Ct BD3 ... 75 D7
Marton Heights HX6 ... 112 A5
Marwood Rd LS13 ... 77 E7
Mary Rose Ct WF7 ... 145 C4
Mary St Bradford BD4 ... 75 C5
Bradford, Carr House Gate BD12 ... 94 C4
Brighouse HD6 ... 115 A4
Denholme BD13 ... 52 E1
East Ardsley WF3 ... 120 E8
6 Oxenhope BD22 ... 51 C2
Pudsey LS28 ... 57 E4
Shipley BD18 ... 54 F8
5 Thornton BD13 ... 72 D6
Maryfield Ave LS15 ... 62 A2
Maryfield Cl LS15 ... 62 A2
Maryfield Cres LS15 ... 62 B2
Maryfield Ct 5 LS15 ... 62 B2
Maryfield Gdns LS15 ... 62 A2
Maryfield Gn LS15 ... 62 A2
Maryfield Mews LS15 ... 62 A2
Maryfield Vale 1 LS15 ... 62 A2
Marygate WF1 ... 216 B2
Maryville Ave HD6 ... 114 E5
Masefield Ave BD9 ... 54 C3
Masefield St LS20 ... 39 F8
Masham Gr LS12 ... 210 A3
Masham Pl BD9 ... 54 F2
Masham St LS12 ... 210 A3
Mason Sq HX2 ... 91 F3
Mason St HX7 ... 89 A3
Mason's Green HX2 ... 91 E5
Masonic St HX1 ... 202 A2
Massey Fields BD22 ... 51 D8
Master La HX2 ... 112 F4
Matherville HD8 ... 175 A1
Matheson Ho BD3 ... 201 C4
Matlock St 9 Halifax HX3 ... 92 A1
Huddersfield HD4 ... 153 C4
Matterdale Cl WF12 ... 118 E2
Matterdale Rd WF12 ... 118 E2
Matthew Cl BD20 ... 18 F1
Matthew Gr HD7 ... 170 C2
Matthew La
Low Bradley BD20 ... 4 C5
Meltham HD7 ... 170 D2
Todmorden OL14 ... 108 E7
Matthew Murray High Sch LS11 ... 213 F4
Matty Marsden La WF4 ... 140 E2
Maud Ave LS11 ... 214 B2
Maud Pl LS11 ... 214 B3
Maud St BD3 ... 75 B6
Maude Ave BD17 ... 38 C2
Maude Cres HX6 ... 111 E3
Maude La HX6 ... 132 D4
Maude St Elland HX4 ... 134 D7
Halifax HX3 ... 92 A3
Leeds LS2 ... 212 A3
Maudsley St BD3 ... 75 B7
Maufe Way LS29 ... 8 B3
Maurice Ave HD6 ... 114 F4
Mavis Ave Dewsbury WF13 . 139 A6
Leeds LS16 ... 41 E6
Mavis Gr LS16 ... 41 E6
Mavis La LS16 ... 41 F6
Mavis Rd WF13 ... 117 F3
Mavis St Bradford BD3 ... 75 B7
Dewsbury WF13 ... 139 A6
Maw St BD4 ... 201 C1
Mawcroft Cl LS19 ... 40 A5
Mawcroft Grange Dr LS19 .. 40 A5
Mawson Ct BD1 ... 201 B3
Mawson St 6 BD18 ... 54 F8
Maxwell Ave WF17 ... 118 C2
Maxwell Rd Bradford BD6 ... 93 F8
Ilkley LS29 ... 8 D3
Maxwell St WF7 ... 145 C5
May Ave BD13 ... 72 E6
May Bush Rd WF1 ... 142 E3
May St Cleckheaton BD19 ... 95 D1
Haworth BD22 ... 51 D6
Huddersfield HD4 ... 153 E4
Keighley BD21 ... 35 C8
May Terr LS9 ... 212 C2
May Tree Cl BD14 ... 73 D5
Mayberry Dr S75 ... 193 F1
Maybrook Ind Pk LS12 ... 210 B4
Maybury Ave WF4 ... 160 A7
Mayfair BD5 ... 74 D4
Mayfair Ave HX4 ... 133 F1
Mayfair Pl WF9 ... 181 D7
Mayfair Way BD4 ... 75 D5
Mayfield Ave
Bradford BD12 ... 94 D3
Brighouse HD6 ... 115 B8
Halifax HX1 ... 202 C2
Huddersfield HD5 ... 154 F6
Ilkley LS29 ... 8 D4
Mayfield Cl Glusburn BD20 ... 16 C6
Ilkley LS29 ... 8 D4
Mayfield Ct WF5 ... 140 E3
Mayfield Dr Halifax HX1 ... 202 C2
Keighley BD20 ... 36 C8
Mayfield Gdns Halifax HX1 202 C2
Ilkley LS29 ... 8 D5
Ossett WF5 ... 140 C8
Sowerby Bridge HX6 ... 112 D5
Mayfield Gr Baildon BD17 ... 38 D3
Brighouse HD6 ... 115 B8
Halifax HX1 ... 202 C2
Huddersfield HD5 ... 154 F6
Wilsden BD15 ... 53 B6
Mayfield Mount HX1 ... 202 C2
Mayfield Pl BD12 ... 94 C3
Mayfield Rd
Hebden Bridge HX7 ... 89 A4
Ilkley LS29 ... 8 C4
Keighley BD20 ... 35 B8
Leeds LS15 ... 81 B8
Mayfield Rise
Bradford BD12 ... 94 D3
Ryhill WF4 ... 162 A1
Mayfield St 8 HX1 ... 202 C1
Mayfield Terr
Bradford, Lane End BD14 ... 73 C3
1 Bradford, Upper Wyke BD12 ... 94 D3
12 Cleckheaton BD19 ... 116 E7
Mayfield Terr S 9 HX1 ... 202 C1
Mayfield View BD12 ... 94 D3
Mayfields Way WF9 ... 182 B1
Mayflower St LS10 ... 80 A2
Maylea Dr LS21 ... 22 D6
Mayman Cl WF17 ... 118 C5
Mayman La WF17 ... 118 B5
Maynes Cl WF12 ... 139 D2
Mayo Ave BD5 ... 74 E2
Mayo Cl LS8 ... 61 D6
Mayo Cres BD5 ... 74 E1
Mayo Dr BD5 ... 74 E1
Mayo Gr BD5 ... 74 E1
Mayo Rd BD5 ... 74 E1
Mayor's Walk Ave WF8 ... 146 D7
Mayor's Wlk WF8 ... 146 D7
Mayors Wlk WF10 ... 125 E7
Maypole Mews LS15 ... 63 D8
Maypole Rd HD2 ... 136 C4
Mayster Gr HD6 ... 135 F8
Mayster Rd HD6 ... 135 F7
Maythorne Ave WF17 ... 118 A4
Maythorne Cres BD14 ... 73 D4
Maythorne Dr BD14 ... 73 E4
Mayville Ave Keighley BD20 .. 36 B8
Leeds LS6 ... 205 E3
Mayville Pl 5 LS6 ... 205 E3
Mayville Rd LS6 ... 205 E3
Mayville St 4 LS6 ... 205 E3
Mayville Terr LS6 ... 205 E3
Mazebrook BD19 ... 95 E2
Mazebrook Ave BD19 ... 95 E2
Mazebrook Cres BD19 ... 95 E2
McBride Way LS22 ... 13 F5
McBurney Cl 2 HX3 ... 92 B2
McLaren Ave WF9 ... 183 D8
McLaren Fields 6 LS13 ... 58 D2
McMahon Dr BD13 ... 73 C2
Mead Gr LS15 ... 81 E6
Mead Rd LS15 ... 81 E6
Mead St HD1 ... 136 A1
Mead View BD4 ... 75 E3
Mead Way HD8 ... 173 E7
Mead Way LS15 ... 81 E6
Meadow Bank
Ackworth M T WF7 ... 146 A1
Dewsbury WF13 ... 138 F8
Holmfirth HD7 ... 189 C6
Ryhill WF4 ... 162 C1
Meadow Bank Cres WF14 . 137 E5
Meadow Bottom Rd OL14 . 108 B6
Meadow Brook Chase WF6 ... 123 C1
Meadow Brook Cl WF6 ... 123 C1
Meadow Brook Ct WF6 ... 144 C8
Meadow Brook Gn WF6 ... 123 C1
Meadow Cl Bardsey LS17 ... 28 E6
Batley WF17 ... 97 A1
Boston Spa LS23 ... 30 C8
Cononley BD20 ... 4 A3
Harden BD16 ... 36 B1
Hemsworth WF9 ... 181 C6
Liversedge WF15 ... 116 F1
Lofthouse Gate WF1 ... 121 D5
Shelf HX3 ... 93 D6
Meadow Cres Halifax HX3 ... 91 E2
Royston S71 ... 179 D3
Meadow Croft
East Keswick LS17 ... 28 C5
Hemsworth WF9 ... 181 E5
Huddersfield HD2 ... 136 F5
Keighley BD22 ... 34 E6
Leeds LS11 ... 211 E1
Lofthouse Gate WF1 ... 121 C5
Shafton S72 ... 180 C3
Meadow Croft Cl BD10 ... 55 F8
Meadow Ct Bradford BD15 ... 54 A4
Brighouse HD6 ... 115 E2
Castleford WF10 ... 125 D6
Ossett WF5 ... 140 C7
Royston S71 ... 179 D3
South Elmsall WF9 ... 183 B3
Meadow Dr Halifax HX3 ... 91 E2
Liversedge WF15 ... 116 F1
Meadow End LS16 ... 24 E2
Meadow Garth
Bramhope LS16 ... 24 F1
Lofthouse Gate WF1 ... 121 C5
Meadow Gn HD7 ... 170 D8
Meadow La Cononley BD20 ... 4 A2
Dewsbury WF13 ... 118 C1
Halifax HX3 ... 91 E2
Leeds LS11 ... 211 F2
Liversedge WF15 ... 116 F1
Slaithwaite HD7 ... 151 F1
Wakefield WF2 ... 141 F7
Meadow Lea BD20 ... 16 C6
Meadow Park Cres LS28 ... 57 B2
Meadow Park Dr LS28 ... 57 B2
Meadow Pk HD5 ... 137 B2
Meadow Rd Bradford BD10 ... 56 E8
Castleford WF10 ... 124 B5
Garforth LS25 ... 83 A7
Leeds LS11 ... 211 E1
Royston S71 ... 179 D3
Meadow Rise WF9 ... 181 C7
Meadow St HD1 ... 153 D7
Meadow The WF6 ... 144 A7
Meadow Vale
Lofthouse Gate WF1 ... 121 D5
Netherton WF4 ... 158 D5
Meadow Valley LS17 ... 43 B5
Meadow View
Barwick in E LS15 ... 63 E8
Bradford BD12 ... 94 C1
Leeds LS6 ... 205 E3
Oakworth BD22 ... 34 D2
Ossett WF5 ... 140 C7
Skelmanthorpe HD8 ... 175 B1
Meadow Way
Ackworth M T WF7 ... 146 A1
East Ardsley WF3 ... 119 D7
Leeds LS17 ... 43 B5
Meadow Wlk
Badsworth WF9 ... 164 E3
Halifax HX3 ... 91 E2
Leeds LS7 ... 204 B2
Meadowbank Ave BD15 ... 54 B1
Meadowcroft
Draughton BD23 ... 1 D6
Honley HD7 ... 171 E4
Menston LS29 ... 22 A4
Meadowcroft Cl WF1 ... 121 D5
Meadowcroft Ct WF1 ... 121 D5
Meadowcroft La HX6 ... 132 E5
Meadowcroft Mews LS9 ... 212 B3
Meadowcroft Rd WF1 ... 121 D5
Meadowcroft Rise BD4 ... 95 C8
Meadowfield Cl WF9 ... 163 A3
Meadowfields Cl WF4 ... 162 A8
Meadowfields Dr WF4 ... 162 A8
Meadowfields Rd WF4 ... 162 A8
Meadowgate WF5 ... 140 C7
Meadowgate Croft WF3 ... 100 B2
Meadowgate Dr WF3 ... 100 B1
Meadowgate Vale WF3 ... 100 B1
Meadowhurst Gdns LS28 ... 76 D7
Meadowlands BD19 ... 94 E1
Meadows The Bradford BD6 . 74 C1
Denby Dale HD8 ... 191 F5
Leeds LS16 ... 42 C3
Meadowside Rd BD17 ... 38 E4
Meadstead Dr S71 ... 179 B3
Meadstead Junior & Infants Sch S71 ... 179 B3
Meadway Bradford BD6 ... 93 F6
Featherstone WF7 ... 144 C5
Meagill Rise LS21 ... 10 E2
Meal Hill HD7 ... 151 F2
Meal Hill La Holmfirth HD7 .. 189 F3
Slaithwaite HD7 ... 151 F2
Meal Hill Rd HD7 ... 187 F1
Mean La Haworth BD22 ... 50 D8
Meltham HD7 ... 170 E2
Meanwood C of E Aided Primary Sch LS6 ... 59 E7
Meanwood Cl LS7 ... 206 B4
Meanwood Gr LS6 ... 42 E1
Meanwood Rd LS6, LS7 ... 206 B4
Meanwood St LS7 ... 206 C2
Meanwood Towers LS6 ... 60 A8
Meanwood Valley Cl LS7 ... 59 F6
Meanwood Valley Dr LS7 ... 59 F6
Meanwood Valley Gn LS7 ... 59 F6
Meanwood Valley Gr 2 LS7 ... 59 F6
Meanwood Valley Mount LS7 ... 59 F6
Meanwood Valley Urban Farm LS7 ... 60 A5
Meanwood Valley Wlk LS7 . 59 F6
Mearclough Rd HX6 ... 112 D4
Mearhouse Bank HD7 ... 189 E4
Mearhouse Terr HD7 ... 189 E4
Medeway LS28 ... 57 C2
Medhurst Ave LS25 ... 83 B2
Medley La HX3 ... 92 F4
Medley St WF10 ... 124 E7
Medlock Rd WF4 ... 141 A1
Medway Kirkheaton HD5 ... 137 B2
Queensbury BD13 ... 92 F8
Medway Ave LS25 ... 83 A5
Medwell Way BD6 ... 94 A6
Meeting House La HD7 ... 152 A4
Meg La HD3 ... 153 B5
Meggison Gr BD5 ... 74 C4
Megnaway 3 BD5 ... 74 E4
Melba Rd BD5 ... 74 B3
Melbourne Ave WF2 ... 120 F3
Melbourne Gr Bradford BD3 . 75 E8
Leeds LS13 ... 58 C2
Melbourne Mews WF2 ... 120 E4
Melbourne Pl BD5 ... 201 A1
Melbourne Rd
Todmorden OL14 ... 108 A1
Wakefield WF1 ... 142 A8
Melbourne St
22 Halifax HX3 ... 92 A1
28 Hebden Bridge HX7 ... 89 A3
Leeds LS2 ... 207 D1
4 Liversedge WF15 ... 117 B3
Morley LS27 ... 98 B4
7 Pudsey LS28 ... 57 D2
Shipley BD18 ... 55 A8
Melbourne Terr BD5 ... 201 B1
Melcombe Wlk BD4 ... 75 E4
Melford Cl S75 ... 178 B1
Melford St BD4 ... 75 C2
Mellor Brook HD7 ... 151 F4
Mellor La HD7 ... 188 B5
Mellor Mill La HX4 ... 134 B4
Mellor St Halifax HX1 ... 202 C1
Todmorden OL14 ... 107 E8
Mellor Terr HX1 ... 202 C1
Mellor's Bldgs WF4 ... 156 D8
Mellwood La WF9 ... 182 F3
Melrose Cl HD5 ... 155 A6
Melrose Ct HX5 ... 134 E6
Melrose Dr LS29 ... 9 E2
Melrose Gr LS18 ... 58 E8
Melrose Pl Horsforth LS18 ... 58 D8
Pudsey LS28 ... 76 D6
Melrose St Bradford BD7 ... 74 A4
26 Halifax HX3 ... 92 A1
Melrose Terr
9 Bacup OL13 ... 106 A7
Elland HX5 ... 134 F6
Melrose Wlk LS18 ... 58 E8
Meltham C of E (C) Junior & Infants Sch HD7 ... 170 E1
Meltham House La HD7 ... 189 F4
Meltham Jun & Inf Sch HD7 ... 170 C3
Meltham Mills Ind Est HD7 ... 170 F2
Meltham Mills Rd HD7 ... 170 F2
Meltham Rd
Huddersfield HD1, HD4 ... 153 F3
Marsden HD7 ... 169 C5
Melton Ave LS10 ... 99 F4
Melton Cl Middleton LS10 ... 99 F4
South Elmsall WF9 ... 183 A5
Melton Garth LS10 ... 99 F4
Melton Rd WF2 ... 160 A4

Melton St WF17 .... 118 B6
Melton Terr BD10 .... 56 E4
Melton Way WF15 .... 116 F1
Melville Cl LS6 .... 206 B3
Melville Gdns LS6 .... 206 B4
Melville Gr LS29 .... 8 E4
Melville Pl LS6 .... 206 B4
Melville Rd LS6 .... 206 B3
Melville St BD7 .... 74 C7
Memorial Dr LS6 .... 59 F7
Mendip Ave HD3 .... 135 A1
Mendip Cl LS25 .... 82 F5
Mendip Rd WF12 .... 118 F1
Mendip Way BD12 .... 94 B6
Menin Dr BD17 .... 38 C5
Menston Dr LS29 .... 22 A3
Menston Infants Sch
LS29 .... 21 F4
Menston Old La
Burley in W LS29 .... 21 F7
Menston LS29 .... 21 F7
Menston PrimSch LS29 .... 22 A4
Menston Sta LS29 .... 22 B5
Menstone St BD8 .... 74 C8
Mercer Cl HD4 .... 171 C7
Merchants Ct BD4 .... 75 A5
Mercia Way LS15 .... 62 E3
Mercury Row LS21 .... 23 A7
Merewood Rd WF10 .... 123 F7
Meriden Ave LS25 .... 82 F5
Merlin Cl LS27 .... 98 C3
Merlin Ct Batley WF17 .... 118 A8
Huddersfield HD4 .... 171 E7
Merlin Gr BD8 .... 73 C7
Merlinwood Dr BD17 .... 38 D4
Merlyn Rees Com High Sch
LS26 .... 99 E8
Merrill Rd S63 .... 194 C1
Merrion Cres HX3 .... 113 E5
Merrion Ctr LS2 .... 206 C1
Merrion Pl LS2 .... 211 F4
Merrion St Halifax HX3 .... 113 E5
Leeds LS1, LS2 .... 211 F4
Merrion Way LS2 .... 206 C1
Merrivale Rd BD15 .... 73 A8
Merry Bent La HX6 .... 132 A5
Merrybents St OL14 .... 108 D5
Merrydale Rd BD4 .... 95 A6
Mersey St 4 OL13 .... 106 A1
Merton Ave LS28 .... 57 D2
Merton Cl LS25 .... 83 C2
Merton Dr LS28 .... 57 C2
Merton Fold 6 BD5 .... 74 E4
Merton Gdns LS28 .... 57 C2
Merton Rd BD7 .... 74 D5
Merton St HD1 .... 154 A5
Merville Ave BD17 .... 38 C5
Metcalfe St BD4 .... 75 B4
Methley CE Infant Sch
LS26 .... 102 C2
Methley Dr LS7 .... 204 A2
Methley Gr LS7 .... 60 C6
Methley Junior Sch LS26 .... 102 D3
Methley La Leeds LS7 .... 204 A2
Rothwell LS26 .... 101 E4
Methley Mount LS7 .... 204 A2
Methley Park Hospl LS26 .. 102 A3
Methley Pl LS7 .... 60 C6
Methley Rd WF10 .... 124 B8
Methley Terr LS7 .... 204 A2
Methley View LS7 .... 204 A2
Methuen Oval 2 BD12 .... 94 C1
Metro Travel Interchange
BD1 .... 201 C2
Mettle Cote OL13 .... 106 A1
Mews Ct WF7 .... 145 D5
Mews The HY6 .... 123 B3
Mexborough Ave LS7 .... 207 D4
Mexborough Dr LS7 .... 207 D4
Mexborough Gr LS7 .... 207 D4
Mexborough House 3
HX5 .... 134 F7
Mexborough Pl LS7 .... 207 D4
Mexborough Rd Leeds LS7 .. 207 D4
Shipley BD2 .... 55 D5
Mexborough St LS7 .... 207 D4
Meynell App LS11 .... 211 D1
Meynell Ave LS26 .... 100 E5
Meynell Ct LS15 .... 81 D7
Meynell Hts LS11 .... 211 D1
Meynell Mount LS26 .... 100 F5
Meynell Rd LS15 .... 81 D6
Meynell Sq LS11 .... 211 D1
Meynell Wlk LS11 .... 211 D1
Meyrick Ave LS22 .... 14 A6
Miall St HX1 .... 202 C4
Michael Ave WF3 .... 121 A5
Mickledore Cl BD7 .... 73 E3
Mickley St LS12 .... 210 A3
Micklefield C of E
Primary Sch LS25 .... 84 A7
Micklefield Ct LS19 .... 40 B4
Micklefield La LS19 .... 40 B4
Micklefield Rd LS19 .... 40 B4
Micklegate WF8 .... 125 D1
Micklegate Sq WF8 .... 125 D1
Micklemoss Dr BD13 .... 72 E7
Micklethwaite Dr BD13 .... 92 E8
Micklethwaite La BD16 .... 36 E7
Micklethwaite Rd WF4 .... 159 F3
Micklethwaite View LS22 .. 13 E4
Mickletown Rd LS26 .... 102 C3
Mickley St LS12 .... 210 A3
Mid Yorkshire
Nuffield Hosp LS18 .... 58 E8
Middle Cl LS25 .... 177 C1
Middle Cross St LS12 .... 210 A3
Middle Dean St 1 HX4 .... 134 D6

Middle Field La WF4 .... 177 F6
Middle Hall Cl WF15 .... 116 F4
Middle La Bradford BD14 .... 73 C5
Collingham LS22 .... 13 C2
Crofton WF4 .... 162 B7
Knottingley WF11 .... 127 A3
Middle Oxford St WF10 .... 124 C7
Middle Rd
Dewsbury WF12, WF13 .... 139 B7
Dewsbury, Earlsheaton
WF12 .... 139 E7
Leeds LS9 .... 80 B7
Middle St Bradford BD1 .... 201 B3
Sowerby Bridge HX6 .... 111 E1
Middle Way BD21 .... 35 E7
Middlebrook Cl BD8 .... 73 E7
Middlebrook Cres BD8 .... 73 D6
Middlebrook Dr BD8 .... 73 D7
Middlebrook Hill BD8 .... 73 D7
Middlebrook Rise BD8 .... 73 D7
Middlebrook View BD8 .... 73 E7
Middlebrook Way BD8 .... 73 E7
Middlebrook Wlk BD8 .... 73 E7
Middlecliffe Dr LS26 .... 200 D5
Middlecroft Cl LS10 .... 99 F8
Middlecroft Rd LS10 .... 99 F8
Middlefield La WF8 .... 166 B4
Middlegate WF17 .... 96 E6
Middlegate Ct BD4 .... 95 B8
Middlemoor LS14 .... 62 B8
Middlestown Junior
& Infants Sch WF4 .... 158 B7
Middlethorne Cl LS17 .... 44 A5
Middlethorne Ct LS17 .... 44 B5
Middlethorne Mews LS17 .. 44 B5
Middlethorne Rise LS17 .... 44 B5
Middleton Ave Ilkley LS29 .. 8 B5
Leeds LS9 .... 207 F1
Rothwell LS26 .... 100 A5
Middleton Cl LS27 .... 98 C4
Middleton Cres LS11 .... 214 B2
Middleton Ct WF15 .... 116 E4
Middleton District Ctr
LS10 .... 99 D5
Middleton Gr Leeds LS11 .. 214 B1
Morley LS27 .... 98 C4
Middleton La
Middleton WF3 .... 99 D3
Rothwell LS26 .... 99 D3
Middleton Park Ave LS10 .. 99 B4
Middleton Park Cir LS10 .. 99 B5
Middleton Park Cres LS10 .. 99 C5
Middleton Park Ct LS10 .... 99 B4
Middleton Park Gdns LS10 .. 99 B4
Middleton Park High Sch
LS10 .... 99 D4
Middleton Park Mount
LS10 .... 99 B4
Middleton Park Pl LS10 .... 99 C4
Middleton Park Rd LS10 .... 99 C5
Middleton Park Sq LS10 .... 99 C4
Middleton Park Sq N LS10 .. 99 C4
Middleton Park Sq S LS10 .. 99 C4
Middleton Park Terr LS10 .. 99 C4
Middleton Primary Sch
LS10 .... 99 B4
Middleton Rd Ilkley LS29 .... 8 A4
Middleton LS10 .... 99 F8
Morley LS27 .... 98 C4
Middleton Rly LS11 .... 214 C1
Middleton St BD8 .... 55 B1
Middleton St Mary's CE
Prim Sch LS10 .... 99 C5
Middleton Terr LS27 .... 98 C4
Middleton Way
Knottingley WF11 .... 126 F4
Middleton LS10 .... 99 F6
Middleway BD20 .... 5 F1
Midge Hall Cl LS29 .... 9 E1
Midgehole La HX7 .... 89 A6
Midgehole Rd HX7 .... 89 A6
Midgeley Rd BD17 .... 38 A1
Midgley Almshouses 10
BD22 .... 51 E8
Midgley Gdns LS6 .... 206 A3
Midgley Junior
& Infants Sch HX2 .... 90 C1
Midgley Pl LS6 .... 206 B3
Midgley Rd Burley in W LS29 .. 9 E1
Hebden Bridge HX7 .... 89 F1
Midgley Rise WF8 .... 125 D3
Midgley Row BD4 .... 75 B1
Midgley Terr LS6 .... 206 B3
Midland Cl LS10 .... 215 D3
Midland Garth LS10 .... 215 E3
Midland Hill BD16 .... 36 F3
Midland Pas LS6 .... 205 F3
Midland Rd LS11 .... 211 D2
Midland Rd Baildon BD17 .. 38 D2
Bradford BD8 .... 55 D1
Leeds LS10 .... 215 E3
Leeds, Hyde Park LS6 .... 205 F3
Pontefract WF8 .... 125 E1
Royston S71 .... 179 D4
Shipley BD9 .... 55 C5
Midland St
Huddersfield HD1 .... 154 B8
Rothwell LS26 .... 101 C6
Midland Terr Bradford BD2 .. 55 E3
Keighley BD21 .... 35 C8
Shipley BD9 .... 55 C5
Midway HD4 .... 171 A6
Midway Ave 1 BD16 .... 54 A7
Milan St LS8 .... 207 F3
Milan St LS8 .... 208 A3
Mildred St BD3 .... 56 A1

Mildred Sylvester Way
WF6 .... 123 E2
Mile Cross Gdns HX1 .... 202 A2
Mile Cross Pl HX1 .... 202 A2
Mile Cross Rd HX1 .... 202 A2
Mile Cross Terr HX1 .... 202 A2
Mile End HD7 .... 170 D2
Mile Thorn St HX1 .... 202 B3
Miles Garth LS17 .... 28 F6
Miles Hill Ave LS7 .... 60 B6
Miles Hill Cres
Bradford BD4 .... 75 C1
Leeds LS7 .... 60 B6
Miles Hill Dr BD4 .... 75 C1
Miles Hill Gr LS7 .... 60 B6
Miles Hill Mount LS7 .... 60 A7
Miles Hill Pl LS7 .... 60 B7
Miles Hill Primary Sch LS7 .. 60 A7
Miles Hill Rd LS7 .... 60 B6
Miles Hill Sq LS7 .... 60 B6
Miles Hill Terr LS7 .... 60 B6
Miles Hill View LS7 .... 60 B6
Milestone Ct LS28 .... 57 F2
Milestone Sch LS28 .... 57 F2
Milford Gr BD19 .... 96 A3
Milford Pl Bradford BD9 .... 55 A3
Leeds LS4 .... 205 D1
Milford St HD1 .... 154 A5
Milgate St S77 .... 179 D4
Mill Ave HD5 .... 155 A7
Mill Bank Cl HX6 .... 132 C7
Mill Bank Rd Meltham HD7 .. 170 F1
Sowerby Bridge HX6 .... 132 D7
Mill Banks BD20 .... 5 E1
Mill Carr Hill Rd
BD12, BD4 .... 95 B5
Mill Cl Ackworth M T WF7 .. 164 A6
Meltham HD7 .... 170 D2
South Kirkby WF9 .... 182 A1
Mill Cotts WF7 .... 145 B5
Mill Croft LS27 .... 97 D7
Mill Ct 8 BD22 .... 51 C2
Mill Dam LS25 .... 30 E5
Mill Dam Jun & Inf Sch
WF7 .... 164 A6
Mill Dam La WF8 .... 125 E2
Mill Farm Dr WF4 .... 160 C6
Mill Fold Way HX6 .... 132 E4
Mill Forest Way WF17 .... 118 F4
Mill Garth LS27 .... 97 D7
Mill Gn LS12 .... 210 C2
Mill Gr HD6 .... 114 F4
Mill Grath WF8 .... 146 C7
Mill Green Cl LS14 .... 62 C5
Mill Green Garth 6 LS14 .. 62 C5
Mill Green Gdns LS14 .... 62 C5
Mill Green Rd LS14 .... 62 C5
Mill Green View LS14 .... 62 B5
Mill Hey BD22 .... 51 D7
Mill Hill Ackworth M T WF7 .. 164 A8
Haworth BD22 .... 51 C7
Normanton WF6 .... 123 A1
Pudsey LS28 .... 76 E5
Rothwell LS26 .... 100 E5
Mill Hill Ave WF8 .... 146 C6
Mill Hill Cl WF8 .... 146 C6
Mill Hill Gn LS26 .... 100 E5
Mill Hill La Brighouse HD6 .. 114 F4
Liversedge HD6 .... 115 F1
Pontefract WF8 .... 146 C7
Mill Hill Rd WF8 .... 146 C7
Mill Hill Sq LS26 .... 100 E5
Mill Hill Top BD16 .... 53 B8
Mill House La HX6 .... 112 A2
Mill House Rise BD5 .... 75 B1
Mill La Ackworth M T WF7 .... 164 A6
Adwick Le S DN6 .... 184 F2
Batley, Carlinghow 7 .... 28 E4
Batley, Hanging Heaton
WF17 .... 118 E3
Batley, Howden Clough WF17 .. 97 B2
Birkenshaw BD11 .... 96 A6
Birkenshaw, Tong BD11 .... 77 A2
Bradford BD4, BD5 .... 201 C1
Bradford, Woodside BD6 .... 93 E6
Brighouse HD6 .... 115 B2
Castleford WF10 .... 103 D1
Cleckheaton BD19 .... 95 D3
Dewsbury WF12 .... 140 A7
East Ardsley WF3 .... 120 E8
Flockton WF4 .... 156 E7
Gildersome LS27 .... 97 D7
Guiseley LS20 .... 38 D8
Halifax HX2 .... 91 D7
Halifax, Boothtown HX3 .... 92 B2
Huddersfield HD5 .... 137 B5
Leeds LS13 .... 58 A3
Low Bradley BD20 .... 4 C6
Mapplewell S75 .... 177 E1
Micketown LS26 .... 102 D3
Middleton WF3 .... 99 D8
Notton WF4 .... 178 D8
Oakworth BD22 .... 34 C2
Otley LS21 .... 23 A8
Oxenhope BD22 .... 51 C3
Pontefract WF8 .... 125 D1
Pool LS21 .... 24 D7
Queensbury BD13 .... 72 C2
Ryhill WF4 .... 162 B1
South Elmsall WF9 .... 183 B4
South Kirkby WF9 .... 182 A2
Steeton BD20 .... 17 C5
Thorp Arch LS23 .... 30 E8

Mill Lane Jun & Inf Sch
WF17 .... 118 D3
Mill Moor Rd HD7 .... 170 C2
Mill Pit La LS26 .... 100 D7
Mill Rd WF13 .... 118 C2
Mill Row BD20 .... 16 E6
Mill Royd St HD6 .... 115 B2
Mill Shaw La HD7 .... 190 B1
Mill St Batley WF17 .... 117 E8
Bradford BD1 .... 201 C3
Bradford, Wibsey BD6 .... 74 A1
Castleford WF10 .... 124 B7
Cullingworth BD13 .... 52 D6
Elland HX3 .... 113 A1
Glusburn BD20 .... 16 D6
Huddersfield HD4 .... 153 E4
Leeds LS9 .... 212 A3
Morley LS27 .... 98 A3
South Kirkby WF9 .... 182 A2
Sutton in C BD20 .... 16 E5
Mill St E WF12 .... 139 D6
Mill St W WF12 .... 139 D6
Mill View Burley in W LS29 .. 9 E2
Hemsworth WF9 .... 181 C6
Knottingley WF11 .... 126 B4
Millacre View HD7 .... 189 C8
Millars Wlk WF9 .... 182 C1
Millbank LS28 .... 76 F6
Millbank View LS28 .... 76 F6
Millbank Fold LS28 .... 76 F6
Millbeck App LS27 .... 98 C4
Millbeck Cl BD16 .... 73 C6
Millbeck Dr BD16 .... 36 A1
Millbeck Gn LS22 .... 29 A8
Millbeck Infants Sch
WF15 .... 117 B4
Millbridge Upper
Junior Mixed Sch WF15 .. 117 B4
Millbrook Gdns WF13 .... 118 A3
Millcroft WF3 .... 121 E6
Millcroft Cl WF3 .... 121 E6
Millcroft Est LS21 .... 24 D7
Milldale Rd WF3 .... 121 E6
Millennium Way LS11 .... 214 B1
Millennium B LS27 .... 4 48
Miller Ave WF2 .... 142 D2
Miller Cl BD2 .... 55 E5
Miller Ct LS27 .... 160 B4
Miller Garth WF7 .... 164 A5
Miller Hill HD8 .... 192 A5
Miller Hill Bank HD8 .... 192 A5
Millergate BD1 .... 201 B3
Millers Cl WF15 .... 117 B2
Millers Dale LS27 .... 97 F6
Millersdale Cl BD4 .... 95 A7
Millfield Cl HD3 .... 153 C7
Millfield Cres WF8 .... 146 C6
Millfield Rd WF4 .... 159 C8
Millfields Ossett WF5 .... 140 C5
Silsden BD20 .... 5 D1
Millgarth St LS2 .... 211 F4
Millgate Ackworth M T WF7 .. 164 A5
Bingley BD16 .... 36 F3
Elland HX5 .... 134 F7
Huddersfield HD4 .... 155 B2
Huddersfield, Yews Hill HD1 .. 153 E5
Millhaigh Ave BD2 .... 56 A5
Milligan Ct BD16 .... 36 A1
Milligans Pl BD20 .... 16 D7
Millmoor Cl BD9 .... 54 D2
Millshaw Leeds LS11 .... 213 E1
Morley LS11 .... 213 E1
Millshaw Mount LS11 .... 98 E8
Millshaw Park Ave LS11 .... 98 D8
Millshaw Park Cl LS11 .... 98 D8
Millshaw Park Dr LS11 .... 213 D1
Millshaw Park La LS11 .... 98 D8
Millshaw Park Way LS11 .. 213 D1
Millshaw Rd LS11 .... 98 E7
Millside LS27 .... 180 C3
Millside Wlk Morley LS27 .. 98 C4
Shafton S72 .... 180 C3
Millstone Cl WF7 .... 146 A4
Millstone Rise WF15 .... 117 B2
Millward St WF4 .... 162 A1
Millwater Ave WF12 .... 139 B5
Millwood La OL14 .... 108 D5
Millwright St LS2 .... 207 D2
Miln Rd HD1 .... 154 A8
Milne Ct LS15 .... 81 D6
Milne St BD7 .... 74 C7
Milne's Ave WF2 .... 141 F3
Milner Bank LS21 .... 22 D6
Milner Cl HX4 .... 134 C7
Milner Gdns LS9 .... 212 C2
Milner House 2 BD15 .... 73 B7
Milner Ing BD12 .... 94 C5
Milner La Bardsey LS14 .... 28 F1
Elland HX4 .... 134 C7
Rothwell WF3 .... 100 A2
Scarcroft LS14 .... 45 F7
Thorner LS14 .... 45 F7
Milner Rd BD17 .... 38 A1
Milner Royal La HX6 .... 112 E3
Milner St Halifax HX1 .... 203 D3
Huddersfield HD1 .... 153 E3
Ossett WF5 .... 119 C1
Milner Way WF5 .... 140 E6
Milner's La HX6 .... 112 E4
Milner's Rd LS19 .... 40 C7
Milnes Gr WF10 .... 125 B7
Milnes St LS12 .... 210 B2
Milnthorpe Cl LS23 .... 30 C3
Milnthorpe Cres WF2 .... 160 D7
Milnthorpe Dr WF2 .... 160 D8
Milnthorpe Garth LS23 .... 30 C3

Milnthorpe Gdns LS23 .... 30 C3
Milnthorpe Gn WF2 .... 160 D7
Milnthorpe La
Bramham LS23 .... 30 C3
Wakefield WF2 .... 142 D2
Milnthorpe Way LS23 .... 30 C3
Milroyd Cres WF17 .... 97 A2
Milton Ave
Liversedge WF15 .... 117 C3
Sowerby Bridge HX6 .... 112 B5
Milton Cl Crigglestone WF4 .. 159 D6
Liversedge WF15 .... 117 C3
Milton Cres WF2 .... 141 C4
Milton Ct WF3 .... 121 F6
Milton Dr Barwick in E LS15 .. 62 F7
Batley WF17 .... 117 C2
Hemsworth WF9 .... 163 B2
Milton Gdns WF13 .... 118 C2
Milton Pl HX1 .... 118 C2
Milton Pl Halifax HX1 .... 203 D3
Ossett WF5 .... 140 D7
Milton Rd Liversedge WF15 .. 117 C3
Wakefield WF2 .... 141 D4
Milton St 1 Sutton in C BD20 .. 117 D5
Bradford BD7 .... 74 C7
Castleford WF10 .... 124 C8
Denholme BD13 .... 71 E8
10 Sowerby Bridge HX6 .. 112 B5
Wakefield WF2 .... 142 A5
Milton Terr
Cleckheaton BD19 .... 116 C8
3 Halifax HX1 .... 203 D3
Hemsworth WF9 .... 163 A4
Leeds LS9 .... 212 C4
Yeadon LS19 .... 39 F7
Milton Wlk 9 WF13 .... 139 C8
Minden Cl WF8 .... 146 A7
Minden Way WF8 .... 146 A8
Minerva St HD4 .... 152 F3
Mini Market 3 HD1 .... 154 C8
Minnie St Haworth BD22 .... 51 C6
Keighley BD21 .... 35 B6
Minorca Mount BD13 .... 52 D1
Minstead Ave HD6 .... 135 D7
Minster Cl HX4 .... 134 B7
Minsthorpe High Sch
& Com Coll WF9 .... 183 A5
Minsthorpe La
South Elmsall WF9 .... 182 E4
Upton WF9 .... 182 E4
Mint St Bradford BD2 .... 56 B2
Huddersfield HD1 .... 153 D7
Miramar HD2 .... 136 D5
Mirey Butt La WF11 .... 126 D3
Mirey La HX6 .... 111 C3
Mirfield Ave BD2 .... 56 A5
Mirfield Free Grammar
Sch The WF14 .... 137 F7
Mirfield Sports Ctr WF14 .. 137 F7
Mirfield Sta WF14 .... 138 A3
Miriam Lord First Sch
BD8 .... 55 B1
Miry La Barwick in E LS25 .... 46 F1
Cleckheaton WF15 .... 116 C5
Hebden Bridge HX7 .... 88 F6
Holmfirth, Netherthong HD7 .. 188 F6
Holmfirth, Thongsbridge
HD7 .... 189 B8
Yeadon LS19 .... 40 B7
Mission St HD6 .... 115 C1
Mistral Cl BD12 .... 94 C2
Mistral Gr WF15 .... 116 B5
Mistress La LS12 .... 209 F4
Mitcham Dr BD9 .... 55 A2
Mitchell Ave
3 Castleford WF10 .... 118 B2
Huddersfield HD5 .... 155 B5
Mitchell Cl BD10 .... 39 C1
Mitchell La Bradford BD10 .. 39 C1
Silsden BD20 .... 5 D1
Mitchell Sq 8 BD5 .... 74 E4
Mitchell St Brighouse HD6 .. 115 A3
6 Hebden Bridge HX7 .... 89 A2
Keighley BD21 .... 35 D8
Sowerby Bridge HX6 .... 112 C4
Todmorden OL14 .... 107 E8
Mitchell Terr BD16 .... 36 F2
Mitford Pl LS12 .... 210 A3
Mitford Rd LS12 .... 210 A3
Mitford St LS12 .... 210 A3
Mitford Terr LS12 .... 210 A3
Mitford View LS12 .... 210 A3
Mitre Ct BD4 .... 75 D3
Mitre St Dewsbury WF13 .... 139 A8
Huddersfield HD1 .... 153 E7
Mitton St Bradford BD5 .... 74 C3
2 Shipley BD16 .... 54 B6
Mixenden Cl HX2 .... 91 D4
Mixenden Ct HX2 .... 91 D4
Mixenden Jun & Inf Sch
HX2 .... 91 A6
Mixenden La HX2 .... 91 D6
Mixenden Rd HX2 .... 91 C5
Mixenden Stones HX2 .... 91 C6
Moat End LS14 .... 45 F5
Moat Hill WF17 .... 97 A2
Moat Hill Farm Dr WF17 .. 97 A2
Mockbar Ave LS12 .... 188 F4
Modder Ave LS12 .... 209 E3
Modder Pl LS12 .... 209 E3
Model Ave LS12 .... 210 A3
Model Rd LS12 .... 210 A3
Model Terr LS12 .... 210 A3
Moderna Bsns Pk HX7 .... 110 F8
Moderna Way HX7 .... 110 F8

Moffat Cl BD6 .... 93 F7
Moffatt Cl HX3 .... 91 F3
Moldgreen Junior
& Infants Sch HD5 .... 154 D5
Moles Head HD7 .... 152 C6
Molly Hurst La WF4 .... 177 F7
Mona St Slaithwaite HD7 .... 151 F1
 Wakefield WF2 .... 141 E6
Mona's Terr LS14 .... 108 A1
Monckton Dr WF10 .... 125 C6
Monckton Rd S 142 B2
Mond Ave BD3 .... 56 D1
Monk Barn Cl BD16 ...... 37 A4
Monk Bridge Ave LS6 .... 59 F6
Monk Bridge Dr LS6 ...... 59 E6
Monk Bridge Gr LS6 ...... 59 E6
Monk Bridge Mount LS6 59 F6
Monk Bridge Pl LS6 ...... 59 E6
Monk Bridge Rd LS6 .... 59 E6
Monk Bridge St LS6 .... 59 F6
Monk Bridge Terr LS6 ...... 59 E6
Monk Ings WF17 .... 96 D1
Monk Ings Ave WF17 .... 96 C2
Monk St Bradford BD7 .... 74 C7
 Wakefield WF1 .... 216 C1
Monkfield WF14 .... 137 E6
Monkhill Ave WF8 .... 125 D2
Monkhill Dr WF8 .... 125 D2
Monkhill La WF8 .... 125 D3
Monkhill Mount WF8 .... 125 D2
Monkhill Sta WF8 .... 125 E2
Monkmans Wharf BD20 .... 5 E1
Monkswood LS5 .... 58 F6
Monkswood Ave LS14 ...... 61 F8
Monkswood Bank LS14 ...... 61 F8
Monkswood Cl LS14 .... 61 F8
Monkswood Dr LS14 .... 61 F8
Monkswood Gate LS14 .. 62 A8
Monkswood Gn LS14 .... 61 F8
Monkswood Hill LS14 .... 61 F8
Monkswood Rise LS14 .... 61 F8
Monkswood Wlk LS14 .... 62 A8
Monkwood Rd WF1 .... 121 B5
Mons Rd OL14 .... 107 F7
Monson Ave LS28 .... 57 B6
Mont Gr BD5 .... 74 D3
Montagu Ave LS8 .... 61 C5
Montagu Cres LS8 .... 61 C5
Montagu Ct LS8 .... 61 B6
Montagu Gdns LS8 .... 61 B5
Montagu Gr LS8 .... 61 C5
Montagu Pl LS8 .... 61 B5
Montagu Rd LS22 .... 14 A6
Montagu Rise LS8 .... 208 C4
Montagu View LS8 .... 61 B5
Montague Cres LS25 .... 83 A7
Montague Ct LS12 .... 209 D3
Montague Pl LS25 .... 83 A7
Montague St Bradford BD5 .. 74 C3
 Sowerby Bridge HX6 ...... 112 A3
 Wakefield WF1 .... 142 F2
Montcalm Cres Leeds LS10 215 E2
 Lofthouse Gate WF3 ...... 121 F3
Monterey Dr BD15 .... 54 A4
Montfort Cl LS18 .... 41 B3
Montpelier Terr LS6 ...... 206 A4
Montreal Ave LS7 .... 204 A2
Montreal St OL14 .... 108 A1
Montreal Terr LS13 .... 77 A8
Montrose Ave LS5 .... 177 F1
Montrose Pl BD13 .... 72 C2
Montrose St BD2 .... 55 D4
Montserrat Rd BD4 .... 75 F1
Monument La WF8 .... 146 E7
Monument Mews WF8 ...... 146 E7
Moody St BD4 .... 201 C1
Moor Allerton Ave LS17 ...... 43 E2
Moor Allerton Cres LS17 .... 43 E2
Moor Allerton Ctr LS17 ...... 43 B2
Moor Allerton Dr LS17 .... 43 E2
Moor Allerton Gdns LS17 .. 43 D2
Moor Allerton Hall
 Primary Sch LS8 .... 43 F1
Moor Allerton Way LS17 .... 43 E2
Moor Ave Boston Spa LS23 .. 30 D6
 Leeds LS15 .... 80 F7
 Lofthouse Gate WF3 ...... 121 E6
Moor Bottom LS27 .... 171 F4
Moor Bottom La
 Bingley BD16 .... 37 B3
 Elland HX4 .... 134 A8
 Keighley BD21 .... 35 B2
 Sowerby Bridge HX2 ...... 111 A5
Moor Bottom Rd Halifax HX2 91 F6
 Ripponden HX4 .... 132 F5
Moor Cl Huddersfield HD4 .. 153 C1
 Leeds LS15 .... 215 D2
Moor Close Ave BD13 .... 92 C8
Moor Close Farm Mews
 BD13 .... 92 C8
Moor Close La BD13 .... 92 C8
Moor Close Par BD13 .... 72 D1
Moor Close Rd BD13 .... 92 C8
Moor Cottage Cl HD4 ...... 171 D7
Moor Cres LS11 .... 214 C4
Moor Crescent Chase
 LS11 .... 214 C4
Moor Crest Rd HD4 .... 153 C3
Moor Croft Bingley BD16 .... 37 B5
 Leeds LS16 .... 42 D4
Moor Dr Leeds LS6 .... 59 E6
 Oakworth BD22 .... 34 C3
 Otley LS21 .... 23 D8
 Pudsey LS28 .... 76 F5

Moor Edge High Side BD16 36 A2
Moor End Ave HX2 .... 91 C1
Moor End Gdns HX2 .... 91 D1
Moor End High Sch HD4 .. 153 D2
Moor End La Batley WF13 .. 117 F2
 Sowerby Bridge HX6 ...... 112 D2
Moor End Rd Halifax HX2 .. 91 B1
 Huddersfield HD4 .... 153 E3
Moor Farm Gdns LS7 .... 60 C7
Moor Flatts Ave LS10 .... 99 C5
Moor Flatts Rd LS10 .... 99 C5
Moor Fold HD7 .... 189 E7
Moor Gate OL14 .... 108 C3
Moor Gr
 Lofthouse Gate WF3 ...... 121 E6
 Pudsey LS28 .... 76 F5
 Shelf HX3 .... 93 C7
Moor Grange Dr LS16 .... 59 A8
Moor Grange Rise LS16 ...... 59 A8
Moor Grange View LS16 .... 59 A8
Moor Haven Ct LS17 .... 43 A3
Moor Hey La
 Elland, Elland Upper Edge
 HD2, HX5 .... 135 C5
 Elland, Sowood Green HX4 .. 133 F2
Moor Hill Rd HD3 .... 134 F1
Moor House Ct LS17 .... 44 B4
Moor Knoll Cl WF3 .... 120 D8
Moor Knoll Dr WF3 .... 120 D8
Moor Knoll La WF3 .... 120 D8
Moor La Addingham LS29 .... 2 B1
 Addingham, Addingham Low Moor
 LS29 .... 2 B1
 Askwith LS21 .... 10 B7
 Birkenshaw BD11 .... 96 C3
 Burley in W LS29 .... 21 D7
 Cleckheaton BD19 .... 96 B2
 Clifton LS21 .... 10 C4
 Collingham LS22 .... 29 F7
 Darrington WF8 .... 147 A2
 East Keswick LS17 .... 28 A5
 Guiseley LS20 .... 22 E2
 Halifax HX2 .... 91 E4
 Holmfirth HD7 .... 187 F4
 Huddersfield HD4 .... 171 D7
 Kirkburton HD8 .... 173 F7
 Kirkburton, Farnley Tyas
 HD4 .... 172 F5
 Menston LS29 .... 21 E4
 Pontefract WF8 .... 146 E4
 Stutton LS24 .... 48 F8
 Thorp Arch LS23 .... 14 D5
 Todmorden OL14 .... 108 B3
Moor Park Ave
 Huddersfield HD4 .... 153 C1
 Leeds LS6 .... 59 D6
Moor Park Cl
 Addingham LS29 .... 6 D8
 Bradford BD3 .... 75 C8
 Leeds LS6 .... 59 E6
Moor Park Gdns WF12 .... 118 E1
Moor Park Gr LS29 .... 6 E8
Moor Park Mount LS6 ...... 59 E6
Moor Park Rd BD3 .... 75 C8
Moor Park Villas LS6 .... 59 E6
Moor Park Way LS29 .... 6 E8
Moor Rd Bramhope LS16 .... 24 D2
 Featherstone WF7 .... 145 D5
 Ilkley LS29 .... 21 C7
 Leeds, Far Headingley LS6 .. 59 D6
 Leeds, Hunslet Moor LS10 215 D2
 Leeds, Hunslet Moor LS10 214 C4
 Littleborough OL15 .... 129 C1
 Lofthouse Gate WF3 ...... 121 E6
 Menston LS29 .... 21 C7
Moor Royd Halifax HX3 .... 113 A4
 Honley HD7 .... 171 E3
Moor Side LS23 .... 30 B7
Moor Side Cotts BD20 ...... 19 B3
Moor Side La HD7 .... 151 D3
Moor St Oakworth BD22 .... 34 D3
  Queensbury BD13 .... 72 E1
Moor Stone Pl HX3 .... 93 C5
Moor Terr BD2 .... 56 C1
Moor Top Birkenshaw BD11 .. 96 D6
 Gildersome LS12 .... 77 C1
 Guiseley LS20 .... 22 E4
 Mirfield WF14 .... 137 E6
 Sliabh.. LS22 .... 22 E4
Moor Top Ave
 Ackworth M T WF7 .... 163 E5
 Kirkburton HD4 .... 172 F2
Moor Top Dr WF9 .... 181 D5
Moor Top Gdns HX2 .... 91 E8
Moor Top La WF14 .... 156 D1
Moor Top Rd
 Bradford BD12 .... 94 B6
 Halifax HX2 .... 112 B8
 Kirkheaton HD5 .... 137 C2
Moor Top Sch WF7 .... 163 F4
Moor Valley Pk LS20 .... 38 C7
Moor View Bacup OL13 .. 106 A4
 Batley WF16 .... 117 E2
 Crigglestone WF4 .... 159 F5
 Leeds LS11 .... 211 D1
 Meltham HD7 .... 170 C3
 Mickletown LS26 .... 102 F3
 Mirfield WF14 .... 117 A1
Moor View Ave BD18 .... 55 A8
Moor View Cl WF10 .... 124 F7
Moor View Ct BD20 .... 36 C7

Moor View Terr BD22 .... 50 D7
Moor Way BD22 .... 34 C3
Moorbank Ct LS6 .... 59 E5
Moorbottom BD19 .... 116 B7
Moorbottom Rd HD1 ...... 153 E4
Moorbrow HD7 .... 189 C2
Moorcock Rd HX7 .... 87 C5
Moorcrest Rise S75 .... 178 B2
Moorcroft WF13 .... 118 A1
Moorcroft Ave Bradford BD3 56 D1
 Haworth BD22 .... 34 E3
Moorcroft Avenues HD7 .... 56 B6
Moorcroft Dr Bradford BD4 .. 75 F1
 Dewsbury WF13 .... 117 F1
 Holmfirth HD7 .... 189 D7
Moorcroft Park Dr HD7 .... 189 E7
Moorcroft Rd Bradford BD4 .. 75 F1
 Dewsbury WF13 .... 117 F1
Moorcroft Terr BD4 .... 95 F8
Moore Ave BD6, BD7 .... 74 A2
Moore St BD21 .... 35 C6
Moore West BD7 .... 73 F3
Moorehouse Gr LS9 .... 207 E1
Moorend C of E First Sch
 BD19 .... 95 C1
Moorfield WF4 .... 97 C7
Moorfield Ave Bradford BD3 .. 56 D1
 Brighouse BD19 .... 115 E7
 Leeds LS12 .... 209 D4
 Menston LS29 .... 21 F4
 Yeadon LS19 .... 40 D6
Moorfield Cres
 Hemsworth WF9 .... 181 C6
 Leeds LS12 .... 209 D4
 Pudsey LS28 .... 76 D6
 Yeadon LS19 .... 40 D7
Moorfield Croft LS19 .... 40 D6
Moorfield Ct LS19 .... 40 D6
Moorfield Dr Baildon BD17 .. 38 C6
 Oakworth BD22 .... 34 D3
 Yeadon LS19 .... 40 D6
Moorfield First Sch BD3 .... 75 C7
Moorfield Gdns LS28 .... 76 D6
Moorfield Gr Leeds LS12 .. 209 D4
 Pudsey LS28 .... 76 D6
Moorfield Pl Bradford BD1 .. 56 A8
 Hemsworth WF9 .... 181 C6
Moorfield Rd
 Huddersfield HD1 .... 136 B1
 Ilkley LS29 .... 8 E4
 Leeds LS12 .... 209 D4
 Shipley BD18 .... 54 A7
 Yeadon LS19 .... 40 D7
Moorfield Sch LS29 .... 8 D3
Moorfield St Halifax HX1 .. 202 C1
 Leeds, Hill Top LS12 ...... 209 D4
  Leeds, Woodhouse LS2 .. 206 A3
Moorfield Terr LS19 .... 40 C7
Moorfield View WF15 ...... 116 F1
Moorfield Way BD19, LS29 .. 115 E7
Moorfields LS13 .... 58 C3
Moorfoot La BD20 .... 4 A3
Moorgarth Ave BD3 .... 56 D1
Moorgate BD7 .... 38 C4
Moorgate Ave Bradford BD3 .. 56 D1
 Kippax LS25 .... 83 A2
Moorgate Cl LS25 .... 83 A2
Moorgate Dr LS25 .... 83 B2
Moorgate Flats HD7 .... 170 D2
Moorgate Rd LS25 .... 83 A3
Moorgate Rise LS25 .... 83 A2
Moorgate St HX1 .... 202 B1
Moorhead CI HD7 .... 170 D2
Moorhead Cres BD18 .... 54 E7
Moorhead La BD18 .... 54 E7
Moorhead Terr BD18 .... 54 E7
Moorhouse Ave
 Bradford BD2 .... 56 A5
 Leeds LS11 .... 213 F1
 Lofthouse Gate WF3 ...... 122 B6
 Wakefield WF2 .... 142 A6
Moorhouse Cl
 Lofthouse Gate WF3 ...... 122 B7
 Normanton WF6 .... 123 C3
 Oxenhope BD22 .... 51 C3
Moorhouse Cres WF2 ...... 142 A6
Moorhouse Ct
 Oxenhope BD22 .... 51 C3
 South Elmsall WF9 .... 183 A1
Moorhouse Dr BD11 .... 95 F7
Moorhouse Gap DN6 ...... 183 F1
Moorhouse La
 Birkenshaw BD11 .... 96 A7
 Hooton Pagnell WF9 ...... 183 D1
 Oxenhope BD22 .... 51 C4
 Ryhill WF4 .... 162 C4
 Woolley S75 .... 177 C5
Moorhouse Terr WF3 ...... 122 B7
Moorhouse View
 Lofthouse Gate WF3 ...... 122 B7
 South Elmsall WF9 .... 183 B2
Moorings The
 Bradford BD10 .... 56 D8
 Leeds, Alwoodley Gates LS17 .. 43 E5
 Leeds, Stourton LS10 ...... 80 B3
Moorland Ave Baildon BD17 .. 38 D5
 Birkenshaw BD11 .... 96 A7
 Gildersome LS27 .... 97 C8
 Guiseley LS20 .... 22 E1
 Leeds LS6 .... 205 F2
 Mapplewell S75 .... 178 B2

Moorland Cotts HX7 .... 131 C8
Moorland Cres
 Baildon BD17 .... 38 D4
 Gildersome LS27 .... 97 B8
 Guiseley LS20 .... 22 C2
 Guiseley LS20 .... 22 E2
 Leeds LS17 .... 43 C1
 Mapplewell S75 .... 178 B2
 Menston LS29 .... 22 A5
 Pudsey LS28 .... 57 A1
Moorland Dr
 Birkenshaw BD11 .... 96 B6
 Crigglestone WF4 .... 159 F5
 Guiseley LS20 .... 22 E2
 Leeds LS17 .... 43 D1
 Pudsey LS28 .... 57 A1
Moorland Garth LS17 .... 43 C1
Moorland Gdns LS17 .... 43 D1
Moorland Gr Leeds LS17 .... 43 C2
 Pudsey LS28 .... 76 A8
Moorland Ings LS17 .... 43 C1
Moorland Leys LS17 .... 43 C1
Moorland Mount BD19 .. 116 B6
Moorland Pl
  Bradford BD12 .... 94 E5
 Lofthouse Gate WF3 ...... 121 E8
Moorland Rd
 Birkenshaw BD11 .... 96 E6
 Bramhope LS16 .... 24 C2
 Leeds LS6 .... 205 F2
 Pudsey LS28 .... 57 A1
Moorland Rise Leeds LS17 .. 43 C2
 Meltham HD7 .... 170 C2
Moorland Terr
 Garforth LS25 .... 82 E6
 Keighley BD21 .... 35 F6
Moorland View
 Bradford BD12 .... 94 E5
 Clayton West HD8 .... 176 A2
 Emley HD8 .... 175 E2
 Leeds LS17 .... 43 C2
 Leeds, Intake LS13 .... 58 B4
 Sowerby Bridge HX6 ...... 111 F3
 Wilsden BD15 .... 53 D4
Moorland Wlk LS17 .... 43 C2
Moorlands Holmfirth HD7 189 C3
 Ilkley LS29 .... 8 A2
Moorlands Ave
 Bradford BD3 .... 56 D1
 Dewsbury WF13 .... 118 C1
 Halifax HX2 .... 91 E3
 Keighley BD22 .... 34 F4
 Yeadon LS19 .... 40 D6
Moorlands Cres
 Halifax HX2 .... 91 E3
 Huddersfield HD3 .... 134 D1
Moorlands Ct HX4 .... 134 B8
Moorlands Dr Halifax HX3 .. 91 E2
 Yeadon LS19 .... 40 D6
Moorlands Pl HX3 .... 203 D1
Moorlands Rd
 Birkenshaw BD11 .... 96 A7
 Dewsbury WF13 .... 139 B8
 Elland HX4 .... 134 B8
 Huddersfield HD3 .... 134 D1
Moorlands Sch Leeds LS16 .. 42 D1
Moorlands Terr BD11 .. 106 A1
Moorlands The
 Bacup OL13 .... 106 A8
 Boston Spa LS23 .... 30 C8
 Leeds LS17 .... 43 E4
 Wetherby LS22 .... 13 F5
Moorlands View HX1 ...... 203 D1
Moorlea Dr BD17 .... 38 C4
Moorleigh Cl LS25 .... 83 B2
Moorleigh Dr LS25 .... 83 B2
Moorroyd St WF5 .... 140 C8
Moors Cl HD8 .... 173 J...
Moorshutt Rd WF9 .... 181 C6
Moorside Baildon BD17 .... 38 C5
 Bradford BD9 .... 54 E2
 Cleckheaton, Hartshead
 Moor Side BD19 .... 116 A6
 Cleckheaton, West End
 BD19 .... 116 C7
 Kirkburton HD8 .... 173 B6
Moorside App BD11 .... 96 F5
Moorside Ave
 Batley WF13 .... 117 F2
 Birkenshaw BD11 .... 96 A7
 Birkenshaw, Drighlington
 BD11 .... 96 F5
 Bradford BD2 .... 56 D2
 Huddersfield HD4 .... 153 D4
 Steeton BD20 .... 17 A5
Moorside Cl
 Birkenshaw BD11 .... 96 F5
 Bradford BD2 .... 56 C4
 Halifax HX2 .... 91 F4
Moorside Cres BD11 .... 96 F6
Moorside Dr
 Birkenshaw BD11 .... 96 F5
 Leeds LS13 .... 58 C4
Moorside End WF13 .... 117 F2
Moorside Gdns
 Birkenshaw BD11 .... 96 F5
 Bradford BD2 .... 56 C4
 Halifax HX2 .... 91 F4
Moorside Gn BD11 .... 96 F6
Moorside Junior
 & Infants Sch HX2 .... 91 F4

Moorside La Addingham LS29 .. 6 E1
 Askwith LS21 .... 10 A...
 Bradford BD3 .... 75 D...
 Oxenhope BD22 .... 50 F...
Moorside Maltings LS11 .. 214 C...
Moorside Mews BD2 .... 56 D...
Moorside Mount BD11 ...... 96 E...
Moorside Paddock BD19 .. 116 B...
Moorside Par BD11 .... 96 F...
Moorside Pl Batley WF13 .. 117 F...
 Bradford BD3 .... 75 D...
Moorside Rd Batley WF13 .. 117 F...
 Birkenshaw BD11 .... 96 E...
 Bradford BD3 .... 75 D...
 Bradford, Haigh Fold BD2 .. 56 C...
 Honley HD7 .... 171 E...
 Kirkheaton HD5 .... 137 C...
 Wilsden BD15 .... 53 C...
Moorside Rise BD19 .... 116 B...
Moorside St Bradford BD12 .. 94 E...
 Leeds LS13 .... 58 C...
Moorside Terr
 Birkenshaw BD11 .... 96 F...
 Bradford BD2 .... 56 D...
 Leeds LS13 .... 58 C...
Moorside Vale BD11 .... 96 F...
Moorside View BD11 .... 96 F...
Moorside Wlk BD11 .... 96 F...
Moorthorpe Ave BD3 .... 56 D...
Moorthorpe Sta WF9 ...... 182 E...
Moortop BD11 .... 96 F...
Moortown Corner House
 LS17 .... 43 D...
Moortown Golf Course
 LS17 .... 43 B...
Moortown Primary Sch
 LS17 .... 43 D...
Moorview Cres BD16 .... 53 E...
Moorview Croft LS29 .... 21 F...
Moorview Ct BD10 .... 39 A...
Moorview Dr Shipley BD18 .. 55 E...
 Wilsden BD15 .... 53 E...
Moorview Gr BD21 .... 35 D...
Moorville Ave BD3 .... 56 D...
Moorville Cl LS11 .... 214 B...
Moorville Ct LS11 .... 214 B...
Moorville Dr BD11 .... 96 A...
Moorville Gr LS11 .... 214 A...
Moorville Rd LS11 .... 214 B...
Moorway LS20 .... 39 C...
Morcar Rd BD2 .... 56 C...
Moravian Pl BD5 .... 74 D...
Morefield Bank HD7 .... 189 C...
Moresby Rd BD6 .... 93 F...
Moresdale La LS14 .... 61 F...
Moreton Cres WF10 .... 124 A...
Morlands Cl WF13 .... 117 F...
Morley Ave Bradford BD3 .. 56 D...
 Knottingley WF11 .... 127 A...
Morley Carr Rd BD12 .... 94 D...
Morley Cross Hall
 Infants Sch LS27 .... 97 F...
Morley Cross Hall
 Junior Sch LS27 .... 97 F...
Morley Elmfield Infant Sch
 LS27 .... 98 B...
Morley Fold HD8 .... 191 F...
Morley Hall La HX2 .... 111 D...
Morley High Sch LS27 ...... 97 F...
Morley La HD3 .... 153 A...
Morley St BD7 .... 201 B...
Morley St Francis
 RC Prim Sch LS27 .... 97 F...
Morley Sta LS27 .... 98 C...
Morley Victoria
 Primary Sch LS27 .... 98 A...
Morley View HX3 .... 113 E...
Morning St BD21 .... 35 B...
Morningside Bradford BD8 .. 55 D...
 Denholme BD13 .... 52 E...
Mornington Rd
 Bingley BD16 .... 37 A...
 Ilkley LS29 .... 8 C...
Mornington St BD21 .... 35 B...
Mornington Villas BD8 ...... 55 D...
Morpeth Pl LS9 .... 212 B...
Morpeth St Bradford BD7 .. 74 C...
 Oxenhope BD22 .... 51 C...
Morphet Terr LS7 .... 206 C...
Morrell Cres WF2 .... 120 F...
Morris Ave LS5 .... 59 A...
Morris Cl WF9 .... 163 B...
Morris Gn BD13 .... 53 A...
Morris La LS5 .... 59 A...
Morris Mount LS5 .... 59 A...
Morris Pl LS27 .... 97 F...
Morris View LS5 .... 59 A...
Morrison St WF10 .... 124 C...
Morrit Ave LS15 .... 62 B...
Morritt Dr LS15 .... 80 F...
Morritt Gr LS15 .... 80 F...
Mortimer Ave Batley WF17 .. 117 F...
 Bradford BD3 .... 56 D...
Mortimer Cl Garforth LS25 .. 82 D...
 Ossett WF5 .... 140 F...
Mortimer Row
 Bradford BD3 .... 75 E...
 Horbury WF4 .... 140 F...
Mortimer St Batley WF17 .. 117 F...
 Bradford BD8 .... 73 F...
 Cleckheaton BD19 .... 116 D...
Mortimer Terr WF17 .... 117 F...
Morton Gn HD5 .... 155 A...
Morton Dr Dewsbury WF12 139 B...
 Keighley BD20 .... 36 D...
Morton La Bingley BD16 .... 36 D...
 Keighley BD20 .... 36 D...
Morton Par WF2 .... 142 A...

Morton Rd BD4 .... 75 D5
Morton Terr LS20 .... 22 D1
Morton Way HX3 .... 134 E1
Morton Wood Gr HD7 .... 189 D3
Mortons CI HX3 .... 113 E3
Morvern Meadows WF9 .... 181 F7
Morwick Gr LS15 .... 62 F6
Moselden La HX6 .... 150 D6
Moseley PI LS6 .... 206 B3
Moseley Wood App LS16 .... 41 D4
Moseley Wood Bank LS16 .... 41 D5
Moseley Wood CI LS16 .... 41 D4
Moseley Wood Cres LS16 .... 41 D5
Moseley Wood Croft LS16 .... 41 D4
Moseley Wood Dr LS16 .... 41 D5
Moseley Wood Gdns
  LS16 .... 41 D5
Moseley Wood Gn LS16 .... 41 D5
Moseley Wood La LS16 .... 41 E5
Moseley Wood Rise LS16 .... 41 D5
Moseley Wood View LS16 .... 41 E6
Moseley Wood Wlk LS16 .... 41 D5
Moser Ave BD2 .... 56 A5
Moser Cres BD2 .... 56 A5
Moss Bridge Rd LS13 .... 57 F5
Moss Carr Ave BD21 .... 35 E5
Moss Carr BD21 .... 35 F5
Moss Carr Rd BD21 .... 35 F5
Moss Dr HX2 .... 91 E6
Moss Edge Rd HD7 .... 188 C1
Moss Gdns LS17 .... 43 A5
Moss Hall La HX7 .... 87 E4
Moss La Halifax HX2 .... 91 E6
  Hebden Bridge HX7 .... 89 A4
Moss Lea [4] LS28 .... 98 B7
Moss Rise Horsforth HD7 .... 188 E5
  LS17 .... 43 A5
Moss Row BD15 .... 53 C6
Moss Side BD9 .... 54 E2
Moss St Castleford WF10 .... 124 C8
  Haworth BD22 .... 51 E8
  Huddersfield HD4 .... 154 B4
  Thornton BD13 .... 72 C7
Moss Syke LS14 .... 45 C8
Moss Valley LS17 .... 43 A5
Mossdale Ave BD9 .... 54 C3
Mosstree CI BD13 .... 72 C2
Mossy Bank CI BD13 .... 72 E2
Mostyn Gr BD6 .... 94 A8
Mostyn Mount HX3 .... 92 A3
Mostyn Wlk WF4 .... 159 F2
Motley La LS20 .... 22 D2
Moulson Ct [1] BD5 .... 74 E3
Moulson Terr BD13 .... 71 D8
Mount Ave
  [1] Batley WF17 .... 118 D3
  Batley, Nunroyd WF16 .... 117 E6
  Bradford BD2 .... 56 C5
  Halifax HX2 .... 112 C7
  Hemsworth WF9 .... 181 D7
  Huddersfield HD3 .... 134 D1
  Wakefield WF2 .... 120 F3
Mount Cres
  Cleckheaton BD19 .... 116 D8
  Halifax HX2 .... 112 C7
  Holme Chapel BB10 .... 85 A8
  Wakefield WF2 .... 141 F3
Mount Dr LS17 .... 43 B6
Mount Gdns
  Cleckheaton BD19 .... 116 D8
  Leeds LS17 .... 43 B6
Mount Gr BD2 .... 56 B5
Mount Jun & Inf Sch The
  WF2 .... 141 F3
Mount La Brighouse HD6 .... 135 E6
  Holme Chapel BB10 .... 85 A8
  Todmorden OL14 .... 86 C3
Mount Pellon BD2 .... 202 B4
Mount Pellon Rd HX2 .... 202 A4
Mount Pisgah LS21 .... 23 A7
Mount PI BD18 .... 55 B8
Mount Pleasant
  Ackworth M T WF7 .... 163 F6
  Addingham LS29 .... 6 F8
  [1] Bradford BD6 .... 93 F7
  Brighouse HD6 .... 135 E6
  Castleford WF10 .... 124 F6
  Denholme BD13 .... 71 D8
  Dewsbury WF12 .... 139 E1
  Emley HD8 .... 175 D7
  Glusburn BD20 .... 16 B6
  Guiseley LS20 .... 22 E2
  Huddersfield HD1 .... 153 F3
  Ilkley LS29 .... 8 C3
  Keighley BD20 .... 36 C7
  [4] Kippax LS25 .... 83 B1
  Kirk Smeaton WF8 .... 166 F6
  Menston LS29 .... 21 F4
  Middleton LS10 .... 99 C5
  Ripponden HX4 .... 132 F4
Mount Pleasant Ave
  Halifax HX1 .... 203 D4
  Leeds LS8 .... 204 C1
Mount Pleasant Dr HX7 .... 89 F1
Mount Pleasant Gdns
  [3] Kippax LS25 .... 83 B1
  Leeds LS8 .... 204 C1
Mount Pleasant
  Infants Sch HD1 .... 153 F3
Mount Pleasant
  Junior Sch HD1 .... 153 F3
Mount Pleasant La HD8 .... 155 C4
Mount Pleasant Rd LS28 .... 76 F8
Mount Pleasant Sports Ctr
  HD1 .... 153 F3

Mount Pleasant St
  Featherstone WF7 .... 145 D6
  [1] Huddersfield HD5 .... 154 D6
  [2] Pudsey LS28 .... 76 F8
  Queensbury BD13 .... 72 E1
  Todmorden OL14 .... 86 A1
Mount Pleasant View [7]
  OL14 .... 108 B5
Mount Preston LS2 .... 206 A1
Mount Preston St LS2 .... 206 A1
Mount Rd Bradford BD6 .... 74 A1
  Bradford, Eccleshill BD2 .... 56 B5
  Huddersfield HD1 .... 153 D7
  Lofthouse Gate WF3 .... 121 F6
  Marsden HD7 .... 168 D1
Mount Rise LS17 .... 43 B6
Mount Royd BD8 .... 55 C2
Mount Scar View HD7 .... 189 D4
Mount St Batley WF17 .... 118 D3
  Bradford, Eccleshill BD2 .... 75 B6
  Bradford, Eccleshill BD2 .... 56 B5
  Cleckheaton BD19 .... 116 D8
  Halifax HX1 .... 203 E3
  Huddersfield, Milnsbridge
  HD3 .... 153 A4
  Huddersfield, Rashcliffe
  HD1, HD4 .... 153 F3
  Keighley BD21 .... 35 A7
  Sowerby Bridge HX6 .... 112 C4
Mount St Mary's High Sch
  LS9 .... 212 B3
Mount St Marys
  RC Primary Sch LS9 .... 80 A8
Mount St W HX2 .... 202 A4
Mount Tabor Rd HX2 .... 91 A4
Mount Tabor St LS28 .... 76 C7
Mount Terr Batley WF17 .... 118 C3
  Bradford BD2 .... 56 B5
Mount The
  Barwick in E LS15 .... 63 D6
  Batley WF17 .... 96 E2
  Castleford WF10 .... 125 C7
  Kippax LS25 .... 83 A1
  Leeds LS15 .... 62 E8
  Leeds, Alwoodley LS17 .... 43 B6
  Normanton WF6 .... 123 B2
  Pontefract WF8 .... 146 C8
  Rothwell LS26 .... 100 F7
  Todmorden OL14 .... 108 C6
  Wakefield WF2 .... 141 F3
  Wakefield, Wrenthorpe
  WF2 .... 120 D1
Mount Vernon Rd LS19 .... 40 C4
Mount View Halifax HX2 .... 91 A3
  Oakworth BD22 .... 34 B2
  Queensbury BD13 .... 72 D1
Mount View Rd HD7 .... 189 E2
Mount Wlk HD7 .... 124 D5
Mount Zion Rd HD5 .... 154 C6
Mountain Cres WF12 .... 139 D2
Mountain Rd WF12 .... 139 D2
Mountain View BD18 .... 55 D6
Mountain Way HD5 .... 155 C7
Mountbatten Ave
  Lofthouse Gate WF1 .... 121 C5
  Wakefield WF1 .... 160 E8
Mountbatten Cres WF1 .... 121 C5
Mountbatten Ct [4] BD8 .... 74 E2
Mountbatten Gdns HD3 .... 153 B7
Mountbatten Gr WF1 .... 121 C4
Mountbatten View LS27 .... 98 B7
Mountfield Ave HD5 .... 155 B4
Mountfield Rd HD5 .... 155 B5
Mountfield Wlk WF9 .... 182 B1
Mountfields
  Brighouse HX3 .... 114 E8
  Leeds LS3 .... 205 F1
Mountjoy Prep Sch HD1 .... 153 F7
Mountjoy Rd HD1 .... 153 F7
Mountleigh CI BD4 .... 95 A7
Mouse Hole La WF14 .... 138 D1
Moverley Flatts WF8 .... 146 E7
Mowat Ct WF15 .... 116 B5
Mowbray Chase LS26 .... 101 B7
Mowbray Ct BD13 .... 52 C5
Mowbray Cres LS14 .... 62 A3
Mowbray Cres LS14 .... 62 A3
Moxon CI WF8 .... 146 D6
Moxon Gr WF1 .... 121 B3
Moxon PI WF1 .... 141 C5
Moxon Sq WF1 .... 121 C4
Moxon Way WF1 .... 121 C4
Moynihan CI LS8 .... 208 B4
Mozley Dr HX7 .... 91 F6
Mucky La HX5 .... 134 D4
Muddy La LS22 .... 13 C8
Muff St BD4 .... 75 B5
Muffit La BD19 .... 117 D8
Mug Mill La WF12 .... 157 E8
Mugup La HD7 .... 189 E1
Muir Ct LS6 .... 205 D4
Muirfield Ave WF7 .... 124 D1
Muirfield CI S72 .... 180 C1
Muirfield Dr WF2 .... 142 A2
Muirfields The S75 .... 178 A1
Muirhead Dr BD4 .... 75 E2
Muirlands The HD2 .... 136 E5
Mulberry Ave Leeds LS16 .... 42 D4
  Ryhill WF4 .... 162 B1
Mulberry Ct HD7 .... 152 E5
Mulberry Garth
  Leeds LS16 .... 42 E3
  Thorp Arch LS23 .... 14 E1
Mulberry House [2]
  WF10 .... 124 C7
Mulberry PI WF4 .... 162 B1
Mulberry Rise LS16 .... 42 D4

Mulberry St
  Huddersfield HD5 .... 154 C5
  [1] Keighley BD21 .... 35 D8
  Leeds LS10 .... 212 A1
  Pudsey LS28 .... 76 F7
Mulberry Terr HD1 .... 154 B8
Mulberry View LS16 .... 42 D3
Mulcture Hall Rd HX1 .... 203 F3
Mulehouse La HA03 .... 134 B1
Mulgrave St BD3 .... 75 B6
Mullberry Gdns LS26 .... 102 B2
Mullins Ct LS9 .... 212 C3
Mullion Ave HD7 .... 171 E4
Mumford St BD5 .... 74 E3
Munby St BD8 .... 73 E7
Muncaster Rd LS25 .... 83 B8
Munster St BD4 .... 75 B6
Munton CI BD6 .... 73 E6
Murdoch St BD21 .... 35 F8
Murdstone CI [5] BD5 .... 74 E3
Murgatroyd St
  Bradford BD5 .... 74 E2
  Bradford BD3 .... 55 B8
Murray Rd HD2 .... 153 F8
Murray St [3] BD5 .... 74 C3
Murton CI LS14 .... 62 A4
Museum Ct BD2 .... 56 C2
Museum St LS9 .... 207 F1
Musgrave Bank LS13 .... 58 E2
Musgrave Bldgs [6] LS28 .... 76 F8
Musgrave Gr [7] WF4 .... 141 D4
Musgrave Dr BD2 .... 56 C2
Musgrave Gr BD2 .... 56 C2
Musgrave Mount
  Bradford BD2 .... 56 C2
  Leeds LS13 .... 58 E2
Musgrave Rd BD2 .... 56 C2
Musgrave Rise LS13 .... 58 E2
Musgrave St WF17 .... 96 E1
Musgrave View LS13 .... 58 E2
Mushroom St LS9 .... 207 E1
Musselburgh St BD7 .... 74 C7
Mutton La BD15 .... 53 D2
Myers Ave BD2 .... 56 A4
Myers Croft
  Huddersfield HD5 .... 154 F6
  Otley LS21 .... 23 A7
Myers La BD2 .... 56 A4
Myrtle Ave Bingley BD16 .... 36 F2
  Dewsbury WF13 .... 138 E5
  Halifax HX2 .... 91 E4
Myrtle CI HD5 .... 36 F2
Myrtle Dr Halifax HX2 .... 91 E4
  Haworth BD22 .... 34 F3
Myrtle Gdns HX2 .... 91 E4
Myrtle Gr Bingley BD16 .... 36 F2
  Halifax HX2 .... 91 E4
  Huddersfield HD3 .... 153 B6
  [4] Queensbury BD13 .... 92 C8
Myrtle Park First Sch
  BD16 .... 36 F2
Myrtle PI Bingley BD16 .... 36 F2
  Halifax HX2 .... 91 E4
Myrtle Rd Dewsbury WF13 .... 138 E5
  Halifax HX2 .... 91 E4
  Huddersfield HD3 .... 153 B6
Myrtle St [1] Bingley BD16 .... 37 A3
  Bradford BD3 .... 75 C6
  [1] Huddersfield HD5 .... 154 B7
  Todmorden OL14 .... 108 B5
Myrtle View
  [2] Haworth BD22 .... 51 F8
  Oakworth BD22 .... 34 D3
Myrtle Wlk BD16 .... 36 F2
Myson Ave WF8 .... 125 F4
Mytham CI HX7 .... 88 E3
Mytholm CI HX7 .... 88 E3
Mytholmes La
  Haworth BD22 .... 51 C8
  Oakworth BD22 .... 34 D1
Mytholmes Terr BD22 .... 51 C8
Mytholmroyd Sta HX7 .... 110 E8

Nab Cres HD7 .... 170 C2
Nab End BD10 .... 94 D2
Nab End La HX4 .... 134 D7
Nab La Batley WF17 .... 97 B2
  Mirfield WF14 .... 138 A6
  Shipley BD18 .... 54 D7
Nab The WF14 .... 137 E6
Nab View BD20 .... 5 F3
Nab Water La BD22 .... 70 C6
Nab Wood Bank BD18 .... 54 D7
Nab Wood CI BD18 .... 54 E7
Nab Wood Cres BD18 .... 54 D7
Nab Wood Dr BD18 .... 54 D7
Nab Wood Gdns BD18 .... 54 E7
Nab Wood Gr BD18 .... 54 D7
Nab Wood Grammar Sch
  BD18 .... 54 C7
Nab Wood Middle Sch
  BD18 .... 54 D7
Nab Wood Mount BD18 .... 54 D7
Nab Wood PI BD18 .... 54 D6
Nab Wood Rd BD18 .... 54 C6
Nab Wood Rise BD18 .... 54 D7
Nab Wood Terr BD18 .... 54 D7
Nabbs La HD7 .... 151 F1
Nabcroft La HD4 .... 153 D4
Nabcroft Rise HD4 .... 153 D4
Naburn App LS14 .... 62 C8
Naburn Chase LS14 .... 62 C8
Naburn CI LS14 .... 62 C8
Naburn Ct [3] LS14 .... 62 C8
Naburn Dr LS14 .... 62 B7

Naburn Fold LS14 .... 62 C7
Naburn Gdns LS14 .... 62 B7
Naburn Gn LS14 .... 62 B7
Naburn PI LS14 .... 62 B8
Naburn Rd LS14 .... 62 B7
Naburn View LS14 .... 62 B7
Nail's Ct BD10 .... 39 B2
Nairn CI HD4 .... 153 C2
Nancroft Cres LS12 .... 209 F3
Nancroft Mount LS12 .... 209 F3
Nancroft Terr LS12 .... 209 F3
Nanny Goat La LS25 .... 82 D8
Nansen Ave [8] LS13 .... 58 C2
Nansen Gr [10] LS13 .... 58 C2
Nansen Mount [11] LS13 .... 58 C2
Nansen St [1] LS13 .... 58 B2
Nansen Terr [3] LS13 .... 58 B2
Nansen View [2] LS13 .... 58 B2
Naomi Rd HD4 .... 154 A2
Napier House OL14 .... 129 A8
Napier Rd Bradford BD3 .... 75 D7
  Elland HX5 .... 134 E6
Napier St Bradford BD3 .... 75 D7
  Keighley BD21 .... 35 D6
  [2] Queensbury BD13 .... 72 F1
Napier Terr BD3 .... 55 B1
Nares St BD8 .... 55 B1
Nares St [9] Haworth BD22 .... 51 E8
  Keighley BD21 .... 35 B7
Nares St Upper BD21 .... 35 B7
Narrow Balk LS25 .... 196 C5
Narrow La BD16 .... 36 B1
Narrows The BD16 .... 36 B1
Naseby Garth LS9 .... 207 E1
Naseby Gdns [4] LS9 .... 212 B4
Naseby Grange [3] LS9 .... 212 B4
Naseby PI LS9 .... 212 B4
Naseby Rise BD13 .... 72 F1
Naseby Terr LS9 .... 212 B4
Naseby View LS9 .... 212 B4
Naseby Wlk LS9 .... 212 B4
Nashville Rd [4] BD22 .... 35 A6
Nashville St [2] BD22 .... 35 A6
Nashville Terr [1] BD22 .... 35 A6
Nassau PI LS7 .... 207 E4
Nat Mus of Photography
  & TV BD1 .... 201 B2
Nathan La HX6 .... 132 C7
Nathaniel Waterhouse
  Homes HX1 .... 203 E2
National Rd LS10 .... 215 E4
National St BD1 .... 201 A2
Natty Fields CI HX2 .... 91 E7
Natty La HX2 .... 91 E7
Nature Way BD6 .... 93 E2
Navigation Gdns WF12 .... 139 B4
Navigation Rd
  Castleford WF10 .... 103 D1
  Dewsbury WF12 .... 139 B4
  Halifax HX3 .... 203 F2
Navigation Wlk LS10 .... 211 F3
Navvy La LS11 .... 118 D1
Naylor Ct WF13 .... 118 D1
Naylor La HX2 .... 90 C1
Naylor Rd Dewsbury WF13 .... 118 B1
  Halifax HX1 .... 202 B3
  Ossett WF5 .... 140 D8
Naylor's Bldgs [5] BD19 .... 115 F8
Naze View OL14 .... 107 F3
Neal PI LS10 .... 212 A2
Neal St BD5 .... 201 B2
Neale Rd HD1 .... 153 F3
Neale St [5] HX7 .... 89 A2
Near Bank HD8 .... 174 B2
Near Crook BD17 .... 38 F1
Near La HD7 .... 170 E2
Nearcliffe Rd BD9 .... 55 A2
Neath Gdns LS9 .... 80 C5
Necropolis Rd BD7 .... 73 F5
Ned Hill Rd HX2 .... 71 F3
Ned La Bradford BD4 .... 75 F4
  Slaithwaite HD7 .... 169 F8
Needles Inn La LS26 .... 101 C7
Nell Gap Ave WF4 .... 158 A7
Nell Gap Cres WF4 .... 158 A6
Nell Gap La Netherton WF4 .... 158 A7
  Netherton, Middlestown
  WF4 .... 158 A6
Nelson Croft LS25 .... 82 D5
Nelson Ct LS27 .... 98 B4
Nelson PI [1] Morley LS27 .... 98 A5
  Queensbury BD13 .... 72 E1
  Sowerby Bridge HX6 .... 112 D4
Nelson Rd Ilkley LS29 .... 8 C4
Nelson St Batley, Birstall WF17 .... 96 F1
  Bradford BD15 .... 54 C1
  Bradford BD5 .... 201 B1
  Dewsbury WF13 .... 139 C8
  [2] Elland HX5 .... 134 F7
  Haworth BD22 .... 51 C6
  Huddersfield HD1 .... 153 F4
  Liversedge WF15 .... 117 B3
  Normanton WF6 .... 123 C3
  Otley LS21 .... 23 A7
  [1] Queensbury BD13 .... 72 E1
  South Hiendley S72 .... 180 E5
  Sowerby Bridge HX6 .... 112 D4
  Todmorden OL14 .... 129 A8
Nene St BD5 .... 74 C4
Nepshaw La
  Gildersome LS27 .... 97 D4
  Morley LS27 .... 97 E5
Nepshaw La N LS27 .... 97 E5
Nepshaw La S LS27 .... 97 E5
Neptune St LS9 .... 212 A3
Nesfield CI LS10 .... 99 F6

Nesfield Cres LS10 .... 99 F6
Nesfield Garth LS10 .... 99 F6
Nesfield Gdns LS10 .... 99 F6
Nesfield Rd Ilkley LS29 .... 7 F5
  Middleton LS10 .... 99 F6
Nesfield St BD1 .... 201 B4
Nesfield View Ilkley LS29 .... 7 F4
  Middleton LS10 .... 99 F6
Nesfield Wlk LS10 .... 99 F6
Nessfield CI BD22 .... 34 F5
Nessfield First Sch BD22 .... 34 F5
Nessfield Gr BD22 .... 34 F5
Nessfield Rd BD22 .... 34 F5
Nest East HX7 .... 110 D8
Nest La HX7 .... 110 D8
Nestfield CI LS25 .... 125 D3
Neston Way WF5 .... 119 D1
Nether CI HD5 .... 154 E8
Nether Cres HD5 .... 154 E8
Nether Hall Ave HD5 .... 154 E8
Nether La HD7 .... 187 C3
Nether Moor View HD6 .... 171 C8
Nether Moor View [18]
  BD16 .... 37 A3
Netherby St LS28 .... 57 D4
Netherby St BD3 .... 75 B7
Nethercliffe Cres LS20 .... 22 D2
Nethercliffe Rd LS20 .... 22 D2
Netherdale Ct LS22 .... 14 A6
Netherend Rd HD7 .... 151 F1
Netherfield Ave WF4 .... 158 D5
Netherfield CI
  Castleford WF10 .... 123 F5
  Kirkburton HD8 .... 173 F6
  Yeadon LS19 .... 40 B7
Netherfield Cres WF4 .... 158 D5
Netherfield Ct LS20 .... 22 D1
Netherfield Dr
  Guiseley LS20 .... 22 D2
  Holmfirth HD7 .... 189 A7
Netherfield Ind Pk WF13 .... 138 E5
Netherfield PI
  Cleckheaton BD19 .... 116 F7
  Netherton WF4 .... 158 D6
Netherfield Rd
  Dewsbury WF13 .... 138 E5
  Guiseley LS20 .... 22 D2
Netherfield Rise [1] LS20 .... 22 D1
Netherhall Rd BD17 .... 38 D3
Netherhouses HD7 .... 188 D5
Netherlands Ave BD6 .... 94 C7
Netherlands Avenue Sch
  BD6 .... 94 D7
Netherlands Sq BD12 .... 94 D7
Netherlea Dr HD7 .... 188 F7
Netherleigh Sch The BD9 .... 54 E2
Netherley Dr HD7 .... 168 E2
Netherly Brow WF5 .... 140 E3
Netheroyd WF7 .... 144 C5
Netheroyd Hill Rd HD2 .... 136 A3
Netheroyd PI WF4 .... 144 B4
Netherthong Junior
  & Infants Sch WF4 .... 188 F8
Netherthong Rd HD7 .... 187 F8
Netherton Fold HD4 .... 171 C6
Netherton Hall Gdns WF4 .... 158 E6
Netherton Infant Sch
  WF4 .... 171 D7
Netherton Junior
  & Infants Sch WF4 .... 158 E6
Netherton Moor Rd HD4 .... 171 E6
Netherwood CI HD2 .... 136 A3
Nettle Gr HX3 .... 92 F1
Nettleton Ave WF14 .... 137 F5
Nettleton Chase WF5 .... 119 C1
Nettleton Cres HD4 .... 154 B4
Nettleton Ct LS15 .... 81 D8
Nettleton Hill Rd HD7 .... 152 B6
Nettleton House WF9 .... 181 D6
Nettleton Rd
  Huddersfield HD5 .... 155 A8
  Mirfield WF14 .... 137 F5
Nettleton St
  Lofthouse Gate WF3 .... 122 B6
  Ossett WF5 .... 140 C6
Nettleton Terr HD5 .... 155 A8
Nettleton's Almshouses [3]
  HD5 .... 154 F3
Nevill Gr BD9 .... 54 D3
Neville App LS9 .... 80 C6
Neville Ave Bradford BD4 .... 75 B1
  Leeds LS9 .... 80 C6
Neville CI LS9 .... 80 C6
Neville CI Leeds LS15 .... 80 C6
  South Kirkby WF9 .... 182 C3
Neville Garth LS9 .... 80 D6
Neville Gr Huddersfield HD5 .... 154 F4
  Leeds LS9 .... 80 D6
  Swillington LS26 .... 82 A2
Neville Mount LS9 .... 80 D6
Neville Par LS9 .... 80 C6
Neville PI LS9 .... 80 D6
Neville Rd Bradford BD4 .... 75 B4
  Leeds LS9 .... 80 D6
  Leeds LS15, LS9 .... 80 C6
  Otley LS21 .... 23 B7
Neville Row LS9 .... 80 D6
Neville Sq LS9 .... 80 D6
Neville St Cleckheaton BD19 .... 116 F7
  [2] Keighley BD21 .... 35 D8
  Leeds LS1 .... 211 E3
  Normanton WF6 .... 123 B1
  Wakefield WF1 .... 142 F4

Neville Terr LS9 .... 80 C6
Neville View LS9 .... 80 C6
Neville Wlk LS9 .... 80 C7
Nevins Rd WF13 .... 138 D6
Nevison Ave WF8 .... 125 E3
New Adel Ave LS16 .... 42 A3
New Adel Gdns LS16 .... 42 A3
New Adel La LS16 .... 42 A3
New Augustus St BD1 .... 201 C2
New Ave HD5 .... 137 B1
New Bank HX3 .... 203 F4
New Bank Rise BD4 .... 75 D3
New Bank St LS27 .... 98 B5
New Bond St WA1 .... 203 D3
New Bridge Rd HD7 .... 170 B2
New Briggate LS1, LS2 .... 211 F4
New Brighton
  Denby Dale HD8 .... 191 B3
  Shipley BD16 .... 54 C6
New Brook St LS29 .... 8 B4
New Brunswick St
  Halifax HX1 .... 203 D3
  Wakefield WF1 .... 216 B1
New Cl Horsforth LS18 .... 58 B8
  Marsden HD7 .... 151 C1
  Shipley BD18 .... 54 D7
New Clayton Terr BD13 .... 52 D5
New Close Ave BD20 .... 5 E1
New Close La
  Marsden HD7 .... 151 C1
  Norton DN6 .... 184 E7
New Close Rd BD18 .... 54 C7
New Clough Rd HX6 .... 112 D1
New Coll WF8 .... 125 B1
New Craven Gate LS11 .... 214 C4
New Cres LS18 .... 58 B8
New Cross St
  Bradford, Lower Woodlands
  BD12 .... 95 B5
  Bradford, West Bowling BD5 .. 74 F3
New Dales La BD20 .... 4 B7
New Delight HX7 .... 69 A1
New England Rd BD21 .... 35 C5
New Farmers Hill LS26 .... 101 D7
New Fold Bradford BD6 .... 93 E7
  Holmfirth HD7 .... 189 A5
New Gate HD7 .... 189 C1
New Grove Dr HD6 .... 154 E7
New Hall App WF4 .... 157 F4
New Hall Cl WF4 .... 159 E4
New Hall La WF4 .... 157 F4
New Hall Rd WF8 .... 125 E3
New Hall Way WF4 .... 157 F3
New Hey Moor Houses
  HD8 .... 173 F2
New Hey Rd Bradford BD4 ... 75 A4
  Brighouse HD6 .... 135 D5
  Elland HD3 .... 152 A8
  Huddersfield HD2, HD4, HD6 .. 135 D5
  Huddersfield, Marsh
  HD2, HD3 .... 153 C7
  Huddersfield, Salendine Nook
  HD2, HD3 .... 152 E8
  Marsden HD3 .... 150 D2
  Slaithwaite HD2, HD3, HD6 .. 151 D5
New Holme Rd BD22 .... 51 D6
New House
  Holmfirth HD7 .... 199 D7
  Slaithwaite HD7 .... 169 F7
New House La BD13 .... 73 B1
New House Rd HD2 .... 136 D4
New Inn Ct LS21 .... 23 A7
New Inn St LS12 .... 209 D3
New John St BD1 .... 201 B3
New Kirkgate BD18 .... 55 B8
New La Birkenshaw BD4 ...... 76 C2
  Blackshaw Head HX7 .... 88 D3
  Bradford BD3, BD4 .... 75 D6
  Burton Salmon LS25 .... 105 D3
  Castleford WF10 .... 123 D5
  Cleckheaton BD19 .... 116 A6
  Crigglestone WF4 .... 159 E7
  East Ardsley WF3 .... 120 C8
  Farnhill BD20 .... 4 F2
  Gildersome BD11 .... 97 B8
  Halifax HX3 .... 113 D4
  Halifax, Copley HX3 .... 113 B2
  Hebden Bridge HX7 .... 110 D4
  Leeds LS11 .... 211 E2
  Marsden HD3 .... 150 D4
  Middleton LS10 .... 99 B5
  Skelmanthorpe HD8 .... 175 B1
  Slaithwaite HD7 .... 152 A3
  Slaithwaite, Scapegoat Hill
  HD7 .... 152 B6
  Sowerby Bridge HX2 .... 111 B5
  Upton WF9 .... 183 A7
New Laithe Cl HD4 .... 154 C2
New Laithe Hill HD4 .... 154 C2
New Laithe La HD7 .... 189 E5
New Laithe Rd
  5 Bradford BD6 .... 74 A1
  Haworth BD22 .... 49 E8
  Huddersfield HD4 .... 154 C2
New Laithes Junior Sch
  LS18 .... 58 A6
New Lane Cres WF9 .... 183 A7
New Leeds LS13 .... 58 B5
New Line BD10 .... 56 E7
New Longley HX6 .... 112 A1
New Longley La HX6 .... 112 A1
New Market LS21 .... 23 A7
New Market Pl BD1 .... 201 B3
New Market St LS1 .... 211 F3
New Mill La LS23 .... 30 E5

New Mill Rd Holmfirth HD7 . 189 B7
  Holmfirth, Brockholes HD7 .. 172 C3
  Honley HD7 .... 172 C3
New North Par HD1 .... 154 A6
New North Rd
  Huddersfield HD1 .... 153 F7
  Liversedge WF16 .... 117 C5
  Slaithwaite HD7 .... 152 A2
New Occupation La LS28 .. 76 C6
New Otley Rd BD3 .... 201 D4
New Park Ave LS28 .... 57 E3
New Park Cl LS28 .... 57 E3
New Park Croft LS28 .... 57 E3
New Park La WF2 .... 141 B7
New Park Pl LS28 .... 57 E3
New Park Rd BD13 .... 72 D1
New Park St LS27 .... 97 F3
New Park Vale LS28 .... 57 E3
New Park View LS28 .... 57 E2
New Park Way LS28 .... 57 E3
New Park Wlk **4** LS28 .. 57 D2
New Pepper Rd LS10 .... 215 F3
New Popplewell La BD19 .. 115 F8
New Princess St LS11 .... 211 E1
New Rd Badsworth WF9 .. 164 D2
  Blackshaw Head HX7 .... 87 F6
  Bramham LS23 .... 30 D3
  Castleford WF11 .... 126 A5
  Cawthorne S75 .... 193 B5
  Denholme BD13 .... 71 D8
  Elland, Greetland HX4 .... 134 B7
  Elland, Old Lindley HX4 ..... 134 C2
  Elland, Slack HD3 .... 152 A8
  Featherstone WF7 .... 144 F7
  Halifax HX1 .... 203 E2
  Hebden Bridge HX7 .... 110 D1
  Hebden Bridge, Hebble End
  HX7 .... 88 F2
  Hebden Bridge, Mytholmroyd
  HX7 .... 110 E8
  Holmfirth HD7 .... 189 A7
  Horbury WF4 .... 141 B1
  Kirk Smeaton WF8 .... 166 D8
  Kirkheaton HD5 .... 137 B2
  Ledsham LS25 .... 84 D2
  Mapplewell S75 .... 178 B1
  Netherton WF4 .... 158 B7
  Penistone S36 .... 192 E1
  Rothwell WF3 .... 100 D3
  Silsden BD20 .... 5 E1
  Todmorden OL14 .... 86 C4
  Todmorden OL14 .... 108 F8
  Todmorden OL14 .... 109 A5
  West Hardwick WF4 .... 145 C1
  Woolley WF4 .... 178 B6
  Yeadon LS19 .... 39 F7
New Rd E BD19 .... 115 F8
New Road Prim Sch HX6 .. 112 A3
New Road Side
  Horsforth LS18 .... 58 B7
  Leeds LS19 .... 40 B4
New Road Sq HD6 .... 135 E6
New Row Badsworth WF9 .. 164 E2
  Bradford BD9 .... 54 E2
  Elland HX4 .... 134 C4
  Holmfirth HD7 .... 189 A5
  Pudsey LS28 .... 57 A3
  Shipley BD16 .... 54 B8
  Wakefield WF2 .... 120 B2
New Row Cotts WF8 .... 147 C5
New Scarbro' Rd **1** LS13 ... 58 D2
New St Ackworth M T WF7 .. 163 F5
  Batley WF17 .... 118 E3
  Batley, Hanging Heaton
  WF17 .... 118 E3
  Bingley BD16 .... 36 E7
  Bradford, Bierley BD4 .... 95 B8
  Bradford, Idle BD10 .... 56 E7
  Bradford, Lower Woodlands
  BD12 .... 95 B5
  Brighouse, Bailiff Bridge
  HD6 .... 115 B7
  Brighouse, Clifton HD6 ..... 115 D2
  Castleford WF10 .... 103 E1
  Clayton West HD8 .... 175 D1
  Denholme BD13 .... 71 D8
  Dewsbury WF12 .... 139 F7
  Elland HX4 .... 133 F3
  Halifax, Pellon HX2 .... 202 A4
  Halifax, Southowram HX3 ... 114 A4
  Haworth BD22 .... 51 C6
  Hemsworth WF9 .... 163 C1
  Honley HD7 .... 171 F4
  Horbury WF4 .... 141 B1
  Horsforth LS18 .... 58 B8
  Huddersfield HD1 .... 154 A5
  Huddersfield, Leymoor HD7 .. 152 E4
  Huddersfield, Milnsbridge
  HD3 .... 153 A4
  Huddersfield, Netherton
  HD4 .... 171 C7
  Huddersfield, Paddock HD1 .. 153 B3
  Kirkburton HD5 .... 155 C8
  Liversedge BD19 .... 116 F6
  Mapplewell S75 .... 178 B1
  Meltham HD7 .... 170 D2
  Oakworth BD22 .... 34 D2
  Ossett WF5 .... 140 E5
  Pudsey LS28 .... 76 E6
  Pudsey, Farsley LS28 .... 57 D2
  Royston S71 .... 179 C3
  Skelmanthorpe HD8 .... 175 A2
  Slaithwaite HD7 .... 152 A1
  South Elmsall WF9 .... 182 E3
  South Hiendley S72 .... 180 D6
New Station St LS1 .... 211 E3
New Street Cl LS28 .... 76 E6

New Street Gdns LS28 .... 76 E6
New Street Gr LS28 .... 76 E6
New Sturton La LS25 .... 83 B7
New Tanhouse **4** WF14 .. 137 F5
New Temple Gate LS15 .... 81 A7
New Toftshaw BD4 .... 95 D8
New Town Ct **16** BD21 ...... 35 A7
New Way Batley WF17 ...... 118 C5
  Guiseley LS20 .... 22 C1
New Wellgate WF10 .... 124 F6
New Wells WF1 .... 216 B1
New Windsor Dr LS26 ...... 100 F6
New Wlk LS8 .... 44 B1
New Works Rd BD12 .... 94 D5
New York La LS19 .... 40 D2
New York Rd LS2, LS9 .... 212 A4
New York St **1** LS2 .... 212 A3
Newall Ave LS21 .... 10 F1
Newall Carr Rd Clifton LS21 . 10 F6
  Otley LS21 .... 10 F2
Newall Cl Menston LS29 .. 22 B5
  Otley LS21 .... 10 F1
Newall Cres WF9 .... 162 F3
Newall Hall Pk LS21 .... 11 A5
Newall Mount Otley LS21 ... 22 F8
  Otley LS21 .... 22 F8
Newall St Bradford BD5 ... 74 D4
  Todmorden OL14 .... 129 A8
Newark Cl S75 .... 178 F2
Newark Rd BD16 .... 36 E5
Newark St BD4 .... 75 B5
Newbridge La BD23 .... 1 D8
Newburn Rd BD7 .... 74 B5
Newbury Dr WF9 .... 183 A5
Newbury Rd HD6 .... 135 F7
Newbury Wlk HD5 .... 137 C1
Newby First Sch BD5 .... 74 D3
Newby Garth LS17 .... 44 B5
Newby Rd BD20 .... 16 E8
Newby St Bradford BD5 ... 74 F4
  Glusburn BD20 .... 16 D7
Newcastle Cl BD11 .... 96 D5
Newcastle Farm Ct WF11 .. 105 A4
Newcastle Ho BD1 .... 201 C3
Newcombe St HX5 .... 135 A6
Newfield Ave
  Castleford WF10 .... 124 E7
  Normanton WF6 .... 123 C1
Newfield Cl WF6 .... 123 C1
Newfield Cres WF6 .... 123 C2
Newfield Dr Garforth LS25 .. 83 B4
  Menston LS29 .... 22 A5
Newfield La LS25 .... 104 D8
Newforth Gr BD5 .... 74 C2
Newgate Mirfield WF14 .. 138 A4
  Pontefract WF8 .... 146 C8
Newgate La HD7 .... 170 E2
Newgate St WF17 .... 118 F3
Newhall Bank LS10 .... 99 D5
Newhall Chase LS10 .... 99 D6
Newhall Cl LS10 .... 99 D6
Newhall Cres LS10 .... 99 D6
Newhall Croft LS10 .... 99 D7
Newhall Dr BD6 .... 94 F8
Newhall Garth LS10 .... 99 D5
Newhall Gate LS10 .... 99 E7
Newhall Gdns LS10 .... 99 D5
Newhall Gn LS10 .... 99 D6
Newhall La WF14 .... 138 B2
Newhall Mount
  Bradford BD6 .... 94 F8
  Middleton LS10 .... 99 D5
Newhall Rd Bradford BD4 ... 75 B1
  Middleton LS10 .... 99 D6
Newhill WF9 .... 182 B1
Newhold **2** HD1 .... 154 A7
Newill Cl BD5 .... 75 A2
Newlaithes Cres WF6 ..... 123 D2
Newlaithes Garth LS18 .. 58 A6
Newlaithes Gdns LS18 .. 58 B7
Newlaithes Rd LS18 .... 58 B6
Newland Ave HD2 .... 135 F1
Newland Cres WF9 .... 159 E7
Newland Ct WF1 .... 142 E2
Newland La WF6 .... 122 F1
Newland Rd HD5 .... 155 B7
Newland St
  Knottingley WF11 .... 126 B5
  Wakefield WF1 .... 142 E2
Newland View WF6 .... 122 F3
Newlands LS28 .... 57 D2
Newlands Ave
  Adwick Le S DN6 .... 184 F2
  Bradford BD3 .... 56 D1
  Clayton West HD8 .... 175 F2
  Northowram HX3 .... 93 A3
  Sowerby Bridge HX6 .... 111 E3
  Yeadon LS19 .... 40 A7
Newlands Cl HD6 .... 115 B1
Newlands Cres LS27 .... 98 E4
Newlands Dr Bingley BD16 .. 36 C6
  Glusburn BD20 .... 16 D7
  Lofthouse Gate WF3 .... 121 E5
  Morley LS27 .... 98 D4
  Northowram HX3 .... 93 A3
Newlands Gdns HX3 .... 93 A3
Newlands Junior Sch HX6 .. 111 E3
Newlands La HD7 .... 188 C5
Newlands Pl BD3 .... 56 B1
Newlands Primary Sch S72 .. 98 D5
Newlands Rd HX2 .... 112 B7
Newlands Rise LS19 .... 40 A7
Newlands The HX6 .... 111 E2
Newlands Wlk WF9 .... 181 E5
Newlay Bridle Path **2** LS18 . 57 C7
Newlay Cl BD10 .... 56 E7

Newlay Gr LS18 .... 58 B6
Newlay La Horsforth LS18 .. 58 B7
  Leeds LS13 .... 58 C4
Newlay Lane Pl LS13 .... 58 C4
Newlay Wood Ave LS18 ..... 58 C7
Newlay Wood Cl LS18 ...... 58 C7
Newlay Wood Cres LS18 ... 58 C7
Newlay Wood Dr LS18 ..... 58 C7
Newlay Wood Fold **9**
  LS18 .... 58 B7
Newlay Wood Gdns **3**
  LS18 .... 58 C7
Newlay Wood Rd LS18 ..... 58 B7
Newlay Wood Rise LS18 ... 58 C7
Newley Ave WF17 .... 117 F8
Newley Mount LS18 .... 58 B6
Newlyn Dr WF2 .... 142 D2
Newlyn Rd BD20 .... 19 A1
Newman Ave S71 .... 179 C1
Newman St BD4 .... 75 B2
Newmarket App LS9 .... 80 B6
Newmarket Gn LS9 .... 80 B6
Newmarket La Leeds LS9 .. 80 B6
  Lofthouse Gate WF3 .... 122 D8
Newmillerdam Ctry Pk
  WF2 .... 160 D2
Newport Ave LS13 .... 58 A2
Newport Cres LS6 .... 205 D3
Newport Gdns LS6 .... 205 D3
Newport Mount LS6 .... 205 D3
Newport Pl BD8 .... 55 C1
Newport Rd Bradford BD8 .. 55 C1
  Leeds LS6 .... 205 D3
Newport St WF8 .... 125 C1
Newroyd Rd BD5 .... 74 E2
Newsam Ct LS15 .... 81 A7
Newsam Dr LS15 .... 80 E6
Newsam Green Rd LS26 .. 81 E1
Newsholme La WF9 .... 159 F7
Newsholme New Rd BD22 .. 34 B4
Newsome Ave HD4 .... 154 A2
Newsome High Sch HD4 .. 153 F1
Newsome Junior Sch
  HD4 .... 154 A1
Newsome Rd HD4 .... 154 B3
Newsome Rd S HD4 .... 154 A1
Newsome St WF13 .... 118 B1
Newstead Ave Halifax HX1 .. 202 A3
  Hemsworth WF9 .... 163 A3
  Lofthouse Gate WF1 .... 121 A5
Newstead Cres WF9 .... 163 A4
Newstead Dr WF9 .... 163 A3
Newstead Gdns HX1 .... 202 A3
Newstead Gr Halifax HX1 .. 202 A3
  Hemsworth WF9 .... 163 A4
Newstead Heath HX1 .... 202 A3
Newstead La LS4, WF9 .... 162 F3
Newstead Pl HX1 .... 202 A3
Newstead Rd Barnsley S71 . 178 E1
  Otley LS21 .... 23 B7
  Wakefield WF1 .... 216 A3
Newstead Terr Halifax HX1 . 202 A3
  Hemsworth WF9 .... 163 A3
Newstead View WF9 .... 163 A3
Newstead Wlk BD5 .... 74 D4
Newton Ave WF1 .... 121 B2
Newton Cl
  Lofthouse Gate WF1 .... 121 B1
  Rothwell LS26 .... 100 B4
Newton Ct Leeds LS8 ...... 61 C6
  Lofthouse Gate WF1 .... 121 B4
  Rothwell LS26 .... 100 B4
  Silsden BD20 .... 5 D2
Newton Dr Castleford WF10 . 125 B7
  Holme Chapel BD10 .... 85 A7
  Lofthouse Gate WF1 .... 121 C3
Newton Garth LS7 .... 204 B1
Newton Gn WF1 .... 121 B1
Newton Gr LS7 .... 207 E4
Newton Hill Jun & Inf Sch
  WF1 .... 121 C2
Newton Hill Rd LS7 .... 204 A1
Newton La Fairburn WF11 .. 104 C4
  Ledsham WF10 .... 104 C4
  Ledston WF10 .... 103 E4
  Lofthouse Gate WF1 .... 121 B4
Newton Lodge Cl LS7 ..... 60 C5
Newton Lodge Dr LS7 ..... 60 C5
Newton Par LS7 .... 204 A1
Newton Park Ct LS7 .... 204 B1
Newton Park Dr LS7 .... 204 B1
Newton Park Mans LS7 .... 204 A1
Newton Park View LS7 .... 207 E4
Newton Pk HD6 .... 114 F6
Newton Pl BD5 .... 74 E4
Newton Rd LS7 .... 207 E4
Newton Sq LS12 .... 77 D3
Newton St Bradford BD5 ... 74 E3
  9 Sowerby Bridge HX6 ..... 112 B4
Newton View LS7 .... 204 A1
Newton Way BD17 .... 38 C4
Newton Wlk LS7 .... 207 E4
Newtown Ave S71 .... 179 B4
Nibshaw La BD19 .... 117 A8
Nibshaw Rd BD19 .... 117 A8
Nice Ave LS8 .... 207 F4
Nice St LS8 .... 208 A4
Nice View LS8 .... 207 F4
Nicholas Cl BD7 .... 73 F7
Nichols Cl LS22 .... 13 C5
Nichols Way LS22 .... 13 C5
Nicholson Cl BD16 .... 37 A6
Nicholson St WF10 .... 124 C7
Nicklebly Rd LS9 .... 80 A8
Nicola Cl **16** OL13 .... 106 A7
Nicolsons Pl BD20 .... 5 E1

Nidd App LS22 .... 13 DE
Nidd Ct BD20 .... 5 E1
Nidd Dr WF10 .... 125 B8
Nidd St BD3 .... 75 B6
Nidderdale Cl LS25 .... 83 B5
Nidderdale Wlk BD17 ..... 38 E4
Nields Rd HD7 .... 169 F8
Nightingale Crest WF2 .. 141 C4
Nightingale St **8** BD21 .. 35 D8
Nile Cres BD22 .... 34 F6
Nile Rd LS29 .... 8 B4
Nile St Haworth BD22 ...... 51 E8
  Huddersfield HD1 .... 153 F5
  Keighley BD22 .... 34 F6
  Leeds LS2 .... 212 A4
Nina Rd BD7 .... 73 F3
Ninelands La LS25 .... 83 A6
Ninelands Primary Sch
  LS25 .... 83 A6
Ninelands Spur LS25 ...... 83 A6
Ninelands View LS25 ...... 83 A6
Nineveh La
  Badsworth WF9 .... 164 E3
  Kippax WF10 .... 102 F5
Nineveh Gdns LS11 .... 211 D1
Nineveh Par LS11 .... 211 D1
Nineveh Rd LS11 .... 211 D1
Ninth Ave WF15 .... 116 B5
Nippet La LS9 .... 212 B4
Nixon Ave LS9 .... 80 B7
Nixon Cl WF12 .... 139 F1
Noble Ct HD4 .... 171 D6
Noble St BD7 .... 74 B5
Nog La BD9 .... 55 A4
Nook Gdns LS15 .... 62 F8
Nook Gr WF12 .... 139 D2
Nook La
  Sowerby Bridge HX6 .... 131 F8
  Wadsworth Moor HX7 .... 89 D4
Nook Rd LS15 .... 62 F8
Nook The
  Cleckheaton BD19 .... 116 E8
  Cullingworth BD13 .... 52 D6
  East Ardsley WF3 .... 119 E6
  Leeds LS17 .... 43 D5
Noon Wlk WF13 .... 138 F8
Nooking The WF2 .... 120 B3
Nooks The LS27 .... 97 D6
Noon Cl WF13 .... 121 E5
Nopper Rd
  Huddersfield HD4 .... 170 F8
  Meltham HD4 .... 170 F8
Nor Wood Rd WF9 .... 181 D5
Nora Pl LS13 .... 58 A3
Nora Rd LS13 .... 58 A3
Nora Terr LS13 .... 58 A3
Norbeck Dr BD22 .... 51 E8
Norbury Rd BD10 .... 56 F6
Norcliffe La
  Brighouse HX3 .... 114 A7
  Halifax HX3 .... 114 A7
Norcroft Brow BD7 .... 74 C6
Norcroft End BD7 .... 74 C7
Norcroft La S75 .... 193 F3
Norcroft St BD1, BD7 .... 74 C7
Norcross Ave HD3 .... 153 B7
Norfield HD2 .... 136 A4
Norfolk Ave WF17 .... 118 B3
Norfolk Cl
  Brotherton WF11 .... 126 C8
  Leeds LS7 .... 204 A3
  Littleborough OL15 .... 129 C1
  Rothwell LS26 .... 101 D5
Norfolk Dr LS26 .... 101 D5
Norfolk Gdns
  Bradford BD1 .... 201 B2
  Leeds LS7 .... 204 A3
Norfolk Gn LS7 .... 204 A3
Norfolk House WF1 .... 142 F3
Norfolk Mount LS7 .... 204 A3
Norfolk Pl Halifax HX1 ..... 202 C2
  Leeds LS7 .... 204 A3
Norfolk St Batley WF17 ... 118 B4
  4 Bingley BD16 .... 37 A3
  3 Hebden Bridge HX7 ...... 89 A2
Norfolk Terr LS7 .... 204 A3
Norfolk View LS7 .... 204 A3
Norfolk Wlk
  6 Dewsbury WF13 .... 139 B8
  Leeds LS7 .... 204 A3
Norgarth Cl WF17 .... 118 F5
Norham Gr BD12 .... 94 D2
Norland CE (Controlled)
  Jun & Inf Sch HX6 .... 112 D2
Norland Rd
  Sowerby Bridge HX6 .... 112 C3
  Sowerby Bridge,
  Upper Greetland HX6 .... 133 D8
Norland St BD7 .... 73 F3
Norland Town Rd HX6 .... 112 D2
Norland View
  6 Halifax HX2 .... 113 A4
  Sowerby Bridge HX6 .... 112 D4
Norman Ave Bradford BD2 .. 56 B5
  Elland HX5 .... 135 A6
Norman Cres BD2 .... 56 B5
Norman Dr WF14 .... 137 F6
Norman Gr Bradford BD2 .. 56 B5
  Elland HX5 .... 135 A6
  Leeds LS5 .... 59 A4
Norman La BD2 .... 56 B5
Norman Mount
  Bradford BD2 .... 56 B5
  Leeds LS5 .... 59 A4
Norman Pl **6** Horbury WF4 .. 141 B1
  Leeds LS8 .... 44 B3
Norman Rae Playing Fields
  BD9 .... 54 F6

Norman Rd Denby Dale HD8 191 F5
Huddersfield HD2 136 A1
Mirfield WF14 137 F6
Norman Row LS5 59 A4
Norman St Bingley BD16 37 A3
Halifax HX1 135 A6
Halifax HX1 202 B1
14 Haworth BD22 51 D7
Leeds LS5 59 A4
Shipley BD18 55 D7
Norman Terr Bradford BD12 56 B5
Elland HX5 135 A6
Leeds LS8 44 A2
Norman View LS5 59 A4
Normanon Pl LS11 214 A4
Normans Way WF2 142 F1
Normanton C E (Aided)
First Sch WF6 123 B2
Normanton Common
First Sch WF6 123 D3
Normanton Cross St WF4 159 C8
Normanton Gr LS11 214 A4
Normanton Ind Est WF6 123 D3
Normanton St WF4 159 C8
Normanton Town Mid Sch
WF6 123 A1
Normanton Woodhouse
First Sch WF6 123 A1
Norr Green Terr BD15 53 D6
Norridge Bottom HD7 189 A5
Norris Cl HD5 155 A4
Norristhorpe La WF15 117 A2
Norristhorpe La WF15 117 B2
Norristhorpe Sch WF15 117 B2
Nortech Cl LS7 207 D2
North App LS24 48 A5
North Ave Bradford BD8 55 D2
Castleford WF10 123 F7
Horbury WF4 141 C1
Otley LS21 23 A8
Pontefract WF8 146 B7
South Elmsall WF9 182 F2
Sutton in C BD20 16 D4
Wakefield WF1 216 B4
North Baileygate WF8 125 E1
North Bank
Batley WF17 118 A6
Huddersfield HD2 135 F1
Shipley BD16 54 B5
North Bolton HX2 91 E7
North Bridge HX1 203 E4
North Bridge L Ctr HX1 203 E4
North Bridge St HX1 203 E4
North Broadgate La LS18 41 C1
North Brook St BD1, BD3 201 C4
North Byland HX2 91 E7
North Carr HD5 154 E7
North Carr Croft HD5 154 E7
North Cl Huddersfield HD7 124 C1
Leeds LS8 61 D6
Royston S71 179 C3
North Cliffe HX6 112 B3
North Cliffe Ave BD13 72 F6
North Cliffe Cl 16 BD13 72 F6
North Cliffe Ct BD13 72 E6
North Cliffe Gr 16 BD13 72 F6
North Cliffe La BD13 72 F6
North Cres WF9 183 B4
North Croft Grove Rd LS29 8 A4
North Cross Rd HD2 135 F2
North Ct LS2 211 F4
North Cut HD6 114 F2
North Dean Ave WF4 159 F7
North Dean Bsns Pk HX3 113 D1
North Dean Rd Halifax HX4 113 A1
Keighley BD22 34 F7
North Dene Rd BD20 5 E2
North Dr Bramhope LS16 24 F2
Garforth LS25 83 B4
Huddersfield HD7 152 E4
North Farm Rd LS8, LS9 208 C3
North Field La HD8 175 A2
North Field Rd DN5 195 D7
North Fold BD10 56 B8
North Gate Wl14 137 E3
North Grange Mews LS6 205 F4
North Grange Mount LS6 59 F5
North Grange Rd LS6 205 F4
North Grove App LS22 13 E7
North Grove Ct LS22 13 E7
North Grove Cl LS8 61 D6
North Grove Cres LS22 13 E7
North Grove Ct LS22 13 E7
North Grove Dr Leeds LS8 61 D6
Wetherby LS22 13 E7
North Grove Mount LS22 13 E6
North Grove Rd LS22 13 E7
North Grove Rise LS8 61 D6
North Grove Way LS22 13 F6
North Halifax Grammar Sch
HX2 91 F6
North Hall Ave BD10 39 A2
North Hill LS14 28 D1
North Hill Cl LS8 61 C6
North Hill Ct LS6 59 F6
North Hill Dr LS16 155 C8
North Hill Rd LS6 205 F4
North Holme St BD1 201 B4
North Ives BD22 51 C4
North John St 16 BD13 72 E1
North King St WF17 118 D4
North La Lawthorne S75 193 A2
Leeds, Headingley LS6 59 D5
Leeds, Oakwood LS8 61 C6
Rothwell LS26 101 C6
Slaithwaite HD7 151 D1
North Lingwell Rd LS10 99 C5
North Lodge Fold WF13 117 F3

North Lodge La WF8 147 F4
North Mead LS16 24 F2
North Moor La HD5 137 C2
North Ossett High Sch
WF5 119 D1
North Par Bradford BD1 55 A2
Bradford BD1 201 B3
Burley in W LS29 9 E2
Halifax HX1 203 E3
Ilkley LS29 8 C4
Leeds LS16 59 A8
Otley LS21 23 A8
North Park Ave LS8 44 A1
North Park Gr LS8 44 A1
North Park La LS8 204 C4
North Park Rd Bradford BD9 55 E3
Leeds LS8 61 A8
North Park Terr BD9 55 C2
North Parkway LS14 62 A6
North Pl BD20 16 C5
North Queen St 1 BD21 35 C7
North Rd Bradford BD6 74 B1
Dewsbury WF13 138 E6
Fairburn WF11 105 A4
Horsforth LS18 41 B3
Kirkburton HD8 173 E7
Leeds LS9 80 D3
Leeds, Cross Gates LS15 62 C2
Royston S71 179 D4
Sutton in C BD20 16 C5
North Rise HD2 136 C2
North Road Terr WF1 216 A3
North Row Shepley HD8 190 D8
Sutton in C BD20 16 C5
North Royd HX4 133 B5
North Selby HX2 91 D7
North St Addingham LS29 7 A8
Batley WF12 118 B6
Batley, Heckmondwike
WF16 117 D3
Bradford, Oakenshaw BD12 95 A4
Bradford, Thackley BD10 39 B2
Castleford WF10 124 C8
Castleford, New Fryston
WF10 104 C3
Dewsbury WF13 118 C1
Elland, Holywell Green HX4 134 D7
4 Elland, West Vale HX4 134 D7
Glusburn BD20 16 D7
Haworth BD22 51 D7
Huddersfield, Paddock HD1 153 D5
Huddersfield, Rashcliffe HD1 153 E3
Keighley BD21 35 C7
Leeds LS2, LS7 207 D1
Mirfield WF14 137 F4
Normanton WF6 144 A4
Otley LS21 23 A8
2 Pudsey LS28 76 E8
Silsden BD20 5 E2
South Kirkby WF9 182 B3
Sutton in C BD20 16 D5
Wetherby LS22 13 E4
Yeadon LS19 40 B4
North Terr Batley WF17 96 F1
1 Leeds LS15 62 C2
Yeadon LS19 40 B7
North View Bradford BD15 54 A1
Burley in W LS29 9 E2
Dewsbury WF12 139 D6
Hemsworth WF9 163 A4
Knottingley WF11 126 E4
Menston LS29 22 A3
Steeton BD20 16 F6
Sutton in C BD20 16 D5
Wilsden BD15 53 C5
North View Rd
Birkenshaw BD4 96 A7
Bradford BD3 55 F2
North View St
N Keighley BD20 18 C1
Pudsey LS28 57 E2
North View Terr
2 Dewsbury WF13 118 B2
2 Dewsbury, Chapel Fold
WF13 117 F2
Haworth BD22 51 C8
3 Pudsey LS28 57 E2
North Way
Huddersfield HD2 136 C4
Leeds LS8 61 D6
North West Rd LS6 206 B3
North Wing BD1 201 C2
North Wlk Harden BD16 36 A1
Hemsworth WF9 181 D8
North's Pl WF14 138 A7
Northallerton Rd BD3 55 F1
Northampton St BD3 55 F1
Northcliffe Croft 1 LS27 204 A1
Northbrook Pl LS7 204 A3
Northbrook St LS7 204 A3
Northcliffe Golf Course
BD9 54 E6
Northcliffe WF13 119 C1
Northcote Cres LS11 214 B4
Northcote Dr LS11 214 B4
Northcote Fold LS23 13 B2
Northcote Gn LS11 214 B4
Northcote Rd BD2 56 B2
Northcote St LS28 57 D2
Northcote Terr BD5 56 B1
Northcroft WF9 183 A3
Northcroft Ave WF9 183 A4
Northcroft Rise BD8 54 E1
Northdale Ave BD5 74 C2
Northdale Cres BD5 74 C2

Nordale Mount BD5 74 C2
Northdale Rd BD5 55 B5
Northedge La HX3 93 D1
Northedge Meadow BD10 56 B6
Northedge Pk HX3 93 D1
Northern Sch
of Contemporary Dance
LS7 207 D3
Northern Cl BD7 73 F2
Northern St 1 LS1 211 D3
Northfield Ave
Huddersfield HD1 153 E4
Knottingley WF11 126 F3
Ossett WF5 140 D6
Rothwell LS26 100 C4
South Kirkby WF9 182 C3
Wetherby LS22 13 E6
Northfield Cl 1 HX5 134 F6
Northfield Cres BD6 54 A7
Northfield Dr WF8 125 F1
Northfield Gdns BD6 74 C1
Northfield Gr Bradford BD6 74 C1
Huddersfield HD1 153 F3
South Kirkby WF9 182 C3
Northfield Jun & Inf Sch
WF9 182 C3
Northfield La Horbury WF4 141 C1
Kirkburton HD8 173 E8
South Kirkby WF9 182 C3
Northfield Pl Bradford BD8 55 C1
Dewsbury WF13 118 C1
Rothwell LS26 100 B4
Wetherby LS22 13 E6
Northfield Rd Bradford BD6 74 B1
Crofton WF4 144 B3
Dewsbury WF13 118 B1
Knottingley WF11 126 F3
Ossett WF5 140 D7
Northfield St
Dewsbury WF13 118 C1
South Kirkby WF9 182 B3
Northfield Terr
Queensbury BD13 73 A1
Slaithwaite HD7 152 A2
Northfields LS13 15 A3
Northgate Baildon BD17 38 C4
Cleckheaton BD19 116 D7
Dewsbury WF13 139 D8
Elland HX5 134 F7
Halifax HX1 203 E4
Heptonstall HX7 88 F5
Honley HD7 172 B6
Horbury WF4 141 A1
Huddersfield HD1 154 B7
Huddersfield, Almondbury
HD1, HD5 154 F3
Liversedge WF16 117 C4
Pontefract WF8 125 D1
1 Rothwell LS26 101 C6
South Hiendley S72 180 E6
Wakefield WF1 216 B3
Wakefield WF1 216 B3
Northgate Cl WF8 125 D1
Northgate La LS22 13 A2
Northgate Lodge WF8 125 D1
Northgate Rise LS22 13 B2
Northgates LS22 13 E5
Northlands LS17 179 C4
Northlea Ave LS16 39 B1
Northolme Ave LS16 59 B7
Northolme Cres LS16 59 B7
Northorpe Ct WF14 138 C6
Northorpe La WF14 138 C7
Northowram Gn HX3 92 E2
Northowram Primary Sch
HX3 93 A3
Northrop Cl BD8 55 A1
Northside Ave BD7 74 A6
Northside Bsns Pk LS7 207 D2
Northside Rd BD7 74 A6
Northside Terr BD7 73 F6
Northstead WF13 138 D7
Northumberland St 1
HD1 154 B6
Northway WF14 137 F7
Northway Cres WF14 137 F7
Northway Gdns WF14 137 F7
Northways Sch LS23 30 D5
Northwell Gate LS21 10 C7
Northwest Bsns Pk LS6 206 B3
Northwood Cl Pudsey LS28 76 F5
Rothwell LS26 101 C7
Northwood Cres BD10 56 C6
Northwood Falls LS26 101 C7
Northwood Gdns LS27 81 E7
Northwood Mount LS28 76 F5
Northwood Pk
Kirkburton HD8 173 E7
Rothwell LS26 101 C7
Northwood View LS28 76 F5
Norton Cl Elland HX5 134 F5
Halifax HX2 112 B7
Norton Dr HX2 112 C7
Norton & Kirk Smeaton Rd
WF8 166 E4
Norton Rd Leeds LS8 44 A3
Wakefield WF1 216 C3
Norton St Elland HX5 134 F6
Silsden BD20 5 D1
Wakefield WF1 142 E4
Norton Terr HX3 173 C2
Norton Way LS27 98 A6
Nortonthorpe Hall Sch
HD8 175 D1
Nortonthorpe Ind Est
HD8 175 D1

Norville Terr LS6 205 E4
Norwich Ave LS10 215 D2
Norwood Ave 147 A5
Norwood Ave
Birkenshaw BD11 96 B4
Burley in W LS29 9 F1
Shipley BD18 55 B6
Norwood Cl LS29 9 F1
Norwood Cres
Birkenshaw BD11 96 B4
Pudsey LS28 57 F2
Norwood Croft LS28 57 F2
Norwood Dr Batley WF17 117 F8
Birkenshaw BD11 96 B4
Brierley S72 181 A3
Norwood Gr
Birkenshaw BD11 96 B4
Leeds LS6 205 E3
Norwood Green Hill HX3 93 F2
Norwood Mount LS6 205 E3
Norwood Pk HD2 135 D1
Norwood Pl Leeds LS6 205 E3
Shipley BD18 55 B6
Norwood Rd
Huddersfield HD2 135 E2
Leeds LS6 205 E3
Shipley BD18 55 B6
Norwood St Bradford BD5 74 D2
Normanton WF6 123 D4
Shipley BD18 55 B6
Norwood Terr
Brighouse HX3 94 A2
Burley in W LS29 9 F1
Leeds LS6 205 E3
Shipley BD18 55 B6
Norwood View LS6 205 E3
Nostell Cl BD8 74 D8
Nostell La WF4 162 B2
Nostell Priory WF4 162 E8
Noster Gr LS11 213 F3
Noster Hill LS11 213 F3
Noster Pl LS11 213 F3
Noster Rd LS11 213 F3
Noster St LS11 213 F3
Noster Terr LS11 214 A3
Noster View LS11 213 F3
Notre Dame
Sixth Form Coll LS2 206 B3
Nottingham Cl WF3 100 A3
Nottingham St BD3 75 E7
Notton La WF4 179 B6
Nova La WF17 96 C2
Nowell App LS9 208 B1
Nowell Ave LS9 208 B1
Nowell Cl LS9 208 B1
Nowell Cres LS9 208 B1
Nowell End Row LS9 208 B1
Nowell Gdns LS9 208 B1
Nowell Gr LS9 208 B1
Nowell Mount LS9 208 B1
Nowell Par LS9 208 B1
Nowell Pl Huddersfield HD5 154 F4
Leeds LS9 208 B1
Nowell St Dewsbury WF13 118 B1
Leeds LS9 208 B1
Nowell Terr LS9 208 B1
Nowell View LS9 208 B1
Nowell Wlk LS9 208 B1
Nowell's Yd WF13 139 B8
Nuffield Hospl HD2 135 E1
Nunburnholme Wlk BD10 56 C6
Nunington Ave 18 LS12 209 F4
Nunington St LS12 210 A4
Nunington Terr 3 LS12 209 F4
Nunington View 2 LS12 59 C1
Nunlea Royd HX3 114 C7
Nunn's Cl WF7 145 D4
Nunn's Croft WF7 145 D4
Nunn's La WF7 145 D4
Nunnery La HD6 115 B5
Nunns Ave WF7 145 D3
Nunns Ct WF7 145 C3
Nunns View WF7 145 C3
Nunroyd WF16 117 D5
Nunroyd Ave Guiseley LS20 39 F8
Leeds LS17 43 D1
Nunroyd Gr LS17 43 D1
Nunroyd Lawn LS17 43 E1
Nunroyd Rd LS17 43 D1
Nunroyd St LS17 43 D1
Nunroyd Terr LS17 43 D1
Nunthorpe Rd LS13 57 F5
Nurser La BD5 74 C4
Nurser Pl BD5 74 C4
Nursery Ave HX3 91 F3
Nursery Cl Baildon BD17 37 E2
Leeds LS17 43 C4
Keighley BD20 18 A1
Leeds LS17 43 C4
Nursery Garth LS22 13 F6
Nursery Gr Halifax HX3 91 F3
Leeds LS17 43 A4
Nursery La Addingham LS29 7 B7
Halifax HX3 91 F3
Leeds LS17 43 B4
Rippenden HX6 132 B3
Nursery Mount LS10 215 E2
Nursery Mount Rd LS10 215 E2
Nursery Rd
12 Bradford, Clayton BD14 73 B4
Bradford, Pickles Hill BD7 73 F2
Guiseley LS20 22 D3
Nursery Sq
Dewsbury WF12 139 C4
Huddersfield HD2 136 A1

Nursery Way
Boston Spa LS23 30 B8
Boston Spa, Clifford LS23 30 D5
Nursery Wood Rd WF17 118 D3
Nussey Ave WF17 96 E2
Nutclough Rd HX7 89 B4
Nutfield St 18 OL14 108 B6
Nuttall Rd BD3 201 D4
Nuttall St 1 OL13 106 B3
Nutter La WF17 96 C2
Nutter Pl BD1 201 B3
Nutter St BD19 116 D7
Nutting Grove Terr LS12 77 E5
Nutwood Wlk BD6 93 F6

O'Cot La HX3 151 B4
O'Grady Sq 4 LS9 212 C3
Oak Ave Bingley BD16 36 F2
Bradford BD8 55 D2
Burley in W LS29 21 F8
Garforth LS25 82 F7
Huddersfield HD5 154 E5
Huddersfield, Leymoor HD7 152 E5
Lofthouse Gate WF3 121 F4
Meltham HD7 170 C3
Morley LS27 98 B3
Normanton WF6 144 A8
Sowerby Bridge HX6 112 B5
Todmorden OL14 108 A7
Oak Bank 7 Bingley BD16 37 A2
Shipley BD18 55 D5
Oak Cl LS29 21 F8
Oak Cres Garforth LS25 82 F7
Leeds LS15 80 F7
Oak Dr Garforth LS25 82 F7
Slaithwaite HD7 152 D3
Oak Gr Garforth LS25 83 A7
Keighley BD21 35 A4
Morley LS27 98 C3
Oak Hall Pk WF4 159 C4
Oak Head Terr BD20 16 D8
Oak House 3 WF10 124 E7
Oak La Bradford BD9 55 C2
4 Halifax HX1 202 C3
Sowerby Bridge HX6 132 E8
Oak Leigh S75 193 C4
Oak Mount Bradford BD8 55 D2
Todmorden OL14 108 B6
Oak Pl Baildon BD17 38 F4
Garforth LS25 82 F7
Halifax HX1 202 C3
18 Sowerby Bridge HX6 112 B5
Oak Rd Garforth LS25 82 F7
Huddersfield HD2 137 A5
Leeds, Halton LS15 80 F7
Leeds, New Wortley LS12 210 B3
Leeds, Potternewton LS7 204 A1
Morley LS27 97 F3
Shafton S72 180 D2
Oak Ridge LS22 13 C5
Oak Rise BD19 95 D2
Oak Royd LS25 82 F7
Oak Scar La HD7 189 D3
Oak St Batley WF16 117 D4
Bradford BD14 73 B4
Crofton WF4 162 A7
Elland HX5 134 F7
Haworth BD22 51 D7
8 Hebden Bridge HX7 89 A4
Lofthouse Gate WF1 121 C4
Morley LS27 98 B7
Oxenhope BD22 51 C8
Pudsey LS28 76 C8
South Elmsall WF9 182 F1
18 Sowerby Bridge HX6 112 B5
Todmorden OL14 108 A4
Oak Terr 2 Elland HX4 134 A4
7 Halifax HX1 202 C3
Huddersfield HD2 202 C3
1 Leeds LS15 62 D3
Oak Tree Ave
Holmfirth HD7 189 D3
Lepton HD8 155 D3
Oak Tree Bsns Pk LS14 62 A7
Oak Tree Cl LS9 208 C3
Oak Tree Cres LS9 208 C3
Oak Tree Ct LS9 208 C3
Silsden BD20 5 D2
Oak Tree Dr LS8 208 C3
Oak Tree Gr
Hemsworth WF9 181 F6
Leeds LS9 208 C3
Oak Tree Meadow WF2 161 A6
Oak Tree Mount LS9 208 C3
Oak Tree Pl LS9 208 C3
Oak Tree Rd HD8 155 D3
Oak Tree Sch WF7 164 A5
Oak Tree Terr HD8 155 D3
Oak Villas LS8 208 C3
Oak View BD20 17 E8
Oak Villas BD5 55 D2
Oak Wood Rd LS22 13 D3
Oakbank Ave BD22 34 F5
Oakbank Broadway BD22 34 F5
Oakbank Cres BD22 34 F5
Oakbank Ct BD22 34 F4
Oakbank Dr BD22 34 F4
Oakbank Gr BD22 34 F5
Oakbank Gr BD22 34 F5
Oakbank La BD22 34 F5
Oakbank Mount BD22 34 F5
Oakbank Recn Ctr BD22 34 F4
Oakbank Sch BD22 34 F4

Oakburn Rd LS29 .... 8 A3
Oakdale BD16 .... 37 A5
Oakdale Ave Bradford BD6 .... 74 B1
Shipley BD18 .... 55 D6
Oakdale Cl Bradford BD10 .... 56 E3
Halifax HX3 .... 92 A2
Lofthouse Gate WF3 .... 121 B6
Oakdale Cres Bradford BD6 .. 74 B1
Huddersfield HD3 .... 153 A8
Oakdale Dr Bradford BD10 ... 56 E3
Shipley BD18 .... 55 E6
Oakdale First Sch BD18 ...... 55 E6
Oakdale Garth LS14 .... 45 B1
Oakdale Gr BD18 .... 55 E6
Oakdale Meadow LS14 .... 45 B1
Oakdale Pk LS21 .... 24 D6
Oakdale Rd BD18 .... 55 E6
Oakdale Terr BD6 .... 74 B1
Oakdean HD2 .... 136 A4
Oakdene Cl LS28 .... 76 F5
Oakdene Ct LS17 .... 44 A4
Oakdene Dr LS17 .... 44 A4
Oakdene Gdns LS17 .... 44 A4
Oakdene Vale LS17 .... 44 A4
Oakdene Way LS17 .... 44 A4
Oaken Bank Cres HD5 .... 154 C4
Oaken Cl OL13 .... 106 B3
Oakenclough Rd OL13 .... 106 B3
Oakenshaw La
Bradford BD12 .... 94 C2
Oakenshaw La
Bradford BD13 .... 95 A3
Crofton WF4 .... 143 A2
Walton WF4, WF2 .... 161 A8
Oakenshaw St WF1 .... 142 F3
Oakes Ave HD7 .... 172 C2
Oakes Fold HD8 .... 156 A3
Oakes La HD7 .... 172 C2
Oakes Rd HD3 .... 153 B8
Oakes Rd S HD3 .... 153 B7
Oakfield LS6 .... 205 E4
Oakfield Ave Bingley BD16 .. 37 C2
Rothwell LS26 .... 100 E6
Oakfield Cl Elland HX5 ...... 134 E6
Garforth LS25 .... 82 F6
Menston LS29 .... 22 A6
Oakfield Cres WF11 .... 126 F3
Oakfield Ct S75 .... 178 A1
Oakfield Dr Baildon BD17 .. 38 D2
Mirfield WF14 .... 137 F3
Oakfield Gr Bradford BD9 ... 55 C2
Skelmanthorpe HD8 .... 175 A1
Oakfield Pk WF8 .... 165 B4
Oakfield Rd
Huddersfield HD2 .... 135 E1
Keighley BD21 .... 35 B4
Oakfield Terr
Horsforth LS18 .... 58 E8
Shipley BD18 .... 55 D7
Oakhall Pk BD13 .... 72 D7
Oakhampton Ct LS8 .... 61 C6
Oakhill Rd HD7 .... 118 A7
Oakhurst Ave LS11 .... 214 A1
Oakhurst Gr LS11 .... 213 F1
Oakhurst Mount LS11 .... 213 F1
Oakhurst St LS11 .... 214 A1
Oakland Ct HD8 .... 173 F7
Oakland Dr WF4 .... 158 D5
Oakland Rd
Netherton WF4 .... 158 D5
Wakefield WF1 .... 142 E3
Oakland St BD20 .... 5 D1
Oaklands Bradford BD10 .... 56 A8
Brighouse HD6 .... 114 F1
Ilkley LS29 .... 8 A3
Rothwell WF3 .... 100 B2
Shipley BD18 .... 54 D7
Oaklands Ave Leeds LS16 .. 42 D3
Northowram HX3 .... 93 B3
Pudsey LS21 .... 57 E5
Oaklands Cl Holmfirth HD7 189 A7
Leeds LS16 .... 42 D3
Oaklands Croft WF2 .... 161 B6
Oaklands Dr Batley WF17 . 118 F5
Huddersfield HD5 .... 154 F5
Leeds LS16 .... 42 D3
Oaklands Fold LS16 .... 42 D3
Oaklands Gr Leeds LS16 ... 42 D3
Pudsey LS13 .... 57 E5
Oaklands Rd LS13 .... 57 E5
Oaklea Cl S75 .... 178 B2
Oaklea Gdns LS16 .... 42 D2
Oaklea Hall Cl LS16 .... 42 D2
Oaklea Rd LS15 .... 62 F6
Oakleigh Ave
Bradford BD14 .... 73 B3
Halifax HX3 .... 113 C3
Wakefield WF2 .... 141 E5
Oakleigh Cl Bradford BD14 . 73 B4
Crofton WF4 .... 144 C4
Oakleigh Gdns BD14 .... 73 B3
Oakleigh Gr BD14 .... 73 B3
Oakleigh Mews BD22 .... 34 C2
Oakleigh Rd BD14 .... 73 B4
Oakleigh Terr
Bradford BD14 .... 73 B4
Todmorden OL14 .... 86 B1
Oakleigh View BD17 .... 38 B3
Oakley Gr LS11 .... 214 C2
Oakley St WF3 .... 99 E1
Oakley Terr LS11 .... 214 C2
Oakley View LS11 .... 214 C2
Oakridge Ave LS29 .... 22 B4
Oakridge Ct BD16 .... 37 A4

Oakroyd LS26 .... 100 F4
Oakroyd Ave BD6 .... 74 C1
Oakroyd Cl Birkenshaw BD11 96 A5
Brighouse HD6 .... 115 B5
Oakroyd Dr Birkenshaw BD11 96 A4
Brighouse HD6 .... 115 B5
Oakroyd Fold LS27 .... 98 C8
Oakroyd Mount LS28 .... 76 E8
Oakroyd Rd
12 Bradford, Brownroyd Oak
BD6 .... 74 C1
13 Bradford, Wibsey BD6 .... 74 B1
Oakroyd Terr
3 Baildon BD17 .... 38 D2
Bradford BD8 .... 55 D2
Morley LS27 .... 98 C8
Oakroyd Villas BD8 .... 55 D2
Oaks Dr BD15 .... 73 C8
Oaks Farm Cl S75 .... 177 F1
Oaks Farm Dr S75 .... 177 F1
Oaks Fold BD5 .... 74 E3
Oaks Green Mount HD6 .. 135 F7
Oaks La Boston Spa LS23 .. 30 D8
Bradford BD5 .... 73 D8
Oaks Rd WF17 .... 118 E4
Oaks The Crofton WF4 ... 144 B4
Guiseley LS20 .... 22 E2
Morley LS27 .... 98 B7
Oaks Wood Dr S75 .... 178 A1
Oaksfield LS26 .... 102 D2
Oaktree La WF7 .... 164 C5
Oakville Rd HX7 .... 88 D2
Oakway BD11 .... 96 B4
Oakwell Ave Batley WF17 .. 117 F6
Leeds LS12 .... 210 A3
Leeds, Gledhow LS8 .... 61 A6
Pontefract WF8 .... 146 C6
Oakwell Cl
Birkenshaw BD11 .... 97 A5
Bradford BD7 .... 74 B3
Hemsworth WF9 .... 163 A2
Oakwell Cres LS8 .... 61 A6
Oakwell Dr LS8 .... 61 A6
Oakwell Gdns LS8 .... 61 A6
Oakwell Gr LS13 .... 58 C3
Oakwell Hall WF17 .... 96 D3
Oakwell Hall Country Pk
WF17 .... 96 D3
Oakwell Ind Pk WF17 .... 97 A4
Oakwell Mount LS8 .... 61 A6
Oakwell Oval LS8 .... 61 A6
Oakwell Rd BD11 .... 97 A5
Oakwell Terr **8** LS28 .... 57 D3
Oakwell Way WF17 .... 97 A3
Oakwood WF2 .... 141 D3
Oakwood Ave
Birkenshaw BD11 .... 96 A4
Leeds LS8 .... 61 B6
Royston S71 .... 179 C4
Shipley BD20 .... 55 D4
Wakefield WF2 .... 141 D6
Oakwood Boundary Rd
LS8 .... 61 B6
Oakwood Cl WF6 .... 122 F4
Oakwood Cres S71 .... 179 B4
Oakwood Ct Bradford BD8 . 74 C8
Leeds LS8 .... 61 C6
Oakwood Dr Bingley BD16 .. 37 A5
Hemsworth WF9 .... 181 E6
Leeds LS8 .... 61 B6
Normanton WF6 .... 122 F4
Rothwell LS26 .... 100 D7
Oakwood Garth LS8 .... 61 C6
Oakwood Gdns WF14 ..... 159 D6
Oakwood Gn LS8 .... 61 C6
Oakwood Gr Bradford BD8 55 A1
Horbury WF4 .... 141 C2
Leeds LS8 .... 61 B6
Oakwood Grange LS8 ...... 61 C6
Oakwood Grange La LS8 .. 61 C6
Oakwood La LS8, LS9 .... 61 C5
Oakwood Mount LS8 .... 61 B6
Oakwood Nook LS8 .... 61 B6
Oakwood Pl LS8 .... 61 C6
Oakwood Primary Sch
LS8 .... 208 C3
Oakwood Rd Batley WF17 . 118 E5
Royston S71 .... 179 B4
Oakwood Rise LS8 .... 61 C6
Oakwood Terr LS28 .... 76 E6
Oakwood View LS8 .... 61 C6
Oakwood Wlk LS8 .... 61 C6
Oakworth First Sch BD22 .. 34 D2
Oakworth Hall BD22 .... 34 D2
Oakworth Rd BD21, BD22 .. 35 A6
Oakworth Sta BD22 .... 34 D1
Oakworth Terr BD22 .... 34 D2
Oasby Croft BD4 .... 75 E1
Oast House Croft WF3 .... 100 B3
Oastler Ave H01 .... 153 F6
Oastler Pl BD12 .... 94 D6
Oastler Rd Pudsey LS28 .. 57 B6
Shipley BD18 .... 54 F8
Oastler St WF13 .... 139 C8
Oatland Cl LS7 .... 206 C2
Oatland Ct LS7 .... 206 C2
Oatland Dr LS7 .... 206 C2
Oatland Gdns LS7 .... 207 D2
Oatland Gn LS7 .... 206 C2
Oatland Hts LS7 .... 207 D2
Oatland La LS7 .... 206 C2
Oatland Pl LS7 .... 206 C3
Oatland Rd LS7 .... 206 C3
Oatland Towers LS7 .... 206 C2
Oatlands Dr LS21 .... 11 A1

Oats St BD22 .... 35 A4
Oban Cl WF3 .... 98 D1
Oban St **5** LS12 .... 209 E4
Oban St LS12 .... 209 E4
Oban Terr **6** LS12 .... 209 E4
Occupation La
Aberford LS24 .... 47 D4
Batley WF13 .... 117 F3
Bramhope LS16 .... 24 B2
Halifax HX2 .... 91 F6
Holmfirth HD7 .... 189 E8
Honley HD7 .... 172 D1
Keighley BD22 .... 34 E4
Pudsey LS28 .... 76 C7
Occupation Rd
Huddersfield HD2, HD3 ... 153 C8
Huddersfield, Sheepridge
HD2 .... 136 C3
Ochrewell Ave HD2 .... 136 E3
Octagon Terr HX2 .... 112 E4
Odda La LS20 .... 21 E1
Oddfellow St LS27 .... 98 A4
Oddfellows Club Houses
WF7 .... 163 D5
Oddfellows' Ct BD11 .... 201 B3
Oddfellows St
3 Brighouse HD6 .... 115 B4
Huddersfield, Scholes BD19 . 115 F8
Mirfield WF14 .... 138 A5
Oddy Pl **6** Bradford BD6 .. 74 B1
Oddy St BD4 .... 75 E1
Oddy's Fold LS6 .... 59 F8
Odsal Pl **8** BD6 .... 94 D8
Odsal Rd BD6 .... 94 D8
Offley La WF4 .... 163 B6
Ogden Cres BD13 .... 52 D2
Ogden La Brighouse HD6 . 135 F8
Denholme BD13 .... 52 D2
Halifax HX2 .... 71 D2
Ogden View Cl HX2 .... 91 D7
Ogilby Cl LS20 .... 101 B7
Ogilby Mews LS20 .... 101 B7
Old Allen Rd BD13 .... 53 B2
Old Arcade The **8** HX1 . 203 E3
Old Bank Halifax HX3 ...... 203 F3
Ripponden HX6 .... 132 E4
Slaithwaite HD7 .... 169 F8
Old Bank Fold **3** HD5 .. 154 D5
Old Bank Jun & Inf Sch
WF14 .... 138 A7
Old Bank Rd
Dewsbury WF12 .... 139 E8
Mirfield WF14 .... 138 A7
Old Barn Cl LS17 .... 43 A5
Old Bell Ct HX1 .... 203 E2
Old Boyne Hill Farm WF4 . 160 A3
Old Brandon La LS17 ...... 44 E4
Old Bridge Rise LS29 ...... 8 A5
Old Canal Rd BD1 .... 201 B4
Old Cawsey HX6 .... 112 C4
Old Church St WF5 .... 140 D5
Old Cl LS11 .... 98 D8
Old Cock Yd HX1 .... 203 E3
Old Corn La BD7 .... 74 A4
Old Cross Stone Rd **17**
OL14 .... 108 C5
Old Crown Rd WF2 .... 141 D3
Old Dalton La BD21 .... 35 D7
Old Earth HX5 .... 135 B7
Old Farm App LS16 .... 58 F8
Old Farm Cl LS16 .... 59 A8
Old Farm Cres BD4 .... 75 B3
Old Farm Cross LS16 ...... 59 A8
Old Farm Dr LS16 .... 59 A8
Old Farm Garth **2** LS16 . 59 A8
Old Farm Par LS16 .... 59 A8
Old Farm Wlk **6** LS16 .. 58 F8
Old Fieldhouse La HD2 .. 136 D1
Old Fold **8** LS28 .... 57 D3
Old Forge Mews LS16 ..... 24 D3
Old Garth Croft WF11 .... 105 A4
Old Gate
24 Hebden Bridge HX7 .. 89 A3
Holme HD7 .... 197 F7
Old Godley La HX3 .... 92 F1
Old Great North Rd
Brotherton WF11 .... 126 D8
Knottingley WF11 .... 126 C5
Old Ground HD7 .... 169 A8
Old Guy Rd BD13 .... 72 C1
Old Hall HX3 .... 113 D4
Old Hall Cl BD20 .... 16 B6
Old Hall Court Yd WF1 ... 143 A3
Old Hall La HD8 .... 175 E5
Old Hall Mews WF17 ...... 118 C7
Old Hall Rd
Adwick Le St DN6 .... 184 F2
Batley WF17 .... 118 C7
Bradford WF17 .... 119 F8
Glusburn BD20 .... 16 B6
Old Hall Way BD20 .... 16 B6
Old Haworth La **6** LS19 . 40 B7
Old Hollings Hill
LS20, BD17 .... 39 C6
Old La Birkenshaw BD11 .. 96 B5
Bramhope LS16 .... 24 B3
Brighouse HD6 .... 115 B3
Cullingworth BD13 .... 52 D6
Gildersome BD11 .... 97 A8
Guiseley LS20 .... 38 E8
Halifax HX3 .... 92 B2
Halifax, Luddenden HX2 .. 90 E1
Haworth BD22 .... 49 F7
Holme HD7 .... 187 C4
Huddersfield HD2 .... 136 D5

Old La continued
Ilkley LS29 .... 8 D3
Leeds LS11 .... 213 F1
Marsden HD7 .... 169 D7
Nesfield LS29 .... 7 C7
Pool LS16 .... 23 F4
Slaithwaite HD7 .... 169 C4
Todmorden OL14 .... 108 A3
Wadsworth Moor HX7 ...... 89 B8
Old Laithe La HX7 .... 89 C5
Old Lane Ct **2** HD6 .... 115 B3
Old Langley La BD11 ...... 38 E4
Old Lee Bank HX3 .... 92 B1
Old Leeds Rd HD1 .... 154 B6
Old Lees Rd HX7 .... 89 A4
Old Lindley Rd HD3 .... 134 D2
Old Lodge Hill
or Hardings La LS29 .... 7 F6
Old Main St BD16 .... 36 F3
Old Malt St **1** BD22 .... 51 C6
Old Marsh LS28 .... 76 C7
Old Meadows Rd OL13 ... 106 A4
Old Mill Bsns Pk LS10 .. 215 F4
Old Mill Cl Burley in W LS29 .. 9 F2
Hemsworth WF9 .... 181 C7
Old Mill La LS10 .... 215 E4
Old Mill Yd WF5 .... 140 E3
Old Mill View WF12 .... 139 B5
Old Mill Yd WF5 .... 140 C3
Old Moll Rd HD7 .... 171 E5
Old Mount Farm WF4 .... 178 A6
Old Mount Rd HD7 .... 168 E2
Old Oak Cl LS16 .... 59 A7
Old Oak Dr LS16 .... 59 A7
Old Oak Garth LS16 .... 58 F7
Old Orch The
Hemsworth WF9 .... 181 D7
Leeds LS13 .... 58 B4
Old Oxenhope La BD22 .. 51 B4
Old Park Ct BD1 .... 201 D3
Old Park Rd Bradford BD10 .. 56 C7
Leeds LS8 .... 61 A8
Old Pool Bank
Bramhope LS21 .... 24 B5
Pool LS21 .... 24 B5
Old Popplewell La BD19 . 115 E8
Old Power Way HX5 ...... 135 A8
Old Railway Goods Yd The
HD3 .... 153 A5
Old Rd Bradford BD7 ...... 73 E2
Denholme BD13 .... 71 D8
Holmfirth HD7 .... 188 D3
Netherton WF4 .... 158 A5
Pudsey LS28 .... 57 D2
Thornton BD13 .... 73 A6
Wadsworth Moor HX7 ..... 69 A2
Old Riding La HX7 .... 90 F3
Old Robin **8** BD19 ...... 116 D7
Old Run Rd Leeds LS10 .. 215 D1
Middleton LS10 .... 215 D1
Old Run View LS10 .... 99 D8
Old Sawmills The HX6 .. 132 C2
Old School Ct WF10 .... 124 C5
Old School Mews **4** LS8 . 98 C8
Old Schools Gdns **14** HX3 .. 92 C1
Old Shaw La HX7 .... 88 A4
Old Souls Way BD16 .... 36 F6
Old South St HD1 .... 154 A6
Old St Hampole DN6 .... 183 F1
Hooton Pagnell DN5 ...... 195 F7
Old Station Cotts S71 ... 179 D7
Old Station Way LS29 ...... 6 F8
Old Town Junior
& Infants Sch HX7 .... 89 C5
Old Town Hall La HX7 ..... 89 B5
Old Turnpike HD7 .... 172 A4
Old Wakefield Rd HD5 .. 154 D5
Old Water Mill The HX6 . 132 D7
Old Well Head HX1 .... 203 E2
Old Westgate WF13 .... 139 A8
Old Whack House La LS19 . 39 F6
Old Wood La BD16, LS20 .. 21 B2
Old Woodyard The WF4 .. 158 C2
Old Yew La HD7 .... 188 E2
Oldfield HD7 .... 171 F1
Oldfield Ave LS12 .... 209 F2
Oldfield First Sch BD22 .. 50 C8
Oldfield Gate BD22 .... 51 A2
Oldfield La Bradford WF16 .. 117 D3
Clayton West HD8 .... 175 F2
Collingham LS22 .... 13 E1
Haworth BD22 .... 51 A7
Haworth, Oldfield BD22 ... 50 C8
Leeds LS12 .... 209 F2
Oldfield Rd HD1 .... 171 F1
Oldfield St Halifax HX3 ... 92 A3
Huddersfield HD4 .... 153 E4
Leeds LS12 .... 209 F2
Oldgate HD1 .... 154 B6
Oldham Rd HX6 .... 150 C6
Oldroyd Cres LS11 .... 213 E2
Oldroyd Rd OL14 .... 108 E4
Oldside Ct BD20 .... 19 E1
Olicana Pk LS29 .... 8 A5
Olive Gr BD8 .... 73 E8
Olive St HD1 .... 136 B1
Olive Terr Bingley BD16 ... 37 A3
Marsden HD7 .... 169 C6
Oliver Ct BD11 .... 96 F5
Oliver Gdns WF13 .... 137 F7
Oliver Hill LS18 .... 58 C7
Oliver La HD7 .... 168 F4
Oliver Mdws WF13 .... 135 B7
Oliver Rd WF16 .... 117 E5
Oliver St BD4 .... 201 D1

Olivers Mount WF8 .... 146 E8
Ollerdale Ave BD15 .... 54 A2
Ollerdale Cl BD15 .... 54 A2
Ollerton Rd S71 .... 178 F3
Olney St HD7 .... 152 A3
Olrika Ct LS7 .... 207 D4
Oltley Rd LS7 .... 22 B5
Olympic Cl **3** BD12 ..... 94 A1
Omar St WF16 .... 117 C4
Onchan Dr OL13 .... 106 B1
One St BD1 .... 74 D7
Onslow Cres WF8 .... 75 B2
Ontario Pl LS7 .... 204 A2
Opal St **10** BD22 .... 35 A4
Orange St Bradford BD3 .. 75 C6
Halifax HX1 .... 203 E3
Orange Terr HD1 .... 154 B8
Orange Tree Gr WF3 ..... 120 C7
Orchard Ave WF3 .... 121 F5
Orchard Cl
East Ardsley WF3 .... 120 D6
Halifax HX2 .... 112 D6
Horbury WF4 .... 141 A2
Mapplewell S75 .... 178 B1
Meltham HD7 .... 170 F1
Wakefield WF2 .... 120 F3
Orchard Croft
2 Leeds LS15 .... 62 B2
Wakefield WF2 .... 120 C8
Walton WF2 .... 161 A7
Orchard Ct Bramham LS23 .. 30 D2
Huddersfield HD3 .... 152 F6
Orchard Dr
Ackworth M T WF7 .... 164 A5
Collingham LS22 .... 13 B3
Crigglestone WF4 .... 159 F7
Fairburn WF11 .... 105 B5
South Hiendley S72 .... 180 D6
Orchard Gate LS21 .... 23 A7
Orchard Gdns WF4 .... 159 F7
Orchard Gr Bradford BD10 .. 56 D6
Menston LS29 .... 22 B4
Orchard Head Cres WF8 125 F4
Orchard Head Dr WF8 ... 125 E4
Orchard Head Junior
& Infants Sch WF8 .... 125 E4
Orchard Head La
Addingham LS29 .... 7 A8
Darrington WF8 .... 147 C5
Pontefract WF8 .... 125 E4
Orchard Lees WF8 .... 125 C8
Orchard Mount LS15 ...... 62 C2
Orchard Rd Kirkheaton HD5 155 C8
1 Leeds LS15 .... 62 B2
Todmorden OL14 .... 107 F7
Wakefield WF2 .... 142 E1
Orchard Rise HX6 .... 111 F2
Orchard Sq LS15 .... 62 B2
Orchard St Dewsbury WF12 139 D6
Huddersfield HD4 .... 154 A4
Otley LS21 .... 23 B7
Orchard St W HD3 .... 153 A5
Orchard Terr
Cawthorne S75 .... 193 F4
Huddersfield HD4 .... 154 A4
Orchard The Boston Spa LS23 .. 30 D8
Crofton WF4 .... 144 A1
Elland HX4 .... 133 F3
Featherstone WF7 .... 124 D1
Keighley BD21 .... 35 F7
Mirfield WF14 .... 138 A7
Normanton WF6 .... 123 B2
Ossett WF5 .... 140 D5
Pontefract WF8 .... 146 F5
Wakefield WF2, WF4 ...... 120 F3
Orchard View
Brotherton WF11 .... 126 C8
Darrington WF8 .... 147 C5
Wetherby LS22 .... 13 E8
Orchard Way
Brighouse HD6 .... 115 A4
Guiseley LS20 .... 22 E1
Rothwell LS26 .... 100 F6
Orchard Wlk HX7 .... 89 F1
Orchards The Bingley BD16 .. 37 A5
Cleckheaton BD19 .... 117 C8
Hipperholme HX3 .... 114 C8
Micktown LS26 .... 102 C2
Orchid Crest WF9 .... 183 A7
Orchid Ct WF3 .... 100 B2
Oriental St **6** LS12 ..... 209 F3
Orion Cres LS10 .... 99 F7
Orion Dr LS10 .... 99 F7
Orion Gdns LS10 .... 99 F7
Orion Wlk LS10 .... 99 F8
Orlando Cl WF13 .... 138 A7
Orleans St BD6 .... 93 F7
Ormond Rd BD6 .... 74 B1
Ormond St BD7 .... 74 A4
Ormonde Dr BD15 .... 73 A8
Ormonde Pl LS7 .... 204 A2
Ormondroyd Ave BD6 .... 94 C8
Orville Gdns LS6 .... 205 E4
Orwell Cl WF10 .... 125 C5
Osborne Ave **2** HX3 .... 141 C2
Osborne Gr **2** HX3 ...... 114 D7
Osborne Pl
22 Hebden Bridge HX7 .. 89 A3
5 Todmorden OL14 ... 108 C5
Osborne St Bradford BD5 .. 201 A1
Halifax HX1 .... 202 B4
18 Hebden Bridge HX7 .. 89 A3
15 Huddersfield HD5 .. 154 D5
Osbourne Ct LS13 .... 58 D1
Osbourne Dr BD13 .... 72 E6
Osmond Ho **9** BD5 ...... 201 B1
Osmondthorpe La LS9 ... 80 C1

smondthorpe Primary Sch
LS9 .... 80 D8
sprey Cl LS17 .... 43 F4
sprey Ct BD8 .... 73 C7
sprey Dr HD4 .... 171 E7
sprey Gr LS17 .... 43 F4
sprey Meadow LS27 .... 98 D4
ssett High Sch WF5 .... 140 D3
ssett Lane WF14 .... 140 A4
ssett South Parade
Infant Sch WF5 .... 140 F4
sterley Gr BD10 .... 56 E5
swald St BD18 .... 55 B7
swaldthorpe Ave BD3 ..... 56 B1
tley All Saints Inf Sch
LS21 .... 23 B7
tley Ashfield Inf Sch
LS21 .... 10 E1
tley Golf Course LS21 ..... 22 C6
tley La WF17 .... 40 B7
tley Mount BD20 .... 19 E1
tley Old Rd Bramhope LS16 24 B1
East Carlton LS16 .... 23 F3
East Carlton LS16 .... 24 B1
Leeds LS16 .... 41 F4
tley Rd Baildon BD17 ...... 38 E2
Bingley BD16 .... 20 B1
Bingley, Eldwick Beck BD16 37 D6
Burley in W LS29 .... 22 B8
Guiseley LS20 .... 22 D1
Harewood LS17 .... 26 C7
Keighley BD20 .... 19 F1
Leeds, Adel LS16 .... 42 A5
Leeds, Far Headingley
LS6, LS16 .... 59 D6
Shipley BD17, BD18 .... 55 B7
tley St Halifax HX1 .... 202 B3
Keighley BD21 .... 35 B6
tley Westgate Inf Sch
LS21 .... 22 F7
ttawa Pl LS7 .... 204 A2
tterburn Cl BD5 .... 201 B1
tterburn Gdns LS16 .... 42 B3
tterburn St BD21 .... 35 C8
tters Holt WF4 .... 159 F7
tterwood Bank LS22 ...... 13 F7
ttiwells Terr HD7 .... 168 F3
uchthorpe Fold WF1 ...... 121 C4
uchthorpe La WF1 .... 121 C2
ueen's Ct LS17 .... 43 C1
ulton Dr LS26 .... 101 C3
ulton Infant Sch LS26 .... 101 B6
ulton Junior Sch LS26 .... 101 B6
ulton La Rothwell LS26 ... 100 F5
Rothwell, Woodlesford LS26 101 C6
ulton Terr BD7 .... 101 B6
unsworth St BD4 .... 75 B4
ur Lady of Good Counsel
RC Sch LS14 .... 62 A6
ur Lady of Lourdes RC
Jun & Inf Sch HD2 .... 136 C4
ur Lady of Victories RC
rimary Sch BD21 .... 35 A7
ur Lady's RC Prim Sch
LS8 .... 62 A6
use Dr LS22 .... 13 D8
use St 2 BD12 .... 51 D7
ut Gang LS13 .... 58 D3
uzel La Emley HD8 .... 175 C7
Holmfirth HD7 .... 188 F8
utcote Bank HD1 .... 154 A5
utfield Cl WF16 .... 117 E4
utgang La LS13 .... 58 E3
utlands Rise BD10 .... 56 D8
utlane Jun & Inf Sch
HD3 .... 134 D1
utside La BD22 .... 50 F2
utwood Ave LS18 .... 58 D7
utwood Grange High Sch
WF1 .... 121 A4
utwood La LS18 .... 58 D7
utwood Park Ct WF1 ..... 121 B4
utwood Wlk LS18 .... 58 C7
uzelwell Cres WF12 .... 139 B3
uzelwell La WF12 .... 139 A3
uzelwell Rd WF12 .... 139 B4
uzelwell Gn WF3 .... 100 D2
val The Baildon BD17 ..... 38 B2
Beal DN14 .... 127 F5
Bingley BD16 .... 37 B2
Bradford BD8 .... 73 E8
Cleckheaton WF15 .... 116 C5
val The LS25 .... 83 A7
val The Guiseley LS20 .... 39 C8
Holmfirth HD7 .... 188 F7
Leeds, Hunslet LS10 .... 215 E4
Leeds, The Oval LS14 ..... 61 F2
Notton WF4 .... 179 B6
Otley LS21 .... 10 F1
Rothwell LS26 .... 100 F5
venden Ave HX3 .... 92 A1
venden Cl 16 HX3 .... 92 A1
venden Cres HX3 .... 92 A2
venden Gn HX3 .... 92 A2
venden Rd HX3 .... 92 A2
venden Road Terr 9
HX3 .... 92 A2
venden Terr HX3 .... 92 A2
venden Way HX3 .... 91 F2
venden Wood Rd HX2 .... 91 D2
ver Hall Cl WF14 .... 138 B6
ver Hall La WF14 .... 138 B6
ver Hall Pk WF14 .... 138 B6
ver Hall Rd WF14 .... 138 B6
ver La LS19 .... 40 C3
verburn Rd BD20 .... 16 D4
verdale HX6 .... 132 E7
verdale Ave LS17 .... 44 A5

Overdale Cl LS22 .... 13 D6
Overdale Dr BD10, BD18 ... 38 F1
Overdale Mount HX6 ...... 112 C5
Overdale Terr 1 LS15 ..... 81 A8
Overend St 3 BD6 .... 74 A1
Overland Cres BD10 .... 56 D8
Overmoor Fold BD10 ...... 56 A7
Overthorpe Ave WF12 .... 139 D1
Overthorpe CE Jun
& Inf Sch WF12 .... 139 D2
Overthorpe Rd WF12 ..... 139 D3
Overton Dr BD4 .... 73 D2
Ovington Dr BD4 .... 73 D2
Owen Ct BD16 .... 37 A6
Owen's Cres HD7 .... 171 E3
Owl La Batley HD5 .... 119 B1
Batley, Chidswell WF12 ... 119 A3
Ossett WF5 .... 119 B1
Owl Mews HD5 .... 155 C6
Owl Ridge LS27 .... 98 C3
Owlar Bars Rd HD7 .... 170 C2
Owlcotes Ctr LS28 .... 57 D1
Owlcotes Dr LS28 .... 76 C8
Owlcotes Garth LS28 ..... 76 C8
Owlcotes Gdns LS28 ...... 76 C8
Owlcotes La Pudsey LS28 57 C1
Pudsey LS28 .... 76 C8
Owlcotes Rd LS28 .... 76 B8
Owlcotes Terr LS28 .... 76 C8
Owler Ings Rd HD6 .... 115 A2
Owler La WF17 .... 96 F3
Owler Mdws WF16 .... 117 C5
Owler Park Rd LS29 .... 7 F6
Owler's La WF9 .... 164 F4
Owlers Cl HD2 .... 136 F5
Owlet Grange BD18 .... 55 C6
Owlet Hurst La WF15 ..... 117 B2
Owlet Rd BD18 .... 55 C7
Owlett Mead WF3 .... 99 E1
Owlett Mead Cl WF3 ...... 99 F1
Ox Heys Meadows BD13 .. 73 A6
Ox Lee La HD7 .... 199 E8
Oxenhope C of E Aided
First Sch BD22 .... 51 C3
Oxenhope Sta BD22 .... 51 D5
Oxfield Ct HD5 .... 155 A7
Oxford Ave LS20 .... 22 D1
Oxford Cl Cleckheaton BD19 117 B8
Queensbury BD13 .... 92 C8
Oxford Court Gdns WF10 124 C7
Oxford Cres Bradford BD14 73 B4
Halifax HX3 .... 113 D4
Oxford Dr
Cleckheaton BD19 .... 117 B8
Kippax LS25 .... 83 A2
Oxford La HX3 .... 113 D3
Oxford Pl Baildon BD17 ... 38 E2
Bradford BD1 .... 201 C4
Huddersfield HD1 .... 153 E3
Leeds LS1 .... 211 E4
Pudsey LS28 .... 76 E7
Oxford Rd Batley WF17 ... 96 E1
Bradford BD2 .... 56 B2
Cleckheaton BD19 .... 96 B2
Dewsbury WF13 .... 118 B1
Guiseley LS20 .... 22 E1
Halifax HX1 .... 203 E2
Leeds LS7 .... 206 C3
Queensbury BD13 .... 92 C8
Wakefield WF1 .... 216 A4
Oxford Row LS1 .... 211 E4
Oxford St
Batley, Mount Pleasant
WF17 .... 118 A4
Batley, Nunroyd WF16 .... 117 D4
Bradford BD14 .... 73 B4
East Ardsley WF3 .... 120 E8
Featherstone WF7 .... 145 C5
Guiseley LS20 .... 22 E1
Hebden Bridge HX7 .... 88 F3
Huddersfield HD1 .... 154 B7
Keighley BD21 .... 35 A7
Normanton WF6 .... 123 C3
South Elmsall WF9 .... 182 F2
Sowerby Bridge HX6 ...... 112 D4
Todmorden OL14 .... 108 B6
Wakefield WF1 .... 142 E3
Oxford Terr Baildon BD17 38 E2
Wakefield WF1 .... 118 D4
Oxley Gdns BD12 .... 94 C7
Oxley Hall LS16 .... 59 C8
Oxley Rd HD2 .... 136 C4
Oxley St Bradford BD8 .... 74 C8
Leeds LS9 .... 212 C3
Oxleys Sq HD3 .... 134 D1
Oxton Mount LS9 .... 212 C4
Oxton Way LS9 .... 212 C4
Oyster Cl LS27 .... 98 C3
Oyster Park Infants Sch
WF10 .... 125 D8
Oyster Park Junior Sch
WF10 .... 125 D8

Pacaholme Rd WF2 .... 141 D8
Pack Fold HD7 .... 170 C8
Pack Horse Cl HD8 .... 176 A4
Pack Horse Ctr 9 HD1 .... 154 B6
Pad Cote La BD22 .... 32 A8
Padan St HX3 .... 113 D4
Paddock BD9 .... 55 B4
Paddock Cl
Birkenshaw BD11 .... 96 E5
Bradford BD12 .... 94 C1
Garforth LS25 .... 83 A6
Mapplewell S75 .... 178 C1

Paddock Dr BD11 .... 96 E5
Paddock Foot HD1 .... 153 E5
Paddock Gn LS17 .... 28 C5
Paddock House La LS22 .. 12 B3
Paddock Jun & Inf Sch
HD1 .... 153 D5
Paddock La LS27 .... 112 C8
Paddock Rd
Kirkburton HD8 .... 174 A7
Mapplewell S75 .... 178 C1
Northowram HD8, S75 .... 92 E5
Paddock The Baildon BD17 38 H4
12 Brighouse BD19 .... 115 F8
Burton Salmon LS25 ...... 105 E3
Castleford WF10 .... 125 C6
Cullingworth BD13 .... 52 D6
Dewsbury WF12 .... 139 F6
East Keswick LS17 .... 28 C5
Kirkheaton HD5 .... 155 C7
Knottingley WF11 .... 126 F3
Leeds LS8 .... 59 F7
Normanton WF6 .... 123 B1
Rothwell LS26 .... 100 E5
Silsden BD20 .... 5 E1
Thorner LS14 .... 45 F5
Woolley WF4 .... 178 A7
Paddock View WF10 ...... 125 B6
Paddy Bridge Rd HX7 ..... 89 D1
Padgum 12 BD17 .... 38 C4
Padma Cl BD7 .... 74 B3
Padmans La LS23 .... 30 D8
Padstow Ave LS10 .... 99 A5
Padstow Gdns LS10 .... 99 A5
Padstow Pl LS10 .... 99 A4
Page Hill HX2 .... 90 E1
Page St HD1 .... 154 B5
Paget Cres HD2 .... 135 D1
Paget St BD21 .... 35 A7
Pagewood Ct BD10 .... 39 A1
Painthorpe House
Country Club WF4 .... 159 E4
Painthorpe La WF4 .... 159 E4
Painthorpe Terr WF4 ..... 159 E4
Paisley Gr 2 LS12 .... 209 E4
Paisley Pl 3 LS12 .... 209 E4
Paisley Rd LS12 .... 209 D4
Paisley St LS12 .... 209 E4
Paisley Terr 4 LS12 .... 209 E4
Paisley View 5 LS12 ...... 209 D4
Pakington St BD5 .... 74 D4
Palace House Rd HX7 ..... 89 A2
Paleside La WF5 .... 140 D7
Palesides Ave WF5 .... 140 D8
Palestine Rd 4 HX7 .... 89 A4
Paley Rd BD4 .... 75 A4
Paley Terr BD4 .... 75 A4
Palin Ave BD3 .... 56 D1
Palm St Halifax HX3 .... 92 B2
Huddersfield HD4 .... 154 B4
Palma St OL14 .... 86 B1
Palmer Rd BD3 .... 75 B8
Palmer's Ave WF9 .... 183 B2
Palmerston St BD2 .... 56 B2
Pangbourne Rd S63 .... 194 C1
Pannal Ave WF1 .... 142 E8
Pannal St BD7 .... 74 A3
Panorama Dr LS29 .... 7 F3
Papyrus Villas LS24 .... 31 C6
Parade The Batley WF17 118 A4
Bradford BD4 .... 75 E3
Leeds LS8 .... 212 B3
Otley LS21 .... 10 E1
2 Shipley BD10 .... 54 A7
Yeadon LS19 .... 39 F6
Paradise Fields WF8 ...... 125 D1
Paradise La Halifax HX2 .. 112 B6
Stutton LS24 .... 48 B5
Paradise Pl 3 LS18 .... 58 B8
Paradise Rd BD9 .... 54 F4
Paradise St Bradford BD1 74 D7
Halifax HX1 .... 203 D2
Pudsey LS28 .... 57 D3
Pariss Mews HD7 .... 189 D7
Paris Rd HD7 .... 189 D4
Parish Ghyll Dr LS29 ..... 7 F3
Parish Ghyll La LS29 ..... 7 F3
Parish Ghyll Rd LS29 ..... 8 A3
Parish Ghyll Wlk LS29 ... 8 A3
Park Ave Bingley BD16 ... 36 F2
Birkenshaw BD11 .... 96 E6
Bradford BD10 .... 39 B2
Brierley S72 .... 181 B3
Castleford WF10 .... 124 E7
Clayton West HD8 .... 175 F3
Crofton WF1 .... 143 D7
Darrington WF8 .... 147 C5
Dewsbury WF13 .... 139 B7
Elland HX5 .... 134 F5
Huddersfield HD1 .... 153 F6
Keighley BD21 .... 35 B6
Kippax LS25 .... 83 C1
Kippax, Allerton Bywater
WF10 .... 103 C4
Leeds LS8 .... 204 A2
Leeds, Lady Wood LS8 ... 61 C7
Leeds, Manston LS15 .... 62 D2
Liversedge WF15 .... 117 A2
Lofthouse Gate WF3 ..... 121 C6

Park Ave continued
Shipley BD18 .... 55 A8
South Kirkby WF9 .... 182 B2
Sutton in C BD20 .... 16 D5
Swillington LS26 .... 82 A1
Wakefield WF2 .... 142 B4
Yeadon LS19 .... 40 A4
Yeadon, Larkfield LS19 ... 40 C4
Park Cl Batley WF17 ...... 118 B3
Bingley BD16 .... 37 A4
Birkenshaw BD11 .... 96 E6
Bradford BD10 .... 56 C5
Brighouse HX3 .... 114 E7
Darrington WF8 .... 147 C5
Halifax HX2 .... 91 B2
Keighley BD21 .... 35 C5
Leeds LS13 .... 58 C3
Normanton WF6 .... 123 A1
Queensbury BD13 .... 72 D1
Shipley HD8 .... 173 F3
Park Cliffe Rd BD2 .... 56 B2
Park Copse LS18 .... 41 A1
Park Cotts LS8 .... 44 B1
Park Cres Addingham LS29 7 A8
Bradford BD3 .... 56 A2
Castleford WF10 .... 125 C7
Gildersome LS27 .... 97 D6
Guiseley LS27 .... 39 C7
Halifax HX3 .... 92 B2
Leeds LS8 .... 209 E4
Leeds, Park Villas LS8 ... 44 B1
Rothwell LS26 .... 101 A6
Royston S71 .... 179 D3
Park Crest WF9 .... 181 D7
Park Croft Batley WF17 118 B8
Dewsbury WF13 .... 139 A8
Park Cross St LS1 .... 211 E4
Park Ct Bradford BD9 ... 55 C2
Featherstone WF7 ...... 124 D1
Ossett WF5 .... 140 F4
Pool LS21 .... 24 D6
Park Dale Castleford WF10 104 C1
Menston LS29 .... 22 A4
Park Dr Batley WF17 .... 118 A7
Bingley BD16 .... 37 B5
Horsforth LS18 .... 58 A8
Huddersfield HD1 .... 153 E7
Lofthouse Gate WF3 ... 121 C7
Mirfield WF14 .... 138 B5
Shipley HD8 .... 173 F3
Sowerby Bridge HX6 ... 111 F8
Sutton in C BD20 .... 16 D5
Park Dr S HD1 .... 153 F6
Park Edge Cl LS8 .... 61 C7
Park Est WF9 .... 182 C2
Park Farm Ind Est LS11 99 B8
Park Field LS29 .... 22 A4
Park Fields WF11 .... 91 B2
Park Gate Bradford BD1 201 C3
Huddersfield HD8 .... 173 F6
Park Gate Cres LS20 .... 39 D8
Park Gate Rd HD7 ...... 169 B6
Park Gdns Ossett WF5 .. 140 F4
Sowerby Bridge HX2 ... 112 D5
Park Gn Normanton WF6 123 A1
Silsden BD20 .... 5 C2
Park Gr Gildersome LS27 97 D6
Horbury WF4 .... 140 F2
Horsforth LS18 .... 57 F8
Huddersfield HD1 .... 153 F6
Keighley BD21 .... 35 C6
Mirfield WF14 .... 138 C4
3 Queensbury BD13 .... 72 D1
Shipley BD18 .... 54 F8
Shipley, Frizinghall BD9 55 C6
Swillington LS26 .... 102 B8
Yeadon LS19 .... 40 A7
Park Grove Rd WF2 ..... 142 A5
Park Head La
Denby Dale HD8 .... 190 F5
Holmfirth HD7 .... 188 E4
Park Hill Huddersfield HD2 136 F6
Kexbrough S75 .... 177 B2
Park Hill Cl BD8 .... 54 D1
Park Hill Dr BD2 .... 54 D1
Park Hill Gr WF1 .... 142 F6
Park Holme LS7 .... 207 E4
Park House BD20 .... 17 C6
Park House Cl BD12 ..... 94 E7
Park House Cres BD12 .. 94 E7
Park House Dr WF12 ... 139 D4
Park House Gn BD12 ... 94 E7
Park House Rd BD12 ... 94 E6
Park House Wlk BD12 .. 94 E7
Park Jun Sch The WF10 124 E7
Park La Baildon BD17 ... 38 F4
Bradford, Holme Top BD5 74 D4
Bradford, Park Lane BD14 73 B4
Denby Dale HD8 .... 191 B8
Elland HX4 .... 133 F1
Emley HD8 .... 175 A5
Guiseley LS20 .... 39 C7
Halifax HX3 .... 113 E2
Hebden Bridge HX7 .... 110 D8
Huddersfield HD4 .... 172 A7
Huddersfield, Town End
HD7 .... 152 D4
Kippax LS25 .... 103 C8
Kippax, Allerton Bywater
WF10 .... 103 C5
Ledsham LS25 .... 104 C8
Leeds LS3 .... 211 D4
Leeds, Roundhay LS8 ... 44 B2

Park La continued
Meltham HD7 .... 170 E2
Mickletown LS26 .... 102 A1
Pontefract WF7, WF8 ... 124 E1
Queensbury BD13 .... 72 F1
Sutton in C BD20 .... 16 A1
Swillington LS26 .... 82 A1
Sicklinghall LS22 .... 12 B5
Sutton in C BD20 .... 16 D5
West Bretton WF4 .... 176 F7
Park Lane Coll of Further
Education LS3 .... 211 D4
Park Lane Mews LS17 .. 44 B4
Park Lea LS10 .... 136 F6
Park Lodge Cres WF1 .. 142 E6
Park Lodge Gr WF1 .... 142 E6
Park Lodge La WF1 ..... 142 F6
Park Mead BD10 .... 39 B2
Park Mews LS21 .... 24 D6
Park Mill La WF5 .... 141 B8
Park Mill Way HD8 ..... 175 F3
Park Mount Leeds LS12 209 D4
Leeds, Kirkstall LS5 .... 59 B4
Pool LS21 .... 24 B5
Park Mount Ave BD17 . 38 E3
Park Mount Terr LS5 ... 59 A4
Park Nook HX3 .... 113 F2
Par Dewsbury WF13 ... 139 B7
Morley LS27 .... 97 F3
Park Pl Bradford BD10 39 B2
Halifax HX1 .... 202 C2
Leeds LS1 .... 211 E3
Pontefract WF8 .... 146 B8
Park Pl E HX3 .... 114 E7
Park Pl W HX3 .... 114 E7
Park Rd 3 Batley WF16 117 D4
Batley, Birks Fold WF17 118 D5
Batley, Healey WF17 ... 118 A5
Bingley BD16 .... 37 A4
Boston Spa LS23 .... 30 C8
Bradford BD6 .... 94 C7
Bradford BD5 .... 201 B1
Bradford, Greengates BD10 56 E6
Bradford, Thackley BD10 39 B2
Brierley S72 .... 181 B3
Castleford WF10 .... 125 A5
Clayton West HD8 ...... 175 F3
Dewsbury WF12 .... 139 C6
Dewsbury, Earlsheaton
WF12 .... 139 F7
Dewsbury, Ravensthorpe
WF13 .... 138 F6
Dewsbury, Westborough
WF13 .... 118 B1
Glusburn BD20 .... 16 C7
Guiseley LS20 .... 39 D8
Halifax HX1 .... 203 D2
Huddersfield, Lockwood
HD4 .... 153 D4
Huddersfield, Milnsbridge
HD4 .... 153 B4
Leeds LS12 .... 209 D4
Leeds, Colton LS15 ..... 81 D6
Leeds, Whitecote LS13 58 C3
Menston LS29 .... 22 A4
Pontefract WF8 .... 125 B2
Shipley BD18 .... 55 C7
Sowerby Bridge HX6 ... 112 D5
Todmorden OL14 .... 108 B6
Yeadon LS19 .... 40 A7
Yeadon LS19 .... 40 A8
Park Rd W HX4 .... 153 D4
Park Rise Castleford WF10 124 F7
Leeds LS13 .... 58 C4
Park Road Jun & Inf Sch
LS12 .... 118 D5
Park Row
6 Brighouse HD6 .... 115 B2
Burley in W LS29 .... 9 F2
Leeds LS1 .... 211 E4
Otley LS21 .... 23 B8
Pudsey LS28 .... 57 E1
Sutton in C BD20 ...... 16 D4
Park Sch The WF2 ..... 216 A1
Park Side
Cleckheaton BD19 ..... 117 A7
Flockton WF4 .... 157 C3
Holmfirth HD7 .... 189 E4
Horsforth LS18 .... 58 A8
Kirkheaton HD5 .... 137 C1
Park Spring Gdns LS13 58 B1
Park Spring Primary Sch
LS13 .... 77 B8
Park Spring Rise LS13 58 B1
Park Sq 1 Bradford BD6 94 A8
Lofthouse Gate WF3 ... 93 A2
Northowram WF3 ...... 140 F4
Ossett WF5 .... 24 D6
Park Sq E LS1 .... 211 E4
Park Sq N LS1 .... 211 E4
Park Sq S LS1 .... 211 E4
Park Sq W LS1 .... 211 E4
Park St
Batley, Brown Hill WF17 118 E8
Batley, Nunroyd WF17 117 D4
Brighouse HD6 .... 115 B2
Cleckheaton, Gomersal
BD19 .... 117 C8
Cleckheaton, Hartshead
Moor Side BD19 .... 116 B6
Dewsbury WF13 .... 118 D1
Glusburn BD20 .... 16 D6
Haworth BD22 .... 51 D7
Horbury WF4 .... 141 A1
Leeds LS12 .... 209 D4

Park St continued
Leeds LS1 .... 211 E4
Leeds, Graveleythorpe LS15 .. 81 B8
Morley LS27 .... 98 C8
Ossett WF5 .... 140 F4
Shipley BD18 .... 55 A8
Slaithwaite HD7 .... 152 C6
Lowertop Bridge HX6 .... 112 D4
Wakefield WF1 .... 216 C1
Yeadon LS19 .... 40 A7
Park Stone Rise HX3 .... 93 B5
Park Terr Brighouse HX3 .... 114 D7
Halifax HX1 .... 202 C2
Keighley, Eastwood BD21 ..... 35 D7
Keighley, Thwaites Brow BD21 35 F6
Leeds LS6 .... 59 D6
Otley LS21 .... 23 B8
Park LS21 .... 24 A5
Shipley BD18 .... 55 A8
South Elmsall WF9 .... 183 A2
Park The S75 .... 193 E4
Park Top Leeds LS6 .... 57 E1
Park Top Cotts BD16 .... 37 B5
Park Top BD22 .... 51 A5
Park Towngate The HX3 .... 114 A4
Park View Brierley S72 .... 181 B3
Castleford WF10 .... 125 B6
Cleckheaton BD19 .... 116 C7
Elland HX4 .... 134 A1
Halifax HX1 .... 202 C2
Hemsworth WF9 .... 163 B1
Holmfirth HD7 .... 189 A5
[6] Kippax LS25 .... 83 B1
Leeds, Beeston Hill LS11 .... 214 A3
Leeds, Bramley LS13 .... 58 C3
Lofthouse Gate WF3 .... 121 C6
Marsden HD7 .... 169 A4
Mirfield WF14 .... 138 C4
Pudsey LS28 .... 76 E7
Royston S71 .... 179 D3
Shafton S72 .... 180 D2
Swillington LS26 .... 82 A1
Wakefield WF2 .... 141 E6
Yeadon LS19 .... 39 F7
Park View Ave
[B] Haworth BD22 .... 51 E8
Leeds LS4 .... 205 D3
Northowram HX3 .... 93 A1
Yeadon LS19 .... 40 C4
Park View Cres LS8 .... 44 A2
Park View Gr LS4 .... 205 D3
Park View Rd Bradford BD9 .. 55 B3
Leeds LS4 .... 205 D2
Mapplewell S75 .... 178 D1
Park View Terr
Bradford BD9 .... 55 B3
[6] Leeds LS8 .... 81 A8
Yeadon LS19 .... 40 B4
Park Villa Ct LS8 .... 44 A1
Park Villas LS8 .... 44 A1
Park Villas Dr WF8 .... 125 B1
Park W LS26 .... 100 F5
Park Way Baildon BD17 ..... 37 F1
Menston LS29 .... 22 A4
Pool LS21 .... 24 D7
Park Wood Ave LS11 .... 98 F8
Park Wood Cres LS11 .... 98 F7
Park Wood Dr LS11 .... 98 F8
Park Wood Rd LS11 .... 98 F8
Parkcroft LS28 .... 57 D2
Parkdale Dr HX6 .... 132 E7
Parker Ave WF6 .... 122 E4
Parker La WF14 .... 138 B5
Parker Rd Dewsbury WF12 .. 139 C4
Horbury WF4 .... 141 C1
Parker St Batley WF16 ..... 117 D4
East Ardsley WF3 .... 120 C7
Glusburn BD20 .... 16 D7
Parker's La BD20 .... 18 A3
Parkfield Ave
[6] Elland HX5 .... 134 F6
Leeds LS11 .... 214 A3
Mirfield WF14 .... 138 C4
Parkfield Cl LS25 .... 83 B2
Parkfield Cres WF14 .... 138 C4
Parkfield Croft WF14 .... 138 C4
Parkfield Ct LS14 .... 61 E3
Parkfield Dr
Boston Spa LS23 .... 30 C8
Ossett WF5 .... 141 A5
[B] Queensbury BD13 .... 72 D1
Sowerby Bridge HX6 .... 112 A2
Parkfield Gr LS11 .... 214 A3
Parkfield La
Featherstone WF7 .... 124 C2
Sowerby Bridge HX6 .... 112 D3
Parkfield Mount
Leeds LS11 .... 214 A3
Pudsey LS28 .... 76 E7
Parkfield Pl LS11 .... 214 A3
Parkfield Rd Bradford BD8 .. 55 D2
Leeds LS11 .... 214 A3
Shipley BD18 .... 54 E8
Parkfield Row LS11 .... 214 A3
Parkfield St LS11 .... 211 F1
Parkfield Terr
[B] Pudsey LS28 .... 76 E7
Pudsey, Stanningley LS28 ... 57 E1
Parkfield View Leeds LS11 214 A3
Ossett WF5 .... 141 A5
Parkfield Way Leeds LS11 .. 61 E3
Mirfield WF14 .... 138 B4
Parkgate Mews WF1 .... 142 E6
Parkgate Ave WF1 .... 142 E6
Parkhead Ct S71 .... 179 A4

Parkhill Cres WF1 .... 142 F6
Parkin Hall La HX6 .... 111 B1
Parkin La Bradford BD10 ... 56 F8
Todmorden OL14 .... 107 E5
Parkin Sq HD7 .... 152 B5
Parkin St WF15 .... 116 C5
Parkin's Almshouses [2]
HD5 .... 154 F3
Parkinson App LS25 .... 82 F8
Parkinson Cl WF1 .... 142 E6
Parkinson La HX1 .... 202 B2
Parkinson Lane Junior
& Infants Sch HX1 .... 202 C2
Parkinson Rd BD13 .... 71 E8
Parkinson St BD5 .... 74 D4
Parkland Ave LS27 .... 97 E3
Parkland Cres LS6 .... 43 A1
Parkland Dr Bradford BD10 .. 56 C7
Leeds LS6 .... 43 A1
Parkland Gdns LS6 .... 60 A8
Parkland Middle
& First Schs BD10 .... 56 D7
Parkland Terr LS6 .... 60 A8
Parkland View LS19 .... 40 B6
Parklands Bingley BD16 ..... 37 B5
Bramhope LS16 .... 24 D3
Castleford WF10 .... 124 E7
Ilkley LS29 .... 8 A4
Ossett WF5 .... 140 F4
Parklands Ave WF4 .... 140 E1
Parklands Cres
Bramhope LS16 .... 24 E3
Horbury WF4 .... 140 E1
Parklands Ct WF4 .... 140 E1
Parklands Dr Horbury WF4 . 140 E1
Sowerby Bridge HX6 .... 111 E1
Parklands Gate LS16 .... 24 E3
Parklands High Sch LS14 .. 62 B4
Parklands Prim Sch LS14 .. 62 B3
Parklands Wlk HD8 .... 173 F3
Parklee Ct BD21 .... 35 C6
Parkmere Cl BD4 .... 95 B8
Parkside Bingley BD16 .... 37 B4
Cleckheaton BD19 .... 116 E7
[10] Halifax HX3 .... 113 B4
Parkside Ave Leeds LS6 ...... 59 F7
Queensbury BD13 .... 72 D1
Parkside Cl Leeds LS6 .... 59 F8
Todmorden OL14 .... 86 B1
Parkside Cres LS6 .... 59 F8
Parkside Ct BD22 .... 51 E8
Parkside Gdns LS6 .... 59 F7
Parkside Gn LS6 .... 59 F7
Parkside Gr Bradford BD9 .. 55 A3
Leeds LS11 .... 214 A1
Parkside Ind Est LS11 .... 214 C2
Parkside La Leeds LS11 ...... 214 C2
Leeds LS11 .... 214 A1
Parkside Middle Sch
BD13 .... 52 E6
Parkside Mount LS11 .... 214 A1
Parkside Par LS11 .... 214 A1
Parkside Pl LS6 .... 59 F8
Parkside Rd Bradford BD5 .. 74 E2
Leeds LS16, LS6 .... 59 E8
Pudsey LS28 .... 57 D2
Todmorden OL14 .... 86 B1
Parkside Row LS11 .... 214 A1
Parkside Terr BD13 .... 52 E6
Parkside View LS6 .... 59 F8
Parkside Wlk LS28 .... 57 E2
Parkstone HD2 .... 136 F6
Parkstone Ave LS16 .... 42 A1
Parkstone Dr BD10 .... 56 C6
Parkstone Gn LS16 .... 42 A1
Parkstone Gr LS16 .... 42 A1
Parkstone Mount LS16 ..... 42 A1
Parkstone Pl LS16 .... 42 A1
Parkview Ct Leeds LS8 ...... 44 A7
Shipley BD18 .... 55 A7
Parkville Pl LS13 .... 58 C3
Parkville Rd LS13 .... 58 C3
Parkway Bradford BD5 ...... 74 F2
Crofton WF4 .... 143 F2
Gildersome LS27 .... 97 D6
Keighley BD21 .... 35 C5
Queensbury BD13 .... 72 D1
Steeton BD20 .... 17 B5
Parkway Cl LS14 .... 61 E4
Parkway Ct LS14 .... 61 E3
Parkway Grange LS14 .... 61 E3
Parkway Mews LS14 .... 62 B5
Parkway Towers LS14 .... 61 E4
Parkway Vale
Leeds, Brooklands LS14 .... 61 F4
Leeds, Parklands LS14 .... 62 A4
Parkways LS26 .... 101 B6
Parkways Ave LS26 .... 101 B6
Parkways Cl LS26 .... 101 B6
Parkways Ct LS26 .... 101 B6
Parkways Dr LS26 .... 101 B6
Parkways Garth LS26 .... 101 B5
Parkways Gr LS26 .... 101 B6
Parkwood Ave LS6 .... 61 A7
Parkwood Cl HD8 .... 173 F3
Parkwood First Sch BD21 .. 35 D6
Parkwood Gdns LS28 .... 57 A6
Parkwood Rd
Huddersfield HD3, HD7 ...... 152 E6
Pudsey LS28 .... 57 B6
Shipley BD18 .... 54 F7
Parkwood Rise BD21 .... 35 C6
Parkwood St BD21 .... 35 D7
Parkwood Way LS8 .... 61 A7
Parliament Pl LS12 .... 210 A3
Parliament Rd LS12 .... 210 A3
Parliament St WF2 .... 216 A2
Parlington Ct LS15 .... 63 E7

Parlington Dr LS25 .... 64 E7
Parlington House LS25 ..... 64 D7
Parlington La LS25 .... 64 C4
Parlington Meadow LS15 .. 63 E6
Parlington Villas LS25 ...... 64 E7
Parma St BD5 .... 201 B1
Parnaby Ave LS10 .... 215 F1
Parnaby Rd LS10 .... 215 F1
Parnaby St LS10 .... 215 F1
Parnaby Terr LS10 .... 215 F1
Parratt Row BD3 .... 75 D7
Parrock La HX7 .... 89 B6
Parratt St BD4 .... 75 D1
Parry Cl BD10 .... 36 A1
Parry La BD4 .... 75 C5
Parson La WF4 .... 178 A8
Parson St BD21 .... 35 D8
Parson's La LS29 .... 6 C8
Parsonage La HD6 .... 115 A2
Parsonage Rd
Bradford BD5 .... 74 E3
Bradford, Tyersal BD4 .... 75 D5
Mickletown LS26 .... 102 D3
Parsonage St S6 .... 92 D1
Parsons Gn LS22 .... 13 F5
Parsons Rd BD9 .... 55 A4
Parsons Pl WF3 .... 121 C6
Partridge Cl [B] LS27 .... 98 D4
Partridge Cres WF12 ...... 139 F1
Pasture Ave LS7 .... 204 A3
Pasture Cl BD14 .... 73 E4
Pasture Cres LS7 .... 204 A3
Pasture Dr WF10 .... 124 A6
Pasture Fold LS29 .... 9 F2
Pasture Gr LS7 .... 204 A3
Pasture La
Bradford BD14, BD7 .... 73 D4
Leeds LS7 .... 204 A3
Pasture Mount LS12 .... 209 E4
Pasture Par LS7 .... 204 A3
Pasture Pl LS7 .... 204 A3
Pasture Rd Baildon BD17 .. 38 D2
Leeds LS8 .... 207 F4
Pasture Rise BD14 .... 73 D4
Pasture Side Terr E
BD14 .... 73 C4
Pasture Side Terr W [4]
BD14 .... 73 C4
Pasture St LS7 .... 204 A3
Pasture Terr LS7 .... 204 A3
Pasture View LS12 .... 209 E4
Pasture View Rd LS26 .... 100 E5
Pasture Way WF10 .... 124 A6
Pasture Wlk BD14 .... 73 C4
Pastures Way HD7 .... 152 D5
Pateley Cres HD2 .... 136 A2
Patent St BD9 .... 55 B2
Paternoster La [10] BD7 ... 74 A4
Paterson Ave WF2 .... 141 E4
Patience La WF6 .... 122 F3
Patterdale App LS22 .... 13 B5
Patterdale Dr HD5 .... 154 D6
Patterdale Rd WF12 .... 118 E2
Patterson Ct WF2 .... 120 F3
Pattie St BD20 .... 18 B1
Paul La Kirkheaton HD5 .... 137 C4
Lepton HD8 .... 156 C2
Paul Row OL15 .... 129 D1
Pauline Terr WF10 .... 124 C7
Pavement La HX2 .... 91 E8
Pavement St [5] BD19 ..... 116 E7
Pavilion Cl S72 .... 181 A3
Pavilion Ct BD4 .... 95 C8
Paw La BD13 .... 92 F7
Pawson St Bradford BD4 ... 75 D6
East Ardsley WF3 .... 120 E8
Morley LS27 .... 97 F3
Rothwell WF3 .... 100 B2
Peabody St [8] HX3 .... 92 A1
Peace Hall Dr HD8 .... 155 C5
Peace St BD4 .... 75 C5
Peach Tree Cl WF8 .... 146 B6
Peach Wlk BD4 .... 75 B4
Peacock Ave WF2 .... 141 F7
Peacock Cl WF2 .... 141 F7
Peacock Ct LS19 .... 40 D6
Peacock Gn LS27 .... 98 D3
Peacock Gr WF2 .... 141 F7
Peak View WF13 .... 117 F2
Pear Pl [B] Halifax HX1 ..... 86 A1
Pear St Halifax HX1 .... 202 B2
Huddersfield HD4 .... 153 E4
Keighley BD21 .... 35 A3
Oxenhope BD22 .... 51 C2
Pear Tree Acre LS23 .... 14 E1
Pear Tree Cl WF8 .... 146 B6
Pear Tree Ct BD20 .... 5 E2
Pear Tree La WF9 .... 181 D7
Pearl St Batley WF17 ...... 118 A6
Pearson Ave [B] LS6 .... 205 E3
Pearson Fold BD12 .... 94 F4
Pearson Gr LS6 .... 205 E3
Pearson La BD9 .... 54 D1
Pearson Rd [B] BD6 .... 94 D8
Pearson Rd W [7] BD6 ...... 94 D8
Pearson Row [B] BD12 .... 94 D3
Pearson St Bradford BD3 ... 75 C6
Cleckheaton, Hartshead Moor Side
WF16 .... 116 A3
Cleckheaton, Marsh BD19 .. 116 E6
Leeds LS10 .... 212 A1
Normanton WF6 .... 123 A5
Pudsey LS28 .... 57 B7
Pearson Terr [14] LS6 ...... 205 E3
Pearson's La WF12 .... 156 F7
Peasons Bldgs LS21 .... 23 B7

Peartree Field La WF8 .... 165 D5
Peas Acre BD16 .... 36 E8
Peasborough View
LS29 .... 21 F8
Pease Cl WF8 .... 146 D6
Peashill Cl LS19 .... 40 C4
Peashill Pk LS19 .... 40 C4
Peaseland Ave BD19 ...... 116 C7
Peaseland Cl BD19 .... 116 D7
Peaseland Rd BD19 .... 116 D7
Peaselands BD18 .... 55 A7
Peat Ponds HD3 .... 134 E1
Peckett Cl HD3 .... 153 C7
Peckfield Bar LS25 .... 83 D4
Peckover Dr LS28 .... 76 A8
Peckover St BD1 .... 201 C3
Peebles Cl HD3 .... 135 B1
Peebles Wlk WF6 .... 123 D1
Peel Ave WF17 .... 118 C5
Peel Cl Bradford BD4 .... 75 E6
Horbury WF4 .... 141 B1
Peel Cottage Rd OL14 .... 108 A1
Peel Cottage St [5]
OL14 .... 108 A1
Peel Ct BD2 .... 56 A2
Peel Dr OL13 .... 106 B1
Peel House BD16 .... 36 E2
Peel Park Dr BD2 .... 56 B2
Peel Park Terr BD2 .... 56 B2
Peel Park View BD3 .... 56 A1
Peel Pl LS29 .... 9 E2
Peel Row BD7 .... 74 A4
Peel St Bingley BD16 .... 37 B3
Horbury WF4 .... 141 B1
[5] Huddersfield HD1 .... 154 A5
Liversedge WF16 .... 117 C4
Marsden HD7 .... 168 F4
Morley LS27 .... 98 B4
Queensbury BD13 .... 72 F1
[8] Sowerby Bridge HX6 .... 112 B4
Thornton BD13 .... 72 D6
Wilsden BD15 .... 53 C4
Peep Green Rd WF15 .... 116 C2
Pegholme Dr LS21 .... 22 D6
Pelham Ct BD2 .... 56 B3
Pelham Pl LS7 .... 60 C7
Pelham Rd BD2 .... 56 B3
Pell Ct HD7 .... 189 C7
Pell La HD7 .... 189 C7
Pellon La HX1 .... 202 C4
Pellon New Rd HX1, HX2 .. 202 B4
Pellon St OL14 .... 108 A2
Pellon Terr BD10 .... 39 B1
Pellon Wlk BD10 .... 39 B1
Pemberton Dr BD7 .... 74 D6
Pemberton Rd WF10 ...... 125 B8
Pembridge Ct S71 .... 179 C4
Pembroke Cl LS27 .... 97 F5
Pembroke Ct HD4 .... 153 B2
Pembroke Dr Morley LS27 .. 97 F5
[5] Pudsey LS28 .... 76 E8
Pembroke Gdns LS9 .... 61 D2
Pembroke Rd LS28 .... 76 E8
Pembroke Rise LS25 .... 83 C2
Pembroke St BD5 .... 74 E4
Pembroke Towers LS9 .... 61 D3
Pembury Mount LS15 ...... 62 F3
Penarth Ave WF9 .... 183 A7
Penarth Rd LS15 .... 62 B2
Penarth Terr WF9 .... 182 F7
Penda's Dr LS15 .... 62 D2
Penda's Gr LS15 .... 62 D3
Penda's Way LS15 .... 62 D2
Penda's Wlk LS15 .... 62 D2
Pendenus Ave WF9 .... 182 F4
Pendil Cl LS15 .... 81 C8
Pendle Ave OL13 .... 106 A3
Pendle Cl OL13 .... 106 A2
Pendle Rd BD16 .... 37 B3
Pendragon BD2 .... 56 A3
Pendragon La BD2 .... 56 B3
Pendragon Terr LS20 .... 39 D8
Penfield Gr BD14 .... 73 C4
Penfield Rd BD11 .... 96 F6
Penistone Hill Country Pk
BD22 .... 51 A6
Penistone La HD8 .... 190 D6
Penistone Mews BD22 ..... 51 C7
Penistone Rd
Denby Dale HD7, HD8, S36 .. 191 C3
Holmfirth, Hade Edge HD7 .. 199 D7
Holmfirth, Lane Head
HD7, HD8 .... 190 C6
Huddersfield HD8 .... 155 C3
Kirkburton HD8 .... 173 E5
Lepton HD8 .... 155 C3
Shepley HD8 .... 173 E5
Shepley, Lane Head
HD7, HD8 .... 190 C6
Penlands Cres LS15 .... 81 D7
Penlands Lawn LS15 .... 81 D7
Penlands Wlk LS15 .... 81 D7
Penlington Cl WF7 .... 181 D5
Penn Cl BD2 .... 56 B4
Penn Dr WF15 .... 116 D6
Penn Gr WF15 .... 116 D6
Penn St HX1 .... 202 C4
Pennine Cl Holmfirth HD7 .. 188 D5
Queensbury BD13 .... 92 D7
Wakefield WF2 .... 141 E3
Pennine Cres HD3 .... 152 E8
Pennine Dr HD8 .... 175 D2
Pennine Gdns HD7 .... 152 D1
Pennine Gr OL14 .... 108 C6
Pennine Rd Bacup OL13 .. 106 A2
Dewsbury WF12 .... 139 E8
Pennine Rise HD8 .... 175 D2

Pennine View Batley WF17 .. 97 A1
Blackshaw Head HX7 .... 87 F4
Kirkheaton HD5 .... 137 C6
Mapplewell S75 .... 178 A5
Slaithwaite HD7 .... 152 D5
Upton WF9 .... 183 A6
Pennine Way
Clayton West HD8 .... 175 D4
Hebden Bridge HX7 .... 88 D6
Hemsworth WF9 .... 181 F1
Heptonstall HX7 .... 88 B8
Pennington Ct [E] LS6 ...... 206 A4
Pennington Gr [E] LS6 ...... 206 A4
Pennington La LS26 .... 101 B4
Pennington Pl [B] LS6 ...... 206 A4
Pennington St LS6 .... 206 A4
Pennington Terr
Bradford BD5 .... 74 C1
[E] Leeds LS6 .... 206 A4
Pennithorne Ave BD17 ..... 38 C2
Pennwell Croft [6] LS14 ... 62 D
Pennwell Dean LS14 .... 62 E
Pennwell Fold LS14 .... 62 E
Pennwell Garth LS14 .... 62 D
Pennwell Gn LS14 .... 62 D
Pennwell Lawn LS14 .... 62 E
Penny Hill Ctr The LS10 .. 215 E
Penny Hill Dr BD14 .... 73 C6
Penny La HD5 .... 155 B6
Penny Lane Way LS10 ...... 215 D0
Penny Spring HD5 .... 154 E
Pennyfield Sch LS6 .... 42 F
Pennygate BD16 .... 37 A7
Penraevon Ave LS7 .... 206 C0
Penraevon Ind Est LS7 .... 206 C0
Penraevon Ind Units LS7 .. 206 C
Penrith Cres WF10 .... 104 E
Penrith Gr LS12 .... 209 F
Penrose Beck Dr WF7 ...... 163 F
Penrose Dr BD7 .... 73 F
Penrose Pl
Crigglestone WF2 .... 159 F
Northowram HX3 .... 93 A
Penryn Ave HD5 .... 155 C0
Pentland Ave
Bradford BD14 .... 73 C
Knottingley WF11 .... 126 E
Pentland Cl BD20 .... 35 A
Pentland County Infants
Sch WF12 .... 139 D
Pentland Dr LS25 .... 82 F
Pentland Gr WF12 .... 141 E
Pentland Rd WF12 .... 139 D
Pentland Way [1] LS27 ..... 98 A
Pepper Gdns LS13 .... 58 E
Pepper Hill HX3 .... 93 A
Pepper Hills LS17 .... 43 D
Pepper La Leeds LS13 ...... 215 F
Leeds, Moorside LS13 .... 58 E
Pepper Rd LS10 .... 215 F
Pepper Royd St WF13 ..... 118 D
Per La HX2 .... 91 D
Percival St Bradford BD3 .. 201 D
Huddersfield HD3 .... 152 F
Leeds LS2 .... 206 C
Percy St Bingley BD16 ...... 37 A
Huddersfield HD2 .... 136 A
Keighley BD21 .... 35 C
Leeds LS12 .... 210 A
South Kirkby WF9 .... 182 E
Peregrine Ave LS27 .... 98 D
Peregrine Ct HD4 .... 171 E
Peridot Fold HD2 .... 136 C
Permain Ct HD4 .... 154 B
Perry Cl BD22 .... 35 A
Perseverance St LS28 ...... 76 C
Perseverance La [7] BD7 ... 74 A
Perseverance Rd
Halifax BD13 .... 72 A
Queensbury BD13 .... 72 A
Perseverance St
Baildon BD17 .... 38 D
[4] Castleford WF10 .... 124 D
Huddersfield HD4 .... 154 A
[8] Sowerby Bridge HX6 .... 112 B
Perseverance Terr
Batley WF17 .... 118 C
Halifax HX1 .... 202 C
Rothwell LS26 .... 100 E
Perseverance St HD4 ...... 153 A
Perth Ave BD2 .... 55 E
Perth Dr WF3 .... 119 F
Perth Mount LS18 .... 41 B
Peter Hill WF17 .... 118 D
Peter La Halifax HX2 .... 112 B
Morley LS27 .... 98 D
Peter Laycock Ind Est
LS7 .... 206 C
Peterborough Pl BD2 .... 56 B
Peterborough Rd BD2 .... 56 B
Peterborough Terr BD2 ..... 56 B
Petergate BD1 .... 201 C
Peterhouse Dr LS21 .... 23 C
Petersfield Ave LS10 .... 99 E
Petersgarth [5] BD18 .... 54 E
Peterson Rd WF1 .... 216 C
Pether Hill HX4 .... 133 F
Petrel Way LS27 .... 98 C
Petrie Cres LS13 .... 57 D
Petrie Gr BD3 .... 75 E
Petrie Rd BD3 .... 75 E
Petrie St LS13 .... 57 D
Petworth Croft S71 .... 179 B
Peverell Cl BD4 .... 75 E
Peveril Mount BD2 .... 56 C
Pexwood Rd OL14 .... 107 F
Pheasant Dr WF17 .... 97 A

Pheasant St BD21 .... 35 D8
Phil May Ct LS12 .... 210 B2
Philip Garth WF1 .... 121 C5
Philip Garth ⬛ WF1 .... 121 C6
Philip's La WF3 .... 147 C5
Philippa Way LS12 .... 78 C3
Philips Rd OL13 .... 106 A7
Phillips St WF10 .... 124 B8
Phoebe La Ind Est
HX3 .... 113 D4
Phoenix Ave HD8 .... 175 D6
Phoenix Ct Batley WF17 .... 118 F5
Todmorden OL14 .... 108 D6
Wakefield WF2 .... 142 A6
Phoenix St Brighouse HD6 ...... 115 B2
Todmorden OL14 .... 108 D6
Phoenix Way BD4 .... 75 E6
Piccadilly Bradford BD1 .... 201 B3
Wakefield WF2 .... 216 A2
Pick Hill Rd HD7 .... 170 D3
Pickard Ct LS15 .... 81 C8
Pickard La BD20 .... 5 E2
Pickard Way WF13 .... 118 B1
Picker St OL14 .... 107 E8
Pickering Ave LS25 .... 83 B8
Pickering Dr WF5 .... 119 C1
Pickering La WF5 .... 119 C1
Pickering Mount LS12 .... 210 A4
Pickering St LS12 .... 210 A4
Pickerings The BD13 .... 92 E8
Pickersgill St WF5 .... 140 C8
Pickford St HX3 .... 153 A4
Pickle Top HD7 .... 151 E2
Pickles Ct ⬛ OL14 .... 108 B6
Pickles Hill BD22 .... 33 F1
Pickles La Bradford BD7 .... 73 F2
Skelmanthorpe HD8 .... 175 B1
Pickles St Batley WF17 .... 118 B2
⬛ Keighley BD21 .... 35 B5
Picklesfield WF17 .... 118 A2
Pickthall Terr OL14 .... 108 D5
Pickwood La HX6 .... 112 E2
Picton St BD8 .... 55 D1
Picton Way HD5 .... 155 A7
Picturevilie BD1 .... 201 B2
Piece Hall Mus HX1 .... 203 F3
Piece Hall Yd BD1 .... 201 B3
Piece Wood Rd LS16 .... 41 D3
Pigeon Cote Cl LS14 .... 62 A6
Pigeon Cote Rd LS14 .... 62 A6
Piggott St HD6 .... 115 A3
Pighill Top La HD7 .... 151 F2
Pike End Rd HX6 .... 150 C7
Pike Law WF7 .... 152 B5
Pike Law La HD7 .... 152 B5
Pike Law Rd HD7 .... 152 B5
Pikers Brow WF5 .... 140 C6
Pildacre Croft WF5 .... 140 C6
Pildacre La WF5 .... 140 B6
Pilden La WF3 .... 120 C7
Pilgrim Ave WF13 .... 138 F7
Pilgrim Cres WF13 .... 138 F7
Pilgrim Dr WF13 .... 138 F7
Pilkington St WF2 .... 142 C4
Pill White La LS21 .... 11 F6
Pilling La HD8 .... 175 C2
Pilling Top La HD8 .... 174 C4
Pilot St BD3 .... 201 D4
Pilmer Ct WF2 .... 141 D4
Pilot St LS9 .... 207 E1
Pin Hill La HX2 .... 90 D1
Pincheon St WF1 .... 216 C2
Pinder Ave LS12 .... 77 F4
Pinder Gr LS12 .... 77 F4
Pinder St LS12 .... 77 F4
Pinder View LS12 .... 77 F4
Pinder's Gr WF1 .... 142 E8
Pinderfields
General Hospl WF1 .... 121 D1
Pinderfields Rd WF1 .... 216 B3
Pinders Cres WF11 .... 126 C5
Pinders Garth WF11 .... 126 D5
Pinders Green Ct LS26 .... 102 C1
Pinders Green Dr LS26 .... 102 C1
Pinders Green Fold LS26 .... 102 C1
Pinders Green Wlk LS26 .... 102 C1
Pinders Prim Jun
& Inf Sch WF1 .... 216 C3
Pine Cl Castleford WF10 .... 124 E6
Wetherby LS22 .... 13 E7
Pine Court Mews HD4 .... 171 D6
Pine Croft BD20 .... 18 A1
Pine Ct Huddersfield HD4 ...... 171 F6
⬛ Leeds LS2 .... 212 A3
Pine Gr Huddersfield HD4 ...... 118 B3
Pine Rd OL14 .... 107 F7
Pine St ⬛ Bacup OL13 .... 106 A1
Bradford BD1 .... 201 C4
Halifax HX1 .... 203 D2
Haworth BD22 .... 51 C6
Huddersfield HD1 .... 154 B7
South Elmsall WF9 .... 182 E1
Pine Tree Ave
Boston Spa LS23 .... 30 E8
Pontefract WF8 .... 146 B6
Pineapple Cotts WF1 .... 143 E6
Pinedale BD16 .... 36 F5
Pinehurst Ct HD3 .... 135 B1
Pines Gdns LS29 .... 7 F3
Pinewood Ave WF2 .... 141 D6
Pinewood Cl LS29 .... 8 A5
Pinewood Gdns HX4 .... 134 B4
Pinewood Pri WF11 .... 126 E3
Pinfold Cl Dewsbury WF12 ...... 139 E2
Flockton WF4 .... 157 C2
Knottingley WF11 .... 126 C5
Mirfield WF14 .... 138 B5
Rippenden HX4 .... 133 A5

Pinfold Cross WF8 .... 166 D5
Pinfold Ct LS15 .... 81 B8
Pinfold Dr WF4 .... 144 A1
Pinfold Gr Leeds LS15 .... 81 A8
Wakefield WF2 .... 142 E1
Pinfold Hill
Dewsbury WF13 .... 139 B7
Leeds LS15 .... 81 B8
Pinfold La
Brighouse HD6 .... 135 D5
Flockton WF4 .... 157 C2
Garforth LS25 .... 82 F7
Kirk Smeaton WF8 .... 166 D5
Leeds LS16 .... 41 F7
Leeds LS13 .... 209 E3
Leeds, Halton LS15 .... 81 A8
Lepton HD8 .... 156 A3
Marsden HD3 .... 151 C5
Mickletown LS26 .... 102 E2
Mirfield WF14 .... 138 C5
Royston S71 .... 179 C2
Slaithwaite HD7 .... 152 A4
Sowerby Bridge HX6 .... 111 E4
Wakefield WF2 .... 142 E1
Pinfold Mount LS15 .... 81 B7
Pinfold Rd LS15 .... 81 B7
Pinfold Rise LS25 .... 64 E8
Pinfold Sq LS15 .... 81 A8
Pingle Rise HD8 .... 192 A7
Pink St BD22 .... 51 C6
Pinnacle La HX7 .... 109 E8
Pinnar Croft HX3 .... 114 A4
Pinnar La HX3 .... 113 F5
Pioneer St Dewsbury WF12 ...... 139 C4
Todmorden OL14 .... 129 A2
Pioneer Way WF10 .... 123 F4
Pipe & Nook La LS12 .... 77 F7
Piper Hill WF11 .... 105 A4
Piper La LS21 .... 22 F7
Piper Well La HD8 .... 190 E6
Pippercroft BD6 .... 93 E6
Piper Mdw LS27 .... 98 C3
Pippins App WF6 .... 123 B3
Pippins Green Ave WF2 .... 120 B2
Pirie Cl BD2 .... 56 C2
Pit Field Rd WF3 .... 100 D2
Pit La Batley WF13 .... 117 F2
Cleckheaton BD19 .... 96 B2
Denholme BD13 .... 52 C1
Mickletleld LS25 .... 83 F5
Mickletown LS26 .... 102 D4
Queensbury BD13 .... 72 C4
Thornton BD13 .... 72 C4
Pitcliffe Way BD5 .... 74 F4
Pitfall St LS10 .... 211 F3
Pits La BD19 .... 115 H6
Pitt Hill La HX4 .... 133 D2
Pitt Row LS1 .... 211 F3
Pitt St Keighley BD21 .... 35 D7
Liversedge WF15 .... 117 B2
Todmorden OL14 .... 108 C5
Pitts St BD4 .... 75 D4
Place's Rd LS9 .... 212 B3
Plaid Row LS9 .... 212 B4
Plain La HX6 .... 111 C2
Plains HD7 .... 169 A5
Plains La Halifax HX5 .... 134 F8
Marsden HD7 .... 169 A5
Plane Gn WF8 .... 146 D6
Plane St Huddersfield HD4 ..... 154 B3
Todmorden OL14 .... 107 E7
Plane Tree Ave LS17 .... 43 F4
Plane Tree Cl LS17 .... 43 F4
Plane Tree Croft LS17 .... 43 F4
Plane Tree Gdns LS17 .... 43 F4
Plane Tree Gr LS19 .... 40 D6
Plane Tree Nest HX2 .... 202 A2
Plane Tree Nest La HX2 .... 202 A1
Plane Tree Rd HX6 .... 112 B5
Plane Tree Rise LS17 .... 43 F4
Plane Tree View LS17 .... 43 F4
Plane Trees CI BD19 .... 95 D3
Planet Earth OL14 .... 106 B4
Planetrees Rd BD4 .... 75 C6
Planetrees St BD15 .... 54 A1
Plantation Ave
Leeds, Blackwood LS17 .... 44 A5
Leeds, Halton LS15 .... 81 A7
Royston S71 .... 179 D3
Plantation Dr HD4 .... 154 A1
Plantation Fold BD22 .... 34 F4
Plantation La LS15 .... 44 B5
Plantation Pl BD4 .... 75 A4
Plantation Way BD17 .... 38 D3
Platt La HD7 .... 152 A1
Platt Sq ⬛ BD20 .... 116 D7
Playfair Rd LS10 .... 215 D2
Playground LS12 .... 77 D3
Playhouse Sq LS2 .... 212 A4
Playhouse The HX1 .... 203 D2
Pleasance The LS26 .... 82 A1
Pleasant Ct ⬛ LS6 .... 206 A3
Pleasant Mount LS11 .... 211 D1
Pleasant Pl LS11 .... 211 D1
Pleasant St Bradford BD7 ..... 74 A4
Leeds LS11 .... 211 D1
Sowerby Bridge HX6 .... 112 C4
Pleasant Terr LS11 .... 211 D1
Pleasant View WF2 .... 120 F3
Pledwick Cres WF2 .... 160 D6
Pledwick Dr WF2 .... 160 D5
Pledwick Gr WF2 .... 160 C5
Pledwick La WF2 .... 160 D5
Plevna St LS10 .... 80 A2
Plevna Terr BD16 .... 36 A4
Plimsoll St Bradford BD4 .... 75 A4
Hemsworth WF9 .... 181 D7

Ploughcroft La HX3 .... 92 C3
Ploughmans Croft BD7 .... 55 E4
Plover Dr WF17 .... 97 A3
Plover Rd HD3 .... 153 B8
Plover St Bradford BD5 .... 74 C3
Keighley BD21 .... 35 C8
Plover Way LS27 .... 98 D3
Plum St Halifax HX1 .... 202 B2
Plum St ⬛ WF9 .... 146 B6
Plumpton Ave BD2 .... 55 F6
Plumpton Cl BD2 .... 56 A5
Plumpton Dr BD2 .... 55 F6
Plumpton End BD2 .... 56 A6
Plumpton Gdns BD2 .... 55 F6
Plumpton Lea BD2 .... 55 F6
Plumpton Mead BD2 .... 55 F6
Plumpton Pl WF2 .... 142 A4
Plumpton Rd WF2 .... 142 A4
Plumpton St Bradford BD8 ..... 74 A4
Wakefield WF2 .... 142 A4
Plumpton Terr WF2 .... 142 A5
Plumpton Wlk BD2 .... 55 F6
Plymouth Gr HX1 .... 202 C4
Poet's Pl LS18 .... 41 C2
Pog Hall HD7 .... 170 C8
Pohlman St ⬛ HX1 .... 202 B1
Pole Gate HD7 .... 151 D4
Pole Gate Branch HD7 .... 151 D4
Pole Rd BD22 .... 33 F8
Pollard Ave Bingley BD16 ..... 37 B5
Cleckheaton BD19 .... 96 B1
Pollard Cl BD19 .... 96 B1
Pollard La Bradford BD2 ...... 56 B1
Leeds LS13 .... 58 C5
Pudsey LS13 .... 58 C5
Pollard Park Middle Sch
BD3 .... 55 B8
Pollard St Bradford BD4 ..... 201 C1
Huddersfield HD2 .... 136 B2
Lofthouse Gate WF3 .... 121 C6
Pollard St N HX3 .... 203 F4
Pollard St WF3 .... 121 C6
Pollard Way BD19 .... 96 B1
Pollard's Fields WF11 .... 126 B5
Pollit Ave HX6 .... 111 F3
Pollums La WF11 .... 105 B6
Polperro Cl WF6 .... 123 B3
Pomfret Cl HD4 .... 153 F2
Pomfret Pl LS25 .... 83 B8
Pond Cl HD4 .... 153 F2
Pond La Bradford BD22 .... 50 A7
Pond St BD21 .... 35 C8
Ponderosa Cl ⬛ BD3 .... 56 A7
Pondfields Cl LS25 .... 83 B2
Pondfields Crest LS25 .... 83 B2
Pondfields Dr LS25 .... 83 B2
Pondfields Rise LS25 .... 83 B2
Ponker La HD8 .... 175 F3
Ponker Nook La HD8 .... 174 F1
Pontefract Ave LS9 .... 212 C3
Pontefract CI WF8 .... 125 E1
Pontefract CE Sch WF8 .... 125 D1
Pontefract General Infmy
WF8 .... 146 D8
Pontefract La LS15, LS9 ..... 80 C5
Pontefract Lane Cl LS9 ...... 212 C3
Pontefract Mus WF8 .... 146 D8
Pontefract Rd
Ackworth M T WF7 .... 164 A8
Castleford WF10 .... 124 E7
Crofton WF4 .... 144 A2
Cudworth S72 .... 180 C1
Featherstone WF7 .... 145 E5
Hemsworth WF9 .... 163 F2
Knottingley WF11 .... 126 A8
Knottingley, Ferrybridge Hill
WF11 .... 126 D4
Leeds LS10, LS26 .... 80 B2
Normanton WF6 .... 123 D3
Pontefract St LS9 .... 212 C3
Pontefract Terr WF9 .... 181 E6
Pontey Dr HD5 .... 155 B5
Pontey Mount HD5 .... 155 B5
Pool Bank Cl LS21 .... 24 D7
Pool Bank Ct LS21 .... 24 D6
Pool Bank New Rd
Bramhope LS21 .... 24 D5
Leathley LS21 .... 24 D5
Pool Cl BD3 .... 75 A7
Pool Hill La HD8 .... 192 D6
Pool in Wharfedale C of E
Primary Sch LS21 .... 24 D7
Pool Rd Leathley LS21 .... 24 B7
Otley LS21 .... 23 C8
Poole Cres LS15 .... 62 B1
Poole Mount LS15 .... 62 B1
Poole Rd LS15 .... 62 B1
Poole Row LS15 .... 105 E3
Poole Sq ⬛ LS15 .... 62 B1
Pools La S71 .... 179 E3
Pope St Keighley BD21 .... 35 D8
Popeley Rd WF16 .... 117 C6
Poplar Ave Bradford BD7 ..... 73 F2
Castleford WF10 .... 125 D8
Garforth LS25 .... 82 E6
Holmfirth HD7 .... 172 C1
Leeds LS15 .... 62 D2
Shafton S72 .... 180 C2
Shipley BD18 .... 55 C5
Sowerby Bridge HX6 .... 112 C5
Todmorden OL14 .... 108 A7
Wakefield WF2 .... 141 E5
Wetherby LS22 .... 13 E7

Poplar Cl Burley in W LS29 ... 21 F8
Leeds LS13 .... 77 F8
Poplar Court LS13 .... 77 F8
Poplar Cres Halifax HX2 ..... 91 F7
Morley LS27 .... 98 C1
Shipley BD18 .... 55 C5
Poplar Croft LS13 .... 77 F8
Poplar Dr Horsforth LS18 .... 57 F8
Keighley BD20 .... 36 C7
Normanton WF6 .... 123 A5
Shipley BD18 .... 55 C5
Poplar Garth LS13 .... 77 F8
Poplar Gdns LS13 .... 77 E8
Poplar Gn LS13 .... 77 F8
Pontefract WF8 .... 125 F1
Poplar Gr Bradford BD7 ...... 73 F2
Cleckheaton BD19 .... 116 C6
Harden BD16 .... 36 A1
Knottingley WF11 .... 126 C4
Pontefract WF8 .... 146 B8
Shipley BD18 .... 55 C5
Poplar House ❸ WF10 .... 124 E7
Poplar Mount LS13 .... 77 E8
Poplar Rd Bradford BD7 ...... 74 A2
Shipley BD18 .... 55 C6
Poplar Rise Leeds LS13 ...... 58 E1
Skelmanthorpe HD8 .... 175 B1
Poplar Sq ⬛ LS28 .... 57 D2
Poplar St Halifax HX3 .... 203 E4
Huddersfield, Fartown
HD2 .... 136 A1
⬛ Huddersfield, Moldgreen
HD5 .... 154 D5
Lofthouse Gate WF3 .... 121 C6
Poplar Terr
⬛ Huddersfield HD5 .... 154 D5
⬛ Keighley BD21 .... 18 D1
Keighley, Crossflatts BD20 .. 36 D7
Royston S71 .... 179 D4
South Elmsall WF9 .... 183 E2
Poplar View Bradford BD7 .... 73 E2
Brighouse HX3 .... 115 B6
Leeds LS13 .... 77 E8
Poplar Way LS13 .... 77 F8
Poplars Farm First Sch
BD2 .... 55 E4
Poplars Park Rd BD2 .... 55 E4
Poplars The Bramhope LS16 ... 24 F2
Guiseley LS20 .... 22 E2
Knottingley WF11 .... 126 D4
Leeds LS16 .... 205 E4
Lofthouse Gate WF3 .... 121 C8
Sutton in C BD20 .... 16 C4
Poplarwood Gdns BD10 .... 56 E5
Popley Butts HD7 .... 170 C1
Popley Dr HD7 .... 170 C1
Popple Wells La HX2 .... 112 A7
Popples HX2 .... 91 F7
Popples Dr HX2 .... 91 F7
Popples Side HX7 .... 88 D6
Poppleton Ct ⬛ WF3 .... 98 E1
Poppleton Dr WF3 .... 98 E1
Poppleton Rd WF3 .... 119 E8
Poppleton Way WF3 .... 119 E8
Porchester House ❹
HD5 .... 154 D6
Porritt St BD19 .... 95 D1
Portage Ave LS15 .... 80 F7
Portal Cres LS15 .... 138 A8
Portal Dr WF14 .... 138 A8
Portland Ave WF8 .... 125 B1
Portland Cl HD3 .... 153 C7
Portland Cres LS1 .... 206 B1
Portland Ct BD21 .... 35 B6
Portland Gate LS1 .... 206 B1
Portland House ⬛ HX5 .... 134 F7
Portland Pl Bingley BD16 .... 37 A2
Halifax HX1 .... 203 E2
Upton WF9 .... 183 A7
Portland Rd Halifax HX3 ..... 203 E4
Leeds LS12 .... 209 F2
Portland St Bradford BD5 .... 201 B2
Halifax HX1 .... 203 E3
Haworth BD22 .... 51 D7
Huddersfield HD1 .... 153 F6
Leeds LS1 .... 211 E4
Wakefield WF1 .... 142 F3
Portland Way LS1 .... 206 B1
Portman St LS28 .... 57 B6
Portobello Rd WF1, WF2 ..... 142 D3
Portobello Rd WF1, WF2 ..... 142 D3
Portree House ❺ BD6 .... 93 E8
Portsmouth Ave BD3 .... 55 F1
Portwood St BD9 .... 54 D2
Post Hill Ct LS12 .... 77 D7
Post Office Rd
Bradford BD2 .... 56 C5
Featherstone WF7 .... 145 D5
Post Office St BD19 .... 116 F6
Postcard Mus HD7 .... 189 A5
Pot La BD20 .... 17 C6
Pothouse Rd BD6 .... 94 B8
Potovens Cl WF3 .... 121 C6
Potovens La
Lofthouse Gate WF1 .... 121 B5
Wakefield WF2 .... 120 F4
Potter Ave WF2 .... 141 E4
Potter Brow Rd BD17 .... 38 C6
Potternewton Ave LS7 .... 60 B6
Potternewton Cres LS7 ...... 60 B5
Potternewton Gdns LS7 ...... 60 C6
Potternewton Gr LS7 .... 60 B6
Potternewton Heights LS7 ... 60 C6
Potternewton La LS7 .... 60 B6

Potternewton Mansion
Coll of F Ed LS7 .... 204 B1
Potternewton Mount LS7 ...... 60 B6
Potternewton Primary Sch
LS7 .... 60 B5
Potternewton View LS7 .... 60 B6
Potters Croft WF3 .... 121 C6
Potters Gate HD8 .... 190 E1
Potters Wlk HD7 .... 152 E4
Potterton Cl LS15 .... 63 E8
Potterton Ct LS15 .... 63 E8
Potterton La LS15 .... 46 E2
Pottery La
Knottingley WF11 .... 126 D5
Rothwell LS26 .... 101 D7
Pottery Rd LS10 .... 215 D4
Pottery St Castleford WF10 .. 124 B8
Huddersfield HD3 .... 152 E8
Potts' Terr WF6 .... 144 B8
Poulton Pl LS11 .... 214 C3
Poverty La HX6 .... 111 A1
Powell Rd Bingley BD16 ...... 37 B2
Shipley BD18 .... 55 D5
Powell St Batley WF16 .... 117 E3
Castleford WF10 .... 124 D8
⬛ Halifax HX1 .... 203 E3
South Kirkby WF9 .... 182 D3
Poxton Gr WF9 .... 182 E1
Prail Cl WF8 .... 125 F1
Pratt La Mirfield WF14 ...... 138 A6
Shipley BD18 .... 55 D6
Precinct The WF7 .... 145 C5
Premiere Pk LS29 .... 7 E3
Prescott St HX1 .... 203 E2
Prescott Terr BD15 .... 54 B1
Preston La Halifax HX2 ..... 91 D2
Swillington LS26 .... 102 E7
Preston Par LS11 .... 214 A2
Preston Pl HX1 .... 202 C3
Preston St Batley WF17 ..... 118 C4
Bradford BD7 .... 74 C7
Dewsbury WF12 .... 139 E6
Preston Terr BD16 .... 36 E5
Preston View LS26 .... 82 B1
Prestwich Dr HD2 .... 135 F3
Prestwick Cl LS21 .... 22 D6
Pretoria St
Castleford WF10 .... 124 E7
Featherstone WF7 .... 145 C5
Slaithwaite HD7 .... 151 F1
Wakefield WF1 .... 142 D3
Priest Bank Rd BD20 .... 16 E8
Priest Hill Gdns LS22 ..... 13 D8
Priest La HX6 .... 132 E4
Priest Royd S75 .... 178 A1
Priesthorpe Ave LS28 ...... 57 B2
Priesthorpe Ct LS28 .... 57 D4
Priesthorpe High Sch LS28 . 57 B2
Priesthorpe La LS28 .... 57 B3
Priesthorpe Rd LS28 .... 57 B4
Priestley Ave Batley WF16 .. 117 D6
Bradford BD6 .... 94 B8
Priestley Cl LS28 .... 76 F8
Priestley Dr LS28 .... 76 F8
Priestley Gdns
Liversedge WF16 .... 117 C5
Pudsey LS28 .... 76 F8
Priestley Gn HX3 .... 93 E1
Priestley Gr HD4 .... 153 F1
Priestley Hill BD13 .... 92 C6
Priestley Pl HX6 .... 112 A3
Priestley Sq WF17 .... 96 F2
Priestley St Bradford BD1 .. 201 C4
Thornton BD13 .... 72 D6
Priestley Terr ⬛ BD6 ..... 74 C1
Priestley Wlk LS28 .... 76 F8
Priestly Ct LS19 .... 76 F8
Priestman Cl BD8 .... 54 F1
Priestman St BD8 .... 55 A1
Priestman Middle Sch
BD5 .... 74 C2
Priestman St BD8 .... 55 A1
Priesthorpe Cl BD16 ...... 37 A4
Priestthorpe First Sch
BD16 .... 37 A3
Priestthorpe La BD16 ..... 37 A4
Priestthorpe Rd BD16 ..... 37 A4
Priestwell St OL14 .... 108 C6
Primitive St
⬛ Huddersfield HD1 ...... 154 B6
Rothwell WF3 .... 100 D3
Primley Gdns LS17 .... 43 C4
Primley Park Ave LS17 .... 43 D4
Primley Park Cl LS17 ..... 43 D4
Primley Park Cres LS17 ... 43 C4
Primley Park Ct LS17 ..... 43 D4
Primley Park Dr LS17 ..... 43 D5
Primley Park Garth LS17 .. 43 D5
Primley Park Gn LS17 ..... 43 D5
Primley Park Gr LS17 ..... 43 D5
Primley Park La LS17 ..... 43 D5
Primley Park Mount LS17 .. 43 D4
Primley Park Rd LS17 ..... 43 C4
Primley Park View LS17 ... 43 D5
Primley Park Way LS17 .... 43 C5
Primley Park Wlk LS17 .... 43 D5
Primrose Hill WF3 .... 118 D5
Primrose Ave ⬛ Leeds LS15 81 A8
Primrose Bank BD16 .... 37 B2
Primrose Cl Leeds LS15 ... 81 A8
Pontefract WF8 .... 146 D7
Primrose Cres LS15 .... 62 A1

Primrose Dene WF11 ..... 126 D7
Primrose Dr Bingley BD16 ..... 37 C2
  Castleford WF10 ..... 125 B6
  Leeds LS15 ..... 81 A8
Primrose Garth [1] LS15 ..... 80 F8
Primrose Gdns
  Batley WF17 ..... 118 E6
  Leeds LS15 ..... 62 A1
Primrose Gr
  Huddersfield HD4 ..... 154 A3
  Keighley BD21 ..... 35 E7
  Leeds LS15 ..... 62 A1
Primrose High Sch LS9 ..... 207 E1
Primrose Hill
  Knottingley WF11 ..... 127 A5
  [5] Pudsey LS28 ..... 57 E1
Primrose Hill Cl LS26 ..... 82 B1
Primrose Hill Dr LS26 ..... 102 B8
Primrose Hill Garth LS26 ..... 102 B8
Primrose Hill Gdns LS26 ..... 82 B1
Primrose Hill Gn LS26 ..... 102 B8
Primrose Hill Gr LS26 ..... 82 B1
Primrose Hill High Sch
  (Annexe) LS8 ..... 207 E2
Primrose Hill Rd HD4 ..... 154 A4
Primrose House WF1 ..... 216 C1
Primrose La Bingley BD16 ..... 37 C2
  Boston Spa LS23 ..... 30 C7
  Crigglestone WF4 ..... 159 D6
  Kirkburton HD8 ..... 173 D8
  Leeds LS11 ..... 214 C3
  Leeds, Halton LS15 ..... 81 A8
  Liversedge WF15 ..... 116 F5
  Mirfield WF14 ..... 138 C7
  Shipley BD2 ..... 55 D4
Primrose Rd LS15 ..... 81 A8
Primrose Row BD17 ..... 38 F4
Primrose St
  [2] Bradford BD8 ..... 74 C8
  Huddersfield HD4 ..... 154 A4
  Keighley BD21 ..... 35 E7
Primrose Vale WF11 ..... 127 A4
Primrose Way HX3 ..... 93 D7
Primrose Wlk LS27 ..... 98 C8
Prince Edward Gr LS12 ..... 78 A4
Prince Edward Rd LS12 ..... 78 A4
Prince Henry Rd LS21 ..... 11 A1
Prince Henry's
  Grammar Sch LS21 ..... 11 A1
Prince St Batley WF17 ..... 118 C6
  Bradford BD4 ..... 75 C2
  [2] Dewsbury WF13 ..... 139 D8
  Haworth BD22 ..... 51 D7
  Huddersfield HD4 ..... 154 B4
  Kippax WF10 ..... 102 F7
  Silsden BD20 ..... 5 D1
Prince William Ct WF7 ..... 145 C4
Prince Wood La HD2 ..... 135 C2
Prince's Ave LS8 ..... 61 B7
Prince's Cres BD2 ..... 55 E3
Prince's Ct LS17 ..... 43 C1
Prince's Gate HX3 ..... 113 B4
Prince's St Bradford BD6 ..... 94 B8
  [4] Bradford, Buttershaw
  BD6 ..... 93 E7
Prince's Way BD1 ..... 201 B2
Princeroyd Way BD7 ..... 74 A7
Princes St WF16 ..... 117 E4
Princess Alexandra Wlk [10]
  HD1 ..... 154 B6
Princess Ave
  Dewsbury WF12 ..... 140 A8
  South Elmsall WF9 ..... 182 F2
Princess Cl WF12 ..... 140 A8
Princess Cres WF12 ..... 140 A7
Princess Ct Leeds LS17 ..... 43 D3
  Normanton WF6 ..... 123 C1
Princess Gdns [9]
  WF13 ..... 139 B8
Princess La WF12 ..... 140 A8
Princess of Wales Prec
  The [4] WF13 ..... 139 D8
Princess Rd
  Dewsbury WF12 ..... 140 A7
  Ilkley LS29 ..... 8 A3
Princess St
  Batley WF17 ..... 118 C6
  Brighouse HD6 ..... 115 B2
  Castleford WF10 ..... 103 F1
  Cudworth S72 ..... 180 C1
  Dewsbury WF12 ..... 140 B8
  [3] Elland HX4 ..... 134 D7
  Halifax HX1 ..... 203 E3
  [3] Huddersfield HD1 ..... 154 A5
  Lofthouse Gate WF1 ..... 121 B4
  Mapplewell S75 ..... 178 A1
  Mirfield WF14 ..... 138 A4
  Normanton WF6 ..... 123 B2
  Sowerby Bridge HX6 ..... 112 C4
  Wakefield WF1 ..... 142 E2
  Yeadon LS19 ..... 40 A4
Princeville First Sch BD7 ..... 74 B6
Princeville Rd BD7 ..... 74 B7
Princeville St BD7 ..... 74 B6
Prior St BD21 ..... 35 D8
Prior's La BD23 ..... 1 E7
Priory [7] Bingley BD16 ..... 37 A4
  Mirfield WF14 ..... 137 E6
  Normanton WF6 ..... 140 D4
  Ossett WF5 ..... 140 D4
  Wetherby LS22 ..... 13 F6
Priory Cl WF5 ..... 140 D5
Priory Ct BD8 ..... 74 D8
Priory Ctr Sch WF4 ..... 143 F2

Priory Estate WF9 ..... 183 B3
Priory Gr BD16 ..... 37 A4
Priory Grange WF8 ..... 125 E2
Priory Mews WF3 ..... 121 F6
Priory Pl HD2 ..... 136 F5
Priory Rd Brighouse HD6 ..... 115 C2
  Featherstone WF7 ..... 145 C4
  Ossett WF5 ..... 140 D5
Priory Ridge WF4 ..... 162 A8
Priory Sq WF2 ..... 161 A7
Priory Way WF14 ..... 137 E6
Priory Wlk WF14 ..... 137 E6
Privilege St LS12 ..... 209 E3
Proctor St BD4 ..... 75 D2
Prod La BD17 ..... 37 E2
Progress Ave BD16 ..... 36 A1
Prospect Ave Halifax HX2 ..... 112 E4
  Leeds LS18 ..... 58 C3
  Normanton WF6 ..... 123 B3
Prospect Bank LS23 ..... 30 D3
Prospect Cl Halifax HX2 ..... 112 E4
  Shipley BD18 ..... 55 C7
Prospect Cotts WF9 ..... 182 E3
Prospect Cres
  Leeds LS10 ..... 215 D3
Prospect Ct HX2 ..... 112 E8
Prospect Dr BD22 ..... 34 E5
Prospect Gdns [4] LS15 ..... 81 B8
Prospect Gr Pudsey LS28 ..... 76 D8
  Shipley BD18 ..... 55 C7
Prospect La BD11 ..... 96 B5
Prospect Mount
  Keighley BD22 ..... 34 E5
  Shipley BD18 ..... 55 C7
Prospect Pl Bradford BD9 ..... 54 F1
  Bradford, Fagley BD2 ..... 56 C2
  Brighouse HX3 ..... 94 A2
  [2] Brighouse, Waring Green
  HD6 ..... 115 A2
  Elland HD3 ..... 151 F8
  Halifax HX2 ..... 91 F3
  Horsforth LS18 ..... 58 B8
  Leeds LS13 ..... 58 C3
  [10] Queensbury BD13 ..... 72 E1
  Rothwell LS26 ..... 100 F4
  Rothwell, Town End WF3 ..... 100 B2
Prospect Rd
  Batley WF16 ..... 117 C6
  Cleckheaton BD19 ..... 116 D7
  Huddersfield HD3 ..... 152 F6
  Liversedge WF15 ..... 116 D2
  Ossett WF5 ..... 140 D5
Prospect Row Halifax HX2 ..... 91 F3
  Menston LS29 ..... 21 C6
Prospect Sq [12] LS28 ..... 57 D2
Prospect St Batley WF17 ..... 118 C6
  Bradford BD4 ..... 201 D1
  Bradford, Bank Top BD10 ..... 56 C5
  Bradford, Woodside BD6 ..... 93 F7
  [1] Cleckheaton BD19 ..... 116 D8
  Glusburn BD20 ..... 16 D7
  Halifax HX3 ..... 203 F4
  [2] Haworth BD22 ..... 51 C6
  Horbury WF4 ..... 159 C8
  Huddersfield HD1 ..... 154 A5
  Keighley BD21 ..... 34 F6
  Pudsey LS28 ..... 76 C8
  Pudsey, Farsley LS28 ..... 57 D3
  Shipley BD18 ..... 55 C7
  Thornton BD13 ..... 72 E6
  Yeadon LS19 ..... 40 C3
Prospect Terr
  [1] Batley WF13 ..... 117 F2
  Bradford BD15 ..... 54 C1
  Leeds LS13 ..... 58 C3
  Liversedge WF15 ..... 117 A4
  Low Bradley BD20 ..... 4 C6
  Mickelfield LS25 ..... 84 A6
  [3] Pudsey, Farsley LS28 ..... 57 D2
  Pudsey, Rodley LS13 ..... 57 E5
  Rothwell LS26 ..... 100 F4
  South Kirkby WF9 ..... 182 B2
Prospect View
  Leeds LS13 ..... 58 C3
  Liversedge WF15 ..... 116 E2
Prospect Villas LS22 ..... 13 E6
Prospect Wlk BD18 ..... 55 C7
Prosper St [1] LS10 ..... 215 E4
Providence Ave
  Baildon BD17 ..... 38 C4
  Leeds LS6 ..... 206 A4
Providence Bldgs HX3 ..... 114 A4
Providence Cres BD22 ..... 34 C2
Providence Ct
  [3] Morley LS27 ..... 98 A5
  Oakworth BD22 ..... 34 C1
Providence Gn WF8 ..... 125 E3
Providence La BD22 ..... 34 C1
Providence Pl
  [6] Bradford BD4 ..... 94 C4
  Brighouse HD6 ..... 115 C1
  Garforth LS25 ..... 82 E7
  Kippax WF10 ..... 103 B3
  Leeds LS2 ..... 206 C1
  [7] Pudsey LS28 ..... 57 E1
  Swillington LS15 ..... 82 A6
Providence Rd LS6 ..... 206 A4
Providence Row
  Bradford BD4 ..... 38 C4
  Halifax HX2 ..... 91 F3
  Keighley BD20 ..... 19 E2

Providence St
  Batley WF17 ..... 118 C5
  Bradford BD1 ..... 201 A3
  Brighouse BD19 ..... 94 E1
  [2] Cleckheaton BD19 ..... 116 E8
  Dewsbury WF12 ..... 139 F7
  [8] Elland HX5 ..... 134 F7
  Leeds LS9 ..... 212 B3
  [5] Pudsey LS28 ..... 57 D2
  Todmorden OL14 ..... 129 A7
  Wakefield WF1 ..... 216 B3
Providence Terr
  Leeds LS2 ..... 206 A3
  Thornton BD13 ..... 72 D6
Prune Park La BD15 ..... 53 F2
Pudding La OL14 ..... 86 C2
Pudsey Bsns Ctr LS28 ..... 76 F7
Pudsey Crawshaw Sch
  LS28 ..... 76 F7
Pudsey Grangefield Sch
  LS28 ..... 76 E8
Pudsey Greenside
  Primary Sch LS28 ..... 76 D6
Pudsey Primrose Hill
  Primary Sch LS28 ..... 57 D1
Pudsey Rd Leeds LS12, LS13 ..... 77 E7
  Pudsey LS28, LS13 ..... 77 B7
  Todmorden OL14 ..... 86 B2
Pudsey Tyersal Primary Sch
  BD4 ..... 75 F6
Pudsey Waterloo
  Infants Sch LS28 ..... 76 C7
Pugneys Central Sta
  WF2 ..... 160 B8
Pugneys Country Pk
  WF2 ..... 160 B8
Pugneys Lakeside Sta
  WF2 ..... 160 A8
Pugneys Light Rly WF4 ..... 160 A8
Pugneys Rd WF2 ..... 142 C2
Pule Green La HX3 ..... 92 C3
Pullan Ave BD2 ..... 56 C4
Pullan Cl BD2 ..... 56 C4
Pullan Dr BD2 ..... 56 C4
Pullan Gr BD2 ..... 56 C4
Pullan La BD17 ..... 39 C5
Pullan St BD5 ..... 74 D5
Pulmans Pl HX3 ..... 113 C2
Pump La Dewsbury WF13 ..... 138 F8
  East Ardsley WF3 ..... 119 E5
  Kirkburton HD8 ..... 174 C7
  West Hardwick WF4 ..... 163 A8
Pump St HD8 ..... 191 B3
Pumphouse La WF14 ..... 138 B6
Punch Bowl Yd
  Brotherton WF11 ..... 126 C8
  Cleckheaton BD19 ..... 116 C7
Pundles HX7 ..... 91 E8
Purbeck Gr LS25 ..... 82 F6
Purcell Dr BD20 ..... 5 D2
Purley Wlk BD6 ..... 94 B8
Purlwell Ave WF17 ..... 118 B3
Purlwell Cres WF17 ..... 118 B3
Purlwell Hall Rd WF17 ..... 118 C4
Purlwell Inf Sch WF17 ..... 118 B3
Purlwell La WF17 ..... 118 C4
Purprise La HX7 ..... 69 A1
Purston Infants Sch WF7 ..... 145 D4
Purston Park Ct WF7 ..... 145 F1
Purston Park La WF7 ..... 145 D4
Pye Nest Ave HX2 ..... 202 A1
Pye Nest Dr HX2 ..... 112 E4
Pye Nest Gdns HX2 ..... 202 A1
Pye Nest Gr HX2 ..... 202 A1
Pye Nest Rd HX2 ..... 112 E4
Pye Nest Rise HX2 ..... 112 E4
Pyenot Ave BD19 ..... 116 E6
Pyenot Dr BD19 ..... 116 E6
Pyenot Gdns BD19 ..... 116 E6
Pyenot Hall La BD19 ..... 116 E6
Pym St LS10 ..... 212 A1
Pymont Ct WF3 ..... 100 C1
Pymont Dr LS26 ..... 101 B7
Pymont Gdns LS26 ..... 101 B7
Pymroyd La HD4 ..... 153 B3
Pymate Rd WF17 ..... 118 A6
Pyrah Fold [6] BD12 ..... 94 C4
Pyrah Rd BD12 ..... 94 D7
Pyrah St Bradford BD12 ..... 94 D4
  Dewsbury WF13 ..... 118 C1

Quail St BD21 ..... 35 D8
Quaker House [9] LS2 ..... 206 A3
Quaker La Bradford BD5 ..... 74 B3
  Cleckheaton BD19 ..... 116 D6
  Liversedge WF15 ..... 116 E3
Quakers La
  Rippenden HX6 ..... 132 D3
  Yeadon LS19 ..... 40 B5
Quarmby Croft HD3 ..... 153 A7
Quarmby Fold HD3 ..... 153 A7
Quarmby Rd HD3 ..... 153 B6
Quarrie Dene Ct LS7 ..... 60 C6
Quarry Ave WF11 ..... 127 A3
Quarry Bank Ct LS5 ..... 58 F6
Quarry Cl HD7 ..... 172 C2
Quarry Cotts BD20 ..... 17 D5
Quarry Ct Halifax HX3 ..... 113 E7
  Huddersfield HD3 ..... 152 F7
Quarry Dene Pk LS16 ..... 59 C8
Quarry Dr HD5 ..... 155 C5
Quarry Farm Rd LS21 ..... 24 B5
Quarry Gdns LS17 ..... 43 A6
Quarry Hill Horbury WF4 ..... 140 F1
  Leeds LS9 ..... 155 B4
  Rothwell LS26 ..... 101 C6
  Sowerby Bridge HX6 ..... 112 B3
Quarry Hill La LS22 ..... 13 E6

Quarry La [10] Batley WF17 ..... 96 F1
  East Ardsley WF12 ..... 119 A6
  Huddersfield HD4 ..... 171 C7
  Kirkheaton HD5 ..... 155 C5
  Morley LS27 ..... 98 B2
  Upton WF9 ..... 183 A8
Quarry Mount Leeds LS6 ..... 206 A4
  Ryhill WF4 ..... 162 B1
  [7] Yeadon LS19 ..... 40 C7
Quarry Mount Pl [7] LS6 ..... 206 A4
Quarry Mount Primary Sch
  LS6 ..... 206 A4
Quarry Mount St [6] LS6 ..... 206 A4
Quarry Mount Terr [8]
  LS6 ..... 206 A4
Quarry Pl Bradford BD2 ..... 56 C2
  Leeds LS6 ..... 206 A3
  Mirfield WF14 ..... 137 D6
Quarry Rd
  Cleckheaton BD19 ..... 116 D7
  Cleckheaton, Gomersal
  BD19 ..... 117 B7
  Dewsbury WF13 ..... 139 B7
  Halifax HX3 ..... 91 E2
  Huddersfield HD4 ..... 153 B3
  Huddersfield, Marsh HD1 ..... 153 E6
  Liversedge WF15 ..... 117 A4
  Pool LS21 ..... 24 B5
  Rothwell LS26 ..... 101 D6
Quarry St
  Ackworth M T WF7 ..... 163 F5
  Bradford BD9 ..... 55 B2
  Leeds LS6 ..... 206 A4
  Shipley BD9 ..... 55 A4
Quarry The LS17 ..... 43 A6
Quarry View
  Ackworth M T WF7 ..... 163 E5
  Dewsbury WF13 ..... 117 F1
Quarrydene Dr WF10 ..... 125 B6
Quarryfield Terr WF3 ..... 120 D7
Quarryfields WF14 ..... 138 B8
Quarryside Rd WF14 ..... 137 F5
Quaver La BD15 ..... 54 B1
Quay St HD1 ..... 154 B6
Quayside BD17 ..... 55 B8
Quayside The BD10 ..... 56 E8
Quebec St Bradford BD1 ..... 201 B2
  Elland HX5 ..... 135 A2
  Keighley BD21 ..... 35 B6
  Leeds LS1 ..... 211 E3
  [8] Todmorden OL14 ..... 108 A1
  Wakefield WF2 ..... 216 A2
Queen Elizabeth Dr WF6 ..... 144 B8
Queen Elizabeth Gdns
  HD1 ..... 153 F6
Queen Elizabeth Gr WF1 ..... 142 E7
Queen Elizabeth Gram
  & Jun Gram Sch WF1 ..... 216 B3
Queen Elizabeth Rd WF1 ..... 142 E7
Queen Elizabeth St LS1 ..... 181 B4
Queen Margaret's Dr
  WF1 ..... 126 D8
Queen Margarets Ave
  WF1 ..... 126 D8
Queen Margarets Cl
  WF1 ..... 126 D8
Queen Sq LS2 ..... 206 C1
Queen St [5] Baildon BD17 ..... 38 C1
  Bingley BD16 ..... 36 F3
  [3] Bradford, Buttershaw BD6 ..... 93 E7
  Bradford, Greengates BD10 ..... 56 D7
  Castleford WF10 ..... 124 E8
  Cleckheaton BD19 ..... 96 B2
  Dewsbury, Chickenley WF12 ..... 140 B7
  Dewsbury, Ravensthorpe
  WF13 ..... 138 E6
  East Ardsley WF3 ..... 120 D8
  Elland HX4 ..... 134 C6
  [4] Haworth BD22 ..... 51 C6
  Horbury WF4 ..... 141 A1
  Huddersfield HD1 ..... 154 B6
  Leeds LS1 ..... 211 D4
  Leeds, Stourton LS10 ..... 80 A2
  Liversedge WF15 ..... 117 C3
  Lofthouse Gate WF1 ..... 121 B4
  Mirfield WF14 ..... 138 A4
  Morley LS27 ..... 98 A5
  Normanton WF6 ..... 123 A2
  Ossett WF5 ..... 140 D5
  Pontefract WF8 ..... 146 C8
  Rothwell WF3 ..... 100 D3
  Silsden BD20 ..... 5 E1
  Skelmanthorpe HD8 ..... 175 A2
  South Elmsall WF9 ..... 182 F2
  Sowerby Bridge HX6 ..... 111 E3
  Steeton BD20 ..... 17 C5
  Swillington LS26 ..... 102 E6
  Todmorden OL14 ..... 108 B5
  Wakefield WF1 ..... 216 B2
  Wilsden BD15 ..... 53 C4
  Yeadon LS19 ..... 40 A4
Queen St S [5] HD1 ..... 154 B5
Queen Tap Yd [24] HD1 ..... 154 A6
Queen Terr [1] WF8 ..... 146 B8
Queen Victoria Cres HX3 ..... 93 B3
Queen Victoria St LS1 ..... 211 F4
Queen's Arc LS1 ..... 211 F4
Queen's Ave Bradford BD2 ..... 55 F3
  Pontefract WF8 ..... 146 A7
Queen's Cres Crofton WF4 ..... 144 C4
  Ossett WF5 ..... 140 D5
Queen's Dr Cudworth S72 ..... 180 C1
  Ilkley LS29 ..... 7 F3
Queen's Drive La LS29 ..... 7 F3
Queen's Gate HX3 ..... 113 B4

Queen's Gdns Ilkley LS29 ..... 8 A3
  Ossett WF5 ..... 140 D5
Queen's Gr LS27 ..... 97 F3
Queen's Park Dr WF10 ..... 125 B8
Queen's Pl LS27 ..... 98 B4
Queen's Prom LS27 ..... 98 B5
Queen's Rd Bingley BD16 ..... 36 E6
  Boston Spa LS23 ..... 30 C8
  Bradford BD1, BD2, BD8 ..... 55 E2
  Brighouse HX3 ..... 93 F2
  Cudworth S72 ..... 180 C1
  Halifax HX1 ..... 202 B3
  Huddersfield HD2 ..... 153 E8
  Ilkley LS29 ..... 8 A3
  Keighley BD21 ..... 35 B5
  Leeds LS6 ..... 205 E2
  Morley LS27 ..... 97 F3
  Pontefract WF8 ..... 146 A7
Queen's Rise [1] BD2 ..... 55 F3
Queen's Road Primary Sch
  HX1 ..... 202 B3
Queen's Sq WF8 ..... 146 A7
Queen's Wlk Leeds LS6 ..... 59 B6
  Ossett WF5 ..... 140 F5
Queens Cl Bingley BD16 ..... 37 B2
  Leeds LS7 ..... 60 C8
Queens Ct Cleckheaton BD19 ..... 96 B2
  [4] Leeds LS14 ..... 62 B5
Queens Dr Halifax HX3 ..... 114 A4
  Pudsey LS28 ..... 76 D8
  Rothwell WF3 ..... 100 D3
  Wakefield WF2 ..... 120 E1
Queens Dr Ct WF5 ..... 140 F5
Queens Gr BD21 ..... 35 B5
Queens Mill WF13 ..... 138 E6
Queens Mill Ind Est HD1 ..... 154 A4
Queens Mill Rd HD1, HD4 ..... 154 A4
Queens Pk Ave [1] LS14 ..... 62 B5
Queens Park Cl WF10 ..... 125 B8
Queens Pl Otley LS21 ..... 23 A7
  Shipley BD18 ..... 54 F8
Queens Rd Castleford WF10 ..... 125 B7
  Shipley BD18 ..... 54 F8
Queens Rd W HD4 ..... 153 B4
Queens Sq HD2 ..... 136 D1
Queens Terr
  Hebden Bridge HX7 ..... 88 F3
  Otley LS21 ..... 23 A7
Queens's Ct LS1 ..... 211 F3
Queensbury Ave WF1 ..... 121 C5
Queensbury Cl WF6 ..... 123 C1
Queensbury Golf Course
  BD13 ..... 93 A8
Queensbury Rd HD3 ..... 92 B5
Queensbury Sq [3] BD13 ..... 72 E1
Queensbury Upper Sch
  BD13 ..... 92 E8
Queensgate Bradford BD1 ..... 201 B3
Queenshill App LS17 ..... 43 C2
Queenshill Ave LS17 ..... 43 C3
Queenshill Cl LS17 ..... 43 C3
Queenshill Cres LS17 ..... 43 C3
Queenshill Dr LS17 ..... 43 C2
Queenshill Garth LS17 ..... 43 C2
Queenshill Gdns LS17 ..... 43 B2
Queenshill Rd LS17 ..... 43 C3
Queenshill View LS17 ..... 43 C2
Queenshill Way LS17 ..... 43 C2
Queenshill Wlk LS17 ..... 43 C2
Queensthorpe Ave LS13 ..... 77 E8
Queensthorpe Cl LS13 ..... 77 F8
Queensthorpe Rise LS13 ..... 77 D8
Queensway Bingley BD16 ..... 37 B2
  Garforth LS25 ..... 82 D7
  Guiseley LS20 ..... 40 A8
  Halifax HX1 ..... 202 B4
  [7] Keighley BD21 ..... 35 A5
  Kirkburton HD8 ..... 174 A5
  Leeds LS15 ..... 81 C8
  Morley LS27 ..... 98 A4
  Normanton WF6 ..... 144 A2
  Pontefract WF8 ..... 125 F3
  Rothwell LS26 ..... 100 E6
  Royston S71 ..... 179 C4
  Yeadon LS19 ..... 40 A8
Queenswood Cl LS6 ..... 59 A6
Queenswood Ct LS6 ..... 59 B4
Queenswood Dr LS6 ..... 59 A5
Queenswood Gdns LS6 ..... 59 C4
Queenswood Gn LS6 ..... 59 A6
Queenswood Hts LS6 ..... 59 C5
Queenswood Mount LS6 ..... 59 B5
Queenswood Rd LS6 ..... 59 B5
Queenswood Rise LS6 ..... 59 B4
Quincy Cl BD2 ..... 56 C2

Raby Ave LS7 ..... 207 D3
Raby Pk LS22 ..... 13 C6
Raby St LS7 ..... 207 D3
Raby Terr LS7 ..... 207 D3
Racca Ave WF11 ..... 127 B4
Racca Gn WF11 ..... 127 B4
Race Moor La BD22 ..... 34 C3
Rachael St WF4 ..... 140 F1
Racton St HD7 ..... 152 E1
Radcliffe Ave BD2 ..... 56 A5
Radcliffe Gdns LS28 ..... 76 E6
Radcliffe Gr [1] LS28 ..... 76 E6
Radcliffe La Halifax HX2 ..... 90 D2
  Pudsey LS28 ..... 76 E6
Radcliffe Pl WF11 ..... 216 B2
Radcliffe Rd
  Huddersfield HD3 ..... 153 B4
  Slaithwaite HD7 ..... 152 B2
  Wakefield WF2 ..... 141 E4
Radcliffe St HD8 ..... 174 F2

adcliffe Terr LS28 .... 76 E6
adfield Rd BD6 .... 74 E1
adford Park Ave WF9 .... 182 B1
adnor St Bradford BD3 .... 75 D7
Halifax LS12 .... 210 B2
adwell Dr BD5 .... 201 B1
ae Ct WF3 .... 121 E5
ae Rd BD18 .... 55 B6
aeburn Dr BD6 .... 94 A7
afborn Ave HD3 .... 134 E1
afborn gr HD3 .... 134 E1
aglan Ave BD22 .... 34 F6
aglan Cl WF10 .... 124 A8
aglan Ct HX1 .... 202 C3
aglan Rd LS2, LS6 .... 206 A3
aglan St Bradford BD3 .... 75 D7
Halifax HX1 .... 202 C3
Keighley BD22 .... 34 F6
Queensbury BD13 .... 72 F1
Todmorden OL14 .... 108 B5
aglan Terr BD3 .... 75 E7
akes La Batley WF17 .... 96 F2
Birkenshaw BD4 .... 76 B2
Birkenshaw, East Bierley BD4 .... 95 E7
Bradford BD4 .... 76 B2
aikes Wood Dr BD4 .... 95 E7
ailes Cl HX2 .... 90 D1
ailgate OL13 .... 106 C1
ailsfield Mount LS13 .... 58 C2
ailsfield Rise LS13 .... 58 C2
ailsfield Way LS13 .... 58 C2
ailway Ave WF8 .... 125 C1
ailway Cotts
Bolton Abbey BD23 .... 2 C7
Burton Salmon LS25 .... 105 D4
Dunford Bridge S36 .... 199 F2
Mickfield LS25 .... 84 A6
South Elmsall WF9 .... 183 E7
ailway Rd Bradford BD10 .... 56 B8
Ilkley LS29 .... 8 B4
Leeds LS15 .... 62 D2
ailway St Bradford BD4 .... 75 C2
Brighouse HD6 .... 115 B1
Cleckheaton BD19 .... 116 D7
Dewsbury WF12 .... 139 D7
Dewsbury, Scout Hill WF13 .... 139 A6
Huddersfield HD1 .... 154 A6
Keighley BD22 .... 18 C1
Leeds LS9 .... 212 B3
Liversedge WF16 .... 117 D3
Todmorden OL14 .... 108 B6
ailway Terr
Bradford BD12 .... 94 E5
East Ardsley WF3 .... 99 C1
Elland HX3 .... 113 A2
Featherstone WF7 .... 145 D5
Hemsworth WF9 .... 163 A3
Lofthouse Gate WF1 .... 121 A5
Normanton WF6 .... 123 A2
ailway View
Castleford WF10 .... 124 B7
Lofthouse Gate WF3 .... 121 F6
aincliffe Gr LS9 .... 80 A8
aincliffe Mount LS9 .... 80 A7
aincliffe Rd LS9 .... 80 A7
aincliffe St LS9 .... 80 A8
aincliffe Terr LS9 .... 80 A7
aines Dr BD20 .... 4 C5
ainsborough Ave WF11 .... 126 C3
aistrick Way BD18 .... 55 D8
ake HX7 .... 109 F8
ake Bank HX2 .... 91 D3
ake Head Barn La OL14 .... 129 A8
ake Head Rd HD7 .... 197 F2
akehill Rd LS15 .... 63 B7
aleigh Gdns OL15 .... 129 C1
aleigh St HX1 .... 202 B1
alph Thoresby High Sch
LS16 .... 41 F4
ampart Rd LS6 .... 206 A3
amsden Ave BD7 .... 73 E5
amsden Cl WF11 .... 126 C8
amsden Ct BD7 .... 74 A4
amsden La Holme HD7 .... 198 B7
Todmorden OL14 .... 128 F7
amsden Mill La HD7 .... 152 E3
amsden Pl BD14 .... 73 B5
amsden Rd Holme HD7 .... 198 C7
Littleborough OL15 .... 128 C1
amsden St
Castleford WF10 .... 124 C5
Halifax HX3 .... 91 F2
Huddersfield HD1 .... 154 A5
Huddersfield, Leymoor HD7 .... 152 A4
Kippax LS25 .... 102 F8
Todmorden OL14 .... 129 A7
amsden Wood Rd OL14 .... 129 A7
amsey Ave OL13 .... 106 A1
amsey Cres WF4 .... 158 A7
amsey Rd WF4 .... 158 A7
amsey St BD5 .... 74 D3
amsey View WF4 .... 158 A7
amsgate WF3 .... 100 B1
amsgate Cres WF3 .... 100 B1
amsgate St HX1 .... 202 B3
amshead App LS14 .... 62 A6
amshead Cl LS14 .... 62 A7
amshead Cres LS14 .... 61 F7
amshead Dr LS14 .... 62 A6
amshead Gdns LS14 .... 61 F7
amshead Gr LS14 .... 62 A6
amshead Heights
LS14 .... 62 A5
amshead Hill LS14 .... 62 A6
amshead Pl LS14 .... 62 A6
amshead Way LS14 .... 62 A6
Rand Pl BD7 .... 74 C5
Rand St BD7 .... 74 C5

Randall Pl BD9 .... 55 A3
Randall Well St BD7 .... 201 A2
Randolph St Bradford BD3 .... 75 E8
Halifax HX3 .... 203 E4
Leeds LS13 .... 58 A2
Randon Cl BD22 .... 34 F5
Ranelagh Ave BD10 .... 56 E5
Range Bank HX3 .... 92 C1
Range Ct HX3 .... 203 E4
Range Gdns HX3 .... 92 C1
Range La HX3 .... 92 C1
Range St HX3 .... 92 C1
Ransdale Dr BD5 .... 74 D3
Ransdale Gr BD5 .... 74 D3
Ransdale Rd BD5 .... 74 D3
Ranter's Fold WF4 .... 141 A1
Range View LS25 .... 64 E8
Rapes Highway OL3 .... 167 A5
Rashcliffe Hill Rd HD1 .... 153 F4
Raspberry Pl BD20 .... 16 D4
Rastrick Comm HD6 .... 136 A8
Rastrick High Sch HD6 .... 114 F1
Rathlin Rd WF12 .... 118 F3
Rathmell Rd LS15 .... 80 E7
Rathmell St BD5 .... 74 D6
Ratten Row Rd HX6 .... 111 C1
Raven Cl WF7 .... 124 A1
Raven La S72 .... 180 A6
Raven Rd LS6 .... 205 E4
Raven Royd S71 .... 178 F1
Raven St Bingley BD16 .... 36 F3
Halifax HX1 .... 202 B3
Huddersfield HD1 .... 153 D5
Keighley BD21 .... 35 B7
Raven Terr BD8 .... 73 C7
Ravens Ave
Dewsbury WF13 .... 139 A6
Huddersfield HD5 .... 154 E5
Ravens Cres WF13 .... 139 A6
Ravens Croft WF13 .... 139 A6
Ravens Gr WF13 .... 139 A6
Ravens Lodge Terr WF13 .... 139 A6
Ravens Mount LS28 .... 76 F7
Ravens St WF13 .... 138 F6
Ravens Way HD7 .... 189 E4
Ravens Wlk WF13 .... 139 A6
Ravenscar Ave LS8 .... 61 A6
Ravenscar Mount LS8 .... 61 A6
Ravenscar Pl LS8 .... 61 A6
Ravenscar Terr LS8 .... 61 A6
Ravenscar View LS8 .... 61 A6
Ravenscar Wlk LS8 .... 61 A6
Ravenscliffe Ave BD10 .... 56 E4
Ravenscliffe First Sch
.... 56 E4
Ravenscliffe High Sch
HX3 .... 113 B2
Ravenscliffe Rd LS28 .... 56 F6
Ravenscourt HD1 .... 153 D5
Ravensdeane HD3 .... 153 D8
Ravensfield Rd WF13 .... 139 A6
Ravenshall Sch WF12 .... 139 A4
Ravenshouse Rd WF13 .... 138 F7
Ravensknowle Rd HD5 .... 154 E5
Ravensmead WF7 .... 145 F5
Ravensthorpe CE
Junior Sch WF13 .... 138 E5
Ravensthorpe Infants Sch
WF13 .... 138 E6
Ravensthorpe Sta WF12 .... 138 F4
Ravenstone Dr HX4 .... 134 C6
Ravenstone Gdns BD20 .... 16 E5
Ravenstone Rd HX4 .... 134 C6
Ravenswharf Rd WF13 .... 139 A6
Ravensworth Cl LS15 .... 62 F3
Ravensworth Way LS15 .... 62 F3
Raw End Rd HX2 .... 112 A8
Raw Hill HD6 .... 135 F8
Raw La Halifax HX2 .... 91 D5
Hebden Bridge HX7 .... 89 D3
Raw Nook Rd HD3 .... 152 E8
Rawden Hill LS21 .... 25 F6
Rawdon C of E Primary Sch
LS19 .... 40 D3
Rawdon Dr LS19 .... 40 B3
Rawdon Golf Course LS19 .... 40 B3
Rawdon Hall Dr LS19 .... 40 B3
Rawdon Littlemoor
Primary Sch LS19 .... 40 C4
Rawdon Rd Haworth BD22 .... 51 C7
Horsforth LS18 .... 57 F8
Rawdon St BD22 .... 35 A6
Rawfield La Fairburn WF11 .... 105 C6
Monk Fryston LS25 .... 105 C6
Rawfolds Ave WF17 .... 96 F2
Rawfolds Way BD19 .... 116 F6
Rawgate Ave WF10 .... 124 A7
Rawling St BD21 .... 35 A5
Rawnsley HX4 .... 134 C5
Rawson Ave Bradford BD3 .... 75 D8
Halifax HX3 .... 113 B3
Rawson Junior
& Infants Sch HX3 .... 92 B2
Rawson Mkt BD1 .... 201 B3
Rawson Pl Bradford BD1 .... 201 B3
Sowerby Bridge HX6 .... 112 A3
Rawson Rd BD1 .... 201 A3
Rawson Sq Bradford BD1 .... 201 B3
Bradford, Thackley BD10 .... 39 B1
Rawson St Bradford BD12 .... 94 D4
Halifax HX1 .... 203 E3
Rawson St N HX3 .... 92 B1
Rawson Terr LS11 .... 214 C3
Rawson Wood HX6 .... 111 E2
Rawthorpe C of E
Infants Sch HD5 .... 154 E8
Rawthorpe Cres HD5 .... 154 E8
Rawthorpe High Sch HD5 .... 154 E8

Rawthorpe Junior Sch
HD5 .... 154 D7
Rawthorpe La HD5 .... 154 E7
Rawthorpe Terr HD5 .... 154 E8
Rawtonstall Bank HX7 .... 88 E4
Ray Gate Holmfirth HD7 .... 189 D8
Huddersfield HD3 .... 152 D8
Wadsworth Moor HX2 .... 89 F8
Ray St HD1 .... 154 B7
Ray Winfield Ind Est WF7 .... 163 E5
Rayfield WF2 .... 141 F5
Raygill Cl LS17 .... 44 B5
Raylands Cl LS10 .... 99 F6
Raylands Ct LS10 .... 99 F6
Raylands Fold LS10 .... 99 F6
Raylands Garth LS10 .... 99 F6
Raylands La LS10 .... 99 F6
Raylands Pl LS10 .... 99 F6
Raylands Rd LS10 .... 99 F6
Raylands Way LS10 .... 99 F6
Rayleigh St BD4 .... 75 A4
Raymond Dr BD5 .... 74 E2
Raymond St BD5 .... 74 E2
Raynbron Cres BD5 .... 201 B3
Raynel App LS16 .... 42 A3
Raynel Cl LS16 .... 42 A4
Raynel Dr LS16 .... 42 A4
Raynel Garth LS16 .... 42 A3
Raynel Gdns LS16 .... 42 A4
Raynel Gn LS16 .... 42 A3
Raynel Mount LS16 .... 42 A4
Raynel Way LS16 .... 41 F4
Rayner Ave Batley WF16 .... 117 D6
Bradford BD8 .... 54 F1
Rayner Dr HD6 .... 115 A4
Rayner Mount BD15 .... 73 A8
Rayner Rd HD6 .... 115 A4
Rayner St WF4 .... 141 A1
Rayner Terr LS28 .... 76 F8
Rayners Ave WF15 .... 116 C4
Raynham Cres BD21 .... 34 F8
Raynor Cl HD3 .... 153 C7
Raynville App LS13 .... 58 E3
Raynville Ave LS13 .... 58 E3
Raynville Cl LS13 .... 58 E2
Raynville Cres LS12 .... 58 E2
Raynville Ct LS13 .... 58 E3
Raynville Dene LS12 .... 58 E3
Raynville Gn LS13 .... 58 E3
Raynville Gr LS13 .... 58 E3
Raynville Grange LS13 .... 58 E3
Raynville Mount LS13 .... 58 E3
Raynville Pl LS13 .... 58 E3
Raynville Primary Sch
LS13 .... 58 E2
Raynville Rd LS12, LS13 .... 58 E3
Raynville Rise LS13 .... 58 E3
Raynville St LS13 .... 58 E3
Raynville Terr LS13 .... 58 E3
Raynville Wlk LS13 .... 58 E3
Raywood Cl LS19 .... 40 A8
Reap Hirst Rd HD2 .... 135 D2
Rebecca St BD1 .... 74 D7
Recreation Ave LS11 .... 214 A4
Recreation Cres LS11 .... 213 F4
Recreation Gr LS11 .... 214 A4
Recreation La HX5 .... 134 E6
Recreation Mount LS11 .... 214 A4
Recreation Pl LS11 .... 214 A4
Recreation Rd Leeds LS11 .... 213 F2
Sowerby Bridge HX6 .... 112 C6
Recreation Row LS11 .... 213 F4
Recreation St LS11 .... 214 A4
Recreation Terr LS11 .... 214 A4
Recreation View LS11 .... 214 A4
Rectory Ave WF10 .... 124 D6
Rectory Cl Garforth LS25 .... 82 F7
Marsden HD7 .... 168 F4
Royston S71 .... 179 D1
Rectory Dr Batley WF17 .... 97 A1
Huddersfield HD5 .... 155 B7
Rectory Garden HD8 .... 175 D7
Rectory Garth WF9 .... 181 D7
Rectory La HD8 .... 175 D8
Rectory Row BD21 .... 35 B7
Rectory St
Leeds LS9 .... 207 E1
Rectory View WF12 .... 139 E3
Red Beck Rd HX3 .... 92 F1
Red Beck Vale BD18 .... 55 A5
Red Brink La HX6 .... 111 B2
Red Deer Park La WF4 .... 156 E5
Red Doles Ind Est HD2 .... 136 C1
Red Doles La HD2 .... 136 C1
Red Doles Rd HD2 .... 136 C2
Red Hall App LS14 .... 45 A1
Red Hall Ave LS17 .... 44 F1
Red Hall Chase LS14 .... 45 A1
Red Hall Croft LS14 .... 62 A8
Red Hall Ct LS14 .... 45 A1
Red Hall Dr LS14 .... 45 A1
Red Hall Garth LS14 .... 45 A1
Red Hall Gdns LS17 .... 44 F1
Red Hall Gn LS14 .... 45 A1
Red Hall La Leeds LS14, LS17 .... 45 A1
Wakefield WF1 .... 121 A1
Red Hall View LS14 .... 45 A1
Red Hall Way LS14 .... 45 A1
Red Hall Wlk LS14 .... 45 A1
Red House Gdns LS29 .... 22 A3
Red House Mus BD19 .... 96 B1
Red La Huddersfield HD8 .... 173 A6
Featherstone WF7 .... 144 E5
Meltham HD7 .... 170 B2
Pudsey LS28 .... 57 C3
Red Laithes Ct WF13 .... 138 E6

Red Laithes La WF13 .... 138 E6
Red Lees Rd BB10 .... 85 A8
Red Lodge Cl LS8 .... 61 D4
Red Vale BD19 .... 96 B2
Redbeck Cotts LS19 .... 57 E8
Redburn Ave BD18 .... 55 A5
Redburn Dr BD18 .... 55 A5
Redburn Rd BD18 .... 55 B5
Redcar La BD20 .... 17 C2
Redcar Rd BD10 .... 56 E6
Redcar St HX1 .... 202 B3
Redcliffe Ave BD21 .... 35 A7
Redcliffe Gr BD21 .... 35 A7
Redcliffe Rd BD21 .... 35 A7
Redcote La Leeds LS4 .... 59 C2
Leeds, Upper Armley LS12 .... 59 B1
Reddisher Rd HD7 .... 169 A3
Reddyshore Scout Gate
OL14 .... 129 C5
Redesdale Gdns LS16 .... 42 B3
Redfearn Ave WF16 .... 117 D5
Redhall Cl LS11 .... 213 E1
Redhall Cres LS11 .... 213 E1
Redhall Gate LS11 .... 213 E1
Redhill Ave
Castleford WF10 .... 125 A6
East Ardsley WF3 .... 119 E5
Redhill Cl WF3 .... 119 E5
Redhill Cres WF3 .... 119 E5
Redhill Dr Castleford WF10 .... 125 B7
East Ardsley WF3 .... 119 E5
Redhill Gdns WF10 .... 125 A7
Redhill Inf Sch WF10 .... 125 C8
Redhill Jun Sch WF10 .... 125 C8
Redhill Mount WF10 .... 125 A7
Redhill Rd WF10 .... 125 A7
Redhill View WF10 .... 125 A6
Redhouse La LS7 .... 204 B3
Redland Cres WF9 .... 163 B2
Redland Dr HD8 .... 173 E7
Redland Gr S75 .... 178 B2
Redlands Cl WF14 .... 138 A7
Redmayne Gr WF11 .... 126 D3
Redmire Ct LS14 .... 62 B4
Redmire Dr LS14 .... 62 A4
Redmire St BD3 .... 75 E7
Redmire View LS14 .... 62 A4
Redruth Dr WF6 .... 123 B3
Redshaw Rd LS12 .... 210 A2
Redthorne Way S72 .... 180 C3
Redthorpe Crest S75 .... 178 B1
Redvers Cl LS16 .... 42 A1
Redwood Ave
East Ardsley WF3 .... 120 A8
Royston S71 .... 179 C3
Redwood Cl Keighley BD21 .... 35 E5
Yeadon LS19 .... 39 F7
Redwood Dr HD2 .... 136 C5
Redwood Gr
Huddersfield HD5 .... 154 D6
Yeadon LS19 .... 39 F7
Reed St LS12 .... 209 F2
Reed St Bacup OL13 .... 106 A3
Huddersfield HD3 .... 153 D7
Reedling Dr LS27 .... 98 C3
Reedsdale Ave LS27 .... 97 C7
Reedsdale Dr LS27 .... 97 C7
Reedsdale Gdns LS27 .... 97 C7
Rees Way BD3 .... 201 C4
Reeth Rd HD6 .... 135 E8
Reevy Ave BD6 .... 93 F8
Reevy Cres BD6 .... 93 F8
Reevy Dr BD6 .... 94 A8
Reevy Hill First Sch BD6 .... 73 F1
Reevy Rd BD6 .... 94 B8
Reevy Rd W BD6 .... 93 E8
Reevy St BD6 .... 74 A1
Reevylands Dr BD6 .... 94 A8
Reform St BD19 .... 96 B1
Regal Cl HX6 .... 132 C1
Regal Dr HX6 .... 132 C1
Regency Ct Bradford BD8 .... 74 B8
Leeds LS6 .... 205 E4
Regency Gdns WF3 .... 120 A8
Regency Park Gr LS28 .... 76 E5
Regency Park Rd LS28 .... 76 E5
Regency Rd WF14 .... 138 A4
Regent Ave LS18 .... 58 A7
Regent Cl Brighouse HD6 .... 135 E6
Horsforth LS18 .... 58 A7
Regent Cres Horsforth LS18 .... 58 A7
Leeds LS18 .... 180 E5
Regent Ct Horsforth LS18 .... 58 C7
Leeds LS18 .... 211 F3
Regent House HX5 .... 134 F7
Regent Mews WF17 .... 118 F4
Regent Park Ave LS6 .... 205 F4
Regent Park Cross Ave
LS6 .... 205 F4
Regent Park Terr LS6 .... 205 F4
Regent Pl Bradford BD10 .... 39 A1
Sowerby Bridge HX6 .... 112 B5
Regent Rd Horsforth LS18 .... 58 B7
Huddersfield HD1 .... 153 E7
Ilkley LS29 .... 8 A4
Kirkheaton HD5 .... 137 C2
Regent St Bacup OL13 .... 106 A2
Bradford BD10 .... 56 D7
Bradford, Thackley BD10 .... 39 A1
Castleford WF10 .... 124 C7
Featherstone WF7 .... 145 C5
Hebden Bridge HX7 .... 89 A3
Hemsworth WF9 .... 181 C7
Horbury WF4 .... 140 F2

Regent St continued
Leeds LS7 .... 204 A3
Leeds, Mabgate LS2, LS7 .... 207 D1
Liversedge WF16 .... 117 C3
Mirfield WF14 .... 138 A3
Normanton WF6 .... 123 C4
Queensbury BD13 .... 72 F1
South Elmsall WF9 .... 182 E3
South Hiendley S72 .... 180 E5
Todmorden OL14 .... 108 A1
Wakefield WF1 .... 142 E3
Regent Terr Leeds LS7 .... 204 A3
Leeds, Burley LS6 .... 205 F2
Regents Pk WF1 .... 142 E6
Reginald Gdns Brierley S72 .... 180 E2
Reginald Mount LS7 .... 207 D4
Reginald Pl LS7 .... 207 D4
Reginald Row LS7 .... 207 D4
Reginald St Bradford BD5 .... 74 D3
Leeds LS7 .... 207 D4
Reginald Terr LS7 .... 207 D4
Reginald View LS7 .... 207 D4
Reid Park Ave WF4 .... 140 E1
Reighton Croft BD10 .... 56 E6
Rein Ct LS25 .... 64 E8
Rein Gdns WF3 .... 119 C8
Rein Mews WF3 .... 119 C8
Rein Rd Horsforth LS18 .... 58 C6
Morley LS27 .... 98 C1
Rein St LS27 .... 98 C1
Reins The LS14 .... 61 F6
Reins Ave BD17 .... 38 B1
Reins Rd HD6 .... 135 E8
Reins Terr HD7 .... 172 A5
Reinwood Ave
Huddersfield HD3 .... 153 B7
Leeds LS6 .... 61 E5
Reinwood Jun & Inf Sch
HD3 .... 153 B7
Reinwood Rd HD3 .... 153 B6
Rembrandt Ave WF3 .... 119 F8
Renee Cl BD4 .... 95 C8
Renfield Gr WF6 .... 123 B3
Renshaw St BD10 .... 39 B1
Renton Ave LS20 .... 22 D1
Renton Dr LS20 .... 39 D8
Renton Lea LS20 .... 39 D8
Reservoir Pl
Dewsbury WF13 .... 118 A1
Queensbury BD13 .... 72 C2
Reservoir Rd Batley WF17 .... 117 F4
Halifax HX2 .... 202 A4
Haworth BD22 .... 50 F6
Meltham HD7 .... 170 E6
Yeadon LS19 .... 118 A1
Reservoir View
Skelmanthorpe HD8 .... 174 E2
Thornton BD13 .... 72 D7
Restmore Ave LS20 .... 22 D2
Retford Pl BD7 .... 74 C5
Reuben Goldberg La BD3 .... 75 D8
Reuben St WF15 .... 117 A5
Reva Cl BD16 .... 37 B4
Reva Syke Rd BD14 .... 73 B4
Revel Garth HD8 .... 174 A2
Revie Rd LS11 .... 213 F3
Reydon Wlk BD6 .... 73 F1
Reyhill Gr BD5 .... 201 B1
Reyner Ho BD5 .... 201 B1
Reyner House Mews BD5 .... 201 B1
Reynolds Ave BD7 .... 73 E5
Rhine St BD4 .... 201 D1
Rhode's Hill La LS23 .... 30 F3
Rhodes Ave WF16 .... 117 D6
Rhodes Cres WF8 .... 146 D6
Rhodes Gdns WF3 .... 121 C6
Rhodes La LS23 .... 30 C6
Rhodes Pl BD17 .... 55 B8
Rhodes St Castleford WF10 .... 124 B7
Castleford WF10 .... 124 B7
Halifax HX1 .... 203 D3
Liversedge WF15 .... 117 C4
Shipley BD18 .... 55 A8
Rhodes Terr Bradford BD2 .... 56 B4
Leeds LS12 .... 210 B2
Rhodesia Ave Bradford BD15 .... 73 C8
Halifax HX3 .... 113 C3
Rhodesia St BD20 .... 16 D6
Rhodesway BD8 .... 73 D8
Rhodesway Sch BD15 .... 73 C8
Rhondda Pl HX2 .... 202 A4
Rhum Cl BD6 .... 93 F6
Rhyddings Ave WF7 .... 163 F5
Rhyddings Dr WF7 .... 163 F5
Rhyddings Gdns LS29 .... 8 D4
Rhyl St WF7 .... 145 D6
Rhylstone Mount BD7 .... 73 F6
Ribble St BD21 .... 35 E8
Ribblesdale Ave LS25 .... 83 B6
Ribbleton Gr BD3 .... 201 D4
Ribstone St HX7 .... 89 E1
Riccall Nook BD10 .... 56 E6
Rice St HD1 .... 154 B5
Rich Gate HD7 .... 189 B2
Richard Dunn Sports Ctr
The BD6 .... 94 D1
Richard Oastler Sch LS4 .... 205 D2
Richard Pl HD6 .... 115 A4
Richard St Bacup OL13 .... 106 A7
Bradford BD3 .... 201 D3
Brighouse HD6 .... 115 A4
Wakefield WF1 .... 216 B3

Richard Thorpe Ave
WF14 .... 138 B5
Richardson Dr LS28 ..... 57 E1
Richardshaw La LS28 .... 76 E8
Richardshaw Rd LS28 .... 57 F1
Richardson Ave BD6 ...... 94 C8
Richardson Cres LS9 ..... 80 C7
Richardson Rd LS9 ...... 80 C7
Richardson Sq 5 HD1 .... 154 A6
Richardson St BD12 ...... 95 A4
Richmond Ave
 Huddersfield HD2 .... 136 A2
 Knottingley WF11 .... 126 B5
 Leeds LS6 .... 205 E4
 Sowerby Bridge HX6 ..... 111 F3
Richmond Cl Halifax HX1 .. 203 E4
 Leeds LS13 .... 58 A2
 3 Morley LS27 .... 98 A3
 Rothwell LS26 .... 100 F6
Richmond Ct Crofton WF4 . 162 A8
 Huddersfield HD4 .... 152 F3
 Leeds LS9 .... 212 C3
 Pontefract WF8 .... 125 D1
 Rothwell LS26 .... 100 F6
Richmond Flats 7 HD1 ... 154 B7
Richmond Garth WF5 ..... 140 F4
Richmond Gdns
 Pudsey LS28 .... 77 A7
 Sowerby Bridge HX6 ..... 111 F3
Richmond Gr BD19 .... 96 B2
Richmond Green St LS9 .. 212 B3
Richmond Hill App LS9 ... 212 B3
Richmond Hill Cl LS9 .... 212 B3
Richmond Hill
 Primary Sch LS9 .... 212 C2
Richmond House Sch
 LS16 .... 59 C7
Richmond Lea WF14 ...... 138 A6
Richmond Mews BD18 .... 54 F8
Richmond Mount LS6 .... 205 E4
Richmond Park Ave
 WF15 .... 117 A3
Richmond Pl Ilkley LS29 .. 8 C3
 10 Shipley BD18 .... 54 F8
Richmond Rd Batley WF17 . 118 D2
 Batley, Nunroyd WF16 .... 117 E6
 Bradford BD7 .... 74 D6
 Halifax HX1 .... 203 D4
 Leeds LS6 .... 205 E4
 Pudsey LS28 .... 57 C2
 17 Shipley BD18 .... 54 F8
 Upton WF9 .... 183 A7
 Wakefield WF1 .... 216 A4
Richmond St
 Castleford WF10 .... 124 D7
 Cleckheaton BD19 .... 116 D7
 Halifax HX1 .... 203 D4
 Keighley BD21 .... 35 B8
 Leeds LS9 .... 212 A3
 8 Todmorden OL14 ...... 108 C5
Richmond Terr Otley LS21 . 22 F7
 Pudsey LS28 .... 77 A7
Richmond Way LS25 ..... 82 F5
Richmondfield Ave LS15 .. 63 E6
Richmondfield Cl LS15 ... 63 E6
Richmondfield Cres LS15 . 63 E6
Richmondfield Cross LS15 . 63 E6
Richmondfield Dr LS15 ... 63 E6
Richmondfield Garth LS15 . 63 E6
Richmondfield Gr LS15 ... 63 E6
Richmondfield La LS15 ... 63 E6
Richmondfield Mount LS15 63 E6
Richmondfield Way LS15 .. 63 E6
Rickard St LS12 .... 210 C2
Ridding Gate LS21 .... 10 E1
Riddings Cl
 Hemsworth WF9 .... 181 D5
 Huddersfield HD2 .... 136 D3
Riddings Rd
 Huddersfield HD2 .... 136 D3
 Ilkley LS29 .... 8 B4
Riddings Rise HD2 ...... 136 E3
Riddlesden C of E First Sch
 BD20 .... 18 F2
Riddlesden Golf Course
 BD20 .... 18 C4
Riddlesden St BD20 ...... 18 F1
Rider Rd LS6 .... 206 B4
Rider St LS9 .... 212 B4
Ridge Ave WF4 .... 158 A2
Ridge Bank OL14 .... 108 B5
Ridge Cl Guiseley LS20 .. 39 C8
 Huddersfield HD4 .... 154 A3
 Skelmanthorpe HD8 ..... 175 A1
Ridge Cres WF4 .... 158 A5
Ridge Gr LS7 .... 60 A5
Ridge Hill HD6 .... 114 E1
Ridge La BD20 .... 5 C7
Ridge Lea HD6 .... 114 F1
Ridge Mount LS6 .... 206 A4
Ridge Mount Terr LS6 .... 206 A4
Ridge Rd Kippax LS25 .... 83 D2
 Leeds LS27 .... 206 B4
 Netherton WF4 .... 158 A6
 Todmorden OL14 .... 108 B5
Ridge St HD4 .... 154 B3
Ridge Terr LS6 .... 59 E5
Ridge The LS27 .... 13 C3
Ridge View Elland HX5 ... 135 C6
 Pudsey LS28 .... 77 C8
Ridge View Dr HD2 ...... 135 D2
Ridge View Gdns BD10 ... 56 C7
Ridge View Rd HD6 ...... 115 A1
Ridge Way LS14 .... 204 C2
Ridgedale Mount WF8 ... 125 D4

Ridgefield St WF10 ...... 124 D7
Ridgemount Rd BD20 ..... 18 E2
Ridgestone Ave WF9 ..... 181 E7
Ridgeway Guiseley LS20 .. 39 B8
 Huddersfield HD5 .... 154 E7
 Queensbury BD13 .... 92 F8
 Shipley BD18 .... 55 E6
Ridgeway Cl
 Huddersfield HD5 .... 154 E7
 Leeds LS8 .... 204 C2
Ridgeway Cres S71 ...... 179 C1
Ridgeway Dr WF17 ...... 97 A1
Ridgeway Gdns HD6 ..... 114 E5
Ridgeway Mount BD22 ... 34 F5
Ridgeway Sq WF11 ...... 126 F3
Ridgeway The WF11 ..... 126 F3
Ridgeways The HD7 ..... 170 D8
Ridgewood Cl BD17 ..... 38 E3
Riding Head La HX2 ..... 90 E1
Riding Hill HX3 .... 93 E6
Riding La HX2 .... 91 D3
Riding St WF17 .... 117 E6
Ridings Bsns Pk HX1 .... 202 B2
Ridings Cl WF3 .... 121 B6
Ridings Croft BD5 ...... 75 A3
Ridings Ct WF3 .... 121 B6
Ridings Fields HD7 ..... 172 C3
Ridings Gdns WF3 ...... 121 B6
Ridings La Holmfirth HD7 . 189 C7
 Lofthouse Gate WF3 ..... 121 B6
Ridings Mews WF3 ...... 121 B6
Ridings Rd WF3 .... 139 D8
Ridings Sch The HX3 .... 91 F3
Ridings St WF11 .... 216 B2
 The BD20 .... 18 E1
Ridings Way Bradford BD6 . 93 E8
 Lofthouse Gate WF3 ..... 121 B6
Ridingwood Rise HD8 .... 175 E2
Ridleys Fold LS29 ...... 6 F8
Rievaulx Ave BD8 .... 74 C8
Rievaulx Cl LS23 .... 30 C7
Rifle Fields HD1 .... 153 F6
Rigg La WF7, WF8 ...... 164 E7
Rightox Rd HD7 .... 172 C3
Rigton App LS9 .... 212 A4
Rigton Bank LS17 ...... 28 D4
Rigton Cl LS9 .... 212 C4
Rigton Dr LS9 .... 212 B4
Rigton Gn Bardsey LS17 .. 28 E4
 Leeds LS9 .... 212 B4
Rigton Lawn LS9 .... 212 B4
Rigton Mews LS9 .... 212 B4
Rigton St BD5 .... 74 D3
Riley La Halifax HX2 .... 91 F8
 Kirkburton HD8 .... 173 E6
Riley Pk HD8 .... 173 F6
Riley St HD4 .... 154 B4
Rill Ct WF9 .... 181 D7
Rillbank La LS3 .... 205 F1
Rillbank St LS3 .... 205 F2
Rillington Mead BD10 ... 56 D6
Rills Mead LS21 .... 23 A7
Rillside HD8 .... 173 F1
Rilston St BD7 .... 74 B6
Rimswell Holt BD10 .... 56 E6
Ring O'Bells Yd 9 WF4 .. 141 A1
Ring Rd Adel LS16 ..... 42 D2
Ring Rd Beeston LS12 ... 78 C3
Ring Rd Beeston Pk
 Leeds LS11 .... 98 F7
 Middleton LS10 .... 99 A6
Ring Rd Farsley LS28 .... 57 C4
Ring Rd Halton LS15 .... 62 C1
Ring Rd (Horsforth) LS18 . 58 E8
Ring Rd Low Wortley LS12 . 78 B4
Ring Rd Meanwood LS17 . 42 F2
Ring Rd Middleton LS10 . 99 F6
Ring Rd Moortown LS17 . 43 D3
Ring Rd Seacroft LS14 .. 62 B6
Ring Rd Shadwell LS17 .. 44 D2
Ring Rd Weetwood LS16 . 42 C1
Ring Rd West Pk LS16 ... 42 A1
Ring Road Bramley LS13 . 77 C8
Ring Road Cross Gates
 LS15 .... 62 C3
Ring Road Farnley LS12 .. 77 E7
Ringby La HX3 .... 92 B4
Ringstone HX4 .... 133 A3
Ringstone Gr S72 ...... 181 B3
Ringway LS25 .... 82 D6
Ringwood Ave LS14 ..... 62 A8
Ringwood Cres LS14 .... 62 A8
Ringwood Ct WF1 ...... 121 D5
Ringwood Dr LS14 ...... 62 A8
Ringwood Edge HX5 .... 134 D6
Ringwood Gdns LS14 ... 62 A8
Ringwood Mount 1 LS14 . 62 A8
Ringwood Rd BD5 ...... 74 D2
Ringwood Way WF9 .... 181 F7
Rink Par 6 WF17 ...... 118 D3
Rink Terr 4 WF17 ..... 118 D3
Ripley Cl WF6 .... 123 D2
Ripley Ct WF6 .... 144 B8
Ripley Dr WF6 .... 123 D3
Ripley La LS20 .... 22 E2
Ripley Rd Bradford BD4 . 74 F4
 Liversedge WF15 .... 116 F4
Ripley St Bradford BD15 . 54 A2
 Bradford, Ripleyville BD5 . 74 F4
 Brighouse HX3 .... 115 A7
 Keighley BD20 .... 18 F1
Ripley Terr HD1 .... 111 D7
Ripon Ave HD2 .... 136 D2
Ripon House 6 HX5 .... 134 F7
Ripon Rd WF17 .... 118 F1
Ripon St HX1 .... 202 A2

Ripon Terr HX3 .... 92 B1
Ripponden Junior
 & Infants Sch HX6 ..... 132 E5
Ripponden New Bank
 HX6 .... 132 E4
Ripponden Old Bank HX6 . 132 E4
Ripponden Old La HX6 ... 132 B3
Rise La OL14 .... 108 A5
Rise The Brotherton WF11 . 126 C8
 Kippax LS25 .... 83 A3
 Leeds LS5 .... 59 A5
 Northowram HX3 .... 93 A2
 Pontefract WF8 .... 146 E7
Risedale Ave WF17 ..... 97 B2
Risedale Cl WF17 ...... 97 B2
Rishworth Ave HD8 ..... 175 D6
Rishworth Cl WF2 ...... 120 E2
Rishworth Hall Cl HX6 .. 132 B1
Rishworth Mill La HX6 .. 150 D8
Rishworth New Rd HX6 .. 132 B1
Rishworth Rd
 Dewsbury WF12 .... 139 D8
 Ripponden HX4 .... 133 A4
Rishworth Sch HX6 .... 132 C2
Rishworth St
 Dewsbury WF13 .... 139 D8
 Keighley BD22 .... 34 F6
 Wakefield WF1 .... 216 B3
Rishworthian Ct HX3 ... 113 A1
Rivadale View LS29 .... 8 B5
Rivalin Rd WF10 .... 124 B6
River Holme View HD7 .. 172 C2
River Pk HD7 .... 171 F5
River St Brighouse HD6 .. 115 C1
 6 Haworth BD22 .... 51 D7
 Keighley BD21 .... 35 C8
 Todmorden OL14 .... 108 C5
River Valley View HD8 .. 192 A6
River View Boston Spa LS23 . 30 F7
 Castleford WF10 .... 124 B8
 Ilkley LS29 .... 8 D5
River Wlk BD16 .... 36 F3
Riverdale LS22 .... 13 F4
Riverdale Ave WF1 ..... 121 F2
Riverdale Cl WF3 ...... 121 F2
Riverdale Cres WF3 .... 121 F2
Riverdale Ct LS21 ..... 23 B8
Riverdale Dr WF3 ...... 121 F2
Riverdale Gdns
 Boston Spa LS23 .... 30 F7
 Otley LS21 .... 23 B8
Riverdale Rd
 Lofthouse Gate WF3 .... 121 F2
 Otley LS21 .... 23 A8
Rivermead WF2 .... 142 D3
Riverside Clayton West HD8 . 175 E3
 Keighley BD21 .... 35 E7
Riverside Ave LS21 .... 11 B2
Riverside Cl LS21 ..... 11 B1
Riverside Cotts BD20 ... 17 D8
Riverside Cres LS21 ... 11 B1
Riverside Ct Leeds LS1 . 211 F3
 Shipley BD17 .... 38 A1
Riverside Dr
 Cleckheaton BD19 ...... 95 D1
 Otley LS21 .... 11 B2
Riverside Est BD7 ..... 55 B8
Riverside Ind Est WF12 . 139 C7
Riverside Junior Sch HX7 . 89 A3
Riverside Pk LS21 ..... 11 B1
Riverside Villas WF2 ... 142 D2
Riverside Way WF13 .... 138 E4
Riverside Wlk LS29 .... 7 F5
Riverwood Dr HX3 ..... 113 B2
Riviera Gdns LS7 ...... 60 C6
Rivock Ave Keighley BD20 . 17 F3
 Steeton BD20 .... 17 D6
 Steeton BD20 .... 17 F3
RM Grylls Middle Sch
 WF15 .... 116 B4
Roach Grange Ave LS25 . 83 A3
Road End 4 HX4 ...... 134 C7
Road Sides HX6 .... 146 D6
Roans Dr BD10 .... 56 C6
Robb Ave LS11 .... 214 A1
Robb St LS11 .... 214 A1
Robbins Terr WF7 ..... 145 D6
Roberson Terr BD19 ... 117 A8
Robert Ct WF15 .... 116 F3
Robert La HD7 .... 189 C7
Robert St N 4 HX3 .... 92 C2
Robert's St BD19 ...... 116 C7
Roberts Ave LS9 ...... 208 B2
Roberts Ct LS9 .... 208 B2
Roberts Pl Bradford BD1 . 201 A3
 Leeds LS9 .... 208 C1
Roberts St Keighley BD22 . 34 C6
 Pudsey LS28 .... 57 E1
 4 Wakefield LS26 ..... 101 C6
Roberts Way WF2 ..... 142 F1
Robertsgate WF3 ...... 100 B1
Robertshaw Rd HX7 ... 88 F3
Robertson Ave HD6 ... 136 A8
Robertson CE (Controlled)
 Jun & Inf Sch WF15 ... 116 E2
Robertson La WF15 .... 116 F2
Robin Chase LS28 ..... 76 F7
Robin Cl Bradford BD2 . 56 C4
 Pontefract WF8 .... 125 D3
Robin Dr Bradford BD2 . 56 C4
Robin Hill WF17 ...... 118 A8
Robin Hood Ave S71 ... 179 D4
Robin Hood Cres WF2 . 141 E4

Robin Hood Gr HD2 .... 136 C4
Robin Hood Hill WF14 . 171 F7
Robin Hood Junior
 & Infants Sch WF3 .... 100 B2
Robin Hood Rd HD2 ... 136 C4
Robin Hood St WF10 .. 124 E7
Robin Hood Way HD6 .. 115 E2
Robin La Batley WF13 .. 118 B2
 Batley, Heckmondwike WF13 117 F3
 Hemsworth WF9 .... 181 A5
 Leeds WF3 .... 76 E7
 Royston S71 .... 179 D4
Robin Rocks HD7 ..... 172 C2
Robin Royd Ave WF14 . 138 A8
Robin Royd Croft WF14 . 138 A8
Robin Royd Dr WF14 .. 138 A8
Robin Royd Garth WF14 . 138 A8
Robin Royd Gr WF14 .. 138 A8
Robin Royd La WF14 .. 138 A8
Robin St Bradford BD5 . 74 C4
 Huddersfield HD1 ..... 153 D5
Robin Wlk BD18 ...... 55 D6
Robin's Gr LS26 ...... 100 F5
Robinia Wlk WF7 ..... 142 A8
Robins The LS29 ..... 21 E8
Robinson Ct BD7 ..... 73 F6
Robinson La Honley HD7 . 172 B3
 Kippax LS25 .... 83 B1
Robinson St
 Huddersfield HD1 ..... 154 C5
 Kippax WF10 .... 103 B4
 Pontefract WF8 .... 125 D1
Robinwood Ct LS8 .... 44 A1
Robson Cl WF8 .... 146 D6
Robson's Rd WF1 ..... 216 A2
Rochdale Rd Bacup OL13 . 106 A1
 Elland HX4 .... 134 B7
 Halifax HX2, HX6 ..... 112 B5
 Ripponden HX6 .... 131 C2
 Slaithwaite HD7 ...... 151 F4
 Sowerby Bridge HX6 .. 111 F1
 Todmorden OL14 ..... 129 B6
 Todmorden, Knowl Wood
 OL14 .... 108 A3
Rochester Ave LS26 ... 82 B1
Rochester Ct WF2 .... 141 D3
Rochester Dr WF14 ... 138 A6
Rochester Gdns LS13 . 57 F4
Rochester House BD15 . 54 B1
Rochester Pl 5 HX5 .. 134 F6
Rochester Rd WF17 ... 96 F3
Rochester St Bradford BD3 . 75 C7
 Shipley BD18 .... 55 C6
Rochester Terr LS6 ... 205 D4
Rochester Wynd LS17 . 44 A4
Rock Cliffe Mount HX2 . 111 D7
Rock Edge WF15 ..... 117 A5
Rock Fold HD7 .... 152 D8
Rock Hill WF10 ...... 125 A6
Rock House Dr WF13 . 118 C2
Rock La Leeds LS13 .. 58 B4
 Slaithwaite HD7 ...... 152 A3
 Wilsden BD15 .... 72 C8
Rock Lea 13 BD13 .... 72 E1
Rock Nook OL15 ..... 129 D1
Rock Rd HD3 .... 135 B2
Rock St 16 Brighouse HD6 . 115 A3
 Huddersfield HD1 .... 152 E7
Rock Terr Brighouse HX3 . 114 D8
 Castleford WF10 ..... 125 A6
 Huddersfield HD1 .... 135 B1
 2 Leeds LS15 .... 80 F8
 Morley LS27 .... 98 B5
 Thornton BD13 ...... 72 D6
 Todmorden OL14 ..... 108 A2
Rock The HD7 .... 152 E1
Rock View Elland HX4 . 134 C4
 Marsden HD7 .... 168 F3
Rockcliffe Ave BD17 .. 38 C1
Rockery Croft LS18 ... 41 C2
Rockery Rd LS18 ..... 41 C2
Rockfield Terr LS19 .. 40 C7
Rockhill Cl WF17 .... 96 F1
Rockhill La BD4 ..... 95 A7
Rockingham Cl LS15 . 62 F3
Rockingham La WF9 .. 164 E4
Rockingham Rd LS15 . 62 F3
Rockingham Way LS15 . 62 F3
Rockland Cres BD7 .. 73 F5
Rocklands Ave 8 BD17 . 38 C4
Rocklands Pl 3 BD17 . 38 C4
Rockley Cl HD5 ...... 154 E4
Rockley Dr WF9 ..... 160 B6
Rockley Grange Gdns
 LS25 .... 82 D5
Rockley St WF13 ..... 139 D8
Rockliffe La OL14 ... 106 A1
Rockliffe Rd OL13 ... 106 A1
Rockmill Rd HD7 .... 171 D1
Rocks La HX2 .... 71 D1
Rocks Rd HD3 .... 113 A4
Rocks View 3 HX2 ... 113 A4
Rockville Terr
 11 Halifax HX1 ...... 202 C1
 Yeadon LS19 .... 40 C6
Rockwell La BD10 ... 39 A3
Rockwood Cl
 Crigglestone WF4 .... 159 D6
 Pudsey LS28 .... 57 A3

Rockwood Gr LS28 .... 57 B3
Rockwood Rd LS28 .... 57 A3
Rockwood Rise HD8 .. 192 A4
Roderick St LS12 .... 209 E2
Rodger La WF2 ...... 120 F4
Rodillian Sch WF3 ... 100 B3
Rodin Ave BD8 ...... 73 D2
Rodley La Emley HD8 . 175 D2
 Leeds LS13 .... 58 A4
 Pudsey LS28, S13 ... 57 D2
Rodley Primary Sch LS13 . 57 F1
Rodney Yd WF1 ..... 216 B3
Rods Mills La LS27 .. 98 B3
Rods View 4 LS27 .. 98 B3
Roe House BD17 .... 38 B1
Roebuck La LS21 ... 10 F1
Roebuck Memorial Homes
 HD5 .... 154 F4
Roebuck St WF17 ... 96 F1
Roebuck Terr LS21 . 10 F1
Roeburn Cl LS21 ... 178 A4
Roger Ct BD2 ...... 56 D2
Roger Dr WF2 ...... 142 D2
Roger Fold 1 LS25 . 83 B1
Roger Gate HX7 .... 89 C7
Roger La HD4 ...... 154 C2
Rogers Ct WF3 ..... 121 F4
Rogers Pl LS28 .... 76 F4
Rogerson Sq HD6 .. 115 A3
Rois Head Rd HX2 . 112 C4
Rokeby Gdns Bradford BD10 . 56 E4
 Leeds LS6 .... 59 C5
Roker La LS28 ...... 77 A7
Roman Ave
 Huddersfield HD3 ... 134 D7
 Leeds LS8 .... 44 A1
Roman Cl HD3 ...... 134 D7
Roman Cres LS8 .... 44 B3
Roman Dr Huddersfield HD3 . 134 D7
 Leeds LS8 .... 44 B2
Roman Gdns LS8 ... 44 A2
Roman Gr LS8 ...... 44 A2
Roman Mount LS8 .. 44 B2
Roman Pl LS8 ...... 44 B2
Roman Rd 5 WF17 . 117 F6
Roman Rise WF8 ... 146 C5
Roman Terr LS8 .... 44 A2
Roman View LS8 ... 44 B2
Romanby Shaw BD10 . 56 D6
Rombald's View LS29 . 8 D5
Rombalds Ave LS12 . 209 F4
Rombalds Cl LS12 .. 59 C3
Rombalds Cres LS29 . 21 F4
Rombalds Dr BD16 . 37 B3
Rombalds Gr LS12 . 209 F4
Rombalds La LS29 . 8 E1
Rombalds Pl 8 LS12 . 59 C3
Rombalds St LS12 .. 59 C3
Rombalds Terr LS12 . 209 F4
Rombalds View Leeds LS12 . 59 C3
 Otley LS21 .... 10 D2
Romford Ave LS27 . 98 A3
Romford Ct BD6 ... 93 F6
Romney Mount LS28 . 77 A5
Romsey Cl HD3 .... 134 F3
Romsey Gdns BD4 . 75 E3
Romsey Mews BD4 . 75 D3
Ronald Dr BD7 .... 74 A2
Ronaldsway Cl OL13 . 106 B3
Roods La HD7 ..... 188 B3
Rook La BD4 ...... 75 C2
Rook St Bingley BD16 . 36 F3
 Huddersfield HD1 ... 154 A7
Rook's Nest Junior
 & Infants Sch WF1 . 121 C4
Rook's Nest Rd WF1 . 121 D4
Rookeries Junior
 & Infants Sch The WF9 . 146 E6
Rookery La HX3 .... 113 D3
Rookery The LS29 .. 6 F8
Rookes Ave BD6 ... 94 C8
Rookes La HX3 .... 94 A1
Rookhill Dr WF8 ... 146 E7
Rookhill Mount WF8 . 146 F7
Rookhill Rd WF8 ... 146 F7
Rooks Ave BD19 ... 116 C8
Rooks Cl BD12 .... 94 D1
Rookwith Par BD10 . 56 E6
Rookwood Ave
 Kippax LS25 .... 103 A8
 Leeds LS9 .... 80 D8
Rookwood Cres LS9 . 80 C8
Rookwood Gdns LS9 . 80 C8
Rookwood Hill LS9 . 80 C8
Rookwood Mount LS9 . 80 C8
Rookwood Par LS9 . 80 C8
Rookwood Rd LS9 .. 80 C8
Rookwood Sq LS9 .. 80 C8
Rookwood St LS9 .. 80 C7
Rookwood Terr LS9 . 80 C8
Rookwood Vale LS9 . 80 D8
Rookwood View LS9 . 80 C8
Rookwood Wlk LS9 . 80 C8
Rooley Ave BD6 ... 74 E1
Rooley Banks HX6 . 111 E3
Rooley Cl BD5 .... 74 E1
Rooley Cres BD6 .. 94 E8
Rooley Hts HX6 ... 111 D3
Rooley La
 Bradford BD4, BD5 ... 75 A1
 Sowerby Bridge HX6 . 111 D3
Roomfield Ct OL14 .. 108 B5
Roomfield St OL14 .. 108 B5
Rooms Fold LS27 ... 98 A6

Rooms La Gildersome LS27 .... 98 A8
Morley LS27 .... 98 A6
Rope Wlk Halifax HX2 .... 90 F7
Knottingley WF11 .... 127 A4
Roper Ave LS8 .... 204 C4
Roper Gdns HX2 .... 91 D4
Roper Gn HX2 .... 91 D4
Roper Gr LS8 .... 204 C4
Roper La Halifax HX2 .... 91 F8
Queensbury BD13 .... 72 B2
Roper St BD21 .... 35 B7
Ropergate WF8 .... 146 C8
Ropergate End 4 WF8 ..... 146 C8
Roscoe St LS7 .... 207 D2
Rose Ave Horsforth LS18 ...... 58 B7
Huddersfield, Marsh HD3 ... 153 C6
Upton WF9 .... 183 A7
Rose Bank LS29 .... 21 E8
Rose Bank Pl BD8 .... 73 E7
Rose Bank Rd OL14 .... 108 A5
Rose Cl WF9 .... 183 A7
Rose Croft LS17 .... 28 C6
Rose Ct LS25 .... 83 A7
Rose Farm App WF6 .... 122 F4
Rose Farm Cl WF6 .... 122 F5
Rose Farm Fold WF6 .... 122 F5
Rose Farm Rise WF6 .... 122 F5
Rose Garth Crofton WF4 .... 143 F1
Menston LS29 .... 21 C7
Rose Gr
18 Hebden Bridge HX7 ...... 89 A4
Hebden Bridge, Mytholmroyd
HX7 .... 110 E8
Rothwell LS26 .... 100 D6
Upton WF9 .... 183 A7
Rose Grove La HX2 .... 112 A5
Rose Heath HX2 .... 91 D7
Rose Hill Dr HD2 .... 135 E1
Rose La WF7 .... 163 D4
Rose Meadows BD22 .... 34 E5
Rose Mount Bradford BD2 ... 56 A3
Huddersfield HD2 .... 135 D1
Rose Mount Pl LS12 .... 210 A2
Rose Pl HX2 .... 111 E5
Rose St Bradford BD8 .... 55 B1
Halifax HX1 .... 202 B2
Haworth BD22 .... 51 C6
Horsforth LS18 .... 58 B8
Keighley BD21 .... 35 F7
Todmorden OL14 .... 108 B5
Rose Terr Addingham LS29 .... 6 F8
18 Halifax HX1 .... 202 C3
2 Halifax, King Cross HX2 . 113 A4
Horsforth LS18 .... 58 A7
Huddersfield HD1 .... 154 B8
Rose Wlk LS26 .... 100 D6
Rosebank LS13 .... 205 F2
Rosebank Gdns LS3 .... 205 F1
Rosebank Ho LS6 .... 205 F2
Rosebank Rd LS3 .... 205 F1
Rosebank St WF17 .... 118 B6
Rosebery St
Oakworth BD22 .... 34 D2
Todmorden OL14 .... 86 C1
Rosebery Ave Halifax HX3 .. 113 D4
Shipley BD18 .... 55 C7
Rosebery Mount BD18 .... 55 D7
Rosebery Rd BD8 .... 55 C2
Rosebery St Elland HX5 ..... 134 F6
Huddersfield HD2 .... 136 C1
Pudsey LS28 .... 76 C8
Rosebery Terr Halifax HX1 .. 202 C4
3 Pudsey LS28 .... 57 F2
Rosebud Wlk LS8 .... 207 E2
Rosecliffe Mount LS13 .... 58 C2
Rosecliffe Terr LS13 .... 58 C2
Rosedale LS26 .... 100 F6
Rosedale Ave
Bradford BD15 .... 53 F2
18 Huddersfield HD5 .... 154 D5
Liversedge WF15 .... 116 D2
Wakefield WF2 .... 160 E8
Rosedale Bank LS10 .... 215 D1
Rosedale Cl Baildon BD17 ... 38 A2
Normanton WF6 .... 123 D1
Upton WF9 .... 183 B7
Rosedale Gdns LS10 .... 215 D1
Rosedale Gn LS10 .... 215 D1
Rosedale Rise LS23 .... 30 C7
Rosedale Wlk LS10 .... 215 D1
Rosegarth Ave HD7 .... 189 C7
Roseleigh Ave WF17 .... 181 C6
Rosehill Cres BD12 .... 94 C4
Roselee Cl HX3 .... 113 E3
Rosemary Ave LS12 .... 210 A3
Rosemary Cl HD6 .... 115 A1
Rosemary La Brighouse HD6 115 A1
Halifax HX3 .... 93 C5
Rosemont LS16 .... 24 E3
Rosemont Ave
7 Leeds LS13 .... 58 C2
3 Pudsey LS28 .... 76 F8
Rosemont Dr LS28 .... 76 F8
Rosemont Gr 3 LS13 .... 58 C2
Rosemont La 2 BD17 .... 38 D2
Rosemont Pl LS13 .... 58 C2
Rosemont Rd LS13 .... 58 C2
Rosemont St Leeds LS13 .... 58 C2
3 Pudsey LS28 .... 76 F8
Rosemont Terr Leeds LS13 .. 58 C2
Pudsey LS28 .... 76 F8
Rosemont View LS13 .... 58 C2
Rosemont Wlk 4 LS13 ..... 58 C2
Rosemount OL13 .... 106 A4
Rosemount Ave HX5 .... 135 A6

Rosemount Cl 2 BD21 ..... 35 B7
Rosemount Ct BD20 .... 16 D4
Rosemount Terr HX5 .... 135 A6
Rosemount Wks HX5 .... 135 A5
Rosemount Wlk 18 BD21 ... 35 B7
Rosendale Ct 8 OL13 .... 106 B3
Rosendale Cres OL13 .... 106 B3
Roseneath Pl LS12 .... 210 A2
Roseneath St LS12 .... 210 A2
Roseneath Terr LS12 .... 210 A2
Rosetta Dr BD8 .... 73 F8
Roseville Rd LS8 .... 207 E2
Roseville St LS8 .... 207 E2
Roseville Terr
Dewsbury WF12 .... 139 F8
4 Leeds LS15 .... 62 D3
Roseville Way LS8 .... 207 E2
Rosewood Ave
Keighley BD20 .... 18 F1
Kippax LS25 .... 82 F3
Rosewood Ct LS26 .... 100 F7
Rosewood Gr BD4 .... 75 D5
Rosewood Sq BD20 .... 16 D4
Rosgill Dr LS14 .... 62 A5
Rosgill Wlk LS14 .... 61 F5
Rosley Mount BD6 .... 93 F6
Roslyn Ave HD4 .... 171 C7
Roslyn Pl BD7 .... 74 B6
Ross Gr LS13 .... 58 B4
Ross Terr LS13 .... 58 A4
Rossall Gr LS8 .... 207 E4
Rossall Rd LS8 .... 207 E4
Rosse St Bradford BD8 .... 74 A8
Shipley BD18 .... 55 B8
Rossefield App LS13 .... 58 D2
Rossefield Ave
Huddersfield HD2 .... 135 E1
Leeds LS13 .... 58 D2
Rossefield Chase LS13 .... 58 D2
Rossefield Cl 3 LS13 .... 58 D2
Rossefield Dr LS13 .... 58 D2
Rossefield Gn LS13 .... 58 D2
Rossefield Gr LS13 .... 58 D2
Rossefield Lawn LS13 .... 58 D2
Rossefield Par LS13 .... 58 D2
Rossefield Pk BD9 .... 55 B4
Rossefield Pl LS13 .... 58 D2
Rossefield Rd BD9 .... 55 A4
Rossefield Sch BD9 .... 55 A4
Rossefield Terr LS13 .... 58 D2
Rossefield View LS13 .... 58 D2
Rossefield Way LS13 .... 58 D2
Rossefield Wlk 8 LS13 ..... 58 D2
Rossendale Pl BD18 .... 55 A7
Rossett Ho BD3 .... 201 C4
Rossington Gr 4 LS8 .... 207 E4
Rossington Pl 6 LS8 .... 207 E4
Rossington Rd LS8 .... 61 A5
Rossington St LS2 .... 211 E4
Rossiter Dr WF11 .... 126 D3
Rosslyn Ave WF7 .... 163 F5
Rosslyn Cl WF7 .... 163 F5
Rosslyn Ct
Ackworth M T WF7 .... 163 F5
Dewsbury WF12 .... 139 F7
Rosslyn Gr
Ackworth M T WF7 .... 163 F5
Haworth BD22 .... 51 C6
Rossmore Dr BD15 .... 54 C1
Rotcher HD7 .... 169 E8
Rotcher La HD7 .... 169 E8
Rotcher Rd HD7 .... 189 A5
Rothbury Gdns LS16 .... 42 B3
Rothesay Terr BD7 .... 74 C6
Rothwell CE Prim Sch
LS26 .... 100 E6
Rothwell Dr HX1 .... 203 D1
Rothwell Infants Sch LS26 . 100 E4
Rothwell La LS26 .... 100 E5
Rothwell Mount HX1 .... 203 D1
Rothwell Rd HX1 .... 203 D1
Rothwell Sports Ctr LS26 . 101 C4
Rothwell St HD5 .... 154 C6
Rothwell St Mary's RC
JMI Sch LS26 .... 100 F4
Rothwell West Jun Sch
LS26 .... 100 E4
Rough Hall La HX2 .... 90 F5
Rough Side La OL14 .... 108 C3
Round Close Rd HD7 .... 199 B6
Round Hill Halifax HX2 ..... 91 F6
Mapplewell S75 .... 178 A1
Round Hill Cl Bradford BD14 . 73 B2
Halifax HX2 .... 91 F6
Round Hill La HD5 .... 137 B3
Round Ings Rd HD3 .... 152 A6
Round St Bradford BD5 ..... 74 E3
Wakefield WF1 .... 142 E4
Round Thorn Pl BD8 .... 74 A8
Round Wood Ave HD5 ...... 155 A6
Roundell Ave BD4 .... 95 B8
Roundhay Ave LS8 .... 204 C1
Roundhay Cres LS8 .... 204 C1
Roundhay Gdns LS8 .... 204 C1
Roundhay Gr LS8 .... 204 C1
Roundhay Hall Hospl LS8 . 61 A7
Roundhay High Sch LS8 ... 61 A7
Roundhay Mount LS8 .... 204 C1
Roundhay Park LS8 .... 44 C1
Roundhay Park La LS8 ...... 44 B4
Roundhay Pl LS8 .... 204 C1
Roundhay Rd LS7, LS8 ...... 207 F3
Roundhay Sch LS8 .... 61 A7
Roundhay St John's C of E
Primary Sch LS8 .... 61 C6
Roundhay View LS8 .... 204 C1
Roundhead Fold BD10 ...... 56 E8
Roundhill Ave BD16 .... 54 B7

Roundhill Mount BD16 ...... 54 B7
Roundhill Pl BD1 .... 201 A3
Roundhill Rd WF10 .... 124 D7
Roundhill St BD5 .... 74 F2
Roundthorn Sch BD5 .... 74 E3
Roundway HD7 .... 172 A3
Roundway The LS27 .... 97 F4
Roundwell Rd WF15 .... 116 C5
Roundwood BD18 .... 54 F7
Roundwood Ave
Baildon BD17 .... 38 F3
Bradford BD10 .... 56 E4
Roundwood Cres WF2 ...... 141 C5
Roundwood Glen BD10 ..... 56 E6
Roundwood Hill Sch
WF2 .... 141 D3
Roundwood Ind Est WF5 .. 141 B5
Roundwood Rd
Baildon BD17 .... 38 E4
Ossett WF5 .... 141 A4
Roundwood Rise WF2 .... 141 D4
Roundwood View BD10 ..... 56 E6
Rouse Fold BD4 .... 201 C1
Rouse Mill La WF17 .... 118 D4
Rouse St 7 WF15 .... 117 A4
Row Gate HD8 .... 190 D6
Row La Marsden HD7 .... 169 C8
Sowerby Bridge HX6 .... 111 D3
Row St HD4 .... 153 E4
Rowan Ave Bradford BD3 .. 75 E7
Huddersfield HD4 .... 171 D6
Normanton WF6 .... 144 A7
Rowan Avenue Mews
HD4 .... 171 D6
Rowan Cl Batley WF17 ..... 97 A2
Knottingley WF11 .... 126 E2
Rowan Ct Bradford BD2 ... 56 C1
Wakefield WF2 .... 141 F8
Yeadon LS19 .... 40 B5
Rowan Dr HD6 .... 115 C3
Rowan Garth BD20 .... 16 D6
Rowan Gn WF8 .... 125 F1
Rowan Pl LS25 .... 83 B6
Rowan St BD20 .... 18 A2
Rowanberry Cl BD2 .... 56 C2
Rowans The Baildon BD17 .. 37 F3
Bramhope LS16 .... 24 F2
Pudsey LS13 .... 57 F3
Wetherby LS22 .... 14 A6
Rowantree Ave BD17 .... 38 B4
Rowantree Dr BD10 .... 56 C6
Rowanwood Gdns BD10 ... 56 E5
Rowe Cl WF9 .... 183 A4
Rowgate HD8 .... 191 B6
Rowland La HX7 .... 89 C4
Rowland Pl LS11 .... 214 B3
Rowland Rd LS11 .... 214 B3
Rowland St LS11 .... 214 B3
Rowland Terr 6 LS11 ..... 214 C3
Rowlands Ave
Huddersfield HD5 .... 154 F6
Upton WF9 .... 183 A7
Rowlestone Rise BD10 ...... 56 E6
Rowley Dr Ilkley LS29 ...... 8 F3
Lepton HD8 .... 155 D3
Rowley La Lepton HD8 ..... 155 C2
South Elmsall WF9 .... 183 A2
Rowsley St 11 BD21 .... 35 D7
Rowton Thorpe BD10 .... 56 E6
Roxburgh Gr BD15 .... 73 B8
Roxburghe Dale WF6 .... 123 D1
Roxby Cl LS9 .... 207 E1
Roxby St BD5 .... 74 D3
Roxholme Ave LS7 .... 204 B1
Roxholme Gr LS7 .... 204 B1
Roxholme Pl LS7 .... 204 B1
Roxholme Rd LS7 .... 204 B1
Roxholme Terr LS7 .... 204 B1
Roy Rd BD6 .... 73 D1
Roy St OL14 .... 86 A1
Royal Armouries Mus The
LS10 .... 212 A2
Royal Birkdale Way WF6 .. 123 D1
Royal Cl Bradford BD7 ...... 73 F3
Leeds LS10 .... 215 D2
Royal Ct Leeds LS10 .... 215 D2
Pontefract WF8 .... 146 B5
Royal Dr LS10 .... 215 D2
Royal Gdns LS10 .... 215 D2
Royal Gr LS10 .... 215 D2
Royal Halifax Infmy HX1 .. 203 D1
Royal London Ind Est The
LS11 .... 214 C3
Royal Park Ave LS6 .... 205 F3
Royal Park Gr LS6 .... 205 F3
Royal Park Mount LS6 ..... 205 F3
Royal Park Primary Sch
LS6 .... 205 F2
Royal Park Rd LS6 .... 205 F2
Royal Park Terr LS6 .... 205 F3
Royal Park View LS6 .... 205 F3
Royal Pl LS10 .... 215 D2
Royal Terr Boston Spa LS23 .. 30 E8
Huddersfield HD3 .... 153 A5
Royd Ave Batley WF16 ..... 117 D6
Bingley BD16 .... 37 C3
Holmfirth HD7 .... 189 E6
Huddersfield HD3 .... 153 A5
Huddersfield, Ainley Top
HD3 .... 135 B3
Mapplewell S75 .... 178 A1
Royd Cl BD12 .... 94 D6
Royd Cres Halifax HX1 ..... 202 B4
Hebden Bridge HX7 .... 89 F1
Royd Croft HD3 .... 153 A5
Royd Head Farm WF5 ...... 140 C5
Royd House Gr BD21 .... 35 E5

Royd House La HD7 .... 152 D1
Royd House Rd BD21 .... 35 E5
Royd House Way BD21 .... 35 E5
Royd House WIk BD21 ..... 35 E5
Royd Ings Ave BD21 .... 18 D1
Royd La Halifax HX3 .... 92 A3
Halifax, Illingworth HX2 ... 91 E7
Holmfirth HD7 .... 188 E2
Keighley BD20 .... 18 B1
Rippondon HX6 .... 132 D4
Todmorden OL14 .... 108 B6
Royd Mill Bsns Pk HD6 ... 115 C2
Royd Moor La WF9 .... 164 C1
Royd Mount 4 Halifax HX3 92 A3
Holmfirth HD7 .... 189 A5
Royd Mount Middle Sch
BD13 .... 72 C6
Royd Pl HX3 .... 92 C2
Royd Rd Meltham HD7 ..... 187 E8
Todmorden OL14 .... 108 B7
Royd Sq 2 HX7 .... 89 A3
Royd St 3 Bradford BD12 .. 94 D6
Huddersfield HD3 .... 153 A5
Keighley BD20 .... 18 B2
Slaithwaite HD7 .... 151 F1
Thornton BD13 .... 72 C6
Todmorden OL14 .... 108 A6
Wilsden BD15 .... 53 C5
Royd Terr
Hebden Bridge HX7 .... 89 A3
Huddersfield HD4 .... 171 E8
Royd View HX7 .... 89 E1
Royd Way BD21 .... 18 C1
Royd Wood
Cleckheaton BD19 .... 116 D6
Oxenhope BD22 .... 51 D4
Roydfield St HD2 .... 136 B2
Roydlands St HX3 .... 114 D7
Roydon Gr BD9 .... 55 A2
Royds Ave Birkenshaw BD11 96 B5
Brighouse HD6 .... 115 B8
Castleford WF10 .... 125 C8
Holmfirth HD7 .... 189 D6
Huddersfield HD3 .... 153 C5
Ossett WF5 .... 140 F4
Slaithwaite HD7 .... 152 D2
Royds Cl Holmfirth HD7 ... 189 D6
Leeds LS12 .... 78 C4
Royds Cres HD6 .... 115 B7
Royds Dr HD7 .... 189 D6
Royds Hall Ave BD6 .... 74 C3
Royds Hall La BD6 .... 94 C8
Royds Hall High Sch HD3 . 153 C6
Royds Hall La
Bradford BD12, BD6 .... 94 B5
Bradford, Moor Top BD6 ... 94 A7
Royds Hall Rd LS12 .... 78 C4
Royds La Leeds LS12 .... 78 C4
Leeds, Far Royds LS12 ...... 78 C4
Rothwell LS26 .... 101 A3
Royds Park Cres BD12 ..... 94 D4
Royds Ho HD6 .... 192 A6
Royds St LS26 .... 101 B2
Royds St HD7 .... 168 F3
Royds The
Clayton West HD8 .... 176 A3
Holmfirth HD7 .... 189 A5
Royds View HD7 .... 152 D1
Roydscliffe Dr BD9 .... 54 F4
Roydscliffe Rd BD9 .... 54 F4
Roydsdale Way BD4 .... 95 B3
Roydstone Rd BD3 .... 75 D8
Roydstone Terr BD3 .... 75 D8
Roydwood Terr BD13 .... 52 D6
Roydwood Terr (Back)
BD13 .... 52 D6
Royle Fold WF16 .... 117 D4
Royles Cl WF9 .... 182 C2
Royles Head La HD3 .... 152 E6
Royston C of E Jun
& Inf Sch S71 .... 179 C3
Royston Cl WF3 .... 120 D6
Royston Comp Sch
S71 .... 179 C4
Royston Hill WF3 .... 120 D6
Royston La S71 .... 179 C2
Royston Midland Jun
& Inf Sch S71 .... 179 C3
Royston Rd S72 .... 180 B1
Ruby St Batley WF17 .... 118 A7
18 Keighley BD22 .... 35 A4
Leeds LS9 .... 212 A4
Rud La HX7 .... 110 A3
Rudd St BD7 .... 74 A4
Rudding Ave BD15 .... 54 A1
Rudding Cres BD15 .... 54 A1
Rudding Dr WF17 .... 117 F6
Rudding St HD4 .... 153 E3
Rudgate Tadcaster LS24 ... 31 D4
Thorp Arch LS23, LS24 ..... 15 A3
Rudgate HM Prison LS23 .. 15 A2
Rudgate Mews LS23 .... 15 A3
Rudgate Pk LS23 .... 15 A3
Ruffield Side BD12 .... 94 C5
Rufford Ave LS19 .... 40 C6
Rufford Bank LS19 .... 40 C6
Rufford Cl LS19 .... 40 C6
Rufford Cres LS19 .... 40 C6
Rufford Dr LS19 .... 40 C6
Rufford Pl 2 HX3 .... 113 B4
Rufford Rd Elland HX5 ..... 134 F6
Halifax HX3 .... 113 B4
Rufford Ridge LS19 .... 40 C6
Rufford Rise LS19 .... 40 B6
Rufford St Bradford BD3 ... 75 C7
Wakefield WF2 .... 141 F6

Rufford Villas 4 HX3 ..... 113 B4
Rufus St Bradford BD5 ..... 74 B3
6 Keighley BD21 .... 35 C8
Rugby Ave HX3 .... 91 F3
Rugby Dr HX3 .... 91 F3
Rugby Gdns HX3 .... 91 F3
Rugby Mount HX3 .... 91 F3
Rugby Pl BD7 .... 74 B6
Rugby Terr HX3 .... 91 F3
Rumble Rd WF12 .... 118 F1
Rumbold Rd HD3 .... 153 D7
Rumple Croft LS21 .... 10 E2
Runnymeade Ct BD10 ...... 56 B7
Runswick Ave 1 LS11 ..... 210 C1
Runswick Gr BD5 .... 74 D1
Runswick Pl LS11 .... 211 D1
Runswick St Bradford BD5 .. 74 D1
Leeds LS11 .... 211 D1
Runswick Terr
Bradford BD5 .... 74 D1
Leeds LS11 .... 211 D1
Runtlings WF5 .... 140 C5
Runtlings La WF5 .... 140 C4
Runtlings The WF5 .... 140 B5
Rupert Rd LS29 .... 8 A5
Rupert St Haworth BD22 ... 51 C6
6 Keighley BD21 .... 35 C8
Rushbearers Wlk HD5 .... 154 E3
Rushcroft Terr BD17 .... 38 C3
Rushdene Ct BD12 .... 94 C1
Rushfield Vale HD8 .... 155 C4
Rushmoor Rd BD4 .... 75 D2
Rushmore Dr LS28 .... 57 C3
Rushton Ave BD3 .... 75 E8
Rushton Hill Cl HX2 .... 91 C1
Rushton Rd BD3 .... 75 E8
Rushton St Halifax HX1 ... 202 B4
Pudsey LS28 .... 57 B6
Rushton Terr BD3 .... 75 E7
Rushworth Cl WF3 .... 121 E5
Rushworth St 18 HX3 ..... 92 A1
Ruskin Ave Bradford BD9 .. 54 D3
Wakefield WF1 .... 121 A3
Ruskin Cl WF10 .... 125 B8
Ruskin Cres LS20 .... 39 F8
Ruskin Ct WF7 .... 120 F2
Ruskin Dr WF10 .... 125 B8
Ruskin Gr HD2 .... 136 D3
Ruskin Gr WF10 .... 125 B8
Ruskin Pl WF10 .... 125 B8
Ruskin St LS28 .... 57 C1
Ruskin Terr 22 HX3 .... 92 A1
Russel Ct LS17 .... 28 D3
Russell Ave
Cragglestone WF4 .... 159 F3
Queensbury BD13 .... 92 E8
Russell Cl Batley WF17 .... 118 C5
Batley, Heckmondwike
WF16 .... 117 E3
Russell Hall Cl BD13 .... 96 B5
Russell Hall First Sch
BD13 .... 72 E1
Russell Hall La 18 BD13 .. 72 E1
Russell Rd BD13 .... 72 D1
Russell St Bradford BD5 ... 201 A1
Dewsbury WF13 .... 118 A1
Halifax HX1 .... 203 E3
Keighley BD21 .... 35 B7
Leeds LS1 .... 211 E4
Queensbury BD13 .... 72 E1
Shipley BD18 .... 55 C5
Todmorden OL14 .... 108 C5
Wakefield WF1 .... 142 C4
Russet Fold WF15 .... 117 A5
Russets The LS7 .... 160 E6
Russett Gr HD4 .... 154 C3
Rustic Ave HX3 .... 114 A4
Ruswarp Cres BD10 .... 56 D6
Ruth St 18 Haworth BD22 . 51 C8
Huddersfield HD4 .... 154 A2
Ruthven View LS8 .... 208 A3
Rutland Ave Pontefract WF8 146 D5
Wakefield WF2 .... 142 C2
Rutland Cl Kippax LS25 .... 83 B2
5 Rothwell LS26 .... 101 D6
Rutland Ct LS28 .... 76 E8
Rutland Dr Crofton WF4 ... 143 C2
Kippax LS25 .... 83 B2
Rutland House 5 BD16 ... 37 A3
Rutland Ind Est WF1 .... 142 D4
Rutland Mount LS3 .... 210 C4
Rutland Rd Batley WF17 ... 118 D6
Flockton WF4 .... 157 C3
Huddersfield HD3 .... 153 A5
Rutland St Bradford BD4 .. 201 D1
7 Keighley BD21 .... 35 B5
Leeds LS3 .... 211 D4
Rutland Terr LS3 .... 210 C4
Rutland Wlk 7 WF13 .... 139 B8
Ryan Gr BD22 .... 34 D8
Ryan Pl LS9 .... 208 A1
Ryburn Golf Course HX6 .. 112 C2
Ryburn Ho 6 HX1 .... 202 B3
Ryburn La HX6 .... 132 E5
Ryburn Pl WF2 .... 216 A1
Ryburn Rd HX6 .... 132 B3
Ryburn St HX6 .... 112 B3
Ryburn Terr Halifax HX1 .. 202 B3
Rippondon HX6 .... 132 C1
Ryburn Valley High Sch
HX6 .... 111 E3
Ryburn View HX6 .... 132 C3
Rycroft Ave Pudsey LS13 .. 58 B2
Shipley BD16 .... 54 A6
Rycroft Cl LS13 .... 58 B1

Rycroft Ct 2 LS13 .... 58 B1
Rycroft Dr LS13 .... 58 B1
Rycroft Gdns LS13 .... 58 B1
Rycroft Gn 1 LS13 .... 58 B1
Rycroft Pl 3 LS13 .... 58 B1
Rycroft St BD18 .... 55 D5
Rycroft Towers LS13 .... 58 A1
Rydal Ave Baildon BD17 .... 37 E1
  Garforth LS25 .... 82 F6
  Shipley BD9 .... 55 C4
Rydal Cres Morley LS27 .... 98 D5
  Wakefield WF2 .... 141 E7
Rydal Dr Huddersfield HD5 .... 154 D6
  Morley LS27 .... 98 D5
  Wakefield WF2 .... 141 E7
Rydal Gr WF15 .... 117 A1
Rydal St Castleford WF10 .... 125 D8
  Keighley BD21 .... 35 A6
Rydale Ct WF5 .... 140 D4
Rydale Pl LS11 .... 210 C1
Rydall St LS11 .... 210 C1
Rydall Terr LS11 .... 210 C1
Ryder Cl WF8 .... 146 B8
Ryder Gdns LS8 .... 61 A7
Rydings Ave HD6 .... 115 A3
Rydings Cl 11 HD6 .... 115 A3
Rydings Dr HD6 .... 114 F3
Rydings Wlk HD6 .... 114 F3
Rye Close La HD7 .... 187 E4
Rye Croft HX2 .... 91 F6
Rye Field La HX4 .... 150 F6
Rye Field La W HX4 .... 150 F6
Rye Garth LS22 .... 13 D8
Rye La HX2 .... 91 C1
Rye Pl LS14 .... 61 F1
Rye St 9 BD21 .... 35 B4
Rye Way WF10 .... 125 B8
Ryebank HD7 .... 189 B4
Ryebread WF10 .... 103 E1
Ryecroft BD21 .... 35 E1
Ryecroft Ave WF4 .... 162 C2
Ryecroft Cl WF1 .... 121 C5
Ryecroft Cres HX2 .... 91 D1
Ryecroft Dr HD3 .... 135 B1
Ryecroft First Sch BD4 .... 75 F2
Ryecroft La Brighouse HD6 .... 136 C8
  Halifax HX2 .... 91 D1
  Holmfirth HD7 .... 189 C3
Ryecroft Middle Sch LS12 .... 77 E6
Ryecroft Rd
  Cullingworth BD21 .... 35 E1
  Glusburn BD20 .... 16 B7
  Harden BD16 .... 36 A1
Ryecroft St WF5 .... 140 C7
Ryecroft Terr HX2 .... 91 D1
Ryecroft Way BD20 .... 16 C6
Ryedale HD5 .... 137 B2
Ryedale Ave
  Knottingley WF11 .... 126 E2
  Leeds LS12 .... 78 B4
Ryedale Cl WF6 .... 123 A5
Ryedale Ct LS14 .... 61 F5
Ryedale Holt LS12 .... 209 F1
Ryedale Pk LS29 .... 8 D3
Ryedale Pl WF6 .... 123 A5
Ryedale Way Bradford BD15 .... 54 A2
  East Ardsley WF3 .... 119 F7
Ryefield Ave BD14 .... 73 B5
Ryefields HD7 .... 189 D4
Ryefields Ave HD3 .... 153 A7
Ryefields Rd HD7 .... 152 E4
Ryeland St BD20 .... 16 D7
Ryelands Gr BD9 .... 54 D4
Ryhill Ind Est WF4 .... 162 B1
Ryhill La WF4 .... 161 E1
Ryhill Prim Sch WF4 .... 162 B1
Rylands Ave BD16 .... 37 B3
Rylands Mdw 17 BD22 .... 51 E8
Rylstone Gdns BD3 .... 56 A1
Rylstone Gr WF1 .... 142 F8
Rylstone Rd BD17 .... 37 F2
Rylstone St BD21 .... 35 D8
Ryndlesdale 4 HD3 .... 134 F1
Ryshworth Ave BD16 .... 36 D6
Ryshworth Bridge BD16 .... 36 D6
Ryshworth Middle Sch
  BD16 .... 36 E7
Ryton Dale BD10 .... 56 E6

Sable Crest BD2 .... 55 F4
Sackup La S75 .... 178 A2
Sackville App LS7 .... 206 C3
Sackville Rd BD20 .... 5 D2
Sackville St Bradford BD1 .... 201 B3
  Dewsbury WF13 .... 138 E6
  10 Hebden Bridge HX7 .... 89 A4
  Leeds LS7 .... 206 C3
  Todmorden OL14 .... 108 C5
Sacred Heart RC Primary Sch
  LS29 .... 8 D4
Sacred Heart RC Primary Sch
  HX6 .... 112 A3
Saddler St 7 BD12 .... 94 C4
Saddler's La WF11 .... 105 C1
Saddlers Croft
  Castleford WF10 .... 125 B6
  Ilkley LS29 .... 8 A4
Saddleworth Rd Elland HX4 134 C7
  Marsden HX4, HX6 .... 150 E5
  Ripponden HX4, HX5 .... 133 C5
Sadler Cl LS16 .... 42 C4
Sadler Copse LS16 .... 42 C4
Sadler Way LS16 .... 42 C4

Sadlers Wlk LS22 .... 13 F6
Saffron Dr BD15 .... 73 B8
Sagar La OL14 .... 86 D3
Sagar Pl LS6 .... 205 D4
Sagar St WF10 .... 124 D8
Sage St BD5 .... 74 C4
Sahara Ct BD8 .... 55 D2
Saint St 1 BD7 .... 74 A4
St Abbs Cl BD6 .... 94 C7
St Abbs Dr BD6 .... 94 C7
St Abbs Fold BD6 .... 94 C7
St Abbs Gate BD6 .... 94 C7
St Abbs Wlk BD6 .... 94 C7
St Agnes Preparatory Sch
  LS6 .... 59 D6
St Aidan's CE (Aided)
  First Sch HD8 .... 175 A1
St Aidan's Rd BD17 .... 38 D2
St Aidan's Sg BD16 .... 36 E6
St Aidans Rd LS26 .... 102 E8
St Aiden's Wlk WF5 .... 141 A4
St Alban App LS9 .... 208 C1
St Alban Cres LS9 .... 208 C1
St Alban Gr LS9 .... 208 C1
St Alban Mount LS9 .... 208 C1
St Alban Rd LS9 .... 208 C1
St Alban's Ave Halifax HX3 .... 113 C3
  Huddersfield HD3 .... 135 A3
St Alban's Pl LS2 .... 206 C1
St Alban's Rd HX3 .... 113 C3
St Albans Croft HX3 .... 113 D4
St Andrew's Ave LS27 .... 97 F3
St Andrew's C of E
  First Sch BD12 .... 35 A7
St Andrew's C of E
  Infants Sch HD6 .... 115 A4
St Andrew's CE Junior
  & Infants Sch BD12 .... 95 B4
St Andrew's Cl Morley LS27 .... 97 E3
  Pudsey LS13 .... 57 C5
St Andrew's Cres BD12 .... 95 A4
St Andrew's Dr HD6 .... 115 A4
St Andrew's Gr LS27 .... 97 F3
St Andrew's Pl
  Bradford BD7 .... 74 C6
  Leeds LS13 .... 210 C4
St Andrew's RC Prim Sch
  LS17 .... 43 D1
St Andrew's Rd
  Castleford WF10 .... 104 D1
  Huddersfield HD1 .... 154 C7
St Andrew's St LS3 .... 210 C4
St Andrew's Terr BD20 .... 16 D7
St Andrew's Villas BD7 .... 74 C7
St Andrew's C of E
  Junior Sch HD6 .... 115 A3
St Andrews Cl Halifax HX2 .... 92 A5
  11 Yeadon LS19 .... 40 C7
St Andrews Croft LS17 .... 43 B4
St Andrews Dr
  Featherstone WF7 .... 124 D1
  Kirkheaton HD5 .... 155 C8
  Knottingley WF11 .... 126 C5
  Leeds LS17 .... 43 C4
  Mapplewell S75 .... 178 A1
St Andrews Rd LS19 .... 40 C8
St Andrews Wlk LS17 .... 43 C4
St Ann's Ave LS4 .... 205 D2
St Ann's Cl LS4 .... 59 C4
St Ann's Gdns LS4 .... 59 C3
St Ann's La LS12 .... 59 C3
St Ann's Mount LS4 .... 205 D3
St Ann's Rise LS4 .... 59 C3
St Ann's Sq Leeds LS9 .... 212 B4
  Leeds, Headingley LS4 .... 59 C3
St Ann's Tower Mews LS6 .... 59 C4
St Ann's Way LS4 .... 59 C3
St Anne's Ave HD3 .... 135 A3
St Anne's Cl WF12 .... 139 D4
St Anne's Dr LS4 .... 59 C4
St Anne's Gn LS4 .... 59 C4
St Anne's Pl HX4 .... 133 E4
St Anne's RC Cath LS2 .... 211 A4
St Anne's RC Sch BD21 .... 35 B8
St Anne's Rd Halifax HX3 .... 113 C2
  Leeds LS6 .... 59 C5
St Anne's St LS2 .... 211 E4
St Anne's St WF4 .... 162 B1
St Annes Villas WF8 .... 125 E2
St Anns Sq HX6 .... 112 C4
St Anthony's Dr LS11 .... 213 F2
St Anthony's RC Prim Sch
  BD14 .... 73 D5
St Anthony's Rd LS11 .... 213 F2
St Anthony's Rd LS11 .... 213 E2
St Augustine's CE Sch
  HX1 .... 202 C4
St Augustine's Terr
  Bradford BD3 .... 56 A1
  Halifax HX1 .... 202 C4
St Augustines RC
  Primary Sch LS8 .... 208 B3
St Austin's Catholic
  RC (A) Jun
  & Inf Sch WF1 .... 216 C3
St Barnabas Rd
  Cleckheaton WF15 .... 116 C5
  Leeds LS11 .... 211 E2
St Barnabas Sch BD9 .... 55 A4
St Bartholomew's C of E
  Primary Sch LS12 .... 209 F3

St Bartholomew's Cl LS12 .... 209 F3
St Bartholomews St WF2 .... 141 C4
St Bede's Grammar Sch
  BD9 .... 55 A3
St Benedict's RC Prim Sch
  LS25 .... 82 F7
St Bernard's Ave WF8 .... 146 B8
St Bevan's Rd HX3 .... 113 C3
St Blaise Ct BD5 .... 201 B1
St Blaise RC Middle Sch
  BD8 .... 75 B1
St Blaise Sq BD1 .... 201 B3
St Blaise Way BD1 .... 201 B3
St Boltophs Cl WF11 .... 127 A4
St Brendan's RC Sch BD10 .... 56 D4
St Catherine's Cres LS13 .... 58 D4
St Catherine's Dr LS13 .... 58 D4
St Catherine's Gn LS13 .... 58 D4
St Catherine's Hill LS13 .... 58 D4
St Catherine's St WF1 .... 142 F3
St Catherine's Villas WF1 .... 142 F3
St Catherine's Wlk LS8 .... 61 A6
St Chad's Ave
  Brighouse HD6 .... 114 E5
  Leeds LS6 .... 59 D6
St Chad's C of E
  Primary Sch LS6 .... 59 B7
St Chad's CE (Aided) Jun
  & Inf Sch HD6 .... 114 E5
St Chad's Dr LS6 .... 59 C6
St Chad's Gr LS6 .... 59 C6
St Chad's Rd Bradford BD8 .... 55 B1
  Leeds LS16 .... 59 D6
St Chad's Rise LS6 .... 59 C6
St Chad's View LS6 .... 59 C6
St Christopher's Ave LS26 .... 100 F5
St Christophers Dr LS29 .... 6 F8
St Clair Gn WF3 .... 141 D8
St Clair Rd LS21 .... 23 B7
St Clair St Otley LS21 .... 23 B8
  Wakefield WF1 .... 216 C2
St Clairs Terr LS21 .... 23 B8
St Clare's Ave BD2 .... 56 D2
St Clare's RC Prim Sch
  BD2 .... 56 D2
St Clements Ave LS26 .... 100 E5
St Clements Cl LS26 .... 100 D4
St Clements Rise LS26 .... 100 D5
St Columba's RC Prim Sch
  BD4 .... 75 D2
St Cuthbert
  & the First Martyrs
  RC Sch BD9 .... 55 A2
St Cuthbert's Ct WF7 .... 146 A1
St Cyprians Gdns LS9 .... 208 B2
St Davids Rd LS21 .... 10 E2
St Edmund's Hall Prep Sch
  LS8 .... 44 A1
St Edmunds Cl WF10 .... 125 C8
St Edward's RC
  Primary Sch LS23 .... 30 D7
St Edward's Terr LS23 .... 30 D5
St Edwards Cl WF11 .... 126 E7
St Elmo Gr 6 LS9 .... 80 A8
St Eloi Ave BD17 .... 38 C4
St Enoch's Rd BD6 .... 93 F6
St Francis Gdns HD2 .... 136 A5
St Francis of Assisi RC
  Primary Sch LS11 .... 214 B3
St Francis Pl LS11 .... 211 E2
St Francis' RC First Sch
  BD2 .... 56 A4
St George's Ave
  Huddersfield HD3 .... 135 A3
  Rothwell LS26 .... 100 C7
St George's Cres LS26 .... 100 C7
St George's Mews WF7 .... 160 A5
St George's Pl
  Bradford BD5 .... 201 B1
  Bradford, Bowling BD5 .... 75 B4
St George's Rd Halifax HX3 .... 92 A1
  Holmfirth HD7 .... 189 D4
  Leeds LS1 .... 206 B1
  Wakefield WF2 .... 141 D3
St George's Sq Elland HD3 .. 152 B8
  16 Hebden Bridge HX7 .... 89 A3
  16 Huddersfield HD1 .... 154 A6
St George's St
  16 Hebden Bridge HX7 .... 89 A3
  Huddersfield HD1 .... 154 A6
St Georges Cres HX3 .... 92 A1
St Georges Ct WF4 .... 162 D2
St Georges Wlk WF2 .... 160 C6
St Giles Ave HD8 .... 146 B8
St Giles Cl HD6 .... 114 E5
St Giles Garth LS16 .... 24 E3
St Giles Rd HX3 .... 114 E7
St Giles' View WF8 .... 146 D7
St Gregory's RC
  Primary Sch LS14 .... 62 D5
St Helen's Ave WF9 .... 181 C7
St Helen's Dr LS25 .... 83 F8
St Helen's Gate HD4 .... 155 A2
St Helen's Gr WF2 .... 142 F1
St Helen's La
  Huddersfield HD4 .... 155 A2
  Leeds LS16 .... 42 C3
St Helen's Pl 3 WF10 .... 124 E7
St Helen's Way LS29 .... 8 D4
St Helena Rd BD6 .... 93 F8
St Helens Ave LS16 .... 42 D3
St Helens C of E Jun
  N & Inf Sch WF9 .... 181 C6
St Helens Cl LS16 .... 42 C3
St Helens Croft LS16 .... 42 C3
St Helens Gdns LS16 .... 42 C3
St Helens Gr LS16 .... 42 D3
St Helens St LS10 .... 212 A1

St Helens Way LS16 .... 42 D3
St Helier Gr BD17 .... 38 C4
St Hilda's Ave LS9 .... 212 C2
St Hilda's Cres 14 LS9 .... 212 C2
St Hilda's Gr 15 LS9 .... 212 C2
St Hilda's Mount 14 LS9 .... 212 C2
St Hilda's Pl LS9 .... 212 C2
St Hilda's Rd LS9 .... 212 C2
St Hilda's Sch WF4 .... 141 A2
St Hilda's Terr BD3 .... 75 E8
St Hildas Cl S63 .... 194 E1
St Ians Croft LS29 .... 6 F8
St Ignatius RC Junior
  & Infants Sch WF5 .... 140 E3
St Ive's Gdns HX3 .... 113 C3
St Ive's Rd HX3 .... 113 C3
St Ives Cl WF8 .... 125 D3
St Ives Cres WF10 .... 125 C5
St Ives Gr Harden BD16 .... 36 C2
  Leeds LS12 .... 209 D4
St Ives Mount LS12 .... 209 D4
St Ives Pl BD16 .... 36 C2
St Ives Rd BD16 .... 36 C2
St James App LS14 .... 62 B4
St James Ave LS18 .... 41 D1
St James Bsns Pk BD1 .... 201 C2
St James C of E (C)
  First Sch WF4 .... 159 F6
St James C of E Sch LS22 .. 13 F6
St James Cl LS12 .... 77 F8
St James Cres LS28 .... 76 B7
St James Ct Brighouse HD6 .. 115 B3
  Halifax HX1 .... 203 E3
  Ryhill WF4 .... 162 C1
  Wakefield WF2 .... 142 B4
St James Dr LS18 .... 41 D1
St James Manston
  Prim Sch LS15 .... 62 D3
St James Pk WF2 .... 141 C4
St James Pl BD17 .... 38 F4
St James Rd Baildon BD17 ... 38 F4
  Halifax HX1 .... 203 E3
St James' Rd LS29 .... 8 A4
St James Sq HX3 .... 93 A3
St James St 1 Batley WF17 .. 118 C5
  Battley, Heckmondwike
  WF16 .... 117 D3
  Halifax HX1 .... 203 E3
St James Terr LS18 .... 41 D1
St James Way WF4 .... 159 F6
St James Wlk LS18 .... 41 D1
St James's Ct LS8 .... 207 E2
St James's Mews WF17 .... 77 D8
St James's Mkt BD1 .... 201 D2
St James's Pk WF1 .... 142 E6
St James's Rd HD1 .... 153 D7
St James's Sq BD5 .... 201 B1
St James's Sq LS12 .... 13 E5
St James's Univ Hospl
  LS9 .... 207 F2
St John Fisher RC
  High Sch WF13 .... 118 B1
St John Par WF13 .... 139 B7
St John St Brighouse HD6 .. 115 A1
  Dewsbury WF13 .... 139 B8
St John the Evangelist
  Inf & Jun Sch BD6 .... 73 E1
St John Wlk WF13 .... 139 B8
St John's Ave Batley WF17 .. 118 A6
  Huddersfield HD4 .... 154 A2
  Kirkheaton HD5 .... 137 C1
  Leeds LS28 .... 205 F2
  Ossett WF5 .... 141 A5
  10 Pudsey LS28 .... 57 D3
  Thorner LS14 .... 45 F5
  Wakefield WF1 .... 216 A4
St John's C of E First Sch
  BD4 .... 75 D1
St John's C of E
  Infants Sch WF13 .... 139 A8
St John's CE Jun
  & Inf Sch HX6 .... 132 C1
St John's CE Junior
  & Infants Sch WF1 .... 216 A4
St John's CE Primary Sch
  HD6 .... 115 C8
St John's Chase WF1 .... 216 A3
St John's Cl Aberford LS25 .. 47 E1
  Kirkheaton HD5 .... 137 C1
  Leeds LS6 .... 205 F2
  Ossett WF5 .... 141 A5
  Rippoden HX6 .... 132 C1
St John's Cres
  Bradford BD8 .... 73 E8
  Huddersfield HD4 .... 154 A8
  Leeds LS6 .... 205 F2
  Normanton WF6 .... 144 A7
  Ossett WF5 .... 141 A5
St John's Croft WF1 .... 216 A4
St John's Cross HX2 .... 91 F8
St John's Ct Keighley BD20 .. 18 A2
  Leeds LS27 .... 207 D4
  Lepton HD8 .... 155 F3
St John's La WF1 .... 216 A4
St John's Mews WF1 .... 216 A4
St John's N WF1 .... 216 A3

St John's Pk LS29 .... 21 F5
St John's Pl BD11 .... 96 A6
St John's Pl 7 BD19 .... 116 E7
St John's Pl HX1 .... 203 E2
St John's RC Jun & Inf Sch
  HX6 .... 123 C2
St John's Rd
  Boston Spa LS23 .... 30 D7
  Huddersfield HD1 .... 154 A8
  Ilkley LS29 .... 8 E4
  Keighley BD20 .... 18 A2
  Kirkheaton HD5 .... 137 C1
  Leeds LS3 .... 205 F1
  Yeadon LS19 .... 40 A6
St John's Residential Sch
  for the Deaf LS23 .... 30 D7
St John's Sq WF1 .... 216 A3
St John's St Cononley BD20 .. 4 A2
  Horbury WF4 .... 140 E1
  Rothwell LS26 .... 101 C5
  Silsden BD20 .... 5 E1
St John's Terr LS6 .... 205 F2
St John's View
  Batley WF17 .... 118 A6
  Boston Spa LS23 .... 30 C7
St John's Way LS19 .... 40 A6
St John's Wlk S71 .... 179 D4
St John's Way LS29 .... 6 F8
St Johns CE Jun & Inf Sch
  HD7 .... 152 D5
St Johns Cl
  Cleckheaton BD19 .... 116 E7
  Dewsbury WF13 .... 139 B8
St Johns Ct HD7 .... 188 F4
St Johns Ctr LS2 .... 211 F4
St Johns Mews WF1 .... 216 A4
St Johns Way BD22 .... 34 F6
St Joseph's Catholic
  Primary Sch LS22 .... 13 E6
St Joseph's Coll BD9 .... 55 C3
St Joseph's Ct LS19 .... 40 B2
St Joseph's Jun & Inf Sch
  BD21 .... 35 B5
St Joseph's Mount WF8 .. 146 B7
St Joseph's Primary Sch
  WF13 .... 118 A2
St Joseph's RC Infant Sch
  BD5 .... 74 D4
St Joseph's RC Jun
  & Inf Sch Brighouse HD6 .. 114 F5
  Todmorden OL14 .... 108 B6
St Joseph's RC Junior
  & Infants Sch WF8 .... 146 C8
St Joseph's RC Prim Sch
  BD16 .... 37 A3
St Joseph's RC
  Primary Sch HX3 .... 203 F4
St Joseph's RC Prim Sch
  Huddersfield HD1 .... 154 F6
  Pudsey LS28 .... 76 F8
St Josephs RC
  Jun & Inf Sch
  Castleford WF10 .... 124 E8
  South Elmsall WF9 .... 182 E3
St Josephs RC Junior Sch
  LS25 .... 23 A8
St Jude's Pl BD1 .... 201 A4
St Jude's St Bradford BD8 .... 74 D8
  Halifax HX1 .... 203 D1
St Julien's Mount S75 .... 193 E4
St Julien's Way S75 .... 193 E4
St Laurence's Cl BD2 .... 55 E5
St Lawrence Cl LS28 .... 76 D7
St Lawrence St LS7 .... 204 A2
St Lawrence Terr LS28 .... 76 E6
St Leonard's Ct 4 BD8 .... 54 F1
St Leonard's Farm Pk
  BD17 .... 39 C5
St Leonard's Gr BD8 .... 54 F1
St Leonard's Rd BD8 .... 54 F1
St Leonards Cl LS29 .... 6 F7
St Lucius's Cl HD4 .... 172 E6
St Luke's CE Primary Sch
  LS11 .... 214 B4
St Luke's Cl
  Boston Spa LS23 .... 30 D5
  Cleckheaton BD19 .... 116 B7
St Luke's Cres LS11 .... 214 A4
St Luke's Gn LS11 .... 214 A4
St Luke's Hospl BD5 .... 74 D4
St Luke's Rd Hospl LS12 .. 153 C3
St Luke's Rd LS11 .... 214 A4
St Luke's Terr BD19 .... 116 B7
St Luke's Terr LS28 .... 36 D8
St Luke's View 4 LS11 .... 214 A4
St Lukes C of E First Sch
  WF1 .... 216 C3
St Malachy's RC Sch
  .... 91 E3
St Margaret's Ave
  Bradford BD4 .... 75 D2
  Horsforth LS18 .... 41 B2
  Leeds LS8 .... 44 B2
  Mickletown LS26 .... 102 D3
St Margaret's Cl LS18 .... 41 B2
St Margaret's Ct WF9 .... 183 B6
St Margaret's Dr
  Horsforth LS18 .... 41 B2
  Leeds LS8 .... 61 A6
St Margaret's Gr LS8 .... 61 A6
St Margaret's Hospl LS26 .. 59 D6
St Margaret's Pl BD7 .... 74 C5
St Margaret's Rd
  Bradford BD7 .... 74 B6
  Horsforth LS18 .... 41 B2
  Mickletown LS26 .... 102 D3

St Margaret's Terr
Bradford BD7 .... 74 B5
Ilkley LS29 .... 8 B3
St Margaret's View LS8 ...... 61 A6
St Mark's Ave LS12 .... 206 A2
St Mark's Flats ⁷ LS2 ...... 206 A3
St Mark's Rd
Huddersfield HD3 .... 153 A6
Leeds LS6 .... 206 B3
St Mark's St Leeds LS2 .... 206 A3
Wakefield WF1 .... 216 C4
St Mark's Terr LS2 .... 94 C5
St Marks View HD3 .... 153 A6
St Martin's Ave LS7 .... 204 A1
St Martin's Cres LS7 .... 204 A1
St Martin's Dr LS7 .... 60 C6
St Martin's Gdns LS7 .... 204 A1
St Martin's Gr
Castleford WF10 .... 124 B6
Leeds LS7 .... 204 A1
St Martin's Rd LS7 .... 204 A1
St Martin's View
⁷ Brighouse HD6 .... 115 A3
Leeds LS7 .... 204 A1
St Martins Ave
Bradford BD7 .... 74 C7
Otley LS21 .... 10 F2
St Martins Cl WF7 .... 145 C4
St Mary St HX1 .... 203 D2
St Martins Ave Batley WF17 . 118 B3
Bradford BD12 .... 94 C2
Holmfirth HD7 .... 188 B4
Mirfield WF14 .... 138 C6
Swillington LS26 .... 82 A1
St Mary's C of E Junior
& Infants Sch HX4 .... 132 C7
St Mary's Cl Bradford BD12 .. 94 B2
East Ardsley WF3 .... 119 D7
✦ Garforth LS25 .... 82 F6
Ilkley LS29 .... 8 C4
Leeds LS12 .... 210 A2
Leeds, Potternewton LS7 .... 204 A1
South Elmsall WF9 .... 183 A2
St Mary's Cres
Bradford BD12 .... 94 B2
Holmfirth HD7 .... 188 F8
St Mary's Ct Kippax WF10 .. 103 B4
Leeds LS7 .... 204 A1
Meltham HD7 .... 188 B8
St Mary's Dr BD4 .... 94 C2
St Mary's Garth LS17 .... 43 D5
St Mary's Gdns ¹ BD12 ...... 94 C2
St Mary's Heights HX2 .... 91 D5
St Mary's Hospl LS12 .... 77 F8
St Mary's La
Kirkheaton HD5 .... 155 C7
Leeds LS9 .... 212 B4
St Mary's Mews HD7 .... 171 F5
St Mary's Mount BD12 .... 94 B2
St Mary's Park Ct ⁹ LS12 .. 77 F8
St Mary's Park Gn ⁸ LS12 .. 77 F8
St Mary's Pl
¹ Castleford WF10 .... 124 D8
Dewsbury WF12 .... 139 D6
St Mary's RC Jun
& Inf Schs WF17 .... 118 B6
St Mary's RC Prim Sch
BD1 .... 94 C2
St Mary's RC Primary Sch
Bacup OL13 .... 106 B2
Halifax HX1 .... 203 D2
St Mary's RC Sch
Guiseley LS29 .... 22 C3
Horsforth LS18 .... 41 C1
St Mary's Rd
Bradford, Manningham
BD8, BD9 .... 55 C2
Bradford, Swain Green BD4 .. 75 D5
Holmfirth HD7 .... 188 F8
Honley HD7 .... 171 F5
Keighley BD20 .... 18 C2
Leeds LS7 .... 204 A1
Normanton WF6 .... 122 F3
St Mary's Rise HD7 .... 188 F8
St Mary's Sq Bradford BD12 .. 94 C2
Honley HD7 .... 171 F5
Morley LS27 .... 98 A4
St Mary's St Boston Spa LS23 30 D8
Leeds LS9 .... 212 A4
St Mary's Way HD7 .... 188 F8
St Mary's Wlk
Mickelfield LS25 .... 83 F7
Mickelfield LS25 .... 84 A7
Mirfield WF14 .... 138 C6
St Marys Ave WF6 .... 122 F4
St Marys CE Fst Sch
BD19 .... 117 B8
St Marys Gate ⁵₂ HX5 .... 134 F7
St Marys Park App LS12 ...... 77 F8
St Marys Park Cres LS12 ..... 77 F8
St Matthew Rd WF13 .... 139 B8
St Matthew's C of E
Middle Sch LS7 .... 60 C7
St Matthew's CE First Sch
BD5 .... 74 E1
St Matthew's Dr HX3 .... 93 A3
St Matthew's RC Sch BD15 .. 73 D8
St Matthew's Rd BD5 .... 74 D1
St Matthew's St ⁴ LS11 .... 211 D1
St Matthews Cl BD15 .... 53 B4
St Matthews Gr BD15 .... 53 C4
St Matthias' Ct LS4 .... 205 D2
St Matthias' St LS4 .... 205 D2

St Matthias' Terr LS4 .... 205 D2
St Michael Ct LS13 .... 58 D3
St Michael's & All Angels
Sch HX3 .... 93 D6
St Michael's C of E Sch
LS6 .... 59 E5
St Michael's CE Prim Sch
WF2 .... 141 E5
St Michael's Cl
Castleford WF10 .... 124 D7
Dewsbury WF12 .... 139 E1
Emley HD8 .... 175 D7
St Michael's Cl ⁶ BD16 ...... 54 B6
St Michael's Cl WF2 .... 142 A5
St Michael's Coll LS3 .... 205 F1
St Michael's Cres LS6 .... 205 D6
St Michael's First Sch BD5 .. 74 B4
St Michael's Gdns HD8 ...... 175 D7
St Michael's Gr LS6 .... 205 D6
St Michael's House WF2 ...... 142 A5
St Michael's La LS6 .... 205 D4
St Michael's Mount WF2 .. 139 E1
St Michael's Rd
Bradford BD8 .... 74 C8
Leeds LS6 .... 205 D4
St Michael's Terr LS6 .... 59 D5
St Michael's Villas LS6 .... 205 D4
St Michael's Way LS29 .... 21 F8
St Michaels Ave ¹ WF8 ... 146 B8
St Michaels Gn WF6 .... 123 A1
St Michaels Way LS29 .... 6 F7
St Nicholas Catholic
Primary Sch LS9 .... 61 D3
St Nicholas Rd LS29 .... 8 A5
St Nicholas St WF10 .... 124 D7
St Oswald Ave WF8 .... 146 B8
St Oswald Rd WF2 .... 141 D5
St Oswald St ⁶ WF10 ...... 124 D8
St Oswald's CE First Sch
BD5 .... 74 C3
St Oswalds C of E
Junior Sch LS20 .... 39 E8
St Oswalds Garth LS20 .... 22 F1
St Oswalds Pl WF5 .... 140 E7
St Oswalds Terr LS20 .... 22 E1
St Patrick's First Sch BD8 .. 74 C8
St Patrick's RC Jun
& Inf Sch Batley WF17 ...... 96 E2
Huddersfield HD2 .... 153 E8
St Patrick's RC Junior
& Infants Sch LS28 ..... 134 D6
St Patricks RC
Primary Sch LS9 .... 80 A8
St Paul's Ave
Birkenshaw BD11 .... 96 B5
Bradford BD6 .... 94 B8
St Paul's C of E Jun
& Inf Sch WF2 .... 141 E8
St Paul's CE First Sch BD6 .. 94 B8
St Paul's Cl WF9 .... 183 D8
St Paul's Dr WF7 .... 141 D8
St Paul's Gr Bradford LS29 .. 94 B8
Ilkley LS29 .... 8 C4
St Paul's Pl LS1 .... 211 E4
St Paul's RC Primary Sch
LS17 .... 43 A4
St Paul's Rd
Birkenshaw BD11 .... 96 B5
Bradford BD6 .... 94 B8
Bradford, Manningham BD8 . 55 C2
Halifax HX1 .... 202 B1
Keighley BD21 .... 35 D6
Mirfield WF14 .... 138 A4
Shipley BD18 .... 55 A7
St Paul's St
Huddersfield HD1 .... 154 B5
Leeds LS1 .... 211 E4
¹ Morley LS27 .... 98 B8
St Paul's Terr WF14 .... 138 A4
St Paul's Wlk WF2 .... 141 D8
St Paulinus Cl WF13 .... 139 B8
St Paulinus' RC
Primary Sch WF13 .... 139 A7
St Pauls Rd HD5 .... 155 B8
St Pauls Rise LS29 .... 6 F8
St Peg Cl BD19 .... 116 E7
St Peg La BD19 .... 116 E7
St Peter & St Pauls RC
Primary Sch LS9 .... 212 A6
St Peter's Ave LS26 .... 100 F5
St Peter's Ave HX6 .... 111 F3
St Peter's C of E Inf Sch
LS27 .... 98 A4
St Peter's C of E Jun
& Inf Sch WF1 .... 121 F5
St Peter's CE Infants Sch
HX6 .... 111 E3
St Peter's CE Primary Sch
LS9 .... 212 B4
St Peter's Ct Batley WF17 .... 96 D1
¹ Mirfield WF14 .... 137 F5
St Peter's Cres
Lofthouse Gate WF3 .... 122 B6
Morley LS27 .... 98 A6
St Peter's Garth LS14 .... 45 A6
St Peter's Gate Dearne S63 194 C1
Todmorden OL14 .... 129 B8
St Peter's Gdns
Dewsbury WF12 .... 139 F7
Leeds LS13 .... 58 C3
St Peter's Gr WF4 .... 141 B1
St Peter's Mount LS13 .... 58 D2
St Peter's Par WF12 .... 139 F7
St Peter's Pl LS9 .... 212 A4
St Peter's RC Prim Sch
BD3 .... 75 B6
St Peter's Sq LS9 .... 212 A4

St Peter's Sq HX6 .... 111 E3
St Peter's St
² Huddersfield HD1 .... 154 B6
Leeds LS2 .... 212 A4
St Peter's Way LS29 .... 21 F4
St Peters Cres HX6 .... 155 B8
St Peters Ct
Addingham LS29 .... 6 F7
Horbury WF4 .... 141 A1
Leeds LS11 .... 214 C4
St Peters Gate WF5 .... 140 D7
St Philip's Ave LS10 .... 99 B5
St Philip's Cl
Burley in W LS29 .... 9 F1
Dewsbury WF13 .... 118 D1
St Philip's Dr LS29 .... 118 D1
St Philip's RC Prim Sch
LS10 .... 99 B5
St Philip's Way LS29 .... 21 F8
St Philips Ct LS10 .... 99 B5
St Philips Ct HD3 .... 135 B2
St Richards Rd LS21 .... 10 F2
St Stephen's CE First Sch
BD5 .... 74 B1
St Stephen's Ct Leeds LS9 . 212 C4
Steeton BD20 .... 17 C6
St Stephen's Rd
Bradford BD5 .... 74 E3
Huddersfield HD1 .... 153 F6
Leeds LS28 .... 212 C4
Pudsey LS28 .... 57 A7
Steeton BD20 .... 17 C5
St Stephen's Sch HX3 .... 113 A2
St Stephen's Terr BD5 .... 74 D3
St Stephens Ct HX3 .... 113 A2
St Swithins Dr WF3 .... 121 F2
St Swithins Gr WF3 .... 121 F2
St Theresa's RC Prim Sch
LS15 .... 62 C4
St Thomas à Beckett
Catholic Comp Sch
WF2 .... 142 E1
St Thomas C of E Jun Sch
WF7 .... 145 C5
St Thomas Rd WF7 .... 145 D5
St Thomas' Rd HD1 .... 153 F5
St Thomas Row LS2 .... 207 D1
St Thomas's Rd ¹ BD1 .... 74 D7
St Thomas's Terr WF8 .... 125 F3
St Vincent Rd LS28 .... 76 F6
St Vincent's Sch LS23 .... 30 D8
St Walburga's RC Prim Sch
BD18 .... 54 F7
St Walburga's RC Prim Sch
BD18 .... 55 A7
St Wilfred's St LS28 .... 57 B7
St Wilfrid's Ave LS8 .... 208 B4
St Wilfrid's Catholic
High Sch WF7 .... 124 C1
St Wilfrid's Cir LS8 .... 208 B3
St Wilfrid's Cl BD7 .... 73 F5
St Wilfrid's Cres
Bradford BD7 .... 73 F5
Leeds LS8 .... 208 B4
St Wilfrid's Dr LS8 .... 208 A4
St Wilfrid's Garth LS8 .... 208 B3
St Wilfrid's Gr LS8 .... 208 B4
St William's RC First Sch
BD8 .... 74 B8
St Winefride's RC Sch
HD3 .... 94 B8
St Winifred's Cl HX2 .... 91 D5
Sal Nook Cl BD12 .... 94 F2
Sal Royd Rd BD12 .... 94 E6
Salcombe Pl BD4 .... 75 E2
Salem Pl Garforth LS25 .... 82 E7
Leeds LS10 .... 211 F2
Salem St Bradford BD1 ...... 201 B4
Hebden Bridge HX7 .... 88 F3
Queensbury BD13 .... 72 E1
Salendine Nook High Sch
HD3 .... 152 F7
Salford OL14 .... 108 A4
Salford Way OL14 .... 108 A4
Salisbury Ave Baildon BD17 . 38 C3
Leeds LS12 .... 209 F4
Salisbury Cl
Dewsbury WF12 .... 139 F8
Normanton WF6 .... 123 B3
Salisbury Ct LS18 .... 41 D1
Salisbury Gr LS12 .... 209 F4
Salisbury Mews LS18 .... 41 D1
St Mary's ⁷ Halifax HX3 ..... 92 B1
Pudsey LS28 .... 57 A7
Salisbury Rd
³ Bradford BD12 .... 94 C6
Brighouse BD19 .... 115 F8
Keighley BD22 .... 35 A6
Leeds LS12 .... 209 F4
Shipley BD9 .... 55 D3
Salisbury St Pudsey LS26 ..... 57 A6
Sowerby Bridge HX6 .... 112 A3
Yeadon LS19 .... 40 B4
Salisbury Terr LS12 .... 209 F4
Salisbury View
Horsforth LS18 .... 41 D1
Leeds LS12 .... 209 F4
Salley St OL15 .... 129 C2
Salmon Cres LS18 .... 41 C1
Salt Drake HX4 .... 132 B8
Salt Grammar Sch BD17 ..... 37 F2
Salt Horn Cl BD12 .... 94 F5
Salt Pie Alley WF2 .... 216 A2
Saltaire ⁴ BD22 .... 51 F8
Saltaire First Sch BD18 .. 54 F8

Saltaire Rd Bingley BD16 ..... 37 D5
Shipley BD18 .... 55 A8
Saltaire Sta BD18 .... 37 F1
Saltburn Pl BD9 .... 54 F2
Saltburn St HX1 .... 202 B3
Salter Rake Gate OL14 ...... 129 B8
Salter Row ⁴ WF8 .... 146 D8
Salter St WF12 .... 118 B2
Salterhebble Hill HX3 .... 113 D3
Saltherbble Primary Sch
HX3 .... 113 D3
Salterlee Jun & Inf Sch
HX3 .... 92 F2
Saltersgate Ave WF11 .... 126 E4
Saltonstall La HX2 .... 90 D5
Salts Mill Rd BD17 .... 55 B8
Sampson St WF15 .... 117 B4
Samuel Dr WF3 .... 121 E5
Samuel St BD21 .... 35 C7
Sand Beds BD13 .... 72 F1
Sand Hill La LS17 .... 43 D3
Sand Hill Lawn LS17 .... 43 D3
Sand Moor Golf Course
LS17 .... 43 C6
Sand St Haworth BD22 .... 51 C6
Huddersfield HD1 .... 154 B5
Keighley BD21 .... 35 C8
Sandal & Agbrigg Sta
WF1 .... 142 E2
Sandal Ave WF2 .... 142 E1
Sandal Castle WF2 .... 142 D1
Sandal Cliff WF2 .... 142 E1
Sandal Endowed C of E
Jun Sch WF2 .... 160 E8
Sandal First Sch BD17 .... 38 C3
Sandal Hall Cl WF2 .... 142 F1
Sandal Hall Mews WF2 ..... 142 E1
Sandal Magna Jun
& Inf Sch WF1 .... 142 E2
Sandal Rise WF8 .... 165 A5
Sandale Wlk ⁸ BD6 .... 93 F7
Sandall Cl LS25 .... 83 B2
Sandall Magna HX3 .... 93 E7
Sandals Rd BD17 .... 38 C3
Sandbeck Ind Est LS22 .... 13 F7
Sandbeck La LS22 .... 14 B8
Sandbeck Way LS22 .... 13 F7
Sandbed Cl LS15 .... 62 D3
Sandbed La LS15 .... 62 D3
Sandbed Lawns ⁵ LS15 .... 62 D3
Sandbeds HD7 .... 171 F6
Sandbeds Cres HX2 .... 91 E1
Sandbeds Rd HX2 .... 91 E1
Sandbeds Terr WF1 .... 91 E1
Sandbeds Trad Est WF5 .... 140 E7
Sandene Ave HX4 .... 153 C2
Sandene Dr HX4 .... 153 C2
Sanderling Ct ⁷ BD8 .... 73 C7
Sanderling Garth ⁶ LS10 .. 99 D5
Sanderling Way LS10 .... 99 D5
Sanderson Ave
Bradford BD6 .... 74 C1
Normanton WF6 .... 123 A1
Sanderson La
Lofthouse Gate LS26 .... 122 B8
Rothwell LS26 .... 100 B5
Sanderson St WF1 .... 216 C2
Sandfield Ave LS6 .... 59 E6
Sandfield Garth LS6 .... 59 E6
Sandfield Rd Bacup OL13 .. 106 A1
Bradford BD10 .... 56 B6
Sandford Pl LS5 .... 59 A4
Sandford Primary Sch
LS13 .... 58 E3
Sandford Rd Bradford BD3 .. 75 C7
Leeds LS5 .... 59 B3
South Elmsall WF9 .... 183 A5
Sandgate ⁸ LS29 .... 22 C7
Sandgate Dr LS25 .... 83 C2
Sandgate La Kippax LS25 ..... 83 D3
Kippax LS25 .... 83 D3
Sandhall Ave HX2 .... 112 D7
Sandhall Cres HX2 .... 112 D7
Sandhall Dr HX2 .... 112 D7
Sandhill Cl WF8 .... 125 D4
Sandhill Cres LS17 .... 43 E4
Sandhill Ct LS17 .... 43 D3
Sandhill Dr LS17 .... 43 E4
Sandhill Gr
Grimethorpe S72 .... 181 A1
Leeds LS17 .... 43 E5
Sandhill Lawn WF8 .... 146 C7
Sandhill Mount
Bradford BD10 .... 56 B6
Leeds LS17 .... 43 E5
Sandhill Oval LS17 .... 43 E4
Sandhill Rise LS17 .... 125 D3
Sandholme Cres HX3 .... 114 D7
Sandholme Dr
Bradford BD10 .... 56 C6
Burley in W LS29 .... 22 A5
Ossett WF5 .... 140 D5
Sandholme Fold HX3 .... 114 D7
Sandhurst Ave LS8 .... 208 A3
Sandhurst Gr LS8 .... 208 A3
Sandhurst Mount LS8 .... 208 A3
Sandhurst Pl LS8 .... 208 A3
Sandhurst Rd LS8 .... 208 A3
Sandhurst St LS28 .... 57 A7
Sandhurst Terr LS8 .... 208 A3
Sandiford Cl LS15 .... 62 D3
Sandiford Terr LS15 .... 62 D3
Sandiway Bank WF12 .... 139 D3

Sandleas Way LS15 .... 62 F2
Sandlewood Cl LS11 .... 211 D1
Sandlewood Gn LS11 .... 211 E1
Sandmead Cl Bradford BD4 . 75 E3
Morley LS27 .... 98 A6
Sandmead Croft LS27 .... 98 A6
Sandmead Way ¹ LS27 ...... 98 A6
Sandmoor Ave LS17 .... 43 D6
Sandmoor Chase LS17 .... 43 D5
Sandmoor Cl Leeds LS17 ..... 43 D5
⁶ Thornton BD13 .... 72 E6
Sandmoor Dr LS17 .... 43 D5
Sandmoor Garth BD10 .... 39 B1
Sandmoor Gdns HX3 .... 93 B5
Sandmoor Gn LS17 .... 43 C6
Sandmoor La LS17 .... 43 D5
Sandmoor Mews LS17 .... 43 C6
Sandon Gr LS10 .... 215 E2
Sandon Mount LS10 .... 215 E2
Sandon Pl LS10 .... 215 E2
Sandown Ave Crofton WF4 . 143 F1
Halifax HX2 .... 91 E4
Sandown Rd HX2 .... 91 E4
Sandpiper App LS27 .... 98 C3
Sandpiper Mews ⁵ BD8 ..... 73 C7
Sandringham App LS17 .... 43 E3
Sandringham Ave
Knottingley WF11 .... 126 C4
⁴ Pudsey LS28 .... 76 E6
Sandringham Cl
Bradford BD14 .... 73 D5
Morley LS27 .... 98 C5
Pontefract WF8 .... 146 D5
Sandringham Cres LS17 .... 43 E3
Sandringham Ct
Bradford BD14 .... 73 D5
Huddersfield HD2 .... 136 E5
Sandringham Dr LS17 .... 43 D3
Sandringham Fold LS27 .... 98 C5
Sandringham Gdns LS17 ..... 43 D3
Sandringham Mount LS17 .. 43 E3
Sandringham Rd
Bradford BD14 .... 73 D5
Byram WF11 .... 126 D7
Wetherby LS22 .... 13 E6
Sandringham Way LS17 .... 43 D3
Sands House La HX3 .... 113 B1
Sands La Dewsbury WF12 .. 139 F2
Lepton HD5, HD8 .... 155 F6
Mirfield WF14 .... 138 D3
Sands Rd WF12 .... 139 E6
Sandsend Cl BD9 .... 54 D3
Sandside Cl BD5 .... 201 B4
Sandstone Cl HD7 .... 171 F3
Sandway LS15 .... 62 B2
Sandway Gdns LS15 .... 62 B2
Sandway Gr LS15 .... 62 B2
Sandwell St HD7 .... 151 F1
Sandwich Cres HD2 .... 135 F3
Sandy Bank Ave LS26 .... 100 F6
Sandy Banks BD16 .... 53 B8
Sandy Beck BD15 .... 54 A3
Sandy Dyke La HX6 .... 132 E8
Sandy Gate Harewood LS17 . 26 E7
Hebden Bridge HX7 .... 89 A4
Holmfirth HX7 .... 189 C4
Sandy Gr LS26 .... 35 A8
Sandy Gate La
Ackworth M T WF7 .... 146 C3
Wadsworth Moor HX7 .... 89 C4
Sandy Gr LS26 .... 100 F6
Sandy La Huddersfield HD4 . 171 A7
Netherton WF4 .... 157 F1
Sandy Lane First Sch
BD15 .... 54 A4
Sandy Lobby LS21 .... 24 C6
Sandy Way ⁸ LS19 .... 40 B7
Sandy Wlk Bramhope LS16 .. 24 F2
Wakefield WF1 .... 216 A3
Sandyacres LS26 .... 100 F6
Sandyacres Cres LS26 .... 100 F6
Sandybridge La S72 .... 180 B4
Sandyfield Terr WF17 .... 118 B6
Sandyfoot HX4 .... 133 B4
Sandygate La WF9 .... 181 C7
Sandygate Terr BD4 .... 75 E3
Sandylands Glusburn BD20 . 16 D7
Huddersfield HD4 .... 171 D6
Sandymoor BD15 .... 54 A4
Sandywood Ct LS18 .... 58 C7
Sandywood St BD21 .... 35 C8
Sangate Terr WF9 .... 75 A1
Sanquah Terr HX1 .... 123 C3
Santa Monica Cres BD10 ..... 56 A7
Santa Monica Gr BD10 .... 56 A7
Santa Monica Rd BD10 .... 56 A7
Santingley La WF4 .... 162 A6
Sawworth St ⁸ OL14 .... 108 C5
Sapgate La BD13 .... 72 E6
Saplin St BD8 .... 55 B1
Sapphire Ct WF17 .... 118 A6
Sarah St WF3 .... 120 D8
Sardinia St LS10 .... 212 A1
Saunders Cl HD3 .... 153 A7
Saunters Way WF6 .... 123 A4
Savile Ave Bradford BD10 .... 56 C6
Leeds LS7 .... 207 D4
Savile Bsns Ctr WF12 .... 139 C6
Savile Cl HD6 .... 115 D3
Savile Cres HX1 .... 203 D2
Savile Ct WF14 .... 138 A6

Savile Dr Halifax HX1 .... 203 D2
Horbury WF4 .... 141 A2
Leeds LS7 .... 207 D3
Savile Glen HX1 .... 203 D2
Savile Gn HX1 .... 203 E2
Savile Gr WF12 .... 139 C7
Savile House ⁊ HX5 .... 134 F7
Savile La HD6 .... 115 D3
Savile Lea HX1 .... 203 D2
Savile Mews WF12 .... 139 C5
Savile Mount LS7 .... 207 D3
Savile Par HX1 .... 203 D1
Savile Park Gdns HX1 .... 203 D1
Savile Park Jun & Inf Sch
HX1 .... 202 C1
Savile Park Rd
Cleckheaton BD19 .... 95 D3
Halifax HX1 .... 203 D1
Savile Park St HX1 .... 202 C1
Savile Park Terr ⁊ HX1 ... 202 C1
Savile Pit La WF12 .... 140 A8
Savile Pk Halifax HX3 .... 113 B4
Halifax, King Cross HX1 .... 202 C1
Savile Pl Leeds LS7 .... 207 D3
Mirfield WF14 .... 138 A7
Savile Prec WF10 .... 124 C8
Savile Rd Castleford WF10 .. 124 C8
Dewsbury WF12 .... 139 C6
Elland HX5 .... 134 F6
Halifax HX1 .... 203 D2
Hebden Bridge HX7 .... 88 E3
Huddersfield HD3 .... 153 C8
Leeds LS7 .... 207 D3
Micklefield LS26 .... 102 D3
Savile Royd HX1 .... 203 D1
Savile Sq WF14 .... 138 A5
Savile St Batley WF17 .... 118 D2
Huddersfield HD3 .... 153 A5
Saw Mill HX6 .... 132 E8
Saw Mill St LS11 .... 211 E2
Saw Yd WF1 .... 216 B2
Sawley Cl WF1 .... 142 E8
Sawley St BD21 .... 35 B6
Sawood La BD22 .... 70 F8
Sawrey Pl BD5 .... 201 A2
Sawyers Garth LS29 .... 7 A8
Saxon Ave WF9 .... 181 F2
Saxon Cl Emley HD8 .... 175 C6
Upton WF9 .... 183 C7
Saxon Ct LS17 .... 43 B3
Saxon Gate LS17 .... 43 B2
Saxon Gn LS17 .... 43 A2
Saxon Gr Leeds LS17 .... 43 A2
South Kirkby WF9 .... 182 A1
Saxon Mount Leeds LS17 ...... 43 B3
South Kirkby WF9 .... 181 F1
Saxon Rd LS17 .... 43 A2
Saxon St Bradford BD8 .... 74 C8
Halifax HX1 .... 202 B4
⁊ Todmorden OL14 .... 108 A1
Saxon Way WF10 .... 125 A8
Saxton Ave BD6 .... 73 F1
Saxton Ct LS25 .... 82 F8
Saxton House LS19 .... 40 B6
Saxton La LS9 .... 212 B3
Saxton Pl HD5 .... 155 A4
Saxton St WF15 .... 117 C5
Sayers Cl LS5 .... 59 B4
Sayle Ave BD4 .... 75 B1
Sayner La LS10 .... 212 B1
Sayner Rd LS10 .... 212 A2
Scaitcliffe View OL14 .... 107 F7
Scale Hill HD2 .... 136 A2
Scalebor Park Hospl LS29 .. 21 D8
Scaley St BD3 .... 75 D7
Scaly Gate Holmfirth HD7 .. 190 A2
Holmfirth HD7 .... 190 A5
Scammonden Rd HX4 .... 133 B3
Scape View HD7 .... 152 E4
Scapegoat Hill
Junior & Infant Sch HD7 152 B6
Scar Bottom La HX4 .... 133 F7
Scar Gr HD4 .... 153 F2
Scar Head Rd HX6 .... 112 B3
Scar Hill Cotts HX4 .... 133 E4
Scar Hole La HD7 .... 190 A3
Scar La HD3, HD7 .... 152 F4
Scar Top HD7 .... 152 E4
Scar Top Cotts BD22 .... 50 B7
Scar Top La HD4 .... 171 D6
Scar Top Rd BD22 .... 50 A7
Scarboro Mdws WF14 ...... 138 A5
Scarborough Gr BD18 .... 55 A7
Scarborough La WF3 .... 98 D1
Scarborough Rd Otley LS21 .. 22 F7
Shipley BD18 .... 55 A7
Scarborough St
Dewsbury WF12 .... 139 D6
East Ardsley WF3 .... 119 D8

Scarborough Terr WF12 ... 139 D6
Scarbro' Junc LS13 .... 58 D1
Scarbro Terr HX5 .... 134 F6
Scarcroft Ct LS14 .... 45 D8
Scarfold HD7 .... 189 A5
Scargill Cl LS9 .... 207 F1
Scargill Grange LS9 .... 212 C4
Scarhouse La HD7 .... 152 E4
Scarlet Hts BD13 .... 72 F1
Scarr Bottom HX2 .... 112 F4
Scarr End La Batley WF13 .. 117 F2
Dewsbury WF12 .... 139 F5
Scarr End View WF13 .... 117 F2
Scarr Green Cl HD7 .... 170 E2
Scarsdale La LS17 .... 28 E6
Scarsdale Ridge LS17 .... 28 E6
Scarth Ave LS9 .... 208 A2
Scarth Terr WF1 .... 122 B6
Scarwood Cl ⁊ BD16 .... 37 A4
Scatcherd Gr LS27 .... 97 F4
Scatcherd La LS27 .... 97 F4
Scatcherd Park Ave LS27 ..... 98 A5
Scawthorpe Cl WF8 .... 125 F1
Sceptone Gr S72 .... 180 C3
Schofield La HD5 .... 154 D6
Schofield St OL15 .... 129 D2
Scholars Wlk BD2 .... 56 B3
Scholebrook La BD4 .... 76 C4
Scholemoor Ave BD7 .... 73 E5
Scholemoor La BD7 .... 73 E5
Scholemoor Rd BD7 .... 73 F5
Scholes (Elmete)
Prim Sch LS15 .... 62 F6
Scholes Junior &
Infants Sch HD7 .... 189 D3
Scholes La Barwick in E LS15 . 62 E8
Brighouse BD19 .... 115 F7
Elland HX4 .... 113 A1
Haworth BD22 .... 33 F1
Scholes Moor Rd HD7 .... 189 C2
Scholes Rd
Castleford WF10 .... 104 D1
Holmfirth HD2, HD7, WF10 .. 189 E3
Huddersfield HD2 .... 136 A2
Scholes St BD5 .... 74 D2
Scholey Ave HD6 .... 136 A8
Scholey Head La BD16 .... 85 A8
Scholey Rd HD6 .... 136 A8
Scholfield St ⁊ OL14 .... 108 B6
School Ave WF13 .... 117 F1
School Cl Crofton WF4 .... 144 B4
Gildersome LS12 .... 77 D3
Halifax HX2 .... 91 F7
Ripponden HX6 .... 132 E4
School Cote Brow HX3 .... 92 B6
School Cote Terr HX3 .... 92 B6
School Cres
Dewsbury WF13 .... 117 F1
Halifax HX2 .... 91 F7
Wakefield WF2 .... 141 D4
School Croft
Brotherton WF11 .... 126 C8
Rothwell LS26 .... 100 E6
School Dr WF11 .... 126 C5
School Fold BD12 .... 94 B6
School Gn Bramhope LS16 .... 24 E2
Brighouse HD6 .... 136 A8
Thornton BD13 .... 72 A6
School Gr WF13 .... 117 F1
School Green Ave BD13 ...... 72 E6
School Hill
Crigglestone WF2 .... 160 B4
Huddersfield HD4 .... 171 A7
Kirkburton HD8 .... 173 F6
School La Aberford LS25 .... 64 E7
⁊ Bradford BD6 .... 74 B1
Castleford WF10 .... 124 F6
Collingham LS22 .... 29 B8
Denby Dale HD8 .... 192 A6
Dewsbury WF13 .... 117 F1
East Keswick LS17 .... 28 C5
Emley HD8 .... 175 D7
Halifax, Illingworth HX2 ..... 91 F7
Halifax, Southowram HX3 ... 114 A3
Harewood LS17 .... 44 C8
Holmfirth HD7 .... 189 B4
Horbury WF4 .... 141 A1
Huddersfield HD4 .... 171 F8
Huddersfield, Hill Side HD5 . 155 B7
Huddersfield, Paddock HD1 . 153 E5
Leeds, Chapel Allerton LS7 .. 60 C6
Leeds, Halton LS15 .... 81 A8
Leeds, Meanwood LS6 .... 59 E6
Leeds, Whitkirk Lane End
LS15 .... 81 E7
Liversedge WF15 .... 116 D2
Marsden HD7 .... 169 C6
Ryhill WF4 .... 162 B1
Slaithwaite HD7 .... 152 B6
Thorp Arch LS23 .... 14 F4
⁊ Todmorden OL14 .... 108 B5
Wakefield WF2 .... 120 E2
Walton WF2 .... 161 A7
School Land La HX7 .... 87 F6
School Pl ⁊ BD12 .... 94 C4
School Rd Keighley BD22 ...... 34 F7
Pontefract WF8 .... 146 F7
Slaithwaite HD7 .... 152 B6
Wakefield WF2 .... 141 D4
Wetherby LS22 .... 13 F6
School St ⁊ Batley WF17 ..... 96 F1
Bradford BD12 .... 94 C6
Bradford BD1 .... 201 B3
Bradford, Barley BD4 .... 95 B8
Bradford, Clayton BD14 .... 73 B4
Bradford, Dudley Hill BD4 ... 75 C3
Bradford, Oakenshaw BD12 .. 95 A4

School St continued
Castleford WF10 .... 124 C8
Castleford, Castleford Ings
WF10 .... 103 E1
Cleckheaton BD19 .... 116 B7
Cullingworth BD13 .... 52 D6
Dearne S63 .... 194 D1
Denholme BD13 .... 52 E1
Denholme BD13 .... 71 E8
Dewsbury WF13 .... 139 D8
Dewsbury, Chickenley WF12 140 B8
Dewsbury, Ravensthorpe
WF13 .... 138 C5
East Ardsley WF12 .... 119 D5
Elland HX4 .... 134 B7
Elland HX5 .... 134 F7
⁊ Hebden Bridge HX7 .... 89 A3
Holmfirth HD7 .... 189 A5
Honley HD7 .... 171 F5
Huddersfield HD5 .... 154 D5
Keighley BD20 .... 18 A2
Liversedge WF15 .... 116 F2
Liversedge, Norristhorpe
WF15 .... 117 B2
Mapplewell S75 .... 178 C1
Mapplewell, Darton S75 ..... 177 E1
Morley, Churwell LS27 .... 98 C8
Morley, City LS27 .... 98 B4
Ossett WF5 .... 119 C1
Pudsey LS28 .... 76 D6
Pudsey, Farsley LS28 .... 57 D3
Shipley BD16 .... 54 B7
Steeton BD20 .... 17 C5
Upton WF9 .... 183 D8
Wilsden BD15 .... 53 C5
School St W HD3 .... 153 B8
School Terr Fairburn WF11 .. 105 A4
Shipley HD8 .... 174 A3
School View LS6 .... 205 E3
School Wlk BD22 .... 34 F7
School Yard View ⁊ HX3 ..... 92 C1
Schoolgate LS15 .... 62 E7
Schreiber Bsns Pk WF1 .... 142 D4
Scissett First Sch HD8 ..... 175 D2
Scissett Middle Sch HD8 .. 175 D2
Sconce La BD16 .... 38 B7
Scopsley Gn WF12 .... 156 E8
Scopsley La WF12 .... 156 E8
Scorcher Hills La DN6 .... 184 E5
Score Croft HD8 .... 175 A2
Score Hill Northowram HX3 .. 93 A4
Shelf HX3 .... 93 A4
Scoresby St BD1 .... 201 C3
Scotch Park Trad Est
LS12 .... 210 A4
Scotchman Cl LS27 .... 97 F2
Scotchman La LS27 .... 97 E1
Scotchman Middle Sch
BD9 .... 55 A2
Scotchman Rd HD7 .... 171 E4
Scotgate Rd HD7 .... 171 E4
Scotland Cl LS18 .... 41 B4
Scotland La LS18 .... 41 B5
Scotland Mill La LS16 .... 42 F1
Scotland St WF17 .... 96 C2
Scotland Way LS18 .... 41 B4
Scotland Wood Rd LS17 ...... 42 F2
Scott Ave WF16 .... 117 D6
Scott Cl Sutton in C BD20 ... 16 D5
Swillington LS26 .... 82 A1
Scott Dr WF4 .... 162 A8
Scott Gn LS27 .... 97 B8
Scott Green Cres LS27 .... 97 C8
Scott Green Dr LS27 .... 97 C8
Scott Green Gr LS27 .... 97 C8
Scott Green Mount LS27 ..... 97 B8
Scott Green View LS27 .... 97 C8
Scott Hall Ave LS7 .... 206 C4
Scott Hall Cres LS7 .... 60 B6
Scott Hall Dr LS7 .... 60 C6
Scott Hall Gn LS7 .... 60 C5
Scott Hall Gr LS7 .... 60 C5
Scott Hall Pl LS7 .... 60 C5
Scott Hall Rd LS7, LS17 .... 60 B6
Scott Hall Row LS7 .... 207 D4
Scott Hall Sports Ctr LS7 ... 60 B6
Scott Hall Sq LS7 .... 60 C5
Scott Hall St LS7 .... 206 C4
Scott Hall Terr LS7 .... 60 C5
Scott Hall Way LS7 .... 60 C6
Scott Hall Wlk LS7 .... 206 C4
Scott Hill HD8 .... 175 F3
Scott House OL14 .... 116 E8
Scott La Cleckheaton BD19 .. 116 E8
Cleckheaton, Gomersal BD19 .. 96 B1
Keighley BD20 .... 18 B2
Morley LS27 .... 97 E3
Wetherby LS22 .... 13 E5
Scott La W BD20 .... 18 E2
Scott Mews LS22 .... 13 E5
Scott St ⁊ Bradford BD6 ..... 94 D8
Keighley BD21 .... 35 C7
Pudsey LS28 .... 76 F6
Todmorden OL14 .... 129 A8
Scott Vale HD2 .... 136 D3
Scott Wood La LS7 .... 206 C4
Scotts Hill CE LS14 .... 45 F5
Scotty Bank ⁊ HD6 .... 115 A2
Scotty Croft La HD6 .... 115 A1
Scout Bottom La HX7 .... 110 F8
Scout Cl HX7 .... 110 F8
Scout Hill Rd WF13 .... 139 A6
Scout Hill Terr ⁊ WF13 .... 139 A6
Scout Hill View ⁊ WF13 ... 139 A6
Scout Rd HX7 .... 110 E8
Scout Rd HX7 .... 151 B1
Scout Road Junior, Middle
& Infants Sch HX7 .... 110 F8

Scrapers La OL14 .... 108 B8
Sculptor Pl ⁊ HD6 .... 115 A3
Seacroft Arc ⁊ LS14 .... 62 B5
Seacroft Ave LS14 .... 62 B5
Seacroft Chase ⁊ LS14 .... 62 B5
Seacroft Cl LS14 .... 62 B5
Seacroft Cres LS14 .... 62 B5
Seacroft Gate ⁊ LS14 .... 62 B5
Seacroft Grange
County Primary Sch LS14 . 61 F3
Seacroft Hospl LS14 .... 62 A1
Seacroft Ind Est LS14 .... 62 B7
Seacroft Park Middle Sch
LS14 .... 62 B3
Seaforth Ave LS9 .... 208 A3
Seaforth Gr LS9 .... 208 A3
Seaforth Mount LS9 .... 208 A3
Seaforth Pl LS9 .... 208 A3
Seaforth Rd LS9 .... 208 A3
Seaforth Terr LS9 .... 208 A3
Seagrave Rd HD4 .... 153 C3
Seaton St BD3 .... 75 B7
Seckar La WF4 .... 178 B8
Secker St WF7 .... 142 B3
Second Ave Bardsey LS17 ..... 28 E5
Bradford BD3 .... 56 C1
Cleckheaton WF15 .... 116 B8
⁊ Halifax HX3 .... 113 B4
Horbury WF4 .... 140 F1
Huddersfield HD7 .... 152 D4
Huddersfield, Dalton HD5 .. 154 F7
⁊ Keighley BD21 .... 35 B6
Kirkheaton HD5 .... 137 C1
Leeds LS12 .... 210 B3
Lofthouse Gate WF1 .... 121 B2
Rothwell LS26 .... 100 F7
South Kirkby WF9 .... 181 F1
Upton WF9 .... 183 A8
Wetherby LS22 .... 13 F5
Sedan St LS9 .... 207 F2
Sedbergh Cl LS15 .... 80 D7
Sedbergh Dr LS29 .... 8 C3
Sedbergh Pk LS29 .... 8 B3
Sedbergh Rd HX3 .... 203 F1
Sedge Gr BD22 .... 51 C8
Sedgewick St ⁊ WF17 .... 96 E1
Sedgfield Terr ⁊ BD1 .... 74 D7
Sedgwick Cl BD8 .... 74 D8
Seed Hill Terr Halifax HX2 .. 91 C6
Steeton BD20 .... 17 C5
Seed St BD12 .... 94 C6
Sefton Ave Brighouse HD6 .. 114 F5
Leeds LS11 .... 214 A3
Sefton Cres HD6 .... 114 F5
Sefton Dr Brighouse HD6 .. 114 F5
Ilkley LS29 .... 8 B3
Sefton Gr BD2 .... 56 B3
Sefton La HD7 .... 170 D2
Sefton Pl BD21 .... 35 C8
Sefton Rise WF12 .... 139 D4
Sefton St Halifax HX1 .... 202 C4
Keighley BD21 .... 35 C8
Leeds LS11 .... 214 A3
Sefton Terr Halifax HX1 .... 202 C4
Leeds LS11 .... 214 A3
Selborne Gr Bradford BD9 ... 55 B2
Keighley BD21 .... 35 B5
Selborne Mount BD9 .... 55 C2
Selborne Terr
Bradford BD9 .... 55 B2
Shipley BD18 .... 55 B8
Selborne Villas BD9 .... 55 B3
Selbourne Ave WF12 .... 139 C5
Selbourne Dr WF12 .... 139 C5
Selbourne Rd WF12 .... 139 C5
Selbourne Villas BD14 .... 73 C3
Selby HX2 .... 91 D6
Selby Ave LS9 .... 80 E8
Selby Rd Garforth LS25 .... 83 C4
Ledsham LS25 .... 84 B3
Leds LS9 .... 212 C4
Leeds LS15, LS25, LS9 .... 81 C8
South Milford LS25 .... 84 B4
Swillington LS15 , LS25 .... 82 B6
Selby St WF1 .... 216 C3
Seldon St BD5 .... 74 B3
Selene Cl BD19 .... 96 C2
Sellars Fold ⁊ BD7 .... 74 A4
Sellerdale Ave BD12 .... 94 D2
Sellerdale Dr BD12 .... 94 D2
Sellerdale Way BD12 .... 94 D1
Selso Rd WF12 .... 118 F1
Seminary St LS2 .... 206 A1
Semon Ave BD2 .... 55 F5
Senior St Dewsbury WF13 .. 139 B7
Huddersfield HD5 .... 154 E5
Senior Way BD5 .... 201 B2
Sentry HD7 .... 171 F5
Sergeantson St ⁊ HD1 ...... 154 A6
Serpentine Rd BD19 .... 116 D7
Servia Dr LS7 .... 206 C3
Servia Gdns LS7 .... 206 C3
Servia Hill LS6, LS7 .... 206 B3
Servia Rd LS7 .... 206 B3
Service Rd LS9 .... 80 D3
Sessions House Yd WF8 .... 125 C1
Seven Hills Primary Sch
LS27 .... 98 B4
Sevenoaks Mead BD15 .... 54 B1
Seventh Ave
Cleckheaton WF15 .... 116 B5
Rothwell LS26 .... 101 A7
Severn Dr LS25 .... 83 B6

Severn Rd Bradford BD2 ...... 56 A3
Leeds LS10 .... 215 F3
Severn Way LS10 .... 215 F3
Sewage Works Rd LS9 .... 80 C3
Sewell Rd BD3 .... 75 B6
Sewerbridge La WF7 .... 145 A8
Seymour St Bradford BD3 .... 75 A6
Wakefield WF2 .... 142 C4
Seymour Wlk HD7 .... 170 E2
Shackleton St OL14 .... 86 C1
Shackleton Terr BD16 .... 36 A1
Shade Junior &
Infants Sch OL14 .... 108 A3
Shade St OL14 .... 108 A3
Shadwell La Leeds LS17 .... 43 C3
Thorner LS17 .... 44 B5
Shadwell Park Cl LS17 .... 44 C5
Shadwell Park Ct LS17 .... 44 C5
Shadwell Park Ct LS17 .... 44 C4
Shadwell Park Dr LS17 .... 44 C4
Shadwell Park Gdns LS17 ... 44 C5
Shadwell Park Gr LS17 .... 44 C4
Shadwell Primary Sch
LS17 .... 44 F4
Shadwell Wlk LS17 .... 43 E3
Shady La BD20 .... 4 A3
Shaftesbury Ave
Beal DN14 .... 127 F5
Bradford BD9 .... 54 D1
Brighouse HD6 .... 114 B7
Leeds LS8 .... 44 B2
Shipley BD18 .... 55 C7
Shaftesbury Ct BD9 .... 54 D1
Shaftsbury Rd LS8 .... 44 A2
Shafton Hall Dr S72 .... 180 B3
Shafton La LS11 .... 210 C1
Shafton Pl LS11 .... 210 C1
Shafton St LS11 .... 211 D1
Shafton Two Gates
Jun & Inf Sch S72 .... 180 C2
Shafton View LS11 .... 210 C1
Shakespeare App LS9 .... 207 F1
Shakespeare Ave
Leeds LS9 .... 207 F1
Normanton WF6 .... 144 A7
Todmorden OL14 .... 108 D6
Shakespeare Bldgs HD1 ... 153 D6
Shakespeare Cl
Guiseley LS20 .... 39 F8
Leeds LS9 .... 207 F1
Littleborough OL15 .... 129 C1
Shakespeare Cres WF10 .... 125 D5
Shakespeare Ct LS9 .... 207 F1
Shakespeare Gdns LS9 ...... 207 F1
Shakespeare Grange LS9 .. 207 F1
Shakespeare Lawn LS9 ..... 207 F1
Shakespeare Primary Sch
LS9 .... 207 F1
Shakespeare St LS20 .... 39 F8
Shakespeare St
Halifax HX1 .... 203 E3
Leeds LS9 .... 207 F1
Shakespeare Towers LS9 .. 207 F1
Shalimar St HX1 .... 202 B3
Shambles The
⁊ Huddersfield HD1 .... 154 B6
Wetherby LS22 .... 13 E5
Shann Ave BD21 .... 34 F8
Shann Cres BD21 .... 34 F8
Shann La BD20, BD21 .... 34 F1
Shann St BD2 .... 56 B4
Shann St BD2 .... 55 D4
Shannon Cl Brighouse HD6 . 135 E7
Ilkley LS29 .... 7 F3
Shannon Dr HD3 .... 134 D1
Shannon Rd
Brighouse HD6 .... 135 E7
Leeds LS9 .... 212 B4
Shannon St LS9 .... 212 B4
Shapla Cl BD22 .... 35 A6
Share Hill HD7 .... 152 C3
Sharehill HD7 .... 152 C4
Sharlston Junior &
Infant Sch WF4 .... 144 B4
Sharnaley Ct WF8 .... 147 A8
Sharneyford Primary Sch
OL13 .... 106 C5
Sharon Cotts WF5 .... 140 D7
Sharp Ave BD6 .... 94 C8
Sharp House Rd LS10 .... 99 F4
Sharp La
Huddersfield HD4, HD5 .... 154 F2
Middleton LS10, WF3 .... 99 F2
Sharp Lane Prim Sch
LS10 .... 99 E5
Sharp Royd HD5 .... 155 A4
Sharp St ⁊ Bradford BD6 .... 74 C1
Dewsbury WF13 .... 118 D1
Sharp's Row LS28 .... 76 E6
Sharpe St Batley WF16 ...... 117 D3
⁊ Bradford BD5 .... 201 B2
Shaw Ave WF6 .... 123 C2
Shaw Barn Croft LS22 .... 13 C5
Shaw Barn La LS22 .... 13 C5
Shaw Booth La HX2 .... 91 C6
Shaw Cl Elland HX4 .... 134 C4
Guiseley LS20 .... 39 F8
Normanton WF6 .... 123 C2
South Elmsall WF9 .... 183 A4
Shaw Cross Bsns Pk
WF12 .... 119 A2
Shaw Cross Infants Sch
WF12 .... 119 A3
Shaw Fields HD7 .... 169 C8
Shaw Fields La HD7 .... 169 C8
Shaw Gate HD7 .... 142 E1
Shaw Gate HD7 .... 169 F6
Shaw Hill HX1 .... 203 E1
Shaw Hill La HX3 .... 203 F1

Shaw La Cudworth S71 .... 179 E1
Elland HX5 .... 135 C8
Elland, Hollywell Green HX4 .. 134 A8
Guiseley LS20 .... 22 F1
Halifax HX4 .... 203 F1
Holmfirth HD7 .... 188 D4
Huddersfield HD7 .... 153 B4
Keighley BD21 .... 35 D3
Leeds LS6 .... 59 D6
Mapplewell S75 .... 178 C2
Marsden HD7 .... 169 A8
Oxenhope BD22 .... 51 B2
Rippenden HX6 .... 132 C2
Royston S71 .... 179 E1
Shelf HX3 .... 92 F6
Slaithwaite HD7 .... 152 C8
Sowerby Bridge HX6 .... 112 C1
Todmorden OL14 .... 86 C3
Shaw Lane Gdns LS20 .... 22 F1
Shaw Leys LS19 .... 40 A8
Shaw Lodge HX3 .... 203 F1
Shaw Rise HX4 .... 123 C2
Shaw Royd LS19 .... 40 A8
Shaw St ◳ Bradford BD12 .. 94 B6
Cleckheaton BD19 .... 116 B7
Elland HX4 .... 134 C4
Mirfield WF14 .... 138 A5
Shaw Wood Ave OL14 .... 109 A6
Shaw's Terr HD7 .... 168 F4
Shawfield Ave HD7 .... 188 D4
Shawmount HX2 .... 111 E8
Shaws La Barwick in E LS15 .. 63 C5
Sowerby Bridge HX6 .... 111 A2
Shay CI BD9 .... 54 E4
Shay Cres BD9 .... 54 E4
Shay Ct Bradford BD9 .... 54 E4
Crofton WF4 .... 143 E1
Shay Dr BD9 .... 54 E4
Shay Fold BD9 .... 54 E4
Shay Gap Rd BD22 .... 34 C7
Shay Gate LS13 .... 53 E4
Shay Gr BD9 .... 54 F4
Shay La Bradford BD9 .... 54 F4
Crofton WF4 .... 143 E1
Halifax HX2, HX3 .... 92 A4
Holme HD7 .... 187 E3
Walton WF2 .... 161 C7
Wilsden BD15 .... 53 D4
Shay Lane Prim Sch WF4 .. 143 E1
Shay St LS6 .... 206 B3
Shay Syke HX1 .... 203 F1
Shay The
(Halifax Town FC) HX1 .. 203 E1
Shayfield La WF3 .... 100 D3
Sheaf St LS10 .... 212 A2
Shearbridge Pl BD7 .... 74 C6
Shearbridge Rd BD7 .... 74 C6
Shearbridge Terr BD7 .... 74 C6
Sheardale HD7 .... 171 E4
Shearing Cross Gdns
◳ HD1 .... 154 B8
Shed St BD21 .... 35 C7
Sheep Hill La BD13 .... 73 B2
Sheepridge Gr HD2 .... 136 C3
Sheepridge Rd HD2 .... 136 C3
Sheepscar Gr LS7 .... 207 D1
Sheepscar Row LS7 .... 207 D2
Sheepscar St N LS7 .... 207 D3
Sheepscar St S LS7 .... 207 D1
Sheepscar Way LS7 .... 207 D3
Sheerien CI S71 .... 178 E1
Sheffield Rd HD7 .... 189 E3
Sheila Terr WF16 .... 117 C3
Sheldrake Ave BD8 .... 73 C7
Sheldrake Rd WF10 .... 124 D6
Shelf Hall La HX3 .... 93 C5
Shelf Junior & Infants Sch
HX3 .... 93 B5
Shelf Moor HX3 .... 93 C7
Shelf Moor Rd HX3 .... 93 C6
Shelf Rd HX7 .... 88 F3
Shelf La LS28 .... 57 B5
Shelldrake Dr LS10 .... 99 D5
Shelley Ave WF16 .... 117 E2
Shelley Cl LS26 .... 101 C3
Shelley Cres LS26 .... 101 C3
Shelley Ct WF4 .... 141 C2
Shelley Dr WF11 .... 126 B4
Shelley First Sch HD8 .... 174 E2
Shelley Gr BD8 .... 73 E8
Shelley High Sch HD8 .... 174 E2
Shelley La HD8 .... 174 A5
Shelley Sta HD8 .... 173 F1
Shelley Wlk WF3 .... 121 E6
Shelley Woodhouse La
Shepley HD8 .... 174 D1
Skelmanthorpe HD8 .... 174 D1
Shelwith Wlk LS14 .... 62 A2
Shepcote CI LS16 .... 41 F3
Shepcote Cres LS16 .... 41 F3
Shepherd St ◳ BD7 .... 74 B4
Shepherd's Gr LS7 .... 207 E4
Shepherd's La LS7, LS8 ...... 207 F4
Shepherd's PI LS8 .... 207 F4
Shepherds Gr HD2 .... 136 E3
Shepherds Thorn La
HD2 .... 136 C6
Shepley First Sch HD8 ...... 190 E8
Shepley Mount WF14 .... 138 B7
Shepley Rd HD4 .... 172 C7
Shepley St WF1 .... 142 E7
Shepley Sta HD8 .... 173 F1
Shepstye Rd WF4 .... 141 A1
Shepton Ho ◱ BD5 .... 201 B1
Sherborne Dr BD22 .... 34 E5

Sherborne Rd Bradford BD7 .. 74 D6
Bradford, Thackley BD10 ...... 39 B1
Sherbrooke Ave LS15 .... 207 F2
Sherburn App LS14 .... 62 C6
Sherburn CI
Adwick Le S DN6 .... 184 E2
Birkenshaw BD11 .... 96 B6
◳ Leeds LS14 .... 62 C6
Sherburn Ct ◳ LS14 .... 62 C6
Sherburn Gr BD11 .... 96 B6
Sherburn Pl LS14 .... 62 C6
Sherburn Rd
Brighouse HD6 .... 135 E8
Leeds LS14 .... 62 C6
Sherburn Rd N LS14 .... 62 C6
Sherburn Row ◳ LS14 .... 62 C6
Sherburn Sq ◳ LS14 .... 62 C6
Sherburn Wlk ◳ LS14 .... 62 C6
Sheridan Cl LS28 .... 76 F6
Sheridan Ct LS28 .... 76 F6
Sheridan St Bradford BD4 .. 75 B4
Lofthouse Gate WF1 .... 121 C5
Sheridan Way LS28 .... 76 F6
Sheriff La BD16 .... 37 D4
Sherwell Br BD15 .... 54 C1
Sherwell Rise BD15 .... 54 C1
Sherwood Ave
Cleckheaton BD19 .... 117 B8
Huddersfield HD2 .... 136 F5
Sherwood Cl Batley WF13 .. 117 F3
Bingley BD16 .... 37 C5
Cleckheaton BD19 .... 117 B8
Sherwood Dr
Adwick Le S DN6 .... 184 E2
Crigglestone WF2 .... 159 F5
Huddersfield HD4 .... 171 C7
Sherwood Gn WF3 .... 100 A3
Sherwood Gr Shipley BD18 .. 54 E8
Huddersfield HD4 .... 171 E4
Sherwood Pl BD2 .... 56 B2
Sherwood Rd HD6 .... 115 C2
Sherwood Way S72 .... 180 A1
Shetcliffe La BD4 .... 95 C8
Shetcliffe Rd BD4 .... 95 B8
Shetland Cl BD2 .... 55 C4
Shibden Dr WF17 .... 117 F6
Shibden Garth HX3 .... 114 A8
Shibden Grange Dr HX3 .... 92 F1
Shibden Hall HX3 .... 113 F8
Shibden Hall Croft HX3 ..... 114 A8
Shibden Hall Rd
Brighouse HX3 .... 114 A8
Halifax HX3 .... 113 F8
Shibden Head First Sch
BD13 .... 92 C7
Shibden Head La BD13 ...... 92 C7
Shibden Head Mews BD13 .. 92 C7
Shibden View BD13 .... 92 D7
Shield CI LS15 .... 62 E3
Shield Hall La HX6 .... 111 C4
Shill Bank Ave WF14 .... 138 D6
Shill Bank La WF14 .... 138 C6
Shillbank View WF14 .... 138 C6
Shilling St WF1 .... 216 C4
Shillinghill La WF8 .... 126 B1
Shinwell Dr WF9 .... 183 D8
Ship St HD6 .... 115 B2
Ship Yd WF1 .... 216 C1
Shipley Airedale Rd
BD1, BD3 .... 201 C3
Shipley CE First Sch BD18 .. 55 B6
Shipley Coll of
Further Education BD18 .. 55 B6
Shipley College Mill Annexe
BD18 .... 37 F1
Shipley Fields Rd BD18 ..... 55 C5
Shipley Glen Cable Rly
BD17 .... 37 F2
Shipley Golf Course BD16 .. 36 E1
Shipley Sta ◳ LS28 .... 55 C7
Shipley Wycliffe CE
Middle Sch BD18 .... 55 A8
Shipton Mews LS27 .... 98 B3
Shire Cl BD6 .... 93 F7
Shire Oak Rd LS6 .... 59 B5
Shire Oak St LS6 .... 59 D5
Shires Gr WF3 .... 121 F5
Shires Hill HD1 .... 153 E5
Shirley Ave Batley WF17 .... 96 E2
Bradford BD12 .... 94 C1
Cleckheaton BD19 .... 117 B8
Shirley Cl LS21 .... 23 B7
Shirley Cres BD12 .... 94 C1
Shirley Dr LS13 .... 58 C4
Shirley Gr Brighouse HX3 .. 115 A7
Cleckheaton BD19 .... 117 B8
Shirley Manor Manor Pk
BD12 .... 94 C1
Shirley Mount BD19 .... 117 B8
Shirley Par BD19 .... 117 A8
Shirley Pl Bradford BD12 .... 94 C1
Cleckheaton BD19 .... 117 B8
Shirley Rd
Bradford, Shearbridge BD7 .. 74 B6
Bradford, Tong Street BD4 .. 75 D1
Cleckheaton BD19 .... 117 B8
Shirley Sq BD19 .... 117 B8
Shirley St Denholme BD13 .. 52 E1
◳ Haworth BD22 .... 51 B7
Shipley BD18 .... 54 F8
Shirley Terr BD19 .... 117 B8
Shirley Wlk BD19 .... 117 B8
Shoe Market ◳ WF8 .... 146 D8
Shoebridge Ave BD20 .... 16 F6
Shoebroad La OL14 .... 108 B4
Sholebroke Ave LS7 .... 207 D4
Sholebroke Ct LS7 .... 207 D4

Sholebroke Mount LS7 ...... 206 C4
Sholebroke Pl LS7 .... 207 D4
Sholebroke St LS7 .... 207 D4
Sholebroke Terr LS7 .... 204 A1
Sholebroke View LS7 .... 207 D4
Shoolaboards La ◳ WF8 .. 146 F8
Shop La Kirkheaton HD5 .... 155 C8
Lofthouse Gate WF3 .... 121 B8
Shore End La HX2 .... 90 A7
Shore Gn OL14 .... 86 C2
Shore New Rd OL14 .... 86 B1
Shoreham Rd LS12 .... 209 F2
Short Cl BD12 .... 94 B5
Short Ct LS27 .... 60 C7
Short St Dewsbury WF12 .... 140 A7
Featherstone WF7 .... 145 C5
◳ Todmorden OL14 .... 108 B5
Shortway Pudsey LS28 ...... 57 A1
Thornton BD13 .... 73 A6
Shortwood La DN5 .... 194 B4
Shroggs Rd LS12 .... 202 C1
Shroggs St HX1 .... 202 C4
Shroggs Vue Terr HX1 .... 202 C4
Shutt The WF4 .... 159 B8
Shuttleworth La BD8 .... 73 E8
Shuttocks CI LS25 .... 83 A3
Shuttocks Fold LS25 .... 83 B3
Shutts La HX3 .... 93 A2
Sickle St BD19 .... 116 E8
Sicklehome Ct HD2 .... 136 E5
Sicklinghall County
Primary Sch LS22 .... 12 B5
Sicklinghall Rd LS22 .... 13 B5
Siddal Gr HX3 .... 113 D4
Siddal La HX3 .... 113 E3
Siddal New Rd HX3 .... 203 F1
Siddal Prim Sch HX3 .... 113 E3
Siddal St HX3 .... 113 E3
Siddal Top La HX3 .... 113 E3
Siddall St LS11 .... 211 E2
Siddal View HX3 .... 113 E4
Siddon Dr HD5 .... 155 A3
Side Copse LS21 .... 23 B8
Side La HD8 .... 152 F6
Sidings CI BD2 .... 55 D3
Sidings The Guiseley LS20 .. 22 D1
Shipley BD18 .... 55 C8
Sidney St LS2 .... 211 F4
Siegen CI LS27 .... 98 A4
Sigget La OL14 .... 107 F6
Sigott St HD3 .... 152 F6
Sike Cl S75 .... 177 D1
Sike La Holmfirth HD7 .... 189 D5
Walton WF2 .... 161 B5
Sikes CI HX5 .... 154 F4
Silcoates Ave WF2 .... 120 E1
Silcoates Ct WF2 .... 141 E8
Silcoates Dr WF2 .... 120 E1
Silcoates La WF2 .... 120 E1
Silcoates Sch WF2 .... 120 E1
Silcoates St WF2 .... 142 A7
Silk Mill Ave LS16 .... 41 E3
Silk Mill Bank LS16 .... 41 E3
Silk Mill Cl LS16 .... 41 D3
Silk Mill Dr Keighley BD20 .. 19 E1
Leeds LS16 .... 41 D2
Silk Mill Gdns LS16 .... 41 D2
Silk Mill Gn LS16 .... 41 E2
Silk Mill Mews LS16 .... 41 F2
Silk Mill Rd LS16 .... 41 D2
Silk Mill Way LS16 .... 41 D2
Silk St BD8 .... 55 A2
Silkstone Cres WF2 .... 160 C6
Silkstone Crest WF4 .... 122 F4
Silkstone Ct ◳ LS15 .... 62 C1
Silkstone La S75 .... 193 F3
Silkstone Rd BD3 .... 75 B8
Silkstone Way LS15 .... 62 C1
Silsbridge St ◱ BD1 .... 74 D7
Silsden Golf Course BD20 .. 18 A8
Silsden Rd Addingham LS29 .. 6 C7
Keighley BD20 .... 18 E4
Low Bradley BD20 .... 4 D5
Silson La BD17 .... 38 E4
Silver Birch Ave BD12 ...... 94 C1
Silver Birch Cl BD12 .... 94 D2
Silver Birch Dr BD12 .... 94 C2
Silver Birch Gr BD12 .... 94 D2
Silver Court Ind Est HD5 .. 154 C5
Silver La LS19 .... 40 B7
Silver Mill Hill LS21 .... 23 B6
Silver Royd Ave LS12 .... 77 F6
Silver Royd Cl LS12 .... 77 F6
Silver Royd Dr LS12 .... 77 F6
Silver Royd Garth LS12 .... 77 F6
Silver Royd Gr LS12 .... 77 F6
Silver Royd Hill LS12 .... 77 F6
Silver Royd Pl LS12 .... 77 F6
Silver Royd Rd LS12 .... 77 F6
Silver Royd St LS12 .... 77 F6
Silver Royd Terr LS12 ...... 77 F6
Silver St Bradford BD8 ...... 55 B1
Fairburn WF11 .... 105 A4
Halifax HX1 .... 203 E3
Huddersfield HD5 .... 154 D6
Leeds LS11 .... 211 D2
Lofthouse Gate WF1 .... 121 B3
Todmorden OL14 .... 129 A7
Wakefield WF1 .... 216 B2
Silver St ◳ HD5 .... 154 C5
Silverdale Ave Guiseley LS20 .. 39 E1
Keighley BD20 .... 18 E1
Leeds LS17 .... 43 B4
Silverdale Cl LS20 .... 39 E2
Silverdale Cres LS20 .... 39 E8

Silverdale Dr LS20 .... 39 E7
Silverdale Gn LS20 .... 39 D8
Silverdale Grange LS20 .... 39 E7
Silverdale Mount LS20 ...... 39 E7
Silverdale Rd Bradford BD5 .. 74 E2
Guiseley LS20 .... 39 D8
Silverdale Terr HX4 .... 134 A6
Silverhill Ave BD3 .... 56 D1
Silverhill Dr BD3 .... 56 D1
Silverhill Rd BD3 .... 56 C1
Silverwood Ave HX2 .... 91 C1
Silverwood Wlk HX2 .... 91 C1
Silwood Dr BD2 .... 56 C3
Sim Royd La HD8 .... 192 D4
Simeon St OL14 .... 129 A8
Simes St BD1 .... 201 A3
Simm Carr La HX3 .... 92 D4
Simmonds La HX3 .... 203 F1
Simmons Ct LS9 .... 212 C2
Simmons Way LS8 .... 208 B4
Simms Dene BD15 .... 54 A4
Simon CI BD4 .... 75 F2
Simon Green Rd HD7 .... 152 B3
Simpson Gr Bradford BD10 .. 39 C1
Leeds LS12 .... 210 A3
Simpson Rd
Hebden Bridge HX7 .... 110 D8
South Elmsall WF9 .... 183 B4
Simpson St
East Ardsley WF3 .... 120 E8
◳ Halifax HX3 .... 92 B2
Keighley BD21 .... 35 A7
Simpson's Lane Junior &
Infants Sch WF11 .... 126 D3
Simpsons La WF11 .... 126 D3
Sinclair Garth WF2 .... 160 E8
Sinclair Rd BD2 .... 55 F5
Sinden Mews BD10 .... 39 B2
Singleton St BD1 .... 201 A3
Sion Hill HX3 .... 113 E3
Sir Francis Crossley's
Almhouses HX1 .... 202 C4
Sir George Martin Dr
LS16 .... 42 D4
Sir Isaac Holden Pl BD7 .. 74 C7
Sir Karl Cohen Sq LS12 ... 209 E3
Sir Wilfred Pl BD10 .... 56 B8
Sisley La OL14 .... 109 A4
Sissons Ave LS10 .... 99 B4
Sissons Cres LS10 .... 99 B3
Sissons Dr LS10 .... 99 B4
Sissons Gn LS10 .... 99 B4
Sissons Gr LS10 .... 99 B4
Sissons La LS10 .... 99 B4
Sissons Mount LS10 .... 99 A3
Sissons Pl LS10 .... 99 B4
Sissons Rd LS10 .... 99 A3
Sissons Row LS10 .... 99 B4
Sissons St LS10 .... 99 B4
Sissons Terr LS10 .... 99 A4
Sissons View LS10 .... 99 B3
Sitka Cl S71 .... 179 B2
Siward St WF9 .... 163 A4
Six Heights HX6 .... 132 E3
Sixrood La DN6 .... 184 F5
Sixth Ave Bradford BD3 .... 56 C1
Cleckheaton WF15 .... 116 B5
Rothwell LS26 .... 101 A6
Sizers Ct LS19 .... 40 A5
Skelbrooke Dr WF8 .... 146 D5
Skelda Rise LS29 .... 8 A3
Skellow Rd DN6 .... 184 F1
Skelmanthorpe Bsns Pk
HD8 .... 175 B2
Skelmanthorpe First Sch
HD8 .... 175 B2
Skelton Ave Leeds LS9 ..... 80 B8
Mapplewell S75 .... 178 B1
Skelton Cres
Huddersfield HD4 .... 153 B3
Leeds LS9 .... 80 B8
Skelton Grange Rd LS10 .. 80 B2
Skelton Mount LS9 .... 80 B8
Skelton Pl LS9 .... 80 B8
Skelton Rd LS9 .... 80 B8
Skelton St LS9 .... 80 B8
Skelton Terr LS9 .... 80 B8
Skelton Wlk BD10 .... 56 D7
Skeltons La LS14 .... 45 C1
Skelwith App LS14 .... 62 A2
Skinner La Bradford BD8 .. 55 C2
Leeds LS7 .... 207 D1
Pontefract WF8 .... 125 D2
Skinner St LS1 .... 211 D4
Skippon Terr LS14 .... 45 B8
Skipton Ave HD2 .... 136 B2
Skipton Rd Addingham LS29 .. 2 D1
Farnhill BD20 .... 16 E6
Glusburn BD20 .... 16 E6
Ilkley LS29 .... 7 F6
Keighley BD20 .... 18 E2
Low Bradley BD20 .... 4 B6
Silsden BD20 .... 5 D1
Steeton BD20 .... 17 B5
Skipton Rise LS25 .... 83 B7
Skipton St HD7 .... 118 C2
Skircoat Gn HX3 .... 113 C2
Skircoat Green Rd HX3 .... 113 A3
Skircoat Moor Cl HX3 ...... 113 A4
Skircoat Moor Rd HX3 ..... 113 A4
Skircoat Rd HX1 .... 203 E1
Skirrow St BD16 .... 36 F5
Skye Rd BD9 .... 54 C4
Slack HD3 .... 152 A7
Slack Bottom HX7 .... 88 E6
Slack Bottom Rd BD6 ...... 94 A8
Slack House La HX7 .... 89 B7

Slack La Crofton WF4 .... 144 A1
Elland HD3 .... 152 A8
Halifax HX2 .... 90 B4
Holmfirth HD7 .... 189 B4
Oakworth BD22 .... 34 B3
Rippenden HX6 .... 131 F5
Rippenden, Barkisland HX4 .. 133 A3
South Hiendley S72 .... 180 B5
Wakefield WF2 .... 160 C5
Slack Top HD7 .... 88 D6
Slack Top La HD7 .... 190 C1
Slacks La Marsden HD7 .... 169 A8
Slaithwaite HD7 .... 169 E5
Slaidburn Dr BD13 .... 92 C8
Slaithwaite CI LS28 .... 30 D7
Slade House BD2 .... 56 D2
Slade La Brighouse HD6 .. 135 F6
Keighley BD20 .... 18 E2
Slade Wlk WF17 .... 96 F1
Sladen Bridge BD22 .... 50 F7
Sladen St HD3 .... 152 D6
Slades St ◳ BD21 .... 35 A1
Slades La HD7 .... 170 E4
Slades Rd HD7 .... 152 B4
Slaid Hill Ct LS17 .... 44 B5
Slaithwaite CE controlled
Junior & Infants Sch
HD7 .... 169 E8
Slaithwaite Nields
Junior & Infants Sch
HD7 .... 169 F8
Slaithwaite Ave LS12 .... 139 C4
Slaithwaite C of E Sch
HD7 .... 151 F1
Slaithwaite CI WF12 .... 139 C4
Slaithwaite Gate HD7 ...... 152 A5
Slaithwaite Rd
Dewsbury WF12 .... 139 D4
Meltham HD7 .... 170 B3
Slaithwaite Sta HD7 .... 151 F1
Slant Gate
Huddersfield HD7 .... 152 E2
Kirkburton HD8 .... 173 E7
Slant La OL14 .... 108 D6
Slate Quarry La BD16 ...... 37 B4
Slater Ave HX7 .... 89 A4
Slater Ing La HX7 .... 88 C5
Slaters Rd LS28 .... 57 E1
Slates La LS29 .... 8 B7
Slaymaker La BD22 .... 34 C3
Slead Ave HD6 .... 114 F4
Slead Cres HD6 .... 114 F4
Slead Gr HD6 .... 114 F4
Slead Royd HD6 .... 114 F4
Slead View HD6 .... 114 F4
Sledbrook Cres S36 .... 200 C6
Sledgate La HD7 .... 169 E5
Sledge Gate HD3 .... 151 A4
Sledmere Croft LS14 .... 62 C6
Sledmere Garth LS14 ...... 62 C6
Sledmere Gn ◳ LS14 ...... 62 C6
Sledmere La LS14 .... 62 C6
Sledmere Pl LS14 .... 62 C6
Sledmere Sq ◳ LS14 .... 62 C6
Sleep Hill La Hampole DN6 .. 184 B6
South Elmsall DN6 .... 183 F7
Sleights La LS17 .... 27 B6
Sleningford Gr BD18 .... 54 E8
Sleningford Rd
Bingley BD16 .... 36 E5
Shipley BD18 .... 54 E8
Sleningford Rise BD16 .... 36 F5
Sleningford Terr BD16 ..... 36 F3
Slicer's Yd BD16 .... 36 F3
Slipper La WF14 .... 137 E7
Slippery Ford La BD22 .... 33 C6
Slippy La HX2 .... 91 C5
Sloan Sq BD8 .... 74 B8
Slutwell La WF8 .... 146 D8
Smalewell CI LS28 .... 76 D6
Smalewell Dr LS28 .... 76 C6
Smalewell Gdns LS28 ...... 76 C6
Smalewell Gn LS28 .... 76 C6
Smalewell Rd LS28 .... 76 C6
Small La Cawthorne S75 .. 193 K1
Huddersfield HD7 .... 152 D4
Small Lees Rd HX6 .... 132 D3
Small Page Fold ◳ BD13 .. 72 E1
Small Shaw La HX7 .... 69 A1
Smallpage Yd WF1 .... 216 B2
Smallwood Gdns WF12 ... 119 A3
Smallwood Rd
Batley WF12 .... 119 A2
Batley WF12 .... 119 A3
Smawell La WF9 .... 183 D7
Smawthorne Ave WF10 ... 124 D7
Smawthorne Gr WF10 ..... 124 D7
Smawthorne Infants Sch
WF10 .... 124 D6
Smawthorne La WF10 ..... 124 D7
Smeatley's La WF8 .... 166 F7
Smeaton App LS15 .... 62 E2
Smeaton Dr LS26 .... 82 A2
Smeaton Ind Pk WF8 .... 165 F7
Smeaton Rd WF9 .... 183 E8
Smeddles La BD5 .... 74 D3
Smiddy Hill LS23 .... 15 A4
Smirthwaite St WF1 .... 216 B4
Smirthwaite View WF6 .... 123 A1
Smith Ave BD6 .... 94 C8
Smith Cres HD6 .... 135 E8
Smith House Ave HD6 ..... 115 A6
Smith House Cres HD6 .... 115 A6
Smith House Gr HD6 .... 115 A6
Smith House La HD6 .... 115 A5
Smith La BD9 .... 54 F2

Smith Rd Bradford BD7 ...... 74 B3
Dewsbury WF13 ...... 117 F1
Smith St Bradford BD7 ...... 74 D7
Bradford, Bierley BD4 ...... 95 B8
Castleford, Castleford Ings
WF10 ...... 103 F1
Castleford, New Fryston
WF10 ...... 104 C2
Keighley BD21 ...... 35 A8
Liversedge WF15 ...... 117 B3
Shipley BD16 ...... 54 B6
Smith Wlk WF9 ...... 183 A4
Smith's Terr WF3 ...... 92 A3
Smitherd's St BD21 ...... 35 C6
Smithfield Ave HX3 ...... 114 C8
Smithies La Batley WF17 ...... 96 E1
Liversedge FW16 ...... 117 D2
Smithies Moor Cl WF17 ...... 117 F7
Smithies Moor Cres WF17 117 F8
Smithies Moor La WF17 ... 117 E7
Smithies Moor Rise
WF17 ...... 117 F8
Smiths Ave HD3 ...... 153 D7
Smithson Ave WF10 ...... 125 C6
Smithson St LS26 ...... 100 F4
Smithville BD21 ...... 18 F1
Smithwell La HX7 ...... 88 E5
Smithy Carr La HD6 ...... 115 A4
Smithy Cl Crofton WF4 ...... 161 F8
Skelmanthorpe HD8 ...... 175 A1
Smithy Clough La HX6 ...... 132 B3
Smithy Greaves LS29 ...... 7 C7
Smithy Hill Bradford BD6 ... 74 C1
Denby Dale HD8 ...... 191 F3
Denholme BD13 ...... 71 E6
Smithy La Burdsey LS17 ...... 28 C2
Burley in W LS29 ...... 21 E8
Denton LS29 ...... 9 B7
East Ardsley WF3 ...... 119 F8
Heptonstall HX7 ...... 88 A6
Holmfirth HD7 ...... 188 C2
Huddersfield HD5 ...... 154 C5
Leeds LS16 ...... 41 E6
Netherton WF4 ...... 157 F6
Ripponden HX6 ...... 150 D7
Skelmanthorpe HD8 ...... 175 A1
Wilsden BD15 ...... 53 C6
Smithy Mills La LS16 ...... 42 D2
Smithy Nook OL15 ...... 129 C1
Smithy Par WF12 ...... 139 F1
Smithy Place La HD7 ...... 172 B2
Smithy St HX1 ...... 203 F3
Smithy Wlk WF12 ...... 139 F1
Smyth St WF1 ...... 216 A2
Snail La HX7 ...... 110 B8
Snape Dr BD7 ...... 73 D2
Snape Fold HD5 ...... 154 F4
Snape St BD21 ...... 35 C4
Snapethorpe Cres WF2 ... 141 D3
Snapethorpe Gate WF2 ... 141 C4
Snapethorpe Jun Sch
WF2 ...... 141 D4
Snapethorpe Rd WF2 ...... 141 D4
Snaygill Ind Est BD23 ...... 4 A8
Snelsins La BD19 ...... 95 C1
Snelsins Rd BD19 ...... 95 C1
Snittle Rd HD7 ...... 199 B6
Snow Hill Cl WF1 ...... 121 A1
Snow Hill Rise WF1 ...... 121 A1
Snow Hill View WF1 ...... 216 A4
Snowden App LS13 ...... 58 B2
Snowden Cl LS13 ...... 58 D2
Snowden Cres LS13 ...... 58 D2
Snowden Fold LS13 ...... 58 D2
Snowden Gn LS13 ...... 58 D2
Snowden Gr LS13 ...... 58 D2
Snowden Lawn LS13 ...... 58 D2
Snowden Rd BD18 ...... 55 D7
Snowden Royd LS13 ...... 58 D3
Snowden St BD1 ...... 201 B4
Snowden Vale LS13 ...... 58 D3
Snowden Way LS13 ...... 58 D3
Snowdens Wlk BD14 ...... 73 C4
Snowdon Ave WF11 ...... 126 C4
Snowdon St WF17 ...... 118 B4
Snowdrop Mews ⑧ BD15 ... 73 B8
Snug La HD7 ...... 190 A1
Snydale Ave WF6 ...... 123 C1
Snydale Cl WF6 ...... 123 C1
Snydale Ct WF6 ...... 123 C1
Snydale Gr WF6 ...... 123 C1
Snydale Rd WF6 ...... 123 C1
Soaper House La HX3 ...... 93 D1
Soaper La Bradford BD6 ...... 93 D8
Shelf HX3 ...... 93 D8
Sod House Gn HX3 ...... 92 A3
Soho Gr WF2 ...... 142 A6
Soho St Bradford BD1 ...... 201 A3
Halifax HX1 ...... 202 B3
Solid HD4 ...... 153 F2
Solomon Hill HX2 ...... 90 D1
Solway Rd WF17 ...... 118 F5
Somerdale Cl LS13 ...... 58 D1
Somerdale Gdns LS13 ...... 58 D1
Somerdale Gr LS13 ...... 58 D1
Somerdale Wlk LS13 ...... 58 D1
Somers Pl 4 LS1 ...... 211 E4
Somers St LS1 ...... 211 D4
Somerset Ave Baildon BD17 ... 38 B4
Pudsey LS28 ...... 136 B7
Somerset Ct WF11 ...... 126 F4
Somerset Rd
Huddersfield HD5 ...... 154 D4
Pudsey LS28 ...... 76 E8
Somerton Dr BD4 ...... 75 E2

Somerville Ave
Bradford BD6 ...... 94 B7
Leeds LS14 ...... 61 F2
Somerville Dr LS14 ...... 61 F3
Somerville Gn LS14 ...... 61 F2
Somerville Gr LS14 ...... 61 F3
Somerville Mount 2 LS14 ... 62 A2
Somerville Pk BD6 ...... 94 B7
Somerville Terr LS21 ...... 23 C8
Somerville View LS14 ...... 61 F2
Sonning Rd BD15 ...... 73 B8
Soothill La Batley WF17 ... 118 E5
East Ardsley WF17 ...... 119 A5
Sorbus Way HD8 ...... 155 E3
Sorrel Cl WF8 ...... 146 D7
Sorrin Cl BD10 ...... 56 A7
Sotheron Croft WF8 ...... 147 C5
Soureby Cross Way BD4 ...... 95 F7
Sourhall Cl OL14 ...... 107 D6
Sourhall Cotts OL14 ...... 107 D6
Sourhall Rd OL14 ...... 107 C5
South Accommodation Rd
LS10, LS9 ...... 212 B1
South App Bramham LS14 ...... 47 C6
Sutton LS25 ...... 48 A3
South Ave Castleford WF10 . 123 F7
Horbury WF4 ...... 141 C1
Huddersfield, Cowlersley
HD4 ...... 152 F3
Huddersfield, Sheepridge
HD2 ...... 136 B2
Pontefract WF8 ...... 146 B7
South Elmsall WF9 ...... 182 F2
South Baileygate WF8 ... 125 E1
South Bank
East Keswick LS17 ...... 28 C6
3 Queensbury BD13 ...... 72 F1
South Bank Rd WF17 ...... 118 A6
South Bolton HX2 ...... 91 E7
South Bradford
Golf Course BD12 ...... 94 F7
South Brook Terr BD7 ...... 201 A2
South Cl Guiseley LS20 ...... 39 B8
Royston S71 ...... 179 C2
South Cliffe BD13 ...... 72 E6
South Clough Head HX2 ... 112 A8
South Craven Sch BD20 ... 16 D6
South Cres WF9 ...... 183 B4
South Croft
Denby Dale HD8 ...... 191 F3
Shafton S72 ...... 180 C3
South Croft Ave BD11 ...... 96 A6
South Croft Dr BD11 ...... 96 A7
South Croft Gate BD11 ...... 96 A6
South Cross Rd HD2 ...... 135 F2
South Crossland C of E
Junior Sch HX4 ...... 171 D7
South Dr Guiseley LS20 ...... 39 B8
Pudsey LS28 ...... 57 D2
Royston S71 ...... 179 C2
Wakefield WF2 ...... 142 E1
South Edge Keighley BD20 ... 35 A8
Shipley BD18 ...... 54 F7
South Elmsall Fst Sch
WF9 ...... 182 F2
South Elmsall Sta WF9 ... 183 A3
South End Ave LS13 ...... 58 E1
South End Gr LS13 ...... 58 E1
South End Mount 2 LS13 . 58 E1
South End Terr 1 LS13 .... 58 E1
South Farm Cres LS9 ...... 208 C2
South Farm Rd LS9 ...... 61 D2
South Gr Brighouse HD6 ... 114 E5
Shipley BD18 ...... 54 D7
South Halifax High Sch
HX3 ...... 113 E2
South Hawksworth St LS29 . 8 B4
South Hiendley
Jun & Inf Sch S72 ...... 180 D6
South Hill Cl LS10 ...... 99 F7
South Hill Croft LS10 ...... 99 F7
South Hill Dr BD16 ...... 37 C2
South Hill Gdns LS10 ...... 99 F7
South Hill Gr LS10 ...... 99 F7
South Hill Rise LS10 ...... 99 F7
South Hill Way LS10 ...... 99 F7
South La Cawthorne S75 ... 193 C1
Elland HX5 ...... 134 F5
Elland, Blackley HX5 ...... 134 F4
Holmfirth HD7 ...... 189 A5
Netherton WF4 ...... 158 D4
Shelf HX3 ...... 93 C7
South Lane Gdns HX5 ..... 134 F5
South Lee LS18 ...... 41 B1
South Leeds Bsns Pk
LS10 ...... 215 D4
South Leeds L Ctr LS11 .. 211 E1
South Leeds Stadium
LS11 ...... 99 C8
South Mead LS16 ...... 24 F2
South Mount LS17 ...... 28 B6
South Nelson St LS27 ...... 98 A5
South Ossett Infant Sch
WF5 ...... 140 E4
South Par Bradford BD8 .... 55 D1
Cleckheaton BD19 ...... 116 C7
Elland HX5 ...... 134 F5
Elland, Stainland HX4 ...... 133 F3
Halifax HX1 ...... 203 F2
Ilkley LS29 ...... 8 A4
Leeds LS1 ...... 211 F4
Leeds, Headingley LS6 ...... 59 D5
Morley LS27 ...... 98 B4
Ossett WF5 ...... 141 A4
Otley LS21 ...... 23 B7
Pudsey LS28 ...... 76 E6
Wakefield WF1 ...... 216 B2
South Parade Cl LS28 ...... 76 D6

South Parade Junior Sch
WF5 ...... 140 F4
South Park Terr LS28 ...... 76 F4
South Park Way WF2 ...... 120 F4
South Parkway LS14 ...... 62 A4
South Parkway App
LS14, LS9 ...... 61 E3
South Queen St LS27 ...... 98 B3
South Rd Cullingworth BD13 . 52 D5
Leeds LS9 ...... 80 C3
Shipley BD9 ...... 55 C4
South Ridge LS25 ...... 83 A1
South Royd Ave HX3 ...... 113 C4
South Selby HX2 ...... 91 D6
South St Bacup OL13 ...... 72 D6
South St Bacup OL13 ...... 106 A3
Bradford, Little Horton BD5 .. 74 C3
Bradford, Oakenshaw BD12 .. 95 A4
Brighouse HD6 ...... 115 A3
Denholme BD13 ...... 71 D8
Dewsbury WF13 ...... 139 C8
Dewsbury, Savile Town
WF12 ...... 139 D6
Elland HX4 ...... 134 B4
Halifax HX1 ...... 203 D2
Hemsworth WF9 ...... 181 E6
Holmfirth HD7 ...... 189 C6
Huddersfield, Netherton
HD4 ...... 171 D6
Huddersfield, Paddock HD1 . 153 D5
Keighley, East Morton BD20 .. 36 D8
Keighley, Knowle Park BD21 ... 35 B5
6 Liversedge WF15 ...... 117 B4
Mirfield WF14 ...... 138 A4
Morley LS27 ...... 98 B4
Normanton WF6 ...... 144 A7
Ossett WF5 ...... 140 D4
Ryhill WF4 ...... 162 D1
Thornton BD13 ...... 72 D7
Wakefield WF1 ...... 216 C1
Yeadon LS19 ...... 40 B4
South Terr Dewsbury WF12 . 139 E6
Ossett WF5 ...... 140 E3
South View 1 Batley WF17 .. 96 F1
Baildon BD17 ...... 56 D7
Castleford WF10 ...... 124 E5
Castleford, New Fryston
WF10 ...... 104 C2
Collingham LS22 ...... 28 F8
Crigglestone WF4 ...... 159 D4
Dewsbury WF12 ...... 139 D6
East Ardsley WF17 ...... 119 D5
Farnhill BD20 ...... 4 D1
Featherstone WF7 ...... 145 D6
Glusburn BD20 ...... 16 D6
Guiseley LS20 ...... 22 E1
Halifax, Snydal HX3 ...... 113 E4
Halifax, Southowram HX3 ... 114 A4
Haworth BD22 ...... 51 C7
Holmfirth HD7 ...... 189 F3
Horsforth LS18 ...... 58 C7
Huddersfield HD1 ...... 153 D5
Keighley BD20 ...... 19 C1
Keighley, Braithwaite BD22 ... 34 E8
4 Leeds LS15 ...... 62 C2
Menston LS29 ...... 22 A3
Pudsey LS28 ...... 57 C1
Pudsey, Crimbles LS28 ...... 76 F8
Rothwell LS26 ...... 100 B6
Shipley BD9 ...... 55 C4
Sowerby Bridge HX2 ...... 111 F5
Wetherby LS22 ...... 13 E8
Yeadon LS19 ...... 39 F7
South View Cl
Birkenshaw BD4 ...... 95 E7
Yeadon LS19 ...... 39 F7
South View Cres LS19 ...... 39 F7
South View Dr BD4 ...... 95 F7
South View Gdns WF8 ... 147 A8
South View Infants Sch
LS19 ...... 40 B6
South View Rd
Birkenshaw BD4 ...... 95 F7
Middleton LS10 ...... 215 E1
South View Rd 9 LS19 ...... 40 B7
South View St Silsden BD20 .. 5 D1
Todmorden OL14 ...... 86 C1
South View Terr
6 Baildon BD17 ...... 38 C4
4 Dewsbury WF13 ...... 138 E2
Dewsbury, Ravensthorpe
WF13 ...... 138 E6
Flockton WF4 ...... 156 E4
Otley LS21 ...... 23 B7
Yeadon LS19 ...... 40 C6
South Way Birkenshaw BD4 .. 95 F7
Wakefield WF1 ...... 143 D4
South Wlk BD16 ...... 36 A1
Southampton St BD3 ...... 55 F1
Southcliffe Dr BD17 ...... 38 C1
Southcliffe Way BD17 ...... 38 C1
Southcote PI BD10 ...... 56 B8
Southdale CE (Controlled)
Sch WF5 ...... 140 E4
Southdale Gdns WF5 ...... 140 E5
Southdale Rd WF5 ...... 140 E5
Southdene HD5 ...... 154 E5
Southdown Cl BD9 ...... 54 E2
Southdown Rd BD17 ...... 38 B1
Southedge Cl HX3 ...... 114 C7
Southedge Terr HX3 ...... 114 C7
Southern Rd HD4 ...... 153 A3
Southfield Ave Bradford BD6 . 94 C8
Featherstone WF7 ...... 145 E8
Keighley BD20 ...... 19 A2

Southfield Cl Horbury WF4 . 141 B1
Wakefield WF2 ...... 120 E1
Southfield Ct HD8 ...... 173 F7
Southfield Dr Keighley BD20 . 19 A2
Leeds LS17 ...... 43 E2
Southfield Fold WF4 ...... 159 B8
Southfield House LS29 ...... 6 F8
Southfield La Addingham LS29 . 6 E8
Bradford BD5, BD7 ...... 74 B3
Horbury WF4 ...... 159 B8
Southfield Mount
Keighley BD20 ...... 18 F2
Leeds LS12 ...... 209 F3
Southfield Rd
Addingham LS29 ...... 6 F8
Bingley BD16 ...... 37 A1
Bradford BD5 ...... 74 C2
Burley in W LS29 ...... 9 E1
Crofton WF4 ...... 144 B3
Huddersfield HD5 ...... 155 A4
Knottingley WF11 ...... 126 F3
Southfield Sq BD8 ...... 55 C1
Southfield St LS12 ...... 209 F3
Southfield Terr
Addingham LS29 ...... 6 F8
Birkenshaw BD11 ...... 96 A6
Brighouse HX3 ...... 93 C1
Southfield Way BD20 ...... 19 A2
Southfields View LS24 ...... 24 F2
Huddersfield HD5 ...... 154 E5
Southfields View WF4 ... 158 D5
Southgate Bradford BD1 ... 201 B3
1 Dewsbury WF13 ...... 139 C8
Elland HX5 ...... 134 F6
Guiseley LS20 ...... 39 B7
Halifax HX1 ...... 203 E3
Honley HD7 ...... 171 F4
Huddersfield HD1 ...... 154 B6
Pontefract WF8 ...... 146 C8
Rothwell LS26 ...... 101 C6
South Hiendley S72 ...... 180 E6
Wakefield WF1 ...... 216 B2
Southlands Baildon BD17 .. 38 B1
Halifax HX2 ...... 71 F1
Kirkheaton HD5 ...... 137 B1
Southlands Ave
Bingley BD16 ...... 37 A1
Bradford BD13 ...... 73 A6
Leeds LS17 ...... 60 C8
Yeadon LS19 ...... 40 E2
Southlands Cl
Badsworth WF9 ...... 164 E2
Leeds LS17 ...... 43 C1
Southlands Cres LS17 ...... 60 C8
Southlands Dr
Huddersfield HD2 ...... 136 A3
Leeds LS17 ...... 60 C8
Southlands Gr Bingley BD16 . 37 A1
Bradford BD13 ...... 73 A6
Keighley BD20 ...... 19 A1
Southlands Gr W BD20 ... 19 A2
Southlands Mount BD20 .. 19 A1
Southlands Rd BD20 ...... 19 A1
Southlea Ave LS11 ...... 99 A8
Southleigh Cres LS11 ...... 99 A8
Southleigh Croft LS11 ...... 99 A8
Southleigh Dr LS11 ...... 99 A8
Southleigh Garth LS11 ..... 99 A8
Southleigh Gdns LS11 ...... 99 A8
Southleigh Gr LS11 ...... 99 A8
Southleigh Grange LS11 .... 99 A8
Southleigh Rd LS11 ...... 99 A8
Southleigh View LS11 ...... 99 A8
Southmere Ave BD7 ...... 74 A3
Southmere Cres BD7 ...... 74 A3
Southmere Dr BD7 ...... 73 F3
Southmere First Sch BD7 . 74 A3
Southmere Gr 8 BD7 ...... 74 A3
Southmere Oval BD7 ...... 73 F3
Southmere Rd BD7 ...... 74 A3
Southmere Terr BD7 ...... 74 A3
Southmoor Hospl WF9 .... 182 D6
Southmoor La WF11 ...... 127 D3
Southmoor Rd WF9 ...... 181 D3
Southolme Cl LS5 ...... 59 A6
Southowram Bank HX3 ... 113 E6
Southroyd Pk LS28 ...... 76 E5
Southroyd Primary Sch
LS28 ...... 76 E6
Southwaite Cl LS14 ...... 61 F4
Southwaite La LS14 ...... 61 F4
Southway Bingley BD16 ...... 37 C5
Burley in W LS29 ...... 9 C3
Guiseley LS20 ...... 39 B8
Horsforth LS18 ...... 41 D3
Ilkley LS29 ...... 8 D3
Mirfield WF14 ...... 137 F7
Southwell Ave HD3 ...... 153 F7
Southwood Ave HD7 ...... 189 F4
Southwood Cl LS14 ...... 62 C4
Southwood Cres LS14 ..... 62 C4
Southwood Gate LS14 ..... 62 C4
Sovereign Cl WF12 ...... 96 F1
Sovereign Gdns WF6 ...... 123 D3
Sovereign St Halifax HX1 .. 203 D3
Leeds LS1 ...... 211 F3
Sovereign's Way WF12 ... 139 B3
Sowden Bldgs BD13 ...... 56 B2
Sowden Grange 16 BD13 .. 72 D6

Sowden La HX3 ...... 93 F3
Sowden Rd BD9 ...... 54 D3
Sowden St BD7 ...... 74 B3
Sowden's Yd 8 LS6 ...... 59 D6
Sowerby Bridge
High Sch HX6 ...... 112 C5
Sowerby Bridge Sta HX6 . 112 C3
Sowerby Croft La HX6 ...... 112 C2
Sowerby La
Hebden Bridge HX2 ...... 111 C6
Sowerby Bridge HX2 ...... 111 C6
Sowerby New Rd HX6 ..... 111 F3
Sowerby St HX6 ...... 112 B3
Sowgate La
Knottingley WF11 ...... 126 B3
Pontefract WF11 ...... 126 B3
Sowood Ave WF5 ...... 140 E3
Sowood Gdns WF5 ...... 140 F3
Sowood La Flockton WF12 .. 157 B6
Ossett WF5 ...... 140 F3
Sowood St LS4 ...... 59 C2
Sowood View WF5 ...... 140 F3
Soyland Town Rd HX6 ..... 132 D6
Spa Bottom HD8 ...... 155 C5
Spa Croft Rd WF5 ...... 141 A4
Spa Fields HD7 ...... 152 B1
Spa Fields Ind Est HD7 ... 152 B1
Spa Fold WF3 ...... 121 F5
Spa Gr WF2 ...... 141 E3
Spa Hill WF17 ...... 118 D5
Spa La Bingley BD16 ...... 37 A5
Boston Spa LS23 ...... 30 E7
Ossett WF5 ...... 141 A4
Slaithwaite HD7 ...... 152 B1
Spa St Batley WF17 ...... 118 D5
Ossett WF5 ...... 141 B4
Spa Well Gr S72 ...... 181 A3
Spaines Rd HD2 ...... 136 A1
Spalding Towers LS9 ...... 207 E1
Sparable La WF1 ...... 142 E3
Spark House La HX6 ...... 112 C3
Spark La S75 ...... 178 A1
Spark St HD3 ...... 152 F7
Sparks Rd HD3 ...... 153 B7
Spartal La LS25 ...... 103 E8
Spartan Rd BD12 ...... 94 D5
Sparth La HD7 ...... 188 B4
Spawd Bone La WF11 ..... 126 E3
Speak Cl WF1 ...... 142 F8
Speakers Ct WF13 ...... 139 B8
Spear Fir LS17 ...... 28 A2
Spearhead Way BD21 ..... 35 C8
Speedwell Mount 6 LS6 .. 206 B3
Speedwell Rd WF10 ...... 123 E5
Speedwell St
Huddersfield HD1 ...... 153 D5
7 Leeds LS6 ...... 206 B3
Speeton Ave BD7 ...... 73 D2
Speeton Gr BD7 ...... 73 D2
Spen App LS16 ...... 58 F7
Spen Bank
Cleckheaton BD19 ...... 116 F7
Leeds LS16 ...... 59 A7
Spen Cl BD4 ...... 95 B7
Spen Common La LS24 ..... 47 F6
Spen Cres LS16 ...... 58 F7
Spen Dr LS16 ...... 59 A8
Spen Gdns LS16 ...... 59 A8
Spen Gn LS16 ...... 58 F7
Spen La Cleckheaton BD19 .. 117 A8
Leeds LS16, LS5, LS6 ...... 59 A7
Leeds, Ireland Wood LS16 ... 42 A1
Spen Lawn LS16 ...... 58 F7
Spen Mews LS16 ...... 59 A7
Spen Rd LS16 ...... 58 F8
Spen Vale St WF16 ...... 117 D2
Spen Valley High Sch
WF15 ...... 117 A3
Spen Valley Ind Est BD19 . 116 F6
Spen Valley Rd WF13 ..... 138 C6
Spen View WF16 ...... 117 F1
Spen View La BD4 ...... 95 B7
Spen Wlk LS16 ...... 58 F7
Spence La LS12 ...... 210 C2
Spenceley St Leeds LS2 ... 206 A2
Leeds LS2 ...... 206 A3
Spencer Ave Bradford BD7 .. 74 A5
Morley LS27 ...... 98 A2
Silsden BD20 ...... 5 E2
Spencer Cl BD20 ...... 16 E7
Spencer La HX7 ...... 89 A1
Spencer Mount LS8 ...... 207 E3
Spencer Pl LS7 ...... 207 E3
Spencer Rd BD7 ...... 74 A5
Spencer St
7 Keighley BD21 ...... 35 B7
Mirfield WF14 ...... 138 A3
Skelmanthorpe HD8 ...... 175 A2
Sutton in C BD20 ...... 16 D5
Spenfield Ct WF15 ...... 117 A2
Spennithorne Ave LS16 ..... 42 A2
Spennithorne Dr LS16 ..... 42 A2
Spennithorne Rd DN6 ... 184 F2
Spenser Rd LS20 ...... 39 B8
Spenser Rise LS20 ...... 39 B8
Spenslea Gr LS27 ...... 98 A2
Spibey Cres LS26 ...... 100 D7
Spibey La LS26 ...... 100 D7
Spicer House La S36 ...... 191 A1
Spicer St BD5 ...... 74 C3
Spiers Garth HD7 ...... 188 A1
Spindle St HX2 ...... 92 A5
Spindles The 3 LS10 ...... 99 D8
Spinks Gdns LS14 ...... 62 C5
Spink Pl BD8 ...... 74 D8
Spink St BD8 ...... 74 D8
Spink Well La WF3 ...... 98 F1

Spinkfield Rd HD2 — 153 F8
Spinks Gdns LS14 — 62 B4
Spinkwell Rd 🖪 WF13 — 118 C1
Spinners Chase LS28 — 76 E7
Spinners The BD22 — 51 C6
Spinney The
  Brighouse BD19 — 115 F8
  Mirfield WF14 — 137 F3
Spinney Rd
  Brighouse HD6 — 115 A5
  Draughton BD23 — 1 D5
  Keighley BD20 — 36 D7
  Leeds LS17 — 212 B3
  Leeds, Moortown LS17 — 43 E2
  Wakefield WF2 — 160 E7
  Wetherby LS22 — 13 D6
  Yeadon LS19 — 40 A2
Spinneyfield HD2 — 136 A3
Spinneyfield Ct LS9 — 212 B3
Spinning Mill Ct BD18 — 54 E8
Spion Kop LS14 — 45 F5
Spire Ct Huddersfield HD1 — 153 E7
  Huddersfield, Marsh HD3 — 153 D7
Spire Hts BD10 — 37 D3
Spitalgap La WF8 — 147 C6
Spittal Hardwick La
  WF10 — 125 C5
Spittlerush La WF14 — 166 F4
Spofforth Hill LS22 — 13 D6
Spofforth Wlk LS25 — 83 B7
Spout Fold WF2 — 141 D6
Spout Hill HD6 — 135 E6
Spout House La HD6 — 114 E6
Spring Ave Gildersome LS27 — 97 C8
  Keighley BD21 — 35 C6
Spring Bank
  Cullingworth BD13 — 52 D5
  Halifax HX2 — 90 E1
  🖪 Leeds LS5 — 59 A4
  Pontefract WF8 — 146 D7
Spring Bank Cres LS6 — 205 E4
Spring Bank Croft HD7 — 188 D4
Spring Bank Dr WF15 — 117 B2
Spring Bank Pl BD8 — 55 D2
Spring Bank Primary Sch
  LS6 — 205 E4
Spring Bank Rd BD21 — 35 C4
Spring Bank Terr LS20 — 22 E1
Spring Bottom OL14 — 128 F7
Spring Cl Bingley BD16 — 37 B2
  Garforth LS25 — 83 B6
  Garforth, East Garforth LS25 — 83 A8
  Keighley BD21 — 35 E6
  Morley LS27 — 98 A7
Spring Close Ave LS9 — 212 C2
Spring Close Gdns LS9 — 212 C2
Spring Close St LS9 — 212 B2
Spring Close Wlk LS9 — 212 C2
Spring Ct BD15 — 54 A3
Spring Dale HD7 — 171 F5
Spring Edge HD1 — 35 C6
Spring Edge N HX1 — 202 C1
Spring Edge S HX1 — 202 C1
Spring Edge W HX1 — 202 B1
Spring Farm La BD16 — 36 A1
Spring Farm Mews BD15 — 53 C5
Spring Garden St BD13 — 72 E1
Spring Gardens La BD20 — 18 A1
Spring Gardens Mount
  BD20 — 18 A1
Spring Gardens Rd BD9 — 55 A3
Spring Gdns
  🖪 Bacup OL13 — 106 A3
  Batley WF17 — 118 B5
  Birkenshaw BD11 — 96 F6
  Bradford BD1 — 201 B4
  Burley in W LS29 — 9 F1
  Harewood LS17 — 27 A7
  Huddersfield HD7 — 188 E5
  Morley LS27 — 98 C7
Spring Gr Halifax HX1 — 202 A3
  Hebden Bridge HX7 — 89 A4
Spring Grove
  Jun & Inf Sch HD1 — 153 F5
Spring Grove St HD1 — 154 A5
Spring Grove Terr 🖪 LS6 — 205 F2
Spring Grove View 🖪
  LS6 — 205 E2
Spring Hall Cl WF13 — 93 B5
Spring Hall Ct HX1 — 202 A4
Spring Hall Dr HX2 — 202 A3
Spring Hall Gdns HX2 — 202 A3
Spring Hall Gr HX2 — 202 A3
Spring Hall La
  Halifax HX3 — 113 D4
  Halifax, Pellon HX1 — 202 A3
Spring Hall Pl HX1 — 202 A3
Spring Head Halifax HX2 — 91 F1
  Shelf HX3 — 93 C5
Spring Head La HD7 — 168 F5
Spring Head Rd
  Haworth BD22 — 51 C8
  Thornton BD13 — 72 E6
Spring Hill Baildon BD17 — 37 F3
  Leeds, Adel East Moor LS16 — 42 E4
  Leeds, Buslingthorpe LS7 — 206 C4
  Shipley BD18 — 55 E7
Spring Holes La BD13 — 72 D7
Spring La Baildon BD16 — 37 D6
  Batley WF17 — 118 B7
  Crofton WF4 — 162 B7
  Elland HX4 — 134 A7
  Holmfirth, Hinchcliffe Mill
    HD7 — 188 D2
  Holmfirth, New Mill HD7 — 189 E5

Spring La continued
  Holmfirth, Upperthong HD7 — 188 E4
  Mapplewell S75 — 178 C3
  Royston S71 — 179 D1
  Wetherby LS22 — 14 C5
Spring Mill Fold HX2 — 90 F8
Spring Mill La WF5 — 140 F6
Spring Mill St BD5 — 74 E4
Spring Mount BD21 — 35 E5
Spring Park Rd BD15 — 53 C6
Spring Pl Bradford BD7 — 74 C5
  Keighley BD21 — 35 E5
Spring Ram Bsns Pk S75 — 177 D1
Spring Rd LS6 — 205 E4
Spring Rise Draughton BD23 — 1 D5
  Keighley BD21 — 35 E6
Spring Row Harden BD16 — 36 B1
  Keighley BD21 — 35 B6
  Oxenhope BD22 — 51 E1
  🖪 Queensbury BD13 — 72 E1
Spring Side Rise HD7 — 152 D5
Spring St Bradford BD10 — 56 B6
  Brighouse HD6 — 115 A2
  Dewsbury WF13 — 118 C1
  🖪 Haworth BD22 — 51 F8
  🖪 Huddersfield HD1 — 154 A6
  Keighley BD21 — 35 C8
  Liversedge WF15 — 117 B4
  Marsden HD7 — 168 F3
  Ripponden HX6 — 132 D4
  Slaithwaite HD7 — 169 F8
  Todmorden OL14 — 86 C1
Spring Terr Halifax HX3 — 203 F4
  Keighley BD21 — 35 E6
  South Elmsall WF9 — 182 F2
Spring Vale Rd WF9 — 182 C3
Spring Valley LS28 — 57 C1
Spring Valley Ave LS13 — 58 C1
Spring Valley Cl
  Leeds LS13 — 58 C1
  🖪 Liversedge WF15 — 117 A5
Spring Valley Cres LS13 — 58 C1
Spring Valley Croft LS13 — 58 C1
Spring Valley Ct LS13 — 58 C1
Spring Valley Dr LS13 — 58 C1
Spring Valley Sq 🖪
  WF15 — 117 A5
Spring Valley St 🖪
  WF15 — 117 A5
Spring Valley View LS13 — 58 C1
Spring Valley Wlk LS13 — 58 C1
Spring View
  Gildersome LS27 — 97 C8
  Holme Chapel BK10 — 85 A8
  Ossett WF5 — 140 F6
  Sowerby Bridge HX2 — 111 D6
Spring Villas 🖪 OL14 — 86 B1
Spring Way BD21 — 35 E6
Spring Wood Ave HX3 — 113 B2
Spring Wood Dr HX3 — 113 B2
Spring Wood Gdns BD5 — 74 F2
Springbank LS25 — 82 C6
Springbank Ave
  Gildersome LS27 — 97 C7
  Pudsey LS28 — 57 E3
Springbank Cl LS28 — 57 E3
Springbank Cres
  Garforth LS25 — 82 C6
  Gildersome LS27 — 97 C8
  Huddersfield HD2 — 136 D1
Springbank Dr LS28 — 57 E4
Springbank Gr LS28 — 57 E3
Springbank Rd
  Gildersome LS27 — 97 C8
  Huddersfield HD2 — 136 D1
  Pudsey LS28 — 57 E3
Springbank Rise LS28 — 57 E3
Springcliffe BD8 — 55 B1
Springcliffe St BD8 — 55 B1
Springdale Ave HD1 — 153 F4
Springdale Cres HD10 — 56 C7
Springdale St HD1 — 153 F4
Springfield Boston Spa LS23 — 30 D8
  Boston Spa, Clifford LS23 — 30 D5
  Elland HX3 — 152 B8
  Queensbury BD13 — 72 D1
  Sowerby Bridge HX6 — 112 A3
Springfield Ave
  Bacup OL13 — 106 A3
  Batley WF17 — 118 B5
  Bradford BD7 — 73 F3
  Clayton West HD8 — 175 E2
  Hemsworth WF9 — 181 E6
  Honley HD7 — 171 F3
  Ilkley LS29 — 8 C4
  Morley LS27 — 98 A6
  Pontefract WF8 — 125 F1
  Slaithwaite HD7 — 169 E7
Springfield Cl
  Clayton West HD8 — 175 E2
  Horsforth LS18 — 41 E1
  Leeds LS10 — 80 A2
Springfield Cres
  Morley LS27 — 98 A6
  Norton WF8 — 166 E5
Springfield Ct
  Keighley BD20 — 35 A8
  Yeadon LS19 — 40 C5
Springfield Dr
  Cleckheaton WF15 — 116 C5
  Denby Dale HD8 — 191 A4
Springfield Farm
  (Riding School) BD21 — 52 A7
Springfield Gdns
  Horsforth LS18 — 41 D1
  🖪 Keighley BD20 — 35 A8
  Pudsey LS28 — 76 F6
Springfield Gn LS10 — 215 E2

Springfield Gr
  Bingley BD16 — 36 F3
  Brighouse HD6 — 115 B5
Springfield Grange WF2 — 141 D6
Springfield House 🖪
  BD19 — 116 E7
Springfield La
  Birkenshaw BD4 — 76 F2
  Cleckheaton FW15 — 116 E5
  Kirkburton HD8 — 173 E7
  Morley LS27 — 98 A6
Springfield Mount
  Addingham LS29 — 2 E1
  Horsforth LS18 — 41 D1
  Leeds, Armley LS12 — 209 D4
  Leeds, Woodhouse LS2 — 206 A1
  South Elmsall WF9 — 182 E1
Springfield Pk WF14 — 138 B5
Springfield Pl
  Bradford BD1 — 201 A4
  Bradford, Springfield BD8 — 56 B6
  Guiseley LS20 — 22 E1
  Leeds LS10 — 215 E2
  Otley LS21 — 22 F7
Springfield Rd Baildon BD17 — 38 B4
  Elland HX5 — 135 B7
  Guiseley LS20 — 22 E1
  Morley LS27 — 98 A6
Springfield Rise
  Horsforth LS18 — 41 D1
  Rothwell LS26 — 100 F4
Springfield St Bradford BD8 — 74 C8
  Rothwell LS26 — 100 F4
  Thornton BD13 — 72 E6
Springfield Terr
  Bradford BD8 — 74 C8
  Brighouse BD19 — 94 F1
  Brighouse, Hipperholme
    HX3 — 114 D8
  Cullingworth BD13 — 52 E5
  Dewsbury WF13 — 118 C1
  Elland HD3 — 134 B1
  Emley HD8 — 175 A7
  Guiseley LS20 — 39 E8
  Halifax HX2 — 90 C1
  🖪 Pudsey LS28 — 57 D3
Springfield View WF7 — 145 A8
Springfield Wlk LS18 — 41 D1
Springfields WF11 — 127 B3
Springfields Ave WF11 — 127 B4
Springhead BD22 — 51 C8
Springhead Park Sch
  LS26 — 101 A6
Springhead Rd LS26 — 101 A6
Springhill Ave WF4 — 162 A8
Springhill Cl WF1 — 121 A5
Springhill Dr WF1 — 144 A1
Springhill Gr WF4 — 144 A1
Springhill Mount WF4 — 162 A8
Springhurst Rd BD18 — 55 A7
Springlodge Pl BD8 — 55 D1
Springmead Dr LS25 — 82 F6
Springroyd Terr BD8 — 73 F8
Springs La Bickerton LS23 — 14 E6
  Ilkley LS29 — 8 C4
  Thorp Arch LS23 — 14 E6
Springs Rd Guiseley LS19 — 39 E6
  Holme HD7 — 187 B4
Springs The WF1 — 216 B2
Springstone Ave
  Hemsworth WF9 — 181 E7
  Ossett WF5 — 140 D7
Springswood Ave BD18 — 55 A7
Springswood Pl BD18 — 55 A7
Springswood Rd BD18 — 55 A7
Springvale Rise WF9 — 181 D8
Springville Gdns WF9 — 183 B7
Springville Terr BD10 — 56 B7
Springwell Ave LS26 — 82 A1
Springwell Cl 🖪 LS19 — 40 C6
Springwell Ct
  East Ardsley WF3 — 98 E1
  Leeds LS12 — 210 C2
Springwell Dr BD5 — 74 E4
Springwell Rd Leeds LS11 — 211 D2
  Ossett WF5 — 140 C5
  Swillington LS26 — 82 A1
Springwell St LS12 — 210 C2
Springwell Terr 🖪 LS19 — 40 C6
Springwell View
  🖪 Batley WF17 — 96 F1
  Leeds LS11 — 211 D2
Springwood Ave
  Bradford BD5 — 74 F3
  Huddersfield HD1 — 153 F5
Springwood Gdns HX3 — 113 B2
Springwood Gn LS8 — 61 C6
Springwood Hall Cl HD1 — 153 E6
Springwood Hall Gdns
  HD1 — 153 F6
Springwood Rd
  Holmfirth HD7 — 189 C8
  Leeds LS8 — 61 C6
  Yeadon LS19 — 40 A3
Springwood Sq 🖪 HD1 — 154 A6
Springwood St 🖪 HD1 — 154 A6
Springwood Terr BD2 — 55 E2
Sprinkwell Cl BD3 — 201 B4
Spruce Ave S71 — 179 B3
Spruce Dr HD4 — 171 D6
Spruce Drive Mews HD4 — 171 D6
Spruce St 🖪 BD21 — 35 D8
Spruce Wlk OL14 — 129 A8
Sprutts La HX7 — 89 B8
Spry La S63 — 194 B3
Spur Dr LS15 — 62 E3
Spur St WF17 — 118 D4

Spurr Gr WF2 — 161 B6
Spurrier's Ave WF11 — 126 C3
Square HX1 — 203 E3
Square Rd Halifax HX1 — 203 F3
  Todmorden OL14 — 129 A8
Square St BD4 — 75 A5
Square The Batley WF17 — 117 F6
  Boston Spa LS23 — 30 E7
  🖪 Bradford BD8 — 55 D2
  Castleford WF10 — 125 C7
  Farnley LS21 — 11 D4
  Harewood LS17 — 27 A7
  Keighley BD20 — 19 D1
  Kippax LS25 — 83 A1
  Knottingley WF11 — 126 C5
  Shepley HD8 — 190 E8
Square View OL14 — 129 B8
Squire La BD8 — 54 F1
Squire La BD8, BD9 — 55 A1
Squirrel Cl WF13 — 118 A3
Squirrel Ct HD2 — 135 C2
Squirrel Ditch HD4 — 154 C3
Squirrel End WF13 — 118 A2
Squirrel Hall Dr WF13 — 117 F3
Squirrel La BD13 — 72 B5
Squirrel Wlk WF13 — 118 A3
Squirrels Drey WF4 — 159 F7
Stable Ct HD7 — 152 A1
Stable Fold BD22 — 94 D2
Stable La HX3 — 92 B1
Stablers Wlk WF6 — 123 A4
Stables La LS23 — 30 E7
Stables The WF2 — 161 A7
Stackgarth HD6 — 136 A8
Stackhills Rd OL14 — 108 C5
Stacks La HX7 — 110 F5
Stadium Rd BD6 — 94 D8
Stadium Way
  Huddersfield HD1 — 154 C7
  Leeds LS11 — 213 E3
  South Elmsall WF9 — 183 B5
Stafford Ave HX3 — 113 C4
Stafford Hill La HD5 — 155 C8
Stafford Par HX3 — 113 C3
Stafford Pl HX3 — 113 C4
Stafford Rd HX3 — 113 C3
Stafford Sq HX3 — 113 C3
Stafford St Bradford BD4 — 75 B4
  Castleford WF10 — 124 C8
  Leeds LS10 — 215 F4
  Morley LS27 — 97 F4
Stafford Terr WF2 — 141 F6
Stainbeck Ave LS7 — 59 F6
Stainbeck Gdns
  Bradford BD6 — 93 D8
  Leeds LS7 — 60 B7
Stainbeck La LS7 — 60 A7
Stainbeck Preparatory Sch
  LS7 — 60 B7
Stainbeck Rd Leeds LS7 — 60 A7
  Leeds, Chapel Allerton LS7 — 60 C8
Stainbeck Wlk LS7 — 60 B7
Stainburn Ave
  Castleford WF10 — 125 A5
  Leeds LS17 — 43 E1
Stainburn Cres LS17 — 43 E1
Stainburn Dr LS17 — 43 D1
Stainburn Gdns LS17 — 43 E1
Stainburn Mount LS17 — 204 B4
Stainburn Rd LS17 — 204 A4
Stainburn Terr LS17 — 204 A4
Stainburn View LS17 — 43 E1
Staincliffe CE Jun Sch
  WF17 — 118 A4
Staincliffe Cl 🖪 WF13 — 118 A1
Staincliffe Cres 🖪 WF13 — 117 F2
Staincliffe Ct BD20 — 5 D1
Staincliffe Hall Rd WF17 — 118 A4
Staincliffe Rd WF13 — 118 A1
Staincross Comm S75 — 178 B2
Staincross Ave HD4 — 153 C2
Staines Croft HD5 — 154 D6
Stainland Dean HX4 — 133 D2
Stainland Rd Elland HX4 — 134 C6
  Halifax HX3 — 113 D1
  Ripponden HX4 — 133 B4
Stainmore Cl LS14 — 62 A3
Stainmore Pl LS14 — 62 A3
Stainton Cl BD6 — 93 E8
Stainton La BD6 — 93 E8
Stair Foot La LS16 — 42 E5
Staircase La LS16, LS21 — 24 D5
Stairfoot Cl LS16 — 42 D5
Stairfoot La LS16 — 42 D5
Stairfoot View LS16 — 42 D5
Staithe Ave LS10 — 99 D5
Staithe Cl LS10 — 99 D5
Staithe 🖪 LS10 — 99 D5
Staithe Gdns 🖪 LS10 — 99 D5
Staithgate La BD6 — 94 D7
Stake La HX7 — 110 F7
Stake Lane Bank HD7 — 189 C8
Stakes Fold WF16 — 117 E4
Stalabrass St 🖪 BD8 — 74 C8
Stalley Royd La HD7 — 199 F3
Stamford Ave WF10 — 124 A6
Stamford St BD4 — 75 B5
Stamford Way S75 — 178 B2
Stammergate La LS22 — 13 C2
Stamp Hill Cl LS29 — 6 E8
Stan Valley WF8 — 166 E6
Stanacre Pl BD3 — 201 C4
Stanage La HX3 — 93 C7
Stanally St OL14 — 107 E8
Stanbury First Sch BD22 — 50 D6
Stancliffe Way HD5 — 137 B1
Stand Bridge Garth WF4 — 159 F5
Standale Ave LS28 — 76 D8
Standale Cres LS28 — 76 D8

Standale Rise LS28 — 76 D8
Standard Dr HD4 — 153 B2
Standard Ind Est BD2 — 56 C3
Standbridge Cl WF2 — 160 A5
Standbridge
  Jun & Est Sch WF2 — 160 A5
Standbridge La
  Wakefield, Kettlethorpe WF2 — 160 B6
  Wakefield, Stand Bridge
    WF2 — 160 C7
Standiforth La HD5 — 154 F6
Standiforth Pl HD5 — 154 D6
Standiforth Rd HD5 — 154 D6
Standish Cres WF9 — 182 C4
Stanhall Ave 🖪 LS28 — 57 D1
Stanhope Ave
  Cawthorne S75 — 193 F5
  Horsforth LS18 — 41 C2
Stanhope Cl LS18 — 41 C2
Stanhope Dr LS18 — 58 C8
Stanhope Gdns WF3 — 99 E1
Stanhope Gr WF3 — 99 E1
Stanhope Rd WF3 — 99 E1
Stanhope St HD8 — 175 D1
Stanks App 🖪 LS14 — 62 D4
Stanks Ave LS14 — 62 D4
Stanks Cl LS14 — 62 D4
Stanks Cross LS14 — 62 E4
Stanks Dr LS14 — 62 D5
Stanks Garth LS14 — 62 E4
Stanks Gdns LS14 — 62 E4
Stanks Gn LS14 — 62 E4
Stanks Gr LS14 — 62 D4
Stanks La N LS14 — 62 C5
Stanks La S LS14 — 62 D4
Stanks Parade LS14 — 62 E4
Stanks Rd LS14 — 62 E4
Stanks Rise LS14 — 62 E5
Stanks Way LS14 — 62 D4
Stanley Ave LS9 — 207 F2
Stanley Cotts WF6 — 123 A2
Stanley Ct HX1 — 202 B3
Stanley Dr LS8 — 44 B2
Stanley Gr LS20 — 39 E8
Stanley Grove Junior &
  Infants Sch WF3 — 121 F3
Stanley La Elland HX4 — 134 A3
  Liversedge WF15 — 117 A5
  Lofthouse Gate WF1 — 121 F3
Stanley Marsh
  Nature Reserve WF3 — 121 E4
Stanley Pl Batley WF17 — 118 D5
  Huddersfield HD7 — 152 D4
  Leeds LS9 — 208 A2
Stanley Rd Bradford BD2 — 55 D4
  Halifax HX1 — 202 B3
  Huddersfield HD1 — 135 C1
  Huddersfield, Amley Top
    HD3 — 135 A3
  Keighley BD22 — 35 A4
  Leeds LS9 — 208 A2
  Leeds, Chapeltown LS7 — 207 D3
  Liversedge WF15 — 117 A2
  Shipley BD2 — 55 C2
  Wakefield WF1 — 216 C3
Stanley Royd Hospl WF1 — 216 C4
Stanley St Bingley BD16 — 37 A3
  Bradford, Greengates BD10 — 56 D7
  Bradford, Idle BD10 — 56 B8
  Brighouse HD6 — 115 B3
  Castleford WF10 — 124 E8
  Cleckheaton BD19 — 116 D8
  Featherstone WF7 — 145 D7
  Haworth BD22 — 51 E8
  Huddersfield HD1 — 153 E3
  Keighley BD21 — 35 B8
  Shipley BD18 — 55 C5
  Sowerby Bridge HX6 — 112 C4
  Wakefield WF1 — 216 C2
Stanley St N HX2 — 92 A5
Stanley Terr Leeds LS9 — 208 A2
  Leeds, Armley LS12 — 209 F3
Stanley View LS12 — 209 F3
Stanmoor Dr WF3 — 121 E6
Stanmore Ave LS4 — 59 C3
Stanmore Cres LS4 — 59 C3
Stanmore Gdns LS4 — 59 C3
Stanmore Hill LS4 — 205 D3
Stanmore Mount LS4 — 59 C3
Stanmore Pl Bradford BD7 — 74 A5
  Leeds LS4 — 59 C3
Stanmore Rd LS4 — 59 C3
Stanmore St LS4 — 59 C3
Stanmore Terr LS4 — 59 C3
Stanmore View LS4 — 59 C3
Stannard Well Dr WF4 — 141 B2
Stannard Well La WF4 — 141 C2
Stannary Pl HX1 — 203 D4
Stannery End La HX7 — 110 F7
Stanningley Ave HX2 — 91 E7
Stanningley By-Pass
  Leeds LS13 — 58 D1
  Pudsey LS28 — 58 B1
Stanningley Ct 🖪 LS28 — 57 F2
Stanningley Dr HX2 — 91 C5
Stanningley Field Cl LS13 — 58 A1
Stanningley Gr 🖪 WF16 — 117 D3
Stanningley Primary Sch
  LS28 — 57 F2
Stanningley Rd Halifax HX2 — 91 E5
  Leeds LS12, LS13 — 58 E1
  Pudsey LS28 — 57 F2
Stansfield Cl
  Castleford WF10 — 125 B8
  Halifax HX1 — 202 C3

Stansfield Ct HX6 .... 112 B3
Stansfield Dr WF10 .... 125 C8
Stansfield Grange HX6 ...... 111 E1
Stansfield Hall OL15 .... 129 C1
Stansfield Hall Rd OL14 .... 108 C6
Stansfield Mill La HX6 ...... 111 F1
Stansfield Pl BD10 .... 39 B1
Stansfield Rd
 Castleford WF10 .... 125 B8
 Todmorden OL14 .... 108 B5
Stansfield St ▪️ OL14 ..... 108 B6
Stansfield Terr ▪️ OL14 ...... 86 B1
Stanwell Ave HD2 .... 135 D1
Stanwick House BD2 .... 55 D4
Stapleford Ct HD2 .... 135 D2
Stapleton House BD2 .... 55 D4
Stapper Gn BD15 .... 53 B6
Star St BD5 .... 74 C3
Starbeck Rd WF1 .... 142 EB
Starkey La BD20 .... 4 E1
Starkie St BD21 .... 35 B6
Starling House WF9 .... 181 D6
Starting Post BD10 .... 55 F7
Starwort Cl WF8 .... 146 D7
Station App
 Burley in W LS29 .... 21 EB
 Honley HD7 .... 172 B7
 Todmorden OL14 .... 108 B5
Station Ave LS13 .... 58 C2
Station Cl LS25 .... 82 F7
Station Cotts LS24 .... 31 C6
Station Cres LS12 .... 209 E3
Station Ct LS25 .... 82 F8
Station Fields LS25 .... 82 F7
Station Forecourt BD1 .... 201 B3
Station Gdns LS22 .... 13 D5
Station Gr Glusburn BD20 .. 16 D7
 ▪️ Leeds LS13 .... 58 C2
Station Ind Est HX2 .... 111 D7
Station La Birkenshaw BD11 .. 96 B6
 Collingham LS22 .... 29 BB
 East Ardsley WF3 .... 98 E2
 East Ardsley, Thorpe on the Hill
  WF3 .... 99 D1
 East Ardsley, Tingley WF3 .. 98 E1
 Featherstone WF7 .... 145 C5
 Huddersfield HD4 .... 171 F8
 Huddersfield, Wellhouse
  HD7 .... 152 D3
 Liversedge WF16 .... 117 D3
 Pontefract WF8 .... 146 E8
 Rothwell LS26 .... 101 D7
 Shipley HD8 .... 173 F1
 Thorner LS14 .... 45 E6
Station Mount LS13 .... 58 C2
Station Par Leeds LS5 .... 59 B4
 Todmorden OL14 .... 85 F1
 ▪️ Leeds LS13 .... 58 C2
Station Plaza LS29 .... 8 B4
Station Rd
 Ackworth M T WF7 .... 164 C7
 Arthington LS21 .... 24 F6
 Baildon BD17 .... 38 D3
 Barwick in E LS15 .... 62 F6
 Batley WF17 .... 118 D4
 Birkenshaw BD11 .... 96 E6
 Bradford BD1 .... 55 E2
 Bradford, Clayton BD14 ...... 73 C4
 ▪️ Bradford, Raw Nook BD12 94 E5
 Bradford, Wyke BD12 .... 94 B2
 Brighouse HD6 .... 115 C2
 Brighouse, Hipperholme
  HX3 .... 114 C7
 Brighouse, Wyke BD12 .... 94 B2
 Burley in W LS29 .... 9 E1
 Castleford WF10 .... 124 D8
 Cullingworth BD13 .... 52 D6
 Denholme BD13 .... 71 E8
 Dewsbury WF12 .... 139 C5
 Dewsbury, Earlsheaton
  WF12 .... 139 F6
 Elland HX4 .... 134 C4
 Garforth LS25 .... 82 F8
 Glusburn BD20 .... 22 D1
 Guiseley LS20 .... 22 D1
 Guiseley, Esholt BD17 .... 39 C6
 Halifax, Holmfield HX3 .... 92 A5
 Halifax, Luddenden Foot
  HX2 .... 111 D7
 Haworth BD22 .... 51 D7
 Hebden Bridge HX7 .... 89 B2
 Hemsworth WF9 .... 181 E7
 Holmfirth HD7 .... 189 A5
 Honley HD7 .... 172 A5
 Horsforth LS18 .... 41 C3
 Huddersfield, Bradley HD2 .. 137 A5
 Huddersfield, Wellhouse
  HD7 .... 152 E3
 Ilkley LS29 .... 8 B4
 Kippax WF10 .... 103 C4
 Kirkburton HD4 .... 173 C2
 Knottingley WF11 .... 126 C5
 Leeds LS12 .... 209 E3
 Leeds, Cross Gates LS15 ...... 62 C1
 Lepton HD8 .... 155 D3
 Liversedge WF16 .... 117 D3
 Mapplewell S75 .... 177 E1
 Marsden HD7 .... 168 F4
 Menston LS29 .... 22 B4
 Mickletown LS26 .... 102 B3
 Methill WF14 .... 138 A4
 Morley LS27 .... 98 B5
 Normanton WF6 .... 122 F3
 Oakworth BD22 .... 34 D1
 Ossett WF5 .... 140 E4

Station Rd continued
 Otley LS21 .... 23 A7
 Oxenhope BD22 .... 51 C2
 Queensbury BD13 .... 72 F2
 Royston S71 .... 179 B4
 Ryhill WF4 .... 162 A1
 Shipley BD18 .... 55 B7
 Skelmanthorpe HD8 .... 175 A2
 Slaithwaite HD7 .... 152 A1
 South Elmsall WF9 .... 183 A3
 Sowerby Bridge HX6 .... 112 C3
 Steeton BD20 .... 17 D6
 Todmorden OL14 .... 86 C1
 Wilsden BD13 .... 53 A4
Station St
 Huddersfield HD1 .... 154 A6
 Meltham HD7 .... 170 D2
 Pudsey LS28 .... 76 D6
 Wakefield WF1 .... 142 E2
Station Terr Kippax WF10 .. 103 C4
 Leeds LS13 .... 58 C2
 Royston S71 .... 179 E4
Station View Leeds LS15 .... 62 C1
 Oxenhope BD22 .... 51 C3
 Steeton BD20 .... 17 D5
Station Way LS12 .... 209 E3
Station Works Ind Pk
 BD21 .... 35 E7
Staups La
 Blackshaw Head OL14 .... 88 A2
 Northowram HX3 .... 92 F1
Staveley Ct BD16 .... 36 F4
Staveley Dr BD18 .... 54 D7
Staveley Gr BD22 .... 35 A3
Staveley Rd Bingley BD16 .. 37 A4
 Bradford BD7 .... 74 B6
 Keighley BD22 .... 35 A3
 Shipley BD18 .... 54 D8
Staveley Way BD22 .... 35 A3
Stavely Mews ▪️ BD16 ..... 37 A4
Staverton St HX2 .... 202 A3
Staybrite Ave BD16 .... 54 A7
Staygate Gn BD8 .... 74 E1
Staynton Cres HD2 .... 136 F5
Stead Gate HD8 .... 174 D2
Stead La WF8 .... 38 F1
Stead La Ilkley LS29 .... 21 BB
 Kirkheaton HD5 .... 155 BB
 Rippenden HX6 .... 132 C2
 Thorner LS14 .... 45 F5
Stead Rd BD4 .... 95 EB
Stead St Halifax HX1 .... 203 D3
 Shipley BD17 .... 55 B8
Stead's Yd LS18 .... 41 C2
Steadman St BD3 .... 75 B6
Steadman Terr BD3 .... 75 B6
Steanard La WF14 .... 138 C3
Steander LS9 .... 212 A3
Steele La HX4 .... 133 C1
Steep La HX6 .... 111 B4
Steep Riding HD7 .... 172 C3
Steeplands HD2 .... 136 F6
Steeple Ave WF4 .... 156 E4
Steeton Gr BD20 .... 17 D6
Steeton Hall Gdns BD20 .... 17 C6
Steeton Primary Sch BD20 17 D5
Steeton & Silsden Sta BD20 17 D6
Stell Hill BD22 .... 34 C5
Stella Gdns HX4 .... 125 F2
Stephen Cl HX3 .... 93 A1
Stephen Cres BD2 .... 55 E3
Stephen Rd BD6 .... 73 F7
Stephen Row HX3 .... 93 A2
Stephen St ▪️ HX7 .... 89 A3
Stephenson Cl WF12 .... 118 E1
Stephenson Dr LS12 .... 77 E7
Stephenson Rd BD15 .... 53 D2
Stephenson St ▪️ BD7 ...... 74 B3
Stephenson Way LS12 .... 77 D3
Stephensons Way LS29 ...... 8 B4
Stepping Stones BD20 ...... 19 E1
Steps La HX6 .... 112 C5
Sterling Ind Pk WF10 ...... 124 F5
Stevenson Ave WF10 .... 125 C5
Stewart Cl BD2 .... 56 C5
Stewart Pl ▪️ LS11 .... 214 B3
Stewart St BD22 .... 51 E8
Sticker La BD4 .... 75 C4
Stile Common
 Infants Sch HD4 .... 154 A3
Stile Common
 Junior Sch HD4 .... 154 A3
Stile Common Rd HD4 ...... 154 B3
Stile Hill Way LS15 .... 81 E6
Stile Rd OL14 .... 108 A7
Stilemoor Rise OL14 .... 108 A7
Stillington House BD2 .... 55 D4
Stillwell Dr WF2 .... 160 EB
Stillwell Garth WF2 .... 160 EB
Stillwell Gr WF2 .... 160 EB
Stirley Hill HD4 .... 172 B7
Stirling Cres Bradford BD4 .. 75 E3
 Horsforth LS18 .... 41 B4
Stirling Rd LS29 .... 9 D1
Stirling St Halifax HX1 ..... 203 D2
 Silsden BD20 .... 5 E2
Stirling Way LS25 .... 82 B8
Stirrup Gr BD2 .... 55 F4
Stirton St ▪️ BD5 .... 74 D3
Stithy St WF5 .... 140 C8
Stock Hey La OL14 .... 109 C6
Stock La HX2 .... 112 C7
Stockeld La LS22 .... 12 D6
Stockeld Rd LS29 .... 8 A4
Stockeld Way LS29 .... 8 A5
Stockerhead La HD7 .... 170 A8
Stockfield La LS15 .... 45 F1
Stockhill Fold BD10 .... 56 D7

Stockhill Rd BD10 .... 56 D7
Stockhill St WF13 .... 139 A8
Stocking La Aberford LS25 .. 65 A7
 Knottingley WF11 .... 127 C4
Stockingate WF9 .... 182 B2
Stockingate Mill
 Primary Sch WF9 .... 182 A1
Stockinger La LS29 .... 6 FB
Stocks App LS14 .... 62 A8
Stocks Ave HX7 .... 110 D8
Stocks Bank Rd WF14 ...... 137 E6
Stocks Cres HX7 .... 110 D8
Stocks Dr HD8 .... 190 E8
Stocks Gdns HX7 .... 110 D8
Stocks Hill
 Leeds, Armley LS12 .... 209 F4
 Leeds, Bramley LS13 .... 58 D3
 Leeds, Holbeck LS11 .... 211 D1
 Menston LS29 .... 21 F4
Stocks Hill Cl
 Keighley BD20 .... 19 D1
 Royston S71 .... 179 C4
Stocks La Batley WF17 ...... 118 C5
 Bradford BD13 .... 73 B1
 Halifax HX2 .... 90 E2
 Hebden Bridge HX7 .... 110 D8
 Kirkburton HD4 .... 173 A8
 Sowerby Bridge HX6 .... 111 E3
Stocks Lane First Sch
 BD13 .... 73 B1
Stocks Moor Rd HD4 .... 173 B2
Stocks Rd LS14 .... 62 C4
Stocks Rise LS14 .... 62 B4
Stocks Way HD8 .... 190 D8
Stocks Wlk HD5 .... 154 F3
Stocksbank Dr WF14 .... 137 D6
Stocksmoor Rd WF4 .... 158 C2
Stocksmoor Sta HD4 .... 173 C2
Stockwell Dr WF17 .... 118 D6
Stockwell Hill HD4 .... 171 F8
Stockwell Vale HD4 .... 171 F8
Stod Fold HX2 .... 91 C8
Stogoen Hill BD13 .... 73 B1
Stone Acre Ct ▪️ BD5 .... 74 E2
Stone Acre Hts HD7 .... 170 F1
Stone Brig Gn LS26 .... 100 D4
Stone Brig La LS26 .... 100 D4
Stone Cliffe ▪️ HX3 .... 113 A4
Stone Ct Keighley BD20 ..... 36 DB
 South Hiendley S72 .... 180 E5
Stone Dene BD16 .... 37 A6
Stone Dene Pk LS22 .... 13 F6
Stone Fold HD7 .... 171 F4
Stone Gr BD20 .... 17 C6
Stone Hall Rd BD2 .... 56 A4
Stone Mill BD16 .... 37 B5
Stone La BD22 .... 51 B2
Stone Pits La LS27 .... 97 D5
Stone St Baildon BD17 .... 38 E2
 Bradford BD1 .... 201 B3
 Bradford, Sandy Lane BD15 .. 54 A3
 Cleckheaton BD19 .... 116 C7
 ▪️ Haworth BD22 .... 51 C6
Stone Wood La HD4, HD8 .. 173 D1
Stonebridge App LS12 ...... 77 F6
Stonebridge Gr LS12 .... 77 F6
Stonebridge La
 Leeds, Farnley LS12 .... 77 F6
 Leeds, Swallow Hill LS12 .... 77 F6
Stonebridge Wlk HX6 ...... 173 F1
Stonecroft Rise LS27 .... 98 C4
Stonecliffe Bank LS12 .... 77 E6
Stonecliffe Cl LS12 .... 77 E6
Stonecliffe Cres LS12 .... 77 E6
Stonecliffe Dr Leeds LS12 .. 77 E6
 Netherton WF4 .... 158 B7
Stonecliffe Garth LS12 ..... 77 E6
Stonecliffe Gdns LS12 .... 77 E6
Stonecliffe Gn LS12 .... 77 E6
Stonecliffe Lawn LS12 ...... 77 E6
Stonecliffe Mount LS12 .... 77 E6
Stonecliffe Pl LS12 .... 77 E6
Stonecliffe Terr LS12 .... 77 E6
Stonecliffe View LS12 .... 77 E6
Stonecliffe Way LS12 .... 77 E5
Stonecliffe Wlk LS12 .... 77 E5
Stonecroft Bradford BD2 ... 56 A4
 Lofthouse Gate WF3 .... 121 E5
Stonecroft Gdns HD8 .... 190 F8
Stonedale Cl LS21 .... 24 E6
Stonedene Ct WF16 .... 117 E3
Stonefield LS14 .... 45 D8
Stonefield Ave HX4 .... 153 B3
Stonefield Cl BD2 .... 56 B5
Stonefield Pl WF17 .... 96 F1
Stonefield Rd HD4 .... 153 B3
Stonefield St
 Cleckheaton BD19 .... 116 A6
 Dewsbury WF13 .... 139 A8
Stonefield Terr LS27 .... 98 C8
Stonegale Bingley BD16 ..... 37 A5
 Leeds LS7 .... 206 C3
 Ossett WF5 .... 140 F3
Stonegate App LS7 .... 59 F6
Stonegate Chase LS7 .... 59 F7
Stonegate Cl LS7 .... 137 C1
Stonegate Cres LS7 .... 60 A7
Stonegate Dr LS7 .... 60 A7
Stonegate Edge LS7 .... 60 A7
Stonegate Farm Cl LS7 ...... 59 F7
Stonegate Gdns LS7 .... 59 F7
Stonegate Gn LS7 .... 59 F7
Stonegate Gr LS7 .... 60 A7

Stonegate La
 Ackworth M T WF7 .... 163 E5
 Leeds LS7 .... 59 F7
Stonegate Mews LS7 .... 59 F6
Stonegate Pl LS7 .... 59 F6
Stonegate Rd Bradford BD10 56 C6
 Leeds LS17 .... 43 C2
Stonegate Sch LS7 .... 60 A8
Stonegate View LS7 .... 59 F7
Stonegate Wlk LS7 .... 60 A6
Stonehaven Ct BD21 .... 35 E5
Stonehurst LS14 .... 62 A8
Stonehurst Rd WF14 .... 138 A6
Stonehyrst Ave WF13 .... 118 B1
Stonelea HX4 .... 133 A5
Stoneleca Ct Leeds LS7 ...... 60 A7
 Leeds, Far Headingley Lo .. 59 D5
Stoneleigh ▪️ BD13 .... 72 F1
Stoneleigh Ct HD8 .... 174 A3
Stoneleigh Gr WF5 .... 140 D5
Stonely Dr OL14 .... 129 A7
Stonely Rd OL14 .... 108 A6
Stones Bank HX6 .... 132 C2
Stones Dr HX6 .... 132 B2
Stones La Huddersfield HD7 152 D3
 Slaithwaite HD7 .... 170 C8
 Todmorden OL14 .... 107 E4
Stones Rd OL14 .... 107 F4
Stones Terr OL14 .... 108 A2
Stoney Back La HX4 .... 153 E2
Stoney Bank La HD7 .... 189 EB
Stoney Bank St WF13 ...... 139 A6
Stoney Battery HD1 .... 153 D4
Stoney Battery Rd HD1 .... 153 D4
Stoney Butts La HX4 .... 133 B5
Stoney Croft BD10 .... 117 B7
Stoney Cross St HD4 .... 153 F2
Stoney Ford La HD5 .... 137 B1
Stoney Garth WF4 .... 159 F3
Stoney Hill HD6 .... 115 A2
Stoney La Batley WF17 ..... 118 D6
 Crigglestone WF4 .... 159 F2
 Halifax HX2 .... 92 A3
 Horsforth LS18 .... 58 BB
 Huddersfield, Longwood HD3 152 F6
 Lofthouse Gate WF2 .... 120 D5
 Menston LS29 .... 21 D6
 Thorner LS14 .... 45 BB
Stoney Lee Middle Sch
 BD16 .... 54 B6
Stoney Ridge Ave BD9 .... 54 B4
Stoney Ridge Hospl BD16 .. 54 C5
Stoney Ridge Rd BD16 .... 54 C5
Stoney Rise LS18 .... 58 BB
Stoney Rock Ct LS9 .... 207 F1
Stoney Rock Gr LS9 .... 207 F1
Stoney Rock La LS9 .... 207 F1
Stoney Royd S71 .... 178 F1
Stoney Royd La HX7 .... 110 A4
Stoney Royd Terr HX3 ..... 113 D4
Stoney St BD20 .... 18 B2
Stoneybrook Cl WF4 .... 176 FB
Stoneycroft ▪️ LS18 .... 58 BB
Stoneycroft La BD20 .... 18 B2
Stoneyhurst Sq BD4 .... 75 E3
Stoneys Fold BD15 .... 53 B6
Stoneythorpe ▪️ LS18 .... 58 BB
Stonlea Dr HD6 .... 135 F7
Stony Croft La HX4 .... 133 B5
Stony Gate HD7 .... 188 E2
Stony La
 Blackshaw Head HX7 .... 88 D2
 Bradford BD15 .... 53 F2
 Bradford, Eccleshill BD2 ...... 56 C5
 Brighouse HX3 .... 114 C4
 Elland HX4 .... 134 A8
 Honley BD2 .... 171 F3
 Rippenden HX6 .... 132 D5
 Todmorden OL14 .... 108 A8
Stony Royd LS28 .... 57 C3
Stony Royd La HX7 .... 110 A4
Stoodley Cl OL14 .... 109 A5
Stoodley Glen OL14 .... 109 A7
Stoodley Grange OL14 ..... 109 B5
Stoodley La OL14 .... 109 B7
Stoodley Pike Mon OL14 .. 109 C5
Stoodley Terr HX2 .... 202 A1
Stopford Ave WF2 .... 160 EB
Stopford Garth WF2 .... 160 EB
Storey Pl LS14 .... 61 E1
Storie Cres WF2 .... 141 E4
Storiths La LS29 .... 6 F7
Storiths La BD23 .... 3 BB
Storr Hill BD12 .... 94 D4
Storr Hill Terr WF5 .... 140 E2
Storrs Hill Rd WF4 .... 152 F3
Storth Ave HD4 .... 153 F2
Storth Pl HD2 .... 135 F1
Storths Hall La HD8 .... 173 D6
Storths Rd HD2 .... 135 F1
Stotfold Rd DN5 .... 194 E3
Stott Hill BD1 .... 201 C3
Stott Hill Rd LS14 .... 62 C5
Stott St LS12 .... 210 A3
Stott Terr BD2 .... 56 D4
Stourton Rd LS9 .... 7 F5
Stowe Gr LS9 .... 80 D8
Stowell Mill St BD5 .... 74 D4
Stradmore Rd BD10 .... 71 E8
Strafford Way BD10 .... 56 EB
Straight La Addingham LS29 .. 6 A5
 Halifax HX2 .... 91 D5
Straightacres La BD10 .... 56 D5
Straits ▪️ BD17 .... 38 C4
Stralau St WF17 .... 118 C6

Strands Ct WF4 .... 158 E6
Strangford Ct BD10 .... 56 D8
Stranglands La WF11 .... 126 B5
Stratford Ave LS11 .... 214 A3
Stratford Cl HD7 .... 152 E5
Stratford Rd BD7 .... 74 B5
Stratford St LS11 .... 214 B3
Stratford Terr LS11 .... 214 B3
Strathallan Br BD17 .... 38 D3
Strathden Rd WF2 .... 142 A7
Strathmore Ave LS9 .... 208 A3
Strathmore Cl BD2 .... 56 B3
Strathmore Dr Baildon BD17 38 B4
 Leeds LS9 .... 208 A3
Strathmore Gdns WF9 .... 183 B4
Strathmore Rd LS29 .... 8 E4
Strathmore St LS9 .... 208 A3
Strathmore Terr LS9 .... 208 A3
Strathmore View LS9 ...... 208 A2
Stratton Pk HD6 .... 115 C1
Stratton Rd HD6 .... 115 C1
Stratton View BD4 .... 75 E4
Stratton Wlk BD15 .... 73 A8
Strawberry Ave
 Garforth LS25 .... 82 E6
 Liversedge WF15 .... 117 A3
Strawberry Bank WF15 .... 117 A4
Strawberry Fields ▪️ BD5 .. 15 C8
Strawberry La LS12 .... 209 F3
Strawberry Rd LS12 .... 209 F3
Strawberry Sq ▪️ WF16 .... 117 D3
Strawberry St
 Keighley BD21 .... 35 C8
 Silsden BD20 .... 5 D1
Stray The BD10 .... 56 A6
Stream Head Rd BD13 .... 53 B2
Streamside LS6 .... 59 E6
Streamside Cl HX7 .... 110 EB
Street 1 LS23 .... 31 A8
Street 2 LS23 .... 31 A8
Street 3 LS23 .... 15 B1
Street 5 LS23 .... 15 B2
Street 6 LS23 .... 15 B2
Street 7 LS23 .... 15 C2
Street 8 LS23 .... 15 C2
Street Furlong La WF8 ..... 147 B7
Street Head La BD22 .... 50 EB
Street Lane Gildersome LS27 .. 97 C6
 Hooton Pagnell DN5 .... 195 F3
 Leeds LS17 .... 19 C2
 Leeds LS17 .... 43 E2
Street The LS29 .... 6 D8
Streethouse First Sch
 WF7 .... 144 C5
Stremall Gn ▪️ BD6 .... 93 EB
Stretch Gate HD8 .... 173 F2
Stretchgate La HX2 .... 202 A4
Stretton Cl WF7 .... 124 A1
Strickland Ave LS17 .... 45 A4
Strickland Cl LS17 .... 44 F4
Strickland Cres LS17 .... 44 F4
Strickland Rd WF9 .... 183 D8
Strike La HX6 .... 174 F3
Strikes La BD20 .... 16 E3
Strines Moor Rd HD7 .... 199 C8
Stringer St LS13 .... 129 A7
Stringer House La HD8 .... 175 A7
Stringer La ▪️ WF4 .... 141 B1
Strong Close Gr BD21 .... 35 E7
Strong Close Rd BD21 .... 35 E7
Strong Close Way BD21 .... 35 E7
Stuart Gr Normanton WF6 .. 123 A1
 Ossett WF5 .... 140 C6
Stuart Pl HD2 .... 136 F5
Stuart Rd WF8 .... 125 C1
Stuart St Castleford WF10 .. 124 EB
 Pontefract WF8 .... 125 C1
Stubbin La Denby Dale HD8 192 B6
 Holmfirth HD7 .... 188 C3
Stubbin Rd HD7 .... 169 B5
Stubbing Brink HX7 .... 88 E3
Stubbing Dr HX7 .... 88 E3
Stubbing Holme Rd HX7 ... 88 F3
Stubbing La Elland HX4 .... 133 E5
 Sowerby Bridge HX6 .... 132 EB
Stubbing Way BD18 .... 55 C6
Stubbings Cl HX7 .... 110 EB
Stubbings Infant Sch HX7 .. 89 A3
Stubbings Rd BD17 .... 37 F2
Stubbings St HX7 .... 110 EB
Stubbings HX6 .... 132 EB
Stubbs La ▪️ WF3 .... 120 E7
Stubham Rise LS29 .... 8 B5
Stubley Farm Rd WF16 .... 117 D6
Stubley Holme OL14 .... 86 A1
Stubley La OL14 .... 86 B1
Stubley La LS6 .... 117 C6
Stubley Rd OL14 .... 86 A1
Stubley St WF1 .... 216 A2
Stubs Beck La BD19 .... 95 D2
Studdley Cres BD16 .... 36 F3
Studfield View LS14 .... 62 A2
Studio Rd LS3 .... 205 E1
Studleigh Terr HD6 .... 114 E5
Studley Ave BD6 .... 93 D1
Studley Cl BD20 .... 19 D1
Studley Rd BD3 .... 201 D4
Stumpcross Cl WF8 .... 125 F3
Stumpcross Ct WF8 .... 125 F3
Stumpcross Way WF8 ...... 125 F3
Stunsteds Rd BD19 .... 96 B1
Sturges Gr BD2 .... 56 B1
Sturton Ave Garforth LS25 .. 83 A3
Sturton Gr HX2 .... 91 E6
Sturton Grange La LS25 .... 83 C7

Sturton La Garforth LS25 .... 83 A8
Halifax HX2 .... 91 E7
Stutely Gr HD2 .... 136 E5
Sty La BD16 .... 36 F6
Styeton Way BD20 .... 17 B6
Styes La HX6 .... 111 D4
Sude Hill HD7 .... 189 F6
Sude Hill Terr HD7 .... 189 F6
Sudforth La DN14 .... 127 F5
Suffolk Ave WF17 .... 118 B3
Suffolk Cl WF5 .... 140 C4
Suffolk Ct LS19 .... 40 B7
Suffolk House WF1 .... 142 F3
Suffolk Pl BD2 .... 55 F4
Suffolk St WF17 .... 118 B4
Sufton St HD2 .... 135 F1
Sugar Hill LS29 .... 6 F8
Sugar Hill Cl LS26 .... 101 C3
Sugar La Dewsbury WF12 .... 139 E8
Wakefield WF1 .... 142 E3
Sugar Well App LS7 .... 60 A5
Sugar Well Mount LS7 ...... 60 A5
Sugar Well Rd LS7 .... 60 A5
Sugarwell Ct LS7 .... 206 B4
Sugden Cl HD6 .... 136 A8
Sugden St Bradford BD12 ... 94 F4
Bradford, Lister Hills BD11 74 C7
Sugden's Almshouses
  BD22 .... 34 E3
Sulby Gr BD10 .... 56 E7
Sullivan Cl HD4 .... 153 D3
Sullivan Gr WF9 .... 182 B1
Summer Fields
  Jun & Inf Sch S71 ...... 179 A4
Summer Hall Ing BD12 ...... 94 C4
Summer Hill La LS26 ...... 102 D2
Summer Hill St BD7 ...... 74 A5
Summer La Emley HD8 ...... 175 D6
  Royston S71 .... 179 B4
Summer Lea BD10 .... 56 A8
Summer Meadow WF8 ...... 146 C7
Summer Rd S71 .... 179 B4
Summer St Halifax HX1 .... 202 B1
  Huddersfield, Netherton
  HD4 .... 171 D7
  Huddersfield, Rashcliffe
  HD1, HD4 .... 153 F4
Summerbridge Cl WF17 .... 118 A6
Summerbridge Cres
  Bradford BD10 .... 56 D5
  Cleckheaton BD19 ...... 96 C2
Summerdale BD19 .... 96 B2
Summerfield Ave
  Brighouse HD6 .... 115 B6
  Leeds LS13 .... 58 A3
Summerfield Cl
  Baildon BD17 .... 38 B3
  Byram WF11 .... 126 E8
Summerfield Ct HX2 ...... 92 A5
Summerfield Dr
  Baildon BD17 .... 38 B3
  Byram WF11 .... 126 E8
  Leeds LS13 .... 58 A3
Summerfield Gdns LS13 .. 58 A3
Summerfield Gn
  Baildon BD17 .... 38 B3
  Leeds LS13 .... 58 A3
Summerfield Gr
  Baildon BD17 .... 38 B3
  Lepton HD8 .... 155 D2
Summerfield Pk BD17 ..... 38 B3
Summerfield Pl LS13 ..... 58 A3
Summerfield Primary Sch
  LS13 .... 57 F3
Summerfield Rd
  Bradford BD10 .... 56 C6
  Leeds LS13 .... 58 A3
  Todmorden OL14 ...... 108 D5
Summerfield Rd W OL14 .. 108 C5
Summergate Pl HX1 ...... 202 B2
Summergate St HX1 ...... 202 B2
Summerhill Ave BD20 .... 17 D6
Summerhill Dr BD20 ..... 17 D6
Summerhill Gdns LS8 .... 44 B2
Summerhill Gr LS25 ...... 82 D6
Summerhill La WF8 ...... 147 D2
Summerhill Pl LS8 ...... 44 B3
Summerhill Rd LS25 ..... 82 D6
Summerlands Gr BD5 .... 75 A2
Summerscale St HX1 ..... 202 C4
Summerseat Pl BD7 ...... 74 C5
Summervale HD7 .... 189 A6
Summerville Rd
  Bradford BD7 .... 74 C6
  Pudsey LS28 .... 57 C2
Summit St BD21 .... 35 B8
Sun Ct WF7 .... 145 C8
Sun Field LS28 .... 57 D1
Sun Fold HX1 .... 203 F2
Sun Hill Dr BD17 .... 37 E2
Sun La Burley in W LS29 .. 9 E2
  Haworth BD22 .... 50 E7
  Wakefield WF1 .... 216 C2
Sun St Bradford BD1 .... 201 C4
  Haworth BD22 .... 51 C6
  Keighley BD21 .... 35 C6
  Keighley, East Morton BD20 .. 19 E1
  Pudsey LS28 .... 57 E1
  Steeton BD20 .... 17 A5
Sun Terr OL14 .... 86 B1
Sun Vale Ave OL14 ...... 129 B7
Sun Way HX3 .... 113 F5
Sun Wood Ave WF3 ...... 93 B4
Sunbeam Ave LS11 ...... 214 B3
Sunbeam Gr 7 LS11 .... 214 B3

Sunbeam Pl LS11 .... 214 B3
Sunbeam Terr LS11 ...... 214 B3
Sunbridge Rd BD1 .... 74 D7
Sunbury Gr HD5 .... 154 E6
Sunderland Ct 6 HD6 ... 115 A3
Sunderland Rd
  Bradford BD9 .... 55 C2
  Low Bradley BD20 ...... 4 D5
Sunderland St
  5 Halifax HX1 .... 203 D3
  Haworth BD22 .... 51 F8
  Keighley BD21 .... 35 B6
Sundown Ave BD7 .... 73 E4
Sunfield Cl LS28 .... 57 D2
Sunfield Dr LS28 .... 57 D2
Sunfield Gdns LS28 ..... 57 D2
Sunfield Pl LS28 .... 57 D2
Sunfield Terr 11 BD19 ... 116 E7
Sunhurst Cl BD22 .... 34 C2
Sunhurst Dr BD22 .... 34 C2
Sunningdale Bradford BD8 73 D8
  Micklefield LS25 .... 83 F8
Sunningdale Ave
  Leeds LS17 .... 43 A4
  Mapplewell S75 .... 178 A1
Sunningdale Cl LS17 .... 43 A4
Sunningdale Cres BD13 . 52 E5
Sunningdale Cl HD2 .... 135 F3
Sunningdale Dr
  Cudworth S72 .... 180 C1
  Leeds LS17 .... 43 A4
Sunningdale Gn LS17 .... 43 A4
Sunningdale Rd HD4 .... 153 D3
Sunningdale Way LS17 .. 43 A4
Sunningdale Wlk LS17 ... 43 A4
Sunningdales WF6 ...... 123 D1
Sunny Ave
  South Elmsall WF9 ..... 183 B2
  Upton WF9 .... 183 A7
Sunny Bank Bradford BD9 . 54 D2
  Hebden Bridge HX7 ..... 89 F1
  Hemsworth WF9 .... 163 A3
  Knottingley WF11 ...... 127 A4
  Leeds LS14 .... 204 C1
  Normanton WF6 .... 144 B7
  Ryhill WF4 .... 162 A1
  Shipley BD18 .... 55 B7
Sunny Bank Ave
  Bradford BD5 .... 74 D1
  Mirfield WF14 .... 138 A8
Sunny Bank Dr
  Mirfield WF14 .... 137 F8
  Sowerby Bridge HX6 .... 112 C4
Sunny Bank Gr Leeds LS8 204 C1
  Mirfield WF14 .... 138 A7
Sunny Bank La
  Batley WF17 .... 118 D7
  Brighouse HX3 .... 114 B6
  Hebden Bridge HX7 .... 110 C4
Sunny Bank Par WF14 ... 137 F8
Sunny Bank Rd
  Batley WF17 .... 118 D6
  Bradford BD5 .... 74 D1
  Brighouse HD6 .... 115 A2
  Glusburn BD20 .... 16 C6
  Halifax HX2 .... 91 C5
  Meltham HD7 .... 170 C2
  Mirfield WF14 .... 138 A8
  Slaithwaite HD7 .... 152 B3
  Wadsworth Moor HX7 ... 69 A3
Sunny Bank St HX6 ..... 112 C4
Sunny Bank Terr
  4 Halifax HX3 .... 92 C1
  9 Todmorden OL14 .... 86 B1
Sunny Bank View LS8 ... 204 C1
Sunny Bank Wlk WF14 .. 138 A7
Sunny Brow HD4 .... 171 F8
Sunny Brow La BD9 .... 54 D2
Sunny Dale BD13 .... 52 D2
Sunny Gr 12 LS27 ...... 98 C8
Sunny Heys Rd HD7 .... 170 D3
Sunny Heys W HD7 .... 170 D2
Sunny Hill WF2 .... 120 E1
Sunny Hill Ave BD21 ... 34 F5
Sunny Hill Cl WF2 .... 120 E2
Sunny Hill Cres BD21 .. 34 F5
Sunny Hill House Sch
  WF2 .... 120 E1
Sunny Mead HD5 .... 155 A6
Sunny Mount
  Brighouse HX3 .... 114 C7
  Harden BD16 .... 36 B1
  Keighley BD21 .... 35 B8
  Keighley, Braithwaite BD22 . 34 E8
  Keighley, Crossflatts BD20 .. 36 C7
Sunny Side St 11 HX3 .. 92 C1
Sunny Vale Country Club
  HX3 .... 114 C6
Sunny View Cres HD2 ... 136 D3
Sunny View Terr 18 BD13 92 C8
Sunnybank Denby Dale HD8 191 F5
Sunnybank Ave
  Bradford BD3 .... 56 F1
  8 Horsforth LS18 ..... 58 B7
Sunnybank Cl BD19 ..... 115 F7
Sunnybank Cres Elland HX4 134 B7
  Yeadon LS19 .... 40 D7
Sunnybank Ct LS19 ..... 40 D7
Sunnybank Dr HX4 ..... 134 B7
Sunnybank Gn BD3 ..... 56 F1
Sunnybank Grange 1
  HD6 .... 115 A2
Sunnybank La Bradford BD3 . 56 F1
  Elland HX4 .... 134 B7
Sunnybank Rd Elland HX4 134 B7
  6 Horsforth LS18 ..... 58 B7
  Huddersfield HD3 ..... 153 D8

Sunnybank St WF5 ...... 140 D5
Sunnydale Croft HD6 ... 115 A3
Sunnybrae Cres BD16 ... 37 B2
Sunnycliffe BD20 .... 36 D8
Sunnydale Ave HD6 .... 136 A8
Sunnydale Cres LS21 ... 22 D6
Sunnydale Croft WF5 .. 140 E4
Sunnydale Gr BD21 ..... 35 F6
Sunnydale Pk
  Keighley BD20 .... 19 E2
  Ossett WF5 .... 140 E5
Sunnydale Rd WF5 ..... 140 D7
Sunnydale Ridge LS21 .. 22 D6
Sunnydale Terr WF5 ... 140 E5
Sunnydene LS14 .... 61 F1
Sunnyfield WF3 .... 120 C7
Sunnyfield Ave BD10 .. 85 A8
Sunnyfield Dr WF9 ..... 163 A3
Sunnyhill Cres WF2 ... 120 D1
Sunnyhill Croft WF2 ... 120 E2
Sunnylea WF4 .... 169 A4
Sunnymead HD8 .... 175 E2
Sunnymount Terr 6 WF17 . 96 F1
Sunnyridge Ave LS28 .. 76 B8
Sunnyside Batley WF16 . 117 D3
  Brighouse HD6 .... 136 D8
  Elland HX4 .... 134 A1
  Huddersfield HD2 ..... 153 E8
  Todmorden OL14 ...... 108 A5
Sunnyside Ave
  East Ardsley WF3 ..... 119 D8
  Liversedge WF15 ...... 116 F2
Sunnyside La BD3 ...... 55 F1
Sunnyside Rd LS13 .... 58 B1
Sunnyvale Mount WF9 .. 182 E3
Sunnyview LS12 .... 120 C6
Sunnyview Ave LS11 ... 213 F3
Sunnyview Gdns LS11 .. 213 F3
Sunnyview Terr LS11 ... 213 F3
Sunroyd Ave WF4 ...... 141 B2
Sunroyd Hill WF4 ..... 141 B2
Sunset Ave LS6 .... 59 E8
Sunset Dr Ilkley LS29 .. 8 D5
  6 Leeds LS6 .... 59 E7
Sunset Hilltop LS6 .... 59 E8
Sunset Mount LS6 ..... 59 E7
Sunset Rise LS6 .... 59 E8
Sunset Terr LS29 ..... 8 C5
  9 Leeds LS6 .... 59 E8
Surat Rd HD7 .... 151 F3
Suresnes Rd BD21 ..... 35 B7
Surgery St BD22 ...... 51 D6
Surrey Gr Bradford BD5 74 E4
  Pudsey LS28 .... 76 E8
Surrey Rd 4 LS28 .... 76 E8
Surrey St Wakefield WF17 118 D5
  Halifax HX1 .... 202 B2
  Keighley BD21 .... 35 E8
  Todmorden OL14 ...... 108 B6
Sussex App LS10 ...... 215 F3
Sussex Ave Horsforth LS18 .. 41 C3
  Leeds LS10 .... 215 F3
Sussex Cl WF9 .... 181 D8
Sussex Cres WF10 ..... 125 E8
Sussex Gdns LS10 ..... 215 F3
Sussex Gn LS10 .... 215 F3
Sussex Pl LS10 .... 215 F3
Sussex St Batley WF17 .. 118 D5
  Leeds LS9 .... 212 C3
Sussex Wlk 2 WF13 .. 139 B8
Sutcliffe Pl 6 BD6 .... 94 D8
Sutcliffe St HX2 .... 202 A4
Sutcliffe Wood La HX3 . 114 C6
Sutherland Ave LS8 ... 44 A2
Sutherland Cres LS8 .. 44 A2
Sutherland Dr HD4 .... 153 C2
Sutherland Mount LS9 . 208 A2
Sutherland Rd
  Brighouse HX3 .... 114 E8
  Leeds LS9 .... 208 A2
Sutherland St LS12 ... 210 B2
Sutherland Terr LS9 .. 208 A2
Sutton App LS14 .... 61 E1
Sutton Ave Bradford BD2 . 56 A4
  Huddersfield HD5 ..... 155 A7
Sutton Cres Bradford BD4 . 75 E5
  Leeds LS14 .... 61 E1
Sutton Dr Cullingworth BD13 . 52 D5
Sutton Fields BD20 .... 16 C6
Sutton Gr Bradford BD4 75 E5
  2 Morley LS27 ...... 98 A3
Sutton La Byram WF11 . 126 E7
  Kippax LS25 .... 83 D8
Sutton Rd BD4 .... 75 E5
Sutton St LS12 .... 210 C2
Sutton-in-Craven
  C of E Primary Sch BD20 . 16 D5
Sutton-in-Craven County
  Primary Sch BD20 .... 16 D5
Suzanne Cres WF9 .... 182 E3
Swain House Cres BD2 . 56 A5
Swain House
  First & Middle Schs BD2 . 56 A5
Swain House Rd BD2 .. 56 A5
Swain Mount BD2 ..... 56 A5
Swaine Hill Cres LS19 . 40 A7
Swaine Hill St LS19 ... 40 A7
Swaine Hill Terr LS19 . 40 A7
Swale Cres LS25 .... 83 B6
Swale Ct BD20 .... 17 E8
Swale Dr WF10 .... 125 B8
Swale Rise LS22 .... 13 D8
Swales Moor Rd HX3 .. 92 C4
Swales' Yd 2 WF17 .. 146 C8
Swallow Ave LS12 .... 209 D2

Swallow Cl Leeds LS17 . 43 F4
  Pool LS21 .... 24 D6
Swallow Cres LS12 .... 209 D2
Swallow Dr Leeds LS17 . 44 A4
  Morley LS27 .... 98 D4
  Pool LS21 .... 24 D6
Swallow Fold BD8 ..... 73 C7
Swallow Garth WF2 .... 160 D5
Swallow Gr HD4 .... 171 E6
Swallow Hill WF17 .... 118 A8
Swallow La
  Huddersfield HD7 ..... 154 A5
  5 Keighley BD21 ..... 35 D8
  Kirkburton HD8 .... 117 D3
Swan Bank La Halifax HX3 . 203 F1
  Holmfirth HD7 .... 189 A4
Swan La Elland HD3 .... 134 B1
Swan St Bradford BD5 . 201 B2
  Leeds LS1 .... 211 F4
Swanhill La WF8 .... 146 D7
Swarcliffe App LS14 ... 62 C4
Swarcliffe Ave LS14 ... 62 D5
Swarcliffe Bank LS14 .. 62 C5
Swarcliffe Dr LS14 .... 62 C4
Swarcliffe Drive E 12 LS14 . 62 D4
Swarcliffe Gn LS14 .... 62 D4
Swarcliffe Par LS14 ... 62 C4
Swarcliffe Prim Sch LS15 . 62 C5
Swarcliffe Rd LS14 ... 62 C5
Swarcliffe Towers 9 LS14 . 62 D5
Swardale Gn LS14 .... 62 C4
Swardale Rd LS14 .... 62 C4
Swarland Gr BD5 ..... 201 B1
Swartha La BD20 ..... 6 A2
Swastika Stone LS29 .. 7 D2
Sweep La HD7 .... 189 B3
Sweet St LS11 .... 211 E2
Sweet St W LS11 ..... 211 D2
Swift Pl HD6 .... 132 B2
Swift Way WF7 .... 160 D5
Swift's Fold HD7 ..... 171 F5
Swillington La LS26 .. 82 A4
Swillington Primary Sch
  LS26 .... 82 A2
Swincar Ave LS19 .... 40 B7
Swincliffe Cl BD19 .... 96 A4
Swincliffe Cres BD19 .. 96 B3
Swincroft WF5 .... 140 E5
Swindon Rd WF13 .... 139 C8
Swine La Keighley BD20 . 36 B8
  West Hardwick HX7 ... 162 D5
Swine Market La HX7 . 110 A3
Swinegate LS1 .... 211 F3
Swineshead La OL14 .. 108 B3
Swineshead Rd OL14 . 108 A3
Swinnow Ave LS13 ... 58 A1
Swinnow Cl LS13 ..... 58 A1
Swinnow Cres LS28 .. 58 A2
Swinnow Dr LS13 .... 58 A1
Swinnow Garth LS13 . 58 A1
Swinnow Gdns LS13 .. 58 A1
Swinnow Gn LS28 .... 77 A8
Swinnow Gr LS13 .... 58 A1
Swinnow La LS13 LS28 . 58 A1
  Pudsey LS13 .... 77 A8
Swinnow Middle Sch LS13 . 77 A8
Swinnow Pl LS13 .... 58 A2
Swinnow Prim Sch LS28 . 77 A8
Swinnow Rd LS13 .... 58 A1
Swinnow View LS13 .. 58 A1
Swinnow Wlk LS13 .. 58 A1
Swinton Pl BD7 .... 74 B5
Swinton Terr HX1 .... 202 B1
Swire Smith Middle Sch
  BD21 .... 35 E6
Swires Rd Bradford BD2 . 56 C1
  Halifax HX1 .... 203 D2
Swires Terr HX1 ..... 203 D2
Swiss St WF10 .... 103 E1
Swithen Hill LS75 .... 177 B3
Swithen's La LS26 ... 100 F4
Swithen's St LS26 ... 100 F4
Swithenbank Ave WF5 140 D8
Swithenbank St WF5 . 119 C1
Swithens Ct LS26 .... 100 F4
Swithens Dr LS26 .... 100 F4
Swithens Gr LS26 .... 100 E4
Sycamore Ave Bingley BD16 . 36 F2
  Bradford BD7 .... 73 F6
  Huddersfield HD3, HD7 . 152 F5
  Kippax LS25 .... 82 F1
  Knottingley WF11 .... 126 D3
  Leeds, Halton LS15 ... 81 A8
  Leeds, Potternewton LS8 . 204 C1
  Meltham HD7 .... 170 D1
  Todmorden OL14 ...... 108 A7
  Wakefield, Brag Lane End
  WF2 .... 120 F3
  Wakefield, Flanshaw WF2 . 141 F7
Sycamore Chase LS28 . 76 F7
Sycamore Cl Batley WF12 118 F2
  Bradford BD3 .... 201 D4
  Bramhope LS16 .... 24 F1
  Knottingley WF11 .... 126 D2
  Leeds LS6 .... 206 A4
  Leeds, Meanwood LS6 . 59 F7
  Leeds LS10 .... 215 F3
Sycamore Copse WF2 .. 141 F5
Sycamore Croft LS11 .. 214 B3
Sycamore Ct Bradford BD3 201 D4
  Huddersfield HD8 .... 152 F5
  Ilkley LS29 .... 8 A5
  Kirkburton HD8 .... 173 F7

Sycamore Dr
  Addingham LS29 ...... 7 A8
  Brighouse HX3 .... 115 A6
  Cleckheaton BD19 .... 116 A5
  Elland HX5 .... 134 D6
  Royston S71 .... 179 A3
Sycamore Fold LS11 .. 214 B3
Sycamore Gn WF8 .... 125 F1
Sycamore Gr
  Normanton WF6 ...... 144 A8
  Steeton BD20 .... 16 F5
  Wakefield WF2 .... 141 F7
Sycamore House 5 HD6 124 E7
Sycamore Ind Est WF16 117 D2
Sycamore La WF4 ..... 176 F8
Sycamore Rise BD7 ... 189 D7
Sycamore Row LS13 .. 58 A4
Sycamore St WF1 .... 142 E4
Sycamore Terr Honley HD7 171 E3
  Horbury WF4 .... 159 C8
Sycamore View BD22 . 34 F6
Sycamore Way
  Batley WF17 .... 96 F1
  Featherstone WF7 ... 145 D6
Sycamore Wlk Dearne S63 194 D1
  Pudsey LS28 .... 57 D2
Sycamores The
  Bramhope LS16 ...... 24 F1
  Dewsbury WF13 ..... 118 B2
  Guiseley LS20 .... 22 E2
  Horbury WF4 .... 141 C1
Sydenham Pl BD3 .... 56 A2
Sydenham Rd LS11 .. 210 C2
Sydenham St LS11 .. 210 C2
Sydney Gdns OL15 .. 129 C1
Sydney St 12 Bingley BD16 . 37 A3
  Liversedge WF15 .... 117 B3
  Pudsey LS28 .... 57 D2
  Rothwell LS26 .... 101 D6
Syke Ave Dewsbury WF12 139 F8
  East Ardsley WF3 .... 119 D7
Syke Cl WF3 .... 119 C7
Syke Gdns WF3 ...... 119 D7
Syke Gn LS14 .... 45 C8
Syke Gr WF3 .... 139 F8
Syke House La HX4 .. 133 F7
Syke Ing Cl WF12 .... 140 A7
Syke Ing Terr WF12 .. 140 A7
Syke La Brighouse HX3 . 93 E1
  Dewsbury WF12 ...... 139 F7
  Halifax HX2 .... 71 E2
  Queensbury BD13 .... 92 F7
  Scarcroft LS14 .... 45 B8
  Sowerby Bridge HX6 . 112 B3
Syke Rd Dewsbury WF12 139 F8
  East Ardsley WF3 .... 119 D7
  Wetherby LS22 .... 14 A5
Syke Side BD20 ...... 18 B2
Syke St WF12 .... 139 F7
Syke Terr WF3 .... 119 C7
Syke View WF12 ..... 139 F8
Sykes Ave Batley WF16 . 117 E5
  Mirfield WF14 .... 138 C6
Sykes Cl 8 Ackworth M T WF7 163 D5
  Batley WF17 .... 96 F1
Sykes Fold BD22 ..... 51 E1
Sykes Gate HX7 ...... 131 C7
Sykes La Batley WF12 . 119 A4
  Bradford BD12 .... 95 A4
  Oakworth BD22 .... 34 D2
Sykes Rd WF17 .... 118 E6
Sykes St
  9 Cleckheaton WF10 . 124 D8
  Cleckheaton BD19 ... 116 D7
Sylhet Cl BD1 .... 74 D8
Sylvan Ave BD13 .... 92 D8
Sylvester Ave WF6 .. 144 A7
Symons St WF2 ...... 216 A1
Syringa Ave BD15 ... 54 A4
Syringa St HD1 ...... 153 D7

Tabbs Ct BD19 ...... 94 F1
Tabbs La BD19 ...... 94 F1
Tadcaster Grammar Sch
  LS24 .... 31 D2
Tadman St WF1 ..... 142 C4
Tagore Ct BD3 ...... 75 D6
Talbot Ave
  Huddersfield HD3 ... 135 C1
  Leeds, Burley LS4 .. 59 C3
  Leeds, Lidgett Park LS17, LS8 . 43 F2
Talbot & Falcon Yd WF1 . 216 B2
Talbot Ct LS8 .... 43 F2
Talbot Gdns LS8 .... 43 F2
Talbot House 2 HX5 . 134 F6
Talbot Mount LS4 .. 59 C3
Talbot Primary Sch LS8 . 43 F2
Talbot Rd LS8 .... 43 F1
Talbot Rise LS17 ... 43 F2
Talbot Row WF17 ... 118 D5
Talbot St Bradford BD7 . 74 C7
  4 Keighley BD21 ... 35 A7
  Normanton WF6 .... 123 A2
Talbot Terr Leeds LS4 . 59 C3
  Rothwell LS26 .... 100 F4
Talbot View Leeds LS4 . 59 C3
  Mirfield WF14 .... 138 A6
Tall Trees Dr WF7 ... 145 D8
Tamar St BD5 .... 74 C4
Tammy Hall St 1 WF1 . 216 B2
Tamworth St BD4 ... 75 E6
Tan House Ct BD4 .. 95 B7

Tan House La
Ackworth M T WF7 ...... 164 B7
Shelf HX3 ...... 93 A5
Wilsden BD15 ...... 53 B6
Tan La BD44 ...... 95 B6
Tan Pit CI DN5 ...... 194 D4
Tan Pit La DN5 ...... 194 D4
Tandem Ind Est HD5 ...... 155 B6
Tandem Way HD5 ...... 155 B6
Tandy Trad Est The LS12 ...... 205 D1
Tanfield CI S71 ...... 179 A4
Tanfield Dr LS29 ...... 9 E2
Tanfield Rd HD1 ...... 153 F8
Tanglewood Ct 2 BD6 ...... 74 A1
Tanhouse Hill
Brighouse HX3 ...... 114 C7
2 Horsforth LS18 ...... 58 E8
Tanhouse La WF14 ...... 156 B7
Tanhouse Pk HX3 ...... 114 C7
Tanhouse St WF13 ...... 138 F6
Tanner Hill Rd BD7 ...... 73 E3
Tanner St WF15 ...... 116 B5
Tannerbrook CI BD14 ...... 73 D4
Tanners HD7 ...... 169 F7
Tannery Ct Bradford BD10 ...... 56 D8
Mirfield WF14 ...... 137 E6
Tannett Gn BD5 ...... 74 F2
Tanpits 25 HX7 ...... 89 A3
Tanshelf Dr WF8 ...... 146 C8
Tanshelf Ind Est WF8 ...... 125 C1
Tanshelf Sta WF8 ...... 125 C1
Tansy End BD22 ...... 51 E2
Tanton Cres BD14 ...... 73 D4
Tanton Wlk BD14 ...... 73 D4
Tanyard Ave HD3 ...... 153 A7
Tanyard Fold WF4 ...... 160 A3
Tanyard Rd
Huddersfield, Milnsbridge
HD3 ...... 153 B4
Huddersfield, Quarmby HD3 ...... 153 A7
Tarn CI WF10 ...... 104 E1
Tarn Ct Keighley BD20 ...... 34 F8
Lofthouse Gate WF1 ...... 121 B3
Tarn Hows Wlk WF7 ...... 163 F6
Tarn La Bardsey LS17 ...... 44 E7
Harewood LS17 ...... 44 E7
Keighley BD22 ...... 34 B8
Tarn Rd WF7 ...... 145 E4
Tarn View Rd LS19 ...... 40 D7
Tarnhill Mews BD5 ...... 74 E4
Tarnside Dr LS14 ...... 62 A3
Tate Naylor St WF13 ...... 118 B2
Tatefield Gr LS25 ...... 83 A1
Tatefield Pl LS25 ...... 83 A1
Tateley CI WF11 ...... 119 D1
Tateley La WF11 ...... 119 C1
Tatham Way LS8 ...... 61 C6
Tatton St WF1 ...... 142 F3
Taunton Ho 11 BD5 ...... 201 B1
Taunton St BD18 ...... 55 A8
Tavern St WF1 ...... 216 C2
Taverngate LS20 ...... 38 E8
Tavistock Way WF2 ...... 160 A5
Tavora St WF1 ...... 216 B3
Tawny CI 1 LS27 ...... 98 D4
Tay Ct BD2 ...... 56 D5
Taylor Ave BD20 ...... 5 D1
Taylor CI WF5 ...... 140 F4
Taylor Cres WF5 ...... 140 F4
Taylor Dr WF5 ...... 140 F4
Taylor Gr LS26 ...... 102 E3
Taylor Hall La WF14 ...... 137 F8
Taylor Hill Rd HD4 ...... 153 C1
Taylor La Barwick in E LS15 ...... 63 B5
Halifax BD23 ...... 72 A3
Slaithwaite HD7 ...... 152 B5
Taylor Rd 10 BD6 ...... 94 D8
Taylor St Batley WF17 ...... 118 C4
Cleckheaton BD19 ...... 116 C7
Huddersfield HD7 ...... 152 E4
Taylor Wood Cotts WF4 ...... 163 B6
Taylor's Bldgs HD4 ...... 154 A2
Taylors CI LS14 ...... 62 B4
Teal CI WF10 ...... 124 D6
Teal Ct BD20 ...... 17 B6
Teal Dr LS27 ...... 98 D4
Teal Mews LS10 ...... 99 D5
Tealbeck App LS21 ...... 23 B7
Tealback House LS21 ...... 23 B7
Tealby CI LS16 ...... 41 E2
Teall CI WF5 ...... 141 A5
Teall St Ossett WF5 ...... 141 A5
Wakefield WF1 ...... 216 B2
Teapot Cnr DN5 ...... 194 B4
Teasdale St BD4 ...... 75 B3
Teasel CI BD12 ...... 95 A4
Technology Dr WF17 ...... 118 E4
Teddington Ave HD5 ...... 154 F6
Tees CI WF10 ...... 125 B8
Tees St BD5 ...... 74 C3
Teesdale PI WF11 ...... 126 E2
Telephone PI LS9 ...... 207 D1
Telford CI Castleford WF10 ...... 124 B7
Leeds LS10 ...... 215 E2
Silsden BD20 ...... 17 F8
Telford Ct BD7 ...... 74 B6
Telford Gdns 2 LS10 ...... 215 E2
Telford PI LS10 ...... 215 E2
Telford St 7 LS10 ...... 215 E2
Telford Terr LS10 ...... 215 E2
Telford Way WF2 ...... 120 F5
Telford Wlk 3 LS10 ...... 215 E2
Telscombe Dr BD4 ...... 75 D2
Temperance Field Ct WF4 ...... 94 D3
Temperance Fields BD19 ...... 115 F8

Temperance St 1 LS28 ...... 57 E1
Tempest PI LS11 ...... 214 A3
Tempest Rd Leeds LS11 ...... 214 B2
South Kirkby WF9 ...... 182 C4
Templar Dr HD5 ...... 154 D5
Templar Gdns LS22 ...... 13 F7
Templar La Leeds LS12 ...... 212 A4
Leeds, Shanks LS15 ...... 62 D4
Templar PI LS2 ...... 212 A4
Templar St Leeds LS2 ...... 212 A4
Wakefield WF1 ...... 142 F3
Templar's Way BD8 ...... 73 E8
Templars CI HX4 ...... 134 C2
Templars Way LS25 ...... 82 F6
Temple Ave Leeds LS15 ...... 81 A6
Rothwell LS26 ...... 100 F7
Temple Bank Specl Sch
BD9 ...... 54 E2
Temple CI
18 Huddersfield HD1 ...... 154 A6
Leeds LS15 ...... 81 A6
Temple Cres LS11 ...... 214 A3
Temple Ct Leeds LS15 ...... 80 F7
Rothwell LS26 ...... 100 F7
Temple Gate LS15 ...... 81 B7
Temple Gate Dr LS15 ...... 81 A7
Temple Gdns WF6 ...... 122 F4
Temple Gn LS26 ...... 101 A7
Temple Gr LS15 ...... 81 A7
Temple La Leeds LS15 ...... 81 B7
Littleborough OL15 ...... 129 D1
Temple Lea LS15 ...... 81 A7
Temple Lea LS15 ...... 81 B7
Temple Moor High Sch
LS15 ...... 81 B7
Temple Newsam Park
Golf Course LS15 ...... 80 F5
Temple Newsam Pk LS15 ...... 81 A8
Temple Newsam View LS15 ...... 80 F6
Temple Park CI LS15 ...... 81 A7
Temple Park Gdns LS15 ...... 81 A7
Temple Park Gn LS15 ...... 81 A7
Temple Rd WF13 ...... 139 B8
Temple Rhydding Dr BD17 ...... 38 C2
Temple Rise LS15 ...... 81 A6
Temple Row
Keighley BD21 ...... 35 B7
Leeds LS15 ...... 81 E6
Temple St Bradford BD9 ...... 55 B2
Castleford WF10 ...... 124 C7
Huddersfield HD1 ...... 135 B1
18 Keighley BD21 ...... 35 B7
Temple View LS9 ...... 100 C1
Temple View Gr LS9 ...... 80 A7
Temple View PI LS9 ...... 212 C3
Temple View Rd LS9 ...... 212 C3
Temple View Terr LS9 ...... 212 C3
Temple Wlk LS15 ...... 81 B8
Templegate Ave LS15 ...... 81 B6
Templegate CI LS15 ...... 81 C7
Templegate Cres LS15 ...... 81 B6
Templegate Gn LS15 ...... 81 B7
Templegate Rd LS15 ...... 81 B6
Templegate Rise LS15 ...... 81 A6
Templegate View LS15 ...... 81 B6
Templegate Way LS15 ...... 81 C7
Templegate Wlk LS15 ...... 81 B7
Templenewsam Halton
Primary Sch LS15 ...... 81 A8
Templenewsam Rd LS15 ...... 81 A6
Templenewsam View LS15 ...... 80 F6
Templestowe Cres LS15 ...... 62 C1
Templestowe Dr 3 LS15 ...... 81 C1
Templestowe Gdns 5 LS15 ...... 81 C1
Templestowe Hill 1 LS15 ...... 62 B1
Ten Lands La WF4 ...... 180 A7
Ten Row HD8 ...... 191 A4
Ten Yards La BD13 ...... 72 A8
Tenbury Fold BD4 ...... 75 E3
Tennants Ct WF11 ...... 127 A4
Tennis Ave BD4 ...... 75 E1
Tennis Way BD17 ...... 38 A1
Tennyson Ave
Lofthouse Gate WF3 ...... 121 E6
Sowerby Bridge HX6 ...... 111 F3
Todmorden OL14 ...... 108 D6
Tennyson Ct
Knottingley WF11 ...... 126 B4
Pudsey LS28 ...... 76 F6
Tennyson PI Bradford BD3 ...... 75 B8
Brighouse HX3 ...... 114 C8
4 Cleckheaton BD19 ...... 116 D8
Tennyson Rd BD6 ...... 94 B8
Tennyson St Guiseley LS20 ...... 39 F8
12 Halifax HX3 ...... 92 A1
6 Keighley BD21 ...... 35 B5
Morley LS27 ...... 98 A4
Pudsey LS28 ...... 76 F6
8 Pudsey, Farsley LS28 ...... 57 D2
Tennyson Terr LS27 ...... 98 A4
Tennyson Way WF8 ...... 125 D2
Tenter CI HD8 ...... 175 A2
Tenter Garth 5 BD17 ...... 38 C4
Tenter Hill Bradford BD14 ...... 73 B4
Bramham LS23 ...... 30 C2
Holmfirth HD7 ...... 189 F4
Tenter Hill La HD2 ...... 136 D4
Tentercroft Ct WF13 ...... 118 D1
Tenterden Way LS15 ...... 62 F2
Tenterfield Rd WF5 ...... 140 E5
Tenterfield Rise HX3 ...... 93 A1
Tenterfield Terr OL14 ...... 108 E6
Tenterfields Bradford BD10 ...... 56 E8
Halifax HX2 ...... 111 E5
Tenterfields Bsns Pk HX2 ...... 111 E5
Tenters CI WF11 ...... 126 D5
Tenters Gr HD2 ...... 136 C3
Tenth Ave WF15 ...... 116 C5

Tern St BD5 ...... 74 C3
Ternhill Gr BD5 ...... 201 B1
Terrace Gdns HX3 ...... 92 B1
Terrace The
Boston Spa LS23 ...... 30 E7
Honley HD7 ...... 171 E3
Pudsey LS28 ...... 76 E4
Terrington Crest BD14 ...... 73 C4
Terry Rd 8 BD12 ...... 94 E5
Tetley Dr BD11 ...... 96 B4
Tetley La HX3 ...... 93 A2
Tetley PI BD2 ...... 55 F3
Tetley St BD1 ...... 201 A3
Teville Ct BD4 ...... 75 E1
Tew St WF2 ...... 142 C4
Tewit CI HX2 ...... 91 F7
Tewit Gn HX2 ...... 91 F7
Tewit Hall Gdns HX2 ...... 91 F6
Tewit Hall Rd BD3 ...... 75 C8
Tewit La HX2 ...... 91 F7
Tewitt St Bingley BD16 ...... 37 B6
Wilsden BD13 ...... 53 A2
Texas St LS27 ...... 98 B2
Thacker Gate Rd HX6 ...... 111 B4
Thackeray Gr HD4 ...... 153 D3
Thackeray Rd BD10 ...... 56 D4
Thackley Ave BD10 ...... 39 A2
Thackley Ct BD10 ...... 55 C8
Thackley First Sch BD10 ...... 39 B1
Thackley Old Rd BD18 ...... 55 D8
Thackley Rd BD10 ...... 39 A2
Thackley View BD10 ...... 39 A2
Thackray Ave WF16 ...... 117 E5
Thackray La WF8 ...... 125 E1
Thackray St Halifax HX2 ...... 112 D7
Morley LS27 ...... 98 A3
Thames Dr LS25 ...... 83 B6
Thane Way LS15 ...... 62 E3
Thanes CI HD2 ...... 135 E1
Thanet Garth BD20 ...... 17 E8
Theaker La LS12 ...... 209 E4
Theakston Mead BD14 ...... 73 C4
Thealby CI LS9 ...... 212 B4
Thealby Lawn LS9 ...... 207 E1
Thealby PI 1 LS9 ...... 212 B4
Thearne Gn BD14 ...... 73 B4
Thearne Wlk 2 LS11 ...... 211 F4
Theodore St LS11 ...... 214 A2
Thewlis La HD4 ...... 153 B1
Thick Hollins HD7 ...... 170 F1
Thick Hollins Dr HD7 ...... 170 F1
Thick Hollins Rd
Holmfirth HD7 ...... 188 A7
Meltham HD7 ...... 187 F8
Third Ave Bradford BD3 ...... 56 C1
Halifax HX3 ...... 113 B6
Halifax HX3 ...... 113 B4
Huddersfield HD7 ...... 152 D4
1 Keighley BD21 ...... 35 B6
Kirkheaton HD5 ...... 137 C1
Leeds LS12 ...... 210 A2
Lofthouse Gate WF1 ...... 121 C2
Rothwell LS26 ...... 101 A7
Upton WF9 ...... 183 A8
Wetherby LS22 ...... 13 F5
Third St 2 BD12 ...... 94 E6
Thirkhill Ct BD5 ...... 74 E4
Thirkleby Royd BD14 ...... 73 C4
Thirlmere Ave
Brighouse HX3 ...... 94 E1
Elland HX5 ...... 135 B7
Thirlmere CI LS11 ...... 98 E8
Thirlmere Gdns
Bradford BD2 ...... 56 B2
Leeds LS11 ...... 98 E8
Thirlmere Gr WF11 ...... 37 E1
Thirlmere PI WF11 ...... 126 E2
Thirlmere Rd Batley WF12 ...... 118 F2
Wakefield WF2 ...... 141 E6
Thirsk CI HD2 ...... 136 B2
Thirsk Dr LS25 ...... 83 A2
Thirsk Grange BD14 ...... 73 D4
Thirsk Row LS1 ...... 211 E3
Thirstin Rd HD7 ...... 171 F5
Thirteenth Ave WF15 ...... 116 B5
Thistle CI HD2 ...... 135 E2
Thistle Dr WF8 ...... 182 F7
Thistle Hill Ave HD5 ...... 155 C5
Thistle St HD1 ...... 154 B8
Thistle Way LS27 ...... 97 D5
Thistlewood Rd WF1 ...... 121 E5
Thomas Chippendale
Prim Sch LS21 ...... 10 F2
Thomas Ct BD6 ...... 74 C1
Thomas Danby Coll LS7 ...... 207 D2
Thomas St Batley WF17 ...... 118 B6
Batley, Heckmondwike HX16 ...... 117 D3
Brighouse HX6 ...... 115 A1
Castleford WF10 ...... 103 E1
Elland HX5 ...... 135 A6
Elland, Holywell Green HX4 ...... 134 B4
Glusburn BD20 ...... 16 D7
Halifax HX1 ...... 203 E3
Haworth BD22 ...... 51 D6
Huddersfield, Lindley HD3 ...... 135 B1
Huddersfield, Yews Hill HD1 ...... 153 E4
Leeds LS6 ...... 206 A3
6 Liversedge WF15 ...... 117 A4
Todmorden OL14 ...... 86 C1

Thomas St S HX1 ...... 202 C2
Thomas St W HX1 ...... 202 C1
Thomas Way WF9 ...... 183 A4
Thompson Ave
Bradford BD2 ...... 55 F5
Castleford WF10 ...... 125 E6
Thompson Dr WF2 ...... 120 F3
Thompson Gn BD17 ...... 38 B1
Thompson La BD17 ...... 38 A1
Thompson St Halifax HX1 ...... 203 D3
Normanton WF6 ...... 123 A2
Shipley BD18 ...... 55 A8
Thompson's Rd WF1 ...... 216 B2
Thongs La HD7 ...... 189 A8
Thoresby Dr BD19 ...... 117 B8
Thoresby Gr BD7 ...... 73 E3
Thoresby PI LS2 ...... 206 B1
Thorn Ave Bradford BD9 ...... 54 D4
Dewsbury WF12 ...... 139 D8
Thorn Bank OL13 ...... 106 A2
Thorn CI 8 Bacup OL13 ...... 106 A2
Leeds LS8 ...... 208 B3
Shipley BD18 ...... 55 E6
Thorn Cres 7 Bacup OL13 ...... 106 A2
Leeds LS8 ...... 208 B3
Thorn Cross LS8 ...... 208 C4
Thorn Dr Bacup OL13 ...... 106 A2
Bradford BD9 ...... 54 D4
Leeds LS8 ...... 208 B3
Queensbury BD13 ...... 92 C7
Thorn Garth
Cleckheaton BD19 ...... 116 C6
Keighley BD20 ...... 18 A1
Thorn Gdns OL13 ...... 106 A2
Thorn Gr Bradford BD9 ...... 54 D4
Leeds LS8 ...... 208 B3
Thorn Hill HX4 ...... 133 F2
Thorn La Bradford BD9 ...... 54 D4
Leeds LS8 ...... 204 C2
Thorn Mount LS8 ...... 208 C4
Thorn Park Sch
for the Deaf BD9 ...... 54 D4
Thorn Rd WF12 ...... 139 C1
Thorn Royd Dr BD4 ...... 75 F2
Thorn St Bacup OL13 ...... 106 A2
Batley WF12 ...... 96 E1
3 Bradford BD8 ...... 55 A1
3 Haworth BD22 ...... 51 E8
Thorn Terr LS8 ...... 208 C4
Thorn Tree St LK11 ...... 202 B1
Thorn View Elland HX5 ...... 135 A6
Halifax HX3 ...... 92 C2
Hebden Bridge HX7 ...... 110 E8
Leeds LS8 ...... 208 B3
Thorn Wlk LS8 ...... 208 C4
Thornaby Dr BD14 ...... 73 C4
Thornacre Cres BD18 ...... 55 E7
Thornacre Rd BD18 ...... 55 E7
Thornberry Dr WF15 ...... 116 B5
Thornbridge Mews BD2 ...... 56 A4
Thornbury Ave BD3 ...... 75 D8
Thornbury Cres BD3 ...... 75 D8
Thornbury Dr BD3 ...... 75 D8
Thornbury First Sch BD3 ...... 75 E8
Thornbury Gr BD3 ...... 75 D8
Thornbury Middle Sch
BD3 ...... 75 E8
Thornbury PI WF2 ...... 141 F4
Thornbury Rd Bradford BD3 ...... 75 D7
Wakefield WF2 ...... 141 F4
Thornbury St BD3 ...... 75 D7
Thorncliff Green Rd HD8 ...... 174 C7
Thorncliff La HD8 ...... 174 C7
Thorncliffe St WF17 ...... 118 A3
Thorncliffe La HD8 ...... 175 D7
Thorncliffe Rd Batley WF17 ...... 118 A3
Bradford BD8 ...... 55 D1
Thorncliffe St HD3 ...... 135 B1
Thorncroft Rd BD6 ...... 74 A1
Thorndale Rise BD2 ...... 55 F4
Thorndene Way BD4 ...... 96 A2
Thorne CI Normanton WF6 ...... 123 C1
Pudsey LS28 ...... 76 B8
Thorne End Rd S75 ...... 178 B2
Thorne Gr LS26 ...... 101 A6
Thorne Rd HD1 ...... 153 E3
Thorne St 14 HX4 ...... 134 A4
Thornefield Cres WF3 ...... 119 D8
Thorner CE Primary Sch
LS14 ...... 46 A6
Thorner Gr BD20 ...... 5 D2
Thorner La Bardsey LS23 ...... 29 D2
Barwick in E LS14 ...... 45 E1
Scarcroft LS14 ...... 45 E8
Thorner Rd Bardsey LS23 ...... 29 E1
Barwick in E LS14 ...... 46 C8
Thornes CI WF9 ...... 182 F1
Thornes Ind Est WF11 ...... 142 C4
Thornes La WF1, WF2 ...... 142 C4
Thornes Lane Wharf WF1 ...... 142 D4
Thornes Moor Ave WF2 ...... 142 A3
Thornes Moor CI WF2 ...... 142 A2
Thornes Moor Dr WF2 ...... 142 A3
Thornes Moor Rd WF2 ...... 142 A3
Thornes Office Pk WF2 ...... 142 B3
Thornes Park CI WF2 ...... 142 B3
Thornes Pk Brighouse HD6 ...... 115 C3
Shipley BD18 ...... 55 D5
Thornes Rd WF2 ...... 142 A3
Thorney La HX2 ...... 90 D2
Thornfield Bingley BD16 ...... 36 E4
Dewsbury WF12 ...... 139 D6
6 Haworth BD22 ...... 51 D7
Thornfield Ave
Bradford BD6 ...... 94 D8
Huddersfield HD4 ...... 153 E3
Pudsey LS28 ...... 57 C3

Thornfield Ct 4 LS15 ...... 62 B3
Thornfield Dr 3 LS15 ...... 62 B3
Thornfield Hall 4 4 BD13 ...... 72 E6
Thornfield Mews
Bingley BD16 ...... 36 E3
Leeds LS15 ...... 62 B3
Thornfield Mount 1 WF17 ...... 97 A3
Thornfield PI BD2 ...... 56 C2
Thornfield Rd
Huddersfield HD4 ...... 153 E3
Leeds LS16 ...... 59 B8
Thornfield Rise 2 HX4 ...... 134 B2
Thornfield Sq BD2 ...... 56 C2
Thornfield St 11 HX4 ...... 134 B2
Thornfield Terr BD15 ...... 53 B4
Thornfield Way LS15 ...... 62 B3
Thornhill Ave
Haworth BD22 ...... 34 E2
Huddersfield HD3 ...... 153 C2
Shipley BD18 ...... 55 D7
Thornhill Bridge La HD6 ...... 115 A3
Thornhill CI Netherton WF4 ...... 158 B2
Pudsey LS28 ...... 57 B2
Walton WF2 ...... 161 A6
Thornhill Croft Leeds LS12 ...... 209 E3
Walton WF2 ...... 161 A6
Thornhill Dr Pudsey LS28 ...... 57 B8
Shipley BD18 ...... 55 D7
Walton WF2 ...... 161 A6
Thornhill Gr Pudsey LS28 ...... 57 B2
Shipley BD18 ...... 55 D8
Steeton BD20 ...... 17 B6
Thornhill Hey HX4 ...... 133 F2
Thornhill High Sch WF12 ...... 139 E1
Thornhill Jun & Inf Sch
WF12 ...... 139 E1
Thornhill Lees C of E
Infants Sch WF12 ...... 139 C4
Thornhill Park Ave WF12 ...... 139 D4
Thornhill PI Bradford BD3 ...... 75 E8
1 Brighouse HD6 ...... 115 A1
Leeds LS12 ...... 209 E3
Thornhill Rd Brighouse HD6 ...... 115 A1
Castleford WF10 ...... 124 E6
Dewsbury WF12 ...... 139 C5
Dewsbury, West Town
WF12, WF13 ...... 139 B2
Huddersfield HD3 ...... 153 A4
Huddersfield, Edgerton BD13 ...... 153 D8
Leeds LS12 ...... 209 F2
Netherton WF4 ...... 158 A8
Steeton BD20 ...... 17 B6
Thornhill St
Dewsbury WF12 ...... 139 D6
Leeds LS12 ...... 209 E3
Pudsey LS28 ...... 57 B6
Wakefield WF1 ...... 216 B3
Thornhill Street Bglws
WF1 ...... 216 B3
Thornhill Terr BD3 ...... 75 D8
Thornhills Beck La HD6 ...... 115 B4
Thornhills La HD6 ...... 115 C6
Thornie View WF12 ...... 139 C6
Thornlea CI LS19 ...... 39 F5
Thornleigh WF12 ...... 139 D6
Thornleigh Ave WF2 ...... 142 C2
Thornleigh Cres WF2 ...... 142 C2
Thornleigh Croft WF2 ...... 142 C4
Thornleigh Dr
Liversedge WF15 ...... 117 B8
Wakefield WF2 ...... 142 C4
Thornleigh Garth WF2 ...... 142 C4
Thornleigh Gdns LS9 ...... 212 C2
Thornleigh Gr 1 Leeds LS12 ...... 212 C2
Thornleigh Mount 3 LS9 ...... 212 C2
Thornleigh St LS9 ...... 212 C2
Thornleigh View 2 LS9 ...... 212 C2
Thornmead Rd BD17 ...... 38 D2
Thornsgill Ave BD4 ...... 75 E2
Thornton Ave LS12 ...... 209 D3
Thornton CI Batley WF17 ...... 96 F7
Hemsworth WF9 ...... 181 D7
Thornton Ct 11 BD8 ...... 73 F8
Thornton First Sch BD13 ...... 72 D6
Thornton Gdns LS12 ...... 209 D3
Thornton Gr LS12 ...... 209 D3
Thornton La BD5 ...... 74 C3
Thornton Lodge Hall HD1 ...... 153 E4
Thornton Lodge Rd HD1 ...... 153 F4
Thornton Moor Rd
Denholme BD13 ...... 71 B2
Oxenhope BD13 ...... 71 B2
Thornton Old Rd BD8 ...... 73 E8
Thornton Rd
Bradford BD1, BD8, BD8 ...... 73 C2
Brighouse HD6 ...... 135 E8
Denholme BD13 ...... 71 F5
Dewsbury WF12 ...... 139 C6
Thornton BD13 ...... 72 C6
Thornton Sch BD13 ...... 73 B6
Thornton St Bradford BD1 ...... 201 A3
Burley in W LS29 ...... 9 E2
Cleckheaton,
Hartshead Moor Side BD19 ...... 116 A6
Cleckheaton, Marsh BD19 ...... 116 D7
Dewsbury WF13 ...... 139 B8
Halifax HX1 ...... 202 B3
Thornton Terr Bradford BD1 ...... 201 A3
Thornton View Rd BD14 ...... 73 C1
Thorntons Arc LS1 ...... 211 F4
Thorntons Dale LS18 ...... 58 B8
Thorntonville BD19 ...... 116 F6
Thorntree Ave WF4 ...... 143 C1
Thorntree CI WF8 ...... 147 D6
Thorntree La WF4 ...... 143 C1

Thornville 5 LS27 ... 98 B7
Thornville Ave 6 LS6 ... 205 E2
Thornville Cres 11 LS6 ... 205 E3
Thornville Ct BD6 ... 55 D2
Thornville Gr 6 LS6 ... 205 E2
Thornville Mount
  3 Dewsbury WF13 ... 139 A6
  5 Leeds LS6 ... 205 E2
Thornville Pl
  Dewsbury WF13 ... 139 A6
  Leeds LS6 ... 205 E2
Thornville Rd LS6 ... 205 E2
Thornville Row LS6 ... 205 E2
Thornville St
  Dewsbury WF13 ... 139 A6
  Leeds LS6 ... 205 E2
Thornville Terr
  Dewsbury WF13 ... 139 B6
  Leeds LS6 ... 205 E2
Thornville View LS6 ... 205 E2
Thornville Wlk WF13 ... 139 A6
Thorp Arch HM Prison
  LS23 ... 15 A2
Thorp Arch Trad Est LS23 ... 15 B2
Thorp Ave HD7 ... 189 B4
Thorp Garth BD10 ... 56 B8
Thorp Pyn Croft HD5 ... 154 E7
Thorpe Ave BD13 ... 73 A6
Thorpe Cl LS20 ... 39 B8
Thorpe Cres LS10 ... 99 C3
Thorpe Ct LS10 ... 99 C3
Thorpe Dr LS20 ... 22 C1
Thorpe Garth LS10 ... 99 B3
Thorpe Gdns LS10 ... 99 C3
Thorpe Gr LS10 ... 99 C3
Thorpe Gr SE Middleton LS10 ... 99 C4
  Thornton BD13 ... 73 A6
Thorpe Green Dr HD7 ... 152 E6
Thorpe La East Ardsley WF3 ... 98 F1
  Guiseley LS20 ... 22 B1
  Huddersfield HD5 ... 155 A4
  Middleton WF3 ... 99 A2
  Thorpe Audlin WF8 ... 165 A4
Thorpe Lower La
  Rothwell WF3 ... 99 F2
  Rothwell WF3 ... 100 A3
Thorpe Middle Sch BD10 ... 56 B8
Thorpe Mount LS10 ... 99 B3
Thorpe Pl HX6 ... 111 C2
Thorpe Prim Sch WF3 ... 99 E2
Thorpe Rd
  East Ardsley WF3 ... 120 C7
  Middleton LS10 ... 99 C4
  Pudsey LS28 ... 76 E8
  Thornton BD13 ... 73 A6
Thorpe Sq LS10 ... 99 D4
Thorpe St Halifax HX3 ... 92 B2
  Keighley BD21 ... 35 C8
  Leeds LS15 ... 81 A8
  Middleton LS10 ... 99 C3
Thorpe View Middleton LS10 ... 99 C3
  Ossett WF5 ... 140 D8
  Wakefield WF2 ... 141 F6
Thorpes Ave HD8 ... 192 A7
Thorpes Cres HD8 ... 175 A1
Thorverton Dr BD4 ... 95 E8
Thorverton Gr BD4 ... 95 E8
Threadneedle St HD1 ... 154 A6
Threap Croft HX2 ... 91 F6
Three Lane Ends WF10 ... 124 A8
Three Nooked Mews BD10 ... 56 D8
Three Nooks S72 ... 180 B1
Three Nooks La S72 ... 180 B1
Three Sisters Sq 11 HD1 ... 154 A8
Threshfield BD17 ... 38 C3
Threshfield Cres BD11 ... 96 A6
Thrift Way BD16 ... 36 F2
Throstle Ave LS10 ... 99 B3
Throstle Bank HX1 ... 202 B1
Throstle Crest WF7 ... 145 A8
Throstle Dr LS10 ... 99 A3
Throstle Farm
  Jun & Inf Sch WF11 ... 126 E2
Throstle Hill LS10 ... 99 B3
Throstle La LS10 ... 99 C3
Throstle Mount
  Middleton LS10 ... 99 B3
  Sowerby Bridge HX2 ... 111 F5
Throstle Nest WF17 ... 118 A4
Throstle Nest Cl LS21 ... 10 D2
Throstle Nest Rd BD20 ... 5 D2
Throstle Nest View 4
  LS18 ... 58 C7
Throstle Par LS10 ... 99 B3
Throstle Pl LS10 ... 99 B3
Throstle Rd Middleton LS10 ... 99 C3
  Middleton LS10 ... 99 E5
Throstle Sq LS10 ... 99 D3
Throstle Sq LS10 ... 99 D3
Throstle St Middleton LS10 ... 99 B3
  Todmorden OL14 ... 129 B6
Throstle Terr LS10 ... 99 C3
Throstle View LS10 ... 99 D3
Throstle Way WF11 ... 126 E2
Throstle Wlk LS10 ... 99 B3
Throxenby Way BD11 ... 73 C4
Thrum Hall Cl HX1 ... 202 B3
Thrum Hall La HX1 ... 202 B3
Thrum Hall La HX1 ... 202 B3
Thrumpton Rd S71 ... 178 F1
Thrush Hill Rd 4 HX7 ... 89 E1
Thrush St BD21 ... 35 A8
Thryberg St BD3 ... 75 A7
Thunder Bridge La HD8 ... 173 D4
Thunderton La HX6 ... 111 C2
Thurgory Gate HD8 ... 155 E3
Thurgory La HD8 ... 155 E4
Thurley Dr BD4 ... 75 B2

Thurley Rd BD4 ... 75 B2
Thurnscoe Gooseacre
  Jun & Mid Sch S63 ... 194 C1
Thurnscoe La S72 ... 194 A1
Thurnscoe Rd BD1 ... 201 A4
Thurrish La HX7 ... 69 B6
Thursby St BD3 ... 75 B7
Thurstonland Bank Rd
  HD7 ... 172 D1
Thurstonland
  Endowed Sch HD4 ... 172 F2
Thurstonland Rd HD4 ... 172 E5
Thwaite Gate LS10 ... 215 F3
Thwaite La LS10 ... 80 A3
Thwaite Mills (Mus) LS10 ... 80 B3
Thwaites Ave LS21 ... 8 C5
Thwaites Bridge BD21 ... 35 F7
Thwaites Brow Rd BD21 ... 35 F6
Thwaites La BD21 ... 35 E7
Thwaites Rd BD21 ... 35 E7
Tichborne Rd 8 WF3 ... 74 E3
Tichborne Rd W BD5 ... 74 E3
Tichborne St FW15 ... 116 E4
Tichbourne St WF17 ... 117 F4
Tickhill St BD3 ... 75 B6
Tiding Field La HD7 ... 151 D2
Tidswell St HD7 ... 117 E4
Tilbury Ave 7 LS11 ... 213 F4
Tilbury Gr 5 LS11 ... 213 F4
Tilbury Mount LS11 ... 213 F4
Tilbury Par 3 LS11 ... 213 F4
Tilbury Rd LS11 ... 213 F4
Tilbury Row LS11 ... 213 F4
Tilbury Terr LS11 ... 213 F4
Tilbury View 6 LS11 ... 213 F4
Tile La LS16 ... 42 D3
Tile St BD8 ... 55 B1
Tile Terr HD6 ... 115 A1
Tilly Sq 5 BD5 ... 74 E4
Till Carr La HX3 ... 115 A8
Tillotson Ave HX6 ... 112 A3
Tillotson St BD20 ... 5 D2
Tillotson's Ct BD20 ... 4 A2
Tim La BD22 ... 34 B1
Timber St 3 Elland HX5 ... 134 F6
  3 Keighley BD21 ... 35 E8
Timbercliffe OL15 ... 129 D1
Timberwood HD8 ... 173 D4
Timble Dr BD16 ... 37 B4
Timmey La HX2 ... 111 F8
Timothy La WF17 ... 118 D7
Tinderley Gr HD5 ... 154 F4
Tingley Ave WF3 ... 98 E1
Tingley Comm
  East Ardsley LS27 ... 98 C1
  Morley LS27 ... 98 C1
Tingley Cres WF3 ... 98 C1
Tinker La Lepton HD8 ... 156 B2
  Meltham HD7 ... 170 D1
Tinkingfield La LS24 ... 15 C8
Tinkler Stile BD10 ... 56 E8
Tinsel Rd WF12 ... 118 F1
Tinshill Ave LS16 ... 41 E3
Tinshill Cl LS16 ... 41 E3
Tinshill Cres LS16 ... 41 E4
Tinshill Dr LS16 ... 41 E5
Tinshill Garth LS16 ... 41 E4
Tinshill Gr LS16 ... 41 E4
Tinshill La LS16 ... 41 E3
Tinshill Mount LS16 ... 41 E5
Tinshill Primary Sch LS16 ... 41 E3
Tinshill Rd LS16 ... 41 D4
Tinshill View LS16 ... 41 E4
Tinshill Wlk LS16 ... 41 E5
Tinsworth Rd WF2 ... 160 A4
Tintagel Ct WF6 ... 123 B3
Tintern Ave Bradford BD8 ... 73 D7
  Huddersfield HD3 ... 152 F5
Tippaty La WF11 ... 127 A7
Tipping La HD8 ... 175 D7
Tisma Dr BD4 ... 95 B8
Titan District Ctr BD12 ... 94 C2
Tithe Barn Fold LS15 ... 63 D7
Tithe Barn La LS17 ... 28 C2
Tithe Barn Rd WF11 ... 127 A4
Tithe Barn St
  Dewsbury WF13 ... 139 D8
  Horbury WF4 ... 141 A1
Tithe House Way HD2 ... 136 E6
Titus La HD8 ... 174 D6
Titus St BD18 ... 54 F8
Tiverton Ho 4 BD5 ... 201 B1
Tiverton Wlk BD4 ... 75 E3
Tivoli Pl Bradford BD5 ... 74 C4
  Ilkley LS29 ... 8 C3
Tivy Dale S75 ... 193 E4
Tivy Dale Cl S75 ... 193 E4
Tivy Dale Dr S75 ... 193 E4
Toby La BD7 ... 74 A5
Toby Wood La HD8 ... 191 D5
Todd Terr 2 BD7 ... 74 B4
Todley Hall Rd BD22 ... 34 A6
Todmorden High Sch
  OL14 ... 107 F6
Todmorden Old Rd OL13 ... 106 B5
Todmorden Rd
  Bacup OL13 ... 106 B4
  Littleborough OL15 ... 129 D7
Todmorden Sta OL14 ... 108 A5
Todwell La BD5 ... 74 C3
Toft La HD4 ... 172 F6
Toft St LS12 ... 210 A2
Tofts Ave BD12 ... 94 C6
Tofts Gr HD6 ... 135 F7
Tofts Grove Gdns HD6 ... 135 F7
Tofts House Cl LS28 ... 76 E7
Tofts Rd Cleckheaton BD19 ... 116 D7
  Pudsey LS28 ... 76 D7
  Pudsey LS28 ... 76 E7

Toftshaw Fold BD4 ... 95 D8
Toftshaw La BD4 ... 95 E8
Toftshaw New Rd BD4 ... 95 D8
Toll Bar La WF17 ... 120 D1
Toll Bar Rd WF10 ... 123 F7
Toller Dr BD9 ... 54 E3
Toller Gr BD9 ... 54 E3
Toller La BD8, BD9 ... 55 A1
Toller Pk BD9 ... 54 F3
Tolson Cres HD5 ... 154 F7
Tolson Grange HD5 ... 154 F5
Tolson Memorial Mus
  HD5 ... 154 F6
Tolson St Dewsbury WF13 ... 118 C1
  Ossett WF5 ... 140 B8
Tolson's Yd 12 HD5 ... 154 D5
Tolworth Fold 1 BD5 ... 74 E4
Tom Dando Cl WF6 ... 123 E2
Tom La HD4 ... 153 B3
Tom Wood Ash La WF9 ... 183 E7
Tombridge Cres WF9 ... 163 B1
Tomling Cote La BD20 ... 18 B8
Tommy La HD7 ... 152 E1
Tonbridge Cl BD6 ... 93 F8
Tonbridge St LS1 ... 206 A1
Tong App LS12 ... 77 D6
Tong Dr LS12 ... 77 D7
Tong Gate LS12 ... 77 D7
Tong Gn LS12 ... 77 D6
Tong Hall Bsns Ctr BD4 ... 76 D2
Tong La Bacup OL13 ... 106 B2
  Birkenshaw BD4 ... 76 D2
Tong Park First Sch BD17 ... 38 F4
Tong Rd LS12 ... 77 C6
Tong Recn Ctr BD4 ... 96 A8
Tong Rd BD4 ... 96 A8
Tong St Birkenshaw BD4 ... 95 F8
  Bradford BD4 ... 75 D1
Tong Way LS12 ... 77 D7
Tong Wlk LS12 ... 77 D7
Tongue La HX6 ... 42 F1
Tool Hill La HX6 ... 111 B2
Tootal St WF1 ... 216 C1
Toothill Ave HD6 ... 136 A7
Toothill Bank HD6 ... 136 A7
Toothill La HD6 ... 136 A7
Toothill La S HD6 ... 135 F6
Top Farm (Mus) WF4 ... 145 B1
Top Fold WF1 ... 105 A4
Top Headlands WF5 ... 140 C5
Top House Farm Mews
  WF11 ... 105 A4
Top La Clayton DN5 ... 194 C5
  West Bretton WF4 ... 158 D5
Top Meadow WF14 ... 137 F2
Top Moor Side LS11 ... 211 D1
Top O' Th' Bank HD7 ... 172 E1
Top o' th' Close Rd OL14 ... 129 C6
Top o' Th' Hill Rd OL14 ... 108 A1
Top o' th' Moor HD4 ... 173 C2
Top of Carr 8 WF17 ... 118 B2
Top of the Hill HD7 ... 169 E7
Top Orch WF4 ... 162 B1
Top Rd HD8 ... 191 E7
Top Row S75 ... 177 E3
Top St Hemsworth WF9 ... 181 C7
  Todmorden OL14 ... 128 F7
Top Stone Cl LS25 ... 105 E3
Topaz Cl HD2 ... 136 C2
Topcliffe Ave LS27 ... 98 C4
Topcliffe Ct 8 LS27 ... 98 D4
Topcliffe Fold LS27 ... 98 C2
Topcliffe Gn 7 LS27 ... 98 D4
Topcliffe La
  Morley, Tingley Common
  LS27 ... 98 D2
  Morley, Topcliffe LS27 ... 98 C2
Topcliffe Mead 6 LS27 ... 98 D4
Topcliffe Wood 9 LS27 ... 98 C4
Tor Ave BD12 ... 94 C1
Tor View HD7 ... 172 C2
Torcote Cres HD2 ... 136 C5
Tordoff Ave BD7 ... 73 E5
Tordoff Gn 8 BD6 ... 94 B8
Tordoff Pl LS5 ... 59 A4
Tordoff Rd 5 BD12 ... 94 E6
Tordoff Terr LS5 ... 59 A4
Toronto Pl LS7 ... 204 A2
Torre Cl LS9 ... 208 A1
Torre Cres BD6 ... 73 D1
Torre Dr LS9 ... 208 A1
Torre Gdns LS9 ... 212 C4
Torre Gn LS9 ... 212 C4
Torre Gr Bradford BD6 ... 73 D1
  Leeds LS9 ... 208 A1
Torre Hill LS9 ... 208 B1
Torre La LS9 ... 80 B8
Torre Mount LS9 ... 208 A1
Torre Pl LS9 ... 208 A1
Torre Rd Bradford BD6 ... 73 D1
  Leeds LS9 ... 80 A8
Torre Sq LS9 ... 208 B1
Torre View LS9 ... 208 B1
Torre Wlk LS9 ... 208 B1
Torridon Cres BD6 ... 93 E6
Torridon Rd WF12 ... 118 E2
Totties La HD7 ... 189 D5
Toulston La LS23 ... 30 F2
Tower Ave WF9 ... 183 A8
Tower Bldgs 11 WF13 ... 117 C3
Tower Cswy OL14 ... 107 B7
Tower Dr The LS21 ... 24 E6
Tower Gdns 2 HX2 ... 112 F4
Tower Gr LS12 ... 209 D4
Tower Hill HX6 ... 112 B4
Tower House St LS2 ... 206 C1

Tower La Leeds LS12 ... 77 F8
  Leeds, Hill Top LS12 ... 209 D4
Tower Pl 6 LS12 ... 77 F8
Tower Rd BD18 ... 54 E8
Tower St Bradford BD2 ... 56 B2
  Todmorden OL14 ... 86 A4
Towers Cl WF4 ... 162 A8
Towers La WF4 ... 144 B1
Towers Paddock WF10 ... 125 A7
Towers Sq LS6 ... 60 A8
Towers Way LS6 ... 60 A8
Towlerton La WF2 ... 120 E2
Town Ave HD1 ... 154 C8
Town Cl LS18 ... 41 B1
Town Cres HD1 ... 154 C8
Town End Bradford BD7 ... 74 A4
  Garforth LS25 ... 82 E8
  Gildersome LS27 ... 97 D7
  Huddersfield, Almondbury
  HD5 ... 154 F4
  Huddersfield, Town End HD7 ... 152 D4
  Ossett WF5 ... 140 D5
Town End Ave
  Ackworth M T WF7 ... 164 C7
  Holmfirth HD7 ... 189 C6
Town End Cl Glusburn BD20 ... 16 D6
  Leeds LS13 ... 58 E1
Town End Cres HD7 ... 189 C7
Town End La HD8 ... 156 A3
Town End Rd Bradford BD14 ... 73 B5
  Holmfirth HD7 ... 189 B7
Town Fields Rd HX5 ... 134 E6
Town Gate
  Bradford, Idle BD10 ... 56 B8
  Bradford, Wyke BD12 ... 94 C3
  Brighouse BD19 ... 115 F8
  Guiseley LS20 ... 22 E1
  Hebden Bridge HX2 ... 90 B1
  Heptonstall HX7 ... 88 F5
  Holmfirth HD7 ... 189 A5
  Holmfirth, Hepworth HD7 ... 189 E2
  Holmfirth, Netherthong HD7 ... 188 F8
  Holmfirth, Upperthong HD7 ... 188 D5
  Kirkburton HD8 ... 173 E8
  Lepton HD8 ... 156 A4
  Marsden HD7 ... 168 F4
  Northowram HX3 ... 93 A2
  Pudsey LS28 ... 57 D2
  Sowerby Bridge HX6 ... 111 E3
Town Gate Cl LS20 ... 22 E1
Town Gn WF12 ... 139 E2
Town Hall Bldgs HX5 ... 135 A6
Town Hall Sq 4 LS19 ... 40 B7
Town Hall St 5 Elland HX5 ... 134 F6
  Holmfirth HD7 ... 189 A5
  Keighley BD21 ... 35 C7
  Mirfield WF14 ... 138 A4
  Sowerby Bridge HX6 ... 112 B4
Town Hall St E 2 HX1 ... 203 E3
Town Hall Way WF12 ... 139 D8
Town Head HD7 ... 171 F5
Town Hill LS23 ... 30 D2
Town Hill St BD16 ... 54 B6
Town Moor HD4 ... 172 F2
Town Pl HD1 ... 154 C8
Town Rd HD5 ... 137 C1
Town St Batley WF17 ... 118 C2
  Birkenshaw BD11 ... 96 A6
  Dewsbury WF12 ... 139 F7
  Gildersome LS27 ... 97 D7
  Guiseley LS20 ... 22 E1
  Hemsworth WF9 ... 181 C7
  Horsforth LS18 ... 41 B1
  Leeds LS7 ... 204 A3
  Leeds, Beeston LS11 ... 213 E2
  Leeds, Moor Top LS12 ... 209 E3
  Middleton LS10 ... 99 C5
  Pudsey, Farsley LS28 ... 57 D3
  Pudsey, Rodley LS13 ... 57 E2
  Pudsey, Stanningley LS28 ... 57 E2
  Rothwell WF3 ... 100 D2
  Yeadon LS19 ... 40 B7
  Yeadon, Rawdon LS19 ... 40 D3
Town Street Mews LS7 ... 204 A3
Town Street Wlk 8 LS7 ... 204 A3
Town Terr HD1 ... 154 C8
Town The WF12 ... 139 D2
Town Top HD5 ... 137 C1
Town Wells Dr LS28 ... 57 B6
Townend Pl Glusburn BD20 ... 16 C6
  4 Pudsey LS28 ... 76 F8
Townend Rd LS12 ... 209 E1
Townfield BD15 ... 53 C5
Townfield La HX7 ... 88 C6
Townhill WF5 ... 140 E6
Towngate Baildon BD17 ... 38 C4
  Brighouse, Clifton HD6 ... 115 E2
  Brighouse, Hipperholme
  HX3 ... 114 C8
  Halifax HX3 ... 114 A4
  Huddersfield HD4 ... 154 A2
  Keighley BD21 ... 35 C7
  Mapplewell S75 ... 178 B1
  Mirfield WF14 ... 138 B6
  Ossett WF5 ... 140 F6
  Shipley BD18 ... 55 B7
Towngate Ave HD6 ... 115 D3
Towngate Gr WF14 ... 138 A6
Towngate House 1 HX5 ... 134 F7
Towngate Junior &
  Infants Sch HX5 ... 140 F6
Towngate Rd WF17 ... 118 A5
Townhead Fold LS29 ... 6 E8
Townley Ave HX3 ... 114 A4
Townley Rd WF12 ... 141 D4
Towton Dr WF10 ... 124 A6
Track Mount WF17 ... 118 B2

Track Rd WF17 ... 118 B3
Trafalgar Cl HD2 ... 136 B4
Trafalgar Rd
  Dewsbury WF13 ... 118 B1
  Ilkley LS29 ... 8 B4
Trafalgar Sq 2 HX1 ... 202 C1
Trafalgar St Batley WF17 ... 118 A4
  Bradford BD1 ... 201 B4
  2 Halifax HX1 ... 202 C1
  Leeds LS2 ... 212 A4
Trafford Ave LS9 ... 208 B2
Trafford Gr LS9 ... 208 B3
Trafford Terr LS9 ... 208 B2
Tramways BD2 ... 94 F5
Tranbeck Rd LS20 ... 22 B1
Tranfield Ave LS20 ... 22 C1
Tranfield Cl LS20 ... 22 C1
Tranfield Ct LS20 ... 22 C1
Tranfield Gdns LS20 ... 22 C1
Tranmere Ct LS20 ... 22 C1
Tranmere Dr LS20 ... 22 C1
Tranmere Park
  Primary Sch LS20 ... 22 C1
Tranquility LS15 ... 62 C2
Tranquility Ave LS15 ... 62 C2
Tranquility Ct 1 LS15 ... 62 C2
Tranquility Wlk 4 LS15 ... 62 C2
Transperience Mus BD2 ... 94 F5
Transperience Way
  BD12, BD4 ... 94 F6
Transvaal Terr WF17 ... 118 B7
Tranter Rd BD4 ... 75 E5
Tranter Pl LS15 ... 80 E8
Travis House OL14 ... 129 A7
Travis Lacey Terr 8
  WF13 ... 139 B8
Tredgold Ave LS16 ... 24 F2
Tredgold Cl LS16 ... 24 E2
Tredgold Cres LS16 ... 24 E2
Tredgold Garth LS16 ... 24 E3
Tree La HX2 ... 90 F5
Tree Top View BD13 ... 72 C2
Treefield Ind Est LS27 ... 97 D6
Trees St BD8 ... 55 C1
Trelawn Ave LS6 ... 59 D5
Trelawn Cres LS6 ... 59 D5
Trelawn Pl LS6 ... 59 D5
Trelawn St LS6 ... 59 D5
Trelawn Terr LS6 ... 59 D5
Tremont Gdns LS10 ... 215 E2
Tremon Park Dr BD10 ... 39 A2
Trenance Dr BD18 ... 54 F7
Trenance Gdns HX4 ... 134 A7
Trenholme Ave BD6 ... 94 B6
Trenic Cres LS6 ... 205 D3
Trenic Dr LS6 ... 205 D3
Trent Ave Garforth LS25 ... 83 B6
  Normanton WF6 ... 123 A4
Trent Rd LS9 ... 208 A1
Trent St LS11 ... 211 E1
Trentham Ave 8 LS11 ... 214 B2
Trentham Gr 7 LS11 ... 214 B2
Trentham Pl 6 LS11 ... 214 B2
Trentham Row 3 LS11 ... 214 B2
Trentham St LS11 ... 214 B2
Trentham Terr 22 LS11 ... 214 B2
Trenton Dr BD8 ... 55 C1
Trenton Rd WF17 ... 118 F3
Trescoe Ave LS13 ... 58 B1
Tresham Ct WF12 ... 118 F2
Trevelyan Sq LS1 ... 211 F3
Trevelyan St
  Brighouse HD6 ... 115 A3
  6 Huddersfield HD5 ... 154 D5
Trevor Terr WF12 ... 120 E6
Triangle Bsns Pk WF17 ... 97 A3
Triangle C of E Infant &
  Junior Sch HX6 ... 111 A1
Triangle The HD1 ... 153 E5
Triath Ct WF17 ... 117 E6
Trilby St WF1 ... 216 C4
Trimmingham A la HX2 ... 202 A2
Trimmingham Rd HX2 ... 202 A2
Trimmingham Villas HX2 ... 202 A2
Trinity & All Saints' Coll
  LS18 ... 41 A3
Trinity Bsns Ctr WF1 ... 216 C1
Trinity Church Gate WF1 ... 216 C2
Trinity Ct HD7 ... 171 F4
Trinity Dr HD8 ... 191 F5
Trinity Gr 2 HD6 ... 115 A4
Trinity House 1 WF1 ... 216 C2
Trinity Pl Bingley BD16 ... 37 A2
  Halifax HX1 ... 203 E2
Trinity Rd Bradford BD5 ... 74 D5
  Halifax HX1 ... 203 E2
Trinity Rise 2 LS21 ... 23 B7
Trinity St Batley WF17 ... 118 C2
  Halifax HX1 ... 203 E2
  Hebden Bridge HX7 ... 88 F3
  Huddersfield HD1 ... 153 F7
  Keighley BD21 ... 35 C8
  Leeds LS1 ... 211 F4
  Mirfield WF14 ... 138 A4
  Ossett WF5 ... 140 D6
  Wakefield WF1 ... 142 F3
Trinity Street Arc 5 LS1 ... 211 F3
Trinity View Bradford BD12 ... 94 E7
  Halifax HX2 ... 202 A2
  Ossett WF5 ... 140 D7
Trinity Wlk Bradford BD12 ... 94 F7
  South Elmsall WF9 ... 183 A4
Trip Garth LS22 ... 13 A2
Trip La LS22 ... 13 A2
Tristram Ave BD5 ... 75 A2
Tristram Ctr The LS12 ... 213 E4
Triumph Cl LS11, LS12 ... 211 D2

Troon Dr HD2 .... 135 F3
Troon Way WF17 .... 142 A2
Trooper La HX3 .... 113 E5
Trooper Terr HX3 .... 203 F2
Trough La
  Cullingworth BD13 .... 52 A3
  Denholme BD13 .... 52 A3
  South Elmsall WF9 .... 183 C3
Trough Well La WF2 .... 120 E3
Troughton Pl LS28 .... 76 F5
Troughton St LS28 .... 76 F5
Troutbeck Ave BD17 .... 37 E1
Troy Hill LS27 .... 98 A5
Troy Rd Horsforth LS18 ..... 41 C2
  Morley LS27 .... 98 A5
Troy Rise LS27 .... 98 B5
Troydale Gdns LS28 .... 77 B5
Troydale La LS28 .... 77 B5
Troydale La LS28 .... 77 B5
Trueman Ave WF16 .... 117 E5
Trueman Ct BD12 .... 94 E6
Trueman Way WF9 .... 183 A4
Truncliffe BD5 .... 74 D1
Trundles La WF11 .... 127 B4
Truro Dr WF6 .... 123 B3
Truro St LS12 .... 209 F4
Truro Wlk WF6 .... 123 B3
Trust Fold LS25 .... 105 E3
Tubby La HD2 .... 136 B1
Tudor Barn Ct BD18 .... 55 D7
Tudor Cl WF8 .... 146 C5
Tudor Croft HD2 .... 136 F5
Tudor Ct [17] Bradford BD5 .. 201 B1
  Pudsey LS28 .... 57 C2
Tudor Gdns LS11 .... 213 E2
Tudor House [4] WF1 ...... 216 B2
Tudor Lawns Leeds LS8 .... 61 C7
  Lofthouse Gate WF2 .... 120 E5
Tudor St Bradford BD5 ..... 74 D4
  Slaithwaite HD7 .... 170 A8
Tudor Way Castleford WF10 125 B8
  Dewsbury WF12 .... 139 B3
Tuel La HX6 .... 112 B4
Tuel Lane Infant Sch HX6 112 B4
Tufton St BD20 .... 5 E1
Tulip Ret Pk LS10 .... 215 D3
Tulip St Haworth BD22 ..... 51 C7
  Keighley BD21 .... 35 D7
Tumbling Cl WF5 .... 140 E6
Tumbling Hill WF8 .... 147 A5
Tumbling Hill St BD7 .... 74 D6
Tun La S72 .... 180 D7
Tunnacliffe Rd HD4 .... 154 B3
Tunnel St Denholme BD13 .. 71 D8
  Huddersfield HD4 .... 171 C7
Tunnicliffe Pl BD20 .... 5 D1
Tunstall Gn BD4 .... 75 E3
Tunstall Rd LS11 .... 214 C3
Tunwell La BD2 .... 56 C4
Tunwell St BD2 .... 56 C4
Tup La WF4 .... 180 C8
Turbary Ave [2] LS28 ...... 57 E2
Turbid La HD4 .... 171 A6
Turbury La Elland HX4 ..... 133 E8
  Sowerby Bridge HX4 .... 133 E8
Turf Ct BD13 .... 52 C5
Turf La BD13 .... 52 C5
Turgate La HX4 .... 111 A1
Turkey Hill LS28 .... 76 E6
Turley Cote La HX4 .... 134 C2
Turn o The Nook WF5 ..... 140 C6
Turnberry Ave LS17 .... 43 B4
Turnberry Cl
  East Ardsley WF3 .... 119 D8
  Leeds LS17 .... 43 B4
Turnberry Ct Keighley BD20 .. 18 A3
  Normanton WF6 .... 123 D1
Turnberry Dr
  East Ardsley WF3 .... 119 D8
  Leeds LS17 .... 43 B4
Turnberry Gdns WF3 .... 119 D8
Turnberry Gr Cudworth S72 180 C1
  Leeds LS17 .... 43 B4
Turnberry Rise LS17 .... 43 B4
Turnberry View LS17 .... 43 B4
Turnbridge Rd HD1 .... 154 C6
Turnbull Ct LS8 .... 61 D5
Turner Ave Batley WF17 ... 118 E5
  Bradford BD7 .... 73 F5
Turner Ave N HX2 .... 91 D5
Turner Ave S HX2 .... 91 E4
Turner Cl WF3 .... 119 E8
Turner Cres LS21 .... 11 B1
Turner Dr WF3 .... 119 E8
Turner La Addingham LS29 .. 6 C5
  Addingham LS29 .... 6 D8
  Halifax HX3 .... 92 D2
Turner Pl Bradford BD7 .... 74 B5
  Halifax HX3 .... 92 E2
Turner St [5] LS28 .... 57 D3
Turner's Ct [1] HX3 .... 92 B2
Turners Yd LS28 .... 57 D3
Turney St HX3 .... 92 A2
Turnip La WF12 .... 139 D2
Turnkey Park LS12 .... 78 C4
Turnpike St HX5 .... 135 A7
Turnshaw Rd Haworth BD22 .. 33 F2
  Kirkburton HD8 .... 174 A6
Turnshaws Ave HD8 .... 174 A7
Turnshaws Cl HD8 .... 174 A7
Turnshaws Special Sch
  HD8 .... 174 A7
Turnsteads Ave BD19 ...... 116 B8
Turnsteads Cl BD19 .... 116 C8
Turnsteads Cres BD19 ..... 116 C8
Turnsteads Dr BD19 .... 116 C8
Turnsteads Mount BD19 .. 116 C8
Turnstone Ct [3] LS10 ..... 99 D5
Turnways The LS6 .... 59 C4
Turret Hall Rd HX7 .... 88 C2
Turret Royd Rd HX7 .... 88 D2
Turton Gn LS27 .... 97 D7
Turton St WF1 .... 216 C2
Turton Vale LS27 .... 97 D6
Turver's La WF11 .... 127 F3
Turvin Rd
  Littleborough OL15 .... 130 D2
  Ripponden OL15 .... 130 D2
Twain Cres WF10 .... 125 C6
Tweed Cl WF17 .... 97 A1
Tweedale Gdns WF13 ...... 139 B8
Tweedale St [1] WF13 ..... 139 B8
Tweedy St BD15 .... 53 C5
Twelfth Ave WF15 .... 116 B5
Twickenham Ct BD8 .... 55 D2
Twitch Hill WF4 .... 141 B1
Twivey St WF10 .... 124 C7
Two Gates HD7 .... 151 E1
Two Laws Rd BD22 .... 49 D8
Tyas Gr LS9 .... 80 B7
Tyas La HD7 .... 151 B2
Tyburn La HD8 .... 175 C6
Tyersal Ave BD4 .... 75 F6
Tyersal Cl BD4 .... 75 F6
Tyersal Cres BD4 .... 75 F6
Tyersal Ct BD4 .... 75 F6
Tyersal Dr BD4 .... 75 F6
Tyersal First Sch BD4 ..... 75 D5
Tyersal Garth BD4 .... 75 F6
Tyersal Gn BD4 .... 75 F6
Tyersal La Bradford BD4 .. 75 F6
  Bradford, Laisterdyke BD4 76 A5
Tyersal Pk BD4 .... 75 F6
Tyersal Rd BD4 .... 75 F6
Tyersal Terr BD4 .... 75 F6
Tyersal View BD4 .... 75 F6
Tyersal Wlk BD4 .... 75 F6
Tyler Cl WF6 .... 123 E2
Tyndale Ave WF4 .... 141 C2
Tyndale Wlk WF16 .... 117 E5
Tyne St Bradford BD3 ...... 201 C4
  [1] Haworth BD22 .... 51 D7
  Keighley BD21 .... 35 D7
Tynedale Ct LS7 .... 60 A6
Tynwald Cl LS17 .... 43 A2
Tynwald Dr LS17 .... 43 A2
Tynwald Gdns LS17 .... 43 A3
Tynwald Gn LS17 .... 43 A3
Tynwald Hill LS17 .... 43 A2
Tynwald Mount LS17 .... 43 A2
Tynwald Rd LS17 .... 43 A3
Tynwald Wlk LS17 .... 43 A3
Tyrrel St BD1 .... 201 B3
Tyrrell Ct WF7 .... 141 D7
Tyson St Bradford BD1 .... 201 A4
  Halifax HX1 .... 202 A2

Ullswater Ave WF12 .... 118 E3
Ullswater Cl Batley WF12 . 118 E3
  Knottingley WF11 .... 126 E1
Ullswater Cres Leeds LS15 .. 80 E7
  Rothwell LS26 .... 101 C6
Ullswater Dr Bradford BD6 .. 93 F6
  Wetherby LS22 .... 13 C6
Ullswater Rd WF12 .... 118 E3
Ullswater Rise LS22 .... 13 C5
Una Pl HD2 .... 153 E8
Underbank Ave HX7 .... 88 C1
Underbank Old Rd HD7 .... 189 B4
Undercliffe First Sch BD2 . 56 B1
Undercliffe La BD3 .... 56 B1
Undercliffe Mid Sch
  Bradford BD3 .... 55 F1
  Bradford BD2 .... 56 B1
Undercliffe Old Rd BD2 .... 56 B1
Undercliffe Pl BD3 .... 114 B7
Undercliffe Rd BD2 .... 56 B3
Undercliffe Rise LS29 .... 8 E2
Undercliffe St BD3 .... 56 B1
Undercliffe Terr [6] HX2 .. 112 E4
Underwood Dr LS19 .... 40 C1
Underwood Rd BD3 .... 201 C4
Union Cross Yd HX1 .... 203 E3
Union Gr WF15 .... 117 B3
Union House La BD13 ...... 73 C2
Union La HX2 .... 71 D1
Union Pl LS11 .... 211 E2
Union Rd Bradford BD12 .. 94 C7
  Bradford, Great Horton BD7 74 B5
  Liversedge WF15 .... 117 B3
Union Sq WF1 .... 216 C2
Union St Baildon BD17 .... 38 E2
  [4] Batley WF17 .... 96 F1
  Bingley BD16 .... 36 E7
  Castleford WF10 .... 124 B7
  Dewsbury WF13 .... 139 D8
  [3] Elland HX4 .... 134 D7
  Halifax HX1 .... 203 E2
  Hemsworth WF9 .... 181 E6
  [6] Huddersfield HD1 ...... 154 B7
  Huddersfield, Oakes HD3 . 153 B8
  Leeds LS2 .... 212 A4
  Liversedge WF16 .... 117 C3
  [1] Morley LS27 .... 98 C8
  Ossett WF5 .... 140 D6
  Otley LS21 .... 22 F7
  [1] Queensbury BD13 ...... 72 E1
  Slaithwaite HD7 .... 151 F1
  Sowerby Bridge HX6 .... 111 E1
  Sowerby Bridge HX6 .... 112 C4
  Wakefield WF1 .... 216 B3

Union St S OL14 .... 108 B5
Union Terr LS7 .... 60 C6
Union Yd BD10 .... 56 B8
Unity Cl LS6 .... 206 B4
Unity Cl WF13 .... 139 B8
Unity Hall Ct WF3 .... 119 F7
Unity St Hebden Bridge HX7 .. 89 A4
  Keighley BD20 .... 18 F2
  Rothwell WF3 .... 100 D3
  Todmorden OL14 .... 129 A8
Unity St N BD16 .... 36 F2
Unity St S BD16 .... 36 F2
Unity Terr HX1 .... 202 A2
Univ of Bradford
  Bradford, Little Horton Green
    BD5 .... 74 C5
  Bradford, Shearbridge BD7 .. 74 D6
Univ of Bradford
  Management Ctr BD9 ...... 55 B4
Univ of Huddersfield HD1 154 B5
University Rd LS2 .... 206 A2
University St WF10 .... 124 D7
Unna Way HD1 .... 154 A7
Unwin Pl BD9 .... 54 E2
Upland Cres LS8 .... 61 A5
Upland Gdns LS8 .... 208 A4
Upland Rd LS8 .... 208 A4
Uplands BD20 .... 18 A1
Uplands Ave BD13 .... 73 B2
Uplands Cl BD13 .... 73 B2
Uplands Cres BD13 .... 73 B2
Uplands Dr WF14 .... 138 A6
Uplands Gr BD13 .... 73 B2
Uplands The WF16 .... 146 C7
Upper Accommodation Rd
  LS9 .... 212 B3
Upper Ada St [8] BD18 .... 54 F8
Upper Addison St BD4 .... 201 C1
Upper Allerton La BD13 .... 72 E8
Upper Armley C of E Sch
  LS12 .... 209 E4
Upper Ash Gr WF9 .... 183 B3
Upper Ashley La BD17 ..... 55 B8
Upper Bank End Rd HD7 .. 189 B3
Upper Bank Hey Bottom
  HX6 .... 132 E3
Upper Barker St WF15 .... 117 A4
Upper Basinghall St LS1 .. 211 E4
Upper Batley La WF17 ..... 118 B8
Upper Batley Low La
  WF17 .... 118 C8
Upper Battye St WF16 ..... 117 D4
Upper Bell Croft HX3 ..... 114 A4
Upper Bell Hall HX1 .... 202 C1
Upper Bolton Brow HX6 .. 112 D4
Upper Bonegate HD6 ..... 115 B3
Upper Brig Royd HX6 ..... 132 E4
Upper Brockholes HX2 .... 91 D8
Upper Brow Rd HD1 .... 153 D5
Upper Butts BD19 .... 116 D7
Upper Calton St BD21 ..... 35 B5
Upper Camroyd St WF13 . 118 D1
Upper Carr La LS28 .... 57 A6
Upper Carr St WF15 ...... 117 A5
Upper Castle St BD5 ...... 74 D4
Upper Chelsea St BD21 ... 35 B5
Upper Clough Rd HD7 .... 170 D7
Upper Commercial St
  WF17 .... 118 C5
Upper Common La HD8 .. 192 F8
Upper Croft Rd WF17 ..... 118 B4
Upper Cross St [8] WF13 . 118 C1
Upper Ellistones Ct HX4 . 134 A7
Upper Exley HX3 .... 113 E1
Upper Ferndown Gn BD15 34 A1
Upper Field La HX6 .... 111 D2
Upper Field La
  High Hoyland S75 .... 176 E1
  Kexbrough S75 .... 176 E1
Upper Fountain St HX6 ... 112 B4
Upper Fountaine St LS2 .. 211 F4
Upper Fyfe La BD17 .... 38 E3
Upper Gate HD7 .... 189 E2
Upper George St
  Batley WF16 .... 117 D4
  [4] Bradford BD6 .... 74 B1
  [3] Huddersfield HD1 ...... 154 A6
Upper Grange Ave [3] BD15 73 B8
Upper Green Baildon BD17 . 38 E2
  [1] Bradford BD7 .... 74 A3
Upper Green Ave
  [1] Brighouse BD19 .... 115 F8
  East Ardsley WF3 .... 119 D7
Upper Green La HD6 ...... 114 E5
Upper Green Way WF3 ... 119 D7
Upper Hagg Rd
  Holmfirth HD7 .... 172 B2
  Honley HD7 .... 172 B2
Upper Hall View HX3 .... 92 F4
Upper Hatfield Pl WF4 ... 162 D2
Upper Hawe Shaw [10]
  HX1 .... 202 C1
Upper Heaton La HD5 .... 137 D2
Upper Heights Rd BD13 ... 72 C8
Upper Hird St BD21 .... 35 A5
Upper Hirst HD3 .... 152 D8
Upper Holme HD7 .... 169 D8
Upper House La WF15 .... 116 C4
Upper House Rd HD7 ..... 199 C8
Upper House St BD4 .... 75 B3
Upper Kirkgate HX1 .... 203 F3
Upper La Cleckheaton BD19 117 B7
  Emley HD8 .... 175 D6
  Netherton HX3 .... 158 D4
  Thornton HX3 .... 92 F3
  Todmorden OL14 .... 87 D1
Upper Langwith LS22 ...... 28 E8
Upper Lombard St LS19 .. 40 A4

Upper Lumb La HX7 .... 110 C4
Upper Marsh HX3 .... 113 F5
Upper Marsh La BD22 ...... 51 A5
Upper Martin Gn HX4 ..... 134 A7
Upper Mary St [5] BD18 .. 54 F8
Upper Maythorn La HD7 .. 200 D8
Upper Meadows
  Holmfirth HD7 .... 188 D5
  Queensbury BD13 .... 72 E1
Upper Mill Row BD20 ...... 19 E2
Upper Millergate BD1 .... 201 B3
Upper Mosscar St BD3 .... 201 D3
Upper Mount HD7 .... 170 F1
Upper Mount St
  Batley WF17 .... 118 C3
  Huddersfield HD1 .... 153 F4
Upper Nidd St BD3 .... 75 B6
Upper Norcroft S75 .... 193 F3
Upper North St
  Batley WF17 .... 118 B4
  Leeds LS2 .... 206 B1
Upper Parish Ghyll La
  LS29 .... 7 F3
Upper Park Gate BD1 ..... 201 C3
Upper Peel St WF13 ...... 118 D1
Upper Piccadilly BD1 ...... 201 B3
Upper Quarry Rd HD2 .... 137 A6
Upper Raglan St OL14 .... 108 B6
Upper Rd WF17 .... 118 B2
Upper Reins HD7 .... 172 A5
Upper Rushton Rd BD3 ... 56 D1
Upper Seymour St BD3 .... 75 B7
Upper South St WF13 .... 118 C1
Upper Station Rd WF17 .. 118 D4
Upper Sutherland Rd HX3 114 E8
Upper Swain Royd Mews
  BD15 .... 53 E4
Upper Town BD22 .... 51 C2
Upper Town St LS13 .... 58 C3
Upper Warrengate WF1 ... 216 C2
Upper Washer La HX2 .... 202 B1
Upper Wellhouse Rd HD7 152 C3
Upper West St WF17 ...... 118 E5
Upper Westlock Ave LS9 . 208 A1
Upper Whitley
  Jun & Inf Sch** WF4 .... 156 E5
Upper Willow Hall HX2 .... 112 D6
Upper Woodlands Rd BD8 55 A1
Upper Woodview Pl [10]
  LS11 .... 214 B2
Upper Wortley Dr LS12 .. 209 E3
Upper Wortley
  Primary Sch LS12 .... 209 E2
Upper Wortley Rd LS12 .. 209 E3
Upper Wortley Recn Ctr
  LS12 .... 77 F7
Upperfield Dr HD7 .... 152 C4
Upperhead Row [2] HD1 .. 154 A6
Uppermoor LS28 .... 76 D7
Uppermoor Cl LS28 .... 76 D6
Uppermoore Junior &
  Infants Sch HD7 .... 188 E4
Upton Jun & Inf Sch WF9 183 C8
Upton St WF17 .... 118 B6
Upton Wlk [8] BD15 .... 73 B8
Upwood La BD20 .... 19 D2
Upwood Pk BD22 .... 51 E3
Urban Terr WF4 .... 156 E5
Ure Cres BD8 .... 74 D8
Ure Gr LS22 .... 13 D8
Usher St BD4 .... 201 D1
Usher Street First Sch
  BD4 .... 201 D1
Utley First Sch BD20 .... 18 A2
Uttley St [4] HX3 .... 92 B2

Vale Ave Knottingley WF11 . 126 D4
  Leeds LS8 .... 44 A3
Vale Cl HD5 .... 154 F3
Vale Cres WF11 .... 126 D4
Vale Crest WF11 .... 126 D4
Vale Gr Queensbury BD13 .. 72 F1
  Silsden BD20 .... 5 D1
Vale Head Gr WF11 .... 126 D4
Vale Head Mount WF11 .. 126 D4
Vale Junior & Infants Sch
  WF11 .... 126 D4
Vale Mill La BD22 .... 34 D1
Vale Rd WF9 .... 163 B1
Vale St Bacup OL13 .... 106 A3
  Brighouse HD6 .... 115 A3
  Keighley BD21 .... 18 E1
  Todmorden OL14 .... 108 B5
Vale The Collingham LS22 . 29 A8
  Leeds LS6 .... 59 F5
Vale View WF7 .... 164 B7
Valentine Ct BD13 .... 72 F7
Valestone Ave WF9 .... 181 C6
Valley Ave Brighouse HX3 115 A8
  South Elmsall WF9 .... 183 B3
Valley Cl LS17 .... 43 A5
Valley Cres WF2 .... 120 F2
Valley Ct Bradford BD1 ... 55 A1
  Castleford WF10 .... 124 A5
  Leeds LS17 .... 204 A4
  Liversedge WF15 .... 117 B5
Valley Dr Dewsbury WF12 . 139 E1
  Ilkley LS29 .... 8 E4
  Leeds LS15 .... 62 B1
Valley Farm Rd LS10 ...... 215 F1
  Wakefield WF2 .... 120 F2
Valley Farm Way LS10 .... 80 A1

Valley Fold BD13 .... 92 E8
Valley Gdns LS7 .... 60 C8
Valley Gn LS28 .... 76 F6
Valley Gr Halifax HX2 ...... 91 F7
  Pudsey LS28 .... 76 F6
Valley Head HD2 .... 135 C2
Valley Mills Ind Est BD10 .. 56 E8
Valley Mount Kippax LS25 .. 83 A2
  Pudsey LS13 .... 77 A8
Valley Par BD8 .... 55 D1
Valley Parade Football Gd
  BD8 .... 55 D1
Valley Pl BD1 .... 55 E1
Valley Rd Bradford BD1 ... 201 B4
  Cleckheaton BD19 .... 116 E8
  Darrington WF8 .... 147 E4
  Dewsbury WF12 .... 139 F1
  [8] Hebden Bridge HX7 .... 89 A3
  Ilkley LS29 .... 8 D5
  Keighley BD21 .... 35 F7
  Kippax LS25 .... 83 A2
  Leeds LS13 .... 58 C5
  Liversedge WF15 .... 117 B4
  Mapplewell S75 .... 178 A1
  Morley LS27 .... 98 C5
  Ossett WF5 .... 140 D4
  [4] Pontefract WF8 .... 146 D8
  Pudsey LS28 .... 76 F6
  Shipley BD18 .... 55 C6
Valley Ridge Kippax LS25 .. 82 F2
  Kippax, Kippax Common S25 82 F3
Valley Rise LS13 .... 58 C5
Valley Sq LS28 .... 76 F6
Valley St WF9 .... 182 F2
Valley Terr LS17 .... 43 A5
Valley The LS17 .... 43 A5
Valley View Baildon BD17 .. 38 B1
  Glusburn BD20 .... 16 C7
  Halifax HX5 .... 134 F8
  Halifax, Illingworth HX2 ... 91 F7
  Harden BD16 .... 36 A1
  South Elmsall WF9 .... 183 B3
Valley View BD22 .... 34 E3
Valley View Gdns [12] BD22 51 E8
Valley View Rd
  Heptonstall HX7 .... 88 F4
  Ossett WF5 .... 140 D4
Valley Way HX2 .... 91 F7
Vancouver Pl LS7 .... 204 B2
Varley Rd HD7 .... 169 F7
Varley St LS28 .... 57 D1
Vaughan St Bradford BD1 .. 74 D7
  [1] Halifax HX1 .... 202 B1
Vegal Cres HX3 .... 91 F1
Venn St HD1 .... 154 B6
Ventnor Dr
  Cleckheaton BD19 .... 96 B2
  Ventnor CI** WF5 .... 140 D5
Ventnor Dr BD3 .... 75 A7
Ventnor Terr HX3 .... 113 B4
Ventnor Way WF5 .... 140 D5
Vento Cl BD6 .... 94 B6
Venture St OL13 .... 106 A3
Verdun Rd BD6 .... 94 A8
Vere Sq [7] BD5 .... 74 E4
Verity Spur LS9 .... 80 E8
Verity St BD4 .... 95 F7
Verity View LS9 .... 61 E1
Vermont St LS13 .... 58 A2
Verner St WF7 .... 145 C4
Vernon Ave HD1 .... 153 F7
Vernon Cl HD1 .... 153 F7
Vernon Ct BD20 .... 35 B8
Vernon Pl Bradford BD2 .. 56 B2
  Leeds LS7 .... 57 E1
  Queensbury BD13 .... 92 C7
Vernon Rd Leeds LS1 ..... 206 B3
  Liversedge WF15 .... 117 C4
Vernon St Haworth BD22 . 51 C7
  Leeds LS2 .... 206 B1
  Todmorden OL14 .... 108 A3
Vesper Ct LS5 .... 58 F6
Vesper Ct LS5 .... 58 F6
Vesper Gate Cres LS5 .... 58 E5
Vesper Gate Dr LS5 .... 58 E5
Vesper Gate Mount LS5 . 58 F6
Vesper Gdns LS5 .... 58 F5
Vesper Gr [2] LS5 .... 59 A4
Vesper La LS5 .... 58 F5
Vesper Mount LS5 .... 59 A4
Vesper Pl [3] LS5 .... 59 A4
Vesper Rd LS5 .... 58 E6
Vesper Rise LS5 .... 58 E5
Vesper Terr [3] LS5 .... 59 A4
Vesper Way LS5 .... 58 E6
Vesper Wlk LS5 .... 58 E6
Vestry St BD4 .... 75 B3
Viaduct Rd LS4 .... 205 D1
Viaduct St
  Huddersfield HD1 .... 154 A7
  Pudsey LS28 .... 152 A1
Vicar La Bradford BD1 .... 201 C2
  Leeds LS1, LS2 .... 211 F4
  Leeds LS2 .... 212 A4
Vicar Park Dr HX2 .... 112 B8
Vicar Park Rd HX2 .... 112 B8
Vicar St WF13 .... 117 A5
Vicarage Ave
  Gildersome LS27 .... 97 C6
  Leeds LS5 .... 59 A4
Vicarage Ct Bradford BD12 95 C1
  Lofthouse Gate WF1 .... 121 C5
  South Kirkby WF9 .... 182 C3
Vicarage Dr LS28 .... 76 D7

Vicarage Gdns
Birkenshaw BD11 96 A5
Brighouse HD6 135 F8
Featherstone WF7 145 D8
Vicarage La Bramham LS23 30 D3
Featherstone WF7 145 D5
Royston S71 179 C3
Vicarage Meadows WF14 138 C5
Vicarage Pl LS5 59 B4
Vicarage Rd
Dewsbury WF12 139 C5
Dewsbury WF12 139 D8
Huddersfield HD3 153 B6
Leeds LS6 205 F2
Shipley BD18 55 E8
Vicarage St LS5 59 B4
Vicarage St N WF1 216 C3
Vicarage St S WF1 216 C2
Vicarage Terr Batley WF17 118 A7
Leeds LS5 59 B4
Vicarage View LS5 59 B4
Vicars Rd LS8 207 F4
Vicars Terr Kippax WF10 103 B4
Leeds LS8 207 F4
Vickerman Cres HD4 153 F1
Vickerman St HX1 202 B2
Vickers Ave Leeds LS5 58 F3
South Elmsall WF9 182 E1
Vickers St Castleford WF10 124 D7
Morley LS27 97 F2
Morley LS27 97 F3
Vickersdale LS28 57 E2
Victor Dr LS20 39 E8
Victor Rd Bradford BD9 55 B2
South Kirkby WF9 182 C2
Victor St Batley WF17 118 D5
Bradford, Bradford Moor BD3 75 E7
Bradford, Manningham BD9 55 B2
Castleford WF10 124 C5
South Elmsall WF9 182 F2
Victor Terr Bradford BD9 55 B2
Halifax HX1 202 C4
Victoria App WF1 121 B3
Victoria Ave Batley WF17 118 C4
Bradford BD2 56 D4
Brighouse HD6 115 C3
Cleckheaton BD19 116 D7
Elland HX5 134 E6
Halifax HX1 202 B2
Haworth BD22 51 C8
Horsforth LS18 58 A7
Ilkley LS29 7 F4
7 Keighley BD21 35 C8
Leeds LS9 80 B7
Menston LS29 22 A5
Morley LS27 98 A5
Rothwell LS26 100 E4
Shipley BD18 54 F8
Sowerby Bridge HX6 112 C5
Wakefield WF2 142 A6
Yeadon LS19 40 D8
Victoria Bldgs
5 Dewsbury WF12 118 E1
Hebden Bridge HX7 110 C2
Victoria Cl Horsforth LS18 58 A7
Ilkley LS29 8 A4
Kippax WF10 103 B4
Yeadon LS19 40 D7
Victoria Cotts LS25 105 D4
Victoria Cres
Dewsbury WF13 118 A2
Elland HX5 134 F6
Horsforth LS18 58 A7
Pudsey LS28 76 C7
Victoria Ct Batley WF17 96 F1
Castleford WF10 124 D6
Keighley BD21 35 B8
18 Shipley BD18 54 F8
Upton WF9 183 A7
Victoria Dr Bradford BD2 56 D4
Dewsbury WF12 139 C4
Horsforth LS18 58 A7
Ilkley LS29 7 F4
Morley LS27 98 B6
Northowram HX3 93 B3
Victoria Gdns
Horsforth LS18 58 B7
Ilkley LS29 7 F4
Pudsey LS28 76 C7
Victoria Gr Horsforth LS18 58 A6
Ilkley LS29 7 F4
Leeds LS9 80 B8
Pudsey LS28 76 C7
Wakefield WF2 141 D3
Victoria Grange Dr LS27 98 A5
Victoria Grange Way 4 LS27 98 A5
Victoria House 6 LS5 59 A4
Victoria Ind Est BD2 56 C4
Victoria Jun Sch LS26 100 D6
Victoria La
Huddersfield HD1 154 B6
Huddersfield, Town End HD7 152 C4
Victoria Mews
Horsforth LS18 58 A7
Keighley BD21 35 B7
6 Morley LS27 98 A5
Victoria Mills WF17 118 B6
Victoria Mills Units HD1 154 B7
Victoria Mount LS18 58 A7
Victoria Park Ave LS13, LS5 58 F3
Victoria Park Gr LS13, LS5 58 E3
Victoria Park Sch LS13 58 E3
Victoria Park St 7 BD21 35 D8
Victoria Park View BD21 35 D8
Victoria Pk Halifax HX1 202 C3
Shipley BD18 54 F7
Victoria Pl Boston Spa LS23 30 D4
Brighouse HD6 115 B1
Castleford WF10 124 E8
Halifax HX1 202 B3
Honley HD7 171 F4
Huddersfield HD4 153 A1
6 Huddersfield, Moldgreen HD5 154 D5
5 Mirfield WF14 137 F5
Yeadon LS19 40 A7
Victoria Primary Sch LS9 80 B8
Victoria Quarter LS1 211 F4
Victoria Rd
Bradford, Eccleshill BD2 56 C4
Bradford, Wibsey Slack BD6 94 A8
Brighouse, Bailiff Bridge HD6 115 B7
Brighouse, Hipperholme HX3 114 D7
Burley in W LS29 9 E2
Cleckheaton BD19 117 C8
Dewsbury WF13 118 C1
Dewsbury, Thornhill Lees WF12 139 C4
Elland HX5 134 E6
Glusburn BD20 16 D6
Guiseley LS20 39 D8
Halifax HX1 202 C3
Haworth BD22 51 D7
Hebden Bridge HX7 89 A4
Huddersfield HD1 153 F4
Ilkley LS29 7 F4
Keighley BD21 35 B5
Leeds LS6 205 E3
Leeds, Camp Field LS11 211 E2
Leeds, Kirkstall LS5 59 A4
Liversedge WF15 117 A3
Meltham HD7 170 D2
Morley LS27 98 A6
Oakworth BD22 34 D2
Pudsey LS28 76 C7
Pudsey, Farsley LS28 57 D2
Rothwell LS26 100 D6
Royston S71 179 D4
Shipley BD18 54 F8
Sowerby Bridge HX6 112 B3
10 Todmorden OL14 108 B6
Victoria Rise LS28 76 C7
Victoria Sh Ctr BD8 74 A8
Victoria Springs HD7 188 E4
Victoria Sq Holmfirth HD7 189 A5
Leeds LS1 211 E4
Ripponden HX6 132 D4
Victoria St
Ackworth M T WF7 163 D5
3 Baildon BD17 38 C1
Batley, Birstall WF17 96 F1
Batley, Carlinghow WF17 118 B6
Batley, Nunroyd WF16 117 D4
Bingley BD16 36 E7
Bradford BD1 201 A4
9 Bradford, Clayton BD14 73 B4
Bradford, Fagley BD2 56 D2
Bradford, Sandy Lane BD15 54 A3
Bradford, Thackley BD10 39 B2
Brighouse HD6 115 B1
Brighouse, Clifton HD6 115 C2
Castleford WF10 124 B8
Clayton West HD8 175 E2
Cleckheaton BD19 116 D8
Cullingworth BD13 52 E6
Dewsbury WF13 138 E6
Elland HX4 134 D7
Featherstone WF7 145 D5
Halifax HX1 203 E3
Hemsworth WF9 181 E6
Holmfirth HD7 189 A5
Horbury WF4 140 F1
Huddersfield HD3 153 C8
Huddersfield, Deighton HD2 136 E3
Huddersfield, Folly Hall HD1 154 A4
Huddersfield, Moldgreen HD5 154 D5
Kippax WF10 103 B4
Leeds LS2 205 F1
Leeds, Chapel Allerton LS7 204 A3
Leeds, Pottery Field LS10 212 A2
Lofthouse Gate WF1 121 B4
Marsden HD7 168 F4
Morley, Churwell LS27 98 C7
Morley, Morley Hole LS27 97 F5
Oakworth BD22 34 D2
Pontefract WF8 125 D3
Pudsey LS28 57 B6
Queensbury BD13 72 F1
Shipley BD17 55 B8
Sowerby Bridge HX6 112 B3
Sutton in C BD20 16 D5
Todmorden OL14 86 C1
Wakefield WF2 142 A7
Wetherby LS22 13 F5
Wilsden BD15 53 C4
Victoria Terr
Addingham LS29 6 F8
Brighouse HX3 114 D7
Clayton West HD8 175 F2
Guiseley LS20 22 E1
Halifax HX1 202 C2
4 Halifax, King Cross HX2 113 A4
Halifax, Luddenden Foot HX2 111 E5
5 Keighley BD21 35 D7
Leeds LS3 205 F1
Low Bradley BD20 4 C5
1 Pudsey LS28 57 F2
Todmorden OL14 109 A7
Yeadon LS19 40 D7
Victoria Theatre The HX1 203 E2
Victoria Way WF1 121 B3
Victoria Wlk Horsforth LS18 58 A7
4 Leeds LS1 211 F4
Victory Ave HD3 153 C5
Victory La WF3 122 A2
Victory Rd LS29 8 B4
View Croft Rd BD17 55 C8
View Rd BD20 35 A8
View St HD5 154 D5
View The Leeds LS8 61 A8
Leeds, Alwoodley Park LS17 43 A6
Viewlands HD2 136 B4
Viewlands Cres LS29 22 D5
Viewlands Mount LS29 22 D5
Viewlands Rise LS29 22 D5
Vignola Terr BD14 73 C5
Viking Ave HD8 175 D6
Viking Rd WF8 146 E8
Villa Cl WF7 164 B8
Villa Gr BD16 37 A4
Villa Mount BD12 94 C1
Villa Rd BD16 37 A4
Villa St HX6 112 C4
Village Ave LS4 205 D3
Village Gdns LS15 81 D6
Village Mews BD15 53 C5
Village Pl LS4 205 D2
Village Rd LS16 25 F1
Village St HX3 94 A2
Village St The LS4 205 D2
Village Terr LS4 205 D3
Village The
Kirkburton, Farnley Tyas HD4 172 F6
Kirkburton, Thurstonland HD4 172 F1
Thorp Arch LS23 14 E1
Vincent Ave BD20 17 A5
Vincent St Bradford BD1 201 A3
Halifax HX1 202 B2
Vine Ave BD19 116 C8
Vine Cl HD6 115 D2
Vine Cres BD19 116 D8
Vine Ct Brighouse HD6 115 D2
Guiseley LS20 39 E8
Vine Garth HD6 115 D3
Vine Gr HD6 115 D2
Vine St Bradford BD7 74 B4
Cleckheaton BD19 116 D8
Huddersfield HD1 154 C8
Vine Terr Halifax HX1 203 D2
3 Thornton BD13 72 D6
Vine Terr E BD8 73 E8
Vine Terr W BD8 73 E7
Vinery Ave LS9 80 A8
Vinery Cl HD8 175 F2
Vinery Gr 3 LS9 80 A8
Vinery Mount LS9 80 A7
Vinery Pl LS9 80 A7
Vinery Rd LS4 205 D2
Vinery St 4 LS9 80 A8
Vinery Terr LS9 80 A7
Vinery View LS9 80 A7
Vineyard HD7 152 D5
Violet St Halifax HX1 202 C3
Haworth BD22 51 C6
Violet St N HX1 202 C4
Virginia Cl WF2 121 A6
Virginia Ct WF2 121 A6
Virginia Dr WF2 121 A6
Virginia Gdns WF2 121 A6
Virginia Rd HD3 153 C7
Virginia St BD14 73 C3
Virginia Terr LS14 45 F5
Vissett Cl WF9 181 B6
Vissitt La WF9 181 B6
Vivian Pl BD7 74 A3
Vivien Rd BD8 73 C8
Vulcan Cl WF13 139 C8
Vulcan Gdns WF13 139 C8
Vulcan Rd WF13 139 C8
Vulcan St Bradford BD4 75 D1
Brighouse HD6 115 C1
11 Todmorden OL14 108 A1

Waddilove's Hospl BD8 55 D2
Waddington St 1 BD21 35 C6
Wade House Ave HX3 93 C6
Wade House Rd HX3 93 C6
Wade St Bradford BD1 201 B2
Halifax HX1 203 F3
Pudsey LS28 57 D3
Wadhouse La WF4 160 A8
Wadlands Cl LS28 57 D4
Wadlands Dr LS28 57 C4
Wadlands Gr LS28 57 C4
Wadlands Rise LS28 57 C3
Wadman Rd HD7 189 D3
Wadsworth Ave OL14 108 A4
Wadsworth Ct HX1 202 C4
Wadsworth La HX7 89 C3
Wadsworth St HX1 202 B4
Waggon La WF9 183 C8
Wagon La BD16 37 A1
Wain Brow HD4 171 F8
Wain Ct HD4 171 F8
Wain Pk HD4 171 F8
Waincliffe Cres LS11 213 F1
Waincliffe Dr LS11 98 F8
Waincliffe Garth LS11 213 F1
Waincliffe Mount LS11 98 F8
Waincliffe Pl LS11 213 F1
Waincliffe Sq LS11 213 F1
Waincliffe Terr LS11 98 F8
Waindale Cl HX2 91 A3
Waindale Cres HX2 91 A3
Waindike Cl WF6 123 C3
Waindyke Way WF6 123 D2
Waingate HD4 171 F8
Waingate Pk HD7 152 D1
Wainhouse Rd HX1 202 B1
Wainhouse Terr HX2 202 B1
Wainman Sq 2 BD12 94 C3
Wainman St Baildon BD17 38 D4
1 Bradford BD12 94 C3
Halifax HX1 202 B3
Shipley BD17 55 B8
Wainscott Cl HX7 89 B6
Wainsgate HX7 89 B6
Wainsgate La HX7 89 B6
Wainstalls HX2 90 F5
Wainstalls La HX2 90 F5
Wainstalls Lodge La HX2 90 E5
Wainstalls Primary Sch HX2 90 F5
Wainstalls Rd HX2 90 F5
Waite St WF2 141 E6
Waites Croft WF2 120 B2
Waites Terr LS21 23 B7
Wakefield 41 Ind Pk WF2 120 F5
Wakefield Ave LS14 61 F1
Wakefield Cathedral CE Sch WF2 142 A3
Wakefield City High Sch WF1 142 F7
Wakefield Coll
Hemsworth WF9 181 E7
Wakefield WF1 216 A3
Wakefield, Thornes Park WF2 142 A4
Wakefield Coll Whitwood Ctr WF10 124 A6
Wakefield Cres WF12 139 F8
Wakefield Eastmoor First Sch WF1 216 C3
Wakefield Gate HX3 112 F4
Wakefield Girls High Sch WF1 216 A3
Wakefield Independent Sch WF4 162 F6
Wakefield (Lupset) Municipal Golf Course WF2 141 E2
Wakefield Meth Jun & Inf Sch WF2 142 C3
Wakefield Mus WF1 216 B2
Wakefield Old Rd 6 WF12 139 D8
Wakefield Rd
Ackworth M T WF7 163 E5
Birkenshaw BD11 97 A5
Bradford BD4 75 B4
4 Brighouse HD6 115 B2
Brighouse HD6 115 D1
Brighouse, Lydgate HD6, HX3 114 E7
Clayton West HD8 175 E2
Denby Dale HD8 192 B7
Dewsbury WF12 139 E8
Featherstone WF7 145 B5
Flockton WF4 157 C4
Garforth LS25 82 C4
Gildersome LS27 97 D5
Halifax HX3 113 B2
Hemsworth WF9 163 B2
Horbury WF4 141 C2
Huddersfield HD1, HD5 154 D5
Leeds LS10 215 F2
Lepton HD8 155 D3
Liversedge HD6 137 A7
Liversedge, Mill Bridge WF15 117 B4
Mapplewell S75 178 C2
Ossett WF5 140 F7
Pontefract WF8 146 B7
Rothwell LS26 100 B6
Rothwell, Royds Green LS26 101 C2
Swillington LS26 82 C4
Wakefield WF5, WF2 141 B6
Walden Dr BD9 54 C3
Walden Howe Cl WF7 145 C8
Walden St WF10 124 D7
Waldorf Way WF2 216 B1
Waldron Ho 8 BD5 201 B1
Walesby Ct LS16 41 E2
Walford Ave LS9 80 A8
Walford Gr LS9 80 A8
Walford Mount LS9 80 A8
Walford Rd LS9 80 A8
Walford Terr LS9 80 A8
Walk Royd Hill S75 177 B2
Walk The Keighley BD21 35 C6
Pudsey LS28 57 C2
Walker Ave Bradford BD7 73 E5
Wakefield WF2 141 F7
Walker Cl BD20 16 B6
Walker Dr BD8 74 B8
Walker Gn WF12 139 E2
Walker La Horbury WF4 141 B1
Sowerby Bridge HX6 112 D4
Wadsworth Moor HX7 89 C5
Walker Pl 7 Morley LS27 98 B7
Shipley BD18 55 D8
Walker Rd Bradford BD12 94 F4
Horsforth LS18 41 B1
Menston LS29 21 F4
Walker St Bradford BD4 95 B8
3 Brighouse BD19 115 F8
Cleckheaton BD19 116 D8
Dewsbury, Earlsheaton WF12 139 F6
Dewsbury, Ravensthorpe WF13 138 D4
Dewsbury, Thornhill Lees WF12 139 D3
Walker Terr Bradford BD4 75 B4
Cullingworth BD13 52 D5
Walker Wood BD17 37 F2
Walker's La Leeds LS12 78 C4
Silsden BD20 5 D7
Walker's Pl BD20 17 E8
Walker's Rd LS6 59 F5
Walker's Terr WF1 216 A2
Walkergate Otley LS21 23 A8
Pontefract WF8 125 E1
Walkers Gn LS12 78 C4
Walkers Mount WF17 118 C3
Walkers Row LS19 40 A7
Walkley Ave WF16 117 D3
Walkley Gr 10 WF16 117 D3
Walkley La WF16 117 D2
Walkley Terr WF16 117 E2
Walkley Villas WF16 117 E2
Wall Nook La HD8 190 D6
Wall St BD22 34 F6
Wallace Gdns WF3 121 B6
Wallace St HX1 202 B2
Wallbank Dr BD18 55 C6
Walled Garden The WF4 178 A7
Waller Clough Rd HD7 151 F4
Wallingford Mount BD15 73 B7
Wallis St
Bradford, Brown Royd BD8 74 A7
Bradford, Green Side BD8 73 F7
Sowerby Bridge HX6 112 B4
Wallroyds HD8 191 F5
Walmer Gr LS28 76 F5
Walmer Villas BD8 55 D1
Walmsley Dr WF9 183 B7
Walmsley Rd LS6 205 E3
Walnut Ave
Dewsbury WF12 140 B7
Wakefield WF2 141 F7
Walnut Cl Dewsbury WF12 140 A6
Leeds LS14 62 C8
Walnut Cres
Dewsbury WF12 140 A6
Wakefield WF2 141 F7
Walnut Dr Dewsbury WF12 140 B7
Normanton WF6 144 A7
Pontefract WF8 146 C6
Walnut Gr WF12 140 B7
Walnut La WF12 140 A7
Walnut Pl WF12 140 A7
Walnut Rd WF12 140 B7
Walnut St Bradford BD3 75 C6
Halifax HX1 202 C3
15 Keighley BD21 35 B4
South Elmsall WF9 182 F1
Walpole Rd HD4 153 D3
Walsden CE Infant Sch OL14 108 B1
Walsden Est OL14 129 B7
Walsden Junior Sch OL14 108 A1
Walsden Sta OL14 108 A1
Walsh La Bingley BD16 37 A7
Gildersome LS12 77 D2
Halifax HX3 92 B1
Walsh St HX1 202 B3
Walsh's Sq 19 HX1 202 C1
Walsham Dr HD3 134 F1
Walshaw La HX7 68 C3
Walshaw St 2 BD7 74 A4
Walter Clough La HX3 114 C5
Walter Cres LS9 212 C3
Walter St Bradford BD10 56 B8
Leeds LS4 205 D1
Shipley BD2 55 D4
Waltham Dr DN6 184 E2
Waltin Rd HD7 188 F1
Walton Cl OL13 106 A1
Walton Croft HD5 154 E6
Walton Dr BD11 96 F5
Walton Fold 2 OL14 108 D6
Walton Garth BD11 96 F5
Walton Grove Infants Sch WF2 161 B6
Walton Junior Sch WF2 161 A7
Walton La Brighouse BD19 115 F6
Wakefield WF2 160 F8
Walton Rd Thorp Arch LS23 14 C4
Upton WF9 183 D8
Walton LS23 15 A3
Wetherby LS22, LS23 14 C4
Walton St Bradford BD4 201 C1
Leeds, Holbeck LS11 211 E2
Leeds, Hunslet LS10 215 E4
Sowerby Bridge HX6 112 B4
Walton Station La WF2 160 F7
Walton View WF4 161 F8
Waltroyd Rd BD19 116 C7
Wansford Cl BD4 75 E2
Wanstead Cres BD15 73 B8
Wapping First Sch BD3 201 C4
Wapping Nick La HX4 134 E3
Wapping Rd BD3 201 C4
Warburton Pl 9 BD6 74 C1
Warburton Rd HD8 175 D6
Warcock La OL13 106 B3
Ward Bank Rd HD7 189 A4
Ward Ct HD6 135 F7
Ward Fall WF4 159 F3
Ward La Leeds LS10 215 D1
Lofthouse Gate WF3 122 A2
Ward Place La HD7 188 F3
Ward Sq 26 HD1 154 A6
Ward St Bradford BD7 74 A3
Dewsbury WF13 118 D1
4 Keighley BD21 35 B6
Leeds LS10 212 A1
Ward's End HX1 203 E2
Wardman St BD21 18 E1

Wards Hill WF17 .... 118 C5
Wards Hill Ct 10 WF17 ...... 118 C5
Wareham Cnr BD4 .... 75 E2
Warehouse Hill Rd HD7 .... 169 A4
Warehouse St WF17 .... 118 D4
Warhurst Rd HX5 .... 135 A8
Waring Way WF12 .... 118 E1
Warlands End Gate
  OL14 .... 129 D5
Warlbeck LS29 .... 7 F4
Warley Ave BD3 .... 75 D8
Warley Dene HX2 .... 112 B6
Warley Dr BD3 .... 75 D8
Warley Edge La HX2 .... 112 C7
Warley Gr Bradford BD3 ..... 75 D8
  Halifax HX2 .... 112 D7
Warley Rd HX1, HX2 .... 202 A2
Warley Road Junior &
  Infant Sch HX1 .... 202 A2
Warley St HX1 .... 202 C2
Warley Town County
  Primary Sch HX2 .... 112 B6
Warley Town La HX2 .... 112 A6
Warley View HX2 .... 112 D7
Warley Wood Ave WF2 .... 111 F5
Warley Wood La HX2 ...... 111 F5
Warm La LS19 .... 40 A5
Warmfield La WF1 .... 143 E7
Warmfield View WF1 .... 142 F7
Warmleigh Pk BD13 .... 72 B1
Warneford Ave WF5 .... 140 D7
Warneford Rd HD4 .... 153 A3
Warneford Rise HD4 .... 153 A3
Warnford Gr BD4 .... 75 D3
Warrel's Ave 4 LS13 .... 58 C3
Warrel's Ct LS13 .... 58 C2
Warrel's Mount LS13 ...... 58 C2
Warrel's Pl LS13 .... 58 C3
Warrel's Rd LS13 .... 58 C3
Warrel's Row 4 LS13 ...... 58 C2
Warrel's St LS13 .... 58 C2
Warrel's Terr 10 LS13 ...... 58 C2
Warren Ave Bingley BD16 .... 37 B5
  Knottingley WF11 .... 126 D3
  Wakefield WF2 .... 142 D2
Warren Cl
  Liversedge WF15 .... 117 B2
  Royston S71 .... 179 D5
Warren Ct WF1 .... 216 C2
Warren Dr Bingley BD16 ..... 37 B4
  Featherstone WF7 .... 145 A8
Warren House WF1 .... 216 B2
Warren House La
  East Carlton LS29 .... 23 D1
  Huddersfield HD3 .... 135 A3
Warren La Arthington LS21 .. 25 A7
  Bingley BD16 .... 37 B4
  Bramham LS24 .... 81 B1
  Mapplewell S75 .... 178 C4
  Woolley S75 .... 178 C4
Warren Park Cl HD6 .... 114 E5
Warren Pk HD6 .... 114 E6
Warren Rd WF7 .... 145 B6
Warren St WF13 .... 139 D6
Warrens La
  Birkenshaw WF17 .... 96 D5
  Cleckheaton WF17 .... 96 D3
Warrenside
  Huddersfield, Deighton
  HD2 .... 136 E4
  Huddersfield, Riddings
  HD2 .... 136 D3
Warrenton Pl BD7 .... 74 A5
Warrington Terr HD7 ...... 168 E4
Warsop WF2 S71 .... 178 E1
Warton Ave BD4 .... 75 B1
Warwick Ave HD7 .... 152 E5
Warwick Cl Bradford BD4 ... 75 B4
  1 Halifax HX3 .... 113 B4
Warwick Cl 1 LS18 .... 58 C7
Warwick Dr BD4 .... 75 B4
Warwick Rd Batley WF17 ... 118 B3
  Bradford BD4 .... 75 B4
Warwick Road Jun &
  Inf Sch WF17 .... 118 C3
Warwick St WF1 .... 142 F3
Wasdale Cres WF2 .... 141 E7
Wasdale Rd WF2 .... 141 E7
Washburn Ct Silsden BD20 .. 5 E1
  Wetherby LS22 .... 13 D8
Washburn Dr BD20 .... 16 C7
Washer La HX2 .... 112 E4
Washer Lane Ind Est HX2 .. 112 F4
Washfold Rd HX7 .... 131 B7
Washington Pl LS13 ...... 77 A8
Washington St
  Bradford BD8 .... 54 F1
  20 Halifax HX3 .... 92 A1
  Leeds LS12 .... 210 B4
  Pudsey LS13 .... 77 A8
Washington Terr LS13 .... 77 A8
Washpit New Rd HD7 ..... 189 B3
Wasp Nest Rd HD1 ...... 136 A1
Waste La Huddersfield HD5 . 154 E4
  Mirfield WF14 .... 137 F3
Mirfield, Lower Hopton
  WF14 .... 138 A3
  Wadsworth Moor HX7 .... 69 A5
Waste The WF14 .... 137 F3
Wastwater Dr BD6 .... 93 F6
Watchit Hole La WF8 ..... 165 C4
Watchley La DN5 .... 195 B3
Water Gn HX6 .... 132 A6
Water Green La HX6 ..... 132 A6

Water Hill La HX2 .... 112 A5
Water La Bradford BD1 .... 74 D7
  Darrington WF8 .... 146 D2
  Dewsbury, Chickenley WF12 140 A7
  Dewsbury, Scout Hill WF12 139 B6
  Halifax HX3 .... 203 F2
  Keighley BD21 .... 35 B6
  Kirk Smeaton WF8 ...... 166 E6
  Leeds LS11 .... 211 F3
  Leeds, Camp Field LS11 .. 211 D2
  Leeds, Gamble Hill LS12 ... 77 D7
  Lofthouse Gate WF3 .... 121 F4
  Netherton WF4 .... 158 D8
  Pontefract WF8 .... 125 F3
  Pudsey LS28 .... 57 D3
  Shepley HD8 .... 174 A3
  South Kirkby WF9 ...... 181 F4
  Woolley WF4 .... 178 A8
  Yeadon LS18 .... 40 F1
Water Lane Cl WF4 .... 158 D8
Water Row HD7 .... 189 E6
Water Royd Ave WF14 .... 138 A6
Water Royd Cres WF14 ... 138 A6
Water Royd Dr WF14 ..... 138 A6
Water Royd La WF14 .... 138 A6
Water Side La HD7 ...... 188 D2
Water St Brighouse HD6 .. 115 B3
  Clayton West HD8 ..... 175 D1
  Holmfirth HD7 .... 188 D3
  Huddersfield HD1 ...... 153 F5
  Huddersfield, Rashcliffe
  HD1, HD4 .... 153 F3
  Sowerby Bridge HX6 .... 112 B3
  Todmorden OL14 .... 108 B5
Water Stalls Rd HX7 ..... 110 F2
Watercock St BD4 .... 201 D1
Watercroft HD5 .... 154 E4
Waterfall Cotts HD7 .... 168 D5
Waterfront Mews BD10 .. 56 E8
Watergate Brighouse HX3 . 114 C7
  Huddersfield HD1 ...... 154 B6
  Mickletown LS26 ...... 102 B1
  Pontefract WF8 .... 125 C1
Watergate Rd WF12 .... 139 B7
Waterhouse Ct 8 LS18 ... 58 B7
Waterhouse Dr WF3 .... 122 A7
Waterhouse Gr WF2 .... 142 A6
Waterhouse St
  Halifax HX1 .... 203 E3
  8 Keighley BD21 .... 35 B7
Waterloo Cl WF10 .... 123 F5
Waterloo Cres
  Bradford BD10 .... 56 F8
  Leeds LS13 .... 58 B3
Waterloo Fold 2 BD12 .. 94 D2
Waterloo Gr LS28 .... 76 B7
Waterloo Junior Sch LS28 76 C7
Waterloo La LS13 .... 58 D3
Waterloo Mount LS28 ... 76 B8
Waterloo Rd Bingley BD16 36 F3
  Brighouse HD6 .... 115 A3
  Huddersfield HD5 ...... 155 A6
  Pudsey LS28 .... 76 B7
Waterloo Rise HD5 ...... 155 A5
Waterloo St Leeds LS10 .. 211 F3
  Wakefield WF1 .... 142 D4
Waterloo Terr HX6 ...... 112 C6
Waterloo Way LS13 ..... 58 D3
Waters Rd HD7 .... 168 D5
Waterside Bingley BD16 .. 36 D5
  Halifax HX3 .... 203 F2
  Huddersfield HD1 ...... 153 F5
  Huddersfield, Salford HD1 153 F2
  Oxenhope BD22 .... 51 C2
  Silsden BD20 .... 17 F8
Waterside Fold HX7 ..... 89 A4
Waterside Ind Pk LS10 .. 80 B2
Waterside Mill BD22 .... 51 C1
Waterside Rd
  Bradford BD8 .... 74 A8
  Leeds LS10 .... 80 B3
Waterside Wlk WF14 .... 137 D5
Waterside La LS23 ...... 14 B4
Waterton Cl
  South Kirkby WF9 ..... 182 D3
  Walton WF2 .... 161 A6
Waterton Gr WF2 .... 141 F5
Waterton Jun & Inf Sch
  WF2 .... 161 A6
Waterton Rd WF2 ...... 141 E4
Waterton St WF10 ..... 124 B7
Waterwood Cl WF3 ..... 119 F7
Waterworks Rd WF17 ... 117 F4
Watery La HD7 .... 197 F8
Watford Ave HX3 ...... 93 F3
Watkin Ave BD13 ...... 72 F6
Watkinson Ave WF4 ... 91 F4
Watkinson Bghws HX2 . 91 E4
Watkinson Dr HX2 ..... 91 F4
Watkinson Rd HX2 .... 91 E4
Watling Rd WF10 ..... 104 E1
Watmough St 2 BD7 .. 74 A3
Watroyd La HD7 ...... 152 B2
Watson Ave WF12 .... 140 B8
Watson Cl BD22 ...... 51 C2
Watson Cres WF1 .... 142 E7
Watson Mill La HX6 .. 112 B2
Watson Rd LS14 ..... 61 F1
Watson St Morley LS27 . 97 F3
  Normanton WF6 ...... 123 A2
Watson's La LS24 .... 31 D5
Watt St BD4 .... 75 D6
Wattlesyke LS22 ..... 29 E8
Watts St BD14 .... 73 A4
Watty Hall Ave BD6 .. 74 A2
Watty Hall La BD6 ... 74 A2
Watty Hall Rd BD6 ... 74 A2
Watty La OL14 .... 107 F3

Watty Terr OL14 .... 107 F3
Wauchope St WF2 ...... 216 A1
Wauds Gates BD17 ...... 38 C1
Waulkmill Cl WF9 ...... 183 A7
Wavell Garth WF2 ...... 160 F7
Wavell Gr WF2 .... 160 F7
Waveney Ave WF2 ...... 209 F1
Waveney Ave Bradford BD7 74 B5
  Keighley BD20 .... 36 B8
Waverley Cres HX3 ..... 114 C7
Waverley Garth LS11 ... 214 B4
Waverley Middle Sch BD7 74 B5
Waverley Pl WF2 .... 74 B5
Waverley Rd Bradford BD7 74 B5
  Elland HX5 .... 134 F5
Waverley St
  Dewsbury WF12 .... 139 C7
  Slaithwaite HD7 .... 151 F1
Waverley Terr
  Bradford BD7 .... 74 B5
  Brighouse HX3 .... 114 C7
  Huddersfield HD1 ..... 153 D7
Waverton Gn BD6 ...... 93 F7
Wavertree Park Gdns 15
  BD12 .... 94 C4
Wayland App LS16 ..... 42 D4
Wayland Croft LS16 ... 42 D4
Wayland Ct LS16 ...... 42 D4
Wayland Dr LS16 ..... 42 D4
Wayne Cl WF17 .... 118 C6
Wayside Ave LS14 ..... 28 D1
Wayside Cres Bardsey LS14 28 D1
  Bradford BD2 .... 56 B5
Wayside Ct BD20 ...... 18 A2
Wayside Mount LS14 .. 28 D1
Weardale Cl BD4 ...... 75 C1
Weardley La LS17 ..... 26 B6
Weather Hill La
  Hebden Bridge HX7 .... 110 E4
  Holme HD7 .... 198 E8
Weather Hill Rd HD3 ... 135 A2
Weatherall Pl DN6 .... 184 F2
Weatherhead Pl BD20 .... 5 F1
Weatherhill Cres HD3 .. 135 A2
Weatherhouse Terr HX2 . 91 D1
Weaver Ct BD10 .... 56 B8
Weaver Gdns LS27 .... 98 D3
Weaver St LS4 .... 205 D1
Weavers Cotts 1 BD22 . 51 C2
Weavers Croft
  Bradford BD10 .... 39 B2
  Pudsey LS28 .... 76 F6
Weavers Ct Leeds LS12 209 E3
  Meltham HD7 .... 170 F2
  1 Pudsey LS28 .... 76 F5
Weavers Grange LS20 .. 22 E2
Weavers Hill BD22 ... 51 C6
Weavers Rd WF8 ...... 125 E1
Weavers Wlk
  Denby Dale HD8 ...... 192 B7
  Silsden BD20 .... 5 E2
Weaverthorpe Rd WF8 .. 75 E1
Webb Dr BD2 .... 56 A2
Webb's Terr HX3 ...... 203 F4
Webber St BD3 .... 75 C7
Webster Hill WF13 .... 139 C8
Webster Pl Bradford BD3 . 75 B7
Webster Row LS12 .... 209 E2
Webster St Bradford BD3 . 75 B7
  Dewsbury WF13 .... 139 C8
Wedgemoor Cl 14 BD12 . 94 C4
Wedgewood Ct LS8 .... 44 A1
Wedgewood Gr LS8 ... 44 A1
Wedgewood Sch BD4 .. 75 F2
Weeland Ave WF4 .... 144 B3
Weeland Cres WF4 ... 144 B3
Weeland Ct WF11 .... 127 A4
Weeland Dr WF11 .... 144 C3
Weeland Rd Beal DN14 .. 127 D4
  Crofton WF4 .... 144 C3
  Knottingley WF11 .... 127 D4
Weet Shaw La S72 .... 180 B1
Weetlands Cl LS25 .... 83 B2
Weetwood Ave LS16 .. 59 D7
Weetwood County
  Primary Sch LS16 .... 59 D7
Weetwood Cres LS16 .. 59 D8
Weetwood Grange Gr
  LS16 .... 59 B8
Weetwood House Ct LS16 . 59 B8
Weetwood La LS16 .... 59 D7
Weetwood Mill La LS16 . 59 D8
Weetwood Park Dr LS16 . 59 B8
Weetwood Rd
  Bradford BD8 .... 74 A8
  Leeds LS16 .... 59 B8
Weetwood Wlk LS16 .. 59 C8
Weetworth Ave WF10 .. 124 F6
Weetworth Pk WF10 .. 124 E6
Weir La OL13 .... 106 A2
Weir Side HD7 .... 168 F4
Weir St OL14 .... 108 A3
Welbeck Dr BD7 ...... 73 E4
Welbeck La WF1 ...... 143 B8
Welbeck Rd Batley WF17 . 96 F2
  Leeds LS9 .... 80 A7
Welbeck Rise BD7 .... 73 E4
Welbeck St
  Castleford WF10 ...... 124 D8
  Wakefield WF1 .... 142 D3
Welburn Ave
  Brighouse HX3 .... 114 D7
  Leeds LS16 .... 59 B7
Welburn Cl WF2 ...... 142 F1

Welburn Dr LS16 .... 59 B7
Welburn Gr LS16 ...... 59 B7
Welburn Mount BD6 ... 93 E8
Welbury Dr BD8 .... 55 C2
Weldon Ct BD4 .... 75 E4
Weldon Dr HD3 .... 152 A8
Welfare Ave LS15 ..... 63 E7
Welham Wlk BD3 ..... 56 A1
Well Bank Rd BD4 ..... 75 D3
Well Cl Swillington LS26 . 102 E8
  Yeadon LS19 .... 40 C3
Well Close Rise LS7 .... 206 C2
Well Close St HD6 ..... 115 B3
Well Croft BD18 ...... 55 B7
Well Garth LS15 ...... 62 C2
Well Garth Bank LS13 .. 58 B4
Well Garth Mount LS15 . 62 C2
Well Garth View LS13 .. 58 C4
Well Gr HD2 .... 136 C2
Well Green La HD6 .... 114 F5
Well Head Dr HX1 ..... 203 E2
Well Head La Halifax HX1 203 E2
  Sowerby Bridge HX6 ... 111 C3
Well Heads HD3 ...... 72 A6
Well Hill Honley HD7 .. 171 F4
  Otley LS21 .... 22 F7
  Yeadon LS19 .... 40 B7
Well Hill Gr S71 ...... 179 C4
Well Holme Mead LS12 . 77 E3
Well House Ave LS8 ... 61 A5
Well House Cl LS8 .... 61 A5
Well House Cres LS8 .. 61 A5
Well House Dr LS8 .... 61 A5
Well House Gdns LS8 .. 61 A5
Well House Rd LS8 .... 61 A5
Well La Batley WF17 ... 118 D5
  Brighouse HD6 .... 115 E2
  Dewsbury WF13 ...... 138 F8
  Guiseley LS20 .... 22 E1
  Halifax HX1 .... 203 F3
  Holmfirth HD7 .... 189 B4
  Kippax LS25 .... 83 A1
  Leeds LS7 .... 204 A3
  Todmorden OL14 ..... 108 B5
  Yeadon LS19 .... 40 B7
  Yeadon, Rawdon LS19 .. 40 C3
Well Royd Ave HX2 ... 112 C7
Well Royd Cl HX2 ..... 112 D7
Well St Bradford BD1 .. 201 C3
  Denholme BD13 ...... 71 D8
  3 Dewsbury WF12 .... 118 E1
  2 Elland HX4 .... 134 B4
  Guiseley LS20 .... 22 E1
  Huddersfield HD1 .... 153 F5
  Keighley BD21 .... 35 B7
  Liversedge WF15 .... 117 A5
  Todmorden OL14 .... 108 B4
  Wilsden BD15 .... 53 C5
Well Terr LS20 .... 22 E1
Well View LS20 ...... 22 E1
Welland Dr LS25 .... 83 B6
Wellands La BD19 ... 116 A7
Wellands Rd BD19 ... 116 A7
Wellands Terr BD3 ... 75 C7
Wellcroft LS21 ...... 23 A8
Wellcroft Gr WF3 .... 119 F7
Wellesley Gr WF7 ... 145 E7
Wellesley St BD1 .... 201 C3
Wellfield Ave LS14 .. 156 E5
Wellfield Bank HD4 .. 153 D2
Wellfield Cl Flockton WF4 . 156 E5
  Huddersfield HD7 .... 152 E2
Wellfield Gdns BD13 . 72 D3
Wellfield Rd HD3 .... 153 C7
Wellfield Terr OL14 .. 108 B4
Wellgarth Bradford BD6 . 93 F7
  Huddersfield HD1 .... 203 D1
Wellgarth Rd WF7 ... 145 C4
Wellgate Castleford WF10 124 F6
  Elland HX4 .... 134 C8
  Mapplewell S75 ...... 178 B1
  Slaithwaite HD7 ..... 152 B3
Wellhead Cl LS16 .... 42 E1
Wellhead Mews WF4 . 159 F4
Wellholme HD6 ...... 115 B3
Wellhouse WF14 .... 138 B7
Wellhouse La WF14 . 138 B7
Wellhouse Cl WF14 . 138 A7
Wellhouse Jun & Inf Sch
  HD7 .... 152 D3
Wellhouse La
  Huddersfield HD5 ... 137 B1
  Mirfield WF14 ...... 138 A7
Wellington Av 7 HD6 .. 115 B2
Wellington Bridge St
  Leeds LS12 .... 210 C4
  Leeds LS12 .... 210 C3
Wellington Bsns Ctr
  HX5 .... 135 A7
Wellington Cres BD18 .. 55 A7
Wellington Ct
  Birkenshaw BD11 .... 96 A6
  Halifax HX2 .... 202 A4
Wellington First Sch BD2 . 56 B3
Wellington Garth 8 LS13 . 58 D4
Wellington Gdns LS13 . 58 D4
Wellington Gr
  Bradford BD2 .... 56 B2
  Leeds LS13 .... 58 D4
  Pudsey LS28 .... 76 C7
Wellington Hill LS14 .. 45 A3
Wellington Middle Sch
  BD2 .... 56 B3
Wellington Mount LS13 58 D4
Wellington Pl
  2 Halifax HX1 ...... 203 F2
  Knottingley WF11 ... 126 D4

Wellington Rd
  Bradford BD2 .... 56 B3
  Dewsbury WF13 ...... 139 C8
  Ilkley LS29 .... 8 B4
  Keighley BD21 .... 35 C7
  Leeds LS12, LS13 ..... 210 B2
  Leeds, New Wortley
  LS12, LS3 .... 210 B2
  Todmorden OL14 ..... 108 B6
  Wilsden BD15 .... 53 C4
Wellington Rd E 10 WF13 . 139 C8
Wellington Rd Ind Est
  LS12 .... 210 C3
Wellington Sq 4 BD21 .. 35 C6
Wellington St Batley WF17 118 C4
  Bradford BD1 .... 201 C3
  Bradford BD15 .... 54 C1
  Bradford BD1 .... 201 C3
  Bradford, Haigh Fold BD2 . 56 B3
  Bradford, Idle BD10 .. 56 D6
  Bradford, Swain Green BD4 . 75 D6
  Castleford WF10 ..... 124 B8
  11 Dewsbury WF13 ... 139 C8
  Huddersfield HD3 .... 153 B8
  Leeds LS11 .... 211 D3
  8 Liversedge WF15 .. 117 B3
  Morley LS27 .... 98 A4
  Queensbury BD13 .... 72 F1
  Wakefield WF2 .... 141 E2
  Wilsden BD15 .... 53 C4
Wellington St N HX1 .. 203 F2
Wellington St W HX1 .. 203 D2
Wellington Terr Leeds LS13 . 58 D4
  Marsden HD7 .... 169 A4
Wellington Wlk 8 WF13 . 139 C8
Wells Croft LS6 ..... 59 E7
Wells Ct Halifax HX3 .. 92 B1
  Ossett WF5 .... 140 D5
Wells Gr LS20 .... 22 E1
Wells Green Gdns HD7 .. 188 F7
Wells Mount
  Denby Dale HD8 ..... 191 A6
  Guiseley LS20 .... 22 E1
Wells Prom LS29 ..... 8 B3
Wells Rd Dewsbury WF12 . 139 E2
  Guiseley LS20 .... 22 E1
  Ilkley LS29 .... 8 B3
Wells Terr HX3 ...... 92 A2
Wells The HX2 ...... 112 D7
Wells Wlk LS29 ..... 8 B3
Wellstone Ave LS13 .. 77 B8
Wellstone Dr LS13 ... 77 B8
Wellstone Garth LS13 . 77 C8
Wellstone Gdns LS13 . 77 B8
Wellstone Gn LS13 .. 77 B8
Wellstone Rd LS13 .. 77 B8
Wellstone Rise LS13 . 77 B8
Wellstone Way LS13 . 77 B8
Wellthorne Ave S36 .. 191 D1
Wellthorne La S36 .. 191 D1
Welton Mount LS6 .. 205 E3
Welton Pl LS6 ...... 205 E3
Welton Rd LS6 ..... 205 E3
Welwyn Ave Batley WF17 . 117 F6
  Shipley BD18 .... 55 F7
Welwyn Dr Baildon BD17 . 55 F7
  Shipley BD18 .... 55 A7
Welwyn Rd WF12 .... 118 F3
Wembly Ave BD13 ... 72 F6
Wenborough La BD4 . 75 E3
Wendel Ave LS15 .... 63 D7
Wendron Cl WF15 ... 116 F1
Wendron Way BD10 .. 56 B7
Wenlock St BD3 ..... 201 D2
Wenning St S71 ..... 35 E8
Wensley Ave Leeds LS7 . 60 C7
  Shipley BD18 .... 55 A7
Wensley Bank BD13 .. 72 E6
Wensley Bank Terr BD13 . 72 C6
Wensley Bank W BD13 . 72 C6
Wensley Cres LS7 ... 60 C7
Wensley Dr Leeds LS7 . 60 C7
  Pontefract WF8 ...... 146 E6
Wensley Gdns LS7 ... 60 B7
Wensley Gn LS7 ..... 60 B7
Wensley Gr Brighouse HD6 . 135 E8
  Leeds LS7 .... 60 B7
Wensley Rd LS7 ..... 60 B8
Wensley St 6 WF4 ... 141 A1
Wensley St E 8 WF4 . 141 A1
Wensley View LS7 ... 60 C7
Wensleydale Ave LS12 . 58 F2
Wensleydale Cl LS12 . 58 F2
Wensleydale Cres LS12 . 58 F2
Wensleydale Ct LS7 .. 60 C7
Wensleydale Dr LS12 . 58 F2
Wensleydale Mews 1 LS12 . 58 F2
Wensleydale Par 2 WF17 . 117 F8
Wensleydale Rd BD3 . 75 F7
Wensleydale Rise
  Baildon BD17 .... 38 E4
  3 Leeds LS12 .... 58 F2
Went Ave WF7 .... 145 C3
Went Croft WF8 ..... 146 D5
Went Edge Rd
  Kirk Smeaton WF8 .... 165 F6
  Thorpe Audlin WF8 .. 165 F5
Went Fold WF8 ...... 146 D5
Went Garth WF8 .... 146 D5
Went Gr WF7 .... 145 C3
Went Hill Cl WF7 .... 164 A8
Went La Featherstone WF4 . 145 D2
  West Hardwick WF4 .. 163 C7
Went View WF8 ..... 165 A5
Went Vale Rd WF8 .. 146 D5
Wentbridge La WF8 .. 165 C6
Wentbridge Rd WF7 . 145 C4

Wentcliffe Rd WF11 .... 126 B4
Wentdale WF8 .... 166 E6
Wentwell Rd WF7 .... 144 D5
Wentworth Ave
　Emley HD8 .... 175 C6
　Leeds LS17 .... 43 C4
Wentworth Cl
　Menston LS29 .... 22 A4
　Woolley WF4 .... 177 F7
Wentworth Cres LS17 ...... 43 C4
Wentworth Ct HD6 .... 135 F7
Wentworth Dr
　Crofton WF4 .... 162 A8
　Emley HD8 .... 175 C6
　Halifax LS3 .... 91 F7
　South Kirkby WF9 .... 182 C3
Wentworth Gate LS22 ..... 13 B6
Wentworth Gr HX2 .... 91 F7
Wentworth Park Rise WF8 147 D5
Wentworth Rd WF7 .... 145 B4
Wentworth St
　Huddersfield HD1 .... 153 F7
　Wakefield WF1 .... 216 A3
Wentworth Terr
　Harewood LS17 .... 163 B3
　Wakefield WF1 .... 216 A3
　Yeadon LS19 .... 40 D3
Wentworth Way Leeds LS17 43 C4
　Wakefield WF2 .... 142 E1
Wepener Mount LS9 .... 208 B1
Wepener Pl LS9 .... 208 B1
Wesley App LS11 .... 213 F2
Wesley Ave Bradford BD12 94 E7
　4 Leeds LS12 .... 209 F3
Wesley Ave S 5 BD12 ...... 94 E6
Wesley Cl Batley WF17 ..... 96 E1
　Leeds LS11 .... 213 F3
Wesley Croft LS11 .... 213 F3
Wesley Ct 3 Halifax HX1 .. 203 E3
　Leeds, Beeston LS11 ..... 213 F2
　Leeds, Woodhouse LS6 .. 206 A3
　Ossett WF5 .... 140 C6
　Yeadon LS19 .... 39 F7
Wesley Dr BD22 .... 94 E7
Wesley Garth LS11 .... 213 F3
Wesley Gn LS11 .... 213 F2
Wesley Gr BD10 .... 39 C1
Wesley Hall Ct WF3 .... 121 F2
Wesley House LS11 .... 213 F2
Wesley Pl Dewsbury WF13 . 139 C8
　Featherstone WF7 .... 145 D4
　Keighley BD21 .... 35 B3
　Leeds LS9 .... 212 B3
　5 Leeds, Armley LS12 ... 209 F3
　Silsden BD20 .... 5 E1
Wesley Rd Leeds LS12 ..... 209 F3
　Pudsey LS28 .... 57 C2
Wesley Row 11 LS28 .... 76 E8
Wesley Sq 13 LS28 .... 76 E7
Wesley St
　7 Castleford WF10 .... 124 D8
　Castleford, Cutsyke WF10 124 C5
　Cleckheaton BD19 .... 116 D8
　Dewsbury WF13 .... 139 C8
　Leeds LS11 .... 213 F3
　Morley LS27 .... 98 A4
　Ossett WF5 .... 140 D6
　Otley LS21 .... 23 A8
　Pudsey, Farsley LS28 .... 57 D3
　Pudsey, Rodley LS13 ..... 57 F5
　Pudsey, Stanningley LS28 .. 57 D7
　South Elmsall WF9 .... 182 E2
　Wakefield WF1 .... 142 E3
Wesley Terr
　1 Bacup OL13 .... 106 A7
　Denby Dale HD8 .... 191 F6
　Leeds LS13 .... 58 D3
　Pudsey LS28 .... 76 E8
　Pudsey, Rodley LS13 ..... 57 F5
Wesley View Pudsey LS28 .. 76 E7
　1 Pudsey, Rodley LS13 .. 57 F5
Wesleyan Terr BD4 .... 75 C3
Wessenden Head Rd HD7 170 D1
Wessenden Rd HD7 .... 169 A1
West Acre Dr WF17 .... 118 E5
West Acres WF11 .... 126 D7
West Ave Baildon BD17 ..... 38 C3
　Bradford BD3 .... 14 C1
　Bradford BD15 .... 53 F3
　Brighouse HX3 .... 115 A7
　Halifax HX3 .... 113 B4
　Honley HD7 .... 171 F4
　Horbury WF4 .... 141 C1
　Huddersfield HD3 .... 135 C1
　Leeds LS6 .... 61 C8
　Pontefract WF8 .... 146 A8
　Royston S71 .... 179 D4
West Bank Bradford BD9 .. 54 F4
　Halifax HX2 .... 91 D4
　Keighley BD22 .... 34 F8
West Bank Cl BD22 .... 34 F8
West Bank Gr BD20 .... 18 E2
West Bank Rd BD20 .... 18 E2
West Bank Rise BD22 ...... 34 F8
West Bolton HX2 .... 91 D7
West Bowling
　Golf Course BD5 .... 75 A1
West Bradford
　Golf Course BD6 .... 54 C2
West Bretton Junior &
　Infants Sch WF4 .... 176 F8
West Busk La LS21 .... 22 D6
West Byland WF2 .... 91 D7
West Carr La HD3 .... 150 E2
West Chevin Rd
　Menston LS29 .... 22 E5
　Otley LS21 .... 22 E5

West Cl Huddersfield HD2 ... 136 B2
　Normanton WF6 .... 123 A3
　Pontefract WF8 .... 146 E5
West Cliffe HX3 .... 113 E6
West Croft Addingham LS29 .. 6 F8
　Bradford BD12 .... 94 C2
　Sutton in C BD20 .... 16 C7
West Ct
　8 Leeds, Bramley LS13 .. 58 C1
　Leeds, Roundhay LS8 .... 61 C8
West Dale LS23 .... 14 C1
West Dene Leeds LS17 ..... 43 F6
　Silsden BD20 .... 5 E2
West Dr Oxenhope BD22 ... 51 C3
　Wakefield WF8 .... 146 E7
West End Boston Spa LS23 .. 14 C1
　Gildersome LS27 .... 97 C7
　Gildersome, New Farnley
　LS12 .... 77 D3
　Hebden Bridge HX7 .... 89 A3
　Queensbury BD13 .... 92 D8
West End App LS27 .... 97 E3
West End Ave
　Featherstone WF7 .... 145 A8
　Holmfirth HD7 .... 189 C6
　Royston S71 .... 179 A3
West End Cl LS18 .... 40 F1
West End Cres S71 .... 179 A3
West End Dr
　Cleckheaton BD19 .... 116 C6
　Horsforth LS18 .... 41 A1
West End Golf Course
　HX2 .... 112 C8
West End Gr LS18 .... 40 F1
West End Junior &
　Infants Sch LS18 .... 40 F1
West End La LS18 .... 40 F2
West End Middle Sch
　BD19 .... 116 C7
West End Prim
　(Jun & Inf) Sch WF9 .... 181 C7
West End Rd Halifax HX1 .. 202 A2
　Huddersfield HD7 .... 152 C4
　Pudsey LS28 .... 57 B6
West End Rise LS18 .... 40 F1
West End Terr Bradford BD2 56 B5
　Guiseley LS20 .... 22 C1
　8 Hebden Bridge HX7 ... 89 E1
　Shipley BD18 .... 55 A8
West Farm Ave LS10 .... 99 B5
West Field Cl LS19 .... 40 F4
West Field La WF17 .... 189 C6
West Garforth Junior Sch
　LS25 .... 82 E6
West Gate Holme HD7 ..... 198 F8
　Holmfirth HD7 .... 189 A7
　Wetherby LS22 .... 13 E5
West Gr 2 Baildon BD17 ... 38 C4
　Royston S71 .... 179 A4
West Grange Cl LS10 ...... 215 D1
West Grange Dr LS10 ...... 215 D1
West Grange Fold LS10 ... 215 D1
West Grange Gdns LS10 .. 215 D1
West Grange Gn LS10 ..... 215 D1
West Grange Rd LS10 ..... 215 D1
West Grove Ave HD5 .... 154 D6
West Grove St 10 LS28 ... 57 D1
West Grove Terr HX1 ...... 203 D3
West Hall La LS29 .... 3 A1
West Hall Sch WF3 .... 122 B6
West Haven WF4 .... 60 C7
West Hill WS1 .... 203 D3
West House 2 HX5 .... 134 F7
West Ings Cl WF11 .... 127 B5
West Ings Cres WF11 ...... 127 B5
West Ings Ct WF11 .... 127 B5
West Ings La WF11 .... 127 B5
West Ings Mews WF11 .... 127 B5
West Ings Way WF11 ...... 127 B5
West La Askwith LS21 ..... 9 E5
　Baildon BD17 .... 38 A3
　Boston Spa LS23 .... 14 C1
　Cleckheaton BD19 .... 96 B1
　Crofton WF4 .... 144 B2
　Halifax HX3 .... 113 F3
　Haworth BD22 .... 51 B7
　Keighley BD21, BD22 .... 35 A7
　Low Bradley BD20 .... 4 C5
　Sutton in C BD20 .... 16 C4
　Thornton BD13 .... 72 D6
　Tea Cl LS17 .... 43 B1
West Lea Cres
　East Ardsley WF3 .... 119 D7
　Yeadon LS19 .... 39 F6
West Lea Dr
　East Ardsley WF3 .... 119 D6
　Yeadon LS19 .... 39 F6
West Lea Garth LS17 ...... 43 B1
West Lea Gdns LS17 .... 43 B1
West Lea Gr LS19 .... 39 F6
West Leeds
　Boys High Sch LS12 ... 209 D3
West Leeds
　Girls High Sch LS12 ... 209 D3
West Leeds High Sch LS12 209 D3
West Leeds St BD21 .... 35 A7
West Lodge Cres HD7 ...... 135 B4
West Lodge Gdns LS7 ..... 204 A3
West Mead WF10 .... 125 A7
West Moor Rd WF9 .... 163 A2
West Moor View HD7 ..... 171 E4
West Moorlands Ave
　WF13 .... 118 B1
West Mount Pl HX1 .... 202 C4
West Mount St LS11 .... 214 A3
West Oaks Special Sch LS23 30 D7

West Par Guiseley LS20 .... 22 E1
　Halifax HX1 .... 203 D2
　Ilkley LS29 .... 8 C4
West Parade LS16 .... 59 B8
　Rothwell LS26 .... 100 F5
　Sowerby Bridge HX6 ..... 112 D4
　Wakefield WF1 .... 216 B2
West Parade St WF1 .... 216 B1
West Parade Flats 2
　HX1 .... 216 B1
West Parade St WF1 .... 216 B1
West Park Ave LS8 .... 44 B3
West Park Chase LS8 ...... 44 A3
West Park Cl LS8 .... 44 A3
West Park Cres LS8 .... 44 B2
West Park Dr
　Darrington WF8 .... 147 D2
　Leeds LS16 .... 59 A8
West Park Dr E LS8 .... 44 B3
West Park Drive (W) LS8 .. 43 F3
West Park Gdns LS8 .... 44 B2
West Park Gr Batley WF17 . 118 A5
　Leeds LS8 .... 44 B2
West Park Pl LS8 .... 44 B2
West Park Rd Batley WF17 . 117 F4
　Bradford BD8 .... 73 F8
　Leeds LS8 .... 44 B2
West Park St
　8 Brighouse HD6 .... 115 B2
　Dewsbury WF13 .... 118 B1
West Park Terr
　Batley WF17 .... 118 A5
　8 Bradford BD6 .... 73 F8
West Parks LS28 .... 76 D7
West Pasture Cl LS18 ..... 40 F1
West Pinfold S71 .... 179 C2
West Pk LS20 .... 22 C2
West Pl HD5 .... 154 D6
West Primley Park Dr
　LS8 .... 43 F5
West Rd LS9 .... 80 C3
West Rd (N) LS9 .... 80 D3
West Royd BD15 .... 53 C4
West Royd Ave
　Bradford BD2 .... 56 B4
　Halifax HX1 .... 202 C2
　Mirfield WF14 .... 138 A6
　Shipley BD18 .... 55 E8
West Royd Cl Halifax HX1 . 202 C1
　Shipley BD18 .... 55 D8
West Royd Cres BD18 ..... 55 E8
West Royd Dr
　Mirfield WF14 .... 138 A6
　Shipley BD18 .... 55 E8
West Royd Gr
　Mirfield WF14 .... 138 A6
　Shipley BD18 .... 55 E8
West Royd Mount BD18 .. 55 E8
West Royd Rd WF14 ...... 138 A6
West Royd Rd BD18 .... 55 E8
West Royd Terr BD18 ..... 55 E8
West Royd Villas 11 HX1 . 202 C1
West Royd Wlk BD18 ..... 55 E8
West Scausby Pk HX2 ..... 91 E7
West Shaw La BD22 .... 51 A3
West Side Ret Pk LS20 .... 39 C3
West Staithwaite Rd HD7 169 C7
West Station BD17 .... 38 C4
　2 Batley, Heckmondwike
　WF16 .... 117 C4
　Batley, Lower Soothill WF17 . 118 E5
　Birkenshaw BD11 .... 96 E5
　Bradford BD2 .... 56 B4
　Bradford, Eastbrook BD1 . 201 C2
　Brighouse, Bailiff Bridge
　HD6 .... 115 B7
　8 Brighouse, Waring Green
　HD6 .... 115 A3
　Castleford WF10 .... 124 C8
　Cleckheaton BD19 .... 116 D7
　Cleckheaton, Gomersal BD19 96 B1
　Dewsbury WF12 .... 139 C7
　Elland HX4 .... 134 B4
　Halifax HX2 .... 202 C3
　Huddersfield HD3 .... 135 B1
　Ilkley LS29 .... 8 B4
　Leeds LS3 .... 210 C4
　Lofthouse Gate WF3 ..... 121 F2
　Morley LS27 .... 98 B3
　Normanton WF6 .... 123 A2
　Pudsey LS28 .... 76 E8
　Royston S71 .... 179 D4
　Ryhill WF4 .... 162 C1
　Shelf HX3 .... 93 C1
　South Elmsall WF9 .... 183 B4
　South Hiendley S72 ...... 180 E5
　South Kirkby WF9 .... 182 A2
　Sowerby Bridge HX6 ..... 112 D8
　Todmorden OL14 .... 108 A6
　Wakefield WF2 .... 141 F5
West Terrace St 9 LS28 .. 57 D1
West Vale Dewsbury WF12 . 139 B6
　3 Leeds LS12 .... 210 B1
West Vale Junior &
　Infants Sch HX4 .... 134 D7
West View
　Ackworth M T WF7 ...... 163 D5
　Arthington LS21 .... 24 F6
　Batley WF17 .... 118 B2
　Bradford BD4 .... 75 A4
　Brighouse BD19 .... 94 F1
　Crigglestone WF4 .... 159 E4
　Elland HX4 .... 134 A4
　Glasshoughton WF10 .... 124 D7
　Halifax, Boothtown Bank HX3 . 92 B2
　Holme Chapel BB10 ...... 85 A8
　Huddersfield HD1 .... 153 D5

West View continued
　Ilkley LS29 .... 8 B3
　Kippax LS25 .... 83 B2
　Leeds LS11 .... 214 A4
　Mickelfield LS25 .... 84 B6
　Otley LS21 .... 23 B8
　18 Pudsey LS28 .... 57 D2
　Rothwell LS26 .... 101 C5
　Silsden BD20 .... 5 E2
　Wakefield WF2 .... 120 B2
　Yeadon LS19 .... 39 F7
West View Ave
　Burley in W LS29 .... 9 E1
　Castleford WF10 .... 125 A7
　Halifax HX2 .... 202 A3
　Shipley BD18 .... 55 E7
West View Cl BD18 .... 55 E7
West View Cres HX2 ...... 202 A3
　3 Low Utley LS29 .... 39 F7
West View Ct HX2 .... 202 A3
West View Rd
　Burley in W LS29 .... 9 E1
　Halifax HX3 .... 92 B2
West View Rise HD1 ...... 153 D5
West View St 11 BD22 ... 51 F8
West View Terr HX2 .... 202 A4
West Villa Rd LS20 .... 22 E1
West Way Leeds LS1 ...... 211 D4
　Shipley BD18 .... 54 D7
West Wells Cres WF5 ..... 140 D5
West Wells Rd WF5 .... 140 D5
West Winds LS29 .... 21 E5
West Wood Cl LS10 .... 99 A5
West Wood Rd LS10 ...... 99 A4
West Yorks
　Transport Mus BD1 ..... 201 B1
West Yorkshire Ind Est
　BD4 .... 95 E8
West Yorkshire Playhouse
　The LS2 .... 212 A4
Westacres HD6 .... 136 B8
Westborough Dr HX2 ..... 112 D7
Westborough High Sch
　WF13 .... 139 A8
Westbourne Ave
　Garforth LS25 .... 82 D6
　Leeds LS11 .... 214 B3
　1 Pontefract WF8 .... 146 C7
Westbourne Cl Otley LS21 . 22 F7
　Wakefield WF2 .... 160 C6
Westbourne Cres
　Garforth LS25 .... 82 D6
　Halifax HX3 .... 113 D3
　Pontefract WF8 .... 146 B7
Westbourne Dr
　Garforth LS25 .... 82 D6
　Guiseley LS20 .... 22 C1
　Menston LS29 .... 22 A5
Westbourne First Sch BD8 55 B2
Westbourne Gdns LS25 .. 82 D6
Westbourne Gr
　Garforth LS25 .... 82 D6
　Halifax HX3 .... 113 D3
　Otley LS21 .... 22 E7
Westbourne Mount
　18 Leeds LS11 .... 214 B3
　2 Pontefract WF8 .... 146 C7
Westbourne Pl
　18 Leeds LS11 .... 214 B3
　Pudsey LS28 .... 57 D1
Westbourne Rd
　Bradford BD8 .... 55 B2
　Huddersfield HD1 .... 153 D7
　Pontefract WF8 .... 146 B7
Westbourne St LS11 ...... 214 B3
Westbourne Terr
　Garforth LS25 .... 82 D6
　Halifax HX3 .... 113 D3
Westbrook Cl LS18 .... 41 B2
Westbrook Dr HX3 .... 203 D4
Westbrook Dr HD5 .... 155 B6
Westbrook La LS18 .... 41 B2
Westbrook Lane
　Primary Sch LS18 ...... 41 B3
Westbrook St BD7 .... 74 D6
Westbrook Terr WF17 .... 118 B6
Westburn Ave BD22 ...... 34 F5
Westburn Cres BD22 ..... 34 F5
Westburn Gr BD22 .... 34 F5
Westburn Way BD22 ..... 34 F5
Westbury Cl BD4 .... 75 D5
Westbury Gr LS10 .... 215 F2
Westbury Mount LS10 ... 215 F2
Westbury Pl HX1 .... 202 A2
Westbury Pl N LS10 ...... 215 F2
Westbury Pl S LS10 ...... 215 F1
Westbury Rd BD6 .... 73 D1
Westbury St Bradford BD4 . 75 D5
　Elland HX5 .... 135 A7
　Middleton LS10 .... 215 F1
Westbury Terr Halifax HX1 202 A2
　Middleton LS10 .... 215 F1
Westcliffe Ave BD17 ...... 38 B3
Westcliffe Dr HX2 .... 112 D7
Westcliffe Rd
　Cleckheaton BD19 .... 116 C7
　Shipley BD18 .... 55 B7
Westcliffe Rise BD19 .... 116 C7
Westcombe Ave LS8 ...... 44 A3
Westcombe Ct 13 BD12 .. 94 C4
Westcroft HD7 .... 171 E4
Westcroft Ave HX3 .... 93 B4
Westcroft Dr WF5 .... 119 C1
Westcroft Rd Bradford BD7 . 181 D7
　Hemsworth WF9 .... 163 B2
Westdale Dr LS28 .... 76 D8
Westdale Gdns LS28 ..... 76 D8
Westdale Gr LS28 .... 76 D8

Westdale Rd LS28 .... 76 D8
Westdale Rise LS28 ...... 76 D8
Westend St BD1 .... 74 D7
Westercroft La HX3 ...... 93 B3
Westercroft View HX3 ... 93 B3
Western Cl BD18 .... 174 A3
Western Cres BD20 ...... 5 C1
Westerley La HD8 .... 174 A3
Westerly Croft LS12 ..... 209 F4
Westerly Rise LS12 ...... 209 F4
Western Way HD8 .... 174 A3
Westerman Cl WF7 ...... 145 D6
Westerman St LS11 ...... 142 E3
Western Ave Batley WF17 . 97 A1
　Keighley BD20 .... 18 D3
Western Pl WF8 .... 125 F1
Western Ct WF8 .... 125 F1
Western Gales Way WF6 . 123 D1
Western Gr LS12 .... 209 E1
Western Mount LS12 .... 209 E1
Western Rd BD11 .... 73 B1
Western Rd
　Huddersfield HD4 .... 153 A4
　Leeds LS12 .... 209 E1
Western St LS12 .... 209 E1
Western Way BD6 .... 94 A7
Westerton Cl WF3 .... 120 B8
Westerton Ct WF3 .... 95 B5
Westerton Prim Sch
　WF3 .... 119 D7
Westerton Rd WF3 .... 119 E7
Westerton Wlk WF3 ..... 120 B8
Westfell Cl BD22 .... 34 F6
Westfell Rd BD22 .... 34 F6
Westfell Way BD22 .... 34 F6
Westfield Brighouse HX3 . 114 D7
　Pudsey LS28 .... 57 D1
　Thornton BD13 .... 73 A6
Westfield Ave
　Brighouse HX3 .... 114 D7
　Castleford WF10 .... 124 C5
　Dewsbury WF12 .... 140 A8
　Huddersfield HD3 .... 153 B7
　Kippax LS25 .... 83 A1
　Kippax, Allerton Bywater
　WF10 .... 103 A5
　Knottingley WF11 .... 126 F3
　Meltham HD7 .... 170 C3
　Pontefract WF8 .... 146 C6
　Skelmanthorpe HD8 ...... 174 F1
　Yeadon LS19 .... 39 F6
Westfield Bungalows
　WF9 .... 183 A2
Westfield Cl Batley WF16 . 117 C5
　Rothwell LS26 .... 100 C4
　Yeadon LS19 .... 39 F6
Westfield Cotts WF8 ..... 146 C5
Westfield Cres
　Bradford BD2 .... 56 B1
　Dearne S63 .... 194 C1
　Keighley BD20 .... 18 F2
　Leeds LS3 .... 205 F1
　Ossett WF5 .... 140 C5
　Ryhill WF4 .... 162 A1
　Shipley BD18 .... 55 E6
　Wakefield WF2 .... 120 B2
Westfield Ct Horbury WF4 . 140 F2
　Leeds LS3 .... 205 F1
　Mirfield WF14 .... 138 A5
　Rothwell LS26 .... 100 C4
Westfield Dr
　Brighouse HX3 .... 114 D7
　Keighley BD20 .... 18 F2
　Ossett WF5 .... 140 C5
　Skelmanthorpe HD8 ...... 174 F1
　Yeadon LS19 .... 39 F6
Westfield Farm WF5 ..... 140 C6
Westfield Gdns
　Brighouse HX3 .... 114 D7
　Kippax LS25 .... 82 F2
Westfield Gn BD4 .... 75 E4
Westfield Gr
　Ackworth M T WF7 ...... 164 C8
　Bradford BD10 .... 56 A8
　Castleford WF10 .... 124 C5
　Dewsbury WF13 .... 138 F8
　Ingbirchworth S36 .... 191 D1
　Kippax WF10 .... 103 A5
　Shipley BD18 .... 55 E6
　Wakefield WF1 .... 216 B4
　Yeadon LS19 .... 39 F6
Westfield Ind Est LS19 .. 40 A7
Westfield La Bradford BD10 . 56 A8
　Bingley BD12, BD19 ...... 94 D1
　Darrington WF8 .... 147 C3
　Kippax LS25 .... 83 A1
　Norton WF8 .... 166 F3
　South Elmsall WF9 .... 183 B2
　South Milford LS25 .... 84 F2
　Thorner LS14 .... 45 E4
Westfield Mount LS19 ... 39 F6
Westfield Oval LS19 ..... 39 E6
Westfield Pl Halifax HX1 . 216 B4
Westfield Pl
　Brighouse BD19 .... 94 E1
　Halifax HX1 .... 202 C2
　Wakefield WF2 .... 120 B2
Westfield Rd Batley WF16 . 117 D5
　Bradford, Clayton BD14 . 73 B4
　Bradford, Girlington BD9 55 A1
　Hemsworth WF9 .... 181 D7
　Horbury WF4 .... 140 F2

Westfield Rd continued
Keighley BD20 .... 18 F1
Knottingley WF11 .... 126 F3
Leeds LS3 .... 205 F1
Morley LS27 .... 98 A4
Rothwell LS26 .... 100 C3
Wakefield WF1 .... 216 B4
Westfield St Batley WF16 .. 117 C5
Halifax HX1 .... 203 D2
Ossett WF5 .... 140 C5
Westfield Terr
Baildon BD17 .... 38 C4
Bradford BD2 .... 56 B1
2 Bradford, Clayton BD14 .. 73 B4
Halifax HX1 .... 202 C4
2 Hebden Bridge HX7 ..... 89 E1
4 Horbury WF4 .... 141 A1
Kippax WF10 .... 103 A5
Leeds LS3 .... 205 F1
Leeds, Chapel Allerton LS7 . 60 C7
Wakefield WF1 .... 216 B4
Westfield View WF1 .... 216 B4
Westfield Villas WF4 .. 140 F1
Westfields
Castleford WF10 .... 124 C5
Royston S71 .... 179 A4
Westfields Ave WF14 ... 138 B5
Westfields Rd WF14 .... 138 A5
Westgarth LS22 .... 13 B3
Westgate Baildon BD17 .. 38 C4
Bradford BD1 .... 74 D7
Bradford, Eccleshill BD2 .. 56 C4
Brighouse HD6 .... 115 E2
Cleckheaton BD19 .... 116 D7
Dewsbury WF13 .... 139 D8
Elland HX5 .... 134 F7
Guiseley LS20 .... 39 B8
Halifax HX1 .... 203 E3
Hemsworth WF9 .... 181 C6
Honley HD7 .... 171 F4
Huddersfield HD1 .... 154 A6
Huddersfield, Almondbury
HD5 .... 154 F2
Leeds LS1 .... 211 D4
Liversedge WF16 .... 117 C4
Meltham HD7 .... 170 D2
Otley LS21 .... 22 F7
Shipley BD18 .... 55 B8
Wakefield WF1, WF2 .... 216 B2
Westgate Cl 5 LS13 ... 121 C8
Westgate Ct WF3 ...... 121 C8
Westgate End WF2 ..... 142 A5
Westgate Gr WF3 ...... 121 C8
Westgate Hill First Sch
BD4 .... 96 A8
Westgate Hill St BD4 .. 96 B8
Westgate La WF3 ...... 121 C8
Westgate Market HX1 .. 203 E3
Westgate Ret & L Pk
WF1 .... 216 A1
Westgate Sta WF2 ..... 216 A2
Westgate Terr
Birkenshaw BD4 .... 96 A8
13 Dewsbury WF13 ...... 139 C8
Westgrove Ct BD19 .... 116 C8
Westhill Ave BD13 .... 52 E5
Westholme Rd HX1 ..... 202 B2
Westholme St BD1 ..... 201 A2
Westland Cl BD20 ..... 16 E6
Westland Ct LS11 ..... 99 B8
Westland Rd LS11 ..... 214 B1
Westlands Dr BD15 .... 54 C1
Westlands Gr BD15 .... 54 C1
Westlea Ave BD20 ..... 18 F1
Westleigh 8 BD16 ..... 37 A4
Westleigh Cl BD17 .... 38 A2
Westleigh Dr BD17 .... 38 A2
Westleigh Rd BD17 .... 38 A2
Westleigh Way BD17 ... 38 A2
Westley Ave HD7 ...... 188 F8
Westlock Ave LS9 ..... 208 A1
Westmead LS28 .... 57 A1
Westminster Ave BD14 . 73 A4
Westminster Cl LS13 .. 57 F4
Westminster Cres
Bradford BD14 .... 73 A4
Leeds LS15 .... 80 E7
Westminster Croft LS13 . 57 F4
Westminster Dr
Bradford BD14 .... 73 A4
Pudsey LS13 .... 57 F4
Westminster Gdns BD14 . 73 A4
Westminster Pl BD3 ... 55 F1
Westminster Rd BD3 ... 55 F1
Westminster Terr BD3 . 55 F1
Westmoor Ave BD17 .... 38 B4
Westmoor Cl BD17 ..... 38 B4
Westmoor County Sch
WF13 .... 117 F1
Westmoor Pl LS13 ..... 58 B3
Westmoor Rd LS13 ..... 58 B3
Westmoor Rise LS13 ... 58 B3
Westmoor St LS13 ..... 58 B3
Westmoreland Mount 1
LS13 .... 58 D4
Westmorland House 3
WF1 .... 216 B2
Westmorland Rd WF1 ... 216 B2
Westmount St 11 WF8 .. 146 C8
Westoff La S72 .... 180 D7
Weston Ave BD13 ...... 92 D6
Weston Cres LS21 ..... 10 E1
Weston Dr LS21 .... 10 E1
Weston La LS21 .... 10 E1

Weston Moor Rd LS21 .. 10 D8
Weston Park View LS21 . 10 D1
Weston Rd LS29 .... 8 B4
Weston Ridge LS21 .... 10 E1
Weston St BD22 .... 34 F5
Weston Vale Rd BD13 .. 92 D8
Westover Ave 6 LS13 .. 58 C3
Westover Gdns LS28 ... 76 C7
Westover Gn LS13 ..... 58 C3
Westover Gr 3 LS13 ... 58 C3
Westover Mount 11 LS13 . 58 C3
Westover Rd LS13 ..... 58 C3
Westover St 2 LS13 ... 58 C3
Westover Terr 1 LS13 . 58 C3
Westover View 5 LS13 . 58 C3
Westridge Dr HD4 ..... 153 C1
Westroyd Clifton LS21 . 11 A3
Pudsey LS28 .... 76 C6
Westroyd Ave
Cleckheaton BD19 ...... 95 D2
Pudsey LS28 .... 76 C6
Westroyd Cres LS28 ... 76 C6
Westroyd Gdns LS28 ... 76 C6
Westroyd Infant Sch LS28 . 57 D2
Westvale Mews LS28 ... 58 E1
Westview Ave BD20 .... 35 B8
Westview Cl BD20 ..... 4 C5
Westview Ct BD20 ..... 35 A8
Westview Gr BD20 ..... 35 A8
Westview Way BD20 .... 35 B8
Westville Ave LS29 ... 8 A4
Westville Cl LS29 .... 8 A4
Westville Rd LS29 .... 8 A4
Westville Way BD13 ... 72 D6
Westward Croft HD3 ... 135 C2
Westward Ho Halifax HX3 .. 92 A4
10 Queensbury BD13 .... 72 E1
Westway Batley WF17 .. 118 F3
Bingley BD16 .... 37 B5
Bradford BD9 .... 54 C2
Garforth LS25 .... 82 D6
Guiseley LS20 .... 39 B8
Keighley BD20 .... 17 F1
Mirfield WF14 .... 137 F7
Pudsey LS28 .... 57 C3
Westways WF2 .... 120 F2
Westways Cl WF2 ..... 120 F2
Westways Dr LS8 ..... 61 C7
Westways Rise WF2 ... 120 F2
Westwinn Garth LS14 . 45 C1
Westwinn View LS14 .. 45 C1
Westwood Ave
Bradford BD2 .... 56 B5
Honley HD7 .... 172 C5
Westwood Cl
Featherstone WF7 ..... 145 D7
Morley LS27 .... 98 B6
Westwood Cres BD16 .. 54 A8
Westwood Dr LS29 .... 7 F2
Westwood Edge Rd HD7 . 152 A3
Westwood Fold HD7 ... 152 B2
Westwood Gr BD2 ..... 56 B5
Westwood Primary Sch
LS11 .... 99 A4
Westwood Rd
Castleford WF10 ...... 124 B5
Ossett WF5 .... 140 F5
Westwood Rise Ilkley LS29 . 7 F2
Morley LS27 .... 98 B6
Westwood Side LS27 .. 98 B7
Westwood St HD5 ..... 137 A6
Westwood Way LS23 ... 30 D8
Wetherby Bsns Pk LS22 . 13 F6
Wetherby County
Primary Sch LS22 ... 13 E5
Wetherby Gr 8 LS4 ... 59 C2
Wetherby High Sch LS22 . 13 F5
Wetherby Pl LS4 ..... 205 D2
Wetherby Race Course
LS22 .... 14 B6
Wetherby Rd Bardsey LS17 . 28 E4
Bramham LS23 .... 30 C3
Collingham LS22 ...... 13 D3
Kirk Deighton LS22 ... 13 E8
Leeds LS8 .... 61 D7
Scarcroft LS14 .... 45 C6
Sicklinghall LS22 .... 12 D5
Thorner LS14 .... 45 C6
Thorp Arch LS23 ...... 14 E4
Wetherby LS22 .... 13 D3
Wetherby Terr 6 LS4 . 59 C2
Wetherhill St WF17 .. 118 B5
Wetherill Terr 4 WF13 . 117 F3
Wetlands Rd HD7 ..... 170 E1
Wetton Cl BD3 .... 75 D7
Weydale Ave HD3 ..... 153 A8
Weyhill Dr BD15 ..... 73 B8
Weymouth Ave
Bradford BD15 .... 73 A8
Huddersfield HD3 ..... 153 B7
Weymouth St HX1 ..... 203 E3
Whack House Cl LS19 . 40 A6
Whack House La LS19 . 40 A7
Whalley La BD13 ..... 52 E2
Wham Bar Dr HD7 ..... 168 F7
Wharf St Bradford BD3 . 201 C4
Brighouse HD6 .... 115 B2
Dewsbury WF12 .... 139 D7
Leeds LS2 .... 212 A3
Shipley BD17 .... 55 B8
Sowerby Bridge HX6 ... 112 C4
12 Todmorden OL14 .... 108 A1
Wharfdale View LS29 . 22 A4
Wharfe Bank LS22 .... 28 E8
Wharfe Cl LS16 ...... 42 D4
Wharfe Cres LS21 .... 24 D7
Wharfe Dr LS22 ...... 13 D5
Wharfe Grange Hospl LS22 . 13 D5

Wharfe Mews LS29 .... 22 B4
Wharfe Pk LS29 ...... 7 A8
Wharfe Rein LS22 .... 28 E8
Wharfe View Pool LS21 . 24 C7
Wetherby LS22 .... 13 D5
Wharfe Way LS29 ..... 8 B4
Wharfe Way WF10 ..... 125 B8
Wharfedale Ave LS7 .. 206 B4
Wharfedale Cres
Garforth LS25 .... 82 F6
Skelmanthorpe HD8 .... 175 B1
Wharfedale Ct Leeds LS14 . 61 F5
Otley LS21 .... 23 A8
Wharfedale Dr Ilkley LS29 . 8 C4
Normanton WF6 .... 123 A1
Wharfedale Gdns LS14 . 61 F5
Wharfedale General Hospl
LS21 .... 10 F2
Wharfedale Gr LS7 ... 206 B4
Wharfedale Mews LS21 . 23 A8
Wharfedale Mount
Leeds LS7 .... 206 B4
Shelf HX3 .... 93 B5
Wharfedale Pl LS7 ... 206 B4
Wharfedale Rd BD4 ... 95 A7
Wharfedale Rise
Bradford BD9 .... 54 C2
East Ardsley WF3 ..... 119 D7
Wharfedale St LS7 ... 206 B4
Wharfedale View
Addingham LS29 .... 6 E8
Leeds LS7 .... 206 B4
Wharfeside La LS29 .. 8 C5
Wharncliffe Cres BD2 . 56 D4
Wharncliffe Dr BD2 .. 56 D4
Wharncliffe Gr
Bradford BD2 .... 56 D4
Shipley BD18 .... 55 B6
Wharncliffe Rd
Shipley BD18 .... 55 B6
Wakefield WF2 .... 160 A4
Wharton St 1 WF15 ... 117 B4
Wharton Terr 3 WF14 . 117 D3
Whartons Prim Sch The
LS21 .... 11 A2
Whartons The LS21 ... 11 A2
Wheat Cl WF13 .... 138 F8
Wheat Field Ave HD3 . 153 A8
Wheat Head Cres BD22 . 34 E5
Wheat Head Dr BD22 .. 34 F5
Wheat Head La BD22 .. 34 E5
Wheat St BD22 .... 35 A4
Wheatcroft WF10 ..... 125 B7
Wheatcroft Ave WF17 . 118 C4
Wheater House WF1 ... 216 B2
Wheater Rd BD7 ...... 74 A5
Wheathouse Rd HD2 ... 135 F1
Wheathouse Terr HD2 . 135 F1
Wheatings The WF5 ... 140 F5
Wheatlands Ilkley LS29 . 8 C4
Pudsey LS28 .... 57 C2
Wheatlands Ave
Bradford BD9 .... 54 E2
Glusburn BD20 .... 16 C7
Wheatlands Cres BD9 . 54 E2
Wheatlands Dr
Bradford BD9 .... 54 E2
Liversedge WF15 ...... 116 F2
Wheatlands Gr BD9 ... 54 E2
Wheatlands La BD20 .. 16 C7
Wheatlands Sq BD9 ... 54 E2
Wheatley Ave Ilkley LS29 . 8 E4
Normanton WF6 .... 123 B1
Wheatley Cl 3 HX3 ... 92 A1
Wheatley Ct HX2 ..... 91 D4
Wheatley Dr WF14 .... 138 A3
Wheatley Gdns LS29 .. 8 E3
Wheatley Gr LS29 .... 8 F3
Wheatley Hill La HD8 . 192 E8
Wheatley La LS29 .... 8 F4
Wheatley Lane Ends HX3 . 91 E2
Wheatley Rd Halifax HX3 . 91 F2
Ilkley LS29 .... 8 E3
Wheatley Rise Ilkley LS29 . 8 E3
Mapplewell S75 .... 178 B2
Wheaton Ave LS15 .... 81 B8
Wheatroyd Cres WF5 .. 140 D3
Wheatroyd La HD5 .... 154 E2
Wheelright Coll WF13 . 139 B7
Wheelwright Ave LS12 . 209 D1
Wheelwright Cl LS12 . 209 D1
Wheelwright Dr WF13 . 138 B2
Wheelwright St 5 WF13 . 139 C8
Wheldale La WF10 .... 104 E2
Wheldon Rd WF10 ..... 104 B2
Whernside Mount BD7 . 73 E2
Whernside Way HX2 ... 91 A3
Wherwell Rd HD6 ..... 136 C8
Whetley Cl BD8 ...... 74 C8
Whetley First Sch BD8 . 74 A8
Whetley Gr BD8 ...... 55 A1
Whetley Hill BD8 .... 74 C8
Whetley La BD8 ...... 74 A8
Whetley Middle Sch BD8 . 74 A8
Whetley Terr 1 BD8 .. 74 B8
Whewell St 4 WF17 ... 96 E1
Whimbrel Cl BD8 ..... 73 C7
Whimbrel Mews LS27 .. 98 C3
Whin Cl WF9 .... 181 D5
Whin Gdns S63 ...... 194 D1
Whin Knoll Ave BD21 . 34 F8
Whin Mount WF6 ..... 144 C8
Whin St BD21 .... 35 A4
Whin View Cl WF4 ... 162 C1
Whinberry Pl WF17 .. 96 F3

Whinbrook Cres LS17 . 43 C1
Whinbrook Ct LS17 .. 43 C1
Whinbrook Gdns LS17 . 43 C1
Whinbrook Gr LS17 .. 43 C1
Whinburn Sch BD20 .. 17 F2
Whincop Ave WF10 ... 124 A7
Whincover Cl LS12 .. 77 F5
Whincover Cross LS12 . 77 F5
Whincover Dr LS12 .. 77 F5
Whincover Gdns LS12 . 77 F5
Whincover Gr LS12 .. 77 F5
Whincover Grange LS12 . 77 F5
Whincover Hill LS12 . 77 F5
Whincover Mount LS12 . 77 F5
Whincover Rd LS12 .. 77 F5
Whincover View LS12 . 77 F5
Whincup Gdns 4 LS10 . 215 E2
Whinfield LS16 ..... 42 B4
Whinfield Ave BD22 . 34 E7
Whinfield Cl BD22 .. 34 F8
Whinfield Dr BD22 .. 34 E8
Whinfield Pl WF5 ... 141 B4
Whingate LS12 ...... 209 D3
Whingate Ave LS12 .. 209 D3
Whingate Bsns Pk LS12 . 209 E3
Whingate Gr LS12 ... 209 D3
Whingate Gn LS12 ... 209 D3
Whingate Gr LS12 ... 209 D3
Whingate Primary Sch
LS12 .... 209 D3
Whingate Rd LS12 ... 209 D3
Whingrove Ave HD7 .. 170 D1
Whinmoor Cl S75 .... 193 F1
Whinmoor Cres LS14 . 45 A1
Silkstone S75 .... 193 F1
Whinmoor Ct LS14 ... 193 F1
Whinmoor Gdns LS14 . 45 A1
Whinmoor La LS17 ... 44 F3
Whinmoor View S75 .. 193 F1
Whinmoor Way Leeds LS14 . 62 D5
Silkstone S75 .... 193 F1
Whinmore Gdns BD19 . 117 C7
Whinney Cl WF7 ..... 144 D5
Whinney Field HX3 .. 113 C4
Whinney Hill Pk HD6 . 115 B5
Whinney Moor Ave WF2 . 141 E4
Whinney Royd La HX3 . 93 A5
Whinny La WF7 ...... 144 D5
Whins La Spofforth HG3 . 12 C8
Thorp Arch LS23 ..... 14 F1
Whins The BD21 ..... 35 A2
Whinside Cres S63 .. 194 C1
Whirlaw Ave OL14 ... 108 A7
Whirlaw La OL14 .... 108 B8
Whiskers La HX3 .... 92 E4
Whisperwood Cl WF1 . 121 D5
Whisperwood Rd WF1 . 121 D5
Whitacre Cl HD2 .... 136 E3
Whitacre St HD2 .... 136 E3
Whitaker Ave BD2 ... 56 C3
Whitaker Cl BD2 .... 56 C3
Whitaker St Batley WF17 . 118 D4
Pudsey LS28 .... 57 D2
Whitburn Way 7 BD15 . 73 B8
Whitby Ave HD2 ..... 136 B2
Whitby Cres WF12 ... 139 F8
Whitby Rd BD8 ...... 55 A1
Whitby Terr BD8 .... 55 A1
Whitcliffe Mount Sch
BD19 .... 116 B8
Whitcliffe Rd BD19 . 116 D8
Whitcliffe Road First Sch
BD19 .... 116 D8
Whitcliffe Sq BD19 . 116 D8
White Abbey Rd BD8 . 74 C8
White Apron St WF9 . 182 B2
White Birch Terr HX3 . 91 F2
White Castle Ct BD13 . 72 B2
White Cross HD2 .... 136 E5
White Cross Gdns S72 . 180 D6
White Cross Rd WF12 . 118 E2
White Ct WF4 .... 162 A8
White Field La HX7 . 110 C8
White Gate HX2 ..... 91 D7
Honley HD7 .... 171 F5
White Gate Rd
Holme HD7 .... 198 D7
Holmfirth HD7 .... 198 E8
Slaithwaite HD7 ..... 151 E8
White Bar HD4 ...... 154 A2
White Hart Fold
South Elmsall WF9 ... 183 B6
6 Todmorden OL14 .... 108 B5
White Hill HD7 ..... 169 C7
White Horse Fold WF10 . 103 B6
White Horse Yd WF1 . 216 B2
White House Bglws WF2 . 142 B3
White La Bradford BD6 . 93 F6
Haworth BD22 .... 33 F3
Hooton Pagnell DN5 .. 195 E4
White Laith Ave LS14 . 62 B8
White Laith Primary Sch
LS14 .... 62 C7
White Laithe App 2 LS14 . 62 B8
White Laithe Cl LS14 . 62 B8
White Laithe Croft LS14 . 62 B8
White Laithe Gdns LS14 . 62 B8
White Laithe Garth LS14 . 62 B8
White Laithe Gr LS14 . 62 B8
White Laithe Rd LS14 . 62 B8
White Laithe Wlk 4 LS14 . 62 B8
White Lands LS19 ... 40 A4
White Lane Top 8 BD6 . 94 D6
White Lee Cl WF16 .. 117 E6
White Lee Croft HX7 . 89 F1
White Lee Gdns HX7 . 89 F1

White Lee Rd WF16 .. 117 E6
White Lee Side WF16 . 117 E6
White Ley Bank HD7 . 190 A7
White Ley Rd WF8 .. 166 E1
White Rose Ave
Garforth LS25 .... 83 A8
Huddersfield HD5 .... 154 F6
White Rose Ctr LS11 . 98 E7
White Rose Way LS25 . 83 A7
White Slack Gate OL14 . 129 A6
White St LS19 ..... 40 C7
White Walls La HD7 . 187 F3
White Wells LS29 .. 8 B2
White Wells Gdns HD7 . 189 D3
White Wells Rd HD7 . 189 D3
White's Cl BD9 .... 54 D3
White's Rd WF1 .... 216 C2
White's Terr BD8 .. 74 B8
Whiteacre St HD2 .. 136 F3
Whitebeam Gn WF8 .. 125 F1
Whitebeam La LS10 . 99 D8
Whitebeam Pk HD8 .. 135 D2
Whitebridge Ave LS9 . 80 E8
Whitebridge Primary Sch
LS9 .... 80 E7
Whitebridge Spur LS9 . 61 E1
Whitebridge View LS9 . 61 E1
Whitechapel Cl LS8 . 61 C6
Whitechapel Gr BD19 . 95 A1
Whitechapel Middle Sch
BD19 .... 116 C8
Whitechapel Rd
Brighouse BD19 ...... 116 A8
Cleckheaton BD19 .... 116 C8
Whitechapel Way LS8 . 61 B6
Whitecliffe Cres LS26 . 82 A2
Whitecliffe Dr LS26 . 82 A2
Whitecliffe Rise LS26 . 82 A2
Whitecote Primary Sch
LS13 .... 58 B4
Whitecote Gdns LS13 . 58 B4
Whitecote Hill LS13 . 58 B4
Whitecote La Leeds LS13 . 58 B4
South Milford LS25 .. 84 F4
Whitecote Rise LS13 . 58 B4
Whitefield Pl BD8 .. 54 E1
East Keswick LS17 ... 28 C6
Halifax HX3 .... 113 D4
Whitegate Dr HX3 .. 113 D4
Whitegate Rd Halifax HX3 . 113 D4
Huddersfield HD4 .... 154 B4
Whitegate Terr HX3 . 113 D4
Whitegate Top HX3 . 113 E5
Whitegates Cl WF1 . 121 A1
Whitegates Gr HD8 . 155 D2
Whitehall Ave
Bradford BD12 ...... 94 C1
Mirfield WF14 ...... 138 A7
Wakefield WF1 ...... 121 A1
Whitehall Cres WF1 . 121 A1
Whitehall First Sch LS26 . 100 F5
Whitehall Gr 1 WF4 . 141 B1
Whitehall Gr
Birkenshaw, Drighlington
BD11 .... 96 B5
Whitehall Quay LS1 . 211 E3
Whitehall Rd
Birkenshaw BD11 .... 96 B6
Bradford BD12 ...... 94 C1
Brighouse BD12 ..... 94 E2
4 Bradford BD19 .... 95 D2
Whitehall Rd E
Birkenshaw BD11 .... 96 A4
Cleckheaton BD19 ... 95 E3
Whitehall Rise WF1 . 142 A8
Whitehall St
Brighouse HX3 ...... 114 D8
Halifax HX3 .... 141 F5
Whitehall Trad Est LS12 . 77 F4
Whitehall Way WF13 . 139 D8
Whitehaven Cl BD6 . 93 F7
Whitehead Gr BD2 .. 56 C1
Whitehead La
Huddersfield HD4 ... 154 A3
Meltham HD4, HD7 ... 170 F6
Whitehead Pl BD2 .. 56 C1
Whitehead St BD3 .. 75 B6
Whitehill Cres HX2 . 91 E6
Whitehill Dr HX2 .. 91 E6
Whitehill Gn HX2 .. 91 E6
Whitehill Prim Schs HX2 . 91 E6
Whitehill Rd HX2 .. 91 D6
Haworth BD22 .... 33 D5
Whitehouse Ave LS26 . 102 D8
Whitehouse Cres LS26 . 102 E8
Whitehouse Dr LS26 . 102 D8
Whitehouse La
Swillington LS26 ... 82 C2
Yeadon LS19 .... 40 F8
Whitehouse St LS10 . 212 A1
Whitelands BD17 ... 38 D3
Whitelands Rd BD17 . 38 D3
Whiteley Ave HX6 .. 111 F3
Whiteley Croft LS21 . 23 A7

Whiteley Croft Cl LS21 ...... 23 A7
Whiteley Croft Garth LS21 .. 22 F7
Whiteley Croft Rd LS21 ...... 23 A7
Whiteley Croft Rise LS21 ..... 23 A7
Whiteley St
  Featherstone WF7 .... 145 C5
  Huddersfield HD3 .... 153 B4
Whiteley Terr HX6 .... 132 C2
Whiteock St LS17 .... 207 D1
Whiteplates St 12 OL14 ...... 108 B6
Whiterose Mead LS5 .... 83 A7
Whiteshaw Mews BD13 ...... 52 D2
Whitestone Cres LS19 .... 40 B7
Whitestone La 2 HD1 .... 154 B8
Whiteways BD2 .... 55 E3
Whitewood Cl S71 .... 179 B3
Whitfield Ave LS10 .... 215 E4
Whitfield Gdns LS10 .... 215 E4
Whitfield Pl LS10 .... 215 E4
Whitfield Sq LS10 .... 215 E4
Whitfield St
  9 Cleckheaton BD19 .... 116 D8
  Leeds LS10 .... 207 F3
Whitfield Way LS10 .... 215 E4
Whitford Freight Ctr
  WF10 .... 123 D5
Whitham Cl LS23 .... 30 D8
Whitkirk Cl LS15 .... 81 E8
Whitkirk La LS15 .... 81 D8
Whitkirk Primary Sch
  LS15 .... 81 C7
Whitlam St BD18 .... 54 F8
Whitley Gdns LS8 .... 207 E3
Whitley Grange Hospl
  WF12 .... 138 F1
Whitley La HX3 .... 114 A5
Whitley Pl HF10 .... 103 B4
Whitley Rd Dewsbury WF12 .. 139 B1
  Keighley BD21 .... 35 A5
  Oxenhope, Common S36 ..... 200 C7
Whitley Spring Cres WF5 ... 140 F6
Whitley Spring Rd WF5 ..... 140 F6
Whitley St Bingley BD16 .... 36 F3
  Bradford BD3 .... 201 D3
  Halifax HX1 .... 203 D2
Whitley Terr S36 .... 200 D5
Whitley Way WF4 .... 156 E5
Whitteron Cl HD3 .... 135 B1
Whittle Cres BD14 .... 73 B5
Whitton Croft Rd LS29 ...... 8 B4
Whitty La HX2 .... 112 B6
Whitwell Ave HX5 .... 135 B7
Whitwell Dr HX5 .... 135 B7
Whitwell Gr HX5 .... 135 B7
Whitwell Green La HX5 ...... 135 B6
Whitwell St BD4 .... 201 D1
Whitwood Common La
  WF10 .... 123 E5
Whitwood Enterprise Pk
  WF6 .... 123 B3
Whitwood La
  Brighouse HD6 .... 115 D7
  Castleford WF10 .... 123 E6
Whitwood Terr WF10 .... 123 E5
Whitworth Rd 1 HD1 .... 139 B7
Wholestone Gate HD7 .... 152 B5
Whytecote End BD12 .... 94 C4
Wibsey Bank BD6 .... 74 D1
Wibsey First Sch BD6 .... 74 B1
Wibsey Middle Sch BD6 ..... 74 B1
Wibsey Park Ave BD6 .... 94 A8
Wicken Cl BD10 .... 56 C6
Wicken La BD13 .... 72 D7
Wicket LS28 .... 57 B7
Wickets Cl BD6 .... 94 D8
Wickets The Leeds LS6 ..... 59 F7
  Leeds, Whitkirk Lane End
  LS15 .... 81 E7
Wickham Ave
  Boston Spa LS23 .... 30 C8
  Bradford BD6 .... 94 B1
Wickham Cl LS23 .... 30 C8
Wickham St Brighouse BD19 . 94 F1
  Leeds LS11 .... 214 A3
Wicking La HX6 .... 132 A8
Wickins La HD7 .... 188 D6
Wickleden Gate HD7 .... 189 D3
Widdop Rd HX7 .... 88 D6
Wide La Morley LS27 .... 98 C3
  Morley, Bantam Grove LS27 . 98 D4
  Oakworth BD22 .... 34 B3
Wigan St BD1 .... 74 D7
Wigeon App LS27 .... 98 C4
Wiggan La HD2 .... 136 D4
Wiggin Cross HD7 .... 152 E1
Wighill La Thorp Arch LS23 . 15 C2
  Wighill LS24 .... 15 C2
Wighill St BD20 .... 16 D5
Wightman St BD3 .... 56 A1
Wignall St BD20 .... 18 B2
Wigton Chase LS17 .... 44 A5
Wigton Gate LS17 .... 43 E6
Wigton Gn LS17 .... 43 E6
Wigton Gr LS17 .... 43 E6
Wigton Moor Primary Sch
  LS17 .... 43 F5
Wigton Park Cl LS17 .... 43 F6
Wike La LS17 .... 28 A1
Wike Ridge Ave LS17 ...... 44 B6
Wike Ridge Cl LS17 .... 44 A6
Wike Ridge Ct LS17 .... 44 A6
Wike Ridge Fold LS17 ..... 44 A6
Wike Ridge Gr LS17 .... 44 A5
Wike Ridge La
  Harewood LS17 .... 44 C7
  Leeds LS17 .... 44 B5
Wike Ridge Mews LS17 .... 44 B5
Wike Ridge Mount LS17 ... 44 B5

Wike Ridge View LS17 ...... 44 A5
Wilberlee Jun & Inf Sch
  HD7 .... 151 D2
Wilby St BD19 .... 116 D7
Wilcock La BD20 .... 4 F5
Wild Gr LS28 .... 76 A7
Wild's Yd WF1 .... 216 C1
Wilday Cl BD16 .... 36 E6
Wildon Hill Gr WF9 .... 189 E4
Wilford Rd S71 .... 178 E1
Wilfred Ave LS15 .... 81 B8
Wilfred St Bradford BD14 .. 73 D4
  2 Leeds LS15 .... 81 B8
Wilkin St HX7 .... 78 A4
Wilkinson Fold 9 BD12 ... 94 C3
Wilkinson Terr BD7 .... 73 F6
Wilkinson Way LS21 .... 10 E1
Willan's Rd WF13 .... 118 C1
Willans Ave LS26 .... 100 E7
Willerton Cl WF12 .... 119 B3
Willgutter La BD22 .... 33 F1
William Ave 2 LS15 ...... 80 E8
William Henry Smith
  Sch The HD6 .... 135 E8
William Henry St
  1 Brighouse HD6 .... 115 A3
  2 Shipley BD18 .... 54 F8
William Hey La LS9 .... 208 B2
William Horsfall St HD4 .. 153 C3
William Prince Gr WF1 ... 142 E4
William Rise LS15 .... 80 E8
William St Batley WF13 ... 117 F3
  Bradford BD5 .... 201 B2
  Bradford, Butlershaw BD6 . 93 F7
  Bradford, Swain Green BD4 . 75 D5
  Bradford, Tong Street BD4 . 75 D1
  1 Brighouse HD6 .... 115 A1
  Castleford WF10 .... 103 D1
  Castleford, New Fryston
  WF10 .... 104 C2
  Denholme BD13 .... 52 D1
  Dewsbury WF12 .... 139 E8
  Dewsbury, Ravensthorpe
  WF13 .... 138 E5
  Elland HX4 .... 134 D6
  3 Huddersfield HD1 ..... 154 B7
  Huddersfield, Paddock Brow
  HD4 .... 153 C4
  Leeds LS6 .... 205 E3
  6 Liversedge WF15 ...... 117 B4
  Morley LS27 .... 98 C8
  Pudsey LS28 .... 57 F2
  8 Pudsey, Stanningley LS28 . 57 D1
William View LS15 .... 80 E8
Williams Dr BD20 .... 17 B5
Williams Rd BD20 .... 17 B5
Williamson St HX1 .... 202 C4
Willis St LS9 .... 212 B3
Willoughby Terr LS11 ..... 210 C1
Willow App LS14 .... 205 E1
Willow Ave Boston Spa LS23 . 30 D6
  Bradford BD2 .... 56 A6
  Leeds LS4 .... 205 E1
Willow Bank Halifax HX1 .. 202 C1
  Todmorden OL14 .... 108 B6
Willow Bank Dr WF8 ...... 125 E3
Willow Beck LS14 .... 179 A6
Willow Cl Bradford BD6 ... 94 C7
  Burley in W LS29 .... 9 E1
  Cleckheaton BD19 .... 117 B7
  Guiseley LS20 .... 22 E1
  Halifax HX2 .... 112 D6
  Leeds LS14 .... 205 E1
Willow Clough HX6 .... 132 D2
Willow Cres
  Boston Spa LS23 .... 30 D6
  Bradford BD2 .... 56 A6
  Leeds LS15 .... 80 F7
  Normanton WF6 .... 144 A8
  Sowerby Bridge HX6 .... 112 C5
Willow Croft
  Cleckheaton BD19 ...... 116 C7
  Menston LS29 .... 22 D4
Willow Ct Castleford WF10 . 124 E6
  Featherstone WF7 .... 124 C1
  Garforth LS25 .... 82 E7
  Pool LS21 .... 24 D6
  Wakefield WF2 .... 141 D7
Willow Dene Ave HX2 .... 112 D5
Willow Dr Bradford BD6 .. 94 C7
  Halifax HX2 .... 112 D6
  Hemsworth WF9 .... 181 D5
  Wakefield WF1 .... 142 E3
Willow Field HD8 .... 156 A3
Willow Fold WF2 .... 141 F7
Willow Garth
  Crigglestone WF4 ...... 159 F6
  Featherstone WF7 ...... 124 C1
  Leeds LS4 .... 205 E1
  South Elmsall WF9 .... 183 B2
Willow Garth Ave
  Bradford BD10 .... 56 D7
  Leeds LS14 .... 62 B8
Willow Garth Cl LS14 .... 62 B8
Willow Gdns Bradford BD2 . 56 A6
  Castleford WF10 .... 125 D5
  Guiseley LS20 .... 22 E1
  Wakefield WF2 .... 141 D7
Willow Glade LS23 ...... 30 D5
Willow Gn WF1 .... 121 B3
Willow Gr Boston Spa LS23 . 30 D6
  Bradford BD2 .... 56 A6
  Huddersfield HD7 ..... 152 E5
  Keighley BD21 .... 35 A3
  Kippax LS25 .... 82 F3
  Ossett WF5 .... 140 E3
  Wakefield WF2 .... 142 E3

Willow Hall Dr HX6 ...... 112 D5
Willow Hall La HX6 ...... 112 D5
Willow La
  Boston Spa LS23 .... 30 D5
  Crofton WF1 .... 143 D7
  Featherstone WF7 ...... 124 C1
  Huddersfield HD1 ...... 154 A8
  Wakefield WF2 .... 141 D7
Willow La E
  Featherstone WF7 ...... 124 C1
  Huddersfield HD1 ...... 154 B8
Willow Mews WF1 .... 141 F7
Willow Mount WF2 ...... 141 F7
Willow Park Dr HX3 ..... 93 D6
Willow Park Junior Sch
  WF8 .... 146 F8
Willow Pk
  Lofthouse Gate WF1 .... 121 B2
  Pontefract WF8 .... 146 F8
Willow Rd Batley WF17 ... 118 E4
  Castleford WF10 .... 124 D6
  Dearne S63 .... 194 D1
  Knottingley WF11 ...... 127 A5
  Leeds LS4 .... 205 E1
  Pudsey LS28 .... 57 E2
  Wakefield WF2 .... 141 D7
Willow Rise Halifax HX2 .. 112 D6
  Skelmanthorpe HD8 .... 175 A1
  Thornton BD13 .... 71 C2
Willow Sq 3 LS26 ...... 101 C5
Willow St Bradford BD8 .. 74 A8
  Cleckheaton BD19 ..... 95 D1
  Halifax HX1 .... 202 C2
  Sowerby Bridge HX6 ... 112 D4
Willow Terr
  Batley WF17 .... 118 E4
  Sowerby Bridge HX6 ... 112 C5
Willow Terrace Rd LS1 ... 206 B1
Willow Tree Cl BD21 .... 35 D5
Willow Tree Gdns
  Bingley BD16 .... 37 C5
  Burley in W LS29 ...... 9 F2
Willow Vale LS22 .... 13 E7
Willow View
  Sowerby Bridge HX6 ... 112 C5
  Wakefield WF1 .... 141 F7
Willow Villas BD2 ...... 56 A6
Willow Way BD20 ...... 16 C4
Willow Well Rd LS15 ... 80 F8
Willowbank Gr HD5 .... 137 B1
Willowbridge La WF10 . 124 A6
Willowbridge Rd WF8 .. 166 F5
Willowbrook DN6 ...... 184 F2
Willowdene La WF8 .... 125 D3
Willowfield Ave HX2 ... 112 D5
Willowfield Cl HX2 ..... 112 D6
Willowfield Cres
  Bradford BD2 .... 56 A6
  Halifax HX2 .... 112 D6
Willowfield Dr HX2 .... 112 D6
Willowfield Rd HX2 .... 112 D6
Willowfield St BD7 .... 74 B6
Willowfield Terr HX2 .. 202 A1
Willowfield View HX2 .. 112 D6
Willowgarth Cl WF4 ... 180 A8
Willowgarth High Sch
  S72 .... 180 B1
Willows The
  Crigglestone WF4 ..... 159 F5
  Halifax WF4 .... 91 E7
  Harden BD16 .... 36 B8
  Horbury WF4 .... 141 A1
  Leeds LS17 .... 43 C2
Wills Gill LS20 .... 22 F1
Willwood Ave HD3 ... 153 B7
Wilman Ave HX4 ...... 140 C6
Wilman Hill 5 BD6 ... 94 B1
Wilman Post WF5 .... 140 C6
Wilmar Dr HD3 ...... 134 A1
Wilmer Dr
  Shipley, Frizinghall BD18 . 55 A5
  Shipley, Heaton BD9 .... 55 A3
Wilmer Rd BD9 .... 55 A3
Wilmington Gr LS7 ... 206 C2
Wilmington St LS7 ... 207 D2
Wilmington Terr LS7 . 206 C2
Wilmur Mount HX2 .. 111 D6
Wilsden First Sch BD15 . 53 C5
Wilsden Hill Rd BD15 . 53 B5
Wilsden Old Rd BD16 . 36 B1
Wilsden Rd Bradford BD15 . 53 F3
  Harden BD16 .... 36 B1
Wilshaw Mill Rd HD7 . 188 B7
Wilshaw Rd HD7 ..... 188 B8
Wilson Ave
  Mirfield WF14 .... 137 F5
  Ossett WF5 .... 141 A4
  Steeton BD20 .... 17 B6
Wilson Ct WF1 ...... 121 C4
Wilson Dr WF1 ...... 121 B4
Wilson Gdns HD3 ... 153 A4
Wilson Rd Bingley BD16 . 36 D4
  Bradford BD12 ...... 94 E4
  Halifax HX1 .... 202 B1
  Mirfield WF14 ...... 137 F5
Wilson St Bradford BD8 . 55 C1
  Castleford WF10 .... 124 C8
  Featherstone WF7 ... 145 C5
  Glusburn BD20 ..... 16 D7
  Pontefract WF8 .... 125 D1
  Sutton in C BD20 .. 16 E5
Wilson Terr WF14 .. 137 F5
Wilson Wood St WF17 . 118 C2
Wilson's Row LS26 .. 102 F3
Wilsons Yd 6 LS28 . 57 D1
Wilton Ave HD2 .... 136 E5
Wilton Gr LS6 ...... 59 E6

Wilton Rd LS29 .... 8 A3
Wilton St Bradford BD5 . 201 B2
  Brighouse HD6 .... 114 F3
  Dewsbury WF12 ...... 139 D7
Wilton Terr BD19 ..... 116 D7
Wimborne Dr
  Bradford BD15 ...... 54 C1
  Keighley BD21 ...... 34 F8
Winbrooke Terr BD6 .. 74 A1
Winburg Rd BD7 ..... 74 A5
Winchester St LS12 .. 210 A3
Winchester Way WF9 . 183 A4
Winden Cl
  Crigglestone WF4 .... 159 D6
  Lofthouse Gate WF3 .. 121 C5
Winden Gr WF3 ...... 121 B5
Windermere Ave LS29 . 22 A6
Windermere Dr
  Garforth LS25 .... 82 F6
  Knottingley WF11 .... 126 E1
  Leeds LS17 .... 42 F6
Windermere Rd
  Bacup OL13 .... 106 A3
  Bradford BD7 .... 37 F1
  Batley WF12 .... 118 E2
  Bradford BD7 .... 73 E3
  Castleford WF10 .... 125 D7
  Meltham HD7 .... 170 C1
  Wakefield WF2 ..... 141 F7
Windermere Terr 3 BD7 . 73 E3
Winders Dale 2 LS27 . 98 A6
Windgate BD20 ...... 17 F8
Windhill Ave S75 .... 178 A3
Windhill CE First Sch
  BD18 .... 55 E8
Windhill Cres
  Mapplewell S75 ..... 178 A3
  Wakefield S75 ...... 142 E8
Windhill Ct WF1 ..... 142 F8
Windhill Dr S75 ..... 178 A3
Windhill La S75 ..... 178 A3
Windhill Mount S75 .. 178 A3
Windhill Old Rd
  BD10, BD18 .... 38 F1
Windhill Rd WF1 .... 142 F8
Winding Rd HX1 .... 203 E3
Winding Way LS17 .. 43 B5
Windle Edge S36 ... 199 D1
Windle La BD20 .... 4 A2
Windle Royd La HX2 . 112 C7
Windmill App LS10 . 99 E8
Windmill Ave S72 .. 181 A1
Windmill Chase LS25 . 100 E4
Windmill Cl LS10 ... 99 E7
Windmill Cres
  Northowram HX3 ... 93 A2
  Skelmanthorpe HD8 . 175 B1
Windmill Ct LS14 .. 62 B6
Windmill Dr HX3 .. 93 A2
Windmill Field Rd LS26 . 100 E4
Windmill Gdns HD8 . 100 E4
Windmill Gr WF4 .. 143 B1
Windmill Hill Bradford BD6 . 74 A1
  Pudsey LS28 ...... 76 C6
Windmill Hill La
  Emley HD8 .... 174 F8
  Flockton WF4 ..... 156 F1
Windmill La Batley WF17 . 97 A1
  Bradford BD6 ..... 74 C1
  Guiseley LS20 .... 22 D4
  Rothwell LS26 .... 100 E4
  Whitley Common HD7 . 190 D3
  Yeadon LS19 ..... 40 C6
Windmill Primary Sch
  LS10 .... 99 E8
Windmill Rd Bramham LS23 . 30 E4
  Middleton LS10 ... 99 E8
Windmill Rise LS25 . 64 E6
Windmill View
  Holmfirth HD7 ... 189 C2
  Knottingley WF11 . 126 B5
  Liversedge WF15 . 117 B2
  Skelmanthorpe HD8 . 175 B1
Windsor Gdns WF1 . 119 B2
Windsor Gn LS25 .. 83 B7
Windsor Gr Oakworth BD22 . 34 B2
  Thornton BD13 ... 72 D6
Windsor Mount LS15 . 81 B8
Windsor Pl HD2 ... 136 C5
Windsor Rd
  Batley, Chidswell WF17 . 119 B2
  Batley, Copley Hill WF17 . 97 B2
  Hebden Bridge HX7 . 89 A4
  Hemsworth WF9 ... 181 E6
  Huddersfield HD4 . 152 F3
  Oakworth BD22 ... 34 B2
  Shipley BD10 .... 55 F7
  Todmorden OL14 . 108 A6
  Wakefield WF2 ... 120 F1

Windsor Rise WF8 ...... 146 B5
Windsor St Bradford BD4 . 201 D1
  Halifax HX1 .... 203 E2
  South Elmsall WF9 .. 183 A2
Windsor View
  Batley WF12 .... 119 B2
  1 Hebden Bridge HX7 . 89 A4
Windsor Wlk Batley WF17 . 97 B2
  Brighouse HX3 ...... 115 A6
Windy Bank La
  Cleckheaton WF15 ... 116 B4
  Liversedge WF15 .... 116 B4
  Queensbury BD13 .... 92 B6
Windy Gr BD15 ...... 53 D4
Windy Harbour La OL14 . 87 B1
Windybank Ave WF8 . 140 F2
Wine St LS1 .... 211 E4
Wine Tavern La HX6 . 111 B3
Wine Tavern Rd HX6 . 111 B3
Winfield Dr HD3 .... 152 E2
Winfield Gr LS2 .... 206 B2
Winfield Pl LS2 .... 206 B2
Winfield Rd BD4 ... 95 C6
Winfield Terr 2 LS2 . 206 B2
Wingate Ave BD22 . 34 F6
Wingate Croft WF2 . 160 F8
Wingate Gr LS12 ... 209 E3
Wingate Gr WF2 ... 160 F8
Wingate Way BD22 . 34 F6
Winget Ave HD4 ... 152 F3
Wingfield Cl BD16 . 37 A4
Wingfield Mount BD3 . 75 B8
Wingfield St BD3 .. 75 B8
Winmarith Ct S71 . 179 B3
Winney Bank La HD7 . 189 C5
Winnipeg Pl LS7 ... 204 A2
Winnow La LS23 ... 30 B7
Winrose App LS10 . 99 E7
Winrose Ave LS10 . 215 D1
Winrose Cl BD12 .. 94 C4
Winrose Cres LS10 . 99 E8
Winrose Dr LS10 .. 99 E8
Winrose Garth LS10 . 99 E8
Winrose Gr LS10 .. 99 E8
Winrose Hill LS10 . 215 E1
Winsford Dr HD5 .. 155 B7
Winslow Rd BD10 . 56 E4
Winston Ave BD20 . 16 E7
Winston Gdns LS6 . 59 C5
Winston Mount LS6 . 59 C5
Winston Terr BD7 . 74 A5
Winter Ct BD15 ... 54 A3
Winter Hill Elland HX3 . 152 A7
  Halifax HX3 ...... 114 A3
Winter St HX1 .... 202 B1
Winter's Cotts HX7 . 88 C2
Winter's La HD7 .. 188 C2
Winterbourne Ave LS27 . 98 B6
Winterburn La HX2 . 111 D8
Winterburn St 3 BD21 . 35 C8
Winterbutlee Gr 13 OL14 . 108 A1
Winterbutlee Rd OL14 . 108 A1
Winterneb HX2 ... 111 E5
Winterset La HX4 . 162 A5
Winterton Dr BD12 . 94 C5
Winthorpe Ave WF3 . 99 D2
Winthorpe Cres WF3 . 99 D2
Winthorpe St LS6 . 59 F6
Winthorpe View WF3 . 99 E2
Winton Gn 2 BD6 . 94 B6
Winton St HD1 .... 153 E3
Wintoun St LS7 ... 207 D1
Wistons La HX5 ... 135 A7
Witchfield Hill HX3 . 93 C6
Witham Rd BD18 .. 54 E8
Witham St S75 .... 83 B6
Withens Ct S75 ... 178 A1
Withens End La HX4 . 133 B1
Withens Hill Croft HX2 . 91 D7
Withens La
  Hebden Bridge HX7 . 109 F3
  Ripponden HX4 .... 150 F8
Withens New Rd
  Halifax HX2 .... 71 B2
  Hebden Bridge HX7 . 109 E3
Withens Rd Batley WF17 . 96 A2
  Halifax HX2 .... 91 A7
Within Fields HX3 . 114 A4
Within Fields Prim Sch
  HX3 .... 114 A5
Withins Cl BD5 ... 74 B3
Withyside HD8 ... 192 A6
Witmore St WF9 .. 183 A3
Witty St 1 HX1 . 216 C3
Woburn Dr HD5 .. 155 B6
Woburn Terr 1 BD4 . 73 B4
Wold Cl BD13 .... 72 D5
Wolfstones Rd HD7 . 188 D6
Wolley Ave LS12 .. 77 D3
Wolley Cres LS12 . 77 D3
Wolley Ct LS12 ... 77 D3
Wolley Dr LS12 ... 77 D3
Wolley Gdns LS12 . 77 D3
Wolseley Rd LS4 . 205 D2
Wolseley St BD14 . 73 C5
Wolsey Ave 2 WF8 . 146 C8
Wolsley Terr 1 HX1 . 202 C3
Wolston Cl BD4 .. 75 E2
Womersley Pl 4 LS28 . 76 D6
Womersley Rd WF11 . 127 B2
Womersley St HX1 . 202 B3
Wonder St WF1 .. 216 C1
Wood Ave WF16 .. 117 D5
Wood Bank Sch HX2 . 111 C6
Wood Bottom La HD6 . 114 E4
Wood Bottom Rd HD4 . 171 C5

Wood Cl Baildon BD17 ... 38 B2
Hemsworth WF9 ... 163 A2
Leeds LS7 ... 60 C7
Low Bradley BD20 ... 4 C5
Normanton WF6 ... 122 E3
Rothwell LS26 ... 100 C6
Wood Cres LS26 ... 100 D6
Wood Croft Brighouse HD6 ... 114 F1
Sowerby Bridge HX6 ... 111 E3
Wood Dr LS26 ... 100 C6
Wood End HD4 ... 153 F3
Wood End Cl HX3 ... 113 B3
Wood End Cotts WF14 ... 137 F3
Wood End Cres BD18 ... 55 D8
Wood End La
Barwick in E LS15 ... 62 E6
Batley WF17 ... 118 D3
Bradford BD2 ... 55 F5
Brighouse HX3 ... 114 D2
Brighouse, Hipperholme
HX3 ... 114 B8
Castleford WF10 ... 123 F5
Crigglestone WF4 ... 160 B3
Denby Dale HD8 ... 191 E6
Dewsbury WF13 ... 118 D1
Gildersome LS12 ... 77 E2
Halifax HX2, HX3 ... 91 E2
Holmfirth HD7 ... 189 A6
Horsforth LS18 ... 58 C8
Huddersfield HD4 ... 154 C3
Kirkburton HD8 ... 173 C4
Kirkheaton WF14 ... 137 E4
Leeds LS6 ... 59 E5
Leeds LS12 ... 78 A3
Leeds, Chapel Allerton LS7 ... 60 C7
Leeds, Farnley LS12 ... 77 D7
Leeds, Whitecote LS13 ... 58 C4
Mapplewell S71 ... 178 E2
Netherton WF4 ... 157 E2
Northowram HX3 ... 93 B1
Pudsey LS28 ... 57 B7
Rothwell LS26 ... 100 D6
Royston S71 ... 179 C1
Slaithwaite HD7 ... 151 F1
Sowerby Bridge HX6 ... 111 E4
Swillington LS26 ... 102 E7
Thorp Arch LS23 ... 14 E1
Wadsworth Moor HX2 ... 90 B5
Wood Land Ct LS6 ... 59 E5
Wood Lea Byram WF11 ... 126 D8
Todmorden OL14 ... 107 E8
Wood Moor Rd WF9 ... 181 F7
Wood Mount
Netherton WF4 ... 157 F6
Rothwell LS26 ... 100 C6
Wood Nook La Honley HD4 ... 171 C2
Sowerby Bridge HX6 ... 112 C5
Wood Nook Terr LS28 ... 57 C1
Wood Pl Bradford BD8 ... 74 C8
❸ Leeds LS11 ... 214 A3
Wood Rd Bradford BD5 ... 74 F4
Shipley BD9 ... 55 C4
Wood Row LS26 ... 102 B3
Wood Royd Hill La HD7 ... 200 B8
Wood Sq HX3 ... 92 B2
Wood St ❹ Baildon BD17 ... 38 C1
Batley WF17 ... 118 C5
Bingley BD16 ... 36 B6
Bradford BD15 ... 54 C1
Bradford, Lister Hills BD8 ... 74 C8
Brighouse HD6 ... 115 B2
Castleford WF10 ... 124 C8
Clayton West HD8 ... 175 D1
Cleckheaton BD19 ... 116 C7
Crofton WF4 ... 144 B3
Dewsbury WF13 ... 118 D1
East Ardsley WF3 ... 120 D8
Elland HX5 ... 135 A6
❹ Haworth BD22 ... 51 C6
Horsforth LS18 ... 41 C2
Huddersfield HD1 ... 154 A6
Huddersfield, Longwood
HD3 ... 153 A5
Huddersfield, Moldgreen
HD5 ... 154 D6
Keighley BD21 ... 35 C6
Morley LS27 ... 97 F5
Ossett WF5 ... 140 D8
Skelmanthorpe HD8 ... 174 F2
Slaithwaite HD7 ... 151 F1
South Hiendley S72 ... 180 F6
Steeton BD20 ... 17 C5
Todmorden OL14 ... 108 B6
Wakefield WF1 ... 216 B2
Wood St N HX3 ... 92 B2
Wood Terr HD4 ... 154 A3
Wood Top Brighouse HD6 ... 114 E5
Marsden HD7 ... 168 F3

Wood Top Rd HX7 ... 89 B2
Wood View Baildon BD17 ... 38 A2
Denholme BD13 ... 52 C3
Huddersfield HD2 ... 135 D1
Morley LS27 ... 98 C8
Wood View Ave WF10 ... 124 A7
Wood View Bglws WF10 ... 124 A7
Wood View Cl WF10 ... 124 A7
Wood View Cres WF10 ... 124 A7
Wood View Dr BD2 ... 56 D2
Wood View Gr HD6 ... 114 F4
Wood Villas HX7 ... 88 C1
Wood View Rd LS28 ... 57 C1
Woodhill Rise BD10 ... 56 E8
Wood's Row LS28 ... 57 E1
Woodacre Cres LS17 ... 28 C3
Woodacre La LS17 ... 28 C4
Woodacre La LS17 ... 28 C4
Woodale Ave BD9 ... 54 D3
Woodbine Ave ❽ WF8 ... 146 C8
Woodbine Gr BD10 ... 56 B7
Woodbine Rd HD1 ... 136 B1
Woodbine St
Bradford BD1 ... 201 D3
❶ Halifax HX1 ... 202 C1
Ossett WF5 ... 140 D7
Woodbine Terr
Bradford BD10 ... 56 B7
Clayton West HD8 ... 175 F3
❼ Halifax HX1 ... 202 C1
❸ Horsforth LS18 ... 58 C7
Leeds, Bramley LS13 ... 58 C3
Leeds, Headingley LS6 ... 59 E6
Todmorden OL14 ... 86 B1
Woodbourne LS8 ... 61 C7
Woodbourne Ave LS17 ... 43 C1
Woodbridge Cl Leeds LS6 ... 59 B5
Wakefield WF1 ... 142 E6
Woodbridge Cres LS6 ... 59 A6
Woodbridge Fold ❷ LS6 ... 59 A5
Woodbridge Garth LS6 ... 59 B5
Woodbridge Gdns LS6 ... 59 A5
Woodbridge Lawn LS6 ... 59 A5
Woodbridge Pl LS6 ... 59 A5
Woodbridge Rd LS6 ... 59 A5
Woodbrook Ave HX2 ... 91 C5
Woodbrook Cl HX2 ... 91 C5
Woodbrook Pl HX2 ... 91 C5
Woodbrook Rd HX2 ... 91 C5
Woodburn Ave WF12 ... 139 F6
Woodbury Rd BD8 ... 55 B2
Woodchurch View HD7 ... 189 B8
Woodcliffe Ct LS7 ... 60 C7
Woodcock St WF1 ... 142 D3
Woodcock Way WF9 ... 183 A4
Woodcot Ave BD17 ... 38 D2
Woodcroft WF2 ... 142 E1
Woodcross LS27 ... 98 A6
Woodcross End LS27 ... 98 A7
Woodcross Fold LS27 ... 98 A6
Woodcross Garth LS27 ... 98 A7
Woodcross Gdns LS27 ... 98 A6
Woodedge Ave HD5 ... 155 A6
Woodend WF10 ... 102 F6
Woodend Cres WF10 ... 102 F5
Woodend Ct BD5 ... 74 F2
Woodend Middle Sch
BD18 ... 55 D8
Woodend Rd WF14 ... 137 F4
Woodfield Ave
Batley WF17 ... 118 A4
Elland HX4 ... 134 B7
Woodfield Ct HD2 ... 153 F8
Woodfield Dr Elland HX4 ... 134 C6
Low Bradley BD20 ... 4 C5
Woodfield Pk WF2 ... 161 A6
Woodfield Rd
Cullingworth BD13 ... 52 E7
Norton DN6 ... 184 E8
Woodfield Terr LS28 ... 76 F6
Woodford Ave HX3 ... 113 D4
Woodford Cl BD15 ... 73 A8
Woodford Dr HD5 ... 155 B7
Woodgarth Gdns BD4 ... 75 F3
Woodhall Ave Bradford BD3 ... 56 E1
Leeds LS5 ... 58 E6
Woodhall Cl
Crigglestone WF4 ... 159 F6
Netherton WF4 ... 158 A6
Pudsey LS28 ... 57 A2
Woodhall Cres HX3 ... 113 A3
Woodhall Croft LS28 ... 57 A2
Woodhall Ct Leeds LS15 ... 81 D6
Pudsey LS28 ... 57 A5
Woodhall Dr
Ackworth M T WF7 ... 163 F6
Batley WF17 ... 118 A4
Leeds LS5 ... 58 E6
Woodhall Gr LS26 ... 102 D3
Woodhall La LS28 ... 57 A2
Woodhall Park Ave LS28 ... 57 B2
Woodhall Park Cres E
LS28 ... 57 B1
Woodhall Park Cres W
LS28 ... 57 A1
Woodhall Park Croft LS28 ... 57 B1
Woodhall Park Dr LS28 ... 57 B1
Woodhall Park Gr LS28 ... 57 A2
Woodhall Park Mount
LS28 ... 57 A1
Woodhall Pl BD3 ... 56 E1
Woodhall Rd Bradford BD3 ... 56 E2
Pudsey, Calverley LS28 ... 57 A5
Pudsey, Upper Fagley LS28 ... 56 D2
Woodhall Terr BD3 ... 56 E1
Woodhall View BD3 ... 56 F1
Woodhead Cl HD2 ... 136 C3

Woodhead La
Brighouse HD6 ... 115 E2
Gildersome LS27 ... 97 C7
Woodhead Rd Batley WF17 ... 97 B4
Bradford BD7 ... 74 B6
Holmfirth, Brockholes HD7 ... 172 B3
Holmfirth, Hinchcliffe Mill
HD7 ... 188 D3
Honley HD7 ... 172 B3
Huddersfield HD4 ... 153 E2
Woodhead St
❷ Cleckheaton BD19 ... 116 E7
Halifax HX2 ... 202 A4
Woodhill Rise BD10 ... 56 E8
Woodhill View LS22 ... 13 E6
Woodhouse Ave
Huddersfield HD2 ... 136 C2
Keighley BD21 ... 35 C5
Woodhouse CE(A)
Infant Sch HD7 ... 136 C3
Woodhouse Cl
East Ardsley WF3 ... 120 B6
Pudsey BD10 ... 39 F1
Scarcroft LS14 ... 45 C8
Woodhouse Cliff LS6 ... 206 A4
Woodhouse Cotts HD3 ... 151 D5
Woodhouse Cres WF6 ... 144 B8
Woodhouse Dr BD21 ... 35 C5
Woodhouse First Sch
WF6 ... 144 A8
Woodhouse Flats LS6 ... 206 A2
Woodhouse Gdns HD6 ... 136 C8
Woodhouse Gr
Huddersfield HD2 ... 136 C2
Keighley BD21 ... 35 C5
Todmorden OL14 ... 108 D5
Woodhouse Grove Sch
BD10 ... 39 F1
Woodhouse Hall Rd HD2 ... 136 C2
Woodhouse Hill HD2 ... 136 C2
Woodhouse Hill Ave LS10 ... 215 E2
Woodhouse Hill Gr ❽
LS10 ... 215 E2
Woodhouse Hill Pl LS10 ... 215 E2
Woodhouse Hill Rd LS10 ... 215 E2
Woodhouse Hill Terr ❺
LS10 ... 215 E2
Woodhouse La
Brighouse HD6 ... 136 B8
East Ardsley WF3 ... 120 B5
Emley HD8 ... 176 A7
Halifax HX3 ... 113 A3
Holmfirth HD7 ... 188 D1
Huddersfield HD2 ... 136 C2
Leeds LS2 ... 206 A2
Woolley WF4, S75 ... 178 B5
Woodhouse Mount WF6 ... 144 A8
Woodhouse Prim Sch
HD6 ... 136 B8
Woodhouse Rd
Keighley BD21 ... 35 C4
Todmorden OL14 ... 108 E6
Wakefield WF1 ... 142 E7
Woodhouse Sq ❼ LS3 ... 206 A1
Woodhouse St LS6 ... 206 A3
Woodhouse Terr ② BD6 ... 94 D8
Woodhouse Way BD21 ... 35 C5
Woodhouse Wlk BD21 ... 35 C5
Woodkirk Ave WF3 ... 119 B6
Woodkirk Gr Bradford BD12 ... 94 C1
East Ardsley WF3 ... 119 D8
Woodkirk High Sch WF3 ... 119 C8
Woodland Ave
Leeds LS17 ... 143 C7
Swillington LS26 ... 82 A1
Woodland Cl Bradford BD4 ... 54 C4
Crigglestone WF4 ... 159 F2
Leeds LS15 ... 81 C8
Woodland Cres
Rothwell LS26 ... 100 D6
Shipley BD9 ... 54 C4
Swillington LS26 ... 82 A1
Woodland Croft LS18 ... 41 C2
Woodland Ct BD16 ... 36 E5
Woodland Dr
Brighouse HD6 ... 114 F3
Halifax HX2 ... 112 D5
Leeds LS7 ... 204 A3
Skelmanthorpe HD8 ... 173 F1
Swillington LS26 ... 81 F1
Wakefield WF2 ... 160 D6
Woodland Gr
Ackworth M T WF7 ... 146 A1
Dewsbury WF13 ... 138 F8
Leeds LS7 ... 207 E4
Shipley BD9 ... 54 C5
Swillington LS26 ... 82 A1
Woodland Hall HX7 ... 88 A4
Woodland Hill LS15 ... 81 B8
Woodland La LS7 ... 204 A3
Woodland Meadow HD8 ... 173 F7
Woodland Mount ❶ LS7 ... 207 E4
Woodland Park Rd LS6 ... 59 E5
Woodland Pk LS26 ... 101 C5
Woodland Rd
Huddersfield HD2 ... 136 F2
Leeds LS15 ... 81 B8
Wakefield WF2 ... 141 D5
Woodland Rise Leeds LS15 ... 81 C8
Wakefield WF2 ... 141 D6
Woodland Sq
Brighouse HD6 ... 115 C1
❶ Leeds LS12 ... 77 F8
Woodland Terr WF17 ... 60 A7
Woodland View
Mapplewell BD22 ... 88 C2
Leeds LS7 ... 204 A3
Pontefract WF8 ... 146 E6
Pudsey LS28 ... 57 A7

Woodlands Crofton WF4 ... 143 F1
East Ardsley WF3 ... 120 C7
Horbury WF4 ... 141 C2
Ilkley LS29 ... 8 D4
Leeds LS17 ... 43 E2
Ossett WF5 ... 140 D7
Sowerby Bridge HX6 ... 111 F2
Woodlands Ave
Castleford WF10 ... 125 C6
Cleckheaton BD19 ... 96 A1
Halifax HX1 ... 92 C1
Holmfirth HD7 ... 189 C8
Lepton HD8 ... 155 E2
Pudsey LS28 ... 57 C1
Todmorden OL14 ... 108 B6
Woodlands CE First Sch
BD12 ... 95 A4
Woodlands Cl
Denby Dale HD8 ... 192 A6
East Ardsley WF3 ... 120 C7
Huddersfield HD2 ... 137 A6
Ilkley LS29 ... 7 F1
Pudsey BD10 ... 39 F1
Scarcroft LS14 ... 45 C8
Woodlands Cres
Cleckheaton BD19 ... 96 A1
Hemsworth WF9 ... 181 E8
Woodlands Croft LS25 ... 103 B8
Woodlands Ct LS16 ... 42 B1
Woodlands Dr
Cleckheaton BD19 ... 96 A1
East Ardsley WF3 ... 120 C7
Garforth LS25 ... 83 B6
Lepton HD8 ... 155 E2
Morley LS27 ... 97 F6
Pudsey LS28 ... 57 C1
Yeadon LS19 ... 40 C2
Woodlands End HD8 ... 155 E3
Woodlands Fold BD11 ... 96 B5
Woodlands Gr Baildon BD17 ... 37 F2
Bradford BD13 ... 73 B1
Halifax HX3 ... 92 C1
Ilkley LS29 ... 7 E4
Kippax LS25 ... 103 C8
Pudsey LS28 ... 57 C1
Shipley BD9 ... 54 B7
Woodlands La WF13 ... 138 F8
Woodlands Middle Sch
WF6 ... 144 A8
Woodlands Mount HX3 ... 92 C2
Woodlands Park Gr LS28 ... 76 D5
Woodlands Park Rd LS28 ... 76 D5
Woodlands Pk LS14 ... 45 C8
Woodlands Prim Sch LS9 ... 208 B3
Woodlands Rd
Batley WF17 ... 118 A8
Bingley BD16 ... 37 C4
Bradford, Girlington BD8 ... 55 A1
Bradford, Little Moor BD13 ... 73 A1
Cleckheaton BD19 ... 96 A1
Halifax HX5 ... 134 F8
Halifax, Woodlands HX3 ... 92 C1
Lepton HD8 ... 155 E3
Woodlands Rd E HD8 ... 155 D3
Woodlands Rise
Haworth BD22 ... 51 C6
Ilkley LS29 ... 7 E4
Woodlands St BD8 ... 74 C8
Woodlands Terr
Bradford, Girlington BD8 ... 55 A1
Bradford, Lower Woodlands
BD12 ... 95 B5
Pudsey LS28 ... 57 C1
Woodlands The
Hebden Bridge HX7 ... 89 A2
Pontefract WF8 ... 146 E6
Woodlands View
Halifax HX3 ... 92 C1
Kippax LS25 ... 103 C8
Scarcroft LS14 ... 45 C7
Woodlands Way HD8 ... 155 E2
Woodlea Boston Spa LS23 ... 30 D8
❷ South Elmsall WF9 ... 182 F2
Woodlea App Leeds LS6 ... 42 F1
Yeadon LS19 ... 39 F6
Woodlea Ave HD3 ... 153 C6
Woodlea Chase LS6 ... 59 F8
Woodlea Cl LS19 ... 39 F5
Woodlea Croft LS6 ... 42 F1
Woodlea Ct
Leeds, Blackwood LS17 ... 44 B4
Leeds, Meanwood LS6 ... 59 F8
Woodlea Dr Leeds LS6 ... 42 F1
Leeds, Meanwood LS6 ... 59 F8
Woodlea Garth LS6 ... 42 F1
Woodlea Gdns LS6 ... 42 F1
Woodlea Gr
❶ Leeds, Beeston LS11 ... 213 F3
Leeds, Meanwood LS6 ... 59 F8
Yeadon LS19 ... 39 F6
Woodlea Lawn LS6 ... 42 F1
Woodlea Mount
Leeds LS11 ... 214 A3
Yeadon LS19 ... 39 F6
Woodlea Pk LS6 ... 59 F8
Woodlea Pl
Leeds, Beeston LS11 ... 214 A3
Leeds, Meanwood LS6 ... 42 F1
Woodlea Rd LS11 ... 213 F3
Woodlea View LS19 ... 39 F5
Woodleigh Ave
Bradford BD5 ... 74 E1
Garforth LS25 ... 82 E7
Woodleigh Cres WF7 ... 163 F6
Woodlesford Cres HX3 ... 91 B2
Woodlesford Junior &
Infants Sch LS26 ... 101 C7

Woodlesford Prim Sch
LS26 ... 101 D7
Woodlesford Sta LS26 ... 101 D7
Woodliegh Gr HD4 ... 153 C1
Woodliffe Cres LS7 ... 60 C7
Woodliffe Dr LS7 ... 60 C7
Woodman Ave Elland HX5 ... 134 F5
Huddersfield HD2 ... 137 A5
Woodman Ct BD6 ... 93 E6
Woodman St LS15 ... 81 A8
Woodmoor Cl WF4 ... 159 E4
Woodmoor Dr WF4 ... 159 E4
Woodmoor Rd WF2 ... 160 B5
Woodmoor Rise WF4 ... 159 E5
Woodnook Cl LS16 ... 41 D2
Woodnook Dr LS16 ... 41 D3
Woodnook Garth LS16 ... 41 D3
Woodnook Rd LS16 ... 41 D3
Woodrow Cres LS26 ... 102 A3
Woodrow Dr BD12 ... 94 E6
Woodroyd HD7 ... 152 C5
Woodroyd Ave
Bradford BD5 ... 74 F2
Honley HD7 ... 171 C1
Royston S71 ... 179 C1
Woodroyd Cl S71 ... 179 C1
Woodroyd Dr HX3 ... 91 F2
Woodroyd Gdns Ilkley LS29 ... 8 F3
Sowerby Bridge HX2 ... 111 F5
Woodroyd Middle Sch
BD5 ... 74 E2
Woodroyd Rd Bradford BD5 ... 74 E3
Bradford, Marshfields BD5 ... 74 E2
Woodroyd Terr BD5 ... 74 F2
Woods Ave HD7 ... 169 B4
Woods Mews LS29 ... 8 C4
Woods Mount HD7 ... 169 B4
Woods Terr HD7 ... 169 B4
Woodside Castleford WF10 ... 125 C8
Denby Dale HD8 ... 192 A6
Keighley BD20 ... 18 A1
Shipley BD18 ... 55 D8
Wakefield WF2 ... 120 E2
Woodside Ave
Crofton WF4 ... 144 C3
Leeds LS6 ... 59 F7
Leeds, Burley LS4 ... 59 C2
Shipley, Cottingley BD16 ... 53 F7
❷ Shipley, Saltaire BD18 ... 54 E8
Wakefield WF2 ... 120 E2
Woodside CE Infant Sch
LS18 ... 41 D1
Woodside Cl LS27 ... 98 A6
Woodside Cres
Batley WF17 ... 118 A4
Crofton WF4 ... 144 C4
Halifax HX3 ... 92 B1
Shipley BD16 ... 53 F7
Woodside Ct
Cullingworth BD13 ... 52 D6
Horsforth LS18 ... 58 E8
Woodside Dr Morley LS27 ... 98 A7
Shipley BD16 ... 53 F7
Wakefield WF2 ... 120 E2
Woodside Gdns LS27 ... 98 A7
Woodside Gr Elland HX4 ... 134 D6
Halifax HX3 ... 92 C1
Leeds LS10 ... 102 F6
Woodside Hill Cl LS18 ... 58 E8
Woodside La
Huddersfield HD2 ... 136 B4
Morley LS27 ... 98 A7
Woodside Lawn LS12 ... 77 D7
Woodside Mews LS6 ... 59 F7
Woodside Middle &
First Schs BD6 ... 94 A6
Woodside Mount HX3 ... 203 D4
Woodside Park Cl LS18 ... 58 D8
Woodside Park Dr LS18 ... 58 D8
Woodside Pl Halifax HX3 ... 92 B1
Leeds LS4 ... 59 C2
Woodside Rd
Boston Spa LS23 ... 30 B7
Bradford BD12 ... 94 C4
Halifax HX3 ... 203 D4
Huddersfield HD4 ... 153 D2
Silsden BD20 ... 5 C1
Woodside St WF10 ... 102 F6
Woodside Terr
❶ Elland HX4 ... 134 D6
Halifax HX3 ... 92 C1
❷ Leeds LS4 ... 59 C2
Woodside View
Halifax HX3 ... 92 B1
Holmfirth HD7 ... 188 E4
Leeds LS4 ... 59 C2
Shipley BD16 ... 54 A7
Woodsley Gn LS6 ... 205 F2
Woodsley Rd
Leeds LS2, LS3, LS6 ... 205 F2
Woodsley Terr LS2 ... 206 A2
Woodsome Ave WF14 ... 137 E6
Woodsome Dr Lepton HD8 ... 155 D2
Mirfield WF14 ... 137 E6
Woodsome Est WF17 ... 118 B4
Woodsome Hall
Golf Course HD8 ... 155 B1
Woodsome Hall La HD8 ... 173 C8
Woodsome Lees La HD8 ... 173 C7
Woodsome Pk HD8 ... 155 D2
Woodsome Rd HD8 ... 155 C2
Woodstock Cl LS16 ... 42 E4
Woodstock Cres HX3 ... 153 B8
Woodstock Wlk BD5 ... 201 B1
Woodthorne Croft LS17 ... 44 A4

Woodthorpe Cl WF2 .... 160 E7
Woodthorpe Dr WF2 .... 160 E7
Woodthorpe Glades WF2 .. 160 E7
Woodthorpe La WF2 .... 160 E6
Woodthorpe Park Dr
  WF2 .... 160 E7
Woodthorpe Terr HD1 ...... 153 F5
Woodvale Cl BD4 .... 75 E5
Woodvale Cres BD16 .... 37 A5
Woodvale Gr BD7 .... 73 E5
Woodvale Rd HD6 .... 115 B3
Woodvale Way BD7 .... 73 E5
Woodview Birkenshaw BD11 . 96 D7
  Bradford BD8 .... 55 D3
Woodview Ave BD17 .... 38 F4
Woodview Cl LS18 .... 41 C2
Woodview Gr LS11 .... 214 B2
Woodview Mount LS11 ..... 214 B2
Woodview Pl LS11 .... 214 B2
Woodview Rd
  Keighley BD22 .... 34 F4
  Leeds LS11 .... 214 B2
Woodview St LS11 .... 214 B2
Woodview Terr
  Bradford BD8 .... 55 D3
  9 Keighley BD21 .... 35 B4
  Leeds LS11 .... 214 B2
Woodville Ave
  2 Horsforth LS18 .... 58 D8
  Huddersfield HD7 .... 152 E4
Woodville Cres 4 LS18 ... 58 D8
Woodville Ct Leeds LS18 .. 44 B1
  Wakefield WF2 .... 142 C2
Woodville Gr
  9 Haworth BD22 .... 51 F8
  5 Horsforth LS18 .... 58 D8
  Middleton LS10 .... 215 E1
Woodville Pl Bradford BD9 .. 54 F4
  6 Horsforth LS18 .... 58 E8
  Huddersfield HD2 .... 136 E6
Woodville Rd
  Dewsbury WF12 .... 139 D8
  Keighley BD20 .... 35 B8
Woodville Sq LS10 .... 215 E1
Woodville St 15 Halifax HX3 . 92 A1
  5 Horsforth LS18 .... 58 E8
  Shipley BD18 .... 55 D8
Woodville Terr
  Bradford BD5 .... 201 A1
  10 Haworth BD22 .... 51 F8
  5 Horsforth LS18 .... 58 D8
Woodward Ct WF14 .... 158 B7
Woodway Horsforth LS18 ... 58 C7
  Shipley BD16 .... 53 F7
Woodway Dr LS18 .... 58 C7
Woodworth Gr BD21 .... 35 B3
Wool Row La HD8 .... 174 C5
Wool St WF16 .... 117 D3
Woolcomb Ct BD9 .... 55 B2
Woolcroft Dr HD7 .... 189 C6
Wooldale Junior Sch
  HD7 .... 189 D6
Wooldale Rd HD7 .... 189 C6
Wooler Ave LS11 .... 214 A2
Wooler Dr LS11 .... 214 A2
Wooler Gr LS11 .... 214 A2
Wooler Pl LS11 .... 214 A2
Wooler Rd LS11 .... 213 F2
Wooler St LS11 .... 213 F2
Woolford Way WF3 .... 121 D6
Woolgreaves Ave WF2 ..... 160 D6
Woolgreaves Cl WF2 .... 160 D6
Woolgreaves Croft WF2 .. 160 D6
Woolgreaves Dr WF2 .... 160 D6
Woolgreaves Garth WF2 .. 160 D6
Woollier Rd BD12 .... 94 A5
Woolley Colliery Rd S75 .. 177 E2
Woolley Edge La WF4 ...... 177 E6
Woolley Hall Coll WF4 .... 178 B7

Woolley Low Moor La
  WF4 .... 159 D2
Woolley Park Gdns WF4 .. 178 A7
Woolley View WF4 .... 159 F2
Woollin Ave WF3 .... 119 E6
Woollin Cres WF3 .... 119 E6
Woolmarket 6 WF8 .... 146 D8
Woolpack HX1 .... 203 E3
Woolpack's Yd WF1 .... 216 A2
Woolrow La HD6 .... 115 C6
Woolshops HX1 .... 203 E3
Woolstocks La S75 .... 193 E3
Wootton St BD5 .... 74 E4
Worcester Ave LS10 .... 99 F4
Worcester Cl WF3 .... 99 C1
Worcester Dr LS10 .... 99 F4
Worcester Gr HD4 .... 154 B3
Worcester Pl BD4 .... 75 A4
Worden Gr BD7 .... 73 E4
Wordsworth App WF8 ...... 125 D2
Wordsworth Ct LS26 .... 101 C3
Wordsworth Dr WF11 ...... 126 B4
Wordsworth Gr WF3 .... 121 F5
Wordsworth Way BD16 ..... 37 A5
Workhouse La Elland HX4 . 134 D6
  Halifax HX2 .... 112 A7
Wormald Row LS2 .... 211 F4
Wormald St
  Dewsbury WF13 .... 139 C8
  Huddersfield HD5 .... 154 F3
  Liversedge WF15 .... 117 C3
Worrall Rd WF2 .... 160 A4
Worrall St LS27 .... 97 F3
Worsley Pl DN6 .... 184 F2
Worsnop Bldgs 18 BD12 .. 94 C4
Worsnop St BD12 .... 94 D6
Worstead Rd BD22 .... 51 F8
Worth Ave BD21 .... 18 E1
Worth Bridge Rd BD21 ..... 35 E8
Worth Valley Middle Sch
  BD22 .... 35 A3
Worth Way BD21 .... 35 A1
Worthing Head Cl 2 BD12 . 94 B3
Worthing Head Rd BD12 .... 94 B3
Worthing St BD12 .... 94 D3
Worthinghead First Sch
  BD12 .... 94 D3
Worthington St BD8 .... 74 C8
Worthville Cl BD21 .... 35 C5
Wortley Heights LS12 .... 210 A2
Wortley High Sch LS12 ... 209 D2
Wortley La LS12 .... 210 C2
Wortley Moor La LS12 .... 209 E2
Wortley Moor Rd LS12 .... 209 D3
Wortley Pk LS12 .... 210 B2
Wortley Pl WF9 .... 181 C7
Wortley Rd LS12 .... 209 E3
Wortley St BD16 .... 37 B3
Wortley Twrs LS12 .... 210 B2
Worts Hill La HD3 .... 151 B4
Worth Hill Side HD7 ...... 151 C4
Wrangbrook La WF9 .... 183 D7
Wrangbrook Rd WF9 ...... 183 D8
Wrangthorn Ave LS6 ...... 205 F3
Wrangthorn Pl LS6 .... 205 F3
Wrangthorn Terr LS6 ..... 205 F3
Wray's Bldgs WF4 .... 141 A1
Wrelton Cl S71 .... 179 B3
Wren Ave BD7 .... 73 E5
Wren Croft WF8 .... 125 D3
Wren Dr LS27 .... 98 B7
Wren Garth WF2 .... 160 D5
Wren Hill WF12 .... 118 A8
Wren Nest Rd HX6 .... 132 A4
Wren St 17 Haworth BD22 .. 51 D7
  Huddersfield HD1 .... 153 D5
  Keighley BD21 .... 35 C8
Wrenbeck Ave LS21 .... 11 B2
Wrenbeck Cl LS21 .... 11 B2

Wrenbeck Dr LS21 .... 11 B2
Wrenbury Ave LS16 .... 41 D5
Wrenbury Cres LS16 .... 41 E5
Wrenbury Gr LS16 .... 41 E5
Wrenthorpe La
  Wakefield WF2 .... 120 D1
  Wakefield, Wrenthorpe WF2 120 E1
Wrenthorpe Primary Sch
  WF2 .... 120 F2
Wrenthorpe Rd WF2 .... 120 E2
Wrexhall Rd WF12 .... 118 E2
Wrexham Rd LS29 .... 9 D2
Wright Ave BD22 .... 34 D3
Wright St 8 Bacup OL13 .. 106 A7
  Oakworth BD22 .... 34 D2
  Sutton in C BD20 .... 16 D5
Wrigley Ave BD4 .... 75 B1
Wrigley Hill HX2 .... 91 E5
Wroe Cres BD12 .... 94 C3
Wroe Pl BD12 .... 94 C3
Wroe St WF13 .... 117 F1
Wroe Terr BD12 .... 94 C3
Wrose Ave Bradford BD2 .. 56 A5
  Shipley BD18 .... 55 D6
Wrose Brow Rd BD18 ...... 55 D8
Wrose Dr BD18 .... 55 D6
Wrose Gr BD18 .... 55 D6
Wrose Hill Pl BD2 .... 55 D5
Wrose Mount BD18 .... 55 E6
Wrose Rd Bradford BD2 ... 56 A6
  Shipley BD18 .... 55 E6
Wrose View Baildon BD17 .. 38 C3
  Shipley BD18 .... 55 D6
Wycliffe Cl LS13 .... 57 D5
Wycliffe Dr LS17 .... 43 D2
Wycliffe Gdns BD10 .... 55 A8
Wycliffe Rd Pudsey LS13 .. 57 D5
  Shipley BD18 .... 55 A8
Wycliffe St WF5 .... 140 D7
Wycoller Rd BD12 .... 94 C4
Wycombe Gn BD4 .... 75 E3
Wyebeck Ave LS9 .... 80 D7
Wyebeck Gdns LS9 .... 80 D8
Wyebeck Gr LS9 .... 80 D8
Wyebeck Mount LS9 .... 80 D8
Wyebeck Pl LS9 .... 80 D8
Wyebeck Primary Sch
  LS9 .... 61 D2
Wyebeck Rd LS9 .... 80 D8
Wyebeck Sq LS9 .... 80 D8
Wyebeck Terr LS9 .... 80 D8
Wyebeck View LS9 .... 80 D8
Wykelea Cl BD12 .... 94 D3
Wyncliffe Gdns LS17 .... 43 D2
Wyncroft Gr LS16 .... 24 F2
Wyncroft Rise BD18 .... 55 D5
Wyndham Ave BD2 .... 55 F3
Wyndy Ridge BD13 .... 72 C7
Wynford Ave LS16 .... 42 B1
Wynford Dr WF9 .... 183 A3
Wynford Gr LS16 .... 42 A1
Wynford Mount LS16 ...... 42 A1
Wynford Rise LS16 .... 42 B1
Wynford Terr LS16 .... 42 A1
Wynford Way BD12 .... 94 E2
Wynmore Ave LS16 .... 24 F2
Wynmore Cres LS16 .... 24 F2
Wynmore Dr Bramhope LS16 24 F2
  Huddersfield HD3 .... 134 F1

Wynne St BD1 .... 74 D8
Wynthorpe Rd WF4 .... 141 B1
Wynyard Dr LS27 .... 97 F4
Wyther Ave 2 LS5 .... 58 F3
Wyther Dr LS5 .... 59 A3
Wyther Gn LS5 .... 59 A3
Wyther La LS5 .... 58 F3
Wyther Lane Ind Est LS5 .. 58 F3
Wyther Park Ave LS12 ..... 58 F1
Wyther Park Cl 1 LS12 .... 58 F1
Wyther Park County
  Primary Sch LS5 .... 58 F3
Wyther Park Cres LS12 .... 58 F2
Wyther Park Gr LS12 .... 58 F2
Wyther Park Hill LS12 ..... 58 F2
Wyther Park Mount LS12 . 58 F1
Wyther Park Pl LS12 .... 58 F2
Wyther Park Rd LS12 .... 58 F1
Wyther Park Sq LS12 .... 58 F1
Wyther Park St LS12 .... 58 F1
Wyther Park Terr LS12 .... 58 F1
Wyther Park View LS12 ... 58 F2
Wyvern Ave HD3 .... 153 C6
Wyvern Cl Batley WF17 ... 118 C6
  Bradford BD7 .... 73 F5
Wyvern Pl HX2 .... 202 A4
Wyvern Terr HX2 .... 202 A4
Wyverne Rd HD7 .... 152 E4
Wyvil Cres LS29 .... 8 E5
Wyvil Rd LS29 .... 8 E5

Yarborough Croft HX3 ... 93 A4
Yard No 1 WF17 .... 118 A3
Yard No 2 WF17 .... 118 A3
Yard No 4 1 WF17 .... 117 F8
Yardley Way BD12 .... 94 E6
Yarn St LS10 .... 215 E4
Yarwood Gr 2 BD7 .... 73 E3
Yate La BD22 .... 51 C3
Yates Flat BD18 .... 55 D6
Yates La HD3 .... 153 B4
Ye Farre Cl 3 HD6 .... 115 A4
Yeadon Dr HX3 .... 114 A4
Yeadon House BD20 .... 16 C5
Yeadon Moor Rd
  Yeadon LS19 .... 40 E6
  Yeadon LS18 .... 41 A8
Yeadon Westfield
  Infant Sch** LS19 .... 39 F6
Yeadon Westfield
  Junior Sch** LS19 .... 39 F6
Yew Gr HD4 .... 152 F3
Yew Green Ave HD4 .... 153 E3
Yew Green Rd HD4 .... 153 E3
Yew La LS25 .... 83 B6
Yew Pk HD6 .... 114 E5
Yew St HD7 .... 136 A1
Yew Tree HD7 .... 169 F7
Yew Tree Ave BD8 .... 54 D1
Yew Tree Cl
  Low Bradley BD20 .... 4 C6
  Shipley BD18 .... 55 D6
Yew Tree Cres BD8 .... 54 E1
Yew Tree Ct
  6 Liversedge WF15 .... 117 A5
  Todmorden OL14 .... 129 A8
Yew Tree Gr BD8 .... 54 E1
Yew Tree La Bradford BD13 . 72 E8
  Holmfirth HD7 .... 188 C3
  Huddersfield HD4, BD7 ..... 152 F3
  Leeds LS15 .... 81 E6
  Slaithwaite HD7 .... 169 F7
Yew Tree Rd
  Huddersfield HD2, HD3 .... 135 B3
  Shepley HD8 .... 173 F1
Yew Tree St WF1 .... 142 E4
Yew Tree Wlk WF11 .... 126 E2
Yew Trees Ave HX3 .... 93 A3
Yew Trees Croft HX2 ...... 90 C1

Yewbank Cl LS29 .... 8 A4
Yewbank Terr LS29 .... 8 A4
Yewdall Rd LS13 .... 57 E5
Yewdall Way BD10 .... 56 C6
Yews Hill Rd HD1, HD4 ... 153 E4
Yews Mount HD1 .... 153 E4
York Ave HD2 .... 136 A2
York Cl WF9 .... 183 A4
York Cres 1 BD16 .... 37 A2
York Dr
  Batley, Bank Foot WF17 .... 118 D6
  Batley, Nunroyd WF16 ..... 117 D6
York Gate LS21 .... 23 C4
York Gr Batley WF17 ...... 118 D6
  4 Mirfield WF14 .... 137 F5
York House Bradford BD10 .. 56 C7
  4 Elland HX5 .... 134 F7
York Pl Ackworth M T WF7 164 B7
  8 Cleckheaton BD19 ... 116 D8
  Leeds LS1 .... 211 E4
  Todmorden OL14 .... 108 B5
  Wetherby LS22 .... 13 F6
York Rd Batley WF17 ...... 118 C6
  Bickerton LS22 .... 14 D7
  Burley in W LS29 .... 9 F1
  Dewsbury WF12 .... 139 F8
  Leeds, Killingbeck LS14, LS9 .. 61 E1
  Leeds, Whinmoor
  LS14, LS15 .... 62 C6
  Mirfield WF14 .... 137 F5
  Wetherby LS22 .... 14 D7
York Road Ind Est LS22 .. 13 F6
York St Bingley BD16 .... 37 A2
  Bradford BD8 .... 73 E7
  Brighouse HD6 .... 115 A1
  Castleford WF10 .... 124 E8
  Dearne S63 .... 194 F1
  Glusburn BD20 .... 16 D7
  Halifax HX1 .... 203 D2
  2 Hebden Bridge HX7 ... 89 A2
  Hemsworth WF9 .... 181 E5
  Leeds LS9 .... 212 A3
  Normanton WF6 .... 122 F3
  Queensbury BD13 .... 72 E1
  Todmorden OL14 .... 108 B6
  York Terr Horsf HX3 .... 92 B1
York Villas WF6 .... 123 B2
Yorkshire Martyrs
  Collegiate Sch BD4 .... 96 A8
Yorkshire Mining Mus
  WF4 .... 157 E6
Yorkshire Sculpture Pk
  WF4 .... 176 C7
Yorkshire Television
  Studios** LS3 .... 205 E1
Yorkshire Way BD7 .... 74 B3
Young St BD8 .... 73 F8
Young's Ct LS26 .... 64 E6

Zakaria High Sch WF17 .. 118 D4
Zealand St BD4 .... 75 D4
Zermatt Gr LS7 .... 60 C6
Zermatt Mount LS7 .... 60 C6
Zermatt St LS7 .... 204 A2
Zermatt Terr LS7 .... 204 A2
Zetland Pl LS8 .... 207 F3
Zetland St
  Huddersfield HD1 .... 154 B6
  Wakefield WF1 .... 216 B2
Zion Cl HD3 .... 135 B1
Zion Dr S75 .... 178 B1
Zion St Bacup OL13 .... 106 A3
  Hebden Bridge HX7 .... 89 E1
  Leeds LS7 .... 212 B2
  Ossett WF5 .... 119 C1
Zoar St LS27 .... 98 A4

Addresses

Name and Address	Telephone	Page	Grid Reference

Name and Address	Telephone	Page	Grid Reference

Ordnance Survey

STREET ATLASES
ORDER FORM

The Street Atlases are available from all good bookshops or by mail order direct from the publisher. Orders can be made in the following ways. **By phone** Ring our special Credit Card Hotline on **01933 443863** during office hours (9am to 5pm) or leave a message on the answering machine, quoting your full credit card number plus expiry date and your full name and address. **By post or fax** Fill out the order form below (you may photocopy it) and post it to: **Philip's Direct, 27 Sanders Road, Wellingborough, Northants NN8 4NL** or fax it to: **01933 443849.** Before placing an order by post, by fax or on the answering machine, please telephone to check availability and prices.

PHILIP'S

COLOUR LOCAL ATLASES	PAPERBACK	Quantity @ £3.50 each	£ Total
CANNOCK, LICHFIELD, RUGELEY		☐ 0 540 07625 2 ➤	
DERBY AND BELPER		☐ 0 540 07608 2 ➤	
NORTHWICH, WINSFORD, MIDDLEWICH		☐ 0 540 07589 2 ➤	
PEAK DISTRICT TOWNS		☐ 0 540 07609 0 ➤	
STAFFORD, STONE, UTTOXETER		☐ 0 540 07626 0 ➤	
WARRINGTON, WIDNES, RUNCORN		☐ 0 540 07588 4 ➤	

COLOUR REGIONAL ATLASES				
	HARDBACK	SPIRAL	POCKET	
	Quantity @ £10.99 each	Quantity @ £8.99 each	Quantity @ £4.99 each	£ Total
MERSEYSIDE	☐ 0 540 06480 7	☐ 0 540 06481 5	☐ 0 540 06482 3 ➤	
	Quantity @ £12.99 each	Quantity @ £8.99 each	Quantity @ £5.99 each	£ Total
BERKSHIRE	☐ 0 540 06170 0	☐ 0 540 06172 7	☐ 0 540 06173 5 ➤	
	Quantity @ £12.99 each	Quantity @ £9.99 each	Quantity @ £4.99 each	£ Total
DURHAM	☐ 0 540 06365 7	☐ 0 540 06366 5	☐ 0 540 06367 3 ➤	
	Quantity @ £12.99 each	Quantity @ £9.99 each	Quantity @ £5.50 each	£ Total
GREATER MANCHESTER	☐ 0 540 06485 8	☐ 0 540 06486 6	☐ 0 540 06487 4 ➤	
TYNE AND WEAR	☐ 0 540 06370 3	☐ 0 540 06371 1	☐ 0 540 06372 X ➤	
	Quantity @ £12.99 each	Quantity @ £9.99 each	Quantity @ £5.99 each	£ Total
BEDFORDSHIRE	☐ 0 540 07801 8	☐ 0 540 07802 6	☐ 0 540 07803 4 ➤	
BIRMINGHAM & WEST MIDLANDS	☐ 0 540 07603 1	☐ 0 540 07604 X	☐ 0 540 07605 8 ➤	
BUCKINGHAMSHIRE	☐ 0 540 07466 7	☐ 0 540 07467 5	☐ 0 540 07468 3 ➤	
CHESHIRE	☐ 0 540 07507 8	☐ 0 540 07508 6	☐ 0 540 07509 4 ➤	
DERBYSHIRE	☐ 0 540 07531 0	☐ 0 540 07532 9	☐ 0 540 07533 7 ➤	
EDINBURGH & East Central Scotland	☐ 0 540 07653 8	☐ 0 540 07654 6	☐ 0 540 07656 2 ➤	
NORTH ESSEX	☐ 0 540 07289 3	☐ 0 540 07290 7	☐ 0 540 07292 3 ➤	
SOUTH ESSEX	☐ 0 540 07294 X	☐ 0 540 07295 8	☐ 0 540 07297 4 ➤	
GLASGOW & West Central Scotland	☐ 0 540 07648 1	☐ 0 540 07649 X	☐ 0 540 07651 1 ➤	
NORTH HAMPSHIRE	☐ 0 540 07471 3	☐ 0 540 07472 1	☐ 0 540 07473 X ➤	